NAVY SEALs

NAVY SEALs

A COMPLETE HISTORY
from World War II to the Present

KEVIN DOCKERY
FROM INTERVIEWS BY BUD BRUTSMAN

BERKLEY BOOKS, NEW YORK

IB

A Berkley Book
Published by The Berkley Publishing Group
A division of Penguin Group (USA) Inc.
375 Hudson Street
New York, New York 10014

Reprinted from three previous Berkley hardcovers
Navy Seals: A History of the Early Years
Navy Seals a History Part II: The Vietnam Years
Navy Seals a History Part III: Post-Vietnam to the Present

Copyright © 2004 by Bill Fawcett and Associates
Cover design by Steven Ferlauto
Text design by Tiffany Estreicher

Berkley hardcover edition: November 2004

Visit our website at www.penguin.com

This book has been cataloged by the Library of Congress

PRINTED IN THE UNITED STATES OF AMERICA

10 9 8 7 6 5 4 3 2 1

Contents

■ Chapter 1

The Navy SEALs

The United States Navy SEALs are the direct action component of the Navy Special Warfare community. Named for the three environments they operate from—the SEa, Air, and Land—the SEALs are highly trained unconventional warfare troops. There are presently six SEAL Teams and two SEAL Delivery Vehicle Teams (SDV Team), with a roughly equal number of men assigned to each coast of the United States. The SEAL Teams are organized into ten sixteen-man platoons, with an additional headquarters platoon and a twenty-man support element. Though each SEAL Team is identified by a number, even numbers on the East Coast and odd numbers on the West, the men who man these units often choose to refer to themselves simply as "the Teams."

These simple statistics do little to illustrate the nature of the SEAL Teams or the unique individuals who are their members. Only in the closing decade of the twentieth century does the story of the SEALs come into public prominence. Since the late 1980s, the SEALs have been the subject of many popular books, movies, television specials, and magazine articles. Few of these information sources have told the history of these men.

The SEAL Teams of today descended from the Underwater Demolition Teams. The UDTs also derived from an earlier unit, the Navy Combat Demolition Teams. Other specialized units that were created during the war years of World War II had a strong influence on today's teams as well.

The SEAL Teams of today have a reputation for being among the toughest unconventional warfare troops in the world. The following pages tell us where they came from.

Chapter 2

World War II: The Origins

World War II was an event that a number of people throughout the world saw coming well before it arrived. But like a giant avalanche, there seemed to be little these few could do to prevent it.

The First World War ended in November 1918, and its repercussions and echoes were felt and heard through most of the twentieth century. A twenty-nine-year-old Austrian-born German who had been less than a success in the business world, had enlisted in the German army and fought through the war, being wounded in battle and cited for bravery twice. Reaching the rank of lance corporal, Adolf Hitler saw his country defeated and brought to her knees. That army corporal would later use Germany's defeat and her fallen status to boost himself to a position of domination. A domination that Hitler spread over almost all of Europe and beyond.

Japan, who had allied herself with Great Britain during the First World War, was given a mandate over many of the islands of the Central Pacific. The Marshalls, Marianas, and Caroline Islands were all ceded to Japan. This mandate allowed Japan to extend her influence almost unopposed across a third of the Central Pacific by 1920. The results of the Russo-Japanese War at the beginning of the twentieth century had Korea in Japanese hands by 1910. Renamed Chosen, Korea gave the Japanese a shared border with Northern China at Manchuria.

In the early 1920s, Mussolini's Fascists gathered power in Italy, eventually eliminating any effective opposition to their rule. Germany suffered under financial reparations she was ordered to pay for her part in the First World War. Inflation brought the country to near-complete ruin, creating the conditions for Hitler's appeal to the poverty-stricken people of the country. On 23 October 1929, the New York Stock Exchange collapsed, beginning a worldwide economic depression.

Unrest swept through the junior officers of the Japanese military in 1930. A group of young officers assassinated Prime Minister Inukai in part because of his support of limitations put on the strength of the Japanese military through treaties. A sabotage incident at Mukden on the South Manchuria Railroad gives the Japanese army an excuse to send in troops. Military action by the Chinese was weak and ineffectual, and by early 1932, the Japanese army had conquered Manchuria, renaming it Manchukuo and quickly exploiting the area.

The early 1930s saw Hitler gaining power in Germany. Violent actions by Hitler's henchmen destroy any effective opposition to him, even in his own Nazi Party. in August 1934, President Hindenburg of Germany dies and Hitler proclaims himself *führer* (leader) and chancellor of Germany soon after.

By the mid-1930s, Hitler's Germany began a policy of expansion in Europe. The Ger-

A UDT naked warrior looking up from the bottom as he swims through clear ocean waters.

U.S. Navy

man seizure of the Rhineland in March 1936 went unopposed by the French or British military. The annexation of Austria and the Sudetenland of Czechoslovakia by Germany takes place in 1938. Mussolini's Fascist regime in Italy has extended relations with Germany and is acting aggressively against countries in Northern Africa. Having joined with Germany, Italy established the basis for what would soon be known as the Axis powers.

Japan conducted operations against China throughout much of the 1930s. Along the Western Pacific rim and deep within Asia, the Japanese Imperial Empire continued enlarging its sphere of influence. In late 1938, Japan announced to the world its establishment of the New Order for East Asia, which firmly placed it as the dominant economic power for the area.

Further expansions by Germany run unopposed by the rest of the world in the late 1930s. On 31 August 1939, the decision is made in Berlin. The next day, 1 September 1939, Germany invades Poland without a formal declaration of war. World War II had begun.

Within a few days of Germany's invasion of Poland, Britain and France declared war against Germany. Within twenty-seven days, Poland surrendered to the new lightning warfare of the German army. The United States tries to remain neutral to the war beginning in Europe while still supporting Great Britain. German submarines begin patrolling the Atlantic, cutting off shipping to the British Isles.

By April 1940, German warships leave their ports for the invasion of Norway. Further actions are taken against the other countries of Europe. Within months, Belgium, the Netherlands, Norway, and eventually France fall. With the exception of a small number of neutral countries, such as Spain, Portugal, Sweden, and Switzerland, Hitler controls or dominates the coastline of Europe along the Atlantic and much of the northern Mediterranean.

Though Germany moved into Northern Africa, Hitler never invaded Britain itself. Instead, the air and sea war against Britain raged hotter throughout 1940. The Japanese move into Indochina in late September 1940, against little argument from the Vichy government of occupied France. By late 1940, the British begin a heavy offensive against the German and Italian Axis forces in North Africa. The United States continues to supply Britain with war material and humanitarian aid, but is not yet at war with Germany. This situation continues through 1941, with Britain leading the active fight against the Axis on the western and southern front. Having attacked the Soviet Union in June, German forces make deep inroads into Russia and the Baltic states.

The diplomatic situation in the Pacific goes heavily against Japan during 1941. By the summer months, Japanese assets are frozen in the United States and Britain. Over three-quarters of Japanese foreign trade is cut off, and the flow of oil to Japan, which has no oil resources of its own within its borders, is cut to 10 percent of what it had been. Restricted to her limited stock of oil already on hand, Japan is being forced to negotiate and change her expansionist policy.

Heavy pressure is brought against the Japanese government by her military forces. War preparations are begun in secret in Japan while minor diplomatic proposals are still put forth by her to the United States. On 7 December 1941, Japanese forces attack the U.S. Navy base at Pearl Harbor in the Territory of Hawaii.

Less than a day had passed after the attack against Pearl Harbor when the Japanese opened their attack on Hong Kong, began landings in Malaya, and initiated air attacks on Luzon in the Philippines. On 8 December 1941, the United States and Britain declare war on Japan. Australia, New Zealand, the Netherlands, Free French, and others do likewise.

Within days of the attack on Pearl Harbor, Germany and Italy declares war on the United States. On December 11, the United States Congress formally declares war against the Axis forces. World War II is now a global conflict. Before the end of the war, more than seventy countries of the world will be directly involved in the conflict.

The Mission: The Target

Prior to World War II, no major amphibious landing had been successfully conducted during the twentieth century. The last time the U.S. had landed on an enemy-held beach was in June 1898, when U.S. forces, including Colonel Teddy Roosevelt and the Rough Riders unit, landed unopposed in Cuba.

The war against the Japanese in the Pacific would require major amphibious landings conducted against all types of fortified island beaches. In the Atlantic and the European theater, the lack of any land-based facilities from which to mount the war would also require amphibious landings. It was in part the major difficulties in conducting an amphibious landing against strong enemy opposition that kept Hitler and his forces from invading England.

The U.S. Navy and Marine Corps had been practicing and developing amphibious landing techniques and planning in the 1930s and into 1941. Navy–Marine Corps Fleet Landing Exercises (FLEXs) recognized a need for specialized groups of men to mark approaches and guide landing craft to the beach; locate suitable beaches and scout out enemy forces, fortifications, and obstacles (both man-made and natural); and deal with mines and obstacles with demolition or other clearing techniques.

One astonishingly prescient U.S. Marine officer, Lieutenant Colonel Earl Hancock "Pete" Ellis, had studied the Japanese and their possible operating areas in the Pacific in the 1920s. Even prior to World War I, Ellis had lectured at the Navy War College. Beginning in 1913, he predicted that the U.S. would eventually be at war with the Japanese and that amphibious warfare would have to be developed soon in order to conduct that fight.

A huge line of Japanese log obstacles off the beach of a Pacific island. As part of their post-invasion work, these and other obstacles would be demolished by the men of the UDTs.

U.S. Navy

When Japan received a mandate over islands in the Pacific that had been under German control after World War I, Ellis and other Marine and Navy officers saw the possibility of interisland warfare in a Pacific conflict become stronger. Before 1920, Marine operations on islands were of a defensive nature. With the changes in the political structure of much of the Central Pacific, plans for attacking an island rather than defending it had to be developed. Continuing his study of the situation, Ellis submitted a complete report of his findings in 1921.

Ellis's detailed report on his researches became "Operational Plan 712H—Advanced Base Operations in Micronesia," the basic doctrine for Marine operations in the Pacific until the end of WWII. Along with a number of other recommendations, one item stands out. Ellis suggested the assignment of trained demolition specialists with wire cutters and explosives. These men would constitute part of the first wave of an amphibious invasion to break up obstacles on the beach and in the shallow waters offshore.

Ellis died within a few years of delivering his report. The war he predicted arrived twenty years later. During the 1920s and 1930s, military planners in Washington, D.C., developed what were called the Orange plans. Modified a number of times, the basic Orange plan had the Navy conducting much of the offensive action against Japan in conjunction with air attacks and the Army's seizure and occupation of islands in the Central Pacific. The major problem with the Orange plan was that it had the United States facing only a single enemy, Japan, in only one theater, the Pacific.

In 1941, it could be seen that the coming war would involve multiple enemies in different theaters. With the final commitment to action in December 1941, the United States was faced for the first time in her history with fighting on two major fronts at the same time. In the Atlantic and across Europe and North Africa against the Axis, and in the Pacific and Asia against the Japanese Imperial Forces.

Japanese forces had been moving rapidly across the Pacific in all directions immediately after the attack on Pearl Harbor: east against the islands of the Central Pacific; south and southwest against the Philippines, Malaya, and the islands of the South China Sea, Burma, Thailand, and Indochina; west farther into China; and even north into the Aleutian Islands that extended out from the Alaskan territory.

In Europe, the target was a little more concentrated than in the Pacific, but it was as well or better fortified. The Mediterranean was almost completely surrounded with Axis-controlled territory. Combat actions would have to drive the Axis forces from Africa as well as Europe. And the only forward base available was beleaguered, isolated England.

World War II was a WAR. And it was fought strategically. It was totally engaging all the military capabilities of this and other countries. It was an all-out war. It went from submarines to the air. And it had a reason to be fought.

CAPTAIN FRANK KAINE, USN (RET.) NCDU/UDT

Admiral Ernest J. King was the new Chief of Naval Operations (CNO) for the United States Navy. The greatest of his tasks was to guide the strategy of the Navy through the war on both fronts. Amphibious warfare was going to be the means the United States would use to establish a toehold in enemy territory.

Of all of the U.S. military services, amphibious warfare had always been a specialty of the Marine Corps. As implied by the name, an amphibious operation began with a seaborne force being landed for the invasion and occupation of a land area. Once the forces had arrived on the land, the operation became normal land warfare with naval gunfire support available as long as the combat area was within range.

It was the actual getting from the transport ships to the beaches that took extra training as well as specialized small craft and tactics. For the large number of amphibious operations that would be needed to fight in Europe and the Pacific, specially trained Army commands had to be developed. Planning for the upcoming war included invasions of enough forces to occupy whole continents if necessary.

The Navy's mission during an amphibious operation would be to transport and protect the landing forces while at sea, land the forces on the target and protect them from attack by enemy naval forces, and keep a constant flow of supplies, materials, and manpower coming in to the invading forces.

To conduct these landing operations, a new class of naval ship was developed and classified as landing craft. As a general Navy rule, anything over 200 feet in length is referred to as a ship, anything smaller is a craft. The one major feature of all landing craft was their ability to run aground on a beach, unload, and get off the beach under their own power. This was true for all such craft, from the 36-foot, 3-inch LCVP (Landing Craft, Vehicle, Personnel) to the 328 foot LST (Landing Ship, Tank).

The industrial might of the United States turned to the production of war materials, even before war was declared. Landing craft were one of the items produced, and built in tremendous numbers. Invasions involving hundreds of thousands of troops, material, and vehicles would be delayed or abandoned without the many simple, ugly, floating plywood boxes known as LCVPs.

To conduct the operations as efficiently as possible, the Amphibious Force was developed. This force would contain the specialized manpower, ships, and small craft necessary to conduct amphibious operations. Amphibious Forces were assigned to each of the fleets that would need them.

Admiral Chester W. Nimitz had been assigned to the post of commander-in-chief of the Pacific Fleet (CINCPAC) shortly after the Pearl Harbor attack. The initial Allied strategy of the war, known as War Plan Rainbow 5, had been prepared in 1941, prior to Pearl Harbor, and focused the initial efforts of the United States on the defeat of Germany. With the European theater under control, a concentrated effort could then be made against the Japanese in the Pacific.

Admiral Nimitz could easily see the problems that would ensue if the Japanese were allowed even more time to consolidate their positions and reinforce the fortifications of islands, some of which they had already held for years.

The newly established U.S. Joint Chiefs of Staff (JCS) consisting first of the Chiefs of Operations for the Army and Navy, organized the Pacific theater into two major commands, the Southwest Pacific Area and the Pacific Ocean Areas. General Douglas MacArthur would command the forces operating in the Southwest Pacific. His area of responsibility contained Australia, New Guinea, the Bismarck Archipelago, the Dutch East Indies, and the Philippines.

The Pacific Ocean Areas consisted of the North Pacific Area, which was everything north of latitude 42 degrees North, and the South Pacific Area, which was south of the equator and east of the Southwest Pacific at longitude 159 degrees East. Extending from the equator north to the forty-second parallel, and including the main islands of Japan, was the Central Pacific Area.

The Pacific area had been organized and the campaign against the Japanese Imperial Empire outlined. With the decision made to conduct the Pacific campaign concurrently with the Atlantic and European campaign, the buildup of men and materials began in earnest.

Detection of a buildup of Japanese facilities on Guadalcanal in the Solomon Islands caused great concern for the Allies. The capacity to launch land-based long-range bombers would give Japan an edge in cutting off the shortest sea routes between the United States and Australia. To prevent this from happening, the first major U.S. offensive of World War II was planned and conducted.

On 7 August 1942, Operation WATCHTOWER begins and the First Marine Division lands on Guadalcanal. Additional detachments land on Tulagi and Gavutu Islands. The Marines are transported by Admiral Richmond Kelly Turner's Amphibious Force. The landings themselves were made against relatively light resistance and few fortifications and obstacles. The fighting for Guadalcanal itself was considerably different. It took four long months of debilitating jungle warfare before the Japanese were defeated and Guadalcanal taken by the Allied forces.

Only a few weeks after the invasion of Guadalcanal, another amphibious action took place in Europe. Allied planners, especially the British, wanted a major landing in Europe as quickly as possible. Resources for such an operation—manpower and available ships and small craft—simply weren't available in 1942/43. Instead, a large raid or commando sortie was planned for mid-1942.

On 19 August 1942, the first major invasion in the European theater was conducted as a large-scale raid by Canadian troops and British commandos along with a small number of American and Free French forces at Dieppe in northern France. Following a British plan, the primarily Canadian force landed with the intention of destroying a German radio location center as well as a number of gun and other installations. The intention was also to learn how the Germans would fight against such an invasion and the nature and extent of their resistance.

In spite of their fighting with tremendous valor, the troops never reached their objectives. Flaws in the basic plan, its organization and support, caused the tide of battle to turn against the raiders as they fought heavy German resistance.

Lessons were learned on how to conduct future amphibious landings in Europe, but they were learned at a cost. Of 6,000 men in the landing force, 3,369 Canadians alone were casualties or taken prisoner. Additional Allied losses included 106 aircraft, a destroyer, 30 tanks, and 33 landing craft. This against a German loss of about 600 men and 50 aircraft. Included in the Allied casualties was Lieutenant Loustalot of the U.S. Army Rangers, the first American serviceman of World War II to die in combat on European soil.

It was now unequivocally clear that the taking of a defended port such as Dieppe would be too costly in terms of men and material. Another site needed to be chosen for the eventual European landings.

Additional forces were going to be necessary in both the Atlantic and Pacific theaters to properly conduct the amphibious campaigns. Material was being developed and produced at an increasing rate by the United States' industrial complex. Men were enlisting and the Selective Service was drafting more to fill out the U.S. military forces. Additional specialized units were created as the needs arose, or had been foreseen by military planners.

Chapter 3

The Naval Construction Battalions: The Seabees

In almost every conflict the U.S. Navy had been involved in, it needed to build, modify, improve, or just repair shore facilities quickly in order to support the fleet. By the early 1930s, the Navy's Bureau of Yards and Docks had started laying the groundwork for the Navy Construction Battalions, but for most of the decade, preparations for the new units never got very far beyond an idea and a name. The beginning of World War II changed that situation drastically.

The international situation at the start of the war forced the U.S. government and military to increase their preparedness. By the end of the 1930s, the U.S. Congress had authorized an expansion of naval shore facilities. In the Caribbean and the Central Pacific, new naval construction projects were begun in 1939. In the Pacific, on Guam, Midway, and Wake Island, as well as at Pearl Harbor in Hawaii, larger naval base construction had begun by the summer of 1941. In the Atlantic, new bases were being built or existing Navy facilities were being enlarged in Iceland, Newfoundland, Bermuda, Trinidad, and a number of other sites.

To aid in the work of these projects, the Navy Bureau of Yards and Docks organized the military Headquarters Construction Companies. Each company consisted of two officers and ninety-nine enlisted men. Instead of their personnel doing the actual construction work, men from the Headquarters Constructions Companies were to supervise the civilian contractors who did the actual work. On 31 October 1941, Rear Admiral Chester W. Nimitz, the Chief of the Bureau of Navigation, authorized the first Headquarters Construction Company. The men were recruited and undergoing Navy boot camp training by the beginning of December 1941.

Four more companies were authorized by 16 December. But by that time the situation had drastically changed after the Japanese attack on Pearl Harbor on 7 December. The men recruited for the Headquarters Construction Companies quickly received another assignment.

With the U.S. having entered a state of war in December 1941, the civilian contractors who had been doing much of the Navy's construction could no longer work overseas. International law kept civilians from fighting an enemy in a combat zone, even in defense of their lives. Any armed civilians who were captured after a fight could be executed as a guerrilla.

In December 1941, Rear Admiral Ben Moreell, then forty-five and the youngest man in the Navy to hold that rank, was the chief of the Bureau of Yards and Docks. On 28 December, Admiral Moreell sought the authority to create a new kind of Navy construction unit to meet the wartime demands. On 5 January 1942, that authority was granted. Men were recruited to form the new militarized Naval Construction Battalions. The men who were originally slated to go to the Headquarters Construction Companies found themselves in the new units.

Command of the new units was given to the officers of the Civil Engineer Corps by the authority of the Secretary of the Navy effective 19 March 1942. Admiral Moreell, who had been an officer in the Civil Engineering Corps, gave the new units their official motto: *Construimus Batuimus*—"We Build, We Fight."

Earlier, in January 1942, at the Naval Air Station in Quonset Point, Rhode Island, some 250 recruits were gathered to man the new Construction Battalions. At the request of the officer-in-charge of the new recruits, plan file clerk Frank J. Lafrate designed an insignia for the new unit. The final design showed a sailor-capped bee in flight, holding a stylized Thompson submachine gun in its front arms and tools in its hands. Below the bee were the initials of the Construction Battalions—CB—and thus the name "Seabee" was coined.

The first groups of men recruited specifically for the Seabees were trained and experienced civilian construction workers and engineers. Selection of the new recruits was based on their experience and skills, not their physical condition. The normal Navy physical standards were lowered in order to bring on board capable, otherwise-qualified individuals. During the first year of the Seabees' existence, the average age was thirty-seven, much older than the average sailor or soldier. The range of age for enlistment into the Seabees ran from eighteen to fifty. But a number of over-sixty men had managed to get through the enlistment boards and were serving in their units.

These recruits were construction men who had built bridges, roads, and dams. Men with experience in building skyscrapers, roadways, and tunnels and in working quarries and mines could all be found among the ranks of the Seabees. Quarrymen, hard-rock miners, blasters, powdermen, and others came into the unit, bringing with them years of invaluable experience in explosives handling and demolition. Military discipline, drill, and weapons handling were taught to the recruits so that they could defend themselves in some of the frontline construction sites they would operate at.

Initial Seabee boat training was given over three weeks at Camp Allen, Virginia. Later the training was moved to a much better site at Camp Peary, located northwest of Norfolk, on the shores of the York River near Williamsburg. Camp Peary soon became the basic training camp for most of the Seabees during the early part of the war.

By December 1942, the older volunteers could no longer directly enlist in the Navy and the Seabees. A presidential order required all of the new men entering the Construction Battalions to have come through the Selective Service System. Experience and skill levels lowered as the age of the new Seabee recruits dropped. An additional six weeks of advanced military and technical training was included in the basic training course. This was over and above all the additional training the new Seabees would receive once they arrived at their new units.

The men of the Seabees quickly earned a reputation for toughness and skill. They operated in every theater of the war. Roadways were cut and airfields opened by the Seabees, even while under the direct fire of the enemy. (Some airfields were made operational and U.S. fighter aircraft worked from them while the sounds of battle could still be heard over the roar of the engines.)

During the war, Seabees filled 151 regular construction battalions, 39 special construction battalions, and a host of additional battalions, detachments, regiments, brigades, and forces. By its end, 325,000 men had enlisted in the unit, along with almost 8,000 officers. These men built and fought on six continents and over 300 islands. The majority of their construction efforts took place in the Pacific, where the Seabees built airstrips, bridges, roads, hospitals, oil tank farms, barracks, and buildings.

Following some of the first waves of landing U.S. forces onto enemy beaches, the Seabees would immediately set to work. Some Seabee volunteers would find themselves going in to enemy beaches even before the first landings took place.

■ Chapter 4

Scouts and Raiders (Joint)

To aid the new Amphibious Force in conducting its mission of landing troops on enemy beaches, a number of specialized units were created. Rear Admiral Henry K. Hewitt was assigned to command the Amphibious Force of the Atlantic Fleet in late April 1942. It would be Admiral Hewitt who would first take the Amphibious Force into combat.

To best prepare the force for future operations, Admiral Hewitt was put in charge of all amphibious training for his command. Even the Army units who were to conduct the actual landings were placed temporarily under Hewitt's command for training. The mission was still a new one, but the military situation in the European theater and the diplomatic situation among the Allies was heating up rapidly by the early summer of 1942.

Landing craft of any type were still few in number in all of the Navy fleets in early 1942. Trained personnel who knew how to operate in the surf zone along the shore, and who could teach others the same skill, were in even shorter supply than the landing craft. Experienced rough-water Coast Guard chief petty officers were among the first instructors at the new Amphibious Training Base (ATB) at Solomons Island, Maryland, on the shores of the Chesapeake Bay.

The Coast Guard chiefs and their students made up what was called the Boat Pool at the Solomons ATB. A number of the Boat Pool's chief specialists had been instructors in the Navy's Physical Training Program, nicknamed "Tunney's Fish" after their commander, former world heavyweight boxing champion Gene Tunney.

The very strong and fit chief specialists quickly learned the handling characteristics of a number of landing craft. All of the Boat Pool people would operate the available landing craft at all hours of the day or night, practicing maneuvering, signaling, and assaulting the beach itself.

Just the year before, fleet training exercises had demonstrated the need to do amphibious reconnaissance prior to a landing. A Marine Scout-Observer group assisted in the landing exercises and was instrumental in developing some of the techniques for amphibious reconnaissance. Additionally, an Army group experimented with various small craft, conducting beach examinations and hydrographic soundings at likely training sights along the Maryland coast. The seven-man inflatable rubber boat was a direct result of the Army experiments, the lead NCO of the unit working with engineers and production people from Goodyear to produce the now common small boat.

By the middle of 1942, the Marine Corps was committed to actions in the Pacific at Guadalcanal and elsewhere. Marines who had been assigned to the Amphibious Force were moved to other assignments, leaving the landing force actions to the Army. With the Marines went their Scout-Observer group, leaving a gap in the intelligence-gathering capabilities of the Atlantic Amphibious Force.

The Army NCO who had earlier worked with the Army group conducting amphibious reconnaissance experiments and who had been instrumental in developing the seven-man inflatable rubber boat was now a commissioned lieutenant. Lieutenant Lloyd Peddicord was called in to the headquarters of the Atlantic Fleet Amphibious Force at Norfolk, Virginia, and given the assignment of developing a new reconnaissance school on an immediate basis. The new school was to be located at the nearby Naval Amphibious Base (NAB) being built at Little Creek, to the east and slightly south of Norfolk.

The decision was made to call the new school the Amphibious Scout and Raider School (Joint). Men from the Army's Third and Ninth divisions would be trained in small boat work, including the new rubber boats, physical training, working with and from landing craft, observation and scouting of beaches and shorelines, and raiding techniques against different types of objectives.

The Navy contingent at the Scout and Raider School would take many of the same courses as the Army students, but with much less emphasis on land combat and raiding. Instead, the Navy personnel would be trained to become experts in the small boat handling, including landing craft and rubber boats. The school emphasized the study of navigation and operations in poor conditions and at night, as well as signaling, communications, and gunnery. Small-arms and hand-to-hand combat were taught to all of the Scout and Raider students.

The new school was formed on 25 August 1942 by the order of Admiral Hewitt. The first training classes began 1 September 1942. Among the first personnel arriving at the new school were forty sailors from the Boat Pool at Solomons, Maryland, as well as ten of the chief specialists. These naval personnel made up ten Scout boat crews of four men and a Scout boat officer. The Navy group was under the command of Ensign John Bell, USNR. Lieutenant Peddicord was the officer-in-charge of the new Scouts and Raider School.

The basic objective of the school was laid out by Lieutenant Peddicord. The Army and Navy men would be trained to scout out and locate landing sites on selected beaches just prior to a planned invasion. The men would go ashore at night, scout the areas, and set up signaling locations. The signals would be used to guide in the waves of landing craft for the invasion.

Both the Army and Navy personnel in the new Scouts and Raiders (S&R) unit conducted a number of exercises and demonstrated their abilities to a number of officers from both services, including Major General George S. Patton Jr. Most of the Navy personnel not only had their own mission to learn, they also had to teach these same skills to the members of the Army contingent. In a very short time the school was closed at Little Creek and all of the S&R personnel assigned to Operation TORCH, the upcoming Allied landings in North Africa.

The doors at the S&R School had hardly been closed when class number two was mustered to begin training. Army troops who were to join the second S&R class were delayed, as was the start-up date of the training. As these events were taking place in the U.S., Operation TORCH was unfolding in North Africa.

Chapter 5

North Africa: Operation TORCH

Operation TORCH would be the first major U.S. and Allied amphibious landing in the European theater. The mission was to place U.S. troops into North Africa, reinforcing the British there, attacking the Germans on the eastern flank, and preventing the Axis from winning an operational base on the Atlantic shore of Africa.

There were three primary targets for the Allied landing forces. The central target was Fedala near Casablanca and just outside of the city's fixed defenses; Safi, 190 miles to the south, was the second; and Mahdia and Port Lyautey, 65 miles to the north, the third. With newly promoted Vice Admiral Hewitt in command, the Amphibious Force Atlantic Fleet set sail from the United States for Africa in spite of the threat from German submarines. As soon as the force was afloat, it was renamed the Western Naval Task Force, or Task Force 34. The Western Task Force split up into three groups as it approached Africa the morning of 7 November 1942.

The Southern Attack Group would land in Safi. The Central Attack Group would go in at Fedala, and the Northern Attack Group at Mahdia. As the U.S. landings were taking place, task forces of primarily British ships and troops in the Mediterranean would be landing at Oran and Algiers in Algeria.

During the intelligence-gathering phase of the planning for Operation TORCH, sea-level photographs of the coastline at the U.S. landing sites had not been available. Such pictures would have facilitated the identification of the proper landing beaches for the incoming landing craft. Instead, the Scouts and Raider detachments would go in and mark the landing beaches just prior to the invasion.

During the invasions on 8 November, the S&R units made heroic efforts to complete their missions. On enemy beaches, without immediate support, the men scouted their areas, set up their signals, and brought the incoming landing craft to their targets. Resistance to the landings by Vichy French forces was almost nonexistent in some areas, and stronger in others. For their actions during the TORCH landings, eight of the ten Scout boat officers were recommended and later awarded the Navy Cross. The eight chief specialists of the S&Rs were commissioned as ensigns.

The Northern Attack Group also conducted its landings on 8 November. In the attack group, a small group of Navy personnel and several platoons of Army Raiders were assigned a special mission. Mahdia was a small community on the Atlantic shore, near the mouth of the Sebou River, called the Wadi Sebou in the local language. Several miles up the winding Wadi Sebou was Port Lyautey along with its very important airfield. The Allied forces and General Patton wanted the airfield captured intact so that it could be used for U.S. P-40 aircraft as soon as possible. The capture of that airfield was considered the primary objective of Mahdia landings.

Intelligence gathered prior to the invasion revealed that the French had put a cable boom and possibly a net across the Wadi Sebou, blocking the river to any attack force. In September, at Little Creek, a special volunteer unit of Navy personnel had been gathered under the command of Lieutenant Mark Starkweather and Lieutenant James W. Darroch. The fifteen enlisted men of the unit as well as the officers all had experience in salvage work for the Navy. Prior to being sent to Little Creek, ten of the men had worked raising ships sunk at Pearl Harbor. Once at the new ATB, the seventeen-man unit received a quick course in demolition techniques, cable cutting, small boat operation, and other techniques. Extensive training was given by the personnel of the Amphibious Scout and Raider School (Joint) before it was closed for Operation TORCH.

The special net/cable cutting team, called a Navy Demolition Unit by some, was attached to the USS *Clymer* for transport to North Africa. The Navy unit was to cast off from the *Clymer* and board a small landing craft, the type known as a "Higgins boat," for the trip into the mouth of the Wadi Sebou, about 4,000 yards upriver to the blocking boom.

During the landings on 8 November, a S&R boat, manned by Lieutenant Peddicord, was on station at the end of the southernmost of the two jetties that bracketed the mouth of the Wadi Sebou. The commander of the Army Fifteenth Engineers, Lieutenant Colonel Frederick A. Henney was in charge of the net cutting crew as they launched from the *Clymer* in the early morning hours and moved through the dark waters to the mouth of the Wadi Sebou.

The sea was very rough and the small Higgins boat was violently driven into the mouth of the Wadi Sebou. Expert seamanship on the part of the Navy crew kept the small craft on course until it reached the much calmer waters between the two jetties. But once it was on the river itself, the situation turned much worse for the small Navy boat.

Machine guns dug into the cliffs on the south side of the Wadi Sebou opened fire on the Higgins boat as soon as it was within range. The U.S. landings down the beach closer to Madhia had alerted the French crews and they were able to mount a serious defense. Incoming fire on the small craft was so heavy that Lieutenant Colonel Henney ordered the boat's withdrawal before it was sunk. The demolition men returned to the *Clymer* to try again later.

The U.S. forces continued their landings at Madhia and elsewhere along the Moroccan coast. It was the evening of 9 November before the demolition party was able to set out again. Pressure was mounting to capture the upriver airfield, which U.S. ground forces had been unable to reach by land. The USS *Dallas* had tried to steam up the river and ram the boom, but had been driven off by cannon fire from the old Casbah fort near the mouth of the river on the southern shore.

At 2130 hours on the night of 9 November, the demolition unit set off again in the Higgins boat. Lieutenant Starkweather had been unable to find Lieutenant Colonel Henney at a planned rendezvous and went forward with the operation under his own authority. The Higgins boat had been stocked with materials the demolition crew needed for its second attempt at cutting the boom. Besides incendiary devices, two light machine guns had been included, one in each of the two forward gun tubs.

Careful navigation got the small boat into the Wadi Sebou under better control than had been the case during the first attempt. Slipping past the Casbah as quietly as possible, the boat reached the cable boom blocking the river without taking fire. The crew cut the inch-and-a-half-thick steel cable and even put a man into the water to confirm that the blockage was breached. By 0230 in the morning, the mission had been accomplished. The ends of the cable drifted apart on their buoys and broke a small signal wire. The guard forces in the Casbah were alerted and opened fire on Lieutenant Starkweather and his small command.

Returning fire with their own weapons, the crew of the Higgins boat turned and made a dash for the open sea. Incoming gunfire was reinforced by small-caliber cannon fire as it tore downriver at its top speed, zigzagging to avoid the searchlights from the old fort. Fire from one of the boats' two light machine guns put out one of the searchlights and discouraged some of the machine gun crews on shore. But one of the machine guns jammed and couldn't be cleared for operation.

The Higgins boat took a large number of hits and several of the personnel on board were wounded as she made her way back out to sea. Demolitions, materials, even the jammed machine gun were dumped overboard to lighten the small craft as she took on water through the many bullet holes in her hull. But the injured craft made its way back to the fleet and none of the personnel on board were lost in the operation.

The next morning, the USS *Dallas* steamed upriver, ramming through the remainder of the cable boom that was held up by its buoys and anchored to the river bottom. A local river pilot had been spirited out of the area earlier by the new Office of Strategic Services (OSS) personnel and was on board the *Dallas* to pilot her through the dangerous waterway. At 0530 on 10 November, the ship entered the Wadi Sebou. The Raider detachment left the *Dallas* in rubber boats when she finally ran aground in the shallow river, near the desired airfield. By 0800 in the morning, the Port Lyautey airfield was in U.S. hands.

French resistance to the U.S. landing in Morocco ended soon afterward. Many of the men from the Scouts and Raiders and the Special Demolition Unit returned to the United States during the following weeks. Over 107,000 Allied troops were now on shore after the landings. The land battle for North Africa had begun and the major fighting was up to the armies now. Six months after Operation TORCH, the last active German soldier in Africa would surrender.

■ Chapter 6

The Establishment of the Naval Combat Demolition Units

The first inroads against the Axis in Europe had begun with Operation TORCH. Afterward, some Scout and Raider Navy personnel remained in North Africa to train additional units for further operations in Europe and the Mediterranean. Other Scouts and Raiders returned to the United States and their training school at the Little Creek ATB in Virginia. The S&R School was re-formed in December 1942 in preparation for its move to a more southern location.

Review of the battle reports on the actions of the Scout and Raider personnel who took part in Operation TORCH resulted in the decision to continue the school. Naval Scout boat crews and Army Scouts and Raiders were considered essential for preinvasion planning and reconnaissance. These men would hold key positions in upcoming amphibious operations. With winter descending on the Norfolk, Virginia, area, it was decided to move the S&R School south to a more year-round training site. The new school would be located at the new Amphibious Training Base at Fort Pierce, Florida, on the east coast of the state, roughly halfway between Miami and Cape Canaveral.

One of the Navy commodores at the TORCH invasions, Captain Clarence Gulbranson, was ordered to expedite the opening of a year-round amphibious training site soon after the operation was over. Captain Gulbranson chose the reasonably isolated Fort Pierce location. At 10 A.M., 26 January 1943, the US-NATB Fort Pierce was officially commissioned. Soon a number of other amphibious support organizations arrived at the Fort Pierce base to set up training programs of their own.

On 14 January 1943, the S&R School was closed in Little Creek, Virginia, and the six officers and seventy-five enlisted men making up the Navy staff and students of class number two moved south to Florida. Originally, the school was going to be set up at Camp Murphy. On 17 January, the convoy of sixteen amphibious DUKW trucks transporting the S&R School received orders to stay in the new USNATB at Fort Pierce overnight. The orders received on 18 January instructed the S&R School to stay where it was and set up training in Fort Pierce. Preparations were to begin immediately so that the first class from the Forty-fifth Infantry Reconnaissance Group could begin training by 24 January.

The DUKW (pronounced "Duck") that the S&R School used for transportation was another invention of World War II. The vehicle was essentially a two-and-a-half-ton truck that could float and drive itself through the water. The DUKW could travel 45 mph on land or 6 mph in the water, all while carrying 5,000 pounds of material or 25 men. A single shaft and propeller drove the DUKW through the water, while its six wheels moved it on land. For the first weeks of training at the new S&R School, the students used the DUKWs as landing craft until more suitable boats were available.

While the Scout and Raider School was running training, additional planning was going forward to prepare the Navy for the next major amphibious operations in Europe. The invasion of Sicily was planned for the early summer of 1943 and major landings on the coast of Europe in 1944.

The building up of the beaches of Europe was known to be under way. Layers of fortifications were being produced that would lead up from the beaches. Prudent planners had to expect beaches thick with obstacles and mines. Heavy weapons would back up machine gun emplacements and mortar pits. Such were just the standard fortifications, already known to exist in other parts of Europe. The specific fortifications of the Atlantic wall portion of Hitler's Festung Europa (Fortress Europe) were not known to the Allies. But there was no question that if it wasn't built now, it would be soon.

In May 1943, Allied strategic planners had made the decision to open the Western Front in Europe by the next year. Only fourteen months were left to prepare what would be the largest amphibious invasion to date. Admiral Ernest J. King, the U.S. Chief of Naval Operations (CNO), had the tremendous task of preparing his Navy for the upcoming campaigns.

The decision to use explosives to breach obstacles had yet to be made. The demolition operation by the net-cutting party at the Wadi Sebou during TORCH was the extent of the Navy's experience in the Atlantic so far. Though their training had been rushed, the men of that unit had completed their mission, though taking much longer than originally planned.

The only certain method to clear a beach was to hand-place explosives on each obstacle to be destroyed. That method was labor-intensive and would

A German Tellermine 43 "mushroom" antitank mine mounted on a post driven into the ground at Normandy Beach. The post is angled so that it's pointing out to sea. Any incoming landing craft striking the post would detonate the twelve pounds of TNT contained in the mine. These were one of the targets the NCDUs were intended to destroy.

U.S. Navy

take many men skilled in demolitions and explosives handling. The Seabees had men trained with explosives, but not in the kind of demolitions needed to face the expected target. Instead, men would have to be trained to do the job. A large number of shoreline demolition experts would be needed, and in a relatively short time.

Admiral Ernest J. King signed and issued a two-part directive on 6 May 1943 to address the problem of obstacle clearance. The first part of the directive required men immediately for an "urgent requirement." The second part called for demolition and obstacle clearance techniques and materials to be developed and for the training of permanent "Navy Demolition Units."

Captain Jeffrey C. Metzel of Admiral King's planning staff was an experienced officer who had a reputation for energy and getting a job done quickly. He had been involved with the establishing of a number of other special units in the Navy and may have been the moving force behind the idea of specialized demolition units. Whatever the reason, it was Captain Metzel who would brief and give the orders to the officer who would create the new unit.

Draper L. Kauffman was a graduate of the U.S. Naval Academy and the son of Vice Admiral James Kauffman. At his graduation from the Academy at Annapolis, Draper Kauffman had to resign from the Navy because of his poor eyesight. It was the middle of the Great Depression and the Navy had raised the requirements for acceptance. There just weren't enough openings for the entire graduating class.

Not one to let obstacles stand in his way, Kauffman went to sea with a civilian steamship company and later joined the American Volunteer Ambulance Corps in France in 1940. In June 1940, Draper Kauffman was captured by the Germans and held until August. From France, he made his way to England, where he joined the British navy and took up duties as a bomb disposal officer.

Twice commended by the Admiralty and once by King George VI, Draper Kauffman was known to be an excellent bomb disposal officer, this no small thing in England during the height of the German bombing campaign. Unofficially, Kauffman was considered to hold the record for the hundred-yard dash by his fellows in the bomb and mine disposal business. Kauffman was witnessed leaving the site of an unexploded bomb that was, apparently, changing its mind about its unexploded status. His speed while traversing the distance between the location of the bomb and the protection of a sandbagged area where another officer was watching was considered something of a record, given the short time delay of the activated fuze.

In November 1941, Draper Kauffman resigned from the Royal Navy to return to the United States and take up an appointment as a lieutenant in the U.S. Navy. That same month he was ordered to duty with the Bureau of Ordnance. Within weeks, he was ordered to Hawaii, where he rendered safe an unexploded 500-pound Japanese bomb at Schofield Barracks. His skills allowed the bomb to be recovered for study and resulted in his being awarded the Navy Cross.

In January 1942, Kauffman, now appointed a lieutenant commander, was assigned to organize a U.S. Bomb Disposal School at the Washington Navy Yard. Besides setting up the Navy school, he assisted the Army in setting up the same type of training at Aberdeen Proving Grounds in Maryland.

Draper Kauffman met his future wife in the Washington area. In the late winter of 1943, he married and took one of his few leaves during his nearly three years of action. Only six days after beginning his honeymoon, Kauffman received a telegram ordering him back to Washington and a meeting at the new Pentagon immediately.

His explosives experience had stood him in good stead, as did his setting up of two schools involved in explosives work. Captain Metzel met with Lieutenant Commander Kauffman and gave him his new assignment. He was to set up a training program, organize, and train a Navy unit to eliminate obstacles on enemy-held beaches and clear the way for incoming landing craft.

His orders gave Kauffman the freedom to go anywhere he wanted, get any men he might want, and set up his own organization and training. What he wasn't given was much time to get the program going. The situation was considered an emergency and time was critical. The reasons for this time crunch were classified and not necessary for the completion of the assignment. But it was easy for a man of Draper Kauffman's experience to see what was coming— the major invasion of Europe.

His orders in hand and having received his instructions, Kauffman left the Pentagon to start examining how to assemble and train this new unit. Officers from his Bomb and Mine Disposal School were among his first volunteers. Because of their experience with explosives, Kauffman looked to the Seabees at Camp Peary in Virginia as his primary source of enlisted men. But as he began putting together his new staff and students, the first part of Admiral King's directive, listing an urgent requirement for specially trained men, was being addressed.

Naval Demolition Unit #1

By January 1943, the prelminary plans for Operation HUSKY, the invasion of Sicily in the Mediterranean, had been completed. It would be six months before the operation would take place, a very short time for a major operation. Combat was ongoing in North Africa, but the Axis forces were already being driven back.

As the campaign in North Africa continued, there was a buildup of supplies and materials at the secure ports along the Mediterranean and Atlantic shores of Africa. As the preparations for the invasion of Sicily went forward, further specialized Navy amphibious units were being prepared on a crash basis.

As Draper Kauffman was leaving the Pentagon and beginning on his new assignment, another group of Navy officers and enlisted men were receiving new orders. At the Seabee training base at Camp Peary, Virginia, six Civil Engineering Corps officers and twelve enlisted men received orders to report to the ATB at Solomons Island, Maryland. All eighteen of the men had background experience with explosives prior to their joining the Navy. Some had been mining engineers, oil field workers, powder monkeys, and just general construction blasters.

The orders all of the men received just had them reporting to the ATB with no details as to just what they would do when they got there. An additional officer, Ensign Jack Fagerstal, from the Navy Bomb and Mine Disposal School, joined the group of men at the Solomons ATB. The senior officer among the group was Lieutenant Fred Wise.

A Navy commander, Joe Daniels, came down to the ATB and explained to the men and their officers just what they would be doing. As one man wrote later, the first words from Commander Daniels's mouth were, "You are all volunteers and you will be shipping out to Africa in ten days." This was actually the first at least some if not all of the men had heard about their volunteering.

The briefing on their upcoming training and mission continued. The British had reported that all of the beaches in Northern Europe that could be used for landing invasion troops were being fortified. The fortifications included steel and concrete obstacles placed from the high tide line to below the low tide mark. The obstacles were intended to damage, sink, or impale landing craft, blocking them from getting to the landing beach. The men were to be trained to examine landing beaches and destroy any obstacles.

To complete their training, the group was going to be supplied with an LCPL (Landing Craft, Personnel, Large) and various military explosives. They had all of a week to get themselves familiar with the explosives and the LCPL. They would be moving and blasting along the beaches of Chesapeake Bay.

The men were experienced with explosives, but none was a very experienced sailor. Training with the landing craft wasn't difficult, but making any sense of the buoys and channel markers in the Chesapeake was almost too much for them. Reportedly, they made the acquaintance of every mud bar and obstacle in their portion of the bay.

The men had a variety of explosives to work with, including tetratol, TNT, shaped charges, and primacord. The explosives were fired in various ways, but the team had no obstacles to practice on. Their previous experience prepared them for the new explosives, and their experiments with primacord in simultaneously detonating multiple charges impressed even the experienced explosives men.

Within the stated ten days, the men were sent on to Norfolk, where they boarded a ship for transport to Africa. Now designated Navy Demolition Unit #1, the men found a lavish amount of equipment on board for their use. As the transport ship, the USS *Alcyon,* arrived at the port of Oran in Algeria, the men started examining their equipment.

The gear included the expected demolition materials and tools. Also found was an inflatable rubber boat and a small outboard motor. And a set of shallow water diving equipment.

None of the men was experienced with the diving equipment, which consisted of a weight, belt, harness, two-man air pump, hose, and faceplate/mask. When the first lieutenant of the ship saw the men with the equipment, he asked if they could check the rudder post of the ship for suspected damage. One of the men geared up and went over the side. The dive proved interesting, not only as the first underwater experience of the demolition man, but also because of the extremely polluted water he found himself in. The ship's steering gear was satisfactory, and a very long shower rendered the diver acceptable for regular company as well.

Several times the demolition crew, who had very little experience with Navy customs and courtesies, "bumped" into the ship's crew and officers. This situation was alleviated when the captain of the ship spoke to one of the men about an infraction of the rules and discovered the individual had been in the Navy all of six weeks.

It was a few days later that the transport whip and the demolition unit set out for Sicily. Operation HUSKY would put a large number of American and

British troops on shore in Sicily at five different beaches. The American Army contingent was Lieutenant General George Patton's Seventh Army with seven divisions. The British army contingent was commanded by Lieutenant General Sir Bernard Montgomery. The naval armada had to set out from a number of ports in Africa, gathering at sea, and approaching Sicily in time for the invasion on 10 July 1943.

All of the invasion beaches were on the southeastern section of Sicily, and the U.S. Western Task Force, under Vice Admiral Hewitt, would split up to land at beaches near Licata, Gela, and Scoglitti. The men of the Navy Demolition Unit broke up into three teams; Group 1 was under the command of Lieutenant Wise, Group 2 was commanded by Lieutenant Bob Smith, and Group 3 by Ensign Harold Culver.

Each of the NDU groups had their own LCPL, which they loaded with their explosives and equipment. As the landing boats went in for the invasion, the job of the three NDU groups was to stand by in their LCPL between the transport ship and the shore, ready to be called to any obstacles that had to be destroyed.

For hours, the men of the NDU bobbed about in the water in their LCPLs. And for hours, they had nothing to do. There were no obstacles in the water offshore or on the beach that needed clearing. Though there was fighting on shore, it was not as heavy as was expected. The only target the men of the NDU were called upon to destroy was some rubble walls blocking the streets of Scoglitti.

Moving to the shore and jumping to their task, the men placed shaped charges to blast holes in the rubble mounds. The holes would then be packed with high explosives to blow the walls to pieces. The only trouble was, the shaped charges obliterated the loosely piled rubble walls and cleared the way. Packing up their gear, the men of the NDU returned to the landing beach.

After two days of little activity, the nearly empty transport ship took on a cargo of German POWs and prepared to leave. Some of the sailors handling the prisoners made more than a few comments to the Germans. One of the Germans answered with: "Don't laugh at us; we're going to New York and you are going to Rome."

With the prisoners and the men of the NDU on board, the transport returned to Oran. The NDU men continued on back to Camp Bradford, Virginia, near Little Creek, to wait for further orders. Most of the men and a number of the officers eventually were sent to Fort Pierce, where the NCDU school was established. One of the officers, Ensign Culver, was later assigned as an instructor on explosives at the new demolition school.

While the men of the NDU had been undergoing their training and conducting their mission, Draper Kauffman had been hard at work developing his training program back in the States. Personally going to various units, he asked for volunteers for a secret assignment. The mission of what would soon be the Naval Combat Demolition Units was so secret, Kauffman himself did not know many of the details. And most of even those few details could not be told to the men who were being asked to volunteer. In spite of this limitation, Draper Kauffman was able to fill the ranks of his first groups of student volunteers without a lot of difficulty.

Robert P. Marshall Jr., Commander USN (Ret.)

Our group went down to Fort Pierce from the Seabee training camp in Virginia. The officers were all from the Civil Engineering Corps and the enlisted men were all Seabees or Seabee candidates. As I remember, we were the second group to go down to Fort Pierce for training in the late spring of '43.

The Seabees had been fine organizations, but some of us wanted to get a little closer to combat in those days. The job they had been doing was important and the Seabees were great. But then Draper Kauffman came along.

Kauffman had been given the mission of establishing a demolition group. It was thought at that time that the best source of people who already had that kind of background would be the Seabees. Draper came up to Camp Peary and gave us a remarkable sales pitch about his new unit. The mission of the new organization couldn't be revealed to us because of security considerations. However, Kauffman did say that it was going to be a very challenging and dangerous kind of group. He also said that we weren't going to receive any extra pay, as some other units such as the submariners and parachutists did, but that we would be getting a lot of medals. That was because we would work in a very dangerous situation.

Most of us were taken with the charisma and personality of this man, Draper Kauffman. He was already experienced in combat and it showed.

Even after we had volunteered, Kauffman would come out to our training. We were still working at Camp Peary until another training base was available. Our training program was still being developed a lot. It was known that we would be working in the water, so it was decided to give us some experience with surface-supplied hard-hat diving equipment. One time, we were out on a diving barge and Kauffman came out to join us.

While we were working with the suits out on the barge, Draper insisted that he go down in the gear and try it himself. That was quite an experience, but not due to the diving. While Kauffman was underwater, he started to become very ill with a malady of the stomach. He shouted, "Get me up! Get me up!" over the communicator. We quickly pulled him up to the surface and were able to get him out of the suit before there were any personal disasters.

That was just the kind of guy Draper Kauffman was. And our opinions of him were proven out later when we served with him in combat. It was because of Draper Kauffman personally that a number of us volunteered for the new unit. In spite of the fact that he was constantly running off to Washington or wherever those first few months, when he was with us, he trained right alongside his men. He led by example.

With the basic manpower coming on board, Draper Kauffman now established his new training site for the Naval Combat Demolition Units at the Naval Amphibious Training Base, Fort Pierce, Florida. The base had been chosen by Kauffman for a number of reasons, among these the fact that the water off the east coast of Florida remained warm enough year-round to allow swimming. In addition, the amphibious forces already at the base allowed interaction with the boats and crews to work out problems in the mission of the NCDUs as they came up. Also, the ATB itself was located on South Hutchison Island. North Hutchison Island was just a short distance away by water, reasonably isolated for security purposes, and experimental demolition work could be conducted on its shores in safety.

On the negative side, the facilities at NATB Fort Pierce were just barely beginning to be developed. Few amenities were available for the troops already in place there. The new NCDU School would begin with tents for housing and all other support to be developed. What stood out to the men of the new NCDUs who would soon arrive at Fort Pierce was the amazing number of mosquitoes, sand fleas, gnats, and other insect life that permeated the area. There would soon be more than one occasion when the men undergoing training would prefer to face the enemy than another night crawling though the bug-infested brush of Fort Pierce.

The Navy Combat Demolition Unit started at Fort Pierce in June 1943. The first class arrived and prepared to begin training the first week of July 1943. The first training courses were literally developed as the men went through them. Much of the information on the possible target of the NCDUs, specifically what they would face, where it was, and what they would have to do on arrival, was highly classified and not known to any of the staff, including Kauffman himself.

The basic unit of the NCDU was determined to be a single officer and five enlisted men. This six-man NCDU would work and live together more closely than any other Navy unit officially had before. The six men would operate a single seven-man rubber boat. The space for the seventh man would be taken up by the explosives and equipment the NCDU would need to conduct their mission.

Draper Kauffman well knew the importance of such a small unit working together as a team. To ensure the teamwork aspect of his training, Kauffman had all of his officers, including himself, go through exactly the same training

Some of the beach obstacles built along the shores of Florida at Fort Pierce. Instead of protecting the beach from invasion craft, these obstacles were built by the Seabees so that they could be destroyed by the NCDUs in training.

UDT-SEAL Museum

as the men under their command. Officers and gentlemen in the U.S. Navy did not normally work hand in glove with their enlisted men. In the NCDUs, if they didn't, they soon found themselves going to another assignment. The NCDUs would not swim in to their targets; instead, they would paddle in a rubber boat and walk to their targets once they reached the shore. Uniforms were boots, dungarees, and steel helmets. Crawling through the sand, brush, and mud soon became very familiar to the lowest-ranking seaman as well as his officers and chiefs as they all went through training together.

Since he had a very short timetable to prepare the NCDUs for their mission, Draper Kauffman decided to create an elimination event at the very beginning of training. Going to the personnel at the Scouts and Raiders School also at the ATB, Kauffman studied their physical training techniques and schedules for a week. He took the physical training program of the S&R School and condensed it down to a single week. That week, originally called Indoctrination Week, later renamed Motivation Week, had another more popular name given to it by the thousands of men who have endured its six terrible days. They call it Hell Week.

During that first week, constant on-the-go training, physical activity, and little sleep soon proved whether an individual had the mental and physical toughness to keep going no matter what. With the very small size of an NCDU, a single man giving up could jeopardize the entire unit and their mission. It is interesting to note that a number of men who went through this early training at Fort Pierce didn't think the first week was as tough as the last week of their eight-week training schedule.

The last week of training involved every aspect of the earlier training received by the men of the NCDUs. Their payoff week was a long tactical problem that kept them in the field constantly. They resolved reconnaissance problems, determined demolition attacks against obstacles of one kind or another—and then they carried out those plans.

Captain Frank Kaine, USN (Ret.) NCDU/UDT

I reported for duty with the NCDU on June 6, 1943. Our training began in Fort Pierce with a combination of instructors, including some from the Scouts and Raiders, some Army Rangers, and a British commando type. These were the men who initiated our training.

Several of us, including myself and my buddy Lloyd "Andy" Anderson, also acted as instructors. We taught things like demolitions, swimming, or anything that we could.

Our concentration in training was on explosive demolitions and rubber boat work. But we did have to teach some of our volunteers how to swim much better than they could when they arrived. That included Draper Kauffman, who was not the greatest swimmer in the world at the start.

Lloyd Anderson and I had been working as instructors at the Navy Bomb Disposal School, which Kauffman had recruited us for months earlier. The idea of spending the whole war in Washington as instructors didn't hold a lot of appeal to us. We wanted at least the chance to see some action.

In the spring of 1943, Draper Kauffman had approached a number of us and told us that he was going to start this new unit. We had no idea what the job was going to be exactly, but we had our suspicions. Kauffman was familiar with the coast of France from his earlier wartime experiences. We figured clearing the beaches of obstacles was going to be a part of this mission. So Lloyd Anderson and I volunteered for the new unit and asked Draper if we could go with him to this new duty station.

Draper agreed with our request and told us we were the first people to sign up with his new unit. As a kind of aside to our volunteering, we had an agreement with Draper. He had agreed that we would be the first to also sign out from the school to see action. Neither of us wanted to be permanent instructors again.

When we finished training, everyone was given the chance to pick the fleet they would be sent to. We didn't know a fleet from anything else and had no idea which one operated where. Kauffman gave us a choice of numbers from one through seven. My buddy and I picked seven just as a lucky number. Number seven turned out to be the Seventh Fleet, serving with MacArthur's forces in the Southwest Pacific.

From our start in action until the end of the war, my unit, NCDU 2, served with the Seventh Fleet forces. We were never relieved or rotated. Ultimately, six NCDUs of six men each were assigned in total to the Southwestern Pacific theater. Later, when the rest of the NCDUs were gathered into Underwater Demolition Teams, our groups remained as NCDUs through the whole of the war.

We remained in the same unit configuration throughout our part of the war. When we finally returned home in late 1945, we were still NCDUs, the last in the Navy. We operated, very carefully, in our six-man units conducting reconnaissance of a landing site prior to an invasion. As many NCDUs as would be needed, usually just two, would be used for an operation.

Our normal operating procedure would be to go in from sixteen days to one day prior to D day, and conduct a reconnaissance of the beaches and offshore waters. We would look for reefs, mines, fishnets, whatever obstacles of any kind. Depending on what we found, we would come back on a later date and conduct our demolition swim prior to the invasion. So the greatest part of our work, and the most dangerous portion, was completed before D day. When we finished, the way was open to get the landing going.

The job was kind of neat to do really. And the support we received from the other Navy units was great. If we received any fire from enemy positions on the beach or in the jungles, the destroyers and other ships would come in and just lower their big guns down on target. When those Navy guns fired right over our heads, we could hear the shells whistling through the air right over our heads.

The other NCDUs who had operated in France weren't really swimming units. The beaches the European NCDUs operated on, especially for D day in Normandy, were wide and shallow. It was much more efficient for them to walk or wade through the water to get to their targets. For us, the situation and the mission were different.

The waters were so shallow off most of the beaches we worked on in the South western Pacific that the larger craft weren't able to come in as close to shore as we might have liked. For an operation, we tended to go from a ship to a landing craft, and then from the landing craft to a rubber boat. Finally, we would swim the last distance in. We had masks and swim fins to work with, a round black rubber mask and heavy black fins. The mask was small and round with no way to breathe except to put your head above the surface. And the fins were not the most comfortable. But that was the gear we had to work with right from the start.

We operated with MacArthur's forces through the New Guinea area, the Philippines, the Schouten Islands, and finally Borneo. Out of all of the operations we did, the landings at Biak early on stand out as probably the hardest. At Biak, one of the Schouten Islands, we had a lot of air attacks come at us from the Japanese forces. And these attacks included kamikazes, which were very hard to defend against.

The next-hardest operation was Leyte Gulf in the Philippines. The only reason Leyte was second in difficulty was that the air attacks at Biak came as a surprise. At Leyte, the kamikazes were expected and the Japanese didn't disappoint us. Also the Leyte attacks came over a period of time; at Biak, the attacks came suddenly and were gone almost as fast. Both operations, Biak and Leyte, involved a lot of strafing attacks against us as well as kamikaze crashes into the ships in the fleet around us. It was something that would get your attention fairly quickly.

In spite of all of the action, we didn't take any losses in any of the NCDUs. Out of the thirty-six men who served with the Seventh Fleet, we all went home in one piece at the end of the war. All of the NCDUs did at least ten or eleven landings while with MacArthur's forces. Some did even more. On some ops, we would split up and only two NCDUs would do one beach. Then the next beach would be done by another pair of NCDUs. We kept busy operating most of the time.

At Leyte I had the opportunity to talk to other UDTs from the CENPAC (Central Pacific) and SOUPAC (South Pacific). Some of those men had never even been on an operation. Others were going on their first or maybe their second. For us, Leyte was something like our sixth invasion. We had joined with the NCDUs intending to see whatever action we could. And we were seeing a good deal of it.

Serving with MacArthur's group was the way we were seeing so much action, but we never even really considered ourselves as working for him. Our commander was Rear Admiral Daniel E. Barbey and the Seventh Amphibious Force, which was under his command. That force was, in turn, part of the Seventh Fleet.

The first invasion we went on was in the Admiralties Islands at Los Negros, a small island that was almost part of the much larger Manus Island nearby. What the higher-ups hadn't known was that Los Negros was home to a batch of Japanese Imperial Marines who were known to be hard fighters. The U.S. Army landed a relatively small group, like a reconnaissance battalion, from the Army's Fifth Cavalry Regiment on Los Negros. The fighting got pretty hot and heavy fast, so command wanted to open up a second front and land troops on the far side of the enemy forces. The troops were already on their way and there was a great bay, harbor really, that could be used to land the troops. The trouble was that the mouth of the bay was blocked by a large coral reef.

The coral reef ran across the bay from about eight feet deep on one side to about twenty feet deep on the other. None of the larger ships would be able to get past it the way it stood. So we were ordered to the other side of the island to blast an opening through the reef.

We had a lot of explosives we hadn't used yet, so all the tools we needed were right at hand with us. There were Mark-8 rubber hose charges, two-inch-thick lengths of hose, twenty-five feet long and loaded with two pounds of high explosives for every foot. In addition, we had boxes of bangalore torpedoes, military-issue pipe bombs, each section made up of five-foot lengths of two-and-a-half-inch-diameter steel pipe loaded with ten pounds of high explosive. Along with those items, we had cases of bulk tetrytol charges and anything else we might need.

When we looked at the reef, we found it was about ten or twelve feet thick. We didn't know what to use to blast the reef to start with; we didn't have enough Mark-8 hose to do the job. So instead, we laid out whole boxes of bangalore torpedoes, ten sections to a case, and draped the chains across the reefs. The box chains lay across the reef every few feet or so the width of the channel we wanted to blast. When the charges were finally in place, we must have had twenty-eight or thirty tons of explosives in the shot.

When we fired the shot, it really went, and the reef went with it. What we hadn't known was that the troop ships were holding detachments from the Army's Fifth Cavalry Regiment on board. The ship didn't even wait until we had a chance to recon the blast site. They just sailed through the channel easily, with enough room on either side and plenty of depth under their keel. We did finally recon the shot, but that was well after the troops were ashore. All told, that was a pretty hairy operation as far as our getting the job done was concerned.

When we fired that big shot, the shock wave swept through the waters around the reef. Every place you looked, fish or something were popping up to the surface. We gathered up a number of huge jewfish (groupers) that were absolutely massive. The heads on these fish were several feet wide, the lips around their mouths were six inches or more thick. These fish may have been hundreds of years old and could eat anything they felt like along that reef.

A Seabee battalion was on shore and they came out onto a floating causeway they had put out to unload ships with a wrecker. Using the wrecker, they could haul the big fish out of our landing craft when we put the tow hook under the fish's jaw. After filleting the fish, the Seabees fed their entire unit from just one fish. We had brought almost a dozen of these monsters in from the blast site and gave them to all of the Army units that were around.

The Scouts and Raiders ran a training program at Fort Pierce at the same time as the NCDUs were training there. At the time we were training there with the first NCDU class, the S&R people were completely separate and weren't involved with our training at all. Later, some Scouts and Raider personnel transferred over to the NCDU school and served as instructors. But I don't know of any who served with the UDTs. The S&Rs themselves had been operating for almost a full year in the European Theater of Operations (ETO) before the NCDU reached the field.

The end of the war for those of us in the Southwestern Pacific was great. We were out there a little over two years, but our units had returned to the States just prior to the Japanese surrender. We had been sent back to California to train for cold-water operations as part of the invasion forces for the Japanese main islands. None of us was very impressed with either the idea of landing on Japan itself or swimming around the waters off Japan during the winter months. There was an advantage to having operated only in the Southwestern Pacific: at least the water was warm.

For the invasion of Japan itself, we didn't have any ideas about what to expect. After two years of combat operations, we had all learned not to anticipate anything. You planned for what you knew and then did your job. The situation would get to be a routine as you knew the people you had, what their abilities were, and what materials you had to work with. Everyone in the unit relied on everyone else and you knew what to expect. The unexpected you couldn't plan for, so worrying about it just wore you down.

Worry was something you did on your first landings. You would wonder about what was going to happen, how much gunfire you were going to take from the beach. In general, you were apprehensive about the coming situation because you really didn't know just what a minimal target a swimmer was in the water. If you knew that ahead of time, you wouldn't worry about it nearly as much.

Five or ten swimmers in the water across 800 yards of beach are little more than dots in the water. That's not much of a target. And the swimmers would be spread apart and constantly ducking under the water and coming up someplace else. It would take a very good shot, or a lucky one, for an enemy to even come very close to hitting one of us while we were swimming. And that hard shot would be made even worse by all of the heavy fire coming in to the beach from the ships offshore. The Navy did a very good job of suppressing Japanese positions when they came in firing prior to an invasion.

Enemy fire just wasn't a real problem for us when we were reconning a beach prior to a landing. The only real problem we had was with our own ordnance. When the rocket-armed landing craft came in to pound the beach with a rain of high-explosive rockets, those bothered us a lot. The 4.5-inch barrage rockets were more of a menace to us than anything else during an invasion.

You could be swimming along and happen to look up, or be swimming on your back, you would see these rockets overhead and one of them would twitch its tail or a couple would bump together, and you knew it was coming down. Wherever that rocket was going to hit wasn't where you wanted to be and we were right under them. None of us was ever hurt by friendly fire. But those barrage rockets could make life a lot more exciting sometimes.

When the war finally ended and we returned to the United States, the story of the UDTs was declassified and the public finally learned of the men who led the invasions in. The term frogman was coined by a magazine writer and adopted by both the public and the teams.

Nicknames were always something that made the rounds in the teams, and once you received one, it tended to stick with you. I was called "MacArthur's Frogman" from having served with the Seventh Fleet in the Southwestern Pacific. General Douglas MacArthur was in overall command of the Allied war effort in that part of the Pacific.

So we came under MacArthur's command in general. Directly, we worked for Rear Admiral Daniel E. Barbey and the Seventh Amphibious Force he commanded. The Amphibious Force did the landing operations for the Seventh Fleet. So when I returned to the United States, the team guys demonstrated their love of nicknames by giving me the "MacArthur's Frogman" title.

At the end of the war, the UDTs and the NCDUs were practically wiped out. As the last of the NCDUs, our units didn't exist past 1945. My understanding was that UDT 27 had just been commissioned as the war ended, so there were a lot of UDTs in operation as the war came to an end. I was finally sent home in January of 1946. When I returned to the service in January 1950, there were only five UDTs left, two on the East Coast at Little Creek and three on the West Coast at Coronado. The teams in 1950 were ten officers and eighty men, still good-sized but smaller than the WWII teams.

The Navy reactivated me for duty with the Naval Beach Group at Little Creek, Virginia, in 1950. I stayed there about six months before going back to demolition work with UDT 4. At UDT 4, I spent about two months as the executive officer of the team. Then I was sent over to UDT 2, where I took the position of CO. UDT 2 was a long assignment; I was there from 1951 to 1958, serving both as the CO and also assigned as the commander of UDU 2. Underwater Demolition Unit 2 was the command structure that both the East Coast UDTs operated under.

While I was the CO of UDT 2, we did operations in the Arctic every year. Construction was ongoing for the Distant Early Warning System (DEW line) and the UDT worked in support of that construction. Those weren't the only cold-water ops we did. There were also Antarctic deployments with operations done on an experimental basis. Jack Connelly and Norm Olsen both were in some of the UDT exploratory operations in Antarctic waters.

Though I personally never went on an Arctic or Antarctic deployment, I never felt I had missed anything. I had been plenty cold enough at other times in my life.

Working in the UDTs was much like operating with my old NCDU, only on a much larger scale. Since I was the commander of a UDT during peacetime, the administrative load was much heavier. There were more people to do the job, but unlike the way it was during wartime, you couldn't ignore the paperwork in order to get the mission accomplished.

And we had a wider mission scope in the UDT at that time. Besides conducting operations in support of the fleet, we ran our own training programs. We also were constantly trying to expand our mission capabilities.

At that time in the mid-1950s we were trying to develop on our limited experience with the British and Italian wartime minisubs. In the UDT we had a division known as Sub Ops, which was really most of the diving operations. For our experiments, we had several British Welman midget dry submarines. And we had an Italian two-man midget wet submarine. The Italian sub I always associate with Joe DiMartino; he always seemed to be on that rig no matter where it went. So we had a lot of good developmental stuff going on in the UDT at that time.

We were using the minisubs to try to develop and keep up-to-date on all submersibles. They were a great attack unit for an organization like ours. So we wanted to know their capabilities and limitations. Depending on where you were and what was going on, the small submersibles could allow a small unit of men to successfully attack even a capital ship.

The Italians had used the minisubs quite successfully during WWII at Gibraltar in the Mediterranean. They had taken a sunken ship in the water across from the British base at Gibraltar and converted it into a hidden base. They stowed their minisubs and equipment in the partially sunken ship, where they could slip out unnoticed and attack ships lying at anchor.

The basic idea of the Italian minisub was that the front end could be loaded with explosives. Within the minisub was a gear train that could release the front warhead. The top of the explosive warhead was magnetic and it could be attached, or even just dropped, underneath the keel of a ship. Men would ride the small craft wearing rebreathers and protective suits against the cold. Once they had the warhead in place, they would just set the fuse and then steam away.

This was very much a mission that could be performed by the UDTs. But we had some trouble with the rest of the Navy in some respects. The Submarine Service decided that the Welmans were true dry submarines, and as such, they belonged to them. So our Welmans disappeared. Since the Italian minisub was a wet type, the men rode on it like a torpedo with seats; those we could keep since only a swimmer could use them.

During the Kennedy administration, the Army Special Forces and Air Force's Air Commandos were looked on favorably. The President was financing the new type of units that were needed to fight an unconventional war. The guerrilla war was looking to be the wave of the future and Kennedy wanted the United States to have the capability to fight one.

Someone in Washington decided that if unconventional warfare was good for the Army and the Air Force, it was good enough for the Navy as well. Up to that point, the Navy was, and still is for the most part, concentrating on very large capital ships and aircraft capable of fighting a major conventional conflict. The other main thrust was for the construction and support of the fleet's ballistic missile submarine as part of the nuclear deterrent force.

To meet Kennedy's desires, a small, specialized unit of men would have to be created that could conduct unconventional warfare in a maritime environment. In 1962, ten officers and fifty enlisted men from the UDTs were gathered on each coast and the SEAL Teams established. Outside of gathering the people and running the units, no one who served with the SEAL Teams themselves had very much to do with their creation.

The men who make up the SEAL Teams today are no different from the men who made up the UDTs or the NCDUs back in WWII. Individuals who go into the Teams are a select group who are able to pass the strenuous training program. These men are also extremely loyal and devoted to their teams and their teammates.

The NCDU mission during WWII was to clear the beaches of obstructions and obstacles so that the incoming landing craft and troops could access the beach. Another part of the job was to determine that the beach could be exited and the troops able to access the hinterland. The UDT mission was exactly the same and included a very detailed survey of the offshore waters so that last-minute charts could be made.

The SEAL mission is the result of an evolutionary process. The NCDU of WWII was originally a foot-slogging, hardworking guy in the water with a lot of demolition knowledge and experience. The UDT swimmer took that same know-how into the water. As we progressed after WWII and into Korea, the UDT man had gone completely under the water to do his job.

In Korea, the UDT operator got back out of the water a little bit and went up on land to destroy bridges and tunnels. So that got the teams back up and out of the water. When the SEALs came along, the teams went to offensive operations for the first time. They became hunters and seekers of the enemy, prisoner takers and intelligence gatherers.

In Vietnam, the SEALs were forced to work almost twenty-four-hour days. When the SEALs were first started, there had been very few of them. But to do the jobs that were given the teams in Vietnam, more and more qualified SEALs were needed.

The actions the teams did during the different conflicts varied as much as the wars themselves did. Korea was a so-called police action. It never got finished. There wasn't a final victory that could be pointed to and described as the end of the war. Vietnam was much the same way. They were both wars of politics. The battles were not the same; there had been no opposed amphibious landings in Korea as there had been in WWII. There were major land battles in Korea, fought with the same kind of fire and maneuver tactics as had been used for centuries.

In Vietnam, there were very few major battles, none of which was like the great land engagements of WWII. The fights in Vietnam were conducted almost on a hand-to-hand basis, units engaging within close proximity to each other because of the thick jungles. And the enemy couldn't be pursued to a final confrontation. The guerrillas vanished into the population. Armed groups could not be chased past a certain point, borders were not to be crossed. Vietnam was a war of frustrations.

There were a lot of jobs and different hats I wore during my career in Special Warfare. I was the head of the training business at Little Creek, running the UDTR School where the new men would get qualified to enter the UDT. And there was an assignment to run a SERE School (Survival, Evasion, Resistance, and Escape) for a year. In 1966, I was sent out to the West Coast to take the position of commander of Special Warfare Group One (SpecWarGruOne) in Coronado.

In the SpecWarGruOne was a SEAL Team, the UDTs, and the Special Boat Unit. All of those units were being used in Vietnam at that time with different levels of involvement. As the commander of the group, I was responsible for carrying forward the training, our fleet commitments, and our new combat commitment in Vietnam. So the position managed to keep me pretty busy.

▓ Chapter 7

NCDU Assignments

By the fall of 1943, the first NCDU classes were graduating at Fort Pierce. Besides a number—NCDU 2, NCDU 127, etc.—each NCDU received a name based usually on its officer-in-charge, such as Kaine's Killers, Andrews's Avengers, etc. Officially, the training time for each of the first five NCDU classes was six weeks; later this schedule was increased to eight weeks in time for the sixth class.

The NCDUs from the first class of graduates were sent to Kiska, Alaska, the Southwestern Pacific, and the Mediterranean. NCDU 1 was sent under very secret orders to San Francisco, where they were to receive further transportation and assignment. NCDU 1 was to take part in the invasion of Kiska and other possible operations in the Aleutian Islands off Alaska. The NCDU never joined with the U.S. invasion forces prior to their unopposed landings on Kiska. The Japanese had gone. The men of NCDU 1 were later sent to the Central Pacific forces at Pearl Harbor. There, they ended as an NCDU and joined into the new UDTs.

The next two NCDUs left Fort Pierce for duties in the Southwestern Pacific as part of the Seventh Fleet on 8 September 1943. They were not to arrive in Australia until early January 1944. They were later joined by four additional NCDUs, making the NCDU detachment six units strong with thirty-six men total.

The first NCDU to arrive in England was NCDU 11, arriving in October 1943. They were the vanguard of what would be the largest concentration of NCDUs of the war. The frustrated men of the NCDU were assigned jobs such as guard duty, officer of the day, and other general tasks. No one knew who they were at the time, or what to do with them. This situation didn't start to really change until early in 1944. Until then, valuable training time was lost.

William L. Dawson, Gunner's Mate, Second Class

We came down to Fort Pierce in July and August 1943. In the group were forty-two men straight from boot camp in Bainbridge, Maryland, thirty-six Seabees from Camp Peary, and our officers, who came out of the Mine and Bomb Disposal School in Washington, D.C., including Draper Kauffman, who was our commanding officer. In spite of his rank, Commander Kauffman trained right alongside the rest of us when he wasn't in Washington taking care of one thing or another.

Originally, I had intended to be a submariner. I had finished my boot camp at Bainbridge and volunteered for Sub School up in New London, Connecticut. While I was waiting to be sent up to school, a pair of officers came in to Bainbridge and gave a bunch of us a talk about this new outfit they were putting together. The mission wasn't exactly described, but you would learn how to blow things up and generally be some kind of cloak-and-dagger man. Getting out of Bainbridge and leaving boot was what really appealed to me right about then. Another man and I went up to the officers later and asked if we could volunteer.

We were told that there were enough volunteers for the new program and no more men were needed right now. This didn't sit too well with the pair of us, so we slipped around to the back of the building where they were checking out the volunteers. There was an open window that we slipped through and quickly got into the end of the line. Out of all of the volunteers they had that day, forty-two men were picked and the pair of us were two of them.

Shortly after that adventure, the bunch of us were sent by train down to Fort Pierce, Florida, to start training. The two officers we had tried to volunteer with may have been from Bomb Disposal School, but we didn't see that pair for a while. But the officers we did have down at Fort Pierce didn't act quite like the others we had seen up in Bainbridge.

The officers in training with us had to do just exactly the same things we did, Commander Kauffman as well. They crawled through the mud and swatted insects right with the rest of us. Seeing that made me feel more like our officers were with me rather than being above me. And they could do the same things I could do. It made us feel a lot more like we wanted to follow them.

But we all had to lead in one way or another. During training, you could be coming in on a rubber boat and suddenly the surf would toss you and the men one way and dump the explosives the other way. Then some of the training officers might come up and say, "You're dead, and you're dead," while they pointed to members from your boat crew.

Then the "dead" guys would have to lie on the beach and let the sand flies and mosquitoes eat on them for a while. The rest of the guys in the boat crew would have to continue on and carry out the mission we were supposed to have been on. They would gather up the explosives, gear, boat, and do whatever they had to do to get the job done.

Before coming into the service, I had played a lot of football and baseball. And I considered myself to be in pretty good shape. By the time the trainers at Fort Pierce were done with me, I had muscles I never knew I had before. And I was certain about them because they all ached.

The training at Fort Pierce was considered pretty tough at the time by those of us who went through it. There were seven Army instructors, all of them sergeants, who had taken the British commando course over in England. It was these Army NCOs who set up our physical training course, setting up the two- or three-mile runs along the beach, log PT, and the obstacle course along with rubber boat drills, swimming, and a lot of calisthenics. They gave us a little bit of everything.

The workouts put me in much better shape than I had ever been in in my life. The people speak about Hell Week, which back then was the first week of training and officially called Indoctrination Week. For myself, I considered every week to be Hell Week. In spite of the heavy physical and mental demands put on us, we managed to make it through the training; at least a number of us did. Some men were dropped and others just couldn't keep up the pace. There were a lot fewer men at the end of training than first went into it. But we managed to make out.

There were about ten or more six-man NCDUs who completed the course with that first group of students. Some of the NCDUs were sent to the Pacific and others to the European theater. Our officer, Frank Kaine, had our unit, NCDU 2, join those heading to the Southwest Pacific and the Seventh Fleet. There, we found ourselves under the command of General Douglas MacArthur as part of his campaign against the Japanese.

For a long time it seemed no one knew who we were or what we were supposed to do. The upper command knew us and our mission, but we were so secret, no one on the local operational level had any idea about us. We would receive our orders, get on a ship, and go on an invasion. Once everything was done, we went back to our base and waited for the next set of orders. The bases changed quite a bit.

It seemed that we never stayed in any one base for more than a few months before we were on the move again. In about two years, we did twelve invasions—four in New Guinea, six in the Philippines, and two in Borneo.

Some of the operations weren't too bad. The troops just kind of walked ashore and there wasn't too much to worry about. We didn't find much in the way of obstacles and the enemy didn't put up a heavy resistance right on the beach. Other invasions were a little different.

But it was always pretty much the same for us. We swam in to beaches, made our reconnaissance, checked out piers for mines or booby traps, and blew open the way to the beach. It depended on what was needed; we blew coral reefs, sandbars, and anything else that was in the way. Personally, I thought we did a very good job.

Originally, we had been told we would be shipped out for six months and then returned to the States. That time grew a little bit and we stayed out in the South-western Pacific with MacArthur's forces until the end of the war. We were the only Navy NCDUs to remain such all through the war. Other NCDUs eventually joined into UDTs, but we stayed the same six-man units for the duration.

We were kept so busy on operations that it didn't seem like two years had gone by when it was all over. We had been very fortunate that none of us were hurt and we all got through the war okay.

Not that what we did was easy at all. Our first invasion was in the Admiralty Islands, and two NCDUs hit the beach right alongside the Army forces. We moved in on an LST along with twelve tons of explosives. We unloaded the explosives on the beach and just waited there. The Army told us to dig in before it got dark and wait until morning. So we dug a good, deep foxhole right there on the beach.

Eleven of us crawled into that hole and spent the night. It started to rain and our hole filled up with a bit of water. But that didn't do much to keep us awake. The noise from the machine gun fire and grenades going off all night long, that kept us from sleeping soundly. But the next morning, we were all there and had all managed to come out of it in one piece.

When we were in the foxhole on the beach that night, the machine guns and grenades just kept going off all night long. And it started to rain pretty hard, filling the hole we were in with water. We could just lie there all night in miserable conditions and listen to what was going on around us. My officer seemed to have a pretty bad cold, and the situation we were in wasn't doing it any good. I was more worried about him than about myself as the night wore on.

When you're lying there like that, under those conditions, a lot of things can run through your mind. It's hard to even say afterward what they were. But eventually, that night ended and we were able to continue our mission the next day.

A couple of days after that long night we were ordered to the harbor on the other side of the island. When we got over there, we found that there was a coral reef about twenty feet down going all the way across the channel into the harbor. The Army wanted the top of the reef knocked off so that the bigger ships could come right up on shore and unload.

It took us about two or three days to lay all of the powder, about four or five tons a day, that was needed to blow that reef down. We used some shallow-water diving gear; the Jack Brown canvas rig, as I remember it, came down over both your shoulders and had a full face mask. The rig was a rebreather and it had baralyme to purify the air you breathed along with an oxygen tank to replace what you used.

We used the diving gear to help us lay all the explosives along the top of the reef. When we fired the shot, we killed a small jewfish (grouper), which we took in to the Army camp up on the beach. They told us that if we could get any more, they would be glad to have them. They were eating combat rations and any kind of fresh food would be a treat.

The next shot we fired to clear the reef, we must have killed a dozen of those jewfish, some of them pretty big ones. It took seven men to pull this one fish into the bow of an LCM, then we dragged in two more. The Army brought a weapons carrier over with an A-frame hoist on the back of it, like a civilian wrecker truck.

The Army dragged the fish out of the boat and hoisted it up to the top of the A-frame. In spite of the nose of that fish being some ten feet in the air, its tail was still dragging on the ground. The next day, we were told the Army fed some 900 men with that one fish, and the two smaller ones fed the Seabee battalion. All told, they were very happy with both our demolition job and our fishing skills.

We were part of invasions at Los Negros, Aitape, Biak, and Numfoor in the New Guinea area. Then there was Leyte Gulf, Mindanao, Lingayen Gulf, Luzon, Zamboanga, and others in the Philippines. And finally Tarakan Island and Bunei Bay in Borneo. Leyte Gulf was one of our big operations. We went in about four days before D day to make our reconnaissance. We checked the depth of the water and made sure that the landing craft could get to the beach.

We were the guys who opened up the way, or made sure the chosen way in was clear. We would swim ashore if we had to and make a reconnaissance of the beach and the offshore waters. We would make notes if there were any obstacles, sandbars, coral reefs, or anything that would be in the way of the incoming landing craft.

Often enough, we didn't have much to do after we had gone in and conducted our recon. There just wouldn't be many obstacles, natural or man-made. The most common things we found were sandbars and coral reefs that were blocking a way in, especially for the bigger boats. Those blockages we had to blow out of the way.

We checked facilities that might already be at a site and that the command wanted to use. Checking piers for mines or booby traps had to be done before the ships could use them to unload.

What we did more than anything else was just to see if the way in to the beach was clear. Fortunately, we never lost anyone on one of our operations. Other teams on other missions in other places had men killed or wounded; we were lucky enough that everyone who was with us also went home.

Prior to one operation we were supposed to go on, we were up in Lingayen Gulf. A PT boat was supposed to pick us up and take us down to Manila, where there was a cable line across the entrance to the bay. Command wanted the cable cut and the buoys holding it up removed. They didn't know if it was a submarine net or what. So the PT that was to transport us would drop us at the cable and pick us up afterward. The only trouble was, the PT that was assigned to us had been shot up pretty badly making a run along the beaches earlier. So our part in that operation was canceled.

When we would be going in to a beach in a small boat, that was when you might think about what might happen. Thoughts of your home and your loved ones would go through your head. But if you think about those things too much, it can get in your mind and work on you. So you have to put such thoughts aside and concentrate on the mission.

We were there to do a job and on the way in to the beach you just had to put the possibilities out of your mind and go do what you had to do. That was the only way to get the whole thing over with.

We didn't have the training to roll over the side of the boats at speed, not like the UDTs did later in the war. What we did was just drop off the side of the boat, usually a small landing craft, and just swim in to the beaches. Depending on the operation we were on, the boat might just drop its bow ramp and we'd go into the water that way. All in all, we were very lucky and we just didn't hit that many places where the invasion beach was a real rough spot.

Later on, when the cast and recovery system had been developed by the UDT, getting in and out of the boat was much faster and safer. For us, we had only the six men in a unit. Two units working together, which was how we often operated, just made ten enlisted men and two officers. We would go in together and keep track of each other, but we didn't operate in assigned pairs or swim buddies. Mostly, we just swam on our own, and tried to keep everyone else in sight.

On one operation, we went in with a rubber boat full of explosives to blast an obstacle clear. On the swim in, a Japanese sniper opened fire on us. You could dive down to escape the fire, but not for very long. Eventually, you had to come back up for air and the sniper was there, ready to open fire. The only place we had to take cover from the sniper was behind the rubber boat and its load of explosives.

We lucked out again during that sniper episode when an Army patrol finally took the shooter out. Once the patrol had heard we were in trouble, they just went on the hunt for that sniper. And we appreciated what they did for us. We now could go back to our job, laying out explosives to blast a coral reef.

Not all of the military units we worked with acted the same. The Australians had their own way of conducting an invasion. They would hit the beach and soon have a fire going. On the fire would go a tin of water and they would brew themselves up some tea. We thought that was a pretty odd way to conduct an invasion. And every now and then, another Jap sniper would open fire and hit a couple of the Aussies. But that never discouraged them from making their tea.

Most of our operations occurred during the day, and we could see everything going on. When we found obstacles on our swims, we could usually see them pretty well. We didn't have the plastic slates and wax markers the UDT had, so we just made note of them being there and continued on.

Anytime we found obstacles that we would have to remove, we would get the explosives we needed to destroy them, usually a tetrytol pack or two, and load the target. If we had to, we would run a primacord main between multiple obstacles so we could fire them all together. The primacord would be set off with a fused cap, though sometimes we used electrical caps and a hell box.

For sandbars and coral reefs, we would lay bangalore torpedoes or Mark-8 rubber hose charges, whatever explosives we had left, and cap them. If we were using electric caps, we would reel out the electric line, clear the area, and blow the charge.

There was one time in the Admiralty Islands when we loaded a coral reef and the charge misfired. We set off the caps and nothing happened. These are not the best times to be a demo man, so we just left the charge until the next day. I made a straight dive down on the charge with a line. Tying the end of the line to the explosive hose charge would let us bring it back up and reprime for firing.

Just before I was to go into the water, a great big sea snake swam by. Sea snakes are among the most poisonous snakes in the world and I wasn't too sure I wanted to share the ocean with him. But after he went out of sight, I had to con-

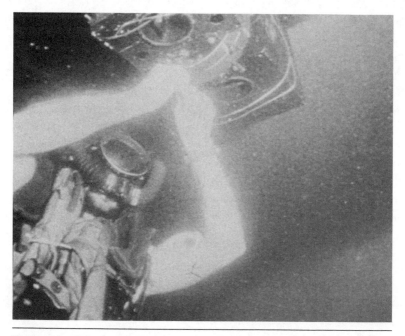

Wearing a closed-circuit rebreathing rig, a UDT operator arms a demolition charge underwater.

UDT-SEAL Museum

tinue with my job. So I swam down to the charge and tied on my line. We pulled the end of the hose back up, recapped it, and set off the charge. Fortunately, we didn't have many misfires, but that one with the snake was rather memorable.

There was often some rivalry between the Army and the Navy back in the States. Most of that was just in good fun. Out in the field during the war, there just weren't any real problems. We got along pretty well with the Army. When we were on the beach with them, there weren't any problems at all, other than some the Japanese might have tried to throw up at us.

We transferred a lot from one ship to another as we went on different invasions. A lot of things happened over those years. We did our jobs and opened the way for the Army. But there was one transfer to a ship that stands out and that was the one we boarded to go home.

Personally, I think the atomic bomb was a great thing. It saved a lot of American lives, ours in particular. We would have been lined up to go into Japan with the first waves. And there's no telling how many men would have been killed on that operation. My understanding is that the Japanese main islands were very well fortified. And we already knew that they were willing to fight to the bitter end. It's a good thing that never had to be tested; a lot of people would have died on both sides.

Most of the men I trained with were up to par. They did their jobs and they did them well, you could depend on them. And we had a lot of variety in the kind of people in our NCDU. One of the men in our unit was a full-blooded Comanche Indian I thought a lot of. His name was Sam Powderpony and he was a very good man to have alongside you in any situation. After the war he went back to Oklahoma. I had liked serving with him very much.

Our officers were all good officers. Sometimes you might not agree with what they did, but someone had to make the final decisions. All in all, you could describe our unit with the word excellence. We did what we had to do, we got the job done. And I think we did a good job.

Doing the kind of work we did, you didn't have a whole lot of time to think about what might happen. With the job at hand to concentrate on, you were just too busy to think about getting hurt or killed. If you were going to think about such things on the job, then you didn't belong in an outfit like ours. You can get killed anywhere and at any time. Just because we had a more hazardous job than the next guy didn't mean we should worry about it.

There doesn't seem to be a whole lot of difference between the basic man of the SEAL Teams today and what we were back during our day. The men today are much more highly trained than we were, and they have a very technical job with a lot of things to learn. But the man underneath all that equipment—he's the same.

■ Chapter 8

Tarawa

The invasion of Tarawa Atoll in late 1943 turned out to be a watershed event in the history of naval special warfare. The operation would remain well known to the Marine Corps and the Navy who took part in its execution. The name "Terrible Tarawa" was remembered through World War II and for some years afterward.

Rear Admiral Richmond Kelly Turner was in overall command of Operation GALVANIC, the invasion of the Gilbert Islands, including Tarawa Atoll. The taking of the Gilberts was planned to be one of the major openings of the Central Pacific campaign against the Japanese. General Douglas MacArthur would conduct his campaign against the Japanese up through New Guinea and the Philippines. The other point of the Allied two-pronged offensive against the Japanese would start with the Operation GALVANIC action. The emphasis on the Central Pacific holding the first major action was placed on Galvanic by the U.S. Joint Chiefs of Staff and the CNO, Admiral King.

Planning for the invasion of Tarawa was based on a number of intelligence sources, including charts, photographs, surveys, and the interrogation of people who were familiar with the area from prewar times. Aerial photographs of Tarawa were taken in September and October 1943. In addition, the submarine USS *Nautilus* conducted surveys of the offshore waters and beach emplacements at Tarawa in late September and early October. These studies filled in a host of missing hydrographic data on the offshore waters at Tarawa. Photographs taken through the submarine's periscope also showed the beaches in great detail.

Plans were made to land the initial waves of troops on Tarawa from tracked amphibious vehicles (LVTs). The limited number of the amphibious vehicles available would require that the follow-up troops be landed in LCVPs. Landings at Makin Atoll in the Gilberts were timed to take place simultaneously with the Tarawa actions.

On 20 November 1943, the landings on Betio, the main island of the Tarawa Atoll began. The first waves of LVTs faced heavy fire from the many Japanese fortifications that survived the preinvasion bombardment. The follow-up waves of LCVPs found a much worse problem than enemy fire. The reefs around Tarawa were covered by much less water than was planned for. An unusual tidal condition left many of the reefs with water far too shallow for the landing craft to cross.

Landing craft ran aground far from the shores of Betio Island. Heavily laden assault troops had to wade in to shore, sometimes hundreds of yards away, in the face of heavy enemy fire. More Marines drowned in the waters off Tarawa during the landings than were killed by enemy fire taking the island itself in over three days of combat. Admiral Turner swore that the mistakes that led to Tarawa earning the nickname "Terrible Tarawa" would not be repeated.

The Creation of the UDTs

In the first week of November 1943, just prior to Operation GALVANIC and the invasion of Tarawa, the Fifth Amphibious Force, under Real Admiral Turner, was directed to begin the organization and specialized training of demolition personnel. The training was to be such that the demolition specialists would be able to clear natural coral formation obstacles as well as man-made obstacles and mines from future invasion beaches. A limited number of men from the Seabees had already been gathered at Waimanolo, Oahu, to form a cadre to train additional demolition personnel. The Seabees were the only Pacific naval unit available at that time that had practical coral blasting experience.

The initiative for this training action was reported to have come from the commander-in-chief, Pacific Fleet, Admiral Chester Nimitz's office, in a letter sent to Admiral Turner dated 11 November 1943.

In the aftermath of Operation GALVANIC, in late November, Admiral Turner pushed forward two directives to prevent a repeat of the offshore problems at Tarawa. Turner's first, and most time-constrained, directive required the immediate formation of two Underwater Demolition Teams. The two teams were to be ready for action by the middle of January 1944. The second directive was for the establishment of a secure base in the Hawaiian Islands for the further training of UDTs. This base would later become the Naval Underwater Demolition Training and Experimental Base, Maui.

By the end of November, approximately 30 officers and 150 enlisted men were in training at Waimanolo, Oahu, for underwater demolition work. These men were divided into UDTs 1 and 2. The bulk of the personnel came from NCDUs sent to Hawaii for operations in the Pacific. The balance of the personnel came from the Seabees, Marines (20), and Army (4).

In a letter to Admiral Turner on 9 December, Admiral Nimitz directed that replicas of known Japanese beach obstacles be included in the training going on at Waimanolo. During a 17 December meeting with a joint-force Reef Obstacle and Mine Committee, founded only a few weeks earlier, Admiral Turner dis-

A UDT combat swimmer tows a floating demolition charge into the beach during an exercise. On the beach are a pair of UDT swimmers already loading steel rail obstacles with explosives. Additional charges will be used to knock down the log wall farther up the beach.

U.S. Navy

cussed the type of unit that would be required to clear coral as well as man-made obstacles from invasion beaches. It was during that meeting that the term *Underwater Demolition Team* was mentioned for the first time to identify the new unit as separate from the existing NCDUs and Seabees.

The new UDTs were formed up and preparing for their first actions by mid December 1943. The new teams consisted of fourteen officers and seventy enlisted men each and were numbered UDTs 1 and 2. UDT 2 was put under the command of Lieutenant Commander J. T. Koehler. On 23 December, UDT 2 was ordered to San Diego. Once in the States, UDT 2 was attached to Task Force 53, under the command of Rear Admiral Richard Conolly, for Operation FLINTLOCK, the invasion of Roi and Namur in the Marshall Islands. UDT 1 remained in training at Waimanolo, where they were to be assigned to Task Force 52. Admiral Turner was in direct command of Task Force 52, which would attack Kwajalein as part of Operation FLINTLOCK.

In a message to the CNO on 26 December, Admiral Turner requested the creation of the UDTs as active units. This was several days after Turner directed that UDT 2 be sent on to San Diego to prepare for Operation FLINTLOCK. The breach in military protocol was ignored and permission was issued.

On 29 January 1944, Operation FLINTLOCK began with the invasion of several smaller islands in the Kwajalein Atoll, the largest coral atoll in the world. By 1 February, the invasion of the two islands of Roi and Namur commenced. Under the cover of darkness, UDT 2 moved in to the islands in rubber boats. Testing the depth of the waters over the reef, UDT 2 operators didn't find any mines or other obstacles. The UDT 2 report to the Marines was that the way in was clear. After a very heavy shore bombardment by naval gunfire, the Marines experienced few difficulties or resistance against their late morning landings.

A further target of Operation FLINTLOCK, the invasion of Kwajalein also started on 1 February. During their offshore reconnaissance of Kwajalein, several members of UDT 1 took to the water, going over the side of their landing craft and swimming in over the reefs to check its depth directly. UDT 1 reported the depth of the water as shallow over large coral heads. Tracked landing vehicles were used to land Marine forces because of the UDT's findings. Postinvasion blasting by the UDTs opened paths in to the beaches at Kwajalein through the coral reefs, allowing faster landing of additional men and material.

In March, after Operation FLINTLOCK had been completed, UDTs 1 and 2 were decommissioned. The men and officers were broken up to supply a training cadre with combat experience for the new Maui training base. They also created an experienced core group for newly commissioned UDTs 3, 4, 5, 6, and 7 to be assembled around. The new UDTs would soon see action during Operation FORAGER, the upcoming invasion of the Marianas Islands. At this

Two UDT combat swimmers place a limpet mine on the keel of a ship during a practice swimmer attack in 1965. The ring of magnets around the base of the mine will hold it securely to the steel hull of the ship.

U.S. Navy

Having been attacked by UDT combat swimmers during a practice live-fire limpet mine operation, this ship splits in half and soon sinks to the bottom.

time it was decided that the UDTs would be completely manned with naval personnel except for liaison officers and observers.

On 14 and 15 March 1944, two basic letters covering the organization of the UDT training base in Maui and the UDTs themselves were issued by Vice Admiral Turner as the commander of the Fifth Amphibious Force, Pacific Fleet. The UDT concept was now established and proven. UDTs would continue to be commissioned to the end of the war.

Robert P. Marshall Jr., Commander, USN (Ret.)

The main part of our physical training at Fort Pierce initially came from the Scout and Raider School. Draper Kauffman had come down to examine the Fort Pierce ATB as a possible NCDU training site. He spent a week with the Scouts and Raiders to see what their physical training program consisted of. Then he returned to his own command and instituted a program that paralleled what the S&R people were doing.

Lieutenant Bill Flynn was the training officer for the NCDU School during its first months. He may have brought in some S&R PT instructors for a limited time. But we had Navy personnel running our PT program fairly early on. Captain Gulbranson, the commanding officer of the Fort Pierce Amphibious Base, had good contacts with various athletic teams and other Navy programs. He was also able to help the

NCDU School get the qualified people it needed to put together a very rugged and complete physical training program.

Our training at the NCDU School began with a lot of the typical physical training exercises. Included with the usual calisthenics and running were log exercises in which a group of us would move a large chunk of telephone pole through different maneuvers. We would also paddle, drag, and carry our rubber boats through the lagoons and swamps, crossing the whole of North Island.

As training continued, Bill Flynn would add his own special touches, mostly by throwing lit half-sticks of dynamite at us.

We also had an old house that stood on posts some two and a half or three feet above the sand that was used as a form of obstacle. We would have to squat down and duck-waddle underneath that building. That's the exercise I most blame for my bad knees today.

But we also marched or ran through the sand and the water a great deal. We would carry M-1 carbines with us on the marches. Although not the largest rifle in the world, even the M-1 carbine could get heavy over a long distance.

There was very little swimming at that time in our training. Most of our actions were done from rubber boats, also called the LCR or Landing Craft, Rubber. The LCPRs (Landing Craft, Personnel, Ramped) we had would take us out to sea out the inlet between North and South Hutchinson islands. When we launched our rubber boats, we would paddle in to shore until the water was about knee-deep. At that point we would get out of the rubber boats and slip in the rest of the way on foot. Then we would conduct our demolition operations against the obstacles a Seabee detachment had constructed for us.

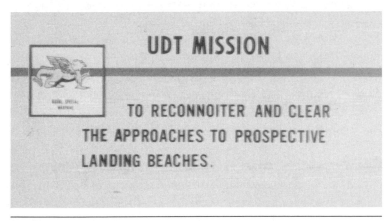

A single slide from an originally classified briefing series on the Navy SEALs and Naval Special Warfare.

U.S. Navy

There was kind of a constant battle between the men of the NCDUs and the Seabee detachment. They were always trying to build obstacles that we couldn't blow up, at least not with the explosives we could carry with us. But they kept building them and we kept blowing them up. With shaped charges and high explosives we could just destroy anything they could make.

At Fort Pierce, we went through training as a group, but hadn't been assigned to a single unit yet. We would work in our rubber boats with a crew picked for that day, normally one officer and four or five men to a crew.

What we called Hell Week then was our final exam, officially called the Jen-Stu-Fu problem. After that weeklong problem, which was the eighth week of training, the next step we took was to join up as an official, numbered Naval Combat Demolition Unit of one officer and five men. The building up of an NCDU was done in a very unique way that was developed and promoted by Draper Kauffman.

All of the group officers who were going to lead an NCDU had the opportunity to interview the people who were going to be available for their units. It was from that pool of qualified people that they would build up their own NCDU. All of the officers, including myself, sat down in front of the stage one afternoon and spoke to the men available.

Each enlisted man would come up and describe himself to us, listing his qualifications and skills. He would tell us where he was from, how old he was, and just what all of his credentials were. We had known these men pretty well already from our earlier training together.

After we had talked to and heard from everyone, we would put down on a list the five men we would like for our boat crew. Then we had to put down five more men that we would accept into our crew. Taking all of our lists with our primary and secondary choices, Draper and his staff would try to give us as many of the specific men we wanted as possible. Not everyone could be satisfied; the best had to be divided up a bit. But it was a good system and it promoted unit integrity.

Usually, an officer would get a couple of the men he really wanted on his crew, and the balance were men who were completely acceptable. But the selection process didn't end there. The enlisted men had the opportunity to turn down their assignment to any particular officer. That was a unique and wonderful way of instilling a team spirit and level of camaraderie right away that no other unit in the service used.

After the men and the officers were selected and the units made up, they were assigned a number and usually made up a name for themselves. The name would be something based on the officer's name followed by a descriptive word such as Kane's Killers, Heideman's Hurricanes, etc. If my NCDU had a name, I just don't remember it. It could have been something like Marshall's Marauders. Our number was NCDU 92.

At the time of our graduation, we had a choice between the European theater or the Pacific. At that time the ETO was considered to be the one that would be the most active. Besides choosing the men that they wanted, Draper also gave each NCDU officer the opportunity to express his preference for which theater he wanted to operate in.

For myself and a great number of other officers, our choice was the ETO. Draper knew a great deal more information than we did as to just what was going on in the war and he knew that the Pacific theater was going to be a very active area. And if he had his way, Draper Kauffman was going to see action in the Pacific with some of the men he trained.

Draper picked and chose a little bit about who would go where. And it was through these machinations of his that I and my NCDU received orders for the Central Pacific area. Looking back at how well things turned out for me in the Pacific, I think I might not be around today if I had gone to the ETO and ended up on the Normandy beaches. When the NCDUs were shipped out, I ended up in the Pacific and my best friend, Ensign George Gallinlock, was sent with his unit to England and eventually Normandy, where he was killed in the landings.

We took a troop train out of Fort Pierce on the first leg of our journey west. The train had something like twelve cars and we were going to be on it all the way across the country. Being resourceful troops, we had secreted about the train a few bottles of beverages to ease the trip for us. But we had forgotten to get any orange juice as a mixer. Warrant Officer "Doc" Barge was the last person to board the train; he was running down the railroad tracks as the train was starting to pull out, a case of oranges on his shoulder.

Doc made it onto the observation deck at the end of the train and we pulled him aboard. It was a long trip, all the way across the country, but we finally made it to our last stop in San Francisco more or less in one piece. There was a layover of some four or five days for us in town while our transportation further west was being arranged. Our party in San Francisco was brought to an abrupt end when it was announced that our ship was ready and we were pulling out.

We left San Francisco Harbor and traveled under the Golden Gate Bridge in fair style. The government had chartered the Matsonia, a civilian cruise ship, to act as a transport for the duration. Not only did we cross the Pacific to Hawaii on a civilian cruise liner, but we had good food and even better company. The living accommodations were crowded, but this was because of all of the troops on board. Included in this crowd was the first contingent of WACs (Women's Army Corps) to serve overseas as well as a thirty-two-woman contingent of Red Cross nurses.

So we spent a very interesting weeklong cruise to Honolulu. For a while we were billeted in one of the great hotels in Hawaii and we managed to conduct some unofficial reconnaissance operations to the area where the Red Cross ladies we had met aboard ship were stationed. After another short week of these adventures, we were placed aboard an LST and taken to Maui, where we would undergo further training.

The invasions at Tarawa had come and gone, but the lessons learned there had not been forgotten. The lack of hydrographic reconnaissance on the offshore waters at Tarawa had been very costly to the U.S. forces. Besides the lack of some very basic information on the reefs off Tarawa, there was no proper way to forecast tides for an unknown shoreline. Between the reefs and the low tides, a lot of landing craft had run aground and a lot of Marines never made it in to the beach.

The high command out in the Pacific, with Admiral Turner in charge of the amphibious operations, told Draper Kauffman that he had to develop the capacity to accurately measure the depths of the water off invasion beaches using swimmers in the water. This information was to be delivered to the high command in the form of accurate charts prior to H hour on D day.

A lot of the reefs that were to be examined could be a mile or more offshore of an island. So the people who were going to do the reconnaissance had to be good swimmers. The plan was to take the men of the NCDUs and reorganize and retrain them into Underwater Demolition Teams or UDTs. The men of the UDTs would have to be good swimmers, and that was the immediate training emphasis at the very new Navy Combat Demolition Training and Experimental Base at Maui.

We found out that we were going to have to do these long offshore recons of invasion beaches when we arrived at Maui. Now, instead of working from rubber boats as we had at Fort Pierce, we were swimming every day. There were long swims of at least a mile in the bay at Maui. There were swims later in our training where we went halfway to Lanai, the next island and some ten or fifteen miles away, before turning back.

Even though he was a very poor swimmer, Draper Kauffman worked right alongside the rest of us, swimming along in the water. Kauffman had come out from Fort Pierce to see some of the action with the men he had trained, and he wasn't the kind of officer to just sit back in a desk job if there was anything he could do about it. But he just wasn't a very good swimmer. In fact, in the group of us who were undergoing training, there was only one swimmer who was worse than Draper, and that was me.

Draper Kauffman was the designated CO of Underwater Demolition Team 5 when we went through training. UDTs 1 and 2 had already done their operations just a short time earlier and some of the men from those teams were our instructors.

The first two UDTs had proved the concept. Now our mission was being expanded with the requirement to do additional hydrographic reconnaissance. While we were training in Maui, Draper Kauffman developed the string reconnaissance method of measuring the water's depth accurately so that charts could later be made.

The string reconnaissance system was developed and refined late in our training. UDT 5 had been formed and we were getting ready to leave for our first operation when Draper finally perfected the system to his satisfaction. We were still making some of the equipment we needed when we boarded our transport ship, the APD Gilmer.

On board the Gilmer, we had all the strings and lead weights the individual swimmers would use. In addition, we had these galvanized steel drums, one-gallon fruit cans really, that we built into reels to hold the guideline. Boards nailed onto the ends of the fruit cans made up the reels, and the lines were knotted in a pattern that let them be used for measuring distance. All of this material had to be finished before we arrived at our target for Operation FORAGER, the invasion of Saipan in the Marianas Islands.

The string reconnaissance system used a base line of heavy sting or light line, much like twine, that we measured, knotted, and wound on reels. There would be 1,000 feet of line on every reel, knotted in a repeating pattern for measurement. After a given length of the line had been measured and knotted, a colored rag would be tied to the line and the knot pattern repeated. This was done every 100 feet for the length of the line.

The line from the reel would be anchored on the reef at one end, and then swum out and unrolled. Swimmers would then swim out on a line, evenly spaced out at known distances along the main line from the reel. Each swimmer had a small line, like heavy fish line, wrapped around his wrist with a small lead fishing sinker on one end. The lead line was only about 10 feet long and was marked in one-foot increments. Each swimmer would drop his lead line at regular intervals and then write down the depth of the water on a plastic (Plexiglas) slate with a grease pencil. Notes would also be taken about any obstacles and other observations the swimmer might make.

This string reconnaissance system was reasonably simple and no one improved on the basic system for decades. Though they were not used at Fort Pierce at all, we had been introduced to swim fins (flippers) at Maui along with diver's face masks, which were very simple round ones with a small plate of glass in the front. No snorkles, breathing gear, or any sophisticated equipment at all.

Many systems used later by the UDTs hadn't been developed when we did our first operations in the middle of June 1944 at Saipan. Cast and recovery was still very basic. We rolled off in pairs from a rubber boat tied to the port side of our LCPR to get into the water. After our operation was over, we were pulled on board the rubber boat with the LCPR stopped in the water during the pickup.

The LCPR simply sitting there while the swimmers were pulled on board made it very vulnerable to enemy fire. It was a sitting duck really for the people on the shore. That was the reason that the sling pickup method was developed, to give the LCPR a way of picking up the swimmers from the water while remaining under way.

Once at Saipan for the operation, UDT 5 was spread out along about 600 yards of beach. Our beach was one of the ones code-named Green and our mission was to map the offshore waters. We conducted a string reconnaissance, the first one done off an enemy-held beach.

The LCPRs from our APD took us in to about 500 to 600 yards from the offshore reefs. Then we swam in to the reef, deployed our string lines, and then swam in to the beach itself.

The enemy forces on Saipan saw us and opened fire almost immediately. Mostly it was machine guns that were firing at us, along with the occasional mortar. That situation really brought it home to me that this was for keeps; those people on the island wanted nothing better than to kill us all.

Most of the machine gun fire would either ricochet off the water, or dig in and then sink vertically. The bullets would only zip into the water a couple of feet and then just sink to the bottom. A number of them dropped past my face as I was swimming underwater.

At that time I had modified my face mask with a toothbrush holder (tube) glued into the top of the mask. The holder acted a bit like a snorkle, long before they were available. Things leaked a bit, but it did work in a way.

We were operating in plain sight of the enemy, well out in the open. But UDT 5 was lucky right from the start. Our commanding officer was Draper Kauffman, which didn't directly affect us. But Draper's father was Admiral Kauffman and he was not only an admiral, he was COMCRUDESPAC (Commander, Cruisers, Destroyers, Pacific). It could have been normal, paternal concern on the part of Draper's father that resulted in our getting very extensive fire support covering us. Especially since most of the fire seemed to come from cruisers and destroyers.

The heavy guns from the offshore ships kept peppering the Jap positions on Saipan all the time that we were operating in the water. The enemy fire directed at us would surely have been much heavier if the ships hadn't been putting out their all to protect us.

We did have one fatality on our first operation, along with seven wounded. Off of Saipan was the only time we deployed what were called the "flying mattresses." These were inflatable rubber mats maybe eight or nine feet long with a storage battery and an electric motor driving a small propeller. The flying mattresses could each carry two men, one to operate the craft and the other to observe.

The idea of the flying mattresses was that the leadership of the UDT, our officers, would be using them. On the mattress would be one enlisted man, a radio, an M-1 carbine, and whatever else they might need. The officer could stay in communication with support while the enlisted man drove the craft. Then the officers could direct the men of the UDT platoons during their operations. What we found out was that the flying mattresses also made marvelous targets for the enemy.

Draper was on one of the mattresses with his enlisted man also acting as something of a Seeing Eye dog, Kauffman's eyesight being so poor. Ensign Bill Running was also on one of the mattresses with his enlisted man (EM), a man named Christensen. A machine gun bullet killed Christensen while Running never received a scratch. That was our only loss during the whole operation, in spite of four of the mattresses being hit.

For the invasion proper, the first waves were planned to be infantry to move in and hold the beach. Soon after the infantry landing, the plan was for tanks to come in and act as close-in fire support to the troops on shore and begin driving in from the beach. This mobile artillery was limited to the depth of the water it could cross after the landing craft had released them. A lot of the water in the lagoon on the island side of the reefs was going to be a lot deeper than the tanks could accept.

During our reconnaissance, we didn't find any man-made obstacles, only natural ones. We measured and charted out the reef, which also wound through the lagoon a bit as well. What we found was a winding path through the reef that was less than the maximum depth the tanks could cross. The path was plain enough on the chart we made, but the tanks couldn't easily follow the route we would put up on the chart.

An ensign by the name of Jack Adams climbed on board one of the lead tanks during the invasion and led the armored column over the path in the reef. Sitting on the turret, Adams told the driver of the tank how to move and went in all the way to the beach, dropping off buoys behind them to mark the path. In spite of his very exposed position, Jack got through his pathfinding experience without being hurt.

Our post-D-day work involved blowing open a path through the blocking reef to allow landing craft to come in and unload right on shore. By using very large charges of Mark-8 explosive hose on D days plus one, two, and three, we were able to blow open direct channels in the coral reef.

After Saipan was secured and our channels blown, UDT 5 was going to move on to Tinian and work on the planning for operations there. Draper was to assist in picking a possible landing beach. The choice was to be made of a beach that wasn't the most obvious one, read that easiest to land on. Instead, command wanted the beach to be usable, but not one that was blocked either naturally or with man-made obstacles and needing demolition to open the way.

The scouting technique was a fast one. Draper was put up in the nose of a torpedo plane and taken on a flight over parts of Tinian. The plane would dive on likely beaches and Draper would note the likelihood of their being used, along with notes on the amount of antiaircraft fire they took from the surrounding jungle.

The enemy we fought was a hard one. At the time we considered the Japanese a very dangerous enemy, one who would go to any lengths to accomplish their goals. And the Japanese troops were very devoted to their leadership, from the emperor to their officers. They would, and did, often fight to the death. Outside of that, we didn't really have any other feelings toward the enemy we were fighting.

All of the Teams, not just UDT 5, showed a cohesiveness that was remarkable. Some have said that we depended on our buddies to help us get the job done. But it was more than that, we depended on the Team as a whole, not just any of its parts. Virtually every man of the Team, with few if any exceptions, would work with any other member of the Team. You knew you would get the full support of your Teammate, and he could expect the same of you.

A WWII UDT person was in good shape, and we worked hard to stay that way so we could do our job. Unlike today, we had the stimulation of an ongoing war to help us give everything we had, plus whatever more was needed. We were in for the duration, until we defeated the enemy. Even with our motivations, we never did reach the level of physical fitness of the SEALs today. But they are also young and enthusiastic, just as we were then.

When the war finally came to an end, I had left UDT 5 and been promoted. I was the CO of UDT 3 when the war ended and we arrived at Japan itself. My Team landed at Wakayama, Japan, at the end of the war and conducted a normal combat operation with a string reconnaissance and the whole works.

When we finally got to the beach, there was a whole local delegation of Japanese to meet us. The group was led by some dignitaries—they may have been the mayor and other leaders for all I know, wearing formal dress including top hats. They were quite friendly as a group and there wasn't any sign of a military presence. The group was led by a young Japanese lady who spoke perfect English. When I later asked her where she learned such good English, she told me, "the University of Southern California."

Such was the world before the war. But we were almost welcomed rather than just politely met by this group of civilians. I think they had had just about enough of the war and were as glad to see it end as we were. Some of us were welcomed into the homes of the local people. The war was finally over and we all seemed pretty glad of it.

■ Chapter 9

Normandy and Southern France

The main target of the NCDUs was always planned to be the invasion of Europe and the breaching of Hitler's Atlantic wall. As NCDU units graduated from training at Fort Pierce, they were assigned in increasing numbers to the European theater of operations. Orders regarding the specific mission of the NCDUs were issued in England and the units gathered for training against more specific targets.

One of the targets facing the men of the NCDUs was known as the Belgian Gate or Element C. This massive steel construction was known to be part of the obstacles scattered along the French invasion beaches. Element C was ten feet high, ten feet wide, and fourteen feet long. Built of six-inch-wide steel angle iron that was one-half-inch thick, a single Element C looked like a huge piece of picket fence and weighed close to three tons. And the obstacles could be linked together in long chains, creating a wall of steel posts.

Element C, the Belgian Gate of Normandy Beach. This replica was used by the NCDUs to train in how to demolish the huge steel obstacles. Demolition techniques and materials first designed to knock down this target in 1944 are still in use in the Teams today.

UDT-SEAL Museum

Long experiments with different demolition techniques finally resulted in a way to blast Element C into a pile of steel rubble without turning it into a lot of lethal flying fragmentation. Lieutenant Carl Hagensen was part of the crew that developed a special charge, sixteen of which could be quickly applied to a single Element C and collapse in one blast. The new explosive charge was made up of Composition C-2, a plastic explosive, packaged in a small canvas bag. During development of the charge, old wool socks were used to hold the explosive before the canvas bags were sewn up.

Now called the Hagensen Pack, the new explosive charges held two pounds each of C-2 explosive and could be very quickly attached to many kinds of targets. The primacord used to detonate the Hagensen Pack could be quickly tied to another long main line of primacord and an unlimited number of charges set off simultaneously. Prior to their operations during the Normandy invasions, men of the NCDUs would spend days assembling thousands of Hagensen Packs for use against the known beach obstacles.

On June 6, 1944, the largest amphibious operation in history began. The target of the huge Allied armada was the beaches of Normandy, France. The U.S. targets were the beaches code-named Utah and Omaha. The initial plan called for waves of infantry and then tank armored support to land first. Under the cover of these units, the men of the NCDUs, reinforced with Army Engineer troops and Navy volunteers, would blast gaps through the beach obstacles. The plan didn't quite go the way it was intended. On Utah beach, the NCDUs and their Army counterparts were able to blast the majority of

From the troop well of an LCVP can be seen the first waves of troops going to shore on Normandy Beach. On the shore ahead of the troops are the men of the NCDUs charging obstacles with explosives.

National Archives/U.S. Coast Guard

their assigned obstacles out of the way quickly. On Omaha Beach, the situation was different.

At Omaha, the German resistance was very heavy and losses among the U.S. troops built up quickly. In spite of the inferno of steel and explosions all around them, the men of the NCDUs worked feverishly to blast open gaps through the beach obstacles. The armored support in the form of tanks never made it to the beach, most either sinking on launch or quickly being destroyed by German fire.

In the first day of the landings, a thousand U.S. soldiers were killed, the large majority on a piece of beach now known as "Bloody Omaha." On that blood-soaked ground, 31 NCDU men were killed and 60 wounded. Over 50 percent of the NCDUs assigned to Omaha were casualties. On Utah Beach, six men were killed and 11 wounded.

In the months after D day at Normandy, the NCDUs from Utah Beach were transferred to the Mediterranean theater to join in Operation DRAGOON, the invasion of southern France. On 15 August 1944, the men of the Utah Beach NCDUs joined with the NCDUs who had already been sent to the Mediterranean. The thirty NCDUs joined with the Allied forces in the landings on the French Riviera. These operations went smoothly, for which the veteran NCDU men were thankful.

Some of the NCDU men who survived the D day invasion at Normandy. Two of the men on the left in the front row have obtained M1 Thompson submachine guns. The two-inch-wide gray band on their helmets identified them as Navy personnel during the invasion.

National Archives

No losses were taken by the NCDU personnel as they completed clearing the landing beaches of obstacles. Soon after some postinvasion demolition, the men of the NCDUs were sent back to the United States. There, a number of the men returned to their original units or remained with the NCDUs and moved on to the Pacific and the UDTs.

Myron F. Walsh, Chief Shipfitter

Up in Camp Peary, Lieutenant Kauffman and another officer came by one day recruiting for a new unit. When he asked me if I would like to be in it, I said yes. Then there were some other questions; What's your name? What's your age? Can you swim? Are you single?

It was that last question I had a problem with. At that time I wasn't single and they told me that I couldn't be used. That got me mad a bit and after some argument I was told that they would get back to me. They did contact me to tell me that I was accepted. It may be that I was the first married NCDU man with a small child at home.

We arrived at Fort Pierce in late July–early August 1943. When we arrived at South Hutchinson Island, where the base was located, there were just a few tents and not much else. Groups of up to ten of us were assigned to a tent and we quickly settled in. The next morning we had another introduction to Fort Pierce when we arrived at breakfast. Breakfast wasn't fancy, just a bowl of cereal served on a table that was just a board nailed on some upright posts.

Before you could even eat your food, the sand fleas would get into it and almost turn the cereal black. That was okay, we could skip the cereal. But after a couple of days you were hungry enough that the bugs didn't matter.

In training, I didn't have a lot of trouble or pain. I figured if someone else had done it, so could I. Some of the workouts could be hard. One day of training they might have a three-mile run along the beach. The end of that run could be a 200-yard sprint to see if you could beat the guy next to you. That kind of thing could tire you out. But so could the log PT and the obstacle course. But none of it really got to me very badly.

Training was rough enough with the PT, the work we had to do, and just the local environment. But the hardest part of training was the mental end. You had to keep yourself going. I was pretty lucky in that my wife had come down to Fort Pierce. During some of our free time, I had her to talk to and get back to my senses. The other guys could only lie in their bunks and think over the events of the day.

During our training, I don't remember ever working with the Scouts and Raiders. We were told that we had to be vigilant at night. The S&R people were known to sneak into our camp and wreak a little havoc as infiltration practice. Personally, I never had any trouble with them at all. Other than their being at the ATB, there just didn't seem to be a lot of contact between the Scouts and Raiders and the NCDU.

I was all of twenty years old when I became involved with the Navy and the NCDU. Like many around me, I was gung ho, ready to do anything and to fight for my country. Most of us couldn't wait to get into combat; we feared nothing. Looking back on it now, I think we were more or less just ignorant about the whole thing.

After we landed in Normandy and saw everything that happened there, and then went on to southern France, well, we weren't ignorant anymore.

All of us in our group, or any of the NCDUs, were like a band of five or six brothers. There wasn't any rank between the officers and the men when it came to doing the job; Commander Kauffman wouldn't tolerate that. The officers had to stand in line for chow just like the rest of us. You double-timed to the chow line, and if you were slow, you were at the end of the line no matter what your rank. Demolition was kind of equal opportunity that way.

On graduation from training, NCDU 127, myself included, was assigned to what they called the JANET board. JANET for Joint Army Navy Experimental Test. The JANET board had their officers off post in the Peacock building in Fort Pierce itself. Lieutenant Padgett, our officer, along with our crew would do the fieldwork for the board. The JANET office would call our officer in and explain whatever experiment it wanted done. Then we would go to North Hutchinson Island and do it.

The board might have some new beach mines in from the Pacific they wanted tested. They might be looking for a certain way that we might be able to get rid of them safely. That was our first assignment with JANET and there were all kinds of other projects following that.

There were other NCDU units assigned to JANET along with us. There was Lieutenant Jeeter's unit, along with Lieutenant Frank Hunds's and Lieutenant Hunt's NCDUs. All told, there were four NCDUs assigned to the JANET board while I was there. After a month or two of working with the JANET board, we were reassigned to the new Demolition Research Unit (DRU). JANET had been a joint Army–Navy project while the DRU was mostly a Navy matter.

While the DRU mostly worked on Navy projects, we did work on some Army jobs. A lot of these jobs involved rockets. We put rocket launchers on tanks and on boats. We fit LCMs (Landing Craft, Mechanized) with 120 launchers for 7.2-inch TNT-filled rockets for close-in fire support at landings. These LCMs full of rockets we called "Woofus" boats.

In March 1944, our NCDU (127) received orders to immediately fly out of Fort Pierce and head to Europe. We flew down to Miami, from there to New York, and then boarded a ship for England. We landed in Wales and were moved through England up to Scotland. We were finally stationed at what was supposedly one of the king's retreats up there.

After several weeks in Scotland, we were transferred to Salcombe way down near the southern end of England. There, we met up with the other NCDUs who had been sent over well before us. At Salcombe, we started our specific training for Normandy, though we didn't know that name yet.

A lot of the experience we had developed at Fort Pierce with the JANET board and the DRU came in handy now. We had worked a lot with the new Composition C and C2 plastic explosive and that's what we were going to use in a new packaged charge.

A Lieutenant Toomey had originally come up with the idea of using Composition C2 explosive in a canvas pack as a demolition charge. Lieutenant Carl Hagensen had taken the original idea and developed it into a quickly attached charge that was primed with primacord. That charge was soon called a Hagensen Pack and adopted as the Mark-20 demolition charge. We used a lot of Hagensen Packs at Normandy. In the small world of demolition, I had previously worked with Lieutenant Carl Hagensen in training at Fort Pierce, and even earlier while with the Seabees up at Camp Peary.

The Hagensen charge was developed from chunks of C2 rolled out into lengths. A couple of folds of primacord would be buried in the center of a two-pound chunk of C2 to prime it for detonation. Then you would stuff the whole charge into a flexible container. We used old socks to start with, then sewed canvas containers were made up for the charges. A length of line would close off the sock or container, with the long primacord lead hanging out of the charge. Some extra length of the tie-off line was left on to quickly attach the charge to the target.

We experimented with tying blocks of wood to the primacord leads on the Hagensen Packs. You'd dive down on a target, tie the charge to it, and let the block of wood float up with the primacord behind it. Then another man with a big roll of primacord would trail it along and attach all of the leads to it. Then all of the charges could be detonated together.

Finally, sometime in late May, we were all moved into a marshaling area. No one could come or go once they were in the area without being on official business. There, we were told that we were all getting ready to go into France. They still didn't tell us about Normandy. We didn't learn that name until the invasion was under way.

But we still had a lot of work to do before leaving for the invasion. There were thousands of Hagensen Packs to be made up to use against the beach obstacles. They let us out of the town, to a farmer's field, about six or eight miles outside of Salcombe. In the field, we set up these long tables with piles of explosive, containers, lines, and primacords. There we spent days making up Hagensen Packs.

One day, the person in charge of the detail gave us a break and told us we were all going into town for lunch. This sounded pretty good to us and there wasn't anyone around to bother our gear. So we just left the explosives and everything and went in to eat. There was this big pile of Composition C2 on the table, just sitting there like a big lump of brown clay.

When we got back from lunch, all of that bulk Comp C was gone. No one could figure out what had happened; the area was secure, so no one had just come up and stolen it. We were puzzled for a time until someone figured out that the local farmer's cows had eaten the sweetish-tasting explosive. That made for an interesting little while as we stayed in the field working, wondering if a cow was going to blow up at any moment.

We not only needed a lot of Hagensen Packs to open the beaches, it had been decided earlier that we also needed more men. So the Army engineers worked with us to get the job done. The Army was going to help us so far, and then we would do our part of the operation. The Army guys would also be a big help just moving all of the explosives we needed.

We were transported to within range of Normandy on an LST (Landing Ship, Tank). About 0130 or 0230 hours the morning of the invasion, we went over the side of the LST and climbed down cargo nets to board our waiting LCVP (Landing Craft, Vehicle/Personnel). There was only one unit to a VP as we called that type of landing craft. Our whole unit was called a GAT for Gap Assault Team and consisted of our NCDU of five enlisted and one officer, three Navy seamen volunteers, and five Army engineers, fourteen men total. With all of our explosives and rubber boat on board the VP we pretty much had a full load.

At the very front of the landing craft, we had hundreds of Hagensen Packs stuffed into knapsacks and carriers. Each knapsack, much like a child's school-book bag today, held ten packs. Each of us also slung a full M-2 ammunition bag that fit over your head and hung down at the front and back. The M-2 bags had a pouch on the front and back, each of which would hold ten Hagensen Packs. That gave each man forty pounds of ready explosives right on him.

As we hit the water, we circled the landing craft until all of the other units had been able to board their boats. When all of the boats were ready, a signal was given and we all started for the shore. We went in under the covering fire of the battleships first. The fire from the big guns was great for keeping the enemy down, but the muzzle blasts from those guns just about knocked us on our butts.

The covering fire from the cruisers that were closer in to shore wasn't quite so bad. As we approached the shore, the ships were getting smaller and their guns were something we could better stand to be near. We had started in from quite a ways out, so the whole trip took a while. Finally getting in close to the beach, there were Landing Craft, Tank (Rockets) (LCT(R)) launching barrages of five-inch high-explosive rockets right over our heads.

One of the things I remember most from those rocket boats was that you could see the rockets flying through the air overhead. Every now and then, some of the rockets would bump together and then start to fall. We had to maneuver our boat around so that we wouldn't get hit by our own falling rockets.

Finally, we got in close enough to shore that the coxswain, one of the two-man landing craft crew, called out: "Okay, this is where you guys get out."

So we threw our rubber boat over the side and filled it up with our explosives. Then each of us went over the side with our own loads. Of course, the rubber boat wasn't big enough to hold us all. So most of us were hanging on to the side of the boat and swimming or walking in. The water was only about five or five and a half feet deep where we started in. But the tide was coming in and the water was rising pretty fast.

As we got closer to shore, the water was shallower and we could start moving faster. German artillery shells were landing all around us and machine gun bullets would snap past and stitch across the water.

As we got about 100 yards from the landing craft that had brought us in, I looked back just as it took a burst of machine gunfire across the bow. It seemed to be okay and was able to back out and return to sea.

As we moved in to shore, we didn't all remain so lucky. One of our men was hit. We helped him into the boat and continued on to shore. Once we finally reached the beach, we pulled the boat up on the sand and pebbles. Then the 88s started hitting all around us. The shells were being fired in salvos, so we would wait until one salvo had landed and then move before the next one came in.

Our target was Utah Beach and we landed in the first wave. When I looked to my right and left, as far as I could see, there wasn't anyone else on the beach. Nothing seemed to be moving at all for the moment.

When one shell landed close to where a seaman and I were, I quickly dove into the hole it left to take cover. As I waited in the hole, the seaman jumped in next to me. When he asked me what we were going to do, I told him that I was waiting for the next shell to land. Then we would move on to that hole.

"Why are you moving from hole to hole?" he asked.

"They always told me while I was in training," I answered, "that the shells never land in the same hole again. So if you get in one that's just been hit, you're on pretty safe ground."

So that was how we moved up the beach, jumping from one shell hole to another. The tide was coming in pretty fast behind us. Once we reached the seawall area at the high-water mark, we sent back a couple of the Army guys and seamen to bring up the boat and explosives. That was how we finally got the bulk of our explosives on the beach.

Then we started loading all of the obstacles we could reach. Our specific job was to blow a 50-yard-wide gap through about 200 yards of obstacles. The length of the gap really depended on the tide coming in and how deep the water was. Where we were working, the water was about four feet deep at the most as we

A group of men move ashore on Normandy Beach during the invasion on June 6, 1944. The heavy strain of fierce combat already shows in their faces as they struggle to pull a rubber boat loaded with their equipment and wounded comrades ashore.

National Archives

loaded up the obstacles. We didn't have to swim at all as we got everything we could loaded and set.

The tide was coming in so fast and raising the water level so high that we probably only blasted about half the obstacles in our area. As we moved up to the seawall, our GAT spread out in both directions. Once we were under whatever cover was available, we fired our charges.

The group to our left was Lieutenant Jeeter's group, called "Jeeter's Skeeters" back during training at Fort Pierce. They cleared their gap at about the same time as we did ours. A couple more groups to our right also blew their gaps. I'd say that out of the fourteen or fifteen units we had on the beach, nine or so of them completed their mission and blew their gaps on schedule.

We had cleared a gap maybe twenty or thirty yards wide in our fifty-yard-wide assigned channel with our initial blast. Some of the obstacles were the big steel "Belgian Gates" we had worked on during training. Most of the rest of the obstacles were a long log braced up like a ramp with the low end pointing out to sea. There was a Tellermine (land mine) on the high end of the log. The incoming landing craft were expected to slide up these ramps and either be tipped on their sides or go up to where they would set off the twelve pounds of TNT in the mine.

Other obstacles included concrete tetrahedrons with steel bars sticking out of the tops of the blocks. All we could do with those was blow the bars off them. Once we had blown the obstacles and opened a gap, the major part of our mission was over.

Taking cover at the seawall, we stayed there for some two or three hours as a number of waves of troops came in and landed. There was still some incoming fire in terms of 88s and machine guns. But it wasn't near as heavy as it had been earlier. After another few hours under cover, we started to move out and attack more obstacles on the beach as we could with the tide in.

We gathered up unexploded ordnance (shells, bombs, mines, etc.) as we found it. Many of the obstacles we were examining didn't have mines on them. So we could just direct landing craft past those obstacles without a lot of danger. For a while there, we acted as kind of traffic cops along the beach as much as we could. When the incoming fire got heavy again, we moved back to the cover of the seawall.

During all of this, so much was happening that you didn't really have time to think about what you were doing and where you were. We were all cold, wet, and miserable. But it was just that kind of day.

We did wonder about just how badly our wounded man was hurt. It was just about that time that another of our men was hit. Now we thought about both of them. By that time the medics had set up an aid station, so we were able to take our wounded man to them and get him help.

Eventually, we were taken off the beach and sent back to England. Some weeks later it was decided to use some of the NCDUs from Utah Beach for the invasion of southern France. Of course, they didn't tell us where we were being sent. But before long, we were being shipped out to Italy.

The camp we finally arrived at in Italy was at Salerno, south of Naples. During our first briefing on the upcoming invasion, they told us that we wouldn't be in the first waves this time. The NCDUs that were already in Italy and had been training for a while would be the ones in the first waves. We would be in the fifth or sixth wave as backups.

We all figured that this was a pretty good thing for us. Back on Utah Beach in Normandy, we had noticed that by the time the fifth wave had landed, the enemy fire had died down a lot. So going in with a later wave sounded just fine to me.

The night before the invasion was to take place, we received our last briefing on our assignment. It seemed that a bunch of equipment on shore had been moved about by the Germans and that there might be a lot more obstacles than were originally expected. So the basic plan for us was changed.

The target was estimated to be bigger than the command felt they wanted to assign to the new NCDU men. So now it was the veterans from Normandy who would be going in first. As one of those "old vets," I didn't care for the change a whole lot.

This was about the only time I really got scared. We pretty much had it made when we were going to be in the later waves. Going in on the first wave again was pushing our luck. But those were the orders and that's how we went in.

During the invasion, we were right up front with the first troops on the beach and cleared the beaches on schedule. The obstacles we ran into in southern France were pretty much all posts or pilings driven down into the seabed about twenty to thirty feet from shore. There in the Mediterranean, the offshore ground sloped down quickly, not like the long, shallow slopes at Normandy. Just twenty feet from shore you were already in pretty deep water. The pilings were in double rows running parallel to the beach, and now staggered in relation to the rows beside it. Sitting on top of each piling was an armed Tellermine.

For this demolition op, we swam down the rows of pilings, the water being too deep for walking, and dove down on each one. About eight or ten feet down from the surface, we would tie a Hagensen Pack to the post, letting the primacord lead float up to the surface on a wooden block. Another swimmer went along laying out a long primacord main line between the posts. We tied all our charge leads to the main line for multiple detonation.

Bringing all of the primacord mains to the beach, we detonated all of the charges from there. The blast cut away all of our obstacles at once, opening our portion of the beach. As we finished with our specific assignment, we would move along to the next section of beach and help the demolition crew there.

After the invasion was over, we spent additional time in the area clearing wrecks, blasting additional obstacles, and destroying unexploded ordnance. Some of the blasts were pretty large as a bunch of HE (High Explosive) would all go up at once. But we didn't pay much attention to explosions we hadn't set off.

Demolition had been experimenting with Apex boats back at Fort Pierce and the southern France invasion was one of the first attempts in Europe to use them to clear obstacles. The Apex boat was something we had developed back at Fort Pierce with the JANET board and DRU. An unmanned, radio-controlled landing craft, the Apex boat was loaded with 8,000 pounds of explosives. Once driven onto the obstacles by a remote operator, the Apex charge could be detonated by radio. Whenever we heard a really big blast, we just figured another Apex boat had gone up.

Though they looked like a good idea, the boats just didn't work right in the field and were quickly dropped. Instead, demolition men would go in and hand-place charges on obstacles, a technique we had used successfully both at Normandy and southern France.

The landings in southern France weren't as heavily defended as they had been at Normandy. It was like a Sunday in the park in comparison to that June morning in Utah. There were hardly any problems at all, it seemed to me. From one of the tall buildings in town, maybe a church steeple, well back from the beach, someone opened fire on us a couple of times. And we did have some machine guns rake across our bow as we were coming in.

A destroyer escort pulled in very close to shore, so close I thought he was going to run aground for sure. Then the DE turned parallel to the shore and opened fire a few times with his guns. That was just about the end of any enemy fire coming at us except for a few strafings later in the day. But there was nothing in comparison to what we ran into at Normandy Beach.

After the invasion, the Navy sent us back to our camp in Salerno. We stayed in Italy until sometime in September, when we were loaded onto transports and shipped back to the States. The Navy gave us a thirty-day leave back home before we all had to report in to Fort Pierce again.

After our leave, my unit, NCDU 127, was immediately asked if we would go back to working with the Demolition Research Unit. Some of the guys had gotten their fill of demolition work and went back to the Seabee battalions. Our officer, Lieutenant Padgett, was one of those men who went back to the Seabees. Lieutenant Hund asked me to join with his NCDU and go over to the DRU on North Island. Agreeing, I went over with them. I stayed with the DRU until my discharge from the Navy at the end of the war.

■ Chapter 10

The Gap Assault Teams at Normandy

Once information on the specific targets at Normandy Beach began to be available to the planners of the beach demolition operation, it became obvious that the numbers of NCDUs available wouldn't be up to the task ahead of them. Because the landing plan called for the beach obstacle demolition operation to be conducted at low tide, on exposed land, the Army Engineers were put in overall command. The NCDUs would work with and under the direction of the Engineers.

Once photographs and intelligence on the landing beaches themselves were revealed to the NCDU planners in late April–early May 1944, a fast reorganization of the demolition teams was required. Each six-man NCDU was reinforced with five Army Engineers. Later an additional three seamen from a personnel pool in Scotland were attached to each NCDU. The seamen were mostly all brand-new to the Navy, being fresh from boot camp in the States. The new men were to be boat handlers for the rubber boats filled with explosives. The boat handlers would free up additional NCDU men to work on obstacle demolition.

The combined Army/NDCU/Navy units were referred to as Gap Assault Teams or GATs. The GATs were part of the Special Engineer Task Force for Operation NEPTUNE, the amphibious portion of Operation OVERLORD, the D-day landings. For Omaha Beach, there were 16 GATs assigned to the landings with an additional 11 support teams acting as backup. In the GATS were NCDUs 11, 22, 23, 24, 27, 41, 42, 43, 44, 45, 46, 137, 138, 140, 141, and 142. Among the support teams were NCDUs 128, 129, 130, 131, and 133. So for Omaha Beach, there were a total of 105 Fort Pierce graduates opening the way through the obstacles.

Each GAT was assigned to blow a fifty-yard-wide gap through the obstacles within twenty minutes of landing. In the horrible conditions at Omaha Beach, only five of sixteen channels through the obstacles were blown clear, with an additional two channels partially cleared. In spite of not getting all of the channels blown clear in the very short time they were given, the Navy recognized the herculean task accomplished by the Omaha Beach NCDUs during the landings. They were awarded a Presidential Units Citation for their actions that day. And a number of NCDU personnel received the Navy Cross for their individual acts that day.

Joseph D. DiMartino, Lieutenant, USN (Ret.)

I wasn't in one of the early NCDU classes. Instead, I was in Navy boot camp at Sampson, New York. In March 1944, 2,000 of us boots were sent to Pier 92 in New York. On Easter Sunday, all 2,000 of us were put on board the Queen Elizabeth and sailed to Rosneath, Scotland. Rosneath was a U.S. Navy base northwest of Glasgow, and we were all scheduled to be assigned as gun crews and boat crews on landing craft for the invasion against Europe.

This dashing, handsome, Hollywood-type U.S. Navy ensign came to the base and announced to us all that he needed 100 volunteers for a demolition outfit. What was explained to us was that after the main force of the invasion had landed, there would be debris on the beaches and roadways that would have to be destroyed. This was what the volunteer outfit would be doing. So I volunteered, even though that isn't what a soldier or sailor is supposed to do; it tends to get you in trouble.

We were packed up and sent to southern England to a training base. The first thing we learned to do was to prime explosives with blasting caps, primacord, and time fuse. Then we were shown how to place the explosives on obstacles. And that was the first time we saw obstacles. But it was far from the last.

Through March, April, and May, every day except Sunday, we practiced destroying obstacles. On June 4, we loaded up our rubber boat with 1,000 pounds of explosives for the upcoming operation. There were also Army Corps of Engineers troops with us. They would attack the obstacles up to the high-water mark and beyond. They also had 1,000 pounds of explosives.

All of our gear, rubber boat, and explosives were loaded on board an LCM, Landing Craft, Mechanized. For ourselves, we boarded an LCT, Landing Craft, Tank, for the trip over to the invasion site. So on June 4 we set off for the invasion, which was promptly called off due to bad weather. When June 5 came up, Ike (General Eisenhower) said go.

Halfway across the English Channel, our LCT broke down. In the middle of the night, in rough weather and choppy seas, we transferred from the LCT to the LCM.

At about 6:30 or 7:00 the next morning, June 6, 1,000 yards off of the beach, it looked like we were kicking the pants off the Germans on the beach. As we moved in closer to 500 yards or so, I could see and hear that the situation was a lot different. The Germans were putting out heavy fire on the beach and our guys were being killed.

Once we got to the beach, Lieutenant Culver told us all to immediately take cover. So there I was, on this pebble beach with the occasional big rock, digging a foxhole for myself.

"Joe," I said to myself, "you're seventeen years old. What are you doing here? You were working in a shipyard making a hundred bucks a week, and now you're going to get killed."

That was probably when I was the most afraid of any time in my life. I experienced combat again later, but never in the same way as those first few hours on Normandy Beach. The unknown was what got to you, when the bomb or the bullet or the shell would get you. You just knew it was coming sometime, so you did a lot of praying. And the big hope was that the Army would go up and get the Germans before they had a chance to get me. Lying there in a shallow hole on a pebble beach was not the best place to be in the world.

Anyway, I managed to survive that morning as we conducted our mission to blast obstacles off the beach. The next day we started clearing obstacles. The Army had moved in and taken control of the situation. We stayed on the beach for three weeks, in that time clearing the beaches and roadways of obstacles and rubble. Then we were returned to England.

We stayed in England for another several weeks before being sent on to Liverpool for transportation back to the United States. The USS Wakefield, a Coast Guard troop transport, took us back to Boston. Boarding a train, we were taken down to New York, where we were all given leave. For me, that meant getting back on the train and heading back to Boston, to get to my hometown of Dedham, Massachusetts.

When September had rolled around, I was told to report to Fort Pierce, Florida, to the NCDU training base. Commander Kauffman said, "All you seamen can either go to a UDT Team or go back to the fleet."

Remaining at Fort Pierce, I went through some of the training they were still giving the NCDUs who were going on to UDTs. The one thing I never did in training was go through Hell Week. Whenever I'm asked, "What class were you in?" and "How was your Hell Week?" my answer is that my Hell Week was June 6, 1944. In the early days, that answer was comprehensible, but today the young SEALs and others sometimes ask, "June 6, '44? What is that?"

"You ever hear of D day?"

That was good enough for Commander Kauffman to accept a number of us from Omaha Beach directly into the UDTs. As far as he was concerned, we could go right into the teams.

I was assigned to UDT 25 as one of the three officers and thirty men who had all been on Omaha that June day. The team began training in October 1944. In February 1945, UDT 25 had completed its training at Fort Pierce and was on its way to Maui, Hawaii, for advanced training. In UDT 25, I was assigned as a boat coxswain. We were working on perfecting the pickup of swimmers from the water. Additional techniques were experimented with and the double-loop snare was retained as the best available system.

In June, our Maui training was completed. Now we had to report back to the

United States to Oceanside, California, to undergo cold-water training. The purpose of that was to get us ready for the invasion of Japan later in the year.

On August 15, six UDTs left Oceanside for Japan. This wasn't going to be for the invasion since we already knew the war was over because of the atomic bombs. We arrived in Japan in the first weeks of September. There wasn't any work for us to do, as several other UDT were already doing recons in the same area as we were. We just didn't have a mission and command had more than enough UDTs available to them.

We never even got to the shore really. As a boat coxswain, I got to the docks at Yokosuka and Yokohama, but I didn't get a chance to go ashore the whole time we were there. Some of the guys from the team did get a chance to go ashore, but not many. We were never called upon to perform any operations. So about three weeks later, we shipped out for Guam, and then back to the States.

Even though I had never fought against the Japanese in the Pacific, I had enough of a taste of active war on the beaches at Normandy. Personally, I felt that the dropping of the atomic bomb was okay. The use of that weapon not only demonstrated it to the world, it proved that perhaps it should never be used again. It also prevented the invasion of Japan from ever being necessary, and the projected U.S. casualties alone for that operation were over one million. Having been through one major invasion, I was glad that President Truman said, "Let's end this."

When we were sent back to the States, we arrived in San Diego and were sent on to the Coronado Amphibious Base. The Navy gave us all leave prior to reporting back to Coronado. UDT 25 was decommissioned on 13 November 1945. We remained at Coronado, decommissioning UDTs and helping to set up the postwar UDTs with Commander Kauffman, who had made the trip back from Japan with us.

In June 1946, the Navy split up the four postwar UDTs, sending half to Little Creek, Virginia, and keeping the other half in Coronado. I went on with UDT 4 to Little Creek. In 1946/47, UDT 4 went on a deployment to Antarctica and the South Pole as part of Operation HIGH JUMP.

Training with scuba gear started about that

A UDT underwater swimmer wears the 1952 model Lambertsen Underwater Respiratory Unit (LARU) during a demonstration in the early 1950s. This was an improved model over the 1940 WWII design.

National Archives

same time. We didn't have the aqualung, open-circuit system that became so common later. Instead, we started with the Lambertsen Amphibious Respiratory Unit (LARU), which is a pure oxygen, closed-circuit rebreather. The LARU is what we used off of Saint Thomas in the Virgin Islands and from submarines in experiments in locking in and locking out while submerged. Prior to this time I had always acted as a boat coxswain; now I was starting to get into the swimming with the new underwater gear.

By 1949, we had started using the aqualung, which released bubbles into the water but was much safer and easier to use than the LARU. For the next ten to fifteen years, I was training primarily with scuba gear, conducting underwater swimming, underwater obstacle clearance, and underwater reconnaissance.

In those days the UDT mission was primarily hydrographic reconnaissance and the destruction of obstacles. The secondary UDT missions were in the marine hinterland, the wetlands, and attacking shipping by placing limpet mines on boats, as the Italians had done during WWII. We also perfected our techniques for locking in and out of submarines while both submerged and under way.

During the Korean War, in the early 1950s, the West Coast teams said that they could handle the UDT commitment to the effort. Our COs volunteered to augment the West Coast teams with platoons from the East Coast. But the command said no and we never took part in that conflict.

In the late 1950s, we started parachuting, using this as another method of infiltrating into a target area. In previous years officers and individual men had gone to parachute jump training as an experiment. Now, under Captain Olsen and some other officers, a group of UDT enlisted men, myself included, became the first UDT "stick," the line of men who jump from a plane, to go to Jump School together as a group. That was about June 1956, as I remember.

As a bunch of fit, qualified Navy frogmen, we found the Army Jump School at Fort Benning to be nothing but three weeks of repetition. All we did from the morning until late afternoon was practice how to jump out of the airplane and how to hit the ground in a parachute landing fall (PLF). After three weeks of that, we were ready to jump out of that plane just to finish with this constant repetition. It was all right, but nothing in comparison to the way you jump today in the Teams with free-falling.

On that first jump, your adrenaline goes and it is exhilarating. Jumping from the old Bumblebee, the C-119 Flying Boxcar, it was loud and noisy while on board. When you leaped out, suddenly it was quiet while you were in the air.

Now I was both a qualified parachutist and a frogman. In 1960, I took another step and received my commission as a limited-duty officer. After 15 years as an enlisted man, I had finally decided to become an officer, since I was going to do at least my 20 years and retire. As an officer, I could do 25 years and retire at a better rate of pay. If I went for the whole 30 years, I could retire at 75 percent of my base pay. And the duty was good, I enjoyed the work with the Teams. Being happy in my career is why I stayed in.

It was in the early 1960s that the Navy found that it needed a maritime environment organization to combat guerrillas and conduct other commando-type operations.

The new organization, the SEAL Teams, had the order of their mission priorities changed from that of the UDTs. Hydrographic reconnaissance and obstacle demolition was now a secondary mission. The primary mission was to conduct operations in the marine hinterland and beyond. The SEALs would go behind the beaches to infiltrate and gather intelligence.

When the new unit came along, I didn't know much about it, but I was ready to join up immediately. One of the reasons I had stayed in the Teams so long was that I loved to operate and stay busy. Roy Boehm was the officer on the East Coast who was putting SEAL Team Two together. I always had a high regard for Roy; he's a great leader and a good boss, altogether an excellent man.

In general, Roy Boehm is the best deep-sea diver, bosun's mate, limited-duty officer lieutenant commander I have ever known. He hails originally from Brooklyn, New York, I believe. He was, and still is, hell on wheels; he can do it all. Roy was probably one of the best men to be among the first SEALs, as he has initiative, integrity, farsightedness, and knows what to do and when to do it. He is a very versatile sailor and has been since his deep-sea diving days as an enlisted man during World War II. He's just a fish in the water.

The first muster for SEAL Team Two was on January 8, 1962. I was on assignment at Great Lakes Naval Training Station in Illinois when the Team was formed up, so I missed the first days. A letter came to me notifying me of the new unit, so I didn't see anything until I returned to Little Creek. The unit had a nucleus of ten officers and fifty men, a tight group of top-notch sailors and operators.

For fifteen years I had been in the Underwater Demolition Teams. I had seen the beginnings of scuba diving, parachuting, and helicopter operations. Everything you see today as a polished skill of the SEALs, we started out back in those formative years. After I had received my commission, I was made aware of SEAL Team Two and the planning that was going into it. That's when I decided that this was something new and that I wanted to be part of it. Just as I had been for all of my Navy career, I always wanted to be part of something new and operational.

The name of the new team came from the acronym for the three environments it would work in, the SEa, Air, and Land. But the hard-charging bunch of operators Roy Boehm picked to fill out its first ranks soon had determined the true meaning of the SEAL name—Sleep, Eat, and Live it up.

The SEALs were new, but they were a Team from day one, in the bigger meaning of the term. The Team as we had known it in the UDTs and now in the SEALs meant that we were a cohesive group. We always worked as a Team. The ideal of the

The Airborne platoon of SEAL Team Two rigged out for an air insertion during the first years of the SEALs. The men are equipped with a mix of equipment, including police ammunition holders for the S&W Model 15 revolvers. Over their shoulders, they have slung the first AR-15 rifles used in the Navy. The platoon is facing their officer, Lieutenant Roy Boehm.

UDT-SEAL Museum

Team, and the idea of teamwork, is instilled in all of us from day one in training. The SEALs were made up of high-quality, skilled, knowledgeable individuals, but its strength came from them all working together.

You can see the teamwork mentality of the SEALs and the UDT in the smallest working unit of the Teams, the swimmer pair, an operator and his swim buddy. A swim buddy is the man you look after, and that man looks after you. No matter where you go or what you do on an operation or exercise, out of the water or in, that swim buddy is with you. You never, ever, leave your swim buddy. That rule is number one in the Teams.

The swim buddy rule especially holds true when you're operating in the field. If you're in the water or in enemy territory, whatever you're in, wherever you are, you take care of each other. You make sure nothing happens to him and he makes sure nothing happens to you. And that basic integrity goes through the whole group. You always take care of your swim buddy.

It was integrity that made the Teams work. Each man had his own personal integrity and would not break from his stand of staying with his buddy and his Team. And you tried to build further unit integrity as an officer, to have the men work together, and play together in both their on- and off-duty time. But no matter what each man did, he had to maintain that personal integrity to always do the right thing no matter what the cost.

The first duties in the new SEAL Team consisted mostly of going out to different training schools. One of the early schools that stands out the most was the E&E School (Escape and Evasion) run by the Marine Corps at their cold-water training center in Bridgeport, California. The first and last lesson every one of us came away from that school with was don't ever be captured.

At the E&E School, they put you in a prison camp where Marine instructors play the part of Communists. At that camp, they put you through the grinder for twenty-four to forty-eight hours. That taste of prison camp life is enough to instill in you the determination that you will never allow yourself to be captured. And to my knowledge, no SEAL has ever been taken captive by anyone.

It was pain that they inflicted on us during E&E School. But it wasn't a long-lasting pain. We knew that there would be an end to it. But what they exposed us to was what could be expected in a prison camp, where you would never know when the pain would end.

After several years of deployments and training, SEAL Team Two had its first chance at direct combat in 1965, when there was a crisis in the Dominican Republic. Along with two Army colonels and other staff from the commander-in-chief, Atlantic's staff, we flew in to Santo Domingo on a C-7 Army aircraft. By the time we got there, things had already quieted down and there were no operations being conducted.

SEAL Team Two already had a platoon in the area prior to my coming down. They had seen some shooting against the Communist rebels down there, but there were no casualties taken on our side. They had conducted some operations and intelligence-gathering missions, so SEAL Team Two had demonstrated their value in the limited action that took place. The SEAL Team wasn't going to see direct action again for several years, until we sent platoons in to Vietnam in 1967.

By 1966, we were preparing to send direct action platoons against the enemy. That year I was the executive officer of SEAL Team Two and was even the commanding officer of the Team from August to September 1966, while we were transitioning from Lieutenant Commander Tom Tarbox to Lieutenant Commander William Earley. Between Commander Earley and myself, we chose and formed up the platoons that would be the first from SEAL Team Two to go into action in Vietnam the next year. SEAL Team One had platoons in combat in Vietnam in 1966, so we would be working with them initially.

When I went over to Vietnam in June 1967, it was for a yearlong tour as a member of the U.S. Naval Advisory Group, Vietnam. We supported the South Vietnamese UDT/SEALs in both training and in an advisory capacity among other missions.

The Vietnamese I was working with made up a good force. But it was hard to keep them motivated and to get them to work with the U.S. Navy SEALs on operations. They would go to briefings and afterward were supposed to stay in the area. They wouldn't do that and went into town or whatever. That could be a very serious security breach and would compromise the operation they had been briefed on.

By this time we knew very well how the enemy, the Viet Cong and the North Vietnamese Army (NVA), were very ingenious in their methods of operating and gathering intelligence. They inflicted a lot of casualties on the U.S. forces and even the SEALs, but we inflicted casualties on them as well.

In late January 1968, I was up in Saigon. That was when the '68 Tet offensive began and the Viet Cong and NVA rose up all through South Vietnam. The action in Saigon got hot and heavy quickly, but I wasn't able to take much part in it. Those of us at the Navy command were restricted to the building during the fighting.

We weren't too far from the U.S. embassy but just couldn't leave the building when the Viet Cong arrived on the grounds of the embassy itself. The building we were in was only a couple of blocks away from the U.S. embassy and I hadn't even realized that it had been attacked. That situation had been pretty rough for the embassy personnel, but we didn't know about it until several days after.

The VC and NVA forces had infiltrated the whole of South Vietnam, stockpiling weapons and munitions, for their Tet offensive. Infiltration was something they were very good at. Direct fighting in the cities and towns was something else again.

We had been ordered by the Army to stay in our building during the first stages of the offensive. After a couple of days we were told it was all right for us to go to our work areas. Mine was down at the Saigon shipyard, where the Naval Advisory Group had its headquarters.

Then I got together with the Vietnamese Navy lieutenant who was my counterpart with their SEALs. We patrolled the Cho Long area to the north of Saigon. So we did that for a couple of weeks as everything quieted down again throughout South Vietnam. Everywhere the VC had captured territory, cities, towns, or hamlets, it was taken back from them by the U.S. and South Vietnamese forces.

In June 1968, I finished my tour in Vietnam and returned to Little Creek and SEAL Team Two.

In World War II, we had carried little more than swim fins, a face mask, a knife, belt, and explosives. In the Pacific, the water wasn't too cold for the most part, so there wasn't a need for suits or things of that nature at that time. The LCPR boats had a couple of machine guns on them. That was about it in the way of gear for the UDTs.

The SEALs in Vietnam, though, had a world of equipment. There were ammunition vests, M-16 rifles, Stoner machine guns, grenade launchers, claymore mines, and all types of sophisticated weapons. The main idea in equipping the SEALs was to give them the most firepower they could carry in a small package.

The change in the enemy from WWII to today is what forced the SEALs to change the way they fought. Now the Teams have to have the equipment and the technical knowledge to use it in order to fight battles.

In spite of all of the differences between the way the UDTs were equipped and the way the SEAL Teams are equipped, and the differences in the missions, the basic men who do the ops are the same today as they were in World War II. There does seem to have to be a bit more intelligence in today's SEALs; they go through a lot more formal schooling than we did. In the early days it seemed to be mostly brawn that was needed; today it's both brains and brawn.

It takes a person who is strong-willed and has a strong mind as well as being physically fit to get into the Teams. To stay in the Teams, he also has to have a good heart and a sense of value. This lets that person become part of a unique fighting force. What makes the SEALs unique is that they can get into a country or target area by all different methods. They can come in by sea, over land, or down through the air. Acting as peasants or generals, they can infiltrate an area, accomplish their mission, and leave without anyone ever knowing they were there.

Back during WWII, we fought a war for patriotic reasons. We were U.S. citizens fighting a war to stop both Hitler and Japan. The war was fought with big numbers, huge forces; the U.S. Army and Marines had more gear and better equipment than any of the enemy forces. We could just overpower them with bombs and bullets. It was putting force against force and seeing who had the most and the greatest will to use it.

Vietnam was unique in that it was jungle, wetlands, and rice paddies with a people with whom you couldn't tell who was who. There were no solid battle lines. In Europe during WWII, there were the enemy lines and our lines on one side or the other of a battle line. In the Pacific, the battle took place on an island for the most part. In Vietnam, the enemy could be in front of you, in back of you, or right in your camp area with you. They all looked the same and the Viet Cong guerrillas just blended in with the population.

To fight the Viet Cong you would have to go out into the jungle and the bushes and fight their kind of war. And you might think you were killing the enemy, but when you went and looked, they might not be the enemy at all.

The SEALs were effective during the Vietnam War mostly because they had a good intelligence net. They knew exactly where they were going, who they were after, and where to find them whenever possible. This was due to the intelligence net that the Teams had developed themselves and matched up with information coming in from other official sources. Fighting as the enemy did allow the SEALs to do their job where no one else could; knowing who the enemy was gave them their target.

■ Chapter 11

The UDTs' Organization and Legends

Almost all of the World War II UDTs were known by simple number designations. One single team, however, had a different designation. This was UDT Able. Among the first NCDUs sent to the Pacific area, several were sent to Admiral Wilkinson's Task Force 31 in the South Pacific. As part of the Third Amphibious Force, these NCDUs took part in a few operations in the Solomons, blasting on Guadalcanal, and landings on Green Island and Emirau Island in February 1944.

The South Pacific NCDUs were brought together and reinforced with additional personnel to form a UDT. This new UDT was UDT Able. There is no available explanation for the unusual designation except for the fact that the base NCDUs used in that UDT were among the first graduates from Fort Pierce. But UDT Able completed its training at Maui in time to be included in the planning for the invasion of Peleliu.

In the early morning hours of September 12, 1944, the APD *Noa* with UDT Able aboard was struck by a U.S. destroyer. The crew and UDT personnel were able to abandon the stricken APD before she sank, but without saving any of the UDT's equipment of explosives. Without the material means to conduct its part in the invasion, UDT Able was sent back to Pearl Harbor. UDT Able was broken up at Maui and the personnel from the unit assigned to UDTs 11, 12, 13, 14, 15, and 16 as they were being formed.

UDTs 6 and 7 continued on to the Peleliu operations, conducting the beach reconnaissance and later demolition swims. Instead of doing a single beach operation, UDT 6 was also assigned the operations that would have been done by UDT Able. Initial recon swims were conducted on 12 September, with the needed demolition swims carried out on the thirteenth and fourteenth. The invasion of Peleliu was successfully begun on 15 September 1944.

An Underwater Demolition Team now consisted of sixteen officers and eighty enlisted men. The personnel were organized into four operating platoons and a headquarters platoon. The operating platoons consisted of three officers and fifteen men each. The Headquarters Platoon had the remaining four officers and twenty enlisted men. The commanding officer, executive officer, technical officer, and mine disposal officer were all in the Headquarters

Platoon. The HQ enlisted men included signalmen, boat technicians and operators, motor machinist's mates, coxswains, and seamen. The HQ Platoon handled all of the needs for the UDT, including medical, supply, repair, and maintenance.

The officers in the operating platoons were assigned as the platoon leader, assistant platoon leader, a boat officer, and a loading officer. This allowed three officers to operate as leaders of rubber boat crews, each with four of the enlisted men of the platoon. The remaining officer and three enlisted men would remain on the LCPR assigned to the platoon, the men being the coxswain and crew.

UDTs were later reorganized in units of thirteen officers and eighty-five enlisted men. Only two officers and fifteen enlisted men were in the four operational platoons. The Headquarters Platoon now held five officers and twenty-five enlisted men. This UDT organization would last for most of World War II.

The UDTs were normally assigned to APDs (Assault Personnel Destroyers) for transportation and basing. The APDs were high-speed troop transports, early versions being converted "four-stacker" destroyers of WWI vintage, remodeled for troop transport by removing two smokestacks and other machin-

Mounted on their davits over the central deck of an APD are the four LCPRs used by a deployed UDT. Each UDT platoon would use a single LCPR for an operation. The two smokestacks between and forward of the LCPRs are the remainders from the APDs conversion from a "four-stacker" WWI destroyer.

U.S. Navy

ery. The APD had her own crew and the UDTs rarely took part in ship's duties. Instead, the APD was to transport the UDTs, their explosives, equipment, rubber boats, and four LCPRs to and from target beaches.

Stories quickly grew among the forces that operated with the UDTs on invasions. The UDTs were known to go onto the beach well ahead of any troops, armed with nothing but a knife and a bag of explosives. The UDTs would conduct their operations and return, and often lead in the first waves of landing craft to the cleared beaches during the invasion.

Some Marines landing on Saipan on 15 June 1944 crossed paths with Draper Kauffman, then the commanding officer of UDT 5. When they passed Kauffman, who was wearing only his swim trunks and other minimum gear, the Marines were said to comment on the summer tourists arriving before the beachhead was secured!

But the most memorable story of the UDTs centers around operations at Guam in July 1944. On 18 July, several UDT operators from Team Four crawled up on White Beach at Guam and left behind a sign. When the Marines landed on Guam near the small town of Agat only a short while later, they were met by the astonishing sight of a sign stating:

WELCOME MARINES

AGAT USO TWO BLOCKS

COURTESY UDT 4

The story of this sign soon made its way through the fleet and the Marine Corps. Additional markers were planted by the UDTs for years to come, including a large one placed on Japan to greet the incoming occupation troops. What isn't widely known is the existence of another sign that may have been planted first. It could be that the signs were a result of a bet or some other challenge between UDTs 3 and 4. But on Asan Beach four days before UDT 4 conducted their operations off of White Beach, a smaller sign was left by UDT 3. This sign stated:

WELCOME

U.S. MARINES

BY

SEABEE

DEMOLITION

7.14.44 U.D.T.3

But it was the later sign by UDT 4 that has received the lion's share of the publicity.

Carrying forward a tradition begun by UDT 4, this is the last of the beach greeting signs put up by the WWII UDTs. It was part of the UDTs' answer to just who was first on the beach during an invasion.

Barry G. McCabe Collection

Edwin R. Ashby, Boatswain's Mate, Second Class

My Team during WWII was UDT 7, considered the last of the full Seabee Teams. The Seabees were the construction battalions, units full of special rates (jobs) that were really something that we were used to every day. The Seabees rates were what they gave the carpenters, tin knockers, and other workers who had joined the Navy from civilian life. These men brought their abilities and skills with them and didn't have to go through much training to be put to use.

There were people in the Seabees who had built roads, tunnels, and railways. So these men already had some knowledge of explosives. These men were considered a good source of manpower for the NCDUs and later the UDTs.

After I got out of Boot Camp, I was sent down to Gulfport, Mississippi, for further training at Gunnery School. I had wanted to be a gunner's mate in the Navy and that was what I managed to do. After being sent to New York, a bunch of us ended up in Little Creek, Virginia. There, we were going to crew landing craft, what they called attack boats.

This wasn't what most of us wanted, but then a group of us were sent down to the ATB at Fort Pierce, where they also had attack boat training. We went down to

Fort Pierce by train along with a bunch of Seabees from Camp Peary. The Seabees were going down for other training, something I was soon to learn a lot more about.

We were all called in to this big auditorium one day and asked if we would like to volunteer for a new unit training at Fort Pierce. I wanted out of the attack boat business and this new unit sounded like a good deal. So it wasn't long before I was undergoing NCDU and then UDT training.

It was quite extensive and really forced you to put out your best. We talk about Hell Week and the roughness of it all, but we were young then and had high spirits. We felt like we were going to beat the Japanese all by ourselves.

So we took to our training pretty well. For myself, I never had any idea of quitting. And it was an all-volunteer outfit. You could quit at any time. All you had to say was, "I want out!" and you would be gone with no prejudice or bad mark on your record. But I never had any personal doubt that I was going to make it.

At Fort Pierce, we trained as an NCDU, five enlisted men and an officer. The seventh "man" in our unit was a rubber boat. That thing went everywhere with us. We dragged that boat over the beaches, carried it over the rocks, and pulled it through the swamps. And swamps are something Fort Pierce had a lot of back then. Swamps and bugs. There were sand fleas and little biters everywhere.

For our final exercise during Payoff Week, what they called the Jen-Stu-Fu problem, we took our rubber boat for miles. Over the islands, through the rivers and inlets we went. With our rubber boat right along with us.

The demolition part of the exercise centered around blowing the channel open down in Saint Lucie, south of Fort Pierce. During that last week, rations were pretty light. Something like a can of C rations per man per day or whatever. Pretty lean cuisine. When we set off our explosives, the fish came up to the surface after the blast and we went out and gathered them up.

Some guy down near the channel had some potatoes, so we "borrowed" them to include in our seafood menu. We had no salt or anything, but that was some of the best fish I ever tasted in my life.

When we got to Maui in Hawaii, the small NCDU groups were reorganized into much larger Underwater Demolition Teams. Several UDTs had already run through the training at Maui, so the idea was pretty well established. When our group arrived from Fort Pierce, we were broken down and rearranged as UDTs 5, 6, and 7.

The NCDUs hadn't really been big enough to tackle the job they were handed during the Normandy invasion. Casualties were high and the command didn't want any mistakes to be repeated. In Normandy, the NCDU men had carried some weapons in to the beach, carbines and pistols mostly. Out in the Pacific, we weren't going to carry any weapons at all except for a sheath knife on our belts.

The new UDTs were supposed to be organized as hundred-man teams with four operational platoons and a headquarters platoon. The reality was Teams of eighty and ninety men each. We had to do all of the work for an operation, handle the boats, do the swim, handle the explosives, ourselves. And the jobs rotated among the platoons.

Say on one operation, Platoon One would be the swimming platoon and they would go in and do the recon. Then Platoon Two would go in and do the demolition work the next day. Platoon Three would be back on the APD making up the explosive packs for the operation. And Platoon Four would remain in reserve.

If a whole platoon was lost during an operation, the reserve platoon would be sent in. It was our good luck that we never had so many casualties that the reserve platoon was ever sent in. Then, on the next invasion or operation, the platoons would rotate their positions: Platoon One would be reserve, Platoon Two swimming, and so on.

The operating situation had changed a lot for us since we had left Fort Pierce. There, we had dressed generally like Army soldiers, in combat boots, fatigues, and steel helmets. In Maui, the working uniform tended to be a pair of trunks or shorts, a K-bar knife, and a plastic pad and wax pencil. At the beginning we didn't wear any life preservers or inflatable belts. By later in the war we were wearing inflatable life belts so that if a man was hurt, he could be floated a bit more easily. The belt was this canvas and rubber affair what went around your waist and you blew it up with a CO_2 cartridge.

The uniform changes had come because at Fort Pierce we had walked, or waded, in to do our job of demolition. In Maui, we were swimming everywhere. They used to take us out of sight of land and practice being picked up and dropped off for something like six or seven hours. That kept us in the water pretty much all day. On one of the pickups, I hit the CO_2 release on my life preserver just as I was being picked up by the boat. The belt inflated just as I grabbed the snare to get into the boat and the sudden drag just about dislocated my shoulder.

If you did the sling pickup right, and your belt didn't inflate, you would be picked up and rolled into the runner boat without any trouble. Then you would scramble into the LCPR to make room for the next swimmer being picked up.

The cast and recovery system using the double-loop snare worked great for us. A man could be snatched up out of the water without the pickup boat slowing down. To the best of my knowledge, a man named Joe B. Davis actually made the first double-loop snare as the pickup system was being developed. Prior to that, the pickup boat actually had to stop and the swimmer was pulled onto the rubber boat for recovery. That made the pickup boat a much easier target for enemy fire. This was found to be pretty disastrous when done during the first couple of UDT operations.

On the fourteenth of June 1944, we started the Marianas operation along with UDTs 3, 4, 5, and 6. Because the Normandy invasion took place on 6 June that same month, it always kind of overshadowed the start of the Marianas campaign. The targets of the operation included Saipan, Guam, and Tinian. It was a big, important op-

During Operation SPRINGBOARD off of Vieques, Puerto Rico, in 1972, the snare man hauls in a recovered UDT swimmer. This technique of recovering UDT swimmers from the water while the boat is moving at speed was first developed during WWII in the Pacific. It is still trained with today.

U.S. Navy

eration, but it just never got the press it should have because of what was going on over in Europe.

But Saipan was our first operation. It was a Team effort throughout, each of us did our job, but it was drilled into us that we did everything as a Team. That, and your swimming partner is the best friend you could ever have. Those were the two greatest lessons and strengths of the UDT, everyone always worked together, and Teamwork got the job done.

There was a lot of resistance to the Team's going in to the beaches at Saipan. The enemy put out a lot of fire against both the fleet and us. In spite of that, the operation went very well; we gathered the information that we were supposed to, and got back to the fleet with it. So we had conducted our first combat operation successfully.

The invasion of Guam took place a few weeks later and that used UDTs 3, 4, and 6. Our next operation was at Tinian on July 24. There was more enemy fire at Tinian, which made it harder than Saipan had been. But we were learning and we still got the job done. People at fleet level were happy with what we had been able to do.

Ours was still a very new operation. The Teams had been built up because of what had happened the year before at Tarawa. The Marines took heavy losses just getting in to the beach. They had gotten hung up on the reefs and hundreds never even made it to the island.

So our mission was to clear the way for the landing craft to get in to the beach. We had worked with UDTs 3 and 5 and done very well; everyone did their job and it showed. Lieutenant Commander Kauffman was out there with us, but he had very little power when it came to how to use us. All of this was still very new and we were learning parts of our jobs as we went along. We didn't look very much like any sailors that had been seen before and that rankled some people in command.

Some admiral made a comment to Kauffman that he considered us "the most unruly bunch of Navy men" he'd ever seen in his life and he didn't know what he would ever do with us.

And Kauffman answered that officer with, "Yes, sir, but they got the job done."

"Yes," the admiral said, "I hate to admit it, but they did."

So even in those early days we were not accepted well by the regular Navy. When we went on board our ships, the APDs, we went around in our shorts. The regular crew had to keep their uniforms and hats on as per regulations. We just didn't comply with that sort of thing very much. That did raise some resentment among the rest of the Navy. And after the war, it wasn't long before they broke us up back in the States.

After having served in the UDT, it was pretty hard to go back to being regular sailors. There was more than one base commander who didn't really want us in his area. Putting what was left of the Teams kind of out of the way may have added a lot to our ending up in Coronado and Little Creek.

But after the Tinian operation, we went on to Peleliu in September. After that operation, we finally returned to Maui. We had been told that we would be sent stateside and given a leave on our return. The UDTs had gone on a number of ops during the invasions. Between all of the Teams involved, the men had gone on ten or more swims into the enemy beaches.

So the Team had been promised a stateside leave, but that was just one of those things that never happened. Instead, we got a ten-day island leave and most of the guys went over to the main island. Afterward, when the Team got back together, they made instructors out of many of us for the new Teams going through training. The Navy kept us in Hawaii for months, running, training, and various other jobs.

Finally, in February 1944, we left Maui for the Western Pacific along with five or so other UDTs. A number of the Teams were heading for Iwo Jima and the operations there. UDT 7 passed Iwo and went on to the Philippines. The invasion of the Philippines had already been completed. We went in to Lingayen Gulf and the straits around there and worked in that area. We did a few recons, but they weren't under hot combat conditions. The Japanese were there, but we weren't facing the enemy as such. It was practice for what was coming later.

From the Philippines, we went on to Okinawa, where we took part in the invasion. As I remember, we came in to Okinawa on the thirtieth of March. The invasion was planned for April 1. You think about what's coming when you're still on the ship. You get hyped up about the upcoming op, you wonder about what you're going to find in the water, what might be waiting on the beach for you, or even if you're going to make it. All of those kinds of things run through your mind.

As soon as I could get off the ship and out of the boat, things were better. The ship wasn't my blanket, the water was my blanket. As soon as I got into the water, things were all right. Everything seemed to calm down and I could concentrate much better on what I was supposed to do.

We dropped the LCPRs into the water from the APD to start the op. A UDT platoon would get into one LCPR to go in on the op. The rubber boat would be tied to the side of the LCPR and we would load up and head in.

Near the target, the man who would signal us to drop off the rubber boat would climb down off the LCPR and take up his position. Then we would go in and make our drop run off of the beach. At whatever distance from the beach had been decided by our mission planners, say 1,000 yards, we would start dropping into the water.

All of us would have lined up in the boat with our swimming partner for the drop into the water. The LCPR would be traveling along at flank speed, paralleling the beach, as we left the boat. The man giving the signal would drop his arm, and a pair of us would roll off the side of the rubber boat. As soon as one pair was gone, the next would scramble up and into place. We dropped off in pairs spaced about fifty feet apart.

The first thing you would notice, especially off of Okinawa, was that the water was more than a little cool. That shock brought you to your senses pretty quick. Then you and your swim partner would take a look and make sure everyone was in line before striking out for the beach.

Moving on to the beach, we would take our soundings and make notes on our pads. We would also keep a lookout for man-made obstacles, coral heads, and whatever we could see. We would take bearings on landmarks on the beaches to show where obstacles were or whatever.

Enemy fire was very light at Okinawa. We drew some small-arms and sniper fire, but it just wasn't much. There was plenty of fire going overhead. Our cruisers, battleships, and whatever were still pounding targets on the island. But there was only light enemy fire directed at us, at least it seemed so to me. No one was in trouble as we formed up our line and moved back out to sea.

Our LCPR moved along and recovered each of us with the double-loop snare. Then we returned to the ship, where we were all immediately debriefed by the old man and several other officers. Our notes and soundings were taken and compiled together. Then all of the information was taken up to higher headquarters. Then the day was basically over for the time being.

We went in during the early morning, and it seemed we were done by 10 A.M. If we had to make a demolition swim, it would be done later that afternoon, the next day, or whenever. It depended on what the higher command decided from the information we gave them.

Each time we went in on an operation, it was a little harder than the time before to get yourself up for the mission. The first time was the easiest. You hadn't been through it before and you didn't really know what to expect, even though you had heard all of the stories from other guys who had already been there. You always had to get yourself in the right state of mind so you were sure you would have the strength and not fall apart when you had to do your job.

As soon as the stuff started flying, the whole situation started to seem a little like a dream. It was happening all around you, but it didn't seem real. You would psych yourself up and even the sound of the shells and rifle fire seemed to get less. They were kind of muffled, though you could still hear everything.

But you just kept going, did your job, and turned back out to sea for pickup. It wasn't until you got back aboard ship and everything was over that maybe your hand would start to shake a bit, or you got the funny feelings in your stomach.

During our second operation on Okinawa, on our swim in to the beach, I remember seeing a white flag up on the seawall on the beach. I used that flag as my marker for the swim in. The invasion had already been going on, but we didn't take any fire at all. It was as if we could just swim right up to the beach and no one cared. We were taking no fire or anything. Then, just as I reached the beach and could look up and see that white flag—kaboom!

Falling back into the water, I was sure I had been shot and killed. What the noise had been was an American tank, on the far side of the seawall where I couldn't see it, that had chosen that moment to fire its main gun. Right after that little noise, I was scared; everything, all the bravery and psyching up, were gone. All I could hear or feel for a moment was the beating of my own heart.

It seems that for just about everybody, until the situation arises where you've been hit or are in trouble, you stay relatively calm. After something serious happens, though, the shock sets in. Many people do a lot of things when they're in shock that they don't remember afterward. Guys will do things, real acts of bravery, and when you ask them about it afterward, they just don't remember.

On any of the operations we had done, we went in anywhere from four days to just the day before the landings. That was how we could get the last-minute information to the planners on the staffs. It was also how we were able to leave a sign now and then for the Marines when they came in to the beach.

The signs were just a joke and I don't want to run down the Marine Corps. Those are a fine bunch of men who did one hell of a job. We did have the "pleasure" of leading the first Marine landing boats in to the beaches on the mornings of the invasion. At Okinawa, I was one of the men from the UDTs who went in with them.

That first boatload of Marines talked a bit with us on our way in to Okinawa. They considered all of us as crazy as they had even seen. They thought the idea of swimming in to the beaches almost naked was insane and they wouldn't have our jobs for anything. I looked at those men and thought about the fact that we only had to go in to the beaches for two or three hours. Then we were able to go back out to our ships. They had to go in and either take the island or die. I couldn't see their logic in thinking we were so much crazier than they were.

Okinawa was going to be our last combat operation, not that we knew it at the time. In a way, it was probably our worst operation. It wasn't that we had high casualties; only one man was killed, but others were wounded. One good friend of mine, Frank Brittain, was working on one of the obstacles near the beach, and one of our own shells landed near him. The blast nearly deafened him for quite a while afterward.

Frank wasn't one to let things slow him down much. After he left UDT, he joined the Army and became an Airborne Ranger. Later he calmed down a bit, and today he's an ordained minister.

Frank's near miss wasn't the bad action for UDT 7 off of Okinawa.

The serious incident happened to UDT 7 and our APD about 4:30 in the afternoon on April 9. A week or so after the invasion of the main island, we had conducted recons off of Tsugen Shima, a small island off the east coast of Okinawa. We were pulling screening duty off the island when a hidden Japanese shore battery opened up on us and our APD took eight hits from armor-piercing shells.

When the UDTs weren't preparing for or on a mission, we had other jobs we did aboard ship. I had been assigned as head count in one of the mess decks. They woke me up one afternoon to get ready to pull my shift. The nap I had been taking made me a bit groggy, so I went out on the fantail of the ship to get a little air. Standing there, I had one foot up on the depth charge rack and was smoking one of my very rare cigars. That was when I saw the first shell splash into the water behind us.

Even though I had seen enough incoming shells to recognize what had happened, I said, "What was that?" to anyone who could hear me. It didn't matter if anyone had heard me at all, as the second round came in right about then and struck one of the stern 40mm guns tubs right behind me.

I had gone through enough of Gunnery School to know where I could be of the most use right then and I headed toward the bow five-inch gun. From that gun, we would be best able to put some fire back out at the Jap guns that were shooting at us. As I headed up the passageway, more rounds impacted on the ship.

Two or three more rounds had hit, one of them close behind me as I was moving in the passageway. The explosion felt just like a big hand had picked me up and threw me right up the passageway. It didn't hurt or anything, it was just like I was floating through the air. But I was one of the lucky ones.

Other men had been badly hurt in the shelling. Guys were lying all over on the deck, hurt and bleeding. The way forward to the five-incher had been blocked, so there wasn't any way I was going to make it to that gun to be of any use. But the men right there on the deck all around me were able to use any help they could get. So I set to trying to give any first aid that I could to the injured men.

UDT 7 and the ship had twenty-three casualties from the shelling, but only one UDT man was killed, a young man name of Buck. Some of the other injuries were very bad; one UDT man lost his leg.

One of the guys in the Team found a Jap shell that hadn't detonated onboard ship. The round was close enough to our forward explosives stores that if it had gone off, we would probably still be going up into the air. There had been something like twenty-five tons of explosives on board in the forward hold near that shell. That guy grabbed up that dud shell and carried it over to the side and dropped it into the sea. He never received a medal for it.

A lot of guys never were recognized for different things they did. The Team as a whole was decorated for our actions; most of us were put in for Silver Star at one time. But the awarding of medals followed Navy traditions and the officers received the Silver Star and the enlisted got the Bronze Star. But that was just Navy protocol. We had a fine bunch of officers in the Team, leading a great unit of men.

We had stopped off in Manu Bay in the Admiralty Islands on our way back to Maui after Peleliu. We had been transferring powder from our ship to the APD Clemson and UDT 6. Early in the evening a fire broke out on the fantail of the Clemson and spread to our ship. The tetrytol explosives that were still out on deck had caught fire and were burning.

A good buddy of mine, Eddie Remeika, was one of the guys who tossed burning explosive charges off of the ship, probably saving both it and us. But he never received the recognition a number of us felt he should have for doing that. It seems to me that it was much harder to be recognized for heroism back then. Not that we were out looking for medals.

Finally, we were sent back to the States. About the first of August, we reported to Oceanside, California, after our leave. The Team was going to take cold-water training for the upcoming invasion of Japan. But President Truman changed those plans when he had the bomb dropped. The war was over at last.

We did end up going to Japan anyway, but as part of the occupation forces rather than invaders. Our first area of operations in Japan was in the Yokohama area. Then they sent us up to Sendai, where we recconned the beaches prior to landing U.S. forces.

Going up to Sendai turned out to be quite a deal for us. I was one of the guys in the boats who went in that day. We showed no weapons but just went in to where we could see a crowd on the beach. There were hundreds of people there to greet us. One old, gray-haired Japanese in his ceremonial robes came down to meet us directly. Our lieutenant went up to the old man and returned his bow.

There were so many people on the beach, we didn't know what to do. That crowd could have done anything they wanted with us, but instead of anything we might have expected, they picked us up, rubber boat and all, and paraded us up and down the beach. This was something I could hardly believe; they were treating

Japanese officers prepare to lead members of UDT 21 into a storage cave on the coast of the Japanese main islands just after WWII. The officers were expected to show the UDT men if there were any boobytraps in the caves, which had been used to store weapons and munitions for the last-ditch defense of Japan.

Barry G. McCabe Collection

us like arriving heroes rather than the enemy. It may have been that they were just as glad the war was over as we were.

On that particular beach, we didn't find anything in the way of obstacles or fortifications. Our Team wasn't like the UDTs further south in Japan. There, the guys found lots of obstacles and weapons. Boats filled with explosives, mines, suicide weapons, all kinds of materials had been built up by the Japanese and made ready for their final defense of the islands. Any Allied invasion would have been a disaster, for both sides.

The plans for the invasion of Japan called for thirty UDTs. Eventually, I got a chance to see the plans for some of the invasions and what our part would have been in them. One of the sites looked like it was just south of Tokyo, in an area full of mudflats and impenetrable terrain. It wasn't very fortified, so maybe the Japanese thought no one would be crazy enough to try a landing there. But it looked like we would have.

But the Japanese would have fought to the bitter end. There were going to be a number of invasions, one after the other. That mudflat action may even have been a diversion, for all I know. But that wouldn't have mattered much. The Japanese people would have kept fighting until they were all gone, and they would have taken an awful lot of us with them. The cost of those invasions would have been astronomical, on both sides.

Back then we were all really gung ho to do our part and win the war. Patriotism ran really high and Roosevelt was God. I experienced three wars—WWII, Korea, and I was still in the service during Vietnam. Older now, I can look back on what we did and why we did it with a different view. And the only question I still have is just why can't mankind settle their differences without violence. Wars have always been such a waste. In spite of bringing out the best in some men, they also show the worst.

The young guys in the Teams had come from most every walk of life prior to joining the Navy. That was one of the fantastic things about them: they had come from everywhere. We had farmers, schoolteachers, people from the city and the country. In UDT 7, we had a number of older guys, all of around twenty-five years old, who had already started life. They were married, some even had kids. All nationalities, all types. One of the really great fighters we had in the team later in the war was a full blooded American Indian, and he was one hell of a fighter.

Some of the guys had come from very poor backgrounds, a few had come from wealth, some with little education, others with degrees. They were all the same type of people in that they wanted the adventure and challenge of being in the Teams. Other than that, they were all different, there was no one kind of person you could point to and say, "That one would be a UDT man."

There was a strong feeling of team spirit among us all. But our job was secret and we couldn't talk about it to anyone except each other. It was a dangerous job and a difficult one. If you were just there for the glory and all, you weren't going to stay very long. What we did wasn't for the kind of person who gets emotional about things. That kind of person who goes out for the glory and all of that, he just wasn't going to stay long.

Our job depended a lot on what the individual could push himself to do. And not just once but over and over again. We didn't have any underwater breathing gear when we went out on an operation. When you dove under the water, what mattered was how long could you hold your breath. We all had to dive down a fair ways, something like twenty-five feet maybe, and tie a certain kind of knot to attach two lines. The knots were the kind we used to attach primacord lines together. If you couldn't do this knot tying, it didn't mean they would wash you out completely. But you would probably be assigned to a boat crew and not be one of the swimmers in the water.

Everyone was important in the Team, and it took everyone working together to get the job done. But the basic job was to get the swimmers within range of the beach. They were the men who went in and got the information and were the spearhead of the invasion force.

It was from in the water that we got our job done. That's why they kept us there for hours at a time during training. And we made mistakes, both during training and on operations. But it was from these mistakes that we learned how to do the job better. Operations changed from day to day; every island was a little different and every invasion had its own problems. When we came up with a better way of doing something that worked, it would eventually get back to Maui and become part of the training.

Friendship isn't really a good enough word for what we felt for each other in our Team back then. What we did and how we did it was a real bond between us. There was a relationship between the members of my UDT that seems to have been even stronger than the bond between a married couple.

It takes a special type of person to have wanted to be in the UDTs back then, and the SEAL Teams now. The training and equipment these guys have is so far *above what we had that there's no comparison. Many of us couldn't have passed today's SEAL training; we just didn't have the education.*

Despite everything that the SEALs have today, it seems that the man underneath all of the equipment and training is the same as we were. It's hard to say for sure about the differences between now and then. Our birth, the UDTs, was under wartime conditions; we had to learn hard and fast how to do our job. The SEALs were created in peacetime. They had the time to learn what their duties were; we went into things pretty fast and made mistakes. But then, we were expendable.

■ Chapter 12

The OSS Maritime Unit

One of the more unusual forces fielded by the U.S. during World War II involved the unconventional combat units of the office of Strategic Services (OSS). The Office of Coordinator of Information (OCI) was started on 11 July 1941 to collect and analyze information for the U.S. government. In June 1942, the Office of Strategic Services took over the mission of the OCI. Both of these organizations were under the direction of General William J. "Wild Bill" Donovan, a colorful individual who put together his organizations at the request of the President of the United States, Franklin Roosevelt.

The OSS soon became known for its clandestine work in gathering information by espionage. The OSS also created and supported guerrilla groups and other unconventional forces. Among these forces was the Maritime Unit, the first underwater combat and sabotage forces in the U.S. military.

The Maritime Unit (MU) evolved from earlier training activities of the OSS. The activities were conducted at a training site known as Area D, near the present Marine Base at Quantico, Virginia. Training centered around the clandestine infiltration and exfiltration of agents by sea but soon expanded to include attacking ships at anchor and other underwater missions.

The OSS Maritime Unit used kayaks and folding boats for overwater operations. Also used were inflatable rubber boats and inflatable two-man "surfboards" that included an electric motor for propulsion. On 20 December 1943, the OSS purchased 30 Lambertsen Diving Units, the first of almost 350 such units purchased.

The Lambertsen Diving Units were closed-circuit pure-oxygen rebreathers designed by Dr. Christian J. Lambertsen. This device, also called the Lambertsen Amphibious Respiratory Unit (LARU) allowed a swimmer to move underwater at up to thirty feet down without leaving a trail of bubbles behind him.

With the LARU, the Maritime Units also used swim fins, waterproof compasses and watches, and a variety of explosive devices.

Donovan's OSS was not looked on with favor by a number of leaders in the military. Admiral Nimitz would not allow the OSS to operate in his areas of responsibility. General MacArthur was even more adamant about allowing OSS activities in his command area. The Maritime Unit saw few active combat operations during WWII under OSS direction. So to put his MU to good use, and to try to get a toehold in a new operational area, Donovan offered some of his MU personnel to the UDT school at Maui.

At Maui, the OSS men were able to help the UDTs use swim fins much more efficiently than they had before. Swim fins were reportedly used prior to the OSS MU personnel arriving at Maui, but the MU had different types of fins than those used by the UDTs. The commander of the OSS Maritime Unit, Navy Lieutenant Arthur Choat Jr., was one of five officers and twenty-one men to be assigned to Maui by the OSS. With the arrival of a contingent of men from class 6A from Fort Pierce, UDT 10 was formed around the Fort Pierce men and the OSS personnel. Arthur Choat was made the commanding officer of UDT 10.

The close cooperation between the OSS and the UDTs of World War II would survive the end of the war and continue in the years afterward. When the CIA, the postwar successor to the OSS, needed special personnel during the Korean War, they turned to the UDTs. The same held true in the late 1960s and well into the Vietnam War with the Navy SEALs.

Charles Q. Lewis, Motorman First Class

A man came around the Seabee training base at Camp Peary in 1943 asking for volunteers for a new unit. The guy was just an enlisted man like us, as I remember, and he couldn't tell us a lot about the unit. What he did tell us was that it was a completely volunteer organization and that there were liberties and freedoms you would receive that you couldn't get in the regular service. I liked that last part and volunteered along with a group of my fellow Seabees.

We knew the unit would involve demolition and that was about all. When we arrived at Fort Pierce, we were already in top physical condition. The Seabee training had given us a lot of PT to build us up. So when we got into the program at Fort Pierce, most of it was a snap.

Swimming was something we did a good deal of, several miles a day, two or three times a week. But when I arrived at Pierce, I wasn't much of a swimmer. The instructors changed that. They took a bunch of us over to North Island, threw us into a tank of water, and told us to swim. That was the rough-and-ready Navy way then.

At Fort Pierce training, a boat crew included six men, five enlisted and an officer. If we had an officer who didn't work with us, we could complain to the CO and we would get a new officer. We didn't have to salute, even on liberty, and the officers pulled their own KP and cleaned their own latrines.

One of the best parts of demolition, and what pounded the meaning of teamwork into us, was that our officers had to work right alongside each of us. And if they didn't do it, they were just gone. It made a lot of difference that our outfit was all-volunteer. We had a number of older men, and a number of young kids. But we were a close-knit outfit and morale was high.

Commander Kauffman was down at Fort Pierce and he had an office near the beach. If we marched, or ran, by and didn't make some noise, even at 2:30 in the morning, he wanted to know why. There was a spirit in us, and Kauffman wanted to hear it. We had a love for each other and a love for the job we had to do.

After the Fort Pierce training, I could swim well enough. During the UDT at Maui, I didn't have any trouble. And swimming in the open ocean didn't bother me. I had my trusty knife in case of sharks.

At Maui with UDT 12, we developed the cast and recovery sling system for getting swimmers out of the water fast. There wasn't any one person who came up with the final idea. It was another of our Team efforts.

With a rubber boat tied to the side pickup boat, an LCPR, we put a man in the front of the boat to pick up the swimmers and swing them on board. We found out fast that you couldn't just grab a swimmer and swing him into the rubber boat—your hands would slip.

First, we came up with a sling that was just a length of rope tied to the LCPL with a knot at the loose end. But the swimmers couldn't always hang on to the knot as they swung aboard. Then we tried a loop of rope. That turned into the double-loop (figure-eight) snare that worked. A swimmer could put his arm through the loop and be swung aboard. This was almost a surefire fast pickup system. During our first combat trials, we only missed one swimmer we had to go back for.

UDT 12's first combat operation was the invasion of Iwo Jima. We had a job to do and that was how we had to look at it. I don't think I thought of anything in particular before we went in to the beach. I even had a wife and kid back home. But for two days off Iwo Jima, I didn't have a thought for anything but the job we had to do.

There was a lot at stake if we didn't do our jobs. If we didn't find the mines, blow the clear channels, and destroy the scullies that would impale the incoming boats, we would have lost a lot of friends and good men. We were proud of the mission we were assigned and what we accomplished, that every man accomplished.

It was great to be in demolition. We had no beef against the Marines, though we would leave them a sign now and then. But I never envied them having to land on those islands.

The hardest part of the job for me came after the invasion. We had to go up on the beach and clear wrecked and breached boats. Blasting the wrecks back into the water quickly cleared the way for more troops and materials to come in and be landed. Up there on the sand wasn't any place that I wanted to be. There wasn't any envy of the Marines for me; they could have that place. I didn't want any part of it.

During the operations, I was not classified as a swimmer. I could swim and work along with my Team in the water blowing obstacles. But my job was as a member of the boat crew of Platoon Three. Along with myself as the motorman, we had Browning as my coxswain and Reese as the signalman. The three of us were responsible for running the boat (LCPL) for Platoon One and getting the men to and from the water.

Considering how cold the water was off Iwo, staying in the boat wasn't as bad as it could have been. We had covered the swimmers with a thick coating of water-pump grease to try to give some protection from the cold. There weren't any cold-water suits for swimmers then. At least not any that we had.

But I still spent my share of time in the water. When my ensign told me it was my turn to get wet, I just put on my mask and fins and rolled into the water. Of course, I managed a little payback. On the pickup, my ensign was the man on the sling. Now, he was a pretty good-sized lad. But that was before we started tying the sling off to the boat. When it was my turn to be picked up, I set my fins against the water and braced myself. It was my ensign who was pulled from the boat instead of me from the water.

UDT 12 also was at Okinawa, but we didn't operate off the main island. Instead, we were one of the UDTs who went in to the Kerama Islands near Okinawa. We had gone in to investigate some of the small island beaches when we saw something suspicious. There were natives on some of the islands, and there were Japanese in there as well. But they stayed quiet. The Japanese acted respectably toward us, or at least they never opened fire.

We were looking for Japanese suicide boats and gun emplacements in the Keramas. We went on land at a few of the islands, but never ran into any trouble. In fact, one of the island natives gave me a big pocket watch that I still have today.

Okinawa was the last combat operation for UDT 12. We went back to the States for cold-water training. Twenty-two of us were picked from the Team to do the training. We were going to be part of the invasion forces for Japan itself, the next planned operation of the war. But the bomb was dropped and the war was over.

As far as the dropping of the A-bomb goes, all I can say is "Amen." For myself, I was glad it happened. I was sorry for the people who were bombed, especially after seeing the pictures sometime later. But it was time to end that war and the bomb was the fastest way. I have no qualms or bad feelings about using the A-bomb today. If I'd had to give the order to use it, I would have.

A line of Japanese Type 1/Improved 4 Shinyo explosive suicide boats being towed out to sea for scuttling just after WWII.

Barry G. McCabe Collection

The A-bomb ended the war suddenly. The bunch of us were on a five-day leave that was suddenly canceled. We were scooped up and shipped out fast. Within a day we found ourselves on a ship for Korea.

The Teams were a great bunch of people. We had our differences among ourselves now and then. But that never added up to anything much and it didn't last long. We had a lot of respect for each other. Each of us had his job to do and that job supported each of our Teammates.

■ Chapter 13

Kamikaze

The UDTs were part of almost every amphibious operation conducted in the Pacific from January 1944 onward. Those landings that did not use the UDTs either went in unopposed or were led in by the NCDUs working in the Southwestern Pacific. Each operation that led the Allied forces close to Japan met fiercer and fiercer resistance. The Japanese brought out weapons that were unheard of in the rest of the civilized world.

The kamikaze, or "Divine Wind," were generally aircraft pilots who had sworn their lives to their emperor and country. They lifted off in their aircraft with no intention of returning. If an Allied ship or target presented itself, the kamikaze would direct their planes to dive into the target. Only heavy antiaircraft fire could defeat the kamikaze attacks, and not all of the time.

Japanese midget suicide submarines are dragged seaward for destruction by U.S. sailors. Locating and disposing of these weapons found along the shores of Japan after WWII was one of the primary missions of the immediate postwar UDTs.

Barry G. McCabe Collection

It wasn't just aircraft that were delivered to their target by Japanese suicide pilots, explosive-laden boats and midget submarines were also used. The men of the UDTs felt safest when they were in the water, even when that water was just off a Japanese-held beach. They had relatively few losses on operations, but there were exceptions.

E. F. "Andy" Andrews, Lieutenant

When I first heard about Navy demolition, I was an officer in the Navy taking some special classes at Cornell University. There were about two hundred of us in the class and all of us had already put in requests for our preferred assignments. I had asked for and received orders for PT boats. Before I left for the PT boat base up in New England, an officer by the name of Draper Kauffman came to the university and asked to address our class.

During his address, Draper told us about his extra-hazardous-duty unit. The one initial requirement, that we be able to swim, was all he could tell us about the unit. Everything else was classified confidential. Out of those two hundred officers, six of us volunteered to join the new unit. Within twenty-four hours, my orders for the PT boat base in New England were changed to Fort Pierce, Florida.

It was Draper Kauffman himself whose demeanor and bearing convinced me to volunteer. He was a great guy and a terrific leader, the kind of man you would be

For the Apollo 11 recovery operation, there was thought to be a real danger of con-
tamination from the moon's surface. These UDT and SEAL recovery swimmers are all
wearing protective masks and coveralls while securing the Apollo capsule. The capsule was later moved unopened to a secure laboratory structure onboard a Navy ship.
The recovery swimmers had to go through decontamination procedures after the
pickup.

U.S. Navy

*willing to follow. He seemed to me to be one of those people who are just impervi-
ous to danger. From his background in bomb disposal, and the fact that he had all
of his arms. legs, and fingers, my opinion may have been close to the truth.*

*Prior to Fort Pierce, I had been an officer in the Navy for all of maybe six
months. So I had a little experience in the traditional Navy service and the distance
that exists between the officers and the enlisted men in most situations. Fort
Pierce and NCDU training was not one of those situations.*

*We had our own officers' tents at the training base, but they were just tents and
nothing better than what the enlisted men had. Our tents were located a little off to
the side and there weren't as many men assigned to the same tent as the enlisted.
But once you left that tent and got into the day's activities, you couldn't tell the difference between the officers and the enlisted men.*

*About the only difference there was during training was that the officers always
sat in the back of the rubber boat as the coxswain. Kauffman never knew exactly
what our assignment would be, so training was kind of being made up as we all
went along. Until the Tarawa invasion, and later, until we received the intelligence*

on the obstacles off of Normandy, we didn't have a specific target. Training was in some ways trial and error until we knew exactly what it was we had to attack.

But the basis of training centered around the seven-man rubber boat. That boat would be taken in to shore as our basic transportation. On board would be a unit of men and the explosives they would need to accomplish their mission. To this end, the Naval Combat Demolition Unit was six men, five enlisted and one officer and the rubber boat. The space and weight of the seventh man would be taken up by the unit's load of explosives.

The preferred manning of an NCDU was an officer, up to a senior lieutenant, a chief petty officer, and four men, usually a first class and several seamen. How Draper came up with that lineup, I was never really sure. But the idea was for the seventh "man" to be the powder or gear or whatever else you had to haul along.

For a short while after I had completed training at Fort Pierce, I was placed on the staff for the NCDU School. Then a group of NCDUs, including one I was in charge of, were sent out to Maui. Very quickly in Maui, our NCDU organization was dissolved and we were formed up as UDTs, my unit being UDT 15. That was when the word really came back for us to increase our swimming.

"Andrews' Avengers": the six-man Naval Combat Demolition Unit under the command of Ensign Andy Andrews (on the left). This was the basic unit of men that trained at Fort Pierce even though these men went on to be part of UDT 15 in the Pacific. They are armed with M1 carbines, the man at the lower left having an M1 Thompson submachine gun. Around the waist of their uniforms are the inflatable canvas and rubber life belts used during WWII.

UDT-SEAL Museum

APD 48: the USS *Blessman* with UDT 15 aboard at D-1, the day before the invasion of Iwo Jima.

UDT-SEAL Museum

Though swimming had been a requirement prior to being accepted into NCDU training, Kauffman never envisioned the NCDUs as a swimming unit during operations. When the requirement was put out that the men in Hawaii might have to swim up to a mile, Kauffman initially didn't believe it. He wasn't sure a man would be able to swim that far, but his judgment may have been colored by the fact that he wasn't a very good swimmer at the time.

But at Maui, swimming was heavily emphasized. Every day the distances swum and the time spent in the water was increased. This was in addition to time spent paddling the rubber boats. Special training was also given in demolition of coral and lava rock. And we learned reconnaissance techniques for offshore waters and enemy beaches.

When we finished training, UDT 15 was ordered to board APD 48, the USS Blessman, a high-speed troop transport converted from a WWI "four-stacker" destroyer. Prior to our departure, we had to load all of our equipment on board. There were thirty tons of powder (high explosive), all the rubber boats, and all of the other gear that a UDT travels with. We didn't know where we were going or how long we would be gone. So we packed for any eventuality.

My chief petty officer came up to me and asked if the men could have liberty and go into town at least one more time. I explained that we had to have all of our gear on board and properly stowed away by sailing time the next morning. The chief assured me that if I allowed the men to have liberty, he'd see to it that the materials were loaded by the deadline. So I let the men go.

It turned out that day was some kind of holiday in Hawaii and all of the bars were closed up solid. My men, being the resourceful types they were, didn't let that stop them from having a good time. They found a source of native "kanakee juice," which was really just fermented coconut milk. It may have been their last liberty for a while, so they certainly made the best of it.

The next morning I had never seen as drunk a bunch of sailors as my men. But true to his word, the chief got them together and they finished loading on time. The UDTs always got the mission done.

On board the Blessman, we didn't have the opportunity to exercise and stay in shape as well as we might have. Swimming was impossible while the ship was under way. Spending a week or two under way wouldn't sap the men's abilities too much, but we needed to stay in shape for any mission that might come up. So when we stopped at an anchorage, we would take the opportunity to get into the water and swim at least a bit.

We were at anchor in Ulithi in the Carolina Islands, a volcanic atoll that had a safe harbor from submarines in its center lagoon. The rim of the volcano was only six feet below the surface, while the center of the volcano, the lagoon of the atoll, was hundreds of feet deep. Outside the rim of the atoll, it was thousands of feet deep as it dropped down into the depths of the Pacific.

So we decided to swim across the reef and do some work on the outside rim of the atoll where there was some surf action. Inside of the lagoon, the waters were protected and there was very little wave action and no surf. Swimming across the rim of the atoll was interesting. Just a few feet below us, we could see maybe a hundred sharks sunning themselves in the shallow water. They just looked at us as we swam overhead.

We went outside the reef and conducted our exercise. Then it was time to swim back across the reef and to the ship. Going over the rim of the volcano again, we saw that about half of the sharks were still there. We didn't know what happened to the rest of the sharks, but we left them alone and they didn't bother us. There may have been kind of a mutual respect sort of thing going on there.

Our first landing operation swimming in the water was at Lingayen Gulf on the west coast of Luzon in the Philippines. Our job of swimming in the water and doing the beach reconnaissance was not as hard as just staying on the ship turned out to be. For at least three or four days the Japanese conducted kamikaze attacks against all the ships of the invasion fleet.

Every day Japanese planes would come up over the hills of Luzon and dive down on the ships. The area was called Kamikaze Alley because of all the attacks. The men of UDT 15 were not part of the ship's crew for the Blessman, but some of our men jumped in to help when the Japanese threatened.

The kamikazes were coming at the ships from all directions as we floated in the gulf waters. All of the fleet ships put out as much antiaircraft fire as they possibly could to try to hold off the planes. It was just by luck that the Blessman wasn't hit.

We had several near misses with planes falling just short of us and passing overhead to fall beyond the ship.

One particular kamikaze pilot stands out as the plane came in very close. He was aiming at our ship and I could see the expression on his face as he approached our ship. He passed over us by just a few feet and impacted on the water on the other side.

In spite of the nearness of that incident, it was such a big theater of war that the actions just didn't seem personal. Without that direct aspect, and the fact that we were usually pretty busy, you just didn't get as scared of the situation as you might think.

It was when you got into the water and swam up onto the beach to gather a sample of sand that things got personal. The Japanese would be firing and you knew they were firing at you, you were the only target on the beach. In a kamikaze attack, it was almost like being just a spectator at an event. The plane would be after everyone including you. But when you'd gone in to the beach with your swim buddy to gather the sand sample, and the mortars and the machine guns opened up, there wasn't much question what the target was.

To aid in the defense of the ship, the guns from our LCPRs, 50-caliber machine guns, were taken and added to mounts on the fantail of the ship. The gunners from the UDT added our firepower to the overall umbrella of steel that was helping to keep the kamikazes off of us. Other UDT men helped in passing ammunition and doing whatever other tasks could aid the ship. We may not have been a direct part of the ship's company, but for the time being, it was our home too.

We survived the attacks off of Luzon and moved on to our next target, the invasion of Iwo Jima. That island was the most godforsaken place I had ever seen in my life up to that point, with the black volcanic ash beach and dingy, foreboding appearance of the land. Our mission was to perform two operations in one day, one in the morning and one in the afternoon. There were only two beaches on Iwo Jima that were suitable for landing, and the Japanese knew that as well as we did.

It had been pretty well decided that we would be going in on the east beach, which put Mount Suribachi down to our left flank and the cliffs on our right flank. That was the swim we did that morning. That afternoon we conducted the same operation on the west beach of the island. But that last swim was strictly diversionary. The intent was to try to keep the Japanese confused as to which beach we would actually land on.

The Japanese gun position opened fire on us as we conducted our recon swims. Another part of our mission was to try to draw the fire of the Japanese to get them to expose their gun positions. The sites would be noted and the big guns of the fleet would then target them for destruction. This was all well and good in the planning stage. But the actuality of drawing Japanese fire was not the best mission we ever had.

The Japanese guns were in the hills near Mount Suribachi and dug into the cliff-side overlooking the beaches. Finding them was well worth the effort. They were so well camouflaged and emplaced that we never would have found them if they hadn't started firing at us. The next day, the big sixteen-inch guns of the battleships made short work of those gun installations well before the Marines hit the beach.

I was one of the platoon officers in the water for Team 15 during that operation. It was my platoon that was up under the cliffs on the right flank at Blue Beach on Iwo, where we were supposed to try and draw fire. UDTs 12, 13, 14, and 15 were working on the Iwo Jima invasion and it was just the luck of the draw that we were assigned the cliffs area. It was in those cliffs that command suspected the Japanese had placed their guns, and it turned out they were right.

Fear is something everyone feels. Anyone who has ever been in war has been afraid at one time or another, and anyone who says he has never been afraid is a fool. A hero is not somebody who does something he isn't afraid to do. A hero is someone who does something he is afraid to do. And I don't know anyone who isn't afraid of being shot at. So in wartime, of course you feel fear. Somebody is out there trying to kill you, and they aren't trying to kill anyone else at that time. Just like off those beaches at Iwo Jima, it gets very personal then.

The operations off of Iwo Jima were expensive in terms of men and material. I give great credit to the LCI(G) gunboats who gave us close-in fire support. We had refined our operations to the point that we knew the heavy, concentrated fire put in right over the heads of the swimmers in the water was what it took to keep the enemy from wiping us out. The gunboats put in 20mm and 40mm shells into the beach not twelve feet over our heads. You could actually feel the shock waves of the bigger cannon rounds as they passed overhead.

The idea was to keep the fire on the beach as the swimmers approached the shore. As we got closer, the gunboats would walk their fire up from the beach and into the jungle beyond. Then, when our mission was done, as we swam out, the gunboats would again concentrate their fire on the beaches to keep the enemy from firing directly at us.

The LCI(G) gunboats were converted infantry landing craft with a number of rapid-fire antiaircraft weapons installed on them. They could come in to the shallow water and put their fire in at point-blank range. And it was those same gunboats that protected us that drew the fire of the Japanese. The fire coming from the boats made the Japanese think our operation was the invasion, so they uncovered their guns.

On the swim in, I was getting to within 200 to 150 yards of the beach and the return fire from the enemy emplacements was getting heavy. I could see that the gunboats just weren't putting the amount of fire we expected in on the beach to keep the enemies' heads down. When I turned and looked back out to sea, I could see why.

There had been twelve gunboats coming in behind us to cover our operation. All of the boats had been disabled or sunk during our swim in. Not one of the LCI(G) boats escaped destruction. Destroyers were ordered in close to pick up the first support for us. But those ships were further out and just didn't have the range needed for the job. For a while we were receiving as much friendly fire as enemy fire.

In spite of the heavy fire from both sides, UDT casualties were very light during that operation. We were able to return to our pickup points and were snared up and on board our LCPRs. Returning to the Blessman, we made our reports and settled in. The Blessman was moved out for screening duty well away from Iwo as night fell.

What came later, on February 18, 1945, was the most expensive situation, not only for UDT 15 but for any UDT or SEAL Team, on any single mission before or since. It was the heaviest casualty count for a single team ever.

Our commanding officer and a few other officers from UDT 15 had left the ship earlier. They had taken our charts and notes on the beach conditions and were briefing the Marine officers on the conditions they could expect in the upcoming landings. Those of us who remained on board had little to do and were able to relax a bit as the Blessman moved into her assigned position in the antisubmarine screen around the fleet.

The captain may have made a mistake as he moved the Blessman out at flank speed to take up her post. The waters off Iwo Jima were heavily phosphorescent and the bow wave the Blessman threw off glowed in the night. Right about nine o'clock, things had eased down and it was time to wait for the next day when the invasion would take place.

A Japanese Betty, their Type-1 2EB twin-engine bombers, spotted the Blessman and targeted her with two 500-pound bombs. One of the bombs was a near miss to the ship and caused relatively little damage. The other bomb was very different.

The Japanese bomb went right down the middle of the ship and detonated level with the mess deck. The blast almost immediately set the ship on fire from stem to stern. On board the Blessman were not only her own ammunition lockers, but 30 tons of high explosives for the demolition teams stored in the aft explosive magazine.

In spite of the fire, the first order of business for the survivors of the blast was to get to the casualties belowdecks. The bomb had detonated in the enlisted men's mess hall. The majority of the men of UDT 15 had been relaxing, playing cards, reading, and writing home in the mess hall when the bomb went off. The carnage was terrible.

The ship was on fire and there was no power whatsoever. With the Blessman dead in the water, we found that none of the "handy billies," a self-powered water pump, would start. Without the pumps, we had no active fire hoses. In desperation, since we knew the explosives were there in the fantail locker, we formed a bucket brigade. When the buckets were thrown over the side attached to lines, they wouldn't fill quickly and just floated on the surface. A Jacob's ladder was tossed over the side and I went down to the water. As the buckets hit, I would push them down with my foot to help fill them. Even helmets were tied to lines that were thrown over the side to gather water to fight the fire.

We were trying to keep the fire away from the fantail, on the deck of which were our wounded. For some reason, I started singing "Anchors Aweigh" as I pushed the buckets down. Pretty soon we had all picked up the song. That story about the UDT who sang while fighting a fire on board their ship made the rounds.

Throwing the buckets on the fire near the explosives locker may have been doing about as much good as spitting in the ocean. But it was all we could do at the time. If the explosives went up, there would just be a big hole in the water where the Blessman, and UDT 15, had been.

The USS Gilmer, an APD that was acting as the UDT command ship, came up to us as we lay there in the water. I had to climb up the ladder and get back on deck as the Gilmer approached so that I wouldn't be crushed between the two ships. Commander Kauffman was on board the Gilmer and he quickly had fire hoses, running off the Gilmer's pumps, sent over to the Blessman.

Now we had water power and could fight the fire with some chance of beating it. One of the Blessman's fire control crew, a hoseman, was standing over the aft hold playing the hose down into where the fire was burning. I told him we had to get the hose down into the hold and fight the fire where it was. He just looked at me and said, "Yes, sir. After you, sir."

So I grabbed the hose and went through the hatch and down the ladder into the hold. Another UDT 15 officer, Bob McCullum, went down the ladder with me. We played the hose across the bulkhead between the fire and the explosives. Thirty tons of tetrytol and other high explosives wouldn't react well to a lot of heat, and the paint on the bulkhead was already blistering.

I didn't have much choice about going down into the hold and fighting the fire. If that much explosives went up, it wouldn't matter where you were aboard ship. Everything would be gone. What the bigger problem was involved the ship's ammunition locker.

The fire had already taken hold in the ammunition locker and the shells and other rounds were cooking off. The ammunition locker was right next to where our explosives were stored. Bullets and fragments were ricocheting off the steel walls of the hold as we fought the fire. The zing-zing of projectiles bouncing around was a bit disconcerting.

That kind of action I don't think took heroism. It was either do it or get blown up. Somebody had to do it. Besides, Bob went with me.

So we fought the fire and eventually won. Later on, the Navy thought a bit about my actions that day and awarded me the Bronze Star and a Navy Citation. For swimming in to the Iwo Jima beaches and drawing enemy fire, as the officer of the group, I received the Silver Star. Between the two, fighting the fire was the harder action.

It wasn't fighting the fire that was hard—that just had to be done. But I knew we had lost a lot of men in the initial bomb strike. We had moved the wounded and as many of the dead as we were able to the fantail deck at the stern of the ship. That was the only place that wasn't on fire at the time. Lying above that explosives locker were twenty-three of the Team's wounded as well as the members of the ship's company who had been hurt. Those men wouldn't have stood a chance if the explosives blew. And they couldn't move themselves to even try to get out of the way.

The shock of that blast had torn men's hands off, amputated legs and arms, and blinded others. They all would have been lost. But putting that fire out would at least give them a chance to live. Going in on the beach during a swim was hard, but at least that was just me and my swim buddy in harm's way.

I felt a considerable burden as I knew we had already lost a number of men from the Team; the number turned out to be eighteen later, as well as those from the ship's crew. If somebody didn't put that fire out, the number of dead would increase a lot.

We did get the fire out and saved the Blessman. She was later towed to Saipan for initial repairs. The blast from the bomb had been so great, it blew a hole in the side of the ship you could drive two large trucks through. The wounded had been removed to the Gilmer soon after we had the fires under control. Those of us who remained on board had to try to make the ship as seaworthy as possible. And there were other tasks that had to be addressed.

Our problem after the fire was in identifying the dead. It was only a day or two after the incident when I had to go into the blasted mess deck and try to identify what was left of my Teammates. That had to be done so that they could be officially declared killed in action. Otherwise, they would have to be declared officially missing in action, as per Navy regulations.

There have been easier jobs than going into that deck. Along with the Team's dead were the ship's crew. To identify them, several members of the ship's staff went in with me and what was left of the Team's staff. The problem was, we had already removed as many bodies as we could during the fire. Now we had to try to identify people by what was left, none of which was a whole body.

The group of us worked through the wreckage of the mess deck, the engine room, and other spaces that had taken damage. Throughout the areas there was just a mass of dead bodies. We looked for dog tags, or a piece of a body with a ring, tattoo, or other identifier.

In spite of our best efforts, there were some men we had to list as missing in action. There wasn't any question in our minds that they had been killed. We just weren't able to identify them.

In my platoon, I had to list two men as missing in action. Others in the Teams

At 9:20 P.M., 18 February 1945, a five-hundred-pound bomb dropped from a Japanese plane went down the stack of the USS *Blessman* and exploded level with the mess deck. In the blast forty men were killed and thirty-four wounded. The explosion also set fire to the ship, coming close to detonating the tons of high explosives in her magazines.

From UDT 15, eighteen men were killed and twenty-three wounded. This is some of the carnage of the ship after the fires were put out. In this twisted steel, the crew of the ship and men of the UDT searched for the bodies of their comrades.

UDT-SEAL Museum

were listed as MIA as well, but these two were particularly my men. After we had returned to the States, I made sure to contact the families of those men. I told those people that their loved ones were missing in action but that I was convinced beyond a shadow of doubt that they had been killed aboard the Blessman that February evening. I felt it was my duty as their officer to make sure that my men's families did not suffer through years of false hope that their missing men would someday walk through the door.

UDT 15 returned to the United States and Fort Pierce after the bombing off Iwo Jima. Fully half of the Team had to be replaced. Besides the wounded and the outright dead, there were other losses to the Team.

When we returned to Fort Pierce, we were all subjected to a battery of psychological tests. Some of the men who had come back with me from the Pacific looked just as fine as anyone else around us. But the doctors later told me that those men could not continue operating. They were perfectly healthy physically, but were mentally scarred inside. My own swim buddy ended up in a mental hospital six months later.

So my Teammates received the help they needed, and UDT 15 was restored to full strength with replacements. We were going to be in on the invasion of Japan itself when the atomic bomb brought the war finally to an end.

We had our orders to get ready for the invasion of Kyushu, Japan, on 1 November 1945, my birthday. A few of the staff officers, myself included, knew the date we were training toward. The operation was very secret, but only the details. Everyone knew it was only a matter of time until we had to invade the main islands of Japan. That would have been a real suicide mission.

Those of us putting together the plans for UDT 18's involvement in the invasion had been told to expect up to 75 percent casualties. In spite of that, we were going ahead with the plans and training. The dropping of the bombs changed all that. As bad as the bombs were in the amount of destruction they caused, it was nothing in comparison to the loss of life an invasion of Japan would have cost. And that would be on both sides.

In spite of the tremendous cost of the war in terms of human suffering and loss, it was worth it. As expensive as the war was, even to me personally, if given the chance, I would volunteer again. Even with what happened, I would conduct myself as I had done before. When I look back on it, I think the price we paid as a nation was high, but the results were also high. And when I say "we," I mean the collective military might of the United States and the free world, not just the men of the UDTs.

As a fighting force, we were able to be a deterrent force to the black plague of Nazism, Fascism, and Japanese Imperialism. That's what we were fighting for, and we knew it.

The SEALs of today are carrying forward the traditions we established and paid for in blood. They are everything we ever were and more. They are far better today than we were, better equipped and better trained. We were in Model-T Fords and the Teams of today are in Corvettes. But in spite of all of their high-tech equipment and support, underneath is still the naked warrior of WWII who swam into the beaches wearing swim trunks, a knife at his hip, and a bag of explosives over his shoulder. Even in training today, the young men who want to become SEALs have to learn to be UDT men first.

When you're looking at a UDT or SEAL operator, you're looking at a man who is dedicated, is in excellent physical condition (or he's not going to last), and has a very high level of tolerance for personal discomfort. He will not quit. That is what they try to get you to do in training—quit.

If you are the kind of person who would quit, they want you out. There's no disgrace, because they don't want you to get into combat and then decide that's where you want to quit. When you've been dropped off and have to swim farther than you planned, are you going to give up? Or are you going to just keep going? That mental attitude is what may save your life or the life of the man next to you.

The invasion stories most people know about usually start as the boats hit the beach and the landing troops pile out into the face of enemy fire. What usually isn't told is the story that unfolds before that. The story of how someone had to go in and open the way through beach obstacles so that the landing craft could make it in to land their troops.

The NCDUs were the first ones sent in to open the way. At Omaha Beach in Normandy, the losses were very heavy among the NCDUs. Utah Beach had lighter casualties but there were still losses. The beaches at Normandy had a very slow gradient up from the low-water mark to the high-water mark. But the tides rose to a fairly high level. This meant the beaches were awash quickly, with the water level rising and covering the obstacles.

The obstacles on Normandy Beach had to be attacked while they were still out of the water. And in spite of herculean efforts on the part of the demolition crews, they couldn't destroy them all. Especially not in the face of the murderous enemy fire. And the NCDUs at Normandy were walking units. They wore standard uniforms, boots, and steel helmets. Since they weren't swimming, they didn't even have the cover of the water.

Those of us in the Pacific UDTs had the safety of the water. We loved it in the water, that was the safest place to be. An individual could duck and swim away if a spot was drawing fire.

The danger for the UDTs was in getting into and out of the water and in riding the boats to and from the beach. Once you were in the water, it helped make you safe. The poor guys at Normandy had to walk right up on the beach to try to outrun the rising tide.

The UDTs and SEAL Teams cannot be easily described. They have skills, courage, perseverance, tolerance for discomfort and pain. What they all are is dedicated. If they weren't, they would never have volunteered and completed the program. They seek out the challenge, they stand in line to get in. A lot of them don't make it, but they all want to try.

You have to like the challenge. Maybe it's the competition in the hardest arena there is. You have to believe in what you are doing and be willing to put yourself to the test.

On Iwo Jima, I had a radioman with me so that our boat could stay in touch with our APD farther out. That radio was what we called a handie-talkie, an SCR 536, about a foot long and five inches square. If we could reach out with that radio half a mile on a clear day, we felt we had pretty good commo.

I spoke to a SEAL sometime back who was wearing a piece of equipment I didn't recognize. It was just a box that could be put in a large shirt pocket. When I asked him what it was, he told me it was his radio. When I asked him how far could it reach, "anywhere in the world" was his answer. That's just one small example of how much the technology has changed.

But it's the same man today who uses that equipment who would have been swimming off the Pacific beaches in World War II. The men themselves are individuals who have dedicated themselves to a mission, recognized its challenges, and *accepted them. They are the guys in white hats, the good guys. And they are the very best we have.*

Just like a good football player or other athlete, the men of the Teams accept that part of the game that includes the danger, the challenge. And there is no single type who can be pointed to and described as "a man who could be a SEAL or UDT." In my own unit, I had all types of men, all of them gung ho, but different.

Of my own six-man NCDU, who all became part of UDT 15, one was a Golden Gloves boxing champion. Another, my own swimming partner, turned out to be a published poet. One became an engineer after the war. And one of the men of UDT 15 who lost his eyesight that terrible night off Iwo Jima, he beat his personal challenges and became a successful attorney-at-law.

■ Chapter 14

Prisoners of War

On 9 July 1944, a very secret UDT mission took place that would turn out to be unique in the history of the teams. The Balao-class submarine USS *Burrfish* (SS 312) on only her third wartime patrol moved out from Pearl Harbor under the command of William B. Perkins Jr. on a special operation to secretly examine the Japanese-held islands of Peleliu and Yap in the Palau group of the far western Caroline Islands. To conduct the reconnaissance of the islands, the *Burrfish* was transporting a volunteer group of men from UDT 10.

The men consisted of two officers, a chief, and five enlisted men, all from UDT 10. The chief was Howard "Dynamite Joe" Roeder, who was already a veteran of UDT 2, and a number of the men had come into UDT 10 from the OSS Maritime Unit group. The reconnaissance operation was to be launched and received from the submarine, the men using rubber boats for transport.

The reconnaissance of Peleliu took place without major incident outside of an early mechanical failure on the submarine *Burrfish*. The men of the UDT-10 detachment were able to help in the repairs on the submarine working on the outside hull of the sub with a skill that surprised the crew of the *Burrfish*.

The next examination was of the island of Yap. The first rubber boat recon was conducted by Lieutenant Massey and a four-man swimmer team who examined the south end of the island. Chief Roeder and four men went on the last recon of the island during rough seas. The rubber boat operator was Chief Ball, who remained with the small craft while the UDT swimmers went into the island. The UDT men never returned.

The UDT swimmer in the center of the photo is wearing the 1940 model Lambertsen Underwater Respiratory Unit (LARU). The two swimmers on either side of the man with the LARU are both wearing early model dry suits for protection from cold water. In front of the swimmers is a stack of tetrytol explosive haversacks and individual blocks. The officer on the left is Vice Admiral Daniel Barbey, the commander of the U.S. Seventh Amphibious Force during WWII. On the right is Commander Francis Douglas Fane who brought the UDTs forward after WWII.

U.S. Navy

With dawn approaching, Chief Ball had to return to the submarine with a single swimmer who had not been able to complete the swim in to shore. In spite of the great danger, the *Burrfish* patrolled just off the reefs of Yap hoping to see some signal of the lost UDT men in her periscope. With the weather deteriorating and the Japanese having possibly detected her, the submarine finally had to leave Yap waters.

The lost men from UDT 10 were Chief Howard Roeder, John MacMahon, and Robert Black. Documents later captured from the Japanese indicated that the men had been taken prisoner by the Japanese garrison on Yap after several days of search. In spite of what were probably serious interrogation techniques, the UDT men told only the cover story they had been given to tell in this eventuality.

Records indicated that the UDT men were shipped out to a Japanese prison camp in the Philippines when all additional records of them end. It is suspected that the men were part of a group of prisoners being transported in a military ship, against the Geneva Convention and other articles of war, that was probably struck and sunk by an Allied submarine.

All of the men of the UDT detachment, including the three men lost, received the Silver Star for their part in the operation. No more submarine-launched UDT operations were conducted for the balance of WWII. These three men are the only known POWs ever captured from the Teams.

Because of Japanese military policies, POWs were guarded by some of the worst dregs in the Japanese military. Besides wounded and disabled soldiers, who would have little love for the men of the forces that injured them, the Japanese also assigned sadists, drunks, and the simply inept as prison camp guards. This resulted in Allied POWs suffering some of the worst treatment imaginable. And the larger, fitter Americans were particular targets for some of the smaller-statured, insecure captors.

The Japanese treatment of prisoners caused the military men who had their comrades imprisoned to feel a deep and lasting hatred. There was a poor reckoning after the war in the war crimes trials of Japanese prison camp guards. It is indicative of how the Japanese treated prisoners that their own people were terrified to surrender, preferring death. Part of this attitude can be blamed on the Bushido code, which forbade surrender over death. But some of the less advanced Japanese troops may have thought they would simply receive the treatment their own people dealt out to the enemy.

Frank Meder Jr., Machinist's Mate, Second Class

We started training in Fort Pierce in September–October 1944 with about 700 to 800 fellows and finished with somewhere around 80. Up in Little Creek, Virginia, while waiting to be assigned to an amphibious ship, the announcement went out that the Navy was looking for volunteers for a suicide squad. This announcement was just one of the list of such things they read out every day. But I had been standing musters and basically doing make-work for a while and just wanted out of Little Creek. So I volunteered for UDT training.

The announcement was actually read off as volunteers for a suicide squad. None of us really believed that and it was probably just the announcer's way of showing his dislike of such units. For me, it was a way out of the area. If you had experienced Little Creek back in those days, even volunteering for a suicide squad wouldn't have seemed a strange way of getting out. Even after I arrived at Fort Pierce and was involved with the rugged training, I still thought that announcement had been a joke.

But the training was tough, though I didn't have a whole lot of trouble with it. Every day I saw more and more of the big guys dropping out and I would just say to myself, "I'm still here." Outside of maybe a stronger will, I don't think I had anything more than those bigger guys who dropped out. Probably much like me, the guys who volunteered for training originally just wanted out of something else. But I decided I wanted the program, so they quit along the way and I made it through. The hardest part of training for me was all of the running. The swimming, PT, and other things didn't bother me at all; I had been raised around the water.

As far as Fort Pierce went, I had been used to small towns, so the lack of facilities didn't bother me. The bugs that were all over the training areas, those bothered me a little bit. You can never get completely used to things like that. Even though I was from the New Jersey shore area and we had biting bugs up there, it was nothing compared to the swarms down in Fort Pierce.

After the final few of us graduated from the Fort Pierce training, we were sent out to Maui to continue with UDT training. At Fort Pierce, we had mostly gone through physical conditioning and demolition training. In Maui, the emphasis was on swimming. Besides swimming every day, we really got into the more sophisticated end of demolition training.

We learned how to blast ramps through lava rock so that amphibious vehicles could climb out of the water, and techniques for blasting coral heads so that incoming amphibs wouldn't dig just one track in and flip over. But the majority of the demolition training centered on lava work, blasting that kind of rock flow out of the way.

Though I had swum a lot as a kid off the Jersey shore, the waters off Maui were a lot nicer. The water was clearer and a whole lot warmer than the ocean off of Jersey ever got. Swimming around the coral was pretty and it held a lot of appeal to me. So did catching lobsters and other seafood. That part of the training I enjoyed a lot.

Back at Fort Pierce, we had been the first Team to leave the post with the designation of UDT. Other units had graduated before us, but they were put together into UDTs at Maui. But my Team, UDT 18, had left Florida with our designation and basic complement of officers and men.

Once we completed training at Maui, UDT 18 was sent to the Southwest Pacific, where we operated with the Seventh Australian Division in retaking Borneo from the Japanese. That turned out to be the last major amphibious operation of the war. At Borneo, we did something unique in the way of an operation that was copied years later in the Desert Storm.

Our operation was what we called a "hit-and-run." We would blast the beach one day, do a recon, and blast another beach somewhere else the next day. We did that action for four consecutive days. By this point in the war the Japanese knew that when the UDT swimmers had come into a beach and blown up the obstacles, an invasion of that site would take place very soon. By blasting different beaches, we were able to keep them off guard so that they never could figure out where we were going to hit. We also did it so they would move forces to reinforce the beaches we weren't planning to hit later.

The last day, we conducted the actual invasion reconnaissance and demolition swim. Then we led the assault troops in to the beach, which was also part of our job. Our deceptions had apparently worked well; the troops landed against relatively little opposition compared to what had been expected.

Though we had been pretty lucky on our operation, some other UDTs hadn't done so well. Even when the enemy didn't hit you, you had to worry about short rounds from friendly fire landing near you. One UDT had been bombed by accident when a flight of U.S. planes mistook them for enemy swimmers. But this was just something that happens in wartime.

For our operations off Borneo, the higher command had changed their tactics a little bit to account for us being in a target area. As we were going in to the beaches in our boats, we had the best fire support available. Naval gunfire came from everything from destroyer escorts to battleships, three-inch to sixteen-inch guns. And they pounded the beaches and the areas inland.

When we neared the beaches and began our real work, the heavy fire lifted. All we had to protect us then was the cover of the water and the LCS(L) (Landing Craft, Support) gunboats with their cannons and rockets which came in very close behind us and pounded the enemy positions. Those gunboats were right behind us and could see us, so they knew where we were and to shoot over us.

When we went in to do our preinvasion work, we were dropped off individually at 150-foot intervals. The swim-buddy concept that is so important now, we just didn't have yet. Our basic unit, what I think of when asked about the Team, was my platoon. That platoon was the unit of men that I was closest to. We worked together and supported each other. But for the operation itself, we operated as individuals with a common goal.

The men in the Teams, then or now, are dedicated men who want to be among the best. For forty years after the war I just didn't speak about what I did. The UDTs were very secret during the war and the habit of not talking just stuck. Now, with the expansion of the UDT-SEAL Museum, our association, and everything, we get together and remember about the good times we had.

Even though we worked very hard during an operation, we had fun during the other times. Going out on weekends when we could, we would go fishing demo-style. Half-pound blocks of TNT were much faster than using a hook and line. Using a PR (landing craft), we would chase whales and fish, catch lobster, and generally have a good time.

The work was tough, and the ops off of Borneo had some very hard aspects. Though we never really thought we had been given a job we couldn't do, there were some parts that were a bit harder than others.

Off of Borneo, I bailed out of the boat that had brought us in to the beach, and they tossed my charges into the water off the other side. Swimming up to my explosives, I would start towing them in to the beach. The packs floated, but there still were a bunch of them. Swimming in with one hundred pounds of explosives behind you is a chore. And with my explosives in tow, and the bullets flying past my head, that was the time I thought, "What am I doing here?"

Concentration on the job at hand keeps you from thinking about just what's going on around you. Swimming in, placing your charges, tying the lines up, swimming out, and getting picked up keeps you occupied. It's later that the thoughts of just where you had been and what you had done come up and you can get a little scared.

After operations, I had buddies of mine come up and tell me how they had seen enemy bullets flying all around me. I had just continued with my job and never even knew someone was shooting at me in particular. But the other guys told me how they had seen this one enemy sniper up in a tree shooting at me. I hadn't seen the guy and just didn't pay any attention to the little splashes around me.

Our job was what we were doing. Swimming in and blasting the beaches open was what we were trained for. There wasn't any fear because we just didn't have the time to think about it. Our thoughts were centered on getting in to the beach, doing our job, and getting out. That's what makes it work. If you have time to think about where you're going and what you're going to face, then you can get scared.

Doing the beach reconnaissance and demolition swim, that was what we did well and the water was our cover. Later, leading in the invasion boats, that was scary. In the boats, you could see all of what was going on around you. And you didn't have a lot to do. That was when you could think about things.

The troops we were working with were great. Mostly they were Australians and were veterans of serious campaigns. The troops we were with had a great deal of respect for us, and we had the same for them. These were the men who had held out against Rommel at Tobruk in North Africa. The Seventh Australian Division was called the "Rats of Tobruk." These were the men who had held out for thirty-three days under siege by the Germans. When they were finally brought out of the desert, they did all of the mopping up in the New Guinea operations and then were the troops at Borneo with us.

Those men thought we were the greatest. We blew open the beaches for them. We thought those guys were great troops and tough fighters. For us, we were just doing the job we had trained for.

Right before we left Borneo, we transferred over eight tons of tetrytol to the beaches for the use of the Australian army engineers. Moving that much explosive was work, but it wasn't something we weren't used to. We knew explosives, how to handle them, and what to expect. Some of the other people who were observing us may have gotten a bit nervous.

While on guard over the supplies, UDT men would take a smoke break. Lighting up cigarettes near a pile of explosive crates might look dangerous, but we knew exactly what we were doing and how to be careful. It didn't bother us and we really didn't care if it bothered them. We tossed around charges like some people just wouldn't believe.

We had been sent back to the States after the Borneo ops to train in cold-water operations. We would be among the first troops to go in against Japan itself. Before we reported for training in California, we were all given a six-day leave. But our leave was cut short and the Navy gathered us all up quickly.

We were rounded up in Los Angeles by the police, firemen, shore patrol, anyone they could send out to find us. We were taken back to Oceanside, California, then moved across the highway to Camp Pendleton, where we boarded a plane for Alameda. In Alameda, we boarded another plane that flew us all the way to Guam.

The Japanese commander of a small fort overlooking Tokyo Bay hands his sword over to Commander Clayton of UDT 21 at the end of WWII. This was the first formal surrender of Japanese soil to a U.S. serviceman, an action that later drew the anger of General Douglas MacArthur.

Barry G. McCabe Collection

That was my first plane ride and it was a long one. In Guam, the Navy had a ship waiting for us with all of our gear on board.

We had been scooped up in dress uniforms and didn't have a thing with us. We were picked up at the airfield in Guam and moved to our ship in dump trucks. There, we finally had a chance to change uniforms while we were under way to Okinawa. Once we arrived in Okinawa, we picked up UDT 21 and continued on to Japan. We joined Task Force 31 of the Third Fleet off of Honshu Island, Japan, and were ready to invade. That's when we learned that the war had ended.

There was a big relief that went through many of us when we heard about the Japanese surrender, and we were all thankful for it. Dropping the atomic bomb was one of the greatest things that could have been done. It saved thousands, if not millions, of lives. Many of those lives would have been members of UDTs, but it wasn't our lives, that were saved as much as hundreds of thousands of Marines and Army soldiers who would have fought to take Japan. Millions of men, on both sides, were probably saved by the dropping of the atomic bombs.

We were the first to go in to Japan from the fleet, us and UDT 21. The only thing in front of us as we went in to the beach was a minesweeper, and it didn't land. Our landing craft went right into the entrance of Tokyo Bay. Things were a little hectic at first during our reconnaissance and we were a little apprehensive about the situation. I don't think everyone quite believed the war was really over, and they sent us in to check things out.

Our main purpose in going in was to demilitarize all of the dock areas. While checking for mines and booby traps, we would also collect up all of the Japanese weapons and make sure any gun emplacements were rendered safe. We secured the area for the troops to come in.

The people of Japan were beaten, there wasn't any doubt of it when we saw the population. My first contact with a Japanese citizen was with a man who spoke English as well as I did. He was a Japanese officer who had gone to the University of Chicago before the war.

Our UDT had gone into Yokosuka Naval Base and that officer was in charge of a group of young men that we would probably refer to as sea cadets. We had walked into them while they were cooking something in a big pot; it looked like a bunch of roots to me, sweet potatoes or whatever. It certainly didn't look any good to me.

All of the personnel at the base had to be rounded up and I stood with the group of cadets and that officer while other UDT men moved through the area. The group of us were standing in the courtyard and I was sort of standing guard while the rest of the area was cleared. That officer and I just had a little general conversation while the buildings were being cleared and everyone else was brought out into the courtyard.

That first day didn't really prepare us for what we found later. As the UDTs moved up and down the shores, it seemed that every little fishing village we went into had its share of suicide submarines and suicide boats. Our mission now was to destroy all those munitions and war materials. We spent weeks just blowing up midget submarines. Among the stuff we found were caves full of torpedoes. There were even caves full of boxes of Belgian shotguns. Anything that the Japanese home guard could possibly have used against invaders, we found in those caves and villages. We found them, took them out to sea, and destroyed them.

The cost to an invading force would have been tremendous. From just what I saw, the cost to us would probably have reached 80 percent casualties. I saw maps of the beaches we would have been assigned to for Operation CORONET, the invasion of the southernmost island of Japan, Kyushu. The Japanese would not have given up one inch of the island without killing as many of us as they could have first.

Later in October, we boarded our APD for the trip home. We arrived in Southern California and our Team was decommissioned within a matter of days. Many of the guys left the Navy and went back home. Because I was a machinist's mate, my rate was frozen and I was returned to the fleet. Being sent from the Pacific to the Atlantic, I made seven trips across the ocean, ferrying troops back home. And that was in December and I wasn't prepared for the cold weather. I didn't even own a heavy Navy peacoat. Finally, I was discharged from the service in June 1946.

Personally, I never had a very high opinion of the Japanese or their military during the war. Most of this was due to their treatment of prisoners of war, which was cruel, to say the least. I had the opportunity to see both Germany and Japan after the war. To me, the Germans were a much humbler people than the Japanese. We really didn't see much of the Japanese fighting man, their combat troops. What we saw in Japan were the young kids and the older men who weren't fit for combat.

■ Chapter 15

The Last Invasion

The final major operation of the UDTs during World War II wasn't done against enemy resistance. Instead, it was the landings of the UDT men ahead of any other U.S. forces on the main islands of Japan. Though Japan had surrendered and the emperor had put out the call to his subjects to lay down arms and not resist, there was a question as to whether those orders would be obeyed.

So, as on so many occasions before, the UDTs went in first. Beach reconnaissance was done on the offshore waters, but a great deal of additional reconnaissance was done on dry land. For their last operation of the war, the UDTs would again be walking instead of swimming, as the NCDUs had done before them.

The men of the UDTs examined the beaches for mines and the docks and harbor facilities for booby traps. In addition, all of the Japanese naval craft that remained in Tokyo Harbor, along with any intact harbor defenses, were to be rendered safe. Some UDT operators pulled breechblocks from shipboard cannon and dropped them over the side. Others peered into dark, wet areas under docks and piers. But there were no incidents and the surrender plans went forward.

Later the men of the UDTs were given other assignments in Japan. And during these operations, the men learned just how expensive the final battles of World War II could have been.

Barry G. McCabe, Lieutenant (junior grade)

About a month prior to my receiving my commission as an officer in the United States Navy in 1944, a request went out for volunteers for an outfit known as combat demolition. They wouldn't tell us a lot about the organization, but they did tell us one of the requirements was that you had to be able to swim. Most of the fellows I was with at Columbia for my officers' training were going into amphibious operations, which meant ship-to-shore movements. That wasn't something I was particularly interested in, and since I could already swim, the demolition outfit sounded interesting.

A chief signed me up, took my information, and that was about it. When I came in to volunteer, the chief asked me how far I could swim. After I told him I figured about three miles, he said: "That's okay, we'll teach you how to swim."

That was the extent of my indoctrination into combat demolition. In the month that followed, rumors were the order of the day. I was about the only person out of maybe 1,500 young officers at Columbia who volunteered for the new outfit. Scuttlebutt quickly had the outfit known as a suicide squad and my classmates referred to me as "Boom-boom."

The thing that was probably the most frightening centered around our leave after graduation. My classmates all received between a week to ten days of leave between the time they received their commission and the time they had to report for duty. I received a month's leave.

My friends all told me that the Navy gave me the long leave because I would never have the chance to go home again. Since I was all of nineteen years old at the time, all of the rumors tended to make me a bit apprehensive.

After my leave, I went down to Fort Pierce by train. It was early in the morning sometime in November and my first exposure to the training was interesting. As the train pulled in I heard all of these bombs going off and various explosions in the distance. When I reported for duty, I was told the unit was now known as underwater demolition. The term combat demolition wasn't heard again.

Getting involved with the training, I quickly learned how tough it was. But I was also becoming very enthusiastic about it. The hours were horrible and there was a lot of physical endurance training. But we also learned a lot about using explosives. It seemed to me that the primary emphasis was on demolitions and using explosives.

One thing that made the training quite unique was that I was right down in the mud with the enlisted men. Even though I hadn't spent any time at all in the regular Navy as a young officer, I knew this situation wasn't a normal one. Whether you had a commission or not, everyone did exactly the same training. You were hungry, you were bitten by bugs, you were dirty, wet, and tired, and so was everyone else along with you.

After about eight weeks of training at Fort Pierce, we all went on to Maui for further training. Once we arrived at Maui, we immediately began concentrating on swimming. We swam just about every day, and there was a five-miles-plus swim at least once a week. We would spend all day in the water sometimes. There was also a lot of additional rubber boat and explosives work.

During our training we had a number of individual tasks that we would focus on for concentrated periods of time. One of these tasks involved the rubber boat training. We would go out in the boats and paddle them over distance. We learned how to get some rhythm to our strokes and see how fast we could move while still going in a straight line. We had to flip the boats over in the water and then move them right side up. Many of the things we had to do in rubber boats training we never expected to do in the field, but we did them until we knew how to do just about anything with the small craft.

A UDT operator attached a Hagensen pack of high explosives to the center of a steel hedgehog obstacle.

The idea was for us to feel totally comfortable with our equipment and abilities. There were hours of drill in things like swimming, rubber boats, and working with explosives. We would tie charges together on land, and in the water, and half in, half out of the water with waves crashing down on you. Then we would blow the things up. You got to the point where you could properly tie a charge into a primacord line in any situation. It became second nature to you.

The hours of swimming were supplemented with other exercise. We had hours of breathing practice. There was no real scuba gear available to us. When we went underwater, it was with the strength of your own breath. On land, we learned you could hold your breath longer than when swimming in the water. So we practiced the one to be better at the other.

We did some unusual training where we had to jump off a thirty-foot-high pier into the water while wearing full combat gear, sometimes even packs. That one we did a number of times. We had to do things that were unusual, things that you wouldn't normally run into during a day's work, not even in the UDTs. It was to help you learn to cope under almost any circumstance. This philosophy had been followed at Fort Pierce as well.

During our explosives training, we had learned how to tie a number of charges together with primacord so that they could all be detonated together. Individual primacord leads from the separate charges were tied into the main primacord line. To make sure we could tie the knots correctly, we had to tie them behind our backs, underwater, while holding our breaths. Once you can get through that exercise correctly, doing the correct knot becomes second nature.

After my graduation from training at Maui, I was sent out to join up with UDT 21.

The Team was on its way back from the invasion at Okinawa and I met up with them on their trip in to the United States. We came back to the States at the end of July 1945.

The UDTs were created because there was a hole in the capabilities of the Amphibious Force to land on an enemy beach. This gap in abilities can be described in one word which is known to everyone who served in the Pacific in WWII: Tarawa.

Even though there was aerial reconnaissance that showed the reefs—intelligence dug out every piece of data that could be found on the area—the details were wrong. The recons hadn't worked and the landing craft were hung up on the offshore reefs. The Marines had had to wade in to Tarawa carrying all of their equipment; many of them drowned and others were picked off by the Japanese. And much of this was because the water over the reefs was too shallow.

An outfit was formed from the Seabees and Naval Combat Demolition Units to scout out the beaches, recon the waters, and blast the reefs. This new outfit was the Underwater Demolition Teams. And the Japanese learned from their errors as well.

The Japanese became clever in making obstacles of all kinds. Where there weren't enough reefs, they put up other blockages. Cribs of logs were built in the water and filled with rocks. Concrete barriers with steel rails pointing outward were put up. And if there was space between the obstacles for landing craft to fit, the Japanese would string wires up attached to antiboat mines. Striking the mines or the wires would cause the detonation of a large charge of explosives.

And in the UDTs, we learned how to destroy these and other kinds of obstacles.

UDT trainees during UDTR basic instruction charge a rock outcropping with high explosives. The individual demolition charges are strung together with detonating cord "mains." The detonating cord will initiate all of the charges at once in a single huge explosion.

U.S. Navy

We filled the need for someone to go and see what the situation was, measure the waters, and chart the obstacles. After the information was delivered back to command, the UDTs could go back to the same area and blast the way free for the landing craft to arrive. When necessary, men from the same unit that went in on the recon swim would guide the first waves of landing craft in to the proper sites. But for myself and my Team, that mission was over.

In spite of not yet having been with UDT 21 on an invasion, I really didn't feel like I had missed anything so far. The

training I had gone through was rigorous and complete. In spite of just having returned to the United States, I was looking forward to going overseas with the Team
when they left again. The Team reported to Oceanside, California, for cold-water
training to prepare for the invasion of Japan.

One of the big differences in the invasion of Japan compared to the rest of the
Pacific campaign was that the waters would be very cold. They took us up to lakes
in the mountains and put us in the water to see how long we could stand it. This
kind of thing really took your mind off of the invasion itself. Then the atomic bombs
were dropped and Japan surrendered. The war was over.

Here I was, a brand-new nineteen-year-old Navy ensign, and I had seasoned
combat veterans under my command. As far as what the war had been like, I really
hadn't experienced any of it yet. But some of my men certainly had. But I had a lot
of learning myself to do yet and I probably didn't take into account that these men
had a tremendous amount of experience among them. Some of the veterans in
UDT 21 had landed with the NCDUs on Normandy Beach. And here I was, a
nineteen-year-old officer telling them to stand at parade rest or whatever. I really
didn't think of the consequences of that, but I learned.

When we heard that the bombs had been dropped, I thought that the war would
be over and I would be going home soon. The war was over, but I wouldn't be seeing home anytime soon. Two UDTs were flown out to Guam, where they met ships
loaded with all of their gear. And UDT 21 and UDT 18 were those two Teams.

We arrived in Tokyo Bay on August 28, 1945. The Japanese formal surrender
was signed on 2 September on board the battleship Missouri. For about a month
following that ceremony, we went up and down the coastline of Japan locating, gathering, and destroying suicide boats, midget submarines, and major weapons. But
that first landing had been different.

When UDT 21 arrived at Japan, we were the first Americans to set foot on
Japanese soil after the war. Before any troops arrived, paratroopers, anything. In a
UDT of around one hundred men in five platoons, we would land in different places
while checking out sites for the upcoming landing craft. One of the platoons had
our commanding officer, Commander Clayton, on board when they arrived on a
place called Futsusaki, a small peninsula at the mouth of Tokyo Bay.

Thought I wasn't with the platoon at the time, I have a copy of the picture of the
Japanese commander at the small fort overlooking Tokyo Bay handing over his
sword to Commander Clayton. That was the first formal surrender of Japanese soil
to an American soldier.

Going in to Japan was an adventure and we were all a bit apprehensive. We only
swam in once, during that first landing. That was to do a normal hydrographic reconnaissance and check for possible obstacles in the water. After that first time we
would go in to shore in landing craft or our rubber boats depending on how we were
conducting the mission.

Japanese midget suicide submarines being removed from their caves along the shores of the main Japanese islands. This Kairyu "Sea Dragon" miniature submarine would have been launched from its rail trolley to attack Allied ships with its several thousand pound explosive warhead. Shown here are just two of the dozens of such suicide weapons destroyed by UDT 21 in their post-WWII operations.

Barry G. McCabe Collection

We checked docks and beaches for mines and booby traps. And after the mission was over, we would return to our ship for the night. Even though the Japanese had said they gave up, the official surrender hadn't been signed yet. So there were mixed emotions about the war being over—maybe not all of the Japanese military had gotten the word everything was over.

There weren't any incidents for us at all. There was probably apprehension on both sides, given that the Japanese had lost and we were landing in their country. But nothing happened where we were. Later there were reports of isolated Japanese units elsewhere in the Pacific that continued fighting after the war was over. But they just hadn't gotten the word yet, or they didn't believe it.

Our role in UDT 21 in going in first was the same as it had been all through the war, to try to make the way in safe for the troops to land. When we got over there and started landing along the coast of the main island of Japan, we found dozens if not hundreds of caves on the shore. In these caves were hundreds of suicide boats. There were also midget submarines. Our job was to get rid of these weapons and it soon turned into a problem because there was just so many of them.

At first we tried burning the boats. Then because of the danger of hidden explosives, we would take them far out to sea and take axes to them. What went through my mind as well as others' was just how horrible any invasions would have been if we hadn't dropped the atom bombs.

With the vast volumes of materials and weapons we found, there was no question that resistance to an invasion of Japan would have been catastrophic. A lot of people on both sides would have been killed in that operation.

All of our troops would have been exposed to the hundreds of suicide boats and midget submarines we were uncovering. Losses among the Allied troops and ships would have been horrendous. The Japanese were terrific warriors. They could fight to the very end and then try to take you with them. And that was not just the soldiers. Every man, woman, and child on the main islands would have done the same thing to the best of their ability. They would have been defending their emperor and their religion.

The atomic bombs had been horrible in and of themselves. But the alternative would have been so very much worse. The alternative to the bombs would have been hundreds of thousands of casualties on both sides. In spite of everything, the atom bombs were the fastest and cleanest way to bring the war to an end.

Once the emperor had said the war was over, the change in the Japanese people toward us was amazing. They were polite and deferential. I walked among them after the war, meeting men who were younger than I was, in their mid teens really. These men had been trained to be the suicide boat pilots for all of those small craft we had destroyed.

Even those young men were polite to us. We were welcomed up and down the coastline. And this was only because the war was over, the emperor had said so. It was like the difference between night and day the way the people changed.

When we finally returned to the United States for the last time, I knew I was going to go to college and finish my education on the GI Bill. I stayed in the Navy a few months longer and received my promotion to lieutenant, junior grade. Then I just left the Navy and continued my life in the civilian world.

It was right after the war that the term frogman was coined, sometime between the end of 1945 and the beginning of 1946. We never used the term at all in the service; we always called ourselves demo men. It was some civilian writer, I think for the Honolulu Advertiser, who came up with the name when he was writing a story about us after we had finally been declassified. But the term stuck as a great name and we've used it for the men of the UDTs ever since.

In the years after the war I didn't even think much about what had happened. In recent years I met the people in the UDT-SEAL Museum where our history is being saved.

Now, I'm active in helping prepare young men for careers in the SEALs. Captain Andrew Bisset set up a program to help these young men who want to be SEALs prepare for the extensive training at BUD/S (Base Underwater Demolition/SEAL training) in Coronado. And we don't just prepare them for the physical part of the training but also the mental part. Becoming a SEAL is probably at least fifty-fifty, half mental and half physical.

As a WWII frogman, I can see that the young men going into the Teams today are a lot better prepared for what they will face than we ever were. But they have to be now, warfare having changed so much over the last fifty years.

The training we had and the training they have today is similar though, in one way: it's really tough. We had Hell Week and they still do today. That's one of the big breakers. And we both had technical training. But ours centered primarily on explosives. Theirs today is generations ahead of what we had.

As a WWII frogman, we only had a pair of swim fins, a face mask, a knife, a watch, and little else. All of a man's gear then would have fit in a small bag. Today they have vast amounts of equipment they have to learn to operate. A single man's gear in the SEAL Teams today can fill a small room, or at least a large closet.

To become a SEAL today, you have to have physical capability, upper body strength, the ability to swim great distances, and the ability to run great distances under any conditions—run, run, and then run some more. Run with boots on, run in sand, run uphill, run carrying things, run doing all of the above at the same time. That physical aspect is the one best known to the public.

But the other aspect, the harder one to build, is the attitude, the mental discipline. People coming in to training have to have the desire to become a SEAL more than anything else. Young men go into Navy recruiting offices saying that they want to become a SEAL, but they want to finish their education first. That's fine, the individual isn't ready quite yet to join the Teams. But it's a good reason and they can grow further as they learn.

Then there's the men who come in to join who say that they're qualified to become a Navy officer, but they want to be a SEAL so badly they're willing to go the enlisted route just to get in. The job is tough no matter what your rank once you get to BUD/S training, but there are more openings available for enlisted men than officers just because of the way the Teams are organized.

The failure rate for young men going into BUD/S from across the country straight from the recruiters and boot camp is about 70 percent. We help recruit for the SEAL Teams up in the northern East Coast. And we have SEAL candidates come up to us from all over the country. We help prepare them for BUD/S both physically, mentally, and psychologically. We tell them that when they get out there in training at BUD/S, it will be some of the most draining and discouraging work they will ever do in their lives. But they must have the attitude to get through.

We help these young men learn how to swim, run, and work out better. And we test them. The reason so many young men fail at BUD/S is not just that it's hard. Rather they were never prepared properly from their first day in the Navy. The recruiter has a quota to fill, and these young men come in saying that they want to be a SEAL and that's just fine with the recruiter. They're in the Navy whether they pass

BUD/S or not. If the young man can pass the standard screening test, he gets in. But the level of the test, we feel, is too low. So we test our candidates at a higher level. And our young men have an 85 percent success rate in passing BUD/S.

That's better for the Teams, and for the Navy.

To have been in the Teams, then or now, is an accomplishment. Accomplishing the objective, no matter how hard, gives you a boost in your own eyes. You can look back on what you had to do and see that you got the job done.

◼ Chapter 16

Scouts and Raiders

The Scouts and Raiders continued their operations in both the Atlantic and Pacific theaters well after their initial operations in North Africa. The actions in the Mediterranean continued with additional personnel being trained at North African bases as well as at Fort Pierce. The Scouts and Raiders operated heavily in support of actions in the Italian campaign, especially during the several amphibious landings in Italy. The emphasis during the Italian operations was on scouting and reconnaissance duties.

A few S&R personnel were involved with hands-on intelligence-gathering operations off the beaches of France in preparation for D day. For the Normandy landings themselves, S&R personnel were available and were primarily involved with leading the initial landing craft waves in to shore. Operating from command ships, the S&R personnel were not able to use the most efficient means at their disposal to guide in the craft by infiltrating the beach areas the night before and setting up signaling stations. S&R personnel in the Mediterranean theater also operated as part of the Operation DRAGOON forces.

Emphasis at the Scout and Raider School after the Normandy and Atlantic operations were completed was on train-

The three Scouts and Raiders officers lost during combat operations at Anzio in the Mediterranean Theater. On the left is Lieutenant (jg) Jerry Donnel, in the center is Lieutenant (jg) Carmen F. Pirro, and on the right is Lieutenant (jg) Kenneth E. Howe.

L. L. Culver Collection

ing an officer corps in Scout and Raider skills. Once qualified, the officers would be able to act in a staff capacity for operations in the Pacific theater. Staff duty not being something that held a lot of appeal to many S&R School graduates, a number of the officers managed to get into the field and operate as often as they could.

Rear Admiral Dick Lyon, USN (Ret.)

During World War II I went from a Yale undergrad to a graduate of the Columbia University Midshipman's School, which made me an officer and a gentleman by order of Congress in all of ninety days—what was then called a "90-day wonder." I enlisted in the Navy while still at Yale on 9 October 1942. It was while I was at Columbia as a midshipman that a special recruiter came to the school shortly before our class's graduation.

The notice on the bulletin board read, "Looking for volunteers, must be strong swimmer." That kind of had my name on it, as I had spent more than a little time on the Yale championship swimming team, including a period as the team's captain.

That little bit of information in the notice was about all we were told about the new unit for some time. A meeting was held with the students who were interested. Those students who continued to have an interest after the meeting were given the opportunity to volunteer. I signed my name and soon after graduation followed my orders down to Fort Pierce, Florida.

Facilities at Fort Pierce were what might be called spartan. There was a tent, some wooden containers which at one point had contained rubber boats, and a cot that I was told would be my bunk. The bunk wasn't the most comfortable thing in the world. But the level of physical activity demanded by training would soon make it a very welcome sight.

Now I was a member of class eight at the Navy Scouts and Raiders School at the ATB in Fort Pierce, Florida. The choice of Florida for the training base, it was later explained to me, was because Florida's topography is the closest in the United States to the land and water we would find in the South Pacific.

The physical training at S&R School was tough. And it has some aspects in common with BUD/S training today. There was a lot of stressful physical exercise. Ensign Bell was running the school while I was there. Rank didn't seem to mean much among the students or the faculty. A young lieutenant (jg) named Phil Bucklew was there and he had been with the Scouts and Raiders since their very beginning.

Being right there on the water at the ATB, we did a lot of swimming. But that wasn't the toughest thing. Lying absolutely still in the sand and grass, not moving at all for extended periods of time, was a lot harder than any of the other physical activities. And the simple reason for this was the hundreds of thousands of sand fleas and other biting insects that swarmed all over the island training site.

For me, the swimming part was okay. But for others in the class it was a lot harder. We helped each other get through the different parts of training, though no one could help in beating the insects.

Part of the original training staff at S&R School had been from an organization called "Tunney's Fish." These men had been Specialist As (Athletic) and they were in the Navy to help develop and run the physical training program for the entire service. They took a particular interest in the Scouts and Raiders training program, so we received some of the most advanced physical training and conditioning in the Navy at the time.

There was another unit training at Fort Pierce right alongside of us that we knew quite well, though we didn't work with them directly. The Naval Combat Demolition Units had come down much earlier from Camp Peary, Virginia, and became the forerunners of the Underwater Demolition Teams for the Pacific theater. These guys were in the camp right next to us and there was kind of a constant friendly rivalry between the two units. Things never got out of hand, but there were varying degrees of mischief performed between the units. Even then, it seemed a fellowship of special warfare was developing between different units who all went into harm's way.

The Scouts and Raiders trained in the same place where Naval Special Warfare had spent its infancy. SpecWar, as it is known today, was really born with the NCDUs at Camp Peary early in 1943. Though the UDTs operated in the Pacific, the Scouts and Raiders and NCDUs had performed critical roles in the actions conducted in the Pacific theater.

My class was a bit unusual in that it was made up entirely of officers. Previous S&R classes had been a mix of officers and enlisted men, but our class was mostly very junior officers; we had some fifty ensigns. Our few very senior guys were at the lofty rank of lieutenant (jgs). The class was all commissioned officers apparently because the graduates were expected to work as independent operators in the China theater. Later, I was assigned to the Seventh Fleet in the China area, acting as the scout intelligence officer for the fleet commander.

The mission of the Scouts and Raiders met the name very closely. We were training to scout an area and perform raids on targets at or near the beaches. As officers, we directed and led these operations, though not a lot of active operations took place during the war. The only real exception to this was in the China theater, where a number of the S&R officers did conduct field operations. Mostly, especially for me, we ended up doing staff work in the scouting field.

It was after the war, when I had extended for a year, that I was able to do some active scouting actions in China. That was a year I performed intelligence-gathering work and scouting, sending back my reports to the commander of the Seventh Fleet.

The early missions of the Scouts and Raiders were not known to us. They were a secret unit and their history wasn't one of the subjects taught during training.

They had been actively involved in the war since Operation TORCH in November 1942. But none of us were given a lot of information as to where the previous classes had been involved. We didn't even know where we would be going.

About half of my class ended up along with me at the Administrative Command, Amphibious Forces, Pacific Fleet in Pearl Harbor, known as ADCOMPHIBPAC. From that command, we were assigned to do our jobs further out in the fleets.

My last assignment, and the one I extended for, was as part of the staff of the commander of the Seventh Fleet in his Intelligence Section. At the time the war ended I was in the Philippines and my job was to conduct reconnaissance and scouting ops in the area of the islands. The target we had been looking at particularly was the island of Mindanao, with an eye to conducting an amphibious assault at Davao.

The war ended and the operation never took place. I eventually found myself in Shanghai with Com Seventh Fleet, after taking troops up and landing them in Japan. We conducted the recon on the beaches off of Wakayama, Japan, where no obstacles were found. The elements of the Thirty-third Infantry Division I had been traveling with landed safely and conducted their occupation duties soon afterward.

The reconnaissance conducted on the beach was done in much the same manner as those done by the UDTs. I swam in to check out the beach and the off-shore waters since I was not only the scout officer, I was all of the scout troops as well.

Scouts and Raiders disappeared at the end of World War II. They had been a specialized unit that existed only during the war years. Any of the S&R men who remained in the Navy and later became part of Navy Special Warfare did so through the UDTs.

The mission of the UDT through World War II and Korea, and to a lesser degree in Vietnam, was making sure that a beach or landing site was cleared for an amphibious assault.

After World War II, I eventually transitioned into the UDT. I had left the Navy after WWII and returned to civilian life to finish my education. When the Korean War broke out, I went back into the Navy and went through UDTR with class two West Coast in 1951. Personally, I didn't have a lot of trouble going through UDTR. I was still a pretty young guy and my S&R training wasn't that far behind me. It was the presence in the water—the water training that was such a big part of Scout and Raider training—that helped me in UDTR. In the UDTs, swimming and water work was the primary mission, so they received a great deal of emphasis in training. That aspect of training hasn't changed to this day.

So to continue my career in Navy Special Warfare, I had joined with the UDTs on the West Coast, and soon was part of the recommissioning crew for UDT 5. The need for additional West Coast UDT operators to operate in the Korean War supplied the push to bring back UDT 5. It was very soon after commissioning that the

Team had deployments on their way to Korea and were performing UDT operations there.

Our skipper in UDT 5 was Lou States, who had been on the original crew of UDT 11 during WWII, eventually becoming commanding officer of that same UDT in time for a number of their invasions. He came back during the Korean War as a reservist and helped in the commissioning of UDT 5. When he assigned me as the intelligence officer for the new UDT, Commander States made his feelings very clear.

"Now, Lieutenant Lyon," the CO told me, "I want to make something very clear. You don't have to be intelligent to be an intelligence officer."

He was looking right at me during that statement, and I wondered if he was trying to give me a message there. But it was a great Team. Many of our crew and officers were experienced WWII UDT men. We had fourteen officers and one hundred enlisted men in our original crew muster for UDT 5. With all of our WWII vets and the experiences they brought with them, I feel it was the best UDT Team the Navy ever had.

At the beginning of the 1950s in Korea, the UDTs were again involved in combat operations, theoretically only to the high-water mark. That was not where many of the missions ended. When UDT 5 was in Korea, I was assigned by my skipper to go into Wonsan Harbor in later 1951/early 1952 on an operation. There were reports that a very small enemy mine had been detected along the beaches in Wonsan Harbor. Wonsan Harbor is a huge harbor; the mouth of it is nearly ten miles across and there are nine beautiful little islands inside of its protected waters. We controlled the islands, waterways, and harbor, but Wonsan is well north of the thirty eighth parallel, in what is now North Korea.

The mission I was given was to spot the suspected mines from a helicopter. The bird took off and landed from a Navy LST; I flew in that and spotted the mines, making note of their location. Then I would later return with a MINERON 3 explosives ordnance disposal officer and a two-man rubber boat. Going over the side of the boat, I would swim down with a pair of twenty-four-inch bolt cutters and shear through the mines' mooring cables. The mines would float to the surface, where they would be secured. We would then tow them to a nearby island and render them safe.

Through that procedure, we recovered some unusual new mines that were loaded aboard the APD Diachenko. They were returned to the States for study and are now on display in a Navy museum at Indian Head, Maryland. The new mine I had been specifically sent to recover we rendered safe and were able to get into the mine's casing to examine it. We found the still-dry packing slips within the mine casing, all written in Russian.

The Korean War started with the invasion of the North Koreans into South Korea on June 25, 1950. The war was fought up and down the peninsular country, with the Allied forces led initially by General Douglas MacArthur. The basic conflict

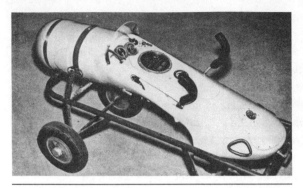

The Mark II SPU (Swimmer Propulsion Unit) as adopted by the UDTs in 1962. This was an improved model over the Mark I SPU, which was first used in the late 1950s. The SPU allowed a swimmer pair to operate over longer distances underwater and take more equipment or explosives along with them during an operation.

U.S. Navy

of the war was never finally resolved. We still face one another in North and South Korea across the demilitarized zone on the thirty-eighth parallel. Weapons are aimed at each other and have been so from 1954 to this day.

The war in Korea was never declared and was the first major armed conflict between the Communist ideologies and the rest of the free world. It is often referred to by people today as the "forgotten war," even though over 50,000 Americans lost their lives in it. For myself, I left Korea in 1952 and watched Pusan fading over the horizon. I said good-bye and I will never go back to Korea. It remains a tragic situation, the constant state of tensions between North and South Korea. Though geographically it certainly appears that Korea should be one nation, politics and ideology prevent that from ever happening.

The most recent descendant of the WWII Teams is today's SEAL Teams. A SEAL is a member of the United States Navy Special Warfare Forces. The name is an acronym made up from the words SEa, Air, and Land. In view of the fact that the seal is a kind of a water animal, the name worked very well, since the SEALs spend a great deal of their time in the water. The mission or work of the Navy SEALs covers all facets of Navy Special Warfare, and there is real meaning to their name since they gain access to their area of involvement from the sea, the air, or on land—for instance by submarine, parachute, or by landing on a beach and moving overland.

UDTs were the Underwater Demolition Teams. Their mission was to conduct beach reconnaissance. Prior to a landing on a beach for an amphibious assault, the UDTs made certain that the beach area and offshore waters could be safely moved across by our armed forces in landing craft. And the UDTs would clear the beach of any obstacles, either natural or man-made, that blocked the safe approach of landing craft.

The NCDU were the Naval Combat Demolition Units and they were the first of the beach clearing units for amphibious invasions. The units were formed from volunteers primarily from the Navy Construction Battalions or Seabees. Assembled first in 1943 in Camp Peary, Virginia, the NCDUs subsequently moved their training site to Fort Pierce, Florida. They later became the Underwater Demolition Teams. Their mission was essentially the same as that of the UDTs.

Scouts and Raiders were to do scouting and intelligence gathering for commands needing the information for the planning of amphibious operations. The raiding portion of the name comes from their ability to quickly strike at objects and installations from the sea and then leave the area. The intelligence-gathering aspect of the S&R mission became important for landing troops on beaches. The Scouts and Raiders did not survive World War II as a unit and their mission became part of that of the UDT.

A Scouts and Raiders beach recon would involve going to examine the beach approaches and the beach itself up to the high-water mark on the shore. Scouts and Raiders worked surreptitiously from submarines, rubber boats, or other small craft to examine a beach area or raid against a target near the water. The missions were done in the dark of night and undercover. The great majority of the UDTs' missions involving reconnaissance work was done in broad daylight.

Though the Scouts and Raiders spent a lot of time swimming in the water during training, actual combat operations done as swimmers was much rarer. S&R people spent the majority of their time on land conducting scouting operations. Scouting would be done to gather intelligence on an area without making contact with the enemy. Raiding took the form of small, fast destructive actions conducted against the smaller enemy installations. The men of the Scouts and Raiders could work in platoon-sized units all the way down to operator pairs, depending on the mission requirements.

The UDT had a much more restrictive and defined mission statement during World War II and the island hopping campaign in the Pacific. Their primary mission was the recon of beaches prior to amphibious assaults. The critically important primary mission of the NCDUs, which they carried out in Europe, was the clearance of beach obstacles.

Even though the UDTs always concentrate on the effort of the Team as a whole, individuals can stand out. Doug Fane is one of these individuals: he was the first man to put together a written history of the Teams, their operations, and their creation in his book The Naked Warrior. As an individual, Doug Fane is one of those people whose mold was broken after he was made.

An integral part of Navy Special Warfare from the early years and into Korea, Doug Fane was one of the forward thinkers who moved to expand the UDTs' doctrine, their missions, and their capabilities. He helped ensure the continuation of the UDTs despite the cutbacks after World War II and their significant participation in any of the Navy's involvements up to and into the Korean War.

The original mission of the Underwater Demolition Teams limited them to operate to the high-water mark during World War II and for some time afterward. In Korea, this changed and we went up on dry land for operations, some of them well *away from the water. Demolition raids were done, tunnels and rail lines were blasted, and prisoners were taken for interrogation. Over time all of that kind of work became part of the UDTs' capabilities.*

The mission that was going to broaden Navy Special Warfare, the creation of the SEAL Teams or someone like them, was something that a number of us could clearly see was coming. When the SEAL Teams were commissioned in the early 1960s, I, like many others, was curious about the name. The SEa, Air, Land acronym made a lot of sense, and led to further training for me.

To become qualified into the SEALs as a Navy captain, I went to Lakehurst, New Jersey, in 1965. There, I received my wings and became jump-qualified. The term pretty cool took on a whole new meaning for me while jumping over Lakehurst from 5,000 feet in the wintertime. Comfortable also wasn't one of the terms I would use to describe that particular course of training.

■ Chapter 17

SACO and Amphibious Group Roger

The Sino-American Cooperative Association (SACO) was part of a 1943 agreement between China and the United States on mutual military cooperation. The target of the cooperation would be the Japanese forces that had been in China since the early 1930s. The United States would provide material and trained personnel to act as instructors and advisers in their part of the agreement. The Chinese would supply facilities, support, and troops.

With U.S. assistance, the Chinese raised a guerrilla force capable of operating against the Japanese. U.S. personnel, considered far too valuable to risk by the Chinese government, were not allowed to even accompany their troops into the field on operations. Allowing the U.S. advisers to fight was completely out of the question. It was not until October 1944 that this order was rescinded by Chiang Kai-shek himself.

Additional trained U.S. personnel were wanted for the SACO project on a priority basis to increase the number of Chinese guerrillas available for the final push against the Japanese empire. Under the code name Amphibious Group Roger, a training program to prepare U.S. volunteers to work with the Chinese guerrillas was established. Supplying men for Amphibious Group Roger was one of the last missions of the Scout and Raider School before it was closed at the end of the war.

Rudy Boesch, Command Master Chief Boatswain's Mate, USN (Ret.)

It was in April 1945 that I arrived in Navy boot camp. The war against Germany ended while I was in boot, but there was still heavy fighting against the Japanese in the Pacific. After we graduated from Boot Camp, they lined us all up and asked if anyone wanted to volunteer for a special outfit. When I put my hand up, I looked around figuring to see a hundred more hands raised. But mine was the only one up. I was told to step out of the formation and very soon I was on my way to Fort Pierce, Florida.

When I arrived in Fort Pierce I reported in to Scouts and Raiders School. At that time I had no idea who they were or what they did, but I eventually found out. The mission we were being trained for was to go to China to organize Chinese guerrillas for actions against the Japanese. In addition, the Chinese would be in on the first waves for the invasion of Japan.

It was a special mission, training guerrillas, and the Scouts and Raiders was one of the first of the Navy's Special Warfare units. While I was at Fort Pierce, the Underwater Demolition Teams were training at the same base, doing most of their active demolition training on the next island north of us. We were separated from the UDT trainees by only the width of a street between rows of tents. There wasn't any real interaction between the two units, besides the normal level of competition between two special outfits. There wasn't any animosity between us and the UDTs, at least none that I ever knew of.

As we got deeper into training, we started to learn how to speak Chinese. At this time I was all of seventeen years old, so all of this was a great adventure to me. The adventure continued as we went out to Lake Okeechobee and conducted inland water training.

It was while we were out in the swamps around Okeechobee that our instructors told us all to come in, that they had some announcements to make. They told us that we were going to stop what we were doing and go back to Fort Pierce. The atomic bombs had been dropped and the war with Japan was over.

Back at Fort Pierce we had all been living in tents. The base was being closed and they told us to start tearing down the tents and burning them. Even with the about five hundred students in my class, it still took us about five days to tear down the entire base except for the original civilian buildings.

Once the Amphibious Base at Fort Pierce was eliminated, we were put aboard troop trains and sent west to California. From California, about three hundred of us were put on board a ship heading for China. It looked like I was going to see China anyway, along with a bunch of my classmates. There was the three hundred of us going west, and we passed about three million U.S. troops coming east and going home.

When I left Fort Pierce and headed for China, I was back in the regular Navy. Go-

ing aboard a ship in China, I spent eighteen months basically guarding Navy assets. Finally returning to the States, I was put on board a destroyer, where I stayed two years. Now I had a chance to put in for some shore duty and I requested Germany, so the Navy put me in London, England.

It was while I was in London that I saw some literature on the UDTs, a write-up in All Hands magazine, and how they were looking for some volunteers. So I applied and was accepted. In 1951, I started UDTR (Underwater Demolition Team Replacement) training with class six on the East Coast at Little Creek. A winter class in southern Virginia.

There were no permanent instructors for the UDT training then. Volunteers and other men would be assigned from the Teams to run the training program. Most of what we did at Little Creek was physical. If the instructor couldn't find anything else for you to do, there was always PT or running. Demolitions training was given, but it wasn't as sophisticated as it became for later classes. What they wanted to know was if you wanted the program badly enough to go through all of the work involved. So the physical end was made the hardest.

Our Hell Week was memorable; it was cold and it was loud. Since we were a winter class, the weather was cold and the wind could come in from the Atlantic like a knife. The instructors didn't have the same restrictions as they do in training today. We didn't use ear protection, and as long as it didn't kill you or mess you up permanently, it was okay. So for training, they exposed us to blasts from twenty-pound demolition charges.

The blasts from those explosions are probably the reason my ears are still ringing today. Those twenty-pound packs would pick you right up off the ground and slam you back down. A bit rougher than the quarter-pound charges they use today. But class six finally finished training, and all of about twenty-five guys finished. From there it was on to the East Coast UDTs.

When Roy Boehm picked his men for the first SEAL Team, I was one of the people he chose. When the SEAL Team was first being put together, Roy wanted everyone in the Team to already be jump-qualified, or at least as many as possible. Not everyone in UDT 21 had gone to Jump School, so his pickings were limited. At that time I was one of the very few, if not the only, chief who was jump-qualified in UDT 21. When the names were called out at the muster on January 8, 1962, to go over to SEAL Team Two, I was the only chief petty officer listed. So I became the chief master at arms for SEAL Team Two, a position I held from 1962 to 1988.

Within a short time we had two more chiefs, a corpsman, Doc Stone, and a storekeeper chief, Hoot Andrews, in the Team. I had been notified prior to that muster that I would be in the new SEAL Team. I had been on a Med (Mediterranean) deployment when I received orders to report back to Little Creek. When I returned to UDT 21, I was told that I would be reporting to the new SEAL Team. My only answer to that was, "What's a SEAL Team?"

But when the Team started, it was a very small, tight unit. Not everyone on the muster list had arrived; there were only about thirty-six men on board at the very start. But we stayed physically active from day one.

When we didn't do PT or running, we played soccer and other games that would build up and keep up our leg strength. At the start there wasn't a lot for the men to do; we were still lining up the schools and the specialized training. Once the training programs had been set up, everybody was going somewhere. When we started going to the Army schools and the Air Force and Marine schools, it seemed like you were going to a different school every week. And I went through my share of the training just like everyone else in the Team.

As the chief master at arms for the Team, I was responsible for keeping a handle on my bunch of hardworking, hard-playing new SEALs. But there really weren't any problems. Most of the men I had known for years in the UDT and I could handle them without any trouble. When it was necessary, I took care of all of the discipline myself and never had to bother the front office (CO) with it. It made it easier on the person that had to be disciplined and it made it easier on me that the officers didn't have to be officially involved.

One aspect of my job at SEAL Team Two was running the daily PT. I enjoyed doing PT myself, and when I was put in charge of the Team's PT, I really enjoyed it. There was a certain amount of fun in the fact that I always knew when I was going to stop doing a certain exercise or run. But the men who were following along never knew. We had a good physical outfit that was in top shape all of the time.

Everyone always made PT, no one got out of it without a good reason. And they all completed the runs, or at least as much as I wanted them to. Sometimes, you could go a bit crazy running and jogging too much. Some games were played too, where guys would try and duck out of a run by hiding from the very end of the line. But those tricks worked only once. And they kept everyone trying which made things fun.

▒ Chapter 18

The Cost

World War II officially ended with the formal surrender of Japan on 2 September 1945. U.S. casualties included over 400,000 dead and almost 700,000 wounded. Of the approximately 3,500 men of the World War II UDTs and NC-DUs, 148 individuals were wounded and 83 lost their lives.

By the war's end, thirty-four UDTs were under commission, with several of the Teams still in training, preparing for Operations CORONET and OLYMPIC, the invasions of the main Japanese islands that never had to be carried out. The almost thirty commissioned and staffed UDTs were gathered in Southern California in the fall of 1945 and decommissioned. Five postwar UDTs were assembled from the remainders of the UDT personnel who didn't go back to the fleet or left the service. Reorganizations kept the new postwar UDTs from being officially commissioned until more than six months after the end of the war.

On 21 May 1946, UDT 1 was commissioned, the first of the post-WWII UDTs. The UDTs were divided between the Atlantic and Pacific Fleets and would be stationed at Coronado, California, and Little Creek, Virginia. Even-numbered Teams would be on the East Coast and odd-numbered Teams on the West. In June 1946, UDTs 2 and 4 arrived at Little Creek after having been transferred to the Atlantic Fleet.

Commander Francis Douglas "Doug" Fane, USN (Ret.)

During a diving equipment demonstration in the early 1950s, this UDT underwater swimmer is wearing the Pirelli Model LS-901 rebreather. Due to the single breathing hose causing a possible buildup on carbon dioxide during use, this system was sometimes called the "Black Death" by the operators who used it.

National Archives

My father was English and drowned in the North Sea just before I was born; my mother was from a well-known family from Aberdeen on the eastern shore of Scotland. Between my two parents, the sea had an effect on my life from the very beginning.

I had become involved in the Underwater Demolition Teams during World War II and was the last wartime commanding officer of UDT 13 prior to it going over to Japan for occupation duties. When UDT 13 was decommissioned on 3 November 1945, I remained with the postwar UDTs, later becoming the commanding officer of UDT 2 stationed in Little Creek, Virginia.

After World War II the UDT had to expand its range of operations if it was to be effective in the modern Navy. One of the first things that had to be done was to take the men of the UDTs underwater. During WWII, the UDTs had worked in a very limited way with some underwater breathing apparatus, but never operationally. Instead, the length of time swimmers could work underwater was limited by how long they could hold their breaths.

During the war, the UDTs could swim in to a beach on the surface of the water because they were being covered by the heavy fire of Navy ships pouring in on the enemy. Without that cover, the swimmers could have been easy targets for light weapons, mortars, and small cannon.

The way to approach an enemy beach, if you are not to be seen, is by coming in underwater. So I had the men under my command learn to swim long distances underwater using oxygen breathing apparatus. That let the men reach the beach unseen, which would keep them from being killed.

Later on, we used the aqualung as invented by Cousteau and Gagnan in France. The aqualung used compressed air and was an open-circuit system; you breathed the air once and exhaled it out into the water. Using air made the system safer and easier to use, with a much greater range of depth, but the bubbles from the air could give away your position.

So to keep from giving away where the swimmers were underwater, we used the closed-circuit oxygen rebreathers. That system reuses the same gas, scrubbing out carbon dioxide and replacing the used oxygen. It is a dangerous system, limited in depth, but leaves no bubbles to track a swimmer. The system we first used was an Italian rig, the Pirelli. With that system, we could swim up to a beach completely undetected, then crawl out and recon the beach itself.

The first real underwater combat swimmers had been the Italians in World War II and even limited attempts in World War I. I had gotten permission from the Chief of Naval Operations to go over to Europe and learn what the British had done during the war, what the French were doing after the war, and to learn everything I could from the Italians. The Italians had conducted successful underwater operations against British ships at Gibraltar and elsewhere. They had sunk British warships, and they had a lot to teach us.

Meeting with the people from all of the different countries face-to-face allowed me to gather the information I wanted firsthand. After over six weeks of travel and study I returned to the U.S., accompanied by one of the Italian swimmers who was willing to work with our people in the UDTs.

Captain Draper L. Kauffman (right), considered to be the Father of the UDTs, and a swimmer from UDT 21 stand on the bow of an LCPR in the 1950s. The swimmer is wearing a Draeger Lt. Lund II breathing rig with the two green-painted oxygen bottles across his stomach.

U.S. Navy

Bringing all of this information back to the United States, we incorporated parts of it into the mission capabilities of the UDTs.

A very good friend of mine was Commander Draper Kauffman, who was both a tremendous man personally and I felt a great swimmer, having spent his time in the water with the UDTs he helped start during World War II. Kauffman was up in the Pentagon at that time and he quickly grasped the importance of what I had learned and what it would mean to the Teams. He helped make sure that my information got to the right people in the Navy and on the Joint Chiefs of Staff. The UDTs received the go-ahead to continue developing their new underwater capabilities.

For our closed-circuit underwater breathing equipment we used the Lambertsen Amphibious Respirator Unit (LARU), which had been developed in 1940 by Dr. Christian J. Lambertsen. The LARU could give a good swimmer one hour underwater without releasing a trail of bubbles. The system had been used by the OSS Maritime Unit during World War II during their very limited operations.

After we had established that underwater operations could be conducted with the equipment we had, we extended the types of operations we could perform. We worked from submarines, locking in and out of the torpedo tubes, though that didn't work very well. And we operated a "Sleeping Beauty" one-man submersible from the deck of a submerged submarine. To prove to those on higher command that we could do the operations as we said we had, we also filmed them underwater. That too was a first for the Navy. These were some of our experiments in 1948.

Now I felt the main thing the UDTs could do was swim long distances underwater. With our new training program, the men could conduct operations covering several miles underwater without surfacing. We learned many of our initial techniques and methods of operating underwater from the British and the Italian swimmers of World War II. It was to those pioneers I felt we owed a debt of gratitude.

Captain Norman H. Olsen, USN (Ret.)

The importance of what the UDTs did during World War II has been borne out by history. For the landings at Tarawa in the Pacific the planners didn't have what proved to be good intelligence on the beach and the waters offshore. When the Marines came in, their boats grounded on reefs offshore and hundreds of men drowned during the assault.

That incident at Tarawa brought home the necessity of reconning the beaches ahead of time and finding out which would be the best for landings. But that was only one factor.

The other factor was that it was well known that we—the Allies—would have to go in to Northern Europe, where the beaches would be heavily defended. There didn't really exist a unit that could go into a beach area like that and open it up for invasion craft. Both of those factors were real missions and the men of the NCDUs and the UDTs performed them.

If there hadn't been any such thing as the UDTs, or NCDUs, World War II would have probably turned out the same. Some organization would have to have been given their mission. The results of not doing the beach reconnaissance and obstacle demolition would have been a much greater rate of casualties and losses among any invading force. Parts of the Pacific-island-hopping campaign would have really had a problem in just getting on the beach. And in parts of the Normandy invasion, particularly on Omaha Beach, the NCDUs took very heavy hits. Those beaches would have been even harder, if not impossible, to secure if someone had not made it possible for the incoming waves of landing craft to reach the shore.

Like so many other things, the UDTs basically went away in the postwar cutbacks. The Teams barely survived that time, and if it had not been for farseeing individuals such as Doug Fane, the UDTs may have disappeared entirely. The Teams had been decimated and he found additional missions and capabilities for them. Then the Korean War came around and suddenly we were in the thick of it again.

People in the military were scrambling to fight a ground war again. Units had to make do with what they had, the UDTs among them. But in Korea too, the UDTs conducted their missions well, including additional ones they hadn't been really trained for. Afterward, it was much the same thing as had occurred after WWII, with cutbacks and restrictions reducing the size of units and the funds available for them.

In the 1960s, the cycle repeated itself. We geared up for Vietnam and the new SEAL Teams showed themselves to be immensely capable and flexible in their operations. But afterward, the small units again suffered reductions, the SEALs and UDTs among them.

Today, Special Operations is a household name. They are at the leading edge of a lot of things that are going on in the world. Back in the earlier days they always seemed to be an afterthought by command. "By the way, we have a lousy job. Let's give it to these guys."

■ Chapter 19

Outbreak of the Korean War

In an act that startled much of the world, the Communist forces of North Korea surged across the thirty-eighth parallel that divided their country from their democratic brothers to the south. At 0400 hours on 25 June 1950, the North Korean People's Army (NKPA) crossed the thirty-eighth parallel in force.

The government of South Korea staggered and almost fell. U.S. President Harry Truman told his Far East commander, General Douglas MacArthur, to support the South Koreans with ammunition and equipment.

As the South Koreans continued to fall back, support was soon ordered in the form of U.S. air and naval forces. A small detachment from UDT 3 was taking part in maneuvers in Japan when the Korean War broke out. These frogmen were soon ordered on emergency behind-the-lines demolition operations to try to slow the NKPA offensive.

The UDT men were now going up on dry land to attack targets that could be approached by the sea. This was the first land combat operations the UDTs performed, but they would be far from the last. The flexibility and adaptability of the UDTs was about to be tried to its utmost.

Lieutenant George Atcheson, USN (Ret.)

While I was an ensign on board a destroyer on the East Coast, I came across an article in a magazine put out by the Bureau of Personnel. As I remember, the article was titled something like "Warriors in Trunks" and was about the Underwater Demolition Teams of World War II. According to the article, the Teams were still active in the Navy, and that sounded like my kind of place to be.

They were accepting applications to the UDTs and I put mine in. My chit was accepted and I was ordered out to Coronado, California, to begin my training. There were no formal training classes then on the West Coast, this being around the spring of 1948, around April. As people arrived, they were assigned to a Team and underwent kind of an intensive on-the-job training.

We went out to San Clemente Island and conducted rubber boat exercises. And we did a lot of swimming, practicing with the dry suits that were to protect us from the cold. There were also a great deal of exercises, long-distance swims, running on the beach, and so on.

When I arrived in Coronado, I reported in to UDT 3. That was always my parent Team of the two, UDT 1 and 3, which were the only two Teams in Coronado at that time. UDT 3 was commanded by Lieutenant Commander Wolmanick, and the CO of UDT 1 was Lieutenant Al Seares, who had been a Fort Pierce/Maui–trained UDT man in World War II.

In spite of there not being a specific class and such, I feel we had pretty good training. And I don't feel I missed much by not going through a formalized course or program. That kind of thing always seems to pick up a lot of Mickey Mouse "make work" parts that should be avoided whenever possible.

Both enlisted men and officers entered the Teams in this manner on the West Coast at that time. I was the only new officer to begin with, but another arrived while I was still being introduced to all of the skills needed for the job. Enlisted men of various ratings came in from time to time as well. As men left the Teams, were discharged from the Navy, transferred, or whatever, new men came in to keep up the unit's strength.

In the spring of 1950, I had taken a ten-man detachment from UDT 3 to Japan. We were going to do some beach reconnaissance in support of some amphibious training the Marine Corps was going to give to various units of the Eighth Army. So my detachment and I were in Japan when the North Koreans crossed the thirty-eighth parallel on 25 June 1950 and invaded South Korea.

The thirty-eighth parallel was a political device that had been cooked up between the Americans and the Soviets at the end of World War II. The Soviets had a faction in northern Korea who were Communist. The so-called South Koreans

In July 1947, UDT operators train for demolition missions off the shores of Little Creek, Virginia. In the center of the IBS are stacks of demolition charges and spools of detonating cord for stringing the charges together.

U.S. Navy

were more democratically oriented, and that made them our kind of guys. All that part of Asia, including Korea, Manchuria, and a good chunk of China, had been occupied by the Japanese for some time. Korea had been practically a colony of the Japanese since almost the beginning of the twentieth century. With the dropping of the atomic bombs and the fall of the Japanese Imperialist Empire, there was a question of how we could even deal with the surrender of all these people.

There were millions of armed people in these parts of Asia. And their arms had to be taken away, they had to be fed, and their economies restarted. So to separate the problem into smaller parts, the politicians decided to divide Korea along the thirty-eighth parallel of latitude. The Soviets would take care of the surrender of the northern part of the country and the Communists there. And we would handle the surrender of the Japanese in the southern portion. That resulted in North and South Korea.

It was at 0400 hours in the morning on 25 June 1950 that the North Koreans made what turned out to be their big mistake. They crossed the thirty-eighth parallel in large force and very quickly took Seoul, the capital of South Korea and the his-

---

toric capital of Korea itself. Then they proceeded to take almost the whole of the Korean peninsula in a very fast series of movements.

The whole world, including the Soviets, probably hadn't expected any such action on the part of the North Korean government, certainly not at the time that they launched the invasion. The Soviet delegation had walked out of the UN in a huff over some quibble they had with us. When the North Korean invasion was brought before the UN Security Council, the Soviets weren't there to veto the vote to support the government of South Korea. That wasn't a mistake they were ever going to make again.

We certainly hadn't expected the invasion. In fact, the then secretary of defense had recently made a speech stating that we didn't really care what happened to Korea. Within a week the north had crossed the parallel and had taken the south away from us. So that was pretty much a complete surprise.

There was some shock that went through the U.S. armed services in Japan, but the overall reaction was not that big a deal at the very start. It sounded like it would be a very tough thing to fight the North Korean army. American forces, such as they were, and South Korean units had collapsed very quickly in the face of the heavy North Korean advance. The People's Army swarmed down from the north until they were finally held up by a line of resistance around Pusan, known as the Pusan Perimeter.

The Pusan Perimeter surrounded a small corner of Korea with Pusan in the middle. The North Koreans pushed up against the perimeter, pressing the remaining U.S. and ROK (Republic of Korea) forces very hard. But with their backs to the sea, the last operating military units had nowhere to go and held their ground.

No one was ready for the sudden outbreak of the war. My men and I had been quartered with the Army's Fifty-second Heavy Tank Battalion in Japan, which had actually been a parade unit and little more than a company-strength unit of light tanks. What the Fifty-second had done during their occupation of Japan was wax and polish their tanks, paint the grease fitting red, keep the markings bright, and see to it that all of the men wore yellow scarves. They turned out for parades and other functions; they were supposed to look good. And these were the men who were suddenly thrust into combat in Korea.

When the news of the Korean invasion arrived where we were stationed in Japan, I may have been excited; I just don't remember. We were quartered with a U.S. Army unit down near the beach, where we had been working in Japan. As the officer in charge of the detachment, I went down to a phone and called the Mount McKinley, which was the command ship of Rear Admiral James M. Doyle, commander of amphibious Group One.

When I asked the commanders on board the McKinley what they wanted me to do, all I got back was some hemming and hawing. Finally I was told to come down to the ship. Going back to our barracks, my detachment gathered up our gear, said good-bye to the soldiers, and all of us piled into a weapons carrier truck that was assigned to us. Going in to Yokosuka from where we were at Camp McGill, we boarded the McKinley. We operated out of there off and on until Team One came out and we could actually join back up with them.

We stayed on board until ordered to Sasebo, Japan, to board an APD there. We were flown from Yokosuka to Sasebo, where we boarded the APD Diachenko.

Very quickly, my unit was put into action against the enemy forces. Command had the idea that if my men and I could do some demolition raids behind the lines in North Korean territory, we might be able to distract some of the North Korean attention on the Pusan Perimeter. The hope was to force the North Koreans to remove some of their troops from the front to police their rear areas, which were vulnerable from the sea.

We were the only demolition men there, so the job fell to us. Our knowledge of demolitions was very good, but our experience on dry land operations was very limited. High command seemed to not have a great deal of experience in choosing targets either. The first target chosen for us was terrible; if we had gone in on it, we never would have survived. The first choice of target would have been like going in to San Diego and trying to blow up the Naval District Headquarters.

The second target was much more realistic for a small group of demolition men like us. There were a small pair of bridges that we were to destroy, a railroad bridge and a highway bridge, near Yosu, which was south of the Pusan Perimeter and now behind enemy lines.

We rode in the Diachenko for the trip to Yosu. Arriving late at night we boarded our LCPRs for the trip in to shore. Two of us were going to paddle in a rubber boat from where the LCPR had released us. Once we had checked out the target, Warren Foley, who had gone in with me, would signal the rest of the men to come in with the explosives to load the target.

The little intelligence photography we had of the area was old, dating from World War II. When we arrived on shore near the bridges, we found there was a thirty-foot embankment that had to be climbed in order for us to get up to the bridges. So we circled around and made the best of our situation.

The North Koreans discovered us and our distraction never worked, as they were able to run us out of there before we loaded the bridges. I threw a couple of grenades that I had brought with me at the ten or so North Koreans who had come out of a tunnel and spotted us. That was about the size of the fight. Heading back to the beach, one of my own men shot my hat off as I approached at the run, mistaking me for the enemy in the dark. But that was our only casualty of the operation. We got off the beach all right, returned to the ship, and went back to Japan.

Very soon after that first mission, UDT 1 arrived in Japan along with a platoon of Marines from the First Marine Division Reconnaissance Company to act as backup. I joined up with them and we went on to do some fairly respectable operations that worked out considerably better than that first one.

Looking back on the situation back then, the demolition of an enemy target was kind of a watershed moment for me. Up until that time everything had been training. Any other time we had blown something up, it had been rocks at San Clemente or something like that. To actually have blown up something that had belonged to the bad guys was a new step in the right direction.

The three demolition raids we conducted kind of run together in my memory, they were so much alike. Even though they were several hundred miles apart, the target sites were similar. They resembled each other in that there was a short stretch of railroad close to the beach, and it ran between two tunnels. The beach would be an open area where the train came out of one tunnel and just went into another.

Usually, we would try to blow up the tracks between the tunnels. A few times we tried to blow down some of the tunnel entrances, but that never amounted to much. You have to prepare a tunnel for demolition a great deal, drilling holes and placing a lot of charges. It's more like mining or construction blasting than military demolitions. We just didn't have the time on target to do that kind of work.

We were out of the water entirely during those three demolition raids. There was a small contingent of a couple of officers and enlisted men who first swam in to look around the bench. We had an infrared sniper scope that would let us look around the beach area in the dark a little bit from the rubber boat, but it didn't work too well. But there was never anyone on the beaches acting as guards or anything during our operations, so we were lucky that way.

On one later operation, we weren't so lucky. With the Koreans, I went back to one of the places that we had gone to earlier with the UDT. On the second trip, there were some North Koreans on the beach and things got hot fast. Several of my Koreans were lost, my interpreter was shot, and it was just a very bad evening.

But that operation during which we finally lost a man wasn't for some time to come. After those first three successful demolition operations in a row, we had been getting kind of cocky about our abilities. On the third op, a group of us had been on the beach talking as if there weren't any problems at all. Being that we were operating at night, behind enemy lines, with very limited immediate support, the lack of problems could have changed very quickly if we had been discovered by the North Koreans.

Marine Major Ed Dupris from the Marine reconnaissance company was in charge of the operation. He became fed up with our nonchalant attitude about where we were, what we were doing, and our talking amongst ourselves. In his best parade-ground voice, that Marine Major called out, "Quiet!" We all quieted down quickly after that.

But those operations were our first real "frogman" ops, in which we got to blow something up that belonged to somebody else. There were veterans of WWII operations in our Team, but a number of us, myself included, were brand-new at this sort of thing. Conducting combat operations behind enemy lines, and getting away with it and not taking any casualties, was kind of exhilarating. So sometimes our enthusiasm got the better of us.

What the command wanted to do was take advantage of our demolition experience and knowledge. A lot of the railway system in Korea had been built by the Japanese during their long control of the country. A great many of the Japanese-built rail lines ran along the eastern coast of the country. To avoid major tunneling through the mountain systems close to the coast, the rail lines were laid out near the shoreline. That made them accessible from the water and that was why the UDTs were chosen to attack them.

We could come ashore in rubber boats and carry our explosives up to the targets. This wasn't much more than an extension of our normal water demolition ops, so the logistics for this kind of operation were already met by the Teams and our APD transports.

Specific targets assigned to us included the rail lines themselves, bridges, and the tunnels. There was somebody in command who thought you could blow up railroad tunnels as easily as any other demolition target. But you can't really demolish a tunnel quickly without a lot of preparation. Setting off even a very large charge of explosives in a properly engineered tunnel isn't much different than firing a big cannon or rifle. The power of the explosives just goes down the tunnel and out the ends.

We could blow up the tracks, but the enemy could fix those fairly quickly. So our operations weren't as long-lasting in their effects as our command planners might have liked. But we did give the enemy something to think about with what was happening in their "secured" areas.

Korea was much like World War II might have been if we had gone in and fought the Japanese in China. It would have been a land war with no real infrastructure as we knew it in Europe. There were small villages spaced out with no good roads between them. It was a pretty primitive countryside. And because of the farming practices of the Koreans, it was tough to get along in the field. If you just cut yourself slightly, it could become infected quickly just from the dust in the air. It just wasn't like anything else. But I had no real experience in land warfare anywhere else in the world.

A frogman was a demolition swimmer initially. He could swim almost anywhere and take care of obstacles in the shallows. Or he would take note of what the obstacles were, measure the beach gradient, and come back to his ship and make a report. That information would be told to the high command and it would tell them what they would be getting into if they tried to land in a particular spot. Like the frog that he's named after, the frogman is an amphibian; he can also get along on land.

Even though we were UDTs and not really intended for land combat, we did not feel at all out of place or uncomfortable during our land operations. During the first little operation we did with only the ten guys from my detachment, we felt a lot more confident going in than we did after we arrived on-site. Our lack of experience kept me from preparing for the operation as well as we could have.

When we first went in, we hadn't prepared to swim in with weapons. Doing that just hadn't occurred to me. We had a fairly long swim in, about five hundred yards, and the tide was ebbing, so the swim must have taken us over half an hour. And we weren't wearing trunks; you don't go ashore in a bathing suit behind enemy lines. You go in wearing clothes you can live in if you have to. So we were wearing fatigues with long pants and shoes, sneakers anyway. I began to realize right away that I would like to have had a lot more training for this kind of operation than I had as I was going in to shore.

In the way of weapons, I was carrying a pistol and some hand grenades. Foley had some grenades along with him as well. We had additional weapons, a Thompson submachine gun, along with us in the rubber boat. That was our primary piece of firepower and it had been my idea to take it along. It wasn't all that good of an idea; we would have been better off taking M-1 carbines along for both of us. Originally, I thought we could swim in with a Thompson, but that didn't work out too well. Neither Foley nor I could swim very far dragging along a ten-pound steel anchor, and that didn't include any ammunition for the weapon, which weighed in at about two pounds apiece for thirty rounds.

So we left the submachine gun behind. It was bad enough swimming with just a pistol and several hand grenades. Weapons are just a dead weight without flotation. But when we ran into an enemy patrol, it was good to have with us what we did. But I wasn't really glad about the situation until we were back on our rubber boat and heading to the ship. Still, I was glad I had something. Later even my limited small-arms experience would come in handy on another assignment.

The Joint Advisory Commission Korea, or JACK, was the cover name for CIA activities in Korea. All the actions of this organization were highly classified at the time and many were done with the cooperation of the U.S. military. But even then, it was fairly common knowledge that JACK was an organization created by the CIA for their paramilitary actions.

Initially, my involvement with JACK was to assist in creating an Escape and Evasion organization in Korea to help downed aviators. No one wanted to be caught by the North Koreans; their reputation for treating prisoners was not a good one. A lot of things that later came out about the Koreans' treatment of prisoners enraged the American public.

The idea was that the aviators would be told where so-called safe areas were and that they should make for those if they had to bail out of their aircraft. Teams of Koreans trained by JACK would be in those safe areas to try to locate the downed aviators before the North Koreans did. Once the teams had the aviators in hand, they could take them down to a beach where a boat could pick them up or get them someplace where a helicopter could come in and snatch them out.

So I was picked to go and work with the JACK organization as a UDT officer. The initial idea was that as a trained UDT man, I was supposed to know how to land rubber boats and how to maneuver them through the surf. So I was brought in to teach the Koreans those skills. The trouble was, we didn't have any rubber boats available to us. We were up in the mountains of Japan, at a place called Camp Drake north of Tokyo, with a hundred or so Koreans and a bunch of various Army, Air Force, and Navy officers, to train these guys.

So I ended up teaching the Korans how to throw hand grenades and shoot various weapons. We didn't have any real curriculum, classes were kind of invented as we went along. The idea was for us to turn the Koreans into kind of a guerrilla force by this time. We were still involved with setting up the E&E units, but there would be other missions for these same Koreans to run.

Later I went to Korea and was attached to a JACK unit over there. They put me to work training a thirty-man group of Korean guys. We ended up doing essentially what the UDT had done when the Koreans first crossed the thirty-eighth parallel.

For our operations, we would land, after maybe a couple of swimmers had gone in to shore first and made sure that no one really serious was on the beach. Pre-designated guys would be sent out to establish a perimeter around the landing site. The rest of us would act as the powder train and pack the explosives up to the target, the little bridge, railroad tracks, or whatever. Once the explosives were set, everyone would withdraw. The fuse pullers would have stayed behind, and when the first boats were back in the water, the fuse igniters would be pulled.

We usually ran a fifteen- or thirty-minute delay on the charges. Once the fuses were burning, the fuse pullers would get on out of there. With the pullers recovered, we would all paddle back out to the ship. This was all done at night and we could usually hear the charges go off. The next day, if it was appropriate, the APD would pull in to the target area and everyone would try to see what we had done.

One time, we blew a little railroad bridge. The next day, as we went in to see the target area, a small train came along and went off the bridge. The Koreans usually put an engine on the back of the train so that they could pull it back into tunnels if the trains came under fire. They managed to pull back part of the train but the front engine stayed on the broken bridge. That was kind of pleasant to see, that our work had made some troubles for the North Koreans right there.

The end of the Korean War was unique in that it never really ended. Instead, it seemed to just kind of fade away. The politicians and military people started negotiations at Panmunjom, northwest of Seoul. Things started to calm down a little bit. The front was well north of the thirty-eighth parallel and it wasn't a line anymore,

more of a conventional-war frontal situation. It was referred to as the bomb line among the American and UN forces. You just didn't go north of the bomb line.

We had stopped bombing the North Koreans pretty much and the amphibious operations had ended. The UDT operations were no longer being conducted. My Korean guys still had work to do, but the ops were intelligence operations rather than demolition raids. And on the ops, none of the Americans, myself included, were allowed to go on shore. The Koreans could go because it was their country. But the active combat just kind of petered out.

Finally, there was a cease-fire that was formally agreed to. It wasn't really even an armistice. And there were some very big loose ends left hanging in the last agreements. They were some large islands in South Korea where there were the UN prisoner-of-war camps.

The camps held thousands of North Korean and Chinese Communist prisoners. A lot of those men didn't want to go back to North Korea or Communist China. Instead, they wanted to stay in South Korea or go on to Nationalist China in Taiwan. There were a lot of really hard-nosed Communist guys among the prisoners and the situation became a very touchy one for the UN forces.

The war just never really was resolved. It's still going on in a very small way. The North Korean operations with their spy submarines that ran aground are just one example of the aggressions that are still felt on both sides of the border.

It seemed to me that maybe some of what we did in Korea helped lead in to the creation of the SEALs. I was never in any strategic thinking sessions after or during Korea. But it was obvious from the start of Korea that the UDTs had been trained for World War II. It was also obvious that World War II was over, that there wouldn't be any more major amphibious operations with beach obstacles, reefs, and things like that.

What we had shown the strategic planners on command staff was that the UDTs had a lot of potential. The demolition skills, the swimming, the gung-ho spirit, and all of that made for a flexible unit. But to make them really useful, they had to broaden the UDTs' capability. They had to be made into a commando unit that was heavily armed, motivated, and very mobile. The SEALs would do parachute jumps and boats, which were first performed by the fifties era UDTs. And the SEALs do the HALO-style parachute jumps, which take steady nerves. From what I have heard, the SEALs have been very effective whenever they have been used, if they were used properly.

It's that last caveat that's important. The armed services have the tendency to use people and units improperly. That puts them in situations that they aren't trained for. I don't know why, but that was the kind of thing that first got the UDTs up on dry land during the Korean War. And sometimes these things work out for the best.

Looking back on the Korean War, I kind of consider it as my war. In spite of my having gone into the Navy in 1943, I spent all my time in training and never saw action. As an aviation cadet, I had just gotten my commission as an air navigator when the war ended. Staying in the regular Navy, I guess I felt the same as a lot of other guys, that we had somehow missed something by not taking an active part in World War II.

So I had felt that, which was a subjective thing. Objectively, I think we had no choice but to get involved in Korea. It would have been a terrible mistake to simply let the Communists take over the entire peninsula, and make the same mess of it that they have made of their own country now. It also would have been strategically bad if we had let South Korea fall. Our whole Far Eastern situation would have been much different if we hadn't gone in there and done what we had to do.

At the start of my operating in Korea, I didn't hold much affection for the people there that I later came to have. I was prepared to like them a lot, as I was born in Beijing, China, and lived there till I was about sixteen years old, my father having been in the diplomatic service. I have very warm memories of the Chinese people. The Koreans have been described as the Irish of the Orient; they are a very stubborn and proud people. That makes it hard to teach them things sometimes. They feel they know how to do it better than you do very quickly, and sometimes they do.

The Koreans that I knew, that I worked with and trained, and got to know well, I have a great deal of affection for. These men were brave and stoic, you couldn't tire them or wear them out. They were just great soldiers. It's a different culture, so it would be hard to say just how tough they really were. But they could stand a lot and just keep going.

The North Koreans as an enemy I didn't really know. They had a good reputation for toughness and held a hard discipline. The troops were also motivated and they believed all of that propaganda that they were told. Or at least they had to pretend to believe it or they would have been killed. It is such a different culture from ours that it's very hard to really compare the differences. But the fact that they were good, tough soldiers isn't argued very much at all.

Being in the Teams was great fun. It was the best duty I ever had while I was in the Navy. I would have liked to have stayed in the Teams for my entire career, but I was a regular officer and had to move out of the UDTs to continue my career advancement. Later this was changed and you could stay in the Teams as an officer and continue your advancement. This was called a career path and there just didn't used to be one in the UDTs.

Now being in the UDTs and the SEALs has become respectable in the regular Navy, or at least it's a lot more accepted than it used to be. Today, being in Special Warfare is almost respectable while back in the old days it was almost a backwater. You were never going to make great rank if you remained in the UDTs back then.

In the Teams you had the comradeship every day. They were good company, those Teammates I served with. There wasn't a lot of spit and polish in the UDTs like in other outfits. And the easygoing camaraderie existed between the officers and the enlisted men, which it didn't anywhere else in the Navy, at least certainly not like it did in the Teams. It wasn't like the respect wasn't there. We weren't buddy/buddy and they didn't call me George. But they thought of me as George and they knew I could do the same job they did. It wasn't like a ship where the officers are very separate from the men by both rank and tradition.

When I think of the Teams, that's what I remember. The congeniality and the fact that it was just fun. We were very proud of doing what we did. You knew you were part of something special when you were in the UDTs. I certainly felt pride in what we did and what we accomplished, and I'm pretty certain everyone else with me felt the same way.

It was great to be in the kind of outfit where you knew you were special. And no one else really knew what you did and they couldn't do your job even if they did know what it was. When you were asked, "Where are you stationed?" and you answered, "I'm with UDT 3," well, then they just looked at you differently. It means a lot, and I think the same thing must be true today, if not even more so.

Gung ho is a Chinese word meaning "togetherness." In general, it means working in harmony. Marine Colonels Edson and Carlson had a lot of experience working with the Chinese and they picked up the term for the First Marine Raider Battalion during World War II. It became their slogan and spread throughout the Marine Corps. Now it has become part of the general vocabulary as meaning a hard-charger, going straight ahead, and working as a team to get the job done.

The SEALs have an enormously high reputation today and they uphold everything we held dear back during the Korean War. They really are Gung ho, with a capital G.

■ Chapter 20

Rotations

As soon as the West Coast UDTs were organized as part of the Korean War effort, the Teams set up a rotation among themselves. In an effort to keep the limited manpower of the UDTs from becoming too exhausted, the deployment time was set at six months. This did not include travel time across the Pacific to the UDTs' staging area in Japan. That long trip could easily add several months to a six-month deployment time.

The UDTs deployed to Korea also operated as part of the Pacific Fleet. Operational platoons would take part in fleet landing exercises and other actions as they were directed. UDTs also conducted their normal reconnaissance and hydrographic survey operations in Korean waters. There was also a new mission they conducted that had them facing an old enemy: water-based mines.

Eugene Poole, Seaman Second Class

In late 1951, I joined the Navy Reserves, where I didn't stay very long. By early 1952, I was put on active duty in the Navy in time for the Korean War. During my civilian work, I had been a lifeguard for Santa Monica. Several of the people who worked for our organization had been UDT operators during WWII. It was they who first introduced me to the Underwater Demolition Teams and caused me to search them out when I was activated.

Doug Fane became my hero, as he was the man who got me into the UDT. When I first went in to the training compound back in 1952, it was really just a group of Quonset huts on the beach in Coronado. Commander Fane was just sitting in his office in one of the huts when I and my friend walked in wearing civilian clothes. There was some first-class petty officer sitting in the front office who asked us what we wanted. When we told him we wanted to see Commander Fane, we were brusquely told that he was busy. We made some pretty unprintable comments to the petty officer and eventually got in to see Fane.

We explained our situation to him, that we didn't want to be where we were on a destroyer. His name had been given to us as the man to talk to about getting into the UDT program. We had references for him and had a few names of individuals we could mention to him. After we told him the rest of our background, he went to see what strings he could pull to get us off our ship and into the UDT.

Within about two months we were off of that destroyer just as it was getting ready to leave for Korea. Then we were officially at the lowest possible rung in the UDTs; we were trainees.

We officially arrived in Coronado in the summer of 1952, barely in time to be part of class six. My friend and I were both from the same reserve unit and it turned out we were the first reservists ever to go into training. The UDTR (UDT Replacement) course was about 16 weeks long back then, with Hell Week being the seventh week of training. The two of us started training during the fifth week, so we had to push kind of hard to catch up. The fact that we arrived in pretty good shape was what helped us catch up with the rest of the class.

The most memorable thing about training was just getting through it. Everyone has heard about the rigors of training; it was tough and it was strenuous. But overall I enjoyed it.

After graduation, we went in to UDT 1. Our first overseas deployment came soon after our arrival, when the Team left for Korea. The Team was stationed at Camp McGill, Japan, just outside of Tateyama and across Tokyo Bay from Yokosuka. We deployed from Camp McGill as units to Korea. The Team operated in different parts of

Korea, up and down the western side, primarily in the Yellow Sea area. We reconned beaches, did some demolition of coral heads, and cleaned obstructions out of harbors. After that, we went back to our base in Japan.

From Japan we were again sent out, but this time to a safe area around Okinawa and the Ryukyu Islands. The work off of Okinawa was similar to what we did in Korea, maybe cleaning out a harbor for the Navy or reconning what had been sunk off some beaches. Then we would go back to Japan. We might be flown out somewhere for an operation of several days, then back again to Japan. Trips were taken on destroyers for shorter operations, just a few days or so. Then again back to our main base.

Most of our work in the Yellow Sea up in Korea centered around a number of beaches and little harbors. The intent seemed to be to examine and chart those areas to see if they were suitable for landings. At my level in the Team, I don't know any of the overall or strategic value of what we were doing. For me, it was simply a "go here and do your job" sort of thing. We were happy just to get back on board or back to wherever we were staying that night after we were done. The waters there were pretty cold.

All of the demolition operations I went on were water-oriented. We didn't do any land operations. There was one platoon that did a demo op that involved blowing up a bridge and that required them to go up on land away from the water. For my Teammates and myself, though, all of our demolition work was on islands that as far as I know were right around the thirty-eighth parallel, maybe a little bit above it. Those islands were supposed to have been in friendly hands. At any rate, we didn't have any incidents.

There was one harbor where some mines were found that we had to deal with. For the operation, the UDT that I was with didn't have to clear the mines or blow them up. Instead, we had to go in and mark the location of each one.

These were large water mines that were floating just beneath the surface. These weren't something that I would have volunteered to swim up on. But we didn't have to do this in order to complete our mission. Instead, we would observe them from the surface and drop a marker buoy nearby. Then we made note of the location of the mine on a chart. It may be that EOD (Explosive Ordnance Disposal) came back later and cleared them out—I wasn't involved in that later operation.

I had some concerns while looking over the side of the boat at a few hundred pounds of high explosive, armed and ready to blow if we struck one of the horns. The thoughts centered on "What am I doing here?" and "Why aren't I up there in the air with that Corsair?" Those mines are nasty things. But you don't think of the danger much, you just go ahead and do your job.

While working off of Okinawa earlier during that deployment, it was hard not to think sometimes about what had happened there not ten years earlier. When you operate in the UDTs, you're part of a Team. You do not do anything on your own:

UDT operators bring their IBS ashore after a mine clearance operation off Wonsan Harbor, Korea. Locations of the mines and other obstacles would be noted down on the plastic slates the men have hanging from their necks. This operation took place on 26 October 1950 during the first year of the Korean war.

National Archives

your Teammates are working right alongside you, even if it's just your swim buddy. So while my Team was functioning in its normal capacity right then, there were thoughts about the Teammates who had preceded us and worked these waters during World War II. They had led the way originally.

The specific Team areas, where they had operated, were unknown to me at that time. Nothing that I was aware of had been written about their operations off Okinawa. Since then, I've seen reports and accounts that have told me a lot more about what happened offshore during that last great island invasion of World War II. As far as I knew, I hadn't been swimming off of any of the same beaches that had been the targets back in April 1945, but then again, I might have been.

You would look at the island now and then and think of what it must have been like back then. Thousands of men died on Okinawa, and many were killed just getting to the island. And there were the occasional reminders of what had happened that made things stand out starkly to you.

For example, we had to do a recon on a harbor off of Okinawa and I found a sunken landing craft down in about thirty-five feet of water. The craft was lying on the bottom, upside down, and had been there since World War II. I wondered just what had happened to that craft, how had she gotten to the bottom? Why was she upside down? And what had happened to the men who had been aboard her?

It was one of our boats and she could have hit a mine or been struck by a bomb

or shell. There was no way to really know. But finding things like that made you wonder about the situation back then and what went on to cause that situation to develop. There isn't any thought of danger to yourself generally. The UDTs had a job
to do and you just did it. That was what we had signed up for.

■ Chapter 21

Recons

The success of the WWII amphibious operations conducted in the Pacific
were very familiar to General Douglas MacArthur. He used this experience to
his great advantage in the audacious landings at Inchon, which turned the tide
of the Korean War and nearly resulted in the defeat of the NKPA. As the North
Korean forces were driven back well past the thirty-eighth parallel and almost
to their northern border with China, the war took an ominous turn when the
Red Chinese People's Army "volunteers" joined with the North Koreans. Now
U.S. and UN forces were faced with one of the largest land armies in the world.

The reinforced NKPA drove the U.S. and UN forces back south past the
thirty-eighth parallel. To maintain his options, MacArthur had earlier ordered
further preparations for possible amphibious operations, both to put forces on
the beaches or evacuate cutoff or threatened units. The demolition skills of the
UDTs were also put to use in destroying facilities that were being abandoned
in the face of the Chinese and NKPA forces.

Rod Griggs, Electrician's Mate, Second Class

Originally, I had volunteered for the service because I was a young fellow and I
wanted to get into the war over in Korea. One of my desires at that time was to do
my duty for my country. My choice of service was the Navy, and one day a call was
issued for volunteers for UDT training. I had been raised on a lake, was an excellent swimmer, so I figured that I could do some good in the UDTs.

Personally, I don't believe in Communism, I never did, and I thought the conflict
in Korea was a just war. They called it a police action, but it was a war no matter
what name they gave it. And I wanted to be more involved. The ship I had been stationed on had been conducting a lot of antisubmarine exercises. I figured there
wasn't much chance we'd chase down any North Korean subs—I don't think they
even had any then—so the Teams looked like a way to get into the action.

The Korean War was the first real armed conflict between the Communists and
the free world. We had to keep the Communists from moving forward, and the Ko-

rean War did that. The later cold war, the Berlin Wall, and other incidents, they weren't active combat. The Korean War was.

In August 1952, I was accepted for UDTR training with class six on the West Coast. Training was a long seventeen weeks that took just about everything you could give. The biggest single week of training was Hell Week, but everything that was demanded of you prior to then made you numb through that ordeal. The first six weeks of training was a lot of physical work. They condition you, get you in shape, and then put you through Hell Week to see if you also have the mental toughness to do the job.

It was after Hell Week that you started to receive the more technical training. Then we had to learn flashing light code, demolitions, gradients, and beach conditions. That last was really the kind of information we would be going after on a hydrographic reconnaissance. And we also received a little bit of training on booby traps, disarming mines, and other explosive studies.

It was the numbness I felt that helped me get through Hell Week. You would get maybe two hours of sleep during the night and then they would get you up for a march through the muck. You're so tired and worn-out that you run solely on stamina. That's what they want to see you show before they spend time teaching you the nuts and bolts of being a UDT man.

After graduation, I was assigned to UDT 1. It was just shortly after we had completed graduation that UDT 1 deployed to operate in Korea. That was about February 1953. We went aboard ship in February and took about thirty days to cross the Pacific to Japan. Our base in Japan was Camp McGill near Tateyama on the eastern side of the mouth to Tokyo Bay, a short trip from Yokosuka where the ship pulled in.

The thirty-day trip across the Pacific was memorable. The ship was an AGC, an amphibious force flagship, basically a converted WWII liberty ship. In the middle of one of those Pacific storms, the ship cracked up both sides of the hull. We had been sleeping in the mess hall when the crew came in, woke us up, and tossed all of us out. Then they stripped off all of the insulation from the walls and welded up the cracks. That was roughly in the middle of the Pacific. I knew the crew could handle the situation; the ship wasn't really breaking in half, just kind of cracking in the middle.

Even when we were in Japan, we hadn't been told where our operations would be. That kind of decision, where the command wanted us, was made well above the Team level. We were a Team of about one hundred people divided into four action platoons and a headquarters. For missions, some platoons would be sent to one place while other platoons would go someplace else. We all went to Korea together as a Team, but this was after we had been in Japan for a few months. We had gone to Hokkaido to recon some beaches there. And we had gone to Okinawa to clear some beaches for practice Marine landings.

After those operations, we returned to Sasebo, Japan, and waited for an APD, a high-speed transport, to pick us up and take us over to Korea. When we arrived in Korea, we received our orders where to send the platoons. All of our equipment, rubber boats, LCPRs, and whatever, were aboard the APDs. So we worked from those ships while off Korea. The major Korean operations that I was involved in consisted of beach surveys, the normal UDT op.

We had different ways of surveying beaches, using swimmers in the water or measuring from boats. On the swimmer beaches, the operations went much like the standard UDT op from World War II. We would work from our WWII-vintage ply-wood LCPRs, putting a number of swimmers in the water. For some beaches, it would be a line of fifty swimmers spaced out at roughly the three-and-a-half-fathom (twenty-one-foot) depth line. The swimmers would raise their arms to help everyone line up for the swim in to the beach.

Going in to the beach, we would have our plastic slates, drop our lead lines at regular intervals, and write down the depth on our slate. Then the line would move in to the next interval and repeat the measuring. What we would do was measure the gradient of the seafloor as it sloped up to the beach. That told the planners what kind of ships could land on that beach.

Ships—the LST, for example—required a depth of 14 to 15 feet under the stern, as I remember, while the bow needed only four feet of water under it. Since an LST was something like 328 feet long, calculating where it could nose in to the beach, drop her bow ramp, and unload while still being able to get off the beach later was easy.

There were two things about swimming in the water off of Korea. First off, the water was never very clean; mud, silt, and whatever suspended in it kept you from being able to see very far at all underwater. Second, the ocean around Korea had something like a 30-foot tide. So we would always conduct our surveys at low tide. The rest of the recon could be done by observing the beach high-tide line.

And the water around Korea was cold. If the temperature was below sixty de-grees, we had to wear exposure suits to protect us. Around Korea, we wore the suits all of the time. The exposure suits were Italian Pirelli rubber dry suits, basi-cally a waterproof rubber suit you wore over a set of long underwear. The suits kept you warm by trapping a layer of air in the long underwear between the suit and your skin. As long as you didn't cut the suit or let any water into it, it worked pretty well.

So the Navy was taking care of us with the equipment we were getting. We had used aqualungs in our operations off of Okinawa, but none of them were used on the Korean ops that I was on. We would just make the swim in and hold our breaths for any time that we had to spend underwater.

I was not involved in any land operations while off Korea. In fact, we were told to stay away from the people who were conducting such things. On some beaches, we would set out a perimeter to maintain the security of our site. On one operation,

I was assigned to go ashore prior to the landing and watch one end of the beach. Another man from my UDT was watching the other end of the beach. We were both armed, but there wasn't any enemy contact or other incident.

The lack of incidents was a good thing for us; we weren't supposed to make contact with the enemy. We were an intelligence-gathering outfit, our information was valuable, and we had to get back with it. Then the cartographers could draw up an accurate and complete chart of the beach. If even one man was missing, then information he had gathered about a coral head or other obstruction might be missed, as well. In that case, a ship coming in to a beach and running aground wouldn't be able to do its job. So we had to do ours to prevent that.

The only time I even heard of any UDT men making contact with the enemy and actually getting into combat was early in 1951. The men were from UDT 1 and they had been getting back from a survey when supposedly friendly Koreans on the shore opened fire on them. Two of the UDT men were killed, an enlisted man and an officer, and five more were wounded. Some of the wounded men were

Two UDT combat swimmers wearing the early model dry suits. It was because of suits like these that the UDTs were first able to operate in arctic and antarctic waters. These suits and improved versions aided underwater operations off the coast of Korea during the Korean War. The suits trapped a layer of air, usually formed by a set of long underwear, to insulate the swimmer from the cold water. The black device below the neck is a flapper valve to allow excess air to escape.

U.S. Navy

later returned to our Team. The UDT men hadn't been armed and weren't able to return fire. The machine guns aboard their LCVP just didn't have the range to cover them.

We—that is, the men just doing the job—never really knew where we were. The job was just to survey the assigned beaches. We could have been above or below the thirty-eighth parallel, with North Koreans on the shore around us. We kept watch on shore but remained sneaky and always avoided contact. That was just part of how we did our job.

There were other actions the UDTs did in Korea, such as cutting the North Korean fishnets, going on shore for demolition raids, and blowing up the dock facilities at Hungnam prior to the time when the North Koreans and the Chinese military forced all of the UN forces back down the Korean peninsula.

In Korea, the UDTs would alternate being on station. UDT 1 might be over there and were relieved by UDT 3, then UDT 5 would relieve UDT 3. The tours were six months long on paper, but you had to add two months of travel time—thirty days to get there and thirty days to return—to the overall deployment. So a UDT was away from Coronado for eight months at a time during the Korean War.

My one tour over in Korea came just before the signing of the cease-fire on 27 July 1953. We were just packing up to return to the United States when they announced over the ship's PA system that the armistice had been signed. So we were the last UDT to do a combat tour during the Korean War. I have the Korean Medal with two stars on it, indicating I was in three different combat zones during the war. So we traveled a lot up and down the coast of Korea during our deployment.

Soon after UDT 1 returned to Coronado, I volunteered for a trip to Alaska. The USS Burton was a Navy icebreaker heading up to Alaska and they always carried six underwater demolition men on board. In case the ship penetrated into the ice fields and was frozen in, we had the capability to go into the water and blast the ice from underneath. That would create a leed of open water that the ship could move through. Building up some forward speed, the icebreaker could then keep going forward, busting through the ice with her heavy reinforced bow.

Another duty we had during that trip was to try to do demolitions under the ice in order to clear channels for boat landings. That was an experiment that didn't work too well. We could do the demolitions, but you couldn't run a normal boat through the heavy slush that resulted.

This was seriously cold water, twenty-eight degrees at the intake of the engine room. Cold enough that some of the salt water would freeze up and become ice, joining up with the snowmelt and other buildup floating on the surface. The operations were very interesting, in spite of the fact that I broke my eardrum on one dive.

For protection from the extreme cold, we wore padded aviator's underwear under our Pirelli suits. Then we put wool suits over that. Vaseline protected the exposed skin of our faces and tight gloves protected our hands. What happened to me was that the Vaseline sealed my ear to the hood of the rubber suit. When you go down with an aqualung on, you try to clear the ear and equalize the pressure on either side of the eardrum. If you can't equalize the pressure by swallowing or blowing into your mask, you try bobbing in the water to open the passages up in your ear. If your ears don't equalize, the pain can get pretty bad.

I had been bobbing and suddenly my ear was clear and the pain had gone away. I thought the ear had cleared, but what had really happened was I had created a vacuum between my ear and the suit and had popped the eardrum outward and ruptured it. So I had a bad ear and couldn't dive anymore on that trip.

Other than the problem I had on that one dive, going under the ice was a very interesting experience. It's very beautiful underneath the ice, with light filtering down through the snow and overhead cover. The water is very clear and there are

A UDT swimmer moves to the edge of an ice pack in frigid Arctic waters. Though his fellow sailors do not appear particularly uncomfortable on the landing craft nearby, without his protective suit, the UDT swimmer would be killed by the cold waters in minutes.

U.S. Navy

very few things floating around or moving through it. There are air pockets under the ice, some of them so large that you can go up into them and breathe out of the water.

The trip was very interesting at the beginning, but after you've seen ice for a week or two, the next two months aren't very interesting. So things became boring after a while and stayed that way. Our path was up the inland passageway, through Canadian waters, and we went from Juneau, Alaska, over to Kodiak.

An interesting incident occurred while we were at Kodiak. The mail was being delivered in large rubber containers for air pickup. One of the bags was dropped in about seventy-feet of water and the ship wanted someone to go down and get it. I and another diver went down to pick it up. There was no problem finding the bag, it was just lying on the bottom right off the pier where it had fallen. But while we were down, a real big fish came along and scared the hell out of me for a moment. But we rescued the mailbag and received a standing ovation from the ship's crew when we surfaced.

My discharge was coming up relatively soon after the Alaska tour. UDT 1 was deploying again, and since my time in the service was almost up, I stayed behind in Coronado. Finally, in November 1954, I left the UDT and the Navy and returned to civilian life.

Life in the UDTs had been good in general. We had quite a few more privileges than the rest of the people in the Navy. We were an elite group and that came with some perks. We had early chow passes, although we had to exercise every day to *earn them. There was less "spit and polish" discipline in the Teams, and the rank consciousness that was so prevalent in the regular Navy you didn't see in the UDTs. Aboard ship, it was "yes sir, no sir." When you were swimming with an officer, you were learning to trust each other with your lives. That makes the command situation quite a bit different, and a lot more relaxed.*

■ Chapter 22

Heat and Cold: Mines and the Korean Winter

The environment of the Korean War ranged from hot and dusty in the summer to blistering cold in the winter. Cold-weather fronts would sweep down from Mongolia and Russia in the winter, bringing with them shattering cold. And it was in this environment that the UDTs operated on land, without the necessary supply line for cold-weather clothing. Few UDT operators who spent the winter months in Korea have a fond memory of the place.

And in the constantly cold waters off Korea were floating mines. These dangerous packages could hold hundreds of pounds of high explosive, enough to blast a hole in the hull of a capital Navy ship. Actions were conducted by the UDTs to search out and mark or destroy these mines—procedures that occasionally led to very close calls as the men met the floating bombs.

The safe handling, disarming, or simple disposal of the floating mines required additional technical training. This gave the UDTs another skill to add to their list, one that proved invaluable as their operations and missions increased in technical complexity.

Louis J. DeLara, Senior Chief Boatswain's Mate, USN (Ret.)

At the beginning of the Korean War, I was a civilian in Pittsburgh, Pennsylvania. I had been in the Navy during World War II, and unknowingly to me, on my discharge from that service, I had signed a reserve clause on my papers. Nothing ever showed up in my mail and I didn't have any drills or anything like that to go to. Still, I was a member of the inactive reserves of the U.S. Navy. The start of the Korean War very quickly changed all that. I was one of the first guys reactivated for service.

The situation was thoroughly miserable and I didn't want to have any part of this thing that was going on over in Northeast Asia. But the Navy took a number of ships as well as men out of mothballs. I was assigned to one of these old rust-buckets as it came out of storage and immediately went to sea.

That ship cruised into the bay of San Diego. All I wanted to do was get back out of the Navy and go home. One day I happened to notice this LCPR in the water with big shark's teeth painted on it and a bunch of suntanned guys running around on the deck.

When I asked one of the other guys aboard ship who those people were, he said, "They're frogmen."

"Where are they stationed?" I asked.

"Over there." He pointed across the bay at the Amphib Base in Coronado, then looked at me and said, "That's a volunteer organization. Are you thinking about joining?"

I thought yeah, it was a way to get off of that ship. So I submitted my request, and it was approved. The ship was getting under way and they called over to the Amphib Base and told them about this man they had on board who would be shortly reporting for training. The ship was leaving about a month early, but they were willing to send me over to the base before we left. The folks over at the Amphib Base agreed and now I was off the ship.

The situation was one that made me at least semihappy. Then I reported in for training. A gentleman by the name of Hughes, who is still a very good friend of mine, did so too. "Lou," he told me, "we're going to get into this training and get a jump on the rest of the class. We're going to get up early and get into some exercise."

This guy was out of his mind as far as I was concerned. I was off of that ship and that was the big thing for me. The upcoming training wasn't something I was worried about. But five o'clock the next morning, here he was rattling me up and out of my rack. Then we were running around that base, and that was the start of it.

Two SCUBA-equipped UDT swimmers are entering the water from the bow ramp of the LCPR. This small craft was one of the famous "Higgins" boat designs of WWII.

U.S. Navy

Then I got into training. And the more I was involved, the more I felt like I was putting money in the bank. Now I had an investment in what I was doing. Then I became semidedicated to it and I found I had put too much time and effort into what I was doing. By that time you couldn't get me out of the program. So that was how I became a frogman.

My class, class six, was a winter class. We graduated in 1952 and immediately were sent over to Korea with UDT 1. The men I was with and the work I was doing drew me in. And the more I was involved with it, the more I became committed to the service. Before I realized it, I had become a dedicated career Navy man.

Originally, training was just a way to get off that ship. But it grew quickly into something that had a life of its own. Guys like Hughes and others like him that I met while in training helped me get through the hard parts. And the extra pay you received as a member of the UDT didn't hurt either.

During an interview with the trainees they had early on, they passed around this questionnaire to find out why we wanted this training. When I looked at the questions, I just said that I wanted the extra money. One of my friends told me not to put that down. He suggested that I write how this was the best way I could serve my country and the Navy. How I was dedicated and my becoming a frogman would be to the best interests of the service. I agreed and put all of that down, but I really did want the extra money initially.

After graduation, I was assigned to UDT 1. There were three Teams on the West Coast then. The Navy had just commissioned UDT 5 to join with UDT 1 and UDT 3 at Coronado. At that time the Teams were made up of about 120 men total, officers and enlisted. Whether we ever were up to capacity, I don't know. But we did average between 75 and 80 enlisted men and maybe 10 to 12 officers. These were broken down into four operating platoons and one Headquarters Platoon.

The whole Team went on combat operations off to Korea. The operating mandate for the Teams calls for us to do reconnaissance and clear obstacles for an amphibious landing. We also tried to acquire intelligence about the trackability of a beach and where its entrances and exits were. That was so that once the landing forces had gotten to the beach, they would know if the surface could hold tracked or wheeled vehicles and how they would get off that thing. And that was our basic mission.

In Korea, as time went on, we found ourselves going inland on missions. That wasn't where we were supposed to be, according to our basic mandate, but it wasn't like we were in violation of the Geneva Convention or anything. But we were getting more and more involved inland. Now we were putting out perimeters to protect our site and blowing up railroads and bridges. That became our more usual mission.

All in all, that kind of inland work, the operational type of things we were doing, proved abilities and helped raise the SEALs years later.

The operations we did took us up and down both coasts of Korea a number of times. For an inland demolition operation, we would go in on an APD at night to within range of our target. We would launch from the APD into our rubber boats for the paddle in to the beach. There would be two boats usually, each with a crew of six, so there would be about twelve people, not quite a full operational platoon, on the op.

Getting in to the beach, we would put a few people out to sneak in and make sure that we could come up and get in there with the boats. Then we would land and set up a perimeter, putting some people out in a circle so that we wouldn't be surprised by someone walking up on us. Then we would make our way up the beach. We had maps and whatever with us to guide us in to the target and we carried our explosives with us.

Once we got to the target, we set our explosives, which were on a timer. Then we armed the timer, retracted from the target, pulled in the perimeter, and beat feet out of there.

Even though we were out of the water, we had no real problems in conducting our missions. We had been doing some land operations training in the years before and during the Korean War. So we certainly felt confident in conducting the ops that we did. And we didn't go that far inland. Most of our operations were directed at targets on or near the water.

Back in World War II, the Naval Combat Demolition Units and the UDTs were assigned primarily to demolish beach obstacles. And beach obstacles usually meant right in the water. It was the Army's demolition people who took care of those targets up on the dry beach itself. The high-water mark was the normal limit of UDT operations.

As the war went on, the UDTs found it to their advantage to conduct some limited land operations. Training was done in handling small arms, setting up command posts and perimeters, and being able to move about on land. Then we could attack targets on the beach as well.

In Korea, we were able to put that training to some use, and we learned more. Few of my memories of Korea are fond ones. Mostly I was there during the winter months, and that is a cold country. Also, we were a poor outfit at that time. I was running around the hills of Korea, a long way from the water, with an old pair of boots on, the soles half-gone and one of my toes sticking out. A wrapping of tape kept the worst of the snow and mud out.

You could line up a platoon of UDT sailors at that time and no two people would be dressed the same way. There would be a Marine hat on one, Army boots on another, and an Air Force flight jacket would be a considerable fashion item. This was where our clothing came from—the other services. We would do training runs to different bases and see what they were willing to trade. This usually was to everyone's advantage. We would offer all of the fish and lobster they wanted if they gave us what we wanted. What really made things bad was that it was just so miserably cold in the winter.

Sometimes we would get a break and go back to Yokosuka in Japan. That was the forward location that the UDTs were based out of. There were barracks at an old Army base in Kamakura where the UDTs, Seabees, and whatever other Navy units were in at that time were housed. Those were some pretty fun times at the base because the camaraderie was great and so were the guys I worked with. But the operations were always cold.

UDT 5 had another mission later in the war that got them pretty cold and wet. Basically, what happened was that the North Koreans had strung fishnets out to sea. This was feeding the enemy forces and keeping the fish from getting to the South Koreans. So UDT 5 was given the assignment of destroying the nets and whatever at sea. That cut down on what the North Koreans getting as well as giving the South Koreans a much better catch.

One of the things we encountered all over the place in Korea were mines, especially in the water. It was the UDTs' experience with mines in Korea that led to a modification of the Teams' manning levels to include qualified EOD people. That school taught men the art of rendering an explosive device harmless or getting rid of it. Qualified members of the Teams, and even the SEAL Teams today, would be sent on to EOD School to learn how to safely handle and dispose of mines.

These UDT operators clamber across the rocks on the shore of Korea during Operation FISHNET in mid-September 1952. Their mission was to destroy or capture North Korean fishing nets to help cut off a source of supply to the enemy.

National Archives

The safest way to get rid of a mine is to blow it up. Just let the mine function, preferably not by striking a ship. For the landings at Inchon, the approaches were mined. The UDTs were sent in there to locate and clear the mines. The water was pretty murky, so just wandering around was not the way to look for a mine. Instead, a helicopter would fly overhead and an observer in it could see a shadow in the water cast by the mine. We would leave our boat and swim over to the mine with a Hagensen Pack.

To destroy the mine, we would put the shoulder strap of the pack over one of its horns. Then you would take the line from the pack and put it around the mine, securing it to another horn. Cinching the line down tight to keep the pack close to the mine, you would then pull the fuse device, step back, and just watch it blow.

After doing that for a while, a number of us, including myself, were sent to EOD School. There I found out that the horn of the mine I was pressing against to secure my Hagensen Pack was soft lead and only required a few pounds to bend or crush it and detonate the mine. That horn had a glass ampule of electrolyte in it. Below the horn were battery plates wired to the mine's detonator and ready to go. Breaking the glass let the electrolyte flow down to the battery plates, create a current, and boom!

Fortunately, no one in the Teams was ever hurt messing with an antiship mine. One time aboard our APD troop transport an announcement came over the PA system calling out a warning about a mine in the water and sending us all to the opposite side of the ship. So naturally, we all ran to the other side of the ship to see the mine.

This one single mine slid along the side of our ship, bouncing several times against the hull and finally slipping past the stern. On the fantail were some men with automatic weapons. When the ship was clear of the mine, they opened fire on it. Not more than half a dozen or so rounds had been fired when the mine blew up. That was about the luckiest day for our UDT and that APD.

In today's schools, the Korean War is taught as having been heavily involved with an air war. There were more than a few ground-pounders involved trying to capture and hold the real estate the planes flew over. One famous piece of dirt was a good-sized bulge of land known as Pork Chop Hill. Both the North Koreans and the UN forces wanted that hill for a strategic advantage over the surrounding area. Each side had determined that the other wasn't going to get it. That hill was fought over for months, with a tremendous loss of life. That hill kind of exemplified the ground combat in Korea.

A lot of the UDT work had to do with the water, but not all of it was offensive in nature. With the heavy involvement of aircraft in the war, there were also a number of air losses. The Korean War was probably the last great war of dogfighting in the air. Now missiles are used; then, it was mostly plane to plane with cannons and guns.

Prior to going out on a mine clearance operation, these UDT operators receive a premission briefing. The cold waters off Korea require the dry suits for underwater operations. The black "ear" on the side of some of the dry suit hoods is a one-way rubber flapper valve to allow excess air to escape as the men enter the water.

National Archives

And we did a lot of pilot recovery. You would stand by on board ship if you saw a plane in trouble over the water. If a plane popped its canopy, you could see the pilot eject. Then we would all make the best effort we could to get to the pilot before the North Koreans did. We had a pretty good success rate in conducting that mission. Taking a fast boat, we could get in to the pilot quickly and pull him out before a larger, slower craft pulled up.

The involvement of the Teams in the war included risky missions, beach reconnaissance, mine clearance, and things of this nature. The Marines and the UDT worked together a lot on operations. The Marine Corps is a dedicated unit of fighting men, professional and extremely capable at their job. We thought highly of them and I like to think they thought a lot of us.

There was an element of danger in everything we did in Korea, maybe a bit higher than what the average soldier or sailor faced. But we had a pretty decent record on our operations. There were UDT operators wounded, and I believe we even had several killed. But for the most part, we conducted our operations with minimum casualties.

The Korean War concluded with a cease-fire and not really an end to the conflict. Though there was still a lot of cleanup work to do off of Korea, the Teams went back to Coronado, and for the most part we were in the States for good. Somewhere along the line during the war, the Navy had changed UDTs 1, 3, and 5, to UDTs 11, 12, and 13.

When I returned from my third tour in Korea, I was assigned to Underwater Demolition Unit One, which was the overall command unit for the UDTs. Commander Doug Fane was the man in charge of UDU 1 at that time. Fane was the equivalent of today's admiral of SpecWar; he was in charge of all of the Teams on the West Coast. There was a group of about ten or twelve of us at UDT 1 that Fane had working on various secret projects and the development of new equipment.

Manufacturers and other companies would send new gear down the line to our unit for testing and possible use by the Teams. It could be a new diving device or swimmer propelling device of some kind. Testing those items is what justified our workday.

An officer by the name of Bill Hamilton, a lieutenant at that time, was always hanging around our unit. I didn't know him as a frogman or as having come through training. He wore flight wings, so I knew he was an aviator. Looking to one of the guys who had been there longer than me, I asked him just who this guy was. "He's our air officer," I was told.

But UDT wasn't conducting air operations at that time. We would jump out of helicopters without parachutes, from 75 to 80 feet in the air. But that was about the extent of our air operations. If you wanted to get back into the helicopter, it would have to drag a Jacob's ladder behind it, down into the water. You caught the ladder and crawled back aboard the bird that way. This was long before the parachuting requirement entered the Teams.

What I came to find out about the "air ops" officer later was that he was with the CIA. In his efforts to expand the operations of the UDTs, Commander Fane had a lot of dealings with the CIA. To the best of my knowledge, Hamilton was one of the men working with Doug Fane on those projects.

Commander Fane was a lieutenant commander when I first met him. He'd had some problems on the East Coast earlier involving a demolition operation and was sent over to Coronado. He was a heroic, brave man who always led from the front. A good example of his attitude was shown when we were locking in and out of submarines.

Subs didn't have a real good system for locking swimmers in and out en masse while the boat was underwater. We could use

During underwater training, a SEAL exits the hatch of a very crowded submarine escape chamber.

U.S. Navy

the submarine escape hatch, which was about the size of a trash barrel, to move a few guys at a time. We would squeeze, literally, four guys into this small steel barrel, to get out of the sub while it was under way.

This was a pretty inefficient way of moving divers in and out of a submarine, so Doug Fane thought it might be a good idea to go out through the torpedo tubes. The procedure would be to crawl into the torpedo tube through the loading hatch inside the submarine. Then you'd flood the tube and open the outer doors. The water could be leaked in reasonably slowly, the pressure would be equalized, and the swimmer would go up the torpedo tube and out into the open water. This sounds easy until you realize that the tube is only twenty-one inches in diameter. A swimmer and his breathing rig would be very crowded inside of that tube. But it did work.

Getting back into the submarine was a little different. First, you had to work your way into that greasy tube, and then crawl down in the absolute dark to the loading hatch. Banging on the side of the tube would tell the people inside the torpedo room that you were ready. They would close the outer doors, blow the water out of the tube, and open the interior hatch.

The problem was, there was no way of controlling the air pressure that was used to eliminate the water and clear the torpedo tube. What they did was hit the button that normally fired a torpedo. The firing button dumped the boat's high-pressure air lines into that tube in a hurry. That air pressure was enough to send a snug-fitting 3,800-pound Mark-14 torpedo up and out of that greasy tube like a cork from a bottle.

During the first torpedo-tube-lock exercise, when we opened the tube holding Doug Fane, we found him bleeding from the eyes, ears, and mouth. It was obvious to all of us that the sudden air pressure had really done a job on him. Standing there in the torpedo room, a little shaky on his feet but standing on his own, Commander Fane said, "I don't think this is going to work too well."

Inside the cramped stern torpedo compartment of a submarine, a UDT swimmer backs into the open torpedo tube. He will don the mask of his Scott Hydro-Pac after getting into the tube and then drag the tanks in behind him. Then the operator's swim buddy will enter the tube face first, pushing his air tanks in front of him.

U.S. Navy

I and quite a number of other Frogmen really learned to appreciate the man. He was a tremendous leader and a real example of what it meant to have guts. There was another occasion when we were out on a diving operation on a wreck and I spotted a big, beautiful lobster—it must have been about ten pounds. When I came up to the boat, I told Fane about the great lobster I had seen on the bottom. "Well, why the hell don't you get it?" was all he said.

"Because right next to it is a real big moray eel," was my answer.

"Goddammit," was all he growled as he went over the side. Fane went down to where that lobster was, pushed the eel aside, and came back up with a really nice dinner. "That's the way you do it," he said to me when he was back on the boat. Doug Fane was a real good man to have leading us in the Teams.

By the latter part of 1961, there were some rumors making the rounds of the Coronado Teams about this new formation, a SEAL Team or something of that nature. We didn't know what it was about. Little by little, it became a reality.

What was done was the UDTs were drawn on to supply the personnel for this new SEAL Team. A lot of people were under the impression that the SEALs were a completely new outfit. What they were was UDT sailors under a new name and mission. Once that was done, the SEALs did go on to a lot more technical training. They were given weapons training, taught languages, they were even taken up into the mountains and taught how to ski.

The SEALs had a new operational mandate that justified their going inland for intelligence gathering and other missions. Whether it was capturing an enemy chief or rescuing hostages, all of this was under the new mandate of the SEAL Teams. The UDT mandate remained the same.

The SEAL Teams continued drawing manpower from the UDTs. When a man graduated from training, he didn't go into the SEAL Team, he went into the UDTs to get some experience first. Eventually, the UDTs were completely absorbed by the SEAL Teams. The last component of the UDTs to go was the Swimmer Delivery Vehicle units. These were consolidated and became the SDV Teams, one on each coast.

As an EOD-qualified individual, I spent time in both the SEAL Teams and the UDTs during the Vietnam War. If there was an accident or a piece of ordnance didn't operate correctly, I was one of the people who was sent in to check things out and investigate what happened. Vietnam wasn't a place that really impressed me at all. The guys in the Team did some beautiful work there, and a lot of the operations weren't fun. It was a lot of very hard work and occasionally very tricky to pull off.

The Teams had some ordnance in Vietnam that they tried to modify in the field on occasions. Normally, you never touch that kind of thing, and you certainly don't modify it. Ordnance is approved of by the Bureau of Ordnance and is controlled. The way they send it to you is the way you are supposed to use it.

But the SEAL Teams had some leeway in those rules. They could alter weapons and ordnance if they felt it would give them some advantage in completing a mission. There were times when some SEALs felt that a piece of ordnance would work better with their design. And sometimes people got hurt.

There was a backpack-carried rocket system made for the SEALs that had three rounds of 3.5-inch bazooka rockets. The fuze system ended up being at fault. The system turned out to be very unstable because in a safe position, where it wasn't supposed to fire, it fired on three occasions. Several of the people hurt in these incidents were friends of mine. The weapons and materials issued to the SEALs were sometimes experimental. And the guys using them earned their extra pay.

■ Chapter 23

The Lighter Side

Only the West Coast UDTs participated in the Korean War. Even though the West Coast had to commission an additional UDT, UDT 5, to meet their commitment to actions in Korea, they continued to decline offers of assistance from the East Coast Teams at Little Creek.

Support personnel were assigned to the UDTs to assist in the completion of their mission. Although these men were usually not qualified as UDT operators, having never gone through UDT training, they had technical skills that the Team needed, skills the UDT operators lacked. These people were the only nonvolunteers in an entirely volunteer outfit.

But the appeal of the UDT lifestyle would draw some of these individuals into trying their luck at UDTR or Underwater Demolition Team Replacement training. When they completed training and joined a Team, they often conducted Team operations in addition to their original technical job. Even though they may not have gone on a single combat tour during their time in the Teams, some of these operators made an impression on the UDTs that would endure long after their own Navy careers came to an end.

Jack Tomlinson, Draftsman Second Class

Prior to enlisting in the Navy, I had been a flooring designer at Armstrong Industries. When I found out that I was in line to be drafted into the Army, I decided to enlist in the Navy. Because of my civilian designer background, the Navy sent me to drafting school. The school was in California and after graduation I was scheduled to go to a Seabee unit at Little Creek, Virginia. Instead, I was issued a set of orders sending me to a unit called UDT 2, also in Little Creek, and was assigned work as a cartographer.

At that time I had no idea what a UDT was or what job they did in the Navy. A cartographer I understood—I would be drawing naval charts and maps. When I first started to work with what I learned were the Underwater Demolition Teams, I did the drafting work from information the swimmers obtained by measuring and observing the offshore waters. Part of my job was to go out with the unit on exercises, so I was able to watch the men go through their paces.

My first thought after watching the UDT in action was that these men had to be crazy to do the kind of work that they did. Rolling out of high-speed boats, swimming off "enemy" beaches and dropping lines into the water, and then being snatched back up by the high-speed boats.

My second thought after watching these actions was that there was no way a skinny little guy like me could ever do it with them. The UDTs were an all-volunteer outfit. I was assigned to UDT 2 not as a swimmer, but specifically as a draftsman and cartographer. After I had been in the unit for a while, I spoke to the commander and found out that there was no way I was going to get a transfer from the UDTs to another unit. So I decided to try out for the next training class.

My class was class eight in 1952 and it took place right there at Little Creek. The training was something I never want to go through again. It was very strenuous, difficult work. Looking back on it now, I realize that much of what they had us doing was intended to test and stretch our mental capacity. This testing reached a climax during Hell Week, kind of the highlight of the training. Once an individual passed through Hell Week, he was pretty much on his way to the Teams. The real hard weeding-out of the volunteers was completed during that week.

What got me through Hell Week personally was probably nothing more than my determination to accomplish it. A young fellow by the name of Wendell Witherow buddies up with me early on, and through most of the course, we poked each other to keep going when one of us flagged a bit.

I graduated with my class and returned to UDT 2. Now I was one of the Team. Probably my most vivid memory of being in the Teams was actually making it through training. Some of the forced marches we had done, I really don't know how I completed. There was pain and discomfort at a level I hadn't experienced before. In spite of the throwing up, the arms and legs aching, the desire to just collapse and give it all up, your buddy would prod you a bit and you would just keep going. And the instructors just kept asking for more, and more, and more.

Individuals who enter the UDT or SEAL Teams seem to me to have to be nonconformists. They're not the image the public holds of giant men with huge muscles. Instead, the average UDT operator got through training because he was a regular guy who had a strong mental capacity. It was an individual's will that got him through training much more than his physique.

Once you had gotten through the training, you became a member of a UDT. Each man in the UDTs had his own specialty, and each man worked as part of a Team, using his skills for the good of the whole. Everything in the Teams is done under the buddy system. The training exercises and swimming exercises were all done as a Team and each man worked with his buddy on the same job. Throughout training and during operations, there was no thought to the individual, only the Team. The stand-alone individual wouldn't have survived in the Teams, much less through training.

So many things were going on in a tactical operation that one man couldn't hope to accomplish the mission. And the water is a dangerous environment. Each man in the Teams had to know he could count on his Teammate to help him if he got into trouble. Just as he would help if needed. You covered each other, always.

We didn't train to operate against any specific enemy. In the UDTs then, our mission stopped at the dune line on the beach. We didn't go inland yet; that was to come later. Our training mostly was to clear paths and to destroy ships. A team of combat swimmers could attack a ship at anchor with explosives, and that was one of the operations we practiced for.

On a mission, we weren't even really armed. Our gear consisted of a knife, a packet of shark repellent, and a plastic slate. This was enough for the operation at that time. The lack of equipment didn't bother us since there was no real need for more. We didn't go on shore, so we didn't need guns or other weapons. Communications were conducted from the boats, so there weren't radios with us in the water. We just did water work and that was enough.

Later I was able to leave something with the Teams that was a bit more permanent than the charts and maps I had been making.

There was an advertisement in a Norfolk paper about a contest for all of the personnel of the Atlantic Fleet. My partner in the chart shop brought it to my attention and suggested I enter. The competition was to design a symbol for the Underwater Demolition Teams. Before then, there had been a number of different signs and kinds of mascots used. During World War II, a stylized octopus with its multiple arms waving explosives had been used a few times. But nobody had come up with something that everyone liked.

Having been a designer and not an artist in my civilian work, drawing wasn't really what I did. But a lot of the guys in the Teams had me do different drawings, cartoons, and whatnot, so my sketching skills had become fairly good. I submitted about four different designs to the contest, which isn't a very large number in most design work. You just don't do you best work right at the beginning. Instead, you kind of warm up to the subject, change things, develop others, and sometimes just turn your back on it for a while.

The early sketches had been all right, but they just didn't really grab me. So I put everything away for a bit. When I picked it back up again, I started making sketches. The first idea that came to mind was based on our name. To the public, we weren't the Underwater Demolition Teams, we were the frogmen, a name that had been coined just after WWII. So my new character sketches centered around a frog.

So I had this little frog down on paper. To make him look a bit more Navy, I gave him a white enlisted man's hat. We had a reputation for being tough in the Teams, so I gave him some heavy muscles and a serious expression. A stock of dynamite in the frog's hand came from my memories of training. The instructors had thrown these little packets of explosives at us during Hell Week.

Freddy the Frog, the official Navy symbol for the Underwater Demolition Teams. In his mouth is a burning cigar and in his right hand, a stick of dynamite with a lit fuse.

The lighting of the explosive came from the fact that during training, we had a bosun's mate by the name of Mark O. Lewis. When we went south for further training, all of the trainees had been put up in the bow of this APD for the trip down to the Caribbean. The rough Atlantic waters bounced us all over the place during the trip. Instructor Lewis used to stand in the door of our compartment smoking a great big smelly cigar, doing his best to make us all sick. It was that memory of Instructor Lewis with his cigar and his throwing explosives at us that gave my design his cigar and stick of dynamite.

That design, Freddie the Frog, became the official insignia of the U.S. Navy's Underwater Demolition Teams. Being its creator was quite an honor, and it would have been an even greater one if I had known about it. No one notified me of anything and the design wasn't accepted as an official symbol until some years had gone by and I'd left the service.

One day when I came down to visit the UDT-SEAL Museum in the early nineties, I found out that my drawing had been adopted. The then curator of the museum, Chief Jim Watson, showed me all of the different ways my design had been used.

As a cartographer in the UDT Team, I was really part of the Intelligence Section. When the Team went out on a predemolition run, the men were dropped off in pairs, spaced out at intervals from the boat. They would swim in, making depth soundings and recording their information down on plastic slates. This was also when they made any notes of obstacles.

When the swimmers were returned to the ship, the intelligence officer interrogated each man on details of their swims. Then they would deposit their plastic slates with me. I would transfer that information onto charts that were used by the

Amphibious Forces to plan their landings. The same charts could be used by our own UDT to plan a demolition swim if we were going to go back in and blast away obstacles.

■ Chapter 24

Cold Waters, Cold Stares, Cold Rides

Besides swimming the cold waters off of Korea, the UDTs conducted operations in the late 1940s and through the 1950s well north of the Arctic Circle. To support distant military facilities across the northern cap of the North American continent, the men of the UDTs opened landing sites on beaches that were covered with thick ice through most of the year. Cold-water diving technology was still in its infancy during these operations and the men of the UDTs suffered through extremes of cold that taxed even their well-known endurance.

Cold wasn't the only threat the men of the UDTs faced. In the warmer waters of the tropics, cold wasn't a problem, but some of the denizens of those waters could pose a definite hazard. Encounters with some members of the ocean's population could be difficult only if you weren't aware of them. Others made you very aware that you were the interloper in their territory.

Even with new diving equipment that allowed a swimmer to remain underwater for hours, the length of a UDT combat swimmer mission was still dependent on the muscle power of the individual. UDT operators were superbly fit, but miles of swimming could tax the most powerful of men. Add to the swimmer's load the weapons, explosives, or equipment needed to complete a mission, and the distance he could cover decreased greatly. Mechanical means for extending a combat swimmer's range and carrying ability were developed throughout the 1950s and into the 1960s. But a new drawback was found in using these aids.

Commander Donald Balzarini, USN (Ret.)

Like so many other people, I probably first heard about the Underwater Demolition Teams by seeing the Richard Widmark movie The Frogmen. *Then there was a Life magazine cover and article called "The King of the Frogmen," with Tiz Moresson in the title role, as I remember. That really looked like something I wanted to do. Having done a lot of swimming and other water sports, I figured I'd give it a try.*

While I was at Navy OCS (Officer Candidate School), they were asking for people to volunteer for UDT training. Passing the screening tests, I asked for the West Coast and received orders for Coronado. Class 17 started in July 1956 and I was a part of it. The sunny Southern California weather doesn't have a lot of effect on the cold-water currents off Coronado. It didn't matter that it was summer; we did our share of shivering.

Particular stories can be told about any number of individual classes, but we all had pretty much the same experiences. We were all cold, wet, and miserable. The instructors beat us with hard work and PT, had us running and rolling around in the sand. Generally, it was an ordeal. For myself, I didn't particularly like to run and I didn't start out in training as one of the best runners. Swimming I didn't enjoy particularly either, but it was a lot easier for me than the running. Paul McNally was our class proctor and he would just go out and run forever. We would be trying to follow him and he was just running and running and running.

Probably the worst run I can remember at UDTR was during Hell Week. Our instructor for that "evolution" was Al Huey, and he was acting as the "good guy" instructor in contrast to the "bad guy" instructors. Just another mind game they played on you in training.

Instructor Huey was going to take us on an easy run, just a half mile over the sand dunes, down to the Del Coronado hotel and back. At least rumor had it that we would be having an easy run. As it turned out, he took us and ran us past the Hotel Del Coronado, down to the North Island fence. Then we went past the Del again and continued halfway to Imperial Beach. It was the most miserable run I had ever been on in my life. What we had been "told" was going to be one mile turned out to be twelve.

So Hell Week lived up to its name for us. You could "fight back" in your own way. We decided on the last night to make our own changes to the route the instructors had laid out for us for an "Around the World" rubber boat trip. We were to start near the Del, go across the land to the bay, paddle around the Amphibious Base and down to Imperial Beach, then cross back over to the ocean and paddle our IBS (Inflatable Boat, Small) north to the Hotel Del. We thought that route was ridiculous and decided to cut it a little short.

When we went around the Amphibious Base, and didn't think we could be seen, we cut into the base and headed overland. Stopping at the BOQ (Bachelor Officers' Quarters) and the enlisted barracks, we grabbed up a couple of six-packs, sandwiches, and things and figured we were going to fool the instructors and have an easy night of it. You get a little ding-y by the end of Hell Week.

Back into the ocean we went and we paddled on toward Imperial Beach. We had gone about a hundred yards when we could see the instructors on the beach. And they were just motioning us in. We went in to shore and there were the other boat crews standing at attention. The instructors, it seemed, were capturing each crew and having them do additional "fun" things on the beach.

We had a slight problem, though. Before taking our boat back into the water, we had taken one guy, Billy Davis, and sent him on another mission. He was going to go and find a friend of his nearby who had a truck. They were going to drive down to Imperial Beach, meet up with us, and drive us back to the base. That way we wouldn't have to paddle back. So when we were captured, Billy was off looking for this truck.

The instructors took us back to the Hotel Del and held a big beach party, and we were the entertainment. We would paddle out through the surf, up to the North Island fence, back in to shore, check in, run down to the Del Coronado, and check in to where the party was going on. Then we would do the whole thing again. This was the evolution we did all night.

So Billy Davis wasn't with us. He was still looking for us in Imperial Beach and had no idea that we were up doing our little circuits. It came to be around 4:00 or 4:30 in the morning and we were allowed to go back to our barracks and get cleaned up and some sleep. About 5:30, we were awakened in time for our morning PT and whatever down on the grinder. It was Saturday morning, the last day of Hell Week. As the leader of our boat crew, I had to turn in a muster report. Billy was in our boat crew, but he still hadn't shown up. I couldn't turn in a false report and I certainly didn't want to report him missing and get him in trouble.

So I went up to Instructor McNally, our class proctor, and told him I had a problem. He asked me what the problem was and I told him that Billy Davis was missing. And about that time Davis came running onto the grinder. He had been looking for us all over and finally just conked out to sleep at about 4:30. The sun woke him up and he came and found us. And we got away clean with our misfired little plan.

About noon that day we were secured from Hell Week. We all went to our quarters, showered, and just absolutely crashed. Some non-UDT guys woke me up around 4 P.M. Getting some of the other guys together, we actually went out and partied after completing Hell Week and being up all week. Finally, I got back to the BOQ about 11 P.M., fell into bed, and woke up sometime Sunday afternoon.

It didn't seem to me that the enlisted men going through training were treated any differently than the officers. The instructors took people that they weren't really sure should be in the Teams and seemed to give them some additional attention. But the rest of us mostly shared the abuse evenly. The officers, of course, had some different evolutions during training that we had to plan and lead. But the general treatment was about the same for us all.

In later classes that I observed in the late 1960s, there seemed to be a lot more verbal abuse from the instructors than we had to face a decade earlier. There was a lot more swearing at the trainees and such. Demeaning more than anything else. That's gone away again; it seemed to have just been around for a few years, perhaps with just a few instructors, and that was their technique. All trainees were scumbags; that was something we learned the first day at training, if not before.

Until the day you got into the Teams, we were all given a goodly helping of misery. Then came the day you graduated and you were welcomed into the Teams as a comrade. We didn't have a big graduation ceremony such as they have nowadays. We had a small outdoor graduation in front of the base theater. There were about twenty-five of us who had made it and there was just a feeling of elation at our accomplishment. We were part of the Team now. It was a wonderful feeling that can't really be described.

To get through UDTR—or what is called BUD/S today—you have to have a certain level of physical ability. That's tested during the screening programs and you have to have it just to get through the quarterdeck. But we've had world-class athletes who didn't make it through. Mentally, it's nice to be able to turn off the pain. But what you really have to have to get through training is that desire to make it to the Teams. That's the heart. You see some scrawny little wiry runt make it through to graduation while some big hulking guy didn't make it to Hell Week.

Physically, I was just kind of typical, five-foot-eleven, 180 pounds. My size was just kind of ordinary. Some of the other guys we had were well-built, muscular quitters. It was the desire—you had to want it. And it was sure worth it when you made it through.

Everything we had done to get to the Teams was worth it. And what seemed to be the best thing about it was that they paid us to do our jobs once we got into the Teams. Some of us would have done what we did for nothing. We lived on the beach in Coronado; you could go and jump out of airplanes, blow stuff up, and they paid us. That was pretty good.

The friends you made in the Teams, your comrades, your pals, these were great people to be with. That carries on to the present day. The men in the SEALs today are real professionals, but they also know how to really enjoy themselves when they can. They fight hard and they can party hard.

A Teammate is someone you can count on for your whole life. These are people you will be able to depend on no matter what the situation is. No matter how difficult the situation or task is, you will not be alone. Your Teammate will be there to help you. And if he isn't enough, more will come. A Teammate will not disappear, he will not bail out on you, he is there, unconditionally.

It's not that you can always recognize a SEAL or a frog in a crowd of people. Truthfully, you can recognize the phonies before you spot the real ones. The guys who are not SEALs or frogs but claim to have been, they stand out more. The big thing that trips up the phonies is the simple truth that once you have gone through training, you will never forget your class number. And that number is not classified. Training isn't what's classified in the Teams; some missions and capabilities are. If a guy claims to have gone through training and he can't remember his class number, he's a phony. If he says his training was classified and secret, he's a phony. Everyone who has ever gone through it is very proud of their class, as well they should be.

Once I graduated from UDTR and got into UDT 11, we did a lot of training ops along the coast of California. We did recons and amphibious landings, learning our craft and polishing our skills. The first real deployment I went on was the Arctic DEW line support operations. The Distant Early Warning System was set up along the far northern edge of North America and it was designed to spot a Soviet attack coming in on the United States over the North Pole. The radar and other sites that made up this line had to be manned and those people needed to be resupplied on occasion.

A detachment from UDT 11 flew from San Diego up to Kodiak, Alaska. From there, we flew on to Point Barrow, the northernmost point of Alaska. From Point Barrow, we used bush pilots to fly us in to different sites all across the North American continent. We would do beach reconnaissance, ice demolitions, and other actions to try to see if these sites could be supplied by ship. We spent about six weeks up north of the Arctic Circle, traveling from Point Barrow to the Boothia Peninsula and back.

UDT 12 operators paddle their IBS in frigid Arctic waters as they return from an underwater charting mission. The ice floes floating about them demonstrate the extreme cold of the water. Even in their insulated dry suits, the UDT swimmers suffered from the cold every time they entered the water.

U.S. Navy

There had been cold water in Coronado, but wet suits weren't available in the Teams back then. You could go and buy your own, which many of us did. In the Arctic waters, we would wear our wet suits under the issue dry suits we had. The dry suits work by keeping a layer of underwear dry that's between your skin and the suit. But dry suits almost always leaked and that got the long underwear wet and you got really cold really fast. The wet suits kept you warmer longer.

Where you really felt the cold was on your hands, because we didn't wear gloves. And your face also got very cold. And this was cold from frigid water. It wasn't very much fun diving under the ice or working in Arctic waters. It was just unbearably cold. But it was beautiful once you went under the ice. The water was this great color, and it was very interesting. But it wasn't something you would do if you didn't have to.

Under the ice, the surface was a light white gray. The water was a very deep blue looking down. Looking around you, the water had a greenish tint, but didn't have any real color to it. The overhead cover of snow is what controlled the amount of light that penetrated the water. It could get dark but not really black.

We had a contest one day with a big tub of half ice and half water. The challenge was to see how long you could stay in the water before you climbed out. I lasted maybe thirty seconds. But the guy after me lasted forty-five seconds. Then the time just kept growing. The final time was something like twenty-five minutes that someone stayed in this ice bath. Again, that was from mental discipline, because the doctors said you couldn't stay in that thirty-two-degree water for that long. But some guys did.

The experience of working the DEW line was enjoyable. Seeing caribou, walrus, small whales, and polar bears, as well as the Eskimo culture was worth the work. But the work was hard and we earned every sight we saw. But we never had any close encounters.

There was one occasion with some Eskimos that was noteworthy. A couple of the guys were on the ice in their wet suits when some Eskimos approached. They must have looked like a couple of seals—the animal kind—and the Eskimos started taking shots at them. It was their arm waving and jumping around that caused the Eskimos to finally stop shooting.

There was another time when a bush plane crashed. The UDT men on board had been wearing their wet suits and were able to get the pilot out. They were all lucky to be alive after that incident.

There was another wildlife encounter I had out in the Pacific that took place in a lot warmer water. It was a night operation and Ron Smith was swimming off to my right. As Ron tells it later, he looked over his right shoulder and just saw this huge mouth in the darkness. Whatever it was, it struck him in the shoulder. He didn't know what it was and swam in to shore pretty quickly. We always teased him later, saying that he hit the beach and kept swimming across the sand until he hit the rocks.

When we checked Ron out later, we could see where he had been bitten on the shoulder. The puncture wounds looked like what a sea lion would leave if it nipped you. As near as we could figure out later, Ron may have gotten between a mother sea lion and her pup. He wasn't hurt real bad, so the situation seemed funny later.

There was another time when we were operating off of Wake Island in the Pacific that didn't seem so funny afterward. The first couple of days out we were doing reconnaissance and prepping a channel where we were going to blast through the coral. There were a few sharks around but nothing seemed bad. We set our shot off and the next day went back to the site. Now there were sharks all over the place. We went out through the surf and they literally chased us back to the shore.

Standing amid floating ice floes, a UDT swimmer comes close to resembling an aquatic seal long before the Navy SEALs were commissioned.

U.S. Navy

We waited another day to let things settle down. The sharks had probably been feeding on fish and whatever our shot had killed. So we went out again to do a recon and see how our demolitions had gone. We paddled in IBS out there and Dick Swenson and I hit the water. We separated a little bit and just skin-dived down the thirty or forty feet or so to the channel we had shot. There were quite a few sharks still around.

I swam back up to the surface and looked down at a shark that appeared to be looking at me. That shark just kind of leveled off and started coming up to where I was. Now I knew how a fly felt on top of the water as a trout came up to eat it; the only trouble was that I was the fly and that shark was a really big trout.

He was about six feet away when I kicked at him with my fins and he swerved away. Then that shark just started circling me. He was about eight feet long and I was spinning around as fast as he was circling to keep my eye on him. The IBS was about fifty-feet away and I was working my way toward it as I spun in the water. The guys in the boat had no idea what was going on.

When I got to the boat, I wanted to get in, but I also didn't want to take my eyes off the shark. Finally, I just about swam straight up out of the water and into the IBS. Swenson was something like a hundred yards away and he too had no idea what was going on. So we paddled over and jerked him into the boat. Then I explained that there was a shark going around who looked very interested in us. So we went back in to shore.

The next day there were still sharks, but fewer of them. There was a cloudy layer in the water where we had blasted the coral. You had to swim down through the cloud layer to get below it and see just what the blast had done. It was a little disconcerting to watch the sharks moving in and out of this cloudy layer when you had to go back through it and not be able to see anything for a moment.

There was only one known incident in which a guy from the Teams was killed by a shark. That was in April 1963, when Lieutenant John Gibson of UDT 21 was attacked and killed by a shark in Megans Bay on Saint Thomas. The shark was later caught and they found parts of Lieutenant Gibson inside its body that proved they had gotten the killer.

But for all of the operations the UDTs and SEALs have conducted in the water, there have been very few attacks of any kind from the critter there. Some guys have been bitten by morays while catching lobster, and more than a few guys have had encounters with sea urchins and jellyfish. There have been guys who have disappeared, though.

When I first came into the Teams, one of the first things I was involved in was a memorial for a lost teammate. This guy had been diving off of Panama and just dis-

A UDT underwater swimmer using the Mark II SPU. His swim buddy would ride along behind him on an operation, being towed above and behind the man operating the SPU.

U.S. Navy

appeared. It could possibly have been a predator or shark attack, but the sea is a dangerous place even without the things that live in it.

The "cruel sea" was an expression we've heard more than once. But the UDT mission is inherently dangerous. We've had more people killed since 1950 in non-combat than combat. Training accidents, equipment testing, or just operations have taken Team lives. It is just a dangerous environment.

Little mistakes when diving, working with explosives, or operating can kill you or your Teammate quickly. But when you're in the Teams, you don't think of the dangers. These things can happen, but you train constantly to see that they don't. When you worry about what can happen too much, it's time to get out.

But there were some interesting times working with new equipment. In the late 1950s, we were developing what were called SPUs or Swimmer Propulsion Units. These were battery-powered electric motors in a waterproof casing connected to a small propeller. The SPU could tow a swimmer a longer distance than he could swim, keep him better rested, and allow him to take more equipment/explosives with him.

The first SPUs in the Team were jury-rigged items the guys had made themselves. The first official SPU came to us in the late fifties. Chief Gagliardi and I went up to the Aerojet General Company in Southern California and picked up our first unit. The device was maybe three and a half or four feet long and a foot or so in diameter.

It was January when we went to pick up the unit. The company had a tank of water outside we could test the SPU in. And that water was cold. Right away we noticed a problem with the SPU, and it has been the same problem they have been struggling with ever since. The vehicles are cold to operate. When you are swimming, you're doing enough work that you'll keep yourself warm, especially in a good suit. When you're just hanging on to an SPU and riding around, you can get very cold, and very, very bored.

Later SPUs became bigger and you could sit inside of them. They were miniature submarines that were flooded rather than being dry inside. The driver would have something to do, but those of us just riding along would get bored and cold. Today they're developing warmer suits, even heated ones. But until they come up with a completely dry submersible to be used by the Teams, people are going to get cold and bored.

The history of the Teams hasn't been well documented over the years. Those of us who were doing the job wanted to be operating and not filling out paperwork. A lot of the history, the personal stories, have been lost. Now we are fortunate to have the UDT-SEAL Museum in Fort Pierce, Florida. The people there are really trying to gather the history through documents, recordings, photographs, and arti-

facts. The experiences of the people even from World War II can be saved now and kept for future generations.

The UDT-SEAL Museum is built on the training land that was used by the first UDTs and their forerunners, the Naval Combat Demolition Units, during World War II. Initially, the training done at Fort Pierce was for the invasion of Europe. Then the Teams were created at Maui and Hawaii and their manpower came from the Fort Pierce training site. Now there is a home for the Teams' history on the site where they really had their beginnings.

■ Chapter 25
Beach Jumpers

In warfare, deception has always been as valuable a weapon as a firearm, vehicle, or ship. A specialized naval deception unit was founded during World War II based on an idea of a man who was well versed in the art of illusions. That man was the actor Douglas Fairbanks Jr., then a Navy lieutenant, and the unit he proposed would become the Navy Beach Jumpers.

The Beach Jumpers were an elite unit that used modern sound effects, electronics, and other tricks to make a group of small craft appear to be a much larger task force. These Beach Jumper units were first used as part of Operation HUSKY, the invasion of Sicily, in July 1943. The German forces were convinced that they had detected and repulsed an Allied landing force. Instead, a Beach Jumper unit had fooled them into directing some of their limited assets to an area that wasn't threatened with a landing.

The Beach Jumpers are among the most unconventional units that ever were active in combat. Though not used for the Normandy invasions, the Beach Jumpers proved their worth in other actions during World War II. After the war, they were retained in the Navy. Eventually, the Beach Jumpers were assigned to the same organizational command as another Navy unconventional warfare unit, the UDTs and later the SEAL Teams.

Commander Peter C. Dirkx, USN (Ret.)

I spent practically my entire naval career in the Navy Special Warfare community, from my first entering UDTR class fifteen, a winter class on the West Coast in 1955, to my retirement in 1981. When I first left boot camp in the Navy, I was assigned to Beach Jumper Unit 1 in Coronado. We were berthed in an adjacent build-

ing to the UDT barracks there. Every payday, we tended to give our paychecks to the UDT men in a crap game. Since our money was going to them anyway, the men finally convinced several of us to join the Teams. So another man and I in the unit started training together, based on our friendship with the UDTs guys.

A Beach Jumper Unit at that time consisted of four aviation rescue and reconnaissance boats along with their crews. Our mission was mainly one of cover and deception. Later it evolved into something more sophisticated, but at that time it was basically about simulating ships that were not ships by making the small boats sound and seem to be much bigger. That system could deceive the enemy into thinking a unit was either landing where there really wasn't anyone, or a much larger force than there really was steaming by offshore.

When we first volunteered for UDT training, we didn't have a clue about what we were getting into. Part of what kept us going was the friends we had in the next barracks. They promised that if we failed training, we would quickly be boarding one of those long, gray ghosts (Navy fleet ships) in the harbor and never see land again. That helped us continue through training when things really got bad.

And things did get pretty bad during training. We didn't have many of the "habitability items" that made working in the water at least a little more comfortable. Wet suits were pretty much unknown and the water could be really hard to get into. The training hasn't changed in its overall goal today, but the Navy has gotten a lot better at running the students through. And the habitability factor has changed.

Does it make you a stronger or better person because you didn't have hot showers, hot meals, a wet suit? That's a question I just don't have the answer to. Comfort level isn't something that comes up a lot in BUD/S, and it didn't in the days of UDTR either. It's all relative to the time anyway.

Some things didn't change noticeably; our Hell Week then was pretty much the same as Hell Week now. There were five and a half days of misery, pain, and pure hell. Swimming, nuisance exercises, paddling the rubber boats, and only an hour or so of sleep each night. The constant movement, constant going, and staying awake all of the time, that was matched only by the constant harassment from the instructors.

It was the teamwork, the fellows in my boat crew, that helped get me through that long week. We hung in there and said we were getting through to each other. And that meant a lot when you were dead tired and just wanted to fall off of the tube (the side of the boat) into the water and just sleep forever. In fact, we did have people fall asleep while paddling the rubber boat and slip into the water. We'd have to grab them and pull them back. That's what got all of us through, our Teammates.

The thought of quitting is always in your mind during training, but I never seriously considered it. There was the thought that all of the misery and cold could be stopped in a moment, but then the thought would go away as you worked with your boat crew through the next evolution.

Cold is something everyone has experienced at one time or another. But then there's COLD. Being cold is dropping off the side of the rubber boat off San Clemente Island In December, when the water is 49 degrees and you don't have a wet suit. That's cold. You are so cold when you come out of the water that you don't have any feeling at all; you're numb all over. We did that to see if we could sustain that kind of cold. And we did those freezing cast and recoveries off San Clemente more than once.

Then comes the time when you hear the phrase "Secure from Hell Week!" Those words cause the greatest feeling of relief in the world. It is probably the best thing you have ever heard in your life. Secure from Hell Week. You just want to lie down and sleep for a week, get warm, take a hot shower, eat. And there's also a sense of accomplishment. You know you've crossed the roughest period of the training.

After many weeks of training, a lot of them spent on San Clemente Island, what stands out in my mind is some of the really great instructors we had. When we went out to that island, we had to erect the tents, the instructors' tents first of course, at eleven o'clock at night. Then we could put our own tents up. And all of this work was done in what felt like gale-force winds. Every morning we would get up and do our PT and then hand-to-hand combat, followed by the day's training. In the evening it was fall out for semaphore and flashing-light drill. Then came the night exercise.

We didn't have showers. So you would come back off an exercise, peel off your wet clothes, and climb into that sleeping bag with all of the sand that came with you, and try to get warm. Walking out of the tent one evening, when we were being rousted out for some more signaling drill, I asked, "What are they trying to prove?"

An instructor, Chief McNally, looked at me and said, "Son, we aren't trying to prove anything. We want you to try and prove something to yourself."

These words stuck with me for the balance of my training and the rest of my military career. That was the single most significant thing I remember from my training.

We had about one hundred people start the class; we graduated thirty. It was a very proud and gratifying moment for me, and that sense of relief again, when we finally graduated. And there was a sense of excitement as well. Now we were looking forward to going into a Team. And I knew the Team I was being assigned to, UDT 11, was leaving for Japan in January. So my next biggest interest was to get my name on that list of men going to Japan.

So class 15 graduated training on December 15. I went over to UDT 11 and we left Coronado for Japan the first week of January 1956. I stayed over there with the Team until May 1957. For our mission we worked off of APDs (Assault Personnel Transports) on advanced force operations all over the South Pacific. The APDs included the Weiss, Bass, and Diachenko, and I rode on all of them at one time or another. We covered the same ground that WWII UDTs had gone to—Iwo Jima, Okinawa, and all of the other islands in the South Pacific. The operations we did were part of the amphibious exercises for the fleet. And we did demolition training.

There was an amphibious exercise off of Iwo Jima one night when we disembarked the ship into our PRs at 3 A.M. We took our PR (Landing Craft, Personnel, Reconnaissance) in and conducted our hydrographic reconnaissance and beach feasibility study from the boat. This was generally the same mission the UDTs had always done and was our part of the advanced force operations. It was around four o'clock in the morning when we were out on the water and a pitch-black night.

Iwo Jima has a black volcanic ash beach with a steep gradient. There were twenty of us from the UDT aboard that PR going in to the beach that night, and all we could hear was the surf crashing on shore. The next thing that happened, the boat had been lifted up on a wave, and we were surfing in to the beach. We hit the beach and the next wave hit our boat. Twenty people were scrambling out of that boat as the waves and surf came in on it. Within a half hour there was nothing left of that thirty-six-foot plywood boat except the engine block. We lost six boats on that particular operation, working in the middle of the night. And that was without any enemy fire or anything coming at us from the island. Just the power of the sea and the steepness of the shore.

In Japan, things went a lot easier for us. We initially stayed at Camp McGill, but it was closed while we were over there. So they moved us to the Yokosuka Naval Base. Each time we deployed on an exercise, it was on an APD, as used by the WWII and Korean UDTs. We spent thirty days one time doing a hydrographic survey of what was Siam then on the same APD. With twenty-some people on that ship, it was a pretty notable exercise. There wasn't any water available for showers or really washing up, so anytime it rained, we stood on the fantail and scrubbed up in nature's shower. When we got into Bangkok after thirty days, the fleet commodore ordered the APD alongside another ship to take on water. He thought we all looked a little scrungy.

I have to give the WWII UDTs who spent months on those same APDs a lot of credit. I never thought much about them, but to spend thirty days on the same class of ship, they had to have been pretty hardy souls. We only had a detachment of some twenty UDTs on board, but there was also an equal number of Marines on the same ship. With roughly forty men on board besides the crew, we stayed on our side of the ship and the Marines stayed on theirs, both groups trying to stay out of the crew's way.

We returned to Coronado and it wasn't long before I was on another deployment. In 1957, I was one of the UDT 11 crew who went on a DEW line deployment to the Arctic Circle. Our job on the DEW (Distant Early Warning) line was to do a reconnaissance on the beaches that the Army was going to use to bring in supplies to remote sites. We would conduct a hydrographic reconnaissance off the beaches and make up charts for the Army. Large ships were bringing in the supplies and the

Army forces were using small lighters to move the materials to shore. It was a little-known fact then that the Army had more small boats than the Navy. But they still needed to know the offshore waters.

Our base of operations was located at Point Barrow, Alaska, but we were taking aircraft inland to a number of the sites. The planes were DC-3, twin-engine prop jobs, and the only way we could get back off the small strips at the sites was with JATO (Jet Assisted Take Off) assists. These were rocket bottles strapped to the outside of the planes, fired to build up speed fast.

The runways we were landing on were so short that we had to touch down on exactly the right spot to safely land. If we overshot the spot, the pilot would often fire off the JATO rockets to get us back up in the air for another try. There were other times when we had to fly low across the strip to chase the herds of caribou away to clear the way for our landing.

On one site in particular, we went in with a Cessna-170 light plane. We loaded our rubber boats, Fathometers, and other gear into the plane. Then the three of us who were going stuffed ourselves into the small cabin. The plane was piloted by a twenty-year-old kid whose father was with the FAA up in Fairbanks. This youngster was an experienced bush pilot who flew into these sites all of the time.

My memories of that trip were pretty good ones. My son was born while I was in Alaska, and I received notification while up there. And going in to the sites was fun. The people would be so glad to see us they would really put out a spread. They were cooking caribou steaks and beef, baking pies, just being wonderful hosts while we were there. So it was a very enjoyable experience.

We had been exposed to very cold water while in training, but this was the Arctic. Landing in the water unprotected would kill you quickly. Every time we flew in to one of these remote sites, we were wearing our Pirelli dry suits. These were the two-piece models worn over long underwear for cold-water protection. We wore those in the aircraft in case it crashed. Those were our survival suits. We wore the Pirellis in the water, and they would let us operate and withstand the temperature for a short period of time at least.

Most of our reconnaissance in the Arctic was done from rubber boats working with a Fathometer. We had to get in the water only when it was absolutely necessary. We didn't do any demolitions on that particular trip. Though we were prepared to, it just wasn't necessary.

Just a few years later there was a new excitement in the UDTs. The SEAL Teams were coming along and a lot of men were interested in just what was going on. Still in UDT 11 at the time, I was selected to be one of the "plankowners," one of the original crew members of SEAL Team One on the West Coast. But I had orders already cut to go to Key West and be an instructor at the Underwater Swimmers School. The assignment was one I couldn't afford to turn down because my *wife was pregnant with our fourth child. She had already delivered three other children while I was deployed somewhere, and she made it very clear to me that I was going to be around when this one entered the world.*

So even though I very much wanted to join this new organization, I had to decline, and went to Key West instead. Later, in 1968, I was back in Coronado and was able to join with SEAL Team One while they were active in Vietnam.

■ Chapter 26

Materials, the Tools of War

The side that can bring the most production to a war is usually the one that wins. In an all-out war of attrition, it's the side that runs out of men and materials last that wins. This was well proven during World War II when a German antitank unit officer was heard to comment how he had run out of shells before the Allied side had run out of tanks.

The UDTs of WWII pride themselves on the fact that they operated in the field with almost nothing in the way of equipment. At that time a full issue of gear for a WWII frogman going in on an op without explosives would fit in the average child's book bag.

After WWII, the UDTs were not as well funded as they would have liked, suffering as they did the same dislike by conventional Navy units as any other service's unconventional forces. The UDTs got by on relatively little and made do with what they had or could get their hands on. In the mid-1950s, this changed a bit among the more farseeing members of the Navy's command structure as the UDTs began to rise in prominence.

New materials and supplies came in to the UDTs along with new missions. It took supply personnel who were not only familiar with how a UDT operated in the field but were qualified to operate themselves to know ahead of time what materials would be needed for an operation or even the day-to-day running of a Team in the field. With the advent of the new SEAL Teams, the need for good supply personnel was even more important, given the wide variety of unusual and exotic weapons and equipment the Teams used. But these supply personnel also had to be familiar with the bureaucracy and red tape of a very large Navy in a peacetime situation.

James H. "Hoot" Andrews, Chief Storekeeper, USN (Ret.)

When I volunteered to go into underwater demolition training, I joined up with other volunteers from all over the fleet. This group is gathered together and that composes a class. In this mob of strangers, I didn't know anyone. The only way I found to get someone's attention—to talk to them or whatever—was to call out "Hey, Hoot!" That would cause them to turn around to see who was calling them Hoot. The spin-off of that was by being nicknamed Hoot.

It was 1951 when I joined up with class seven on the East Coast at Little Creek. We started training in May and finally graduated in August. I was only twenty-four years old at the time, and I would never go through it again. The instructors we had were volunteers from the UDTs there at Little Creek. There wasn't a trained cadre of instructors like they have today in Coronado. Each Team, UDT 2 and 4 then, would just supply a number of experienced UDT men to act as our instructors. These individuals would vary from day to day, so we never knew just who might be running what evolution.

The Amphibious Base at Little Creek back then was hardly as built up as it is today. There were long stretches of mudflats, stagnant water, and the instructors made sure we were put through every inch of it. I always tried to make sure I was up in the front of the group when we plowed through the muck. After 160-some guys during the early days of the class had run through the same patch of mud, it would be so churned up that the guys at the back of the pack ran the risk of sinking totally out of sight.

And there was a lot more to occupy your training time at Little Creek than just mud. Going across the obstacle course would give you a new experience of the word pain. Or crawling through the mudflats on your elbows and knees, with just your chin, nose, and eyes barely above the surface of the slime.

The Seabees had been one of the first sources of manpower for the Teams back in World II. And they seemed to still be mad about our taking their men when they built our obstacle course at Little Creek. They seemed to have taken every Seabee who was sadistic and had him design part of the obstacle course. It was terrible! It was awful! And we had to go through it every day during training.

The instructors even added a bit of competition to the obstacle course. They would see who could go over it the fastest, timing the whole thing. I never was one of the faster people. I was just about in the middle of the pack. But I did finish; a lot of others never did.

Class seven started with 169 men and we graduated 34. When I graduated with that proud few, I was assigned to UDT 2, later redesignated UDT 21. UDT 4 was also later redesignated as UDT 22. During the early 1950s, we still worked with the same limited equipment the Teams had used in World War II. The salvage yards were hit often to help us keep our boats and other equipment up and running. As far as individual gear went, they were issuing a pair of coral shoes, a web belt, K-Bar knife, face mask, and a pair of fins. During training, we had to qualify to earn those fins by swimming a mile under a certain time.

But those fins we had were a synthetic rubber WWII type that wouldn't bend and they just didn't last very long. But that's what we had to live with.

In 1954, I was sent to the Bureau of Ships to help formulate and implement an allowance list for one Underwater Demolition Team. Prior to my leaving on that assignment, I went around to all of the department heads in the Team. They were told to give me a complete list of everything they needed to operate, from screwdrivers to toothpicks or whatever.

Taking those lists, I collated them to eliminate the duplication factor. And that was the basic set of information I used to put together the allowance list. Each department, or code, as they would say at the bureau, had an allotment of equipment to begin operations. And then a listing of consumable materials to continue operating. These codes had to explain why something was needed and how much it would cost to purchase and maintain.

There were more than a few problems with some of the materials I ordered. The 5 or 10 gross (720 or 1,440) of condoms I ordered from the Naval Supply Center in Norfolk caused me to get a phone call. Some woman in the requisitioning department at the supply center wanted to know what we were going to do with 10 gross of condoms. I had to explain to her that these materials were necessary to waterproof firing assemblies used to detonate explosives in the water. She accepted my explanation and said that I should include on all my future requisitions for this item the words For Government Use Only.

Another item on the allowance list caused a little more stir in some offices. We had to go to the various bureaus that were concerned with all of the different items on the lists. For each bureau, we had to give a presentation justifying why we needed the things on the list. At the Bureau of Medicine, they wanted to know why I had listed 460 two-ounce bottles of brandy. The doctor who asked the question said he was wondering what we were going to do—outdrink the enemy?

We had a very good reason for the request. For our mission, we were responsible for the entire hemisphere that included the North Atlantic and the Northern European area. If we were tasked with a mission up in the Arctic, then we would have a platoon, twenty-five men, in the water in the morning and possibly again that afternoon. When the men came in from such a swim, the corpsman would issue each of them a two-ounce bottle of brandy. That could easily amount to fifty such bottles a day, and if there was a night operation, the total was seventy-five bottles a day.

We had to operate on the premise that we needed to supply ourselves independently for 90 days, until an auxiliary train came up and bought us a resupply. Adding all of the numbers together and using the equations the Bureau of Supply had come up with, that gave us 460 bottles for a platoon. And that answer satisfied the medical officer.

Later, in the fifties, I went over to the Nuclear Navy and became qualified to work as a chief of the watch on the new nuclear submarines. Before going aboard the George Washington, one of the first of the operational Polaris missile boats, I had gone through the initial outfitting, loading, location system, and records on board. It had been a very trying time and everything was starting to go very smoothly. Since I had been in underwater demolition before, I still carried that job code as part of my record. Even though I was a storekeeper chief, I still had that UDT code.

When Roy Boehm took the assignment of setting up the SEAL Team, he was having a very hard time getting anyone to respond to his needs for equipment. He had just written out a list on a pad and was trying to get some cooperation in filling it. That was when he got in touch with ComSubLant (Commander, Submarines, Atlantic) and went up the line to track me down.

When the George Washington pulled in to Holy Loch, Scotland, on what was my third patrol with her, there was a set of orders for me to report to SEAL Team Two. I didn't even know what that was. I had just received my qualifications as chief of the watch on the George Washington and the captain called me up to his stateroom.

He wanted to know if I had put in for a transfer to this new duty on my orders. My answer was simply no, and that I didn't even know what a SEAL Team was. So he said he was going to do everything he could to squash the orders. That started a flurry of messages and paperwork crossing the Atlantic from Washington, D.C., to Holy Loch. When the final message came in with year, date, and time group stamped on it, it said, "Negative, transfer." So I went back to Little Creek.

When I had gotten back to Roy, whom I had known well in my UDT 21 days, I learned what was going on. I have absolutely no regrets about my transfer. All of the guys I had been in Underwater Demolition with before were part of the new Team. Roy had brought them over, picking and choosing his men carefully. Some of the guys had been out on operations when they received the word that they would be reporting to SEAL Team upon their return. They were still plankowners, they just had to complete their operational commitment before they could ship over.

Plankowner is a uniquely Navy term. The term dates back to the days of the sailing Navy and wooden ships. It refers to a member of the original crew for a newly commissioned ship or shore activity. Each plankowner is qualified as such when he is assigned to the new unit by order. The name comes from the Navy tradition according to which each sailor owned one foot of the deck planking of the ship. In this way, the crew and the new command were brought that much closer.

So at SEAL Team Two, I was back making up new allowance lists. My first attempt was to try to get us more money, but that didn't go over too well. The SEALs were a new concept and the traditional Navy didn't like the idea very much to begin with. What the Navy at large wanted was seagoing men and ships to carry them. They wanted conventional warfare, and our type of unconventional warfare wasn't seen as the kind of thing that would enhance anyone's career at the Pentagon or elsewhere. But President Kennedy had been the one to start the idea going forward. He wanted the military to have these new capabilities and that meant we were going to have them.

To set up an allowance list, you first take the mission statement that is issued by the higher authority in the Navy and usually comes out of the CNO's office. That statement is matched up with the personnel complement, the number of people you are told it will take to carry out this mission. That's the basic piece of hard paperwork you have to have before anything else comes up. Equipment, clothing, weapons, everything is dependent on your mission statement and personnel.

At the beginning, the SEALs didn't really have anything. The Team was doing the beg, borrow, and steal routine from everywhere, including the UDT right across the street. Gear would be checked out from UDT, used for an operation, and then returned. There was no real paperwork kept to help them out or to be used as a guide.

ComPhibLant (Commander, Amphibious Force, Atlantic) was our command, and the supply types didn't know what we were or what we were doing. The folks over in command just considered us a bunch of misfits. In 1962, everything was top secret, even the name "SEAL," so we couldn't explain anything in very much detail. From the time I got to the SEAL Team, I went through the same procedures I had gone through before. They worked and we could at least eventually get what we needed.

Part of what I was doing really was repeat work. Besides using the mission statement and personnel lists, I picked up a copy of the UDT allowance list to use as a base. And that was the same list I had written years earlier. There were elements in the two units' mission statements that overlapped—Sub Ops, Air Ops, diving equipment, recharging compressors, things like that were the same whether it was for the SEALs or the UDT.

The armory with our weapons in it, that was a very different story from what was used over in the UDTs. We had to come up with a lot of different, exotic stuff to stock those shelves and racks. So to get the Team everything it needed, I took my paperwork over to ComUDU (Commander, Underwater Demolition Unit) and the both of us traveled back up to Washington to visit with bureaus up there.

We talked to every one of the heads of the different codes and we came back with an allowance list for the SEALs. The UDTs had been hard enough to explain to these guys; the concept of the SEALs was beyond them. The different bureau people had never heard of unconventional warfare, counterinsurgency, guerrilla warfare, or marine sabotage. And all of those things were parts of our mission statement. Those conventional Regular Navy sailors were all still out in the fleet firing fourteen- and sixteen-inch guns at sea. That was the Navy to those people. They preferred conventional warfare, like the WWII battles in which the sixteen-inch guns slammed between battleships and the Marines would move in to take and hold the beach.

In unconventional warfare, you would go in, hit a target, and run. Or slip in quietly and overrun an area and secure it. The training for unconventional warfare is very different from a normal training routine, and so Roy Boehm had to set up a cross-training program. We would be assigned to different elements that would be going to different training sites, such as Fort Bragg and the Army Special Forces School there.

With the Army Special Forces, we trained in foreign weapons, reconnaissance, sneaky-pete work, and specialized training. Our communications people went to the Special Forces communications courses. Our corpsmen went through some of the SF medics training, where they learned the more advanced field surgery techniques and so on. And we all went through the HALO (High Altitude, Low Opening) parachute training.

That kind of training prepared us to conduct some of our unconventional operations and marine sabotage. At that time we had only one type of submersible craft. And like the UDTs, we used them to attack ships at anchor, slipping up on them and attaching limpet mines to their hulls. That was the training and that was the job. And we needed the tools to complete that mission. Getting most of those tools was my assignment.

Roy Boehm came up with some real exotic pieces of hardware he wanted for the SEALs. Instead of going through the normal ordnance channels, which would have turned him down anyway, he went out and bought AR-15 rifles, enough to outfit both SEAL Team One and Two. We had the funds, he mostly had the authority, and he certainly had the attitude to just get what he needed to get the job done.

One of the strangest pieces of equipment Roy wanted was thirty or forty crossbows. In spite of the fact that we were trying to build a modern unit in 1962, Roy wanted crossbows. And he had some suggestions for sources in his request. The manufacturer was in England and supposedly they made the best crossbow then on the market. It wasn't my place to ask questions. They just told me what they wanted and I went out and got it.

So I submitted the crossbow request to the Navy purchasing office. That began a week or a week-and-a-half runaround. Jut because I wouldn't ask questions didn't mean that anyone else wouldn't. They wanted to know why we needed the crossbows and I would answer that we were still in a classified state, had a Priority 2 for equipment, which was pretty high in their ranking. This was what was on the allowance lists and we wanted them. About a month or so later forty crossbows and a whole bunch of arrows showed up at SEAL Team Two.

In spite of the exotic nature of much of what was wanted for the new SEAL Team, it all made sense to me. And that was because of my experience in underwater demolition. If there was a bastard outfit in the Navy, that's what the SEALs seemed like. No one without a real need to know, knew what we did, what we were, or why we needed what we needed. It was a never-ending argument every time the request went forward about another piece of equipment or parts and materials to keep what we did have going, going.

They wanted to know what, why, and where. And we could only tell them the barest essentials, if that, because of security reasons. Even the name "SEAL" couldn't be openly used on unclassified documents.

At the same time I was going through all of the work of preparing the allowance list and requisitioning gear, I had to get ready to do my own training to operate. Like all of the rest of the Team, I had to go to Fort Benning for Jump School; I had to make my dive qualifications, and every other element that was required to earn and maintain the SEAL job code.

Missions and deployments were something we all did. The officer or commander assigned a task would usually post an announcement on the bulletin board on the Team quarterdeck. The note was usually pretty simple; this is the trip, this is who's in charge, and then it would ask for volunteers. Every time, the list was filled up completely. So the officer in charge of that operation could pick the men he knew would best fit the job.

You didn't always like what you had to do, but you had to do it. For myself, I hated parachute jumping. I have no trouble saying I was scared every time I went out the door. But it was part of the job, so I did all of my training and kept up the jumps needed to remain qualified.

But the training you received in the Teams took over when you were doing a job. It didn't matter if you were scared, you would have been drilled often enough that whatever needed to be done, you did it automatically. But none of the SEALs were machines when they worked on a job. Everyone was a thinking, feeling man. The emotionless Hollywood lone-wolf type just didn't exist in the SEALs or UDTs.

There are men in the Teams who are extremely intelligent, and they have good common sense to go along with it. They are very good at making individual decisions when called on to do so. There are just no stereotypes in the Teams.

I met a guy who asked me if I had been a SEAL. When I told him yes, he looked at me puzzled.

"You don't look like a SEAL," he said.

"Well," I said back, "what's a SEAL supposed to look like?"

He didn't have an answer for that one. What he had been thinking of was the movie image of a huge, muscled guy coming up from the water with a black bandana around his head and a blazing machine gun in each hand. That's not a SEAL, that's just ridiculous.

Underneath all of the equipment, camouflage paint, weapons, and ammunition is a dedicated, committed warrior. Well trained, he knows exactly what to do to get the mission done. And he will carry that mission out. That attitude goes everywhere in the Teams, from the highest-ranking officer to the most junior seaman. Whatever the mission calls for, they will do it.

The men I worked with I could depend on for anything. Putting your life in your Teammate's hands was common. And he would do the same with you. When you had a Teammate next to you, you knew you would be all right. And he knew the same thing. There was no fear with your Teammates beside you.

The SEALs are a group unlike any other in the world that I know of. There's a bond between the men that you can't explain. It stems from the Underwater Demolition Teams of World War II who went in to the beach with no weapons at all except for a K-Bar knife. Then it came on up to the SEAL Teams. The difference in the kind of warfare and missions conducted just grew. From just underwater reconnaissance and beach blowing of obstacles to going in to the jungle, swimming up the rivers and streams of Vietnam, and going ashore to seek out the VC. Hit them first rather than let them ambush you.

Regular forces had to go in to an area, dig in, and wait. They secured an area and pacified it. The SEALs would slip into an area and seek out the enemy, and either capture the leadership or just wipe them out.

The UDTs and the SEALs were very much the same; the only real difference between the two units was their mission statement. Both units started from the same beginnings and went through the same basic training. When a UDT man came over to the SEALs, that's when he received the additional specific training called for by the type of missions SEALs did. By the 1980s, the missions of the SEALs and the UDTs were recognized as being so close that it was a duplication of effort. So the names changed and the UDTs became the SEAL Teams.

The man who joins this kind of unit has a high level of commitment to what he is doing. The willpower has to be there so that the individual will never give up, never ever give up . . . never.

■ Chapter 27

Leaders and Losses in the Teams

For a long time there was no career path for officers who had gone through UDT training and wanted to remain in the Teams. A career path meant the opportunity to make rank and move up in positions. But there were very few higher-ranking slots in the Teams, especially in the 1950s and into the 1960s.

Officers who wanted to move ahead in rank much past lieutenant often had to return to the regular Fleet Navy to pull their time on board ships and in staff positions. And there was a stigma that went along with having been a "frogman" in the regular Navy, especially among those who didn't understand the UDTs' mission. Not surprisingly, in some circles, volunteering for training and an assignment to a UDT was considered a career killer.

The Fleet Navy was also ignorant of the dangers that the men of Navy Special Warfare faced every day. Even without enemy activity, training and practicing for operations was often dangerous, sometimes even deadly.

Captain Thomas N. Tarbox, USNR (Ret.)

The first time I learned of the UDTs, I believe, was when I saw the movie The Frogmen starring Richard Widmark. To me, it was just another movie at the time. Although I swam quite a bit most of my life and was very good in the water, I didn't give the UDTs another thought until I was in OCS.

While I was at Officers Candidate School for the Navy, I think the student body was shown a short presentation on the UDTs. At that time I was a frustrated naval aviator more than anything else; I was just too short. There wasn't any way I was going to get any taller in time to fly the Navy's planes, so I had to look to other avenues for my time in the service. In OCS, your choices were small ships, big ships, or something other. No one wanted to be on a big ship, and a lot of people wanted to be on the small ships. So I decided to give the UDTs a try.

In January 1958, I began training at Little Creek, Virginia, with class 19. The fact that we were a winter class was in my favor. My home had been in Montana and Colorado; I could not have stood that swampwater summer so common in Virginia. Busting ice off my pants or cracking through the ice to get to the mud was okay for a young lad from Montana.

Training was everything that could be expected—a lot of harassment, a whole lot of physical training, and we learned a great deal about demolitions. But that last only happened after we had gone down to Puerto Rico.

At that time the heavy demolition training for a winter class was done down in Puerto Rico. A summer class was trained right there at Little Creek. It turned out to be pretty awesome; I still can't believe the number of windows we broke along the beach.

It didn't appear that the instructors were any harder on those of us who were officers than they were on any other student in the class. They might have had greater expectations of us. It's tough to go into a Team as an officer when you're the same as any other trainee. It takes about a year and a half for an officer to start to know more about what you are doing than the men around you. That knowledge comes from working at a different level, from being aware of the op plans and specific orders which the men under you are not.

But before I could get to the Teams, I had to complete UDTR training. The hardest part of training for me was the deep, soft sand. Not being a great runner at the best of times didn't help me, but after a few hundred yards of running in the sand, my leg muscles would start to knot up. After that, just putting one leg in front of the other was about all I could do.

In spite of the trouble with the sand, at no time during training did I give much thought to quitting. Sometimes I feared that they might throw me out. And at that time the instructors could do that very easily. But I never thought of quitting the

The UDT naked warrior slips up on a beach to attach a demolition charge to a concrete tetrahedron obstacle. Outside of his bag of explosives, he is armed only with a knife at his hip. It is from these beginnings that the lavishly equipped and thoroughly trained SEALs of today come from.

U.S. Navy

course. You develop kind of a love/hate relationship with the instructors, or maybe more of a hate/hate one. But I figured that if they could make it, so could I.

What got me through training was probably just looking at the instructors. And I just didn't see any reason to quit. As a fresh-cut ensign just out of OCS, you have no incentive to quit. If you did drop the course, the Navy might just have a worse place they could send you.

Even though I never considered quitting training, graduation day was still pretty good. We had our picture taken with an admiral and we knew were going to the Teams. But I had a little different situation—I was going to immediately leave for a Med (Mediterranean) tour. The reason was that the officer-in-charge of that deployment was Jim Wilson.

Jim Wilson had come down to our UDTR class right after we had gotten back from Puerto Rico. We still had a few weeks to go in training, but Jim came down to shop around the new officers and pick an assistant OIC (Officer in Charge). He picked me, and he did so for a very good reason. He figured we could wear each other's clothes since both of us were about the same size.

When you go to the Med in the summertime at the exalted rank of ensign, you use up a lot of white uniforms. You're assigned as boat officer, beach officer, import officer of the day—all those nasty jobs fall upon an ensign's shoulders. And you have to do them all in whites. Jim figured if we could wear each other's clothes, it might put us ahead of the pack. And he turned out to be right. While one officer was working with the platoon, the other could be standing duty in clean white, whether the clothes were his or not.

Officers had a real problem in the UDTs at that time, as there was no career path. You couldn't be promoted past a relatively low rank without leaving the Teams. So I left the service after my time was up and went back to college. In early 1962, I had already received a letter from the Navy trying to get me to come back into the Teams. Not only were the SEAL Teams being formed up at that time, they were also forming UDT 22. But I still couldn't see any future in it, so I turned the Navy down.

Then I received a letter from a friend of mine who was still in the Teams. Steve Young wrote to tell me about this new Team that was being created. He told me there was something called the SEALs coming along, and he thought the name meant Sink Enemy And Leave. But it looked like it might be something exciting up on the horizon.

Still being in the Navy Reserves, I spent my two weeks active duty at Little Creek. Sure enough, they had something called a SEAL Team. I figured that if I played my cards right and was lucky, I might be able to make a career of it and still make some rank. I did and it worked.

Arriving at SEAL Team Two on 27 August 1962, I was not a plankowner of the new Team. But I became the executive officer (XO) fairly quickly. When I first returned to the active Navy I had said that I wanted to go to the SEAL Team. They told me that wasn't going to happen because at that time I would have been senior to the then XO, Roy Boehm. So instead, I was sent over to UDT 22 and told that I might be able to go over to SEAL Team Two on my next duty rotation.

In between the time that I was accepted back into the Teams and my actual arrival, Roy Boehm had ticked off enough people that he had to go someplace else for a while. So I was able to go into SEAL Team Two as their new XO. Within two years I succeeded John Callahan and became the Team's commanding officer.

Because I had been a reserve officer, the Bureau of Personnel asked me if I would like to extend my active duty time. I said that I would, but that I would like to have SEAL Team Two. So I was assigned and started spending my time at SEAL Team Two.

Those first few years we were spending a lot of our time doing new things, things the UDTs never did. It was kind of funny in a way because many of the men in the new SEAL Team had been very conservative operators while in UDT. Every time something new came along at UDT, these same guys would say how it had been tried before and didn't work then, so it wouldn't work now. In the SEAL Team, the same people were willing to try anything.

That first year at SEAL Team Two was full of new experiences, not all of them good. While on a training exercise in Turkey, we lost Lieutenant (jg) William Painter in a diving accident. Ensign Painter had been a plankowner of the Team, coming in to the Team directly from his training class. He was the officer-in-charge of a detachment sent to Turkey from SEAL Team Two in early 1963. During a diving exercise, Painter put on a rig and went into the Bosporus by himself, which was a big no-no, and never came up. As far as I know, his body has never been found.

We were very sorry to lose him. But to go down without a swim buddy was anathema to us—you just don't do that. He broke the rule and proved why it was a rule. It was our first loss, made worse for having been the result of a mistake.

By 1964, I was a lieutenant, and I had been a lieutenant while I was the XO. That year I became the commanding officer of SEAL Team Two. It sounded a lot more impressive than it looked at the time. I was in the same office, with the same people, and I don't think I even changed desks. There was a formal change of command, and the ceremony which the Navy calls for is pretty awesome, but other than that, it wasn't that big a change.

We lost another man from SEAL Team Two in May 1965 in a parachuting accident. Mel Melochick was one of the guys conducting a rehearsal for Sea Week, a big festival we have in Norfolk every year with shows and everything for the families. The SEAL jumpers were practicing over Willowby Bay, a little arm of Chesapeake Bay that's enclosed by Naval Air Station, Norfolk. About five jumpers bailed out of the aircraft on a water jump.

The jumpers did some maneuvering in the air and then Melochick pulled his rig (released his chute). I don't know if he waved off or not, but when you pull your rig and your canopy opens, you stop in the air in relation to everything around you. Jerry Todd, who was the jumper above Mel, couldn't maneuver out of the way in time and he crashed through Mel's canopy.

Melochick was probably killed instantly from the crushed vertebrae in his neck. That he was dead when he hit the water is fairly certain. Jerry survived the crash with a broken arm and I think a broken leg as well. But he recovered and had a full career afterward.

Joe DiMartino obtained a DC-3, a Navy C-46, to take us from NAS Norfolk to near Pottstown, Pennsylvania, where we took Mel's body home for burial. There was a full military funeral, with an Army firing squad and the presentation of the flag. His mother was very distraught, as were most of Mel's relatives. When the ceremony was over, we all left for the local American Legion hall and started drinking and having a party. I think if you have to go, it's a good thing to have your Teammates celebrate your life afterward.

The accident taught us that in parachuting, it is always important to give a wave-off, move your arms so that everyone around and above you knows you're going to open your parachute. We also learned how the press reacts to such a death. The guys had been talking in the airplane prior to the jump. And they didn't get wild, but their joking around was reported in the press later. From the journalism class I took in college, I knew how the press works and how anything you say can work against you, and I explained this to the men. And that no matter how the guy, or girl, acts, the media people are there on business and they aren't your friends.

Another thing I did in SEAL Team Two was get to be the first SEAL CO to send his men into a contingency, an active combat situation, when I dispatched a SEAL detachment to the Dominican Republic for the crisis there in 1965. At that time the Team was organized into assault groups, what would be called platoons now. And several assault groups were sent down to take part in the U.S. aid action there.

Sending my men into harm's way was a difficult part of the job. The Dominican Republic thing was much like many of the contingencies have been since. You couldn't tell the enemy from the friendlies. And we were obviously being Yankees in a place where not too many of the people liked us. There was a lot of sniping activity in the capital, Ciudad Trujillo. Our guys were out in the weeds more, but the actual combat turned out to be pretty light.

The incident was just one of those things that turned out to be like Vietnam and a lot of other places, though it hardly lasted as long as Vietnam. It was, however, the forerunner of Vietnam. The SEALs did some hairy things, but they did them very well and everyone got home safely.

A little less than a year after the Dominican Republic action, I left SEAL Team Two. It was August 1966 and I went up to the Defense Intelligence School. From that school, I went on to Okinawa and duties there. I never did get back to the UDTs or the SEALs. SEAL Team Two was my last experience with an active Team. I spent time in staff positions within Special Warfare and was the later CO of BUD/S. But nothing was ever quite the same as those early years at SEAL Team Two.

■ Chapter 28

The Creation of the Navy SEALs

The serious development of the U.S. military's ability to combat the worldwide increase in Communist-supported guerrilla warfare began in the late 1950s during the Eisenhower administration. Development of these capabilities was slow and consisted of little more than studies and discussions among high-level military officers, politicians, and political appointees. It was not until the 1960s and the Kennedy administration that the development of these capabilities was pushed forward. Under President Kennedy, the military received the stimulus necessary to actively create unconventional warfare units.

Op-003/rer
Op-00 Memo 00242-01
3 May 1961
SECRET
MEMORANDUM FOR OP-01
Subj: Guerrilla Warfare

1. We should have a record of all naval personnel, particularly officers, who have been specially trained in guerrilla warfare, UDT, psychological warfare, and what the Army calls "Special Forces Training." We should get more people below the age of thirty-five trained in this field.
2. Training is of course one of the key factors in guerrilla warfare. We will need such things as training pamphlets on this subject. We should take a look at the Army pamphlets. We should send people through other Service schools as well as our own survival courses and probably set up courses at the amphibious schools.
3. I know this is going to be difficult, but we are going to have to take over such operations as river patrol in the Saigon Delta, in the Mekong River, and other areas. Our people will have to know thoroughly how to live and fight under guerrilla conditions.
4. Will you please give me a list of equipment that has been developed such as silent motors, etc., along with things that we might need now? It might be beneficial to look at the Army's list of equipments.

Arleigh Burke

[The above is one of the first official documents produced by the CNO's office during the earliest development of the SEAL Teams]

On 11 July 1960, Admiral Arleigh Burke, the Chief of Naval Operations, directed Deputy CNO (Fleet ops and readiness) Admiral Wallace Beakley to study possible contributions by the Navy to unconventional warfare. Admiral Beakley responded to the CNO's directive by August 12 and included his suggestion that, because of their extensive training in small-unit actions of this type, the Navy's Underwater Demolition Teams and Marine reconnaissance units were the logical organizations for expanding the Navy's capability in unconventional warfare.

Four weeks after Admiral Beakley's response to the CNO, the Unconventional Activities Working Group was established within the Office of the CNO under the Deputy Chief of Naval Operations (plans and policy). The group was to consider "naval unconventional activity methods, techniques, and concepts which may be employed effectively against Sino-Soviet interests under conditions of cold war." This group was later succeeded by the Unconventional Activities Committee, which turned in the final report.

The year 1961 brought a large number of changes for the world in general and the United States military in particular. President Eisenhower was replaced by a new, young President who thought differently than others had and had experienced war in a very up-close and personal way. There was also a serious threat to world peace in the form of the Soviet Union, which was aggressively seeking to export its style of Communism to the rest of the world.

On 6 January 1961, Nikita Khrushchev, the premier of the Soviet Union, publicly announced that his country would "support just wars of liberation and popular uprisings... wholeheartedly and without reservations." The developing struggle in Vietnam was mentioned as an example of such a just war. A few weeks later, on 29 January, John F. Kennedy became the thirty-fifth President of the United States. At the age of forty-three he was also the youngest person ever to hold that office.

Admiral Burke maintained his advocacy of unconventional warfare in a response to Admiral John Sides (CINCPACFLT). In correspondence, Admiral Burke stated that unconventional warfare did constitute a proper mission for the Navy. In another memo issued in early February, he again suggested that the Navy "do as much as we can in guerrilla warfare... even if it is not our primary business." Burke proposed emphasizing UDT groups, escape and survival training, and the creation of a nucleus of young naval officers trained by the Army in guerrilla warfare. At that time the Army Special Forces at Fort Bragg were the only experienced guerrilla warfare group in the U.S. military.

President Kennedy met with the Joint Chiefs of Staff on 23 February. The President stressed the importance of guerrilla and counterguerrilla warfare responses to Communist actions. He wanted present capabilities increased and new counterguerrilla warfare concepts established and put into place as quickly as was practicable. On March 10, Rear Admiral William Gentner Jr., the

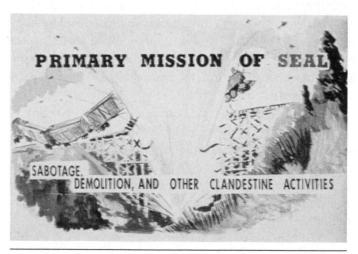

A slide from an originally classified briefing series showing one of the primary missions of the U.S. Navy SEALS.

U.S. Navy

director of the Strategic Plans Division, approved the preliminary recommendations of the Unconventional Activities Committee. The recommendations were to involve the Navy more directly in the lower levels (direct action) of counterguerrilla actions.

Specific proposals of the group included the recommendation that new units be established, one for the Atlantic and another for the Pacific command. The proposed units would be known by the acronym SEAL, "a contraction of SEA, AIR, LAND . . . indicating an all-around, universal capability." Initially, the units would consist of 20 to 24 officers and 50 to 75 men. Each detachment would have a three-faceted mission:

1. develop a specialized Navy capability in guerrilla/counterguerrilla operations to include training of selected personnel in a wide variety of skills
2. development of doctrinal tactics, and
3. development of special support equipment

It was during that March 10 meeting that the name SEALs was used for the first time. The acronym was coined in Admiral Gentner's office. It is not known if the term originated with the admiral himself or one of his staff.

President Kennedy continued a CIA-run operation against the Communist government of Cuba that had begun during the Eisenhower administration. The CIA had been arming and training Cuban exiles to return to Cuba and lead a revolt to oust Fidel Castro. This would have removed a major Soviet-backed Communist threat from U.S. shores and Caribbean waters. Some of the personnel the CIA used as trainers had been recruited from UDT 21. From 17 to 19 April 1961, the Bay of Pigs operation took place as Cuban expatriates tried to take back their country from Fidel Castro and his Communist regime. Without proper support from U.S. military and clandestine forces, the Cuban invaders were stopped almost at the shoreline of the Bay of Pigs. The invasion was a complete failure.

Secretary of Defense McNamara met with the Joint Chiefs of Staff and civilian heads of the military services on 21 April, only a few days after the Bay of Pigs debacle. The meeting was to discuss the implications of the Cuban situation. During the meeting, McNamara suggested that "what is required is a new idea on counteraggression [guerrilla warfare] of the type we are seeing around the world."

Within a day or two of this statement, President Kennedy directed General Taylor of the Army to head the Cuban Study Group, which included Admiral Burke, Attorney General Robert Kennedy, and CIA Director Allen Dulles. The objective of the group was to determine what lessons were to be learned from the Bay of Pigs fiasco. Additionally, the group was to explore ways the United States could strengthen its capabilities in military, paramilitary, guerrilla, and antiguerrilla activities without going on to an active war standing.

By the end of April, the CNO's office had begun to seriously consider the direct participation of the Navy in guerrilla and counterguerrilla warfare and the creation of units specially trained and suited to that type of conflict. The first week of May, Admiral Burke issued a directive calling for an increase in the training of naval personnel in guerrilla warfare. The directive also announced an appraisal of the Navy's equipment to determine what would be suited to operations to be conducted in the swamps and rivers of South Vietnam.

In mid-May, Admiral Beakley reiterated the 10 March proposal by the Strategic Plans Division that the Special Operations Teams (SEALs) be established as separate components of the Atlantic and Pacific UDT commands. The SEAL mission statement was enlarged to include greater emphasis on conducting actual combat operations rather than training and support for them. Admiral Arleigh Burke decided to retire from active duty in the summer of 1961 prior to the implementation of his idea for the SEAL teams. His successor as CNO, Admiral George Anderson Jr., was not the proponent of unconventional warfare that Admiral Burke had been.

On 1 August 1961, Admiral George Anderson Jr. was sworn in as the new Chief of Naval Operations. He replaced Admiral Arleigh Burke, who had held the office for six years. By the end of August, Admiral Anderson was questioning the creation of the new SEAL Teams. Studying the plan for their creation with the intention of curtailing the program, Admiral Anderson felt that the manning requirements (20 officers and 100 men total) for the new Teams could not be immediately met. Encouragement was given by the CNO's office to "enhance and augment present naval support capabilities in the area of paramilitary operations by developing the existing capabilities within the Underwater Demolition Teams for demolition, sabotage and other clandestine activities. . . ."

In the fall of 1961, tensions between the Soviets and the United States increased rapidly with the Berlin Crisis in East Germany. The building of the Berlin Wall and additional actions by the Soviets and the Soviet-backed East German government distracted the Kennedy administration from Southeast Asia. This too retarded the establishment of the Navy SEAL teams.

During that time, specialized training for naval officers in unconventional warfare was not being well implemented. At the end of October, only four Navy officers, two from Underwater Demolition Team 21, were attending courses in unconventional warfare at the Army's Special Warfare Center at Fort Bragg. The push to create the SEAL Teams was now getting more emphasis from the CNO's office. On 13 November, a letter was written at the CNO's office outlining the size and organization of the two proposed SEAL Teams. A month later, on 11 December 1961, Admiral George W. Anderson Jr. signed CNO Speedletter Serial # 697P30. The letter activated SEAL Teams One and Two and UDT 22 on 1 January 1962. The document also contained the intended mission statement for the SEALs as well as a description of their organization, command, and logistical support.

Captain William Henry Hamilton Jr., USN (Ret.)

Just toward the end of World War II, I joined the Navy as a midshipman by virtue of going to the US Naval Academy. I heard about the UDTs after I had been on active duty for some years. Since I had been a naval aviator who had flown some of the service's earlier jets as well as having served aboard a number of ships, my career leaned toward the more active duties when I could manage it. It was suggested to me that the UDTs might be a good idea. So I volunteered in Little Creek, Virginia, and was accepted into the program.

But I didn't start training with the East Coast UDTs in Little Creek. Instead, the Navy ordered me to Coronado. Arriving there, I was able to join my training class in the early winter of 1953 and we graduated in July of that year after a long five months of hard work. Being a little older than the average trainee, I was all of twenty-four or twenty-five and a lieutenant (junior grade) when I went through UDTR.

That week of training that everyone speaks of, Hell Week, isn't any fun for anyone. But it's something everyone must go through to reach the Teams. The instructors wouldn't throw you out of training if you couldn't meet the standards. Instead, they seemed to leave it up to the individual. If you found that you couldn't do what they wanted you to do, you had two options. You could either drop out and quit. Or you could try to continue on, but in some cases the people who tried to stay on had some physical disability that kept them from making the grade. It was rare that someone was just thrown out.

For myself, I never considered quitting. There was no other thought in my mind but to complete the course. When I graduated from training, the Team I was assigned to had already left on a Far East deployment. So I was ordered to meet with the Team in Japan and caught up with them at Camp McGill. There, I reported aboard UDT 5, which later became UDT 13.

It was mid-1953 when I was first assigned as the platoon leader of Platoon One. Later I became the operations officer after UDT 5 had become UDT 13. In Japan, we were training our people to do underwater work and further explosives work. In general, our men were trained to do most any job that no one else in the Navy wanted to do.

The Korean War was not technically over. But the fighting had diminished to the point that nothing was going on actively any more. The truce had only been signed on 27 July 1953, so active combat in Korea was still a very recent memory for many.

Just before I left to go over to Japan and join UDT 5, I had met Commander Doug Fane, the commanding officer of Underwater Demolition Unit 1, the command element controlling the West Coast UDTs. The only first impression you could have of Doug Fane was that he was a very difficult, very hard-nosed, and dynamic person. If you didn't see him that way, you were missing the point. He was a very tough guy.

Later I had a great deal more involvement with Doug Fane when I was ordered from UDT 13 to become the chief staff officer to the Commander, Underwater Demolition Unit One (COMUDU1)—at the time Commander Fane. That position wasn't one I had asked for, but then the Navy doesn't often ask its personnel what they want to do.

My dealings with Fane always left me with the impression that I had to try harder to get along with him. He had some attitudes about regular Navy officers that didn't include me. So I did my best to get along with him and we both somehow succeeded well enough.

About nine o'clock on a Wednesday night one time Commander Fane invited me to go along with him to Tijuana and have a drink or two. It struck me that maybe I had been wrong in my opinion of him and that he was much more of a nice guy than I thought he was. After a night in TJ, having more than a few drinks, we eventually returned to the States and went to his house in Coronado. At the house we had more of a real disagreement than we ever had in our time together. It was my holding my own with him that night that made us close friends. We had finally gotten over any problems there were between us. But it had taken a real frogman's night together to do it.

Without question, Doug Fane was a real leader in the Teams. In my opinion, he's the only reason that the UDTs continued to exist after World War II. Even though there were a lot of other people who had a great deal to do with keeping the Teams going, he had the most to do with it. It's ridiculous for anyone to think that the Teams would be where they are today, and that includes their evolution into the SEAL Teams, without Doug Fane. He was the reason all that growth started in the first place right after World War II.

Largely because of Commander Fane, the UDT ended up with financial and operational support from the fleet that other units, such as the Scouts and Raiders of WWII, did not receive. It was through Fane's work that the UDTs developed and flourished while other units just disappeared at the end of World War II.

Doug Fane and I had many conversations about what should happen to the UDTs down the road. We discussed what we both should do to help the UDT become better known and better able to serve the Navy. We didn't discuss any specific new unit and we certainly didn't talk about a possible SEAL Team, as that term hadn't even been coined yet. But Fane thought we should have something further than what the UDT was doing in the later 1950s, and I certainly agreed with him. As things developed, and I make no claims to originating the term, the SEAL Teams came about to fit much of what Doug Fane and I had envisioned.

What one really has to remember is that Doug Fane was the man who really kept things going when there were fewer than 200 active UDT men in the whole of the Navy. And he is the guy who triggered me to make the moves that I made when President Kennedy made his speeches in the early 1960s.

President Kennedy made a speech on 1 June 1961 recommending that the armed forces of the United States have a greater paramilitary and counterguerrilla warfare capability. The President made that speech while I was the commanding officer of UDT 21 and we were stationed on Saint Thomas in the Virgin Islands. I had heard about the speech and it struck me that this was precisely what Commander Fane and I had been talking about years earlier.

So I took it upon myself to begin putting together a letter to Admiral Arleigh Burke, the Chief of Naval Operations, proposing that the Navy create an organization like what the President was suggesting. Admiral Burke was an avid supporter of swimming and underwater work for the Navy. Of course, he was also very much a supporter of driving destroyers around for the Navy as well in conventional operations.

Going ahead with my letter, I kept in mind that if the Army was going to do something, the Navy might be able to work with them to do what we wanted to do. That proved to be true. The Army Special Forces people that I had been working with before in Key West at the Navy's Underwater Swimmer School, where I had been the executive officer, proved to be as supportive as they could be, and we in turn were supportive of them.

While we were in Saint Thomas, I had started to draft my letter to the CNO. By the time UDT 21 had returned to its base in Little Creek, I had the letter pretty well in the shape I wanted it to be in. One of the men in the Team, Charlie Watson, helped me revise a part of it before I submitted it. The letter was addressed to the Chief of Naval Operations via the commander of the Amphibious Force of the Atlantic Fleet and also via the commander of the Atlantic Fleet.

The letter went first to the three-star admiral who was the Amphibious Force commander, then it continued on to the four-star admiral who was the Atlantic Fleet commander. It went through their offices and in each case they called me and asked if I had written it. When I answered that I had, I was told to come over to their offices and write their endorsements. So that was precisely what I did in both cases. I wrote their endorsements and then the paperwork went on to Admiral Burke.

Now I found myself being approached by a captain from the Office of Naval Operations. He informed me that I was going to be ordered to the Pentagon. That wasn't something that I had asked for, nor was it something that I was that anxious to be doing. But I was going to be ordered to the Pentagon and they were going to tell me to start building the SEAL Teams.

You aren't given any options in this Navy, you do what the man tells you to do. And that was what I did. The first time I heard the word SEALs was from that captain who told me I was moving. That term had been invented in the Pentagon and I had nothing to do with its creation.

When I arrived in Washington, D.C., and the Pentagon, I was assigned as part of a small organization called OP343E. When I first reported in, I was given a copy of a letter written by Admiral Don Griffin to the Vice Chief of Naval Operations, Admiral Claude Ricketts. Admiral Griffin had been the commander of the Destroyer Navy at that point, as well as a supporter of the UDT concept. He wrote this letter to Admiral Ricketts saying that he thought we should go ahead and do this, that the Navy should build the SEAL Teams.

In the margin of the letter he received from Admiral Griffin, Admiral Ricketts wrote a notation to go ahead and build the SEAL Teams, recommission UDT 22, and to keep him posted about what was going on. That was the letter that I finally received and that I had volumes of copies of to show around. Anytime I would run into a destroyer sailor who complained that he didn't have any money or support to give for our project, I would just show him the letter and tell him that this was what your boss said you were going to do.

It was amazing, but after that letter, I had no trouble getting the money I needed to do the job. For the building and commissioning of two SEAL Teams and the recommissioning of UDT 22, I was given $4.2 million to work with.

That was around July 1961. I was given until December 1961, six months, to build the two SEAL Teams. What I found was that I was able to put them together by the eleventh of December, 1961. They were authorized at that time but then were not commissioned until 8 January 1962.

In those six months I had to build the SEAL Teams, I found the job was anything but easy. And everyone I had to work with wasn't necessarily on my team. I found people in the Pacific Fleet who thought that they wanted to do the job their way. And that was not the way that I wanted things done. And I found people in the Office of the Chief of Naval Personnel who wanted to do things differently from how I wanted them to be done. What I did find was that the biggest support I had was from Admiral Griffin. When I ran into a difficult situation, I remembered what he had told me at the very beginning of the project.

"Bill," Admiral Griffin said to me, "come and see me if you have problems that you can't handle."

At the time I was all of a lieutenant commander and he was a three-star admiral. All I could do was say, "Aye aye, sir" and continue on. So when I had a problem that I couldn't handle, I would go and see Admiral Griffin. There wasn't a lot of time to meet because of the admiral's schedule and delays were not something that could be easily afforded. After I explained the situation, Admiral Griffin would pick up his phone and call the "offending" party. Suddenly things would be straightened out, and it was all due to his phone call.

When I reported to the Chief of Naval Operations' office, I found that there was a letter that had been written by Admiral Griffin to Admiral Ricketts, who was then the Vice Chief of Naval Operations. Admiral Ricketts had told Admiral Griffin to go ahead and build the SEAL Teams and recommission UDT 22. What this told me was that I had an awful lot of things to do and not much time to do them. Therefore, I should get all the help I could.

So I drove down to Fort Bragg in order to get together again with my Army Special Forces friends whom I had trained to scuba-dive in Key West some years before. They could help me in putting together the new Navy units. They allowed me access to their documents regarding unconventional and counterguerrilla warfare.

While at Fort Bragg, I asked for all of the manuals and training paraphernalia, everything that I could use to build a SEAL Team. And I made it clear to them that I wasn't competing with the Army. Instead, I wanted to take everything that they had learned in building the Army organization, add to that the things that applied to the Navy, and go ahead and build the SEAL Teams.

The Army guys were terrific. They came through and gave me everything I could possibly have imagined wanting. And it was largely because of what they did that the job I had was done In the short six months that I knew I had.

In the Navy in those days, I wasn't able to control totally who would be coming aboard the new SEAL Teams. The Office of the Chief of Naval Personnel determined which officers would go to the Teams. I couldn't control that situation, though I did have a lot of input. Lieutenant John Callahan, who would be the first commanding officer of SEAL Team Two, was one of the officers that they found. One of the men that I found was Lieutenant Roy Boehm.

Lieutenant Boehm at that time was with UDT 21 and I had been the command-ing officer of that Team. So I just picked up the phone and called him.

"Roy," I said, "let's get this thing going here. You've got a lot to do down there and we don't have a lot of time."

"Aye aye, sir," was what he said, "whatever you want, I'll do it."

And he did.

It was only a few days after I turned in some of the paperwork to personnel and they gave me Dave Del Guidice and John Callahan to be the commanding officers of SEAL Teams One and Two respectively that I called Roy Boehm. I didn't know Calla-han or Del Guidice personally, but I had known Roy Boehm and I knew I could count on him.

Roy Boehm is one of the finest people I have ever known. He is an ex–destroyer sailor and he knows what's going on. If you have a problem that you can't solve easily, you go to Roy and he'll solve it.

It was Boehm who had something to say to President Kennedy when there was a problem with the weapons we were using after the SEAL Teams were up and running. As I remember, Roy told the President that he could line up a dozen of his people with any other weapon and he would line up a dozen of his people (SEALs) with this weapon (the AR-15) and we'll beat you to death. And apparently President Kennedy respected that.

Roy Boehm was, and is, a very unique person. He's a guy you can really count on. And that is what I needed then. To create a SEAL Team, you would be starting out with people who were Underwater-Demolition-Team-trained. In order to become SEALs, they would have to be further trained. And we had no way of knowing at the beginning who would be the best one from the UDT to become a SEAL with the additional training. There were no guidelines and certainly no experience I had to draw on.

So I couldn't speak for either of the two lieutenants who would be the commanding officers of the Teams. But I knew that once we put the program together, the system we built would be able to determine who could hack and who could not.

After that first authorizing letter, I wrote everything that was officially written about the SEAL Teams, including their mission statement. I started the Teams, put the people together, and got the mission rolling. The Navy has a booklet that tells a commanding officer what he's supposed to do. The SEALs had such booklets,

Four modern-day SEALs rise up from the water, ready to move in silently and complete their mission.

U.S. Navy

called Naval Warfare pamphlets, which I wrote, and which described precisely what everybody was supposed to do in the Team.

So Callahan, Roy Boehm, and all of the new officers had this information to draw on. The information for the mission statement came from my conversations with Doug Fane, my Army friends, and whatever else I could think up myself. There was input, but not influence, from the Army Special Forces. And I wanted to take advantage of everything they could offer us. But we would be a Navy unit and we had to put Navy things in our mission. And we did just that.

So with complete confidence, I can say that I started the SEAL Teams for all practical purposes. There are others who will say that they would have happened anyway as a natural evolution. Well, I'm sorry about what they might say. They didn't make the Teams as a unit; I did.

Later I became the Chief of Maritime for the Central Intelligence Agency. This meant I ran the CIA's Navy worldwide. I should emphasize that I went to the CIA well after the Bay of Pigs fiasco; I was not there when they made that mistake. But after the Bay of Pigs, I was invited to join the CIA and I went in as their number three guy in their maritime structure. After a few months I had become the number-one guy when I took the position as chief.

There were three wars going on at the same time when I took the position. There was the war in Vietnam, the war in Cuba, and the war in Africa. We didn't win the war in Vietnam, and the war with Cuba turned into what I call a Mexican standoff. But we did win our war in Africa against the Soviets.

Off and on, the SEAL Teams worked with the CIA in various areas. But I came along into the Agency well after that. They were my creation, but I never worked in the field with them.

When I received the order to start the SEAL Teams, first and foremost I felt proud and honored in being chosen, even though I hadn't asked for it. And I feel I was being honored because of the Navy in effect saying to me, we feel you are the best guy to start the SEAL Teams. That's an honor and a responsibility.

Jumping with one of today's steerable parachutes, this SEAL is able to fly his rig over long distances and land with great accuracy. His equipment is a long way from the improvised parachutes and rigs used by the UDTs and SEALs in the late 1950s and early 1960s.

U.S. Navy

A squad of SEAL trainees conduct field operations as part of their land warfare training. From the lessons the SEALs learned in Vietnam come many of the techniques and skills taught to the SEALs today.

U.S. Navy

I wanted to do the best I could with the assignment. And I think that I did do that. The SEALs have proven themselves because of the beginning that I was able to give them. For all of what the Teams have done that is good, I am very proud of them. And you have to recognize that everything doesn't work all of the time. They have made mistakes and they have learned from them and been made stronger because of them.

The SEALs have become one of the most elite forces in the history of the United States military. And I am very proud of my part in their creation. Almost never in the history of the Navy has someone come along with an idea, and it wasn't totally my idea, been authorized to go ahead develop that idea into an existing capability, and then lived to see that capability become so well recognized and approved of. I had that honor.

The Trident was developed after I had been involved with developing the SEAL Teams. But I am authorized to wear it and I proudly do on my uniform. Some people in the Navy, especially the aviators and the submarine sailors, consider the device a little too ostentatious. Personally, I think they're right—it is a bit large—but it's what we have. The men of the Teams wear the Trident proudly, as they should. It is a proud thing to have.

The term SEAL is an acronym; it means SEa, Air, and Land. I don't find that it means anything different to me than UDT did. There is a brotherhood, and a very strong one, that goes with having been in the UDTs or the SEALs.

■ Chapter 29

The Commissioning and Mission of the SEALs

On 27 December 1961, Rear Admiral Allan Reed issued "SEAL Teams in Naval Special Warfare," Naval Warfare Information Publication 29-1 (NWIP 29-1). Based on the experience gained in South Vietnam and elsewhere during 1961, the report was the basic SEAL directive for operations during most of the Vietnam War.

The following is a declassified excerpt from the still-classified Naval Warfare Information Publication. This forty-plus page document listed for the first time the capabilities of the new SEAL Teams and their mission statement.

The SEAL Mission Profile (NWIP 29-1)

(1) *Primary:* To develop a specialized capability to conduct operations for military, political, or economic purposes within an area occupied by the enemy for sabotage, demolition, and other clandestine activities conducted in and around restricted waters, rivers, and canals, and to conduct training of selected U.S., allied and indigenous personnel in a wide variety of skills for use in naval clandestine operations in hostile environments.

(2) *Secondary:* To develop doctrine and tactics for SEAL operations and to develop support equipment, including special craft for use in these operations.

(3) *Tasks:* Tasks may be overt or covert in nature.

    (a) Destructive tasks—These tasks include clandestine attacks on enemy shipping, demolition raids in harbors and other enemy installations within reach; destruction of supply lines in maritime areas by destruction of bridges, railway lines, roads, canals, and so forth; and the delivery of special weapons (SADM) to exact locations in restricted waters, rivers or canals.

    (b) Support tasks—The support tasks of SEAL Teams include protecting friendly supply lines, assisting or participating in the landing

and support of guerrilla and partisan forces, and assisting or participating in the landing and recovery of agents, other special
forces, downed aviators, escapees and so forth.

(c) Additional Tasks:

   1. Conduct reconnaissance, surveillance, and intelligence collection missions as directed.

   2. In friendly areas train U.S. and indigenous personnel in such
   operations as directed.

   3. Develop equipment to support special operations.

   4. Develop the capability for small boat operations, including the
   use of native types.

1 January 1962 is the official date of the commissioning of SEAL Teams One
and Two. On 8 January, SEAL Team One, at NAB Coronado, California, and
SEAL Team Two, at NAB Little Creek, Virginia, mustered for the first time at
1300 hours local time. The official commissioning date for the two Teams was
eight days earlier, but there were no main actions until the first muster. This
has caused some confusion as to the actual date of the SEALs commissioning.
The date of 1 January is the official paperwork date. The 8 January date was the
practical day that work actually began.

SEAL Team One was placed under the command of Lieutenant David Del
Guidice and took its personnel as volunteers from UDTs 11 and 12. Lieutenant
John F. Callahan was put in command of SEAL Team Two, which took the majority of its personnel from the ranks of UDT 21. Thirty-seven men and officers
of the initial complement for SEAL Team Two were at the 1300 muster on 8 January. The balance of the ten officers and fifty enlisted men would arrive over
the next several months as they completed training or were released from previous commands.

Lieutenant Roy Boehm was the officer-in-charge of SEAL Team Two prior
to its commissioning and was responsible for selecting the initial complement
of men and setting up their training and equipment. He was given the assignment to make the first SEAL Team and has earned the name "First SEAL."

Lieutenant Commander Roy Boehm, USN (Ret.)

*Back in 1962, I was the officer-in-charge of SEAL Team Two, waiting for someone
senior enough to be the commanding officer of the team; this turned out to be Lieutenant John Callahan. He came in and relieved me, taking the position of CO while
I moved to the XO's slot.*

It was the actions of Lieutenant Commander Bill Hamilton, who was the com-

mander of UDT 21 at the time, that got the SEALs started. He wore two hats, being the commander of Underwater Demolition Units, Atlantic Fleet, at the same time. Both gave him a hands-on role as a Team leader and put him in a position to see more of the strategic picture.

We were in Saint Thomas in the Virgin Islands with UDT 21 at the time and I was the Team's operations officer, acting as Hamilton's second-in-command during advanced UDT training. He ordered me to organize and give him a commando outfit, a group of men that would go anyplace, at any time, in any way, and do any thing. I asked Commander Hamilton to give me a line of guidance for the unit. His answer to me was, "When you're called upon to do anything, and you're not ready to do it, then you've failed."

That was a pretty wide scope. So I started to assemble a group from the men within UDT 21. They were sent out to different types of training, as I wasn't sure of where were going at that particular time. I had read books by Che Guevara, Mao Tse-tung, Sun-tzu, Admiral Milton Miles, and others for much of my life. And I knew the Underwater Demolition Team had so much more potential than our country was using.

In those days (the late fifties, very early sixties) we were restricted to the berm line on the beach. That mark was as far as we could go as underwater demolition-eers. From the berm line on belonged to the Marine Corps. That was a rule violated a bit more than observed pretty much continuously. Still, in the Teams, we had all of this talent going to waste. To make more use of it, I had been pushing for just such an opportunity to break all of the rules. Bill Hamilton's wonderful order for that group of "anywhere, anytime" commandos freed me.

This was what I started out to do. Well before the SEALs were begun, requests for surgical type precise operations were sent down to us from the "up-there" types. These requests were to perform certain of these missions on a very covert basis.

At that time each operation could be choreographed, trained for, and built up on just the single mission itself, whether it took two, three, five, or seven men. That commando group I thought would be nothing more than just a special group. Bill Hamilton was going to be the skipper and I was going to be his exec. This was well prior to the commissioning of the SEAL Teams.

We found out that we were working for the President of the United States. Since he was our commander-in-chief, all of us in the military were officially working for him already; now we'd just be a little more under his direct control. Our special team was for specific surgical strikes and was assembled on a mission-by-mission basis. We were a "dirty dozen" well prior to any book or movie.

The cadre of men in UDT 21 from among whom I would choose a mission team were always adding to their skills because of the schools they were being sent to.

There were men who knew how to hot-wire cars, crack safes, and get in and out of buildings without being noticed. This raised more than a few eyebrows around the base, but it added to our mission capabilities.

Men were sent to Jump School for training. Prior to the commissioning of the SEAL Teams, I was trying to get all of my men airborne-qualified. After the SEALs were a functioning unit, the airborne qualification could just be made mandatory for them.

Some of the missions we did from the special group at UDT 21 included training some people who came out of Panama City, Florida. The Cubans were watching that area fairly closely, as a number of expatriates were training there. We taught the people assigned to us demolitions, how to take out generators, some of the tricks that we had in our repertoire.

This group was going to act as a training cadre for their fellow expatriates in techniques that would help them retake their country from the Communists. Whatever other arrangements had been made for these individuals wasn't something I was privy to. My job and that of my men was to teach them the mechanics of operating.

When I first put together my operating group, I didn't know how many people I could get from UDT 21. The Underwater Demolition Team at that time only had about 115 personnel in the ranks. These men were spread out all over Europe, South America, and the Caribbean Islands. With using my special group as the reason, I was able to get about 80 percent of the Team special training of one kind or another. It was when it came time to commission the SEAL Team that the manning issue became very critical.

Prior to the official commissioning of the SEALs, I had been told to prepare for a much smaller group than was finally created. Originally, I was told to come up with a group of about twenty or thirty men. To make that number, I figured I couldn't go wrong by trying to arrange additional training for all of UDT 21. About the time that the SEAL Team finally did go into commission, I was so relieved and happy that the original group of people I had put together as a special group at UDT 21 had been used extensively. When I heard that the SEAL Teams would contain ten officers and fifty enlisted men each, and one Team to each coast, I couldn't have been happier: we needed all of the help we could get.

There were some problems with filling out the ranks of SEAL Team Two. On the West Coast at Coronado, where SEAL Team One would be, they had the men from UDT 11, 12, and 13 to draw from. They could fill their Team without hurting their parent units. At Little Creek, we had UDT 21, just 115 men to be our qualified manpower pool. If I had taken 10 officers and 50 enlisted men to fill out the SEAL ranks, I would have gutted our parent Team. I was far too good a sailor to do that.

So I did have my fifty all earmarked, but I couldn't take them all immediately. They had to finish the operations they were already on in order to shoulder our responsibility to the Atlantic Fleet. There were a few rules I had to break or bend seriously to get some of the men I needed. To build the SEAL Team, I had a Presidential Priority, just as Admiral Rickover had had to build the Nuclear Navy. If you're nothing but a lieutenant junior grade, but you have the same priority as an admiral's unit, why not use it? I needed the best storekeeper chief in the United States Navy and that was James "Hoot" Andrews. So I stole him from Admiral Rickover's high-priority nuclear submarine project.

To be the keel of the new SEAL Team, I had to have a good master-at-arms who was also an operator. To fill that job I had Rudy Boesch over in UDT 21. I had first met Rudy back when I was a first-class bosun's mate and he was a third class. All I saw over the years was Rudy getting better and better. He stayed longer in the Teams that anyone else ever has. At the time that Rudy finally retired in 1988, there was only one commanding officer at SEAL Team Two who hadn't had him as their master-at-arms.

Not everyone was available for some time after the SEAL Team was commissioned. Some openings in the ranks were filled with a small group of fresh graduates from the most recent UDTR class at Little Creek. Others I just waited for. There was Robert "The Eagle" Gallagher. When I first met the Eagle Gallagher, he looked at me and said, "Boehm, I'm going to be better than you ever thought of being." And this was when he was fresh out of boot camp and I was his instructor in UDTR. He didn't give up easily and was one tremendous man. If I had to list the people who fit the image of the true warrior, in the Teams or elsewhere, I would have to put Gallagher at the top of the list.

There was no way I was going to take too many men from the ranks of UDT 21 and risk destroying that Team as a functional entity for a while. That Team was the wellspring whence we came. It was also going to be the support group we were going to need to build and polish the SEAL concept of commandos.

It is interesting to note that at the time the SEALs went into commission, I strongly protested the difference between them and the UDT. As far as I was concerned, we should all be SEALs and receive the same training to conduct the same mission. For myself, I could see no good reason for there being a difference. It took the United States Navy from 1962 to 1983 to realize that I was right. In 1983, the UDTs were all decommissioned and made into SEAL Teams. We can be a little slow sometimes and many times it seems we have to learn the same lessons over and over.

There were still more than a few difficulties in getting the SEALs up and running even after the men had been chosen and were on their way. The equipment we needed in order to operate was a constant problem. The Army had just recently adopted the M-14 rifle, an improved version of the M-1 Garand that the U.S. forces had carried since just before WWII. The weapon was large, heavy, had a thousand-yard range, and was just far more than we needed. The M-1 carbine was a lot less than I wanted. What I needed for the new Team was a weapon that was light, had a 500-yard maximum range, and was lethal. We were going to operate up close, move fast, and if we got into a fight, make it a quick, savage one.

To fill my needs I opted for the new AR-15 rifle, which had not been adopted by BuWeps (Bureau of Weapons). It fired a small, fast bullet that destroyed its target through hydraulic shock. Short version: it was a deadly bullet if it hit you. The small, light 5.56mm rounds fired by the AR-15 let you carry a full third more ammunition than an equivalent weight of 7.62mm ammunition for the M-14. This gave me more rounds per unit of weight, something we needed to consider for the fast, long-range operations I might have to ask my men to conduct.

The AR-15 was what we wanted, and O'Connor, who was the head of BuWeps at that time, told me I didn't need it. Besides, the weapon wasn't in the supply system then. I suppose I can't really blame the bureaucrats for the way they did their jobs, though I still do; we were so secret an organization that I couldn't explain to them the kinds of missions we were actually going to do. They just weren't in on the secrecy involved with our Teams.

A small group of us from SEAL Team Two had watched a demonstration of the AR-15 at the Cooper-McDonald facility near Baltimore, Maryland. The weapon looked like what I wanted for the Team. I was given several to examine, so we ran them through the mill. One was frozen in a block of ice in an icehouse. Another was thrown into the Chesapeake Bay and allowed to sit in the surf, locked and loaded with a magazine and ammunition. Within my group of people, we tested and examined the weapons extensively.

The results of our testing were submitted to BuWeps. They ignored both our tests and further requests. When I went up there to face them down on the question of the AR-15, they said that we were not a recognized testing facility and that we didn't need it. But I was determined to get my men what they needed, as judged by an operator and not a bureaucrat.

So to outfit the SEALs with the best weapon available at that time, I used the open purchase allowance I had available, money I could just spend to buy equipment, and bought the AR-15. This deal was basically done on a handshake with the Cooper-McDonald people from whom I bought the weapons. And this was also what led to one of my formal board of inquiries leading to a possible court-martial.

Before dealing with those consequences, I had taken my storekeeper along with me to Cooper-McDonald and bought the weapons I wanted. SEAL Team One, commanded by Dave Del Guidice, had told me that whatever I did for my Team they wanted done for themselves. So I ordered 132 brand-new AR-15 rifles with spare parts, accessories, and ammunition. The magic number came from the needs of two SEAL Teams of 60 men each and a 10 percent spare rate.

Another weapon I had trouble getting for my SEALs was the specific sidearm I wanted. We needed the capability of taking out some of the "hands-across-the-sea" outboard motors our State Department had been handing out to developing countries. The VC had received a number of these motors for their sampans by simply taking them. The bullet from a .357 Magnum would crack the block of such a motor, so that's what I wanted.

The weapon I asked for was the Smith & Wesson Model-19 Combat Magnum. Some gun enthusiast someplace along the line decided we could have the Smith & Wesson Model-15 Combat Masterpiece, a .38 Special revolver. He had fired the Model 19 on the range, but someone had put .38 Specials in it to make the recoil easier. He figured there was no difference, so gave us the cheaper weapon.

It seemed that all of our procurement fit into this kind of reasoning somewhere along the line. If they hadn't used it before, we didn't need it. Another example of this was when we ordered parachutes for the SEALs. The chute we needed had to be able to support a combat-laden man and have a steerable capability. The only such parachute on the market at that time was the HALO rig made and patented by the Pioneer Parachute Company. It was a beautiful rig and even had a safety feature, a barometric release, that made it even better for our purposes. The barometric release opened the chute automatically when it reached a set altitude even if the jumper was unconscious.

We couldn't get the parachutes we wanted; again, the proper bureaus said we didn't need them, they hadn't been accepted, they didn't like them, they were too expensive. . . . So instead, my crew modified the parachutes we did have, cutting out sections of canopy and sealing the nylon back up with soldering irons. These worked, made what we needed, and had the steerable capability we needed.

Modifying the parachutes was a no-no in two ways. First off, we were using salvage parachutes because they were what we could get. Second, we were doing unauthorized modifications to salvaged chutes. This, and a few other parachute-related difficulties I had, led to another formal board of inquiry investigation pending a court-martial.

Another weapons-oriented situation involved my wanting something we could use to take somebody out silently. I wanted to be as sneaky as I could be and I didn't bother trying to follow Hoyle's rules. You can't play by the rules when you're the only person reading the book. The kind of enemy we would be fighting would be sneaky, underhanded, and fight as dirty as he could. So we had to be better at that than he was.

First, we tried to get some silencers, but those were very hard to come by. The people who had them didn't want to admit it and they certainly didn't want to give them up. But there were some drawbacks with using a silencer on a weapon: it left that smell of gunpowder in the air and could be noticed. But we still wanted a silent way to take out a sentry now and then, so I investigated modern crossbows. England put out the best sporting crossbow, according to my research. So with my Presidential Priority, we again drove the supply people into fits by ordering crossbows.

We did get the bows and my people practiced with them. They were getting pretty good with the bows and were able to target in on the right spot so that a sentry wouldn't make any noise. This was going fine and they were kept sealed up in our armory. Then someone brought in an outside inspection team and they looked at our armory.

We shouldn't have had to pass a regulation inspection since we weren't doing regulation things. But the Navy had a problem with that, so we had an inspection. Some supply officer came into our armory, found out we had crossbows, and looked them up to see what they were. He had no idea about what we were doing. Hoot Andrews was leading the guy around when he found the crossbows and apparently thought they were against some Geneva Convention or other agreement. They weren't, but he couldn't be convinced of this.

The name of the game for us was do the mission and make sure everyone has a round-trip. Anything that made it more likely that all of my men would come home after an operation was fine by me. But this officer was convinced the bows were illegal and took them away. Another case of a little knowledge along with some authority being a bad thing.

Finally, the higher-ups had a whole series of charges they wanted to lay at my feet. It seemed that getting the job done wasn't in their vocabulary if it went outside a very limited viewpoint. It looked like I was going to face a series of courts-martial, but at least my men had what they needed for the most part.

There were always risks that had to be taken to achieve real results. My problems seemed petty compared with what my men and I might have to face out in the field.

As soon as the SEAL Team was in commission, I started losing people. Some men were being lost to assignments with the Agency, others were getting overseas assignments. H. R. Williams went over to Southeast Asia and became the head of the Junk Force in Vietnam for a while to see what was needed over there. The cold war was rolling right along and Cuba was coming to heat things up a bit.

We did a recon of Cuba and I led the Team in. It was a group of SEALs and UDT men. Myself, J. C. Tipton as my swim buddy, and H. R. "Lump-lump" Williams made up part of the recon Team that came from SEAL Team Two. The other half of the team was taken from the ranks of UDT 21 and included George Walsh, Chief Schmidt, and Gene Tinnin. What I was trying to tell the Navy was that a mix of UDT and SEALs could work very well and that there shouldn't be a difference between the Teams. My team went in to Cuba, launching from the submarine Threadfin for an underwater swim in.

The people up in Navy supply had done their best to sabotage the mission before it began, and that was with them working on our side. I had ordered the German Draeger closed-circuit breathing rigs for our mission. The rigs were completely silent, released no bubbles into the water, and were very dependable. Some bureaucratic problems with the head of Bureau of Ships ended up giving me the rig that he felt was suitable. The time constraints of our operation forced me to go ahead with what we had for the operation. And it almost cost me some of my men.

The rigs we were given lasted long enough for us to lock out of the submarine. Almost as soon as we hit the water, one of my men's rig flooded out, the rebreathing bag taking on water. In a rebreather, a closed-circuit system, a mixture of caustic chemicals called Baralyme chemically scrubs the CO_2 from the air you breathe. Getting this chemical wet causes what we call a "caustic cocktail." The diver ends up sucking in something like wet lye into his lungs. This does not make for a safe situation.

While we were dealing with one of our team strangling on chemicals, to complicate matters, two Cuban Komar-class missile boats came into the area at high speed. The boats appeared to know that we had been launched from the submarine. Perhaps our secrecy somewhere up the line hadn't been everything that it could have been.

As the boats came out to us, we had to dive under them. As the Cuban patrol boats passed over us, all I could imagine were the series of events occurring on them that would result in our all being killed. I could see the Cubans taking out grenades, pulling the pins, the grenades arcing though the air, striking the water, sinking to our level, the fuses burning down. . . .

George Walsh's rig was completely flooded out by this time. The situation was more than tense. An explosion in the water would cave our rigs in, bust our eardrums, and generally work us over more than if we had been in a heavyweight prizefight. And that was if the blast wasn't close to us. Then the Komars continued on their way. They may have been a lot more interested in the sub than us, or they might have just been passing by.

Now all I had to deal with was being off a hostile foreign coast with at least one of my team having severe troubles with his breathing rig. It was a very good thing that I didn't lose anyone on that operation. I just might have had to make a visit and look someone up at BuShips.

Our intelligence for the operation listed an obstruction in the water that caused the current to eddy back against the normal flow. That wasn't quite the way the situation was, so we had to swim against the current all of the way in. We reconned about two miles of beach and charted it in case there had to be a U.S. invasion of Cuba itself. Going back out, we had trouble with that same obstruction in the water. It made the water too shallow for the submarine to come in and pick us up.

H. R. Williams spoke to me and asked what would we do if they didn't come in and pick us up? I told him not to worry, that I had the situation all figured out. We would just swim out to sea and drown. That made my team a little bit angry and they threw a bit more into their kicks as we swam out past the obstruction. We had a line stretched between the two groups of us to catch the buoy line the submarine was supposedly trailing.

When we reached deep enough water, there was that submarine with her gallant crew and their very cool commanding officer. They had avoided the Komars and were as close in as they dared to be to pick us up. We snagged onto their buoy line and had located the boat underwater.

The only problem now was the same one we had started with. The 'lungs we had were pretty much crapped out, flooded, not working, in general everything I thought they would be. You can only lock three men into the escape trunk at a time, and all six of my men had followed the buoy line down to the forward escape trunk. Now I had to signal three of them to go back up to the conning tower while the other three of us went into the trunk.

Ducking into a flooded escape trunk is like going into a bucket underwater that's only half-full of air. You duck under the hatch coaming and then you can stand up in an air bubble while you shut the hatch behind you, blow out the water, and open the hatch in the deck that lets you into the sub itself. There's also an intercom at the top of the trunk that lets you communicate with the interior of the sub.

As soon as I ducked into the trunk, I was on the intercom to the captain. He told me to move as quickly as I could, that the Komars were making another sweep back. I told him I had men on his conning tower and it was going to take time to clear both groups through the trunk. He understood the situation and knew what I had meant when I told him the ball was now in his court. He surfaced the sub enough to clear the conning tower and pulled my men in. As soon as I was told they were aboard, we started locking in through the trunk. And the boat was diving as we were clearing out the water.

We all returned to the United States and came out with the information we had been sent in to get. It would remain to be seen if the landing site we had been sent in to recon was really secret to the Cubans. Those Komar missile boats had been Johnnies-on-the-spot waiting for us when we were in the area.

President Kennedy came down to Little Creek to inspect the SEALs and see what the unit he had wanted built looked like and what our capabilities were. I wanted to show him just how good we were, so I built a sand-charged "bomb" with a flashbulb and timer. The bomb was concealed where President Kennedy would be. I later set off the "charge" and told the Secret Service what had been done and how. They weren't too happy about it, but it did show that we could slip past almost anyone.

Vice President Johnson was a gun enthusiast and he got with just the right man in my team—A. D. Clark, who also was a firearms expert. Clark had been one of the men who had helped me test and evaluate the AR-15 rifle. Vice President Johnson was talking to A. D. about the selection of our weapons that were spread out for viewing. They got to talking about the AR-15 rifle, which was still very rare at that time.

A. D. Clark picked up the AR-15. "Now, you take this," he said. "This is the weapon that we want and this is what my boss got me."

"Well, what's the problem?" the Vice President asked.

"My boss is getting a court-martial for buying them for us."

Vice President Johnson went and got President Kennedy's naval aide, who in turn got the President. President Kennedy went over and examined the weapons, speaking to A. D. Clark and looking at what we were doing.

Shortly after that visit, Admiral Edmund B. Taylor, who was the commander of the Fifth Naval District and out of my chain of command, contacted me. Admiral Taylor was a personal friend of President Kennedy from his days as a senator. Admiral Taylor called me up and asked me if I had a civilian suit. After I told him I did have one, which hadn't been worn very much, he told me to get my suit and meet him at the naval air station.

President John F. Kennedy inspects men from SEAL Team Two. In spite of the existence of the SEAL Teams being a secret at this time, the presidential visit had a large number of cameramen record the event. President Kennedy is examining the semi-closed circuit Mark VI breathing rig worn by Louis A. "Hoss" Kucinski on the right.

UDT-SEAL Museum

It doesn't really matter if an admiral is in your direct chain of command or not; when one asks a lieutenant to meet him somewhere, the lieutenant shows up. When I asked Admiral Taylor where we were going, he told me I couldn't ask. When I asked him who we were going to see—I already had my suspicions—he again told me I could not ask that either. So I said, "Aye aye, sir," and climbed on board the aircraft.

The flight to Washington, D.C., wasn't a long one. The drive from the air station to the Blair House, right across the street from the White House, wasn't a very long one either. Sitting at that house, waiting for whatever heel was going to land on me and grind me into the dirt, that was a long one. Then President Kennedy came in.

I was so startled to see the President walk into the room that I blurted out probably one of the most stupid things I ever said in my life. "I didn't vote for you, Mr. President."

It only took a moment for me to realize just how dumb that sounded, so I quickly tried to save face by saying, "But I'm willing to die for you."

It wasn't that I really wanted to do that either. But he was graceful about it. He asked me if I knew what a Presidential Priority was. I told him that I did and how it was supposed to allow me to gather the materials and men I needed to do the job that was assigned to me. And I may have also mentioned something about being stonewalled by bureaucrats and so-called experts.

At that time I had five formal boards of investigation hanging over me. I felt there was no way I was even going to get out of the Navy with an honorable discharge, let alone continue my career.

The President then said something I found unusual at the time. He said, "Roy, you'll make your number."

What he had meant was that I would make my promotion to lieutenant commander later. And my five formal boards of investigation went away as well.

Someone could probably have put together the SEALs a lot more smoothly than I did. But the problem was that we had immediate missions that had to be performed, and we had equipment that wouldn't do the job. The only way I could get the materials for my people, to ensure that they would do their missions as a round-trip and not one-way, was to turn up the heat. After doing that, I couldn't complain about the heat.

There were a lot of people without whose work there wouldn't have been a SEAL Team. Bill Hamilton organized the paperwork and took a concept and made it a reality. I took that reality and give it manpower and equipment.

There was a time when I called the Team together during the Cuban Missile Crisis. I needed fifteen people to prepare to jump in to Cuba on a possible mission. Our skipper, John Callahan, was coordinating the Cuban effort from both SEAL Team One and Two. So I was running the Team while John was coordinating the entire naval unconventional warfare mission. So I called the Team together and asked them all for fifteen volunteers. Then I said I really needed only thirteen volunteers. My swim buddy, Lump-lump Williams, was going in with me and that made two of us.

When I asked for the thirteen volunteers to step forward, the whole of SEAL Team Two took one step forward. That was probably one of the highest honors I have ever been paid.

What could I say to them but, "I'm in charge of the dumbest bunch of people I have ever met in my entire life."

I already had their names because I had a hunch that they would all step forward, and they all did.

Chapter 30

The First CO

Though Roy Boehm was the first officer-in-charge of SEAL Team Two, he was not the first commanding officer. That position was assigned to Lieutenant John Callahan. Like so many of his counterparts in the UDTs, Callahan had no idea who or what the SEALs were. Given all the work involved to qualify to join the UDTs, transferring out of them into a new and unknown unit did not hold a lot of appeal.

But orders are what a sailor follows and John Callahan moved his family from the West Coast to the East Coast. After arriving at the new SEAL Team's headquarters, greeting the men, and then leaving for training and meetings with higher command, Lieutenant Callahan still had to learn just what this new SEAL Team of his was all about.

Lieutenant John F. Callahan, USN (Ret.)

Officially, SEAL Team One is the older of the two Teams by twelve minutes. There was a document that had to be signed and sent to the Chief of Naval Operations' office stating that the command was manned and ready. The receipt of that document was the official beginning of the team. David Del Guidice beat me to the CNO's office with his paperwork by twelve minutes. But that was okay; we got all of the publicity.

Back in November 1961, I was just returning to the United States after a nine-month detachment in WestPac (West Pacific). I arrived in time to see my wife and, for the first time, my three-month-old child. Then I was informed that it was fine for me to see my family, but that the admiral would like to see me at three o'clock. So much for coming home.

When I arrived at the admiral's office, he told me that he had a set of orders for me and that I would be proceeding to Little Creek, Virginia, to form and commission Navy SEAL Team Two. My first question was, "What's a SEAL Team?"

The admiral explained the acronym to me. Then I said that I really didn't want to leave UDT. He informed me that eventually all UDTs would become SEALs and then said that I would still be in the (Special Warfare) community. He finished by telling

The artwork approved to be the unit patch by Lieutenant John F. Callahan, the first commanding officer of SEAL Team Two. The seal is superimposed over the number 2 to signify the Team. Under the seal is a pair of swim fins bracketing an open parachute. Above the crest of the parachute is the oval of a swimmer's face mask while below is a stylized M3A1 submachine gun.

U.S. Navy

me that the orders were very impressive and that I should be very happy to take them. "Yes, sir, Admiral," I said. "I'm ready to go."

My wife was from La Jolla in Southern California, and her question was, "What's Virginia Beach like?"

"It's just like La Jolla," I told her. I paid for that last remark for years. But we were a Navy family and moving was part of the package. One thing that didn't go with me to the East Coast were any people from the West Coast UDTs. Upon arrival at Little Creek, I was immediately informed that I couldn't take any of the people from UDTs 11, 12, or 13 for my new Team. Everyone for SEAL Team Two had to come from the East Coast, and that meant UDT 21.

Names were run by me as possible people for SEAL Team Two, and I didn't know a one of them. So I told the people running the personnel pool that I would like the source of the men split. Part of the officer core I wanted to be mustangs, who had a lot of experience in the Navy and the Team prior to receiving their commission. The rest of the officers could be ensigns, fresh new officers who would work and learn. The men were to be the same way, a core of very experienced Navy UDT men and the balance fresh new people who could learn from the others.

A mustang officer was someone who had gone into the Navy as an enlisted man and then specialized in his rate. After spending time in his rate, developing rank and learning his skills, some men would put in for and receive their commission as an ensign. In another program, these men would become warrant officers and remain in their field. But the mustang officer would be a fully commissioned officer and he could expect to go on to be a lieutenant or lieutenant (jg) fairly easily, depending on how much time he had left that he could spend in the service. These men would broaden themselves to become a complete officer rather than stay in a single discipline. These men had a tremendous background in skills and knowledge.

The young officers who were fresh graduates were very gung ho. The world was theirs and they wanted to take it on. That was also what we wanted because it gave the Team its heart and a lot of life. But this enthusiasm could be tempered by the experienced mustang officers. They were also in a position to teach the new en-signs, who had to learn more and more as things went on. So I looked at my mus-tangs as teachers who could spread their wealth of knowledge throughout the Team.

There was some consideration made for my family and I was able to spend the holidays, Christmas and such, with them prior to the move. So I arrived at Little Creek the first week of January 1962. Arrangements had been made ahead of time to house the new SEAL Team and some buildings, Quonset huts and such, had been made available for us on the base. The structures had to be cleaned up and reconditioned a bit before we could use them. So I asked that some of the person-nel who were going into the new SEAL Team be detached from their UDT and as-signed to our area to help get things ready. At that time, Roy Boehm, Joe DiMartino, and about ten or twelve men went over to what would be the SEAL compound. The buildings we were assigned hadn't been used in some time, so there was plenty of work to do.

Then I arrived and we started to put some things together. I have always tried to be an up-front man, but when I sent that message to the CNO saying we were manned and ready, I had no idea what we might be ready for. We had a few dozen K-Bar knives between the bunch of us, didn't have an armory, and there was already some yelling from the UDT since many of the guys had brought their fins and gear from UDT and those had to be replaced.

During those early days in the Team, we were fortunate in that a lot of our en-listed men who came over from UDT were more senior than you normally saw in a commissioning crew. During my first three days at the Team, I didn't really talk to anyone except Rudy Boesch, SEAL Team Two's master-at-arms. I knew him by repu-tation and also knew that the UDT really hated to lose him. But they sent him and I was very glad to have his experience. I got to know him as he did me. Rudy soon learned what I was willing to put up with and what I wouldn't. That gave him the guidance he needed to work with the enlisted men. That was a fantastic relation-ship.

There we sat in the middle of the base at Little Creek, Virginia, calling ourselves SEALs. None of us really knew what a SEAL was yet; we hadn't done anything to build up the name. At that time the biggest thing that we were sure of was that we were going to get parachute training. The UDTs still weren't sure they would all re-ceive parachute training. That was one of the reasons some of the guys volun-teered for the new SEAL Team: it was the only way they were sure to get parachute training.

Initially, the new Team had come about and was thrust on the Amphibious Base without a lot of prior discussion. We didn't have our financing fully organized yet and there wasn't anything in the base's budget for the SEALs. So the base would take some money from Special Services, a little money from the Seabees, and some from other organizations to build us up. We were very close to being

McHale's Navy at that time. We were secret and no one could talk to us. Not that they'd have learned much; very few people in the Team knew anything about what we would be actually doing. There were a few missions that were going to start very soon, but little beyond that.

Everything that came down to us at the SEAL Team followed a single channel of communications. But there were several different people feeding the channel. Someone had planned out what we would be getting into in the way of small boats and riverine warfare. Another guy was talking about HALO operations, but it wasn't the same person. Another guy was talking about the special delivery units for the submarines. But none of these people seemed to be talking to each other. All of these things were coming at us from different areas. There wasn't a single man at the top looking at everything and funneling us directions with some kind of priority.

The equipment we had at the very beginning was almost a bad joke. We didn't have much of anything in the way of gear. Guys were going into civilian stores and buying their own gear, even their own handguns. I never really wanted to know the full story, but Roy Boehm went out with some of the men and came back with AR-15 rifles. Later enough AR-15s came in to equip the whole Team and SEAL Team One as well. Those were the first AR-15s in the Navy. The Army wasn't going to see the M-16 for several years yet. And Roy just bought them through an account he had available. Then the ammo was made available.

There was one big thing that we were sure of—schooling. Everyone had to go to school. That put us in very different areas of the country at any one time. I think that Joe DiMartino, Roy Boehm, Chief Boesch, and I passed each other every few months and said hello, asked who was around, and if anyone new had shown up. This was because we were being sent everywhere.

They sent me to the Royal Canadian Air Force Survival School in Edmonton, Alberta. Then I was sent to the Army's Jungle Warfare School in Panama. Then it was off to the Marine Corps Escape and Evasion School in Pickle Meadows, California. And I was sent to a Code School in San Francisco. All of these things were four and five weeks long and you were away for all of them. I would come home, my wife would do my laundry, and I would go into the base for a few days. So everyone was cross-training.

The Marine School at Pickle Meadows, California, was one of the real eye-openers of training. It was unbelievably effective. First off, we took a bus out of Reno, Nevada, up into the mountains to where the school was located. You were tired when you finally got there and the instructors told us just to throw our equipment into our rooms and that they would give us an orientation speech.

Just a few minutes into the speech, the doors flew open and guys stormed in wearing Soviet uniforms. They gathered us all up as prisoners and stacked us in the back of a truck like cordwood. Then they drove off, traveling for hours over back trails, kicking up dust, and winding and turning through rough roads. Then they took us from the truck, stripped us of our belts, shoelaces, and whatever else we had with us, and threw us into compartments.

They had different-size compartments they put us in depending on what they wanted to do. When they wanted to talk to you, they had this one container that was about the size of a coffin. They would put you in there and pile heavy rocks on top of the box and just let you go for a few minutes, only you didn't know how long the wait would be. Another of their devices was a big pipe in the ground full of water.

There was a wire mesh above the pipe that they closed once they slipped you into the water. The water was about up to your chin. All of a sudden they would throw a whole bucket of water into the pipe and you would crash your head into the mesh trying to rise above it. The water would cover your head, but what you didn't know was that there were a number of holes all around the pipe that drained the water away in something like 30 seconds.

They would ask you questions and dump water in on you. This was great training. All of their techniques had been taken from people who had faced it firsthand in prison camps in the Soviet Union and North Korea. They gave us about a day and a half or more of the prison camp treatment, then we were "released" and had half a day off. Then the classroom work started and the instructors showed us what we had done wrong.

Those of us from the Teams knew nothing, or very little at most, about how prisoners had been interrogated during the Korean War. There were simple tricks that had been used. If it was cold and you asked for a blanket, you first had to sign for it. This was not anything unusual for someone who was in the service—you signed for everything. The next day they showed the propaganda documents about how we had signed confessions about the atrocities we had committed. That wasn't what had happened, but they showed us how it could be made to look that way.

So after three days of classroom training, they took us up into the hills in groups of four and chased us. We could come in every morning and they would give the group of four people a couple of hot dogs and a cup of rice. We had lucked out because of some maneuvers that had been staged in the training area. One of the men with me was a SEAL corpsman and we found two boxes of C rations that had been buried by the troops. Checking the dates on the boxes, we saw that they were fine. So we sat up there for two days eating regular Army chow, so that wasn't too bad.

The lesson I learned during that school was if you were captured and they were going to kill you, they would have already done it. Nothing was worse than dying, so just take the abuse you were going to get. Don't fight it, don't make a big deal, do nothing. The only way to beat the system at all was to do nothing.

No one back at the Team ever said, "What do you do if you get captured?" And that was simply because everyone said it didn't matter how many they were fighting, they were not going to be captured. And the question never had to be answered. No SEAL was ever taken, alive or dead. It would have been a huge propaganda coup if a SEAL had been taken in Vietnam or wherever. He would have been paraded through villages and shown off. There were rewards placed on a SEAL's head in Vietnam, and it was never collected. What every man in the Teams knew was that you never gave up, and you never left anyone behind. It didn't matter who you were, what your rate or rank was, everyone knew that. Everyone was important, and everyone was a Team player.

But we still had a lot to learn about being a SEAL. That first year at SEAL Team Two, I don't think that anyone could tell you anything about what happened at SEAL Team Two as a whole. No one was around long enough to find out. Then we started to sit down and find out more about where we were going. People started to plan more about what would happen with us operationally.

One day I received orders for four officers and twenty-eight men who were going to arrive. Two of the officers were senior to me and I thought I was going to be replaced. Finally, I received a phone call from Lieutenant Knight, who was one of the officers. He asked if he could come over and meet with me and I quickly agreed. This sounded like a chance to find out just what was going on. Then Lieutenant Knight arrived and the first thing he asked me was, "Why am I here?"

Now it was time for a call to Washington. When I got through to higher command, they told me the situation was highly classified and that I would have to go up to D.C. for a meeting. So I flew up to D.C. and was told that I would be receiving boats within the next two weeks. Two of the boats would be PT boats that were being taken out of mothballs in Philadelphia and reactivated. Another two boats would be brand-new craft coming in from Norway. The enlisted men and officers were going to be my boat crews.

The boats were late in coming, so I found things for the extra men to do. They were a little bummed out because we made them do calisthenics right along with us every day. Some of those men had been on ships for years, so it was a good idea to try to condition them and get things ready.

Finally, the boats arrived, and they came with a package that contained information about riverine warfare. That made sense. We were Navy divers and combat swimmers. What was going to be used in the rivers and shallow waters? You could tell that at that time they were thinking about Southeastern Asia. We weren't really going full bore in Vietnam yet, that was still some years away. But you could tell that was the direction things were pointing.

These boats did not have torpedo tubes, so we were not a part of the regular Navy and were not going to attack large ships. Instead, these boats were going to be used to move people in and out of areas, make quick raids along coasts and up rivers. Everything on the boats was geared toward making as much speed as possible. What we did was discuss which weapons would go on them, where they would go, and why. How could explosives be safely stored on them? Could you take along a limited amount of diving gear if you needed it for an op?

We made a lot of mistakes initially. The diving gear question was reexamined and it was asked what it would be used for in the first place. Those boats were for running and fast striking, not supporting an underwater operation. Everything was trial and error, since there was nothing written up on how these boats would fight.

We finally came up with the information to write up the manual for using these boats. A Commander Clay gave me a great book compiled by the IRA, of all people. Another book I used was on guerrilla warfare and it was from the CIA for dropping into Cuba. The works of Che Guevara were used. All of these things pointed at the jungle as a place to fight.

We started to get more information from the Army Special Forces. We had a lot of people who wanted to fight in the jungle, but no one really knew how to do it. How was a patrol conducted? How many people did you need in one? What were their jobs, their equipment, their support? All of these questions had to be answered and we had to obtain the equipment we needed to conduct the operations once we had the answers.

We tried to take a look at each situation and get the best people the new Team had on it. Joe DiMartino was told to take a look at the dive locker. He was not only to make note of what we had on hand but also to take a look around in the industry and see what else might be available. We started to work with the Emerson as our new rebreather rather than the old system which had been in-house at UDT for a while.

Another officer was a lieutenant (jg) who had also been a mustang and a gunner's mate when he came up through the ranks. He was asked what we were looking at in the way of weapons. One man was very experienced with parachutes, so he was asked to make his recommendations.

The guys in the armory were told that they weren't just to polish equipment. They had to come up with whatever weapons we were going to need. What were we going to do with them? And where were we going to get them? We had to study foreign weapons, since we might have to use them.

That sort of thing got a lot of people thinking in the Teams. You could see the enthusiasm build up during those first few years. Everyone had something to contribute, and it wasn't things that had just been passed on by others who had learned about them years before. Assigning the men projects that they had to research stretched them and made them learn more than they would have learned any other way. And we started learning more about what we were going to do and where we were going to go.

It was very tough in the beginning in part because some of the other services saw us encroaching on their mission. The Army Special Forces helped us, but wondered if we were going to take some operations away from them. Marine Force Recon felt the beach and hinterland was their territory and now this new Navy unit (us) was taking that away. That's the way it was and that was the way it was going to be.

The regular Navy had gotten behind the SEAL concept for one reason: money was being sent to Special Warfare units. The Army had the Special Forces, the Air Force had the Air Commandos, and the Navy didn't have anything. What they had was the UDT, which they now made into a Special Warfare unit. That meant we would be getting special funding, and in the next year the money came from Special Warfare.

In the early years there was a lot of rivalry between the SEALs and the UDT. It was like brother against brother. That took its toll along the way and we had to work hard and quick to repair the break.

The backbone of the UDTs, the SEALs, the Scouts and Raiders, or whoever is the individual. It was high-quality individuals put together that made the Team. We were worried about the training units. Would they be able to maintain the quality of their graduates and increase the numbers to fill the new Teams?

The training units always had pressure on them from outside the community to ease up, change things, make a quota in the number of graduates. That was one of the things that we felt we could not give in on, no matter what else we did. That pressure never went away. My last year and a half in the service, I ran BUD/S training in Coronado. It was a continual battle against outside forces who tried to change the way we did training.

Noncommunity people wanted to know what made some trainees quit and if we could talk them into coming back. As far as I was concerned, I didn't want to talk them into coming back. They had quit, they didn't want the program, and that was enough.

That constant pressure to change training was a much bigger concern than the rivalry between the UDTs and the SEALs. As far as the rivalry went, in a short period of time, as we worked together more, it became a benefit. The competition drew the best from both sides. But there were some jealousies that also came up.

We had started with nothing at the SEAL Team. But then all of the money and all the new toys started to arrive. Now the UDT didn't have everything and they were feeling left behind. Now they were borrowing from us and we were happy to share. I like to kid Richard Marcinko about the time he came to me while he was a third class at UDT 21. And he was in the UDT parachute locker, only they really didn't have much in the way of parachutes compared to us. So we would take many UDTs with us when we went jumping. Again, this was for a building up of the individuals who made both Teams.

Now we started to build up our supply of equipment and increase the skills we needed to operate. The boats were developing in application and people were brought in to do that job. Now the whole Special Warfare unit began to take shape.

The boats would take us in and out, and we wouldn't have to worry about that. That freed up men in the Teams, and qualified personnel were in short supply to begin with.

Then we started building a staff, and that took a lot of the paperwork burden off those of us in command. Dave Del Guidice and I were the commanders of SEAL Teams One and Two, but were just lieutenants. My knowledge of office procedures was limited. I had never really been behind a desk during my time in UDT. The second month I was at SEAL Team Two, they assigned me a first-class yeoman. That was the best thing that happened to me. Not only did he know procedures, he could type. Everyone wanted a report on what the new SEAL Team could do, what we were learning, and when we could do whatever. We could not operate and do all of the paperwork. Now it was starting to get done.

President Kennedy had a lot of influence on the creation of the SEALs, even if not directly. He wanted a force that could fight the wars that he could see coming up, not the major land battles where tanks slugged in out on the plains, but the little guerrilla fights that could bleed a country dry and make it fall. During the president's visit to Little Creek, I had the privilege of talking to him for twenty minutes about the Teams and what we were to do. An unheard of amount of time in his schedule. But he had an enthusiasm for what we were and what we were going to do. That came in part from his own Navy background in PT boats during WWII.

President Kennedy knew what a small group of determined men could do. And he wanted that capability for his armed forces. Why were the first two commanding officers of the SEAL Teams lieutenants? Because he did not want the new units to be led by men who had been brainwashed by the traditional Navy. If full commanders had been put in charge like the Navy wanted originally, it would have been a, "We're going to do it this way because this is the way we do it on a destroyer or cruiser or whatever."

Del Guidice and I used to kid each other that what was wanted was a couple of dummies who could just stand up there and take it. I hadn't been involved in any of the creation and planning of the new SEAL Teams. But I was open to new ideas and new things, so that was why I was put in charge of SEAL Team Two. And the same general thing is what led Dave Del Guidice to be put in charge of SEAL Team One. If things had been done any other way, the SEALs could have been just another unit. And they never were.

■ Chapter 31

Skills

The men who filled the ranks of the first SEAL Teams were chosen for a variety of reasons. All were competent operators and most had long proven themselves in the UDTs. Others had already received training that the rest of their teammates would receive at formal schools. And some had skills they could teach to their Teammates. Among the plankowners of the SEAL Teams were a number of individuals who possessed all of the above characteristics.

Leonard "Lenny" Waugh, Senior Electronics Chief, USN (Ret.)

As a plankowner of SEAL Team Two, I was one of the original crew to man the Team, handpicked by Roy Boehm from the ranks of UDT 21 back in 1962. Rudy Boesch and I were both over in Europe on a deployment when the orders came out for us to report to SEAL Team Two. We were flown back to Norfolk and were met at the airport by Harry Beal. He was the one who told us that we were no longer frogmen, we were SEALs. I had always wanted to be a frogman; now I'm a SEAL.

It was the next day, January 8, 1962, that we found out what the SEALs were. We mustered at UDT 21 and were moved over to this little place that had been set aside for SEAL Team Two. I was impressed to be there, but all we were told that first day was that SEAL stood for Sea, Air, and Land. And that was about all we could be told.

For myself, and a number of others, we wanted to know a little bit more about what we were going to do. We were told that we would be parachuting, and that pleased me because I like jumping. Then we were told that we would be working underwater. That also pleased me since I liked diving. It sounded like my kind of thing, but I still had no idea what we were going to do.

I had joined the Navy back in 1951. By 1954, I had volunteered for the UDT and went through training with class thirteen. We started in August 1954 and graduated that December. My classmates included Roy Boehm, Jake Rhinebolt, Bill Sutherland, Bill Bruhmuller, and a number of others who stayed with the Teams. My class had a very good retention rate, our guys mostly stayed with the Teams throughout their Navy career. I stayed with the UDT from 1954 until 1962, when I was moved over to the SEAL Team.

When the first class of frogmen went to Jump School down in Fort Benning, I was in Europe on a deployment. But I was back in time to get to Jump School with the second group from UDT. From the moment of my first jump, I knew this was something I liked.

We came back from Jump School in November 1958, and within a month or so I was the first frog on the East Coast to make a free fall. We knew nothing about how to do it; I had bought a parachute and just strapped it to my back. In fact, I had to wear two harnesses to jump. The reserve chute wouldn't fit on my parachute harness, so I had to wear a second one just to hold the reserve chute.

After that first free fall, everyone in the Team seemed to get the bug and we all started parachuting. It may have been my parachuting skills that helped get me picked for the first SEAL Team, but I was also a brown belt in judo, an electronics technician, and maybe some other things that may have gotten me picked, or at least pushed me in the new Team's direction.

Later I was one of the first two SEALs to go to the Air Force's Judo School in Nevada along with Jim Wilson. We were both to feel out how that school was set up and whether it would be a good place to send the SEALs. I felt the Air Force had done a fine job in their training and we both recommended the school. The first martial art studied at SEAL Team Two was judo. There was a Marine who came down to our training and taught judo to the UDTR students. After several of us received our belts, we started teaching the art to our Teammates. But the Air Force course was our first organized martial art training school.

It wasn't very long after the SEALs had been commissioned that I was sent over to Vietnam. Bill Burbank and I were sent to the West Coast to join with a SEAL Team One detachment and we went to Vietnam in early 1962. That detachment was MTT (Mobile Training Team) 10-62. I had no idea what we were going to do over there. The mission turned out to be training Vietnamese naval personnel. But I loved the country very much and came back from the deployment with a Vietnamese bride.

Personally, I thought we were doing a bang-up job over there. We were in Da Nang teaching their personnel to do underwater work, demolitions, and sneaking and peeking. Eventually, our training helped develop the Vietnamese Junk Force, their Biet Hai. Later the West Coast SEALs helped train and set up the Vietnamese LDNN, their Lien Doc Nguoi Nhia—"soldiers who fight under the sea"—the South Vietnamese version of the SEALs.

Five years later, in January 1967, I returned to Vietnam with SEAL Team Two's Third platoon. Larry Bailey was our platoon leader and I was with him in first squad. Bob Gormley was the assistant platoon leader and he had second squad. Second platoon from SEAL Team Two also deployed with us, with a fresh young ensign Richard Marcinko as assistant platoon leader.

Everyone from SEAL Team Two had wanted to go to combat in Vietnam with the first deployment. SEAL Team One had been in operation incountry for almost a full *year before we arrived. I felt very good about coming back and being able to fight for my wife's country. We thought we were doing some good and were going to win the war against the VC.*

This wasn't really my first combat in Vietnam. Back with the MTT in Da Nang, we had gone out on several ops with the Army Special Forces. They had wanted to see a little bit of us and we wanted the same of them. So we kind of cross-trained each other a bit.

But that first deployment was different. We knew we had the best group going from SEAL Team Two. We were all handpicked and enjoyed working with each other. What we called a crackerjack group.

We didn't win the war, though we did think we might at the very beginning. But the SEALs certainly carried their share of the load. We did well in the operations we did and left our mark on the Viet Cong.

■ Chapter 32

First Combat

No matter how well trained, how experienced in other ways, or how old and mature, a SEAL or UDT man can never be certain about his reactions to combat until he has experienced it firsthand. That experience allows the operator to know and be certain of the confidence he can have in his training. He knows how to react and has proved it to himself.

During the first years of the SEALs' direct action involvement in the Vietnam War, combat veterans were few in number. Initial deployments could be nerve-racking when platoons finally went out on their first operations. To ease a new platoon into operating in Vietnam, members of a previous platoon that had been incountry for a while or were from a platoon rotating back to the States would introduce a new platoon into an operational area.

Breaking-in ops became a standard procedure for the SEALs throughout the Vietnam War. Experience could increase an operator's confidence in himself, his training, and his teammates. And actions during combat could draw out the finest in men.

Frank Toms, Boatswain's Mate Third Class

A brother of mine had been in the Navy before I joined. He left the service just as I finished high school. There wasn't a job I could find and so I decided to join the

Navy, as he had done. My brother had told me that I would be bored to death in the Navy if I didn't get into something exciting like a UDT or SEAL Team. And that was where I first heard of them. It was my second or third week of boot camp in San Diego in 1964 when a person came around recruiting for UDT.

The person that I happened to interview with was Bud Jurick, who was well known to all of the instructors I was soon going to meet. Bud had been in just about every Special Warfare group the services had to offer. He had been a Marine, an Army Ranger, and looked like a Sergeant Rock from the comic books. He had this deep voice, square jaw, and immaculate appearance. He was impressive, and I took one look at him and thought I wanted to be one of those.

He tried his best to talk me out of volunteering for UDT training. I had done fairly well on my entrance exams and could have gone to an A School. But I was adamant and wanted to be a frogman.

My UDTR training was with class thirty-four, a winter class in Coronado. And of course, mine was the last hard class. At first the place scared me to death. I wasn't sure I could get through training, but I definitely knew I wanted to. Every day in training on the Amphibious Base—and this was back when we were training out of a Quonset hut on the eastern edge of the base itself—when we marched to chow we would see frogmen and SEALs in their starched fatigues. Later, when some of us were in the Teams, they would make us get dressed and stand there for the trainees to see us.

By far the hardest part of training for me was the last three weeks, which were spent on San Clemente Island. We went out there in a large landing craft with everything we would need for our stay. We lived in tents, had cold-water showers, and worked a lot. Those three weeks on San Clemente you use and practice everything that you've learned in training. For the past eighteen weeks, you had been training for San Clemente. And when you got to the island, you put it all together.

Sinking deep into the mud of Vietnam, this SEAL operator keeps his Stoner Mark 23 light machine gun well clear of the mud. Having just stepped off the insertion craft, this man has sunk to his hips in the thick, brown mud. It is situations like this that proved the value of the mud flats training during UDTR and BUD/S.

U.S. Navy

Every night we had a night problem. You would go to your briefing first. Then go and do the problem. And then return and do your debrief on the problem. And if you didn't do things right, you did the whole thing over again. In the three weeks we were there, we did every problem over again except one, and that was because it was daylight by the time we finished it.

Hell Week was rough. But you kind of go into automatic pilot during that week. I was fortunate enough to be in a very good boat crew. Everything was competition between the crews. A boat crew was seven people, and that moved over into SEAL Team with you since a squad was also seven people.

But during that week, we had races every night carrying and paddling our rubber boats. Everything was competition and mine was a good boat crew—that and we cheated a lot. But cheating was encouraged. We were going into an unconventional unit; unconventional thinking was something we were going to have to practice. But you didn't snivel about things when you got caught cheating during training either.

Winning Hell Week was worth it for my crew and me. We secured a half day before the rest of the class, and we didn't have to help clean everything up either. That week was tough and we did lose a lot of people. Other folks quit, but I was just too focused on the competition to think about quitting. It wasn't that difficult for me, though it was very hard just to stay up during that week. We were always falling down almost asleep. Guys would slip facedown into their food while eating.

And I thought about quitting—there was no shame in that. But it wasn't during Hell Week. Instead, it was at San Clemente Island. Whenever the instructors told us to hit the beach, of course we all did. And a buddy of mine and I were convinced that the instructors were going to kill us. And that was crazy, so we were going to quit right there. Then the instructors told us to hit the beach and we jumped right in along with everyone else.

The cold was miserable. I was from Texas and had seen blue northerns before. But I'd only seen the ocean once before joining the Navy. And that was the Gulf of Mexico, which is nothing like the big, blue, cold Pacific.

The last day of training was wonderful. It's very hard to put into words what it feels like to graduate from UDT training. All of these people that we'd seen during our training, all of these impressive frogmen and SEALs—and you always knew the SEALs because the UDT wore a patch on their sleeves—these people all made an impression on us.

And then there were the instructors. For twenty-one weeks they had been trying to kill you. And then at graduation, they put their arm around you and said, "Welcome aboard." For me, it was just incredible. It had seemed such a lofty goal, and I was sure I would be struck down by lightning or something before I graduated. But there I was standing with my class that last day. My brother was extremely proud of me.

After graduation, I was assigned to UDT 11. At that time there were UDT 11 and

12 on the West Coast, and UDT 21 and 22 on the East Coast. SEAL Team One was in Coronado and SEAL Team Two in Little Creek. Basically, we had the odd numbers and they had the even ones.

But once I was at UDT 11, I couldn't wait to make a deployment to the Philippines. That first trip was great, especially for a youngster from Texas. It was just incredible to go to the Philippines, do the diving there in the tropical waters, and meet the girls in Olangopo town. We even got to go to Vietnam and practice a bit of what we had learned.

Our Vietnam deployment was the hardest I worked in my life. We were stationed in Da Nang, but were going someplace up and down the coast every day to do beach surveys. Frequently, we would be out on an APD for up to two weeks reconning beaches. We would be in the water from 8:00 in the morning to 5:00 or 6:00 at night. Just swimming and taking depth soundings was the basic job, along every inch of landable beach in Vietnam.

More often than not, at the end of the day, we couldn't take a freshwater shower because the ship only made enough fresh water for the crew. It seemed the UDTs were always extra baggage aboard the APDs. That was the toughest I ever worked. And it wasn't due to any enemy action. We just didn't see a lot of that in the UDTs at that time. It was because we reconned more shoreline than I care to think about.

After I did that first deployment with UDT, I was able to go over to SEAL Team One. It was 1966 and they were stepping up the SEAL commitment to the Vietnam War. SEAL Team One had the only combat deployments to Vietnam that year. SEAL Team Two wouldn't be in-country with platoons until early 1967. They needed people for the SEAL Team and I was torn between volunteering and staying with UDT. I didn't have to worry about things much since I was one of the guys soon drafted into the SEAL Team.

They came up with a list of names that was posted that basically said we need you in SEAL Team One. So as much as I would have liked to go back to Olongapo and further adventures with UDT 11, being invited into the SEAL Team was quite an honor.

So I went into SEAL Team One in 1966. After arriving in the Team we all had to first complete SEAL cadre training and then get put into a platoon. We were one of the earliest full platoons to go over to Vietnam. Previously, the detachments that were sent over were as groups of SEALs. All of us were pretty much in our regular Team platoon as we went through cadre training. There were no veterans of Vietnam in our platoon, just fifteen very green rookie SEALs.

So we just had to kind of step out into the waters of combat in Vietnam. And that first stepping out, our first operation, was terrible. The SEALs who had been over there before us took us to a fairly secure area for our "break-in" op. Being rookies, we didn't know a secure area from anything else. So we had about a five-hundred-yard patrol that took us all day to conduct. We were positive that there was a VC behind every tree.

After you had been over to Vietnam and been on a number of operations, you started to learn about what was, and wasn't, there around you. By the end of our six-month tour, we knew that there were certain parts of the jungle you could run through. And there were other parts where you had better get down on all fours and crawl.

It was kind of tough breaking in to combat. But that was our job and we did it. The first combat engagement we were involved in could easily be described as total confusion. Until you have been in a SEAL seven-man fire team and heard all of the noise when we initiate an ambush, you can't believe anything can be that loud. Personally, I always tried to think of what it would be like to be the other guys, and I think I would have been just as terrified as they looked.

Frequently—like 99 percent of the time—we saw the expression on their faces because we always tried to take prisoners. There was a saying in the Team that dead men wouldn't talk. So we wanted them alive. Where we were operating in the Rung Sat Special Zone, prisoners were very valuable.

We always tried to take prisoners rather than just kill the enemy. If there are two expressions in Vietnamese that I will never forget, they are dung lai, which means "stop," and lai dey, which means "come here." So we always said those words, unless of course they were pointing a gun at us. Even when we initiated an ambush, we tried to start it with those words first.

More often than not, the VC would be terrified looking up and seeing seven people with green and black face paint on. And that would be if they could see us at all, since we were always well camouflaged. Most of the time they would dive into the water and all hell would break loose as we opened fire. The blast of fire and noise would just seem to be total confusion. Your job during an ambush was to cover your sector of fire and just empty your weapon at whatever target was there. And that would usually be the time when the VC's heads would come bobbing up in the water. I often felt sorry for them, especially during that first operation of ours. We operated at night and used a lot of tracers, so seven men with automatic weapons would put out a lot of noise, muzzle flashes, and streaks of red light zipping through the air.

What stands out most in my mind about that first tour is how we matured and operated before we left Vietnam. Most of the SEALs I knew wanted to stay over there and just not go back to Coronado. Even some of those who went back quickly tired of the regimen and wanted to join with the first platoon they could find that was going to Vietnam.

But during that first six-month tour, the platoon all grew as a team. And I stress that word Team because I think that's where the SEALs and UDTs have excelled. Other Special Operations units gradually incorporate the team concept into their actions. But with us, it was drilled into you from the first day of training. You were part of a Team and you always did what was best for the Team. The very few people we had in the unit who really didn't know the meaning of fear stood out a bit for the rest of us. I personally knew the meaning of fear, and I have no trouble saying so. But you put seven of us together, and we forget the word.

During that first tour, my platoon, Kilo Platoon, had been ambushed badly by the VC. It was 7 April 1967 and we were going back up the river to Nha Be and our home base when we started taking some fire from the shoreline in the Rung Sat. That was pretty much what we had been looking for, so we turned the boat around and headed into the fire, giving them all we had from the weapons we carried and that were mounted on the boat. As luck would have it, they dropped a mortar round right into the boat.

When the mortar shell went off, I and my closest friend, Jan Halderman, were manning one of the forward .50-caliber machine guns. The blast knocked us both away from the gun. Jan was down on the deck, hurt pretty badly in the neck. I was down there with him trying to get a pressure bandage out to put on his wound. Then I felt something running down my eyes, reached up, and found out it was blood. So I panicked a little bit myself. First I got Jan taken care of, then I was trying to get somebody to look at my head.

I thought maybe I had been wounded pretty badly in the head. I could see my helmet lying on the deck and there was a big hole in it. The corpsman or one of my other Teammates just kind of told me to shut up, that there were other people who were really hurt in the boat. Later I found out that Lieutenant Dan Mann was killed along with Don Boston, who had gone through class thirty-four with me, and Ron Neil.

That was one of the SEAL Teams' worst single losses due to enemy fire during the Vietnam War. Not only were three men killed, but a large number were wounded as well. In fact, I'm not sure anyone on the boat escaped some kind of injury. Mine was pretty light, though my helmet didn't look like this was so. I spent one night in the hospital, then got up and hitchhiked back to the base.

The Stoner machine gun was the SEALs' weapon of choice in Vietnam. It was a belt-fed small machine gun that fired the same round of ammunition as the M-16 rifle. It carried a 150-round belt and could put out its ammunition at 850 rounds per minute on the average. Each squad tried to have at least two Stoners with it on every mission.

On my second tour, we were going in on an ambush, transporting in an LCPL. We had probably an hour or so to go to get to our landing site and I was doing what a lot of combat men do in such a situation. I was asleep. You get up about 1 A.M. to prep yourself and your gear. Then get on board the transport going in to the insertion point. I just always liked to grab a little extra sleep before insertion time.

Since I had experience in that part of Vietnam, I was helping to break in a new platoon. Three other guys from my platoon were helping as well. We were going in on a predawn ambush. My fire team was in the front of the LCPL, which is a small cabin maybe eight by fifteen feet. There were eight of us in the cabin and one of the guys, Walter Pope, had stacked his Stoner right next to where he was sitting on the deck.

We must have hit the wake of a sampan or some other wave. But the motion knocked Walter's Stoner over; it hit the deck and the retaining pin fell out of the action. The retaining pin holds the bottom trigger mechanism to the weapon, letting the trigger and sear hold the bolt in the cocked position. When the weapon opens up, there's nothing to keep the bolt from going forward and the weapon just starts firing uncontrollably.

From what the doctors tell me, I was immediately hit by six to ten rounds from that Stoner. What was later explained to me was that Walter Pope grabbed up his weapon and pulled it to his chest to try to control it. And that has to be so since there were eight of us in the front of that boat and only Walter and I were hit. The six to ten rounds that hit me were bad, but Walter took over forty rounds when he pulled the gun into himself. He died instantly and I passed out.

Before I slipped away, I cried out, "Ambush!" When that sudden firing woke me up, I fully believed we were being ambushed by the VC. Only later did I realize what had happened. If it hadn't been for Walter pulling that weapon into himself, I don't see how any of us in that cabin could have escaped. He sacrificed himself for his Teammates.

In spite of our losses, the SEALs were very successful in their operations in Vietnam. We operated in small groups and could move very quietly through the night. We could sneak up on a position, or just hide in the darkness, and wait until the enemy practically came within arm's reach. And the VC weren't expecting us, they weren't listening for us. And we could get close enough to kill them with a knife, and we did.

The SEALs of today should know the debt they have to the Teammates who came before them. The men like Roy Boehm, who started the Teams, and others who opened the way in Vietnam. We all come from frogman stock, so there's a big debt to those men from before the SEALs, back to World War II, who started it all.

I was one of the men lucky enough to have been in the Teams during the Vietnam War, during which the SEALs made their name known. But the men who came before then are the ones who made me. And the SEALs of today were made by those of us back then.

Even when we didn't have a separate insignia to wear, people on a Navy base knew who a SEAL was. Today it's the same man, but he also has the Trident he can wear. But all of the SEALs are the same underneath. We are all tough. You put seven of us together and we're a Team. Those guys are my brothers. You put seven of us together and nobody can whip us.

■ Chapter 33

The Job

In the SEAL Teams and the UDTs, men were often asked to volunteer for some very unusual assignments. A single operator with a long career in Navy Special Warfare could find himself in a number of unusual situations. It is to the SEALs' credit that all missions and assignments were considered and no worthwhile idea was left unacted upon.

The kinds of missions and assignments that were offered to the Teams include learning an esoteric skill, qualifying on an unusual piece of hardware, or participating in a scientific study or experiment. All of these were conducted at one time or another in the Teams.

One thing that is always a constant in the Teams is the level of trust between Teammates. Each man knows the others can be depended on completely. When one man cannot complete a job, others will join in until the job is finished. It is their sense of brotherhood that causes many men in the SEALs and the UDTs to risk everything for a Teammate. Though these men are patriotic to the extreme, they do not always accept the hardships and do the difficult for their country, or even the Navy or their families. But they always do it for each other.

There is a bond between partners in the Teams that is hard to explain to the outsider. Even when that partner isn't human. . . .

Bill Bruhmuller, Master Chief Boatswain's Mate, USN (Ret.)

A strange set of happenings led me into the UDTs and then SEAL Team Two. When I came into the Navy in January 1953, the Korean War was still going on and I wanted to be active and do my part like so many of my peers did. At that time I only thought the Navy owned things like battleships, aircraft carriers, destroyers, and submarines. I didn't know anything about the Amphibious Force or the minesweeping force.

As luck would have it, I did not get my requested assignment aboard a battleship. Instead, I ended up in what was called a receiving station in Charleston, South Carolina. For about 15 months all I did was the general work assigned to new untrained sailors in the Navy. Mess duty in the galley and all the other jobs the low man on the totem pole does. It didn't take too long for me to notice the guys being transferred from the jobs that I was doing onto the little wooden minesweepers. During my Charleston tour, I had the occasion to ride one of these minesweepers and I quickly became satisfied that it was not what I wanted to do.

Fortunately, the plan of the day came out prior to my getting orders to the minesweeping fleet and it had a request out on it for volunteers for underwater demolition training. I didn't know anything about UDT but thought it sounded good and that I should check it out. One of the first requirements for UDT was that you had to pass a swimming test. That didn't sound like any problem for me; I had always been a good swimmer.

Going over to the testing area, I took the PT test and swimming test, passed them, and thought this was going to be a piece of cake. Then I talked to several of the older guys who had been around awhile. All they could tell me about UDT was that going to UDT was crazy and that I didn't know what I was doing. But they would never tell me what UDT was all about.

My orders came in and I was on my way to Little Creek and UDT training. This was what I had wanted, to go to a Navy school. My parents had always told me that the Navy had the finest schools of all of the services and to get into as many of them as I could.

Arriving in Norfolk on a Sunday, I had to take a taxi down to Little Creek, which was basically all farmland in those days. Dropped off at the main gate, I had to walk a couple of miles with my seabag on my shoulder, down to a building where I checked in with a guy. He told me to grab a bunk and that they would get with me in the morning. I stayed in that building for three days without hearing from anybody. Finally, I started searching around and found out where I really was supposed to be. There was a receiving station that was a holding billet for a couple of weeks until the next training class started.

Then training started and I got the surprise of my life. I was waiting for my little copy of the curriculum and the class agenda, and my book and pencil. That was not what I received. What I did get was a boot in the fanny, a couple of sharp words, and the orders to fall in smartly.

The class was something like 138 people at the start. Within a matter of weeks we were down to 60 men, then 50, then 40, and the class size continued to drop. Hell Week was the third week of training then. Fortunately for me, just a class or two prior to my training, Hell Week had been the first week of training. If I had gotten off of that taxi, stepped onto that base, and gone right into Hell Week, it would have really been a shocker. Three weeks later was enough of a stunner.

There really wasn't any preparation, at least not enough to get you ready for that intense training. That was probably what caused a lot of people to drop the program: they weren't physically prepared. Being eighteen years old and in fairly good shape worked in my favor, so running, push-ups, and such didn't bother me as much as they could have. And as training went on I got better and better.

But Hell Week was the real eye-opener as far as sitting in a classroom and learning things from an instructor standing on a platform was concerned. But I was going to learn a lot from the group of instructors who were running around beside me, booting me in the pants and yelling and screaming at me, belittling me, and doing everything they possibly could to make me want to go away.

Now I was in the position of still not wanting to get aboard that minesweeper, and seeing what the Amphibious Forces had in the way of ships. LSTs, AKAs, APAs, and other landing ships I also certainly didn't want to go aboard. So the only option I had was to try to stick this training out and see where it led. I am very glad I did this. It set up the rest of my Navy career, for which I am extremely thankful.

My class was class thirteen and there were 21 of us standing there that last day at graduation, seven officers and 14 enlisted men. Along the way, 117 people had quit, so that made us a very proud and select few. In those days we had two Teams, UDT 21 and 22 on the East Coast, and UDTs 1, 3, and 5 on the West Coast. Each coast ran its own training then and the graduates stayed in their respective areas.

My fellow graduates and I were given the option of UDT 21 or 22, and I selected 22. Several of the people I had come to know during training were at Team 22 and that's why I selected it. My class was almost split in half between Teams 21 and 22.

There's no question, of course, that the East Coast had the harder training. Now, before my West Coast Teammates start sniping at me, I should really say that both coasts had equally hard training. The quality of graduates from either program stands on its own. The whole objective of UDTR, and later BUD/S, training was to try to get the student to graduation mentally prepared for whatever his career in Special Warfare might hold for him. Neither coast had the option of relaxing its standards when it came to training. This resulted in fit, prepared men who had gone through the hardest training available in the U.S. military. This level of fitness also resulted in some strange assignments for UDT operators.

In 1957, the United States still hadn't gotten into space proper. We had launched gondolas from balloons and rocket planes had gotten men up to 150,000 feet or so, but a man hadn't really gone into space yet. There was a difference of opinion between scientists as to what kind of person, from a technical and physical perspective, it would take to get into space and survive the trip. The scientific people felt that the person would have to be superior technically because there was so much involved in the instrumentation and all the other factors involved in going into space. The other, much smaller group felt that the individual had to be a physically superior specimen to do the job and have the best chance of returning safely.

There was an Air Force Captain McGuire who was able to convince the powers that be to let him go out and find the best physical specimens he could. That captain received permission to basically shop through the services for men. He ended up coming to the Underwater Demolition Teams at Little Creek, where twelve men were selected for the program.

The twelve of us who were chosen were transferred to Wright-Patterson Air Force Base in Ohio, initially for two weeks. We went up to the base in groups of four to a cordoned-off, secure area. From 6:00 in the morning to 6:00 in the evening, we worked, doing just as many tests as the scientist could possibly do.

For example, we sat in a heat chamber at 140 degrees for three hours. They wanted to see our reactions—would we remain stable, get antsy, or just what the exposure to heat would do to the human mind and body. They had a series of serums they injected into us and then a scientist would sit there and talk to you for probably about 60 seconds. He would tell you your mouth was getting watery and then your whole body would seem to turn red and you felt that you were burning up inside. Then they would immediately stick your feet into a pan of ice water. It was our reactions to sudden extremes that many of the tests were examining.

The cordoned-off section of the base prepared for us had its own barracks and private mess hall. There were MPs guarding the roads so no traffic or anything else could come near us. We were not to be disturbed at all. You take four UDT sailors who are used to a lot harder schedule than 6:00 to 6:00 and park them on an Air Force base: they will become a little bored. There was not that much of a physical demand put on us, certainly nothing compared with our initial training. So for the first week we pretty much adhered to their rules. By the second week the TV, which really wasn't all that great in those days, wore thin fast.

We would get up and maybe go for a little run in the mornings, something the guys would mostly just do on their own. By the second week we decided to venture out a bit and see what town was like. All we had with us was one Navy white dress uniform and the rest of our clothes were our regular green UDT fatigues. Since we didn't have a car, we would have to hitchhike into town anyway, so why not wear the white uniform? It would be easier to get a ride, since people in those days would readily pick up a serviceman.

There wasn't a real big problem for us to get past the guards at the base and around our building. We hit the road and started thumbing our way into town. We discovered an amazing number of young ladies who wanted to give young sailors a ride. This turned out to be a pretty good exercise for us. We would dance and have a few drinks, just a generally good social evening, and probably get back to the barracks around 1 or 2 A.M.

It was quite evident to Dr. McGuire that something was different about us the next morning. The procedure was, if you were going to make a high-altitude run in the pressure chamber, you had to prebreathe pure oxygen before the test. So they put a flight suit helmet on you and you breathed oxygen for a couple of hours to take all the nitrogen out of your system. Having your head in that helmet put you in a closed, tight compartment with little noise surrounding you. And the several hours of just breathing was pretty boring, and the extra sleep didn't sound too bad after the longish night before.

The scientists were not used to having their test subjects react as we did. The tight helmets often caused claustrophobia. To us, it wasn't much different than wearing a face mask on a dive. We just went to sleep. And when they woke us up, we would tell them to leave us alone. It was when we went into the test chamber that things changed a little bit.

When we were all wired up to record our reactions, the doctor would look at his readouts and ask us what we had done the night before. He would ask us if we had gone out on the town the night before and we would just tell him we watched a little TV and went to bed. But that we woke up about midnight and just couldn't get back to sleep.

There wasn't much question that he knew what was going on. When he asked us if we had been drinking, we could easily tell him that there wasn't anyplace in our limited area where we could go drinking. And that we were staying religiously dedicated to the program. It was to his credit that he never tried to discourage what was going on. He knew what we were doing. But the combination of our daily activity and our nightly escapades made answering his questions even better.

There wasn't much question that we were fit enough to take on the doctor's daily physical activity. And our enthusiasm for our nighttime activities gave him an end result that was even more than he had expected. And the results were rewarding for us as well. You knew that you were doing something worthwhile. As well as learning things about yourself that you probably never would have otherwise gotten the chance to learn.

We were "flying" in the big centrifuge, all of us pulling about eleven Gs. One of the guys, Tom McAlllister, passed out. And the reason Tom passed out was that he was too relaxed. That sounds unusual, but normal anxiety can keep some of the muscles twitching more, keep the blood moving better, and push more of it up to your head. Full relaxation will let the blood drain from your head and you'll just pass out.

Even though we were high-level physical specimens, it didn't prove necessary to be like us to go into space. The recent space flight by John Glenn helps prove that. He's a kind of national hero who has taken care of himself over the years. His attitude is so positive that there didn't seem to be anything bad that could happen to him on his space shuttle flight. And it's a great example for those people in the population who are reaching sixty and seventy years old. It shows there may be some life in the old body yet.

And being one of the people who helped to literally open the door on the manned

Bill Bruhmuller during a SEAL demonstration at St. Thomas in the U.S. Virgin Islands in 1964. He is wearing a Rolex watch as well as a Mk 1 Mod 0 compass on his left wrist. In his left hand is the transducer for the AN/PQC-1 UTEL underwater telephone hanging from his right hip. His breathing rig is the closed-circuit Draeger Model LT. Lund II.

Richard Brozack Collection

space program feels pretty good. And I'm sure the other individuals who were up there with me feel equally good about it. The small part we played was one of the stepping-stones for what we are doing today. It's nice to know you were a contributor to that. And what seems particularly fitting is that Captain Bill Shepherd is going to be the first commander of the space station, and Bill Shepherd was also a SEAL. So the group of us back then helped pave the way for Bill, and I let him know it every time I see him. But that's just friendly in-house harassment.

It was only a few years later that I had another first adventure in the UDTs. Prior to the commissioning of SEAL Team Two, there were some indications that I was going to be selected by this new special organization. Nobody would tell you what its members were going to do, what the mission was, or even how big the units were going to be. We didn't even know if it was going to be located at Little Creek. No information was coming out on the new Team. All that was told to some of us was that after the first of the year (1962) we were going to be assigned to this new unit. You did have the option of refusing the assignment. But any guy in the Team, if you give him the chance to try something new or something that's going to be a challenge, he's going to be very reluctant to turn it down. So I certainly wanted to take the new assignment on, and that was the only way I could learn about what it was going to be.

The original group was only about ten people. Roy Boehm was our officer-in-charge and we had yet to be officially formed up, but we were getting close to it. We met in a little office over in UDT and stood around wondering what we were supposed to do. So we tried to at least look busy, really just kind of fake it through the day until commissioning came through. When Rudy Boesch came out during a muster on January 8 and read the names of the members in the new Team, we were all excited to have been selected. By that formation, we had some twenty-five guys and that number soon jumped up to fifty.

There was still a lot of anticipation about what we were going to do. And that was the big question, what was our mission? All we could find out was that we were going to be an unconventional warfare unit. That kind of set your mind to working. That assignment meant we would have to be sneaky, and we would have to be trained in a lot of other special areas that we hadn't studied for our UDT mission.

Roy Boehm, being the crusty old gentleman that he is, knew that if the Navy was going to start an organization like this, the best way to keep its members strong and get them ready for what might be coming was to get them trained in whatever and wherever they possibly could. So he arranged schools all over the country. This was when we really got our interface with the Army Special Forces down at Fort Bragg. A lot of the young SEALs today don't realize this, but if it hadn't been for Special Forces, I'm not sure we would have gotten off of dead center as easily as we did. We owe a lot of thanks to them. And I don't hesitate to convey that to the young lads in the Teams today.

Some of the materials we trained with over the years involved some really exotic hardware. And eventually, a few of us worked with the most exotic piece of hardware there was. The weapon was called the SADM—Small Atomic Demolition Munition. It was a nuclear weapon that could be delivered by a couple of people to an objective area. The SADM could be swum in submerged, towed by a swimmer pair, or parachuted in. Both individuals were trained on setting up and arming the device. Then they were to exfiltrate and there would be a nuclear blast.

As I recall, the bomb was maybe a maximum of three feet long and probably between twenty-four and thirty inches in diameter. This was after it had been taken out of its large, sealed packaging of course. When I was selected to participate in training on the activation of the device, and we were given the briefing on what it was and its capability, it really scared the hell out of me. There was a really great potential here for a massive screwup.

I just thought that things go wrong sometimes. But if this one went wrong, I wouldn't be around to know about it. I think I had kind of mixed emotions about working with the SADM. One thing was that I wasn't afraid to get involved with the thing. But I was very afraid to make a mistake with it. This was something really highly technical. It wasn't like another explosive charge or demolition technique, nothing of that nature. This was something that could cause massive destruction. So I was just very con-

Silver, one of SEAL Team Two's German shepherd Scout Dogs demonstrates the view an unwary Viet Cong could expect to see.

U.S. Navy

cerned that I might do something wrong so that it wouldn't explode, wouldn't do its job. What it could do to me didn't really enter my thoughts. I had to learn how to handle it, and to do that properly.

Prior to SEAL Team Two's direct involvement in Vietnam, I had watched the news clips of the war and what had been going on in that country. In a number of the clips, I saw Marines and Air Force personnel going on patrol, and there were dogs in the scene. So I had the idea that maybe there was a mission involving dogs with the SEALs. By this time we pretty well knew we would be doing patrolling, ambushing, and things of this nature. A dog offered something beyond what the human was capable of, and that was their senses of hearing and smell. If that was going to be an advantage to us, to help us in our missions, I felt that we should examine its feasibility.

So I went to our commanding officer at the time, Bill Earley, and talked to him about the idea. He agreed that if I could get a dog and get the training needed, we would give the idea a try. There wasn't enough time before I was scheduled to deploy to Vietnam to go to the formal military dog school at Fort Benning. So if I could get some basic training from the Norfolk police force, Bill agreed to back my suggestion.

There were only about ten weeks before I was to deploy. I called the Norfolk police, the K9 force; Bob Bouchard was their training officer at the time. After explaining my idea to him, I asked if there was any possibility of coming up with a dog. He wasn't quite sure if he could do that, but he promised to call me back inside of twenty-four hours with some kind of an answer.

Fortunately, Officer Bouchard called me back and said that someone had just donated a dog we could have. After talking the situation over with his command, he had found out that the idea was okay with the police if the Navy would release me for the standard six-week K9 police training. That was okay with everyone involved and I went out for the training.

The dog was a big German shepherd named Prince and we went through training very well. The police had attack training, search training, and things of that nature that still looked like they would fit our mission. There isn't a lot of difference between a house and a hooch as far as searching goes. So I saw some value in all of the training. There was the opportunity to fire on the range with the dog lying beside you to see if the animal had any problems with the loud noise. Prince had no anxieties about the firing and that was another plus for him since I wouldn't have time to worry about the dog once the shooting started.

Prince was an exceptional dog and he learned very quickly. On graduation day, he graduated number one in his class and I think I came in number two. But we became very close and we deployed to Vietnam together. What I hadn't known was that we would be deploying to the Mekong Delta area of South Vietnam. That is a very muddy area.

During the dry season, everything was fine. The dog would go with us on patrols and we could use him very well. When we set up an ambush I could have the dog lying right beside me. He knew when something was coming down the trail or canal well before any of us. You could tell by the way his ears moved, and the way he would look in a particular direction and his nose would go up in the air. He gave us the early warning system that was so valuable in the performance of our jobs. We would know what direction something was coming from and surprise tended to be on our side.

We used the dog on patrols and hooch searches as well. Prince found several weapons caches in hooches just because of the smell. I did have him out on a patrol one day when his searching abilities became something of a bother. During our training together at the police K9 unit, we always trained for a length of time together and then took a break. Just like a human, the break allows the dog to relax and come down from what he was doing. The dog remains in a work profile until you tell him that you're going on a break. You just change your voice and tell him, "Take a break!"

Now, this is play time, and Prince would wander off to do dog things. He would never go very far and would always immediately return when called. So there I was, just kind of sitting there, leaning up against a tree, and Prince came back and dropped some toy he had found right between my legs. It was a hand grenade.

That scared me to death. He just backed up and looked at me. In his mind, he had just found a ball and he wanted me to throw it so he could chase it. So I took it away and said, "No!" He went away, and came back with another one. Again, he dropped it between my legs and I took it away again. He did this three times and dropped all three grenades between my legs.

Something was going to blow eventually if I didn't find out where the dog was getting the grenades. So I followed Prince and found where he had uncovered a fairly large weapons cache. He was pulling out the hand grenades and bringing them to me, thinking they were balls.

Prince was later awarded a Purple Heart for his actions while we were on a standard patrolling operation one day. We were looking for some North Vietnamese who had supposedly infiltrated down into the delta. We ran into a small ambush while patrolling. It was quite surprising that he didn't pick up on it before the ambush was triggered. Prince was acting strange, but he didn't do the normal alert indicating that someone was to the right, left, or directly in front. I think this might have been because the enemy had been there for some time.

They initiated the ambush and there were a lot of hand grenades being thrown back and forth. Prince didn't get shot or hit with a grenade. I think it was a 40mm grenade that went off very close to us that hit him with some fragmentation in his side. That wasn't enough to stop him during the action and he was later awarded the Purple Heart.

Chief William Bruhmuller and Prince after their first tour in Vietnam. Prince is wearing the Purple Heart he received for being wounded during an ambush in Vietnam. The action took place during the first SEAL Team Two combat deployments of the Vietnam War.

U.S. Navy

In this deployment, Prince and I were part of the first SEAL Team Two platoons deployed to Vietnam. People have different impressions of what it's like to go into combat. I was in the Dominican Republic operation some years earlier and some people consider that to have been active combat. But when you get into a country like Vietnam where the fighting is really very serious, you have thoughts about what you may run into and how big a force you may have to fight.

The SEALs sometimes operated in three-man or six-man groups, depending on the mission. We all had the inherent confidence in ourselves and our abilities that we could handle most anything that was tossed at us. But when it comes right down to seeing a mass of people firing at you, and you have to shoot them before they kill you, there are some anxieties you are going to have. I can still remember the first guy I ever shot. It was in a river. And I swear I can still see him today. There was probably a fraction of a second of hesitation on my part before I pulled the trigger. There was still that quick reaction in my mind where I wondered if there was something else I could do besides kill this guy. My common sense won out before he was able to open fire.

Once you have passed through that first incident, you realize that this is the job that you have been trained to do. And you try to do your job to the very best of your ability. Every SEAL I know, or at least the very great majority of them, develops a mind-set that; regardless of how horrendous the situation might be and what the end picture looks like, they all possess the ability to do what they have to. That's probably the reason why the majority of the SEALs who served in combat in Vietnam don't have the flashbacks and things that so many of the other military forces have had.

These were young kids who fought in that war. And these were horrendous experiences to many of them. To see body parts flying around and battle taking place can be quite shattering to someone who places a value on human life. And seeing how fast that life can be taken away will affect many people. So in order to maintain the peace of your own mind, just do your job and forget about it. And I think everyone possesses that ability.

■ Chapter 34

The Testing Ground

The Vietnam War was to prove to be the crucible that would test the SEAL Team concept. All that had gone before with the UDTs, the actions in Korea, WWII, the Scouts and Raiders, and finally the NCDUs on Normandy Beach laid the groundwork for the SEALs. Vietnam would prove what they had become, the finest unconventional fighting force of the United States military.

Every skill the SEALs had would be tested to the utmost in the rivers, streams, and canals of a small country at the outermost edge of the Southeast Asian mainland. They would soon prove worthy of the legend that grew up around their actions during seven years of active combat.

And the story of the SEALs was just beginning.

The Trident

The only outward sign of a uniformed Navy man being a SEAL, besides his high level of fitness and air of cool assuredness, is the Navy Special Warfare Breast Insignia he wears on the left breast of his uniform. The Trident, as it is called by the men who wear it, can be properly worn only by an individual who has completed the Basic Underwater Demolition/SEAL (BUD/S) course of instruction or the earlier Underwater Demolition Team Replacement (UDTR) course and a six-month probationary tour with a SEAL Team.

Receiving their Trident is a significant moment for all of the men of the SEAL Teams. Some of these men can put their feelings into words, while others have a hard time expressing their emotion at such an event. And a very few others can describe the Trident in very proper SEAL terms understandable to all members of the Teams.

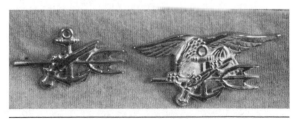

The UDT breast insignia on the left and the Naval Special Warfare uniform breast insignia on the right. The UDT insignia was only issued for a few years before it was decided that both the UDTs and the SEALs would wear the same uniform device.

Kevin Dockery

Barry W. Enoch, Chief Gunner's Mate, USN (Ret.)

When we first became SEALs, we were given our Tridents. The Tridents for enlisted men were silver at that time and the ones for officers and chiefs were gold, to match our uniforms. Later on, the gold Trident became standard for all Navy SEALs and Navy SEALs only.

The Trident itself is a breast insignia. The lower part of it displays an anchor, indicating the branch of service, the United States Navy. Neptune's scepter—trident spear—is crossed with the anchor, indicating that we work from and under the sea. There's a half-cocked pistol, an old flintlock type, showing that we're always at the ready. But to me the most important part of it is the American eagle, which stands watch over the anchor, standing on the trident and holding the pistol.

The American eagle was selected because of his keen eyesight. He's a bird of prey that flies higher than any other bird. The stronger the winds and higher the air currents, the better he likes it. He selects a mate for life and he builds his home and returns to it each year. That nest he rebuilds each year.

And he feeds his mate while she's on her nest. When the young are hatched out, he helps feed them. He's one of the only birds that helps teach his young to fly when they're ready to leave the nest.

You'll find the American eagle in a lot of places. You'll find him on the President's Seal. You'll find him on guard over the Ten Commandments behind the Supreme Court. And you'll find the American eagle at the top of a flagstaff and on an officer's hat device.

In all of these places, you'll find the eagle standing tall and proud. But only on the Trident does he bow his head. And when I think back on the men in combat, the ones who are always standing on the edge ... the ones who have been wounded, and the ones who have died ... I think I can understand why he bows his head.

And that's what the Trident means to me.

The U.S. Navy's UDT Combat Swimmer.

U.S. Navy

Today's Navy SEALs proudly carry forward the traditions laid down before them in the deserts of the Middle East, the swamps of Vietnam, the frozen wastes of Korea, and the beaches of the Pacific and Atlantic Oceans.

Andre Dallau

■ Chapter 35

The Arena

Southeast Asia is made up of the Indochinese and Malay Peninsulas as well as a number of large island groups. The area is bordered on the north by China, to the west and south by the Indian Ocean and the Indian subcontinent, and to the east by the Pacific. Countries contained within Southeast Asia include Brunei, Burma, Cambodia, Indonesia, Laos, Malaysia, the Philippines, Singapore, Thailand, and Vietnam.

At the easternmost edge of Southeast Asia is Vietnam. Bordered to the west by Cambodia and Laos, and to the north by China, Vietnam's entire eastern and southern boundaries lie along the South China Sea and into the Gulf of Thailand. Prior to the end of World War II, the entire area of Laos, Cambodia, and Vietnam was part of Indochina, popularly called French Indochina. With the fall of France to the Germans early in the war, the French government's control of Indochina grew loose.

The power held by Japan over French Indochina had grown stronger even before France's fall to the Germans. By March 1941, the Japanese dictated a peace settlement regarding Indochina in order to end an invasion by Siamese

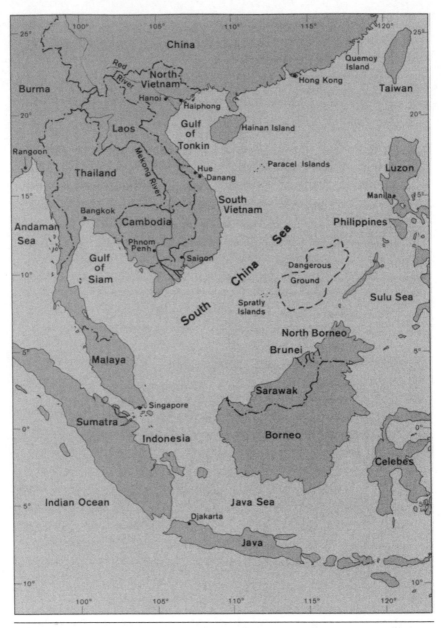

Southeast Asia.

U.S. Navy

(later Thai) forces into what was later to become Laos and Cambodia. The Japanese had encouraged Siam's invasion . With the peace settlement, French Indochina became, in effect, a Japanese protectorate, complete with occupying troops.

The people of Indochina had suffered through a war between the French and the Germans before. During the First World War, 100,000 Vietnamese labored in France to help the French war effort. During that time, Nguyen Tat Thanh, from Hanoi, was living in Paris. Becoming politically active for his people during the First World War, Nguyen changed his name to Nguyen Ai Quoc, which translates to "Nguyen the Patriot."

Fascinated by the Communist revolution in Russia and their overthrow of the czars, Nguyen went to Moscow. After studying there during the early 1920s, he became a staunch Communist and believer in the Communist doctrine. Struggling for the independence of his people from French rule, Nguyen eventually returned to Indochina after the beginning of the Second World War.

Back in his home country, Nguyen established the Viet Nam Doc Lap Dong Minh, the League for Independence of Vietnam, commonly called the Viet Minh. The Viet Minh was a coalition of both Communists and nationalists who wanted to see their country become independent. Nguyen also changed his name, this time for good. It was by this name that he would be identified for decades to come —Ho Chi Minh.

The Viet Minh fought both the Vichy French and the Japanese forces in Indochina during the war. Ho Chi Minh even met with representatives of the OSS in April 1945. In exchange for training and weapons, the Viet Minh combined forces with the United States in their campaign against the Japanese Empire.

With the Japanese surrender in August 1945, the Viet Minh moved quickly to secure their own country before the return of the French. The Democratic Republic of Vietnam was established on 2 September 1945 with Ho Chi Minh as president.

But Chinese and British forces moved in to occupy the new Vietnam in preparation for the return of French rule. The British secured the area of Viet nam south of the sixteenth parallel while the Chinese moved 200,000 troops into the north area. The Viet Minh agreed to allow French troops into the north area in order to help get rid of the Chinese, but after the Chinese had left, the French remained.

By November 1946, war had broken out between the Viet Minh and the French. Fighting the same kind of guerrilla war they had conducted against the Japanese, the Viet Minh operated under Ho Chi Minh's military commander, Vo Nguyen Giap. The Viet Minh were winning out against the French forces until the United States responded to French requests for aid in late 1949.

During the early 1950s, the United States recognized the Bao Dai govern-

Ho Chi Minh.

U.S. Navy

ment of Vietnam, based in Saigon. Bao Dai had been the puppet ruler of the area during the Japanese occupation. But Bao Dai was not a Communist, and anti-Communist feelings were running strong in the United States, especially with the beginning of the Korean War in 1950.

In spite of their situation, the Viet Minh successfully fought the French in the north of Vietnam until the Battle of Dien Bien Phu in 1954. With the defeat of the French during that epic conflict on 7 May 1954, the Viet Minh won the first Indochina war.

With the Communist government under Ho Chi Minh in control of Hanoi and the Bao Dai government in Saigon, the country was divided into North Vietnam and South Vietnam along the seventeenth parallel according to an agreement reached in Geneva in mid-1954. This was intended to be a temporary situation until nationwide elections could be held the next year.

But Bao Dai left Vietnam before the agreement went into effect, appointing Ngo Dinh Diem as prime minister. The United States, never having signed the cease-fire accords, supported the democratic government of South Vietnam over the Communist one to the north. By early 1961, the U.S. was backing the Diem government with military support. In the countryside and jungles of South Vietnam, the Viet Minh, veterans of years of conflict with the Japanese and the French, moved in to conduct a guerrilla war against the government of South Vietnam. These guerrilla fighters would soon become well known to U.S. troops as the Viet Cong.

■   ■   ■

PHYSICALLY, the whole of North and South Vietnam is over 1,000 miles long with a wide northern and southern area connected by a "waist" fewer than forty miles wide at one point. The country is shaped roughly like the letter *S*, and both parts of it total only about 128,000 square miles, roughly the size of the state of New Mexico.

Geographically, the two countries range from mountains in the north, snowcapped throughout the year, to a huge area of mangrove swamps and flat river-delta terrain to the far south. The land in between these two extremes includes jungle areas and triple-canopy rain forests that contain a wide variety of animal, reptile, and insect life.

All of Vietnam has a tropical monsoon climate. Seasonal temperatures in North Vietnam range from about 62 degrees F. in the winter (January) to 100-plus degrees F. in the summer months (from mid-May to mid-September), the hot and humid wet season.

Temperature changes in South Vietnam are less severe, averaging from 78 to 84 degrees throughout the year. But the humidity level is high, especially during the rainy season, which lasts from May to November. Torrential downpours are constant occurrences during the height of the monsoon season. During June and July, the average monthly rainfall is normally over a foot, peaking again in September.

This heavy rainfall, combined with the rich soil of the Mekong Delta, makes the southern part of South Vietnam some of the most fertile land on earth. The Mekong Delta makes up close to a quarter of South Vietnam's landmass, with an area of some 14,000 square miles. As the Mekong River passes through the delta, it splits into two major tributaries, the Bassac River to the south and the Mekong to the north. About halfway through the delta on its trip to the sea, the waters of the Mekong split again into three smaller tributaries, the My Tho River to the north, the Ham Luong River in the center, and the Co Chien River to the south. The major rivers of the Mekong Delta are interconnected by various smaller tributaries, which are themselves connected by a vast network of streams and canals. In all, there are nine major tributaries in the Mekong Delta, dozens of streams, and hundreds of canals. Almost no area of the delta is more than a mile or so from a waterway that eventually connects to the South China Sea or the Gulf of Thailand.

The alluvial sediment that makes up the Mekong Delta is the reason the area is so fertile. Rice paddies are seen throughout the producing farmland. In between them are areas of twisted mangroves, especially along the banks of the many waterways. But there are also fields of huge elephant grass, which can grow ten feet high and completely block any view of the land. Banana groves are also scattered throughout the area, along with pineapple fields and areas of bamboo, nipa palm, and even full-sized forests.

Southeast of the South Vietnamese capital of Saigon, bordered on the south by the Soirap River, on the north by the Long Tau River, and on the east

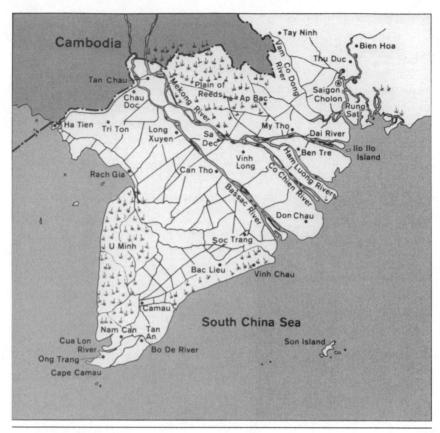

The Mekong Delta.

U.S. Navy

by the South China Sea, lies the Rung Sat (Vietnamese for "dense jungle") swamp. Known to the Vietnamese as the Forest of Assassins, the Rung Sat Swamp was called the Rung Sat Special Zone or RSSZ by U.S. forces.

The almost 400 square miles of the Rung Sat contain rich soil that encourages plant growth, a fact illustrated by the heavy jungles found throughout the region. Twisted mangrove roots line the banks of the hundreds of waterways that crisscross the Rung Sat. Among the mangroves grow nipa palm and other hardy plants, making penetration past the banks lining the water very difficult in areas. This same heavy plant growth conceals the areas of land in the Rung Sat between the waterways. For hundreds of years, pirates, smugglers, and other criminals used the Rung Sat for concealment, giving them a base from which they could safely prey on river shipping going into and out of Saigon.

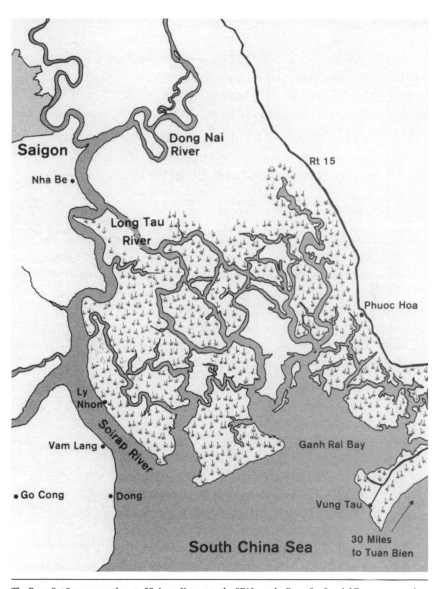

The Rung Sat Swamp, southeast of Saigon. Known to the SEALs as the Rung Sat Special Zone, or more simply, just the Rung Sat.

The Viet Cong used the Rung Sat as a safe haven just as the pirates before them had done.

This was the area where the SEALs would first see active combat in Vietnam. Within months, their actions would spread farther south from the Rung Sat into the Mekong Delta. In the steaming jungles and thick mud, the abilities of the SEALs would be tested to extremes. And it is there where the legend of the Teams would first be written.

Scott R. Lyon, Lieutenant Commander, USN (Ret.)

In 1952, I enlisted in the U.S. Navy, and that was also the year I first heard about the Underwater Demolition Teams. When I learned about the UDTs during boot camp, I tried to go directly from boot to UDTR training at Little Creek. The trouble was, I wasn't twenty-one years old yet. Because the Korean War was going on, anyone under the age of twenty-one had to have their parents' consent in order to volunteer for the UDTs. I didn't have that consent, so I had to wait.

There was a movie I saw one time that showed me the Navy Frogmen; in fact, I think that was the title of the film—The Frogmen. Since I liked to swim, and I had heard about the adventure you could experience as a Navy Frogman, and I always liked adventure, the UDTs sounded like just the place I wanted to be.

The view of the Rung Sat Special Zone from a helicopter flying overhead. Far off to the upper left is Saigon. It was in this maze of rivers, streams, and canals that the SEALs first took on the Viet Cong on their home ground.

U.S. Navy

My route to the Teams was interesting. In those days, the 1950s, there wasn't a lot of paperwork involved in the Navy. I had just completed Explosive Ordnance Disposal school and hardhat diving school. Two classmates of mine, Eve Barrett and Charles Neirgarth, both said that I should go to the Teams. Since I was over twenty-one now, I didn't need anyone's consent, and the Teams still looked very good to me.

My friends and I went down to the Long Branch bar that Friday and had a couple of brews, discussing the situation. My wife and children were both in Washington, D.C., where the hardhat divers' school was located. But without my family even knowing, I went down to Little Creek and was put into UDTR training with Class 25 that night.

I had been looking forward to UDTR training for some time, and now I suddenly found myself right in the middle of it. Having always been kind of a fun person, I just jumped right in and loved every minute of it.

Personally, I didn't have any real trouble with any of the UDTR training. When we graduated, we had the usual party. When someone at the party asked me what I had thought of training, I said I thought it was pretty easy. And I really meant that. But that caused a little conflict among some of the guys who were already in the Teams.

But the simple fact was that I really loved what we did, even in training. Class 25 at Little Creek was a winter class in 1960–61. The second day I was there, it snowed. But in January, we went down to Puerto Rico for further training and that was great. In PR, the water was great, the weather was the same, and it was just fun training.

One night down in Puerto Rico, I had the midwatch in the students' barracks. It was the middle of the night and I was in this building full of sleeping students, making sure the place didn't catch fire and burn down around them.

During that long night, I just decided that everyone else should be up. So I put the lights on in the barracks. With the help of another student on midwatch, Chet Langworthy, I proceeded to wake up everyone there.

Waking the people up, we gave them the instructions to form up in the classroom. Each person was to bring with them one swim fin, one black sock, and their bathing suit. And they were to fall in to class for instruction. These weird instructions were something the instructors had been throwing at us for weeks. So everyone just got up and did what we had told them.

I thought that was a really funny joke. The rest of my class might not have thought so. But they were all so sleepy, they never did figure out who had played that trick on them.

Going through training, I learned something about myself; everyone does. I always thought I had the drive to go forward, to never quit. Whenever I'm given a task to do, I follow through and complete the job to the best of my abilities.

Sam Bailey gave us a lesson in the general attitude toward completing a mission when we first got into the UDTs. When we were being sent out, Sam asked us if we all had some dimes in our pockets. Of course we asked him what for and his answer has stuck with me. Sam said, "Well, we're going to send you out on an operation. And I want you to take that dime and call your mother, because you may not be back."

So I always have a dime in my pocket, because of Sam Bailey.

But in the Teams, we always follow through. It's just part of the job, what we do. The thrill of doing something, of completing something that you haven't even been trained to do. That gives you some real satisfaction and a good feeling of accomplishment.

Class 25 graduated in May 1961 and I was assigned to UDT 21. Working in the UDTs was everything I thought it might be. We deployed all of the time, spending relatively little time back at Little Creek. One very interesting mission was when we were tasked to go and pick up some special boats the Navy was having built and take them down to South America on a mission. Rudy Boesch and I went down to the Bertram Boat Company in Miami, Florida. There, we helped finish up outfitting some special boats and we took them down to Venezuela. There, we conducted what were basically counterguerrilla operations, chasing Che Guevara and his group.

There were weapons aboard the boats and we knew how to operate them. There was a lot of terrorist activity around the oil lines, especially around Lake Maracaibo, near the western border with Colombia, near a little town called Lagunillas on the eastern shore of the lake.

This was a UDT operation, sometime before the SEALs were even created. It was definitely unconventional warfare, and I didn't know why a detachment from UDT was chasing a guy around the swamps and on land in South America. What I did know was that I was very glad to go. What little I knew directly about Che Guevara I had picked up just by reading various articles. He seemed to be quite an adventurer, and I admired him for that. But there was no way I could accept his trying to spread communism through Latin America. We never caught up with him while Rudy and I were down there, but his luck ran out in the end.

We weren't really trained to operate in a riverine environment then. None of us had any prior experience in this kind of counterguerrilla work, but we had the will to get the job done. We had the boats and moving through the waterways was something that came naturally to us. But we did a lot of things we weren't formally trained to do in the UDTs. Whatever we were told to do, we did, to the best of our knowledge. And that usually worked out fine. That may have been a forerunner, a spearhead, of what was to come in Navy Special Warfare.

When the orders came down from higher command, you didn't know who had made them, or even why they had been made. They just said "do this." You didn't always know where you were going, but you knew you were being sent to do something. And when you got there, you just figured out a way to get the job done. Flexibility is always the key, one way or another, we'll figure it out.

Just a few years after joining UDT 21, I was on a Med [Mediterranean] trip with UDT 21 when I first heard about the new SEAL Team that they were forming. That sounded like something even more adventurous than working with the UDT, but when I asked if I could volunteer for the new organization, I was told I had to wait until I returned to the Creek from my Med deployment.

So as soon as we returned to the States, I volunteered to go over to SEAL Team. I was the first person to go from UDT 21 to SEAL Team Two after it was formed. Being in the second group of men going to the SEAL Team meant I wasn't a plankowner, but that difference wasn't much.

Getting into the SEALs was great, I knew it was what I wanted right off the bat. Very quickly, we got into all kinds of training—land operations, weapons, and specialized parachuting. I was already jump-qualified, but in the SEALs we also learned free-falling and other methods of infiltrating from a high-flying aircraft. And we finally got a chance to utilize all of this training when SEAL Team Two deployed direct-action platoons to Vietnam.

In June 1967, I first deployed to Vietnam as the platoon chief of Fifth Platoon. That deployment was a real eye-opener as to just what it meant to fight an unconventional war. My first impression of Vietnam was that it was really hot, and that impression never changed.

Fifth Platoon was in only the second group of direct-action platoons to go to Vietnam from SEAL Team Two. We came in to relieve Third Platoon, which had been in-country since January. Some of the guys from Third Platoon—J. P. Tolison was one of them—took us out on our initial operations, to kind of break us in to operating in their area. At that time I was a chief petty officer and I chose to go out on point for that first operation.

Moving along, I went through some very thick bamboo. After finally penetrating the bamboo, I walked right into a native hooch, just flat put my nose right up against the thatch wall of the building in the dark. Calling back quietly, I told the patrol, "We're here."

So much for quietly sneaking up on a target. Instead, I walked right into it in the dark. So that seemed pretty funny to us, and it helped break the tension we were all feeling from our first operation in a combat zone. But we had a lot of good operations on that deployment.

All the times we went out on operations, I was never really what I would call scared. More like what I would call energetic. And that was probably because of all the adrenaline pumping through my system. Even the first time I was shot at, I wasn't scared—I just reacted quickly. The enemy opened fire and I instantly dropped down, flat to the ground. Then the platoon moved up and we went forward

Paddling their IBS (Inflatable Boat, Small) toward a surfaced nuclear submarine, these SEALs are coming in from a practice operation launched from this same submarine. Constant practice like this makes the SEALs able to perform real-world operations with minimum notice.

U.S. Navy

and took out the target. And in all of that, I didn't feel any real fear—more excitement than anything else.

There was one time on a later deployment back in Vietnam when I was scared. Of all of the times I went out on operations, this one time I felt fear. At the time I was one of the first PRU (Provincial Reconnaissance Unit) advisers operating in Vietnam from SEAL Team Two. My unit was 187 men strong and we operated nearly every night. Advisers were told not to go out on operations in the field with their PRUs at that time. But there was no way I could lead these men, earn and maintain their respect, without going into harm's way with them. So I went out into the field on operations with my PRU.

One night, I had my interpreter with me and we were going to meet an NVA snitch who had some information for us. The meeting was to take place in a house, and my interpreter and the NVA informer met easily enough and started their discussions in Vietnamese. After I had gotten the information I wanted from the conversation, I went outside. At that time I was smoking a cigar and I just walked along slowly, enjoying my smoke and thinking about the information and how it could lead to an operation.

I had walked about fifty meters from the house, not going in any particular direction, when the house exploded behind me. Suddenly I was all by myself, just

NAVY SEALs: A COMPLETE HISTORY

standing on the dike of a rice paddy, and it was obvious that someone hadn't cared for what was going on in that hooch. My PRUs had been spread out in another area and they weren't immediately available to give me any support. Then the bullets started flying.

Diving into the rice paddy, I flattened myself out in the dirty, muddy water as bullets flew by overhead. That was the one moment when I was literally scared in Vietnam. I had no idea how I was going to get out of that situation, but I did get out and I never allowed myself to be cornered like that again.

The SEALs supplied individuals to act as leaders for the PRUs. We were advisers who would direct operations and see to it that our PRUs were supplied, supported, and paid. We handled the money for them, lived with them, saw to it that their needs were met, and traveled with them.

The basic objective of the PRUs, who were the operational arm of the Phoenix Program, was to capture the high-ranking individuals, the infrastructure, of the Viet Cong. These captures would result in intelligence that could be used by higher command to send in forces against major VC targets. It could be to break up a VC troop movement, uncover caches of weapons and materials, or just to learn the VC's plans for greater operations.

The Phoenix Program was a good program, though I have a hard time saying if it was a major success or not. I operated on a lower level, as a PRU adviser in the field with my unit rather than at a high enough command level to be able to say just how great a success the whole program was. But for its purpose, for as long as it ran, the program, I felt, was a success. But as the war escalated, I felt that the Phoenix Program just couldn't keep up with the speed of the war's operations.

As a SEAL adviser to PRU portion of the Phoenix Program, I can say that our mission was to flat-out kidnap the Viet Cong leadership, not to go out and assassinate them. We could get a lot more information from a living person than we could get from just a body.

The Chieu Hoi Program had been started well before the Phoenix Program, but the two worked so closely together it was almost impossible to separate them sometimes. The Chieu Hoi Program allowed VC and ex-NVA personnel to "rally" or defect from the Communists and receive an amnesty from the South Vietnamese government. Many of the VC and NVA who defected gave intelligence that led directly to PRU operations. Some of the individuals who gained amnesty through the Chieu Hoi Program joined various PRUs and actively operated against their former comrades.

Working with the Chieu Hois, ex-NVAs and VC, didn't really bother me. I thought both the Chieu Hoi and PRU people were very good troops. As far as being fighters went, they were much superior to the regular ARVN [Army of the Republic of Vietnam] troops. In my experience, the ARVNs were very lazy and reluctant to engage the enemy in battle.

My experience with the ARVN troops and their leadership led me to believe that they weren't trustworthy at all. At least not the ones I had direct experience with. Toward the end of my tour, we wouldn't even give the ARVN commanders the locations where we were going to operate. We knew that if we did, the information would be leaked out to the VC.

And this wasn't just paranoia. There had been several incidents in which the information was leaked about where my PRU was going to conduct an operation. When I quit telling the ARVNs where we were going to operate, our targets quit disappearing and the VC weren't waiting for us to arrive on-site.

When I received my commission to warrant officer in early 1968, I was transferred out to SEAL Team One in Coronado out on the West Coast. Before 1968 was over, I would be back in Vietnam, doing a tour with Alfa Platoon of SEAL Team One. There has always been a good-natured rivalry between the Teams stationed on either coast. Most of the joking around is just in good fun. But having served in both SEAL Team Two and SEAL Team One, I noticed some differences between the two Teams.

Since I had primarily been an East Coaster, it seemed to me that the East Coast Teams, both SEAL and UDT, were always together. We did everything together and even our families lived in the same neighborhoods. When I went to the West Coast, I noticed a lot of diversity among the men of the Teams. Everyone had different things that they did—some went bike riding, running, or even horseback riding. On the East Coast, we didn't seem to have all of those opportunities. So we had to stick together and drink beer.

I am very proud to have been a SEAL. Today, I wear a miniature Trident, the insignia of Navy Special Warfare, on the lapel of my suit coat. I don't brag about having been a SEAL, but when people ask me what that is on my lapel, I am glad to tell them. Personally, on the inside, it means a great deal to me to be able to wear that insignia.

Out of my three combat tours in Vietnam, in two of them I led SEAL platoons. During those tours, I went out on probably over 300 operations. On my second tour, when I was a PRU adviser, I had one operation that was a particularly memorable one, even though I couldn't pull it off until my third tour.

Through various sources, I kept getting intel on the existence of a VC-run POW camp somewhere in IV Corps. The sheer volume of intelligence told me that there had to be something to it, and we spent a lot of nights going out and looking for it. It was never there.

On my third tour in Vietnam, this one with SEAL Team One, I was the assistant platoon leader of Alfa Platoon, and directly in charge of Second Squad. In early October 1968, we had just come in from a big cache op when I was called down to get a report of some new information from another SEAL PRU adviser. I was told that two women had just walked into a PRU camp with information about an active VC

The main armament of the PBR, its twin forward .50-caliber machine guns, are shown in this photograph. The gunner from the River Division has his two weapons aimed outboard to the port side of the boat. The large searchlight is attached to the mounting for the guns. Wherever the light is shining, that's also where the two big machine guns are aimed.

U.S. Navy

POW camp. In fact, the women had apparently just come from the camp, where they had visited their husbands, who were detained there. My ears perked right up at that and all I wanted to know was where the camp was and where the women were.

Very soon I got hold of the women and was able to interrogate them with the help of an interpreter. I learned exactly where the camp was, or at least exactly where the women thought the camp was. This was very hot intelligence and not something that could be allowed to just sit and wait. Right away I put together an operation to raid the POW camp.

For air support, I called in the Seawolves. There was going to be another large ship, the USS Harnett County (LST 821), down in the area of the suspected POW camp that would act as a platform for the Seawolf helos. River Division 51 would supply the insertion boats in the form of PBRs. A company of ARVN forces were brought on board for a postoperation sweep of the area of the POW camp the day after the operation. And a platoon from the local PRUs would work directly with us on the op. And topping off the action team was my squad of SEALs from Alfa Platoon.

Since the intel was hot, the operation was put together very quickly. We took the women with us on board the PBRs well before dawn and they led us in to where they thought the POW camp was located. Inserting at the ladies' direction, we landed on Con Coc Island, part of the Dung Island complex in the Bassac River. But we searched and found nothing. Withdrawing, we moved farther along the shore of Con Coc Island until we came across something the ladies said looked familiar. Then we inserted again.

Inserting from a PBR into enemy territory is quite a problem. Anything could be waiting for you there in the dark. And we had set procedures we followed to maintain security and as much safety as we could. But still, inserting over and over in the same area is pushing your luck.

But this time we had found the right area. We were on the right path on only our second insertion. According to the women, we only had about 200 meters to go inland before we came across a path that supposedly led to the POW camp.

At that point I sent the women back to the PBR. Whether there was anything around or not, I just didn't know for sure. But I didn't want the women around when we tried to sneak up on the camp. And sending them back prevented our having any problem with them if they reacted badly.

As we all went up the path, I stopped the patrol when we came to a rise in the ground. It was sort of a knoll, a rise in the ground, that kept us from being able to see what was ahead of us on the path. Since there could be almost anything waiting for us, I didn't want us walking into any surprises.

With the men crouched down on alert, I slipped up to the edge of the knoll to take a look. It was just daylight now, and there was more than enough light to see. And what I saw was the POW camp right in front of me. Vietnamese prisoners were shackled together, and two of them were secured in bamboo cages. The guards were just getting up, preparing breakfast and getting into their morning routine.

Daylight was brightening rapidly and I wanted to get the raid over with before the guards were all up and moving around the camp. Only one of the guards I could see at that time was armed. As I was looking into the camp, the cages were out on my right-hand side. There were two small buildings in the camp, hooches really, but I didn't see any activity coming from either of them.

Withdrawing from the knoll, I went back and briefed my people. The PRUs, I sent over to my left flank. I didn't want them going in ahead of my SEAL squad. It wasn't that I didn't trust them, but once they saw the prisoners in the camp, there was a good chance they would go a little crazy and wipe out any chance of us getting prisoners for interrogation.

So I sent the PRUs over to the left flank and told them not to come in until the firing stopped. Then I took my squad and formed a skirmish line.

When we hit the camp, there was almost no resistance from the guards at all. They were unprepared and we surprised them completely. The interpreter I had with me shouted through a bullhorn he was carrying to all of the prisoners to drop down to the ground, otherwise they might get shot. Several of the guards made attempts to get to their weapons, and a bunch of them just ran off into the boondocks.

In the short firefight, we killed about seven guards and captured another guard and a VC tax collector who just gave up immediately. Facing seven SEALs, three of whom had Stoners and one who had an M60, was looking at a lot of firepower.

Probably the most exhilarating moment of that whole operation was when we unshackled the prisoners and took those two out of the cages. The men just couldn't do enough to show their gratitude. They were kissing our feet and bowing so much it looked like their backs would snap. This went on for more than five minutes. Finally, we had to stop them, since we had searched the camp and the VC could come back and overrun it, just like we had.

We took twenty-six liberated prisoners, and our own two captives, back to the PBRs. The POWs hadn't been fed very well during their captivity, so we gave them the C rations we had available. They thought that food was great and we were glad to get rid of it, so everyone got something out of that.

We took the liberated prisoners back and turned them over to the Vietnamese at Tra Vinh. Some of the prisoners had been at that camp since the Tet offensive, which had been eight months before. The ARVN sweep of Con Coc the next day indicated that there had been a lot of VC on the island, as many as two battalions' worth. So it was a good thing we pulled out when we did, even though we practically had to drag some of those liberated POWs out, them bowing all of the way.

That was a very successful and satisfying operation. Even though we hadn't liberated any American POWs, it had been a good day for Alfa Platoon.

I was one of the two officers in charge of Alfa Platoon. As the lower-ranking officer, I held the position of assistant platoon leader. But the relationship between officers and enlisted men in the Teams stems from their training together in BUD/S and it's different than I've seen in any other service branch. Everyone, no matter what their rank, would be doing the same things, day and night, during training. Officers and enlisted men did the same exercises, completed the same evolutions, and experienced the cold, the mud, and the water, all together.

This background in working together gave everyone a respect for one another's abilities, experience, and knowledge. Enlisted men in the Teams would often be assigned jobs that required them to lead groups of men, both U.S. and foreign. Sometimes the size of these groups was so big that in any other service, it would require a commissioned officer to do the job "properly." But that wasn't how things happened in the Teams.

When I was a warrant officer in Vietnam with my platoon, after a couple of months of operating, I allowed the petty officers to run ops completely. That meant they did everything—from gathering the intelligence and planning the operation, to giving the patrol orders, and to making sure that all of the equipment and munitions were ready for the op.

When their mission was ready to go, I would go on the op as well. But I went as just another member of the patrol, just a rifleman, M60 carrier, or radioman. The petty officer who had put the operation together would be the man in charge. He would run the op from start to finish. And that would give the platoon, and the Team, a great pool of very experienced petty officers to draw on in the future.

We could work that way. It was just another aspect of the camaraderie among Teammates, and the mutual respect we had for one another. That was the kind of united men we were in the Teams.

The camaraderie stood out sometimes, even in funny ways. One of the ops we went out on involved us swimming in the Cua Lon River, right at the tip of South Vietnam. We swam the width of that river, and some part of its length, looking for mines. All of this done on Christmas Eve. Since it was the season, while we were swimming, we were all singing "Jingle Bells." We all got along pretty well together.

In the Teams, leadership was much more important than rank. We had some very good leaders among the officers, and we also had some outstanding leaders among the enlisted community. The situations we found ourselves in during missions often called on the most experienced man being in charge. There were several times in the Teams when a detachment was sent off with an officer in charge for the record, but the leading petty officer was the one who was really in charge.

A commanding officer would call both the officer and that leading petty officer into his office and speak to them about the detachment or operation. And that officer could easily be told that he was expected to listen to the leading petty officer. And there was no problems with that situation whatsoever. One time while I was an enlisted man, it happened to me.

There was always close cooperation among the men of the Teams, and this started during our very first days of training. We have the idea of a "swim buddy" in the Teams. This concept is introduced to the students at BUD/S right at the start of their training. A swim buddy is the guy you will eat, sleep, and work with. He is hooked to you, literally sometimes, during training swims. You depend on your swim buddy, and he depends on you. When you get in trouble in the water, you can't call for help easily, and there isn't always time for someone else to show up anyway.

When we used to swim with the early Pirelli and Draeger breathing rigs, we found they were very hard to use and took a lot of experience to operate them safely. A lot of swimmers passed out underwater while training with those rigs. If you had problems or went unconscious, it was up to your swim buddy to make sure that your life was saved. He got you to the surface, and you would do the exact same thing for him.

On actual operations, your swim buddy is the guy who covers your "six" [back, six o'clock position] all of the time. And he expects you to do the same for him. He's the guy who literally turns into your mental twin. He knows how you think and you know how he thinks. When something happens, you already know what your swim buddy is going to do, so you just concentrate on the job at hand.

Probably the best tour of duty I ever had in the Navy was as a BUD/S instructor. I had first phase in Coronado and I did that job for three years. Why I say that was the best tour of duty had to do with the students. Everybody who we put through training had the same problem—they didn't like the instructors, mostly because we were harassing them all of the time.

But later, after the students had graduated and moved on to the Teams, done a tour, and found out what it meant to be an operator, then they would come back. Individuals might call me at my home and ask if they could bring their wives and children over to meet me. And I usually agreed and they would come over with their families.

And to a man, every one of them thanked me for training them the way I had. And that just made me feel very good in my heart, and I've felt that way about it ever since.

While in Vietnam on my last tour I had made a film, just a simple 8mm one, on going into a hooch, exactly how you would do that. I made the film as a training device, and I would show it to every class that went by.

What I emphasized to the students was that they were seeing an actual combat situation, though the person we dragged out of the hooch was really my interpreter. But we showed how we came up to the hooches, how we deployed our people, how we went through the door, pulled the prisoners out, and how we handcuffed and searched them. And I had my own experience that told me how important it was that they all knew how to do this kind of operation.

During that last tour of mine in Vietnam, we had gone into a village and waited for a Chinese guy to show up. We had heard he was coming to this particular village and was giving the people there aid and support, and training them in operations against us. So we went in and literally waited all night right outside of his hooch.

When he finally showed up, we jumped in there and grabbed him up. Wrapping him up and bringing him out, we suddenly started taking fire. So it was time to run. I had the prisoner with me, up in front of the patrol. Since I wanted to be sure there wouldn't be any problems with my having the prisoner up in front, I passed him back to one of my men and told him to "take care of him."

Well, the SEAL I passed the prisoner to passed him on again to the man behind him. And with the prisoner went the instructions to take care of him. Finally, we reached the boats and I turned, looking for the prisoner.

"Well," I asked, "where is he?"

"We took care of him," was the answer.

We never got that particular prisoner back for interrogation. And that was why I

A Vietnamese "hooch" or bamboo structure. Made of bamboo framing covered with palm
frond thatching and woven matting walls, this basic construction was common throughout
the Mekong Delta.

Greg McPartlin Collection

decided to make that film on how to do a snatch, secure, and transport of a prisoner. And why I showed the film to my students, to tell them how to correctly do it
and not take things too literally.

My strategy about training at BUD/S developed because of the quantity of
students we had. We used to get about 180 young men in a class, four times a
year. Many of these students were "wannabes"—they really didn't belong at
BUD/S. They wanted to be SEALs, but they weren't going to be. That isn't to say
that they weren't good men, but they just didn't have what it took to get there.

The people who "got there," made the Teams, were the people who knew mentally, deep in their hearts, that being in the Teams was where they wanted to be
more than anything else. Physical prowess doesn't really have a big part in getting
through training. The larger men had trouble with pull-ups. So you sometimes had
to kind of look the other way a bit while they did them. The smaller—framed trainee
could do pull-ups all day long; they could scale walls and leap where the larger men
couldn't.

But the larger man was stronger, and he could do push-ups or do whatever was
a show of pure strength. We had good swimmers, who couldn't do other things well.
But the people who got through the course made it through everything, whether it
was easy or hard for them. They were the ones who wanted it the most.

As an instructor, it was kind of interesting to watch the students grow as individuals. The first couple of weeks, you didn't really look at anyone in particular much. During those days, the students kind of weeded themselves out for the most part. That was where the wannabes found out what they were really letting themselves in for, and they were gone fast.

Then you started looking at people more closely as individuals. And when you looked at that same person ten or twelve weeks later, you would see a completely different person. They would grow inside, get more aggressive, and feel better about themselves and what they were doing.

Lots of times a student would hurt himself during training. And he would just push it away and keep going. But other trainees might hurt themselves and that would be the end of the program for them.

We tried to make competitions among the trainees. Such as when we had a real fast runner and a slow runner. An instructor would try to pair those two as much as he could, and then just get on that slow runner. And you could just watch that man go. He would get to, and go through, that wall that was keeping him from speeding up as fast as he could. And all of a sudden that slow guy was now one of the fastest runners in the class. I enjoyed doing that immensely, watching these young kids grow to be men.

Nobody likes to be harassed. What it does is bother a person's mind. First off, people feel like you're picking on them, and no one likes that. If they can overcome that, it helps move them forward, teaches them how to ignore what isn't important and focus on the job at hand.

I always wanted to know how the U.S. Marines got their people so motivated during training. We did a very good job, but the Marines do an excellent job in motivating their people. I went over to the Marine training camp several times just to watch them and see how they handled their charges. If I could have instilled that motivation in the trainees at BUD/S, we'd have had even more qualified people for the Teams. But that skill remained a Marine one for me.

One of the things we concentrated on as instructors at BUD/S was building up the camaraderie, the teamwork, of the students. To that end, we had them singing songs and shouting out phrases while they worked. Just like the instructors at boot camp or basic training would teach their students how to march—they would have them mark time and build enthusiasm as a unit by singing cadence songs. That same technique worked for us at BUD/S.

When I was at BUD/S in the early seventies, we didn't really prepare the students for combat. They were taught things that were purely combat-oriented, such as how to do warning orders, patrol orders, and do basic patrolling and maneuvers. It was after they graduated BUD/S that they went on to more specialized training, after they were assigned to a Team. In training areas such as out at Niland, the new

During a capabilities demonstration during one of their reunions, the young men of the Teams re-create a tradition of their UDT forefathers.

Kevin Dockery

operators became efficient in conducting warfare. They would use live ammunition, live demo [demolitions—explosives], and would jump in for an operation. BUD/S gave them the basics, and that was built on later.

Some of what we did with the students at BUD/S was dangerous, though as instructors, we knew it was our job to keep things as safe as possible. Rock portage, where we had the students learn to land a rubber boat and cross jagged rocks while the pounding surf drove down on them—that scared me.

For rock portage, we would put the students, broken down into boat crews of six, into inflatable boats and send them out to sea. Right outside the Hotel Del Coronado, on the shore, are a bunch of large rough rocks. And the students would come in and land at those rocks.

Back during WWII, they had done rock portage as part of the training of the very first UDTs. Later, during the Korean War, the UDTs often had to land on rocky beaches where there was no flat sand or smooth surfaces to ground a boat on. So rock portage remained in BUD/S training because of that history.

But every time we did rock portage with the students, my heart was up in my throat. Someone would come very close to being hurt on almost every landing.

Luckily, no one was ever seriously hurt on my watch, but there were a good share of bumps and bruises to go around in spite of that. I have seen broken legs and arms happen during rock portage, but you had to complete that evolution.

Surprisingly, we had people quit rather than face rock portage again. And this was after they had completed Hell Week and some of the more strenuous parts of BUD/S first-phase training. But you never could tell where you might be going in on an op, so rock portage remains a part of training to this day.

The demo (demolition) pits were another important part of training. They were our best chance, as instructors, to expose an individual to the noise and concussion of combat. When you put a man in on a beach someplace during an invasion or operation, he's got a real good chance of being shelled with either mortars or artillery. Some people are deathly afraid of that—the sudden blast of an explosion. And some of them don't even know that they are. The demo pit is a place where we would weed out people like that. If they didn't like being in the demo pit, they really wouldn't like what could happen later on.

The demo pit was this sunken area of black, muddy water and churned-up sand. The students had to crawl around this area while we set off explosions all around them. We even made them eat standing waist-deep in muddy water, trying

Like all of the Special Warfare operators before and after them, these trainees learn how to take their rubber boat through the rocks. Since the days of the Scouts and Raiders in WWII, rock passage has been an integral part of UDT and SEAL training. Even in calm waters such as these, the trainees could easily injure themselves or their Teammates through a mistake. No man likes this work, and every man in the Teams does it.

U.S. Navy

to shield their food from the dust and debris kicked up by the explosions constantly going off.

The reason for having the students eat while all of that was going around them? Well, that's a harassment. It's hard, miserable, and they have to get through it to graduate. They learn that nothing matters unless you let it matter.

We had a trainee at BUD/S once who I had personally gone out and recruited. That was something we had to do now and then, go out and recruit at the different Navy training centers. When this one young man came to BUD/S, he was the fastest swimmer I had ever seen, and was the best runner I had ever seen as well. When he had to face the obstacle course, he went through it like it wasn't even there. And he was a very good leader, already a third class petty officer when he checked in.

Just before Hell Week, we would gather all of the students and instructors together. In the meeting, we critiqued each student separately. Each man would get information on whether he was considered good or bad, and why, from every instructor there. And then I would speak to him as well.

For my recruit, all of the instructors said the same thing. To a man, they considered that trainee the best person they had ever seen. And when I asked him if he was ready to go to Hell Week, that student just looked at me and said, "No, I quit."

Just like that. He just didn't want the program. And he didn't have a reason. So I just said, "Fine, put your helmet outside."

Being a BUD/S instructor was hard work, and it was very rewarding. That's what helped make it my best tour in the Teams. And I feel privileged to have been part of the BUD/S training unit.

Today, I've been out of the Navy for quite a few years. And people will look at me and say, "Oh, you were a SEAL." And I sometimes correct them and tell them that I had been in the Teams. That was the key to our success: we were the Teams, we were Teammates. And that is the heart of where we come from.

Most of the people in the Teams don't like a lot of publicity. Especially back in my day, I had a lot of chances to have my picture taken, be the center of newspaper articles. But I chose not to do that. I'm not bashful, but it just didn't strike me as right to advertise that I was in the Teams. I don't publicize it, but when people ask me what the Trident is that I'm wearing, I'll tell them. But they have to ask.

In my opinion, the guy in BUD/S today doesn't have much in common with the operators from World War II or even from my day. In a practical sense, things have changed so much as to be almost unrecognizable in terms of the kind of missions performed and the gear they do their ops with. In my day, we still trained with a lead line and slate, measuring the waters' depth just as they had in WWII. Today, these young men are computer-oriented. They have all the gimmicks that can be found. They're smarter than we were, and have accomplished a lot.

If there is something missing from today's SEAL Teams, it's maybe that they *aren't as battle-tested as we were. But I think they have a lot more going for them today. Back when I started in the Teams, we were learning how to do everything. The men of the Teams today have built on what we did, and gone much further with it than we even thought possible.*

If there is one thing that everyone who serves in Navy Special Warfare has in common, it is that they are all part of the Teams. And once you have completed that long road to get into the Teams, and have served with your brothers, you will never completely leave. I know I will never leave the Teams behind—never.

■ Chapter 36

The History of the Teams

Naval units and organizations are required to maintain a log or history of their units. These documents are sent in yearly to higher commands as the unit's official command and control history for the reported year. Even units as secret as the Navy SEAL Teams have had to maintain these historical records.

Initially classified confidential or secret, the command and control histories list the Teams' actions throughout the year, the officers and men, who they were and what they did. They are the best single source of data on just what happened to the Teams, especially during years of active combat in Vietnam. These are excerpts from those records:

SEAL TEAM ONE
Excerpt from SEAL Team One, Command and Control History 1967
Enclosure (1)
SEAL Team ONE, COMMAND HISTORY UPDATED TO DECEMBER 1966
Pages 1–3. [DECLASSIFIED from CONFIDENTIAL]
SEAL Team ONE was commissioned on 1 January 1962 at the U.S. Naval Amphibious Base Coronado, California, under the command of Lieutenant David DEL GUIDICE, U.S. Naval Reserve. Five officers and fifty enlisted personnel from Underwater Demolition Teams ELEVEN and TWELVE comprised the initial personnel complement.

SEAL (Sea-Air-Land) Teams are identified as Navy units trained to conduct unconventional or paramilitary operations and to train personnel of allied nations in operations involving the naval or maritime environment. As with every fleet unit, the ultimate goal of SEAL Team ONE is to serve as a superior weapon in time of war and to attain maximum combat readiness in time of peace. This posture of readiness is particularly crucial since military efforts in a "COLD WAR" situation often preclude any clear-cut distinction between war and peace.

Lieutenant James H. BARNES, U.S. Naval Reserve, relieved Lieutenant DEL GUIDICE on 19 June 1964, as Commanding Officer. At that time, SEAL Team ONE consisted of six operating platoons. Each platoon was assigned administrative responsibilities, but was primarily an operating entity, capable of a diversity of skills and tasks. Personnel were extensively cross-trained to ensure the maximum efficiency of each platoon in the field.

Although young in years, SEAL Team ONE has matured rapidly into a close-knit, highly trained force of dedicated officers and men. Almost from its very beginning, SEAL Team ONE has played an active role in various trouble spots of the world. The first actively employed SEAL units in Southeast Asia were deployed in July 1962. There have been SEAL detachments in Vietnam ever since. In February 1966, SEAL Team ONE sent a pilot group of three officers and fifteen enlisted men to Vietnam, under the operational control of Commander Naval Forces Vietnam. From 26 March through 7 April 1966, these personnel were employed in Operation "JACKSTAY," the first amphibious landing in the Rung Sat Special Zone (RSSZ). Operation "JACKSTAY" was also the first joint UDT/SEAL and Marine operation in Vietnam.

On 15 July 1966, LCDR Franklin W. ANDERSON, USN, ******, took command of SEAL Team ONE. Since that time, SEAL Team ONE has intensified its operations in Vietnam and has increased the size of the RSSZ detachment [Detachment Golf] to five officers and twenty men. Operations conducted in the RSSZ include, but are not limited to, harassment of the enemy, hit-and-run raids, reconnaissance patrols, intelligence collection, and curtailment of guerrilla movements by ambush/counterambush tactics. The intensification of these operations afforded by the increased detachment size has proven the value of SEALs in combat situations.

Ambushes make up a high percentage of the operations conducted by SEAL detachments in the RSSZ. Although the enemy kill rate is not high, the SEALs have placed a great psychological burden on the Viet Cong and have provided an effective deterrent to all VC travel.

On 19 August 1966, SEAL Team ONE had their first combat casualty. Petty Officer Billy W. MACHEN, who was point man on a reconnaissance patrol, triggered a Viet Cong ambush and sacrificed his own life in order to save his comrades. He was posthumously awarded the Silver Star for his gallant action.

On 7 October 1966, SEAL Team suffered one of their most unfortunate casualties. Two SEAL squads were transiting one of the smaller rivers in the RSSZ on an LCM-3 when they were attacked by a large number of Viet Cong. The boat received a direct mortar hit and sixteen of the nineteen men on board were wounded. LTJG William PECHACEK, Petty Officer First Class HENRY, and Petty Officer Third Class PENN were subsequently retired from Naval Service for disability due to their extensive wounds. Despite the adverse conditions, intelligence reports later indicated that during the firefight forty VC were killed by this gallant group of men. In October 1966, the commitment for SEALs in Vietnam increased to a total of seven officers and thirty men.

One of the basic missions of the SEALs is the gathering of intelligence information. This information is utilized by the SEALs and by higher authority to more effectively combat the enemy. Although not wholly indicative of the intelligence gathered, the following figures do show the result of SEAL operations conducted during 1966:

VC KIA	86
VC KIA (PROB)	15
SAMPANS DESTROYED	21
JUNKS DESTROYED	02
HUTS/BUNKERS DESTROYED	33
RICE CAPTURED OR DESTROYED	521,600 pounds

Numerous enemy documents have also been retrieved.

On one of the operations [Operation CHARLESTON, 3–4 December 1966], SEAL intelligence led to the capture of a weapons cache including 57MM Recoilless Rifles, 7.92 German machine guns, two U.S. Carbines, one U.S. M3A1 Submachine gun, and 10,000 rounds of assorted ammunitions. SEAL intelligence has been and is being used by friendly forces conducting operations throughout Vietnam; additionally, SEALs have aided these forces by locating VC base camps, helo landing zones, high ground for friendly base camps, and determining VC commo-liaison routes.

In the wake of the increasing manpower commitments to Southeast Asia, SEAL Team ONE has had their manpower increased to 21 officers and 105 enlisted personnel. This increase was projected for fiscal year 1967, but due to the outstanding performances of SEAL personnel, the increase was accelerated to help meet pressing requirements.

There have been other achievements and activities of SEAL Team ONE, outside the combat zone of Vietnam, that have contributed significantly to the defense posture of the United States Military services. Among them have been the conduct of the operational evaluation phase of the Aerial Recovery System "SKYHOOK." During the evaluation, SEAL personnel made live, two-man pickups during both daylight and darkness utilizing an S2F-type aircraft flying at speeds of approximately 110 knots [127 miles per hour]. Additionally, in August 1966, SEAL Team ONE personnel participated in the first live-man pickup in the evaluation of Air-Sea Rescue system utilizing the DRONE antisubmarine helicopter (DASH).

SEAL Team One's performance since its commissioning has been outstanding. This performance is directly attributable to the devotion to duty and superior capability of the officers and men assigned. Their contributions to the war effort in Southeast Asia and the overall national defense posture have earned distinction for themselves, their unit, and the United States Navy.

Excerpt from SEAL Team One, Command and Control History 1969
Enclosure (3) (b)
Subj: Presidential Unit Citation; recommendation for (U)
Pages 1–3. [DECLASSIFIED from CONFIDENTIAL]
2. SEAL Team ONE was commissioned on 1 January 1962 by direction of the late President John F. KENNEDY, with an allowance of 5 officers and 50 enlisted men. Since that period, due to increased demand and requirements placed on SEAL Teams, they have increased in numbers and presently have 32 officers and 132 enlisted personnel on board. Since July 1962, SEAL personnel have been deployed in Vietnam under the operational control of Commander Military Assistance Command, Vietnam and/or Commander U.S. Naval Forces Vietnam. It is strongly felt this small elite unit has fully lived up to the expectations and reasons for its formation. Recommendation for this award is based on the achievements of SEAL Team ONE for duty, primarily in the Republic of Vietnam.
3. One of the primary missions of SEAL Team ONE has been to conduct Naval Unconventional Warfare operations against the Viet Cong in the Republic of Vietnam. There are four separate detachments presently located in Vietnam. Detachments ALFA and GOLF consist of seven officers and thirty enlisted each. These detachments are located in the Mekong Delta and Rung Sat Special Zone (RSSZ) respectively. The Rung Sat Special Zone contains the primary sea access to Saigon, and therefore is an area of great strategic importance. It is imperative that the RSSZ remain under direct government control in order to maintain this vital logistic channel. To assist in the insurance of that control,

there is a constant requirement for factual and timely intelligence data. This task is one of the main objectives of detachment GOLF. Detachment BRAVO is assigned to MACV and operational in III and IV Corps for special operations, and Detachment ECHO, also under MACV, is assigned to Danang for special operations; these detachments consist of one officer and twelve enlisted men and two officers and twelve enlisted men, respectively. Due to the limited number of trained personnel available, the austere operating conditions, and the casualty rate, personnel have been required to rotate on a port and starboard basis, and in many cases much more rapidly. In some instances these fast turnarounds are voluntary; others are dictated by personnel requirements and increased operational commitments. A large number of SEAL Team members have completed as many as five to six tours in Vietnam and some with as little time as one month in CONUS between tours. Additionally, these men are required to be away from their families a great amount of the time while in CONUS, attending schools and other training functions.

4. The environmental conditions in Vietnam that SEAL Team personnel are subjected to in the conduct of their operations is extremely difficult and hazardous. Exposure to almost impenetrable mangrove swamps, mud, tidal flats, prolonged immersions in water, and infestations of crocodiles, snakes, and other tropical animals, insects, and diseases, in conjunction with enemy booby traps, punji stakes, and direct contact, have become a matter of routine on patrols, ambushes, and listening post operations. In areas of the RSSZ, a hardworking, well-conditioned squad can cover no more than a few hundred yards in one day. On occasion, ambush and observation teams have had to wait quietly for over four days in these insect- and reptile-infested jungles and swamps in order to successfully carry out their assigned mission. SEAL Team members usually operate in small units, i.e., two to six men on listening posts, where stealth and concealment are paramount. Intelligence gathering missions take these units/squads within very close proximity of enemy forces, often within earshot and/or a few yards distance. Should a larger enemy force ever detect a SEAL unit of this size, deep within this terrain, outside assistance would be virtually impossible. In spite of the severity of the operating conditions, SEAL Team members have maintained a heavy operating schedule, with many personnel having participated in over forty combat missions in a single deployment. All detachments have been highly successful in carrying out their respective missions, whether they be gathering intelligence data, training indigenous personnel, or interdicting Viet Cong operations . . .

SEAL TEAM TWO

Excerpt from SEAL Team Two, Command and Control History 1972

Enclosure (1)

SECTION V—OVERALL HISTORY OF SEAL TEAM TWO

Pages 1–5. [DECLASSIFIED from CONFIDENTIAL]

REPORT ON THE U.S. NAVY'S SEAL TEAM

1. (C) History

a. SEAL Team was established in J[anuary] 1962 to fill a need for military combat units specializing in unconventional warfare. President John F. Kennedy was one of the principal initiators behind the organization of counterguerrilla forces. These forces were needed not only by the U.S. Army but also by the U.S. Navy to counteract guerrilla activity in the world's rivers, harbors, and inshore areas.

b. The Navy had one unit oriented toward these areas already, the Underwater Demolition Teams. However, their primary mission was hydrographic reconnaissance and demolition of beach obstacles, mainly for the successful operation of an amphibious landing by the Marine Corps. SEAL Team was formed for a more exclusive mission, namely "clandestine operations in maritime areas and riverine environments." The name SEAL was chosen to signify the methods of entry into a hostile environment capable by this unit: by sea, by air, and by land.

c. In 1962, SEAL Team became involved in the growing Vietnam conflict. An advisory group from SEAL Team, called a Mobile Training Team (MTT), was sent rather than a combat unit. MTTs were sent to I Corps region of Vietnam until 1968. In 1967, SEAL Team combat platoons also became involved. They operated mainly in the MEKONG DELTA region until the necessity for combat platoons ended in 1971. SEALs served as Provincial Reconnaissance Unit (PRU) advisers in the IV Corps region from the time of the PRUs inception in 1966 until late in 1970. SEAL advisers to the Vietnamese are still being sent at this time [1971].

2. (C) MISSION.

a. The mission of SEAL Team is stated in reference NWIP 29-1 (A).

b. A SEAL Team is a Navy fleet tactical unit commissioned to conduct naval special warfare in the following areas:

1. Unconventional warfare.

2. Counterguerilla operations.

3. Clandestine operations in maritime areas which include sabotage,

demolition, intelligence collection, and training and advising of friendly military or paramilitary forces in the conduct of Naval Special Warfare.

c. Some of the possible tasks of a SEAL Team are:

1. Destroy or sabotage enemy shipping ports and harbor facilities, railway lines, and other installations in riverine environments.

2. Infiltrate and exfiltrate agents, guerrillas, evaders, and escapees.

3. Conduct action undermining the military, economic, psychological morale, or political strength of the enemy forces.

4. Conduct reconnaissance, surveillance, and other intelligence tasks and capturing key personnel.

5. Ambush, counterambush, and interdict enemy waterway lines of communication.

6. Accomplish limited counterinsurgency civic action tasks such as medical aid, elementary civil engineering, boat maintenance, and basic education of the indigenous population.

7. Organize, train, assist, and advise U.S.-allied and other friendly military or paramilitary forces in the conduct of the above tasks.

3. (C) TRAINING

a. Training for prospective members of SEAL Team is located at the Naval Amphibious Base in Coronado, California. A twenty (20) week course called Basic Underwater Demolition/SEAL Team (BUD/S) Training begins several times each year. Applicants must pass an initial screen test and be physically and mentally qualified to undergo one of the most rigorous training programs in the world. A normal training class has an attrition rate of 66 to 75 percent. In addition, officers and enlisted men must train together, creating an atmosphere of camaraderie. Graduates of BUD/S training go to either UDT or SEAL Teams on both East and West Coasts. BUD/S training consists of these phases:

1. Phase I (five weeks): consists entirely of physical training, runs, swims, obstacle courses, night problems, IBS training, and climaxes with "HELL WEEK": a physical endurance test that allows no sleep all week.

2. Phase II (eight weeks): concentrates on SEAL and UDT operations, i.e. hydrographic reconnaissance, demolition training, weapons, patrolling, and land warfare.

3. Phase III (seven weeks): teaches the trainee diving operations, including SCUBA, Mark IV, and Emerson diving apparatus, diving medicine, and diving physics.

With his oxygen mask firmly in place, this SEAL practices a free fall as part of a HALO jump.

U.S. Navy

b. A graduate of BUD/S Training who goes on to SEAL Team gets even more extensive training including:
1. Parachute Jump School
2. Basic Intelligence
3. Naval Gunfire Support
4. Combat Medicine
5. Survival, Evasion, Resistance, and Escape
6. SEAL CADRE Training

In addition, six (6) months observation and experience are required before a team member is officially qualified.

c. Numerous other schools are available to Team members in their specialties and in special warfare operations. Some of these are:
1. Jumpmaster
2. Parachute Rigger and Packer
3. Ranger School (U.S. Army)
4. Instructor School
5. Leadership School
6. Foreign Weapons

7. Explosive Ordnance Disposal
8. Language School
9. Raider School (U.S. Army)

d. In addition to these schools several joint operations within the U.S. Army and our foreign allies are held each year. Some of these Fleet Training exercises are:

1. FLINTLOCK. An annual NATO exercise in which SEAL Team TWO provides personnel for various joint staffs and operating platoons working in conjunction with the operating forces of our various NATO allies and taking place throughout the European Theater.

2. EXOTIC DANCER. An annual Atlantic Fleet Exercise conducted in the vicinity of Camp Lejeune, North Carolina, in which the scenario involves a combination of both conventional and unconventional warfare forces of the Army, Navy, Air Force, and Marine Corps. SEAL Team TWO provides personnel for various joint staffs, operating bases, and several platoons for the operating forces.

3. STRONG EXPRESS. An additional NATO exercise recently begun in August 1972 that possibly will develop into an annual exercise. SEAL Team TWO provides personnel for various joint staffs and one operating platoon.

4. (C) Organization

a. A SEAL Platoon consists of two (2) officers and twelve (12) enlisted men which can be divided into two (2) squads of one (1) officer and six (6) enlisted. Each platoon is intended to be a self-sufficient unit, and therefore has at least one man from each specialty area. These areas are: ordnance, submersible operations, intelligence, communications, engineering, air operations, and medical.

b. SEAL Team TWO is organized into ten platoons and is supported by the aforementioned departments. Each officer is both a department head and a platoon commander (or assistant). SEAL Team TWO has seventeen (17) officers and one hundred and fifteen (115) enlisted men [NOTE: these are 1972 numbers]. Administrative control is diagrammed in figure (1). It should be noted that SEAL Team ONE is located in California and is larger in size.

5. (C) OPERATIONAL CONTROL

a. Operational control of a typical SEAL platoon is shown in figure (2). Operational control is difficult to diagram because it was constantly changing in the Vietnam situation. At one point in time, two (2) SEAL platoons working in the Mekong Delta were responsible to their respective detachment commands, who, in turn, reported to COMNAVSPECWARGRU "V" in

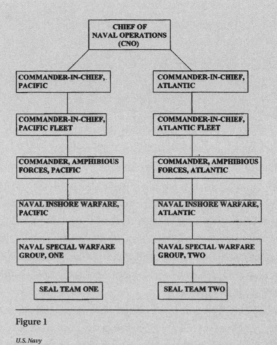

CHIEF OF
NAVAL OPERATIONS
(CNO)

COMMANDER-IN-CHIEF, PACIFIC — COMMANDER-IN-CHIEF, ATLANTIC

COMMANDER-IN-CHIEF, PACIFIC FLEET — COMMANDER-IN-CHIEF, ATLANTIC FLEET

COMMANDER, AMPHIBIOUS FORCES, PACIFIC — COMMANDER, AMPHIBIOUS FORCES, ATLANTIC

NAVAL INSHORE WARFARE, PACIFIC — NAVAL INSHORE WARFARE, ATLANTIC

NAVAL SPECIAL WARFARE GROUP, ONE — NAVAL SPECIAL WARFARE GROUP, TWO

SEAL TEAM ONE — SEAL TEAM TWO

Figure 1

U.S. Navy

Saigon. Because of the distance between commands, SEAL platoons for the most part operated independently. Status reports were sent up a dual chain of command as illustrated (figure [2]).

6. (C) CONCEPT OF OPERATIONS

a. SEAL Team began sending combat platoons to Vietnam early in 1967 and were used almost exclusively in the Mekong Delta. Their mission, as stated above, in many cases evolved into a single objective: to identify and neutralize paramilitary units, i.e. sapper teams. Usually this involved obtaining intelligence on one person who after his capture would then lead you to the next senior man. This activity required an extremely accurate and quick intelligence collection system.

b. SEALs utilized a variety of intelligence sources:

1. Provincial Reconnaissance Unit
2. Static Central Grievances
3. Revolutionary Development Teams
4. District Intel and Operating Center
5. Police Special Branch

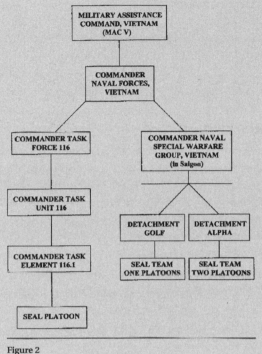

Figure 2

U.S. Navy

6. Civil Operations Revolutionary Development Support
7. Province Chiefs
8. District Chiefs
9. U.S. Military Intelligence
10. Vietnamese Military Security Services
*11. Hoi Chan Center
12. U.S. or VN S-2 Dept.
13. SEAL informants
14. Naval Intelligence Liaison Officers
15. Regional Forces
16. Popular Forces

The Hoi Chan Center and SEAL informants provided the most accurate and most recent intelligence, and therefore proved to be the best SEAL platoon usage. Two (2) independent sources of intelligence were needed before it would be considered reliable information.

c. SEAL Teams achieved very good results by organizing missions on the basis of captured intelligence from these sources. The main reason for this success must be attributed to the organization and readiness of the SEAL platoon. In most cases all necessary equipment was ready and quickly available on short notice, and a full SEAL squad remained on base, ready to respond to new information at all times. After several months of operating together, platoon members needed only the most basic information about any imposed operations, which eliminated the need for lengthy briefings and preparations.

d. The platoon leader was responsible for keeping himself current on all intelligence in his area of operations. When critical information was received at any time of the day, he could clear a mission quickly through the Tactical Operations Center, coordinate necessary support (boat, air, artillery), gather his squad together, and be on his mission within an hour.

Excerpt from SEAL Team Two, Command and Control History 1966
Enclosure (1)
COMMAND HISTORY OF SEAL TEAM TWO
CHRONOLOGY
Page 1. [DECLASSIFIED from CONFIDENTIAL]
20 September 1962–30 January 1963 MTT 4-63 Under direction of Ensign DORAN and coordinated with LTJG A. C. ROUTH (SEAL ONE) SEALs instruct Republic of Vietnam Biet HAI (Junk Force Commando Platoons) in UDT/SEAL type operation.

Excerpt from SEAL Team Two, Command and Control History 1966
Enclosure (1)
COMMAND HISTORY OF SEAL TEAM TWO
2. OPERATIONS, ACTIVITIES, AND SPECIAL TOPICS (NARRATIVE) 1962
Pages 6–7. [DECLASSIFIED from CONFIDENTIAL]
DM2 WAUGH and SK2 BURBANK were the first to see action in Vietnam as part of Mobile Training Team 10-62, which was under the command of LTJG HOLTZ of SEAL Team ONE. It was the purpose of the MTT to establish an indigenous training staff capable of maintaining training and operational readiness of the Vietnamese Navy Commando Platoons, with a minimum of U.S. assistance. They were further to act as advisers in the development of tactics, equipment,

Surrounded by crates of supplies and ammunition, these SEALs are conducting a final briefing before going out on an operation. Their tiger-stripe camouflage uniforms and heavily made-up faces will help these men disappear into the jungle and the shadows on their operation.

U.S. Navy

and operating procedures of these Vietnamese Junk Force Commando Platoons, or Biet Hai. MTT 10-62 was relieved by MTT 4-63, which was composed of one officer and seven enlisted men from SEAL Team TWO; personnel were ENS. DORAN, BM1 KUCINSKI, HM1 SCHWARTZ, CS1 TOLISON, BM2 TOLISON, HM2 McCARTY, AO3 BUMP, MN3 CLARK, and AT3 GOINES. The detachment was under control of LTJG A.C. ROUTH of SEAL Team ONE. Training for Biet Hai was coordinated through LTJG NINH, Vietnam Navy, and was similar to that conducted by MTT 10-62 with emphasis on land navigation, guerrilla fare, ambush and counterambush, and raiding techniques . . .

Both SEAL Teams had now entered Vietnam; they would not leave completely until more than ten years had passed.

Barry Enoch, Chief Gunner's Mate, USN (Ret.)

Back when I was a young man going to a military school, the Columbia Military Academy, there was a magazinelike book in the library that showed the men from the WWII UDTs, what they did, and how they did it. It was probably from the moment of my reading that book that I wanted to be a Navy Frogman.

In 1955, I enlisted in the U.S. Navy specifically to volunteer for the UDTs. But at that time you couldn't go directly to the Teams right after your enlistment. So I spent several years on board a heavy cruiser and then another two years as a crewmember of a destroyer escort. It was when I reenlisted that I was able to put in for UDT training and was accepted.

Class 24 UDTR, West Coast, was exciting, tough, and something I had been waiting a long time for. I was really glad to have been able to get into it and I really enjoyed it overall. There wasn't a question of what I was letting myself in for; I pretty much knew the training would be hard. But I didn't know how bad it would hurt.

Like for so many others, the hardest single part of training for me was Hell Week. During that week, I injured my knee and just had to reach down into myself and grab up that little bit of extra to get through.

We had been doing night rock portages on the beach behind the Hotel Del Coronado. I was the number-one man starboard, which meant I was the guy who was

While being observed by their American SEAL advisers, these Biet Hai commandos train with IBS's near Danang in the early 1960s.

U.S. Navy

supposed to clamber out on the rocks and pull the line in to start securing the rubber boat. Only our boat bent in the middle and suddenly straightened out, flipping me forward and into the rocks. My knee hit the rock hard and took some damage. At any rate, I had a lot of swelling in it. So I just had to tough out the situation and keep on going. All of the swimming and cold water must have helped it a bit, as it healed up and I was fine.

The thing that got me through that long week was what I think gets so many others through; the desire to want to do that, to be a member of the Teams, more than anything else in the world. What I wanted was to be a Navy Frogman, a diver, and that was something I had wanted for a long, long time.

Like so many other training classes, not many of the students had the desire to get all the way through to the end. Class 24 started with sixty-three officers and enlisted men, and when we finally graduated, it was with six enlisted men and two officers. Our graduation ceremony wasn't very long. But it was a nice day, and we were all wearing our white uniforms under the Southern California sun.

After graduation, we were assigned to UDT 12. Going into First Platoon, I soon found myself one of the volunteers picked to join a small contingent of UDT operators going to the arctic for Project IceSkate. A few men were chosen from three different UDT platoons and we were flown up to Point Barrow, Alaska. From there, we caught an icebreaker, the Staten Island (AGB-5), which took us 800 miles into the arctic ice pack until we hit the solid kind of pack ice they call "gray ice."

On board the ship were some civilians from Washington, D.C. Our mission for Project IceSkate was to test a new kind of explosive and explosive device, what is now called HBX-3. The device had a special container with a standoff that would let it float up and breach the ice from the bottom.

What they were trying to do was develop an explosive device that could be released from a submarine to open a hole in the ice. The target was to blast a hole through eighteen feet of ice, a hole large enough to let the submarine's sail slip through to the surface. The thickness of the ice was determined by the height of the sail. The idea was to give the submarine crew a means to escape in case of a nuclear accident while they were under the ice cap.

So we swam these devices back under the ice and fired a number of shots. What we soon found was a twenty-pound charge would make a hole big enough to let the whole submarine come up through the ice. It was cold stuff to work in, but we all had a lot of fun on that trip.

Diving under the ice is absolutely beautiful. The water is a clear blue that you can see through for over 180 feet and still recognize who you're looking at. But as you look down, the blue of the water just turns darker and darker underneath you, until it's almost a purple color.

Under the ice, way down below you, you could see these massive icebergs floating with just a slight negative buoyancy. Those huge bergs just slowly slid by, and you would wonder just what would happen if that sucker started to float up to the surface, where you were under the ice cap.

But the underneath of the ice cap is very rough. The surface of the ice might be flat and scoured down by the blowing snow, but under the water, the ice is rough. There were pressure ridges built up from where ice floes moved together, and those ridges could go down as deep as a house, sixty feet or more. Up where we were firing our shots, it was only eighteen feet thick. But it was like swimming against the surface of a cave, so many ice projections stuck down into the depths.

Close to the edge of the ice pack, the water would be slushy with ice, it seemed to be like swimming in a milkshake. And the water was cold, but we had special wet suits made for it that kept us protected.

It was when we came out of the water that we had a problem. The wind was blowing and it was drifting the snow pretty hard. Those conditions made the air feel super cold. When we surfaced and climbed out, or Teammates would quickly pat our faces dry with towels. Then they would put big parkas over us and hustle us into the boat. They got us aboard the icebreaker and into the warmth as quickly as they could. Because once we were out of the water, the cold would quickly freeze us solid. It was so cold that as they patted your face dry, the seawater that dripped off would freeze well before it hit the ground.

It was that coming out of the water into the arctic blast of cold that was more of a shock than getting in to the water in the first place. But we continued with our operations and then headed back to the much warmer climate around Coronado.

It was a few years later, in 1962, when I was deployed with UDT 12 on a Western Pacific tour. During our stop at Okinawa, a number of us were selected to go to parachute jump school. The U.S. Army First Special Forces Airborne Unit had a jump school at their base on the island. So for a while a number of Navy Frogmen learned how to jump out of a perfectly good airplane well before it landed.

After we completed jump school, we climbed aboard another plane that we were allowed to ride in all the way to its landing. That landing was in Yokuska, Japan, where another surprise showed up for a number of us.

It was around Christmastime, and I'm sure of that because I was coming back to the base from a Danny Kaye USO show. When I passed some of my Teammates on the beach, they told me to get over to the Quonset hut where the UDT 12 headquarters were. That wasn't any big deal, but then they told me that there was a set of transfer orders waiting for me there.

That last was something that had me a little bit upset. I had treaded water in the regular fleet Navy for four years waiting for my chance to become a Navy Frogman. And when I arrived in the office, I found out that sure enough, there were sets of orders for a bunch of us. We were all being transferred to something called "SEAL Team One."

No one there knew what a SEAL Team was, and I was raising more than a little racket about being transferred out of UDT 12. Our executive officer at the time was a man by the name of David Del Guidice. He told me that he didn't know what a SEAL Team was either. But Del Guidice went on to say that he was going to be my commanding officer when we got there. So I shut up right quick.

Men from both UDTs 11 and 12 formed the West Coast SEAL Team, SEAL Team One. The East Coast had men from UDT 21 drawn out to form up SEAL Team Two. Both Teams had sixty men, fifty enlisted and ten officers each.

We were flown back to Coronado, where we formed up into the new SEAL Team. At first, we didn't know what it was or what we were going to do. Confusion was pretty common and we were all a little lost. Six months later and the situation hadn't gotten a whole lot better.

We were fish out of water, literally. We had been told that President Kennedy had wanted people from the Navy to create a unit like the Army Special Forces. We were going to be able to train indigenous forces and operate in a riverine-type environment as well as operate there ourselves. And to meet our new responsibilities, we were going to receive a lot of training.

We went to all kinds of schools. We were commissioned as a SEAL Team in January 1962. And we went to schools almost from day one. Within a week of becoming a plankowner of SEAL Team One, I was at Camp Pendleton, going through basic infantry combat training.

Navy, Marine Corps, Army—all of them had training that we went to. Antiguerrilla and guerrilla warfare training from the Marine Corps; Fort Benning and Army Ranger training. Five days after I graduated from Ranger school, I was down in Panama going through jungle warfare school. Navy schools as well; assault boat coxswain training was one we attended. And after that we went to the Berlitz School of languages. Exotic demolitions training, such as atomic demolition munitions school. Almost anything that was available had some SEALs going to it. We had a Priority 2 and could get a billet for a student just by asking for it.

And we went across the country to Fort Bragg and attended Army Special Forces schools such as foreign weapons or kitchen table demolitions. And Special Forces operational techniques were not ignored as we learned how to operate as unconventional forces.

That last training was closer to what we were going to be doing within just a few years. But Vietnam was still down the road a ways, at least for some of us.

Within about a year of the SEALs Teams being founded, a group of us deployed to Da Nang to train commando-type troops. This was my first exposure to Vietnam. It was all brand-new to me and I was pretty excited. I had a new job and I didn't really know what the job was going to be. But all of us always tried to do the best we could with whatever job we were assigned.

Eventually, I became one of the men teaching the Vietnamese weapons handling, marksmanship, and other skills. This course went on for a while. My job was just to be their instructor. Once they were trained, the Vietnamese commandos were taken away and I never did learn what they were going to be used for.

That was in 1963, and I remember the year well as I had returned home just a short time before my son, our third child, was born. And there wasn't much question in my mind that the SEALs were going to be back in Vietnam.

The SEALs had both a cold-war and a hot-war mission to perform. Those first years after our commissioning, we were operating in a cold-war mode, acting as advisers and instructors. None of us really had any idea that by 1965–1966, the war in Vietnam would escalate to what it did. Once it became a hot war, it stayed that way through 1970 and beyond. But we were ready for it when the time finally came around for us to go into direct combat.

During the first several years of the Teams' existence, we continued to go to all kinds of schools in between the times we deployed as detachments to different assignments. By 1966, SEAL Team One was sending detachments to Vietnam to conduct direct-action combat missions against the Viet Cong. It had become a hot war.

For myself, I didn't go out on my first combat deployment until 1968. In 1965, after I had completed my first enlistment with SEAL Team One, I reenlisted to be an instructor at Underwater Demolition Team Replacement training, what was later to be known as BUD/S for Basic Underwater Demolition/SEAL training.

My tour as a UDTR instructor would be three years long. And after that tour was over, I would go back to SEAL Team One. It was with Class 42 in 1967 that I finished my tour as an instructor, and I ended up taking some of those boys overseas with me.

Things were continually changing during those years I spent as an instructor. When you first went in as a young man to be an instructor, you wanted to do everything to those students that you thought had been done to you when you went through training. Fortunately, there were some old vets who worked alongside you as instructors, and you were assigned to one another.

Those experienced instructors would hold you back and prevent you from tearing a student down completely. Because you were supposed to pick the man back up by the end of the day. And they also kept you from getting too extreme with the students. As my stint as an instructor went along, I learned how to do it right. And there were several things that personally happened to me to adjust my thinking.

Since my Navy rate was as a gunner's mate, my specific assignment was to teach demolitions, weapons, and land warfare. One of the experienced instructors who was there had actually taught me when I went through UDTR. Bud Jurick was someone you could look up to easily. He had parachuted into Normandy during D day when he was in the Army. And he had seen combat in Korea. He was kind of my idol, and he taught me how to be an instructor, and kept me from beating up the students too badly.

A BUD/S instructor points out a fine point involved in the cleaning of the M16A1 rifle. The student, with his disassembled weapon in his arms, looks intently at what his instructor is showing him.

U.S. Navy

Time had gone on in the Teams while I was helping to create new SEALs and Frogs. The SEAL combat commitment in Vietnam had started in 1966 and grown throughout the year. And the cost of that commitment also grew.

A young man that I had gone through training with in Class 24, who had jumped from planes with me over Okinawa, and had even bought the house behind mine in San Diego so that our families could grow up together—he was the first SEAL killed in Vietnam.

On 19 August 1966, Billy W. Machen was killed during an ambush of his platoon in Vietnam. He had been walking point during a patrol and opened fire on a VC ambush before his Teammates moved into the kill zone. He saved his platoon, and it cost him his life.

When that time came, I think it shocked the whole SEAL community. It brought us to the reality that we were fighting a hot war over there, and it could cost. So to try and hold down the cost, we started to do different things to improve our skills and knowledge. We would interview any SEAL who had just come back from Vietnam. We learned what they had been exposed to, how the enemy was fighting, what worked, and what didn't.

Training at UDTR didn't really change; instead it was added onto. When I had first stepped on board as an instructor, UDTR training was sixteen weeks long. When I left, it had increased to eighteen weeks long. It was continually growing, as nothing was taken away from the original course of instruction but more was being added all the time. It became harder because we were trying to teach those things that would help the Teams to deploy as soon as possible.

Our own success was coming back on us in a way. Vice Admiral Elmo R. Zumwalt Jr. was the commander naval forces, Vietnam, as of 30 September 1968. And Admiral Zumwalt wanted more SEAL in-country as soon as he could get them. We had already been sending augmentation platoons to Vietnam, platoons that arrived in-country not to relieve another platoon but to start up operations in new areas. And SEAL Team Two had been sending platoons to Vietnam since early 1967.

All of this added up to making that last year of my tour as an instructor the longest dress rehearsal I was ever on. I wanted to be a SEAL, I wanted to go back to my Team, and I wanted to go back to Vietnam.

Every time I went to Vietnam, it was a learning experience, especially in the beginning. Any individual who goes into combat experiences the fears of that first night. Just because a SEAL is highly trained for combat doesn't mean he won't be scared. And the same fear that was in my heart, I'm sure was in the hearts of the young men I had with me. But you also have to overcome that fear pretty quick or you won't be any use to yourself or your Teammates.

Arriving in Vietnam, I was the leading petty officer (LPO) for Alfa Platoon, following Platoon Leader Rip Bliss and a fine assistant platoon leader, Warrant Officer Scott Lyon. The platoon had another first class petty officer, Harlen Funkhouser, who had done tours up in the Rung Sat, north of the delta, where we were now. Outside of the three of us, all of the rest of the platoon had just graduated from UDTR only six months before our arrival in-country. We had trained as a platoon ever since their graduation.

You worry about kids like that, and I suppose they might have worried about me a bit. They called me the "Old Man," being all of the ripe old age of thirty-two. While we were getting ready to deploy, I remember my daughter going up to my wife crying "How come they're calling Dad the Old Man?"

Those "kids" of mine in the platoon were all of twenty or twenty-one-year-old men. But they did a great job during our deployment—fabulous, as far as I'm concerned. And I think that one of the reasons we did so well was that my platoon hadn't been exposed to the Rung Sat Special Zone and the tactics used there.

The Rung Sat is an almost 400-square-mile area of nipa palms, mangrove swamps, rivers, streams, canals, and mud between Saigon and the South China Sea. Called the Forest of Assassins by the Vietnamese after the hundreds of years of pirates and smugglers hanging out in it, the Rung Sat, as it was known to us, was the first area of Vietnam where SEAL Team One had begun combat operations back in 1966. That jungle mud and swamp needed a particular style of operating and movement for us to get around in it. Where we were for this tour, the Mekong Delta, it had a different way of making you move through it.

So now our platoon was developing new tactics. It did seem that every time you deployed to Vietnam, you were fighting a new kind of war. Things just changed constantly.

It may have been a little different, this tour for Alfa platoon. It may have been made up mostly of new graduates from training. But they also had their old instructor leading them. They would have to say themselves whether or not that made a difference. But I did notice that they did whatever I said without much trouble at all.

Early on during that deployment, Scotty Lyon went out on an operation that stands out in my mind from that tour. He took his squad, all green men, down to the north edge of the Ba Xuyen province, to the Cu Lao Dung Island complex near the mouth of the Bassac River. Mr. Lyon developed one of the finest operations that I have ever seen.

He had an LST offshore with helicopter gunships on board. From somewhere, Mr. Lyon brought somewhere in the neighborhood of eight to ten PBRs on the Bassac River at the same time. And they all went in and hit a POW camp, liberating twenty-six Vietnamese POWs who had been captured during the Tet offensive over six months earlier. And Scotty did all of this without one single casualty or accident among his men. That was a tremendous job.

We were all proud of how the Second Squad from our platoon had conducted that operation. There is no question that the success of that operation was due to Warrant Officer Scott Lyon and the way he was able to put the operation together and plan it out. That op was probably the highlight of the whole trip to me.

For our first operation, things were a little different. We inserted from an LCPL (Landing Craft, Personnel, Large), one of the older boats. One of the officers from Mike Platoon, who we were relieving, was taking us out into the area for a "breaking-in" op.

We inserted and patrolled in probably some 3,000 meters until we approached a hooch. A light inside the hooch caught the attention of our point man, so we spread out to surround the building. A couple of the guys went into the building and surprised the single VC inside. He didn't want to be taken prisoner and didn't get away fast enough. So Alfa Platoon had its first confirmed kill. Our platoon was now blooded.

One of our next operations went much the same. Only, on it we were chasing a mortar tube all night long. It was a heavy mortar and we could see the muzzle flashes from it every time the crew set it up and fired. The flash would reflect on leaves from trees and we knew we had to be close to the firing position. We also

A group of heavily armed SEALs on patrol in Vietnam, with his back to the camera in the center of the picture is Greg McPartlin, armed with a Stoner Mk 23 light machine gun. Attached to his carrying harness is an assortment of ammunition, fragmentation and white phosphorus grenades and medical equipment.

Greg McPartlin Collection

knew that a heavy mortar was usually protected by a dozen men or so with AK-47s. But every time we could get close to a suspected firing position, they would have moved and were firing from another location.

Finally, we found a large canal and figured out that they must have had the mortar mounted on a large sampan. Beaching the sampan, they would fire a few rounds on the nearby town of Vung Tau. They would fire three rounds and then move to another position. There, they would fire three rounds again and move on. After the third cycle of firing, the mortar stopped completely.

We never did find them, so we went back to our original mission. Again, we found a hooch with a single VC in it. And yet again, the man didn't want to be taken prisoner and we ended up taking him out.

Continuing our patrol, we came across a small bunker that we intended to blow. I had the demolitions with me and set the charge to destroy the structure. When the shot went off, the explosion was a lot more powerful than we expected. There was some VC ammo or other ordnance that my demolition charge had detonated. Just an average Saturday night in Vietnam.

We had no losses during that first tour, and few in the way of injuries. Our first op went down on 18 August 1968, and our last was on 9 February 1969. Alfa Platoon had 101 combat operations during that tour. And within a day or so of our last op, we were on our way back home to Coronado.

My second tour of duty to Vietnam was really more involved than that first one. I was again the LPO, this time of Charlie Platoon. On 31 December 1969, we arrived in Vietnam and Charlie Platoon started operating out of Ben Luc, a small Navy base on the Van Co Dong River. But that assignment wasn't going to last. Within a few months, Charlie Platoon was sent to the Ba Xuyen province as an augmentation platoon assigned to Coastal Group 36, right across the Bassac River from Dung Island.

Dung Island was a complex of nine different islands that had more or less been left alone during the war to that point. It was, of course, the same place to which Mr. Lyon had led Second Squad of Alfa Platoon to liberate that VC POW camp. But we were in the area to take advantage of the information that had been built up about the area.

Up in Saigon, the intelligence folder on the local area was about two inches thick. There was a tremendous NILO (Naval Intelligence Liaison Officer) officer down there who had an individual working for him who was a big help. The man working for the NILO was a Vietnamese civilian who was very good at getting into the Chieu Hoi circuit and gathering intelligence from them.

The Chieu Hoi (Open Arms) Program offered amnesty to Viet Cong defectors. People who wanted to leave the Communists could "rally" into a local Chieu Hoi center, where they gave themselves up with no risk of reprisals. There, they would be interrogated and debriefed on the operations they had done and what they knew about the area.

So we ended up on the shore at Coastal Group 36 living in tents. The situation wasn't the best in the world; we didn't even have a supply of food, or any regular way of getting any. Every now and then a Coast Guard cutter would come up and drop off some supplies, but for the most part, Charlie Platoon was eating off the land and what the local market offered.

The tents were our home for about three months. Then the Navy Seabees came in and built us a regular base. And I've loved the Navy Seabees ever since. The first thing they did was build a mess hall to feed us. And the second thing they did was build us a barracks, even before they built living quarters for themselves.

The base was an old French outpost, set up in a typical triangular formation. There was a small detachment of riverine forces at the base, a Vietnamese unit using a number of the old gray junks with a few machine guns on them for defense. The Vietnamese just kind of patrolled up and down the river in those junks.

We in Charlie Platoon didn't have anything much better in the way of equipment. We had little in the way of reliable boat support; there was no MST (Mobile Support Team) support with their specialized SEAL craft for us then. Instead, we had one

Three heavily armed Navy SEALs share a cigarette with a South Vietnamese. It was from their experiences in the early part of the Vietnam War that the SEALs learned prisoners and the information they supplied was one of the most valuable things they could bring back from the jungle.

U.S. Navy

Boston whaler with an outboard motor, IBSs, and sampans. That's what we had and it was what we used. The support may have been light, but Charlie Platoon operated.

In my first platoon back in 1968, we had spent 180 days in-country and ran 101 combat operations. In Charlie, my second platoon, we spent 180 days in-country and ran 71 combat operations. And in both platoons, we had over 80 percent enemy contact on our ops.

The operations for Charlie Platoon weren't as big in numbers, but we had learned a little more over the years. Now we went strictly after the VCI, the infrastructure of the Viet Cong, their leadership and support. Our training had emphasized that "dead men don't talk." And that was the lesson that had been driven home with everyone in the Team over and over again. Now we tried everything we could to capture prisoners and to gather information.

Back the year before, during Tet of 1968, we didn't know just how badly we had hurt the VC when we stopped their attacks and drove them back. The North Vietnam Army had put a lot of the leadership of the VC in the forefront of the attacks during Tet. When those VC leaders were killed, their places were taken by NVA officers from up north.

But when an NVA officer came down to take up an important position, he was usually a colonel or something like that, unless he was a tax collector. That officer would bring along his own security team, medical personnel, and other support staff. Capturing one of these guys would almost always turn into a firefight because of all the people they kept around them.

We started running into light force, company-sized combat units that were NVA. These troops were dressed like VC, but there were telltale signs we picked up quickly. Their packs and ponchos were different. And their sandals were very noticeable as high-quality NVA sandals rather than the local market products.

And the weapons these NVA units carried were better and more powerful than the norm had been with the VC. Instead of the bolt-action rifles we had seen before, now we were finding the troops armed with AK-47s and SKS carbines. The ammunition and grenades they carried also indicated that they were a well-equipped army rather than a purely guerrilla force.

Probably the thing that stands out most in my mind from that second tour is the end results from the whole tour. The capture of a number of VCI members and the intelligence that we drew from them helped us operate. Some of this information led us to jungle workshops where they had a junk factory hidden. This was a camouflaged factory where the VC had been making huge junks to transport their equipment and people from the South China Sea up the Bassac River to other parts of South Vietnam. It was a big factory, but we demolished it with explosives. On a bunch of operations, we ran into a lot of personnel who were shooting back at us. So during that tour, we had our hands full from time to time.

The most major action for me personally during that last tour took place with only a few of my Teammates around me. One night, we went in with three Americans, including myself, and a ten-man LDNN platoon. The LDNNs were then known as the Lein Doi Nguoi Nhai, South Vietnamese SEALs, the name translating to "the team of soldiers who fight under the sea."

The LDNNs were very good fighters in my opinions. But we went along with them on operations for a number of reasons, one of the big ones being to give them support. Without us—that is, Americans—on the operation, they couldn't call for air support or whatever else might be available from the U.S. forces.

We went in on some intelligence that told us about the location of a Viet Cong infrastructure meeting. We had both the time and probable location of the meeting and started our infiltration at night.

Going in from our insertion point, we slipped through the nipa palm for about three hours. The water we were moving through was so deep sometimes that some of us had to pick the shorter Vietnamese up from the water and pass them along

Two SEALs put out fire toward a camouflaged VC bunker hidden under the hooch in the distance. The SEALs are working in support of Operation CRIMSON TIDE near Vinh Binh in December 1967.

U.S. Navy

from one clump of nipa palm to another.

Just before daylight, we arrived at the target site. There was a small dike between us and a clearing. On the edge of the clearing was a hooch. Besides the clearing and the hooch, we also spotted an armed guard, sitting down and leaning against a tree, his weapon in his lap. He may have been asleep, but as soon as we came up over the dike, he jumped up.

When the guard jumped up, he was immediately knocked down. Of course the noise from that alerted the rest of the enemy. When we reached the hooch, there was a short, fierce firefight that resulted in our VCI targets being killed. Later two of the dead VCI were identified as Tu Day, a district security chief and chapter party secretary, and Nam Meo of the People's Revolutionary Committee. Some additional NVA got away, running from the back of the hooch into the jungle nearby.

With my Stoner carbine, I laid down fire on the VC running from the hooch. Other NVA were running toward a bunker at the same time and some of the LDNNs chased them. On the patrol, I was carrying the radio, and when the fighting broke out, I wanted to get that radio to the patrol leader as fast as I could.

As I was running across the field to where the patrol leader was located, something smashed into my back, knocking me down. I smacked into the ground but wasn't hurt. The adrenaline was pumping right then, so I just got up and kept going.

The patrol leader for the LDNNs was a petty officer named Tich. When I saw that young man next, he had been killed, shot right under the left arm near his heart. Ronnie Rodger, the SEAL LDNN adviser, had Tich over his shoulder. When he laid Tich on the ground, we could see that there wasn't anything we could do for him.

That death hit me pretty hard. There had only been ten months between my combat tours to Vietnam. The year before, Tich had been with me. During that deployment, I had even made it to Tich's wedding. And now I was going to attend his funeral.

There were no exit wounds in Tich's body. So I tied his hands together and slipped them around my neck so that his body could hang down across my back. I would carry my friend back out to his people. While I set off to the hooch with Tich, Rodger started gathering up our platoon and pulling them back to the building as well.

Later I thought Tich's body kept breaking my radio antenna. But as we dropped back to the hooch, we could see that the NVA on both sides were jumping into the nipa palm. So we laid down a base of fire with our machine guns.

Now it was time to get some support in there to help us. After unhooking Tich's body and laying it down, I took the radio off from my back, figuring the antenna might have been broken or bent from the weight against it.

After examining the radio, I now knew what had knocked me down when I ran through the clearing earlier. The battery pack of the radio had two holes in it where bullets had struck. The antenna was broken as well from a third bullet's impact. But when I tried it, the radio worked great.

The first thing I tried to do was to call in 81mm mortar fire from the Swift boats we had in the river after our insertion. But that didn't work since we were out of their range. There were some Army Cobra gunships that picked up my signal. They came in and offered what fire support they had available. But they were running short of fuel and ammunition and had to leave while the VC were still around us.

Now our small platoon of LDNNs and SEALs were surrounded by what was later determined to be an NVA light force company. They had us surrounded and we were already down two men, Tich and another LDNN who was wounded in the face. So the situation was starting to get more than a little tense for us.

But there was some additional support that came in over the radio, some of the OV-10B Broncos with U.S. Navy pilots. These were the armed Broncos of the Black Ponies Squadron. We couldn't have received much higher-quality help right then. The two planes had the call signs Pony 102 and Pony 106.

The NVA forces were all around us, cutting off any escape for the platoon. When the Ponies were overhead, I took out a magenta-colored silk "T" ground-marker panel. With the panel indicating to the Black Ponies exactly where we were, I told them that fifty meters in front of the T were the NVA.

The Black Pony pilot called back down to me, questioning the fifty meters' distance between us and the NVA, a dangerously close distance for them to unload their ordnance on a target and not risk hitting us. The pilot understood the situation immediately when I answered him, "Roger that, fifty meters. And if you don't hurry up, it'll be twenty-five."

Those planes came right down to the deck, flying just overhead to minimize hitting us. That was the closest support I ever had. And it was the best support I ever

In flight, a pair of OV-10A Bronco "Black Ponies."

had, too. The heavy five-inch Zuni rockets from those Black Ponies were like hitting the NVA with heavy artillery.

When the first of those big rockets went off, the blast shook us all hard, and I said a few choice words to reflect my feelings. It wasn't that the pilots had made a mistake, but the rocket had hit a palm tree close by over our heads and detonated early. So I called up to the pilot and asked: "What was that?"

"Five-inch rocket," was the answer that came back over the radio.

Well, I had been used to the 2.75-inch rockets from the Seawolves and other helicopter gunships. These were a lot larger, and louder. But their power was something we would be able to put to use.

The planes just pushed back the jungle in front of us. Then we would catch fire from the enemy coming in from the other side. So I would move the marker T and the Ponies would hit the jungle in front of it again.

Those two planes just stayed with us for what seemed like forever. Finally, Pony 102, the flight leader, called down to me over the radio. He said that they were running low on ammunition, so every other run or so would be a dummy run, with the planes not firing their weapons but still keeping the NVAs' heads down.

So those little OV-10s came in on a strafing run, and the NVA would dive behind whatever cover they had available. Only the planes wouldn't shoot. So when the Bronco passed, the NVA would jump up to try and shoot at the plane, and the next guy coming in would open up on them.

In Vung Tau, an airman carefully watches the underside of an OV-10A Bronco. His left hand is on the muzzle of one of the aircraft's four (two to a side) wing-mounted 7.62mm M60 machine guns. In front of the unconcerned airman is a pod of four 5-inch Zuni rockets and their large high-explosive warheads. Just visible to the left is an empty 7-round pod for 2.75-inch rockets. This is just some of the ordnance and weapons normally carried by a Black Pony for an operation.

U.S. Navy

The Black Ponies went back and forth like that for a while, then the flight leader got back in touch with me. He said that they had to leave soon but that two Marines (aircraft) were coming down from Vung Tau and he would stay with us until they arrived.

Soon there were two more OV-10s; these were Vipers from the Marine Corps, flying overhead, and the Black Ponies went back to refuel and rearm. Those Marines might have been different pilots, but you couldn't tell by the way they flew. They were call-signed 106 and 108. And those numbers were the only difference between those Marines and the Black Ponies.

Those Marines flew just as close and as accurately as the others had. The planes flew by so closely that I could tell you whether those pilots had shaved that morning or not. That was how low to the ground those little fixed-wing aircraft flew. Prior to that operation, Black Ponies had always been fighting for us from way up in the sky. That day, they had been right there in the jungle with us. And I wouldn't be here today telling of the action if it wasn't for them.

When the two Marine aircraft showed up from Vung Tau, the Black Ponies had already quieted down the NVA a bit. So I told those pilots to save their five-inch rockets. On the ground, we were getting low on ammunition, with the LDNNs only having about two magazines apiece for their M16s.

Di Croce, one of the SEALs from my platoon, had a Stoner light machine gun with him. So I had him break out part of his ammo load and pass it out to the LDNNs. Since the Stoner fired the same ammunition as the M16, the LDNNs were able to break down the belts and use the loose ammo to load up two more magazines apiece.

Now we had a medevac come in, and we were able to get our wounded and dead out. But the extraction birds wouldn't come in to get the rest of us out. So I told the Marine pilots to use their five-inch rockets and blow me a hole through the nipa palm.

Once that hole opened up for us, any NVA near it would be down for more than a moment from the blasts. So we took off through the hole and just about ran the 400 meters to the nearest water. But the tide had gone out and the water was low. In spite of the low water, as soon as my damaged radio got wet, it quit talking. But I had managed to turn over air-ground control of the aircraft to my lieutenant, who was on a Swift boat nearby.

Before we hit the water, the Swifts wanted to come in and give us fire support. But I had to tell them not to. They would have had to fire at the enemy right behind

PCF-11, a Navy Swift boat of Coast Division 11 making a high speed run. At the stern of the craft is a sailor manning the over/under Mk 2 81mm mortar and .50-caliber machine gun. Above the cabin, another sailor mans the twin .50-caliber machine guns in the gun tub. These boats were able to give rapid service and heavy fire support to SEALs during a mission.

U.S. Navy

us. We already had enough stuff coming at us. For the Swifts to have given us support, their fire would have had to come right at us as well.

But that's what happens when you're encircled.

We finally got out far enough that the boats were able to pick us up. Extracting, the patrol pulled out without any more casualties. Besides the VCI we had killed, we had also captured weapons, ammunition, and documents. And that was probably the most exciting mission I was on.

Ron Rodger and I took Tich's body back to Saigon, to the big cathedral they had there. Then we escorted it to the LDNN base and extended our respects to his comrades and family. Finally, we grabbed a helicopter heading back and returned to work.

That was an expensive operation for us; Tich had been a good friend. But it was pretty expensive for the NVA as well. Later reports added to the body count we had of twelve NVA KIA and fifteen WIA. Reports from NILO a few days after the op told of the NVA forcing the locals to produce forty coffins.

That was a memorable operation for me, and apparently the Navy thought highly of it as well. Sometime later, I was awarded the Navy Cross, our nation's second-highest award for valor, for the actions I took part in that day.

But I have mixed emotions about that medal. Of course you always feel very proud when someone hangs a medal on you for something that you did. And that wasn't the first one that anyone had ever hung on me. But the feeling of humility also comes in very strongly when I think about the medal.

I don't know of any medal that anybody could give anyone, for any action, in which somebody hadn't done more, or even lost their life, and didn't receive one. As I think about that day, I remember those guys up in the sky with their planes, the Black Ponies and Vipers. I wouldn't be alive today if it wasn't for them. And yet I was the one who received the Navy Cross.

My mentor back during my instructor days, Bud Jurick, explained to a student once what heroics were. Bud said that heroics were when the right man saw you at the wrong time, doing the job that you were trained to do. And I think that's what happened to me.

But a Black Pony will never have to buy a drink while I'm around. Just a short time ago I was able to make contact with the fellow who was the lead pilot of that flight of Black Ponies that day. And I am personally looking forward to seeing him.

Physically, a Navy SEAL can be almost any kind of man. There's heavyweights like me, and skinny ones. There's boys from Brooklyn and boys from Oklahoma, from Texas, Kentucky, California, and all of the other states of the Union. And with them come as many different backgrounds as there are places to come from. And each of them is an individual who has made the decision that "I quit" will not be a part of his vocabulary.

Navy SEALs have been portrayed as being kind of superhuman. And some of that might be their own fault. When you don't talk about something, even to end the rumors, the public tends to answer its own questions with whatever story might come along.

What the men of the Teams are, simply, are well-trained, devoted individuals who are, in a combat sense, workaholics. The Team they belong to is more of a huge family than anything else.

In my records are dozens of addresses of men I know and remain in contact with. There are many more who contact me, by phone, mail, or in person, every year. An old Teammate might call me at 2 A.M., and I'll still be glad to hear his voice.

Our reunions are where we get together on a scheduled basis once a year. And it's tremendous to see all of the guys together like that. You might run into a guy at a reunion who you haven't seen for twenty years, but all at once he shows up and it's like the time didn't happen.

I never did have a brother when I was growing up. But I've got hundreds of them now. And that's the reason I say it's a family. Even our higher command refers to the Teams as being a big family. And we react as one.

Sometime back, I went to Las Vegas to visit with an individual who knew that he had terminal cancer. And he knew that he was going to go. But he made a statement that stuck with me. "I don't care how big and how tough a Navy SEAL is," he said. "They'll always be able to say, 'I love you.'"

And that kind of summed it up to me. I may not be able to say that to another man, but inside the family, it's easy.

When a young man stands in front of the Naked Warrior statue, the monument in front of the UDT-SEAL Museum to the UDT men who went before us, I can't tell you exactly what he sees there. But there is something inside those bronze eyes that he does see, and it's not visible to those people who haven't served in the Teams.

What I do hope they would feel is the determination of spirit, the "I'm going to make it. I'm going to do it until I drop, nothing is going to stop me from being a SEAL."

Usually, guys come to that conclusion sometime during training. And by the time they reach that point, where they know inside their soul that they will not stop, usually by then, all of the others who hadn't made that decision have fallen away and are gone.

Chapter 37

First Combat

Vietnam was not the first place where the SEALs were sent in to combat as direct-action platoons. Though they were involved in a number of actions during the Cuban Missile Crisis in October 1962, the men of the SEAL Teams did not see active combat at that time.

The Dominican Republic is a country in the Caribbean that shares the island of Hispaniola with Haiti, taking up the eastern two-thirds of the island. In early 1965, rebel factions in the military rose up against the Ried Cabral government, causing it to fall on 25 April. Further uprisings of political groups and citizens added to the uproar of the coup in the country.

The United States Navy prepared to evacuate U.S. citizens from the Dominican Republic within a few days of the initial coup. Fears of a Communist takeover of the rebel movement prompted the United States to act. Without consulting allies in the surrounding countries of Latin America, the U.S. sent in Marines and other troops to the Dominican Republic. Among the troops that were sent in during May 1965 were Army Special Forces and Navy SEALs from SEAL Team Two.

The SEALs were highly trained, but most had never seen active combat. Actual fighting was limited, primarily taking place in Santo Domingo, which was the rebel stronghold. The rebels were not dominated or controlled by Communist forces, and the situation was later turned over to peacekeeping forces from elsewhere in Latin America. But in the Dominican Republic, the men of SEAL Team Two saw for the first time the tremendous destructive power of their still-new AR-15 rifles, the first ones of their kind in Navy hands. It would be several years before the SEALs would use those same rifles, along with a wide assortment of other weapons, in combat again, this time in Southeast Asia.

Excerpt from SEAL Team Two, Command and Control History 1966
Enclosure (1)
COMMAND HISTORY OF SEAL TEAM TWO
CHRONOLOGY

Mike Boynton, Master Chief Aviation Ordnanceman, USN (Ret.)

In early 1965, I wasn't married yet, though I was dating Mary, who would later be my wife. I was living out in Virginia Beach with a Teammate in a trailer. My transportation was a motorcycle and I considered myself really something hot, zooming into the base every day. Tom Cruise lives, a cool life.

One Saturday, I received a phone call from the quarterdeck at SEAL Team Two. The message was that I had to come in to the Team, that the CO wanted to see me. There was no question that I was going in as quickly as I could, but the thoughts that were going through my head were along the lines of: Oh, geez, what have I done?

I was only a third class petty officer, and I couldn't think of anything I had done recently to deserve the attention of the CO. And it had to be serious if he called me in to the Team on a Saturday.

I had only been in SEAL Team Two for about three months, having transferred over from UDT. It had been a job getting to the new SEAL Team; I couldn't just ship over from the UDT. Instead, I actually had to get out of the Navy and reenlist just to get over to SEAL Team Two. It had been a real hassle, but the end result was worth it.

Most of the guys were long familiar to me; I had known them back in UDT 21. And when I arrived, I started going through the mill, heading out for the various training courses to get my qualifications behind be. Now, three months later, I had most of my quals behind me. The only thing I hadn't done was go to HALO school yet.

So I was qualified to operate, and heading it to SEAL Team Two on a Saturday to see the CO about something that I had no idea about.

Okay, fine, I was heading in on my bike, wondering just what in the hell I had managed to do in the last two weeks since I had gotten back from training. It wasn't like they were going to tell me anything over the phone. It never dawned on me that we might be going somewhere. But that changed the moment I pulled in to the Team.

Here it was a weekend, liberty time, and a whole bunch of the guys were in at the SEAL Team. Oh, it's an op, I thought to myself as I pulled in. There wasn't actually anyone walking around the area, but the parking lot was full of cars. Something was up, no question about it.

Heading inside, I was told to head on back to the briefing room. I went on back to the briefing room and there was the CO, Tommy Tarbox, telling us that we were going to take two platoons down to the Dominican Republic. And we were going to leave tomorrow. And then we got a list of the gear we were supposed to take with us and who was supposed to get what. The rest of the talk was an outline of which platoons were going, how they were being transported—generally, a basic operational briefing.

It wasn't really two specific platoons that were going—we were organized into assault groups then anyway, which was really just a name change. A detachment the size of two platoons, twenty-four men, was being sent out on the deployment. There were guys like me, Bob Gallagher, Frank Moncrief, Swede Tornblum, and Jack Rowell among others, basically just a bunch of the guys from Team Two. Among our officers was Black Jack Macione and Georg Doran.

So we started breaking out the gear and packing it for transportation by ship. Our breathing rigs were these pieces of shit called Westinghouse Emersons. Opinions of the rigs were not high. But they were what we had, so they got packed up. Beans, bullets, this and that, whatever was on the lists, all went into our gray cruise boxes.

One of the new items we had was the first-model starlight scope. This was the newest thing on the market, and we had it mounted on an M14 rifle. That big-ass AN/PVS-1 scope added about six pounds to the rifle, but it let us see in the dark, which was pretty cool.

In a staged recruiting picture, Mike Boynton stands dressed in a camouflage beret and jacket, armed with an M16A1 rifle. With his face camouflaged, Mike Boynton is representing a SEAL. His Teammate stands behind him, geared for an open-circuit underwater swim as a UDT operator.

U.S. Navy

Okay, so we had all of our gear ready to go. We mustered again to get further instructions. Basically, we were going to muster at the Team Sunday and fly out. Then we were told not to tell anyone where we were going.

Tell anyone where we were going? I barely knew where we were going. And I wasn't going to tell anyone anyway. But I wanted to tell Mary something. So I took her out to dinner that night and said that I had to leave the country but couldn't tell her where I was going. There wasn't much more I could say than that. It was kind of stupid, but I was just a third class, what the hell did I know?

So the next day, we all jumped on a plane and flew on south. Landing in the Dominican Republic, we proceeded to stay at the airport all day and that night. Army Special Forces guys were hanging out at the airport along with us. It looked to me like mass confusion, but I guess somebody knew what was going on.

Macione, Doran, and a couple of others went off for briefings, so they had something to do and were gone all that day. For us, all we did was sit on our asses at the airport doing nothing. All we could do was stay in this hangar. You could tell there had been some kind of combat going on already because a lot of the planes were broken and you could smell things. It was the usual disarray of a battlefield, though not as intense as some I would see later.

But our officers finally came back and told us they were going to hold a briefing. So we all piled on this old plane, that we would never want to get on again, to have some kind of privacy. And the officers started to brief us on the situation. Then some yahoo official of the Dominican Republic came up and told us to get the hell off the plane.

So we had to go somewhere else and complete the briefing. Basically, we were told we were going to go into town and do some fighting. And they had some other things lined up for us. And we were all going to get into civilian clothes so that we could blend in. The only thing was, none of us had any civilian clothes with us. We were all running around in greens; nothing unusual about that for us.

So we went to this one place to get outfitted, the local haberdashery. It was a big setup by the Army Special Forces to issue plain clothes to their men, a "sterile issue," and we were now part of the party. What a joke that was; none of the clothes fit us; the only thing that fit me was the shoes because I have small feet.

Drawing our clothes—it was a regular military supply-room kind of setup. We walked along a table and an Army supply type tossed items at us according to our answers about size. When we came to the part where we received civilian shoes, the sergeant barked, "What size?" So I answered, "Five and a half."

Now I'm kind of a big guy, so this sergeant looked up at me, leaned over the table, and looked down at my feet. Then he kind of leaned back up and asked me, "Do you fall over a lot?"

Ha, ha, very funny. Everybody's a comedian. But at least the shoes fit.

So we put on our blue jeans and whatever. And we looked like a real motley mob. Dressed like some kind of refugees, we were going to go into town now, incognito. This was another carefully planned ruse; it really was a great big joke. To transport us into town they were going to use Army six-by-six trucks. So there we were, in Army trucks with all of this military equipment and us, standing up in our civilian clothes, with American weapons in our hands. Subtle. We really had to have looked like a bunch of idiots.

And our weapons were not the most common thing around. We had brand-new AR-15 rifles that Roy Boehm had got for the SEALs right after they were commissioned. The Army only had a handful of those rifles for their airborne and Special Forces. So that helped us really blend in as well.

But the trip into town confirmed what we had seen at the airport. This wasn't a joke; there had been some real fighting going on between the [reportedly] Communist rebels and the government forces. The first clue we had was the bodies we could see beside the road. Going over the bridge into Santo Dominoo, we had a real clue that the fighting wasn't done yet when our trucks started taking fire.

It was exciting trying to get underneath those cruise boxes. There isn't a whole lot of cover in the back of a flatbed truck. We couldn't go anywhere and there was nothing else for us to do. What could we do, jump off the back of the truck? And we didn't know where the fire was coming from, so we didn't have any target we could shoot back at.

All we knew was that the fire was coming from town and heading our way. All of us were a lot more disciplined than to just shoot back randomly. And the fire wasn't that close; it wasn't like the bullets were pinging off the truck. But you could hear the zing of rounds going by. It did manage to concern us a bit.

Our little convoy made it over the bridge and into town with no losses. Our final stop was at this big building. The bottom part was this showroom kind of thing, as if for cars. And there was the parts storage area in the back. The whole place was a two- or three-story job. And the rebels had already been there. The building was shot up a bit and looted.

There was a lot of confusion in town. But we linked up with some Army SFs. What we were supposed to do then, I had no idea. The general plan called for us to do some body snatches among the rebels to gain intelligence on their actions, strength, and intentions. And they had some other shit for us to do on kind of an individual basis.

Two of the guys, Georg Doran and Jack Rowell, were taken out and sent up into the mountains somewhere. Their mission was to search some caves along the shore of a bay to try and find some rebel supply caches or signs of where they were smuggling in gear.

But the situation was a little funny for us, besides the lack of specific direction. We had previously trained some of the Dominican Republic's military people, and apparently they were the nucleus of this uprising. That situation kind of made for some general directions to us about not shooting anybody that we recognized.

That struck me as great. What kind of deal was that? If we met these guys, we were supposed to act like we didn't know them? The training had taken place before my time had begun with the Team. It wasn't like I was going to know anybody. So I just said fine, if I knew the guy, I wouldn't shoot at him.

We camped out in this damned building for two or three days. Everything was dark; there wasn't any power. There were artillery pieces, 105 howitzers, somewhere within range. They were on our side, but sometimes it was hard to tell. The Army would crank off a round at the bad guys now and then, even though they might only be a block or two away from where we were. It was almost like what has been going on in Bosnia today, or it seems close to it, I think.

The population in the city had the good sense to stay out of the line of fire. That is, if there was anybody still in that town after the fighting had been going on. When I manned our sniper position up on the roof of our building, I could see the occasional armed rebel running around down the street. You could time one of the runners moving from place to place and then pop him off.

The Dominican Republic was the place where we first saw just what our AR-15s could do to somebody when you hit them with that small, fast bullet. As far as I was concerned, the M14 was better for the kind of shooting we were doing down there. It had more power and could punch through a wall if you wanted to.

I never really had any preference for the AR-15 or M16 over the M14, except for the weight of the gun and the ammunition you could carry. For myself, I didn't see any of the "explosive" power of the AR-15 bullet. It stopped people, but that was just like any other weapon. Once, in Vietnam, I hit a Viet Cong with eight rounds of

.223, and he just kept on trucking. None of the shots hit a vital spot and he might have bled to death later on, but those bullets didn't stop him from moving.

And there was a chance to do a little firing during our deployment. More than a few shots came our way as we went from room to room during house searches. And we had to stand watch to secure our own area. There was a password system set up and everything. Though in an outfit as small as ours, the idea of passwords seemed pretty ridiculous. More than once the challenge came back in a familiar voice: "Password, what the hell are you talking about? You know it's me."

During pre-deployment training, this SEAL carefully aims his heavy-barreled bolt-action sniper rifle. Sitting to the right of the shooter is another SEAL spotting the bullet strikes. Though most enemy engagements in Vietnam were at 30 feet or less, the SEALs practiced long-range shooting and a limited amount of sniping as part of their combat preparations.

U.S. Navy

I took things kind of lightly because, well, basically I thought it was a farce. The Special Forces didn't, though. They were really pissed at us because of what they thought was our blasé attitude.

The Army Special Forces did have some missions they wanted us to perform because of our special skills. The best one was when they wanted us to go through the sewer system of the city wearing our Emersons. And they wanted us to crawl through the sewers dragging all this demolition [explosives] along with us. That way, we could plant it underneath the building and blow up the radio station. The radio station was a problem because the rebels were in control of it and were broadcasting propaganda to the population at large.

That idea was kind of insane. First off, the sewer system wasn't very big. And there was no telling what was inside of there, besides that stuff that's normally in a sewer. I thought they should just take a helicopter and a pallet full of C-4 and drop it on the station. That would have taken care of the rebel broadcasting problem. I think they did do that bomb drop.

There wasn't a chance in hell that I wanted to go into one of those sewers and run into an alligator or whatever might be down there in the tropics. And that wasn't the only weird thing they were trying to get us to do. But what bothered me was that there was somebody, someplace, thinking up this weird shit. Some second lieutenant probably, straight out of West Point and trying to make a name for himself. Who knows?

There was one operation they had us do that involved us going down to a beach on an inlet of the ocean. Our mission was to render the beach safe so that the Army could take out some politicos or whoever. They had arranged for safe passage to get them out of the country or whatever.

For that one, I had an M14 with that starlight scope of ours. My position was across the river from the inlet. One of the guys was acting as a spotter for me and we had set up a little sniper position where we could see a good part of the beach. If anyone got in the way of the beach group, I would be able to pick them off without much problem.

Personally, I thought the starlight was great. Even later in Vietnam, I liked them in spite of their weight. They were heavy, but that ability to see in the dark was great. There was a problem when I actually fired that M14 with the starlight scope on it. When you fired, the muzzle flash would bloom out the scope, causing the whole thing to just go green for a while. Then it would kind of calm down and you could see through it again.

There wasn't much in the way of action, though I did take a shot or two as those days went on. We got put on a couple of missions, but they all fell through before we could act on them.

One platoon went back to the Creek while another one stayed on. I was in the group that stayed on, so my little adventure continued. Larry Bailey was there as one of the SEAL officers, the officer in charge. All in all, I think I was in the Dominican Republic for over a month, about five weeks or so.

We hooked up with an explosive ordnance disposal unit that was down there and we did a few things with them, but nothing particularly exciting. Then we were told to pack our shit, that we were all going home. Being the low man in the ranks, I took a ship back with all of our gear on board. A boat ride back to the States and my Dominican Republic deployment was over.

■ Chapter 38

The UDT Deploys

Before the SEAL Teams had been commissioned, the UDTs were operating in Vietnam. By the end of 1961, the USS *Cook* (APD-130) had been assigned the task of surveying certain beaches along the South Vietnamese coats. The *Cook* had aboard her a detachment of UDT operators, the men working off the APD as their forebears had done during World War II and Korea. On 4 January 1962, the *Cook* was moving to her assigned objectives along the coasts of South Vietnam.

In 1963, the conning tower of the USS *Sea Lion* is exposed as the submarine moves across the surface off Saint Thomas Island in the Caribbean. Waving from the bridge is the submarine's skipper, Commander Bob Bills. The *Sea Lion* was one of the diesel-electric submarines that worked a great deal with both the SEALs and the UDTs during the 1960s.

U.S. Navy

The UDT operators on board the *Cook* conducted the same hydrographic reconnaissance they had been trained for and that had been a UDT mission for years. Beach configurations, gradients of the shore and underwater seafloor, tides, and underwater obstacles were all located, measured, and recorded. Charts were created from the UDT data that would allow landing craft to conduct amphibious operations with little difficulty. By the end of January, the *Cook*'s mission had been completed.

But this was hardly the end of the UDTs' operations in the waters off, and in, South Vietnam. Detachment Bravo from UDT 12 was conducting survey operations off the northern coast of South Vietnam, near Danang, in late February 1963. Working with a team from the Third Marine reconnaissance battalion on board the USS *Weiss* (APD-135), the men of the UDT were the only ones allowed to carry weapons ashore. These arms were for self-defense only, and the UDT operators were not to go farther inland than the high-water line.

On 24 February, the Marine detachment from the *Weiss,* working onshore, started taking sniper fire from the jungle. There were no casualties among the Marines or other boat personnel as the group left the beach area. The Marines from the *Weiss* again came under fire some weeks later, now operating off the Mekong Delta. Again there were no casualties, but the mission was drawn to a close before the men's luck ran out.

Further hydrographic surveys and other missions in South Vietnam were conducted by UDT detachments operating out of Subic Bay in the Philippines. Clandestine UDT ops were conducted using the submarines *Perch* (APSS-313) and *Sealion* (APSS-315). Operations conducted from these two craft allowed the concealment of the UDT detachments aboard. Extensive use was made of the two craft by the UDTs.

In 1965, a detachment from UDT 12 continued forward a tradition from the World War II UDTs.

Detachment Delta, UDT 12 at Camp Tien Sha
A detachment of Frogs from UDT 12, working as part of Naval Beach Group 1, were on Red Beach II, just to the north of Danang, on 8 March 1965. They had a sign hanging between two rubber-boat paddles reading:

WELCOME U.S. MARINES
UDT 12

The landing Marines were also met by a number of Vietnamese schoolgirls who put garlands of flowers around the Marines' necks.

Throughout the Vietnam War, the UDTs would be operating in and around South Vietnam. Inshore UDT operations included demolition, reconnaissance, and diving ops. Though they were not expected to conduct direct-action operations against the Viet Cong, the men of the UDTs saw their share of combat. Three men from UDT 13 and one from UDT 12 lost their lives due to enemy action in Vietnam.

Dee Van Winkle, Boatswain's Mate Third Class

Back around 1960, Reader's Digest ran a story about the UDTs of the Navy. It was such a powerful story to me that I knew what my life was going to consist of from that point on. The story discussed what the Underwater Demolition Teams had done during World War II, and stressed how they were among the toughest men in the world. From that time on, I just wanted to be one of those Frogmen.

As everyone has to, to get to the UDTs first I had to enlist in the regular Navy. For six to seven months, I served as a lowly compartment cleaner, sweeping bar-

racks out. Then my paperwork had gone though, and in 1963, I was picked up for Class 30, UDTR, at Coronado.

Class 30 started with 143 students; we graduated in January 1964 with 30 still there, the Dirty Thirty. When I first started training, every day was exciting, and so was every night. It was a great bunch of guys to be with, and we sort of stuck together. There's five or six of us who still communicate to this day.

For me, the training was sheer excitement; I loved every second of it. There were aspects of the training that weren't very fun. Fatigue was the big one. It was just very tiring, exhausting really. Lack of sleep was something that everyone suffered from. Had we been able to sleep more, I think we could have performed on a higher level. But of course that's part of the training, to teach your mind as well as your body.

I remember being so tired that I fell asleep in my food a number of times in the chow hall. And I was hardly the only one to do that. It was startling to wake up with my face down in my plate.

Since I was from Arkansas, the Pacific Ocean was something new to me. But at UDTR, it was something you got familiar with very quickly. Arkansas has a serious winter, and I spent more than a few days in the snow growing up. But the cold of the Pacific was something new.

Crouching down on watch, this UDT operator keeps a lookout for enemy activity along a small stream in Vietnam. Behind the UDT operator, his Teammates are preparing demolition charges to destroy a VC bunker.

U.S. Navy

During training, the cold sank into you. Once it got into your bones, into your entire system, it took a long time for it to get out. After training, I remember being cold for weeks. It was like a mild case of hypothermia, and it's hard to explain to someone who hasn't been exposed to it. But it stays with you for a long time.

Hell Week was one of the big hurdles you had to complete early on in training. I remember the lack of sleep and being constantly on the move. The instructors would have us do things that required a lot of intense physical exertion. The memory of being very, very cold, all of the time, is also something that sticks with me about UDTR.

But one of the really great things about the Teams also started during UDTR. And that was the bond that started forming with all of us. It was a very strong bond, and immense respect, for all of us who went through that experience together. Hell Week was great; I actually really liked that whole week.

It was the people I was with who made getting through Hell Week possible. I felt I could have done more than one of those intense weeks of training, as long as I could have my Teammates with me.

It's not so much your own strength you feel, your own power or ability to handle any situation. When you're really into it, you feel like when you're with these certain people, you can just go on, and on, and on, forever. It's quite an amazing thing that not too many people understand.

Hell Week is where you learn to get the job done, but you can't do the job by yourself. You obviously have to have help, and you learn to rely on your Teammates. Just as they rely on you. It is absolutely where you learn the importance of being in a Team.

There were things that were just physically tough in training. Probably the runs in soft sand while wearing boots and after having rolled around in the surf for a couple of hours are a good example of what was physically tough to do. And one of the big reasons for this was not just the running, or the being wet. While you were rolling around in the wet, your crotch filled up with sand. The abrasion of that beach sand against the more tender portions of your body as your legs went back and forth during a run was pretty painful.

We ran for different lengths of time, different distances, and constantly built up our legs for the long swims we would have to do later. In spite of all the physical output, I never reached the point where I felt my body was just giving out. That just didn't happen with your friends around you. You could be in pain, but you were still invincible.

In my estimation, the extraordinary thing about the people who make up the Teams is not the physical aspect. People who look at the UDTs from the outside think about the big, strong guys, just the physical strength. But that isn't the really important part to me.

In our class, we had a guy who was bigger than most of us. He could outrun us, out PT us. He was just stronger and faster than the rest of us. Many of us looked up to him as a hero. But in spite of all of this guy's abilities, he was the last one to quit from our class. He never graduated. It wasn't the strength, or the speed—it was the heart. He wasn't the same on the inside as he was on the outside. And you have to be that, or it just doesn't work.

The respect that you give after you learn just how strong a person is inside is unlike anything you may have felt before. You know absolutely that nothing, nothing at all, is going to stop that man. He could be a big man, a little man, ugly or hand-some. But when you've learned what's inside that person, that shows you real strength. And it is only people like this who make up the Teams, who are your Teammates.

For years, I had been thinking of being in the Teams, or being a Navy Frogman. The thought of quitting just never entered my mind. I wanted to be with these men, to serve and work with them. Nothing was going to make me quit, but 110 other trainees in Class 30 did.

Part of our instruction included learning the traditional cast and recovery tech-niques developed by the UDT operators of WWII. Rolling off the rubber boat se-cured to the side of a speeding LCPR was neat. That wasn't the time for me when I looked at myself and said, "I'm a Frogman now." But later, we all received pictures of ourselves doing that training evolution. It was when I saw that picture of myself doing cast and recovery, rolling off the boat into the foaming water, that it hit me. It wasn't doing the act, it was seeing the picture that made me realize, hey, this is pretty cool, I'm a Frogman now.

Standing on the grinder that last day and graduating from UDTR was terrific. It made me feel special, and I still do. It was just an honor to be with such great guys, and to be accepted by them was an even greater one.

After graduation, I was assigned to UDT 12, stationed right there in Coronado. After training, I went on to complete Army jump school at Fort Benning, Georgia, and was parachute-qualified. My first deployment came soon after, to Southeast Asia and Vietnam.

This was before the full deployment of U.S. troops to Vietnam. But the situation there was still a serious one. Instead of doing much in the way of beach surveys, our main function was river stuff. We did a number of river patrols and river recons. During the deployment, we did do some beach recons off of Vietnam in the South China Sea, but only a handful of them.

The UDT mission in Vietnam was mainly the river work, the river recons. We served a couple of different purposes, conducting beach recons, especially before the war escalated. Clearing waterway blockages and obstacles with demolitions. And some general diving, sometimes for intelligence and equipment recovery.

Most of my time was spent on the Hue River conducting recons with my Team-mates. The river recons we did consisted of doing soundings and recording the

UDT trainees cast off over the side of a rubber boat during their BUD/S training. As did their UDT forefathers, these men are operating with a minimum of equipment to conduct beach surveys. Around the neck of the swimmer still on the boat to the left is a plastic slate and wax crayon for making notes.

U.S. Navy

depth of the waters, ensuring that boats and ships could make it up and down the river. We also charted the locations of fishing nets, the details of possible embankments. All in all, pretty simple stuff, but done in a very scary environment.

We probably weren't the first ones doing that kind of work in the river. But we were the only ones there at that time. And we were operating from an LCPR (Landing Craft, Personnel, Reconnaissance), which was just a wooden boat. On either side of us were fairly high banks where anyone could have been hiding. We were looking over our shoulders a lot.

This was well before the Swift boats were around. There were no helicopter gunships to call on, no gunfire support from offshore ships, or artillery support from local units. There were no other support craft around.

We were armed with some AR-15 rifles, .45-caliber M3A1 "Greasegun" submachine guns, and some M1 Carbines. In other words—nothing. The LCPRs each had one .30-caliber machine gun, and we usually operated in pairs. That's not very much armament. By today's standards, it's no armament. It was a scary situation.

Going down the river, we felt like ducks in a pond, only we didn't know where the hunters were, and the possibility of enemy fire coming in from both sides was pretty bad. Going out of the river to get back to the USS Cook out offshore was even worse.

Right at the mouth of the Hue River was an island. So that meant we could take fire from three sides. Which happened to us; that was where we got hit.

Much later I returned to Vietnam with another deployment for UDT 12, but this one was a combat assignment. The mission involved more river work, only this time we ran into a few firefights. It was a hard time for us; we lost a few men. Those days are still etched in my mind. I still think about them a lot and simply wish they had never happened.

During my first combat op, I was afraid. I think that most people, if they are totally honest with you, will say that they were fearful for their life in combat. But at the moment that the action is occurring, you don't really have time to be very afraid. You just do what you were trained to do. It's only later that you experience the fear about what you just encountered.

The men we lost during that tour were not Teammates; that is, they were not members of the UDT. They were teammates in the sense that we were working together, but they were members of the crew of the USS Cook (APD-130), the ship we were operating from. One of the men was a .30-caliber machine gunner and another was the coxswain of our LCPR, the boat we took from the Cook to our operating site.

While we were on a river operation, our boat was ambushed at the mouth of the Hue River. During the fight, our coxswain and gunner were both killed the same day. That wasn't the only loss we experienced. In another firefight, a U.S. Marine First Force recon guy who was working with us was also killed. I never experienced the loss of an immediate UDT Teammate while in Vietnam. But the men who were killed worked right alongside of us, and it could just as easily have been one of our own who was killed.

There were friends of mine in the Teams who were lost, but not in combat. These men were lost during training exercises after graduating from UDTR. Our duties in the Teams are hazardous, and they proved the point. We lost one of our Teammates during helicopter operations off of Camp Pendleton. His name was Aden Marshall.

The situation was that we were doing helicopter insertions with an inexperienced man at the controls. The pilot didn't realize that every time a 200-pound man with his gear went out of the bird and into the water, the helicopter would increase in speed and altitude. Generally, the insertion ops were 20/20, that is they were twenty miles an hour in speed and twenty feet in altitude. We would go about 10/10, going ten miles an hour faster and up ten feet, every time we deployed an operator. By the time the whole stick was out, the bird was probably doing seventy miles an hour at the seventy-foot level.

An APD, or High Speed Transport converted from an early-model Destroyer. These APDs were made the floating bases for the UDTs, one UDT to an APD. Two of the four UDT Platoon LCPRs can be seen hanging from davits toward the stern of the craft. During WWII, some UDTs spent eighteen months and more aboard the same APD.

U.S. Navy

That pilot just didn't have the proper training or experience to fly the bird on that kind of operation. Aden Marshall was the last guy in the stick, and he hit the water like a ton of bricks. We didn't recover the body until sometime later, and it was just a mess, a huge mass of black-and-blue bruises.

That was one of our bad situations. But it wasn't the only one. Another time, we lost a couple of divers off the Silver Strand during underwater operations. We were conducting a mock attack on a target ship offshore from the Strand. We were using the Emerson rebreather, a real death trap, as our breathing rig.

In reality, the Emerson can be a very good unit to operate with. But at the time we were T&Eing (Testing and Evaluating) this particular piece of equipment. We were not aware that you should not go beyond a certain depth with it. We also weren't aware that if you overworked (breathed too hard) the rig, you had a bad CO_2 buildup.

Carbon-dioxide buildup in a breathing rig was insidious; it would sneak up on you and kill you before you even noticed it. That was what was thought to have happened to two of our Teammates on that attack swim. Cliff Walsh and Samuelson were two of our better Teammates as far as operating goes, and we lost them both. The sea just took them; we never found the bodies.

This was part of the cost of being a Frogman. We worked in a dangerous environment during almost any job we did. That's why the job was so exciting. The danger is like a drug to some people, to do something exciting every day.

Once you've experienced something like this, the constant danger and risk in your everyday work, that level of excitement is something you miss. When you get

A SEAL combat swimmer enters the water having jumped from the "Hell Hole" of a CH-46 Sea Knight helicopter.

U.S. Navy

out of the Teams, there are just a lot of the guys who don't handle it very well. They miss the life and don't handle the civilian world very well because of that. After I got out of the Teams, I was very fortunate in that I was still playing rugby a lot. That gave me back something of what I had in the Teams and made the transition a little easier.

In the early 1960s, while I was in UDT 12, the SEALs were still pretty much in their infancy. We just didn't know much about them and I personally didn't really have any feeling one way or the other about them. I didn't feel that I wanted to be a SEAL because the UDTs were still doing the main bulk of the operating. Being an operator, that's what I wanted to do. What I didn't want to do was spend my time going to school, learning everything new. I just wanted to do what I had already been taught.

No one in the UDTs seemed to envy the SEALs very much in the beginning, at least not from what I could see. We had all worked very hard to get into the UDT, and the SEAL Teams were very much an unknown.

And the UDTs had some really exciting and interesting jobs going on. The space capsule recovery operation had been assigned to the UDT. Though I never served on one of the recovery teams myself, a number of my friends did. Every manned space shot NASA put up was met by a unit of men from the UDT when it splashed down. I would have loved to have been on one of those teams myself, but just never had the chance.

A modern SEAL takes aim with his M4 carbine while moving forward from cover. His uniform, gear, weapon, and skills were directly developed from the SEALs' experiences in Vietnam.

Kevin Dockery

Being in the Teams was the high point of my life. I have no regrets at all about having served in the UDT. As I look back on it, it was a great adventure, a terrific ride. And I'm just happy to have been a part of it. It was awesome.

The connection I feel with the older UDT operators is probably no different from what I feel toward my own Teammates. That is, we both basically did that same thing. I'm a little bit more in awe of those World War II UDT operators than I am of even my own guys in some respects. They had a real lack of equipment, and much of their training was being developed as they operated. But inside, they were the same guys then as we have today.

After having seen some of the older equipment, especially the diving rigs, I'm amazed the older operators aren't all dead. Even something as simple as the face-plates (masks) they wore were horrible in comparison to what we had. The rubber rotted, and they were small, uncomfortable, and leaked a lot.

Then of course, having seen the modern equipment they use in the Teams to-

day, I'm stunned we did as well as we did back in my day. With the weapons and gear they have now, the comparison is just unbelievable.

There are a lot of misconceptions about the Navy SEALs, and about the Frogmen before them. The public image of a SEAL seems to be that they are these "bad" guys who walk the streets. And the last thing you want to do is screw with a SEAL.

That's not the way it is at all in my eyes. From what I've seen, a Navy SEAL is probably the most polite guy you'll meet in a roomful of people. And he's probably the most humble person in there as well. That Navy SEAL knows himself and his capabilities. And he doesn't have to prove himself to anyone.

Navy SEALs are no different from anyone else when it comes down to being a person. They have the same feelings, the same emotions, the same blood. They're only different in that they're able to control themselves a little more than most.

The public hoopla about the SEALs just confuses me a bit. I don't know what the public expects the men of the Teams to do, other than be themselves. They have no need to do anything to impress people. In fact, they have no need to impress anyone at all.

I think it's important that everyone knows that the men of the Teams are just normal people. We're just people who have been selected and trained to do a certain thing, and hopefully do it very well. And that's it. The special feelings we have for each other are created by the hardships we all had to endure during our training. Personally, I don't want anyone to look at me as anything other than a regular guy.

When the young SEAL of today looks at the older men of the Teams, I hope he does so with some respect for that person's accomplishments. That respect is probably the only thing I would really hope for, and maybe a little curiosity to get to know that person, and what he did in the past.

The thing that binds all of us together in the Teams, then and now, is the feeling of invincibility, the capability we all have to just get the job done, any job. It doesn't matter if it's just a bunch of us repairing a car together, or lending a hand moving someone's household, or just chopping wood. You know you can do anything better than you normally could when you're with your Teammates.

If the Navy SEALs were a football Team, they wouldn't lose a single fucking game. The reason I can say that is that every football team I was ever on when I was in the Teams, we won. I was on the original Navy rugby team back in the early 1960s. And we didn't really know what we were doing at first. But that didn't matter; we still won almost every game we played. We would just put all of the other players out of the game, knock them right off the field. Nobody wanted to play us after a while.

Chapter 39

The SEALs Deploy for War

On 1 November 1963, President Diem of South Vietnam was attacked and the government threatened in a coup. The military and the government of South Vietnam staggered and almost fell during the turmoil of the Diem assassination, which took place only a few days later. Diem had been a staunch anti-Communist, and he had received the support of the United States for some time. There were only a few thousand U.S. military advisers in Vietnam at the time of Diem's assassination, among them a handful of SEAL and UDT operators.

Though the situation in South Vietnam was of concern to the U.S. government and the general public, the news of Diem's death was overshadowed by the assassination of President Kennedy only a few weeks later. The government of North Vietnam hoped to take advantage of the situation to their south before the United States could further support South Vietnam. In the year following Diem's death, several more coups and power struggles took place in South Vietnam. And North Vietnam increased its support of the Communist guerrillas in the south. The Viet Cong started receiving a greater flow of materials, weapons, munitions, and even manpower from the north.

The hoped-for general uprising of the population in South Vietnam never took place, much to the disappointment of the commanders in Hanoi. The increase in the flow of supplies to the south caused the United States to begin a bombing campaign along what would soon be called the Ho Chi Minh Trail.

MTT detachments of SEALs continued in South Vietnam, and a new mission increased the SEALs' mission in Vietnam. Admiral Harry D. Felt had put forward a plan of action against North Vietnam in June 1963. Felt's Operational Plan 34A (OP 34A) centered on conducting covert operations against North Vietnam. South Vietnamese commandos, trained and equipped by the United States, would conduct these operations. For the maritime portion of OP 34A, the Navy SEALs would train the South Vietnamese commandos to conduct operations against the north from a variety of watercraft, including Norwegian "Nasty"-class fast patrol boats.

Though the SEALs themselves would not be allowed to go on the northbound OP-34A missions, they trained the men who did conduct the operations. A number of missions were conducted, with some successes. In early August 1964, in the Gulf of Tonkin off the shore of North Vietnam, Swatow motor gunboats of the North Vietnamese Navy attacked the US Navy Destroyers *Maddox* and *Turner Joy*. The Swatows would have been a match for the "Nasty"-class fast patrol boats of OP-34A, but they were not a match in firepower against American destroyers. In spite of this, the Swatows attacked the *Maddox* and the *Turner Joy* on two different occasions during those early August days.

Torpedoes fired by the Swatows did not impact on the destroyers during either engagement, but some heavy-machine-gun fire and small-cannon fire did hit the American craft. The Swatows came under heavy fire from the Navy ships, taking heavy damage in some cases. But the worst damage of the incident would be the political fallout soon to take place in the United Sates.

President Johnson called on the U.S. Congress to respond to the attack against the ships of the U.S. Seventh Fleet. The Congress and Senate passed the Southeast Asia (Tonkin Gulf) Resolution, which gave President Johnson the power to escalate the war in Vietnam as he needed without there actually being a declaration of war. The buildup of U.S. military forces in South Vietnam was now allowed.

Further actions had taken place in Vietnam during 1964 that would greatly affect the SEALs' actions in Southeast Asia. Admiral Felt created a study team to learn about the movement of supplies to the Viet Cong through the Mekong

A Norwegian-built "Nasty"-class fast patrol boat moving at high speed through Pacific waters. Six of these boats were obtained for operations off the coast of North Vietnam. The crews of the boats first received their training at Little Creek, Virginia, from the instructors of SEAL Team Two.

U.S. Navy

Delta as well as about guerrilla actions in South Vietnam. The nine-man team was led by Captain Phil H. Bucklew, a highly decorated naval officer who had served with distinction with the Scouts and Raiders during World War II.

Officially known as the Vietnam Delta Infiltration Study Group, the team arrived in Vietnam in January 1964 to begin their work. The final study of the team became known as the *Bucklew Report*. The *Bucklew Report* identified the Ho Chi Minh Trail as the primary route used to get supplies from the north down to the guerrillas in the south. But the report also identified the rivers, streams, and canals of the Mekong Delta as primary routes of movement for the Viet Cong.

To stop the flow of men and supplies through the Mekong Delta area, new naval task forces would have to be established, equipped, and trained to operate both in the offshore waters of South Vietnam and in the inland waterways of the Mekong Delta. Task Force 115 was established on 11 March 1965. Its mission would be to conduct Operation MARKET TIME, the coastal blockade of South Vietnam against smuggling from the north.

Blocking the movement of Viet Cong men and supplies in the inland waterways of the Mekong Delta became the mission of Task Force 116 and their leading of Operation GAME WARDEN. The River Patrol Force became the active component of TF 116 when it was created on 18 December 1965.

The ships and small craft of both TF 115 and TF 116 would operate against the Viet Cong throughout the waterways of South Vietnam. But they would be most active in the Mekong Delta area. To attack the Viet Cong on land, and gather intelligence on their movements and operations, a detachment of SEALs from SEAL Team One arrived in Vietnam in February 1966. Operating primarily in the Rung Sat Special Zone, the SEALs from Team One became Detachment Golf. By the next year Detachment Alfa of SEAL Team Two would be established to operate primarily in the Mekong Delta.

SEALs deploying to Vietnam from 1966 forward would now be primarily part of the direct-action platoons operating against the Viet Cong. The SEALs would now show the world just how they could conduct unconventional warfare. The Teams had found their war.

Robert Gormly, Captain, USN (Ret.)

While I was growing up in Virginia Beach, Virginia, I saw some of the movies that had come out about the UDTs of World War II. The one with Richard Widmark, The Frogmen, is one of the few I remember. But because I lived in and grew up in Virginia Beach, only a few miles from Little Creek, the UDTs were something that was always in the background.

I finally decided that I wanted to become a member of the UDTs one time while

I was out on a surfboard off Virginia Beach. While out on the water, I ran into the then executive officer of UDT 21, a fellow by the name of Ron Smith. He told me a bit of what he did, and when I found out that he could be out there surfing whenever he wanted to, it sounded like it wouldn't be a bad life for me either. So that was how I joined the program.

Eventually, I was an ensign with East Coast Class 31, a winter class that started in January 1964. The fact that I had a wife and a kid to support did a lot to help me get through training. My college degree and Ron's help got me into the Navy's Officer Candidate School. So when I reported to the Teams, it was as an officer—a very young, very junior officer.

That incentive of my wife and child did help push me through UDTR training, and I didn't particularly want to go aboard a ship for what I intended to be my three-year stint with the Navy. But once you start something like that training program, you get caught up in it. That, and it just wasn't in my nature to quit.

In spite of the difficulties of training, I can honestly say that I never thought of quitting. The fact that Ron Smith had helped get me so well prepared, with an exercise program, running, and swimming, also helped get me through the tough parts. There were just too many incentives not to quit for me to even think about it. But I didn't know what was coming in the program.

Hell Week was cold, and hot, it was rainy, and it snowed. In other words, a typical East Coast winter Hell Week. It was bad, but mostly it was the weather that made it physically miserable for me. People who know say that the East Coast winter training course was one of the hardest, and coldest, you could go through. But I'm not sure that an East Coast summer class—with the heat, mosquitoes, and all the other things unique to that swampy part of Virginia that you just can't get away from—wouldn't have been worse.

Sometime during training, the word came down to us about the existence of the SEAL Teams. In those days, the SEALs were a very classified outfit. Even people in the UDTs didn't know everything about what they did. So I only really learned about the SEALs well after I had gotten into the Teams.

After spending some good years with UDT 21, I went to SEAL Team Two in March of 1966. There was no inclination at that time for SEAL Team Two to deploy to Vietnam. SEAL Team One had sent only a single detachment to Vietnam the month before to conduct direct-action operations against the Viet Cong. SEAL Team Two was pretty much in the doldrums in terms of money and training opportunities. The major shortcoming was money; guys were having to pay their own way to get training done. Our turn to even think about going to Vietnam wasn't going to start happening until late in the summer of 1966.

When deployments to Vietnam finally did start coming up, I did my best to break a few legs and twist some arms in order to be one of the first people going over there from SEAL Team Two. And this isn't just a figure of speech. The CO finally had

Fast patrol boats PTF-3 and PTF-4 move at high speed near Pearl Harbor, Hawaii. The boats will be deployed to Vietnam to conduct operations as part of OP-34A within a few years of this photograph being taken.

U.S. Navy

to cancel our regular Friday-morning soccer games—too many guys were receiving unexplained injuries. And it seemed the injuries were particularly happening to the men selected to be the first to deploy to Vietnam.

But I was lucky; I tried to get into one of the first two platoons deploying to Vietnam and I made it. Third Platoon deployed in January 1967 with Lieutenant (j.g.) Larry Bailey as the platoon leader and Lieutenant (j.g.) Robert Gormly as the assistant platoon commander.

Starting operations in Vietnam was not what we expected. We had a tough time getting going as the first SEALs in the Mekong Delta. SEAL Team One had been conducting operations for about a year up in the Rung Sat Special Zone, very near Saigon. The Rung Sat had a very different kind of terrain than the delta area did. And it required a different method of operating.

The Mekong Delta is a wide-open rice-paddy kind of area, large flat open areas surrounded by bands of jungle and trees. The Rung Sat was a mangrove-swamp, dense kind of jungle area saturated with water and dozens of canals, streams, and waterways.

When SEAL Team Two's Second and Third Platoons arrived in the Mekong Delta

A helicopter view of the smaller rivers, canals, rice paddies, and paddy dikes that covered the majority of the land in the Mekong Delta.

Greg McPartlin Collection

area, the people for whom we would be working, the River Patrol Force, weren't really too sure what they wanted to do with us. Operations started out with our riding river patrol boats as sort of bodyguards. That was a waste of time and talent.

It took about a month really of hashing with the leadership of the River Patrol Force to determine that (a) we would be operating independently, in support of their mission, which was to keep the rivers clear of the Viet Cong; and (b) we would be pretty much calling our own shots on what kinds of operations we did.

It was when we finally got those things ironed out that SEAL Team Two went to work in Vietnam.

During that first tour, the operation where I was dinged (wounded) is the one that stands out the most vividly in the memory. But it was only one of many.

We really didn't know anything about the delta yet. I think that up to the last minute before we deployed, we still thought we would be sent to the Rung Sat. When we went down to the middle of the Mekong Delta instead, we had to learn the territory. So we started off doing ambush patrols in areas that were designated free-fire zones. Which meant that supposedly everyone who moved in that zone was an enemy. Whether this was actually true or not, I just don't know. But those were the designated areas in which we could operate freely.

Some of us got a little tired of taking shots at the local fishermen trying to beat curfew in the morning. So we branched off into running combat patrols in the areas that we knew were completely controlled by the Viet Cong. Anyone we saw in those areas, we could be certain was the enemy.

The first three or four months we were operating, it was really in an intelligence gathering capacity, mainly for the platoons that were to come after us. We learned what areas might be the best possibilities for conducting successful operations, how to operate, and how to coordinate with the available support.

From about the middle to the end of my tour, we started trying to run operations off of the intelligence net we developed. This was information we received either from people we had captured or from the intelligence structures that existed in the delta, on both the U.S. Navy's and South Vietnamese sides.

So we switched from just going out and doing ambushing to actually trying to target specific Viet Cong leaders in their home hamlets, villages, or whatever.

Operating from our own self-generated intelligence was kind of a unique situation for us as the first SEAL to operate in the Mekong Delta. In fact, we were the only U.S. forces actually doing ops on the ground in the delta area for a while. The U.S. Army's Ninth Infantry Division didn't arrive in the delta until several months after we started operations.

Every time we went out on an operation, we gathered further intelligence for ourselves as well as for others. An area could be checked off as a good place to go or not. Or maybe we should go over to this area over here since we've heard a lot of sampan traffic moving over to that spot.

Of course moving about and operating like this only happened after we had gathered some experience. My first combat operation in Vietnam wasn't in the Mekong Delta, it was up in the Rung Sat Special Zone. This was just a few days after we had arrived in-country, and the notion was for some of the guys from SEAL Team One, guys who had already been there for a while, to take us out on a "breaking-in" op.

The operation was okay, with the high point really being the chance I had to work with an old friend of mine, Lieutenant Irve C. "Chuck" LeMoyne, and with his SEAL Team One squad. That first night, we did an ambush, which was pretty much the standard operation for the Rung Sat at that time. All we did was see a crocodile swim by, then a dolphin swam by, and watched the tide come in. No Viet Cong showed and we ended up treading water in a mangrove swamp.

In spite of the discomfort and lack of action, the op was good. I liked to operate, that was just what I wanted to do in those days. The more miserable the better. Of course, when the croc swam by, I was happy to have an M16 rifle in my hands.

What we all learned over there was what the most vulnerable point in any mission was. And that point was at the interface between the river and the land, where we had to get off the river and onto the land. It didn't matter if you were swimming in or coming in off a grounded boat, the first time you went up on the land, you just didn't know what was there.

There were a lot of butterflies flying around stomachs and a lot of adrenaline surging through our systems at that stage in an operation. For myself, after I had gotten on the land and knew what was around me, I felt I was pretty much in control of the situation. After the insertion, it was a matter of continuing on with the op. The adrenaline stayed up, but it peaked and ebbed. Mostly, it hit a high again as you made contact, or were extracting.

The men I was operating with were great. Any SEAL officer will tell you that the men working for him were the best that were in the Team. And I would expect him to say that. But my guys were a great group, mature and skilled. I had no problems with them at all; they were all smart, aggressive, and confident. I relied on them all quite a bit. When we set up a mission, we would plan the thing together. Their input was important and something I listened to closely. And a lot of times I would do what they suggested.

In my squad was Jess Tolison, one of the finest men I've ever known. He was a tremendous leader himself, and having him working for me just made my job a lot easier. If Jess said to go right during an op, then I turned right.

Any group that you go into combat with, you develop a special affinity for. Each of those men will hold a place in your mind from then on. And the men I led were memorable even before we ever went to war.

Toward the end of our tour, we had a series of operations that all resulted in us doing nothing more than spending time walking around and seeing nothing. All of us were itching to do something that had a greater chance of contact. The operations officer from the River Patrol Force, the guys that ran the PBRs up and down the river, came to me with the suggestion for a good op.

He said that there was an island complex down on the Bassac River that the cruising PBRs had been taking a lot of heavy caliber fire from lately, both machine guns and mortars. He suggested that we might want to go in and look around, maybe destroying some of the offensive bunkers that the VC were firing from. That sounded like a good mission to me, so I agreed and an op was quickly put together. I grabbed up my squad and off we went.

We moved into the area, inserted, and set up a security perimeter. After we had a feel for what was going on around us, we started patrolling along a canal. Along with our normal weapons, we had a load of C-4 plastic explosives with us, each man carrying a twenty-pound demolition charge. Out in the canal nearby, I had a boat with a lot more explosives on board.

As we patrolled, we came across a number of bunkers and blew them up—using the SEAL formula for precise demolition work: if a bunker looked like twenty pounds of C-4 would destroy it, we used forty pounds. That way, we were always sure of complete destruction of the target. I think we had about two resupplies from our boat out in the river.

As we continued the operation, we started setting up a pattern in our patrolling for targets. This was my mistake, and I knew we were making it, as did every man with me. But we hadn't seen anyone on the op except for a few old women and some kids. Things seemed so quiet that we even stopped for a moment so that our corpsman, Fred McCarty, could treat a child who had a bad eye infection. Things were just going easy, and that's what should have warned me to be a lot more alert.

The squad's point man, Charlie Bump, contracted something from one of the nasty ditches we had crossed along the way. He came up to me and both his legs were badly swollen and he was having a hard time breathing. The corpsman gave him a shot of antihistamine and we sent him out to the boat on the next re-supply run.

There were only about five of us on the operation now. Jess Tolison had been sent back to the States early for a well-deserved promotion to warrant officer. Now we had Quan, a South Vietnamese SEAL, attached to our squad. That left Bill Garnett as my second in command (leading petty officer), Fred McCarty as the squad's corpsman and radioman, and Pierre Birtz as a grenadier.

Since Bump had been working as our point man, I took his position. After mede-

Patrolling along a Vietnamese waterway, these two Mk II PBRs are running slow and low in the water. The gunners in the forward gun tubs man their twin .50-caliber machine guns as they each watch opposite banks for signs of enemy activity.

U.S. Navy

vacing Charlie, we moved out of the area with me taking the lead. As I moved down the trail in the point position, I caught a glimpse of some grass moving just off to the side of the trail. Stopping, I looked down and could see where someone had just passed by; the grass was still rising up from their footprints.

Concerned for the moment, I directed the squad to hang a left off the main trail and we headed inland. The grass was lower and lower as we moved along, pressed down by someone's feet just a moment before. About fifty meters from where we turned, I stopped and crouched down to look about. There, about five meters in front of me, I saw a head move, and then a rifle. When I leaned up and opened fire, all hell broke loose.

As near as we could determine later, we had walked down the short leg of a L-shaped ambush that the VC had set up for us. If we had continued walking about another ten or fifteen meters past where we turned off the trail, we would have been right in the middle of their killing zone. As it was, only one man was injured, and that was me: I was shot through the wrist within moments of opening fire.

All in all, we were very lucky. We got out and called in a lot of fire. A bunch of people had a good time for the rest of that afternoon, firing up the area we just left. After I received some quick attention from Fred McCarty, and a shot of morphine for the pain that was building fast, we pulled out in our support boat. I was medevaced soon after we returned to base, and I feel very lucky that none of the rest of my men got dinged that day.

A lot of us had discussed combat, and what can happen during it, well before we left for Vietnam. There weren't any illusions about our being bulletproof, outside of the feelings you have along those lines when you're young. We knew about the UDT casualties back in WWII, which was about all we had to draw on in our history. SEAL Team One had taken some casualties up in the Rung Sat, including a whole boatload that had been hit right before we arrived in Vietnam. And after I was hit, I knew I wasn't bulletproof.

The wound was bad enough to take some time healing. And I had some therapy and surgery to correct the damage done to my wrist. But I wanted to get back over to Vietnam as soon as I could. As soon as the hospital okayed it, I snuck back over there, this time in charge of my own platoon.

On my second tour in Vietnam, I relieved Dick Anderson, who was the platoon leader of Ninth Platoon. Dick was the only officer senior enough in Vietnam to be rotated into position as the officer-in-charge (OIC) of Detachment (Det) Alfa, the SEAL Team Two unit in Vietnam that our platoons operated under. So that was my opportunity to go back.

SEAL Team One had Detachment Golf in Vietnam. During all my time in Vietnam, I never saw any difference between the men of SEAL Teams One and Two. A lot of good friends of mine were officers in SEAL Team One. In fact, a number of SEAL Team One officers had transferred there from SEAL Team Two after they re-

A squad of SEALs move through the waterways of Vietnam while on a patrol. The man at the rear is armed with a Stoner light machine gun, belts of ammunition for the weapon draped around his shoulders.

U.S. Navy

ceived their commissions. In spite of the good-natured rivalry between the two Teams, we were all operators.

My opinion of the enemy we were fighting, and the allies we had in Vietnam, was close to being the same. The rank and file of the Viet Cong struck me as being good troops working under hard conditions. The South Vietnamese we were working with, once you got past a lot of the higher leadership, were also decent fighters. They just weren't led very well from the higher levels. Though some of the younger South Vietnamese officers fought hard for their country.

We worked a number of times with South Vietnamese SEALs, their LDNN. An LDNN probably saved my life during that operation earlier when I was wounded.

Quan had been close behind me on that patrol and he shot the VC who had first shot me. And I have a lot of time for people like that.

It was only a few years later that the Vietnam War wound down for the SEAL Teams and the U.S. military. My second combat tour had been my last. But a number of other SEALs spent four or five tours in Vietnam. Officers just couldn't always go back as often as they wanted. Instead, I went on to be the XO of UDT 22, also at Little Creek.

There was, wrongly in my view, blame put on the military for the war we fought in Vietnam. This showed in the antimilitary sentiment that was prevalent during the 1970s. A lot of our senior officers were taking a real beating in the press, and maybe from some of the politicians in Washington, over the fact that we hadn't "won" the war. There was sort of a "back off and let things happen" attitude from the higher command.

What was more immediately noticed was that the funding, which had been very good during the Vietnam days, dried up very quickly. SEAL Team One, which had the much larger commitment of platoons to Vietnam, had grown very large during the war. SEAL Team Two had grown, but it still wasn't half the size of Team One.

Both Teams were drawn down considerably in size after the war. And that was very noticeable in SEAL Team One, which had to actively send men out of the Team to reduce their numbers.

In the SEALs, we hadn't done a very good job in explaining to the Navy hierarchy just what we had done for them in conducting unconventional warfare in Vietnam. Everyone understood what the UDTs did; their mission was tied in to the amphibious force and hadn't changed drastically since World War II. They had their place; the SEALs had lost part of theirs.

We didn't need much in the way of funding; the SEALs just didn't cost as much as the other units in the Navy. But that also meant that taking any money away from us had a much greater impact.

From 1972 to 1974, I was the commanding officer of SEAL Team Two, a big step for someone who originally expected to do only a single enlistment in the Navy. And just like when I had come on board SEAL Team Two back in 1966, the men were forced to pay their own way to get training done. Everyone knew that they had to keep their qualifications up, but we just didn't have any money to send them off to schools. For all the military, the 1970s were hard times financially and otherwise. And that was particularly true for the Teams.

When I was the CO of SEAL Team Two, one of the hardest things I had to contend with was having a whole command filled with Vietnam veterans. The guys were super people; all of them were great operators. But we just didn't have a mission then. Of course we had our historic mission of supporting various Navy commands with an unconventional warfare capability, but we just didn't have a war.

The low silhouette of the Light SEAL Support Craft is shown as this LSSC noses in to the shore for an insertion.

U.S. Navy

Trying to keep a highly trained group of combat veterans happy after there was no war, particularly SEALs, wasn't enjoyable work. Unlike a lot of Vietnam-era veterans I see who didn't want to be there and bemoan the fact that they were in combat, every one of our guys had wanted to be there. So the biggest challenge for me as their CO was to keep them challenged. And the only way I found to do this was to keep involving them in exercises that pushed the envelope a bit. The only way to keep these men occupied was to keep them challenged, keep the adrenaline flowing.

And that adrenaline flow also extended to the CO; only it didn't always come from the fieldwork we were doing. One time while I was out on one of these exercises, the Navy almost decommissioned SEAL Team Two right out from under me.

We had an exercise in Denmark with some of our NATO allies in 1973. After the war had ended, the SEAL community underwent a significant organizational change. Now an organization known as the Naval Inshore Warfare Command had been formed. Ostensibly, all SEALs—explosive ordnance disposal, harbor defense units, and inshore undersea warfare groups—were put underneath this large one-star admiral billet.

The SEAL Teams lost a lot of our clout in the political arena under the new system. There wasn't anyone looking out specifically for the Teams' interests. So, in the process of looking for things to cut because of constantly reduced budgets, the SEALs came under the blade.

While I was in Denmark, the phone rang with a call from my XO, who was still back at Little Creek. He told me that I had better get back as quickly as I could. The news was that the then chief of staff at the Inshore Undersea Warfare Command had just offered up SEAL Team Two as compensation in the next budget POM (Program Objective Memorandum) drill. My answer was short and terse, and I had to quickly find my way back to Little Creek.

The trouble was, we still didn't have any money to just get on a plane. So in the time-honored method of the Teams, I used whatever contacts I had to get the job done. The U.S. Army Special Forces 10th Group commander in Germany listened to my situation and told me that he would just get me back there. I was stuck on a plane en route to the 10th's headquarters in Fort Devens, Massachusetts. And that commander himself bought a commercial plane ticket for me to get from Boston down to Norfolk. In a day and a half, I was back at Little Creek.

The cutting of SEAL Team Two was indeed about to happen. And I couldn't stop it from my level in the command structure. I ended up making a phone call to an admiral whom I had done some business with up in the Pentagon. He was the op O6 at the time, the deputy for plans, policy, and operations for the Navy. He was coming down to Norfolk at his next change of command to become the amphibious-force commander.

When I told him what they were trying to do to the SEALs, his response was to the effect of "don't worry about it." About twenty minutes after that conversation ended, my phone rang again. This time it was the admiral I reported to and he asked me to come into his office for a while. It turned out he didn't know anything about the SEALs being cut either. When I explained the situation, he just told me that it wasn't going to happen.

That was maybe my scariest moment as a CO of SEAL Team Two—when I felt that the command was going to be killed.

Richard Marcinko, Commander, USN (Ret.)

A movie in the 1950s called The Frogmen was where I first learned about the Underwater Demolition Teams. I saw that movie when I was still in high school. In 1958, I had already quit high school and was planning to enlist in the service. The first Lebanon crisis was taking place and I was looking forward to seeing the action. The Marine Corps recruiter I spoke to told me that I wouldn't see any of that action, so I just said "the hell with you" and went to the Navy.

The UDT looked like it promised real action, which is what I wanted. I couldn't see myself being what my rate was, which was radioman, which is "clickety-clack, clickety-clack, here come the girls to the radio shack." In other words, carrier wave operation, listening to the dits and dashes of Morse code for hours on end.

But it was later, after I had been in UDT and learned about the SEALs, that I saw where the real action was going to be. SEAL Team Two was where I wanted to be.

When I received my orders to go to Vietnam, my first reaction was one of thanks. The reasons were several. One, because it had been a long dry spell between wars. The last real war the United States had been involved in was the Korean War during the first half of the 1950s.

When "Cuba" broke out—which was not a war, but we prepared for it as if it was going to be—the West Coast SEALs came east to help us out. Our numbers were small then and every SEAL counted a lot. So when Vietnam broke out, the East Coast Team went west to help in the fighting there. I had just come back to the Teams as a commissioned officer. So I went to war as the only SEAL ensign going out there, all of the other officers being lieutenants.

But that's what the SEALs were all about, being able to go to war. So my finally being able to go to combat was a situation I looked forward to.

My first day in Vietnam was really a surprise, though it was hot and that was something I had been expecting. We had flown all the way across the United States, from Little Creek, Virginia, to San Diego, California, aboard a C-130 cargo plane, basically riding on cargo straps. We stopped in California because we had to learn how to fight the war according to someone's decision at higher command.

So we went up to the Chocolate Mountains and fired all of the different weapons, and generally showed the West Coast that we knew how to find the on/off switches on our weapons. Then we went down to Tijuana to work on our escape and evasion plan, and liberty. That means we had a good time, and is why SEALs stands for Sleep, Eat, And Live it up, not SEa, Air, Land.

But going in to Vietnam wasn't quite as much fun. When we were flying in to the airfield at Binh Thuy, the C-130 banked hard and started circling. The air crew told us that they had to circle the field at high altitude to check the situation out, since they had been shot at a number of times.

Just about all of us aboard the plane had cheated and put our M16s in our hanging bags rather than securing them in the cruise boxes. As we were coming down to the airport to land, magazines were being locked and loaded so that we would be ready to engage the enemy the moment we hit the ground.

Well, when that big cargo ramp came down, the only thing we engaged was Jess Tolison, one of our chiefs who had been in the advanced parts. He had some trucks and cold beer waiting for us. So it was really quite a civilized way to start off fighting a war.

As far as details went, we had no idea where we were going to live. Most of us were ready to live in tents out in the jungle. But instead, quarters had been arranged for us and all the amenities put on. This was not immediately the all-out shooting war we had expected; that was going to come later.

I was the assistant platoon leader of Second Platoon, SEAL Team Two, in charge of Bravo Squad. This meant that Ensign Marcinko had five highly motivated, thoroughly trained, experienced SEALs to help him beat up the Viet Cong.

SEAL Team Two had sent two platoons over to Vietnam to establish Detachment Alfa, assigned to the Game Warden forces down in the Mekong Delta. Jake Rhinebolt was with us to command the new det. During our first few weeks in-country, the rest of Second Platoon and Third Platoon went up north to operate with the SEAL Team One guys who had been in-country for a while. As the SEAL junior officer in the det, I stayed behind with my squad in Ben Thuy.

Bravo Squad was made up of myself with Eagle Gallagher, Patches Watson, Ronnie Rodger, Ron Fox, and Jim Finley. The rest of the detachment had gone up to work with the SEAL Team One guys up in the Rung Sat. And while they were gone, Bravo Squad was supposed to sit quietly at the base. Not much chance of that happening after we had trained for this moment for months, if not years.

To operate in the area, we first had to learn the river, so we went out with the PBRs and went up and down the Bassac. We were shown where the VC normally crossed and all kinds of aspects of the daily river life in the Mekong Delta. We also went out in our own STABs (SEAL Tactical Assault Boats) to test-fire weapons and run the boats out a bit. We actually engaged the enemy in an all-out firefight during one of our test runs. The fact that the other guys were still up in the Rung Sat Spe-

A Mark II STAB speeds along the Bassac River in the Mekong Delta. The small, fast boats proved their worth in Vietnam but the fiberglass hulls couldn't stand up to the rigors of the area.

U.S. Navy

A SEAL sits at the coxswain's position in a Mk 1 STAB during the Team's early years in Vietnam. SEAL Team Two converted several civilian boats to this configuration for their initial operations in Vietnam.

cial Zone learning how to fight the war while we had met the Viet Cong let us have a little jump start on them on operating in the delta.

The first combat mission that we were assigned involved us going downriver from our base on the Bassac. We did an insertion off of our own boats, the STABs, that we had developed back at Little Creek. Penetrating inland from our insertion point, we didn't find anything, so the mission came up a dry hole. But there's a learning curve to operating, and we were going to start climbing it fast.

There were some funny things that happened that showed little bits and pieces that we had to learn as well. The Viet Cong were known as "Charlie," a short version of their initials in military lingo, "Victor Charlie." Our detachment had two platoons, Second and Third, from SEAL Team Two. In Third Platoon was a guy named Charlie Bump.

Charlie went out on the perimeter one night, and on his way back in, somebody let us know that he was coming. "Here comes Charlie!" That caused some thought about whether or not it was our Charlie or the one we're supposed to shoot, Charlie. So we decided that Charlie wasn't a good name for our Teammate right then.

The insert and extract are the two most critical points during any mission. When you start the mission, you're thinking about Murphy, what things can go wrong. And you are mentally preparing yourself for the actions you will take. When you first get to the jungle, and you're sitting there all night long, a palm frond sways, and you look at it and wonder if that's a bad guy moving. If you stare at things long enough, they start taking shape. Things can fool you when you let your imagination run.

When we first went out there in the jungle on patrol, we were told to take stay-awakes, or No-Doz pills. We queered that in a hurry, as people began to see things that just weren't there. I was jumping into the water and killing snakes. The little lights you could see in the hooches—well, they had angels coming out of them. So we didn't take drugs after the first time or two.

In the jungle, you learned very quickly that the human responses were the best. And the hell with the drugs and medications to try to keep you moving.

So you learned on every patrol. People ask the usual question: "Weren't you scared?" But you were so busy doing things, carrying out your mission and surviving, that you really weren't scared. It wasn't until you were back in the base, cleaning up your gear and sitting down to write up the report, that you realized that you almost lost a load out there.

During the action, you don't realize how close you are to losing it, because you're just too busy. When you're inserting, you're worried about all of the things you're going to do. When you're extracting, you're just trying to get everybody home. And the realization of what just happened doesn't hit you until you're relaxing and just writing up the report.

It's very hard to express the relationship all of the men had with one another in the Teams to someone who hasn't been in (1) the military, and (2) any special operations units. The relationship is somewhat like a pro-football-team locker-room experience. That is, we all have a common experience and a common mission. We all want to win, and the important thing you remember is that the probability statistics of where you're going to die are with your Teammates and not with your family.

Your Teammate is your comrade-in-arms. You'll go back-to-back with him in a bar, and you'll go back-to-back in combat. The trust is there about everything. The SEALs came out of the water of the UDT. In the water, we always had swim buddies. And that philosophy just went up onto dry land with the SEALs, we share everything—girlfriends, booze, and whatever—knowing that we might die together as well.

The camaraderie of the Teams was shown when I built SEAL Team Six. I hand-selected everybody in the Team, including the support people. The only way I could really do that was by being able to know a lot about all of the men in the Teams. You can get that in a closed community where everybody knows everybody else.

Across all of the Teams, we know the grandchildren, we know the wives, and we know the girlfriends of our Teammates. We know this because when we were at home and our Teammate deployed, we took care of his family. If the car broke down or the garage door didn't work, we backed that man up while he wasn't there.

Maybe the best way to describe the Teams is to say that we're kind of a "military Mafia." There's a bond between all of us that's very hard to break or slip in on. We take care of our own, and we really don't care if there's somebody else from the outside there to help us.

We trained so much together that we could read one another without using language. When I watched my point man, it got to where he didn't even have to signal me that he'd seen something. The way he carried himself and moved his body told me that he had spotted something or that something was about to go down.

When we lived together so long, developed that comradeship that is so much a part of the Teams, we learned to think alike, do alike. It was like a symphony; we would just flow together and do things in harmony.

If someone was to draw a bead, take aim with their weapon, on the Teammate next to you, naturally, you were going to kill them. We weren't there to make friends. We were there to wipe out the bad guy. In fact, it took a while before we realized that it was good to save a couple of the bad guys for the intelligence that could be learned from them.

But that was part of the evolution of war, of realizing that you are there and what you can do. When you first got there, you had to kind of "vent your spleen" before you knew what you could do. And then you had to finesse the target from there.

You had to learn from the mistakes you made, chew up its ass and make sure you didn't do it again, but knew why. Like some people went out on patrol and were sick. Later the patrol was disrupted by their barfing all over the jungle.

SEALs just think that they're invincible in terms of not having to go see a doctor. They're sure that they can take care of themselves, or just gut it out. And I've had a lot of guys go out who shouldn't have been on patrol. But they didn't want to miss going out on an op.

These are just some of the things you learn about. You also learn about the en-

With the coxswain of their LSSC insertion craft looking on from the lower left, these SEALs insert for an operation. The Point Man on the right is armed with an Ithaca pump-shotgun.

U.S. Navy

emy, his booby traps, and how he operates. And you pass that information on. It's when someone makes the same mistake twice that you either get rid of them, or they're dead.

Nothing supplants being in combat. It's the ultimate challenge. It takes all that you know and all that you have. And when you win—and that's the name of the game—you feel the best about it.

During my first tour to Vietnam, I was an assistant platoon leader for Second Platoon. During my second tour, I was the platoon leader for Eight Platoon. There was actually very little difference between the two jobs for me. The platoon leader I had in Second Platoon, Fred Kochey, was a passive leader. He led by example, but he wasn't a barking dog; he had no ego.

So Fred kind of gave me a free rein. Of course my squad was kind of a wild bunch, in terms of being ultra-aggressive and ultraconfident. We didn't have to worry about being self-starting. Self-containing maybe, but not self-starting.

Actually, in the beginning of the war, that aggressive attitude was one of my biggest problems. After an engagement, I had to stop people from running down the trail and chasing more VC. I was afraid that they would be sucked into an ambush.

The main difference when I was actually the platoon leader was that I picked my own missions. I felt that instead of having to be in the rivers, the maritime environment we were expected to operate in was anywhere I had my canteen, since I had water in it. That's how my platoon operated up on the Cambodian border, down in the Tranh Forest, and up in the Seven Mountains area.

My expanding of the area where we operated not only let me get Charlie where he felt the safest, but I was also getting major kills. Our platoon wasn't getting just couriers and local runners, we were taking down much bigger targets. If you were to compare my operations with today's drug war, Eighth Platoon wasn't taking out the local street dealers with a nickel bag, we were taking out the truckloads.

To accomplish that meant that we had to go deeper inland. And we had to take bigger chances. But that's what we were built for. And no one stopped me. If somebody tried to stop me while I was out on an op deep in bad-guy country, my radio wasn't on.

Operating like that scares the hell out of the bad guy. Particularly in an Asian culture. We had the green faces from our camo makeup. And there were little things you picked up on after you had been over there for a while.

In the villages we passed through, the little kids used to come out and grab our legs. Being an American, you would just think, as I did, Aw, isn't that cute?

It wasn't until after I had been there awhile that I learned the kids were passing their evil spirits on to me. So once I saw that, I would take my green smudge and rub their heads with it. That would cause them to come back in the next life and do the same things again—at least it did according to their superstitions.

Doing that psychological warfare with them could give you an edge. When you were first in-country, you didn't even understand what they were doing to you. But you learned, and then you used what you learned against them. In any combat situation, jungle or urban, when you can go after the enemy where they feel safest, you upset them.

And Asian cultures can be superstitious ones. Odd things, such as running a small deer through a campfire, is taboo for them. So you learned these things, not to believe in them, but to think as your enemy thought. And then you could use those weaknesses against them.

My own weakness centered around the men I was leading. When one of them was hurt or wounded, that weakness was turned back against the enemy. Having a man injured just pissed me off, as it did the rest of his Teammates. We went into retribution mode in a hurry. He would be protected as best we could, and we would kill as many of the enemy as we could on our way out.

The Vietnam War was fought in the kind of place where neither the Army nor the Marine Corps regular units wanted to really fight. They fought the Viet Cong with the same fire and maneuver tactics that had worked during earlier wars, but Vietnam was a place of guerrilla war, fighting in the dark against an almost unseen enemy. And that was where the SEALs could show their best.

If you look at the cloth of those men who joined the Teams, you see that the harder the job they had to do, the better they felt about it. From a managerial, team-leader perspective on the war in Vietnam, the SEALs were given a shitty job in rough terrain. And that meant no staff puke was going to want to come and see you. So all you had to do was fight the bad guy.

There's something to be said about the purity of a small war. For the SEALs, it was instant gratification. You would write up a patrol order, go out there, and shoot the bastard. Either you'd win, or you'd lose. It was black and white, no gray. And that's music, that is the epitome of life for a warrior. It was us against them, and we got an instant readout; we didn't have to wait for a report to come out every six months.

Vietnam was a hard job. And the Teams were ready for that job because (1) Everybody was geared up for it; (2) We felt better about it than anyone else; and (3) No staff puke was going to be on our ass, riding around with us looking for his own medal.

■ Chapter 40
Support from the Sea, Air, and Land

In spite of their wide range of abilities and skills, the SEALs could not have enjoyed the level of success they did in Vietnam without receiving support of an equally high quality. The three environments listed in the name—Sea, Air, and Land—are the same three environments from which the SEALs of Vietnam received support during their operations.

From the sea and the water came the small craft that moved the SEALs in to their target, pulled them out when the mission was over, and would come in with guns roaring if the Teams ran into trouble. This aid included naval gunfire support from large Navy ships such as destroyers and cruisers offshore. And small craft like the thirty-one-foot Mark I and Mark II PBRs (Patrol Boat, River) of

The Medium SEAL Support Craft, another converted landing craft, moves down the river in Vietnam. A number of .50-caliber machine guns, mounted with shields to protect the gunners, can be seen lining the sides of the boat. On top of the overhead cover is a 57mm M18A1 Recoilless rifle.

U.S. Navy

The early Mark 6 LCM, or "Mike" boat conversion to a Heavy SEAL Support Craft in Vietnam. Two .50-caliber M2HB machine guns can be seen under the overhead cover. On top of the cover is a 106mm M40 Recoilless Rifle. Many modifications were done to the three boats of this type during the war.

U.S. Navy

the Brown Water Navy would answer when the SEALs called, carrying firepower that seemed almost too much to be coming from such small and lively craft.

From their own commands, the SEALs received specialized watercraft support from the boat support units (BSUs). These units operated and maintained small craft that were unique to the SEALs' operations. Such craft as the HSSC (Heavy SEAL Support Craft), a converted LCM Mk 6, commonly called the Mike boat, worked with the Teams throughout their years in Vietnam. The Mike boat was heavily converted from its original configuration, carrying weapons and ammunition in bulk behind armor plating, rather than the large numbers of troops it was originally intended to take into the beaches for landings. Big and slow, the Mike boat would just move in like a lumbering giant, spitting out various kinds of fire from its many mounted weapons, to get the SEALs free of an overwhelming enemy force.

From the air came the most agile and destructive force at the SEALs' command. Air support could be in the form of "fast movers"—jet aircraft armed with a mix of bombs, rockets, cannon, and napalm that could rip apart major enemy formations, the fire from the sky being directed to the target by the SEALs on the ground. The helicopter gunship, originally a UH-1 or "Huey" helicopter with gun packages mounted on the sides, was a unique development of the Vietnam War.

A "fast mover" in this case, an F-4 Phantom II aircraft from the carrier USS *Coral Sea*, drops a load of bombs over a target in North Vietnam.

U.S. Navy

Though they could receive helicopter gunship support from the Army and Marine Corps, the SEALs had their favorite unit in one of their own from the Navy, the Seawolves of Helicopter Attack Squadron (Light) 3. Commissioned on 1 April 1967 in order to provide Task Force 116 with its own organic means of aerial fire support, observation, and medical evacuation, the Seawolves quickly became as legendary as the SEALs.

There seemed to be no situation so dire, no enemy so big, or no terrain so bad that the Seawolves wouldn't come in to support the men on the ground. The men of the Seawolves flew thousands of air sorties. When no one else would come in to give the SEALs what they needed, the Seawolves would fly. At times when the men on the ground had no other way to survive an enemy situation, the Seawolf crews would strip off their weapons, their primary means of protection, in order to have room to come in and pull the troops out.

The SEALs of Vietnam have nothing bad to say about the Seawolves of Vietnam, except perhaps that there should have been more of them. The men of the Teams readily admit a deep debt to the Seawolves. "If it wasn't for them, there would be a lot fewer of us," is the way many SEALs have put it.

The Seawolves were not the only specialized form of Navy air support dur-

The insignia of Helicopter Attack Squadron, Light—The Seawolves as shown on a flag displayed at a Seawolf reunion.

Kevin Dockery

ing the Vietnam War. Activated in April 1969 was Light Attack Squadron 4 (VAL 4), known by their call sign, the Black Ponies. Flying small propeller-driven OV-10 Bronco aircraft, the handful of Black Ponies in the skies above the Mekong Delta could loiter on-site for hours. And when a target was available, the Black Ponies could swoop in with unbelievable firepower for their size. Rockets, both 2.75-inch and 5-inch Zunis, would roar out from under the wings of the Black Ponies and blast huge holes in the jungle, or in the enemy formations underneath. Cannon fire from 20mm guns and bullets from 7.62mm machine guns would rip through the ground that had been torn up by the rockets. The power of the Black Ponies even impressed the SEALs, some of whom had seen a great deal of other firepower already.

Ground support in the form of military formations and troops, both U.S. and South Vietnamese, came in to the SEALs across the land. But the most common ground-based support the SEALs received came in the form of artillery fire from batteries of cannon. Given their training in gunfire support, the biggest gun in a SEAL squad was the man with a radio on his back. At the other end of that radio could be 105mm and 155mm howitzers and other cannon. At the SEALs' command, steel shells would come whistling out of the sky, having been fired from miles away. Directed to their target, the shells would tear apart the jungle with high explosives and buzzing steel fragments.

Clyde Christensen, Commander, USN (Ret.)

Before I myself was in the Seawolves, I was in another squadron in San Diego, and I remember there was a lot of talk about the Seawolves going about in the various air units. I had been a helicopter pilot with HC-1 (Helicopter Combat Support

With his PRUs alert and a SEAL Teammate armed with a Stoner just to the left of the picture, Frank Thornton speaks over the radio. The radioman and his backpack radio remained within close reach of the PRU adviser at all times so that he could call in the big guns (support) when needed.

Frank Thornton Collection

Squadron One), which had been renamed in July 1965 from HU-1 (Helicopter Utility Squadron One), the first helicopter squadron in the U.S. Navy.

Even in the mid-1960s, pilots from our squadron had been going over to Vietnam to work with the U.S. Army helicopter units on an advisory basis. It seemed to me that the intent of that advisory work was to get us into the Seawolf mission from early on, but I have no evidence of that.

A lot of stories came back to the squadron about working with the Army and operating their helicopter gunships. Interesting things happened with Navy pilots working with the Army and using their armed helicopters.

Following on from the HC-1 detachments, Helicopter Attack Squadron (Light) Three, HAL-3, began operations in Vietnam in June 1967, flying borrowed Army UH-1B helicopter gunships with Navy crews. It was under the call sign Seawolves that HAL-3 really began developing a reputation for itself, and it was the stories of these exploits that piqued my interest in joining the unit.

Things had been heating up in Vietnam and the Seawolves were operating on a

HAL-33, Detachment 7, Dong Tam, Vietnam, 1971 (back row, left to right) LTJG Schilling, John Orth, Fred Whitlock, L. St. Jaques, AOC James Osterburg, LTJG T. Ziemer, Terry L. Mize (front row, left to right) LCDR Christensen, LTJG Reid, Lt. Joe Sullivan, LTJG Schull, Lt. Harrison, Rick Bogle, LTJG Todd, John Ross.

continuous basis in support of Navy operations while I was working as the naval instructor at the University of Nebraska in their NROTC program. When I completed that tour of duty, I requested to go to Vietnam and be part of the Seawolves. My request was accepted and I would soon find myself back in the air at the controls of a helicopter.

My arrival in Vietnam occurred in the fall of 1970 when I was assigned as the assistant officer-in-charge (OIC) working off the USS Garrett County (LST 786). After about six weeks of training, I was put in command of my own detachment of Seawolves, Det 7 based out of Dong Tam.

HAL-3 was an established squadron with its headquarters in Binh Thuy. It conducted its mission in smaller units—detachments, or dets—that were spread out around the countryside. That way, Seawolf gunships could fly in support of Navy forces quickly and arrive as soon as possible.

The basic Seawolf mission was to support the riverine forces in Vietnam. In addition, the squadron was to support any ongoing SEAL operations. It soon developed that the Seawolves also were being used to support Vietnamese troops in the field. There was a large Vietnamese Army base in Dong Tam, and so if we got a call

A Seawolf helicopter gunship and a Mark II PBR move along a waterway in South Vietnam. These two crafts were the most common air and water support used by the SEALs in Vietnam.

U.S. Navy

from one of their units who was in trouble, we would take off on a support mission for them.

The Seawolves operated in a different manner than the Army helicopter units. For one thing, it was very common to see an Army helicopter operating singly on a mission. At other times, I've observed so many Army helicopters out on the same mission that it looked as if a swarm of bees had been let loose.

For us, we were always in a pattern where we could put in support for the ship (helicopter) that was making the run in on a target. It was a mutual support thing that worked very well for us. Every detachment had two gunships, and if the det didn't have two operational birds, then you just sat there until you had two craft ready to fly. Only if an emergency came up where you had to answer with just your single ship did you go out alone, and that did happen a couple of times.

We operated primarily as a light helicopter fire team, two birds working together. In Det 7, we had two UH-1s armed with 2.75-inch rocket pods fired by the pilot. The lead ship had a heavy machine gun, a .50-caliber, mounted as the door gun. In addition, there was a minigun mounted outboard, next to the rocket pods, that could be directed and fired by the copilot. The trail ship was armed in much the same way, except the door gunners had 7.62mm M60 light machine guns.

Even before I arrived in Vietnam, I had heard about the SEALs. Their reputation preceded them and it was an impressive one. The SEALs to me were always a highly professional, well-trained group of people. But I personally didn't have any direct experience with them until after I arrived in Vietnam.

In the Dong Tam area, we were fortunate to have a SEAL platoon that we worked with on a regular basis. In spite of their reputation as hard chargers, the SEALs struck me as wholly professional in their approach to a possible mission. It was my experience that we simply never went out on a joint mission with the SEALs unless the intel for the operation had been done extremely well. The SEALs just weren't going to go out on an operation unless they felt they had a maximum chance of success.

Everything that I observed the SEALs do during our joint operations was extremely professional. It was just a pleasure to work with them. Their reputation for working hard, and playing hard, was one I'm sure they earned, especially from what I observed firsthand. But I never saw anything they did off duty get in the way of an operation. When the day of a mission came, they were always ready to go and completely professional about it.

The typical mission that we did in Vietnam in support of the SEALs would usually start with the SEAL commander coming in to talk to me about his plan. "Clyde," he would say, "I've got this type of a mission. Here is where we're going to have to go.

Before a mission, Lieutenant Commander Roland Habicht, in charge of HAL-3 (Seawolf) Det 1, gets a final information briefing from a SEAL.

U.S. Navy

NAVY SEALs: A COMPLETE HISTORY

Here is how we want to do it. Here is how many men we're going to want to put in on the ground. And here is how long we think we're going to be on the ground."

The mission would be stated first so that we knew what we were going in for and what the objective was. That would then tell me what we had to do first; perhaps we had to put the SEALs in on the target and then leave the area, something we had to do on occasion because of the type of mission they were going to do.

On other missions, we were required to be overhead during the whole operation. In some cases, a SEALs mission lasted so long that we just didn't have the fuel supply to stay on top of them. Then we had to go back and refuel and return.

Once the original mission was over, we could be called on to come in and get the SEALs out, extract them from the target. And if contact was made, we could come in with very heavy firepower in their support.

The best thing about the helicopter gunship support was that we could put our fire in almost any place it was needed. If a team was in trouble, we could come in almost directly on top of them and either suppress the enemy forces or land and get someone out or in. Our biggest advantage to the SEALs was in being their dedicated close air support.

Aviation Ordnanceman Michael Draper slips a 2.75-inch rocket into one of the 7-round rocket pods mounted on this Seawolf helicopter gunship. To the right in the picture can just be seen the mechanisms of the two M60C machine guns that are part of the Seawolf's mounted weapons system.

U.S. Navy

Even though our units were called light attack teams, we could pack a big wallop. Our machine guns had thousands of rounds of ammunition available to them. Our rockets were limited to fourteen, seven to a pod, one pod on each side of the aircraft. But we fired them in pairs and each rocket carried either a six- or ten-pound high-explosive warhead. Those rockets had the impact of an artillery strike, and we could put them in exactly where they were needed.

Our firepower was one of our greatest defenses, but there were times when we had to give up a lot of it to complete a mission. A number of times, just because of the place where we were and the conditions there, such as being very hot and humid, we were limited in what we could carry and still lift off. We would have to strip down the craft, take some of the weapons or ammunition off, and maybe reduce the fuel load to make sure we could go in and do what we had to do.

When we were the only helicopters available, and the SEALs were in a tight spot, we would strip off all of the ship's weapons and ammunition to have enough capacity to lift out the SEALs. That was just something we had to do. And we called that going in "slick," i.e., not having any armament whatsoever.

According to where you were operating from, adjustments had to be made as to just how much fuel and ammunition you had on board for any operation. When I originally arrived in-country, the LST Harnett County was down in the Ca Mau Peninsula, the southernmost point of Vietnam. Flying off that ship, we always had to work with a reduced fuel load. In that case, we were taking off athwartships—sideways, from the middle of the deck.

When you flew like that, the minute you were airborne and

Slipping a long belt of 7.62mm machine gun ammunition into place, Navy Airman Robert Nunes loads one of the four ammunition boxes for a Seawolf's outboard machine guns. Each of the four long boxes will hold 600 rounds of ammunition for the M60C mounted guns. In front of the airman's knee is an ammunition box with a dozen rounds of 40mm high explosive grenades set nose-up. The grenades would be fired by the Seawolf's crew from an M79 grenade launcher, just visible behind the long ammunition boxes on the far right center of the picture. This is just a small part of the ammunition and weapons load carried aboard a Seawolf helicopter gunship.

U.S. Navy

went off, all you had was water below you. The hot, humid air limited the lifting capacity of the rotors and engines, so we never were able to lift off with a full fuel, or ammo, load.

Once I arrived at Dong Tam, I found we were operating off a fairly long strip—it was just PSP (Pierced Steel Planking)—but it was still long enough to give you a forward run on takeoff. Moving a helicopter forward for takeoff increases the amount of lift available to it. So we could operate with a lot more fuel and ammunition on board.

On certain occasions, when the weather was not the most agreeable, we actually had to physically bounce the helicopter down the runway until we could finally get it airborne. And there were still times when we couldn't get the bird up in the air with a full load on board. In those situations, we had to go back and take off some of the fuel or ammo and try it again.

Though it never happened to me, there were times when you had to get the helicopter moving forward under a lighter load, and then suddenly increase the load as soon as it was airborne. The way you did this was by having the crew chief and door gunner run alongside the bird as she went down the runway. As soon as the helicopter was airborne, the crew chief and gunner would jump aboard. That usually resulted in the bird bouncing back off the ground, but she would be airborne. As I say, that never happened to me, but there were a few times when I was mighty tempted to have my crew run alongside.

The enemy we were facing in the south of South Vietnam were a kind of hit-and-run force. We really never knew just what to expect on a given day. That was when you were speaking of the Viet Cong. Things were much different farther north, where you could be facing North Vietnamese Army (NVA) forces.

We never knew when we would be called for a sudden operation, or what kind of op it might be. It could be a small skirmish someplace or a fairly large engagement in another place. We had a group of Vietnamese Army people, more militia really than anything else. One of the Vietnamese officers in that group had been trained in the U.S., so he spoke English very well.

That officer described to me that his situation was more of a "Hatfields and McCoys" feud situation than a war. He had a running gunfight with a Viet Cong unit, and it was almost like they would tantalize each other, each unit trying to draw the other one out into a fight.

This situation resulted in a planned meeting of the two units. They were going to face each other down and fight it out. But the officer told me he had, in effect, to promise the VC that he wouldn't bring in the Seawolves. And then he told me that he wanted me there anyway. And we were overhead at the time that Vietnamese unit needed us. So they won that engagement.

So we did operate in support of the Vietnamese Army. But we worked even more in support of the riverine forces. And this was true even though the makeup of the riverine forces had changed. By the time I had arrived on the scene, the manning of the riverine boats had been largely turned over to the South Vietnamese Navy as part of the Vietnamization program. Now, instead of a U.S. Navy crew on board, there would be just a single U.S. Navy adviser. So that took some of the feeling out of the situation for us.

We had much preferred working for the U.S. forces in-country. We knew that when a call came in from Americans—SEALs or whoever—there really was a need for us. Unfortunately, sometimes, when we got a call requesting support for a Vietnamese Army unit, we learned when we arrived on target that there really hadn't been a need for our services. But we still had to go up, and put everyone in my crews at risk.

But the Navy rewarded the risks we took in their traditional way. The Seawolves received a lot of decorations in spite of being a rather small unit. There was a point system based on the number of missions flown, how they were reported, and a variety of other factors. I really never understood the system completely. But with the accumulation of a certain number of points, you received an Airman's Medal. When I received my eighteenth medal award, I wondered just why I had received it. Sometimes, it seemed that the reporting system almost overshadowed the event itself. But we did do a lot of missions.

Several of the operations we did during my time there stick in my memories of Vietnam. The first of these was soon after I had first arrived in-country and was still down in the Ca Mau area. As the assistant OIC there, I was not in on all of the whys and wherefores of the integral planning for a mission, even one with the SEALs. But planning was done carefully and completely. In spite of that, this one op didn't go too well.

We had stripped down a couple of the available gunships to a slick configuration for the insertion and extraction of the SEALs. It was a joint operation, so we had additional detachments, three in all, working on the op. So we had plenty of firepower while still being able to move the SEALs in and out with our own assets.

But for some reason, the intel on this operation was not as good as it could have been. As soon as the SEALs were inserted, they were hit pretty hard. Though the exact numbers escape me, I know several of them were wounded. And we had one of our gunships badly shot up, with both the pilot and copilot being wounded.

The crew capacity I was working in at that time was as a copilot. I just hadn't been in-country long enough to act as the aircraft commander. But that was one of my first major operations. And to see it not go well, and not know why, has kept it sharp in my memory. There are a lot of reasons things don't go well sometimes. The intel might have been great, but something else happened to change the situation before we arrived. I just don't know.

After I had moved up north to Det 7 at Dong Tam, it was just so refreshing, after that bad experience in Ca Mau, to deal with the SEALs. To see those folks do their homework so carefully and completely made me very comfortable about going out on a mission with them. And after I'd gone out with the SEALs a number of times, and seeing just how professional they were, that feeling just grew more solid.

But the other mission that really sticks in my mind took place out of Dong Tam, and it wasn't a SEAL operation. We had our own radio set up so that we could respond to calls as quickly as possible. One night, a call came in from a couple of American advisers who were north of Dong Tam. They were surrounded, under heavy fire, and needed air support badly.

It didn't matter to us that it was the middle of the night. We were up and off the deck as quickly as we could. To complicate matters, this was the time of year when the Vietnamese burned off their fields to clear them for the new plantings. Now it was nighttime, with no lights and a smoke haze dimming whatever light there was. Vietnam at night was dark; there were no light grids on the ground and electricity was a nonexistent commodity in the rural countryside. And we were flying through this darkness to an unknown position.

The Viet Cong had set up a heavy-machine-gun trap, where they could get an incoming helicopter in a murderous crossfire. And as a detachment, we flew in and put down close air support as directed by the Americans on the ground. And the situation reminded me of the old WWII movies with the flak coming up to take out the bombers. Only this time the flak was the glowing green lights of tracers, and they were coming up at us.

Belts of ammunition for machine guns were not normally loaded just with tracers. There would be four, five, or six rounds fired for every tracer launched. So between the rounds we could see, there were maybe six others we couldn't.

With all of that fire coming up at us from all sides, I figured there had to be some of it hitting the helicopter. But it wasn't hit, and we stayed in the air, putting out our own fire all around the Americans' position.

Finally, we ran out of fuel and ammunition and had to go back for a hot reload. Our ground crews did their jobs quickly and we took off again with another load of fuel and ammunition. We returned to the advisers' position and again put the enemy under fire with directions from the ground. And again, those green tracers rose up to meet us.

But we were finally able to drive the enemy back, and got the situation to the point where the Americans on the ground were no longer under attack. And all during that time, my knees shook. Normally, a helicopter doesn't face heavy ground fire in the form of .50 caliber or better. A fire team is just a poor weapons system against such fire. And we normally wouldn't have fought against that kind of a position unless the situation was as grave as it was that night.

But we had people on the ground who needed our help, and they needed it badly. So it really didn't matter that any of us were scared, and I'm certain we all

A final pre-op briefing for SEALs ready to go in Vietnam. The SEAL at the top right, wearing the cammo bush hat, is armed with the T223 rifle, a version of the HK 33 tested by the SEALs in Vietnam.

were. But we had a job to do and our people down there desperately needed us to do it.

You could see tracers floating through the air around us; they appeared to move by unnaturally slowly. And you could hear the occasional round strike the aircraft. But we were all very well trained, and we just continued to do what we had to do.

The Navy figured we had done something pretty well in that night's operation. At least, as the officer-in-command, I was given the Distinguished Flying Cross for leading the attack. But I'll always remember those green tracers, and how my legs shook.

Each helicopter burned through fourteen 2.75-inch rockets, 3,000 rounds of ammo for the miniguns, and another thousand rounds of ammunition for the door guns. But the overriding factor for our remaining in the fight was our fuel situation.

But in spite of the fear that came over you in a firefight, you could also have a real good feeling come over you as well. You knew in your heart and mind that the people you were working with were really well trained. And they weren't going to be cutting out on you when things got hot. In fact, they were going to be doing everything they possibly could to make that mission a go. Those things added up to a really great feeling, and I'm sure this was as true for the SEALs as it was for the Seawolves.

Anyone who has been in combat will tell you, if they really think about it seriously, that you grow very close to the people you serve with. When you work that closely with people in that stressful a situation, they become your family. Those men become your brothers, and you don't cut out on your brother. You do whatever you have to do to make the situation work. Yeah, you're scared, but you have to do it.

I was surprised a bit when I first learned just in how high a regard the SEALs held the Seawolves. Surely, I had never considered myself anywhere close to their equals when you took into account the amount and kind of training they went through. And the kind of job they did was incredible. In all of my working with them, I think I only understood maybe ten percent of the job they did. So their thinking well of us is a high honor indeed.

During our flight operations, we always had to worry about going down in enemy territory. It could be while on a SEAL operation, supporting the Riverines, or working with the Vietnamese army. But there was some comfort in the thought I had in the back of my mind.

Without being told in so many words. I knew that if we went down, it wouldn't be very long before there would be some SEALs out there looking for me. And that was a great feeling.

After my tour in Vietnam, I returned to the States. The feeling of being there faded somewhat over time. And then I received the honor of being awarded the Distinguished Flying Cross. But you also had to keep in your mind the other people who may have done a lot more than you did, and they never received a medal for it. Yes, it was an honor, but I know I wasn't doing anything other than what almost every other pilot was doing when they were stationed in Vietnam.

Mark Schimpf, Chief Warrant Officer, U.S. Army

In Vietnam, I was a helicopter gunship pilot for the U.S. Army. My bird was a Huey UH-1B, an aircraft that was first introduced into Vietnam as a troop carrier. The birds were later outfitted with weapons systems and flew as helicopter gunships, the same configuration as those first flown by the Navy Seawolves.

The configuration we used was a thirty-eight-rocket setup, two nineteen-round 2.75-inch FFAR (Folding Fin Aircraft Rocket) pods, one on either side of the aircraft. There were also two door gunners, each man armed with a flexible M60 machine gun. Generally, we didn't fly with any externally mounted machine guns, giving up the weight of the guns and their ammunition in order to carry the larger nineteen-round rocket pods rather than the smaller seven-round versions.

Small arms were available for everyone on board the helicopter. The personal weapons were in case we had to put down someplace and defend ourselves on the ground. On our bird, the copilot also had a 40mm M79 grenade launcher. When he didn't have anything to do on a mission, he would lean out of the bird and conduct miniature bombing missions with 40mm HE grenades.

With those birds, I flew missions all around the Mekong Delta. I was based in III Corps, not too far from Saigon. But every morning, we did about an hour's flight down to the delta region to fly support missions for whoever might need them.

During our missions, we supported a wide variety of people. You never really knew when you started a flight just where you might end up. Vietnamese, Army Special Forces, Navy SEALs, all of them could call us in when we were in the area. It was kind of an open grab bag as to just who we were going to work with.

SEAL missions obviously weren't advertised as to just when and where they would take place. And we never knew when we were going to work with them while I was in Vietnam. Once we had gotten down into an operational area, we could find

A U.S. Marine Corps Bell AH-1G Cobra gunship in Vietnam. Under the stub wings, this lethal aircraft has mounted both a 19-round (inboard) and 7-round (outboard) 2.75-inch rocket pod. In the chin turret under the nose of the aircraft is a 7.72mm minigun and a 40mm machine grenade launcher. The gunner sat in the front of the cockpit with the pilot sitting at the rear in the slip helicopter.

U.S. Navy

out that today we would be working with a group of people on the ground who might not be specifically identified. But we would recognize the SEALs because of their unorthodox appearance and selection of weapons.

The first time I met SEALs in the field, my impression of them was that they were a little comical, since I was used to seeing people in uniforms and with standard-issue weapons, and the SEAL units tended to be a little more "ragtag" in their choice of operational uniforms. Simply put, there probably weren't two of them dressed alike; some might be wearing blue jeans, black cotton tops, bandannas, floppy hats, boots, sandals, or even barefoot. And certainly there wouldn't be two of them in a group armed with the same weapon. All in all, a very wild group and more than a little entertaining, from my point of view.

Generally, we didn't get involved with the SEALs on a fire support mission until they had made contact with the enemy and were in maybe over their heads. Our unit didn't normally start out a mission with the expectation of giving air support to the SEALs unless they were going into an area they expected to be hot. If the SEALs suspected they might be facing a larger target than their normal support could handle, then we would be brought on board to stand by. SEALs preferred to go in to a target quietly, and didn't want a bunch of helicopters flying around drawing attention. We only got called in when things had gone "south" for them and they needed some help.

Since so much time has gone by since those days, all of the missions kind of blur together. Separating one SEALs mission from all of the ops we flew is hard, but there is one that stands out. A SEAL team had been inserted by boat and had run into a lot of trouble on the ground. A Seawolf helicopter fire team had been assisting the beleaguered SEALs, but the Seawolf birds had expended their ordnance almost right off the bat and they had to go back for a reload.

The call went out for more fire support. Fortunately, we still had full loads of everything at the time. Because of the mission that the SEALs were working, they really needed precise, close air support since the bad guys tended to be right in on top of them when a fight broke out. As an Army gunship pilot, I can say that we were pretty good at precise fire support. We could put rockets exactly right where they needed to be. And that was just what those SEALs wanted right then.

Our load of ammunition and rockets was a large one, actually a bit more than regulations allowed. But rules were made to be broken. And I think I can safely say that in Vietnam, any rule there was got broken in every possible way. On our missions, we always wanted to carry as much armament as possible.

The doors were left off our birds, since they really wouldn't do anything; by getting rid of their weight, we could carry more ordnance. The door gunners had several cases of ammunition for each of their M60 machine guns, one on each side of the helicopter. We also had a selection of hand grenades, including white phosphorus. And the M79 would have a nice selection of ammo on board. Our personal weapons consisted of M16s, CAR-15s, and even AK-47s, whatever was available. You just hauled as much as you could to fight with.

Sometimes, this heavy load made it difficult to get a helicopter off the ground. On a hot day, after around noon, a refueled and rearmed bird would barely be able to hover. The hot air caused the rotors to lose lift and the engine would be straining to get the bird in the air. She would be hard to move even on the skids. But once the helicopter was moving, the forward motion gave added lift and the bird could be on her way.

It was common practice in these hot, hard lift situations for the crew chief and door gunner to get out of the helicopter. We would begin a slow forward motion, sliding along the leading edge of the skids. As the bird gained a little speed, the crew would decide when it was time to leap aboard. The helicopter would usually bounce off the ground, but it would manage to lumber into the air. Once we got flying, it was okay.

All of the helicopters and their crews shared the same kind of dangers throughout Vietnam. It didn't matter if you were Army, Navy, or Marine Corps. We flew the birds that went right in where the action was and slugged it out with an enemy that could shoot at us with anything they had. So there wasn't much in the way of serious rivalry between ourselves and, say, the Seawolves.

There was a certain amount of envy about the meals the Seawolves had, though. They seemed to eat very well indeed. Whenever we had the opportunity to stop at the Navy base at Nha Be, near Saigon, we ate with them. The kidding from our side got pretty serious. We used to tell them to come on up to our base and see what the real war was like, C rations and all.

The Seawolves didn't have the opportunity to get involved in as many different kinds of things perhaps as we did. And they were champing at the bit; those Seawolf pilots and crews wanted even more action than they actually got into. They did work under a somewhat more restricted, controlled environment than we did. The Army guys were pretty loose.

We had our own little jokes, games, and traditions in our aviation company. Probably the most spectacular of these was the tradition of "Bomb of the Day." That was a little game we played when things got boring. And it's a bad thing to have bored young men and explosives in the same place. That's a really dangerous combination.

Generally, the Bomb of the Day was something like a couple of 2.75-inch rocket warheads wired together. We had the M151, what we called the ten-pound warheads, and the bigger M229 seventeen-pounders. But even the bigger seventeen-pounders only had about five pounds of Composition B-4 high explosive inside of them. But that could be fixed by securing one or two two-and-a-half-pound sticks of C-4 plastic explosive to the assembly. And you might add a hand grenade, probably white phosphorus for light and smoke, to the bomb. And whatever else you felt would make for a better effect.

What you wanted was a good flash and bang so the crowd could see it. The bomb would be dumped out over a hooch in an area where we had been doing some shooting. When you were getting ready to throw out your bomb, you would call all of the other pilots' attention to the area of the explosion. That way they could all grade your bomb.

The object was to try and duplicate a miniature nuclear blast. Sometimes, the Bomb of the Day turned out to be more effective than you had planned. Usually, your helicopter was fairly low when you dropped the thing out, and you got a little concussion from the explosion. That's what happens when young boys have a lot of explosives.

Bomb of the Day could be a significant event. If your blast was graded well by the other pilots, you could plan on drinking free that night. That increased the value of the Bomb of the Day considerably.

The playing around sometimes made the dangerous situations we found ourselves in every day a little more bearable. You went over to Vietnam with the thought that perhaps you were going to win the war for America and her allies, and carry the flag. What you quickly found out was that the war was a day-to-day survival event of trying to just keep everybody alive for the year and be done.

There was no distinction at all about working with other services. When you needed help, you didn't really care where it came from. And that held true for everybody there. We were always pleased to help out any of the other services. Assisting the SEALs was even more important sometimes, because they were hanging out there pretty far. When we could help them out, we were happy to do so.

There's a mystique about the SEALs. And being an Army pilot, I have an opinion of them formed by the things I've seen of their training. And they went through an entirely different kind of operating than I did. Since the SEALs are a closed group and not a whole lot is known about them, the mystique and legend of the Teams built up in Vietnam continues to live on today.

You get used to getting shot at. And some people have a very hard time accepting that if they've never been exposed to it. But when you get shot at on a regular basis, that's what becomes the norm for you. As a result, it just doesn't impact on you as much. So when someone is in trouble and you go in to get them out, you don't give a great deal of thought to the danger of the situation.

"Oh, I might get shot" or "There's a lot of lead coming up here. Maybe I shouldn't do this." That kind of talk just doesn't enter your mind. All you do think about is the fact that you have to go and get that person out of trouble. And you do this because you know that if you were that person on the ground, you would want someone to come and help you. And that was done by everyone in the war. It was a normal course of events.

■ Chapter 41

SEAL and UDT Detachments

Both the UDTs and the SEAL Teams operated in detachments, commonly called dets, when they deployed from their bases at Coronado or Little Creek. Dets were normally identified by an alphabetical designation according to the Navy phonetic alphabet: *A* was Alfa, *B* was Bravo, and so on. These dets were not of a standard size, but were adjusted to fit the needs of the mission. Det Golf, the largest SEAL detachment of the Vietnam War, grew from an initial allotment of 3 officers and 15 enlisted men (3/15) to a group of six deployed platoons and a command element totaling 13 officers and 75 enlisted men. This was more men than were in SEAL Team One at its commissioning.

At close to the peak of Navy Special Warfare's involvement in Vietnam in January 1970, the numbers of detachments in Vietnam and their assigned personnel were as follows:

PERSONNEL DISPOSITION AND NUMBERS, JANUARY 1970

UNIT	LOCATION	PERSONNEL
NAVSPECWARGRUV	Saigon	10/11
SEAL Det SIERRA	Cam Rahn Bay	1/7
SEAL Det ALFA (HQ)	Binh Thuy	1/2
Fifth Platoon	Dong Tam	2/12
Sixth Platoon	Ca Mau	2/11
Seventh Platoon	Nha Be	2/13
SEAL Det GOLF	Nam Can	1/3
Delta Platoon (A Squad)	Rach Soi	1/6
Delta Platoon (B Squad)	Kien Son	1/6
Echo Platoon	Nam Can	2/8
Foxtrot Platoon	Nam Can	2/12
Golf Platoon	Nam Can	2/11
Hotel Platoon	Sa Dec	2/11
Juliett Platoon	Long Phu	3/12
SEAL Det ECHO	Danang	0/3
MST One	Danang	3/16
MST Two	Binh Thuy	1/11
MST Two, Det ALFA	Sa Dec	1/8
MST Two, Det BRAVO	Nam Can	1/7
MST Two, Det CHARLIE	Nam Can	1/11
MST Two, Det DELTA	Dong Tam	2/21
MST Two, Det ECHO	Rach Soi	1/8

MST Two, Det FOXTROT	Ca Mau	1/7
MST Two, Det GOLF	Long Phu	1/7
BJU One TM 13	Binh Thuy	3/16
UDT Det DELTA	Nha Be	1/5
UDT Det GOLF	Nam Chan	1/7
UDT Det HOTEL	Danang	1/8

Detachment identifiers could be confusing. Both the UDTs and the SEALs could have a detachment with the same letter designator in-country in Vietnam at the same time. The mobile support teams (MST) who ran the special boats also used the same system. Only the beach jumper units (BJU) avoided this particular area of confusion.

SEAL DETS

- DET ALFA: SEAL Team Two detachment of direct-action platoon in Vietnam.

- DET BRAVO: combined SEAL Team One and Two detachment under the control of COMUSMACV to supply advisers to the PRU program primarily in the IV Corps area. Expanded on 4 October 1968 from 1/12 to 13/21.

- DET CHARLIE

- DET DELTA

- DET ECHO: combined SEAL Team One and Two detachment under the control of COMUSMACV to supply advisers and trainers to the South Vietnamese unconventional warfare units.

- DET FOXTROT

- DET GOLF: SEAL Team One detachment of direct action platoon in Vietnam. The largest single SEAL detachment of the Vietnam War.

- DET HOTEL

- DET INDIA

- DET SIERRA

UDT DETS

- DET ALFA: UDT 12 detachment.

- DET BRAVO: UDT 12 detachment; conducted hydrographic reconnaissance along South Vietnamese shores including clandestine missions launched from the submarine USS *Perch*. Assisted in amphibious operations and major landings.

- DET CHARLIE

- DET DELTA: UDT detachment stationed at Camp Tien Sha near Danang.

- DET ECHO: UDT detachment assigned to Amphibious Ready Group conducting standard UDT reconnaissance missions.

- DET FOXTROT: UDT detachment assigned to Amphibious Ready Group conducting standard UDT reconnaissance missions.

- DET GOLF: UDT detachment assigned to riverine forces in the Ca Mau Peninsula.

- DET HOTEL: UDT detachment assigned to riverine forces in the Ca Mau Peninsula.

- DET INDIA: UDT detachment assigned to riverine forces in the Ca Mau Peninsula.

- DET SIERRA

Frank Sobisky, Electrician's Mate, Third Class

In August 1966, I joined the Navy specifically to enter the UDT Teams. When a group of us went down to the Navy recruiters' office, I went along really just to watch my two friends enlist for the Seabees. While at the office, I learned about the UDTs for the first time. Originally, I was thinking about enlisting to go to the war in Vietnam, but as a member of the Army Special Forces. I just had that mentality then, I guess.

But once I was at the Navy office, the recruiter hooked right into me and suggested the UDT. When I asked him what it was, he told me about the Frogmen. The Navy Frogmen were something I had known a little about, at least from popular movies and magazines. Then the recruiter played me along a bit, telling me I could enlist and not have to go for ninety days.

Back when I was that young, ninety days sounded like forever. So I told the recruiter to just sign me up, and I found myself in the Navy. When I first arrived in Coronado months later, I was assigned to Class 42, a West Coast winter class. Training was still called Underwater Demolition Team Replacement training then, and it was a little scarier than I expected. And the training was a lot harder than I expected.

It turned out I wasn't in as near as good a shape as I thought I was once those

Coming up from the escape hatch, this UDT swimmer is just clearing the deck grids of a submerged submarine. He is using open-circuit SCUBA gear during this well-lit training exercise off Key West, Florida, in 1959.

U.S. Navy

instructors got hold of me. But I held up and went through Hell Week with my class-mates. Class 42 was a winter class, and it was very cold. Everyone jokes about the lack of snow in Southern California, but it did indeed snow on our class at least one day. And for San Diego, that was really cold.

A lot of things helped get me through the training, my classmates and just my own stubbornness. But what probably got me through all of that training more than anything else was that I wanted to impress my father. Any thought of quitting was just something I had to push back and ignore and just keep on going.

There was the fun of the mud flats during Hell Week. Those stinking stretches of thick black mud that the instructors had us roll around in. And this mud had a very pungent smell to it. We were covered from head to toe in thick, stinking mud. We were crawling in it, sitting in it, and even doing somersaults in it. Then it was time for lunch.

So with us standing waist-deep in the muck, the instructors, being the kind-hearted souls they were, gave each of us a nice, nutritious sack lunch. Each of the paper bags held an orange, a hard-boiled egg, and a piece of fried chicken.

We had to eat everything with our mud-covered hands. Peeling open some of the package was interesting—you couldn't set the bag down without it sinking out of sight. And all that was visible of our bodies in the mud was white teeth and eyeballs. It was funny to look around and see all these guys daintily trying to peel their oranges with their teeth so at least they didn't have to eat that mud as well. Here were all these big, bad, tough future Frogmen trying their best to keep these bits of dirt out of their food.

We were all pretty much exhausted, and looking around at these guys trying to eat just struck me as funny. So I just lost it and started laughing. That became contagious, and soon enough we were all looking at one another and busting up. The instructors didn't seem to understand what was striking everyone as so funny, but it was a lighthearted moment during a really miserable time.

I made it through Hell Week, but I didn't make it through training, at least not with Class 42. During land warfare training, I injured my left arm and couldn't continue. Since I was already post–Hell Week, the instructors decided to give me a chance to heal and I was rolled back to wait for the next class to go through training.

So when Class 43 began training, I was right in there with them. But the instructors started me right at the beginning with my new class, and I had the honor of going through Hell Week a second time.

Two classes, two Hell Weeks. But at least my second time through, it was a summer Hell Week. And I thought I had an advantage because I knew some of the mind games the instructors would ruin on us during training. That not only helped me get through, it helped my boat crew as well.

But I never had an easy time of it during training. I'm a big guy, and there's a lot of difficulty being a big guy in training. Just by being big, when you step in the sand, you go in deeper than the others. And when you do log PT, you're reaching higher than the others. And if you have a smaller guy next to you, well, he may be trying to pull his own weight, but you usually end up lifting part of his share of the load as well as your own.

The hardest part of training for me was the runs. I just wasn't a good runner. Swimming came much easier for me, as I was already a good swimmer right off the bat at training. And my swimming is probably what saved me during training. At least it helped make up for my slower times during runs.

But all of the work, and both Hell Weeks, were worth it in the end. Standing there on graduation day and getting into the Teams was probably the highlight of my life. And that thought continues to this day. Completing that training was an accomplishment that relatively few others had done. And my father said that it was his proudest moment to see me there that day. For me, it was a very fulfilling moment.

To be a member of the UDT is to have joined a brotherhood. Of the fifteen or sixteen guys who completed training with me that day, any one of them could call me today and I would drop whatever I was doing to assist him if I could. Since I've gotten out of the Navy, I've done a lot of things in my life. But I have never had the camaraderie that I had while in the Teams.

The training then was done on the bay side of Coronado. Once you graduated training, you were sent to the Teams, who were located across the road on the ocean side of the base. So once you had made it through training, you "crossed over" to the Teams.

Once I had been assigned to UDT 11 for several months, I learned about the SEAL Teams for the first time. To me, the SEALs were the elite of the elite. And at that time in my life, I had the mindset that being with the very best was what I wanted to do. But before I could get to the SEALs, I had to prove myself in UDT 11.

We didn't start operating with our respective UDTs right away. Once the graduates of Class 43 had been assigned to their Teams, we all went off to Fort Benning, Georgia, for army jump school. That was another adventure because I don't particularly care for heights. But the training was part of the job. And it was a lot easier than going through UDTR.

Once we arrived at Fort Benning, the instructors broke us up and spread us out among the other students. But we still had our fun. The very first night we got there, we were just kind of wandering around trying to figure out where we were supposed to be. One of the instructors jumped on us as a group and had us start doing push-ups for him. We were being wiseasses about the whole thing, and I think he was trying to make a point about discipline.

The "hooyah" yell we had learned in UDTR came in handy to organize us against the Army in a way. When you screwed up at jump school, the instructors would have you immediately drop and give them twenty push-ups. Every time one of us was dropped down to "start pushing on Georgia," he would yell out "hooo-yahhh!"

When we heard that yell, all of the rest of us would pick up on it, yell out, and drop for push-ups ourselves. No matter what we were doing or where we were, if a Teammate dropped, we all dropped. We had decided this among ourselves after that first-night episode. The instructors all acted frustrated by our shenanigans. But I think that deep down inside, they really got a kick out of it.

I mean, we were in great physical shape. We had all just completed one of the hardest physical training courses in the world, and here we were with these Army instructors trying to punish us with a handful of push-ups. It was nothing for us to do twenty push-ups. And even though I wasn't one of the best runners in the Team, far from it, I could outrun the Army troops in our class. When our jump school class went for a run, the six of us from my UDTR class would literally run rings around them. As the group was running along, we would be circling them on the outside. That pissed them off and was more than a little fun.

There was an incident in the chow line when we disagreed with the Army way of doing things. Volunteers had to serve chow to everyone going through the line. You didn't serve yourself—the volunteers loaded up your tray. And as far as we were concerned, the Army was feeding these guys insufficient portions.

So we volunteered for server duty during chow. I don't think they allowed anyone from the Teams to serve chow at jump school for a while after that. We filled those guys trays so full, they had a hard time carrying them to the dining tables. The civilian cooks said we were going to run out of food, which we did. So we ended up not getting anything to eat, but we still had fun with the situation.

Still, the first time I heard that phrase—"Stand up, hook up, stand in the door"—I was probably in a daze. Even though I didn't like heights, that first jump didn't bother me all that much. But that was only because I was too stunned to react to it. That made my second jump even harder. But I completed jump training and maintained my jump status while in the Teams.

But every time I had to make a qualifying jump in the Teams, I would tell myself that I might not do it this time. You had to jump so many times a year to keep receiving jump pay. But I figured I would finally just not go out the door. But I always did.

The parachute jumping was something I didn't like about the job. But the camaraderie in the Teams was something I really liked. And that aspect of life in the Teams is something that's very hard to explain to someone who hasn't experienced it. It isn't just the danger, or the working close together. I've been a fireman and I've been a policeman since I left the Navy. And both of those jobs hold a certain amount of danger, and there is a feeling of brotherhood among the men who share that danger.

But as much as we got along together in those jobs, it never came close to

The first parachute jumps of Jump School are memorable, even for recent graduates of BUD/S. One parachutist is landing just in front of another, blocking view of his body but not the round canopy of his parachute in this shot.

U.S. Navy

what was felt every day in the Teams. For example, only in the Teams did you have the concept of a swim buddy. A swim buddy was the guy you were teamed up with for any kind of swim or dive in the water. They would usually try to pick two guys who were pretty close together in terms of skills, but that didn't always work out.

No matter what, you never left your swim buddy, you never parted. You just stuck with each other, and if he got in trouble, you were there to help him out, just as he was there to help you if the situation was reversed.

While in UDT 11 in 1967–68, I did my first deployment to Vietnam. I remember thinking it was god-awful hot there the moment the plane's doors were opened. Stories about what Vietnam was like had made the rounds of the Teams back in Coronado. So when we stepped off the plane, I was ready for someone to start shooting at us at any moment. It took a while before I finally learned to relax a bit and not expect a bullet to snap by at any moment.

Once we had arrived in Vietnam and got set up, we started conducting a lot of beach reconnaissance operations as part of our mission. At one point during the deployment, I was assigned to an ARG repair ship for a while. All that ship seemed to be doing was just going around in circles out in the ocean.

But I made it back to my Team soon enough, and we continued carrying out the UDT mission in Vietnam. The SEAL Teams had a lot more training in the land warfare aspect of combat and they really did the Navy's inland operations during the Vietnam War. The UDTs did more along our traditional operation of beach and river recons, measuring the water's depth and making note of any obstacles.

But what kind of operations you would conduct depended on just where your UDT platoon was assigned. There were a lot of river trips and demolition operations conducted. Not only water obstacles were blown out of the way, a lot of shore-based bunkers and hooches were dealt with by the UDT as well. We just didn't get into a lot of the patrolling and close-in combat type of operations is all. That we left up to the SEALs.

In 1969, I volunteered to go over to SEAL Team One and operate as a SEAL. After being assigned to a platoon, I went through tactical training with my Teammates and we deployed to Vietnam later in the year.

The SEALs went out in what were probably smaller groups than we had worked with in the UDTs. And the SEALs had a little more freedom in choosing the operations they would conduct than we did back in the UDT. It seemed to me that our lieutenant would go get an op and come back and give us a briefing on it. We would sit and hash out the details, each man giving his opinion or suggestions as his experience dictated. Then we usually just went out and did the op.

Hopefully, what we had decided to do worked out during the mission. If it didn't, we would

SEALs listen intently during a pre-mission briefing.
U.S. Navy

try and determine just what had gone wrong. Then we could adjust our game plan to fit.

During my first combat operation, my spoken Vietnamese was very limited. I knew a few things, like bookoo (French beaucoup) meant "many." We were working with some South Vietnamese, trying to teach them a little unconventional warfare, and the language difference was a real problem for me.

I heard the South Vietnamese troops going "bookoo, bookoo," quite a bit while we were out in the middle of this defoliated area. Not knowing exactly what we were running into, I took cover behind this little stump when the patrol leader signaled. Or at least I tried to take cover. That stump was small and I stuck out from all sides of it.

There was just nothing there for me to hide behind really, and I was thinking, Oh, God, I'm going to get killed here. Just then, three guys came walking down the edge of a little canal near us. One of the guys was a North Vietnamese Regular by the look of his uniform. The other two were the classic, black-pajama Viet Cong.

Even though I had those three guys in my sights, I didn't shoot them. That was my first chance to really engage the enemy and I just didn't take it. Had somebody else opened fire, I would have joined right in. But I didn't think I could just open fire.

The three men just walked right by us and climbed into a sampan stuck onto the canal's bank just a short distance from us. As they paddled away, I was thinking they acted just like they owned the country. Reflecting back on it, I guess they did.

Some thought about taking another life kept me from opening fire on those three men. My mind had been occupied heavily for some time with the thoughts of killing my fellow man. But I'd have never let down my Teammates through inaction if things had come down to that.

There were a lot more chances for me to fire before that tour was over. The first time we got into a heavy firefight, the situation was much like you would expect it to be. The air was filled with the sounds of small-arms fire and the bullets were snapping by overhead. It was like hell, and that proved even more so when the SEAL next to me was shot.

I had a kind of a funny reaction to the situation. When the SEAL next to me was shot, he called over to me, saying, "I think I'm hit!"

All I said back was "What do you mean 'you think'? Keep shooting."

I just didn't want to talk to him at the time. The situation was pretty intense; there was a lot of fire going back and forth. The fight seemed to go on for quite a while. But it was actually probably over with in just a short time.

It was situations like this that kind of showed the difference between a veteran and a new guy. It depended on the circumstances, but a veteran had been there awhile and knew his training would carry him through. The new guys still had to learn that.

I did two tours in Vietnam, one with UDT 11 and one with SEAL Team One. I spent enough time over there to build up a different view of the enemy we were fighting: I kind of envied him. It was a strange thought and I never talked about it to anybody, but I always thought they had kind of a better war to fight. They could see who the enemy was, and where he was.

A lot of the time we were shooting at nothing solid—smoke from where someone had fired, or maybe a muzzle flash at night. They had ships to shoot at, the river craft, helicopters, and us. It just seemed like they had a better deal.

But one of the things we had really going for us was the quality and volume of support we could call on. The Brown Water Navy, the guys who ran the river patrol boats and other small craft, they were absolutely top-notch, fantastic. They probably had a job that I wouldn't ever have wanted to do. During my tours in-country, I had worked with the Marine Corps, Army, and different Navy units as well as with the South Vietnamese.

For myself, I felt so lucky, and so secure, knowing the guys I was with. Because of my Teammates and our support people, I knew that if something happened to me, I would be taken care of.

We had really great air support as well. The air unit that sticks out to in my mind is the Black Ponies and their OV-10 aircraft. When I left the service, one of my desires was to buy one of those OV-10 aircraft. It amazed me what they could do when they flew in support of us. It appeared as if the small twin-tailed craft could turn on a dime up in the sky. And the pilots who flew those craft were terrific.

When we called in the Black Ponies, they showed up fast and hung around a long time. All you had to do was tell them over the radio where you wanted them and they were right on target. They would lay down cover fire and just eliminate a target. They really impressed me.

Depending on what they carried under their wings, they could put out a blizzard of fire. They would cover an area and just suppress anything you were worried about. With a Black Pony covering you, you could make some distance if you had to and no one would show themselves to fire at you. If they did, the Black Ponies made them go away, permanently. While we were stationed down at SEAFLOAT, the Black Ponies were our primary air support. And we were very glad to have them.

The funny thing is, during the one operation we did in Vietnam that really stands out in my memory, we didn't fire a shot.

There was supposed to be a few VC or NVA at a little bend in a river. Our Team went on the other side of the river and set up an ambush position. Another regular military unit, it was either the Marines or the Army, was going to approach the suspected position of our targets.

With the regular troops coming in and raising a lot of noise moving through the area, they would flush out our targets and drive them across the river toward our ambush. When they came out of the water, we would dump them. It was a classic hammer-and-anvil ambush, with my SEAL unit acting the part of the anvil and the regular troops moving through the area as the hammer.

We were all set up, spaced out on the bank, and waiting for this handful of VC to enter our kill zone. Then we got our little surprise. Instead of a handful of VC, maybe just a couple of guys, it looked like a whole town was crossing the river right in front of us. There weren't just a few guys—it looked like a thousand people were starting to cross that river. I know that's an exaggeration, but there were a whole lot of them coming in on us.

That was one of the few times I thought I would eat it [be killed] on an operation. In my mind, I was listing how I could possibly slide into the water after we opened up and all of these VC started to return fire. If I could get into the water when all hell broke loose and we bugged out, then I had a chance of swimming away. But that never happened.

All of those enemy troops just landed on the shore and walked by, only ten or fifteen feet from us. None of us fired a shot; we just let them go by. They all went right over the bank and walked away, none of us making a noise all the while. Even the SEALs use their brains on occasion.

In Vung Tau, Vietnam, a Black Pony of Light Attack Squadron 4 takes off. Eight pods of rockets and guns are visible below the wings as the small craft lifts into the air.

U.S. Navy

On thing about the men of the Teams, they almost always look to the water as the best avenue of escape. For myself, I always considered the water my best way out. I was always a pretty good swimmer, and working in the Teams always made you think about the water. Even when I was riding in a helicopter, I always wanted to sit by the door. As silly as it sounds, I figured if that bird was going down hard, I would jump out and take my chances in the water. In Vietnam, I had a chance of making it to a pond or canal, any body of water.

The water had always been where the Teams worked. Before the SEALs there were the UDTs and the Teams of World War II. Each unit worked in the water, and they were all stepping-stones to where the SEALs evolved to during the Vietnam war. I can remember one of the instructors telling me during training to just keep my mouth shut. That way no one would know how stupid we were and we could just live off the earlier guys' reputations.

That wasn't true, of course, but the men who had built the Teams before us had raised the bar pretty high. And we had to work hard to live up to that reputation, and maybe raise the bar a bit ourselves.

There's an expression in the Teams: "The only easy day was yesterday." I first heard that back when I was going through training. It means that yesterday is over with, so you don't have to worry about it and you don't know what's coming today, but it's probably going to be worse than yesterday. SEALs are a fatalistic bunch sometimes. And this particular expression seems to be true; at least it certainly was during training.

Things were always growing in the Teams. You were always trying to improve yourself, help your Teammates, and make the Teams better. Sometimes, this meant we didn't play by the rules of the regular military so much. And that had its place, too.

Back when the SEALs were first being developed in the early 1960s, there wasn't any rule book to speak of. The Teams just kind of wrote it as they went along. You would try something to get a job done, and if your technique didn't work, you pulled the good points out and tried something new. When we did break the rules, it wasn't to just buck the system, it was to get a job done.

The SEALs of today are an evolved machine, having come from where my generation was back in the 1960s and the Frogmen before us, all the way back to World War II. From looking at these youngsters in training today, I can see that they're in a lot better shape than even we were. And they are certainly much better equipped. The whole focus of training is different than it was when I went through. Today, training is geared to help get you though, without making the final product any lower in quality. In my day, training seemed to be directed toward getting you out, to get you to quit.

But if you were to join the Teams back then or today, you would get some of the

This class gift from Class 89 plainly states one of the most quoted expressions at BUD/S. And the only reason that yesterday was easy is that it has to be over to become yesterday.

Kevin Dockery

same things out of it as we did. A confidence will develop that's almost impossible to find anywhere else. And you will find yourself, you will know what you can do. Quitting will not be an option any longer. Anything you're going to face in life after having been in the Teams, you will know that you can conquer.

■ Chapter 42

Losses, the Cost of War

In 1968, over sixty SEALs from both Teams were wounded, and fourteen lost their lives. Some platoons deployed to Vietnam and returned without a single man being injured by enemy action. But these platoons were the exception. Most deployed SEAL units suffered at least a few men injured during their actions against the enemy. Some returned from their deployments with almost every SEAL in the platoon having been wounded at least once.

Some SEALs were hit multiple times on different operations during a deployment. Often, a wounded SEAL left the hospital where he was recovering as soon as he could. And SEALs sometimes left before their doctors released them. These men simply wanted to continue operating with their Teammates back in their platoon.

But some injuries were simply too serious. Men from the Teams were paralyzed, lost limbs, eyes, or hearing. These men usually had to leave the Teams and the Navy. But this did not mean they weren't successful later in life. The lessons the SEALs learned about overcoming obstacles during their UDTR or BUD/S training helped them overcome any physical limitations they might have received.

Lieutenant (junior grade) Joseph Robert Kerrey, the first SEAL Medal of Honor recipient of the Vietnam War.

U.S. Navy

A SEAL or UDT man could be stopped, but that usually meant he was dead. During their years of active combat in Vietnam, forty-nine men of Navy Special Warfare made the ultimate sacrifice. Thirty-nine men from SEAL Team One were killed during the course of the war. Nine were lost from SEAL Team Two, three from UDT 13, and one from UDT 12. An additional two men were lost, one while attached to SOG and another who had been assigned to Detachment Golf.

The cost of operating with the Teams could be high, but many were willing to pay it. Even the three Vietnam SEAL Medal of Honor holders had all been wounded, two while performing the actions that led to their receiving the Congressional Medal of Honor.

The first SEAL Medal of Honor recipient was Lieutenant (j.g.) Joseph R. "Bob" Kerrey of Delta Platoon, SEAL Team One. On 14 March 1969, while leading his squad against a Viet Cong meeting on an island in the bay of Nha Trang, Kerrey came under fire as he and his SEALs were detected by the Viet Cong. In the fierce firefight that followed, Kerrey was severely wounded when a VC grenade exploded at his feet. In spite of his wounds, he continued to direct his men, call in support, and secure an extraction site. Without further loss to his squad, Kerrey got his men out of the area, almost eliminating the enemy force in the process.

As a result of his injuries, Bob Kerrey was to lose his leg and left the Service, but his loss did little to slow him down. He became a successful businessman and then entered politics. Elected governor of Nebraska, Kerrey later moved even further up the political ladder, becoming the Democratic senator from his home state of Nebraska.

Lieutenant Tom R. Norris was not injured during his extraction of a downed U.S. pilot from well behind enemy lines. But during his sampan-mounted patrol behind enemy lines from 10 to 13 April 1972, he was in more than a little jeopardy on a constant basis. In spite of the difficulties of the operation, and the overwhelming enemy forces the men in his unit slipped through, Lieutenant Norris successfully recovered both downed pilots.

Even for a SEAL, this was a harrowing mission. With only a single Vietnamese LDNN to go with him, Norris paddled a sampan to recover the second of the two pilots. Slipping past North Vietnamese patrols so closely that they could hear them speaking, the SEAL and LDNN made it through with their passenger. Lieutenant Tom Norris was later awarded the second SEAL Medal of Honor for his actions. For his bravery and actions during that rescue, the LDNN with Norris, Nguyen van Kiet, became the only South Vietnamese LDNN to receive the U.S. Navy Cross.

The last SEAL Medal of Honor recipient was Petty Officer Michael E. Thornton of SEAL Team One. During the evening of 31 October 1972, Thornton was working with Tom Norris during an LDNN operation well behind enemy lines in the north part of South Vietnam. During their action, Tom Norris was horribly wounded when an AK-47 bullet struck him in the side of the head.

In spite of being told that his Teammate was dead, Mike Thornton did the only thing that seemed possible to him at the time: he went back through heavy enemy fire to recover his Teammate's body. No SEAL, living or dead, had ever been left behind. Everyone in the Teams always came home.

Finding the apparently lifeless body of his Teammate, Thornton lifted up Norris and ran back through enemy fire. In spite of being wounded across his back and legs by an enemy grenade, he ran with Norris as naval gunfire started landing behind them.

When he was blown off his legs by an exploding shell, Thornton was shocked to hear his dead Teammate speak to him. Norris was alive. Now there was no way that Thorton could leave him behind.

In spite of his own wounds, Thornton carried his Teammate to the sea and swam offshore. In addition to pushing Norris ahead of him, Thornton towed one of the badly injured LDNNs. Even for a SEAL, this was an incredible feat of endurance and strength. The Navy and the Congress of the United States agreed and a year later Michael Thornton became the last SEAL to receive the Medal of Honor during the Vietnam War. And standing next to him was his Teammate, Tom Norris. In its entire history, this was the only time the Medal of Honor was awarded to an individual for saving the life of another Medal of Honor recipient.

Norris recovered from his severe wounds, but he left the service because of them. He continued an above-average career by becoming an FBI Special Agent and setting a high standard even for that agency. Mike Thornton continued his Navy and SEAL Career, later becoming a BUD/S instructor. He was selected to be a plankowner of the very secret antiterrorist unit, SEAL Team Six, when it was commissioned in 1980.

SEALs can be injured, and they can be killed. But they never lose the love they hold for their Teammates and their Teams.

Curtis Williams, Quartermaster, Third Class

In Vietnam, I carried the radio and packed an M79 grenade launcher, which had absolutely nothing to do with my Navy rate of quartermaster. Instead of directing a boat, I was putting out high-explosive grenades and maintaining contact with our support over the radio. That aspect of Team life did cause trouble sometimes with promotions, because you just didn't work in your rate. But the job you did and the people you worked with easily made up for that.

I grew up in Chula Vista down in Southern California. Being relatively close to the Navy base in Coronado, I had a number of friends who were in the UDTs. This was in 1966 and most guys my age were getting drafted if they didn't have some kind of deferment. To pick where I wanted to go, I would have to enlist, and the Teams sounded like a great place to be. So to beat the draft, I enlisted in the Navy.

When I first got into the service, I had no idea that anything like the SEAL Teams even existed. They were only around five years old by then and were still listed as secret. What I did know about was the UDTs and that I wanted to be a Navy Frogman.

When I arrived in Coronado, I became part of Class 41, which started in March, close enough to be a winter class. One thing I hate is the cold, and training exposed me to a lot of it. Even after I left the Navy and became a commercial diver, I still hated cold water. But it was just part of the job and you just tolerated it.

It was really willpower that pushed you through training. There was nothing I've ever experienced like the cold we were exposed to. But you just had to gut it out and keep going. It was probably that exposure to cold that made it possible for me to be a successful commercial diver. You didn't have to like it, but you had to keep going.

Each graduating BUD/S class for years has met the tradition of leaving a class gift. The gift from Class 63 shown here has been one of the more memorable ones.

Kevin Dockery

For myself, I don't think I ever had any real thoughts of quitting. On my first day of training, I looked around at the over 100 guys we had there at the beginning. And it was while I looked at them all that I made the personal commitment to myself that if only one guy was going to be standing at the end of our training, that guy would be me.

It wasn't that I could shrug off everything the instructors put us through and just keep going. There was a point during Hell Week, something like the third or fourth night, that really got to me.

Training and the pace of Hell Week had been rough and we were all pushing hard to keep going in spite of our exhaustion. And the instructors allowed us to put on dry greens, the fatigue uniforms we wore, and lie down a moment.

Lying in bed, I was just starting to get warm. We weren't falling asleep—it was much more like just passing out. It hadn't been more than fifteen minutes or so when the instructors blasted through the barracks, firing blanks and blowing on whistles. They were screaming at us to get up and get back out on the line. So we all had to get up and move out again.

The closeness and comfort of the dry clothes and warm rack made it hard. And our staggering level of exhaustion sure didn't help build any enthusiasm for getting up and moving again. But there was no way I wasn't going back out that door; it was the only way in to the Teams.

In spite of how I felt, I dragged myself out of my rack. Right next to my bunk was my friend's rack, and he wasn't getting up. He just wouldn't do it, no matter how hard I shook him and hollered at him. It seemed that there were fifteen or twenty guys who just wouldn't leave their bunks, to get up and keep going.

When I finally gave up trying to rouse my friend and left the barracks, it seemed like hardly anyone was left in the class. Class 41 had been a fairly big crowd before the instructors had given us that chance to clean up and get warm. But afterward, we were a lot smaller. From something over 100 guys on our first day of training, we ended with only about 25 guys still standing there on the last day.

And I was one of those twenty-five guys, and the feeling was pretty much indescribable. It was a high; I felt I had finally done it, accomplished my goal in the Navy. All I wanted was to be a Frogman, to put that UDT patch on my shoulder. It just felt so good to know that I had made it.

Then, on that same graduation day, I was called into the main office. "Williams get in here," sounded out, and I thought I was in real trouble.

What I found out was that I wasn't in trouble, far from it. Instead, a number of us were receiving a singular honor.

There was a big board in the office up where the instructors had listed everyone in the class and their standing at graduation. And next to my name was the number one. I had graduated at the top of my class.

All during my training, I figured I was just making it through. I had done my best, but never thought that much of it. Everyone, all of my classmates, was doing the same thing. But that wasn't the only thing the instructors told me at graduation.

"By the way," one of them told me, "we want you to go straight to the SEAL Team."

It turned out that the top six graduates of my class were all being asked to go over to SEAL Team One after graduation rather than report to one of the UDTs.

For myself at the time, I was thinking that the UDTs deployed to the Philippines. Based near Olongapo, the Frogs would deploy over to Vietnam every once in a while. But the SEALs were doing some pretty heavy-duty stuff in Vietnam. And the instructors told me that was pretty much the situation.

So I said that I would prefer to go over to a UDT first.

"No, we want you to go to SEAL Team One now," I was told.

There wasn't a whole lot of point in arguing. So off to SEAL Team One I went. And, outside of those first moments of concern, I never regretted going. The caliber of guys I lived with and operated beside in the SEALs was the best. That time is something I wouldn't trade for anything.

But I was still a young man, and had a young man's thoughts and concerns. On my first deployment to Vietnam, I remember sitting on the plane and, frankly, being a little scared. I was really doing it; I was going to war.

The situation was more than a little scary, but it was also very exciting. Nothing I had experienced up to then had prepared me for the adrenaline rush that comes over you in combat. The level of anticipation that comes over you as you move into a combat situation is incredible. But the discipline that had been driven into us from that first day of training helped us get through all of the excitement and do our jobs.

The other part of training, the teamwork, that is the lifeblood of the Teams. And it was the guys I operated with, my Teammates, who made everything we did possible. These were characters that the most vivid imagination in the world would have a hard time inventing.

At that time I was the youngest guy in the SEAL Team. Going straight from high school to the Navy hadn't allowed me much time for life experiences. But all of my Teammates around me made every day a major experience.

These guys lived large, and did things that I hadn't really considered possible. Whether we were fighting the war or partying, everything was done at an all-out level. High speed and low drag.

It felt really good to have these men around me. Looking back on it, I wouldn't have wanted to fight in that war if I couldn't have the Teammates that I did. It was their professionalism, their skill, and their courage that helped bring out the best in me. And it was those same characteristics that helped bring a young kid back home.

Though I didn't have a "sea daddy"—an older, more experienced SEAL who shows you the ins and outs of being in the Teams—there are individuals who really stand out in my memory. One of these men is John Fietsch.

"Killer John" Fietsch was so cool under fire. Nothing seemed to faze him. The confidence and air he had about him just spread. And that really meant a lot to me. Just being with men like him made you know that you were going to come home.

Then there was tobacco-chewing Lewis. "Competent" and "warrior" just don't seem to be enough to describe him. He carried the M60 machine gun when most other SEALs wanted the much lighter, and less powerful, Stoner. He was unbelievable, both in combat and off duty. When it came to party time, Lewis made the top of the list. When he blew off steam, everyone around knew it.

Those two men stand out in my memories, but there were a lot of things that happened in Vietnam that I'll remember for the rest of my days. My first combat operation is one of them.

The people who were taking us out on the operation were making sure it was an easy one. They were from the platoon we were relieving and knew the area very well. So they were taking us out on a relatively simple op to kind of "break us in" to the area. The only thing was, when it's your first time in combat, nothing is easy or simple.

All we did was patrol in, set up an ambush at a likely crossing spot, and then patrol out or extract if the ambush went down. We didn't make contact, there were no shots fired, supposedly an easy day.

But it wasn't easy for me. I was scared shitless through the whole thing. There were people in that jungle who would have liked nothing better than to kill me, and I just knew they could see or hear me.

It was during the first op that I was introduced to another new thing, using drugs to help you stay awake and alert during a long night ambush. For myself, I had no idea what any kind of drugs really were. But the corpsman came around and asked me if I wanted something to help me keep awake.

It was going to be a long night, and everyone else seemed to be accepting what the corpsman was offering. So I took what turned out to be Dexamil, and the next thing I knew, I was wired.

Here I was sitting on my first ambush with my adrenaline already racing along, and I take an amphetamine on top of it. I was positively electric—"alert" just isn't a strong enough word for it. I could hear everything—the lapping of the water, the soft sounds of the swamp—and smell the mud and the water—clearly. The drugs and the situation made for a long, tense operation.

But we didn't make any contact. The ambush was broken down on schedule and we patrolled back out to our extraction point. All of my other operations kind of blend into a blur over the years since then. But that very first one will always stand out sharply in my mind. And I don't think I ever took that Dexamil again.

Though I can't remember the specific operation where we first made contact with the enemy, I'm sure it was an ambush. Almost all of our ambushes were river ambushes, though sometimes we would set up along a trail in the jungle. And we followed the same general procedures for each one.

The patrol would insert along the riverbank a distance away from the planned ambush site. Then we would patrol in and set up along the river or trail. With our weapons facing out into the kill zone, we would then wait for the target to come along. On a river, it would be a sampan that eventually came down and entered the ambush.

The sampan would have two or three guys in it. Even though we operated almost entirely at night, we could still see well enough to make out the weapons in the sampan that identified the men as VC. And when the target was centered in the kill zone, the ambush would be triggered.

When we all opened fire at once, it looked like the whole world had turned to flame. It wasn't until we did that first active ambush that I really saw just how much firepower we had. When the muzzle flashes died away, our night vision would be pretty much gone along with them. But there really wouldn't be much to see anymore. The high-velocity slugs from our machine guns and rifles tore that sampan apart—there just wasn't anything left.

I think we had three Stoners, an M60, and a bunch of M16s all open fire at once. They all just blew that wooden boat apart—I had no idea up until then just how powerful all of our weapons together really were. It was pretty amazing.

When we went through all of our training, preparing for that first moment of combat, there was a certain amount of anticipation that built up. Then the sitting

In 1968, this SEAL waits cautiously along a stream in Vietnam. He is armed with a Stoner 63A light machine gun fitted with a 150-round ammunition drum. Across his chest are additional belts of 5.56mm ammunition for his Stoner. Slung from his shoulder, across his back, is a 66mm M72 LAW antitank rocket. Lastly, clipped to his belt is an M26A1 fragmentation grenade. His hair is held in place by a 40-inch olive drab triangular bandage which cannot easily slip down across his eyes. The bandage also prevents sweat from running down into the SEAL's eyes.

U.S. Navy

on the ambush site just built up the tension even more. The waiting and waiting would just go on, and then, when the action finally happened, the tension release felt like some kind of high.

That was the reward that came from all of our training. We were able to leave as victors, could feel the victory. That was what I had trained for, why we all sat for hours on end waiting for our target to come along; the sudden burst of action was like finally getting the cookie from inside the jar. You had heard about it for weeks and months, and now it had finally happened.

It was just an unbelievable feeling, and there wasn't any thought given to the fact that someone else was dying. Besides that, they had been the enemy and would have just as easily shot and killed all of us.

The VC did manage to get a piece of me toward the end of the first tour in Vietnam. I was blown up and wounded pretty well during an operation. But I lived and recovered from my injuries. Not all of my Teammates were as lucky.

We had patrolled in on one operation and set up an ambush overlooking an empty riverbed. When the tide was up, I'm sure that riverbed was filled with water. But when we were setting up, there wasn't much more between its banks than mud. There wasn't much question that we were well into the VCs' backyard. Where we set up, there were about four or five hooches in back of us, each complete with a VC flag. If the locals were bold enough to put up a VC flag, you knew you weren't in friendly territory.

That situation alone made for an eerie feeling. But we had moved in very quietly under the cover of darkness and set up our ambush. There was no sign at all that we had been detected. But in spite of that, we left nothing to chance. According to our standard operating procedures, one of the members of our patrol set up as rear security. This man, Saunders, was facing the other way, away from our ambush site, just in case someone tried to sneak up on us while we were waiting.

During the middle of the night, we almost nailed a target with our ambush, and it would have been the wrong one, though it might have tasted good.

While we were all sitting there, primed and ready to fire, a pig came rooting along in the kill zone. It was a near thing, for the pig. We almost opened fire, and if we had, that pig would have been shredded pork. But our fire discipline held and we continued waiting for a real target.

The night passed and dawn was coming up as we all held our positions. The plan was that by dawn, if we hadn't made any contact with the enemy, the Seawolf

Frozen in flight by the camera, a Seawolf launches a high explosive 2.75-inch rocket. The symbol of the Seawolves can be seen painted on the nose of this helicopter.

U.S. Navy

helicopter gunship support we had for the mission would come into the target area. The Seawolves would put out rockets, into the jungle, about fifty yards upriver away from us. That fire should flush any VC returning to their hooches directly our way.

Whether we were in the wrong place or the Seawolves put out their fire on the wrong target, I never did find out. But the helicopters dumped their rockets right into the hooches behind us.

The explosions from the high-explosive warheads on the rockets blew Saunders in between me and the SEAL setup next to me. Now there were people running out of the hooches toward us. It seemed we couldn't get our weapons off safety fast enough to take on all of the targets. The situation was a turkey shoot as all of these VC ran around in confusion.

Those VC must have thought we really had our stuff together to be able to blow up their hooches from the air and nail them when they came running out of the door. They never noticed that we had been facing the wrong way to start with.

We had our own wounded, but nothing on the level of what the VC had. Saunders had been hurt in the face, but it wasn't too bad and he was being bandaged up by his Teammates. I had the radio with me and quickly remade contact with the Seawolves.

Those helicopters were turning around and preparing for another pass. "How'd we do?" the pilots asked. "We're coming around for another run."

"No, you're not," I called back. "Do not fire another thing."

When we walked out of there, you could hear the sounds of wounded VC throughout the area. The groans and moaning of the wounded blended in with the almost supernatural appearance of the landscape. The exploding rockets had put kind of a fog all around the area, just a white mist about two feet thick over the ground. The sun was breaking over the horizon and the pink light of dawn gleamed across the fog. The whole effect looked like something from The Twilight Zone.

We walked through the fog, stirring it up with our legs as we stepped over bodies. The sounds of the wounded carried over everything as I led Saunders out. He couldn't see what was all around us, only hear it and be concerned about his own situation. But I could see everything, and it left a picture that won't soon leave my mind.

On that op, Saunders was hurt. But for the most part, we got away pretty clean. On a later op, I was blown up myself, and one of our officers was killed.

We had prepared for that operation carefully. During the day, we had done a helo recon, where we checked out the area in daylight and made certain where everything was. What we saw told us that we were going to have to go in with a larger force than we usually did.

On a normal mission, we operated in units of five or six guys. For that last op, we were going to take ten SEALs in. The target was a sleeping area that the VC would use to lay up. There was a pagoda, a small Buddhist temple, and a hooch at the target. We were going to go in and ambush both targets at the same time. One group of four of us was going to set up around the hooch. The larger, six-man group, which I was a part of, would set up our ambush around the pagoda.

Gene Tinnin was the officer I was with on the op. Since I carried the radio, I moved along right behind him in the patrol. As we moved in, we came up to a small building just visible in the dark. Tinnin turned to me and whispered, "I think that's probably the hooch; I think it's too small to be the pagoda. The point man and I are going to go out and look for it [the pagoda]."

So I gave the signal for everyone to set down on alert, just in case we were sitting around the wrong thing. We hadn't separated into our two ambush teams yet. But after about twenty minutes had gone by without any sight of Tinnin, the other officer with us decided to move out with the smaller element. They went ahead and set up their ambush around the structure right in front of us. There wasn't anything I could do and just watched them leave.

About another twenty minutes went by when I received a call over the radio. The other element had set up around the hooch and was waiting for us to initiate the ambush. According to the plan, the pagoda element would initiate the ambush and the hooch element would open fire on our signal. The only trouble was that we still hadn't found the pagoda.

"Hey, look," I said into the radio, "the patrol leader is still out looking for the objective. You guys aren't even supposed to be set up yet. You may be sitting around the pagoda."

And I left the conversation at that since I didn't want to be talking long. The other patrol wasn't supposed to have moved out yet, but what happened next I'm only guessing at.

What I think happened is that the other radioman didn't relay my message to the other patrol leader. But that was only the second mess-up. The first mistake was that they shouldn't have gone over and set up an ambush in the first place.

But the time went on and the mission continued. After another twenty minutes or so had gone by, Tinnin finally came back. But he was moving in from the opposite direction from where he had left. He had left, moving off to my right. But because there was a tree line just behind us, it was much easier for him to move around the long way and he ended up coming in from my left.

As Tinnin walked up, he whispered to me, "There's nothing over there. That has to be the pagoda," and he pointed out in the direction of the hooch. "The hooch must be somewhere over there." He pointed off in another direction.

Now our point man, Nap, was a big guy, even for a SEAL. He was something like six feet four inches tall. But that night there was no moon, no anything, just darkness. Our conversation was taking place in whispers, the talker putting his lips right up to the other's ear and keeping his voice as soft as possible. As he walked up, Tinnin had noticed that the other guys were missing, "Where's the other guys?" he whispered to me.

I was just getting ready to tell him that they had already set up when we heard the thud of an object hitting the ground near us. Whatever had hit, it seemed to me to be some five or six feet away. Tinnin and I just looked at each other as if to say, "What was that?" We had no idea that it was a hand grenade.

The other four guys had just seen two figures come up from the darkness. And it was too dark for them to make out that our big point man was one of them. So they had thrown a grenade at what they thought to be two VC coming up on them.

Then the grenade exploded.

The blast threw me backward, and as the explosion echoed around, the other guys opened up with their weapons.

Stunned by the blast, I started pulling at the grass, trying to get away. Then a round hit me in the chest and I immediately began gushing blood from out of my mouth.

The other guys must have heard our screams because they stopped firing and came over to help us. In spite of our support, it took maybe an hour to get us all out of there.

At one point I heard one of the guys say that there was no use in working on Tin-

A Mark II PBR speeding along during tests. Only the twin .50-caliber machine guns in the bow gun tub and single .50 at the stern are mounted on this PBR. Only half of the keel of the boat is in the water as this small craft planes across the surface.

U.S. Navy

NAVY SEALs: A COMPLETE HISTORY

nin, that he was dead. So that was when I knew he was gone. But I didn't know how many of my group had been injured. One of my fears was that the VC had come in and everyone had been hurt. But that didn't turn out to be the case.

Our patrol had inserted from PBRs, and the guys in the boat were lying up in the water not too far away. The PBR sailors could hear our conversations over the radio. And when they learned that a bunch of us had been hurt, they came in at a dead run to pick us up and get us out.

At one point the guy on the other radio was talking to a helo when I came around enough to make out what he was saying. And what he was saying was "If you don't bring that helo in here, I'm going to shoot you down."

So apparently, the extraction birds couldn't find a place to set down close enough to pick up the wounded and get us out. Finally, they did find a place and our Teammates got us out. What I remember is two guys each holding me under one arm and just dragging me along with my feet trailing behind.

When I was hit, I thought it had been a concussion grenade going off. The blast had made it feel like every bone in my body had been broken. Immediately following the blast, I tried to drag myself out of the fire zone. But soon after that, every time I tried to move, everything just felt like limp noodles.

Then we reached the helicopter and my Teammates threw me on board first. Tinnin was put in next, his body, or what was left of it, landing on top of me. Then our big point man, Nap, was tossed in on top of Tinnin.

Among the wounded in the bird then, I was the only one still conscious. So I grabbed up Nap's hand and kept talking to him, telling him that it would be all right. Of course I already knew that Tinnin was dead.

Later the corpsmen told me that if I had passed out instead of trying to reassure Nap, I might have died myself. Apparently, I had lost so much blood that it was a wonder that I made it back at all.

Afterward, the incident was investigated and the blame for the accident was placed on Eugene Tinnin. For myself, I think that was just the easy way out and it certainly wasn't Tinnin's fault. As far as I am concerned, the patrol should never have split up without the senior patrol leader, Tinnin, telling them to.

And I had told the other radioman that we were still right where we had been when they moved out. But the message may never have been passed out among the other patrol. I am certain that otherwise they would never have opened up on us.

So two major mistakes caused a SEAL warrant officer to lose his life and the rest of our element to be wounded. And Tinnin had been a real good guy. The three of us—Tinnin, Nap, and myself—were wounded the worst because we had been the only guys standing up when the grenade went off. But all the other guys, even though they had been lying prone in the grass, were still hit, mostly in the upper body and head.

For myself, I had been hit in sixteen different places. All in all, I was very messed up. My right kneecap was blown pretty much off, and the doctors told me that I'd probably never walk right again.

My injuries were so severe, they kept me in-country for more than a month just trying to stabilize me for transport. Things were pretty bad; the heaviest dose of Demerol they could give me only cut the pain for about two hours. But they could only give that to me every four hours. So for two hours out of four, I was in immense pain.

Time blurred a bit, and I couldn't tell how long I was on that two-hours-of-relief-and-two-hours-of-pain cycle. But it seemed to be almost the entire time I was in-country. Finally, they shipped me out to a hospital in Japan, and finally back to the States.

For the next four months I was in the hospital trying to heal. And the Navy wanted to give me a medical discharge. I was considered so bad off that they had the papers ready to give me a medical discharge with a 50 percent disability.

But I was getting real tired of being in the hospital, and I was missing being with my Teammates back at my SEAL Team. So I finally walked into the office and told them that nothing hurt anymore and I wanted to go back to the SEAL Team.

Then they told me that they weren't certain that they could do that.

"Well," I said. "That's where I'm reporting for work tomorrow, okay?"

So they canceled the paperwork for my medical discharge and I went back to SEAL Team One. But I didn't have a whole lot of time left in my enlistment. The Team didn't want to send me back out with a deploying platoon, and they had another assignment I could do.

Across the street, on the amphibious base proper, there was kind of a research and development platoon working with the four-man swimmer delivery vehicles (SDVs). The guys that they sent over to the R&D platoon had mostly come back from a real hard tour in Vietnam. Gary Gallagher, a SEAL who later received the Navy Cross, was one of the guys in the platoon along with me. Most of us had been hurt and were out of the hospital at one stage of recovery or another.

And I stayed with the R&D platoon until my enlistment was up and I left the Navy and the active SEAL Team. But in spite of the injuries I received during my one combat tour in Vietnam, I never regretted my time in the Teams.

Of course there had been times—sitting in the mud next to some slow flow of brown water in Vietnam, waiting on an ambush and being eaten alive by mosquitoes, or having fire ants crawling up my pants—when other thoughts would cross my mind. Usually, they were along the lines of what my old friends back home might be doing.

My old civilian friends would have been in college, dating the girls and having fun. Then the question of just how I had gotten where I was would cross my thoughts. But that never lasted long. Being with my Teammates meant a great deal. It was the sort of experience you can't buy for any amount of money. And I have no regrets at all that I did it.

In spite of my being badly hurt, nothing would have been worth my not being with my Teammates. The experience was unbelievable. Even if I had to be wounded all over again, I would not avoid going. All of that was part of what we did, who we were.

Now, if I could go through my experiences with the SEALs, do it all again, and not be wounded, well, that would be nice. But that's not how it is. In fact, I feel pretty lucky about just being here. It was Teammates like Tinnin, and the other losses in the Teams, men who were killed, who I do hold regrets for. I hated to see anyone get killed over there, but there's a special pain in the loss of a Teammate.

In spite of it all, I came back alive. I might have been blown up, but I later worked through my injuries and recovered. A lot of things still hurt, but I'm walking and not in a wheelchair. And my mind still works, in spite of what my Teammates might say.

What each man carried for an operation, in terms of weapons and ammunition, varied a bit from squad to squad. In our squad, our point man carried a CAR-15, a shortened M16 only about thirty inches long. The point man led the squad through the bush, watching for boobytraps and any enemy forces. He was usually the first person to come into contact with an enemy while we were patrolling. The short, handy length of the CAR allowed him to swing that weapon into action even faster than he could a rifle.

The patrol leader usually came next in the order of march. Gene Tinnin, my pa-

Wearing a set of mottled camouflage, this SEAL is directing his 40mm M79 grenade launcher toward something that has caught his attention off in the brush.

U.S. Navy

trol leader, usually carried a regular M16 rifle. Then I walked behind him. The radioman always tries to stay close to the patrol leader. For a weapon, I carried the M79 40mm grenade launcher along with all different types of rounds.

For my M79, I carried a number of high-explosive, fragmentation grenades, buckshot rounds that turned it into a close-range shotgun, fléchette rounds, which were the same as the buckshot rounds but launched a swarm of finned, steel darts rather than shot. And different-colored flare rounds.

We all carried pistols as well as our primary weapons. Most of us carried a Smith & Wesson 9mm Model 39. In case your main weapon jammed or whatever, it was nice to be able to grab up a handgun and keep fighting. This was particularly true in my case, as the M79 is a single-shot weapon. If something happened and I missed a close-in shot, I didn't have time to put another round in my grenade launcher. I just grabbed up my 9mm.

Sometimes, Tinnin carried a Stoner instead of an M16. A Stoner is a belt-fed light machine gun that fires the same round as the M16 and is much lighter than an M60. It puts out an amazing number of rounds in a minute, or even a second, and you can carry large amounts of ammunition for it.

Behind me usually was Lewis, and he carried an M60 machine gun. The M60 was a very heavy weapon that most guys didn't want to drag around. But Lewis was an animal who could just keep going. He carried not only the M60, but all his own ammunition, hundreds of pretty big rounds. That was a lot of weight for one man, but he liked the M60. In the Army, an M60 gunner would have other guys carrying rounds as well, but Lewis packed all his own.

To augment the firepower of Lewis's M60, the next man behind him in the patrol usually had a Stoner. Rear security, the last man in line, kept a close watch behind us, making sure no one crept up along our trail and surprised us. He carried either another Stoner or an M16.

Our ammunition loads were heavy. I carried rounds strapped all over me, across my front and on my back. A man armed with an M16 had at least seven or eight magazines minimum, each one holding twenty or thirty rounds depending on their size. For the M60, Lewis had crossed bandoliers as well as big pouches on his belt, same thing for the Stoners. We were all pretty well loaded for bear. Any spare place a man had to strap on some ammunition, he usually had it.

If we went in a straight firefight, we had about fifteen or twenty minutes' worth of ammunition. But that would be fired under discipline. Weapons were used in short, aimed bursts rather than just spraying an area with unaimed fire. That fire discipline made our ammunition last longer.

The men I was with in the Team were some of the most unbelievable people I have ever met in my life. And it started with the men who put me through training. Barry Enoch, a SEAL who later won the Navy Cross for his actions in Vietnam, was one of my instructors. Another was Olivera, a big, hook-nosed American Indian.

On line along the shore, these SEALs test-fire their weapons. The SEAL in the center is armed with a Stoner 63A light machine gun, the rectangular pouches on his back holding extra ammunition belt boxes. The SEAL just half visible on the right is armed with an AK-47.

During our runs, Olivera would pick out a trainee as his target in the group. Then he would run alongside that trainee, sometimes even running backward, while smoking a big cigar. And all along that run he would blow cigar smoke in that trainee's face. All you could do was hope it wasn't you he picked that day.

It may have been Olivera who held a record at that time for running the longest time without stopping. But he was just one of my instructors, all of them an amazing bunch. Another instructor was Chief Allen, a five-time heavyweight boxing champion.

And when I passed training and got to the Teams, the guys there were no less impressive. They all worked hard, and they played harder than anybody else I have ever run into in my life. Plus, the loyalty was intense; we would all have given our lives for one another.

When I went to Vietnam, I knew I was going with some very high-caliber guys. These were men I trusted a lot, had confidence in. And that really helped me a lot as a first-timer.

If there was one word for my time in the Teams, it would probably be "unbelievable."

Chapter 43

TET 1968

As early as July 1967, the Communist leadership and military strategists in North Vietnam were preparing their biggest blow against the forces in the south. Ho Chi Minh and General Vo Nguyen Giap had decided to stage a series of attacks all across South Vietnam. Their intention was to overwhelm the South Vietnamese military and their U.S. allies, hopefully causing the collapse of the South Vietnamese government of President Nguyen Van Thieu.

The enemy used a number of feints and deceptions to decoy the U.S. forces as well as the U.S. government. With offers to go to the peace table diverting the attention of President Johnson, attacks such as the siege of Khe Sanh forced the military to concentrate their forces in the countryside and away from the cities. At the same time NVA forces and supplies were moved down the logistics track known as the Ho Chi Minh Trail.

Stockpiles were built up in the safe areas of Laos and Cambodia. Caches in South Vietnam were filled and more were established. As many as 84,000 Viet Cong and NVA troops were in position to conduct the campaign, scheduled to coincide with the lunar new year in 1968.

The Communist Tet offensive was masterfully planned and executed with the primitive communications and supply means available to the VC forces. The NVA and Viet Cong forces' various feints and deceptions caused the American military command to concentrate their forces along the borders of South Vietnam. The staged NVA border battles at Song Be, Loc Ninh, and Dac To worked. However, intelligence reports and suspicions led U.S. commander General William Westmoreland to investigate the buildup of Viet Cong forces that had been noted for over six months.

A number of Game Warden assets, including PBRs, Seawolves, and SEALs, were dispatched to the Cambodian border in Chau Doc province as part of Operation BOLD DRAGON I. The mission of these units was to locate and interdict men and supplies that were suspected to be crossing into Vietnam from Cambodia. These Game Warden forces located a great deal more than they expected.

The Tet lunar new year is a very significant holiday to the Vietnamese. It is a period of revelry, fireworks, and time spent with family. It is also a time of rev-

A Mark II PBR slowly cruising along a waterway in South Vietnam. The firepower of the 31-foot boat is visible in the three .50-caliber machine guns and single 7.62 mm M60 machine gun that can be seen mounted on the boat. Additional small arms would also be on board for the use of the boat's crew.

U.S. Navy

erence for the ancestors of a family. The Viet Cong and the North Vietnamese decreed a truce to cover the period of Tet, 27 January to 3 February, 1968. The actual beginning of the Tet holiday was before daylight on 31 January. North Vietnam decreed that their people would begin their celebration on 28 January and hold their normal three-day celebration before the south held theirs.

In 1789, the Tay Son Montagnards had attacked Chinese troops who were securing Hanoi. Their attack worked only because it was such a surprise to the enemy, coming as it did at the beginning of the sacred Tet holiday. The leadership of the north knew their history, and planned to have it repeat itself.

On 31 January, prior to sunrise, North Vietnamese Army units and the majority of all available Viet Cong units launched attacks throughout South Vietnam. Out of the forty-four provincial capitals of South Vietnam, thirty-six were attacked. Of the six major cities in the country, five became targets that first day. Military airfields and bases also came under fire, with twenty-three of them trying to hold off heavy enemy attacks. Even Saigon, the capital city of South Vietnam, was attacked by eight battalions of Viet Cong.

The attack was sudden and fierce. South Vietnamese forces, many of whom had been recalled from their holiday, wavered and lost ground. U.S. forces were under heavy fire throughout the country. And smaller units in the field who had not been in constant contact with higher command quickly found themselves facing huge numbers of the enemy.

Harry Humphries, Draftsman, First Class

It was in the early 1960s, when I was a sailor in the fleet serving on board a destroyer that I first learned about the Navy's Underwater Demolition Teams. I was doing experimental underwater work with an underwater sound lab out of New London, Connecticut. There was a group of scientists on board our ship who kept talking about these great guys they worked with in their experiments with underwater equipment. The guys they were talking about were the operators from the UDTs.

This was something that I personally found very exciting. I had been a civilian diver before coming into the Navy, possibly the first one in my town. The thought that I could do the same kind of underwater swimming in the Navy that I had done in the civilian world had a lot of appeal to me.

As a result of my desperate desire to get off of that destroyer, I volunteered for the BUPERS (Bureau of Personnel) request for UDT candidates. Nine chits later, I got off the vessel and was sent to Little Creek, Virginia. There, I became a trainee with Class 29, East Coast, a winter UDTR class.

Looking back on things now, I can see that when both the East and West Coast Teams were running their own replacement training, each was a very difficult program. Each coast had its own disadvantages for the trainee, and neither made things easy for the prospective Frogman.

Training was without question the most difficult mental and physical thing I've gone through in my entire life. There is just a black period in my memory, where every moment was a year and every second a week. But at the end of every day, when we did finally roll into our racks, the thought was there that another one was down. And the next day was another down, and another. And we finally all became Frogs.

Hell Week is one of those things that I just don't remember a lot about. Maybe I have a mental block about remembering something that's tremendously horrible. And Hell Week was all of that. It was really demanding, and probably the closest I came to quitting anything in my life.

But maybe it was the pigheadedness and tenacity in my genealogy that wouldn't let me quit. So I stuck it out and graduated with my class.

I don't think that I have ever experienced a greater thrill in my life than I did when Class 29 graduated. It was, first of all, a tremendous monkey off your back— you're there, you'd finally made it. Looking around, you could see that compared to your first views of the surrounding class, there weren't many folks left.

Without question, to be with those people, and to have suffered what you suffered with them, bound everyone together. Even today, we are all the closet of friends. One of my classmates, John Roat, has written a book called Class 29. And he tried hard to portray the humor, personalities, the difficulty, and all of the things that go along with the UDTR or BUD/S training experience. Everyone in the Teams can relate to the descriptions in that book.

Parts of training still stand out. Cast and recovery, the rolling off a rubber boat on the side of a speeding craft, and later being snatched up with a rubber snare, I think was probably the most dynamic thing that I did during the water phase of UDTR training. By the time we did cast and recovery, and the more technical underwater work, we had moved from Little Creek to Roosevelt Roads, Puerto Rico.

That training was when you really started to feel that you were getting into the advanced stuff. That was real Frogman stuff. But the bottom line was that cast and recovery was really used operationally only during the Second World War, and maybe a little bit during Korea. But you just can't make the boats go quickly enough during high speed combat.

The SEAL Teams were something I really heard about for the first time when I reported aboard UDT 22. During training, there had been rumors about this new Team that had being formed up, but no one really knew what it was. Class 29, which had started up in January 1963, was just getting under way when the SEALs turned one year old.

The scuttlebutt was that it was some top-secret operation and that these guys were doing something very special. No one knew what it was really about, so rumors flew. We had just finished going through the Cuban Missile Crisis less than a year before, just a few months before Class 29 had started training. So there was

During a swimmer recovery, a combat swimmer has just had the rubber snare slipped over his arm by the snare man as the pickup boat moves along. In this particular system, the snare will pull the swimmer around to the back of the rubber boat where he will clamber aboard, like his swim buddy is just beginning to do at the lower left of the picture.

U.S. Navy

still fallout from that situation. All sorts of potential warlike clouds were floating around. And we looked at the whole thing as being pretty exciting stuff. The limited rumors about the SEALs just blended in with everything else.

Once I got aboard UDT 22, I did a couple of platoon deployments. The future CO of SEAL Team Two, Tom Tarbox, had become a friend of mine. He and I had both played football on the amphibious fleet championship team. We kind of hit it off and I asked him about coming over to SEAL Team Two if a billet became available.

My CO at the time was Dave Schaible, who was also my sea daddy and showed me what it was to operate in the Teams. Dave was probably also the sea daddy of 10,000 other SEALs during his career. But in a quiet meeting, I told the skipper that I really would like to go over to this new command. And Dave looked at me in that closed session and said, "I don't blame you, Harry. I'd like to go myself."

Eventually, Dave Schaible did go over to the SEAL Teams, as the skipper of SEAL Team One. But for me, he sent me over to SEAL Team Two when a billet opened. And I became a SEAL.

My arrival at the SEAL Team was the climax of my career in the Navy. When I was at UDT 22, my platoon officer had been a super leader, Irve C. "Chuck" LeMoyne. He was a lieutenant j.g. at that time, and later rose in rank to become one of the first SEAL admirals to serve in the special warfare community. God rest his soul, he passed on a few years back and left a legacy in the Teams that will be a hard one to follow.

Chuck's platoon chief was a man by the name of Dave Casey. The combination of Dave Casey and Chuck LeMoyne made my tour as a new platoon member one of the finest experiences that I can imagine. They were both excellent leaders and true Navy Frogmen. You would die for both of these men, and I was hardly the only one to hold that opinion. They made my break-in period as a new Frog one of the better things that ever happened to me.

After I was broken in to the UDT platoon, I was looking for more. I wanted to advance in my career. And I also wanted to get inland more, because I really did like the inland stuff. The new SEALs were all about inland operations, working from the water and going up on land to conduct operations.

When I came aboard SEAL Team Two, I thought that this was it for me. These men did everything that I ever wanted to do in my military career. Now that I was there, I was going to die at this command. This is where the action was going to happen, and I wasn't going to go anywhere else.

When I first arrived at SEAL Team Two in 1964, I was greeted by the master-at-arms, Chief Rudy Boesch. Rudy was a well-known, top-gun senior NCO in the community. He was probably the most respected bullfrog, and he still is, taking many a new SEAL under his care and making sure they start out right.

As I was one of these very new SEALs, Rudy read the rules to me very clearly and concisely and in a manner that let me know that I was a grown-up now and that I wasn't expected to do anything other than be a grown-up. I would be expected to stand watch every thirty-five days, whether I wanted to or not. Here I was, a guy who had been in the fleet not a long time earlier, and just doing three-section liberty was a lot of fun for me.

But this was when I realized that these men were true professionals. The men were treated as equal to the officers. There really was no difference between commissioned and noncommissioned ranks. The mutual respect between the enlisted and the officers was such that there needed to be no difference. The leader was clearly known, and things moved along from there quite efficiently.

Working in SEAL Team Two the years before Vietnam was extremely different than it was during and after Vietnam. Those years, from 1962 to 1967, were quite a unique period, the formative years of the SEALs. As an E-5 twenty-three-to-twenty-six-year-old in the Team, you were a young kid. Most of the other guys were in their thirties and forties. They had all been career UDT operators, selected as long-term career types because of the intensive training they were going to get. Training was going to be of long duration and cost lots of bucks. And the command wasn't about to waste money on this kind of training on a man who was only going to be in for five or six years.

So the Navy needed to have a career-designated individual, and preferably one with a good deal of prior experience. The Team was still starting up when I arrived, and it needed the collective experience of a lot of veteran individuals to get off and running.

In those days, we were organized into the "assault group" system. Assault groups were similar to platoons. My first assignment was to Assault Group 2. Again, I was extremely fortunate in working under two of the finest leaders that I can think of, though in a different way than back in UDT. These men were a more hardened, combat type. Lieutenant Henry J. "Jake" Rhinebolt was my assault group leader. Jake, who is a dear friend even today, is without question a fine man and great leader.

The guy who I respect and love still today, and would follow to the death, was the assault group chief. That was Bob Gallagher. Without question, Bob Gallagher was the warrior of the SEAL Teams on the East Coast. All of us did our share during an operation, but Bob did his, yours, and everyone else's share of the work on an op. And I am sure that many, many people will remember some of their experiences under Bob's leadership in combat.

Bob set the trail clearly for me as to how a SEAL should operate, and how he should conduct himself, especially in a combat environment. I was fortunate to have that kind of leadership and instruction. It probably helped get me home alive from Vietnam.

Bob Gallagher was called the Eagle by just about everyone in the Team. Maybe because he was just about as tenacious and nasty as an eagle. But he was also a bald-headed son of a gun. In recent years when I've seen him, he's just getting balder. Sorry about that, Bob.

The assault group was organized pretty much like a platoon is today. We thought in terms of boat crews, so that there's at least a coxswain and four or five strokers or paddlers in a rubber boat. So we were organized into twelve-man units in those days. Definitely, there would be one officer in a group, not always two. We often deployed with one officer and one chief, or one officer and one first class petty officer, in a group. That was due in part to the very small number of men in the SEAL Team at that time. There were only around fifty enlisted men in all of SEAL Team Two then. So a lot of assault groups just weren't fully staffed.

As an assault group, you were split up into two IBS crews, manning two IBSs on an insertion. Each boat crew was capable of operating as a fully independent unit. It was as part of an assault group that I went on a mission to France, where we crossed-trained with the French combat swimmers and were tested on our intelligence-gathering capabilities.

After we returned from that mission, I had an opportunity on the outside, out of the Navy, that was very important. So I took that offer up and left the Teams, without knowing that our assault group would soon be deploying to Southeast Asia as a platoon. That information hadn't gone out to much of anyone yet.

So I got out, and after I left, the word came out that SEAL Team Two was going to be deploying to Southeast Asia. That bothered me a lot; I couldn't sleep at night. And there was no way I was going to let this happen and not get a piece of the action. Combat would be the ultimate test at my training and abilities. And seeing action with my Teammates held more appeal than can easily be explained to an outsider.

So I got on the phone and started calling everybody I knew. I was trying to get all of my old buddies to pull strings or whatever it took to get me back into SEAL Team Two so that I could deploy as if I had never left the Team in the first place.

So along came Dick Marcinko, who had gotten out of Officer Candidate School as a brand-new ensign just a year or so before. Dick had recently returned from deploying with the first SEAL Team Two platoon that had deployed for combat in Vietnam.

Because of his performance on that deployment, now lieutenant (j.g.) Dick Marcinko was assigned a platoon. He was now the platoon leader of Eight Platoon. Dick went out of his way to do the Marcinko thing and pull strings left and right with

SEALs slip in during an insertion from a Zodiac rubber boat fitted with an outboard motor. Wearing a ghilly suit as camouflage, the SEAL at the bow of the craft maintains watch while armed with his M60 machine gun. The SEAL radioman, just stepping of the side of the boat in the center of the picture, is armed with an M16A1/M203 combination rifle and 40mm grenade launcher.

U.S. Navy

the Navy detailers in Washington. He made everybody believe that I was the most brilliant thing that ever walked the face of the earth, and that the Navy absolutely couldn't continue without me. Of course we all know that that's a lie, but it worked.

And I came back into the Navy and the Teams. What the point is, is that Dick had the willingness to bend a little bit, and push, and shove, and coerce, if you will, to do what he thought was best for his men and his Team. The next thing I knew, I was climbing off of a helicopter and charging through a rice paddy somewhere in the Mekong Delta. This was only a matter of weeks after I was having my martini lunch with my executive cohorts in the local pub back in the civilian world.

We were starting to take rounds from the tree line. The cracks of the supersonic bullets were snapping by overhead. And as all of this took place, I had the feeling that it was about time for lunch.

But that was how Marcinko operated, how he got things done, and it was also how I got back into the Teams. Now I was on my first deployment to Vietnam, arriving with the Eight Platoon in December 1967. The officer-in-charge was Lieutenant (j.g.) Dick Marcinko, his assistant was Lieutenant (j.g) Gordy Boyce, and the platoon chief was Chief Boatswain's Mate Louis A. "Hoss" Kucinski. That was quite a team.

The surprising thing to me was that we had a large proportion of kids, young men really, in the platoon, something we had never had before. And that was simply a result of the necessity of SEAL Team Two having to beef up the platoons. We did not have as many of the older, more experienced guys around to staff up and keep a three-platoon rotational system going.

There were three SEAL Team Two platoons doing combat tours in Vietnam at any one time from about the middle of 1967 on. When a platoon deployed, it replaced a platoon that was already operating in-country. That platoon in turn rotated back to Little Creek. Three platoons were in the training cycle to deploy to Vietnam while three platoons were already there. And several platoons were in the process of remanning and reorganizing as well as taking care of other SEAL Team Two commitments in the world at the same time. That took a lot more than the fifty enlisted men who were in the Team with me earlier.

So SEAL Team Two was immediately taking people right out of training to build up the numbers. I didn't like this at first. I didn't think these kids needed to be there yet; they didn't have enough experience. But after I did one combat tour, I realized that those were the guys I wanted with me, not the older guys. And that is what the SEALs became, more of a younger group, and less of a Navy fleet–experienced group. And for our mission in Vietnam, that's exactly what should have happened.

Because of our technique of operating, the ferocity of how we did our job, and the tactics we used, we were very much like the VC themselves, only better. We were much more aggressive. Since we had learned just how the VC were successful, and saw that it worked, we copied it. That action resulted in extremely high kill ratios of VC to SEALs lost during the war—in our favor. SEAL Team Two had zero losses, until Eight Platoon went into Chau Doc during the Tet offensive of 1968.

Eight Platoon had been up on the Cambodian border in January 1968. Our orders had come from a communiqué from General Westmoreland regarding a possible large enemy crossing of the Cambodian border during a given time period. Certain units in the area were to go up and observe whether the crossing was indeed happening.

So Dick had Eighth Platoon up in Chau Doc, which was a border city, on the Cambodian border on the west side of Chau Phu province. Eighth was operating along with about eight PRU individuals, mercenaries really, mostly Cambodians and some Chinese. With these men, we patrolled the border, looking for activity and any signs of crossings.

What we didn't realize was that the activity had already occurred. Our patrol was picked up by an advancing company of NVA—North Vietnamese Army regulars—or Viet Cong. We weren't sure of who we'd run into, but it was a group of company strength.

Prior to our patrol going out, we had set up fire support from two 105-howitzer fans. These were angled cones of fire that the howitzers could put out to cover

As two PBRs pour in fire toward the shoreline, a Seawolf helicopter gunship close by overhead launches a 2.75-inch rocket from its rocket pod. The PBRs are part of River Section 523 while the gunship is part of HAL-3, Det 3.

U.S. Navy

known zones in our patrol area. So when we made contact with that heavy concentration of enemy forces, we called in artillery fire support. The tubes [guns] came back to us that we could not be supported because all tubes were turned to defending the city of Chau Doc. So we had no artillery support.

Eight Platoon performed a strategic withdrawal. Calling for extraction, we got the hell out of there. Luckily, we didn't lose anyone in that encounter. For a time, it was extremely intense. When the entire tree line opened up with enemy fire, it was nothing but Kalashnikov-colored tracers coming at us. These were green traces, not the red tracers used by the U.S. and its allies.

The PBRs we had called up came in to extract us and we returned to Chau Doc. On the way back, the local PRU adviser, who had been with us on the op along with several of his men, got on the radio to report what had happened and get an update on the local situation.

The PRU adviser in Chau Doc was an army sergeant named Drew Dix. He was the only Army PRU adviser in the whole of the IV Corps area, the rest mostly being SEALs. Drew had called his safe house to see about the situation. The PRUs were run by "the Company," and the local Company guys maintained their own safehouse facilities in Chau Doc. What Drew was trying to get was a sitrep—a situation report—on just what was going on.

The reports that came back over the PRC-25 radio, on the Company's own secure circuit, were not good. All of the American strongholds in the area had been overrun. The local Army Special Forces C Team, their battalion headquarters detachment, was in a barricade situation trying to hold off the enemy forces. Basically, the Viet Cong had overrun the entire city of Chau Doc.

One of the concerns was that all of the U.S. AIDs (Agency for International Development) nurses were being held captive by Viet Cong. Drew was clearly distressed about this, in part because one of the nurses was an old friend of his. So we just kind of looked at one another as we all agreed that we had to go in and get them.

Going over to Dick, I said that we had to put a group together to try and get these civilians out. Dick wanted to do the very same thing, but he was restricted to doing his job, directing all of the platoons operations from the TOC (Tactical Operations Center) and maintaining the flow of information to keep all of us alive. He wanted to do the very same thing, but instead he gave me permission to split off from the platoon and go in with Dix to support him.

Our PBRs pulled in to the beach and we all piled off, while taking only sporadic sniper fire. We quickly patrolled up to the TOC, where the poor officer who had the duty that day was located. That was a sight I'm never going to forget. As we entered the TOC, I could see that officer lying on a couch, staring up at the ceiling, with the focus of his eyes some 2,000 feet beyond it. He was a very cool and collected, experienced old Army soldier.

In the background, I could hear the voices coming in over the radio, voices from soldiers at the Army Special Forces bases scattered throughout the area. And those voices were screaming about thousands—5,000 from one voice, 6,000 from another—of enemy troops crossing the Cambodian border. Those SF troopers were out there counting the heads of the enemy as major units were passing their locations. And they couldn't get artillery support to attack the incoming VC.

So this Army officer was just as cool as he could be. Because he knew that in about four hours, all those thousands of enemy troops were going to be here, in Chau Doc, and we were all going to be dead. There were all of like twenty of us there in the city to run the defense. And I was impressed with his aplomb in what appeared to be a hopeless situation.

Drew went out to the back area behind the TOC, where he had parked his jeep before we had all gone out on the op just the night before. It so happened that Drew's jeep had a .50-caliber machine gun mounted on a pedestal standing up from the center of the floorboard. I had already committed myself to accompanying him when he came up to me and waved to me that we were going.

So I jumped up into the back of the jeep and checked out that big gun, firing off a few practice rounds to make sure it was operating correctly, that the headspace was set right and the timing was on. The Browning .50-caliber machine gun is a massive weapon. It puts out a half-inch thick projectile the size of a little finger at around 2,700 feet per second. The rounds can chop down a concrete wall as they fly out of the car-axle-size barrel. The blast of a big .50 has authority; it is loud and distinctive. And I was very glad we had that gun with us.

As we were leaving, I could see the look on Dick's face as he came out of the TOC to watch us go. This was the first time I had ever seen that serious an expression on him. And as he saw I was looking, he said, "Watch yourself, asshole."

Then he smiled with that big grin of his. "Who knows, maybe you'll get laid," he finished.

There's nothing much that can be said to that. But it wasn't the last thing that happened. As Drew and I were leaving, into the jeep popped another SEAL. It was Frank Thornton, who jumped in carrying his M16. And we hadn't gone more than a few feet when another volunteer jumped aboard. This time it was Wally Schwalenberger, Eighth Platoon's dog handler. Only Wally didn't have his dog with him; he had a Stoner instead.

I was absolutely tickled pink with having these two volunteers, these Teammates, aboard. There wasn't much question that two guys in the jeep by themselves just weren't going to make it. But what they did was what the Teams are all about. Volunteering to do the things that you wouldn't expect, and during the most traumatic periods you can imagine. The best in men comes out in these situations.

But these guys just jumped in. Nobody told them to, but there was no way they

Frank Thornton (right) and Drew Dix (back to camera) discuss the situation at Chau Doc during Tet 1968. To the left is Drew's jeep with its pedestal-mounted .50-caliber machine gun.

Frank Thornton Collection

were going to let me go by myself. And out we went from the TOC compound, into the raging firefight that was Chau Doc city.

How we made it through those streets I don't know. God was with us. It was just one firefight after another. As we were cruising on down the highway, I was looking around and trying to see the sources of the fire that was coming at us. All I could see was the little smoke and muzzle flash of the guns from those pockets of VC troops all throughout the city.

As I spotted the enemy, I would return fire with the big .50. While I was putting out fire, I noticed the jeep was doing this fantastic job of countersniper maneuvering. The jeep was going through these sinuous curves and bouncing off the gutters and so on.

While I was firing here and there, watching my tracers going through windows and blowing walls out, I was thinking, This guy can really drive this thing! He was really impressive, I thought as I tripped off another series of shuddering kabooms from my .50. The knocking thunder of that huge Browning completely blanketed the firing sound of the 5.56mm weapons of my Teammates.

All of a sudden I noticed that we were coming up to a bridge and that the jeep was heading straight at one of the parapets. Oh my God, I thought, Drew's been hit!

Looking down at the driver's seat, I could see Drew with both his hands up to his head. He wasn't hit; he had clapped his hands over his ears. He hadn't touched the steering wheel since I had started firing that .50, the muzzle of which was only about three feet over his head. It turned out that the muzzle blast from that gun blew his eardrums out. To this day, he can't hear worth a shit.

Seeing how much fun Drew was having, I stopped firing the .50 over his head; the VC had pretty much stopped showing themselves anyway. And we continued on our drive, pulling up to the Company safe house a short time later. The safe house had a number of Company types there—spooks, really—as well as some PRU bodyguards. They had held out in their compound well enough and were able to give us some intel on the local situation. The nurses weren't at the safe house, so we decided to continue on to their quarters in another part of the city.

We regrouped and picked up two other civilian types, spooks, as well as another jeep. Drew kept on as the peerless driver of the first jeep, and Frank and Wally jumped over to the other jeep with the two CIA guys. I maintained my position as the .50 gunner. From the safe house, we headed off into the inner city.

The inner part of Chau Doc was saturated with pockets of VC. Every time we turned a corner, there would be five or six of the enemy in front of us. When they got over their surprise at seeing us, the VC would open up on us, and we would of course return fire. Sometimes, we fired first. But before the firefights could turn into much, we would be around a corner and going down another street. And there we would come across another pocket of VC.

But Chau Doc was giving us the cover of a congested city. We had the narrow streets and short blocks of Chau Doc to thank for being able to duck around and past the firefights the way we were doing. Of course, the surprise of the VC at suddenly seeing our two jeeps appear, fire spitting out from a half-dozen weapons in our rapid passage, gave us an edge.

Eventually, we got to the nurses' house. There, our big advantage had disappeared because now we were stopped. Around this house were several pockets of VC, all of them in upper building areas looking down on the nurses' house. The house was an old French colonial building, with a small courtyard in front of the house proper. Stopping the jeeps, the bunch of us dove into the courtyard and scrambled up to the front door of the house. Then we ran into another problem.

The front door of the house itself was open, but across the opening was an accordion type of steel gate, as you see in the front of some jewelry stores. And of course the gate was securely locked.

Hitting the deck in the courtyard, we were immediately taken under fire by the VC all around us. We were pinned down. But we had fairly decent cover in the courtyard with the concrete walls that surrounded it.

Drew yelled into the house, "Maggie, are you there?"

In kind of a whispering tone, Maggie called back, "I'm here. I'm under the bed, and they're inside!"

The fear in her voice was obvious to us all; she was panicked but called out to us in kind of a distressed whisper. Since the door was open, but with the gate across it, we had visual access to the building; we just couldn't get inside of it.

So as soon as the VC heard the voices of Maggie and Drew, they reacted. We could see three or four VC come running down the stairs and out of the kitchen. As soon as that happened, we yelled to Maggie, "Get down and stay down!"

Then we opened fire and just swept the area. We continued sweeping the area until we figured all of the VC were down or gone. We killed five or six, maybe as many as eight, inside of the house. They just piled up like cordwood right in front of us. Then things were quiet in the house.

But things were anything but quiet around us. Now the VC in the buildings nearby were really ticked off and the shooting down into the courtyard increased. Maybe they thought we had been shooting at them. But it didn't matter—we were still in front of that closed gate and unable to get to Maggie.

The whole point now was for us to get into that house and pull out Maggie and whoever else was in there with her. Calling through the locked gate, we told Maggie to come on out to where we were.

When Maggie came running out, Drew immediately asked her where the key to the gate was. So Maggie started searching for the key in this big pile of furniture that must have been five or six feet high. But she knew exactly where to go, into this one little cubical thing that was at the bottom of the pile. Pulling open a drawer, she removed this tiny little key and came up to the gate. Now, with the gate unlocked, I reached up and grabbed her, pulling Maggie out of the line of fire that was spraying all around us.

Of course all of this last action was moot. The comedy of the situation was that we could have blown the lock off that door in about two-tenths of a second. But no, we had to have Maggie get the key and let us in. We were too polite to break into the nurses' house.

But that was how we got Maggie out from under the noses of the VC. Luckily, the other nurses who were living there had gone out on an inland visit, an aid visit, the night before. In reality, I think some Vietnamese friends took those nurses out of the town without telling them what was going to happen. But the other nurses didn't suffer from any of the actions that were taking place in Chau Doc.

Since we had Maggie, that was all we really cared about. After getting her to a safe, secured area, we went back into the city that afternoon. Our mission was ostensibly to try and locate the command center for the Viet Cong forces who had over-run the city. The province chief, who was in fact the military governor of the province, came up to us and asked if we would go back in and try to get his family out.

Frankly, we didn't give a big care about going into town. The province chief's request was just another reason to get into town. We had already broken the enemy "code." We now knew that we could surprise the VC and accomplish a lot without an unreasonable risk to ourselves. We had seen that the VC were not an organized, well-centered, controlled military entity. The VC were instead in sporadic groups that were not in contact with one another. And that meant they could not get fire support from one another except by chance.

Getting into town, we patrolled down the street. There was no enemy activity, but we stayed as sharp as possible. Looking high and low, watching the shadows and corners, doing all the things we would be doing in the jungle, only without the trees; there were houses and buildings instead.

During the patrol, I noticed a wonderful thing. As we were moving into the heart of Chau Doc, all six of us, I noticed that on either side of us, the ARVN troops were now beginning to advance with us. Our SEAL squad had become their leading stick. That was all that they needed, some direction to get moving, and they moved on in with us. I thought that was tremendous. It showed that the ARVNs wanted to take their city back, but they just needed to know how to do it.

Much like the Viet Cong troops, the ARVNs were in little pockets of individuals who had been hiding here and there in the city. They weren't organized, but were beginning to be so as they gathered together around our squad.

Going deeper into the city, we located an area that was supposed to be the VC command area, which was on the way to the province chief's house. The VC command site happened to be in a movie house. In the backyard of this movie theater was a large walled courtyard. And that was the location of the command center. From the outside, you could see all these radio antennas sticking up into the air.

From our limited elevation, you couldn't shoot or otherwise get through the walls around the courtyard. So we needed to climb. Frank Thornton, Ted Rischer, and I, we all went up on a building nearby. Ted Risher was right behind Frank as we went into a duplex structure about twelve stories high near the movie theater.

We climbed up the shorter building of the duplex, making the entire structure a shield between ourselves and the VC command area. After we reached the roof, we crossed it to the larger building. Now Frank jumped over onto a balcony on the taller of the duplex structures. We had to get to the top of that in order to have a good firing position and be able to shoot down into the command courtyard.

The second guy over was Ted, and then it was my turn. But by the time it was my turn to jump over to the balcony, we had been discovered. The local VC had spotted Ted jumping across, so when I tried it, there was no more surprise. As I jumped across, there were a few cracks of gunfire to either side of me. Then I flew off the roof and landed on the balcony.

As soon as I landed, I went flat. There was a low wall around the balcony, of maybe crotch height, that I could hide behind. That wall just started to disintegrate in front of me from all of the incoming fire.

Dropping down, I was now on top of my two Teammates who had gotten there ahead of me. Now we were on a balcony with a locked door in front of us. But this wasn't going to be as much of a problem as it had been at Maggie's. We knew the procedure now, and we just shot the lock off the door.

Going through the door, we made our way to the rooftop of the taller building. From the roof, we could see down into the courtyard of the theater, and the VC command element who had set up there. The M16s we had with us weren't going to supply the firepower we needed to take out that courtyard. We needed something heavier. Drew, being the PRU adviser, had access to an M18 57mm recoilless rifle, which was not too far away.

We contacted Drew, and he brought the 57 recoilless up to where we were. Having brought a line along with us, we threw it down to Drew and the rest of our squad. With that line, we first pulled up the 57 and then the containers of canister shot rounds. The canister shot round for the 57 mm recoilless rifle fires 133 cylindrical steel slugs to a lethal range of about 175 feet. Effectively, they make the weapon a five-foot-long shotgun. That was a devastating weapon to use against the VC down in that courtyard, which was exactly our plan.

In the process of getting the ammunition up on the roof and setting up to fire, we had some delays. I remember Ted yelling, "Goddammit, hurry up. We're trying to do something up here!"

Well, as soon as he said that, the VC located our position from the rooftop across the street. They started firing at us and down we went. Ted was still standing up and I shouted over to him, "Ted, get down."

As soon as I yelled his name, he dropped as if someone had hit him with a sledgehammer. He had taken a head shot, apparently from a carbine fired from across the street. It wasn't even an aimed shot probably, just one of those things we called a magic BB.

And that was how Ted Risher died, the first SEAL Team Two combat loss of the Vietnam War. He went out like a hero, and I think of him every day.

We had lost another guy earlier. But he hadn't been from SEAL Team Two. He was a West Coast SEAL from Team One who was killed going out on an operation with us.

In that Tet period, action was going on all over the place; there was lots of activity. We were lucky that our own losses were so few. The month before, on 21 January, Gene Fraley of SEAL Team Two's Seventh Platoon had lost his life while making a boobytrap that detonated prematurely. Just a week earlier, on 18 January, Arthur "Lump-Lump" Williams had been shot while operating with Sixth Platoon. His wound was eventually fatal, but he didn't die until some months later. So 1968 started out kind of hard for SEAL Team Two, and we would lose three more Teammates before the year was out.

But that was the cost of war, and we were good enough that we could keep that cost down. Operations continued. The SEALs were audacious and innovative in the way we operated against the enemy. And we ran into our share of problems, not always from the other side either.

Prior to today's Joint Special Operations Command (JSOC) and USSOCOM (United States Special Operations Command), and the joint services training and operational cross-training, there were interservice problems. It was just that we did things differently in each of the services. What was SOP for one community was taboo for another.

Because of that situation, working with nonnaval SOF units in Vietnam could be very difficult. Regarding the complications that I had working with other services, the first situation that comes to mind was when I was a PRU adviser. Since I was the only American out there in the bush with a bunch of mercenary types, it was up to me to coordinate our support.

For this one PRU operation, I had set up a 105mm howitzer fan along with a number of concentration points. The points were predetermined locations, their coordinates already known to and plotted by the artillery unit. We could reference those points in such a manner—such as "Bravo One" or whatever—that the enemy couldn't tell where we were shooting if he was tapping into our communications net.

On this one operation, I was out in the field with only about eight or twelve of my PRUs with me. We were all out in a hide and could see a large concentration of the enemy coming up in the distance. The enemy saw our location and started charging us. They knew they had a superiority in numbers and were just going to overrun us. So I started calling in artillery fire from that battery of 105s we had on call.

As they were coming in, I was calling in fire over the radio and walking the rounds in to the target. The guys manning the guns were exceptional. Rarely do you get a good artillery battery that follows the forward observer's directions so quickly and accurately. And this was an ARVN battery, with a U.S. Army adviser group in charge. And I was talking to the Army people of course.

The fire was completely covering the area the enemy were in. The rounds were walked in on target and just obliterated the oncoming troops. My PRUs and I were going to make it out of this one, and I had watched the entire scene play out in front of my eyes. That doesn't happen very often, and the power of that artillery at my beck and call raised my excitement level quite a bit. When the enemy forces were gone, in my excitement, I yelled into the radio, "That's enough! That's enough!"

But the incoming fire didn't let up. Those thirty-four-pound projectiles just kept landing on target, their five-pound of high-explosive filler shattering the casings into flying shards of steel. The only thing was, there wasn't anything left of the target. And it just kept coming in, and coming in, and coming in.

"That's enough, goddammit, that's enough," I shouted into the radio.

"Do I understand cease-fire, cease-fire?" the voice at the other end of the radio link said calmly.

"That's what I'm saying," I still said rather loudly. "That's enough, goddammit!"

The adrenaline had just kind of taken over completely; I was just so excited and out of sorts really that I hadn't been able to think clearly. But the operation was a success, with no losses on our side.

When I got back to the compound, the situation was a little less happy than it had been in the field. The local battery commander came running up to me all kinds of ticked off. He had stood a chance of putting effective rounds downrange on my fire mission. And he hadn't been able to fire to his satisfaction based on my inability to communicate effectively. So he chewed on me for a while about my inability to correctly call in artillery fire support.

The fact was that I was an excellent forward observer (FO). It was just that I'd had a very anxious moment there. But this guy was really getting into my face. "Well, when I said, 'That's enough,' you'd killed them all," I told the red-faced artillery officer. "So I figured that was enough."

Then he chuckled, slapped me on the back, and just walked away.

That little conversation took place while I was working as a PRU adviser with the Phoenix Program. The Phoenix Program was an extensive South Vietnamese nationwide program run in South Vietnam by a major intelligence organization.

The SEALs were chosen to be the advisers of choice for the PRUs in the area where the SEALs operated. That was IV Corps, the Mekong Delta area south of Saigon. The action arm of the program consisted of a province combat team that was known at its inception as a counterterrorist unit. And the philosophy during the early days was that they would counter the terror of the VC with terror of their own.

The personnel who belonged to these units were strictly mercenaries, former ARVNs, probably criminals, and former military types from other Southeast Asian nations including China, Cambodia, and so on. So there was a complete potpourri of nationalities in the unit.

And these units were a very effective way of stopping the infrastructure from doing their terrorist thing during the early stages of the Viet Cong movement. But these units developed a very bad name for themselves as a result of their tactics. As Nietzsche says, "Beware of the dragon slayer, lest you become the dragon." That may have been the case with the early PRUs.

So the program was revamped, and became the provincial reconnaissance units, or PRUs. They became more of a paramilitary, well-trained organization. The men of the PRUs went to a boot camp that was run by Army Special Forces A-Team types. It was only after they went through this training that they were assigned to their PRU.

Each PRU was assigned to a specific province, the South Vietnamese version of our states. Each PRU had the responsibility under the Phoenix Program of collecting intelligence and responding to intelligence. They would enforce what needed to be enforced in the area and forcibly obtain members, or infrastructure types, from the hidden government that was existing or being built in each province by the Viet

Cong movement. In essence, we were the secret police that were dedicated to elim-inating the political infrastructure, command element, of the Viet Cong. Very rarely did we go after military leaders. The political leaders of the VC were our primary targets.

The PRUs were run, led really, by individual SEALs in the IV Corps area. In the II and III Corps areas, the Army SF types had them; up in I Corps, the Marines had the PRU adviser assignments. So every service had a piece of the Phoenix Program based on the intensity of their particular service's involvement in that corps' the-ater.

For myself, I had the good fortune to be a PRU adviser for two different provinces, Chau Doc and Phong Dinh. At that time I was an E-5 in military rank. But in the Phoenix Program, no one knew just what I was. That was because we were working in a detached capacity from the military. Instead, we worked directly for the O officer and P officer of the province. These men are the contract guys who are working directly for the company. So in effect, we became company operators, un-der the O and P officers. Although we still got paid by the Navy, we took our march-ing orders from the O and the P.

As the adviser of a PRU, you became the company commander of the unit. As an E-5 SEAL, I was running 135 well-trained killers, if you will, all of them excellent Asian military types. They were so good that they managed to get my keister out of the fire when I got hit very badly. They didn't have to do that—they could have left me behind. But they risked their lives to get me out. Those were good troops. And to this day I respect and love them.

The PRU mission was to neutralize the Viet Cong infrastructure, particularly the political infrastructure. The objective was not necessarily to kill, it was to obtain and capture critical members of the infrastructure. To in fact neutralize, and dis-suade the building of this hidden government.

The PRUs were extremely efficient in their operations. In IV Corps, very few hard-core Viet Cong units were even operational because of the efficiency of the PRUs and the Phoenix Program.

In spite of stories and exaggerations that have been spread and have grown up regarding the Phoenix Program, it was not a systematic program of assassination at that time. The first phase of what became the PRU program, the counterterrorist-team phase, had used assassination as a tool. But it was deemed to be an unsuc-cessful attempt at accomplishing something that the American public was just not going to accept. At least that's my understanding of it.

The acronym SEAL stands for Sea, Air, And Land. It identifies the three methods we have of operating—by sea, land, or air. The individual who is a SEAL is someone who has been put through probably the most intensive selection process that any military type goes through in the world on a regular basis.

Almost hidden in the deep grass, these SEALs lay down for cover while one calls out on the radio carried on the other SEAL's back.

U.S. Navy

The concept of selection is to drive the individual down to a common denominator of what his inner animal is, devoid of the personality facades and defenses that he has built up in society. He has none of that left and he deals with one thing, his will to survive and continue. If his will is strong enough, and passes that test, then he does continue and becomes a candidate for the balance of the selection process. Once he has completed this process, he becomes trained. That period can extend for several years of constant learning, until he is truly accepted by his Teammates.

After the conclusion of Vietnam, the Navy took a close look at the success of the SEAL program. The military leadership viewed the concept of special warfare much differently than they had before. They eventually saw the value in a small unit that was able to accomplish great things. The situations the smaller units would go into were high risk. But if you lose a small unit, you haven't lost a battleship.

Accomplishing great missions with little risk was considered a good way to go. After an immediate post-Vietnam cutback, the SEALs gradually became larger. This took a number of years but was inevitable, as there was now a recognized use for them.

The missions that followed this buildup included Grenada; where the SEALs were very effective in getting into Governor Scoon's mansion and bringing him out alive. A very dear friend of mine, Duke Leonard, led that mission in. They held the facility for a number of hours longer than they were supposed to. But they did a super job, and one they can easily be proud of.

After Grenada, one of the most publicly known SEALs actions was Panama. That was more of a search, an urban warfare mission, for the special operators, the "six" guys, in the pursuit of Manuel Noriega. Along with about 10,000 other posse members, they chased him all over the city. But they chased him quite effectively and eventually cornered him in the Vatican embassy, I believe. Noriega was finally extracted and arrested and Panama returned to democratic rule.

Desert Storm, the next major conflict, was primarily a conventional war of fire and maneuver. The field commander, General H. Norman Schwarzkopf, was very conventional in his thinking in the use and application of the forces at his command. But he had been a tanker, a tank commander, and Desert Storm was a tank war.

So Schwarzkopf did not use a lot of the SOF (Special Operations Forces) individuals, both Army and Navy. SEALs did conduct a large number of reconnaissance missions along the beaches of Kuwait and Iraq. And the SEALs did excellent diversionary work just prior to the commencement of the ground war. They did exactly what had been done during the Second World War, they swam in to beaches, set off explosives, and created the image that a beach was being opened for major amphibious landings. That trick caused the diversion of at least one division, maybe two divisions, of Iraqis to the beaches to defend against a potential landing that was never going to occur.

There have been many "brushfire" wars around the world that detachments from the SEAL Teams have reacted to. Fairly recently, it has been considered very fashionable to put a 300-man unit on the beach and get somebody politically corrected. The SEALs, like the other SOF units, are the men who respond to those kinds of missions.

We're headed for a continuing, and greater, use of SOF forces than ever before. The development of JSOC and USSOCOM has created the concept of using the services jointly, or joint service. This is where the best that all of the services have to offer has been brought together in order to conduct precision warfare on the small-unit level.

It would be realistic to say that SOF forces will be used forever in terms of warfare. It just makes sense. The use of electronics is being maximized in the aerial delivery of force. But what a ground force can, and must, do on the target area cannot be replaced. After an air strike had been completed, either large ground forces are sent in, and the lives of many possibly sacrificed. Or a much smaller surgical unit is sent in that is very adept at moving around in a clandestine manner, and they accomplish the same thing as the larger force. Small-unit penetrations can take and hold, or get in and corroborate, the results of other actions.

While on patrol in Vietnam, two SEALs from SEAL Team Two's Sixth Platoon take a short break. Standing, drinking from his canteen, is the Platoon Chief, J. C. Tipton. Keeping watch, armed with an M16A1/XM148 combination rifle/40 mm grenade launcher, is Tipton's Teammate Art Hammond.

U.S. Navy

Dick Marcinko is an extremely controversial fellow SEAL in the community. There are those who love him, and those who hate him. I'm one of those who love him, and for good reason. He has been a brother warrior to me. As a field commander who I operated under, he was excellent. As a fellow E-5 petty officer, he was an excellent shipmate on the beach. And as a fellow older guy, he still is an excellent shipmate on the beach.

In any case, Dick Marcinko is an extremely bright individual. He has a way about him that is disturbing to the status quo. People who want a much more regimented approach to military problem solving have a lot of trouble with his style. However, his technique does work, though I wouldn't recommend it to the entire leadership core.

It is the mental aspect of a SEAL, his personality and drive, that is more important than people realize. The physical aspect of a Navy SEAL is not as great an asset as his mental one. If the mental strength is not there, then the physical is not driven. A case in point is a lot of the students who show up for training.

At BUD/S training, a number of bodybuilders show up, expecting their strength to get them through. Bodybuilders who are very much into themselves but don't give two hoots about anybody else are not Team members. And they probably won't complete training because they just can't put themselves through that much physical, and mental, stress and discomfort. There are some bodybuilders who turn out to be Team members, and they exercise to perfect their physical machine.

But it isn't the physical aspects of a person that gets them into the Teams. It's the drive, that mental aspect, the desire. Guys who have never lifted weights in their lives, never swam, never run before, who have the tenacity to get through. They just won't quit, and it doesn't matter if there's only 150 pounds of individual there. Many men like that have made it through training. Far more than the bulky, strongman types. It's what the mind is all about, not the body.

In terms of intelligence, there's a need for the above average in the Teams today. The concept of the SEALs mission, and the equipment that they are tasked to work with, demand someone who can understand their complexities. The men in the Teams today are given extremely advanced technology to use in support of their own mission or that of other forces.

Today's SEAL is a calculating individual who can take command. If the rest of his unit is knocked out, he can still, if necessary, accomplish the mission by himself. It is that kind of tenacity, the "cannot quit" mentality, that was the heart of a SEAL yesterday and remains the heart today.

One of the results of the selection process, the basic training, of a SEAL is just getting through the program. When you have gone through that, you feel a tremendous amount of self-pride, a strong sense of accomplishment. You have accomplished some extremely difficult stuff. And you have been shown that you could do things you never even dreamed you could do.

As a result of all of that training, you develop a positive attitude. Nothing really seems impossible; the attitude is one of "can do" toward everything. And the Teams are just that, men who work together, are one unit. And they all have that positive attitude. The Teams win.

To accomplish a mission, you conduct your observation first; that's part of the training. What has been observed is processed and understood. With understanding comes the solution to complete the mission successfully.

Our success in our battle against the Viet Cong came about because we looked at how they operated. Our combat experience was very limited prior to Vietnam and there was a lot for us to learn. But we did learn it. We saw how our enemy operated, and we saw how good they were. And we adopted their ways and did what they did. And building on our successes, we developed new techniques, and we became better still.

The Aftermath of Tet

The Tet offensive lasted for weeks. But in spite of the initial successes, the campaign was a stunning defeat for the Communist forces, especially those of the Viet Cong. The U.S. and allied losses included 1,536 killed, 7,764 wounded, and 11 missing. ARVN losses included 2,788 killed, 8,299 wounded, and 587 missing.

Estimated losses among the NVA and VC forces include 45,000 killed, 6,991 prisoners captured, 1,300 crew-served weapons captured or destroyed, and over 7,000 individual weapons captured or destroyed.

The failure of the ARVN forces to defend their country never took place. In spite of early withdrawals, the men of the ARVN forces fought back against the invaders form the north and their own guerrillas from the south. The VC/NVA forces had not been able to bring down the South Vietnamese government. Nor had they been able to hold on to any of the cities, towns, and villages they had captured.

Within a week of the beginning of the Tet offensive, the tide of battle had turned against the VC/NVA. But the north did win the political battle. The American viewing public saw the U.S. embassy in Saigon attacked and breached by VC sappers. A guerrilla force had attacked in a major military engagement, under conditions of almost complete secrecy, something they had not been considered capable of doing.

The Viet Cong never fully recovered from their losses during the Tet offensive of 1968. Whole VC units were almost wiped out to a man. The political and command structure of the Communist forces in the south now changed, with the NVA leadership taking a much greater role. This condition remained until the end of the war.

■ Chapter 44

Hoi Chanhs, PRUs, the SEALs, and the Phoenix Program

Both North and South Vietnam were divided into provinces, administrative units that act as states do here in the United States. Provinces were not large, more the size of an average U.S. county than a state, but they had their own local government and leadership that reported on to the national government in Saigon.

For military purposes, the forty-four provinces of South Vietnam were divided into four military regions or corps. Farthest north was I Corps (pronounced "eye-corpse"). The center of South Vietnam held II Corps, covering the largest land area. III Corps included the Rung Sat Special Zone as part of its area as well as Saigon. And to the south, the Mekong Delta made up IV Corps ("four-corpse").

The Hoi Chanh or "Open Arms" Program operated throughout South Vietnam. Unique to Vietnam, it was initiated by the South Vietnamese at the request of the U.S. government in 1963. As part of the Hoi Chanh Program, Viet Cong or NVA troops in the south could surrender, using leaflets scattered by government forces as safe passes. Paid a bounty for any weapons or major information they might bring over with them, the Hoi Chanhs, as they were known, were given amnesty by the South Vietnamese government. VC and NVA who "Chieu Hoied"—rallied to the Hoi Chanh Program—were also expected to deliver information to the SVN and U.S. authorities. In exchange, local VC would be returned to their homes and families. The program was amazingly successful during the ten years of its existence from 1963 to 1973, and almost 160,000 VC and NVA took advantage of it, according to U.S. records.

The Hoi Chanhs supplied a wealth of intelligence to the South Vietnamese and U.S. forces. Locations of arms and munitions caches, enemy troop movements, and leadership meetings all came out of the Hoi Chanhs. Many of the VC who came over through the program were high-ranking members of the Viet Cong Infrastructure, the VCI. They were the political and military leadership of the Viet Cong in the provinces of the south.

To attack the VCI, the U.S. intelligence community established the provincial reconnaissance units, or PRUs. The action arm of the Phoenix Program, the PRUs were paramilitary organizations made up of local militias, indigenous people, and foreign mercenaries from Cambodia, Laos, and other areas. The PRUs were armed, supplied, trained, and paid by the U.S. intelligence service and military personnel assigned to them. The PRUs came in various sizes, up to an infantry company in number, and were assigned one to a province. The province chief gave the PRUs their directions and they were led by a U.S. military adviser.

In the sixteen provinces of IV Corps, the PRU advisers came from one source almost exclusively. This was Det Bravo, the Navy SEALs. The successes of the PRUs under SEAL leadership were remarkable. Excesses that were known to occur in the Phoenix Program throughout the rest of South Vietnam were a rarity in IV Corps. In some provinces, the Viet Cong ceased to be a functioning entity because of the actions of the PRUs and their SEAL advisers. Many of the men who served in SEAL led PRUs were ex VC and NVA fighters and officers who had come over through the Chieu Hoi Program.

Excerpt from SEAL Team Two, Command and Control History 1968

Enclosure (1) to ST-2 Ltr, ser 04 of 7 Feb. '69

Pages 9–10. [DECLASSIFIED from CONFIDENTIAL]

IV. Provincial Reconnaissance Unit (PRU)

This year found certain members of SEAL Team TWO operating not as members of a platoon but as Provincial Reconnaissance Unit Advisers. The program has been found to be more than satisfactory, especially as it provides enlisted men with a great opportunity to develop their leadership qualities.

The PRUs were established to eliminate VC infrastructure in the local provinces, villages, and hamlets, with the emphasis placed upon the gathering of valuable intelligence. The concept is unique in that Hoi Chanhs are employed as guides, intelligence agents, and combatants against their former comrades.

SEAL Team officers and enlisted men are qualified for duty in this program

---

A detachment from a PRU listen to their American SEAL adviser as they discuss the mission while sweeping through a suspected Viet Cong village. The woven matting and palm frond construction of one of the villages' hooches is detailed to the right of the photo.

Frank Thornton Collection

once they have completed a five-week special operations course in California. This course is run under the direction of the Commanding Officer of SEAL Team ONE. After one has completed the course, he is fully prepared to handle all responsibilities and problems associated with isolated duty. The concept, which involves SEAL personnel on attached duty with indigenous, combative personnel, has produced gratifying results and clearly shows SEAL Team TWO's ability to organize, train, and lead friendly foreign forces.

Excerpt from SEAL Team Two, Command and Control History 1969
III. SEAL TEAM TWO COMMAND HISTORY—NARRATIVE
Page 7. [DECLASSIFIED from CONFIDENTIAL]
3. (C) Detachment BRAVO consisted of specially trained enlisted men who advised the Vietnamese Provincial Reconnaissance Units (PRU). The Provincial Reconnaissance Unit was developed to gather intelligence about, and to eliminate the VC infrastructure in the provinces, villages, and hamlets of IV Corps. As advisers to these units, the SEALs of Detachment BRAVO not only assisted in planning and coordinating operations, but also actively led most of the combat missions. The advisers' experience and training, coupled with the

aggressiveness of these Vietnamese forces during the past year, continued to produce the high degree of success achieved in previous years. Two advisers lost their lives while leading their PRU in combat missions during 1969. They were GMG1 Harry A. MATTINGLY and AE1 Curtis M. ASHTON.

Excerpt from SEAL Team Two, Command and Control History 1970
III. SEAL TEAM TWO COMMAND HISTORY—NARRATIVE
Page 7. [DECLASSIFIED from CONFIDENTIAL]
3. (C) For the first two months of this year detachment BRAVO was composed of specially trained enlisted men. These men were advisers to the Vietnamese Provincial Reconnaissance Units (PRU). These units were trained to gather intelligence about and to eliminate the VC infrastructure in the various provinces of IV Corps. As advisers to the PRU, the SEALs planned and coordinated operations, but were not permitted to actively participate in the combat missions. The aggressiveness of these Vietnamese forces continued to produce results at a high level.

Excerpt from SEAL Team Two, Command and Control History 1970
Enclosure (2) CHRONOLOGICAL OUTLINE

DATE	EVENT
16 MAY 1970	BM1 RODGER returned from Vietnam, thus ending SEAL Team TWO's commitment to DET "B"

Excerpt from SEAL Team One, Command and Control History 1969
Enclosure (2) (b) BASIC NARRATIVE
OPERATIONS
Pages 1–2. [DECLASSIFIED from SECRET]
    b. Detachment BRAVO is under the operational control of the Ministry of the Interior, Republic of Vietnam, and the personnel assigned to it are in direct support of the Provincial Reconnaissance Unit (PRU) Program. During this reporting period [March to December, 1969], with the turnover of control from the Military Assistance Command and the overall Vietnamization of the war effort, this program has decreased from a high of four officers and twenty-four enlisted to its present level of three officers and ten enlisted. This is congruent with the design to completely reduce the SEAL Team commitment to the PRU Program. These personnel are assigned as advisers throughout the IV Corps Tactical Zone, Republic of Vietnam. PRU are armed reconnaissance units of indigenous personnel that have the pri-

mary mission of gathering intelligence on key members of the Viet Cong political infrastructure and indicting or eliminating them whenever possible . . . The notable success of the IV Corps PRU Program can be attributed to the professionalism and dedicated leadership and drive of the SEAL advisers.

Excerpt from SEAL Team One, Command and Control History 1969
Enclosure (2) (c) BASIC NARRATIVE
SPECIAL TOPICS—INTELLIGENCE COLLECTED
Page 1. [DECLASSIFIED from SECRET]
2. The significance of the SEAL Team One PRU effort is reflected in the statistics which follow. The success of the PRU Program has often been traced directly to the leadership and professionalism of the officers and enlisted advisers, a small percentage of the total program. The figures listed here are even more significant when one considers that they are the result of targeting the Viet Cong infrastructure, the core of the enemy's command and control structure:

KILLED	CAPTURED
2120 Body count	2718

Excerpt from SEAL Team One, Command and Control History 1969
Enclosure (2) (C) BASIC NARRATIVE
SPECIAL TOPICS—SPECIAL TRAINING
Page 5. [DECLASSIFIED from SECRET]
1. Special Operations training, a five-week course for experienced officers and senior petty officers to prepare them to conduct covert and clandestine operations as advisers to indigenous personnel, experienced significant changes both in content and the practical application in an effort to remain current with the world situation and SEAL employment. In the immediate future, it is likely that the basic course will also increase in duration to ten weeks. In addition to the curriculum revision, semipermanent buildings were provided for training at Camp Billy Machen, the Special Operations field training facility at Julian, California.

Leonard "Lenny" Waugh, Senior Electronics Chief, USN (Ret.)

After my first tour in Vietnam with Third Platoon from SEAL Team Two, I didn't return to the States with the rest of the guys when they rotated back in June 1967. Instead, I went over to the PRUs to become one of the first East Coast SEAL advisers to that program.

The PRUs were the provincial reconnaissance units. In South Vietnam, they had provinces, much like the states or counties as we have them here in the United States. The PRUs were assigned one to a province and they went out and conducted reconnaissance missions throughout that area. The PRUs themselves were conceived as paramilitary organizations and were manned with mostly Vietnamese personnel, but also had Humong (Montagnards), Cambodians, some Chinese, and even some repatriated ex–Viet Cong.

The West Coast (SEAL Team One) was running the PRU training program at that time and the question was whether a PRU adviser would work to increase the capabilities of the PRUs. What the adviser would do was plan out a mission for the PRU from intelligence gathered from different sources. The NILO (Naval Intelligence Liaison Officer) gave us good bits of intel when he came in with something that he thought we would be interested in. The South Vietnamese junk force would also bring us intel. And we also had our own spies out among the population in the field.

All of these sources and more would bring us information that we would kind of hold back "in escrow," and then combine it later with other information. When we

A group of PRUs move through an open area of grassland while on patrol.

U.S. Navy

---

had a good picture of a given target or situation, we could plan out an action to take.

Information might come in about somebody being somewhere at eleven o'clock in the evening. And that person might be a target we wanted to get other information from. So we would plan a mission to go out and snatch him up. Sometimes, we would operate with as many as thirty people from the PRU. Other times, we might go out on an op with as few as two people.

Probably the most basic goal of the PRU operations was to capture individuals for interrogation and to gather further intelligence on even higher-level targets. One of our big targets was to capture a VC tax collector. A tax collector would come into a village and force the people to pay him money or goods as VC-levied taxes. He had to know a lot about the province to be able to do his job. And that put him high up in the Viet Cong infrastructure (VCI). That was the higher organizational command and control structure for the Viet Cong.

So capturing a tax collector was a good op. And since he was high up in the infrastructure, we could get good information from him. And that was our basic objective, eliminating the VCI and gathering information on the higher-ups and their operations.

The Phoenix Program was the umbrella organization that the PRUs operated under. But when I was a PRU adviser, I wasn't told that we were under the Phoenix Program. Knowledge about the Phoenix Program was something I learned later.

The VC tax collectors were the big target we went out for a lot while I was a PRU

A PRU member proudly pulls a secured Viet Cong prisoner from hiding in a hooch in Vietnam.

Frank Thornton Collection

adviser. We really wanted to stop them. This would not only give us a good deal of information, it would also help choke off one source of supply for the VC. But we never passed up other targets if they made themselves known to us. If we found out about a major enemy movement—say, a VC battalion crossing the Mekong at a given point at a certain time—that was something we gave over to the Army or the Navy so that they could handle it.

In my PRU, we weren't equipped for major engagements. What we were set up for was the "sneak and peek" kind of op with five or six people. My PRU could set up and sit at an ambush site and watch the enemy movement. If the enemy forces were small enough, and they usually were, we could try and engage them ourselves. If there were too many of them, we would just watch and come back with the information.

We didn't want to shoot anyone if we didn't have to. In fact, we preferred not even to fire our weapons. Coming back with, say, six prisoners and not a shot fired on our part was a really good op. This was much the same basic philosophy that the SEALs developed in Vietnam. And the adviser program using SEALs and the PRUs was a very successful one, in part because of this approach.

What we did as advisers was work right with the PRUs, down on their level. We ate with them, drank with them, and went out on operations with them. They were really our kind of people. I trusted my PRUs and they trusted me. By the time I left my assignment as a PRU adviser, my men thought the sun rose and set according to my desires.

One measure of our success as PRU advisers was that the VC put out a bounty on our heads. I had a price on my head that the VC were willing to pay anyone who could take me out. My PRU team leader came back with the priority listing the VC had put out in our province. He was very happy that I was ranked as the number-two most wanted man in the province, and that he was number one, with the larger bounty offered for his head.

The exertion and heat have sweated the camouflage facepaint from this SEAL as he comes in from an operation. The camouflage was a distinctive headgear worn by some SEALs during the Vietnam War.

U.S. Navy

If outranking me on the VC most-wanted list made my PRU team leader happy, that was fine with me. The VC wanted him worse than they wanted me. That was good; I could sleep more easily that night.

The price on my head was something like 50,000 piastres. At an exchange rate of roughly 75 piastres to the U.S. dollar, I was worth in the neighborhood of $670 dollars. But the piastre went a lot further in those days. Thankfully, no one managed to collect my bounty, or that of any other SEAL adviser that I ever heard of.

One of the things we tried to do in Vietnam was build up a reputation among the Viet Cong. I'm not talking about any kind of bravado. What we wanted to do was actually make the Viet Cong fear us. When they did that, they would make mistakes. And they might surrender a lot faster, rather than trying to fight things out with us. But the Viet Cong probably didn't know our real designation—SEAL—for a while.

What we did was encourage the rumors about us. When we went out on operations, we cammied up with green, black, and brown face paint. That not only helped us hide in the shadows and among the plants in the jungle, it really made us look a little "unhuman" to the Vietnamese.

The VC took to calling us the "men with green faces." It was just our makeup, but we did make use of the situation. "Watch out for the men with green faces" was a phrase that troubled the sleep of many a VC, we found out later. And that fear was something we wanted out there.

■ Chapter 45

To Fight a War

The SEALs went in to their first deployments in Vietnam fully trained and more than competent to do their job. But the one thing the Teams were lacking was a great deal of experience fighting a jungle, counterguerrilla war of the type found in Vietnam. But the Teams were more than up to the challenge, and they developed new techniques and applications of old tactics continually as they fought.

But no matter how highly trained an individual was, combat left a lasting impression on anyone who went through it. The men of the Teams were no exception. As they gathered the experience that increased their combat efficiency, they also gathered memories of combat, some of which were so vivid, they would last for the rest of their lives.

Excerpt from SEAL Team Two, Command and Control History 1967
Pages 6–7. [DECLASSIFIED from CONFIDENTIAL]

III. Development of Tactics

During the deployment of Detachment "A" to Vietnam, many valuable contributions have been made to the development of operational tactics for small units such as those employed by SEAL Teams in direct action against the Viet Cong. Being unique in topography and climate, the Mekong Delta offers considerable opportunity for imaginative development of small-unit operations. Various methods of ingress, for example, were tried and proved, such as insert by STAB or Boston whaler (thirteen- or sixteen-foot length), launch by PBR and LCM, and insert by helicopter during hours of day or night. Successful ingress was also made by swimmers carrying full combat loads under tow. Such tactics as simulated withdrawal by water and then the establishing of a double-back ambush were tried and in many instances found effective. Generally speaking, it was discovered that the effectiveness of a small unit of eight men is limited only by the imaginations of those involved.

Gene E. Peterson

One of the operational techniques we developed in Vietnam was a leave-behind ambush. One of the reasons we developed the technique was that a lot of the time when we did an operation or an ambush we failed to capture a lot of the people at the target. In the sudden confusion, a lot of people disappeared back into the bush. Since we operated a lot at night, it was very hard to follow or track them.

The escaped people could come back on their own to see where we had gone. Or they might come back and bring other VC with them as support. To counter this, we would go in and set up on a place and conduct the ambush as usual. But when we extracted, only half of the troops would be pulled out.

Whether we left the men at the ambush site, or they took up positions around our extraction site, their job was to ambush anyone who followed along our trail. The extraction boat would pull out and travel some distance away from the extraction site. If the leave-behind ambush worked, we would come blasting back in with the boat as soon as we heard the shooting. If it turned out to be a "dry hole," we circled around and came back to pick up the leave-behind troops after a short time had passed.

This kind of creative operation worked very well for us sometimes. One of the times that I remember us using this technique was right after we had hit an ammo dump. Once we blew up the dump, everyone in the area knew we had been there. After the blast, the rest of the platoon pulled out, and five of us stayed behind.

There was a kind of little mud ditch, maybe two or three feet deep and about four feet wide, running alongside our target area. The bottom of the ditch was filled with a soft, gooey mud that we sank into when we hid in the ditch. Once we had settled in, the mud was well up on my chest as I lay there.

Once you have situated yourself in a muddy site like that, you really can't move much. Any movement on your part will send waves through the mud, sloshing it around and making enough noise to alert anyone coming up. So we stayed silent and still in that mud for about ten or fifteen minutes.

Somebody started coming into the target area from up in the bushes behind us. We really couldn't see him at all clearly, but we could hear him moving through the jungle. The first thought going through our heads was that maybe we had been compromised. If someone had detected our position, they could be setting up to ambush us.

As we watched what was going on, suddenly this man disappeared. And then all hell broke loose.

Apparently, a company of North Vietnamese had set up across the river from us. The water was only about forty feet wide and they must have detected our position. Instead of us ambushing someone coming into the destroyed ammo dump, we ourselves were now the targets for someone else.

The situation almost didn't seem real; it was almost like watching a movie. That was kind of funny for me; I had been in Vietnam long enough to have experienced my share of firefights. But this time I was watching and could actually see the bullet hit the mud in front of me.

It was sort of like slow motion when you saw the bullet hit the mud. There would be the hit and the mud seemed to slowly spurt up. Then it would settle back down again and the dimple in the surface would collapse. Then another one would hit and the same thing would happen. This was like watching TV, only the bullets were real.

It absolutely fascinated me for a moment. I may even have said out loud, "Wow, it looks just like TV." Suddenly the realization hit me. Damn, this wasn't TV, it was real.

Sinking down, I settled into the mud about as far as I could go and still be able to breathe. Hanging on, I got on the radio and called for our boat to come in and pick us up.

As soon as I called for the extraction boat, it seemed that you could hear their engines fire up, even though they were a mile or more away. They were coming to get us with their throttles wide open.

It was night, the normal time for us to operate in the Teams, and the extraction boat might have a hard time finding us. One of the unusual pieces of ordnance we had with us was a special grenade with luminous material inside it. When one of these grenades went off, it spread this material that glowed with a blue-green light all over its burst radius. That light would be the signal that marked our spot to an overhead Seawolf helicopter. Hopefully, the Seawolves would see the light and not shoot at us.

All you had to do was take the grenade and toss it. When it fired it spread this chemical all over the tops of the foliage above us. The glow was much like you see on the dial of a watch. Not enough to really see by, but hopefully enough to alert the incoming Seawolves.

The choppers started coming in to our position as I began to hear the boat roaring down the river in our direction. The rockets from the Seawolves were being fired right over our heads—you could see them being fired and feel the heat blast from their exhausts, the Seawolves were that close. As the rockets were blasting through the trees over our heads, limbs the diameter of your legs were being broken off and dropping down on us. But that wasn't anything in comparison to those same rockets going through the trees and detonating on the other side of the river.

These Seawolf gunships were also armed with miniguns, mounted outside of their rocket pods. The minigun is a multibarreled machine gun that spins its six barrels as it fires 7.62mm ammunition at high rates of speed, on the order of 3,000 rounds per minute for those mounted on the Seawolves.

While the Seawolf was firing over our heads, and the rockets were blasting out, the miniguns were firing. The bullets came out of the front of those weapons like a steel spray. But the fired ammunition casings were also pouring out from the sides of the guns. Those hot brass casings rained down on us, literally like metal rain-

A port-side helicopter mounted outboard minigun rains fire down on the Viet Cong below. The heavy blast of muzzle gases appears as a huge, white cloud of flame a few feet in front of the weapon.

U.S. Navy

drops. But it was a hot metal. Just like the bullets hitting the mud earlier, the fired minigun casing would smack into the mud, and then there was an audible sizzle as the metal cooled suddenly.

It was kind of exciting.

As the Seawolves poured fire into the NVA positions, our extraction boat was coming up the river and getting closer and closer. I could hear the .50-caliber machine guns mounted along the side of the boat chopping up the countryside. And the bursting 40mm grenades being put out by the grenade launchers on the boat made a constant string of explosions. And over it all was the deep thrumming roar of the 7.62mm minigun near the bow of the boat, pouring out its ammunition at several thousand rounds a minute.

As the boat came closer, I started getting worried that they would take our position under fire as well. In the excitement of the fight, they might forget where our position was. So at just the last second, as the boat approached, I started shouting into the radio for them to stop shooting.

Just as it seemed as if our own people would destroy us, the guns on the boat stopped firing. The boat turned into the bank and headed right for our location. As soon as it touched the bank, we pulled ourselves up out of the mud we were lying in and clambered aboard.

Just as the last man climbed aboard, the coxswain slipped the engines into reverse and pulled away from the bank. Now the guns were firing again as we left the area. But we all got out okay. No one was hit, and no one was hurt, except for the bangs and bruises we got from landing in the boat.

Later we learned that a whole company of North Vietnamese had set up on the bank of the river, directly across from us. There had been at least forty or fifty guys over there, dumping fire into our position. But they were badly chewed up by the rocket fire from the Seawolves overhead, and the heavy gunfire of our own support boat.

The men who crewed our support boats have my respect for the job they were doing. First of all, they had to pull away from where they had inserted us, and then move some distance upriver. Once they were a safe average distance away so as not to compromise our insertion, they would quietly nose into the bank. Then they just sat there and waited for our call for extraction or support.

The fortitude of those men was amazing to me—to just silently sit there, being still and quiet, just waiting for us. And then whenever they actually had to come in and get us out of a hot situation, they immediately jumped into action. Forgetting about their own safety or anything else that was going on, they came and got us.

I don't know how the boat drivers were doing what they did. It was pitch-dark out there on the river in the middle of the night. And they couldn't use a light without making a target of themselves. The drivers would just tuck their faces up against the rubber hoods on the radar scopes and watch the glowing green traces of the riverbank on either side of them. With these as a guide, they would race their boats at top speed to get to us.

They never spoke about the jeopardy they were putting themselves in. Those boats and crews were there to help and support us, and that is what they did.

Without them, we couldn't have done many of the things we have been credited with. And a lot fewer of us would have come home intact or lived to operate another day. Those boats and crews helped make the difference for us countless times.

The Seawolves are another unit we owe a lot to. You would get into a situation on an op where you needed air support, and you needed it right now! And on some of the occasions when we called in Army helicopters, they were ten or fifteen minutes away. That can be more than enough time for even a unit of SEALs to be overrun, wiped out, and the enemy long gone before the helicopters show up.

But when we did an op with the Seawolves on call, they knew where we would be and when. If we called for air support, they were just right there. I don't know where they came from or how they got off the ground that fast. But it seemed like as soon as we made the radio call for the Seawolves, they were right there overhead within three of four minutes.

And those Seawolf pilots and crews weren't afraid to do what we needed. They would come right in and actually touch the tops of the trees to make sure that they protected us. The crews would drop ropes to pick us up if there was no other way out for us.

How the Seawolves got into the position they did with their birds, and flew they way they had to, I don't know. But the support that we received from the Seawolves brought a lot of men home to the Teams who otherwise wouldn't have made it. They were unbelievable.

■ Chapter 46

To Save a Life, the Corpsmen

In the Teams, one experience is shared by all, and that experience is training. It is while undergoing BUD/S, or the earlier UDTR, that a man demonstrates that he has that drive, determination, and heart to make it through some of the hardest military training in the world. Teammates share training stories with each other all of the time. Everyone has a favorite.

But some individuals served in the Teams who never went through UDTR or BUD/S. They simply were not allowed to do so because of an interpretation of the regulations and international agreements of war. But every SEAL or UDT operator who served with these men considers them full-fledged Teammates.

A hospital corpsman is an enlisted man trained to give first aid and basic medical treatment, particularly while under combat conditions. The U.S. Navy Hospital Corps is the only enlisted corps in the Navy, and has a history of service and valor dating back to the corps' founding on 17 June 1898. This valor is well illustrated by the fact that hospital corpsmen have received over half of the Medals of Honor awarded to enlisted men in the Navy.

When the SEALs were first commissioned, a number of hospital corpsmen were among the plankowners of both Teams. But by the time the SEALs were sending direct-action platoons into combat in Vietnam, corpsmen were no longer allowed to go through UDTR training. This had to do with the fact that corpsman going through training had to work with demolitions as well as small arms.

The 1949 Geneva Convention allows Navy hospital corpsmen to be classified as noncombatants. This allows them to be armed for their own defense and that of their patients. But they are not allowed to carry weapons for any other reason. With these restrictions came protections, centering on corpsmen's treatment if they are taken prisoner, among other things. But the corpsmen of the Teams relinquish any protections given them by the Geneva Convention in order to serve fully with their Teammates.

After receiving their full training to qualify as hospital corpsmen, those men who also volunteered to join the SEAL Teams underwent a special course of training before they were allowed to enter the Teams. The special-operations-technician course made the corpsmen who went through it fully qualified divers and parachutists. When they arrived at their respective SEAL Teams, pre-deployment training with their platoons also made the corpsmen proficient with weapons and able to move on patrol effectively.

Each deployed SEAL platoon going to Vietnam was to have a hospital corpsman assigned to it. Corpsmen are most often called simply "Doc" in the Navy or Marine Corps. But in the Teams, they were also called something even more significant—they were called "Teammate."

Jack Salts, Senior Chief Hospital Corpsman, USN (Ret.)

In January 1978, I retired from the Navy after twenty-one years, four months, and seven days of active duty. And during that time, I had the privilege of serving as a hospital corpsman in the Teams.

In 1960, I was a Navy hospital corpsman going though the X-ray technicians' school at a naval hospital. While at the hospital, I met a lady who eventually married Delmar "Freddie" Fredrickson. Sometime later, while I was going through an advanced hospital corpsman school on the West Coast, I again ran into her, and through her, met Freddie.

The stories Freddie told me about life in the Teams made them sound like something I really wanted to be part of. But the Navy had other plans for me at that moment and I was soon stationed in Seattle, Washington. I volunteered for UDT training, but was quickly turned down.

As a corpsman at that time—the mid-1960s—I was not allowed to go through BUD/S training. There had been a window of opportunity back in the early 1960s when corpsmen were allowed to go through UDTR training and join with the UDTs or SEAL Teams. But that was stopped after it was determined that the Geneva Convention prevented hospital corpsmen from being allowed to handle demolitions. Or at least that's how I remember the reasoning.

But I knew the Teams had to have hospital corpsmen, especially since they were getting ready to go to Vietnam and see active combat. Corpsmen are the field medical personnel of the Navy. We go out into the combat area to help the wounded. We're right there where the bullets are flying, trying to save the lives and ease the pain of the wounded.

There were some people I knew who were plankowners of SEAL Team One and still in the Team in Coronado. I had spent three years in Seattle, working in the hospital and trying to get into the Teams. All my requests were denied, so finally I just called down to SEAL Team One and contacted Freddie Fredrickson directly. He told me he would talk to Lieutenant Del Giudice, who was the CO of SEAL Team One at the time, about the situation.

That was about all I could expect. But when Freddie called me back, his news wasn't what I wanted to hear. "Jack, I'm sorry," Fred told me. "There's no way that you can do it. The only way you can get to the Teams is by becoming deep-sea-diver [hardhat] qualified, completing jump school, and underwater swimmer school."

"So," I asked back, "how do you do that?"

"You apply for special operations technician."

If that was the only way I could go to get into the Teams, so be it. So I did that, and my first stop was deep-sea divers' school at the Washington Navy Yard in Washington, D.C. Six months later I was a qualified hardhat diver.

There was a two-week break between my graduation from deep-sea-divers' school and the beginning of my jump school. During the break, I was assigned to UDT 22 in Little Creek. So that gave me a very short taste of life at a UDT, but I still had the balance of my training to complete.

My short stay at UDT 22 was followed by three weeks at Fort Benning, Georgia, and the Army jump school there. Then came eight weeks of underwater swimmer school in Key West, Florida.

All of this training resulted in my being assigned back to Underwater Demolition Team 22 at Little Creek, Virginia, as one of their hospital corpsmen. It was January 1966. This was the long way around, but at least I had finally made it to the Teams.

Lieutenant Commander David Schaible was the CO of UDT 22 during the beginning of my time there. Getting to a SEAL Team was what I really wanted to do, but Commander Schaible told me that he had a working agreement with the Navy detailers up in Washington regarding hospital corpsmen. The detailers were the men who assigned people to posts throughout the Navy, and what they said was pretty much the last word on assignments.

What Commander Schaible told me was that he would receive all of the hospital corpsmen when they graduated deep-sea divers' school. Once the corpsmen were assigned to UDT 22 and arrived in Little Creek, he'd put us through some pretraining and physical conditioning to prepare us for jump school.

The conditioning and training I remember well. But what I didn't know was that Commander Schaible was also picking out the people he wanted to have in his UDT. So even though I had asked to be assigned to SEAL Team One so that I could be with my friend Freddie, I ended up on Commander Schaible's want list and was assigned to UDT 22.

Maybe being in the UDT first would be a good thing, I thought. Spending time in the UDT would teach me the ropes better and I could then move over to a SEAL Team. That worked out, eventually. But it took me three years to get to a SEAL Team.

But life in UDT 22 had its adventures as well. In 1968, I was part of a crew that was sent from Little Creek, on the shores of the Atlantic Ocean, to a demolition job at Midway Island, half a world away in the middle of the Pacific. On the way back from that job, we landed in San Diego for a stopover.

It just so happened that the day we arrived in San Diego was the same day that Commander Schaible was relieving Commander Anderson as the CO of SEAL Team One. I was there at the ceremony and right afterward, while they were cutting the cake, I looked up to see this big guy just spreading the crowd apart as he approached me.

"Doc," he said when he saw I was looking, "come here."

This didn't look like the kind of guy I would say no to. So I walked over to him and he just said, "Come with me."

I followed the man to his office; inside, Commander Anderson was changing into civilian clothes. Then he picked up the phone and called Washington. He was talking to some officer there, but I could only hear part of the conversation. The part I could hear involved him asking about a corpsman in UDT 22 and how he would like to have him in his unit.

Looking over at me, Commander Anderson asked, "What's your rank and horsepower?"

"I'm a second class hospital corpsman," I told him. And then I told him my Social Security number and other pertinent data.

He chitchatted with the man at the other end of the phone for a while and then hung up. Turning to me, he asked, "How much leave do you have built up?"

"A week," I answered.

"Well, when you get back to UDT 22," he told me, "your orders will be there."

And when I got back to UDT 22, my orders were there, along with a little surprise. The minute I walked into the office at UDT 22 to turn in my leave papers, the yeoman there told me that the XO wanted to see me immediately.

So I walked in to see John Ferruggiaro, who was our XO at the time. He let me into his office, shut the door, sat down, and put his feet up on the desk.

"Mister," Ferrugario said to me, "I don't know who you think you are, jumping the chain of command, going behind everybody's back, and getting yourself a set of orders to SEAL Team One. But I'm here to tell you, don't unpack your bags."

"Why's that, sir?" I asked, more than a bit puzzled.

"The day after tomorrow, you're going to the Med [Mediterranean]," he told me. "I've got an operational hold on you."

So he had the last say-so. I made a Med cruise for UDT 22. After I got back, I transferred to SEAL Team One and the West Coast.

Even though I had wanted to get to a SEAL Team for so long, initially I was a little reticent about operating as a corpsman with them. There was always that feeling I had, and maybe it was an unfounded one, about not having gone through BUD/S training; even though I'd had to go through a much longer period of training to get to the Teams, there was that question of was I good enough? Could I measure up?

But I think people realized that most of the other corpsmen who were in the Teams and hadn't gone through BUD/S were pretty good at their jobs. We worked hard at what we were supposed to do. And over time, virtually every one of us was accepted as a Teammate.

The big test for a Team corpsman came when he was deployed to a combat tour in Vietnam. My first deployment to Vietnam was in January 1970. It was an exciting time, to say the least.

While building up for the deployment, during the weeks of predeployment training, you got to know everyone in your platoon. You actually reached a point where you could tell what any of your teammates in the platoon would do in almost any given circumstance. The camaraderie that was built up during that time is something that we will live with forever. It just can't be taken away from us. It is uniquely ours.

Actually being a hospital corpsman in combat was unlike anything I had experienced before. I'd think back to all of the movies I'd seen as a teenager, before joining the service. Those films, following the Korean War and WWII, showed a corpsman as someone who wore a red cross on his arm and on his helmet. They made you wonder if you would just be a big target when you finally became a corpsman.

But it wasn't that way at all in Vietnam. We didn't wear the big red crosses. Instead, we wore what everyone else wore. And in the Teams, we did what everyone else did. When you were operating in a platoon of two officers and twelve enlisted men, or when they were split into squads of one officer and six enlisted, everyone had a number of jobs to do. The radioman handled the radio and maintained communications. But he was also a rifleman, grenadier, or automatic-weapons man.

A hospital corpsman, if there was nobody to patch up, had to add his firepower to that of his unit; he had to do his share. And he could carry any weapon that he was familiar with and confident about handling. Generally, the corpsman not only carried his own medical kit, but each member of the platoon also carried some medical supplies with them. That way, if I was working on someone who was hurt over here, someone else could be tending to another injured person over there.

Every member of the platoon was trained in some lifesaving skills. Each platoon went through some formal medical training. Nothing as sophisticated as what a hospital corpsman had to go through. But each man knew enough that he could jump in and help when he was needed during a lifesaving situation. And if the corpsman got hit, then there was somebody to help work on him. So our guys were pretty well trained.

Just being there and going out on a patrol, making contact with the enemy, and everyone doing just what they were supposed to—that came from all of our training. Whether a man would jump to the right, or to the left, and what the corpsman would do in a given situation, that had all been covered long before. And being able to come out of the fight later made all those long hours of training worth it.

But that first time in combat is never quite like training. The first thing that went through my head when the bullets started to fly was for me not to let my Teammates down. The second thing that went through my head was to get back home alive myself; I had a couple of sons and a family back there waiting for me.

I was scared, but I don't think I acted scared. Instead, I just did my job alongside my Teammates. Fortunately, we all got out in good fashion. My platoon never lost anyone in combat. Though one person was badly wounded—by accident of all things.

We had captured a village chief or some kind of important VCI character. Taking our prisoner away in a sampan, we had the chief secured with plastic riot cuffs in the boat as we were paddling away. The village chief managed to break loose of his handcuffs, which were secured behind his back. And he tried to make a break for it over the side of the sampan.

As the village chief suddenly went over the side, the Teammate who was assigned to keep the prisoner covered swung his weapon around onto him. But as the prisoner went over the side, the light sampan rocked violently from side to side. Our Teammate went rolling over onto his back, his feet rising into the air, as he tried to fire. And he managed to nail himself right in the foot.

So that was the worst injury of our deployment. While the rest of the guys dealt with the prisoner, I treated our wounded Teammate. Though his wound probably wasn't nearly as bad as the razzing he would be getting for some time to come.

There was never any conflict for me personally in my being both an operating SEAL and a corpsman. When it was time to fight, I could use my weapon to kill. When there was a need for my other skills, I would work hard to help heal.

Periodically, we would have what we called downtime. That was when we would get in out of the field and not have any operations scheduled for a while. During this time, I had three or four guys within the platoon who just loved going out with me to the surrounding villages on what were called "Medcaps." During a Medcap visit, we would do whatever we could for the children, the women, whoever needed medical attention.

Illnesses and diseases didn't care that there was a shooting war going on, and we would treat these maladies as best we could. That work was rewarding as well.

On one particular Medcap, up one of the canals in IV Corps, we pulled into a little village and started taking out the candy we had brought for the kids. The villagers began coming out, and through one of the Team interpreters we had brought with us, we explained what we were trying to do. All we did was tell them we were there to help in any way that we could. Anyone in need of medication or treatments for sores, or anything else, would get it.

The villagers liked what we were offering, and the people just started swarming around like they were coming out of the woodwork. They needed what we had and we were glad to give it. That work was just something we could thoroughly enjoy.

What we didn't know was that there was someone in that village passing information along to the VC. This enemy informer would tell them just what we were doing and who we were doing it for. After we left, there would be retributions against the village as a whole and also specifically against some of the people we had treated.

All we had been trying to do was help the local people, just do a job that didn't cost anyone anything. And here there was someone who would rat on them and just make their lives that much more miserable. And things were done and said to make us look like the bad guys to the villagers. And instead of good, we would bring down more harm on those people we were trying to help.

The situation was a perplexing one, and we were caught in the middle. The question was whether we should continue conducting our Medcaps or just wash our hands of it. What finally came about was that we had to be a lot more selective as to how we medically treated the locals.

In my opinion, the Vietnamese people were really under a gun, literally, during that war. They didn't know who they could turn to for help. If they turned to the Americans, they would be persecuted by the Viet Cong and the North Vietnamese.

And if they turned to them, we wouldn't be getting any assistance from them and they'd just make a target of themselves from our side. There just wasn't any simple answer for them.

I'm sure that there are some misconceptions about just who the Navy SEALs were back in the Vietnam days, and what our job was about. None of the men I worked with during my thirteen years in the Teams appeared like the Rambo of the movies. In fact, there was no standard kind of SEAL. Everybody was different.

There were times when everybody would have the macho, get-up-and-go attitude of taking the war to the enemy. And there were also times when these same men could hold a baby in their arms with obvious tenderness. These men who could sit in a swamp silently for days also loved going out on a picnic with a bunch of their kids. SEALs are human, and no different from anyone else in all that being human means.

A man in the Teams has just been trained to do a particular, and difficult, job. And we do that job to the best of our abilities. When it's over, we go back to being family men.

A SEAL Team is effective because it's a close-knit group. When it comes time to do a job, there may be differences between the men of a platoon or team. But those differences are put aside for the greater good. The job gets done, and you don't often hear of a job that was given to a SEAL platoon or SEAL Team that doesn't get done. When I think of the Teams, that's the word that comes to mind first—"team." There's no one person in the SEALs; there's a group of people working together. "Team" is a big word, and it's a big group of individuals who come together to make us a SEAL Team. We can work as individuals on an assignment, but we can also come together as a cohesive unit and accomplish anything.

Greg McPartlin, Hospital Corpsman, Second Class

My enlistment in the Navy began in June 1967, when I started boot camp at the Great Lakes Naval Training Center just north of Chicago. It was interesting just how I settled on the Navy as the service I would be in. My brother Fred was an A4 pilot in the Marine Corps and had already seen action in Chu Lai, Vietnam. Originally, I was going to play football for Notre Dame, but when my scholarship was turned in to Parsegian by Terry Brennan, it was just lost in the shuffle when a large influx of players came in from the South Side of Chicago.

Since I was already classified 1A by the draft board, I figured I would go ahead and rush up to the Marine Corps recruiter in Waukegan, go over to Vietnam as a Marine, and take care of my brother's ass. But when I drove up to the recruiting center in an ambulance, the recruiter had other ideas.

At the time I was earning my living as an ambulance driver in Lake Forest, Illinois. The recruiter asked me just why I was there to join the Marines. When I told

SEAL Team One, Alfa Platoon prior to deploying to Vietnam. Kneeling on the far right in the front row is Greg McPartlin, the platoon's corpsman.

Greg McPartlin Collection

him I wanted to be with my brother, he told me there was a real need for hospital corpsmen. Okay, I'll be a Marine hospital corpsman, I told him.

Then he floored me a bit. Pointing across the room, the recruiter told me I had to talk to another recruiter in the office. When I saw who he was pointing at, my immediate comment was "But that guy's a squid!"

But the Marine recruiter promised me that it would be in my enlistment contract that I would go directly to the Marine Corps from hospital corpsman school. He said they would put it in writing, so I believed him.

The Navy supplied the corpsmen for the Marine Corps, so I soon found myself in the Navy, now a squid myself. And just like it said in my contract, after I finished corps school, I went right on to field med school and then was assigned to the Third Marine Force Recon at Camp Lejeune. Arriving in time to be sent over to Vietnam for the Tet offensive of 1968. During the heavy fighting, most of my platoon was either hospitalized or killed. So we were rotated back to the States early.

When I was being interviewed about a new assignment, my detailer asked me if I could swim. Not knowing where the man was going with his question, but having had my fill of Marine Corps life, I told the man that I could walk on water if it would get me out of the Marines. And I quickly found myself volunteering for a new assignment.

The powers that be put me in a new program called special operations technician. It was for hospital corpsmen and was in Key West, Florida, where we would be trained to be SEAL operators. Back during the Vietnam era—at least the early part of it—corpsmen were still considered noncombatants. That was kind of a holdover from World War II and Korea, where the corpsman only carried a sidearm for his own and his patient's protection. Those corpsmen never operated as straight infantry types.

The rules in force at the time that I was serving precluded any corpsmen from attending UDTR because of the demolitions and weapons phases of training. So the Teams had to get their corpsmen from the fleet, and that wasn't too appealing to the operators in the UDT and SEAL community, since they wanted men with a little more specialized training. So the program in Florida was started as an addition to the underwater swimmers' school in order to give corpsmen the necessary additional training.

The program in Florida consisted of a lot of physical-fitness training, a lot of diving and underwater swimming, and small-unit work. After the rest of the UDT trainees from the East Coast left—they had been there for the underwater-swimmer-school portion of the training—the rest of us continued with instruction in diving medicine and field medicine.

Getting to the special operations technicians' school wasn't just a matter of my volunteering for it. I had to take a number of tests to qualify. The training was tough; nineteen corpsmen began the program and only four of us graduated. And this was where I learned about the UDTs, how they picked up the Mercury and Gemini space capsules as well as conducted the same missions as they did during World War II. The SEAL Teams were completely unknown to me; their operations were still listed as secret.

After we finished special operations technicians' training in Key West, we were sent up to Lakehurst, New Jersey, for parachute training at the Navy school there. Now I was a corpsman, underwater swimmer, and jump-qualified. Finally, they assigned me to UDT 21 in Little Creek, Virginia, late in 1968. The UDTs were also short of corpsmen, so I ended up operating with both UDT 21 and UDT 22 out of Little Creek. This meant that I pulled two deployments in a row, both of them UDT winter deployments to Roosevelt Roads, Puerto Rico.

By the time I returned from Puerto Rico, it was May 1969. One of my counterpart corpsmen with the West Coast Teams had been killed just the month before in Vietnam. My XO at the time, Fred Kochey, called me in to his office and told me that I was going over to the SEAL Team. I told him that wasn't a problem and I would go and get my gear. Then he told me that the Team I would be going to was SEAL Team One.

"What?" I said. "SEAL Team One, Hollywood UDT? You're going to send me over to those guys?"

Apparently he was. There was a pretty good rivalry between the East Coast and the West Coast Teams. But I wasn't going to be able to change anything. They transferred me to Coronado, California, in May 1969.

Arriving in Coronado was kind of interesting. First of all, I was a numerical replacement for Alfa Platoon, which was already in predeployment training. Dick Wolfe, a corpsman who was later killed in Vietnam, met me at the SEAL Team One headquarters and said, "Gosh, Greg, you're so lucky. You get to deploy in September. In fact, your platoon's out in Niland right now undergoing training."

It was all of late June, so in a few months I was going back to Vietnam. But Coronado had their Fourth of July parade coming up, and since I was free-fall-qualified, I was going to be part of the demonstration team for the show. This resulted in my going out to the platoon with there only being a little over a month of predeployment training left.

When I arrived at the platoon, what I hadn't expected was the cold-shoulder routine I received from the guys. They thought I was just some guy coming right off a ship. It was about 114 degrees out at Niland, the SEAL Team One training area out in the California desert near the Salton Sea. Sitting there in my greens, holding my orders, I was sweating from the heat. The lieutenant finally reached over and took my orders from me. As he was reading over my records, he called over the platoon's leading chief petty officer.

The lieutenant proceeded to explain to the LCPO that I had already been to Vietnam, that I spoke the language, and had more than just the experience they would expect someone straight from the fleet to bring with them.

So the situation improved a bit right there. Within a month Alfa Platoon was ready to go, and I had adapted fine. There was some minor question about outfitting me properly as a SEAL corpsman. The platoon found out that my shooting skills weren't up to their level. And it didn't look like I was going to improve a whole lot really quickly. They issued me a Stoner light machine gun. I think they wanted to be sure that I would remain a good corpsman and be surgically correct on all of my shots.

Basically, they didn't want to trust me with any less firepower. With a Stoner, I could put out a whole lot of rounds very quickly. The fact that I missed every few rounds didn't matter much when I could put out a few hundred rounds at a time.

They didn't even hold my having been a Marine against me. In fact, they thought it might have been some good training.

Since I was already familiar with being in-country in Vietnam, going over with Alfa Platoon held no real surprises for me. It had only been about a year and a half since I had been on the soggy shores of Vietnam. Now I was a seasoned combat veteran, an old man with all of twenty years of living behind me.

When I arrived in Saigon, the first thing that hit me was the smell. No matter how many movies they come out with, they will never duplicate that smell of rice paddies, muddy river water, and the ocean. All of it overlaid with the odors of the jungle and decaying organic matter.

We settled down in a little base in IV Corps, right there on the water, a floating base on the river called SEAFLOAT. Our platoon saw action right away, beginning with our first operation. That proved to be a forerunner for the other SEAL platoons that would be following us. We had both good ops and bad ones. Some people were lost and we raised a lot of havoc with the enemy's troops.

One of the things I tried to teach everyone in both of Alfa's squads was enough first aid to keep me alive in case I was hit. If someone else was hit, it was okay as long as I was there to help them. Most of the guys were always very cool and very calm. My previous experience in Vietnam had made me used to the situations that arise in combat. Most of the rest of the platoon had a combat tour behind them and they operated with a tremendous amount of poise and presence of mind.

If somebody was wounded and went down, the platoon immediately set up a perimeter around the wounded man and me. Then a medevac would be called up for an immediate extraction of the wounded. My job was to take care of the casualty, and I concentrated on that while my Teammates did their jobs.

Fortunately, in Alfa Platoon, not one of us was ever seriously hurt. There was an incident in October '69 where another SEAL platoon walked into our ambush. Their officer, Lieutenant (j.g) David Nicholas, was killed along with their scouts.

A squad of SEALs move ashore from their insertion boat. They are operating in Kien Hoa Province, fifty miles southwest of Saigon.

U.S. Navy

That terrible day was Alfa Platoon's breaking-in op for the deployment. Lieutenant Nicholas stood up to try and stop the firing when his platoon walked into our ambush site, and it cost him his life. I worked on him for forty-five minutes, until I almost passed out from heat exhaustion myself. But there was nothing that could be done.

The incident was investigated and no one was found to be at fault. The loss was chalked up to the fog of war that takes place so often in combat. But the loss did shatter the morale of both platoons. Captain Dave Schaible came over to SEAFLOAT and we all went through extensive debreifings. From that incident, we learned that you don't separate units in the field and have them walk toward each other; the chances of killing your own man are just too great. The technique is called a hammer-and-anvil ambush, and it immediately fell out of favor in the Teams.

But not everything we did involved carrying a weapon and dropping the bad guys. Part of the old cliché—that we were over there to win the hearts and minds of the peasants—was something I helped work on directly. We would go into villages that were controlled by the Viet Cong. You always knew they were Viet Cong villages because by the time you went in there, there would be no men around, just the elderly, women, and children.

Unarmed, I would go in wearing just a plain green uniform, no cammies. A couple of boat-unit guys would usually be with me for my security. The area we were in was south of the U-Minh Forest. Usually, the old folks would come up to us first and start talking in French. These people hadn't seen a round-eye since the French were there back in the 1950s.

With my stethoscope around my neck, and a tongue depressor in my pocket, I would be called Bac Si, Vietnamese for "Doctor," by the villagers. We came bearing gifts for the children—candy, small toys, that kind of thing.

Besides treating the locals for whatever ailments and injuries they had, we also gathered information. We could ask a child where their father was, what he was doing, who or what they might be afraid of, things like that. And the answers could tell us a lot about VC activity in the area.

After a few trips into the same area, the kids would get all excited about our showing up as soon as they saw the boat. And the best intel you could get came from little children; they didn't know how to lie about politics and the war.

The villagers would receive Phisohex [antibacterial] soap, vaccinations, bandages, and antibiotics. A lot of my time was spent with the midwives in an area. Whenever they were having a problem with a birth, they would send a message up to SEAFLOAT and I would come down to help. In my two tours, I probably assisted in 150 births. During one incident, I even performed a C-section to save the life of the child and the mother. I may be the only Navy corpsman to have performed that operation during the Vietnam War.

That woman had been in labor almost thirty-six hours. I had asked for permission to bring her back to SEAFLOAT, but the "black-shoe" [regular Navy] officer at the time said that I couldn't bring her aboard. Instead, he wanted me to send her to the nearest Vietnamese hospital, a three-day journey by sampan. Both the woman and the child would have been dead long before they ever got to the local hospital.

So I went into the village during the early evening. That was when the VC were operating, so a squad of SEALs went along with me. The operation was satisfactory, the baby and the mother were saved, and my CO congratulated me in the morning for delivering a new VC. I think I received a Navy Commendation for that.

Several days later I was on an ambush where I was in a position to fire on three VC who were moving in on us. I gave them a chance to surrender, but they weren't having any of that. So I ended up killing all three. Later I received the Bronze Star for my part in that operation. The joke among my Teammates was that I received a Bronze Star for killing three VC and a Navy Comp for saving one.

So when Admiral King was giving out the awards after we were back from that tour, I spoke up about the incident. Captain Schaible knew I was going to do it, but when I received my Navy Commendation medal, I didn't say anything. But when Admiral King pinned the Bronze Star on me, I spoke up asking if that medal meant I was up one and down three, or down one and up three. He never got the joke, and Schaible just shook his head at the whole thing.

Corpsmen did a lot of humanitarian actions, both during Vietnam and elsewhere. Only in the Teams you did your actions usually with a weapon in your hands. The SEAL Teams consist of many different rates [jobs] from the ranks of the Navy. The only man in his rate who is certain to work in that job is the hospital corpsman. Boatswain's mates, gunner's mates, enginemen—they all work as an operator in a platoon.

A hospital corpsman is going to be called on to use all of the skills he has been taught. A good corpsman will be a preacher, mortician, and savior. But in the Teams, a corpsman is also going to be a fighter.

Separating these two jobs—that of a fighter and that of a healer—is not real easy. But much of the ability to do this comes from the basic philosophy of the men of the Teams. SEALs do not fight for their country; we fight for each other. We don't care what the politicians back in Saigon or Washington might have been saying. When you were in the field and the bullets were flying, it didn't matter what Nixon might have been saying—you fought for the man on either side of you. And that was all that mattered to me.

When a Teammate was hurt, then it was the corpsman's job to get him out. But the corpsman is also responsible to see to it that he doesn't get killed getting that wounded man out of danger. No corpsman did anyone any good by being a hero and running out into the middle of a firefight to save a man only to be killed before he got two steps. That's no help to anyone.

For myself, I always tried to assess the situation. And that was also why I carried a big gun. I could go out and lay down a base of fire and do what was necessary to get to my patient. And if that meant I had to let him bleed while I helped the squad suppress the incoming fire, that was just how it was.

We operated in very small units. In a big firefight, every weapon counted. Of course our hope every day was that each one of us would make it back from an op. And during that six-month tour, we all did get out alive, and we still got our job done. Though we did get dinged once or twice.

The only trouble with being a hospital corpsman in the SEALs is when you're hit and call out "Doc!" Then nobody knows what to do and all of your Teammates forget all of their medical training.

During one operation, I took a hit in the arm. It wasn't a bad wound at all; it wasn't even worth the Purple Heart they gave me. But it did hurt like hell, and I still have the scar to remind me. After I was hit, suddenly I had two guys wanting to give me morphine, and one guy trying to start an IV in my arm.

Greg McPartlin (upper left) prepares to sling his Stoner Mk 23 machine gun as he and his Teammates move through the tall grass to approach an extraction helicopter. Greg was struck moments later by a single enemy bullet.

Greg McPartlin Collection

Here I was, already with a wounded man in my arms, holding an IV in my teeth leading down to the patient, and I take a bullet in the upper arm. There was just this trickle of blood down my right arm as we headed for the medevac bird.

By the time we got on the bird, three guys were trying to give me morphine and two were setting up IVs. And a third was trying to strap a tourniquet onto my right arm and damned near twisted it down to the bone. As he twisted the tourniquet tight with his knife, I started losing the feeling in my right hand. The medevac took me to the hospital, where they put in some forty stitches to seal up my wound, and it got me away from my Teammates before they turned me into a one-armed morphine addict swollen up from too many IV drips.

It was just that my Teammates liked me so much. The good thing about being the corpsman in the SEAL Team was that it made you a cumshaw artist. A good corpsman can get his hands on anything, and everything, he needs. Like in the movie The Green Berets, the medic got everything. We had control of the shot rec-

Wearing a SEAL/UDT blue and gold T-shirt, Greg McPartlin poses for the camera while holding an M3A1 submachine gun. The bandage on his upper right arm covers the wound he received during an extraction.

Greg McPartlin Collection

ords, the brandy, the pills. So we were usually pretty well respected by everyone in the platoon. Not even a big tough SEAL likes to have his shot [inoculation] records mishandled and end up having to go through all those needle sticks again.

But as a SEAL corpsman, I also had a Stoner light machine gun. The hardware the Teams have today, as I have seen on static displays, is light-years ahead of what we worked with then. But there's still nothing that they've come up with that's better than the Stoner, in my opinion.

The Stoner Mark 23 light machine gun was the deadliest weapon that you could have in a close firefight—up to maybe 100 to 200 meters' range. That's true if you kept it clean and it was used properly. The Stoner fell out of favor as they became worn and the guys played around with them. Pulling off the stock and putting on a short barrel does not make it a pistol, but guys would try and handle it like one.

My point man would take his stockless Stoner and try to hit a target, and end up shooting up the sky. Then my platoon leader would call out, "Doc, get 'em," and I would track in on my target while it was crossing a rice paddy. You just took aim and the Stoner made targets go away. The bullets would just walk in on a target and make a big shield in front of you. The rounds from a Stoner were absolutely lethal.

A Stoner could fire at a rate of up to 1,000 rounds per minute and held a box of 100 or 150 rounds underneath it. You could change a box of ammo in about fifteen seconds. A Stoner would just scare the dickens out of anybody.

One time, when we were coming in on a helo, we started taking some ground fire. A Navy lieutenant was on board the bird carrying some orders from Ben Thuy. As we flew along, I saw these green tracers start coming up from the ground. The lieutenant was sitting on the door gunner's flak jacket, while I was just wearing my blue-and-gold T-shirt, swim trunks, and coral shoes.

As those tracers started to rise, I pulled up my Stoner and cocked back the bolt. As I looked out the side of the bird, the door gunner pointed out the spot

A fully camouflaged SEAL demonstrates the weapons used by the Teams in Vietnam. On the table in front of him are (from left to right) a China Lake modified Ithaca shotgun with an extended magazine and duckbill choke. Then there is an M79 grenade launcher, an M166A1 rifle, a bolt action heavy barrel sniper rifle, and a pump-action 4-shot 40mm grenade launcher. In front of the SEAL is an M60 light machine gun and he is holding up an M16A1 rifle with an XM148 40mm grenade launcher mounted underneath the barrel. The SEAL has slid the barrel of the XM1448 launcher forward for loading as part of his demonstration.

U.S. Navy

where the tracers were coming from. So I pointed down with my Stoner and pulled the trigger. The lieutenant managed to be just in the spot where my weapon was ejecting its hot, empty brass.

Then we were past the target and out of danger. The pilot refused to go back to let me shoot some more. The lieutenant, his nice, starched and pressed uniform a bit sweat-soaked now, didn't want to go. When I told him that it was the enemy shooting at us and we could shoot back, he said his orders had to go through. So that ended my Stoner fun for that trip.

We didn't always treat officers with such a lack of discipline; sometimes we were worse.

There was one time when carrying a Stoner didn't play to my advantage very well. Admiral Elmo Zumwalt was the COMNAVFORV (Commander, Naval Forces, Vietnam) in 1969 and he paid a visit to SEAFLOAT. He had with him a reporter, who has since become a big-time anchorman, and a small entourage of news types. According to our base security, this group of reporters basically had carte blanche to go anywhere they wanted.

A group of us were coming off an all-night ambush where we had made contact. It had been a long night, as our boat crew had been shot up pretty badly. For myself,

I smelled pretty bad, had already been doing CPR on one of our guys, and one of our three prisoners was seriously wounded. So things were kind of in disarray. Needless to say, we were all hungry, tired, cold, and dirty.

When we entered the mess hall, there were tablecloths laid out on everything. Guys with gold braid up and down their arms were running all around. Salutes were being given and returned. Not at all what our normal SOP looked like on SEAFLOAT. Gold braid and salutes can mark you as a target big time in a combat zone.

We were all coming back and just beginning to wrap up what we had to do. I had just finished securing a prisoner in the SEAL Team area when I left the compartment and ran right into a cameraman. When he asked me what I was doing, I told him that I was just putting some prisoners away and that he wasn't supposed to be in that area.

Like so many other reporters, he continued with his questions. He asked me if I was a SEAL, then asked me my rate. I told him my rank instead and he insisted on knowing what my rate was. When I finally told him I was a hospital corpsman, he just lost all expression in his face.

Then he asked me what it was I was carrying slung from my shoulder. Continuing my "dumb little me" routine, I told him it was my first-aid kit. He wanted to know what was on my other shoulder, so I told him it was my Stoner, my machine gun.

"Isn't it against the Geneva Convention for a medic to carry a weapon?" he asked. "Shouldn't you have a helmet with a red cross?"

With that last stupid line from him, all the fun went out of the situation and I just about lost my temper. Stepping right up into his face, I told him in some graphic detail just what he could do with his Aqua Velva–smelling fat ass and that he should immediately leave our area before he saw what a Stoner could really do.

Just about then, one of Admiral Zumwalt's aides came around and saved that reporter. I was also told that I probably wouldn't be the PR man for the SEALs anymore. And I didn't have much of a problem with that.

All of us tried to answer questions about our rates, or anything else really, as little as possible. There were people out and about who didn't know who we were, and we liked to keep it that way. And there were some who were quite jealous of us when they did know who we were.

At that time in Vietnam, the SEALs had pretty much all of the good deals. My mom never had to send me canned turkey for Christmas or Thanksgiving. We never went without steak, beer, or cigarettes when we wanted them. Even that day I ran into the reporter, we had our steaks.

Coming in from an operation, we cleaned our weapons before we cleaned up ourselves. The day that I ran into the reporter, we followed our usual procedure, but something got between us and our postoperation showers.

We could smell these steaks cooking, and being as hungry as we were, the smell was very tempting. Going up to the back door of the chow hall, we asked if we could get something to eat. The cook had no problem with that and we tramped into the chow hall, dirty camouflage uniforms, muddy boots, general aroma of the swamp, and all.

Some clown came up and asked if we would mind waiting until the officers came in and ate first. That didn't go over very well. Dave Langlois, one of the guys in our squad, had a few choice words with the gentleman who wanted us to wait. And with that, the individual left the chow hall to tell the aide, who in turn passed the message on to the admiral that the SEALs were in the chow hall.

The thing was, Admiral Zumwalt loved the SEALs. So he came into the chow hall and went around introducing himself to everyone. Things were pretty jovial and relaxed. The guys all shook his hand and said hello, but we were all a lot more interested in the food right then. We hadn't eaten in a day and the smells had raised our appetites quite a bit.

Then Admiral Zumwalt, COMNAVFORV, the boss of every U.S. naval asset in Vietnam, met Dave Langlois.

"Hello," Admiral Zumwalt said to Dave. "What's your name?"

"Dave," Langlois replied. "What's yours?"

Not taken aback a bit, Admiral Zumwalt answered, "Elmo."

"Hey," Dave said, shaking the admiral's hand, "how yah doing, Elmo? You gonna eat with us?"

With that invitation, Admiral Elmo Zumwalt sat down and ate lunch with the SEALs he thought so much of. And his aides waited nervously, hovering about the chow hall while we had our steaks.

Admiral Zumwalt's son was one of the boat drivers at SEAFLOAT. So the admiral made periodic visits down to our neck of the woods. Some years later Admiral Zumwalt felt personally responsible for losing his son to cancer. Our operational area around SEAFLOAT was heavily defoliated with Agent Orange and that later cost Elmo Jr. his life.

But Admiral Zumwalt has kept in touch with us over the years. And he still remembers eating lunch with that "colorful" bunch of SEALs at SEAFLOAT.

The camaraderie of the Teams then just can't be duplicated today. It's a solid example of the fact that you just can't go home again, things change. Back in 1969, 1970, the Teams were small, not much more than a few hundred of us total in the whole Navy. Each man knew almost every member of his Team. And we all took it very personally when we lost one of our own. And we celebrated with such zeal that we became famous for some of our antics.

Unfortunately, that reputation for hard partying has cost the SEAL community on occasion. Out at Niland, in the desert east of San Diego, we had our training camp. This training camp wasn't quite completed in 1970–71. We had a warrant officer by the name of Jess Tolison who was in charge of the camp. As one of Tolison's instructors, I would spend two weeks out at the camp and one week back in Coronado.

In the fall of 1971, we were ordered to build a pop-up range out at the Niland camp. Pop-up targets can react to bullet impacts and they can be electronically held down only to pop up again when a button is pushed. This lets classes run small-unit tactics and react to targets, knocking them down, as they patrol along.

Doctors back then had a different way of dealing with the high heat of the desert than we do now. Instead of the hydration that is done today, we dealt with the heat by taking salt tablets to replace the minerals lost through sweat. Instead, we should have been replacing the water lost. But the tablets were what was prescribed at that time.

One day, we had been working on the pop-up range for some twelve or fourteen hours. It was hot, sweaty work. Going into a small local town, we had dinner after work. Myself, Frank Bomar, Jess Tolison, and a number of other instructors were just relaxing a bit.

After dinner, Mr. Tolison said he was going to drive out to the camp and pick up several of the students who were still straggling along out there. Chief Bomar said he and I would go out in my car and meet up with Mr. Tolison later. About fifteen minutes later Frank Bomar and I had finished off the pitcher of beer we were sharing and headed out along the twisting road to camp.

We came around the curve near the camp and spotted the camp's six-by truck up ahead of us lying upside down. I grabbed up my medical kit and a flashlight and went up to the truck. There were no students in the back of the vehicle, but Mr. Tolison was trapped in the front cab, and he was severely injured.

Frank went back to get help. Mr. Tolison's injuries were so severe that just seeing them made me sick to my stomach. Because I vomited by the side of the road, some beer was left on the ground. When the state highway patrol came out and saw Mr. Tolison and the state of the car, and then got a whiff of the smell, they immediately jumped to the wrong conclusion.

They thought we had been partying pretty hard that night. And I couldn't convince them that we had just been coming back from dinner where a bunch of us had drunk nothing more than a few beers. And they wouldn't believe that Mr. Tolison hadn't had anything to drink at all.

Jess Tolison had been killed when that truck rolled over on the curve. The state police put in their report that the accident was alcohol-related. That was never the case that day. When I got back to the Team area, I told Captain Frank Kaine that the accident had certainly not been alcohol-related. But the state police even used a picture of the truck from that accident to illustrate how alcohol could kill.

That situation sent me a little bit ballistic. Our commanding officer at the time was not giving me a lot of support. The situation had left the hands of the SEAL community and others were making their own statements about it. But Mr. Tolison's friends and family should know that he never did anything wrong that day. Jess Tolison was a highly decorated SEAL with some five tours to Vietnam to his credit.

My CO got upset with my stance on that situation. And I pretty much just told him where to go. And he had the last word—he was going to send me out of the SEAL Team. But serving in the SEALs was strictly voluntary, so I told him that I was done. There wasn't a lot of time before my enlistment was up anyway, so I went over to UDT 13 for the few days it took to put my paperwork through.

Though we did party hearty, Mr. Tolison did not lose his life in an alcohol-related incident. The loyalties that built up during service with a SEAL Team did not come lightly. There wasn't one of us who wouldn't have laid his life down for his Teammate. And we might face a life and death situation every day. There is no "I" in SEAL Team; we were all members of the same family, the same Team.

That camaraderie is what makes the reunions and associations of the older SEALs so important for the SEAL Teams of today to see and experience. In today's Navy, there are thousands of SEALs. A member of the Teams today just doesn't have the opportunity to meet and know everyone today as he might have in the past.

And this is where McP's Irish Pub in Coronado comes into play a bit. This is a place where everyone in the Teams has a chance to meet Teammates from the past and the present, East Coast and West Coast.

In 1982, I was tired of the real estate business and I bought a bar in Coronado—now McP's Irish Pub and Grill at 1107 Orange Avenue. When the place opened in 1982, it was not the "kinder and gentler" military people speak of now. We had the Marines coming in from one base, and the SEALs coming in from another area, and the regular black-shoe Navy guys coming in from all over.

Boys being boys, the mix at McP's turned into a scuffle now and then. So I put up a Trident on the wall and told everyone that I was a former SEAL. More and more of the old Team guys came in. Gradually, we've become world famous as a watering hole of the SEALs in Coronado. From the time they're done with training until they retire as an admiral, you'll find SEALs dropping in at McP's. But the instructors won't let the students come up to my place until after they graduate.

A Navy SEAL today is probably the smartest, strongest of mind and fittest of body, young man who's ever come out of high school or college. Back when I became a Navy SEAL, the joke was that we were the ones who forgot and just stood there while everyone else stepped back when the call went out for volunteers. The SEAL of the 1960s is different from the SEALs of today, with two exceptions, and those are the physical fitness and the endurance.

But it doesn't matter whether you were a Navy SEAL, UDT operator, Marine Recon, or Army Special Forces, from then or now, we all put our pants on one leg at a time. There's a fair amount of teasing and good-natured ribbing between the services, and even among the SEALs of the different coasts, but there is an inherent camaraderie as well.

Back when the SEALs were first starting, they received a lot of their training from the U.S. Army Special Forces. And the SEALs gave a lot of the initial swimming training to the Marine Force Recon outfits. Today, the missions overlap so much that the lines between the units can get pretty blurred. We are all fellow warriors.

The men I served with in the Teams are probably the finest individuals I have ever known in my entire life. Unfortunately, after serving in the Teams, we all went our separate ways. The reunions help us catch up, but we sometimes don't stay as close as we should. But the guys I worked with are never far from my mind.

We gather sometimes just by chance, which is one of the great advantages I have in owning McP's. And then we'll rehash the old stories. And I'm sure some of the new kids are tired of hearing the same old lines from the dinosaurs of the Teams.

But the history of the SEALs is important if only for one reason. And that is to try and set straight some of the myths about the rootin'-tootin', rape and pillaging snake eaters of the Teams. These men are intelligent and hardworking. The men of the Teams today are doing one heck of a job of putting themselves in harm's way every day.

Far from what can ever be shown in books or on television, these guys are doing stuff around the world that just isn't for us to know about. They are out there on the sharp end, and talking about what they do, even generally, could increase the danger they face.

Popular fiction, TV shows, and movies portray a SEAL that isn't like the men I knew in the past or see today in the Teams. The term "Rambo" has been thrown around for years and refers to a loaner, a man who accomplishes anything by himself. That's just something that's made up; it's a fantasy. There is no such thing as a Rambo in the Teams, and there never will be. There just isn't a place for someone who will not make himself part of the Teams and work together with his Teammates.

There are some men from all the branches of the military who served during the Vietnam era who didn't fare well in civilian life. From what I've seen, most of the SEALs were just the opposite. The men of the Teams were not "Saigon cowboys." They saw things and did things that were very fierce and more than a little scary. But you don't see them sitting on a street homeless, crying their eyes out. Most of them have done very well on the outside. Partly because you never completely leave the Teams behind. They become a part of you.

As a corpsman, I could be in the middle of a firefight and suddenly have a man down. Once I knew my other guys had me covered, the perimeter was secured, and they had a base of fire laid down, then I was in on the wounded man. I just wouldn't see or hear anything else; I didn't have to. If a bad guy was to come up and kill me, *it would be because my other Teammates didn't protect me, and that just wouldn't happen while they were alive.*

All I was concerned with was getting the wounded man stable and assessing his situation. The combat would be taken care of. It's scary at first when you look back on it. But when your adrenaline gets flowing, just your job becomes important. I could see and hear my patient, and nothing else.

When I operated with my Teammates, my level of confidence was so high that I thought I was a neurosurgeon and all of my Teammates were Superman. There's was nothing I wouldn't do to save a life in that situation. Sometimes, I may have screwed up a bit, but I always gave it my best. My Teammates deserved no less.

There was nothing I was ever scared of when I had my other guys around me.

The stigma a corpsman has to overcome right away is that he's not as good as everyone else because he doesn't have a BUD/S-class number. I graduated as a special operations technician at the same time that Class 45 did. We were trained to be operators; we couldn't have functioned in the field otherwise. The only thing we were lacking in our training was a formal Hell Week, and they really made up for that in Key West, during the demolition phase of training.

Honestly, if I had had to go through regular BUD/S training, I don't know if I'd have graduated or not. I don't know if I'd have had that desire to continue that you just have to feel. I had already been to Vietnam with the Marines before I joined the Teams. But I do know that I was a good operator and I was a hell of a good corpsman for the Teams.

As a corpsman, I felt capable of doing anything my three books would have allowed me to do. Those books are the PDR [Physician's Desk Reference], the Merck Manual, and Current Therapy. Even for a doctor, if it isn't in those three books, chances are you don't need to do it.

■ Chapter 47

To Bring Them Home: Bright Light and the POWs

The SEALs in Vietnam were in a unique position to take immediate advantage of any intelligence that came their way. Using their own intelligence networks, as well as information brought to them from other sources, the SEALs could quickly put together as complete a picture as possible of a given target. And with their experience, organization, and support, the SEALs could react to a sudden target faster than any other U.S. military organization.

Within hours of confirming a target, a SEAL leader could assemble his operating unit, support, transportation, and communications. Authorization for an operation was often not needed for some of the SEALs' operational areas. This let the SEALs react to some of the hardest, and to some the most important, targets of the Vietnam War—the rescue of POWs.

Though no U.S. POWs were ever successfully rescued from enemy hands during the war, the SEALs conducted a number of operations that released South Vietnamese prisoners, some of whom had been held in horrible conditions for extended lengths of time.

The small size of the SEALs' operational units gave them the speed to act on fragile, time-sensitive information. Any SEAL in Vietnam would drop everything in order to go on a POW op. The power of the desire to release fellow soldiers held by the VC or NVA is something only someone who has been in combat can completely understand.

On several occasions, the SEALs put together swift yet complex operations to liberate POWs. The U.S. military considered the POW issue so important that they eventually gave the POW liberation missions their own code name— BRIGHT LIGHT.

In addition to operating in very small, independent units, the SEALs and the UDTs worked as part of much larger operations. One of these missions was

In a haunting illustration of the Vietnam War, this exhibit was set up in the Pentagon. Depicted is the environment of a North Vietnamese prison cell where 178 Navy men spent up to eight and one-half years in captivity. Thirty-six of these men died while imprisoned, and almost all of the POWs suffered regular torture. The small oval lumps are roaches, the larger one to the left is a rat.

U.S. Navy

the rescue of American POWs held in North Vietnam. It was a huge and involved operation, cloaked in secrecy. But every effort was worth the cost as far as the men on the ground were concerned, the Teams among them.

Philip L. "Moki" Martin, Lieutenant, USN (Ret.)

When I was about five or six years old, growing up in Hawaii, I remember seeing the UDTs training off of Maui, blowing up the old concrete obstacles. There were several men I got to know just briefly who told me that if I was ever to join the Navy, the job they did was what I would want to do.

My entire life has been spent in the water. I began scuba diving after only five minutes of instruction and enjoyed it right away. It was the Richard Widmark movie The Frogmen *that pretty much sealed up my adult life. I was only about ten or twelve years old, but after seeing that movie, I knew that being a Frogman was what I wanted to do.*

A few years later my plan was to enlist in the Navy right after graduating from high school. Once in the Navy, I would volunteer for the UDT, and that was exactly what happened, though it took a little longer than I would have liked. I enlisted in the Navy in 1960, and it took me about four years before I received orders for UDT Replacement training (UDTR). I was assigned to Class 35, and we began training in January 1965.

My sole intention in volunteering for the Teams back then was to join the UDTs. The SEAL Teams were new at the time and very little was known about them. There had been some very brief articles about them in the Navy's All Hands magazine and almost nowhere else. The SEALs were kind of a super-secret thing, and supposedly they carried guns and crawled around in the mud. That wasn't what I wanted to do. I wanted to be a Frogman. That had been my goal and my dream for a long time.

UDTR training was fairly easy for me—in the water. Having practically grown up in the sea, I was a very good and powerful swimmer. Handling the surf was nothing new; I had been surfing for years. And being from Hawaii, I hated the cold water. So I became a much faster swimmer than I had been, just to stay warm.

It was my dislike of the cold water that made me the fastest swimmer in the class. Moving hard and fast just helped keep me warm. But there were a couple of times when I outdistanced my swim buddies, swam off and left them behind. That wasn't something that was allowed in the Teams, and the instructors had ways of dealing with it.

Barry Enoch was one of Class 35's instructors. And when I left my swim buddy behind on one swim, he dealt with my transgression. He had a rope, a really heavy one, that was about five feet long and had loops at each end. Instructor Enoch looped one end of the rope around my neck, and the other end around my swim buddy's neck. Now if I wanted to outswim my swim buddy, I would have to tow him along. And if he wanted to lag behind, he would have to put up with strangling. But I still remained a good swimmer.

There was some trouble in the water for me during my first cast-and-recovery training. The trick, they told us, was to kick real hard with your fins as the pickup boat was approaching and try to get up to where your waist was out of the water. I was trying so hard in the kicking that I forgot that you were also supposed to lock your arm and shoulder into one position so that the rubber loop [snare] wouldn't give you too strong a jerk when it went over your upraised arm.

Well, I forgot, and the loop jerked, and it just about ripped my arm out of its socket. But since we had to do cast and recoveries eight or ten times that day, I kept going. In fact, I was surprised that no one dislocated their shoulders during that evolution.

But once we got the hang of it, cast and recovery was really fun to do. This was something only the UDT did. It was straight out of the Widmark movie, and the UDTs had been doing it consistently since WWII. For me, being a part of that was kind of the culmination of a dream. Now I was really connected to those UDT men who had gone before me. And propably they had also thought it monotonous to do after having done it ten or twelve times in one day.

What I did have trouble with was the runs. Running had never been my sport. And PT, the physical training part, got tougher and tougher as UDTR went along. But I just kept hanging in there, sometimes making it through on just pure guts alone.

The hardest parts of training for me were the long field operations during the last phase of training. These were training evolutions that went on for several days. They just seemed to go on and on, and caused tremendous physical breakdown. But you just had to keep going.

The long field operations didn't take place until after we had already completed twenty weeks of training. Now we were doing these final exercises and they just seemed to go on forever. Those last three weeks of training were, for me at least, actually worse than Hell Week.

We were operating from a ship off San Clemente Island, and there was never enough rest. It was just go, go, go . . . constantly, without stop.

But that last day of training, when we all stood on the grinder during graduation, that was worth all of our work. That feeling of accomplishment was unlike anything else. Even though I was only twenty-two years old at the time, and including everything that has happened to me since, there has been nothing to compare to it. While still a young man, I had accomplished the dream of my life, I was a member of the UDT, I was a Frogman.

After graduation, I went on to UDT 12. It wasn't long before I was making deployments to Vietnam. At that time, in 1965, Vietnam was really just starting. The West Coast UDTs were sending just some short detachments, operating from

Subic Bay in the Philippines to Da Nang and to ships working off the coast of South Vietnam.

But off of Vietnam, we were able to do all of the things that I had been trained to do as a UDT operator. We did hydrographic recons up and down the Vietnamese coast. We were even assigned to do two underwater demolition jobs. Those were kind of rare in UDT at the time; most of our jobs involved doing surveys of beaches and rivers all over the place. But we actually had a chance to go in and blow up some rocks and other obstacles to clear the way for some U.S. Marine landings.

In April 1967, I joined SEAL Team One after I had completed several deployments to Vietnam with UDT 12. My entire platoon from UDT 12 was transferred over to SEAL Team One to become a SEAL platoon and augment the Team. As I remember, this happened three or four times during that period of the war. SEAL Team One had the

On the coast of South Vietnam, two UDT operators hold flagpoles so swimmers off-shore can align with the beach. They are conducting beach surveys for likely landing beaches for U.S. forces. These surveys were conducted well before the U.S. committed large numbers of ground troops to the Vietnam War. The men are armed against possible Viet Cong attack.

U.S. Navy

major commitment of manpower to the Vietnam War and they needed to build up the SEAL Team fairly quickly. Transferring over an entire UDT platoon allowed the platoon to maintain its cohesion as a unit and also helped to speed up its training as a SEAL platoon.

The only integration done with the UDT platoon was to add to our number a few—maybe three or more—SEALs who already had Vietnam combat experience behind them. Those experienced SEALs helped season the UDT platoon and provide them with additional leadership. Then the UDT platoon went through SEAL basic indoctrination training—what was called cadre training back then.

The eight-and-a-half-to-nine-week-long cadre training program had the entire platoon working together on everything from communications to insertions and extractions. We also received a lot of weapons training and some "kitchen" [improvised] demolitions. But most of the training cycle concentrated on small-unit tactics.

For small-unit tactics, we worked together initially as a whole platoon of fourteen men. Then we would break down into smaller six-and seven-man squads. This was where we learned the SEAL methods of operating in Vietnam—how to conduct patrols, ambushes, and other operations.

My first SEAL deployment to Vietnam was in August 1967 with Alfa Platoon. Our platoon commanders were then Lieutenant Joe DeFloria and Lieutenant (j.g) Tom Nelson. Tommy Nelson and I had been in the same UDTR training class and Joe DeFloria had been in the class right after mine. Besides those two officers, everyone else in the platoon had either been in my training class or was from the classes of that era, 1965–1966.

Alfa Platoon deployed straight to Nha Be, a little Navy base about fifteen miles or so south of Saigon, on the Long Tau River just above the Rung Sat Special Zone. Most of our operations in the Rung Sat were ambushes. We ran a lot of ambushes against waterborne traffic to try and interdict the VC chains of communication and supply in the Rung Sat.

For our first combat operation in Vietnam, Alfa Platoon was taken out on an ambush, led by one member of the SEAL Team platoon we were relieving. I believe the SEAL Team One operator leading us that op was Chief Ted Kassa. Chief Kassa stayed with us for several operations. Kind of "getting our feet wet" and becoming a little used to the operating area.

That system of introduction to an operating area was very well done, I thought. It got everyone in the right frame of mind and gave us a lot of confidence in operating as a platoon and smaller squads or fire teams.

Doing the work I had trained for was something I enjoyed. The platoon had trained on all different kinds of ops before leaving for Vietnam. But the ambush was the one we had spent the most time on. So when we did our first combat ambush, I thought, This is it! I'm getting to do what I was trained to do.

Little did I realize that just sitting in ambush and shooting at the enemy was really not my idea of SEAL Team work. After a while I thought there were a lot of other kinds of operations that we should be doing—more intelligence gathering, for example. Of course a good ambush could result in gathering hot intelligence on an area. But it was the sneak-and-peek kind of thing that I really wanted to be doing.

There are a number of operations from that first combat tour that stand out in my memory. Mostly, they're the ones where we went out on a straight patrol looking for things. On one such op, we not only found some ammunition caches, we uncovered a whole ammunition factory.

We had been just patrolling through the jungle, looking to confirm some of the things that our intelligence people had told us were happening in that area. Moving from point to point to point though the jungle, we just kept checking things out. Eventually we reached a place where it got really muddy and we just couldn't move any farther.

The mud ended up being our biggest enemy in the Rung Sat. The whole area was a big tidal zone, and for several hours every day when the tides were out, you would find large areas of mud stretching out all over. Almost all of our travel in the Rung Sat was in the mud. Most of the time it was only about waist-deep. But on this particular op, the mud was up to our chests, and we just couldn't move anymore.

We tried to bring some equipment from the ammunition factory back out with us. But we were already so loaded down with weapons and ammunition, we couldn't add any more weight to our loads. The patrol had already gone 2,000 maybe 3,000 yards into the Rung Sat. To get to where we needed to be to extract by boat would have taken another 2,000 or 3,000 yards of travel. It had taken us half a day to get to where we were; it would have been well into the night before we could have gotten out on foot.

The mud training we had all received during UDTR really helped. We learned to kind of slide across the top of the stuff rather than actually walk through it. But you could only do that for so long before you were completely exhausted. And in the Rung Sat, you also had to contend with the nipa palms and the mangrove swamp. The plants all kind of grow together and you can't really go across that kind of terrain, you just have to go around it.

It was during the daylight hours on that patrol when we finally bogged down in the mud and had to call for extraction. There wasn't anywhere the extraction helicopter could set down to pick us up, so we used the McGuire rig in combat for the first time.

The McGuire rig was named after the Army Special Forces sergeant major who designed it, Charles McGuire. It was a 100-foot rope with a loop on the end and a padded canvas seat. You sat in the seat and rode it like a child's swing. The extraction bird we had come in only had three rigs—or "strings," as they were called—and only one guy could ride on a rig at one time.

The trip on a McGuire rig was a wild one. The helicopter would drop the lines, you'd get in the seat, and it would lift you up like a giant elevator. But the rigs couldn't be drawn into the helicopter. So you stayed in the seat until the bird could set you down someplace safe. And that seat would be moving through the air at something like ninty knots, hundreds of feet above the jungle canopy.

It was kind of neat to have that happen, but it was kind of hairy at the same time. Since the helicopter only had three McGuire rigs, it could only pull three people out at one time. As we had nine people in the patrol, that meant three trips. When it got down to just the platoon leader, the radioman, and myself, the ten or fifteen minutes it took the extraction bird to leave and come back seemed to go one for an eternity. In spite of our working in small groups, we weren't used to being just three SEALs alone in the jungle, right in the middle of VC territory. Especially not in broad daylight.

I did three tours of duty in Vietnam with UDT 12, all of them operating out of Subic Bay in the Philippines. Then I went back for three more tours with SEAL Team One, the last one being from the submarine Grayback for Operation THUNDERHEAD.

Along with a number of the older SEALs who had been operating in the Rung Sat and the Mekong Delta, I had always thought that the intelligence-gathering missions were of primary importance. The ambush really wasn't the best way to gather intelligence; we should have been working more along the lines of abduction of key enemy personnel. It was when you snatched up a target that you could interrogate him at length and learn a lot more than you could learn from just a body. And so eventually the Viet Cong infrastructure, the VCI, did become the primary target of a number of SEAL operations.

As we started our first tours in Vietnam, the SEALs did a lot of mud sloshing, walking around and setting ambushes up. Occasionally, we hit a tax collector or somebody who was kind of low in the Viet Cong infrastructure. But as we continued to operate, we got smarter and smarter and learned how to fight that war. In the latter part of 1967 and onward, we started hitting more intelligence-rich targets. These were things that had more to do with the coordination of VC operations, the leaders who knew more about what went on in a province than just an average VC would. And this intelligence could lead to bigger and better targets, even the location of active Viet Cong POW camps where American prisoners were being held. That was the big target for a lot of us.

I was with Delta Platoon on my second tour in-country; we were based out of Cam Ranh Bay and operating in the area of Nah Trang Harbor on the shore of the South China Sea. Specifically, we were looking for VCI leaders, high-level Viet Cong. And we had a working relationship with the Army Special Forces in the area that gave us an excellent intelligence net. So we tried to target specific individuals we had heard about, catch them alive while they were on the move or holed up in what they thought were safe areas.

Right about the time when we had the operations going, my fire team, the first squad of Delta Platoon, moved down to the Nam Can area, the very southern tip of South Vietnam. We set up a little operating base with the help of an Army MAT (Mobile Advisory Team). The operations we conducted in the area were in preparation for the Navy's setting up SEAFLOAT and then, later, SOLID ANCHOR.

While we were down in the Nam Can, the rest of our platoon, under the direction of our platoon leader, Lieutenant (j.g.) Joseph "Bob" Kerrey, continued the operations out of Nha Trang. On 14 March 1969, Delta Platoon conducted an operation that was kind of a culmination of all the little intel-gather ops up until then. Delta Platoon—Second Squad really—had built up a tracking record of sorts for this one VCI's movements. Now they had a chance to target this one individual for capture.

Final intel for the op showed up late at night, and the squad had to hustle to get the operation under way in time. The SEALs just dropped what they were doing and headed for Hon Toi Island in Nha Trang Harbor.

The VC on the island, we later learned, were setting up to conduct a limpeteer attack [a swimmer attack using limpit mines] against U.S. shipping in the area. But that wasn't what the SEALs were going in for. The VC were assembling a really high-level VCI and NVA meeting for that night, and that was the SEAL target. Delta was in the right place at the right time, but things didn't go well for them when they hit the VC group.

The island wasn't much more than a very large rock sticking up from the water. When the SEALs inserted into the island, Lieutenant Kerrey took the team up and over the main rock cliff that made up the island. The squad broke up into fire teams for the attack. While they were sneaking around the VC base on the island, some noise alerted the base and all hell broke loose.

Lieutenant Kerrey rallied his men and they were pouring in fire on the VC when a grenade went off near him. The blast just about destroyed his leg. In spite of his wounds and pain, he directed everyone to set up a perimeter and secure a helicopter landing zone. The team extracted after raising real havoc with the VC.

Later Kerrey was medevaced back to the U.S. But the next day, when they went back in to check the VC camp, they found a bunch of limpet mines, made in either China or North Vietnam. So that was how we learned that they were getting ready for a major limpeteer attack against our shipping. There was also a bunch of intel picked up during the fight and the next day that showed the SEALs had broken up a really high-level meeting.

If that limpeteer attack had gone through, it would have been a big surprise operation against our forces. Nha Trang and Cam Ranh Bay were located in relatively calm areas, so a swimmer limpeteer attack would have done some real damage. And it was prevented because the SEALs were going in on another target on the island.

Delta Platoon returned to Coronado in July 1969. As the war was winding down in the early 1970s, the SEAL platoons were slowly being moved out of Vietnam. Some platoons were stationed aboard ships and others were sent to Okinawa as their base of operations. For my third tour to Vietnam, in 1972, I was sent to Okinawa as a member of Alfa Platoon. We were the Naval Special Warfare Western Pacific Detachment (WESTPAC), a SEAL detachment placed at the disposal of the Navy's Third Fleet.

We were just in Okinawa as a contingency platoon, just to be ready in case

In San Francisco Bay, California, the LPSS-574 *Grayback* moves out to sea. Traveling on the surface, the two rounded hangar doors on her bulging bow are in plain sight in this picture.

U.S. Navy

something came up. So we trained out of Okinawa and Subic Bay in the Philippines. We also spent some time doing cold-water training in Korea. But it was down in Subic Bay that our most interesting operation came about.

Station at Subic Bay was the LPSS 315 Grayback, originally commissioned as the SSG 574 back in 1958. The Grayback was a conventionally powered diesel-electric submarine that had originally been intended to carry the Regulus nuclear missile. Up on the bow of the Grayback were two large hangars, intended to house that missile.

Back in the 1950s, the Grayback would have had to surface to fire her missiles. Once the deck was out of the water, the clamshell doors on the hangar would open and the Regulus missiles could be taken out on their launch trolleys. The Regulus missile wasn't a rocket; it was more of a winged cruise missile. So the wings had to be unfolded before the missile could be launched. Once the Regulus was off the deck, the hangar doors could be closed and the Grayback could dive back under the surface.

In the 1960s, the two bow hangars on the Grayback were converted to lockout chambers for the SDVs, the four-man Mark VI, Mod II swimmer delivery vehicles used in the Teams at that time. These SDVs, known as the Two Boats, were wet-type underwater vehicles that could carry a crew of two men and two passengers much farther than the men could swim. Because they were wet-type vehicles, the passengers and crew were exposed to the water that flooded the hull, and had to wear breathing equipment during their trip.

The Grayback's bow hangars had two parts, what was called a wet side—it was from here that they launched the boats—and a dry side. The SEALs lived on the dry

Though much lighter when under water, these SDVs have to be manhandled along the deck of the *Grayback* while being loaded. The size of the hangars and their massive doors is illustrated by the UDT operators walking through the open hatchway.

side of the bulkhead. On the other side of the bulkhead, on the wet side, where you had access to the hangars up on the deck, lived the UDT platoon that crewed the SDVs with drivers and technicians.

As far as we knew, we were just going to be the SEAL contingency platoon assigned to the Grayback. We would be available if an operation came up that called for our skills. As it turned out, an operation had been in the planning stages, but we knew nothing about that when we went aboard the Grayback at Subic.

As the others were planning the operation, we were working with the UDT platoon and their SDVs, mostly just riding as passengers aboard the Two Boats. The SDVs would leave the Grayback while the mother submarine was still underwater. They would carry us to a certain point, we would get out, and the SDVs would then leave. Returning later, the SDVs would rendezvous with us for the return trip. We then got aboard and returned to the Grayback.

What we were training for was Operation THUNDERHEAD. The mission was basically to liberate some U.S. prisoners out of North Vietnam. Intelligence gathered by U.S. aircraft and other means had indicated that some Americans were going to escape from the Hanoi Hilton. The escaping POWs were to travel down the river

An artist's rendition of the USS *Grayback* releasing SDVs while underwater.

U.S. Navy

to the Gulf of Tonkin. Once there, the men would signal anyone who could pick them up.

During our briefing on the operation, we were told that the Grayback *would be going in close to some islands that were offshore from certain rivers. The submarine would just sit there offshore while we went in to the island to try and spot the escaping POWs.*

The SDVs and their UDT crews were going to transit from the Grayback *to this one island. Once the SDVs reached the island, the two SEAL passengers were to get out and insert onto the island while the SDV returned to the* Grayback. *On the island, the SEALs would set up an observation post where they could observe the mouth of the river off on the mainland.*

The SEALs were just to sit there on the island for one or two days and then get relieved by another pair of SEALs from the Grayback. *The object was to watch for a signal from the escaped POWs and render them all assistance possible. The specific signal we would be watching for would be a series of red lights set up in a certain configuration at night. During the day, the signal would be red flags.*

We would hardly be the only people on the lookout for these signals. The U.S. Fleet had helicopters flying up and down the shoreline of North Vietnam, as close as they dared to come to the NVA antiaircraft defenses. But the island where we were going to set up our observation post had the best view of the mouth of the target river.

The day the prisoners were supposed to escape was known, and we went in to the island a day or so ahead of that. That way, we'd be in position well before the escaping POWs should be able to arrive on scene.

We had no real idea as to the size of this mission. Our part was well known to us and we had been thoroughly briefed. What we didn't know was that there was a large chunk of the U.S. Fleet also offshore watching for these POWs to come out. We didn't know if there was going to be just one POW or more. Later I learned that between two and five POWs were supposed to be in on the breakout. But we were prepared to get out as many as we could.

Our job was to secure the POWs and get them back to the Grayback or call in one of the helicopters to extract them. We would do anything we had to in order to get the men out before the NVA knew what had happened.

But no prisoners escaped from North Vietnam during Operation THUNDER-HEAD. And the operation proved very costly to us. We lost our platoon commander on a helicopter insertion on the day after we started the first operation.

On the first underwater insertion, we lost an SDV. The vehicle had bad problems negotiating the tremendous current coming out of the target river. At the time we were using all of our newest systems to try and get us to a certain point. What the systems told us was that we were fighting this heavy current.

We had to get to the blind side of the island, where the helicopters couldn't go. That was where we were going to set up our op. But the SDV ran out of battery power and ended up dead in the water. All of us from the SDV were picked up by a search-and-rescue helicopter and returned to the U.S. Fleet. Most of the ships off-shore didn't even know the Grayback was in the area, so our appearance came as a surprise to some people.

That night, we were going to cast off from a helicopter to get back to the Grayback and kind of rethink our insertion plans for the island. It was during the helicopter insertion in the vicinity of the Grayback that we lost Lieutenant Dry.

The platoon commander for Alfa Platoon in 1972 was Lieutenant Melvin S. "Spence" Dry. He ended up being the last SEAL loss of the Vietnam War. During our helicopter insertion, we jumped from the bird into the water and Lieutenant Dry broke his neck when he impacted on some flotsam in the water. Because of the heavy secrecy regarding Operation THUNDERHEAD, his loss wasn't reported as being due to a combat operation. Instead, his family was told he was lost in a training accident.

It has only been in the last several years that I've been able to speak openly about what happened to Lieutenant Dry, how he actually died. All of us in the platoon were disappointed that more wasn't made public about Operation THUNDER-HEAD. Even though no POWs were ever rescued during that op—much, much later it came out that the POWs never made it out of the prison in the first place—we felt it was a tremendous effort.

I've always believed that a lot of the success of the SEALs in Vietnam and else-where was due to their methods of insertion and extraction from a target. They would go in where no one would expect anyone to be able to go. And they went in quietly, and came out just as quietly.

The insertion on the night that Spence Dry died, a lot of things happened that we, as SEALs, would not have done if it had been left entirely up to us. The helicopter insertion, even at night, was something we had done before. But the height and speed of the bird was questionable. And this isn't just my opinion; everyone who exited the bird that night had the same thought. We learn from our mistakes, but in the Teams, those mistakes can be very costly.

The Navy SEALs are not perfect; we make mistakes. I've never thought of the SEALs as a perfect specimen of a weapons system or a group of individuals. We were probably the best-trained men available to do that kind of work—basically, unconventional warfare, as it was first called; now it's referred to as special warfare.

As we saw in Vietnam, the SEALs had more of their own destiny within their control than most other units. The young platoon officers were almost totally in charge of an operation. If they ran across something that was not in the original plan or patrol order, they had the option to make the decision right there in the field to take care of the bigger or better target.

It was very important that the officers could do that. And keeping that "can-do" tradition of the Frogman and the SEALs alive helps them make the decision to take on the bigger target.

A Frogman is now a state of mind; it is someone who has volunteered to do any-thing—to go anywhere and do anything they have to do in order to get the mission done. And they will get the mission done before anyone expects them to. Our shared training in BUD/S helps give us all a base experience to build on. And the brotherhood of the Teams supports each man doing his best in support of his Teammates.

The hierarchy in the Teams is different from any other place in the Navy, or even in most of the military. Officers and enlisted men all go through training together, and that makes us all the same as far as being an operator in the Teams goes. But we're still in the Navy, so there has to be a distinction between the officers and the enlisted men.

But my experience in the Teams has shown me the neat thing about the officers in the UDT and the SEALs is how they always asked the opinion of the men they led. Everyone, from the old, grizzled, experienced chief to the young, shaved-headed, new seaman, was asked at one time or another how they thought some-thing would work, or what they thought of a situation.

The officer always made the final decision about how something would be done. But officers were never above learning from their men.

What I came away with from the SEAL Teams was the belief that I can go on, in spite of things like a disabling injury. During my basic UDT training class, and while serving in the UDT and SEAL platoons, I learned that the toughest thing to face is adverse conditions. Whether it is in your job, or your family, or in your life outside of the Teams, once you have been in the Teams, you learn how to reach down inside yourself and get through the toughest times.

You can't stay in the Team your entire life. But I love the guys who are serving today just as I do the men I served with so long ago. It is a great organization, and a great place to learn, both about the world and about yourself.

Today, I work in a field very separated from what I did in the Teams, and that's art, painting. And I think it's neat that I can look at art today from another set of eyes, those of an operator from the UDTs and the SEAL Team. And it was my experience in the Teams that gave me the ability to do that.

We worked on the sharp end, faced dangers and overcame them in the Teams. Vietnam was the ultimate test of the fighting ability and spirit of the Teams, and some of us reveled in it. It was where we served best, in combat. I've known SEALs who had just come off the plane from Vietnam and they immediately went over to the platoon officer of the next deploying platoon back to Southeast Asia. All they wanted to know was if there was any way they could join that platoon, trade with somebody, in order to go back over.

■ Chapter 48

The Last Detachment

SEAL detachments had been in Vietnam since their earliest deployments. Detachment ECHO had been part of the SEALs program of instruction to South Vietnamese unconventional warfare units. The men trained by the SEALs from this detachment were some of the Vietnamese individuals who conducted the maritime operations of OP-34A.

Excerpt from SEAL Team One, Command and Control History 1969
Enclosure (2) (b) BASIC NARRATIVE
OPERATIONS
Page 2. [DECLASSIFIED from SECRET]
   c. Detachment ECHO is under the operational control of Commander U.S. Military Assistance Command, Vietnam. SEAL Detachment ECHO presently [December 1969] consisting of two enlisted personnel acts in the

But Det Echo ended along with a number of other SEALs detachments as the conduct of the war was turned over to the South Vietnamese in the early 1970s. The training and advising of the LDNN—a brother unit of warriors who also worked in a maritime environment—had been part of the SEALs mission.

Originally, LDNN stood for Lien Doc Nguoi Nhai, meaning "soldiers who fight under the sea." Later, though the initials didn't change, LDNN stood for Lien Doi Nguoi Nhai, and later still, it was changed to Lien Doan Nguoi Nhai. *Doi* means "team" and *doan* means "group"; the name change reflected the growth of the LDNNs, the South Vietnamese SEALs, during the war.

The final full detachment for the SEALs, Det Sierra, was an advisory group for the LDNNs.

With the disestablishing of MACV-SOG in April 1972, the Strategic Technical Directorate Assistance Team (STDAT) 158 was commissioned to replace it. The last SEALs from Det Sierra went over to STDAT 158 when Sierra was ended. The mission of STDAT 158 was to assist and advise the Vietnamese. It was as a member of STDAT 158 that Lieutenant Tom Norris conducted his behind-the-lines operation to rescue downed pilots.

With this final assignment, the SEALs were again working with their Vietnamese brothers, the LDNN, as they had at the beginning.

There is some difficulty with describing the Navy SEALs and some of the individuals who have performed their actions so well. The term "hero" is not used in the Teams; in fact, it is considered a very serious insult in some situations. To the men of the Teams, a hero is someone who goes out of his way for his own glory, not for the betterment of his fellow warriors. In doing so, a "hero" can put the rest of his unit in jeopardy because he isn't concentrating on doing his job.

In the SEALs and the UDTs, the Team is everything. Whether it is your squad, platoon, Team, or just your swim buddy, the individual does what is best for the whole. An operator serves the greater good, not himself.

A Teammate is someone you trust with your life, just as he trusts you with his.

Michael Thornton, Lieutenant, USN (Ret.)

Back in the 1950s, I saw the movie The Frogmen *starring Richard Widmark. This was where I first learned about the UDTs. Since I already loved the water, that movie helped me decide that I wanted to be a Navy Frogman. The reason I wanted to be in the Navy was that I had seen the movie about the five Sullivan brothers who were all assigned to the same ship during World War II.*

Those five Sullivan brothers all drowned while trying to save one another after their ship was hit. I've always been a tight-knit-family type of person and that story helped make the Navy appeal to me. And being a Frogman looked like it would be the best job in the Navy.

I didn't know anything about the SEAL Teams when I enlisted in the Navy; no one did. They were still so secret that very little real information had come out about them. And I still had to go through the regular Navy channels to get to the UDTs.

When I first came into the Navy, you had to spend some time in the fleet before you could volunteer for UDTR. But I was kind of lucky in that my ship was decommissioned after I'd been on her only a few months. Since I had already passed the UDT screening tests, I went straight to Coronado.

So in 1968, I became a member of Class 49, West Coast. That was a cold winter class; in fact, it snowed in San Diego that year. Training for me was hell. Our instructors were people like Vince Olivera, Terry Moy, and Dick Allen. These were just super guys. You could tell these men had a lot of power in them just by looking at them, and a tremendous amount of knowledge. You might not have loved these in-

Engineman First Class Michael E. Thornton, the last SEAL Medal of Honor recipient of the Vietnam War.

structors while you were going through training, but there was no way you couldn't respect them.

Everyone tends to remember some specific incidents about when they went through training. For me, that incident was when we were coming back from the mud flats during Hell Week. One four-man boat crew had called some girls up and told them where we would be and when. They came down in a flatbed truck and picked us up along with our IBS.

We were driving back down the Strand from the mud flats, more than covered in mud ourselves. While all of our classmates were paddling along in that cold ocean, we were riding in the back of that truck drinking hot coffee. That didn't last too damned long though. Vince Olivera and Terry Moy pulled up behind us in an ambulance. That was when all hell broke loose. It pays to be a winner; it does not pay to get caught pulling a fast one.

It was probably my own fear of failure that got me through Hell Week. For myself, I had always tried to set goals in my life. Before going to UDTR, the goals I had set were always smaller ones, set one at a time, and I had never pushed out there too far. But UDTR pushed you to your personal limits, and far beyond that. Passing that training was a huge goal I had set for myself. But I knew I could do it, and I wanted to prove to myself that I could indeed complete it. I didn't want to fail, to quit.

As far as I'm concerned, everyone thinks about quitting during training. Anyone who says they never thought about quitting is either lying, or they've just forgotten about it. The time I really wanted to quit, Vince Olivera had a water hose down my throat and I couldn't say that I wanted to quit. I just couldn't speak; if I did, I would have drowned. And I have to thank Vince Olivera for getting me past that moment of weakness.

Graduation was a great day of accomplishment for me and my fellow classmates. Class 49 had started with 129 guys, and we graduated with only 16 of us standing there that day. I think there was a great feeling of satisfaction in our whole group. There was a strong feeling of togetherness, brotherhood, a kind of family atmosphere in the knowledge that we had reached that day, that goal, through all of our efforts.

There was the additional plus for me in that I knew I had been selected to go to SEAL Team One. A lot of the instructors during our training had been in SEAL Team. So they spoke about the SEALs to us. Everyone was saying the SEALs were kind of the elite of the elite, so naturally that was where I wanted to go. But there were a lot of guys in my class who still wanted to go to the UDT; they wanted to be Frogmen. But I felt very comfortable on land, just as I did in the water. So the SEALs held a great deal of appeal to me.

A number of us arrived at SEAL Team One and immediately left for jump school. When we returned, it was time for SEAL indoctrination training. Little time was wasted between my arrival at the SEAL Team and my being ready to be sent over to Vietnam with a platoon.

Once we had it together as far as general training went, we got it together as a platoon. A number of the guys from my training class were in Charlie Platoon, and we had leadership in the form of men like our leading petty officer (LPO), Barry Enoch, and Lieutenant Tom Boyhan.

The bulk of Charlie Platoon was made up of men from either my UDTR class or the class that had graduated just behind ours. This group included one of my best friends, Hal Kuykendall. So we started working as a platoon, and a family basically. Then we deployed to Vietnam.

Deploying to combat was frightening in some ways. But I've always said that fear is good for you in some ways. You can use fear in a positive manner, taking the fear and using it to make you more up on the situation around you, and sharper about everything else. It can make you more aware of your fellowman, those on both sides of the fight. You have to learn to use fear, because it will be there. If you're not afraid about going into combat, then you're not quite right in the head.

During my first combat operation, I was scared to death. It was supposed to be a simple breaking-in op. Something we were taken out on to show us the area and teach us some of the local ways of operating. The only thing was that we stumbled in on a district-level meeting of some serious Viet Cong leaders. And when we showed up, all hell broke loose. The simple patrol turned into a serious firefight.

None of our guys were injured, but I think we ended up with something like a seventeen body count on the enemy. All of our guys were pretty well psyched up after that, but it was a strange way of introducing ourselves into that type of situation.

Being a big guy, I carried a big gun and was assigned as an M60 gunner in the platoon. And I carried a lot of ammunition to feed that big gun. On an op, I would pack anywhere from 1,200 to 1,800 rounds in belts to feed my M60. I never wanted to run out of ammo, which I had seen happen to other guys. It wouldn't be too much fun to be out on an op and discover that your weapon had turned into not much more than a twenty-three-pound club.

Out at Ben Luc, where we were operating at the time, we always had fire support. But later, when we moved down south to Dung Island and to other places, we didn't have the fire support we would have liked. And in that situation, you never want to run out of ammunition.

Carrying 23 pounds of machine gun, between 78 and 117 pounds of ammunition, and the rest of my web gear and clothes, I didn't float very well at all. I don't know why I even bothered to carry one of the small inflatable life jackets we had; it wouldn't have held me up very long at all. Maybe I just wanted to have a pillow along, is all.

But the tour went well, and I never sank out of sight at least. After we returned to the States, I only remained at Coronado for about a month. Inside of thirty days, a detachment of us were sent to Thailand to train their Frogmen in SEAL tactics and techniques. Then we went up on the border between Thailand and Laos and Cambodia. There was a lot of unconventional warfare taking place on the border against Communist infiltrators.

We were a small detachment. There was Al Huey, Captain (then Lieutenant, j.g.) Dick Flanagan, Doc Schroder, and myself. Just the four of us were training this foreign unit. A petty officer such as myself running operations just wasn't unusual in the SEALs. We had junior petty officers and a lot of Navy chiefs running operations as PRU advisers during Vietnam. If you were capable of doing the job, and had proven yourself during a deployment, the Teams would use you. It was just that simple. And our ability to do that allowed small detachments such as the one I was on in Thailand to accomplish all that we did.

In the Teams, if you could do the job, you were given the job. "Cannot do" shouldn't even have been in a Teammate's vocabulary. If it was, you'd be going into a situation with a negative working against you right from the start. You always had to look at the positive side of a situation. No matter how dim or how bad a situation gets, always look at the positive side. You were still alive, still moving, and you could always affect your situation.

After I returned from Thailand, I still had more deployments to Vietnam ahead of me. When I returned to Vietnam with another platoon, some of us were broken off into smaller units and sent off to work with other groups. I was sent to work with the KCS, the Kit Carson Scouts, along with several other SEALs. Then I worked with Al Huey and the PRUs down in My Tho for a while. So we were always moving around. If someone got hurt in one of the other platoons, or in another area of operations, we always went and supported them in any way we could.

That moving around made my second tour to Vietnam a very interesting one. I had worked with a wide variety of men in the different units. But the Vietnam War was winding down for us; the U.S. involvement in the war and combat operations was becoming less and less as more of the fighting was turned over to the South Vietnamese. By 1972, it was very hard to get in on a deployment to Vietnam, and I was part of one of the last SEAL platoons to go over there.

By September 6, 1972, nearly all of the U.S. combat troops had been pulled out of Vietnam. The only U.S. servicemen still out in the field were advisers. The SEALs I was working with weren't down in the south of Vietnam, with IV Corps, south of Saigon, our old stomping grounds. Instead, we were working in I Corps, operating in Quang Tri province, way up northeast of Hue City. Our base was actually in a place called Tuy Not, which was on the ocean.

Primarily, we were working with different units of the South Vietnamese LDNNs. We were providing them with advisers as well as whatever support we could bring to bear. We were basically doing recons and other intelligence-gathering missions. The NVA was crossing the thirty-eighth parallel at the time and we were providing some eyes-on intelligence on their movements.

We were still trying to break up the infrastructure and intel-gathering means of the NVA forces as well as collect information on them. So we ran quite a few different operations, either eliminating enemy personnel or outright capturing them. And the information we gathered helped us set up bigger operations as well as developed targets for bombing missions, which were really running heavily at that time.

By the fall of 1972, we were trying to see just how far south the infiltration of the NVA had reached in Quang Tre province. In the areas that we reconned, we found abandoned American tanks that had been given to the South Vietnamese. These tanks were still full of fuel and ammunition, fully capable of running and fighting. And they had just been left on the sides of the roads and trails. The NVA force that was sweeping down from the south was just overwhelming the South Vietnamese units in the field.

Higher command had planned a reconnaissance operation to come in by sea on a specific target area, the Cua Viet River base up in Quang Tre province. Our job was to do a reconnaissance of the base and gather all the intelligence we possibly could.

Based on our information, an amphibious unit would come in to try and cut off logistical support to the rest of the NVA forces down south. With a stranglehold on the fastest NVA supply route to the south, Command and the South Vietnamese government were hoping to force a treaty onto the North Vietnamese and get our guys out of Hanoi, to free our POWs and bring them home.

Ryan McCombie and William "Woody" Woodruff had originally been tapped to conduct the recon operation up on the Cua Viet. But everyone kind of got shuffled about when Dave Schaible picked Tommy Norris to go on the op. As the most senior and combat-experienced man immediately available, Tommy chose me to go along with him. Give the way things turned out, he's since said he was very glad he picked me.

This operation was taking place in one of the lowest morale times of the war for us. There was still a lot of SEALs in-country and everyone was eager to operate. But there just weren't very many operations available. So a rotation system was set up to try and give everyone a chance to go out on missions.

There were three officers in our group—Tommy Norris, Doug Huth, and Ryan Mc-Combie. So whenever an operation came up, a different officer went out on it and picked a different enlisted man to accompany him. At the end of October 1972, an operation came up, but Tommy jumped the rotation a bit since he was scheduled to go back to the States in a few weeks and was running short of time.

So Tommy Norris pulled rank on Ryan McCombie, who was up for that op, according to the rotation. Then Tommy chose me to go with him instead of Woody Woodruff, who was the next enlisted man up for an op. But Woody went with us and stayed on the insertion boat. And I thank God that he was there, because if it wasn't for Woody, we'd all still be out there floating around, or shark meat.

On the operation, we were inserting from a Vietnamese junk. Two U.S. Navy destroyers were supposed to be vectoring us in, directing us as they saw us on their radar screens. Something went wrong, though—a destroyer was off-line on his vector or whatever—and when we took the vectors in to the beach, it was obvious we had missed the target.

The bunch of us going in on the op hit the water and went in to the beach, leaving the insertion junk behind us. When we landed on the beach, we were supposed to be able to see the mouth of the Cua Viet River. But there was no river in sight.

I told Tommy that we were in the wrong place. But the skipper of the Vietnamese junk that had brought us in said he was sure we were in the right place. That skipper ran his boat all up and down the shore in that area, so Tommy decided to go ahead on the op.

Tommy's decision was for us to go ahead and patrol along the beach a bit and see just what we had gotten into. It turned out the junk had just about put us into North Vietnam. We were far north of where we were supposed to be.

As we patrolled along the beach, we were passing huge bunkers that had obviously taken some time to build. The situation was unbelievable. There were camp-fires everywhere and we could hear people talking, laughing, and walking around. We were right in the middle of a North Vietnamese Army unit.

So we had myself, Tommy, and three Vietnamese LDNNs. Tommy was the right size—he could pass for a Vietnamese at a distance. And of course the three LDNNs wouldn't stand out. But I make a pretty big Chinaman. So I stayed bent over, trying to keep a low profile.

We continued patrolling; since we were already there, we thought we might as well gather as much intelligence as we could. Then we would move out to the beach and find an area to hide for the evening and call for an extraction later that night. We didn't have the slightest idea where we were. So we figured we would move up and make comms [communications] and then extract later that evening. Then we'd be reinserted and try the op again in the right place.

Things pretty much happened that way. We got to the beach and patrolled out. There were tanks there, and heavy artillery guns, fire support—all of the materials of a standard army. Pulling out to the beach, we moved along to a better tactical position, one where we had a swamp on one flank. Now we had a position where we had the ocean on one side and a big swamp and waterway on the other. So with both our flanks covered by natural obstacles, we only had to worry about our north and south flanks.

So I was placed out on point with one of the LDNNs. We set up a perimeter and Tommy got on the radio. He was trying to make comms with the destroyer lying offshore. It turned out the admiral of the Seventh Fleet was riding on that very destroyer at the time. His normal flagship, the Newport News, had damage to one of her gun turrets and was going to return to the Philippines for repairs. So the admiral had just moved his command flag to one of the destroyers a short time earlier.

We got comms with the destroyer finally, but they didn't know where we were any better than we did. And there was no way to really find out exactly where we were located along the shore.

During that period of time, two North Vietnamese came moving down along the beach toward our position. They were looking for a number of things all at the same time. One of the ways the VC and NVA in the south resupplied themselves was from packages tossed into the water offshore. The surf brought the packages to shore, where they could be found on the beach.

The strain of long days operating show on the SEAL's face as he waits for action during training. In his left hand, he holds a Mark 79 Mod 0 pencil flare kit for signaling.

U.S. Navy

The NVA patrol was also looking for any signs of infiltration, footprints along the sand or anything like that. One of the pair was walking right along the waterline, about 100 yards in front of the other guy. The other guy was walking up and down through the sand dunes, the same dunes where we were hiding farther down the beach.

So it was obvious that our hiding place was about to be compromised. A plan was quickly put together where I would take care of the one NVA guy who was moving through the sand dunes. The young LDNN officer who was with us was given a hush puppy, and he would use the suppressed pistol to eliminate the man walking along the waterline.

In order to maintain complete silence, I was to take out the man in the sand dunes with my hands. And then the LDNN officer would have his chance to take out the beach walker with a suppressed gunshot. The NVA walking among the sand dunes came around one dune and I took up the CAR-15 I was armed with and struck him with the butt. He fell to the ground unconscious.

When I had taken care of my man, I gave the high sign to the LDNN officer so he could take out his target. That young officer walked out from where he was hiding and spoke up, demanding that the beach walker surrender!

That LDNN officer was armed with just a pistol pointing at the NVA soldier. He wasn't supposed to threaten the guy with it—he was supposed to shoot him. The NVA soldier was carrying an AK-47, and when the LDNN told him to surrender, he just giggled, swung around with his own weapon, and opened fire.

The LDNN officer jumped behind a sand dune and took cover. I grabbed up my weapon and started chasing the NVA guy down the beach. Hopefully, the noise wouldn't give away our position, especially since I was armed with the same kind of weapon the NVA were carrying. If I could eliminate that NVA soldier, he couldn't tell anyone where we were or how many of us there were. Then we could pull out and move back into the swamp or something.

I chased that guy up the beach, down along the tree line, and almost to a village we had spotted earlier. Finally, I ended up shooting the guy, but by then it was too late. An NVA quick-reaction team of about seventy-five guys had started coming to his rescue.

So now I had this NVA team shooting at me while I was running back out of the tree line to where Tommy and the others were. Now Tommy started getting us supporting fire from the ships offshore. We set the perimeter up again, and I was put up on point. Tommy was back in the sand dunes, where he could watch the flank where the swamp was.

There were two LDNN enlisted men with us who had been with me on two previous tours. I had handpicked those men, and I was glad I did. One of them was with Tommy at the radio. The other was down on my left flank, up behind me.

While I had been chasing that escaping NVA up the beach, the others had gathered up the man I had knocked down with my weapon and started interrogating him. They found out that he was able to point out on a map exactly where we were. While I was trying to hold the NVA elements down, Tommy had gotten back in touch with the destroyers and given them our position. That was when they came in to give us gunfire support.

As those destroyers came in on the target, they started drawing fire from the NVA artillery we had spotted along the shore. The heavy NVA guns actually out-ranged the five-inch guns of the destroyers. So as the ships came in, they took on fragments as one of the destroyers was hit.

The firefight that we were involved in with the quick-reaction force got very hot and heavy. The NVA soldiers were trying to encircle us, and they came into very close range during the fight. At one point I was on one side of a sand dune while an NVA soldier was on the other side. I would shoot from one area, roll over, and come up and shoot from another area. Then I would roll again and move before shooting. You didn't want to come up in the same spot twice.

The NVA didn't quite operate like that. I would see a guy come up, and as soon as I saw his head, I took aim at that area. When I finally saw the top of his head, I just shot right through the sand. The high speed CAR-15 bullets would zip through the few inches of crest on the sand dune and nail that NVA in the head. But before I saw that happen, I was already rolling to another shooting position.

The NVA had moved up on both sides of our flanks. I was on the sand dunes ahead of my guys while Tommy was farther up on the sand dunes. We had brought several M72A2 LAW rockets with us, and Tommy had already put one of them into the tree line. The explosion of the rocket warheads seemed like incoming artillery fire and helped keep the NVA from moving forward.

The blast from the LAW stopped the NVA advance, but they were already too close. A grenade came flying over the dune to land near me. I grabbed it up and threw it back. Then that same grenade came over the dune again, and I threw it back—again.

It was one of those lousy Chicom [Chinese Communist] grenades with a fuse that was anything but dependable. Which turned out to be a good thing for me. The fifth time it came over the dune, I just knew it was going to blow. I crouched down and tried to make myself small as the grenade came back over the dune and deto-nated behind me.

Seven fragments hit me in the back. I yelled, and I guess that NVA thought I had been killed. When he came over the top of the sand dune, he saw where I was lying on my back at the base of the dune. Then the last thing he saw was the muzzle flashes of my CAR.

After I flattened that NVA, Tommy yelled over and asked if I was all right. I called back that I was okay. Then he asked if I had been hit and I told him I had been, but that it was nothing major.

Almost 500 yards behind us, was a sand dune all by itself. In front of us were a bunch of sand dunes where the NVA troops were doing fire-and-maneuver. The NVA would get behind one sand dune, then fire in our direction as another group moved up. Then the other group would cover the first group's advance.

By that time I figured we had already killed anywhere from twenty to twenty-five NVA. But there was still plenty of them left to take us out. But then they just stopped advancing in on us. They weren't moving forward anymore; they had just stopped and were holding their ground.

We found out later that at that moment an NVA company, the 288th, had moved in to the area and were surrounding us. It was at that point that Tommy made the decision that we would all fall back to that one solitary sand dune. He had made contact with the Newport News who was still offshore. The Newport News was a Salem-class heavy cruiser that mounted eight- and five-inch guns.

Tommy had called in gunfire support from the Newport News right in on our own position. We only had a few minutes before the 260-pound, eight-inch and fifty-five-pound, five-inch shells started making our section of beach cease to exist. So I took myself, Quon, one of the LDNN enlisted men, and Tai, the young LDNN officer, back to that solitary sand dune while Tommy gave us covering fire.

Once at the sand dune, we turned to give covering fire to Tommy and Dang, the last LDNN. But then Dang came back by himself. He looked at me and just said, "Mike, da-uy's [dah-whee's] dead, da-uy's dead."

I wouldn't take that as an answer, I looked at him and said, "Are you sure?"

"Yes, Mike," he answered back. "He was shot in the head."

I took no time to consider the situation. Actually, I didn't give any thought to anything but one course of action. You never leave your friends behind, even less so a Teammate. I had to make the decision to go back for Tommy, knowing that he was dead. When I got to him, I thought he was dead, but I still had to recover his body. What the NVA would have done to him in the way of mutilating his body—that I couldn't have lived with. It didn't matter if I died; I couldn't have lived with myself if I had left him.

I looked up and could see that the NVA were close to overrunning the position where Tommy was. I jumped up and ran over to Tommy's last known position. As I approached the area, several of the NVA were already starting to overrun the dune. I opened fire and killed several of them coming over the dune. Then several more were around the dune and I shot them down, too.

Tommy was lying on the side of the sand dune, crumpled down in the sea grass. He had been hit in the left side of the head and the wound was terrible. So I grabbed him up and threw him over my shoulders and started running back with him.

These NVA troops saw me running and started chasing me. If they had any RPGs or heavy machine guns with them, it would all have been over. Instead, they just had their small arms, and sand was kicking up all around Tommy and me as the bullets impacted nearby. Then the first of the eight-inch rounds from the Newport News *hit the ground.* Ka-boom.

The concussion from the shell picked me up and threw me about twenty feet. As I was flying through the air, I could see Tommy actually leaving my shoulders. Then he fell and hit the ground. God almighty, I thought as I climbed up from where I had hit. Shaking off the effects of the concussion, I struggled over to where Tommy lay and grabbed him up again.

And he looked up at me and said, "Mike, buddy."

Tommy had spoken to me. The son of a bitch was alive! That made me happy. And at least if we were going to die now, we would be going together. But I didn't want us to go just yet.

Tommy blacked out again. So I picked him back up onto my shoulders and again started running back with him. Other rounds from the Newport News started landing all around us. I was glad I had gotten up and run that little distance I had at first because those incoming rounds were dead on target, exactly where Tommy had called them in. Both of us would have been dead from our own side's rounds if we hadn't gotten away from those dunes.

The Newport News *was bombarding the beach as I ran on to the rest of our people back at the sand dune. The LDNN were looking to me to tell them what to do, and I just told them that we would swim for it. Whenever a SEAL or Frog looked for a means of escape, we always turned to the water. And that was what I did now.*

I had Tommy's AK-47 with me; I had picked it up back when I grabbed him up at the dunes. I knew we had been running low on ammunition. The whole time of the firefight, Tommy had been on the radio keeping our communications channels open and getting our fire support on target, so his magazine pouches and weapon were still pretty much full.

So, like I said, I picked Tommy up and put him on my shoulder again. He hadn't said anything since that one line back after the explosion. With Tommy solidly in my grasp, I said "go!" and we all started running.

At just about that time the incoming barrage ceased. The Newport News *had started taking fire and pulled off the firing line. They had lost contact with us when Tommy was hit, and all they could see through their big eyes [binoculars] was NVA troops running around on the beach. The* Newport News *also wasn't supposed to be that far north, so when they figured we were lost, they moved back farther offshore.*

When the Newport News *pulled out, they also called back on the radio to Da Nang. The report that went out to Ryan McCombie and all of the rest of our guys was that we had all been killed. The message was garbled a bit—the story was that Tommy was dead, but had gotten back to the ship, the LDNNs were all dead, and I was supposed to be missing in action. That wasn't quite the actual situation.*

As we were running to the shoreline, the NVA moved in as soon as they saw us moving. The enemy was coming in from both sides now. They had surrounded us; some of them had come up and around the intercoastal waterway and were moving in from our south. The original troops that had been coming in were closing from the north and west. That only left the open sea to our east as an avenue of escape.

We jumped into the water and started swimming out to sea. I had fired off every round of ammunition I had for my CAR-15 and Tommy's AK. I was swimming out with Tommy in front of me, pushing him ahead of me. Quan, who was just a little guy, not much more than four foot nine or ten, had been shot in the butt, losing almost his whole cheek. So he wasn't in any shape to swim.

Slinging the AK-47 across my shoulders, I took my life jacket and put it over Tommy's head. For some reason, that dumb SEAL Team Two guy had put his jacket around his right ankle or something—however they do it on the East Coast. Maybe he wanted to float upside down or something; it never did make any damned sense to me. At any rate, I couldn't find it and I was a little too busy to look around for it.

So I inflated my life jacket around Tommy and pulled the H-harness over my head as well. That secured Tommy across my back with his head above water. Then I put Quan in front of me and just started breaststroking out to sea.

In the movies, you see bullets just flying through the water, splashing up all around the target. Well, that's what the water looked like around me. And I was praying that they wouldn't hit me now, because if they did, we would all be going down.

So we swam out of their range of fire and the bullets slacked off completely. Then we could see the Newport News floating away, heading south and out of the area. But we had swum well out of the range of the shore fire, and the guys on shore were just jumping up and down.

I never could understand why those NVA didn't call in for support craft or something to come out on the water and get to us. Or maybe they did and the craft didn't show up until later. Because we didn't hang around to find out. I started swimming south with Tommy on my back and Quan in front of me. And the other two LDNNs just came right along.

After we got out of the surf area and beyond the range of the NVA's small arms, I had stopped and attended to Tommy. He had been coming in and out of consciousness and I had to attend to his wound as best I could. The swells were lifting us up and down and we would probably have been very hard to see from shore. Maybe the NVA thought we had drowned. But at least they were leaving us alone for the moment.

Taking two four-by-four-inch battle dressings, I stuffed one into the wound on Tommy's head and wrapped the other one over the top of it. The injury was so big that the dressings still didn't cover it. It was a devastating wound; an AK-47 slug had entered just under his left eye and exited out the left side of his head. I could feel him shivering as he started slipping into shock, and I thought we were going to lose him for sure.

But there wasn't anything more I could do. When one of the LDNNs asked me what we were going to do, I told him we were just going to keep on swimming. So that's what we did, just kept swimming . . . and swimming . . . and swimming . . . and swimming.

Sometimes you just have to continue on; it's instinct that keeps you going. Could I have easily just stopped and died right there? Yes, I could have. But that wasn't the way I lived, never has been. I had a wife and kids back home, and I wanted to see them again. And I had friends I wanted to see again as well. So I just kept going.

Finally, I saw a junk off in the distance. Pulling off my AK, I started firing rounds into the air. When I started shooting, I couldn't tell for sure if that junk was one of ours or theirs. But we were all pretty close to total exhaustion. And Tommy had to get some real medical attention. And when that junk heard my fire, it started to approach us, and I could see it was one of ours.

It was one of the junks that had brought us in for the op. Woody Woodruff hadn't given up on us. After talking to the Newport News over the radio, he had spent the night searching up and down the coast, forcing both junks to remain in the area. And they had found us.

The junk picked us up from the water we had been in for hours. Woody had picked up Tai, the young LDNN officer, earlier. Tai had left our position when I had run up to get Tommy. He had moved out to sea on his own while the other two LDNNs, Dang and Quan, had held their position to give us covering fire.

But we had gotten out to the boats at last. We got Tommy up on deck, and then I helped get Quan and Dang on board. But I was now just so exhausted I couldn't pull myself up into the boat. There were three Vietnamese trying to pull my fat ass out of the water and it just wasn't going to work. So I told them to just throw a hawser over the side, which they did. I twisted a bow into the line, stepped in it, stood up, and kind of rolled myself over and into the junk.

As quickly as I could, I got to the radio and called Woody to tell him that we were all alive. And I told him we had all been hit. Tommy was the worst by far, but little Quan had lost the whole right cheek of his ass; even Dang, the radioman, had been hit right in his backpack radio and he had fragments all over his back. And I had seven grenade fragments all over my back.

The next message went out to the Newport News and told them the situation. They had a doctor aboard and would get back to us as quickly as they could. The CO of that ship had them turn around and head for us at full speed.

When the Newport News came alongside, we climbed aboard. I carried Tommy down to medical, where the doctor looked at him and told me he didn't have a chance to live. They called in for a medevac bird and got Tommy back to Da Nang, where Ryan McCombie was on hand waiting for them.

There wasn't a U.S. brain surgeon in Vietnam then; all of them had already been sent back to the States. A C-141 with a full medical team on board left Clark Air Force Base in the Philippines, headed for Da Nang. They picked Tommy up and flew him back to the hospital.

Tommy's first operation lasted eighteen and a half hours, and they didn't expect him to live. The Navy flew his mom and dad over as well as his brothers. But Tommy didn't know how to quit. He went through operations for two and a half years, and he's still alive today.

We finally flew back home just a few months later. Then the POWs were released by North Vietnam. That was also one of the greatest days of my life. We brought all of our guys home; there were just no more operations to do. Ryan and a couple of the others had gone out on a few ops after that Halloween [1972], but the SEALs' involvement in Vietnam was pretty much over.

Sometime later, after I was back in Coronado, I received a phone call with some startling news. I was told that I had been put in for the Congressional Medal of Honor. My answer was a little brusque; actually I think I just called it a bunch of BS, and I just blew off the whole thing. But the person on the phone kept trying to convince me that I had been put in for the Medal.

That operation and long swim had taken place on Halloween eve, October 31, 1972. The next year, October 15, I was expected to be in the White House, receiving the Medal from President Richard Nixon. Tommy was in the D.C. area. He was up in Maryland, in the military hospital in Bethesda. The people in charge there wouldn't let him go. So I went up to Bethesda and kidnapped him, and took him to the White House with me.

The greatest honor I have ever had was when they hung that Medal around my neck and Tommy was standing right at my shoulder. That Medal was half his. And it belongs to all of the men and women who have ever supported our country. It doesn't belong to Mike Thornton.

SEAL Team One was my home again for a while. We did a lot of traveling, going up north to Fort Greeley, Alaska, to open up our new arctic training center. Later I went over to BUD/S, where I became an instructor under Captain Anderson. At BUD/S, my philosophy of training was to put the students under every mental stress that we possibly could. There wasn't much question that physically, the students would be in shape to handle whatever came their way. But I wanted to know what mental capability they had, just how much they could handle.

In our job, if you can't handle the mental problems, the fear, the anguish, you're no good to us. So I was more on the mental side, that kind of toughness, than on the physical end. But the students probably just thought I was an asshole, or at least that's what everybody tells me.

But the students who were going to graduate from my classes would be as good as, if not better than, any that had graduated before. I was very proud to be a part of the family of the Teams. Terry Moy, Dick Allen, Vince Olivera, they had all done their jobs in helping to make me a SEAL. The other guys in SEAL Team One, who had given me my training, they, too, had made me proud to have been a part of their group.

It was an honor to have been part of that group, that family. There really isn't any other way to put it—it was a family. We lived together, we died together. We loved, and we cried—we did it all together.

My natural family all lived closer to the East Coast than to Coronado. And I finally wanted to be closer to them after a few years. My father was getting older and I liked the idea of being able to spend some time with him. So I transferred to Little Creek, Virginia, and SEAL Team Two.

I spent about a year there. It didn't seem to matter what I had done, or what my qualifications were, when I arrived at SEAL Team Two, I was a West Coast puke. The men who were there—the likes of Bob Gallagher, Rudy Boesch, and Mikey Boyn-

The crowded conditions aboard an LSSC as a SEAL squad settles aboard. The fact that the SEALs were given a lot of leeway in what they wore as a uniform is shown in this picture. The rounded bulge below the radio on the one SEAL's back in the center of the picture is an inflated flotation bladder. The bladder, originally intended to float demolition charges, will also help keep this SEAL's radio afloat if he slips into the water.

U.S. Navy

ton—they just figured you had finally decided to get over to where the real work was done. They never did tell me why they put their UDT life jackets in their pants cargo pocket while on patrol, though.

After spending time at SEAL Team Two, I moved even farther east. As part of an exchange program, I went over to England and spent a tour with the British SBS (Special Boat Service) while they sent one of their men to take my place at SEAL Team Two. That was a lot of fun. And the tour gave you a whole different outlook on how British techniques worked as compared to our operational techniques. It was a very enjoyable tour.

And as far as I'm concerned, the quality of the SBS is excellent, really outstanding. I think they are the best special warfare unit in Great Britain. We went against the SAS (Special Air Service) several times. And we seemed to win what I called the "shoot-outs" every time.

Back at Little Creek, I was going up the ladder in the enlisted ranks. My goal of making chief was reached, and then I was made E-8 (senior chief). Later I knew was going to be selected for E-9 (master chief). I had to decide just how long I was going to stay in the Teams. I could stay for twenty or thirty years, and I already had fifteen years in when I had to make a choice.

Master chief is just about as high as you can rise in the enlisted ranks. But I could rise further still as an officer. So I went for my commission and the Navy declared me an officer and a gentleman.

Under the tutelage of Dick Marcinko, I became a plankowner of SEAL Team Six in 1980. Six had the mission of conducting counterterrorism actions for the Navy. And that was a great bunch of guys and a great tour of duty. The men Dick Marcinko started that organization with were some of the best Navy guys I ever worked with in my life. I was proud to have been a part of it.

The new enemy for Six was a scary one. The SEALs fought unconventional war in Vietnam; antiterrorism is even more unconventional. What one terrorist can do with a single bomb is unbelievable. And he will give up his life to complete his mission, use his own body as the delivery system for a bomb. This is something that everyone has to be aware of in this country, that such terrorists exist, even among our own people.

But there are units of men, such as SEAL Team Six, whose mission is to protect the people from terrorists and their actions. And they do their jobs very well.

To the young men who might want to take the challenge of becoming a SEAL, I would like to say, Never give up! Always look forward because the past is gone behind you. And don't be afraid to make decisions.

Tommy Norris is one hell of a man, a workaholic, but also a very brilliant, loving, and caring individual. And he continued to serve his country after he left the Teams. In spite of his injury, he went on to make a great second career for himself in the

FBI. There, he's made some of the biggest undercover hits anyone has ever done. And he is also a true friend; we're closer than brothers. And I know the feelings are mutual.

Under all of the training, the equipment, the ammunition, under all of that high-tech material of today's warrior, there's flesh, a body, a soul. Just like all men, SEALs are people who care, who feel. That ridiculous Hollywood image of a SEAL as a fighting machine couldn't be further from the truth. The men of the Teams are men who want to be remembered by one another.

In Vietnam, we were literally facing death every day. So we wanted to fulfill our lives. We lived large and partied hard; that's where a lot of the stories of excesses of the SEALs came from. Maybe we reached too far sometimes; I don't know. But deep down inside, we knew each day might be our last.

Lieutenant Thomas R. Norris, the second SEAL Medal of Honor recipient of the Vietnam War. This photograph was taken after Norris suffered his severe wounds while operating on the mission that resulted in Michael Thornton receiving the last SEAL Medal of Honor awarded from the Vietnam War.

U.S. Navy

And sometimes, it was the last day for some of our Teammates. Before we shipped out to Vietnam, we all threw some money into a kitty. If you lost it on that tour, the rest of the platoon would take that money and go down to the Tradewinds, our hangout at that time. There, we would drink all of the beer we could consume on our Teammate's money. And we would celebrate his life.

It wasn't a sad thing, though we felt some sadness. Instead, we just tried to celebrate him as we had known him. We had lived with him, known him, and knew just what type of person he had been. We had known a Teammate during the best times of his life, and that life had been cut short young. So that was how we saluted a lost Teammate, how we demonstrated the honor we felt in having known him.

The kind of man who becomes a Navy SEAL, or UDT man before him, is an individual who wants to be there. That's the only thing that's the same in every one in the Teams. We have people from all walks of life in the Teams—small men, big *men, it doesn't matter what they are on the outside, it's what's on the inside that counts in the Teams more than anything else. You had to want to be a SEAL, and you had to want it hard. Otherwise, you would just never make it through training.*

And when I was an instructor, I made sure of that. And that's the same feeling the instructors at BUD/S have today.

■ Chapter 49

War's End: The Aftermath of Vietnam in the Teams

The Secretary of the Navy takes pleasure in presenting the NAVY UNIT COMMENDATION to

THE NAVAL ADVISORY GROUP, Vietnam

and

THE MARINE CORPS ADVISORY UNIT, Vietnam

for service as set forth in the following

CITATION:

For exceptionally meritorious service from 10 May 1965 to 28 March 1973 in connection with combat operations against enemy forces in the Republic of Vietnam. During this period, advisors from the Naval Advisory Group and the Marine Corps Advisory Unit, attached to Commander United States Military Assistance Command, Vietnam, provided guidance and assistance to the Vietnamese Navy and Vietnamese Marine Corps throughout the Republic of Vietnam. These advisory teams successfully achieved the transition of the Vietnamese Navy from a fledgling force of 8,000 men to a strong, dynamic, and aggressive force of 42,000 men; concurrently the Vietnamese Marine Corps was reorganized into a first-class combat force. Participating in hundreds of combat, psychological and pacification operations, U.S. Navy and Marine Corps advisors contributed to the high state of training and readiness of the Vietnamese Navy and Marine Corps and their notable record of achievement. Through a concerted effort, the ACTOV (Accelerated Turnover to Vietnamese) Program was completed and all logistic and intermediate support bases were turned over to the Vietnamese Navy. The courage and devotion to duty displayed by the U.S. Navy and Marine Corps advisors throughout this period reflected great credit upon themselves and were in keeping

With the end of the Naval Advisory Group, Vietnam, the last major U.S. Navy commitment to Vietnam was over. The Navy SEALs and the last UDT detachments had left Vietnam much earlier. During the peak of their deployments, only a few years earlier, nine SEAL direct-action platoons of 2 officers and twelve enlisted men had been in Vietnam at any one time. This didn't include the number of SEALs and UDT men assigned to other detachments. All told, there were almost 200 SEALs in-country at one time.

This huge number of SEALs in combat dramatically shows the growth of the SEAL Teams from their initial allotment of 60 men each. SEAL Team One had the greatest share of the Vietnam commitment, and also saw the largest growth in manning allotments. At its peak in 1971, SEAL Team One had over 350 officers and men in its ranks. SEAL Team Two also saw a time of rapid growth, but not on the same scale.

With the end of the war came the end of the need for such large manning levels in the SEAL Teams. SEAL Team Two reduced its levels through normal attrition. A number of SEALs from Team Two decided to retire from the Navy after the Vietnam War.

SEAL Team One comprised a younger population. This made retirement and normal attrition insufficient to meet the Navy's demands for a smaller postwar Team. Setting up their own criteria, SEAL Team One and its Command released a number of men from the ranks back into the Navy fleet. One result of this reduction was that a number of younger SEALs did not extend their enlistments and left the Team when their service commitment expired.

MANNING—PERSONNEL ALLOWANCES/COMPLEMENTS

SEAL TEAM ONE—INITIAL MANNING (1962) 5 OFFICERS / 50 ENLISTED

1966	1967	1968	1969	1970	1971	1972	1973
25/97	29/155	29/182	37/225	53/225	52/310	39/274	25/170 to 25/178

DETACHMENT GOLF—PLATOONS DEPLOYED TO VIETNAM

1966	1967	1968	1969	1970	1971 (End 7 December 1971)
2	3	3	5	6	6

SEAL TEAM TWO—INITIAL MANNING (1962) 10 OFFICERS / 50 ENLISTED

1966	1967	1968	1969	1970	1971	1972	1973
20/100	23/115	27/116	23/115	23/115	23/103	20/123	20/128*

DETACHMENT ALFA—PLATOONS DEPLOYED TO VIETNAM

1966	1967	1968	1969	1970	1971 (End 14 June 1971)
0	3	3	3	3	3

*Organized as 7 Platoons, HQ Platoon (3/13) Training Platoon, 5 operating platoons (2/12)

Excerpt from SEAL Team One, Command and Control History 1972
Enclosure (2) (C) SPECIAL TOPICS
SEAL TEAM ONE MANPOWER REDUCTION
Page 1. [DECLASSIFIED from CONFIDENTIAL]
REDUCTION IN AUTHORIZED MANPOWER MANNING LEVEL
In response to the requirement levied by higher authority for SEAL Team ONE to reduce its on-board strength to the authorized complement, due to a cutback to peacetime operating manning levels, thirty-one enlisted personnel were made available for transfer to fleet units and received permanent change-of-station orders during the month of May 1972. Impartial criteria for the selection of these individuals was as follows: (1) first enlistment, (2) more than one year remaining prior to EAOS, (3) have not made a deployment (RVN, Okinawa, Korea). It was emphasized that selection was not based upon individual performance while attached to SEAL Team ONE, but rather on the impartial criteria set forth above. Personnel were able to retain NEC 5326 and it is expected that some of these men will be returning to SEAL Team ONE when released from their ships or stations as billets in this command become available within its authorized manpower manning level.

James Janos, Storekeeper, Third Class (Governor Jesse Ventura)

Even though he told me not to, I followed my brother Jan somewhat in my decision to first join the Navy. I'd had a swimming scholarship to the University of Northern Illinois and it fell through because of some of its rules and regulations. Being an ex–competitive swimmer, I joined the Navy to become a Frogman, a member of the UDT, just like my brother was. So the decision was, in part, an extension of my swimming.

There isn't such a thing as a professional swimming career. Being an ex–com-

petitive swimmer, you can do nothing to become a professional one. The closest thing there is are the Teams in the Navy. Since I was all of eighteen years old, and not sure of what to do with my life, enlisting in the Navy just seemed like the right thing to do at the time.

My brother Jan had graduated high school in 1966; I graduated in 1969. I think it was about 1968 or so that Jan decided to enlist in the Navy. He had worked a couple of years after school and then enlisted with the intention of becoming a Frogman because both of us had been scuba divers as kids. We had spent a lot of time scuba diving as teenagers and we were both qualified sport divers.

Since Jan wanted to be a Frogman, and he was the older of us, he went through training first. When I followed a few years later, I probably had as much insight about what it took to get into the Teams as an outsider could have in those days. But, training was, and is still, a lot more than anyone ever tells you.

The hardest part of training for me was running. I had always hated running but was a natural swimmer. So when there were swimming evolutions, I enjoyed those a lot more because I excelled at them. But thinking about the things I didn't like about training, I think duckwalking, with your knees bent and your body down low, while carrying the rubber boat on your head—that wasn't something I cared much for either.

That kind of thing was always tough for me because I'm six-foot-four. So when I carried an IBS, there was no way I didn't get the full weight of the boat on my neck. And it always seemed that I had these little shits up front, guys five-foot-three, who had six inches between the IBS and the top of their heads. Then they would tell me later how tired they were carrying the raft, and it never touched their heads to begin with. I'm probably bald today because of those rubber rafts pounding on my head.

But it was the running I didn't like that much. And you run at BUD/S a lot. For years and years after I got out of the Navy, I didn't run. But I've taken it back up now.

My class was Class 58 and I think we started June 22, 1970. I arrived in Coronado for training on Friday, and class started Monday. So I didn't have the benefit of any pretraining whatsoever. When I got there, I was given my gear and a rack, and started with the class right away. I had never run the obstacle course before, and that was what I did for the first time on Tuesday.

Generally, after you've gotten good at running the O-course, you can do the course in about ten minutes. Some guys were faster; we had Ray Holly in the class and he ran it in about six minutes. For a tall guy like me, nine or ten minutes would be a respectable time after you had experience at the course. For me that Tuesday, the first time I ran it took me forty-three minutes. And it was forty-three minutes of pure hell because the instructors would make you do things over and over again, whether you did them right the first time or not.

The part that sticks out to me about that particular ordeal was finishing up that day. Since I didn't have any pretraining, my hands weren't ready for the demands that I put on them. The skin hadn't toughened up. So I had four big flapping loose bits of skin on each hand from blisters that had formed and broken open. They were bleeding around the sand that had been driven into them. Infection was starting in fast, so they were kind of a mess.

Terry "Mother" Moy, my first-phase instructor, came out at the end of the day and set up a table with a first-aid kit on it. Moy asked if any of the trainees had flappers, and I was dumb enough to volunteer the information. "I do, Instructor Moy," I said.

"Come on up here, boy," Moy said in his most pleasant growl.

So I ran on up there and Instructor Moy asked me if I was right-or left-handed. When I told him I was right-handed, he told me to hold that hand out.

When I held my hand out, I figured that he was just going to pour the Mercurochrome on it. But when I held out my hand, he grabbed each flap of skin and just ripped them off.

Then, when he was done doing that, he told me the reason he asked me which hand I used. "Now you do the other hand," he said.

There wasn't much point to arguing with an instructor—Moy the least of them—when I was going through BUD/S. So I had to stand out in front of the class and tear off all of the loose, hanging skin on my left hand.

"Now get back in line, you big dummy," Moy growled.

As I scurried back into line, I realized the training lesson of that little incident. Never volunteer for anything. Be as inconspicuous as you can be, blend in with the group, and don't bring any undue attention to yourself. That is a lesson that stands out clearly in my memories of training.

But going through BUD/S is more than just training you, and testing you, to go into the Teams. That training also helps prepare you for life. No matter what you do later in life, no matter how tough it is, or how depressed you may get, or how sorry you start feeling for yourself, you will always think back to BUD/S. That will help carry you through. It's something you'll always take with you. Once you've become a Team member, you're always one. It never leaves you.

That course of training helps create a benchmark in your life. It gives you a barometer, a gauge, or a level, which you can measure everything else against. There has been nothing that I've encountered in life that has been worse than that training. And I passed that; I completed it. That makes it the benchmark. No matter how tough my pro wrestling and all of that stuff could be, it was never as tough as BUD/S. No matter what you do in life, you can match it up to BUD/S, and you will prevail.

It seems to take an eccentric person to join the Teams. Maybe someone who is off-the-wall a little. But it's people with an inner strength who get through the training. You'll see a lot of people who come to training, and they look like Arnold

Schwarzenegger. And then you'll see some scrawny guy standing next to them, and you'll wonder what that guy is even doing here. He doesn't look like anything.

Then, twenty-two weeks later, the guy who looked like Arnold Schwarzenegger is long gone and you can't even remember who he was or even his name. And that little guy will be standing there, soaking wet and covered with mud and sand and salt water and wanting more. He will be your Teammate.

So you learn very quickly to never judge the book by its cover. It's what the guy carries inside of him that makes him what he is, not the muscles and looks on the outside.

We have a term—Banana—we use to describe someone who's soft on the outside and soft on the inside. Well, sometimes you'll see people who're soft on the outside, but they're rock hard on the inside. And I think in the Teams we're people who are very motivated, very focused, and who don't accept the word "can't."

All of this made the day you graduated from training one of tremendous import to your life. You felt what can only be described as the pride of the Teams. It was an accomplishment built over the twenty-two weeks of the most rigorous training that anyone can imagine. And a feeling of gratification comes over you at graduation.

But then, in good Team fashion, during graduation, I was also thinking about my Teammate Platt. His two cousins had come down for the graduation. They were re-

BUD/S trainees crawl through the mud during training. This experience served the men of the Teams well during their missions in the swamps and mud of Vietnam.

U.S. Navy

ally good-looking babes and we were all heading down to Tijuana that night, some-place we weren't supposed to go. So in good Team spirit, I was already a pirate who was going to break the rules. And I hadn't even been assigned to a Team yet. My instructors had taught me well.

The only thing was, the instructors turned out to be right about going down to TJ. Platt ended up being tossed in jail down there and we had to pass the hat back at the barracks to bail him out. And the instructors had told us specifically that after graduation, we weren't supposed to go to Tijuana to celebrate.

In spite of our can-do attitude, there were some things we just weren't supposed to do. The ocean could teach you very quickly that you couldn't take her on and expect to win. But we operated in the ocean almost every day.

During my first deployment to the Philippines, I had the opportunity to work off the Grayback, a very special submarine used by the Teams. The Grayback was the only submarine of her kind, adapted for the special uses of the UDTs and SEAL Teams. She had these two large hangars on her bow, each one waterproof, with a hatch leading into the front compartments of the sub. You could flood the hangar compartments and lock out a minisub [SDV], IBS, or about eighteen combat swimmers at a time.

The big hangar chambers each had a single huge domed clamshell door, hinged at the top. The big doors could open or close while the Grayback was underwater. We were under the water one night, having completed our operation for the evening. Everyone was switching off from their own breathing rigs to the "hooka" units that were hanging from both sides of the hangar. The hooka rigs let you breathe off of boat air from the submarine. But once you were on one, you could only move the short length of the air hose.

The patrol leader had communications with the crew inside the submarine and they were the ones who opened and closed the big doors. For whatever reason, the big doors couldn't be stopped once they had started to open or close. At least that was the situation then.

This wasn't any big deal for us; we were all inside the hangar, breathing off of the boat air, and the patrol leader had them start to close the door. As the big door started its downward travel, all of a sudden there was about a nine-or ten-foot shark, certainly big enough to get your attention, up on the deck of the Grayback. And he was swimming right toward us.

The hatch was closing, and the shark was heading right toward the compartment. I didn't know sharks very well, but I didn't think he would like being closed in with us very much. That pointy nose of his just headed straight toward us as the big hatch was still on its way down. And at the very last moment, the shark turned away and went on with his business.

The hatch closed, without any uninvited guests coming in. But that wasn't going to be the last time we had a run-in with a shark.

We were doing a 212-foot bounce dive off of the coast of Point Loma, right outside of San Diego. A bounce dive is where you go down for a minimum amount of bottom time so that you don't have to decompress. We didn't have more than thirty seconds or so of bottom time, so most of the dive was just going up and down in the water.

All ten or twelve swim pairs were done with the dive. The IBS had just been pulled in from where it had been tied to the side of the PL [patrol launch]. A couple of the guys were lighting up cigarettes when up from the stern of the PL came an eighteen-to-twenty-foot-long great white shark. The dorsal fin seemed to be sticking up a couple of feet from the water.

This was long before the movie Jaws had been released. So we hadn't seen Quint, or the shark, or anything like that. That huge shark just cruised on by

Looking down and forward from the bridge on the sail of the *Grayback* can be seen the two huge doors sealing the forward hangars. The tracks along the deck outside of the doors are used to move the SDV cradles during launching and recovery operations.

U.S. Navy

the PL, not more then ten feet or so from the side of the boat. We just looked at him and thought, Boy, he's big. That shark was almost the length of the boat. And we hadn't been out of the water, the last swimmer pair, maybe forty-five seconds to a minute. I wouldn't have cared to have been in the water with him; it was his chunk of ocean right there.

Back in our training, someone asked Instructor Moy what we should do in case of a shark attack. And Moy just told us to make sure that our swim buddy was smaller than we were. That way we could pull him in front of the shark.

He didn't mean it really, and there has never been a known shark attack on a Frogman or SEAL during a combat or training swim. But there are things that tell SEALs and Frogs that they're only visitors to the sea.

But in spite of the work and the risks you accept in order to be in the Teams, it's all more than worth it. Many have said that you never leave the Teams. Even after you get out of the Navy, you're still a Team member. You hear the word "hoo yah" from anyone, and right away, your ears perk up. You never completely lose track of the people you served with.

You might go on with your life. But whenever you come back and are reunited with your Teammates, it's like time has stood still. Even though many of us are more than a little gray now, and maybe a bit overweight as well, and we can't run four miles like we used to, we're still the same people inside.

Many of us have families now, and children of our own. I have a son who's three inches taller than I am. But when I meet with my Teammates, all of the other people in my life go away for just a little while. It's kind of like stepping into the Twilight Zone. You're back with the men you spent the greatest part of your lives with.

When you get among three or four, or maybe just one or two, of your old Teammates, you go back to being who and what you were then. Sometimes, it can be a little embarrassing, when you're in your late forties, to be acting like you did at nineteen or twenty. But it's a very good time.

The new guys going into the Teams today are phenomenal to me. They're probably a lot better athletes than we were. Today, they also incorporate sports medicine into training a lot. And the instructors work hard at keeping the students from becoming injured during the evolutions and activities they have to complete.

But some things have never changed. You still have to have the heart to get through training. That remains the same from the first day, so many years ago, until today. And, God willing, it'll stay that way in the Teams for a long time to come.

You can leave the Navy, but you can never really leave the Teams.

If there was one person in the Teams who I look to as my sea daddy, the man who showed me what it meant to be in the Teams, it's Frank Perry. We called him Superman. He was between forty-one and forty-four years old when I served with him at UDT 12. He was actually with the first UDT 12 detachment that went into Vietnam. And Frank was the epitome of physical strength, and yet the most quiet, well-balanced, and fair man there could possibly be.

Frank Perry kept those of us in his platoon in great physical condition; I was in as good a condition in the Teams as I had been at the end of BUD/S. Frank had been a former BUD/S instructor. And he didn't harass anyone; he just did the normal PT as he worked out for himself. And the rest of us tried to keep up.

This guy was remarkable, even among a large group of remarkable men. He was one of the few guys who could climb up this hanging rope that was near the grinder, with a pair of twin-ninety air tanks on his back. And he did the climb with only his arms. Just a wiry-built guy, and among us, he was the one called Superman. The softer the sand got for a run, the faster Frank became. Or at least it seemed that way. Running on the hard pack, Frank would be great. But once he got down in the soft sand, he would pass even other runners. He was probably one of *the top five runners in the entire Team, and that was running against some twenty-year-olds.*

And those were the kind of men I served with. People like that are just some of the reasons you can never really leave the Teams.

And I would like to thank the older guys who let me be a part of the greatest military fraternity in the world. And to the young guys today, I would say, "Welcome. You've got big shoes to fill. No matter what you've done, there's a Teammate who's done it before you."

If you make it into the Teams, you have entered a fraternity of people who you can be very proud of—for what they have done, and for the path they have laid out for you new guys to follow. And it's for the new guys to go beyond that path, to go farther. That's the nature of things and that's the way it will always be.

■ Chapter 50

A New Rebuilding

By the middle of the 1970s, the manning levels of the SEAL Teams were no longer being lowered. The number of qualified SEALs who left the Teams had been a pool of experience and knowledge that had been taken away from the Teams. In 1974, a reorganization of the Navy resulted in an opportunity for the SEALs who had left the Teams.

Reserve SEAL Teams were developed as part of the Navy Reserves in 1975. The idea of SEALs in the Navy Reserves was to augment the active Teams in case of national emergency or war. Originally under the command of the director of the Navy Reserves, the SEALs in the new units trained once a month for two days over a weekend and for two weeks during the year.

Old Teammates who had left the SEALs came streaming back. Men who had gone on to very successful civilian careers would travel for hundreds of miles to be part of their Teams again. Doctors, lawyers, police officers, schoolteachers—all leaped at the chance to once again run, shoot, jump from planes, dive, and blow things up. They were an invaluable resource in the form of highly qualified, experienced, and capable Teammates.

John Sarber, Captain, U.S. Navy Reserve (Ret.)

For four years of active Navy service, I was a member of the Navy Special Warfare community. Once I left the active service, I didn't leave Special Warfare, as I joined the Navy Reserve. As so many others had done, I found being a member of the Navy Reserve SEAL Team a classic excuse to spend one weekend a month and two weeks a year falling out of airplanes, diving, and blowing things up.

To qualify to do all of this, I first had to pass training, which I had done no more than a few years earlier with Class 13, West Coast, a nice, cold winter class.

In someone's infinite wisdom regarding my training class, it was decided that we would benefit from receiving some basic infantry skills in addition to UDTR. So about 130 Navy students went up to Camp Pendleton for a week of training with the Marine Corps.

Those instructors ran us all over that base, up and down the hills, with M1 Garand rifles and tin hats [M1 steel helmets]. The swimming-pool training was a bit brisk in the cold weather. It was so cold that one night the water in our canteens froze. So it was decided to only expose us to one more day of the Camp Pendleton training, but since the surf was up and crashing so nicely on shore, that was where our training took place.

We put the class in eight or nine rubber boats and all of us entered the surf zone. And not one of the boats came back. Instead, we were all flipped over from the surf action and washed on down shore. When we finally came ashore, it certainly wasn't where the instructors wanted us to be.

It may have been decided that it was just a bit too cold for our training at Camp Pendleton. Not because the instructors were that worried about us, but because out of the 130 students who had started that week, sixty or seventy had quit by the next day.

So the remainder of the class was sent to another training unit, this one in Hawaii. They loaded us on board an LST and we traveled to the islands. But the Hawaiian Islands were anything but a sunny place for relaxation for Class 13. Once there, we had to begin training all over again, including going through the whole of Hell Week. And we had already completed three days of Hell Week back in California.

It was during training that we all developed the fraternity that existed in the Teams. That feeling came from every man knowing that another man, no matter whether he had trained in 1950, '70, or '90, had gone through the same experiences. Details are different. But each man had to reach deep down within himself and find what was necessary to get him through. For myself, I just decided that the instructors would have to kill me to make me quit. And I think that I was hardly the only one to think this over the years. Men like that I think a great deal of.

As a by-product of this attitude, those of us who completed the ordeals of training don't hold a lot of sympathy for those who quit along the way. Even while Class 13 was still undergoing training, we held that view. When we all reached Hawaii, the instructors talked about bringing back those who had quit during the frigid days at Pendleton. And the rest of us didn't want to see that done.

The day we were told that we had completed training became something of a high point in my life, and I'm sure that's true for a number of others. Nothing else I had ever done took as much work to achieve, and I really appreciated the accomplishment.

From graduation, the group of us walked across the street and reported in at UDT 12. For us, it was a great big deal. For the men who were already at the UDT, well, they had been there before. Besides, it's always fun to mess with the new guys.

When we reported in, the officer, the commanding officer, and executive officer just looked up from their desks and said, "Here we go again." Myself and the other handful of officers from Class 13 received our assignments and out we went into the UDT.

It seemed that serving in the UDT, and later the SEALs, wasn't like even being in the Navy. We were always in some sort of uniform, not quite the same as the rest of the service. For us, blue-and-golds (T-shirts) and swim trunks were a normal uniform of the day. So was a wet suit or just the swimming trunks. We just didn't have the typical shipboard regime found in the rest of the Navy.

Each day was something new in the UDT. We could be sitting in a bar in Coronado on Saturday afternoon when the phone would ring with the skipper or XO at the other end of the line. I could be told that my platoon and I were needed in Anchorage, Alaska, by Monday morning. Back to the base and a quick grab of a prepacked war bag and then a group of Frogmen would be on their way to a northbound flight. By Monday afternoon, the bunch of us would be swimming under the arctic ice.

It was intriguing, it was hard work, and it was fun. We had to go here, or we had to go there. The whole of the world's oceans were the operating theater of the UDT. And the jobs could sometimes be very difficult, and dangerous. The ocean does not easily allow men to operate under her waves. But the Navy saw to it that we all received some extra money for our hazardous duties.

The arctic is a good example of the kind of missions we were asked to perform. Just getting there was kind of a high for me my first time, because it took us fourteen days just to get up to Fairbanks. From Fairbanks, a plywood-bodied bush airplane flew the bunch of us farther north.

Sitting in the right seat, I could look out the window. Behind me were a number of my guys all crammed into the back of the plane. In the left seat was the pilot, a missionary to the native tribes living in the north. Looking out the window and seeing oil spewing from the engine, or the wings flapping up and down as the air took them, I could see why the bush pilot was a man of God. Religion can come quickly to you when you are in that kind of situation.

There were no radios or tower instructions. Instead, we found ourselves lifting off and flying out over the tundra, trees, and snow. Then came a landing out on an iceberg somewhere with a tractor or some other vehicle appearing out of the white to meet us.

It was interesting work, and we had a job to do that involved demolitions, underwater surveys, and other water work. At one point I was fortunate enough to travel from Point Barrow across the arctic to Cambridge Bay. For a while I was flying along just south of the North Pole before moving down to points farther south. For four months, I and my men moved throughout the arctic, a cold adventure but a rewarding one.

After ten years of good time in the Navy, which included my time in the Teams, flight training, and some of my college, I decided to leave the active service. The Navy Reserves required one drill weekend a month in a regular Navy environment. But for my two-week active-duty requirement, I was able to go back to Coronado and requalify with the Teams in parachuting, diving, and things like that. On top of the qualifications, I was able to spend time with my friends who were still in the active-duty Teams.

That was the start of my Special Warfare reserve career. But just going back to the Teams for those two weeks a year wasn't enough. More could have been done to create a reserve component of the Teams, something that just didn't exist. Several of us who had been in the Teams started politicking with the Navy, both in San Diego and in Washington, D.C., in order to start a reserve SEAL Team. In February 1974, our efforts were rewarded and an authorization was issued to form a reserve UDT.

That was great news for a lot of us. This now meant that we would have our own reserve unit and do our monthly drills as a unit. We put the word out mostly to the eight Western states about the formation of the new unit. The Western states were chosen because they were the most likely to have enough men who were close enough to Coronado to gather there for the monthly drills.

The first meeting ended up with around ten officers and fifty enlisted men, an unheard-of number of civilians coming back into a reserve unit. There were doctors, bankers, attorneys, police officers, cinematographers, producers, and others, all wanting back into a Special Warfare environment.

These were men who had made a success of their careers outside of the Navy. But the lure of the Teams was always there for them. In a reserve Team, they could exercise that desire to be back in the Teams, and not have to give up a lucrative career outside of the Navy.

Now we were able to gather once a month, for a weekend, and do all of the things that we had been so used to during our active time in the Teams. As the commanding officer of the reserve Team, I found it very difficult to combine the civilian aspects of my reservists with the discipline and basic requirements of the Navy.

For one example, I had three police officers who worked undercover duties in their full-time careers. That meant they had long hair, considerably past the Navy's grooming standards. The unit had to pass inspections, but these men were not in a position to cut off their hair to meet regulations. And some of the people who inspected us, such as Captain Schaible or Admiral LeMoyne, just didn't like the long hair very much at all.

But a lot of fast footwork, and the introduction of wigs, hats, and hair grease, got the grooming problem down to a manageable level. At least we were able to pass the required inspections.

Most of the guys didn't have a set of dress blues for the inspections. Even in the active Teams, you rarely wore that traditional Navy uniform. So our being able to conduct our inspection in standard camouflage uniforms came as a relief to the men under my command.

But though they didn't wear dress uniforms much, the men in that reserve unit had a lot of materials to go on their uniforms in the way of decorations. A large number of Bronze Stars and Purple Hearts were scattered among that first group. That was a fact that I was always proud of.

But the active-duty and reserve forces of the Navy didn't really know what to do with us for some time. Here we were, a group of veterans with a lot of experience in-country both in Vietnam and elsewhere, a valuable resource to the Navy. In the active Teams, and even in the Navy as a whole, men with combat experience were something in short supply.

But after they spent some time getting used to us, the Teams learned to use our combat experience to their advantage. Our guys would come in on their own time, even their vacation time, to serve with the active-duty Teams. They were involved with exercises all over the world. Korea and other theaters saw reservist personnel operating right alongside their active-duty counterparts. And that helped keep their skills up-to-date, and their experience added to the overall quality of the Team.

There wasn't really any friction between the active-duty Special Warfare community and the reserve Team. But there were some initial teething problems with incorporating my unit with the rest of the reserves.

Here I was with 100-plus guys, all qualified Special Warfare operators, and the reserve command wanted us to spend our drill weekends with the regular reserve forces. What that meant at the time was spending a weekend in classrooms at the San Diego Naval Training Center. This was not something that would go over big with men who were used to operating in all the environments of the world, the outside environments.

Classroom drills were something that didn't happen. Instead, we moved in with the active Teams in Coronado for our drills. First, I went over and met with the command staff for the UDTs and asked them how we might be able to move my unit onto the base to use the UDT facilities. Besides the portable gear we needed to use for our drills, such as diving gear, weapons, and such like, we also needed to have easy access to the unmovable items, such as the obstacle course, the surf, and the beach.

The Navy wanted to issue my unit funds for it to operate, and of course we accepted them. So when I went over to the active-duty community, I was able to make some offers to them. Instead of us just using and putting wear and tear on their aqualungs, rubber boats, and other gear, we would pay them for their use and the replacement of any consumables we used up. With money being in short supply after Vietnam, this was something of a benefit to the active community.

The next thing we needed was an actual facility, a building. The base offered us what was called a Butler building. A Butler building was a temporary structure intended for rapid set-up in the field. It was little more than a bunch—maybe ten or twelve—of large shipping containers stacked on each other and interconnected.

So we had our building, if you could really call it a building. But a number of us in the reserve Team went into Coronado on our own time—and that covered a lot of weekends—and reconfigured our Butler building into what became the reserve SEAL Team facility. And it worked out pretty well.

The reserve Team conducted a lot of trips during our weekend drills. In the swampy, reed-filled area where the special boat unit trained with their small boats, we would field-train on weekends. Only instead of trucking or walking in, we would jump in for the exercise. Squaw Valley up near Lake Tahoe was another place we jumped in on.

So we quickly developed a very good training program. And the Navy Reserve hierarchy really took a liking to us. The head of the reserve contingent in Coronado became more directly involved with our training. They loved to go on rides in the helicopters and watch us jump out over the target area. The politicking worked out well, both for us and for the Navy.

The Navy Reserves are a completely different organization from the active Navy, a separate element really, and the active and reserve Teams were just as separate in an organizational sense. But we interacted with our brothers in the active Teams to a great extent and were treated as equals. Our capabilities remained sharp and up-to-date and we could augment the active Teams as needed.

A good UDT man or SEAL is a dedicated man, capable and skilled at his job, physically and mentally strong, and a levelheaded thinker. This man is willing and able to get along with other men who are like him and different at the same time. This is an individual who understands what it means to be on a team and what it takes to work together. And old saying is that a team is only as good as its slowest member. But in the UDTs and the SEALs, the rest of the team is willing to help that slowest member get a little faster.

The mission of the Teams grew in complexity over the years. From the hydrographic surveys of WWII to the bridge demolition attacks of Korea, the UDT developed more capabilities and skills as the scope of their missions grew wider. When counterguerrilla warfare became a more important aspect of combat, the SEAL Teams were commissioned from the UDTs. This was another natural progression of skills and capabilities.

Individuals made themselves part of the whole in the Teams. And people didn't seem to try for much in the way of personal recognition. There were a number of highly decorated individuals, but even they mostly just wanted to be considered as operators who just did their jobs.

There were individuals you learned about, historical figures in the story of the Teams. Admiral Draper Kauffman, who was the father of the UDTs during World War II. Frank Kaine was also one of the men who developed and guided the Teams through the postwar years and on through the 1960s. One man who I consider the father and architect of the SEAL Teams is Captain Wendy Webber, though his contribution had more to do with instigating and moving forward the SEAL team concept and figuring out the administrative details, allocating resources, operational commitments, and things along those lines.

When I think of the Teams, it's not individuals who come to mind. Instead it's the pride I feel in being one of these men, a member of that group of accomplished individuals. It's a fraternity, a group of people who had an equal beginning in adversity and who went on past that to become part of the whole.

Garry Bonelli, Captain, U.S. Navy Reserve

My thirty years in the Teams started almost from my first moments in the Navy back in 1968. After my enlistment, I was placed in the first-ever UDT-SEAL boot camp up at the Great Lakes Training Center north of Chicago. After I graduated boot camp, I went on to Coronado, where I started UDTR (Underwater Demolition Team Replacement, later called BUD/S) training with Class 50 on 3 January 1969. But that wasn't the class I graduated with. Right after Class 50 had completed a winter Hell Week, I broke my collarbone.

The instructors must have figured I was worth the trouble, as they rolled me back to complete my training with Class 51. That gave me the time I needed for my collarbone to knit. Training was tough, no matter what class I was with. I was one of those guys who barely held on through the hardest of the training. The only reason I made it was the instructors. At nineteen years of age, I was terrified of those men and there was no way I was going to walk up to one and tell him "I quit."

I just hung in there during training. The only thing I could do passably well was the swimming. Neither running nor the constant push-ups was something I was very good at. But I was a body, and they needed qualified people in the Teams.

At least I was motivated enough for the instructors. After I had been rolled back to Class 51 because of my injury, the instructors told me that I "probably" wouldn't have to go back through Hell Week again.

There was that little word "probably" in the conversation, though. When I asked what "probably" meant, the instructors told me to just take them at their word.

So I started training again on day one with Class 51. When that Sunday night before Hell Week rolled around, I mustered out with the rest of my class, standing there on the grinder facing those long, dark days. And I was all ready to be secured from Hell Week when the instructors pulled their little surprise. "No, you're going to go through Hell Week again," they told me.

So I was pretty well shocked, but there wasn't anything to say about it. There was no way I was psychologically prepared, but I faced another Hell Week. And I hung in there again. It wasn't until Tuesday that the instructors decided that I was motivated for the program and they dismissed me for the balance of Hell Week.

It's kind of hard for me to figure out just exactly what it was that got me through that first Hell Week, or both first phases, since I when through that part twice. Probably, it was my buddies, my boat crew, holding us all together, that got me through that first part of Hell Week the first time. By Wednesday or Thursday, I was just a zombie and whatever the instructors could do didn't matter. They couldn't hurt me, I was just numb.

When I was finishing Hell Week, the instructors had let the winning boat crew, that group who had done the best, be secured the night before the rest of us were. It was part of the Team's philosophy of "it pays to be a winner."

My own head was still straight enough, or at least I was cognizant enough that I would have loved to stop Hell Week right then as well. But the rest of us had to keep going. But at least we knew we were getting close to the end of our trial.

The next morning, when the instructors told the rest of us to secure from Hell Week, I kind of had mixed feelings. For one thing, I was really glad that I had personally made it through. Class 50 had started with maybe 136 guys. By the time we had gotten to Hell Week, the class was down to about 36. At the far end of Hell Week, there were 24 of us still standing on the grinder.

By that time we were only about a third of the way through training. The greatest single trial was behind us. But I was still worried about the training that was still in front of us. Could I keep going?

But I did keep going. Even though I was rolled back to another class, I still kept moving ahead. Class 51 graduated in June 1969. Only when I realized at graduation that I was holding a certificate that said I had passed UDTR did the reality of my situation begin to sink in.

Here I was, a seaman apprentice, and all of nineteen years old. And I could walk up to a Navy captain who I didn't know, and feel like God. I was in the Teams, there was no task too tough, nothing I didn't feel I could do. I wanted to take on the world.

We had started training with guys from all walks of life. There were farm boys from the country, some without a lot of formal education. And there were sophisticated guys with Ivy League backgrounds. But the best thing about the Teams centered on the name. One you were out there, in a platoon or a squad, all of those differences among the men—morals, values, knowledge, and backgrounds—were going to blend together. We were going to make a very flexible fighting force that could take on a wide variety of missions and be able to complete them like no one else could.

We graduated on a Friday, and had our class party that same night. Even though we were still half in the bag, the next morning we had to take a bus from Coronado to El Centro. Once at the Navy air facility there, we got on a plane bound for Army jump school at Fort Benning, Georgia.

My plan was that once I finished the three weeks of jump school, I was going to take some leave and go back to New York City. There, I would spend some time with my parents and walk around the Bronx a bit, seeing the place where I had grown up.

But things were happening pretty fast. We graduated jump school on a Friday and my platoon commander called me up and said we had to get back to Coronado by Sunday. So much for my leave back home. We got back to Coronado that Sunday, and by the following Wednesday, I was in Vietnam.

Now I was a member of Underwater Demolition Team 12. I had gone from UDTR to jump school, was assigned to a Team, and then went straight to Vietnam. Here I was, a kid all of nineteen years old, and suddenly I was stationed at Da Nang. In spite of the rush and confusion of everything, I remember my first impressions of Vietnam very well.

Stepping off the aircraft at Da Nang, I fully expected to be right in the middle of a shooting war. Instead I found myself in kind of a small, metropolitan airport. The guys who picked us up were driving jeeps with "UDT" printed all over them. It seemed pretty strange to me that we were advertising to everyone just who we were.

But that was the way they did things. We piled into the jeeps and drove around the bay, Da Nang Harbor, until we got to our base. It was just like a desert island or some kind of retreat, a number of Quonset huts near a nice chunk of beach.

In spite of appearances, the seriousness of our situation hit me that first evening. One of the more senior petty officers, a guy by the name of Chet Osborne, gave me my H-harness [web gear, weapon, ammunition, magazines, and hand grenades]. Then he told me to drape them over the foot of my bed. The idea was that if we had to go somewhere real fast, I could just grab my gear and move.

So I had my rack, gear, and weapon, and a memorable first night in Vietnam. One thing I wasn't used to was the sound of mortars exploding in the distance and the wavering light of flares dangling from parachutes. All of that made for a pretty tough first night's sleep. But I wasn't sleeping in the mud and was staying in a pretty secure area, seemingly far removed from the war.

The next morning, I was awakened by one of the guys from the unit. Immediately I grabbed for my H-harness, thinking we were going somewhere. Well, sure enough, we were going somewhere, but not exactly where I had thought.

"No, no, no," the Teammate who woke me up said. "Leave your harness here. We're going to an R&R center."

"An R&R center?" I asked. "Rest and relaxation? What are we going to do there?" "

"We're going to go surfing."

So my first full day in Vietnam, I had a surfboard under my feet and was working the waves of the South China Sea. That wasn't really how I pictured that the war was going to be.

But it was only a few days later that another of the many faces of this quick-moving conflict was shown to me. On that same beach where we had been surfing, a detachment of us were doing a beach recon and search. What we were looking for where the bodies of several U.S. Army guys who had gotten so drunk, they had fallen into the surf and drowned. That was my first real shock of the war.

My UDT detachment were fortunate in that we really were detached from the shooting war. To even get to the war, you had to leave the UDT base by jeep and go to either a boat or a helicopter to move out to the active combat zone. And most of the operations we were doing at the time didn't involve much direct combat.

Seawolf 301 of HAL-3, Det 5, lifts off from the USS *Harnett County* (LST-821) in the Mekong Delta area of South Vietnam.

U.S. Navy

The UDT was doing some river reconnaissances, checking the clearance for watercraft, looking for enemy bunkers, and blowing the ones we found. We did set up out in the jungle looking for the bad guys. But we weren't interdicting or ambushing them, just making note of their numbers and points of passage and reporting it back to command. Essentially, the SEALs were doing a lot more of the direct action against the Viet Cong while we in the UDT were still trying to get into the shooting portion of the war.

At least that was my perspective on things as a nineteen-year-old. So my first tour in-country was relatively easy. And I was pulled out of Vietnam fairly soon after I had arrived. I was sent back to Subic Bay in the Philippines, where UDT 12 had their headquarters. There, I attended hardhat divers' school.

So I wasn't in on the bigger UDT operations of the Vietnam War. Things like Operation DEEP CHANNEL, or what the old Frogs called the Big Blow Job. Lieutenant (j.g.) Harvey, a reservist like myself, was in charge of part of that operation, the blasting of a channel wide enough for a PBR to travel through part of the Plain of Reeds within sight of the Cambodian border. That operation was the largest combat demolition job in the history of the Navy. UDT 12 used 60 percent of the free world's supply of Mark 8 high-explosive hose to blast almost six miles of channel open.

Those were the stories that made the rounds of the UDTs. The SEALs were more the hard chargers, at least to me. The SEALs were the guys who went out and picked a fight with the enemy. The UDTs were more related to the beach and the water. We did recons and demolitions. And usually you had to do your time in the UDTs before you could go over to the SEAL Teams, something a lot of the guys in my Team aspired to do.

I spent the entire time of my first active-duty hitch in the Navy with UDT 12. I did another deployment to Southeast Asia, this time down to the Mekong Delta, and was based on SEAFLOAT, just as they turned it into SOLID ANCHOR. SEAFLOAT had been a cluster of barges that the Navy developed into a floating support base. SOLID ANCHOR was the replacement for SEAFLOAT and was a shore facility at Nam Can.

SOLID ANCHOR was a totally different war environment than the one I had experienced up at Da Nang. You didn't have to go far to find the enemy areas; they were in the free fire zone, which was everything outside of the barbed wire and sandbag walls of the base.

We went out and operated a lot differently in the Mekong area than we had up at Da Nang as well. We were far removed from what I would call civilization. At SOLID ANCHOR, we rested up during the day and operated at night. Using patrol boats, we traveled the rivers looking for the enemy.

Essentially, we were trying to help the boats navigate the delta. Only instead of blasting channels, we were blasting bunkers and the enemy. The PBRs would run

With his M16A1 rifle near at hand, this UDT operator prepares demolition charges to destroy a series of VC bunkers. The light-colored cord is detcord that will be used to connect the various C4 explosive charges together. Once the detcord is fired, all of the charges will detonate at the same moment.

U.S. Navy

into a lot of trouble from rocket [B-40] attacks from the VC along the shore. So our job became one of finding the enemy and stopping the attacks.

We still used our diving skills quite a bit in the Mekong. The boats and ships would run aground and bend driveshafts or props. And we would be diving in that terrible brown water to repair the boats since no dry-dock facilities were available.

One of the easy things we did was get a bent prop off a shaft. Normally, this operation required lifting the boat out of the water with a sling or dry dock. Instead, we went into that brown water, with a maximum visibility of about six inches in front of your mask, and removed bent props the UDT way. After we had loosened the nut holding the prop on the shaft, just a few turns of detcord were enough to knock the prop loose. Then we removed the bent prop, sent it up on a line, and they sent down a clean prop for us to install.

The water was warm, but it was like swimming in coffee. Your face mask would fill with liquid and you would clear it. Only you didn't have a leak, that was the sweat coming off your face and filling up the mask.

The Mekong Delta is the "rice bowl" of Southeast Asia. It is some of the most fertile land on earth. And it gets that way from all of the organic runoff coming down the river from the jungles and mountains far upstream. On top of that, the rice paddies throughout the area were fertilized with human waste. And this water also ran off into the delta.

We didn't take much in the way of casualties from enemy fire. But almost everyone I knew

A UDT operator gets ready to place a single block of C4 explosive on a VC bunker. His M16A1 rifle is kept within easy reach even though several of his Teammates are on watch.

U.S. Navy

in that UDT detachment came down with some kind of infection from working in that water. Ears and noses were the victims from germs rather than arms and legs from bullets. We were young studs who didn't think about being vulnerable to such things as infections, and we were very lucky that none of us came down with any kind of lasting injuries or disabilities.

The Vietnam War was winding down, with Vietnamization, the turning over of operations to the South Vietnamese, taking over more and more. But even though I didn't see a lot of heavy combat, I never felt I missed anything. There was more than enough to do just trying to take care of myself and keep myself and my Teammates alive.

It was our platoon officer who really spent his time making sure the rest of us stayed alive. I never knew it for a fact, but the word was that if we had a mission come down that he thought was a little too crazy, he would improvise and not do exactly what he had been told. Our flexibility in how we conducted our operations let him get away with that. And it may have helped a number of us come home again.

I have two very different memories about what it was like to come home to the States after my deployments to Vietnam. Coming home after that first tour, we flew in and landed at the Coronado Air Station. As a young man, I felt that I had just helped save the world from communism, but as I walked down the ramp from the plane, I wondered where everyone was to greet us. The tarmac was empty, no crowds of family and friends, Navy bands, or anything. Instead, a single petty officer came up and told us to get on the bus and it would take us to the base.

So that was it, no big greetings or anything like the Navy units had received coming back from WWII. Instead, there was just a bus ride back to the base. I wasn't a returning hero, just another member of the Teams who had done his job.

Time helped make me a little bit smarter before I returned from my second tour. I had been home on leave before I deployed to Vietnam again. Going back to New York and the Bronx and seeing friends I had grown up with and gone to high school

After an operation in the Rung Sat, SEALs and Vietnamese hand up their weapons to the extraction boat.

U.S. Navy

with and talking to them was an education. My old friends who had gone on to college told me that things had changed a lot. They were telling me that the war was unjust, that men like me weren't doing the right thing in fighting there.

This was a shock for me. As far as I was concerned, I had just come back from helping to save that piece of the world from communism. But what really hit home were the mixed feelings about the war. This wasn't like my dad's combat in World War II. There, we had 100 percent support from all of America. For Vietnam, there wasn't a fraction of that, especially among the young.

That saddened me in a way. I even started questioning myself to some degree. What I was doing and how was I doing it? This was a big thought because I knew I was going back overseas again. And on the next deployment, I already knew that I would be going down to the Mekong Delta and SEAFLOAT/SOLID ANCHOR.

Were we doing the right thing?

Although I had those questions in my mind, what gave me the support I needed was just looking around at my Teammates. These were great guys I was working with. They were doing the right thing, supporting each other. And I was fortunate to be serving with them. I didn't have a lot of questions as to what the right thing was after that. It was to be in the Teams and with my Teammates.

But you couldn't stay in the Teams forever, though some have tried. By the early 1970s, Vietnam was winding down and the Teams were being reduced in size. Within a few years guys were being pulled from the Teams and told to report to the regular fleet Navy or other standard diver units. I could see which way things were going and I left the active Navy and the UDTs in 1972 when my enlistment was up.

The first-ever SEAL reserve unit was started up on the West Coast in 1974. A lot of the guys who had left the Teams because of the postwar cutbacks had been pretty pissed off. They had worked hard to qualify to join the Teams. You don't go through Hell Week and everything else just to sail on ships.

Without those big, gray, steel ships manned by sailors with pride in their work, there wouldn't be a Navy. There certainly wouldn't be the SEALs or UDTs. But the men who had been in the Teams didn't want to just be told to go back to manning a ship, no matter how important it was. There had to be another way of using their skills and giving those who wanted it a means to operate again.

But some bright men had gotten together and convinced the naval reserve force to start a SEAL reserve force. The big pool of qualified SEAL and UDT operators both in the Navy and in the regular reserves could be drawn on to man the new Team. And those skills that had been so hard-won during wartime wouldn't be lost as easily as they might have been.

Initially, we had about thirty-six guys in the reserve Team. In the beginning, it was much like a professional athletic club, where we could come in one weekend a month and keep up our qualifications. What that meant was that we had the chance to do one more jump out of an airplane, dive to the bottom of the ocean, and blow things up. And we got paid to do it. It was a good deal for both the Navy and for us, and we didn't even have to get our hair cut to do it.

Back in those days, I was going back to college and had let my hair grow out quite a bit. In fact, I had an Afro-style cut and looked like Linc from the old Mod Squad TV show. But as long as we could fit our hair under a wig, we were good to operate.

At that time in the midseventies, there was definitely the active-duty side and the reserve side to the Team community. On the weekends when we would come in, it was pretty obvious that we would use their equipment, instructors, and assets to have what appeared to be just a good time. And it was, too.

That did cause some friction between the reserves and the active-duty SEALs. A number of the active-duty SEALs and UDTs were wondering just what they were getting from having a reserve unit. But we had a lot of good operators, and they let us stick around.

And the reserves were a good place for me to be. I remain in the unit to this day. Receiving my direct commission in the reserves, I had stayed in the Teams and moved up to a position of command. In the summer of 1990, I received the big phone call when Special Warfare Group One contacted me about bringing the reserves up. After eighteen years of being off of active duty, suddenly I was being activated back into the regular Teams.

Frankly, I thought the situation was just a drill and someone was having a joke at my expense. But that wasn't the case. A number of senior officers were called in and command told us the situation.

What was needed was extra manpower to augment the SEALs. Command wanted men who were qualified snipers, who were good with outboard engines, who were hot on the fast attack vehicles (FAVs), the stripped-down, armed desert patrol vehicles. The Teams were going to Desert Storm.

For myself and most of the reserves who were called up, we didn't forward-deploy to Saudi Arabia. Instead, we filled empty posts in Coronado. A very select few, maybe less than two dozen of the hundreds of reserve SEALs called up, actually forward-deployed to the Persian Gulf and Saudi.

What seemed to have come full circle in Desert Storm was the development of the UDTs into the SEALs. Many of the missions performed in the Persian Gulf were the same kind of hydrographic reconnaissance that would have been familiar to the Frogs of WWII. The cycle seemed to have become complete.

When I think of the Teams, a rush of different feelings come with the memories. There's patriotism and pride that come with having served my country. There's the satisfaction and well-being that goes along with having a team of fighters at your side. And there's just the pleasure of having a bunch of good guys with you that make up the family of Navy Special Warfare.

NAVY SEALs: A COMPLETE HISTORY

■ Chapter 51

The End of an Era

The Vietnam War had been a testing ground for the SEALs where they not only proved that the concept behind their creation was sound, but that it was outstanding. The SEALs had officially been incountry in South Vietnam within weeks of their commissioning, and remained there during the entire run of the U.S. involvement in the war. Direct action platoon began arriving in South Vietnam in early 1966. The Team's direct involvement with the Vietnam War ended with the last of SEAL Team One's platoons rotating back to the United States without relief in December 1971.

The date of 30 April 1975 does not hold a specific place in the history of the SEALs, but it is significant to many of them who served in Vietnam. At 10:15 A.M., 30 April 1975, South Vietnamese President Duong Van Minh, who had held the post only two days, announced that he was ready to transfer power to the North Vietnamese–backed Provisional Revolutionary Government. By noon that same day, Communist forces entered Saigon. South Vietnam had surrendered.

The almost legendary success of their combat actions in Southeast Asia did very little to spare the SEAL Teams and Naval Special Warfare as a whole from the postwar cutbacks in the U.S. military. After conducting thousands of combat operations in Southeast Asia, the Teams found themselves facing only a relatively few training operations and deployments during the year. In spite of their cutbacks in size and especially in funding, the Teams rose to the challenge and continued to better themselves in skills and abilities. This was to prove extremely valuable to the United States and its allies as the 1970s drew to a close and the world entered the 1980s.

Rick Woolard, Captain, USN (Ret.)

The standard deployment length for SEALs from both the east and west coasts in Vietnam was 179 days. As the platoon commander, I felt it was my job to stay around for another month or so to break in the platoon that was coming to relieve my platoon. So I had basically two seven-month tours in Vietnam.

We ran a lot of patrols during my first tour and conducted a lot of operations.

A group of SEALs from Team Two move on shore in Spain as part of an exercise. The kneeling Scout-swimmer at the front left is armed with an HK MP-5N submachine gun with a flashlight-mounted fore-arm. He would have been the first man on shore. The following SEALs are armed with M4 carbines. The automatic weapons man at the back of the column is watching to the rear and is armed with an M60E3 light machine gun.

U.S. Navy

The only person who was seriously wounded in my platoon was a guy named Skip Isham, who lost an eye due to a grenade. There were a few other fragmentation wounds. A guy by the name of Al McCoy took a piece of shrapnel in the gut the second time I got shot, which eventually forced him to be retired medically from the Navy. That was ten days after I was shot for the first time during an op.

The thing that sticks out in my mind about that first tour of duty in 1968 was how well John "Bubba" Brewton, my assistant platoon commander, I, and Third Platoon as a whole operated together. We really fit well together. The enlisted troops supported us completely, as we supported them. The conditions were great, and we had a good, solid, and fairly safe base from which to operate.

All the support we could have needed to run any kind of operation in our area was available. There was everything—we even had naval gunfire on call at one stage. Artillery support was available for some of the areas we went to. There were fixed-wing and helicopter gunships on call as well. And we had all the river patrol boats as well as our own boats to get us in and out again on an op. All in all, it was an ideal situation.

The first night I got shot, we needed gunfire support. Seawolves, I believe, only had one gunship up for a just a short period of time at that stage; they normally fly them in pairs. The guy who was able to fly flew for us running or air cover with only a single ship. You don't get a lot of people to do that, because it isn't safe—for good reason. But this was a man who knew us. We had eaten with him, we'd drunk with him, and we'd lived in the same place with him for months by that time. We were friends, and he wasn't going to let any SEAL get hurt if there was anything he could possibly do to prevent it.

These guys, the Seawolves, flew with us and for us all the time in Vietnam. You won't find a SEAL who was in Vietnam who won't say that those guys didn't bail our bacon out any number of times. We went places and did things that we wouldn't have dreamed of doing otherwise, just because we knew the Seawolves would be there if we needed them.

One thing that sticks in my mind, one particular operation that I didn't see personally, but some of my troops witnessed it, didn't involve a lot of SEALs. One of the river patrol boats, a PBR, got shot up fairly badly and they needed to evacuate a man as quickly as possible. He was in the far reaches of the Rung Sat Special Zone, and it would have taken hours to get him to medical attention by boat. The quickest way to get him out was for the Seawolves to pick him up; there were no other helicopters available.

A lieutenant by the name of Al Billings was flying one of the Seawolves. As the boat with the wounded man aboard was going down the waterway, Billings steadied his Seawolf perpendicular to the direction the boat was going. That pilot set one skid on the bow of the boat, forward of the twin fifty-gun tub, which had been deflected to the side. He just hovered there as the boat was moving until they could get the wounded guy onboard the Seawolf. Then he took off and took him away to a field hospital.

They were still in enemy territory, and I don't know if they were getting shot at during the time of the rescue. But anybody who could do that from both a courage and an airmanship standpoint, deserves a lot of respect.

In Vietnam, if the SEALs heard a call that a Seawolf was shot down, they would drop whatever they were doing and get to that location as fast as they could. We didn't have any Seawolves shot down during my first tour, but we did during my second tour in 1969. A Seawolf did crash right after takeoff at Nah Beh during my first tour. We immediately dropped what we were doing, and I just ran through the platoon and shouted what had happened.

You didn't have to tell people what to do. If any SEAL thought there was any way he could help a Seawolf, that immediately became his highest priority. We went out and saw that the gunship had crashed in the water. By the time we were able to get to the site, there was no hope of saving anybody. But we dove on the downed bird and got the bodies out, doing whatever we could to help things.

After my first tour was over, I came back to Virginia Beach and volunteered to go back to Vietnam a second time. I wanted to go back; I had experiences my first time that made me absolutely certain that this (the Teams) was a group of people I wanted some more time with. A lot of people from the same platoon I had taken over the first time were going back again as well. I wanted to go back with them. So we built a new Third Platoon around the core of the original Third Platoon. I took that platoon back to Vietnam in October 1969. We came back in April 1970.

The core of the platoon was the same. Bill Garnett, Bill Burwell, Jerry Todd, and a few others had been in my first platoon. Then there were some great new guys who were on their first combat deployment, guys like Bill Beebe, Larry Rich—a really fine SEAL—and a number of other men who had gone through training after I had gone to UDT (Underwater Demolition Teams) for a while and then come to SEAL Team.

For our second tour, we were at the far end of the country, on the shores of the Gulf of Thailand at a place called Song Ong Doc. It was a mobile tactical support base, which meant that it was a series of floating barges that had been lashed together and were anchored offshore of this very small town at the far end of the Ca Mau province that had no roads leading to it. This was basically the boondocks of South Vietnam.

We ran patrols through the whole surrounding area. To the north of us was the U Minh Forest, which was a Viet Cong and North Vietnamese Army (VC and NVA) stronghold. To the south of us was a large no-go area, at the center of which was a SEAL Team One base called SEAFLOAT. We did the same thing there that we did on my first tour—we sought out the enemy and killed or captured him.

My opinion of the enemy was a good one. I felt in many ways that they were fighting for their own cause, what they considered the right reasons, and I respected them. We did not kill or capture a single person who did not conduct himself well in captivity. Most of these people were ideologically motivated I think. Many of them had a little card from Uncle Ho wishing them season's greetings for their new year, their Tet.

The enemy's fighting ability varied from being very good for the NVA type and more highly trained VC, to being just sort of locals without much formal training. Tactically, some were good and some weren't. As a group, you always have to respect and never underestimate your enemy.

On both of my tours, we did not often see men from other platoons because they were located throughout the country. For a good part of the time SEAL Team Two was in Vietnam, there were only three platoons from the Team incountry at any one time. This was ramped up to a larger number—I think maybe six—by the end of the war.

But it's a big country, and we were scattered all over the place. There had been other platoons incountry for four months, overlapping my tours for that time. We were sent over at two-month intervals. I may not have ever seen a single guy from one of the other platoons. At most, we tended to see one other platoon at a time, and that was while we were relieving them or they were relieving us.

On my second tour, we were basically running straight SEAL operations. We had many interesting adventures. We were threatened by everything from a cobra snake we ran into in a field one night to the enemy. Primarily, we operated at night, just as most SEALs did.

On one operation that sticks in my mind, we were transiting along the Song Ong Doc River when we were ambushed by some rockets and a little bit of small-arms fire. At the same time the fire was opening up on us, there were about half a dozen sampans with civilian farmers or fishermen in them all around us in the river. The Vietnamese were just taking their goods to market, going home for the day, or whatever. We went by them in this big boat, and when we came under fire, we turned to go back and return fire. Our wake was enormous, and it swamped a number of the sampans.

The people were drowning in the water. Several of the other guys and I jumped into the water and rescued some of the people who were going to drown if we didn't pick them up. That event stands out in my mind, but we ran so many operations that I wouldn't care to try and pick out any particular one now.

There are several SEALs who I'd heard of as being superlative operators. One, of course, was Bob Gallagher. Mike Boynton was another superlative operator. Bob Gormly in the officer ranks along with Pete Peterson were great operators, too. But I wouldn't want to put out just those names as if they were the only good ones. Everybody did his job; it was not as if there was anybody in the Team who didn't give his all to making sure that everything went as well as possible.

On my second tour, there was one incident where we had a target that was in a very tough place to get to. We ended up patrolling through miserable terrain—lots of mud, lots of deep water, just a horrible, long slog to try and get to this particular place. To top it off, we were running late. It was starting to get to the point where we had to think about getting out of there because it was going to be daylight in the not-too-distant future.

We were patrolling along and, at the same time we were miserably slogging through this wretched terrain, we had to watch out for booby traps. One of the Vietnamese SEALs, an LDNN (Lien Doan Nguoi Nhia), was walking point and he tripped a grenade boobytrap that went off. I was about two people behind him and we all ran up to him to see how he was. I expected this guy to be shredded.

The LDNN was lying on the ground on his side in the fetal position with his eyes closed. The guy was totally scrunched up within himself. We rolled him over to see just where he was hurt, but we couldn't find any blood on the guy anywhere.

In spite of his lack of obvious wounds, the guy was still tightly balled up on the ground. One of the other LDNNs sort of looked at him and shook him a bit, moving him around. Then the guy we thought was wounded opened his eyes and looked around. He felt himself a little bit, then smiled because he knew he wasn't hurt. That's when the other LDNN kicked the guy on the ground as hard as he could, telling him to get up and get moving again.

I don't know how he got away without a scratch. This grenade booby trap detonated, but it must have gone off low-order. As sometimes happens with grenades, a piece that's not supposed to get you because you're out of range will get you in the worst place. Other times, you can be standing almost right next to the thing and the fragments will avoid you entirely. That LDNN just lucked out.

After I came back from my second tour in Vietnam, I wasn't thinking about a career. I had been in the Navy and commissioned less than three years at that point. In the Teams, I had already had three platoons over that time, one UDT platoon and two SEAL platoons with the two combat tours. I was assigned to the training unit on the East Coast. My experience in Vietnam, I believe, was the reason I was selected to go to the training unit and be the training officer.

As the training officer at Little Creek, I put through the last four East Coast training classes from May 1970 to September 1971. When I first left SEAL Team Two, I was not seriously considering staying in the Navy, but I knew that I had to serve out my committed time. I had extended for a year to make my second tour to Vietnam, so that still left some time for me to stay in the Navy.

What finally helped me decide to make a career of the Navy was one event with a lot of background. The background was that I had done two tours to Vietnam with the best people I'd ever met in my life up to that stage. Many of the salient and defining moments of my life took place while I was with these men. The second thing was that the man who had been my assistant platoon commander on my first tour had returned to Vietnam for his second tour with another platoon, been wounded, and died of his wounds.

The Navy named a ship after him. Even though I wasn't in SEAL Team Two at the time, I was invited to attend the launching and commissioning ceremony of the USS John C. Brewton in New Orleans, Louisiana. Attending that ceremony brought my experience into sharp focus. It was shortly after that event that I came back in and requested augmentation into the regular Navy—in other words, to go from being a reservist to a regular Navy officer. The reason I ended up augmenting into the regular Navy was that I knew there was no group of people on this earth with whom I would rather spend my life than the men of SEAL Team Two.

During my first tour in Vietnam, I was still single. I met the woman who is now my wife about a month before I left for that first tour. We lost track of each other for a bit. Her mom wasn't wild about her dating a SEAL and intercepted my letters, so she never knew where I was. We managed to find each other after my first tour, and we were married two weeks before I went back on my second tour.

The first thing you have to understand about being a SEAL is that, to me, it's an obligation. To be a SEAL means that whatever you do any time in your life reflects not just upon yourself but also upon everybody who has been, is now, or will be a SEAL. I take that very seriously. So it's an obligation to do well and be a good example in your life, not just to others, but to yourself. To be a SEAL also means having standards, high standards. You have to have very high expectations of yourself.

Going through basic SEAL training is tough. Training is very difficult from both a physical and a mental standpoint. You're subjected to a lot of adversity, and you come to learn certain fundamental truths that sound very obvious when you hear them said. But you come to really understand what these things mean during training. They're very simple things, such as it's better to be rested than to be tired, it's very much better to be fed than to be hungry, it's much, much better to be warm than to be cold, and it's much, much better to win than to lose.

Having said that, once you go through training, you develop a certain underlying confidence. In some forms it can be a bravado. In other forms, as time goes on, it matures into a kind of quiet confidence, a knowledge that you have way back in the back of your mind that you've seen some nasty times and whatever you're likely to be seeing at the moment, even though it might seem rather urgent or dire, in the perspective of what you have undergone before, it probably really doesn't make that much difference.

You end up having a certain nonchalance, a certain "don't-give-a-damn" attitude about things that some people might really consider problems. This doesn't just apply to when you're in the service or a military situation. My friend Larry Rich was a SEAL in the second platoon that I took to Vietnam and I actually work for him now. We're turning around his manufacturing company in Ohio. We have to borrow some money to do this—millions of dollars. Two weeks ago, we were talking to a banker who had the money we wanted.

We were nervous about it to a degree, but Larry handled himself superbly. I had told the banker that Larry and I had been in the Teams together. The banker asked, "What does that do for you?" Turning to Larry, the banker continued, "You seem to be a rather nonconforming specimen."

And Larry is. He does what he wants to do. So I joked and said that he had always been that way, which was true. But I also told the guy very frankly that having gone through training together and having been in combat together in a SEAL Team, there's a lot of stuff that you just don't give a damn about and don't get excited about. That's what training can do for you.

When I think of the word SEAL, I get a composite picture of the finest people I have ever known. The Trident to me doesn't mean quite what it might mean to newer SEALs. It's our badge, but I'm not too caught up in the symbolism of it. When the Trident originally came out, there was one for SEALs and one for the UDTs. The one for the UDTs did not have the eagle on it. And there was a different colored one for officers and enlisted. The officers wore a gold insignia, and the enlisted wore a silver one.

That has all been done away with, and the SEALs and UDTs, officers and enlisted, all now wear the same gold Trident. But I remember when the Trident that everybody is so proud of now first came out. A lot of people, myself included, were somewhat horrified that the thing was so damned big. There was a very strong movement after it first came out to reduce it to the size of parachutists' and aviators' wings or the submarines' dolphins. There's a more or less standard size for naval insignia, but this thing was twice as big as any of the rest of them.

So a smaller Naval Special Warfare insignia was designed, which I quite liked. But by the time that the Trident had gone through its design process and had gotten out to the Teams for evaluation, everybody had pretty much gotten used to the big one. So that's how it ended up staying as our insignia. So when you say Trident, a little history comes to my mind, not just this feeling of pride in the symbolism like Old Glory or anything. To me, it's a badge.

People often ask, "Why do people become SEALs?" Often, there's a very long, convoluted, and complex psychological reason cited. The answer is very simple in my mind: I think people become SEALs because they want to see if they can do it. There's a certain number of people in the world who just need to go to the limits. They don't necessarily choose to be that way; that's just the way they are. They need to go to the limits, and being a SEAL is one way of doing that.

The great thing about being a SEAL is that you get to go to the limits in the service of your country. It's a powerful argument for being a SEAL as far as I'm concerned.

Today, I think it's tougher to be a SEAL. I would love to be a new guy coming out of BUD/S (Basic Underwater Demolition/SEALs) right now. Being twenty-two years old and coming straight out of BUD/S and into the Teams would be the beginning of a great adventure. But I think they have a tougher road ahead of them from the moment they graduate than people did back in my time some thirty-odd years ago.

When I went through training in 1966, very few people outside the Navy and the services knew anything at all about the SEALs. Even for quite some time after that, SEALs were just not well known. I remember talking with my little English grandmother in New York at a family reunion in the mid-1980s after SEALs had been around for more than twenty years. She said, "Well, Rick, tell me, are you still with that Navy outfit? What was it? The snails?"

For a long time, a lot of people hadn't heard of the SEALs. Today, it's completely different. A guy who graduates from BUD/S automatically gets saddled with a whole load of baggage the moment he steps off the parade ground in Coronado.

There's so much public knowledge about the SEALs, so much information and mis-information about them, that it's just daunting for anybody.

All these books that are out there—some of which are quite good and a lot of which are just total rubbish—give the public an image of a SEAL. The movies are even worse in giving a slanted image of a SEAL. There are impostors and wanna-bes all over the place. You can't help but run into them. So a guy who becomes a SEAL today has a lot more to worry about and a lot more hanging off him than did a man who was a SEAL thirty years ago. I think there's more expectations now, for better or for worse, when a guy graduates from BUD/S.

Getting back to books and the publicity that's been given to the SEALs—much of it by guys who are in the Teams—I'd like to say that generally, SEALs divide them-selves into two categories. The first category—and there are many, many more of these than in the other category—are those men who love the Teams. They love what they do in the Teams, and they love to help their Teammates and their country. That's why they are SEALs. That's why they do what they do.

The second category are those guys who love the Teams for what the Teams can do for them. They love themselves more than they do the Teams, and their fo-cus is on how the Teams and being a SEAL can help them in their lives for one rea-son or another. There are only a few of those, and they make a lot of noise. I think they get undue publicity in some quarters.

There are two ships in the U.S. Navy that are named after SEALs or naval Spe-cial Warfare type people. One is the guided-missile frigate Kauffman, FFG 59, named after Draper Kauffman, one of the men who helped start it all back in 1943. The other is the guided-missile destroyer McFaul, DDG 74, named after Donald L. McFaul, a man from SEAL Team Four who was killed on the Paitilla Airfield in Panama.

There was also a ship, a Knox-class Frigate, the FF 1086, the USS John C. Brew-ton, named after John "Bubba" Brewton, my assistant platoon commander on my first tour in Vietnam. He was a fine man and a fine SEAL. He survived his first trip with me and was extremely lucky on several occasions.

On my first tour in Vietnam, I was wounded twice. Each time, if I had not been positioned exactly where I was, the bullets or the fragments that hit me would have hit Brewton and might have killed him. He just laughed this off each time, and I'd of-ten remind him of the situation. We'd joke about how, when we got back to the States, he would be walking down the street one day and a safe would fall on him or something like that. He never took it too seriously.

John was wounded on Thanksgiving Day, 1969, during his second tour in Viet-nam. His platoon patrolled right into an enemy base camp and he was right near the front and was hit three or four times. They didn't even realize how many times he'd been hit until much later. He went to the hospital and I basically watched him die over a few weeks.

At first, he was not expected to live until Christmas. When John survived until Christmas, they said he wasn't going to make it to New Year's. He finally passed away on 11 January 1970. I was stationed in a different part of the country when John passed away. He was in the Third Field Hospital in Saigon. It had been very difficult for me to get up to see him, but I did it as often as I possibly could.

My memories of John in the hospital are poignant for me. The first few times I went to visit him, John was very lucid and able to express himself. He was in a fair amount of pain, but he knew what was going on. The doctors had to take off his leg at the knee, then they had to remove more of it higher up. The third time, they ended up taking it off at the hip. That's where they found a bullet that had been lodged in John's hip that they didn't even know was there. It was shortly after that last surgery that he died.

The thing that struck me most about the situation was where in the hospital John had been all that time. He was in the renal ward of the Third Field Hospital. I didn't realize it until I went there, but the renal ward is where they put the people who really weren't going to survive.

I just can't say enough about what fine people the Army nurses who took care of John and all the guys in the renal ward were. It must have been tough for them to serve a full tour of duty, in their case a year, in that ward just seeing these fine young men come in all shot up or blown up. I don't think more than one or two of the patients in any given year's time actually walked out of that place under their own power. Most of them died.

Every time I would go up to visit Bubba, the beds would be filled by a completely different cast of characters. I would go around and talk to them and ask them where they're from, just kind of put them at ease. These guys had been wounded badly, and many of them were draftees, although that didn't make any difference. And you could tell, without a word being said, that they weren't going to make it, and they knew it.

When the Navy ended up naming that ship, which was already scheduled to be named after another man, the Chief of Naval Operations (CNO) Admiral Zumwalt, it decided to name the ship after John Brewton. He had known John in Vietnam. I went to the commissioning ceremony. That's when I decided that I was going to stay in the Teams.

I live right in Washington, D.C., and every time I go to the Wall—I went there just a few weeks ago with Lee Barry from New Hampshire, a friend I'd gone through training with—I look up on panel 14 West and see John C. Brewton. Every time, it's tough to keep a tear back. He passed away thirty years ago.

You depend on your friends and your Teammates to keep your memory alive. My assistant platoon commander, Bubba Brewton, who I went through Ranger School, all of my pre-deployment training, and my whole first tour in SEAL Team Two with, got killed. I haven't spoken to him since 1970, and I'm sure I've forgotten things.

Bubba and I had an awful lot of shared history together—things that only happened in Ranger School or SEAL Team Two or things that only the two of us really knew. I have nobody to help stir my memory of those things.

There are a couple things that SEALs are very good at right now, three things actually that I think are very essential to what SEALs are. One is being good combat swimmers. Another is being very good at cold-weather operations. And third is being excellent scout-snipers or marksmen. I'm very pleased to have been able to help develop these capabilities within the Teams.

When I commanded SEAL Team Two from 1982 to 1984, we put a lot of emphasis on combat swimming. In fact, we developed the model for the combat swimmer course that's now still in operation in the Teams. There was a training event in 1983 that illustrates just what combat swimmers can do.

It took place in Denmark and Germany in April 1983, during an exercise called FLINTLOCK. Our mission was to conduct a ship attack in Olpenitz, a heavily defended German harbor on the eastern side of the Jutland peninsula, just south of the Danish border in northern Germany.

The people who were chosen to do the mission were four Kampfschwimmers, who were the German SEALs, and four men from SEAL Team Two who we had

Captain Rick Woolard, commanding officer of SEAL Team Two at the time, to the left, looks on with a smile as one of the new SEAL snipers is examined by a visiting foreign officer. The SEAL is wearing a ghillie suit for camouflage and is armed with a bolt-action 7.62mm rifle.

U.S. Navy

trained to do this sort of mission. They had undergone the first combat swimmer course. The men from SEAL Team Two were Joe McGuire, Ron Pierce, Caleb Esmiol, and Chuck Johnson.

The operation unfolded with a warning order issued on the day they were going to attack the harbor. The harbor was heavily defended by both German National Guard and Home Guard troops standing on a full wartime defense posture. The harbor had a very narrow mouth on the eastern side and was a mile deep in an east-to-west direction, heading toward the west. The target ships that were to be attacked were at the farthest point inside the harbor.

The four SEALs and the four Kampfschwimmers parachuted from an MC-130 aircraft with their dive gear and their wetsuits and nothing else. They dropped into the North Sea at a precise spot and rendezvoused with a German coastal submarine that was waiting for them there. They swam into the sub's torpedo tubes—which are barely large enough for a man to get in to—with their dive rigs on, the first man going in fins-first, the second man going in face-first. Then they could meet face-to-face and breathe from the same mouthpiece.

In a torpedo tube, it isn't a gradual lock-in, lock-out environment. Instead, you go from thirty-three feet of sea water pressure—the depth of the torpedo tubes—to atmospheric pressure in just inside of a second. So if your ears aren't nice and loose, you blow an eardrum right away.

But they all successfully locked in—that was the easy part. They spent the next twenty-four hours waiting while the submarine approached the drop-off point near the harbor. All the while, the submarine was being looked for by the exercise "enemy." The men didn't get much sleep—they didn't have any racks to sleep in and they were in their wetsuits, still wet from the insertion, for that whole twenty-four-hour period. I think they did get a salami sandwich or something like that during their wait.

The lock out of the submarine was made the same way as the lock in: just after dark a mile or so off the harbor they were meant to attack. The two pairs of SEALs and two pairs of Kampfschwimmers swam in on the surface. The Kampfschwimmers were caught up in some kind of currents, swept away, and were never able to make the attack.

The four SEALs swam to a tactical distance outside the harbor so they could visually verify where they were. Then they submerged and, using their attack boards with their underwater clocks and compasses, they worked their way to the target. The entire distance was covered underwater, and they had to change course five or six times while staying submerged. They surfaced, just barely breaking the surface so the water was still filming over their face masks, to make sure the targets were still there. Then they approached the targets, attached their limpets mines to the ships, then swam out again.

By this time, they had gone through all the oxygen in their Draeger rebreathers, or at least some of them were running on empty. They had to surface, and two of them came up under a pier where German guards were walking around looking for them. The guards knew they were coming, they just didn't know when or how.

One of the SEALs, Pierce, was getting a CO_2 hit, which made him nauseated. He had to throw up, so he put his head back into the water, vomited, then surfaced again, put his mouthpiece back in, and the pair swam a short distance away to where they could get out of the water. From there, they exfiltrated over land. They climbed the fence, got outside the harbor, made their way back to the water, and swam out to a fishing boat, a mile and a half to two miles offshore, waiting to pick them up.

This was in April, so the water temperature was thirty-nine degrees at the surface and thirty-six degrees at a depth of three meters, where they were swimming. The SEALs were in wet suits, were in the water for probably twelve to fourteen hours, and swam a total of five to six miles.

That's a world-class combat swim. The fact that these guys were able to do that caught the attention of others throughout Naval Special Warfare. Today, SEALs are trained to do that sort of thing. Not every SEAL can do it to that extreme, but there have been several operations in Panama and elsewhere that have featured this type of skill and endurance. I was happy to be the guy who was in charge of SEAL Team Two when these skills were developed.

There had been a combat swimmer course before I became involved, but it hadn't been well conducted and didn't have any cohesiveness. About two weeks after I became CO, I was supremely fortunate to have come across the quarterdeck of SEAL Team Two a young Frenchman by the name of Francois Devoux. Francois was a member of the French Navy SEAL equivalents, the Nageurs de combat, or French combat swimmers, based in Toulon, France. He was on exchange with SEAL Team Two and was the first French officer who had come to SEAL Team Two to be on exchange with us, although we had sent several SEALs to Toulon to be on exchange with them.

Francois came on board and quickly proved himself a wonderful man, a great SEAL, an excellent ambassador for his country, and a superlative teacher as well as being a very hard taskmaster. I put him in charge of the combat swimmer course and basically gave him carte blanc for the equipment, people, and organization he needed, and he ran one hell of a combat swimmer course for the entire time he was here.

The people who graduated from this course—and not everybody did—went on to train the people who did the attacks in Panama and other places. I have to give myself a little bit of credit because, although Francois taught the course and developed his own cadre of instructors, I did not allow any of the people who thought

In front of an awestruck crowd, this night-ops clan SEAL rapidly scales the fence surrounding the UDT-SEAL Museum in Fort Pierce, Florida, as part of the Veteran's Day demonstration of Team abilities.

Kevin Dockery

they already knew about combat swimming to go though the course. These were the SEALs who had been on exchange with the Germans or elsewhere and had cross-trained with those units and thought they knew about combat swimming. They were not the ones chosen for the training, in part because they generally were too senior to go through the course. What I did was take the young, hard, tough guys, who seemed numerous in SEAL Team Two at that time, and put them through the combat swimmer course instead.

Guys like Perry Bruce, Andy Tafelski, Vinnie Naple, Mike McCarthy, Clell Breining, and a dozen or two others were the ones from SEAL Team Two who went through that first combat swimmer course. The names I just mentioned are all men who have been master chiefs of various SEAL Teams or even Naval Special Warfare Commands. Andy Tafelski is the Command Master Chief of the Naval Special Warfare Command right now (1997), maybe not because he went though the combat swimmer course, although it did make him a better man, I'm sure of that.

■ Chapter 52

A New Mission

"Terrorism" . . . premeditated, politically motivated violence perpetrated against noncombatant targets by subnational groups or clandestine agents, usually intended to influence an audience.

— United States Code, Title 22, Section 265f(d)

With the advent of the 1970s, the world entered a new decade and faced an old adversary in a new war. Terrorism had been around since the days of the Romans. With the creation of the State of Israel in 1948, a new form of terrorism began to grow in the Middle East. Political turmoil in other parts of the world, such as India, Ireland, Spain, and Europe, gave rise to regional variations of terrorists and their groups. But it was out of the Middle East that terrorism grew the most and entered the world stage.

Aircraft hijackings were almost old news by the 1970s. Along the East Coast of the United States, the hijackings of aircraft to Cuba became almost common. Soldiers returning to base from leave on the holidays spoke about having a "Cuban Extension" on their furloughs. But it was at the 1972 Olympics that Middle East terrorism really took its place on the world stage.

The 1972 Munich Olympics was the first time the West Germans had hosted the Games since the 1936 Games were held in Berlin during the days of Hitler and Nazi Germany. The Germans were particularly sensitive about not showing a hard front in the way of security guards, police, and especially the military during the Games. On September 5, terrorists from the Black September organization climbed the fence surrounding the Olympic village and took the Israeli team captive after shooting two of them during the attack.

After a seventeen-hour standoff, the terrorists and nine Israeli Olympians were taken to the Munich airport to board a plane that would take them to Cairo. Bavarian police marksmen opened fire on the Arab terrorists in poor conditions and were unable to hit their targets before the terrorists opened fire on the captives. In the end, all the terrorists, the Israeli hostages, and two German helicopter pilots were dead. This horrific spectacle took place before the cameras of the world's news agencies, which were there to film the Olympic Games.

Germany established Grenzschutzgruppe-9 (GSG-9) to see to it that the horrors of the 1972 Olympic Games would never be repeated. In a relatively short time, GSG-9 became one of the world's great antiterrorist organizations, one that was to be emulated by a number of other governments. Great Britain also established a significant counterterrorist organization when it allotted the resources necessary to establish a permanent Counter-Revolutionary Warfare (CRW) unit within the renowned ranks of the Special Air Service. France established the Groupe D'Intervention De La Gendarmerie Nationale (GIGN).

In the United States, several special counterterrorist organizations were established and in place by the end of the 1970s. The U.S. Army Special Forces established Operational Detachment Delta, commonly called Delta Force by the public, to be the primary counterterrorist organization of the U.S. military.

To counter terrorist actions in a maritime environment, SEAL Teams One and Two both created specialized platoons within their respective Teams. On the East Coast at SEAL Team Two, the counterterrorist platoon was known as MOB-Six, for Mobility Platoon Six. On the West Coast at SEAL Team One, the counterterrorist platoon was Echo Platoon.

The two specialized SEAL platoons were tasked with conducting counterterrorist actions in a maritime environment. Possible actions could range from a ship or shore facility being taken over to an ocean oil rig suffering the same fate. The SEALs trained in how to board a ship while it was under way, climbing aboard ships, structures, and buildings, and close-quarter battle, fighting from room-to-room or compartment-to-compartment within feet of the enemy or a hostage.

The SEALs on the West Coast at least used the venerable M191A1 .45 automatic as their primary handgun for such operations. The fourteen-inch barreled version of the M16 was also a favorite. On the East Coast, and later on both coasts, the stainless steel Smith & Wesson M66 .357 magnum revolver became the handgun of choice.

In the late 1970s, the Shah of Iran was overthrown and a revolutionary Islamic fundamentalist government under the iron hand of the Ayatollah Ruhollah Khomeini took his place. The diplomats and staff of the U.S. Embassy in Teheran, Iran, were taken hostage by militant Iranian students on 4 November 1979. The fifty-two American hostages were to suffer for more than a year at the hands of their captors. From 24 to 25 April 1980, the men of Delta Force conducted Operation EAGLE CLAW to rescue the American hostages and bring them home.

A number of other counterterrorist units had conducted very successful operations to rescue their captured countrymen. The Israeli Unit 269 conducted Operation THUNDERBALL on 4 July 1976, rescuing more than 100 hostages at minimum loss to the hostages or the rescue forces. Operation FIRE

MAGIC was the GSG-9 rescue of the passengers and crew of a hijacked 737 at Mogadishu, Somalia, on 18 October 1977. The eighty-six passengers and the plane's crew were rescued with the only losses being among the terrorists. In Great Britain, the men of the SAS B Squadron conducted Operation NIMROD, the retaking of the Iranian Embassy at 16 Princes Gate on 5 May 1980 after a six-day siege. These operations were all conducted successfully, with the far greater number of casualties being on the side of the terrorists. Operation EAGLE CLAW was not to see a similar fate.

On 25 April 1980, the C-130 aircraft and RH-53D naval helicopters of the rescuing forces arrived at the "Desert One" covert forward refueling base in the Iranian desert. The difficult desert conditions forced the officer in charge of the rescue forces to abort the mission when too few helicopters were functional after a sandstorm. During the return to base takeoff attempt, a helicopter collided with a tanker aircraft, killing five airmen and three soldiers. The resulting fire and disastrous withdrawal from Iran left four helicopters abandoned in the desert, along with the hopes for the mission.

The hostages in Teheran were eventually released by their captors, shortly before Ronald Reagan took office as the president of the United States. The military was smarting from the failure of EAGLE CLAW and the damage it did to the standing of the U.S. military around the world. In the aftermath, new organizations were created to prevent such a chaotic organizational mess as EAGLE CLAW from ever happening again. And the Navy decided to create a counterterrorist organization of its own as well.

The flamboyant, charismatic, and extremely creative SEAL Lieutenant Commander Richard Marcinko was tasked with creating the new Naval CT (counterterrorist) unit. Marcinko saw to it that the new organization would be a command unto itself, and instead of being a unit or detachment, it would be a stand-alone SEAL Team. To sow confusion among outsiders who would be trying to find out about the new and very classified unit, Marcinko gave the new SEAL Team the identifying number Six. SEAL Team Six would make outsiders wonder where SEAL Teams Three to Five were.

Gathering the best talent he could find from all of the special warfare community, Marcinko gathered his new SEALs at Little Creek, Virginia, in the late summer of 1980. By November 1980, SEAL Team Six was commissioned. The small number of enlisted men and officers of the new SEAL Team, about the same number of personnel who originally manned SEAL Teams One and Two, were eventually broken down into two smaller units, Gold and Blue Teams, in the Navy tradition of a nuclear submarine having two operational crews of the same name. Instead of the several years Delta Force had to get operational, the proposal for SEAL Team Six submitted by Richard Marcinko allotted only six months for the Team to reach operational capability.

The training schedule of SEAL Team Six was brutal. In his own words, Richard Marcinko was trying to fit 408 days of training into 365. He decided that his men could sleep onboard planes. The training regime was successful, and SEAL Team Six pioneered techniques for close-quarter combat, ship boarding, and other skills that are used in all the SEAL Teams today. Weapons first used by SEAL Team Six, such as the nine-millimeter Heckler and Koch MP5 submachine gun, became standard issue in all the other Teams. Eventually, a special model of the weapon was produced specifically to fit SEAL specifications.

For SEAL Team Six to conduct some of its operations, particularly undercover or infiltration ops, they had to be able to blend in with a local population. The physical fitness standards for the Team made a group of the

The upper illustration is of the left side of the MP-5N submachine gun modified to Navy SEAL specifications. The collapsing stock is slid forward and the weapon is loaded with a 30-round magazine. In front of the 30-round magazine is the more compact 15-round magazine used for concealment purposes.

The lower illustration is the right side of the MP-5N submachine gun with the collapsing stock locked in the extended position. One of the SEAL features is shown by the ambidextrous selector lever on each side of the weapon above the trigger. On the threaded muzzle of this N model is attached a stainless steel suppressor for reducing the sound of a shot.

Kevin Dockery

operators standing together look like part of a professional football team. But there was nothing that could be done about their size.

One of the means Richard Marcinko used to help his Team blend in was to choose people that had skills and work experience beyond those of a SEAL. Men who had worked on railroads, carpenters, construction workers, and heavy equipment operators were all viewed as having a plus in their ability to blend in on a dock, construction site, or other common locations.

Another aspect of the problem of blending in with a civilian population caused some friction between Team Six and the other SEAL and UDT Teams. As a practical matter, it would have been much easier to cut someone's long hair to fit a local style than it would have been to grow it out to match another style. A wig could slip at a very inopportune moment, possibly exposing an operator and putting an entire mission at risk. To eliminate this problem, SEAL Team Six adopted modified grooming standards.

An example of the modified grooming standards in place at SEAL Team Six during the early 1980s. This SEAL is firing an M79 40mm grenade launcher. At his feet to the left is an M203 40mm grenade launcher with the barrel slide forward in the open position for loading and safety.

Dennis Chalker Collection

Different from the Navy or military norm, or even what was accepted at MOB-Six or Echo Platoon, the modified grooming standards at Six encouraged long hair and facial growth. Ponytails, moustaches, and long sideburns were all common in the ranks at Six. This caused a little heartburn among the operators and those at Six. Not only could the men of SEAL Team Six grow their hair out, they appeared to be constantly traveling for exotic training and they had all the best toys in the way of weapons and equipment, materials they were constantly using to push the limits of their operational envelope.

Red Cell, the Navy's Own Terrorists

A new SEAL unit was established in 1984 at the direction of Vice Admiral James A. "Ace" Lyons, deputy chief of Naval Operations for Plans, Policy, and Operations. The official designator for the new unit was OP-6D and its name was the Naval Security Coordination Team, but it was referred to simply as Red Cell.

The 23 October 1983 suicide truck bombing of the U.S. Marine barracks in Beirut, Lebanon, credited to Islamic Jihad, killed 241 Marines and others and wounded 80. A smaller truck bomb that same day killed 58 French Legionnaires at their barracks. Earlier that same year, on 18 April, a terrorist suicide truck bomb targeted the U.S. Embassy in Beirut. That blast killed 63 and injured 120.

The terrorist actions helped point out the seeming lack of security at some U.S. installations. Admiral Lyons directed the creation of a new unit capable of realistically testing and directing the improvement of security at Navy installations. For the leadership and creation of the new units, Admiral Lyons looked to Commander Richard Marcinko.

Having rotated out of his position as the commanding officer of SEAL Team Six, Marcinko was enthused about the opportunity to create another unique organization. For the primary manpower of Red Cell, Marcinko looked to the SEALs of Team Six. The final personnel roster for Red Cell consisted of eleven enlisted men and three officers—Marcinko included. The offices for OP-6D were on the E Ring of the Pentagon.

After about four months of training, Red Cell was declared operational. The men of Red Cell had learned defensive driving at a racing school. They had become even more proficient with firearms, unusual shooting situations and state-of-the-art weapons. Demolition skills were increased as the knowledge base of the operators grew in the field of IEDs (improvised explosive devices). Even State Department and Secret Service assets were included in the Red Cell training curriculum. Red Cell became a very proficient and dangerous antagonist—effectively a Navy-supported terrorist unit.

Navy bases and other specified facilities would receive a briefing and instructions on generally what to expect of a Red Cell training exercise, but they would not be told the specific time of the upcoming incident. Navy base commanders disliked having their routines and schedules disrupted by a Red Cell security exercise, and they hated it when Red Cell made their security procedures seem lax and ineffectual.

Red Cell would attack a base surreptitiously, infiltrate the facility, and secure IEDs on high-value targets. Or the men would penetrate what had been considered very secure facilities—some of the most secure in the Navy. In spite of Red Cell taking every precaution, even to the point of filming their infiltrations for later post-action briefings, commanders still looked on the Red Cell actions as something personal.

After several years of operations all over the world, Red Cell was ordered to stand down while an investigation was conducted amid accusations of corruption among some of its personnel. Finally, the unit was brought back into action under very restrictive guidelines.

Richard Marcinko, Commander, USN (Ret.)

The postwar cutbacks in the 1970s under President Carter had relatively little impact on Special Warfare, primarily because we're so small. When you cut a carrier from the Navy budget, you save a lot of money. When you take that carrier out, you also lose all the destroyers that have to escort it. You take out a squadron of planes and all of their support needs and personnel, too. If you take away one SEAL Team, you're taking away body count, but there's no support tail to it. So the money you save if you took out a Team wouldn't even be parking meter money to the Navy.

What removing or cutting back on the Teams would do is slow down research and development and maybe slow down the procurement of new buys of equipment. But Special Warfare is supposed to be a force-multiplier; it's suppose to live off the ground. So whatever you get hold of, you use to fight with, and you steal it from anywhere you find it.

Vietnam was our small-unit war. I might hear a lot from the Vietnam Vets by saying this, but the Army had problems with discipline and general leadership. I can understand their problems. Army officers in Vietnam would generally spend only six months with the troops and then six months on staff. They weren't there on the line every day. In the Teams, we were on the line together every day. We flew in together, we stayed together, we fought together, and we came home together. That makes a big difference.

Vietnam was our war. It was the first time the Navy went public that the SEALs existed and about what they did. There had been a long spell between the Korean War and Vietnam. There were little incidents along with the war—the Cuban blockade, the Dominican Republic, things like that—that were really just flash-in-the-pan, two-week jobs that didn't amount to much.

After Vietnam, the next target that showed up that was of any value to a SEAL was of course terrorism. It was everywhere in the 1970s.

For years, way back in Underwater Demolition Team days, there was an exercise called a Zulu Five Oscar. In that exercise, every ship had to repel attempted boarders from getting onboard. That became a cosmetic jerk-off.

Rules were established for the exercise that were very staged and artificial. You had to do the action between sunset and a certain hour. And if you scored a hit on a ship, they backpedaled, explaining how they had really done it and gotten us out of the water. Then we would come back with our version of what we would have done in those circumstances and we would have gotten them. It was like two kids playing a game of "I can do it, you can do it."

No one gave much credibility to the problem of repelling boarders. Then terrorism came along. Suddenly, we were doing embassies and other U.S. property instead of just ships. That was an expansion of Zulu Five Oscar. The powers-that-were said there were bad guys out there now, and we had to do something.

When the raid to rescue the Iranian hostages failed, we learned a lot. In any major conflict, every service has to get involved, otherwise there's no reason for them, there's no budget. It's a money thing. So you have to throw people at the problem to prove that what you have is worth what it costs.

When you start flying Navy helicopters across the desert, they aren't happy. When you start flying Army helicopter pilots across the water, they aren't happy. So it ended up that there were probably thirty-some options written up for the first raid that just didn't go anywhere.

The Chairman of the Joint Chiefs of Staff at the time was an Air Force general who had never commanded troops. He was one of those very bright McNamara brain kids who didn't know about war but knew about books. So we didn't get very far in all of those planned options.

In training for the operation, garbage was left all across the United States. It fell out of the sky, it got broken, or it just didn't work right together. Then, when Operation EAGLE CLAW, the raid into Iran, didn't work, it went bad big-time. At Desert One, the refueling base in Iran, it was Murphy who caused the helicopter to fly into the C-130 in the dust storm. But those helicopters that lifted off left classified materials behind them.

The situation translated to specific service standard operating procedures, which is what the guys did when the shit happened. They could practice the joint operation thing, but they fell back on what they had been doing all of their military lives when things got bad.

The white paper written up after Operation EAGLE CLAW said that the United States needed a full-time force to do counterterrorist operations and to see that such a debacle as EAGLE CLAW never happened again. That's what made counterterrorism the in-vogue thing, and the funded thing, being pushed on all the services.

And we did train together later. Army helicopter pilots took us across water, low and all while running with night-vision devices. Then there were the Air Force refueling services that could refuel us en route. There were dedicated C-130 and C-141 crews to move us and our gear. We now had a package from all the services that worked together, and we knew each other.

I'll tell you flat out that a shooter is a shooter is a shooter. And any of the shooters from any of the services can work for me, and there would be no problem. There's no difference in the cloth they are all cut from.

Harry Humphries said it very well when he said that the Vietnam era was a breeding ground for new types of fighters who might not have existed in prior wars, especially in the Pacific during WWII. But we saw a new sailor in Vietnam; we adopted a new brother during that era. That brother was the Brown Water sailor and the PBR sailor, of the inland rivers and streams, and the Seawolf pilot.

Why is that? How could we have possibly accepted somebody who hadn't gone through our training as a fellow combatant, a fellow warrior? Because when you're in trouble and there's nowhere to go—our back door has always been the water, and there's nowhere to go from there—a firefight is going down. It's an unbelievably difficult situation, and you just know you aren't going to get out.

Then, suddenly, over the horizon comes a small boat, a PBR or whatever, to support us. They came in under those conditions for us. Those guys didn't have to do that. They could have radioed back and said the gunfire was too intense or whatever. But they always came in, snatched us off the beach, and got us out of there.

The Seawolves did the same thing. How can we not accept them as brothers?

There is no question that between the Seawolf pilots, the PBR sailors, and the guys who were in our special boat support units at the time, we were snatched from the jaws of death many, many times.

I think getting us in was probably the easier part for them. When they came in to get us, we had really stirred up the hornet's nest, so they were always coming in to a lot of lead heading their way. And they were putting down fire of their own so that we could get onboard. Once onboard, we fought right alongside them to increase the fire we could throw back at the enemy.

You took those slow-moving Mike boats, or those faster plastic PBR boats, and they faced dumb odds when they had .51 calibers and RPGs coming at them. But they certainly thrived on doing that. And they never said, "Gee I don't want to." It became a new Team in terms of all of us working together.

I started off with the Chief of Naval Operations, who gave me the green light to form the Team that was SEAL Team Six. Admiral Ace Lyons was then the Ops Dep, the operations boss of the Navy in the Pentagon. He protected me in terms of his being a three-star admiral who did the Joint vote. As the commanding officer of SEAL Team Six, I had a reporting chain of command that went to the Army, who owned me. The Joint Commander was an Army general. Administratively, I reported to the Navy.

This caused problems in that the Navy paid for me, but the Army Joint Command took me to war. Every time the Navy said no to something, I could play the Army Joint Command against them. I may be a helluva brain surgeon, but I flunked bedside manner.

I did rub the commanders' noses in it. I did power play more than a little. Taking a message I had written to myself, I would take it to the Pentagon and have it come down gravity feed—everything slides downhill. The admiral found out that I was bending the chain of command, and he certainly didn't like that. But he was the key that allowed me to do that, and he remained that way after I left SEAL Team Six and created Red Cell.

I think SEAL Team Six was my military thesis. Having picked everyone there, it truly was a military mafiosa. I had psychological tests run on all of us, and we had the perfect community—we had the bell curve. We were normal. That satisfied the Navy. What they screwed up on was whether I was normal or not. I had picked those guys. And among the guys that I picked, we all looked normal. So if I was a sick puppy, we all were. But the Navy never caught on to that one. That was giving the bureaucracy what they wanted. They wanted an answer, and I gave them one—we were normal. But they missed the real question—was I normal?

I tried to use all the information Roy Boehm had taught me, the lessons he had learned putting together the first SEAL Team. General Wegner in Germany at GSG-9 was a friend of mine. He told me what would happen as I got bigger.

I listened to everybody who had similar units and learned about their degradation over time. That let me jump-start everything at SEAL Team Six. I used the military magic numbers to make everything at least 300 percent more. Having the Chief of Naval Operations support the development of SEAL Team Six allowed me to be creative in how I did things. That also showed me why it was good to be at the top, working out of the Pentagon versus a lesser staff position where somebody can easily nit-pick at me.

I was asked where I would get the manning numbers from. Those who are history buffs will remember that the cruiser Belknap had suffered a collision at sea. Those billets that had been on the Belknap were ashore now, because a ship hadn't been brought in to replace her.

So I borrowed those Navy billets to build SEAL Team Six until the normal programming cycle had gotten the body count we needed through Congress and all the appropriations committees and whatever. The cycle did go forward, and we had the billets we needed within five years.

When I was asked what it cost to outfit SEAL Team Six, I explained that the Navy plans on losing twelve F-14s a year. These are losses from landings on carriers, training missions, and whatever. I said that for the price of three of those F-14s, I was going to build them SEAL Team Six. I took their planned loss and gave them a planned gain.

When I had done that, I was given access to the storekeeper of the Navy, the admiral who ran all the budgets in the Navy. He sat down with me afterhours. When I told him what I thought I was going to spend, he did his magic Ouija-board work and came back with what he said I would really be spending.

He took me through the process of outfitting and budgeting, showing me what I would not have thought about, things like the out-years, for example, when you know you're going to have to replace bent and expended equipment. When you outfit a command, for example, I had learned that you buy all the parachutes at the same time. The chutes are all going to die, or reach the end of their service life, at about the same time, so you had better start incrementally building in spare parts that you can replace as you need to.

All he did was break out that Ouija board of his and his fingers flew, then the magic numbers showed up. Of course, he was the budget man of the Navy, they were his figures, and who was going to say no to him? Being at the top and seeing and doing that helped make things work. The dichotomy was that the little shooters, the chiefs I picked, chose their gear. And the Operational Boss of the Navy, and the Beancounter of the Navy, paid for it.

So I had both spectrums covered—the highest ranks in the chain of command as well as the lowest ranks. Of course, everybody else who was in the middle just got mad at me. I was considered an asshole because I cared so much about the guy who was going out there to be a shooter. But then I was going to war with those men, the other guys weren't. The mission counts.

This was my benchmark in terms of what I would take. I used secondary buildings until I got Department of Defense money to build a brand-new compound. I leased civilian airplanes, and we drove civilian cars. We got Motorola to make satellite communications gear for us.

I went out and got the best guys and bought the best toys. And at that time, terrorism was the best mission. Nothing wrong with that.

Why did we need Red Cell? Again, it was Admiral Ace Lyons, who had been a ship driver, who knew the Navy was ready to fight the Soviet bear over the horizon. But he knew that the Navy was not geared to do anything about terrorism. When was the last time a terrorist bothered anybody on a ship? So Admiral Lyons thought that there ought to be a unit like Red Flag, where they practice Soviet tactics against U.S. forces, only the new unit would do terrorism.

So Red Cell is an outgrowth of the Zulu Five Oscar exercises. Only now I had the funding to hire civilian analysts so I wasn't doing the score cards myself. I also hired a company that did video work to document our exercises. They hired ex-SEALs who could keep up with us and knew where we were going so they could keep up with us and catch us on film. Not only did we penetrate these bases, but it was all documented on film. There was no longer the "I got you before you could've gotten me" argument.

I certainly pissed off people again. Even though a four-star admiral out of the Pentagon told me to do something and a four-star CinC (Commander-in-Chief) in the area would say, "I want you to attack that base," people in command of the bases were less than happy. Those base-command positions were natural flag-builders, a step to making admiral. When I penetrated their bases and demonstrated their weakness, that ruined it for them and they didn't make flag rank. But, that was my problem, and no one was smart enough to say, "Hey admiral, you sent these guys and they ate me alive. Here's what I need."

Prior to Red Cell, the magic solution was to ask for more people and more money. When I went out to a base, I showed them how to stop us for now with what they had. It was a big change in policy and rules, and it took people to think about the terrorist as the enemy.

That was alien to the Navy back then. When you increase security, you reduce the creature comforts available to your personnel. The base people are unhappy, they can't go to the theater, the hospital is restricted, and on and on. On an exercise, we would be on the base for ten days, and for those ten days we ate them alive.

Red Cell was an embarrassment to the Navy, and the Navy as an entity, not just the people, doesn't wear embarrassment very well. If you look at it from the bean-counting realm, when you're spending $2 million a year for someone to eat your socks up, somebody else asks, "Why am I paying for that pain?"

They didn't really take the negatives that Red Cell pointed out and make them positives. It was always a negative-negative situation. That was their loss. In today's world (1998), we have the same installations in terms of size, the same mission, but one-third less the people. So if I could attack a facility with ease with Red Cell in 1984 and 1985, ten years later and one-third less the people, you could drive a Mack truck through and nobody is going to know what's going on.

We are very vulnerable today to a terrorist attack here in the United States and against our bases overseas. If I had been one of the commanders of a base that Red Cell attacked, the first thing I would do after the exercise is go see the four-star admiral who sicced them on me. Then I would tell him what Red Cell had made me look like, what they say I needed to prevent such a thing from happening again, and ask for it.

An example of what happens on a base is how the hospitals report to one location while the exchange system reports to another location. These are what I call "stovepipe commands." Within a base structure, not all people report to the commanding officer.

So out in the Pacific, where Admiral Ace Lyons went to be a four-star, he made the ultimate responsibility of the bases, under terrorist event, rest with the base commander. But it was one of those things that, administratively and bureaucratically, didn't happen. If there was only one guy in charge, the powers would have eaten him alive after an incident. No one had the guts to raise their hands and say, "I'm going to break the rules under these conditions and do it this guy's way."

■　　■　　■

An oil rig, by law, is considered an island. Therefore, any terrorist action that takes place in it is in the jurisdiction of the FBI. We have some offshore oil rig pump stations that control a lot of the oil flow that's coming in. Destroying or damaging one can cause a tremendous amount of damage. So if you have a perpetrator, a terrorist, who's holding an oil rig for ransom, ultimately the prosecution of that terrorist has to go through the FBI.

But the FBI can't get out to the rig because of all of the water. So the taking down of the oil rig would fall on my men at SEAL Team Six. The feds wanted me to preserve the crime scene when my guys took down that oil rig. That way, they could come in and investigate it and build their case against the terrorists. They also wanted me to turn over the weapons from my guys who had done the operation— risked their lives, busted their asses—to see if any of our bullets had hurt a friendly or done other damage.

"Wait a minute," I said, "that doesn't go." First, as the commanding officer, I will be on the ground, I will be on the rig, and I will turn over the crime scene when I'm ready. If that meant I was going to stack bodies and make sure none of my guys were going to be caught in this BS, that's what my job is. Let the guys fight and I'll preserve their safety. I'm not going to allow someone who wants to put a feather in their cap to hang one of my guys for doing the job no one else would do.

Rules of engagement are there because of lawyers; they aren't there because of war. War says kill the bad guys.

War is another acronym that stands for We Are Ready. That's why it should be War Department, like it used to be, not Department of Defense. But that's better marketing.

Where we sit today, we have the opportunity to say how blessed we were by being in the Teams and how blessed we were for being able to go to war. We're just lucky, and there's a message there. I'm very thankful that the world's as screwed up as it is. That lets me write a lot of books now. But also it shows a need for better training. Harry Humphries and I both were doing the police training recently. It's sad that we don't train our cops enough or the right way. There are no SWAT standards. You end up with the city bureaucracy looking at them as "goon platoons" and actually tying their hands behind their backs.

Somewhere, you have to draw the line and protect the American citizens. We have to have standard training and help out the police in policing the bad guys. There are more bad guys than good guys, and there's more money in being a bad guy than a good guy. They have better equipment, and they can throw more money at it. Thank God they don't have a centralized training program, either.

We're fortunate, Harry and I, in that we can both pass on things that we learned in war to the police today. If you look at where in the world we have sent our military for police actions—Somalia, Haiti, and Bosnia, for example. We're sending *killers to do police jobs, and the cops are in the street now going to war against gangs.*

As a nation, we have to take a hard look at that. Either we change the cops for the better, or we change the Posse Comitatus law and let the military help the police when they get into a heavy gang-influenced area.

Twenty-six weeks is a long time to be a trainee. And that's hard on the students. I think perhaps there ought to be a level where the students are treated more as Teammates and not as stinking trainees. However, I don't think them quitting and then trying to talk them back into the program is right. If they want to be there, then they can stay. If they don't want to be there, then let them get the hell out.

It's a society problem that comes well before they even get into the Navy. As a society, we have made quitting acceptable, if not even honorable. We have CEOs who screw up so we fire them and give them $12 million to go home. Well, how about letting me screw up for only a million dollars and I'll go home?

It used to be that if your family declared bankruptcy, you didn't even look your neighbors in the eye. Now it's considered an administrative tool and if you don't use it, people think you're dumb because it's so available. We raise kids who quit playing a sport or an instrument, then we buy them a new one. We've made quitting a way of life. It's at least acceptable, if not the norm. So when you get these young men in the Navy and into BUD/S (Basic Underwater Demolition/SEALs), it's not the first time society has to take over and correct the problem.

If the students don't have the fortitude and character to stay in training and if there aren't circumstances that warrant it, as an instructor, I shouldn't have to talk the students into staying. I mean flush them and go, we'll go get more.

We don't need people who know it's okay to call time-out in the services. I go to military bases on book signings and find it very appalling. Not only is it hard for me to talk without those four-letter adjectives, but the drill instructors can't curse at them anymore to break them out of their comfort zone.

Training has to be progressed at the pace of the slowest or the lowest. They have now even introduced a yellow card, called a stress card, that the trainee can pull out that forces the drill instructor to back up six feet until the student regroups. How do you meet the hated enemy? Time-out, sweetie, I'm not ready yet?

We're nailing guys for sexual harassment and putting more pressure on that than on proper training. So the youngsters who come into the service and want upward mobility, to be challenged, are just turned down by that. It sets a bad example.

In March 1998, I did a book signing at West Point. The plebe class, the freshmen class of the Academy, was the first class that had stress cards. They could call time-out with those cards. These are the future generals of the Army who are learning that quitting, or calling time out, is okay. However, when the news that the new Secretary of Defense found out about stress cards he had the situation changed.

But that gives you an example of just how far that kind of thinking, that quitting is honorable, has permeated. We who are of the old school, and we who are special, don't have to conform.

If you want to be there, that's what they pay you for. If it was easy, you wouldn't get paid that hard money. You need to keep BUD/S training special.

As Harry Humphries says, there's a misconception in the civilian world about the healthy competitiveness between the militaries. That all disappears when you go into combat, when you go to war, because the guys in the air are supporting you on the ground. If you're in a combined operation and you're with some Force Recon guys, you'll find them to be excellent people and good shooters. If you're working with Special Forces A-Teams, you're going to find them to be totally dedicated and also good shooters. They're all people who you would want to have on your side, and were glad they were on your side when you needed them. There's a shooter camaraderie that exists between legitimate combatants, and the lines drawn by what branch uniform you wear disappear. When the EAGLE CLAW raid failed, we developed the Joint Special Operations Command. JSOC included what are called "trash haulers," the big Air Force transports with dedicated crews that worked with us all the time. They were specially screened and would do some nasty things with those big aircraft. And there were Army helicopter pilots, Air Force pilots, and Army Rangers who secured airfields. It was a family of shooters.

When you get into counterterrorism and really expand it, you learn from the other units around the world. These are units you share intelligence with, and they share it with you. Our FBI used to get annoyed with me when I would arrive in a country, not check in, and be getting intelligence from that mechanism, that shooters group, when I hadn't been screened by my own government.

And the real, true intelligence came from the shooters. We would go sit and drink beer and they would tell me who they took down, what was going on, how it happened, and the lessons they had learned. That didn't usually come up in an official intelligence report.

With most intelligence that's gathered officially, the real meaningful stuff to a shooter is left on the cutting-room floor. The report writers are all trying to get the Pulitzer Prize in writing for their briefs for the president, so they do a strategic overview. The kind of stuff I worry about—who's on the pier, what kind of doorknob it is, what the lethality of the weapons they're carrying is, that kind of thing—doesn't get anyone the Pulitzer Prize, so we don't find out about it.

You can take a shooter from any of those foreign elements, any of the services or branches, cross-pollinate them, and find that they're all great guys. In fact we do that now.

The Air Force Combat Control Teams (CCTs) went and jumped in to hot targets with the SEALs. When tactical air support was coming in, those CCTs had the radio equipment to bring that tac air right to the target. I could worry about kicking ass, and the CCTs would talk to those birds up there. But they were on the ground with me, they ate the same stuff, locked out of submarines with me.

The same thing held with the Army guys with the birds. They came in more than once and saved my ass. A shooter is a shooter, and they're all USA. It doesn't matter what branch they're from, they all want to meet the challenge. And that's what's great about Special Operations. With the establishment of the Special Operations Command in Tampa, now they all even wear the same cloth. The procurement process is working for the operator more. They get the mass buys and everyone wears the same or virtually the same uniforms.

The Navy, in its tradition, somehow took the lead in funding, procuring, and developing an officer core for special operations and research programs for special operations. The other services did not at the same level. That was something that the Navy had the lead in.

The Air Force has been very good at incorporating their reserves into an active role and in special programs. The Navy still doesn't know how to use their reserves in an everyday, fold-them-right-in-and-put-them-to-war manner. Look at DESERT STORM. A lot of National Guard and Reserve units who thought they would never be going anywhere ended up on the front lines.

We have a smaller team now in the armed forces, and we have a vaster role in terms of policing the world. More and more it's going to come down to the individual. Training is going to come to the floor, and we're going to have to be good at it.

Let's look at a realistic target, Saddam Hussein.

In the United States, we send people to West Point to study history and war. They read Clausewits and study the actions of all the big wars. Then we go to a place outside Bagdad, to an operation called Desert Storm. General Patton once said something along the lines of, "Send me fuel, and in five days I'll be in Moscow." If we had stayed three more days in Desert Storm, we could have been in Bagdad and we wouldn't have the problem we have now. There's a political argument that says that we finally had our troops on Saudi Arabian soil, we would have upset the Arab brotherhood, and politically it wasn't a smart thing to do. I say that's tough. They weren't going to like us anyway.

Then there's the question that if we kill Saddam Hussein, who would be next in succession in Iraq? Saddam may be a madman, but at least we know what he is. How about Saddam's son? If we kill Saddam; is his son going to say, "Shit! I'm not going to let that happen to me!" We've never reached across the pond and punched anybody in the nose, so they're going to keep pushing us until we do.

But just how close could we get to a target like that? There's a bigger problem. I could take a team in, get close to Saddam Hussein, or anybody who looks like him, and find the right time to do it. Getting there, watching him, and setting up for a target of opportunity is a lot easier than getting the hell out of there after I got him, because once he goes down, everybody is right on my cheeks. The mission almost becomes a kamikaze.

You don't have to be crazy to be in the Teams, but it does make life easier. As a breed we are a dichotomy. You come to BUD/S as an individual, who has to be individually motivated and has the drive and ambition to be a Team member. Then you are a Teammember. The result is people who are outstanding as individuals, but who work even better as a team.

Then, because you want to go to war, you are trained to survive by yourself and go on and complete the mission by yourself. The Team is that lovely, glowing body that draws you to it. But you brought your toolbox with you, and if everybody dies en route, you're still going to finish the job. The Team is a flow point and a comfort zone for us. It's a thing we enjoy.

Bronze Bruce, the bronze statue of the World War II UDT operator in front of the UDT-SEAL Museum in Fort Pierce, Florida, like other statues, is a symbol. It's a symbol of where we came from; it's a benchmark in the history of the Teams. We have no idea of how far we're going yet in terms of the SEAL program and what kind of enemy we're going to face tomorrow.

As Harry Humphries says, we have our origins with a slate and lead line, a pair of fins and a face mask, a kabar knife, and that's it. That's the beginnings of our group, where we all came from. In fact, that's where operators our age did come from. But we lose sight of the fact that the real, real tough days were those days during the Second World War. That was when these guys were going in to the beaches, and the attrition rates of the invading forces could go into the 80 percent range of wounded and killed on the beach while executing impossible missions.

These guys had an extremely difficult job to do. These were the men who we looked to as a goal to strive for. Their story is what pulled us into the program. Where we are today with the equipment and so forth, is icing on the cake. The real individual is that guy out there in the water in swim trunks and fins.

That statue of the WWII UDT operator brings back memories for me, because what the statue is wearing is all that I was issued. We didn't have the latest and greatest toys they have in the Teams today. When I got there out of Class 26, the Plexiglas—the slate we wrote on—was taken from the salvage yards of the Naval Air Station. We went over there and took old airplane canopies and cut those slates. We poured our own lead for the weights and used colored signal flags to mark the fathoms on the line we tied to the weights.

The guns we shot were a WWII Greasegun and M3A1 submachine gun. The kabar was the only weapon we were issued. We didn't get to fire it very often. We had to qualify a thirty-eight caliber pistol. That was it in the way of our weapons in UDT.

Starting from scratch, with the basics, is what I see in that statue. That was us in those early days. We had trouble talking to the amphibious ships we could see on the horizon because of the radio gear we had. In that same era that we had trouble talking to the ships with our radio gear, we were already talking to men in space. (We should have had those radios!)

Where this program has gone in thirty years in terms of force multiplier is phenomenal. In terms of dollars, new equipment, and capabilities of the Teams, the programs have been built up a lot, yet everything goes back down to that bronze statue. That's all we started from, and that's what will make things work. If the guy is stripped down to that lowly point, he will find something on the ground to do his job.

That's what we were designed for—to live off the ground, live off the land, and make the bad guy's stuff work for us. There are no supply trains arriving in the nick of time. If you don't have it on your back, you don't have it. That's the way SEALs have to operate today, and that's the way we grew up in the Teams back then.

We call Bronze Bruce the Naked Warrior. And naked as he is, the mission will still get done. He is our root. He is our basic form. He's where it all started from. He was the warrior. As spartan as he was in terms of equipment and basic training, he did the mission of his day. And that's our bottom line, getting the mission done.

Thomas N. Tarbox, Captain, USNR (Ret.)

I left SEAL Team Two in August 1966, prior to our involvement in Vietnam, and went up to the Defense Intelligence School. From there, I went to Okinawa and other staff work assignments and never did go back to an active Team. So Team Two's part in the Dominican Republic operation in 1965 was the closest I came to action with the Team.

My involvement with the SEALs was far from over though. I was assigned to running BUD/S for a while in the early 1970s and at the very last of my service, I was the commander of the Navy Security Coordination Team, better known as Red Cell. The Navy brought me back for Red Cell after I had been retired for six years.

I didn't run the East Coast BUD/S training. It had already been consolidated by the time I was assigned. The last East Coast training class, Class 7102, graduated at Little Creek in August 1971. From that point on, all BUD/S training was conducted on the West Coast at Coronado.

The first consolidated class at Coronado, Class 62, graduated in September 1971. At that time, the West Coast was running six classes a year while the East Coast had been running only two classes a year. So the numbers were quite different.

It's not well known, but there was a period of about a year and a half during which they didn't have Hell Week in the West Coast BUD/S classes. The commander of BUD/S had arrived there and was soon told to knock off Hell Week due to the attrition of students during that single week of training. The CO at the time was being banged about the head and shoulders by the weenies back in Washington, D.C., because attrition is inefficient and they needed a lot of people for Vietnam in the West Coast Teams. So it was sometime in 1970 that Hell Week was knocked off the training schedule.

I went to Vietnam in March 1971, and Dave Schaible relieved Dave DelGudice as Naval Special Warfare Unit—Vietnam in December 1971. When I came back and took over BUD/S in March 1972, I immediately put Hell Week back into the training schedule.

At that time, BUD/S was a department of the Amphibious (Phib) School at Coronado. So should I tell them that I was going to put Hell Week back into training? If I told them I was thinking about it, I probably would have had to get their permission first, so I didn't tell them.

Hell Week is part of our training. I feel that, and I think everyone in the Teams feels it. Those kids who didn't get exposed to it were cheated, really cheated. Hell Week is one of the things that we really all have in common, and it really belongs as part of training. At that time, the Phib School was doing a lot of formal curriculum work and writing up stuff. So we did that with Hell Week and nobody ever questioned it.

There were a number of staff positions I took after leaving the command position at BUD/S. But the best thing I did during the 1970s was replacing Hell Week.

By the early 1980s, it was time for me to retire. But even that didn't last long, as the Navy had more plans for me.

The Navy Security Coordination Team, also known as Red Cell, was started in late 1984 sort of as a response to the Marine barracks being bombed in Beirut. Red Cell went everywhere there was a Navy base and conducted antiterrorism exercises and training. The unit was started by Commander Dick Marcinko, and I took over Red Cell in May 1988, well after Dick had left. I was the thirteenth commanding officer of Red Cell.

Red Cell had some problems, which is one of the reasons why I was recalled to active duty from a retired status. I was commander for two years and then Tom Mosure took it over from me in May 1990. He was the last CO before the Red Cell unit finally folded in October 1991.

The mission of Red Cell was to conduct antiterrorism training and exercises at Navy bases worldwide. We tried to increase the awareness of Navy installations to their vulnerability to terrorist attack. The first thing we would do when we went to a base was have an antiterrorism awareness seminar game. We would gather people from the FBI, Coast Guard, local law enforcement, state cops, customs, or whoever would have a role to play in law enforcement around a table and play this game.

These people should have been talking to each other all along to prepare for a possible terrorist incident, but our seminar games were often the first time these area representatives all really got together. I hoped they continued this seminar awareness game, because it was an excellent teaching tool.

After the seminar "war game," if you will, we would hold a practical exercise with events that would stress various parts of a base's defense. The base would typically have its own security people, plus they would muster the auxiliary security force. The auxiliary force was made up of sailors in other jobs who had a collateral duty to be on the auxiliary force.

The exercise would stress the bases. It had to go into a higher threat condition, which meant that all the IDs of people going into the base had to be checked. The exchanges lost sales and all kinds of complaints would come in from the support people and the families of the base personnel. Yes, the exercise was inefficient for the normal running of an installation, but at least they learned something about protecting the base.

We also had hostage barricade situations where we would take over a barracks or building and hold the people inside hostage. Then we would have negotiations between our "terrorists" and the base or law enforcement.

We found that these hostage barricade situations, if they lasted long enough, that we could start turning the people to "our" side and against the base—the old "Stockholm Syndrome." We would tell them how bad their base was because they hadn't been able to protect them and that they weren't getting food in to them or not doing this or that. The reaction of the hostages, as they would come over to our way of looking at things, was very interesting.

But the Navy didn't want to "train" terrorism victims, which is how you could look at our simulations. I still think that if Robert Stethem and the others who were on TWA Flight 847 in 1985 when it was hijacked to Beirut had gone through one of our exercises, they might have all survived that terrorist incident. But who knows.

What kind of a man is a Navy SEAL? He's an ordinary American with an ordinary background, perhaps a little smarter than the average person who comes into the Navy. He has something within him, or can be motivated, so that he can withstand a lot of pressure and a lot of physical duress, and still keep his cool.

I'd like to think that all of us who have been in the Teams, in the past or today, are pretty much the same although the Teams have changed. When I went through training with Class 19 back in 1958, very few of the enlisted men had completed high school. Most of them were high school dropouts, who then came into the Navy and got their GED. A lot of them eventually went on to college.

Fifteen years later, when I ran BUD/S, all the kids were high school graduates, and some of them had attended college. The officers had completed college and had maybe a year or so of graduate school behind them. Realize that the draft was still going on back then and the draft was a real equalizer in the ranks.

Today the kids who come in all have high school diplomas, and most have some college behind them. Quite a few even have college degrees—they remain enlisted men because it's easier to get into the SEAL program as an enlisted man rather than as an officer. Most of our officers now come from the Naval Academy, something that wasn't true twenty years ago.

Some of the enlisted men can't get in as officers with degrees because there are so few volunteers for the program taken from NROTC and OCS. But essentially, they are all the same young men, driven and hopeful to make a challenging career in the Teams.

The statue of Bronze Bruce, the Naked Warrior, is an example of a UDT operator prepared for a combat swim during World War II. He's wearing swim fins, trunks, a face mask, and little else. I think he represents all of us, but especially the WWII Frogs. The World War II generation, nationwide, was the finest generation this country has ever had, including the founding fathers. Those people who went through the depression and on to win the war are a shining example of just what an American can be. When I see that statue of the Naked Warrior, I think of them.

When we created the Teams, there wasn't a lavish amount of equipment available for us to do our jobs with. Instead, we often had to bend the rules to get what we needed. In the early days at SEAL Team Two, we had sixty people total—ten officers and fifty enlisted men. Of everything we wanted to get, we would order sixty plus 10 percent more, so we ordered in amounts of sixty-six.

We had a problem getting the jungle fatigues when they first came out. The Navy didn't have any in the supply system, but the Army had them—a lot of them—so we worked out a little cumshaw, a wonderful Navy term, with the Army down at Fort Bragg.

They always needed paint in the Army, because they had to paint all those damned rocks down there, and they liked Kabar knives. So we would give them paint and Kabars, and they would give us jungle fatigues.

The supply officer at the Naval Operations Support Group, the predecessor to Naval Special Warfare Group, took the Group credit card with him on a trip up to New England. There, he charged a set of tires on the government credit card. The FBI found out about that little purchase, and they came around to check out our supply system. Of course, they uncovered what we had been doing. But the thing that saved us was that we took the fatigues that we had traded for and put them in our stock records as we issued them out. So there wasn't anything illegal going on and no private person was making any kind of profit on our trading, we were just bending the rules to get what we needed. And the FBI guys fully understood that, so we ducked any trouble over that one.

We just wanted enough gear so everybody could be prepared and have enough clothes, weapons, and equipment to do any of the varied missions we were supposed to be able to do. Everything was new and we were learning as we went along, *and the supply people were learning as well, because a lot of the things we needed just weren't normal Navy issue.*

We ended up with very little at all compared to what the kids have now. We were really in the process of determining what a SEAL Team was. We didn't know, and no one else did, either. If Vietnam hadn't come along as the proving ground for the Navy SEALs, we might have turned out a little different than we did. But Vietnam did come along, and both Teams went there. And we came out pretty well.

The word I think of whenever I think of the Navy SEALs is professional. That's the key to being a good SEAL, being a professional. There are really three things that make up a good SEAL—being professional, the need to bring the youngsters along and teach them, and the need to make a difference. If you have those three things in your makeup, you're a real good SEAL.

In spite of the instructors' best efforts at BUD/S, we have a few Rambos in the Teams, but they're damned few in number. Being a Rambo isn't being a professional.

There's a photo that ran in the San Diego Union Tribune *around the anniversary of Pearl Harbor some time back of the Pearl Harbor veterans who visited the USS Pearl Harbor. It showed three or four of the vets talking with maybe six sailors. Everyone was grinning in the shot; they were all just pleased to be talking to each other. They shared a history as well as a present. That photo epitomizes what I hope will always happen when the older SEALs and Frogs meet the young kids today. They share a history, a present, and probably a good future as well, and I hope they always remember that.*

■ Chapter 53

Boat Support

The long cooperation between the Boat Support Units, Brown Water Navy, and the SEALs did not end with the finale of the Vietnam War. The value of such an efficient meshing of skills, equipment, and manpower was recognized by the Navy and maintained after Vietnam ended. The Brown Water Navy had started in 1965 with little equipment and no recent unit background to build on. By the end of the Vietnam War, the Brown Water Navy had grown to a force of more than 700 small craft and 38,000 men.

In early 1967, another more specialized small-craft unit was estabiished specifically to support the needs of the Navy SEALs. Designated Boat Support Unit One, the sailors of BSU-1 were tasked with developing, modifying, testing, evaluating, and operating small craft in support of the SEAL detachments

The main armament of the PBR, its twin forward .50 caliber machine guns, are shown in this photograph. The gunner from the River Division has his two weapons aimed outboard to the port side of the boat. The large searchlight is attached to the mounting for the guns. Wherever the light is shining, that's also where the two big machine guns are aimed.

U.S. Navy

in Vietnam. A component of the Naval Operations Support Group commanded by Captain Phil H. Bucklew, BSU-1 did outstanding service for the Teams and the Navy operating heavy, medium, and light SEAL support craft in the waterways of Southeast Asia.

Sailors in both the Brown Water Navy and the Boat Support Unit underwent an eleven-week River Assault Craft training program. During this program, the men were exposed to various aspects of riverine warfare, joint operations, counterinsurgency, small arms, and survival, evasion, resistance, and escape (SERE) training. They went on to further training in their prospective watercraft, notably the Mark I and Mark II Patrol Boat, River (PBR) for the Brown Water sailors and the various specialized SEAL support craft for the BSU-1 sailors.

After the end of the Vietnam War and the turning over of a number of river and coastal patrol craft to the South Vietnamese navy, the remaining small craft and personnel of Task Force 116 (river patrol), Task Force 117 (river assault), and Task Force 115 (coastal surveillance) were reorganized into Riverine/Coastal Divisions and Squadrons and divided between the East and West Coasts to their support of Naval Special Warfare. In May 1983, the last Boat Support Unit was redesignated a Special Boat Unit and fully integrated into a Naval Special Warfare Group.

As part of a NATO exercise in Spain, a group of SEALs from SEAL Team Two approach the shore tactically as they disembark from their RIB insertion boat. The wet suit-clad scout swimmer, who would have been the first man on shore to check the beach, is kneeling to the left. He is armed with an MP-5N submachine gun with a flashlight-equipped forearm. On his left ankle is strapped his combat knife. On the scabbard of the knife, secured with rubber bands, is a sealed chemical light in a plastic pouch as well as a pyrotechnic flare/smoke signal.

U.S. Navy

To maintain and increase the skills and abilities of the Special Boat Units, the Special Warfare Combat Crewman training course was established at the Naval Special Warfare Training Center in Coronado, California. For eleven weeks, students in the SWCC training course are pushed to achieve a very high physical standard. In addition, they receive instruction in swimming, first aid, maritime navigation, basic seamanship, engineering, communications, combat and basic tactical skills, small arms, and special operations. As of 1995, students who completed the course and successfully served in a Special Boat Unit received the SWCC designator and its accompanying promotion points. As of October 2002, the names of the Special Boat Units and Squadrons were officially changed in order to prevent confusion with other amphibious forces with the same names. The two Special Boat Squadrons, One and Two, became Naval Special Warfare Groups Three and Four respectively. The Special Boat Units were renamed as Special Boat Teams.

The Mini-Armored Troop carrier as used by the Special Boat Units.

U.S. Navy

On the West Coast at Coronado is stationed Naval Special Warfare Group Three, which concentrates its operations in the Pacific and Central geographical areas. Under the command of Navy Special Warfare Group Three is SEAL Delivery Vehicle Team One, based at Pearl Harbor, Hawaii. SDVT-1 conducts operations in support of Naval Special Warfare throughout the Pacific and Central commands areas of responsibility. In addition, there is Special Boat Team Twelve, which is primarily equipped with RIBs and Mark V Special Operations Craft. Special Boat Team Twelve conducts its operations throughout the Pacific and Central commands.

In addition to SDVT-1 and SBT-12, SpecWarGru Three has four of the 170-foot Cyclone-class Coastal Patrol Ships (PCs) assigned to it. These ships are designed and equipped to support a SEAL detachment on extended special operations missions throughout the world. They are commissioned naval craft with a crew of four officers and twenty-four enlisted men. The West Coast is assigned the *Hurricane* (PC 3), *Monsoon* (PC 4), *Squall* (PC 7), and *Zephyr* (PC 8).

On the East Coast at Little Creek is Special Warfare Group Four, which concentrates its operations geographically in the Atlantic, Southern and European areas. SpecWarGru Four has under its command SEAL Delivery Vehicle Team Two. SDVT-2 concentrates on being able to support the Sixth Fleet Commander with both a SEAL Delivery Vehicle capability as well as a Dry Deck Shelter (DDS) capability. The DDS can be attached to a modified or specially built submarine to allow it to transport either an SDV or a CRRC and lock out or recover SEAL units while underwater. The DDS includes a hyperbaric chamber to treat combat swimmers for decompression after particularly long or deep dives.

SpecWarGru Four also has under its direction Special Boat Team Twenty. The primary operation part of SBT-20 is Detachment Caribbean, based in Roosevelt Road, Puerto Rico. Special Boat Team Twenty-Two is also under the command umbrella of SpecWarGru Four but is based in Mississippi at Bay Saint Louis. The Coastal Patrol craft assigned to the East Coast and SpecWarGru Four include the *Tempest* (PC 2), *Typhoon* (PC 5), *Sirocco* (PC 6), *Chinook* (PC 9), *Firebolt* (PC 10), *Whirlwind* (PC 11), *Thunderbolt* (PC 12), *Shamal* (PC 13), and *Tornado* (PC 14).

■ ■ ■

THE Special Boat Teams also operate a variety of special operations craft, including rigid inflatable boats, Mark V Special Operations Craft, High Speed Boats, the light patrol boats, Mark IV PBRs, Mark II PBRs, and the mini-armored troop carrier. All these craft are in addition to the standard Combat Rubber Raiding Craft (CRRC), the latest incarnation of the rubber boat, a SEAL and UDT staple since its earliest days in World War II.

The Mark V Special Operations Craft (SOC). The slim, fast-moving boat can be transported aboard aircraft for rapid deployment. Capable of mounting a variety of weapons, including 25mm Mark 38 cannon, miniguns, .50 and 7.62mm machine guns and 40mm grenade launchers, the Mark V can transport and support a SEAL unit in a threat environment.

U.S. Navy

The Special Boat Teams are tasked with conducting coastal and riverine interdiction operations as well as supporting naval and joint special operations. Specific SBT missions include unconventional warfare, direct action, special reconnaissance, foreign internal defense, counterterrorism, and psychological and civil affairs operations support—all in a maritime or riverine environment. They operate on a worldwide basis, both with Naval Special Warfare assets and on their own.

The men of the Special Boat Teams have developed an illustrious reputation in the few years since their origins in the 1960s. They have and are still proving themselves a very valuable asset to Naval Special Warfare.

■ Chapter 54

The End of an Era, The New Beginning

The Underwater Demolition Teams had performed their missions with professionalism and skill since their first days in December 1943. The operators of the UDT had blown open countless beaches during World War II, conducted demolition raids and other missions behind enemy lines in Korea, looked at nuclear missiles in Cuba, and even greeted returning space capsules during the *Mercury, Gemini,* and *Apollo* space missions.

After almost forty years of operations, the UDT had reached the end of its useful service life. The mission preformed by the UDTs—primarily that of beach and hydrographic reconnaissance and obstacle clearing—could be conducted by the SEAL Teams. The men of both the SEALs and the UDTs shared the same basic training, crawled through the same mud, and proved themselves through the same ordeals. It would be a much better use and application of manpower and resources to give the mission of the UDTs to the SEALs.

But that was not to indicate that the Teams would be made any smaller. On the contrary, while there would be no more Underwater Demolition Teams, new SEAL Teams would rise up in their place.

On 1 May 1983, the Frogmen ceased to be, but only on paper, as the Navy conducted the first major reorganization of Naval Special Warfare since the early 1960s and the commissioning of the first SEAL Teams. The Navy retired the UDTs and put SEAL units in their place. In most cases, this meant little more than a new issue of equipment and reorganization of personnel.

UDTs Eleven and Twenty became SEAL Teams Five and Four. UDTs Twelve and Twenty-Two became SEAL Delivery Vehicle (SDV) Teams One and Two.

A Mark VIII "Eight-Boat" approaches its holding cradle on the deck of a submerged nuclear submarine. The Eight-Boat will be secured to the cradle, which will then be winched into the open hatch of the DDS secured to the access hatch of the submarine. The entire launch and recovery operation can be conducted underwater.

U.S. Navy

The new SDV Teams would concentrate their training and efforts to support the other SEAL Teams with longer range underwater transportation.

The SDVs were wet-type underwater vehicles. The interior of their fiberglass hull would be filled with water, and the occupants needed to wear breathing equipment. With its silver-zinc batteries, the electric motor of an SDV could drive its SEAL crew and up to four passengers for much longer distances than even the SEALs could swim for themselves. In addition, cargo, including heavy demolitions, could be transported by an SDV while a pair of swimmers would be hard-pressed to do more than move such a charge into position.

The Mark VIII SDV, called the Eight-Boat, was the workhorse bus for the underwater work by the Special Warfare community. The Eight-Boat looked like little more than a short, fat, black whale when it moved through the water. The other SDV used for a number of years had a much more sinister appearance and mission.

The Mark IX SDV was a wide, flat boat that could be used for reconnaissance operations or surgical underwater attacks. The Mark IX SDV only held a crew of two, and those operators, a pilot and a navigator, lay flat to work their craft. So no extra personnel could be moved in the Mark IX. What could be done was mount the Mark 38 Standoff Weapons System to the Mark IX. That gave the SDV two torpedoes that it could fire at a target thousands of yards away. Now the small fiberglass SDV could take on a capital ship, sink it, and

A crewman in the drivers' section of a surfaced Mark IX SEAL Delivery Vehicle looks to the rear of his craft. The low, flat SDV maintains a very small cross-section, either above or below the surface. The navigator and driver of the SDV have to lie flat during normal operations.

U.S. Navy

move away before anyone could think to look for such a small underwater craft—if they could even find it.

So new SEAL Teams were in existence, and they now had the secondary mission of conducting beach reconnaissance and obstacle clearance. The Frogmen were not gone; they had just changed their designations. With the commissioning of two more SEAL Teams, Three and Eight, by the end of 1983, there were three SEAL Teams and an SDV Team on each coast. Each SEAL Team consisted of eight operational platoons of sixteen men—fourteen enlisted and two officers—as well as a headquarters platoon.

George R. Worthington, Rear Admiral (lower half), USN (Ret.)

In 1955, at the age of 18, I joined the Naval Reserves. For two years, I was on inactive service while I went to Brown University as a NROTC student. Following that, things got a little interesting. While at Brown, I was one of the school swimmers. My swimming coach used his contacts at the Naval Academy to help me get in there. So my next four years were spent at the Naval Academy, and those were followed with thirty-one years of active duty.

We have a second-class summer at the Naval Academy called tramid—train a midshipman. A number of us went down to Little Creek as part of this program. At the Little Creek Naval Amphibious Base, a Frogman in a nice white uniform came into the room and threw an M80 firecracker into the wastebasket.

After getting our undivided attention, this Frogman went on to tell us all about the Underwater Demolition Teams (the commissioning of the SEAL Teams still being a few years in the future). That was the first time I ever heard about the Teams. Afterward, we were told never to join the Teams, because it would be a career-killing move.

In the Navy as it was then, joining the UDT could be the end of a young officer's career. The "regular" Navy looked down on the UDTs as not really being regulation Navy. They didn't move in fleets and do combat on the high seas; instead, they swam in and blew things up. Any officers who would be willing to lead such a group of men couldn't be expected to later "drive a boat"—the normal course of a career for a Navy officer.

The next time I heard about the UDTs was in 1963, when I had rejoined the CISM, the Conseil International du Sport Militaire (International Military Sports Council), Naval Pentathlon team. When I did that, the CISM was being held out of UDT Twelve at Coronado. I believe Ted Lyon was the XO of UDT Twelve at that time and the commanding officer was Bill Robinson, who is now deceased.

During the CISM stuff, you couldn't help but meet all the guys at the Team. They were in and around the town as well. I was on a destroyer staff at the time, which kept me from being with the UDTs constantly.

The mission the UDTs performed and the job the men did at Coronado looked interesting to me. My athletic interests weren't being met by my work in the surface Navy. Besides, after a couple years as a flag officer's aide-de-camp, I was ready to do anything to get to other duties. Eating sand with the UDTs looked fine to me.

A time later, while a trainee at Underwater Demolition Team Replacement (UDTR) training, which later became BUD/S, I was down in the front learning rest position on the beach, when I remembered what I had said earlier.

Okay, Worthington, I said to myself. You wanted to eat some sand, now do it. And I happily ate the sand. It was much more pleasurable than taking brownies to the Third MATH general in Da Nang in April 1965.

I was part of UDTR Class 36, West Coast. It was a summer class, so the traditional cold wasn't as bad as it could have been. We only lost one man during Hell Week, and he came back in to UDTR later and completed training, finishing his tour in the Navy as an E-9 Master Chief.

The hardest part of training for my class was the last three weeks we spent at San Clemente. It had gotten cold and rained every day, so Neptune paid us back for the good weather and warm time we had enjoyed up to then. Although I refer to our training as an "easy day," the work was difficult. UDTR was everything I had expected and more.

You think you can get in shape for the physical demands of training, but you really can't. The course was grueling. Back then, they had an additional two-week training session for officers. As I recall, we had about thirty-five officers show up. After the two weeks were over, we were down to something like fifteen officers left.

The Hell Week we went through was a test, just as it is for all the other classes who go through it. Hell Week was an opportunity to perform, succeed, and show that you could hack it. It might sound foolish, but frankly, I felt I got stronger as the week went on. In that long week of maximum output and minimum rest, you're kind of flatlined by Tuesday.

Our Hell Week went from midnight on Sunday until noon on Saturday. But because my boat crew was the first to finish most of the evolutions—we did all the exercises as hard as we could—the instructors rewarded us by pulling my boat crew out of Hell Week about 9 o'clock Friday night.

To try to get our boat back to the base and the showers that awaited us was nothing more than a three-hour hallucination trip. We were exhausted and in a state of mind that let us see anything we could imagine out on the dark waters.

The expression in training is "It pays to be a winner." That expression means, in the parlance of the time, that they didn't put the "ee-ties" on you, that if you were the last boat all the time, the instructors made things worse and worse for you. It was a very difficult position to pull yourselves out of.

Being a winner didn't give you any privileges, but you did get a lot more respect from the instructors. Once you set a winning path for yourself and your teammates, the instructors expected you to win and they didn't ride you as much. And being secured from Hell Week early was a big reward on its own.

There was a time during my Hell Week that I considered quitting. Barry Enoch was one of my instructors, and we learned to dread Enoch's Time. Tuesday night, he gave us time on Enoch's swimmer line. Wearing heavy, red canvas kapok life jackets at 10 o'clock on the second full night of Hell Week, we didn't think it was too bad. We knew we could hack it.

The instructors lined us up, tied us together, and gave us our paddles from the rubber boats. In those days, training was often conducted on the bay side of Coronado. There was a nice long pier extending out into the bay that we marched along, off of, and into the waters of San Diego Bay.

We would swim out into the water in a straight line, then do wheeling movements and turns. We sang songs and treaded water for about an hour while wearing our kapok life jackets. It was fun.

Then we were ordered back in and marched out of the water and back to our barracks where we took everything off and were allowed to hit our racks. Sleep—that looked to be a really great thing.

Twenty minutes after hitting the racks—bam! An M80 firecracker was tossed into a wastebasket and we were all out of our racks and on our feet. We were out and moving again. The time in the racks had been enough for most of us to fall into a serious sleep, and now we had to get moving again. So with heavy confusion in our heads as we tried to shake off the alpha waves of sleep that we had sunken in to, we had to get dressed in our clod, wet, clammy uniforms, boondocker boots, and kapoks. That hurt.

Okay, now we sang some songs for half an hour, out into the water and back in. Then, back to the barracks, strip, and into the racks. Ten minutes after we laid down—bam—here it comes again.

We marched down to the end of the pier and held position for a moment. I thought to myself, If I have to get into that water again, I'm quitting.

Who knows if I would have actually quit or not. I don't. But as that first man hit the end of the pier, the next step was into the water. Then the instructors called an about face.

We turned and went back onto the base to Turner Field where we were run through PT for the remainder of the night.

I managed to dodge the bullet on that. I never again thought about quitting and got through that Hell Week and the balance of training. I have no idea what really got me through Hell Week. I can't say it was courage, because all I did was hang in there and keep on going.

The instructors exhort you to hang in and not to quit. They were very positive, which is in contrast to some recent stories and films. I don't recall the bad language you hear in the films. I cannot remember any time while I went through UDTR

BUD/S trainees move across the grinder with their rubber boats on top of their heads. In spite of the uncomfortable appearance of this situation, this is the most effective way to carry the boat over any real distance—something the students learn over the long weeks of BUD/S.

U.S. Navy

when an instructor used foul language—ever. They were absolute professionals, and they forced us to bring out everything we had and then some.

You have to have the desire to complete the BUD/S or UDTR course. Your heart and your brain both have to want it. Second, you hope your body holds together enough to get you through.

When I went through training, once something happened to you, whether you were seriously injured or even got a serious set of blisters, you could be turned out. Then you were sent back to the Fleet and had to go through the whole application process again to even have a chance at returning to training. Today, I think we're a little bit more sage in our handling of this kind of situation.

If a fellow is a good person—the kind of man you would like to have in the Teams—he can be rolled back to heal from an injury. Once the man has healed, he can return to training with another class. But back in the days of Class 36, it was back to the Fleet.

So your heart and mind have to be together in order for you to complete training. Having your body together and the ability to keep pushing it forward is also important. Another thing that helps you get through the training is the support of your boat crew. The leadership that's exhibited within that crew, not just the officers but also the senior petty officers, can keep a man going when he flags a bit.

We've seen in BUD/S that when an officer trainee goes by the wayside, he can take a number of the troops with him. By the same token, a petty officer can keep things together and help both the men and the officer. We had a number of first class (E-6) petty officers in my class who were tough guys. They hung in there and were a good adhesive for the rest of us, officer and enlisted alike.

The "secure from Hell Week" phrase, that line that ends that week-long torture and test of your personal mettle, is a tremendous relief. But I've associated that sort of relief with lots of things throughout my Naval career. There's the "thank God it's open," or "survived the landing," or "passed the finals at the Naval Academy." "Secure from Hell Week" is another in a continuing series of Navy experiences that I can look back on and just think, thank God it's over and that we survived.

Both the low and high points during my UDTR training was Enoch's Swimmer Line. That was a very, very depressing period of five minutes during which we stood on the pier contemplating going back into the water. Then, when we about faced, I thought I was home free. By then, we were pretty much numb and I had faced enough things in my life up to that point that I was hopeful now of getting through the balance of training.

Other than that moment, I didn't really have a low point during my training. Even that time on the pier was relative in being a downturn because it happened so fast that I didn't have enough time to make up the excuses I would have to lay out as to just why I was quitting. At that time, I was a full lieutenant, and my leaving would have stood out.

Even though I was an officer, I didn't feel that the instructors chose us out for any kind of personal attention because of our ranks. The officers do have a little more responsibility than the enlisted men during training, though. We would have to work up the operations during training and such.

But I saw no favoritism on the part of the instructors, good or bad. It was an equal-opportunity situation; everybody got it, and we were all equally miserable.

Here I was, a Naval Academy graduate with time in the Fleet, where the officers are treated separately from the enlisted men. And at UDTR, I was right down there, crawling through the mud, sand, and surf with the lowest seaman in the class. I had no problem with that whatsoever. You would have to ask some of the other men in my class if I was a snob or not—I don't think I was.

We got into training and did what we had to do. If you're an officer, you have to show leadership and you expect the fellows to come along. The instructors told us very precisely and clearly what we were to do in each evolution, so setting out the plan for the men was a no-brainer. It was just, "Guys, here's what we have to do." And the senior instructor was always there to ask for help, if you really needed it.

Bosn's Mate Second Class Vince Olivera was my senior instructor. He was a man straight out of the backlots of Hollywood, the image of a Navy Boatswain's mate. They could not have picked a finer man to lead training than that classic character. He was the epitome of cool, of suave. His whole act of addressing the class made you almost want to throw yourself into the bay if that was what he wanted. And when Olivera told us to do something on an evolution, I had no burden of proof to give to the men. Just do it because Olly said to. It was fun sacrificing your life for Olivera. If Olivera said to do it, it had to be okay. That was leadership.

The experiences of UDTR were good, but the graduation from training held no particular excitement for me. The pain was over, but only for the time being. It would start again when I was operating in the field with a UDT. Four years of New England prep school had been kind of rigorous. Plebe year at the Naval Academy hadn't been pleasurable, and later-class years are even harder in terms of the aca-demics. So UDTR graduation was another phase in my Naval career. The taste of completion and accomplishment is something you learn to enjoy—after all, the training has made masochists out of the bunch of us.

My first assignment after graduating UDTR was a strange one: I was made the Operations Officer of Underwater Demolition Team Eleven. As a full lieutenant, I was sent over there to relieve the lieutenant holding the position. That officer, in turn, went on to become the executive officer of the Team, taking the space John Callahan had been holding. The illustrious commanding officer of the Team was none other than Stormin' Norman Olsen. So my initiation into the active UDTs went from UDTR straight into Norman Olsen's span of control. Sure I could swim, but I was stepping into the deep end right away.

My first deployment with UDT Eleven came along rather fast. It was in April as I recall. We reported to UDT Eleven after graduating near the end of December 1965. During March and April 1966, Bill Robinson, who was a staff officer in the CTF 76 staff, worked up an operation called Operation Jackstay. That operation was to take place down in the Mekong Delta region of South Vietnam.

Our mission was to go over there, which involved fifty-two hours of flight and travel time. Once we got to town, Jim Barnes was already there with a detachment of SEALs, and some Marines were there, too.

We received our briefings on the op. The plan involved was putting four-man groups up little tributaries in the southern section of the Rung Sat Special Zone. That was just about in the Vung Tau area down there. We would go in during daylight, insert, then spend the night there in the nipa palms and tidewaters. The funny thing about the operation was to listen to Norm Olsen talk about it the next day after spending a whole night in water up to his nipples.

We went to get some information from the staff intelligence officer and were asked to bring back some incidental information about the local fauna. The intel officer had heard about a local fish that actually climbed out of the water to move on the (more or less) dry land. It was supposed to be a true amphibian, and the intel officer wanted us to bring him back a specimen.

Here we were, operating off of the Weiss where we weren't even getting showers. During our operations, we were looking for places to set up ambushes against the Viet Cong. And now this intelligence officer wanted a fish. We tried to be as kind to him as we could, because he was a commander and we were just peons. But the general opinion was that we would probably eat one of those fishes before we would ever give one to him.

The deployment for Operation JACKSTAY did involve some direct combat for the UDT in Vietnam. We did a bunch of ambushes in the Rung Sat against VC hiding in the huge swamp. This had not been my first visit to Vietnam, but it was the first time I was there squatting in the mud and brown water.

I had received my first impressions of Vietnam earlier in 1965 when I accompanied the admiral in charge of Comcrudesflot 7 (Commander Cruiser Destroyer Flotilla 7). We flew the length of the South Vietnamese coast, stopping off at various places. The staff I was with were responsible to the Seventh Fleet for developing the Operation Market Time plan.

Our first night incountry, we hit Saigon and went to the Top of the Rex, I guess it was. I made reservations for us at the Paprika Restaurant. We went out there and spent an interesting time.

I looked at the area as being the old French colonial village, a minor city. Culturally, I was kind of looking at how we could help the people there, maybe even some of the French. Our job was to see how we could better stop the infiltration of the Communist forces coming down from the North and slipping into the area from the seacoast. The powers-that-be thought the seaborne infiltration was true due to the Bucklew report. The 1964 Bucklew report had established that the Viet Cong were using the waterways of the Mekong Delta to move personnel and smuggled supplies. It was used as part of the reason for sending direct action SEAL Platoons to Vietnam in 1966.

Some of the Communists and their supplies came down on the Ho Chi Minh trail, with the majority of the stuff coming in to Vietnam from Sihanookville across the Cambodian border. The situation for us was kind of the blind leading the blind. The MAG Navy guy had an airplane that he flew us around in.

The SEALs' first direct combat operations in Vietnam were when Jim Barnes brought his detachment from SEAL Team One over into South Vietnam in early 1966. They conducted ops as part of Operation Jackstay. Jim didn't like Jackstay, and I don't think he participated in the operation much. But once he and the SEALs were over there, they started doing things, active combat operations and such, after that.

Barnes and company were scheduled for Jackstay, but he opted out of it, leaving the support of that operation to the men of UDT Eleven and the Marine Recon guys. On one of the missions, I had a Marine unit operating in close support of myself and a detachment of UDT.

My UDT men and myself were the Team farthest up this little river, which was almost all mud really. About 400 meters away from my UDT team was a Marine team. Mike Troy, who was an Olympic swimmer before he joined with the UDT, was there, leading his detachment. Troy's group was overrun by the Viet Cong, and we all held our breath until, thank God, we heard he was in the clear. We were operating in the jungle and mud of the Rung Sat, and that wasn't something we had been trained for.

Things became a little tight for us, doing those sorts of missions but we worked the situation and figured that we could pull off what was expected of us. Basically, we were trained to do beach recons and dives to blow up obstacles. We were very experienced in working with demolitions, not crawling through the jungle and waiting to conduct an ambush while chest-deep in muddy water.

The remainder of that tour in Vietnam consisted mostly of the more traditional UDT operations. Working with the amphibious guys while on the Dagger Thrust operations, the UDTs checked out sandbars along the coastline of South Vietnam to see if they could be eliminated or if channels could be blasted through them. Beach recons were run and the areas were charted for the national authorities in case amphibious forces had to be brought into an area quickly.

We came back from that deployment in September 1966 and found that we had a new commanding officer at UDT Eleven. At this time I was fleeted-up to the position of executive officer of the Team. The following February (1967), after only about five months back home, UDT Eleven again deployed to South Vietnam, this time with me in the position of XO.

The plan this time was to deploy the full UDT to the operational area of the deployment. There was a lot of administrative mashing about because of the plan to try and develop White Beach, Okinawa, as the headquarters area for forward-deployed UDTs.

We Teams argued that we should keep the preponderance of the guys close to the amphibious forces they worked so closely with. The amphibious forces operated out of Subic Bay in the Philippines, the closest major U.S. Naval facility to the operational theater in Southeast Asia.

So the UDT Eleven CO and his personal staff were located in Okinawa for the 1967 cruise. As the XO, I stayed back in Subic and ran things from there. We took certain officers and gave their platoons specific assignments. One officer would be told that he was the ARG (Amphibious Ready Group) platoon who would operate with the Marines, another officer would take the submarine detachment, and so on.

Some operations had to be conducted down in the IV Corps area. Surveys had never been done of the beaches in IV Corps—basically the Mekong Delta and points south in Vietnam. So the discussions went around about who should go in command of the detachment to conduct the surveys.

The first person suggested was the CO of the Team, but that was immediately denied. Then it was suggested that the XO of the UDT—myself—go as the OIC. Well, I could have gone but at the time I was in the business of training lieutenants to work in the Team.

Mike Collins, one of the officers at UDT Eleven then, was on the Weiss with his platoon. They had a pretty good CO of the boat, a former Frogman himself. So Mike was put in as the OIC, and his platoon went down and conducted those first surveys along the shore of IV Corps.

Training still didn't stop as UDT Eleven was deployed. During that summer, quite a few of us went to HALO (high altitude, low opening) school and learned military free-fall parachuting at the U.S. Army Special Forces–run school in Okinawa.

At one point, we put together some training instructions did some new training of our own. Taking a new UDT platoon, we put them through the U.S. Army jump-training syllabus, the training being run by our own UDT Instructors.

Two days before UDT Eleven was to redeploy back to the United States, I was involved in a parachute accident and managed to do a number on my left ankle that basically put me in a leg cast for four months. One thing you can't do is run around and undergo SEAL training with a cast on your leg.

Only in fairly recent years has command been operating lieutenant commanders in the field, and that only with SEAL Team Six at the beginning. As a lieutenant commander by that time, with a hurt leg, the rank and injury kept me out of the active SEAL Teams during the balance of the Vietnam War.

So I left the Teams for a length of time, and went back to the Fleet to serve time aboard ship. As the ops (operations) officer on a destroyer, I participated in a

Mediterranean cruise. After that, I made a career choice and told BUPERS (Bureau of Personnel) that I wanted to go back to Naval Special Warfare. My request was approved, and I was told to go back to Vietnam.

So I went over to Vietnam, first as the ops officer and later as the XO of Naval Special Warfare Group—Vietnam. Toward the end of our Vietnam involvement, things became very competitive between the Teams and the Navy. When I became the commanding officer of SEAL Team One, I had only one platoon deployed to Vietnam. Now I felt my mission was to do some interesting, if arcane, training for my Team while at the same time trying to find more work for them.

I hear people today talking about great morale problems that existed in the Teams then. I didn't see those problems, except maybe for some lieutenants who weren't able to deploy to combat. I had guys come to me and ask to be able to make some parachute jumps. These were the older operators, and I had no trouble helping make arrangements for them to go out and do what they needed. But I couldn't get a platoon for an officer who wanted to deploy. It's interesting that fifteen years later, I've heard just the opposite. What I heard from lieutenants then were things like, "I've had five platoons and I'm tired of deploying." There is a balance there that needs to be reached.

But that balance certainly wasn't reached back then in the five or six years following our drawdown from Vietnam. Opportunities to deploy, to go out and operate, were few, and the order of the day was to stand in line. That's when guys would do whatever they could to stay working, stay busy, and keep a challenge in front of them.

SEALs were intended to be men for all seasons, so they trained in skills that could prove valuable in the field. Those years following the Vietnam War were when guys were doing things like traveling the Colorado River in rubber rafts. I even sent a platoon down to get sailboat training. I set up course of ski training for the SEALs and started a little bit of winter warfare training. Anything to keep things interesting.

For the younger guys in the Teams, time goes slowly without action to keep them busy. For the older chiefs, a quarter-year could seem to go by in an instant. So the challenge was to find a training cycle that was, if not equitable for all concerned, at least something that everyone could learn from and work with. If the young kids, those SEALs on their first tour of duty, start to feel that things are dragging at the Team, they could get in trouble on their own, so we had to keep them interested.

From 1976 to 1978, I was the commanding officer of something called Inshore Undersea Warfare Group One (IUWG-1). That was a hodge-podge of expertise from electronics people, Marine Mammals and SEALs. Many SEALs loved to be involved with the Marine Mammals program, if for no other reason than they were in bathing suits most of the day and at the farthest point in the base from the "flagpole" (command). There, no one ever really bothered them.

The work was starting to get the Marine Mammals involved in amphibious operations like mine recovery. The Mammals seemed to enjoy the work. We also had a sensor group in the Inshore Warfare Group. But the Navy hadn't funded sensors for four years, so we worked with older sensor systems that were contained in these shielded Army Battle Area Surveillance System (BASS) vans.

I had an idea to take all the sensor electronics out of the BASS vans and put in communications gear and radios and make it an organic Command, Control, and Communications (C3) suite for the Group commander. That idea ultimately sold, and today it's called the Mobile Comm Teams. We used it during Desert Storm. We could talk from the Group command in Coronado all the way to the SEAL commander on site with our own equipment.

So my morale was fine in the late 1970s, and I suspect the morale of the men in the Teams wasn't bad either—at least I never got the sense that it was.

Things were changing at the IUWG. A lot of gals were starting to come over into the unit from other parts of the Navy. How to use them and work them into the scheme of things wasn't too difficult. There wasn't any grousing about the women being here.

Some of the women new in the unit were pregnant, and that wasn't a problem I had faced in the Teams before. But I took a little section from the personnel department, kind of a lounge area, and turned that into a nursery. That way any of the female yeomen who were nursing their kids could just bring them to work. They could type the letters and watch their kids—no problem, everyone was as happy as rain, and the situation didn't bother me.

One activity we had was something we called Monster Mashes. Two teams, blue and gold, made up of equal numbers of SEALs and Fleet sailors, would do things like negotiate the obstacle course. It was kind of fun to watch some of the women sailors negotiate the CISM obstacle course. Then they would go into the swimming pool, turn an IBS (inflatable boat, small) over, then conduct a race. All of this was done on a Friday, and a barbecue was held afterward.

There was a question about some of the women not being happy at having to wear swimsuits. So I said to watch some of the films of the Olympics and get those suits for the women to wear. If someone wanted to file a complaint, then they were free to. But no one complained, the gals all participated, and it was fun. Then by 1700 (5 o'clock), everyone got to go home. I can't speak to what it was like aboard a Navy ship at that time but we kept up the morale at the Group and all the organizations that were part of it.

By the late 1970s, I was attending the National War College from which I graduated in June 1979. Then I reported in to our OPNAV for a staff position. I moved in on 15 July 1979. Ted Lyon and Jim Barnes were there then, but Barnes was moving out because he was retiring as I remember. That meant the staff was made up of only two people, Ted and myself.

On 24 December 1979, I got the piece of paper signed that established Naval Special Warfare Unit 2 in Macrihanish, Scotland. There had been a Unit 2 earlier, but it had been put down due to some objections by a Fleet admiral. He might not have liked how the SEALs creased their pants as far as I knew.

So we had reestablished a SEAL forward-operating unit with NSW Unit 2 in Macrihanish. The following year, Ted Lyon got an opportunity to be the commodore down at Naval Special Warfare Group Two in Little Creek, Virginia. He left, and that basically left me in charge of the office for a period. There was another fellow, Maynard Wires, who came in to relieve Ted, but I held the fort on my own for four months or so. While all of this was going on, a new operations code (opcode) class, Op 09-5, was established.

This new organization was to be the honest broker for the Navy. They would look around and see if things like the sonars that were used in the Navy's aircraft were the same as those used on the surface ships and submarines. They were looking for any commonality in the technologies of the Navy that could be used by other organizations or services, such as air, surface, or subsurface. The new organization needed a SEAL in their office, so I ended up working for their amphibious desk.

While I was at Op 09-5, I was working as 09-54, strike warfare (amphibious), and created the "master plan." A master plan meant that you laid out what you wanted and then you'd fund toward it.

A bunch of people looked at my Naval Special Warfare Master Plan and said that it was daunting and that it couldn't be done. Well, in the Reagan years, if you were going to get any piece of the pie for your people, you couldn't think that just crumbs from the Surface Warfare table were going to get you where you wanted to go. So we created a master plan to encompass the entire special warfare community and asked for what we needed to really initiate the plan.

I was then sent back down to the Op-03 desk, Surface Warfare, when Wires left. So in essence, I had three back-to-back Pentagon tours.

Contrary to popular opinion, your job gets easier in the Pentagon the longer you're there. You learn the operations of the building and how to get things done. Knowing where to get your view-graphs for briefings, your charts, and even just the phone numbers for the right people to call for a problem all come once you get some time in the building.

I think there's a law or regulation in place that an officer cannot spend more than six years in the Pentagon at a stretch. That might be to prevent the more experienced people from staging a coup or something.

So I went from writing the Master Plan, which stated our requirements in Special Warfare and where we were and where we wanted to go, to the desk that was responsible for funding the plan. Part and parcel of this was that we got some things done, including getting SEAL Team Eight.

About that time in 1983, we had a conference in Washington of most of the Naval Special Warfare high command. At the meeting, Irish Flynn said he thought it was time that all the UDTs became SEAL Teams. As the Action Officer on the Chief of Naval Operations Staff, I said that if the Group commodores all agreed, and they were all at the table, that they should start the action. Then I would run it to ground and make sure that the name change happened.

At that time, it was rather simplistic, but I thought, Okay, we'll change the name. Of course, it wasn't just a name change. The primary and secondary missions of the SEALs and the UDTs were different. Now the SEALs had both their own and the missions of the UDTs. That meant there were equipment requirements. If you were doing beach recons, you needed flutterboards and things like that. If you were doing ambushes, you needed face paint and all the other types of things that went along with a direct combat mission.

But that's where it happened, in that meeting in Washington. The Teams changed officially in 1983, and the UDTs became SEAL Teams. In addition to that, we had to set up Swimmer (later SEAL) Delivery Vehicle Teams because operating SDVs is probably the hardest thing we do in Naval Special Warfare. The care, shepherding, and husbandry required by the SDVs are beyond the normal training of a SEAL. Keeping them moving, and the SEALs within them breathing, is a very technical and demanding specialty.

Lynn Reilander came to me and asked how we did with the growth of Special Warfare. I thought we had done fine to the extent that we were able to get things from the Surface Warfare barons, whose main mission in life was to see the Arleigh Burke class get commissioned.

Lynn said we were going to fix what was missing and showed me a piece of paper that outlined where he was going in terms of special ops, including Naval Special Warfare and Army Special Forces. Lynn intended to correct all the shortcomings of the special operations community in one fiscal year.

I had to tell him that it was going to be impossible to spend or accomplish everything it would take to get all the spec ops community healthy. You just couldn't grow these kinds of operators overnight.

Every available engineer who could work on our problems was already working on other priority projects. The only way to get an engineer to work on our projects would mean taking him off another project and then that project would languish until someone else could come in and get it back up to speed. And it would take time to get even an experienced engineer smart in terms of what SEALs needed or even what their warfare capabilities were all about.

So a program would have to be shown that went over what was then called the Five Year Defense Plan. It would have to start in 1986 and finish in 1990. Of course, we all knew that once it started, it would never really be finished.

Lynn wrote a paper for the then Secretary for Defense. The Secretary came out with his own memo on 3 October 1983. The memo was to all the services and all the staffs in the Pentagon to fix special operations, and the action was to be completed by the end of fiscal year 1990. That made 1996 the first year to begin a new rebuilding of the Special Operations Forces for the U.S. military.

To get more SEALs, we had to look and see what we needed in the standard SEAL Team. So we redid the numbers on that. You can't get these men in just one year, but you would have to start growing them right away. In order to grow them, you had to fix the schoolhouse, the BUD/S training center.

I called a contact of mine up at BUPERS, told him we had a hot problem on our hands, and asked him to come down to a meeting. When he arrived, we told him we had to grow the schoolhouse. In order to get more students through training, we had to have a bigger facility. To make a long story short, we got the pool and other facilities, including more instructors, to increase the numbers of SEALs available for the new Teams.

The first year of the buildup was 1987, so 1986 was the planning year. With some rapid military construction, the new schoolhouse compound at BUD/S was built. In 1987, they were able to ramp up to five or six classes a year, and soon we would have the manpower we needed to build up the Teams.

Other questions came up, such as the level of readiness and whether the demographics would match the number of students we needed to come into BUD/S.

Well, the kids were nearly standing in line to try and complete BUD/S and go on to the Teams. The raw numbers were there, and we weren't going to sacrifice the quality of training just for numbers. And I don't think the increase in the numbers of students going through BUD/S lowered the final quality of the graduates.

We had some great minds working on the problems of getting quality students through the training program. It was suggested that, if we had a good man, we try harder to keep him rather than just let him go, as had been done in earlier training.

I used to talk to the classes as they graduated. I asked one graduating lieutenant, junior grade, how long he had been at BUD/S.

"Eighteen months," was his answer.

That young officer had been a UDT/SEAL trainee for a year and a half. That man wanted the program, and we would have lost him earlier just because of a bad throw of the dice. Someone had dropped an engine or rubber boat on his leg and injured him. In earlier years, that would have sent him back to the Fleet and he would have had to reapply and try to just get to BUD/S all over again.

But the new idea was to offer worthwhile individuals the chance to stick it out at BUD/S. If some want to call that liberal, okay, but I call it conservative because you're assuring that BUD/S is less of a crap shoot as to just who's going to make it or not due to an injury. The guy who sticks it out is the kind of guy we wanted.

We renamed the schoolhouse the Naval Special Warfare Center in 1987. We brought Phil Bucklew out to the ceremonies in a wheelchair and named the new structure after him. He had been a highly decorated veteran of the World War II Scouts and Raiders and was influential in first getting the SEALs directly involved in the Vietnam War.

At about the same time, there was also a change in the overall command structure for U.S. Special Operations Forces, a change that affected the SEALs along with all the others. An amendment to the 1986 military authorization bill ordered that the U.S. Special Operations Command (USSOCOM), a command that put all the Special Operations forces under the same umbrella, be established in Tampa, Florida.

At SOCOM, flag officers would be in charge of each of the different service's special operations forces. Chuck Lemoyne was one of the thinkers behind the idea and was the first SEAL admiral at SOCOM. This gave a command a push to make sure that what was needed to conduct special operations received the necessary priorities.

The shield of the Special Operations Command, based on the spearhead patch of the World War II OSS, surrounded by its unit commands. To the upper left is the arrowhead and dagger of the Army Rangers. At the upper right is the U.S. Navy Special Warfare Command symbol. At the lower right is the Joint Special Operations Command shield. At the lower left is the Air Force Special Operations Command shield.

USSOCOM PAO

Now the Air Force could be asked why the Combat Talon aircraft was number 83 on the priority list. The small unit numbers of specialized equipment needed for spec ops support didn't make them as appealing as a new class of destroyer for the Navy or fighter plane for the Air Force. But with the establishment of USSOCOM, that situation could be better dealt with.

With the establishment of the Special Operations Command, there was now an infrastructure, an organization, in place that was able to monitor the health of all the special operations forces. The new organization had the knowledge and experience to know what was required to carry out these sorts of missions, what was needed in the care and feeding of the SEALs and the Special Forces. SOCOM is still evolving and growing to this day.

All the U.S. military forces are evolving and changing as the world has become such a different place after the fall of the Soviet Union. The U.S. Navy Submarine forces are an example of such changes. When the Russian subs were tied up at the docks, the Navy subs had to extend their mission parameters to keep operating. Suddenly, Navy SpecWar were the recipients of more offered submarine services after the Berlin Wall came down than we ever would have hoped to get, and the sub fleet was looking for spec ops missions.

Even the Air Force B-52 people were looking for a change of missions—not in terms of migrating away from their strategic bombing role, but to look for additional reasons for being. They were suggesting that special ops could have low-level attack missions they could do. Everyone has a vested interest in what their branch or part of the service did; that was what they had learned and what they knew. And now these skills and abilities were being applied in new ways. Everyone benefits from such a situation.

It is possible that the Special Operations Command may evolve into a separate branch of the service, standing alongside the Army, Navy, Air Force, and Marines. That possibility was argued back when the idea of something like SOCOM was being discussed. There are people in SOCOM now who say that the antecedent of the command was the OSS of World War II. That is only true when you consider the operational side of the OSS. The later CIA doing covert operations has had mixed reviews over the years. They, as the direct descendants of the OSS, have more of an intelligence-gathering mission as a holdover from the World War II days.

In my view, it would be hard to see SOCOM as a separate service today. But could it grow to something like that? I just don't know. My crystal ball is a little too foggy to make that future out, but it is certainly possible. That kind of conjecture is easy to make here in CONUS (continental United States), but out in the field, it can be harder to see.

Duplicity of missions and operations could easily be a problem. Would some future Secretary of the Navy see someone from SOCOM swimming in to their target and decide that the mission should be given to the Marines just because it was moving from water to land? And besides, the Marines probably wouldn't want the additional mission; their plate's pretty full right now.

SOCOM's present position as a central command and infrastructure for all the different service's special operations forces is probably the best situation it could be in for the foreseeable future. Whether something becomes a separate service or not ultimately depends on how that would help the man at the end of the rifle. If it would help him do his mission, then that has to be shown and justified.

That man on the ground, the operator, the eyes on the target, that man is the ultimate ground-truth guy for what is happening in a situation. That is the person who the public visualizes when they think about the special operations forces. The public image of the SEALs, and the special operations forces in general, is usually far from the truth. With the secretive nature of most special operations, the public doesn't have the information to build a correct image, and so the gap is filled with images from movies and television.

There is no Rambo in the SEALs. There cannot be. The mythical image of the SEALs is precisely that, a myth. SEALs are looked up to as military athletes, as really tough guys. But I can't see anyone taking a movie, say such as GI Jane, seriously. When the trainees stood in ranks in that movie, you saw people from different U.S. services. In my 30-some-odd years of associating with the Teams, I've never seen a Marine or an Army guy go through SEAL training. Foreign sailors or allied UDT guys, yes, they have gone through training at BUD/S. But to be a SEAL, you have to be in the Navy, period.

Only people who have gone through the rigors and testing of BUD/S and on to the Teams are entitled to wear the Naval Special Warfare breast insignia—the Trident. To me, the Trident is a symbol of respect and honor. It very much represents something to the rest of the Navy. We took a lot of jibing about it from the Fleet when it was first adopted. There were comments about how we should have had some SEALs on the selection board in order to have made it a little smaller. Truth was, SEALs would have probably made it bigger. It represents what we do; it's a symbol of all the skills held by the SEALs.

When I was going through training and for some years afterward, I had nothing on my uniform to show my association with the Teams. Those were the days when few Naval officers had distinguishing devices on their uniforms other than the Dolphins of the Submariners or the Wings of the Fliers. Then Admiral Zumwalt brought in the Surface Warfare pin and it was decided that the SEALs and the UDTs needed a uniform device.

The only unique thing worn on a SEAL's or UDT's uniform for a long while was parachute wings. Then two pins were designed, one for the UDTs and another for the SEALs. The difference between the two pins was the presence of an eagle on the SEAL pin. There were gold and silver pins respectively for officer and enlisted personnel.

But finally someone said wait a minute. Everybody took the same dose of medicine (BUD/S) to get to the Teams. Everyone, UDT and SEAL, officer and enlisted, had to do the same stuff and crawl through the same mud to graduate BUD/S. There should be only one pin, gold with the eagle, for all the Teams and all the qualified personnel, officer and enlisted alike.

One comment on the history of the Teams, past, present, and future. The misnomer that the SEALs, Underwater Demolition Teams, and the Naval Combat Demolition Units (NCDUs) somehow evolved from out of the Scouts and Raiders—which were a separate unit—is not accurate. These units did evolve one from the other, not from the Scouts or Rangers.

The reason there were NCDUs and then the Frogmen (UDTs) was that in 1942 and 1943 the Navy didn't have good charts for many of the areas the U.S. Navy would have to conduct landings on to put forward the war effort. They didn't know what the beaches were like, so recons would have to be run to supply the most up-to-the-minute intelligence. It was the men in the water—men like the Naked Warrior—who conducted these recons. They swam in and checked the bottom to see if ships and boats could get in and where any mines or other obstacles might be. If necessary, the men could then blast a pathway through the obstacles for the landing forces.

The secondary mission of the UDTs included land warfare centering around demolition raids. The UDTs did a lot of those raids behind enemy lines during the Korean War. In 1962, the SEALs were established as a separate unit from the UDTs because President John Kennedy wanted more work to be done in counter-guerrilla-type missions.

In 1983, the missions came back together. For twenty years, the SEALs' primary mission was above the high water mark, while the UDTs' primary mission was below that point. But the men who conducted the operations were the same animal.

You look at a SEAL, Marine Recon, Army SF, or Ranger, and they're all pretty much the same red-white-and-blue 98.6 guy. He might put on a different uniform or train differently perhaps, but underneath it's all the same person.

Individuals stand out in all of the services. Barry Enoch was one person I remember meeting for the first time back in 1965 when he was one of the petty officer instructors at UDT Replacement training for Class 36. There were a lot of very colorful instructors at UDTR, and Barry was one of them.

The enlisted people who went over to UDTR to train us were all very top-notch guys. In some cases, the officers weren't necessarily the equivalent of the enlisted instructors. The enlisted guys were the ones we spent the most time with, and these were some of the best people on Earth.

As I remember, Barry Enoch was a Second Class petty officer at the time, and he managed to make me question my presence at UDTR through one of his evolutions as I recounted earlier regarding Enoch's Swimmer Line. He was, and is, a great guy. Went on to the SEAL Teams and won a Navy Cross during one of his tours in Vietnam.

Another colorful guy in the Teams was Norm Olsen. He was my first commanding officer in UDT and as such made quite an impression on this very new Frogman. They call him Stormin' Norman because when you went to see him about something, you had better make sure that all of your facts were correct and the answer was right. You had to give him the answer, and it had better be a good one. Explain things to him and there was no problem. The "Stormin' " part came if you had the numbers wrong or if you had the spelling wrong on your papers. He would not abide sloppiness.

Norm Olsen was an avid skydiver, one of the original guys who was doing an awful lot of it back when everyone was still learning. I remember one day, some guys had a night jump out of UDT Eleven and some people missed the muster. Word got back to the people who were providing the airplanes that they weren't full on the jump. Norm hit the overhead on that and said "Hey, if you need space filled, you call me and I'll do a string [static line] jump." Up to that time, Norm was doing a lot of free-fall jumps. He was one of the original guys who got a parachute demonstration team going—what later became the Leap Frogs.

There are people in the Teams today keeping the community moving ahead. Admiral Ray Smith is a great guy, someone I consider to be a natural leader. His personality and drive and just the way he is with people makes you want to follow him. He is a very cordial and congenial guy as well as being a very capable man.

Admiral Tom Richards is the same kind of man. Nicknamed "the Hulk," Tom was my ops officer when I was running Group One, and he did a superb job for me. He was also an ops officer for me at SEAL Team One. He's just overall a great guy. If I was asked to write a fitness report for him, I could give him nothing less than all A's.

■ Chapter 55

Aircraft: The "A" in SEAL

The SEALs used aircraft to a large extent both to insert and extract men from a target as well as to provide fire support when and where needed. In the jungles and swamps of Vietnam, the primary aircraft used by the Teams for both purposes was the rotary-winged helicopter. The Huey, the workhorse bird of the Vietnam War, could put SEALs into a target area half the size of a football field, pull out their wounded without even touching down if necessary, and place machine gun and rocket fire within yards of a beleaguered SEAL position.

The SEALs found a liking for any chopper pilot who would come in and help them when needed. But it was the Navy Seawolves who were the Teams' favorites. Close behind the Seawolves were the pilots of the fixed-wing OV-10 Broncos, the Black Ponies. Both of these units were Navy assets, and the SEALs worked with them on an almost daily basis in Vietnam.

As the SEALs downsized and changed to a nonwar footing, training became the primary activity. All forms of Navy helicopters were used for training, and several new techniques were developed. Because most of the larger Navy helicopters are fitted with an external hoist mounted above one of the side doors, capable of lifting either equipment or rescue slings, they are a ready-made securing point for a heavy line.

Rappelling from hovering choppers was, and is still, practiced by the SEALs as a viable insertion technique. But a new system called "fast roping" has developed. In fast roping, a heavy line is attached to the helicopter's rescue hoist and the SEALs simply slide down the line. Little more than a pair of leather gloves to protect the hands and a crash helmet are used in the way of special equipment, and the speed of the insertion is incredible with a practiced team. In five or six seconds, a four-man fire team can be on the ground from a single rope, the men just using their hands and legs as the braking force on the rope. Resembling the climbing rope used in school gym classes, the descender rope is a special thick, tri-weave polyester line with a tensile strength of 35,000 pounds (15,876 kilograms). The rope is used in either 50 (15.24), 90 (27.43), or 120 foot (36.58 meter) lengths.

The speed of the fast roping technique makes it a preferred method for many types of insertions, especially when boarding a possibly hostile ship at sea. Care does have to be taken by the SEALs so that they do not impact on each other as they hit the ground—a very real danger as the men are coming down at something like one-second intervals.

Once you got into an area, it was nice to have a method of extraction if things got too hot. The SEALs developed the SPIE (Special Patrol Insertion/Extraction) rig for their own use. The SPIE or Spyrig uses a single 120-foot (36.58-meter) length of 1-inch-diameter (2.54 cm) nylon line with a polyurethane core as the lifting rope. With a tensile strength of 24,000 pounds (10,886 kilograms), a single rope can lift out an entire six-man team at one time. With spaced attachment D-rings secured to the main line ahead of time, the SEALs just have to attach their personal SPIE harnesses to the D-rings for extraction. The SPIE harnesses are generally worn as part of the combat uniform.

Again made much the same as a parachute harness, the SPIE harness is made from 5,000-pound (2,268-kilogram) tensile strength nylon webbing with a single attaching point above and behind the SEALs' neck. Used in conjunction with a 12-foot safety line that would be attached to another person using the rig, the SPIE system allows the user's hands to remain free for stabilization or using weapons. The SEALs would attach to the SPIE rig in pairs, with one man on either side of the line. Attachment is quick, and a team can be removed to safety in a very short time. The SPIE rig is particularly useful in inserting or extracting a team in tight spaces such as on the deck of a ship at sea.

With the wide range of techniques available to them, the SEALs are able to operate effectively from most Navy asset helicopters. But for the best efficiency, the SEALs should be working with air crews trained in Special Warfare operations. Many of the Navy's helicopters are fitted for specific missions, and the equipment packages limit the amount of room onboard. This cuts down on the number of SEALs who could be employed from the aircraft. This situation is particularly true in those helicopters assigned to antisubmarine warfare duties.

Fleet helicopter assets today generally consist of SH-3, CH-46, SH-60, and CH-53 aircraft. With the sixteen-man size of SEAL platoons today, the CH-46 is the preferred aircraft for many Special Warfare insertions, and especially on VBSS (Visit, Board, Search, and Seizure) operations, as it can carry a fully equipped platoon along with two EOD (explosive ordnance disposal) men. However, the CH-46 is a very large aircraft and is not as suitable for clandestine insertions.

■ ■ ■

SEAL airborne capabilities received a strong upgrade with the increase of all Special Operations forces under the Reagan and later administrations. Besides

A line of armed A/MH-6 "Little Bird" helicopters of the Army's 160th Aviation Regiment. The agile little helicopters are modified versions of the Hughes MD500 helicopter.

USSOCOM PAO

increasing the strength of the SEALs with new Teams and men, several air units were created that greatly added to the overall capabilities of all the Special Operations units, including the SEALs. These new units came under the direction of the new Special Operations Command (SOCOM), consolidating all the Service's Special Operations forces under a single umbrella organization.

The Army added the 160th Aviation Regiment, called the Night Stalkers, to the rolls of Special Operations forces. Today, equipped with MH-6F Little Birds, AH-64A Apache gunships, and other rotary-wing aircraft, the men of the 160th train heavily in night flying and all forms of special operations support. In addition to the special capabilities of the 160th Regiment, the SEALs can also rely on regular Army support in the form of AH-1G Cobra gunships for fire support and UH-60A Blackhawks for transportation. Marine air units also have the AH-1J Sea Cobra for air support, and this aircraft is also available to the SEALs.

In addition to support from the Army, SOCOM had new Air Force assets

An aircraft crewman prepares to push a rubber boat out the rear of a C-130 cargo plane as the SEALs who will man the boat line up to the left. This is the rubber duck insertion and the SEALs will release the inflated rubber boat from its cardboard-padded pallet once they are in the water. The cavernous interior of the C-130 is illuminated for this training operation. In a combat jump, this procedure would be conducted under very dim light conditions.

that are also available to support the SEALs. In the 23rd Air Force/Special Operations Command, MH-53J Pave Low III Enhanced helicopters are used along with fixed-wing aircraft such as the MC-130E Combat Talon and AC-130H Spectre gunship. All these craft work in close cooperation with Navy assets, including the SEALs, in conducting special operations today.

■ ■ ■

EARLIER transport planes, such as the famous C-47, were used as jump platforms by several generations of military parachutists. The UDT and SEALs were no exception to this and jumped from the C-47 and other craft often during tactical training. But the side-door exit point of the C-47 made it unsuitable for jumping a team and airdropping large pieces of equipment at the same time. Inserting combat swimmers by parachute would limit the equipment the swimmers could carry, or tow, through the water to their target. The distance they could swim effectively was also a limiting factor. Using the rear cargo ramp of the C-130 as an exit point, a technique unique to the Teams was developed called the "rubber duck."

A rubber duck insertion is where a team of SEALs jumps from an aircraft along with an inflated rubber boat. Attached to a shock-absorbing platform and rigged with large cargo parachutes, the rubber duck, as the complete package is called, is pushed out ahead of the parachuting SEALs. With the inflated rubber boat immediately at hand and ready to go, the SEALs can climb aboard and move out on their mission, covering a much longer distance over water and carrying a great deal more equipment than they could if they were just inserting as combat swimmers.

■ ■ ■

THE cargo aircraft were used for considerably more than just jump platforms or airborne trucks. An idea born prior to the Vietnam War was for a cargo plane to be armed with rapid-fire machine guns aimed out of the side of the aircraft. With the plane circling over a target in what was called a pylon turn, the guns would shoot to the side and strafe the ground. The first of these aircraft was the venerable CH-47 fitted with three 7.62mm miniguns aiming out of the plane's port side. The three guns, each firing at 2,000 or 4,000 rounds a minute depending on their settings, could place a 7.62mm bullet on every four square inches of a football field in a single pass. The designation for the new flying gunship was AC-47, but it was better known by its common name—Puff the Magic Dragon.

The AC-47 aircraft suffered from the limited range of its weapons. For accuracy, the gunships would have to circle over their target at an altitude no greater than 3,500 feet, making them vulnerable to ground fire. As the Viet Cong and NVA forces became more sophisticated with their antiaircraft weapons employment, the threat to the gunships became very serious. Orbiting as they would over a target area, the rather slow-moving cargo planes were particularly vulnerable when their port (gun) side was facing away from the enemy's guns. To help relieve this situation, and utilize a more modern airframe, the C-130 Hercules was looked to as a possible gunship platform.

Initial tests were conducted with a C-130 armed with four M61A1 20mm Vulcans and four M134 7.62mm miniguns. The AC-130E Spectre so armed was sent to Vietnam for field testing in the late 1960s. The AC-130 quickly came online as a much heavier-armed gunship. Two 40mm Bofors cannons were installed in place of two each of the Vulcans and miniguns. The Bofors fired full automatic at a very slow rate of 100 to 120 rounds per minute. The magazine of the weapon held stacks of four-round clips, and the gun crew could top-up the magazines as the weapons were being fired.

Flame projects out from the muzzles of two roaring M61A1 20mm Vulcan cannons as they spew their rounds out at a rate reaching 6,000 rounds per minute. The two 20mm multibarrel cannons are only part of the armament of the awesome AC-130H gunship. Other weapons include the 40mm M2A1 Bofors cannon toward the rear of the aircraft and finally, the modified M102 105mm howitzer that can launch a 33-pound high explosive shell with extreme accuracy.

USSOCOM PAO

The Bofors was a welcome addition to the firepower of the gunship, and C-130s so armed were designated AC-130H. During tests for heavier armament to be added to the gunship, the M40A1 106mm recoilless rifle was considered but then dropped due to difficulties with the weapon's backblast. Further research resulted in one of the heaviest weapons ever consistently mounted in an aircraft. A modified M102 105mm howitzer was put in place next to the 40mm Bofors. Even firing a relatively light charge, the 105mm would launch a 33-pound high-explosive projectile that could eliminate any normally encountered ground target. Even buried bunkers could be vulnerable to the incredible firepower of the AC-130H Spectre. The gunship was, and is, an awesome sight in the skies of Vietnam, Grenada, Panama, Afghanistan, and elsewhere.

Specially trained crews of the Air Force Special Operations Squadrons operate their craft with consummate skill. When absolutely necessary, the crews of the gunships could put their shells literally within yards of a SEAL position.

■ Chapter 56

Grenada

Grenada is a small island nation in the southern Caribbean. Only about 133 square miles in size and boasting a population of about 110,000 native people, Grenada was a place little known by the average American. A small medical school on the island was the place of study for a number of American students, and the island's two major industries, tourism and spice exports, were not something to attract the attention of more than travelers and gourmets. All this changed in late October 1983.

The announcement was made on public television by President Ronald Reagan on 25 October 1983. In short, the president told the American people that the U.S military had invaded the island of Grenada. The operation, backed by a small military contingent from several Caribbean nations, was named URGENT FURY.

Communist forces based out of Cuba had been working on Grenada for some time prior to the October action. Moscow had sent large shipments of military stores, arms and ammunition, to Grenada because an agreement had been reached between the two countries in 1980. Cuban workers were extending the island's airfield, making it suitable as a way station for bombers and cargo planes heading for Nicaragua.

The final incident for the Reagan administration was the execution of the island's prime minister, Maurice Bishop, by the hard-line Marxist Deputy Prime Minister Bernard Coard on October 19. Control of the island was seized by the Revolutionary Military Council, and a 24-hour curfew was imposed. The announcement was made that anyone violating the curfew would be shot on sight. This made things very dangerous for the nearly 1,000 Americans on Grenada, most of them at St. George's Medical College in the island's capital. The invasion forces moved in at dawn, roughly 0530 hours Grenada time on 25 October. But there had already been losses among the incoming forces even before the invasion began.

On what was to be SEAL Team Six's first hot combat operation, a team of eight SEALs would be inserted into the waters off Grenada along with a pair of Boston Whaler fiberglass-hulled boats. Aboard a Navy destroyer well over the

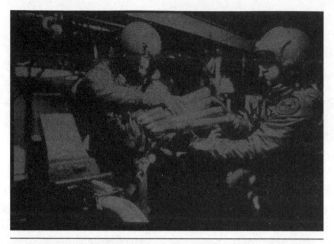

Under the eerie red illumination used to preserve night vision, these AC-130 gunship crewmen handle the four-round clips of high explosive 40mm cannon shells for the M2A1 Bofors cannon. Originally designed for antiaircraft use, the 40mm Bofors is seeing a new life as the medium-sized armament of the AC-130 Gunship.

USSOCOM PAO

horizon from Grenada was a four-man Air Force Combat Controller Team (CCT).

The CCT was trained and equipped to manage forward air traffic control for the combat forces coming in to Grenada. What they would immediately do on the island would be to place radio beacons to guide in the MC-130 Combat Talon aircraft that would be carrying U.S. Army Airborne Rangers who would jump in and seize control of the Point Salines Airfield. It would be the SEALs' mission to take the CCT in to the beach and establish security for the unit.

Delays for the SEALs' jump into the waters near Grenada began almost immediately. Late on the afternoon of 23 October eight SEALs were in two C-130 aircraft along with their Boston Whalers rigged for an air drop. For security considerations, the Air Force crews of the C-130s had not been told that they would be conducting a combat operation. Instead, they thought they would be doing only a slightly unusual administrative water drop.

One plane got lost on its way to the rendezvous point with the Navy destroyer, and both planes were late arriving on site for the drop. Instead of an expected daylight drop, the lateness of their arrival, combined with errors in computing times, put the SEALs over their target in the dark.

In spite of being rigged out for a daylight drop, the SEALs decided to go ahead with their insertion. What they didn't know was that one of the aircraft was several miles off-course. The inexperienced Air Force crew knew how to operate their aircraft, but night water jumps were something new to them. But the SEALs were not going to allow their situation to cause them to fail in their first hot operation. Eight SEALs—four per aircraft—and two boats—one per plane—fell into the night skies of the Caribbean.

What the SEALs had no way of knowing was that a sudden squall, common in that part of the world during that time of year, had blown in below them. Instead of relatively calm seas, the SEALs jumped into six- to eight-foot-high waves. Parachutes tangled with equipment. Boats smashed into the water, and one capsized and was lost.

Four of the SEALs disappeared into the dark ocean. Their bodies were never recovered. The rest of the SEALs struggled with their parachutes and gear in the high waves and 20-knot winds. They somehow managed to get to the one upright Boston Whaler and regrouped with the destroyer.

The first SEAL combat operation since the Vietnam War, and the first hot op for SEAL Team Six, had begun badly. Four SEALs became the first losses to the Teams on a combat operation since 1972. They were Senior Chief Engineman Rudolph Schamberger, Machinist's Mate First Class Kenneth John Butcher, Quartermaster First Class Kevin Lundberg, and Hull Technician First Class Stephen Leroy Morris. In spite of the pain of their losses, the SEALs continued with their operation. Regrouping on the destroyer, they gathered the Air Force CCT and continued with their mission.

On their way into Grenada that same night, the men spotted a Grenadian patrol boat and cut power to minimize their chance of discovery. The single Boston Whaler was overloaded with men and equipment. Water swamped over

Parachutes collapse down into the water after a successful SEAL water jump. The seas are very calm in this daylight practice operation.

the stern of the boat, flooding out the motor. Unable to restart it, the SEALs were running out of darkness as dawn was approaching. Finally, they limped their way back to the destroyer, wet, angry, and ready to try again.

The night of 24 and 25 October, the eve of the planned invasion, the SEALs and their CCT companions tried again to get in to the beach near Point Salines. Their attempt resulted in the timetable for the invasion being changed. It was moved back several hours, but the difficult mission was never completed. On their way in to the beach, the Boston Whaler swamped again. The CCT radio equipment was lost, and the floating Whaler was swept out to sea. The first SEAL mission of Urgent Fury was a failure.

The 22nd Marine Amphibious Unit that had been on its way to Beirut before being ordered to Grenada had a detachment of SEALs as part of its normal mission complement. The SEALs from Team Four went in on a normal reconnaissance operation at 2200 hours local time on 24 October. They conducted a recon of the beaches on the north end of the island in spite of bad conditions of driving rain and poor visibility. Working first from Seafox boats and then going on to rubber boats, the SEALs conducted a hydrographic survey of the beach within hearing of a Grenadian work party on the shore.

The SEALs found the beach area and offshore waters too difficult to bring the Marines in by anything but very shallow-draft vessels. So the Marines began coming in and landing on Grenada by helicopter at 0520 hours, Tuesday, 25 October. They quickly captured Pearls Airport and took control of the nearby town of Grenville.

Two additional operations were to be conducted by SEAL Team Six while the rest of the invasion forces, including the Army Rangers and units from Delta Force, came in to the island. The SEALs would simultaneously take over the transmitting facilities of the Grenadian radio station as well as rescue the island's appointed Governor-General Sir Paul Scoon.

Being an independent nation within the British Commonwealth, the Queen of England is the titular head of State for Grenada and had appointed Sir Paul Scoon the governor-general. Scoon was being held with his staff under virtual house arrest in the governor's mansion, and his rescue had a high priority with the U.S. government. The SEALs of Team Six assigned to the governor's rescue expected to be on the ground quickly and away with Scoon inside an hour or two. Although their mission was successful and without any casualties on the part of the SEALs or the governor-general's party, they were on the ground in Grenada for more than a full day.

Delays cost the SEALs the element of darkness for their insertion. Instead of coming in before dawn, the SEALs were over Grenada in full daylight. That allowed the Grenadian ground forces to more effectively open fire on the in-

SEAL Team operators practice fast roping from the open doorway of a hovering SH-3G Sea King Helicopter. The very quick fast-roping insertion technique works only because of the strong grip of the leather-glove–wearing SEALs.

U.S. Navy

coming helicopters with antiaircraft cannon. The SEALs fast roped in to their target and almost immediately lost another helicopter to ground fire.

Limping away, one of the Blackhawk birds had the commanding officer for SEAL Team Six, Robert Gormly, onboard. The bird also had the long-range radio for the unit that had gone in with the other Blackhawk and were already on the ground. In spite of not being wounded during the insertion attempt, Gormly was never able to get back to the SEALs at the governor's mansion.

The SEALs on the ground, under the leadership of Duke Leonard, were able to rescue Scoon and maintain security for the grounds around the mansion. Several times, Grenadian troops and armored vehicles looked to be about to overrun the trapped SEALs, but their own firepower, and that of an overhead AC-130 gunship on one occasion, drove off the island forces. Eventually, the SEALs were able to link up with Marine forces and return Governor-General Scoon to safety.

In flight over water is the rocket-pod armed A/MH-6 Little Bird of the 160th Army Aviation Regiment.

USSOCOM PAO

The SEAL unit attempting to capture the radio station had a much worse situation on their hands. Intelligence about their target had been in error, and the SEALs captured only a transmitter site, the actual studios were some distance away in St. George. A large number of Grenadian troops and armor showed up before the SEALs were able to extract by helicopter. Using their weapons, the SEALs were able to halt the Grenadian troops and badly damage a BTR-60PB armored personnel carrier in the process. When the Grenadian troops began to assault the site again, the SEALs saw that their firepower could not hold off the troops and abandoned the position. Using their escape and evasion training, the SEALs withdrew safely in spite of two men being wounded. Several of the escaping SEALs commandeered a small sailboat from a local marina and sailed out to sea until they were picked up by a Little Bird helicopter.

In spite of their losses, the SEALs completed the majority of their mission assignments during URGENT FURY. Several SEALs were among the crews of the Seafox boats that helped patrol the island's offshore waters after the invasion was over. The situation had been a major learning experience for both the SEALs and the U.S. military as a whole.

Robert Gormly, Captain, USN (Ret.)

Frankly, we were fighting terrorism in Vietnam. The Viet Cong were capable of doing some horrendous things that make some of the Palestinian groups look pretty tame in comparison. To me, and to a lot of us who've been in the Vietnam conflict, terrorism was just another enemy. At the time it reared its head in the 1970s,

SEALs started getting sort of tasked with "What do you do about this if this happens?"

Our big problem was not so much a lack of capability among the people; there was enough foresight to understand what had to be done against terrorism. The problem at the time (mid- to late 1970s) was that we didn't have enough money to buy equipment to do certain things.

Community-wide, I don't think we viewed the terrorists much differently than any other enemy we had to go up against. Operations were pretty much the same, and they really weren't that unique to begin with.

At the time the UDTs were decommissioned in the early 1980s, I happened to be the Chief of Staff at Special Warfare Group One in Coronado. Rear Admiral, then Captain, Irish Flynn was the Commodore of the Group, and I worked for him. We were sitting around one day batting around the notion of maybe some better ways of doing things. We took a look at what was going on operationally with the UDTs and the fact that we had an awful lot of people tied up doing a very small mission.

So we thought about what would happen if we decided to make them all SEALs. This wasn't a new idea; we'd also run this around back in the early 1970s right after Vietnam. It didn't get very far then, but we figured this would economize more the people and their use if we all became SEALs and then made the UDT mission part of the SEAL mission.

Eventually, that's what happened in 1983, and all the UDTs were decommissioned and SEAL Teams and Swimmer Delivery Vehicle Teams were formed. From what I can determine, we never missed a beat in fulfilling any of the requirements we had. It was a good idea.

The creation of SEAL Team Six was something I thought was a good idea as well because we needed to have a well-equipped, well-funded SEAL entity to be able to do SEAL-like things. And that's what that command could do.

One thing I never expected was to receive the position of commanding officer of SEAL Team Six. That came as a big surprise to me. I'd escaped pulling duty in Washington, D.C., for about eighteen years and I figured I was due, so I was fully prepared to go to Washington after my tour as a Chief of Staff at SpecWarGru One. Instead, I ended up the CO of Team Six.

It was under my watch as the CO that Six saw its first combat operation at the island of Grenada in October 1983. Even given what I know now about what went on during that operation, I don't think there's much that could have been changed. I know you can't go back and rewrite what happened.

I inherited a command that we all—the members of the command as well as myself—learned wasn't ready to go into combat. We were lacking some training, and we certainly lacked equipment. The boats at the time were horrendous; they were in terrible shape. When I relieved Richard Marcinko, we all knew this, but there was nothing we could do about it. You can't just go out and get boats at the drop of a hat.

So we had equipment problems that I couldn't have changed, and wouldn't have had time to change anyway. Frankly, I don't know of anything that I could have changed that would have mattered.

I had no idea of where Grenada was until I was called out of my breakfast one Saturday morning to go learn something about it and to do something about it. To make a long story short, in 1983, Grenada was a British Crown Protectorate with a governor-general appointed by the Queen and a Parliament elected by the people.

During the spring and summer of 1983, the Parliament had been taken over by hook or crook—I'm not sure which, and frankly I don't think it matters—by the Communist element. The Parliament had their own internal problems, not to mention the Communists. One of their men was killed in a coup and another group of Communists took over. While all this happening, Cubans made their way onto the island at the behest of the Parliament.

One of the things the Cubans were doing was improving an airfield on the southern end of the island. It had been a civilian airfield capable of handling small aircraft, but the Cubans were enlarging the runway and making it capable of handling bombers and fighters. Politically and strategically, that wasn't acceptable to our government, nor should it have been.

The other factor in the mix at the time was a medical school where quite a few American citizens were as students. So when the chaos developed on Grenada in early October, President Reagan was faced with a large Cuban presence on the island plus the threat to the American citizens on the island. He decided that he needed to send some forces down there to deal with that.

The joint organization, of which I was a member as the CO of SEAL Team Six, was one of the units tasked to do something about it. I first learned about the situation on 22 October 1983. Our initial mission was to put some members of an Air Force team on the beach to determine whether the airfield the Cubans had been working on was sufficient to land C-130 and C-141 aircraft on. At the time, we had no satellite coverage of the island and overhead photography apparently wasn't doing enough good. That was the task for the group that ended up losing four people.

The first part of the mission was to go to Port Salinas and check it out to see if it was capable of handling our aircraft. So we put about three guys on a plane, flew them down, and got them on a Navy ship that was at an island nearby. The plan was for the ship to drive them around, and the SEALs would then get in a rubber boat and take the Air Force guys in there to get a look at the airport.

Once the SEALs got to Grenada, my boss decided that he wanted to look at another airfield at the other end of the island. We needed more people down there to do that, and we had to conduct the missions simultaneously.

This was a pretty fast-moving train, and we had a very short time frame to operate in. It was Saturday, and they wanted to do the operation starting out at 0200 on Tuesday, 25 October. The only way to get people down there quickly enough was to fly them down and jump them in with boats.

We picked a spot well away from the island and planned to do a daylight drop, what I would call an administrative-type drop. And it would be far away from anyone who could have seen us. That was the plan as we sent them out.

They were supposed to have jumped at 1600 hours local time. The whole thing was planned on local time, not the normal military ZULU (Greenwich mean) time. But because the east coast of the United States and Grenada were both in the same time zone then, it was done that way.

At 1600, I walked into Command Center at the joint headquarters and asked how the drop went. The Air Force planned said, "Well, it didn't go. We had some problems and had to route them a different way . . . dah . . . dah . . . dah. But don't sweat it, they're time on target is 1800, and it's still daylight."

Well, it wasn't daylight. Daylight saving time had come into effect, and 1800 hours our time was 1900 hours down there. And there was no moon so it was dark. The jumpers came in on two C-130s. We had the people on the ship who had been put down there earlier and had communications with the aircraft. The aircraft came in, and in the aftermath we learned that instead of dropping in trail as they were supposed to have done, the first aircraft broke in right on the ship and the people went out of the plane. The second aircraft, for some reason, went two more miles past the ship and then turned and dropped.

To complicate matters further, anyone who has ever been in the Caribbean will understand that sudden squalls pop up down there. It can be bright and sunny and five minutes later it can be raining with thirty miles an hour blowing winds.

That's apparently what happened. A squall overcame the drop zone just before the jumpers went out. Nobody on the ship noticed it, and the jumpers went out at night, rigged for a daylight drop, in the squall. The best we can determine, four men from Team Six couldn't get out of their parachutes and probably ended up drowning. We never recovered a body or the equipment, so we don't know for sure what happened to them.

Being the commander of a Team that suffered the first combat losses since Vietnam affected me deeply. Murphy's Law certainly took over that operation—anything that could go wrong did.

I use the saying "It wasn't pretty, but we got the job done" in referring to the operations at Grenada. We did two other operations later. I will call one of them completely successful, and the other one was successful, but at the wrong place. So it wasn't pretty, but the missions were completed.

The State Department and everyone else were telling us that Grenada would be a cakewalk. Grenada had no military, but everyone underestimated the role of the

Cubans there. In fact, I had a State Department gent look me in the eye and tell me that the Cubans would be in the barracks during this mission. Had I not been so sleep-deprived at the time, I probably would have said, "How do you know?"

In the aftermath of the operation I figured this out: Every place there were Cubans down there, there was pretty heavy fighting. They motivated the Grenadians into putting up a defense. We found out later that the Cubans, nearly to a man, were combat veterans from their fighting in Angola. They had brought in antiaircraft weapons and shot down a bunch of helos. In fact, one of the ones I was on was almost knocked out.

But the enemy, as it were, were a lot stiffer than anyone gave him credit for being. But where there weren't any Cubans around, like at the governor-general's house, there were only Grenadians who gave up their weapons as soon as they saw our guys. For the Grenada operation, the Cubans were the stiff resistance factor.

For the next combat operation of SEAL Team Six, we were to engage the enemy that we were originally intended for—terrorists. When the cruise ship Achille Lauro was seized by Palestinian Liberation Front terrorists, a detachment from SEAL Team Six was sent in to take back the ship. Would the plan have worked? I don't know, because it never happened.

I never heard of any aspect of the operation going down where the credit for the capture would have been given to the Italians or any other unit. That was not in my mind. In those days, supposedly everything Six did was unknown.

From my level in the command structure on down, as I remember, to give credit for the operation to another unit for political reasons was not the notion. We were just going to go and do our job. We had a good plan for taking back the ship, but unfortunately, we didn't get the opportunity to carry it out.

When I was at Six, I never felt that I was not able to go out with the men if the situation called for it. I wasn't that old, and frankly, my notion and philosophy of command was that I was going to be at the scene of the hottest action. And that's what I pretty much tried to do. Even though my job as the commanding officer is to direct the whole of an operation, my philosophy was to do that directing from the front line. I didn't believe in sitting in the back and letting others do it. So for every one of our planned missions, that's where I was going to be—and was in some cases.

If you ever lose that sort of a mentality in the SEAL business, if you ever think that you're a rear-echelon so-and-so, then you need to get out of that business. Every SEAL officer, from an admiral on down, ought to be thinking that he should be at the front. SEALs lead from the front, we don't lead from the rear.

What I would tell someone about the history and future of the Teams is that first of all, know the history of the Teams. Hopefully, this book will help a lot in that *direction. Since the time I first became involved with the SEALs, the SEALs and UDTs have been excellent at never writing anything down on paper. I tell people we're like an Indian tribe: information gets passed down to the younger troops from legends being told around the fires.*

That's okay, but when all your old chiefs go out, their experience goes with them. This is particularly true in the present-day SEAL Teams. I doubt there's anybody with any combat experience in Vietnam still on active duty, and I'd be very surprised if there were any more than one or two here and there.

I think I would first tell the young men of today that they need to understand their history and where they came from—the UDTs of World War II, then Vietnam, as that was the first proving ground for the SEALs, then the many other situations since then—the latest being the Persian Gulf and maybe Bosnia, but I'm not certain about what went on or is going on in Bosnia.

I would tell the troops that they need to have a sense of history, that they should understand that they're part of something that is very proud of its existence, which hasn't always been easy to maintain. They need to consider themselves professionals and not some Rambos running around with knives in their teeth. They have a job to do, and they should be committed to their Teammates, the Command, the military, their country, and all of that which, believe it or not, used to factor into a lot of our minds.

A lot of people would say that it was just flag-waving and BS, but it wasn't. A lot of us back in the old days actually thought that we were part of something bigger. We knew we were. I think the young men today need to understand that.

I'm speaking before a BUD/S graduation class on Friday, and I'm going to tell them just what I said here. They need to know where they came from and what's expected of them once they get to the Teams. And I'll tell them to never compromise their professionalism and to always maintain their honor, integrity, and just be good citizens.

I never thought SEALs were anything unique. To me a SEAL was just a guy, myself included, who just had some unique training and did a specific type of mission. That's how it is for naval aviators who fly on and off aircraft carriers, too. That scares the hell out of me and is something that I definitely wouldn't want to do.

My advice to a guy in the Teams, or someone just coming in to them, is this: You're going to be a professional and part of a professional organization, and you're going to have a lot of fun in the process.

I wouldn't use the term "bad ass" to describe the SEALs, although a Hollywood type might because SEALs are tough. We go through tough training and have a tough mission, and individually we're mentally tough, which is probably our biggest attribute. Physically, we're a lot like anybody else walking on the street. Whatever your definition of "bad ass" is, I don't know. If the connotation of that is negative, then I would definitely say it doesn't describe the SEALs. When I watch movies like Rambo, yeah, I laugh. It's funny, some of it really is.

The SEAL Teams are a team; it's the only full-time military organization that has that designation of being a team. And that's just what it is—a bunch of guys pulling together to do the job. It's inculcated into everyone who comes through our basic training course. They never lose that mentality when they leave. They aren't just individuals, they are part of a larger group that has to function like a team to get the job done.

First, JFK said "Let there be unconventional warfare forces in all the military services." The Navy leadership looked at that and said, "Well, we kind of have the UDTs who did some of these sorts of things in Korea. We'll form something out of the UDTs." And that's what happened—the SEALs formed directly out of the UDTs.

The Marines have a saying: "Once a Marine, always a Marine." I think that's even more true for the SEALs. Once you're in a Team, that's your life, and you'll do what you have to do to keep it going. The notion after Vietnam was sort of "put them back in their cages until the next war." Of course, our guys weren't going to put up with that, and we did what we had to do to keep the Commands going. I've bought my own equipment when I had to, and a lot of other guys did as well when the money wasn't there. That's just the way it was.

Frankly, there were two reasons for this. First of all, we knew that what we could offer the country and the military was something no one else could. No other unit could do the job we did. Second, I think our guys had too much pride to just throw up their hands and quit, that's about the bottom line.

If the SEALs were suddenly ordered to become a professional football team, we would probably win the NFL championship. I'm serious. I used to take a lot of ribbing from some of the regular Naval officers, the blue water types, about how the SEALs could only do one thing and could never go out and run a ship. I would tell them to give me a ship and give me my men from SEAL Team Two, and in a month, we would have the best ship in the Fleet. I fully believe that the guys can do anything. So if we had to be a professional football team, we would figure out a way to do it and win.

In my own book, Combat Swimmer: Memoirs of a Navy SEAL, I talk about a "lock and load" mentality. Lock and load is a term everybody uses to mean be ready, but in a SEAL Team, it's a reality.

Wellington T. "Duke" Leonard, Lieutenant Commander, USN (Ret.)

I joined the Navy in 1966. After spending a year in the Fleet, I had the opportunity to go through BUD/S training in 1967. I had a step-uncle who had been in UDT Eleven from 1959 to 1961, so when I joined the Navy, thanks to my step-uncle, I

In the surf zone at the edge of the Pacific, BUD/S students continue the most common activity they will be doing during training—push-ups.

knew about the UDTs and wanted to be a part of them. The SEALs were still very classified back then, and I personally know nothing about them. The SEALs were classified even as we went through training.

My BUD/S class was 6702, Class 40 in the sequential numbering system. That was an East Coast class—a summer one, thank God—conducted at Little Creek, Virginia. I didn't have any problem getting through training, none at all. Fortunately, thank God, I stayed healthy through the course and just kept moving. Quitting wasn't a thought that ever crossed my mind.

Hell Week was just a lot of harassment and no sleep. We were cold and wet, but moving forward was all I had to keep doing. All the memories of training are kind of clumped together now. Probably the strongest memory I have is that there were only two real written tests when we went through training. There was a demolition test and a cartography test. That was about it, other than doing a lot of push-ups.

To me, it's simple. To get through training, you have to have the will to keep going. If you don't have it, you won't make it. You can be the biggest, strongest, fastest guy in the world, but if you don't have the will to complete the training, you're not going to get there.

Class 40 might have been the largest class that ever went through training. I want to say that there were 355 guys who started training, and we graduated 54. The line of helmets from the quitters went around the block. Once we got everyone thinned out, normally that was after Hell Week, we got on with the real training. That class had more retirees in it, more men who spent their career in the Navy and the Teams, than any other class that had gone before it.

When we checked in to Underwater Demolition Team Twenty-One, we started to get the word on the SEAL Team. That sounded like just what I wanted to do, so I started putting in a transfer chit once a week to get over there.

Finally, I made it over to SEAL Team Two on 11 May 1968. It was my birthday, so I remember the date exactly. My first deployment to Vietnam was with Seventh Platoon in January 1969. My first impression of Vietnam was that it was great. It was everything I hoped it could be. It was warm, the people were great, and there was all the operating you could possibly do. That's why I had gone through all the training—to be out in the field operating.

Mind you, I was just a seaman when I started my evolution into combat. Fortunately, when I came back, I had been promoted to E-5. To help break in the next SEAL platoon that had come in to relieve us, I volunteered to stay in Vietnam an extra three months when the rest of my platoon went back home. My time in Vietnam was basically spent conducting operations and taking liberty.

On my first tour, there were so many operations that picking out just a few is hard. There was Bob Thomas's op—he went down in a helo and ended up winning a Navy Cross for holding off the VC with nothing more than a couple of pistols.

My first combat mission in Vietnam was supposed to be just a "break-in" op, where the new platoon was broken in to the area of operations. We went out and I was walking point. Talk about being wired, I thought there were bad guys behind every tree and bush. Al Ashton and Paul Schwartz caught three guys walking up behind us. When they took them out the noise compromised us, so the VC now knew we were there. We extracted.

As we extracted, we started taking mortar rounds from the VC around us. The platoon officer at that time was Ron Yeaw, and he did an outstanding job zig-zagging us out of there.

The first six operations I ever went out on, we got hits—we made contact with the enemy. I think it was the third operation that I got blown out of a door by a grenade. After all this, I thought this was what was going to happen every time we went out into the field.

Unfortunately, Admiral Zumwalt thought Seventh Platoon was doing so well that we should go to the Cambodian Border for interdiction operations there. We didn't get a hit for two months—nothing, no contact. Here we were, netted a lot of action after our first six operations, then all of a sudden, dry for two months. That just destroys you.

We were a platoon operating on the border between South Vietnam and Cambodia, trying to interdict North Vietnamese coming across. And we did stop some. One time, a squad of us, Al Ashton, Dick Moran, myself, and others, were out on an op. We were sitting on the border and had intelligence that 120 North Vietnamese were going to cross. Yeah, right, we thought.

The group of us were sitting on the north side of a canal, surrounded by open terrain, nothing but low grass. Looking across to the south about thirty yards away, we could see three guys crawling on their hands and knees. We were looking through a starlight scope so we could see them clearly, but they couldn't see us. Then, about thirty yards behind the three guys, came this mass of NVA troops moving along.

Sitting there, we contemplated opening up on them. There were only seven of us. We would just hose them down and then run. And the only place we could run to was into Cambodia. So we backed off from that idea and just watched them cross by. Then we gave a sitrep (situation report) when we got back. The Intel had been good, and the report was all we could do.

It was on my second tour, with Jim Watson and Sixth Platoon beginning in April 1970. Jim and I had some great operations. One op I love telling about had Watson and I going out after an individual who had opened up the gates of Hy Yen in 1962 or 1963. With the gates open, the Viet Cong came in and killed every man, woman, and child in the place.

In 1970, I, Watson, Chuck Fellers, John Porter, Bud Thrift, and others were advisers for a Chinese company, for lack of a better description. We located our target, and Watson and I went out on the op along with five of the Chinese guys to snap this guy up.

It was a perfect op. We snatched the guy up without a shot being fired. Watson got more Intel that there were more bad guys off in another direction, and he told me that he was going to take three of the Chinese with him to check out the situation and that I was to stay where I was with the other two Chinese and the prisoner. Then he put a set of S&W handcuffs on the guy and handed me the keys, with the instructions to see to it that nothing happened to our prisoner, because he was going to be a valuable source of Intel for more ops.

So I was just sitting out there, and Watson had been gone about thirty minutes when the Chinese came up to me and told me that they wanted to talk to our prisoner. They wanted to see if there were any more of his buddies around.

My thoughts were that this guy had left the gates open to a civilian village that was wiped out by his VC buddies. Besides, I had the key and I knew they weren't going to do anything with the handcuffs on the guy. So I said they could go and talk to him.

About two minutes went by and I suddenly heard the bam . . . bam of a pair of gunshots. Oh, my God, I thought, just what's going on? Then one of the Chinese came back and handed me the handcuffs.

Not very long after that, Watson came up and asked what was going on. I said that he wasn't going to believe it anyway, so I handed him back the handcuffs. I still hear about that every once in a while.

While I was in Vietnam, I was a Stoner man. In the squad, I carried the Stoner light machine gun. We had the best and the brightest weapons and equipment at that time; the SEALs were on the forefront of all the new equipment. The Stoner was an outstanding piece of weaponry. It could put out fire at a rate of more than 1,000 rounds a minute and was loaded with a 150 round drum. Normally I would carry eight bandoleers on an operation, with 100 rounds of linked ammunition for the Stoner in each bandoleer, depending on the op. There were a few times during that tour that we would come back with less than fifty rounds in the Stoner. Things got a little tenuous on some operations, I will say that.

But, digressing to training for a second, you had to have the will to get through training. When you go out on these ops, you have to have the will to complete the operation. That's the beauty of training—it separates those who have the will from those who do not have it.

In spite of the difficulty sometimes, I was always comfortable on an op. In fact, I felt more secure out in the field, and I'm sure a lot of guys will say the same thing. We would go out and lay down in an ambush and just wait. But we felt so comfortable out there, in spite of the situation, because nothing could really get to us. We were on their territory, on bad ground, with bad guys all around, and they've got to find you. That's pretty hard.

After we pulled out of Vietnam, things changed. We came back and it was basically "lock them up, throw the key away, and we'll call you when we need you again." That was a rough period. There was a big cut in RDT&E (research, development, training and equipment) money and pay. There were a lot of exercises that we went on all over the world, but everything seemed kind of superfluous after going to Vietnam.

I left the active Navy in 1972, but stayed in the Navy Reserves. I had decided that I was going to get my college degree, become an officer, and go to OCS. My feelings were that I could accomplish more going this route than by slamming away at the promotion exams. My enlisted rate was mineman, which was really a closed rate with promotions being few and far between. After they got through with Vietnam, the Navy really shot it down.

So I spent three and a half years in the Navy Reserves and then came back in, receiving my commission in 1976. As an officer returning to the Teams, I didn't have to go through any refresher training and was able to report back without any problems.

A new enemy had developed during the 1970s, and the SEALs had to address a new kind of conflict. During the Vietnam conflict, basically, the enemy left the cities and went to the countryside where they started beating up on the farmers. That's where the VC got their resources. In the early 1970s, the enemy left the countryside and went back to the cities. There, they began pulling off their operations in the cities, hence the word urban in Urban Warfare. So that's where we had to adapt. We were good at chasing them around out there in the countryside; that was guerrilla warfare. But once they started going back into the cities, blowing up airplanes, hijacking, kidnapping, and assassinating, we had to change our warfighting skills to adapt to the city.

And it wasn't hard for us. The same principles that applied in the guerrilla theater of war also applied in urban warfare. We just had to change various tactics to operate in buildings, planes, and other vessels.

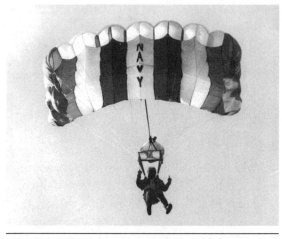

Sailing into a soft landing under the fully inflated canopy of a high performance parachute is this SEAL member of the U.S. Navy Parachute Team. His free-falling skills were gained through hard practice for a much more serious use of a parachute, the clandestine airborne insertion of SEALs to a target area.

U.S. Navy

In the late 1970s, I was the operations officer at UDT Twenty-one. Lou Boink was the CO, and Tom Richards was the XO. MOB Six, the mobilization platoon tasked with the counterterrorism mission for the Teams on the East Coast, was doing its thing over at SEAL Team Two. There was going to be either an expansion of MOB-Six or there was going to be another SEAL Team created. When the decision was made to create a new SEAL Team, each East and West Coast Team was to pony up so many men to fill the ranks.

Lou Boink was a supporter of what Captain Marcinko was trying to do in developing SEAL Team Six. So he ponied up his best and brightest guys who wanted to go to the interviews. I really didn't interview or anything, they just snapped me up for the new Team. I was glad they did. I figured I was a lot older than a lot of the other guys in the new Team, plus I was a lieutenant, j. g. (junior grade) at the time.

The new assignment was something I was really excited about, simply because we were going to be on the pointy end of the spear again. I wanted to get back into combat; that's the reason I volunteered. The training they were doing was all new. It was some wild stuff and state-of-the-art operations. The Teams to this day are better for what we did because we passed on all the information we developed on the new ways of operating.

At SEAL Team Six, we really developed our insertion and extraction skills. We learned new skills, like room entry. Actually, we developed these skills, because nobody before us and including us really knew how to do it. So we just jumped in with both feet and learned it from scratch.

We learned some intensive parachuting skills. By intensive, I mean jumping out of a plane and HAHOing, which is high-altitude, high-opening, a hop-and-pop, at 32,000 feet. We would be running on oxygen and traveling thirty, thirty-five miles across the ground on a jump. It's cold up there, sixty-five degrees below zero.

So we pushed the envelope on everything. In diving, we pushed working with the Draeger to where we were doing four-and five-hour dives, because nobody really understood just how far we could go with these things. And we had the flexibility to go out there and push it.

There was a cost to this high-speed work. Yes, we had some training accidents. That's going to happen, and it's not going to stop happening. Rodney Cheuy was killed early on in a shooting accident, we lost Gary Hershey on a parachute accident, and there were follow-on accidents. The deaths had no effect on the commitment of the men in the Teams. If anything, it made them work even harder.

Our training schedule was pretty incredible. For four years, I spent roughly 300 days a year training. I'd be home 60 days a year to see my family, and I never knew just when I was going to be home. It was usually just an in-and-out situation.

It was very intense and on-step. I can remember going up to A.P. Hill in Virginia to do fire-and-maneuver problems with Blue Team. It was Hell Week all over again. In seven days, we got roughly twelve hours of sleep. We were doing around-the-clock ops.

Our first combat operation with SEAL Team Six came in October 1983 with the invasion of Grenada. I was the team leader for Governor-General Scoon's house. It was great leading all the young guys into combat for the first time, and that was due, in part, to our training.

They always told me that at twenty-five yards you had to be able to shoot two rounds into the black. I said that there were going to be a few things that are going to interface with your theory. One's going to be adrenaline, and two's going to be some bumps and scrapes. You've got to expend a lot of energy before you can fire that first round.

So we were tasked with securing Governor-General Scoon's mansion while he was under house arrest. We fast roped in from a hovering Blackhawk helicopter. I went down and went right through a tree. Fifteen guys right behind me all went through the branches of this big oak tree as well. That tree beat us up bad, and everyone had scrapes and bruises. Then we hit this retaining wall in Scoon's front yard and rolled down the hill to Luke Street.

The bad guys were all on the outside of the fence surrounding the governor-general's place, so we had to have it out down there, run back up to the retaining wall, and wait for Bob Gormly, our CO, to come in.

We were taking rounds from all over the place when I saw some movement at the mansion. I told Dennis Chalker to cover me and we crossed the driveway. Introducing myself to the man who was just coming out of a doorway, I find out that the man was Governor-General Scoon.

The governor-general handed me an AK-47 he had and we shook this other man down who was with Scoon. The other man had a pistol on him, so I took it and passed him up to Johnny Johnson. Scoon looked into the cellar door behind him, motioned, and out came eleven more people—his wife and ten of his staff. That situation had deviated from the intelligence we had received on the situation.

My guys were really pumped up with excitement. Coming in on the helicopters, we had been taking a lot of 23mm flak. Rich Hanson had been hit and he didn't even know it yet. Then we had been hanged up by the tree on the insertion. The young guys' eyes were like saucers.

This was a handful, so into the house we went. I asked Scoon if the house was clear. He said that he thought so, that all the guards had run away when they saw us come in. Because we were taking rounds out in the yard, everyone was much safer in the house. So after getting everyone in the house, we started clearing it room by room. I was walking with Scoon, and I suddenly yelled out, "Everybody freeze!"

Everybody froze in place. "What do you see, Duke? What do you see?"

Their hearts had to be racing right about then. The adrenaline of combat pushes nerves to the limit. They were all excited and ready to pop.

"Now tell me about that twenty-five-yard head shot," I said. "Now go ahead and keep clearing."

Basically, we had no intelligence going into the operation on Grenada. What I

Under normal lighting, this crewmember of an AC-130 gunship loads a high-explosive shell into the breech of a modified M102 105mm howitzer. The cannon is the largest piece in the arsenal of the AC-series of gunships and is the biggest gun normally carried by any aircraft in the world.

USSOCOM PAO

was told was that on the island there were four BTR-60s, an armored vehicle armed with a 14.5mm machine gun, and only the Grenadian troops that had been trained by the Cubans to oppose us.

When I got there, we had four BTR-60s at the front gate, two on one side of the driveway and two on the other. I thought, My God, I've got all four of them right here. Then I watched all of these trucks going up and down Luke Street. These guys might be a little more organized than we thought. Then we took an RPG rocket off the roof of the mansion, then a round came through a window.

Our Intel had been atrocious. Nobody knew really what we were going to be facing.

We had fast roped about ninety feet down to the ground from the helicopter. Each SEAL probably weighed 100 pounds more than normal with all his equipment on. We hit that retaining wall, then the tree. We were banged up pretty good coming in. In all of that crashing about, our only antitank weapon, an M72 LAW, was bent. At one point, I think Johnny Johnson told Dennis Chalker to get ready to fire the LAW. It was bent enough that I think Chalker was very glad he never had to fire it.

When we first got to the mansion, we didn't have any communications. We ended up setting up a link with Gormly's troops down at Port Salinas through our MX-360 handheld radios.

I talked to them, and they told me that they had something to take care of the armored vehicles we were facing. They had an AC-130 gunship on the horn. I thought that was great. The miniguns, vulcan cannon, 40mm cannon, and 105 howitzer of an AC-130 gunship could easily deal with everything we were facing.

The BTR-60s were coming in toward the house, and behind them were about ten or fifteen troops. The troops would then try to circle around to the backyard. They made something like four runs, and it wasn't very long until we were totally surrounded. They were conducting reconnaissance by fire and just trying to get us to crank off a round so they could figure out where we were. Everyone in my team held their fire. They did very well.

Then I got the AC-130 up online. But it wasn't a direct line. I had a three-step communications drill with the gunship. First, I had to talk to Master Chief Dennis Johnson on the hill. Then he had to relay my directions to the support personnel who had a PRC-77 radio. That radioman radioed up to the gunship, and they would start firing. Then I would tell them when to stop.

With our communications drill, I walked in the rounds to about twenty-five yards of the house. Then I had them do a 360-degree firing run around the house, then go over and hit Bishop's house some 200 meters away.

Even though we got things to work after a fashion, commo did not work well during the op. When we had first arrived at Scoon's place, we hadn't heard from anybody. We were totally surrounded, and we had four BTR-60s in front of us. The op *had called for us to be at the mansion for only forty-five minutes. And I hadn't seen hide nor hair of Bob Gormly. Later we learned that he had been shot out of the sky.*

Things were looking a little grim.

I got on the phone at the governor-general's mansion and called down to the airfield. I didn't want to give away anything over the phone, OPSEC (operational security) and all. When a young Army Ranger, a private, answered the phone, I spoke rather cryptically.

"Look, Private," I said, "do me a favor. Have you seen any of those long-haired guys running around down there? You know, the ones that are always wet?"

"Yeah, I did," he said. Then he did exactly what I didn't want him to do—he set down the phone and ran away.

A minute-and-a-half later—I was sweating bullets the whole time—Wally Stevens was on the phone. I started chewing him out, asking just what was going on.

"It's not pretty down here at this end," he said.

"Well, you ought to see it at this end!" I said rather sharply.

But everything worked out and we did establish communications. That was a tough situation, especially for the troops. I was very fortunate, because I had some Vietnam vets with me—Johnny Johnson, Bobby Lewis, and Timmy Prusak. I put them out on the perimeter around the house, trying to balance the situation.

When I was setting the guard around the house, I had Bob Lewis and Rich Hanson with me. As I was walking out, two guys popped over the fence and cranked off a round. This thing lands about six inches from my face, peppering me with a bit of shrapnel. All I said was "Get them."

Lewis, without any hesitation, opened up on those guys—picked them up and laid them right out on the picket fence down there. Those are the kind of reactions you want in a combat situation.

It hadn't quite been like that on the helicopter coming in. That helo ride was absolutely fantastic for me. We flew treetop level all the way into the target zone, then popped up as we approached the mansion.

The birds were crowded. I had to squat for the whole sixty-one-minute flight. Nobody could move. We had fifteen guys in the bird—all combat troops—and everybody was jammed in place. Myself and the older guys, Bobby Lewis, Timmy Prusak, and Johnny Johnson, we were just bored and only wanted to get off that flight. Everybody else was mostly just staring eyeballs.

Then we started taking flak from the ground. It was a lot of fire. Gormly's bird ended up taking more than we did. Ours was the lead bird in and the ground gunners must have gotten a better silhouette of the bird behind us. I think Gormly's bird ended up taking forty-six rounds—heavy hits.

But we did the mission, successfully pulling out Governor-General Scoon and his people without any losses after something like twenty-six hours on the ground.

The men I had to work with in Team Six were absolutely outstanding. That gets right back to that level of will needed to be in the Teams.

All the guys at Six had volunteered to be where they were, knowing they were going to be on the pointy end of the spear. The training we went through was incredibly intense. Then we had a shot at taking our training to war. That was the highlight. Those guys performed admirably, and you can expect that.

For the SEALs, the mission always comes first. But then there's always your Teammates. No one is ever left behind. Mike Thornton demonstrated that better than anyone. Mike's a good man, and what he did with Tommy Norris is just incredible. I'm glad to say that Mike's a good friend of mine; Tommy is a good friend of mine as well.

Here was Tommy in Vietnam, shot and left for dead. Mike, with complete disregard for his own personal safety, ran back to Tommy and got him. He killed three of the enemy on the spot, then he picked Tommy and ran him off the beach along with several LDNNs. They jumped into the water while gunfire from a cruiser ripped up the beach behind them. Then Mike just swam straight out to sea.

Tommy Norris was only semiconcious, bleeding from the head, and had lost his eye from the injury. But Mike saved him—a superhuman act. Mike received the Medal of Honor for his actions that day. But that kind of action, although maybe not to that degree, was pretty common among the SEALs. Mike was recognized for it, and I'm glad he was.

Bob Thomas did something very similar. Only he was in a helo that crashed in Hy Tien, near the Cambodian border. He ended up saving at least the co-pilot of the bird, also an incredible thing. Here was Bob, all banged up from the crash. And all he could find was a .45 pistol. He ended up shooting one Viet Cong at something like one-hundred yards with that .45. He received the Navy Cross for that action, and we in the Teams are all very proud of him.

There were times we saved people and times we lost them. During the first SEAL action at Grenada, the insertion was plagued with bad timing. The guys were looking to do a daylight, administrative drop from an aircraft, a "rubber duck" insertion where men jumped along with a boat. Things didn't go as planned, and somehow, something got delayed. The guys ended up jumping at 1830 hours. It was dark and they were not rigged for a night jump. The seas had picked up from around two feet to four feet to six feet, and the winds had risen from around eight knots to around twenty-two or twenty-four knots.

The SEALs mentality is, Hey, we've got to get down. We have a job to do. So they jumped. I would have done the same thing. Four men, close Teammates of mine, drowned on that insertion.

The operation at Grenada happened so fast that there wasn't any time for any real hard rehearsals or anything like that. It was more of a "let's do it" situation. I would say that the thing that hurt us most was the lack of intelligence of what was on the ground.

The development of the Special Operations Command, SOCOM, has solved many of the problems we faced back then. The Grenada problem, as far as the lack of intelligence, has been cleaned up three-fold. Panama, with the exception of Noriega taking off, went pretty well, too.

We were tasked with getting Noriega in Panama. He had run up to Colon to give a speech and just disappeared. Once he disappeared out of Colon at 4 o'clock in the afternoon, the U.S. forces basically began knocking on doors in Panama, trying to find the guy. We ended up chasing him into a Catholic church.

The bottom line was that we couldn't get Noriega because we just didn't know where he was.

He had flown up to Colon to give this speech, then got in a car and drove back to Panama City. Intel didn't know he had done this, so he just disappeared from our view.

A SEAL is your basic, normal guy. You can't tell one by looking at him; they look the same as everyone else—some are thin, some are big. The differences center on the will. These guys have the mental will to get through the training, get through the operation, and ensure mission success. That's the difference.

Quite honestly, the SEALs are so busy doing various training scenarios and exercises that they just don't have the time to go out and act like the Hollywood image of a SEAL. Basically, they don't want the visibility, the Command doesn't need it, and the personnel don't need it. They just do their job and play like everyone else.

The uniqueness of a SEAL Team centers on the camaraderie between all of its members. These guys spend more time with each other than they do with their families. I was deployed 300 days a year, so I spent a lot more time with my Teammates than I did with my own family—and I did this for ten years.

This makes all the members of the Team very close to each other. They're so close that they really don't have to verbally communicate—they can almost do it through osmosis. As a group, they tick like a Swiss watch. And that's what you want.

You put a challenge before them and everybody knows what everybody else is thinking. They should, they've practiced with each other a hundred times for every problem. Then, after the work's done, you'd think everybody would go home. No, they all go out and have a couple beers. Then they go home.

There is a tradition of going out and having a few beers for a Teammate who's been lost. I've had more than a few beers in that particular tradition, and that's unfortunate. Basically, you get a keg. Normally the family of the lost Teammate will provide that keg. After a number of SEALs were lost at Paitilla Airfield, Ross Perot came in, brought a beer truck, and parked it in the compound. We all went from the memorial service right to the beer truck. When I punch out, I hope that's what happens for me.

These guys in the Teams are self-motivating. President Kennedy formally started the SEAL Teams back in 1962. There were the underwater demolition teams back then, which were the same guys just with different names. They took the ball Kennedy handed them and ran with it. There were some creative officers, such as Bill Hamilton and Roy Boehm, who started the ball rolling and brought the idea of the Teams to fruition.

The reason why you have to expend the energy to keep training is because you know you're going to have to go back to war again. It might not be in two months, or it might not be in ten years, but it's going to happen. A conflict is going to rise up. And if it happens on your watch, you want to ensure that you're ready.

So you get very creative. You try to put up some of the slickest training exercises that you can think of. And all that time, you're still searching for the right equipment. You always want to have that edge that technology can give you.

The SEALs are a small unit. We have flexibility. We have our oversight, our commanding officers, and our staff. That's where the ability to apply our skills and our latitude to go out and try different things lies.

Back in my early days, we didn't put on the Trident because we didn't have it yet. The only unusual insignia we wore on our uniform was Navy Parachute Wings. Earning them wasn't a big deal—you had to complete ten jumps. Just going through Army Airborne training gave you five jumps right there.

Where I was, it wasn't a real big tradition. If you had ten jumps or you had fifty jumps, you just kept jumping. You had sky guys and other guys who really didn't like jumping, but they still had to do it. It was part of the job.

There wasn't any big moment when I knew I was a SEAL. I didn't do anything more than walk onto the quarterdeck at SEAL Team Two on 11 May 1968. Master Chief Rudy Boesch was right there on me, telling me to go get a haircut and then get ready to take over the quarterdeck. That was my first day.

Of course, when you went across the street to SEAL Team Two, the guys at UDT Twenty-One said that you were leaving them, that you were abandoning ship. And they beat the holy crap out of you. You end up looking like the ragman in off the street. Then you go across to the SEAL Team, and Rudy's standing there waiting for you. He jumps all over you with orders to get a haircut and get cleaned up and all of that so that you can assume the watch.

I ended up standing the quarterdeck watch my first thirty days at SEAL Team Two. But that's probably the best way to learn the Teams, the organization, the faces, and all that stuff. But you're so intimidated by checking in to that command that you just don't think of those things.

I was a seaman who had been hearing all these great war stories about the men over at SEAL Team Two. And here I was with Bob Gallagher and Scotty Lyon walking around. These guys have eight rows of ribbons on their chests, and here I was with my National Defense ribbon on. I just told myself that I had to get some of those ribbons myself. I just didn't know how yet.

It's a very intimidating situation for a new guy. And I pretty much stayed intimidated for a year until I came back from Vietnam. After I came back from my first combat tour, I was finally comfortable at SEAL Team Two.

The first word that comes to my mind when I think about the SEALs is aggressiveness. That goes back to what I said about training, that you have to have the will to get through training. You have to have the will to be a SEAL. Once you get into that platoon, you're with fourteen guys who have that same will. And all they're doing is waiting and watching. They want to act, to apply that will of theirs. Hopefully, something will come up.

Pride is an inherent trait in everyone, although some people have more pride than others. As far as I'm concerned, it's a quiet pride that we have in the Teams. Everyone is really proud of each other. The competitiveness of most SEALs will probably hold them back a little from showing their pride for another Teammate, but they normally love to see each other succeed, especially if that success furthers the Team's goals.

The individual SEALs in the Team are there to do one thing—complete the mission successfully. It's a Team evolution. One guy doesn't go out and do an op. It's fourteen, twenty, or a hundred guys, who pull it off. And without each and every one of those guys, the Team wouldn't be complete, it wouldn't be whole.

The guys in BUD/S right now and the UDTs from World War II are the same guy, the same faces, just different names. We've evolved since then, training's different. Plus the guys today are a little smarter. But they are all the same guy. They're just going to be introduced to some different skills then the guys from UDT Twenty-One, or UDT One for that matter.

During World War II, they needed somebody to do something hard. That's the bottom line. The Navy needed some work done, and it was hard work. They went out and found some guys who could do that hard work, and they didn't complain. Those men were the first UDTs.

I don't have any idea what the needs will be for the SEALs in the future, what their hard work is going to be exactly. What I do know is that the Teams will adapt. I can guarantee you that.

One of the SEALs I've known is Captain Bill Hamilton. Bill's a great guy, a real sweetheart, a prince of a gentleman. He's had one heck of a career. He had a career on the civilian side, and he retired from Naval Special Warfare. I had the good fortune to work with him for about three years.

Tom Richards is also great man. We call him the Hulk. Tom is one of these guys who puts his nose down and goes to work, and he doesn't quit until the work is done. Whether it's lifting weights or pushing paper or operators, he concentrates on the job at hand and gets it done. I first met Tom in 1970 in Ca Mau, Vietnam. He's a big guy—240 pounds, the Hulk just sitting there. I walked in, weighing 148 pounds, and just looked at him. Where did this guy come from? I wondered.

He was at SEAL Team One down in Ca Mau, working with Leon Rauch. He was just passing through. That was the first time I met him. The next time I ran across him, he was the XO at UDT Twenty-One. It's a small community in the Teams.

But I can't say who's the best operator I ever met. I think that they all are. Once again, to have that successful mission, you have to have all the members of a Team in sync, ticking like a Swiss watch.

I think that there are a lot of guys who have had the same experience I have. You're in your forties and all of a sudden you've got a seventeen-year-old with you. This guy is a hard-charger. He's got the hairy-chested, antimagnetic, you-can't-hurt-me type of mentality. What you have to do is basically slow him down a bit and just get him focused. That takes some time. And you might have to jerk his collar every once in a while, but he will come into line over time.

The maturation hits fast when they start getting troops under them. These guys have gone from seventeen to twenty-two or twenty-five, and now they have a seventeen-year-old to command. I got a great deal of satisfaction seeing how they handle the younger men. Dennis Chalker, Rich Hansen, Mark Stefanich, and others were my "seventeen-year-olds," if you will. Chalker was only a third class when he started under me. We grew together. Some of the great things these guys have done now makes me very proud of them.

Mark Stefanich, Signalman First Class

It was when I was just getting ready to graduate from high school when a good friend of mine, Mike Hall, had me meet his brother. Mike's brother was an Army Green Beret home on leave. I had always been intrigued by the military; I watched all the TV commercials about the Marine Corps and other services. Those images stirred something inside of me for some reason, and I was really interested in joining the service.

When Mike's brother came home, I sat around the table and talked with him about just what we were going to do with our lives. Here we were, Mike and I, about to graduate from high school in Highland, Indiana, and neither of us wanted to go into the steel mills and do all that regular midwestern thing. We wanted to do something with our lives that would be fun and interesting. So we asked Mike's brother just which would be the most elite military unit out there. We expected him to tell us the Green Berets, Army Special Forces. What he turned around and said was, "The Navy SEALs."

I'd never heard of the Navy SEALs before. So I just said, "Excuse me?"

"Yeah," he said, "the Navy SEALs. A branch of the Navy, a special operations team. They do everything—operate in the sea, air, and land. They are considered the best operators and the meanest soldiers out there."

Mike and I both thought this sounded interesting and decided to check into it. Going down to the Navy recruiter, we both got a bunch of information on the Navy SEALs. Eventually, we joined the Navy together under the buddy system for the purpose of going through BUD/S and hoping we could both make it to the same SEAL Team.

The Navy shipped us off to get qualified before we could go to BUD/S. I was trained as a signalman, and Mike became a hull technician. Mike went on to hull tech school while I was shipped off to Orlando to signalman's school. I passed the fitness test to go on to BUD/S, and later found out that Mike hadn't passed the test.

That really devastated me. I didn't want to go on to BUD/S without my friend; we had joined the Navy together just to go on to the Teams. After reflecting on the situation for a bit, I decided that I should try for BUD/S anyway. That was really something that I wanted to do.

At BUD/S, I ran into more than the usual surprises. Looking across the grinder, there he was, shaved head and running across the grinder with a green team class. Mike had made it to BUD/S. So we linked up and managed to get into the same room together. Later on, we ended up going through Hell Week together—at least part of it.

Mike ended up having really bad shin splints and, unfortunately, he finally rang out of Hell Week. I managed to hang in there and made it through, but I didn't graduate with that class.

I went through Hell Week as part of Class 97, but came down with a really bad case of dysentery during the week. The corpsman had already recommended that I not start Hell Week with Class 97. I had a really bad blister on my heel that was infected, and the infection was traveling up my leg. So I was on medication already, and he recommended that I roll back and go through Hell Week with Class 98. That would have meant staying at the base, training, and doing grunt work until the next class started.

The night of breakout, I was lying in my bunk and thinking that I didn't want to go through the workup to Hell Week all over again. What I wanted to do was go through Hell Week with my buddies, the guys I knew and who I had gone through the Green Team training with. So I looked at my boots and just said the hell with it.

Cutting the heel off my boot, I put it on and thought it just might work. So here I was, wearing a boot with the heel cut off of it and pondering just what I would do now. Then all hell broke loose.

Instructors kicked the doors in with M60 machine guns blazing and flash-crash grenade simulators going off. Everything was chaotic, and I just jumped into the mess with the rest of my class. Somehow, I managed to make it through the week.

During the time in the demo pits, we had to cross this stagnant pool using two ropes hanging one above the other. Who knew just how long that stinking water lay in the bottom of that pond, or just what diseases were growing in it. And we had to wallow around in that water. We even ate our food in it a few times.

It just might have been the demo pits that did it, but I came down with a real bad case of dysentery. I lost twenty-seven pounds, and the last two days of Hell Week were a bigger mess than usual. I was running, having bad cramps and diarrhea, and just was weak. I have a picture of me, crawling under barbed wire during Hell Week, and I look like a long-term POW—my head was shaved and I weighed only 140 pounds. At six feet tall, that's not much weight, and my cheeks were sunken in.

But I had to get through; I had to make it. Just to prove a point if nothing else. Many times I thought of quitting. The reason I didn't quit was kind of strange, but kept me going. I thought of all of the people I had told that I was going to make it. What would they think if I quit? Plus, they were always stating that Team members didn't quit—ever. Teammates never quit at anything, no matter what. You just had to reach deep down inside yourself to achieve your goal.

Those were the principals I grew up with, the same ones that I continue to hold to this day. Besides, I got to hear those words that secured Class 97 from Hell Week.

At least, I think I heard the words. I was pretty much in a daze by the end of that long week. "Secure from Hell Week" is a term I don't really remember the instructors saying. All I remember is collapsing onto my bunk and being glad, very glad, that it was over and that I made it. There was also some thought about never wanting to do that week again—it had been a bit much.

Reflecting back now, I can see that completing Hell Week made me a better person. So many times I had just wanted to quit, and I saw so many friends quitting, just ringing out. I was wet, cold, tired, and miserable—and for what reason was I doing this? I had no idea what lay ahead in my years to come in the Teams. I thank God I persevered with that challenge, because it led to the most incredible time in my life. I wouldn't trade it for anything in the world.

My first cast-and-recovery during training was interesting. Luckily, we had the opportunity to watch people do it first. That allowed us to try and figure out just what not to do and what to do. When you do it your first or second time, there's always somebody or yourself, who maybe anticipates too much and screws up a little bit. Then you hook your arm into the sling and catch it in the wrong place, maybe causing a rubber friction burn along the bottom of your arm.

After you get picked up a few times, you figure out the technique that works the best for you, and you can clamber into the boat without much trouble. Cast-and-recovery was something that I've never done since BUD/S, but it was something we had to learn. It is an old UDT technique for inserting for shore reconnaissance or loading obstacles, and it's not much used anymore. That part of operations for Navy SEALs is kind of a thing of the past I believe.

The old cast-and-recovery is an incredible ride, and it connects so much to our history. For some guys, that is the time in training when they really feel like a Frogman. For me, it was the live-fire operations on San Clemente Island that made me feel that I was a SEAL for the first time—going out to the island and actually having real demolition blowing up all around you, setting off the charges, going through the woods with live ammunition in the M16s and M60s, and seeing the tracers going by at night. That was when I said to myself, Wow, I'm here now, and this is for real.

What's next? was about all I could think of at graduation, the final day of training, that and wondering about where I might be going, which Team I would be ordered to. Would it be SEAL Team One, SEAL Team Two, or the UDTs? I wanted to go to a SEAL Team. Eventually I did receive orders to SEAL Team One, but I wanted to go to the East Coast and SEAL Team Two, so I found another graduate who would trade assignments with me.

It was right after Jump School at Fort Benning that I was sent on to my assignment at SEAL Team Two. Jump School immediately followed our graduation from BUD/S. It was a great time working with the Army there, jumping, drinking, and carrying on.

I arrived at SEAL Team Two in September 1978. When I went to SEAL Team Two, I met people like Rudy Boesch, a legend in the Teams. Richard Marcinko was the commanding officer when I checked in. All these people around me kind of kept me in awe of them. These guys had done so much, and they had so much to teach, so much knowledge. And they enjoyed their jobs.

A lot of times as a civilian back then, you heard all the negative stuff about soldiers and their experiences in Vietnam. Most of those people hated being there, because they were drafted into the service. The people I was with wanted to be warriors; they chose to go out there and fight for our country. There was pride in just knowing that these people had gone there and fought, put their lives on the line, and enjoyed it.

Most of these guys couldn't wait to go back during Vietnam. Some of these guys had three or four tours—they just kept going back and back. They got shot, healed, and went back to war. It was their job; that was their thing in life. It was handed down to them from somewhere on high. They just found out one day that they were going to be warriors, some of the most ultimate warriors in the world, and there they were. And I was among them. It was quite an honor.

I don't remember if Rudy Boesch met me at the quarterdeck when I first arrived at SEAL Team Two, but he probably did. And what he said was probably along the lines of, "Get your UDT trunks on. We're going for an eight-mile run."

Here you had this fifty-year-old guy, built like Arnold Schwarzenegger but thinner. What, an eight-mile run? Yeah, it's going to be slow. Then he took off. Six-minute miles. Wow, I want to be like him when I grow up. But I grew up and I'm not like Rudy—it's too much work.

My first assignment at SEAL Team Two was to go to Copenhagen, where we cross-trained with the Danish Frømandskorpset, their frogmen. That was a great group of people. We did a lot of kayak work and a lot of running. Those Danes were really into their running, and they were very good at it. The Europeans' training was mostly running with a little bit of swimming. Then we showed up, Navy Frogmen, and we have a tendency to be jacks-of-all-trades. We like to incorporate all kinds of different types of training to our schedule so you're never completely inexperienced in one area or another.

So we introduced PT to our Danish counterparts. Boy, were they hurting. They kicked our butts big-time running—they took us on these eight-mile runs, up hill. But we figured we could get even. Let's get on the grinder and start doing 100 four-count flutter-kicks, push-ups, sit-ups, and all the other little exercises we have in our workouts. That got to our hosts. We taught them about the folly of taking us on an eight-mile run—after drinking all night.

While at SEAL Team Two, I didn't get in on the mobility platoon, MOB-Six, which had been developed to train for counterterrorist work. And I wasn't a plank owner of SEAL Team Six, which took up the job that MOB-Six had been intended to do. Instead, to my knowledge, I was the first person asked to join SEAL Team Six after the plank owners had come aboard and started training.

I had been away on a Med Cruise deployment in the Mediterranean when SEAL Team Six was created. They had commissioned the new Team in November 1980. My platoon didn't come back from deployment until January 1981. As soon as I came back, I went into a meeting and was selected for SEAL Team Six. Myself and Billy Staff never had to go through Green Team training at SEAL Team Six. Green Team training was for the new guys, and when we got there, everyone was still new guys.

When I first got to SEAL Team Six, it was an experience all over again. Just the amount of knowledge that Marcinko had mustered together in that one Team was incredible. And it wasn't just the knowledge pool that was there; the people were some real, true warriors. They might not have been the best dressed or had the best attitude, but these were the guys you wanted to go to war with.

That first group of people at SEAL Team Six was incredible. I still look back on it and know we were the best in the world at that time. I don't know how it is now; I've been out for quite a while. But those guys were something else. We volunteered to go into situations where we knew there was a small possibility of our coming back.

But Marcinko was such a great leader, and our just wanting to go and do this job made any risk seem doable. We wanted to do this job that we had been training for. Not having combat experience felt like having a sheet of paper in a typewriter and just typing away for years and years—without any ink. Then finally, you got some ink. You didn't want to just sit there, you wanted to start knocking on those keys.

We were all there with the same attitude: Who cares, let's just go do the job and not worry about it. Plan for the best and then go to kick ass and take names. And we had the men to do it.

Duke Leonard was one of the guys I met at SEAL Team Six. He was a really good leader and a lot of fun. And he had a lot of knowledge. The way he taught the younger guys, his attitude toward the right way to instruct somebody to do a certain operation or style of shooting, came across well and made you want to learn more from him. You just wanted to gain more of what he could teach you, and he didn't deliver the material in a harsh manner. A lot of people can be harsh and just tell you to do something "this way" and that's about all.

Duke wasn't like that. You could sit down and just ask him why we were doing something a certain way. If you had a point about coming across a different situation and addressing the problem in a new way, he would sit down and talk to you. And he listened. But he would also explain why something wasn't done a given way.

He always wanted us to learn the basics and learn them well. Then we could change for a different scenario and adapt to the situation as it occurred. We could do that in a split second, but only because we had studied and trained hard. The ability to adapt the training to different situations came later in our advanced training. Duke Leonard was very good at bringing that point across and explaining it to eliminate any questions you might have. Knowing him was very beneficial to me.

There were other very impressive men who had been picked by Marcinko to fill the ranks of Team Six. Mike Thornton was one of our officers, and he held the Congressional Medal of Honor. At first, I was startled to meet him. The Medal of Honor! You don't get any better than that. That's the pinnacle. I liked to sit down and listen to his stories about him and Tommy Norris, what had happened, and what it would actually take to receive a Medal of Honor. Most people who receive one aren't alive to talk about it. I was very impressed, as I am to this day.

It's not really just the Medal of Honor that makes you look up to Mike Thornton. It's what he had done for his Teammate. He had jeopardized his life for his Teammate, without question or hesitation.

A Teammate is your fellow warrior, your fellow friend, your brother. I hate to say this, but I love my Teammates more than my brothers, because I don't spend as much time with my brothers as I had with my Teammates. We bled together, we sweated together, and we froze together.

There's this bond that we created by mutual experience, suffering, and accomplishment, and I can trust them with my life in a combat situation and not have to worry about it. To me, that's a true Teammate, not having to second-guess what this person next to me is going to do if a situation becomes hazardous. All I have to do is worry about what my job is, because I know that he knows what he has to do. That leaves your mind open to be focused on the operation at hand.

Master Chief Denny Chalker is a really, really, good friend of mine, and our wives and daughters are friends. We hit it off very well together at SEAL Team Six, which works well because he was my door partner—we went through the door together on ops. We were also drinking and workout buddies. Basically we were inseparable for about the four or five years I was at SEAL Team Six.

Denny has done a lot. Right now, when I tell civilians about Master Chief Chalker, I say that he's probably the most experienced and highly decorated Navy SEAL of the post-Vietnam era that I know of. He's a hard-ass, but that's what it takes.

When I say that Denny is my door partner, that means he's the guy that I'm partnered up with during Close Quarters Battle (CQB). I was usually number one in going through the door, and Denny was usually number two. But we would flip-flop the order so we'd be used to either position. We were usually at each other's side, like swim partners.

Navy SEALs operate on the buddy system. It's not like the Rambo movies. Nobody is an individual—it's called SEAL Team. There aren't any individuals in a Team, and everybody works together and supports each other. Our Teams are broken down into partners. You know your partners as closely as anyone you have known in your life.

There are several instances that I remember going in to the Kill House for training, kicking the door in, and engaging multiple targets. Coming in to a second room and stepping in to the side, I would feel a muzzle blast next to my head and not worry about it. I knew that the blast was Denny right next to me, engaging targets while I was engaging others. Normally, a situation where a gun is going off just to the side of you would raise some kind of scare in you, but I knew it was Denny.

I could actually feel what he was thinking, and I think he could feel the same thing about me. You train so much together and you have to trust your partner so completely, that you just don't have to worry about him. I have all the confidence in the world that Master Chief Chalker would take care of his responsibilities and expect me to deal with mine.

Training was hard and fast, and it was dangerous. We lost a guy during training more than once. We lost Rodney Cheui when we were first training at Eglin Air Force Base while going through a door. He was shot in the kidney, I believe, and passed away. We learned a lot from that incident, but unfortunately, somebody lost their life for us to learn the principals of operating Close Quarters Battle (CQB).

Then there was Rich Horn, a great SEAL and a flawless operator. It was just one of those days; fate or whatever it was had him at the wrong place at the wrong time. A bullet went through one of the partitions and creased his vest. It went though a joint in the vest and entered his lungs. The odds of that happening were like winning the lottery twice in a row. It just shouldn't have happened, but it did. That was a really sad moment, but we had beers to him.

That was a thing about Navy SEALs when one of us passed away. We had kind of a wake for our missing Teammate. We always looked at each other and questioned just how many people could actually die doing something that they loved to do. So if we lost a Teammate, that was okay, because they went out doing the job they loved. Not too many people can say that in this world, because most people hate their jobs. But as a Navy SEAL, you love it so much that you can drink a beer to your friend and miss him for the fact that he's gone, but you know he died being happy. And if you can die being happy, then you've done something right in your life.

I was on the Grenada op, but I didn't make it to the island right away. A group of us finally got to Grenada after we treaded water for a few days. I went in ahead with the CIA, went to a nearby island, and got on the recovery ship where jumpers from Team Six were supposed to come in on a C-130. They would jump into the water and we were to pick them up afterward, plan our operation, and launch into Grenada from there. Unfortunately, things went a little off from what was planned.

We lost four of the eight jumpers, four good friends, in the high seas, winds, and darkness off Grenada. That was another very sad day.

In spite of the losses, we planned to still go in to Grenada on a modified plan. We lost several boats on the drop, and the others we had with us were barely operating. The seas were really bad, with seven-foot swells and twenty-some-knot winds. We still had our old Boston Whalers intact onboard the ship, so we packed the two boats that were left full of people, weapons, and ammunition. Our mission was to go straight in to the airstrip and continue with our job.

We got all of halfway to Grenada when the boats just died on us. They filled up with water, and we treaded water for two days until someone came by to snag us up. It was something to watch the firefights from the surface of the water.

A couple of the guys, myself included, were even thinking about swimming in to the island. But twenty miles or so of open sea is a bit much. There never was any concern that our Teammates or somebody would come along and get us, though sooner would have been better than later.

A Cuban patrol boat came by really close to us. We were sitting in the whalers, filled with water, and a lot of us were seasick. Two-cycle oil was floating on the surface from our fuel tanks, and the waves kept us moving up and down. So we were puking, wet, cold, and miserable—just like during Hell Week. All of a sudden, this Cuban patrol boat from Grenada came along and started shining its light toward us.

Oh, shit! We couldn't go anywhere, we were just sitting ducks in the water. Then somebody said, "Stefanich, get up front with the M60."

So I crawled up to the bow and sat there with my M60 machine gun and about two thousand rounds of ammunition all linked together. And all I wanted was for those guys in the Cuban boat not to shine their light on me. Then the light swept by us and they left. I like it when that happens. But we did miss the big party on Grenada.

My time in the Teams was kind of strange for me. I took a lot of it for granted. I chose to be a Navy SEAL, and I loved doing it, but I just looked at it as my job, something that I was gifted at doing. What I never did was get into the ego bit, thinking that I was a great warrior. I was around some really great people who had some very good backgrounds and a lot of training.

MOB-Six was SEAL Team Six before it became a whole Team. There were all these different names that we had for the job of countering the terrorist threat. Specifically, MOB-Six was a source of manpower when Marcinko was first commissioned with putting together the best of the Navy SEALs for counterterrorism. They were officially part of SEAL Team Two. It was an elite team that dealt more with counterterrorism than with special operations.

Eventually, SEAL Team Six was formed and we moved to behind the old wooden Cub Scout buildings on the base at Little Creek, Virginia. Most people didn't really know that SEAL Team Six even existed. A lot of people in the military would drive by our buildings and wonder what these guys with the long hair and the cigarette boats were doing. The boats were long-bodied, sharp-nosed, powerful-engined racing craft. They had gotten their name from one of the first successful open-ocean racers. The trucks full of boxes of weapons, grenades, and other odd gear also kind of stood out a bit. But they just thought it was SEAL Team Two doing their thing, or maybe an offspring of SEAL Team Two, which we were in a way.

Actually, we didn't even call ourselves SEAL Team Six for quite a while. We kept as low a profile as we could. It wasn't until probably around 1982 or so that our name even made the rounds. Very few people even knew who the Navy SEALs were, and an even smaller percentage of those knew about SEAL Team Six. We didn't go out and advertise ourselves.

The Green Berets, Army Special Forces, were like that at first. Then John Wayne did the movie The Green Berets, and they quickly became the most popular thing around. Everyone wanted to be a Green Beret, and there was a lot of press about them.

But the Navy SEALs were still relatively unknown to the public well into the 1980s. What was a Navy SEAL? Nobody really knew what we were or what we did. Even today, a lot of people still think that as a Navy SEAL, we must spend a lot of time in the water, that we must do a lot of diving. That's not true; it's only a small portion of our operational experience and capabilities.

Once you finish basic training and complete BUD/S and Jump School, you are still a long way from being a Navy SEAL. When you first go on to a Team, you're on probation. You still don't really become a Navy SEAL until you prove yourself. And you're always proving yourself. Even after you earn your Trident and are walking around like a big, hairy-chested Frogman, you can still lose it in an instant. Screw up badly once, and it's "See ya," you're back in the Fleet.

So you're really always trying to better yourself so you can continue to be a Navy SEAL, because you know it's a privilege and that privilege can go away fast, and then you become a shitbird. We always try very hard to focus on our jobs and not get a big ego. What you have to understand is that being a SEAL is a job, just as other people have jobs. This is our work, and we're good at it.

To do our job takes a lot more training than we get just at BUD/S, Jump School, and even at our Teams. Advanced training and schooling goes on indefinitely. I look at Rudy Boesch—he's the walking bible on Special Operations. Every day, you can learn something new from him, or others around him. Tactics change, and so does the world's situation. Every day of your life as a Navy SEAL, you try to better your-self through advanced training to keep up and even stay ahead of what's going on around you. You learn new things, new ways of improvising explosives, going into a room dynamically, skydiving, or getting guys together and patrolling. It never stops. You can't get to the point that you say you know everything. If you do get to that point, then it's time to say "I'm outta here."

They'll draw us together for advanced training and say they have these military schools available. Sometimes, there's cross-training available, schools conducted by another country's military forces. That's advanced training, and it can be jungle warfare in the Philippines or Borneo, jump training with the German jump team, technical rock-climbing at Lake Tahoe, or diving practice at Key West.

We always had these schools available to us. If you were on stand-down and in your training cycle, then you could go to these schools. It would be up to the officer in charge to sit down with the executive and commanding officers to look at what was available, then he could say that he thought his platoon needed to bone up on this or this.

We also had advanced training in-house, where we had the facilities to conduct the course as needed. There was the close-quarter battle house that we could set up in different configurations. The walls could be moved around or we could have moving targets. You could even go into another room and have a screen up where different scenarios would be projected, and you could go through hostage situations or be forced to draw your secondary weapon as part of transition drills.

The training was endless. It would be up to the person in charge at the time to determine what he felt was an advanced training aid or technique that we could use. Then we would sit down, analyze it, and practice it. You would do that and might go home and just think about it. Anyone could remember something that we used, say eight months ago, and think of how it could be incorporated into what we were doing now. Then you could go back and talk about it. Even training was a joint effort, a Team effort. No one person knows everything. And in the SEALs, we would put all our heads together and make the best of a situation that we could.

Our training was so dangerous that it could kill us, absolutely. Our training had killed several of our good friends, because we train for real. And that wasn't just in SEAL Team Six; it happened in the other SEAL Teams as well. If you train as if it's a real situation, when that situation actually comes up, then you just have to work from muscle memory. You don't have to think about what to do.

You train like you fight and fight like you train. That prevents mistakes. In police training on the range, they used to reload their revolvers by opening up the cylinder and dumping the brass into their hand. Then they could just drop it in the bucket and not have to pick it up off the ground later. They used to find cops shot dead after an engagement with a handful of empty brass and an empty gun. They were so used to going to the range and shooting like that, that it became a habit, and those habits became instinctive. In a hot situation where multiple people were shooting at them, the cops reverted to muscle memory—and it got some of them killed.

Our training prevented situations like that from ever happening. When you've trained for something, you didn't have to think about what you had to do next, it was instinctual and you got it done, then you moved on to the next step. If someone was injured or killed in training, what happened was very closely looked at and studied. If a mistake had been made, it was never allowed to happen again. Lessons like that were painful and expensive, but they were never forgotten.

Navy SEALs train and operate at their peak 110 percent all the time. So when we partied, we partied at 110 percent. Everything we did in life, we did all out, 100 percent and more. That's just the way we are, because we're not afraid of the consequences. SEALs and Frogs know what they're up against, and they like being on the driving edge, a little bit more ahead of everyone else. Why? I don't know. It just seems to be something we have in us.

Nowadays, the first thing I think of when I think about the Navy SEALs are the experiences I used to have. There were things I'd done that I took for granted during the nine years that I was in. I really never gave it much thought before because I knew I was doing something I loved to do. I was good at it, and I had the best guys in the world around me.

Then I got out and became involved in the entertainment business. I haven't really looked back for going on fifteen years now. It was only within the last year that I've looked back at what I've accomplished with the Teams. Now, I'm starting to hook up with a lot of my old Team friends, and that's bringing back some very fond memories of life in the Teams and of some really excellent individuals.

Once you've gotten out into the civilian world, it's hard to have friends like the friends you had in the Teams. There's something missing. I've been out for more than fifteen years now, and I probably have only one good friend, and that's my wife Barbara. It's hard to replace the caliber of person you meet in the Teams.

The Navy Trident isn't something I've ever really put much emphasis on. It was our badge, the symbol that we earned by going through a lot of pain and a lot of hard training. We earned that badge, and some of my friends died wearing it. But it's still just a piece of metal. It's the man wearing it that really stands out.

The term "Frogman" isn't really used that much today. It's more or less a name from the past, and one that I love. I think it sounds great—"Frogman." When they first created the UDT, they mostly operated in the water environment. A lot of their time was spent underwater blowing up obstacles or placing demo charges on ships as part of sneak attacks.

Today, there are no UDTs left; they're all SEAL Teams now. We still have that beach recon and obstacle clearance job, but when I heard the term "Frogman," I think of one of the older guys, the old frog. I really never hear about the newer guys using the term to describe each other. Now, he's a SEAL, or he's in a SEAL Team.

Then there's the BullFrog. Physically, Rudy Boesch was the pinnacle of what a Navy SEAL would hope to be. Here was this guy who had been through a number of wars, was highly decorated, and had seen so much action and history—and he drinks beer with the best of us. But he'll be there at 5 or 6 o'clock in the morning, hair cut, perfect uniform, and his voice would growl out, "Let's go, guys."

Oh nooooo. I hope he's feeling a little tired today. We regretted drinking so much the night before and hoped he might feel the same way. Not a chance in hell. Rudy was out there and was what we always looked up to. Rudy was what we wanted to be as a twenty-year-old, or as a fifty-year-old. There was no difference with him. He was outrunning twenty-year-olds, nineteen-year-olds. And not just outrunning them, he was going through the obstacle course faster, or outswimming them. He was incredible, and I'm sure he still is to this day.

The thing that you would find in the Teams that you might not find anywhere else, especially in that kind of job environment, is truly loyal friends. These are people who you know, who you have something in common with. These aren't people who are trying to buddy up to you to get ahead somehow or get something from you. You're both there in the Teams on an even playing field.

To me, the best single word that describes the Teams is camaraderie. Just the friendship, the trust that was there, that's hard to find in the world these days, and I've looked very hard for it. And a lot of times I've been disappointed in my search. I think I see a quality in somebody that could come close to what I had in the Teams, and nine times out of ten, I'm eventually let down. But that's life. You live and you learn and you move on.

The saturation training program that we went through at Six was a result of the mission. Marcinko was tasked with a job that not too many people in the world probably could have accomplished. He took a group of Navy SEALs and turned them into one of the most unique counterterrorism organizations in the world—and he did it in a matter of a year.

During our first year of training at Six, we had two days off—Christmas and Thanksgiving. The rest of the time we were training fourteen or sixteen hours a day, then drinking and relaxing perhaps four hours after training while we cleaned up and prepared for the next day. That was our schedule, seven days a week. Marcinko wanted to have the best counterterrorist organization in the world, because that was the task that was given to him by Admiral Lyons. He was told, "You will not fail, Dick. This is what you have. Make it happen."

And he did that. Marcinko is an incredible leader, he did a great job and put together a phenomenal group of people. The selection process for those people was very good, too. It wasn't just him and the executive officer looking at a list of names and records. He would also get all the Teams guys together in a room, something like the Knights of the Round Table, and he would ask them about an individual candidate.

Dick wanted to know if anyone knew the man personally, what his qualifications were, and if he was wanted in the Team. Everyone had a say. That resulted in a very good group of people, because we liked and knew each other. That helped us operate that much better because there was no personal tension there. It was amazing how your operational level would go up notches just because you didn't have to worry about any bullshit, just the job at hand.

Marcinko wanted us to think like the enemy, to live like him—not to the extreme, though. We didn't become terrorists, but that let us have the mindset of what a specific terrorist or group was doing, and why. That helped us learn to hate them that much more.

I was there to protect the United States of America. I love my country. The most beautiful thing in the world to me is the American flag flapping in a stiff breeze. I was willing to give my life for my country, because we have the best one in the world. That was my level of dedication at the time. Thank God I didn't have to, but I would have made any sacrifice that was demanded of me.

What I couldn't stand was to see this country be ruined by people who hate, are greedy, or just have their own stupid little beliefs and violently try to do something about those beliefs. When they kill innocent people, there's no need for them to continue on in this world. There's only one thing to do with people like that, and that's to neutralize them.

■ Chapter 57

Central America

The SEAL losses off Grenada were their first combat losses since the Vietnam War, but earlier that year, there had been another SEAL lost to enemy fire, but not in combat. On 25 May 1984, Lieutenant Commander Albert A. Schaufelberger III was assassinated in El Salvador by what was later declared to be a unit of the FMLN (Farabundo Marti National Liberation Front).

Schaufelberger had been sitting in his armored Ford Maverick, provided to him by the U.S. Embassy. As a Navy SEAL, Schaufelberger was the senior Naval representative at the U.S. Military Group, El Salvador, at the time of his death. Faulty air conditioning had caused Schaufelberger to roll down the window of his armored car. While he was stopped to pick up his girlfriend, a Volkswagen Microbus stopped nearby. Jumping from the Microbus were a number of terrorists. One of the terrorists ran up to Schaufelberger's window and pumped four rounds from a .22 Magnum into the SEAL. Then the group escaped in their vehicle. They were never captured.

By the early 1980s, Naval Special Warfare had begun to increase its activity in Central and South America. Schaufelberger's loss had been a result of the severe unrest in not only El Salvador, but also many locations throughout Central America at the time.

Only a few SEALs—less than four at any one time—were stationed in El Salvador, supporting the Military Advisory Group's activities there. Primarily, the SEALs advised and helped train the El Salvadoran naval units on a variety of subjects from maritime operations to land combat. The SEALs worked under very strict rules of engagement and were not able to take an active part in the fighting against Communist insurgents in the country. This was a severe irritation to the SEALs on duty in El Salvador, as they were used to taking a much more active role in the surrounding situation.

SEAL operations extended through the 1980s to include missions in Honduras and along the Nicaraguan border. The situation turned into a learning experience for both the Honduran forces as well as the SEALs and Special Boat Squadron assets that were assigned to the areas.

The political defeat of the Sandinista Government in Nicaragua in the early 1990s began to settle the turmoil in the Central American area. The SEAL and U.S. military presence as a whole was reduced as the guerrilla movements lost support with the failure of communism in the Soviet Union and elsewhere in the world.

Steven Scott Helvenston, Quartermaster First Class

When I was sixteen years old and a junior in high school, I was struggling somewhat with my family life and just life in general and I looked into going into the Navy. When I went to the recruiters, I told them I was very interested in joining the Navy, and that was when I was made aware of what the SEAL Team was all about.

At that time, my SEAL recruiter basically told me that I would be a crazy man to even try out, but I went for it anyway. Later, I was part of Class 122, a winter class, with our Hell Week starting 6 December.

Because El Niño—although they didn't call it that at the time—happened to hit, the storm, surf, and cold weather that was involved with our training class stands out the most to me from those days. Sandbag PT—filling, lifting, and stacking all those bags of sand to protect the officer's quarters barracks, the Country Store, and even helping out at the Coronado Cays from water—was an exercise Class 122 did a lot of. That was a very unique element to SEAL training at that time.

Hell Week was cold and miserable. Class 122 was the next class after a no-bell Hell Week class—no one from the class before us had quit during Hell Week. The thing I remember the most about our Hell Week was that I think initially, the instructors were going to make sure that Class 122 was not going to have a no-bell Hell Week.

I remember the first six hours of Hell Week being probably a little bit more miserable than they should have been. Going through Hell Week on 6 December, at that time of the year with El Niño making it so windy and so cold, the instructors gave us field jackets when we were at Camp Swampy. I think the decision had been made that things were just too cold and we had to have some kind of covering. Shivering in the miserable cold—that's the thing I remember the most. Sure, that's probably the case with every Hell Week, but that's what I remember the most.

There were a lot of things in my life leading up to that point. I grew up in kind of a broken environment—I lost my father when I was young and I didn't really see eye-to-eye with my mom too much. So the survivor element was established in me well before I joined the Navy and decided to become a SEAL. I just knew that, no matter what, in training anyway, I wasn't going to die. These guys, the instructors, weren't going to kill me. I just wasn't going to quit, no matter what.

Sure, I thought about quitting. I thought about what it would be like to be labeled a quitter, or how negative or bad I would feel about myself because I quit. In a way, that's what inspired me not to quit. But I don't think I ever came anywhere near really quitting. That bell was nowhere near in my mind, and I wasn't going anywhere close to it if I had a choice.

It's weird, but that last day of BUD/S, graduating training, was the biggest accomplishment of my life to that point. I'd never achieved something that arduous. Now, fifteen years in the future, I look back and think how that was really just the beginning. Really, truly becoming a Navy SEAL happens after two or three predeployment trainings and three platoon workups. That's when you become a real Navy SEAL, when you shed all the T-shirts and get rid of all the images in your mind. You realize that becoming a Navy SEAL is a very professional job.

The training after BUD/S, at least going to Fort Benning and Army Jump School, did seem like kind of a joke. It was a lot of fun. There was one situation at Benning that I'll never forget. We were in our stick, the formation of paratroopers that line up to jump from the plane. The jump sergeant, whatever they call that guy who's in charge at that Army school, was running down the stick checking us over on a prejump inspection.

For some reason, I don't remember why, I failed his inspection. That sergeant dropped me down for whatever amount of push-ups he told me to do, and I started banging them out. Being a cocky young graduate of BUD/S, I told him that there wasn't anything that he could do to hurt me, that there weren't enough push-ups he could have me do that would hurt me, I started banging out some more push-ups.

That sergeant kept walking down the stick to inspect the rest of the students. There were Army people and other Navy SEALs in the line. Todd French, two people away from me in the stick, was a classmate of mine. We look kind of alike, though not exactly.

Finally, I got maxed out after banging out one hundred or one hundred and fifty push-ups in a row. I asked Todd to help me out. So as soon as I got maxed out, I jumped back up and stood at attention while Todd dropped to the ground and started doing push-ups. He was banging them out hard.

That airborne instructor came back and I peeked out at him from the side of my eye. He had an expression on his face like he had known that Navy SEALs were badasses, but he hadn't thought they were that bad. Between the two of us, Todd and I must have banged out almost five hundred push-ups in about five minutes. And I'll never forget that, because that must have been the biggest joke played on that guy ever. SEALs are in great shape, but 500 push-ups? So that's how Jump School was. It was fun.

Not everything at Jump School was quite as funny, though. There's something wrong with anyone who jumps out of a plane for the first time and isn't a jar-full of eyeballs. Of course, I was scared, but I was excited at the same time, excited and exhilarated about doing it—jumping from a plane. I really had a liking toward parachuting and skydiving, so I became a free-fall jumpmaster and a free-fall instructor. Later, I became a parachute rigger (packer) and senior rigger for the FAA. Now I work in the civilian community, packing parachutes and teaching people how to jump.

But I won't lie to you. Jumping out of an airplane that first time makes your eyes bulge out of your head. It is a big relief looking up at that big, open canopy above you for the first time. There's no doubt about it, that's the best skirt you'll ever look up. I think you feel that way every time it opens, but there's definitely something about that first one.

Right out of BUD/S, I was given orders to UDT Eleven, which shortly thereafter became SEAL Team Five. I like calling myself an original Frog [Frogman], but the reality of it is that I checked into UDT Eleven then six days later it became SEAL Team Five. So I was a UDT Frogman for less than a week before becoming a SEAL.

The mission didn't really change that much in the beginning, but the consolidation of the UDTs into SEAL Teams was happening then, as it should have. When you look at the entry-level training in BUD/S and then where you are eventually sent, it's obvious that everybody should have been ready to do either job. All Teams should maintain something of the same responsibilities, in my opinion.

I guess I had the opportunity to experience that in the beginning. UDT Eleven/SEAL Team Five wasn't much different in the beginning except for the name change. After about a year or so, they picked up SEAL Team operations and so forth.

And I don't believe we ever really went through a plankowner process at SEAL Team Five. Basically, we were still the same command, they just changed our title. It really wasn't a new command, so I don't consider myself a plankowner of SEAL Team Five. It was definitely a different transition to the SEAL Team status than the earlier cases with SEAL Teams One and Two.

I spent roughly eleven months at SEAL Team Five and then the opportunity came up for me to transfer to the East Coast. It was very evident to me at that time that a lot of West Coast Frogs were going to hate me for this, but East Coast Teams at that time in the early 1980s, were operating quite a bit more than the West Coast Teams were. Within three weeks of checking in to SEAL Team Four, I was gone. I was in a platoon deployed to Honduras in Central America and doing real-world stuff.

Being that I sat at SEAL Team Five for eleven months and went through SERE (Survival, Escape, Resistance, and Evasion) school and one other technical school on dive maintenance, I'll be the first to say that was happy to have made that move.

While I was at SEAL Team Five, there was a list of people who would be deploying. After having been at the Team for eleven months, I was not slated to be in a platoon for another eight months. That's why I did a coast transfer. It was ridiculous to me that I was at a Team for almost a year and wasn't going to be in a platoon for another eight months. Then, I was going to do a workup that could last over a year until we went out on a deployment. So that was really my motivation for going to the East Coast. There, I was operating in the field after only a short time.

Operating in Central America was swampy. Central America was like a third-world country, and working in that environment definitely makes you appreciate being a U.S. citizen, that's for sure. I guess the thing that sticks out in my mind the most about working in Honduras and El Salvador was being involved in training kids.

Having joined the Navy at the earliest opportunity, I was young at the time. At that time, I was the youngest student to have graduated BUD/S, having completed the course at seventeen. When I was working in El Salvador and Honduras, I was eighteen to twenty years old, and the kids I was training were thirteen, fourteen, and fifteen years old.

The biggest thing I struggled with was the fact that these kids had seen more action than I had. They'd been out there and trading bullets with the bad guys, and now I was there teaching them how to do it.

At the risk of sounding like a warmonger, I think in a way I missed that opportunity to see active combat because I was training. When you train, and train intensively, to do something, I think it's just natural desire to put that training to the test. I spent tours with four different platoons, working up to putting that training to the test. I saw a little bit of combat action, but I never really had the opportunity to put my training to the test. It becomes fatiguing to practice, practice, practice, and then never really see that practice put into use.

I did once hear a bullet crack by, one that was fired in anger. I'm not going to claim to be anything like one of the Vietnam veterans or experience some of the things that happened back then. We've all heard the stories, and I have the utmost respect for the men who fought for our country in Vietnam and other wars. When I experienced combat danger, it was very minimal and just sniper fire.

My part of the combat was pretty much just covering, but I do wonder what it would be like to go out on patrol in hostile territory. To this day, I wonder what it would be like to be dealt the situation of having to enter into a firefight or a major conflict.

In Central America, the rules of engagement were definitely much more stringent and restrictive than probably what they were in Viet-

Striking a pensive pose, this SEAL trainee listens intently during tactical training. This is only a small part of the almost full year of training that BUD/S students undergo to go on to the Teams as qualified SEALs.

U.S. Navy

nam or any other previous war. It was a very frustrating experience for me. Here we were allowed to train the El Salvadorans and Hondurans, and we were even allowed to go out on patrol with them, but if we were taking enemy fire, we weren't even allowed to shoot back. That's kind of frustrating. But I'm not saying that we never shot back.

Still, it was a difficult situation. The political environment around the mission was always hard to work with. A very good friend of mine, Arthur Fusco, died in Honduras, not because of war, but because of a political agenda. At the time, I was very young, and remembering affects me now more than it did then. I'm a little bit more seasoned and mature now, so I reflect on it differently.

Arthur had been a classmate of mine. Actually, he was rolled out of the class, but he remained a very good friend. He died trying to improve Honduran relations.

Central America was a job, and we did it. Overall, the mission we did in Central America was a good job. It's so hard, so difficult, to get into the big, political, Washington, D.C.–Pentagon environment, to get into their heads and see what their agenda is. But when we go on a deployment like this, we're tasked to do a certain job and we do it.

As a SEAL Team, we did our job. There are certain things that we did that could have probably been done a little better, and there are other things that probably could have been done better by the Army Corps of Engineers. Certain demolition jobs we were involved with were kind of ludicrous, but we were asked to do it and we went in there and did the best job that we could.

The thing that I looked for the most in the SEALs Teams in the beginning was the challenge. I'm a very goal-oriented person, as most Navy SEALs are. Some are more goal-oriented than others. I found a lot of reward in challenging myself. The thing that I looked forward to the most in the Teams was the next challenge.

When you look at the arena of what the SEAL Teams offers a person, what comes first, the man who accomplishes SEAL Team or SEAL Team, the organization? I think it's somewhere in between. SEAL Team afforded me the opportunity to achieve a goal and to pursue something that was a criteria. Within that criteria, it allowed me to become a part of a really special organization.

I'm still a Navy SEAL. I spent twelve years in active duty, and I've been out for roughly four years now. The things I learned about myself and the things I accomplished definitely affect everything I do in my life now. The key ingredient I've learned is tenacity. There's nothing that will substitute for tenaciousness. If you feel strongly about something, passionately about something, pursue it and don't ever give up. I learned that in SEAL Team, and I learned that about myself because of the SEAL Teams.

During part of my time in the Teams, I was an instructor at BUD/S in Coronado.

My focus as an instructor when training students was to push them to reach all that they were able to and more. I didn't get a lot of gratification or pleasure out of being a real mean, hard, in-your-face, critical, and insulting instructor.

What I did take a lot of pleasure in was maintaining a really high standard physically. I was a big stickler for physical standards, and I was a huge stickler for anything that was somewhat skill-related. I was a First Phase instructor from Class 157 to Class 171, then I moved on to teach free-fall, which is an advanced skill.

Free fall is not a physical evolution. When you look at skydiving and free fall, it's an evolution that's really an issue of teaching an individual how to compose himself in a stressful, somewhat death-defying evolution. If they mess up, they die, which is a very important element in SEAL Team. In a fire-fight—which we can never really simulate, we can simulate with paintball, paper targets, but we can never really throw live ammo at each other—you are in the ultimate, stressful, life-threatening situation.

What we can do is put an individual in a life-threatening situation such as skydiving and rock-climbing and see how he's going to respond. (I was a rock-climbing instructor as well.) What I placed a lot of value on during that training was seeing how an individual responded in those particular curriculum environments.

When I hear about some of the veterans of the Teams, the first thing that comes to my mind is respect. That's the first thing I have for those men such as Mike Thornton, Barry Enoch, and others. They performed in a wartime environment, and they performed well. There's no taking that away from them. I respect them for it big time.

At the same time, I'm very envious of those individuals. I don't want this to sound wrong; there's a fine line between envy and jealousy. Throughout my twelve years as a Frog and a SEAL, I never really had the opportunity to really put my training to the test, other than in the pentathlon, which was probably one of the most rewarding things I ever did in the Navy, competing for my country in a peacetime environment. But you get a little ridicule, a little shit run at you by some of the guys who say that you're a new-school Frog and you've never really been put to the test. That part becomes a little irritating after a while. You know that you would have tried and possibly have done just as well as the guy giving you shit, but you just didn't have the opportunity.

But again, respect is the first thing I have for anybody who fought for our country in a wartime environment. But envy and maybe a little jealousy, I'm not going to lie about that, is also in the background.

When I reflect on my training, I covered thirteen Hell Weeks as an instructor and of course went through one Hell Week myself. The fitness element kind of just comes, and it comes easier to some than to others. People who come to training not in as good shape as others have to work harder to reach the the fitness levels the others have.

The thing that probably sticks out the most in my mind about going through Navy SEAL training is the misery. There's no way you can really explain that to somebody. They have to go through it to understand it. If I have to explain it to you, you'll never really understand. I know that's cliché, but the reality is that it's true. BUD/S training is miserable.

In First Phase, which is the first eight weeks of training, the IBS, the inflatable boat, small, is glued to your head. You travel everywhere with it. There's a number of reasons for that. The main reason is for team-building. Obviously, you need to learn how to paddle the boat, but if you're not utilizing good teamwork, that boat can really work against you.

The pressure on your neck and your spine from carrying that boat around like that for eight weeks can be excruciating. But the one thing that probably influences an individual to quit more than anything is cold and lack of sleep. No sleep, and being cold, wet, sandy, and miserable, along with wondering what it would be like to just be in a dry set of clothes and living a normal life, saps your will. You have to set your mind to get through the evolution and continue on.

One night of no sleep is kind of painful. Try it three times over. And then when you're three nights into Hell Week and we give you just two hours of sleep—just two, just enough to piss you off—then we wake you up and it's "Oh my God, all those dreams I was just having . . ."

As an instructor, it's hilarious to watch students wake up after three days of no sleep. They look around in a delirium. It's kind of funny.

Because I'm a physical guy, I'm one of those CISM (Conseil International du Sport Militaire) pukes, those pentathlon guys, I've always had a lot of respect for the older guys in the Teams who, for one, achieved a lot in a wartime element but still maintained a heck of a physical standard. Rudy Boesch was one of those guys.

When I transferred to the East Coast, I went to SEAL Team Four and heard stories about Rudy Boesch at SEAL Team Two. There would be guys who would check into SEAL Team Two right out of BUD/S. You're in pretty top condition when you graduate from BUD/S. When you go to SEAL Team Two and on a conditioning run, you can't keep up with, let alone beat, Rudy Boesch, that's when the stories build up.

When I checked in at SEAL Team Four, I think Rudy was in his mid-fifties, and he was still whipping guys half his age and younger. And if they didn't beat him on a conditioning run, they were stuck on the quarterdeck for a weekend duty. I have a lot of respect for Rudy Boesch, and I hold a couple senior officers and enlisted guys in the same regard. I think Admiral Raymond C. Smith is the same way, he lives by a pretty high Team standard. I think it's always kind of frustrating how some Team guys let themselves go a little bit. It disappoints me, because I think we have a standard to live by. Whether you're in or out of the Navy, you have to maintain that standard.

My association with Admiral Tom Richards was through the pentathlon. He was the officer-liaison, the international office liaison with CISM. Their motto is "Substitute the playing field for the battlefield," and when you look at what that organization does, it is easy to see how Admiral Richards was such a strong supporter and proponent of the SEALs being involved with that. I hold him in high respect for that.

I wish that CISM was embraced more as a whole by the Special Warfare community. Look at what it's doing—we're out there, representing our country. And no, we're not in a physical, confrontational war, but we're a part of the peacemaking process, maintaining relations with other countries and representing our country. It's just unfortunate sometimes when some people don't understand the priority of what that part of the military is all about—competing at an international level in something other than war.

In white camouflage, to include white tape on his M16A1 rifle, this SEAL from SEAL Team Two conducts winter training.

U.S. Navy

I think our mission as SEAL Teams is definitely changing. It's probably going to consistently change. Whether it's a desert environment, a jungle environment, or a winter warfare environment, we will train and adapt for that arena. I think right now we're looking at a lot of counterterrorist issues that we really need to be specialized in. It's not just an issue of going out and doing fire-and-movement exercises in the woods anymore. It's a lot more complicated than that.

SEAL Team's mission is changing to meet the new threats. I've been out for four years (as of 1998), doing what I'm doing, which is still being a SEAL, only in the civilian world now, so I'm not as well versed as I would like to be to make a comment about where SEAL Teams' mission is going. But I will say that I think that it's a heck of a lot more complicated than it's ever been.

I'm not very familiar with SEAL Teams' involvement in the drug-interdiction program. I think they should play a role, because we're qualified to do so. When you

The shield of the United States Special Operations Command.

USSOCOM PAO

look at how much involvement the Coast Guard has had with drug interdiction and where their qualifications fit in with that task, it's kind of ludicrous that we SEALS aren't doing the job. From what I hear, we are cross-training quite a bit with the Coast Guard, but why cross-train? Why not just give the job to SEAL Team? That's what we're qualified to do.

When I think of the SEAL Teams, the first word that comes into my head is win. SEAL Team is built on a competitive environment, and it pays to be a winner. It doesn't just translate into one thing; that attitude translates into every aspect of my life. In the business world, I'm an entrepreneur now and have my own business. I'm still competitive. Even while I'm raising a family, I compete in events athletically. But the winning mentality, that stays.

Chapter 58

U.S. Special Operations Command

The lessons learned in Iran at Desert One were not forgotten by the U.S. military or the political leaders of the country. Also remembered were the problems that cost four SEALs their lives off Grenada during URGENT FURY. The Goldwater-Nichols Department of Defense Reorganization Act of 1986 was the most significant change to the organization of the U.S. military since 1947. For the Naval Special Warfare, and special operations forces in general, the major effect of the act was the creation of a central command structure for all special operations forces in the U.S. military.

The U.S. Special Operations Command was activated on 16 April 1987 at MacDill Air Force Base in Tampa, Florida. SOCOM is commanded by a four-star flag or general officer. All the Special Operations Forces in the U.S. military are under the SOCOM command umbrella—Army Special Forces, Rangers, and the 160th Special Operations Aviation Regiment; the Naval Special Warfare Command, which includes all the SEAL and SDV Teams as well as the Special Boat Teams; and the Air Force Special Operations Command with the Special Operations Wings and Groups.

Close to 50,000 enlisted men and officers from the three different branches of the service operate under the direction of SOCOM. The different units work together on joint operations on a constant basis. This raises the skill levels of all of the units and makes their ability to conduct difficult operations much greater than before. The men who operate the aircraft know what the men on the ground or in the water need because they've worked directly with them.

Funding is less of a problem, as SOCOM manages procurement for its forces and commands. New equipment is brought online and put into the hands of the operators much more quickly than was possible earlier. Programs for the different forces can be combined where possible to give all the men the best support available.

Rudy Boesch, Command Master Chief Boatswain's Mate, USN (Ret.)

At SEAL Team Two in Little Creek, Virginia, I was the Command Master Chief forever. Actually, I was a plankowner at SEAL Team Two, which was formed in 1962, and remained at the Team until I left in 1988. I was at SEAL Team Two for a total of twenty-six years.

One of the things I enjoyed doing was physical training (PT). Once I was put in charge of it for the Team, I really enjoyed it. I knew when I was going to stop, but the men didn't. We had a good physical outfit, no doubt about it.

The men followed my lead in PT, and I led them through the exercises and the run or swim that followed. This was the order of the day for all of my time at SEAL Team Two. Once, it did cause some trouble for me and a little for the men, too.

Back in the early 1970s, after we had finished in Vietnam, we were making a two-mile swim after PT and I wasn't feeling well. We had been swimming awhile, covering about a quarter-mile or so, and I had been swallowing salt water. I decided to get out of the water and walk back to the Team. There were probably about fifty people in the water following my lead, as we were all swimming together. When I got out of the water, they all followed me, and we all walked back to the Team.

When I asked them why they were following me and told them that I was sick, they just continued following me anyway. The commanding officer, Bob Gormly, got in and asked me why we had all gotten out of the water before the planned swim was over. I just told him that I had gotten sick and they had all followed me in. Why? I didn't know. He said that they could all follow me Friday afternoon at liberty call, so we had to do the swim again—and finish it this time.

In 1968, I first went to Vietnam, leaving Little Creek on Easter Sunday as I remember. It didn't matter what day you left the States, because you didn't get to Vietnam until the last day of the month. That was the way the pilots who flew the transports over there figured things out. If they did a month in Vietnam, they received combat pay. So they would plan to land a plane about 11:30 at night on the last day of the month and they would take off at 12:30 the next month—an hour later—so they got two months' combat pay. The Air Force probably doesn't want to hear that, but that's the way it was.

My first tour of duty in Vietnam was with Tenth Platoon. The second time I went over, I ended up not doing any operating in the field with a platoon. On my second tour of duty, four of us trained and went over to Vietnam late in 1970. Usually, we would report in to Saigon and they would tell you where to go. I reported in to Saigon, where Captain Schaible was in charge. I knew him, so he told me that I was going to Cam Ranh Bay, and the other three SEALs with me were going down to Solid Anchor, which was a floating base down in the swamps of the southern delta.

I asked why I couldn't go with my Teammates since we had just gotten done training together. All Schaible said was, "Shut up. You're going to Cam Rahn Bay."

So I got on the airplane and flew up to the huge navy base at Cam Ranh Bay. As we were coming in on our approach run, I looked down and it looked like we were flying over Miami Beach—big, white-sand beaches and clear water. When I finally got down to where I was supposed to be, I found out that my job was to be training LDNNs (Lien Doan Nguoi Nhia by that time in the war), Vietnamese SEALs.

We were running the LDNNs through a training course. Actually, they were running their training themselves by 1970, we just advised them on how to do things. They administered their own discipline and things like that. By this time, the Vietnam War was winding down for us. Dave Schaible had told me that if the LDNNs wanted something, such as a roll of toilet paper, they had to fill out the paperwork themselves. Earlier, we had just handed them over a roll when they asked for it.

Now, we were supposed to make them do things by the book because we were going to turn everything over to them. The LDNNs didn't like that, so they went back to using a handful of leaves just like they used to.

There were still a lot of SEALs operating incountry when I was on my second tour in Vietnam. Lieutenant Joe DiMartino was in Saigon. Where I was in Cam Rahn Bay, the Navy had the dolphins, which were trained to guard the ammunition pier. The dolphins were kept in a pen with a paddle sticking down into the water. When the dolphin sensed something in the water, like an enemy swimmer—they could sense them hundreds of yards away—the dolphins would bang their heads on the paddle. Then the person on watch would turn them loose, and the dolphins would go out and push the swimmer to the surface if he was underwater. Or they would just nudge a swimmer on the surface and push them onto the beach. Then the handlers and guards would take charge of the prisoner. That's how they would catch these enemy swimmers before they could do any damage.

Anyway, I believe Joe DiMartino was eventually assigned as the officer in charge of this dolphin program at Cam Ranh Bay. Before that, though, he came over to see me one day. I took him over to where the dolphins were and told him all about what they did. He didn't believe it, so the people who took care of the dolphins told him to go out into the bay the next morning around 5 o'clock and start swimming in toward the ammunition piers and see what happens for himself.

So Joe went out the next morning and started swimming in. The dolphins nailed him before he got very far. According to Joe, they hit him so hard they almost broke his ribs. But he was a believer in the program after that. That's how he got involved with that outfit.

It wasn't much longer after my tour was over and I got back to Little Creek that things really started to wind down for SEAL Team Two in Vietnam. By 1972, our last platoons had come home. Things really slowed down at the Team after that. During the war, we had ten platoons at SEAL Team Two, all coming and going all the time. With the end of the war, all that stopped.

We tried to get back to normal after our commitment to Vietnam was over. A lot of people were dissatisfied and got out of the Team or retired from the Navy. They liked the war. That's what we trained for, and they preferred the action to a peacetime Team.

At SEAL Team Two in the mid-1970s, we just participated in Med (Mediterranean) trips and started working with the British and Germans in Europe. Things finally did get busy again, but it was a different kind of busy than we had during Vietnam.

In about 1978 or 1979, MOB-Six at SEAL Team Two was formed. MOB-Six meant Mobility Group Six. They took the people for the unit from Headquarters platoon at SEAL Team Two. These people were always there. If command needed them, they could call the people of MOB-Six away in a hurry. I was part of MOB-Six.

Our mission was to conduct counterterrorist actions for the Navy and SEAL Team Two. We went to Europe, and the British commandos (SAS) taught us fast roping and stuff like that. These were new things to us, and we learned from all the different foreign national counterterrorist units.

Then, around 1980, SEAL Team Six was formed, and most of the people from MOB-Six went over to the new Team. I went back to SEAL Team Two because I didn't want to go to Six. There, we went back to doing all of our conventional missions while Six continued with the new, high-speed, more unconventional stuff.

In 1988, the military formed the United States Special Operations Command (USSOCOM). They didn't have the Navy in it yet, and although the SEALs weren't part of it at the beginning, they soon became part of the new organization. A four-star Army general was put in charge of SOCOM, and he interviewed Army, Navy, and Air Force people to be his senior enlisted advisor. I was the Navy person who was put up as a SEAL for the new position.

The general was in California, so I went out there to be interviewed personally by him. Before the interview, I was briefed all morning about the kind of things he would ask me. I was told to expect questions like who was the president of Zimbabwe and things like that.

"Look," I said to my briefers, "if I don't know it by now, I'm not going to learn it this morning."

Anyway, I got in to see the general that afternoon. The first thing he asked me was how had I managed to stay in the Navy so long. At that time, I had forty-two years in the Navy, most of them with the UDTs. From 1951 and my joining up with Class 6 to 1988, I had spent thirty-seven years with the UDTs or SEAL Team Two.

So when that general asked me how I had stayed in the Navy so long, I told him that if I got the job, he was going to find out, because he would have to write the next letter to keep me in the Navy. After thirty years, the Navy wants you out, and I was already well past that.

But I got the job. Overnight, I was in charge of the enlisted men of the SEALs, the Army Special Forces, the Rangers, and the twenty-third Air Force, approximately 45,000 enlisted men. And I was the head Non-Commissioned Officer (NCO).

Not everything went smoothly during my time in the new position. I was put on the awards board at SOCOM at its new headquarters on MacDill Air Force Base in Tampa, Florida. The rest of the people on the awards board were all colonels, captains, admirals, generals, and so on. I was the only enlisted man, so I just asked them what I was supposed to do.

The officers told me that every month, they were going to give me the paperwork on the guys they were going to give the awards to. I read the first batch of papers and said that these guys weren't doing anything out of the ordinary, they were just doing their jobs, and I didn't see why they should get an award.

The Air Force general in charge of the award board didn't like it when I said that I probably wouldn't recommend the men on the list for an award. He said, "I tell you what, Chief. You might not recommend them, but I know nine people who will."

That meant that he would just tell the rest of the board to give out the awards. It didn't really matter to me very much, it just showed me how the different services worked and sometimes bumped heads. The Air Force would give medals for successfully going to certain schools and things like that. The Navy doesn't do that.

Finally, it came time for me to get my last extension for my time in the service. That last extension letter was written by General Lindsay. I had told him that if I got the job, he would have to write that letter to keep me in the Navy, and he did. About a week later, he told me that I had the extension, but that he hadn't written the letter. Instead, General Lindsay told me that he had called Frank.

So I just asked him, "Frank who?"

It turned out Frank was Admiral Frank Kelso, the Chief of Naval Operations. What the CNO told General Lindsay was that he could keep me as long as he wanted me. There was somebody a bit higher up than the CNO who signed my paperwork. On my final application for an extension, I had the signature of Ronald Reagan, the president of the United States and Commander-in-Chief of all the armed forces.

When I first started my Navy career, President Franklin D. Roosevelt was sitting in the White House. When I finally left the Service, the president was Ronald Reagan. During my Navy career I stood watch under the administrations of Roosevelt, Truman, Eisenhower, Kennedy, Johnson, Nixon, Ford, Carter, and Reagan. Nine presidents—not a bad run.

The SEALs are made up of good, dedicated men, and you know what they can do, because they've already been through it. That six months of training put the men through some hard stuff. You can depend on the men who graduate that training. They're smart enough to improvise. If they can't do the job one way, they'll come up with another way to do it. I attribute a lot of the SEALs' capabilities to their physical well-being. If you're in physical shape, you can do anything you want to do.

The guys you see in the movies, the ones who don't show their feelings and act like hard cases all the time, those aren't SEALs, they're just actors. Real SEALs have a lot of feelings. I saw a guy cry just a few days ago just at the thought that an argument that was going on among the Teams could result in his being sent out of the community. At the thought of his being cut away from the rest of us, tears came into his eyes. That's showing feeling, a lot of it.

And SEALs can be scared, just like anyone else can. Every night in Vietnam was scary. Ninety percent of the time we conducted our missions at night, and every night we went out, we were scared—excited, but scared. At least I was.

You never knew what was going to happen or what it was going to take to get you through the mission. Usually we went out on intelligence—you go to this place at this time and you can catch these guys. Most of the time, it worked because the intelligence was good. But there were a lot of times that the mission fell through and nothing happened. You were prepared for anything, but there wasn't anything there. You had just gone out for a walk in the dark.

If the SEALs hadn't been in Vietnam, I don't think things would have turned out any differently. What we did was operate like the Vietnamese did, like the Viet Cong did. They went out at night and would ambush people and then disappear. We went into the Viet Cong's backyard and did the same thing to them. Now they were afraid of us because we had become the aggressor. Instead of sitting back and waiting for them to come to us, we went out and hunted them down in their own safe areas.

The whole Navy today has come out with a lot of new equipment. The Landing Craft, Air Cushion (LCAC) doesn't even sit on the water or the land, they just go right over the beach. One day, there might not be a need for a UDT-type mission any more, but there will always be a need for a SEAL. SEALs work in the rivers, swamps, and lakes. They do a different line of work than the old UDT did, and they do it very well. And the SEALs can adapt to whatever they have to.

If you're in good physical shape, you can do anything you want to do. I'd bet my life on that, and I have. In the SEALs, we're not going to beat the New York Giants *in a football game. We might not win that game, but we'll win in the end some other way. That's due to the mental attitude we guys have, and our physical abilities. We go into battle thinking that we'll win.*

Right now [1997], I'm seventy years old and I exercise every day. I'd feel lost if I didn't do something every day, but there's always something new to try.

■ Chapter 59

The Iran-Iraq War and the Persian Gulf, 1980–1988

The Persian Gulf extends inland from the Arabian Sea, northwest for more than six hundred miles. A wide, shallow body of water, the Gulf is more than two hundred and fifty miles wide at its widest point, while at its mouth in the Strait of Hormuz, it measures only twenty-nine miles wide. The average depth of the Gulf is only one hundred and fifty feet, the waters reaching a maximum depth of not over three hundred feet.

The major significance of the Persian Gulf are the countries that border it. Those eight countries, most on the Arabian Peninsula, are Bahrain, Iran, Iraq,

Aboard the USS *Guadalcanal*, a group of heavily armed SEALs escorts Iranian prisoners captured from the minelaying ship, the Iran *Ajr*. After treatment and interrogation, the Iranian prisoners were eventually returned to their countrymen.

U.S. Navy

The Colt M4 carbine fitted with the M203 40mm Grenade Launcher. The sliding buttstock of the M4 is in the forward (collapsed) position, and the safety of the grenade launcher is in the On position, blocking the trigger finger of a firer from entering the trigger guard of the grenade launcher.

Kevin Dockery

Kuwait, Oman, Qatar, Saudi Arabia, and the United Arab Emirates. All these countries are major oil producers. The area produces and ships more than half of the world's supply of oil, most of it going to the free world.

Long an area of conflict, the lands surrounding the Persian Gulf have seen wars and the ebb and flow of history for millennia. Today, anything that affects the flow of oil, and with it the energy it produces, can rock the world.

In January 1979 the Shah of Iran fell from power and a fundamentalist militant Islamic government moved into its place. The new government was a theocracy run by mullahs, the ultimate leader of which was the Ayatollah Khomeini. The Iranian theocracy became the founders and first major leaders of militant Islamic fundamentalism, exporting their world views, enforced by terrorism, throughout the world. Iran makes up the entire northern shore of the Persian Gulf, so can exert a strong control of the Gulf waters. That put the mullahs into a very powerful position both economically and politically.

The lack of an apparently stable leadership and government in Iran caused Saddam Hussein in Iraq to seriously consider the situation. Not only was his country now facing a border shared with an Islamic fundamentalist country—and Iran made no secret of the fact that it felt it should export its form of Islam—but the country also appeared to be at its weakest level ever. Khomeini had spent fourteen years of his life in Iraq, all of it under close house arrest. He had no fond thoughts of the Iraqi people or their leader.

Saddam Hussein felt he could strike a blow for his country and not only extend his own sphere of power, but also take back some lands traditionally considered Iraqi. If the government of the Ayatollah should fall in the process, that would be considered a plus by Saddam.

Carefully climbing onboard the subdued Iranian minelayer Iran *Ajr*, are SEALs and EOD personnel moving under the watchful eyes of armed Teammates. The Iran *Ajr* was caught during the night by Little Bird helicopters that witnessed the Iranians laying mines. Immobilized by helicopter gunfire, the abandoned *Ajr* was boarded during the early morning hours.

U.S. Navy

On 12 September 1980, Iraq launched an attack across its border with Iran. Expecting a fast and easy victory, Saddam was astonished when the fighting quickly bogged down after some quick advances by the Iraqi forces. The stalemated fighting resulted in Saddam utilizing chemical weapons to try and defeat the masses of fanatics that Iran would throw against his forces. Soon, Iraq learned how to maneuver and use chemical weapons to a greater advantage.

Now the fighting between Iran and Iraq took on global proportions, not because of Saddam's use of outlawed weapons, but because both countries tried to choke off the oil exports of the other. Stopping the flow of oil would stop the incoming flow of money, and along with it influence, support, and weapons.

The Iranian Pasdaran Islamic Revolutionary Guard Corps ran high-speed gunboats through the Gulf waters to try and stop Iraqi tanker traffic. These attacks were against almost any tankers in the Gulf waters and increased in frequency during 1986. In December 1986, Kuwait officially asked the United States to supply aid and support in preventing the attacks on their shipping. The nature of the Kuwaiti request was to allow eleven of the countries' tankers to be registered as American ships. By 10 March 1987, President Reagan agreed with the Kuwait request and Operation EARNEST WILL was planned out.

The U.S. naval vessels patrolling the Persian Gulf did not stop the Pasdaran gunboat attacks. To increase the Navy's response flexibility in the region, assets of the Navy's Special Boat Unit Eleven along with a SEAL detachment were dispatched to the Gulf in the spring of 1987.

More deployments of Naval Special Warfare assets were continually sent to the Gulf. On 6 September 1987, two oil-servicing barges, the *Hercules* and the *Winbrown 7* were leased for six months and set up as floating Special Warfare bases in the Gulf. The barges could each house ten small boats, three helicopters, more than one hundred and fifty men, and the necessary ammunition, fuel, and service support for their operations.

Looking forward of the superstructure of the Iran *Ajr*, nine Soviet Mark M-08/39 contact mines stand in line on the deck. The large mines are being examined by Navy SEALs and EOD technicians.

U.S. Navy

The U.S. Navy frigate *Stark* was struck by two Iraqi Exocet missiles on 17 May 1988. Although Iraq claimed the missiles were fired in error, that did little to make up for the thirty-seven U.S. sailors who were killed in the attack. The Persian Gulf was a dangerous place to operate in—and it was going to become more dangerous.

During the first reflagged escort mission of EARNEST WILL, the tanker *Bridgeton* struck a floating naval mine. The blast tore a fifteen-by-thirty-foot hole in the over-inch-thick steel hull of the *Bridgeton*. The ship remained afloat and there were no casualties, but the incident established that the Gulf waters were mined.

The Navy recalled six old Acme-class wooden-hulled minesweepers to duty in the Gulf. SBU (Special Boat Unit) crews would spot mines in the water and destroy them with small-arms fire. The same thing was done from the decks of larger Navy ships. SEAL marksmen also had a hand in shooting the very large reactive targets found in the Persian Gulf. On at least one occasion, a

Captured intact during Desert Storm, a Chinese-manufactured Iraqi CSS-N-2 Silkworm missile is transported by a U.S. Army truck. China sold a number of the Silkworm missiles to both Iran and Iraq as well as other foreign buyers.

U.S. Navy

SEAL swimmer entered the water and approached a floating mine to better examine it. Within a short time, the SEALs and the Navy would get a much better look at the Iranian mines.

On 21 September, deployed helicopters from the Army's Task Force 160, the Nightstalkers, spotted an Iranian ship in the act of laying mines in the Gulf. The helicopters, as were all the U.S. forces in the Gulf, were operating under very strict rules of engagement. When they received radioed permission to open fire, the helicopters fired guns and rockets at the Iranian ship, the Iran *Ajr*. As the ship tried to flee, further firing by the helicopters drove the Iranian crew to abandon ship.

A SEAL platoon from the amphibious assault ship *Guadalcanal* boarded the Iran *Ajr* along with a Marine force reconnaissance team and a detachment of EOD (Explosive Ordnance Disposal) technicians. They found a number of old Soviet M-08/39 moored contact mines, each containing some 253 pounds of TNT. Along with the mines, twenty-three Iranians were rescued from the Gulf waters. The Iran *Ajr* was examined closely, then taken out and sunk in deep water on 26 September.

Besides floating mines, Chinese-supplied HY-2 Silkworm antiship missiles became a threat when, on 16 October, an Iranian Silkworm struck the reflagged tanker *Sea Isle City* just outside Kuwait City. Seventeen crewmen and the American captain were injured by the attack. On 19 October, during Operation NIMBLE ARCHER, four destroyers shelled the two Rashadat oil plat-

A view of the complicated deck of an Iranian oil platform, partially obscured by smoke during a SEAL takeover. The elimination of several Iranian oil platforms, used as Command and Control platforms for Pasdaran speedboat attacks in the Persian Gulf were part of Operation Praying Mantis in 1987.

U.S. Navy

forms in the Rostam oil field. Through loudspeakers, the Navy officers had told the Iranian crews that they had twenty minutes to abandon the platforms. After the platforms were shelled, SEALs boarded them to search for intelligence materials. Demolition charges were planted and the platforms destroyed. In addition, the SEALs boarded and searched another oil platform two miles away. Documents and a radio were removed for examination.

After the U.S. frigate *Samuel B. Roberts* struck a mine on 14 April 1988, the United States responded vigorously. On 18 April, during Operation PRAYING MANTIS, U.S. forces attacked the Iranian frigate *Sabalan* and oil platforms in the Sirri and Sassan oil fields. After a naval gunfire bombardment, a SEAL platoon onboard a UH-60 helicopter tried to board the platform, but the heat of the burning oil fires prevented them from landing.

On 18 July 1988, Iran accepted the UN cease-fire offer. On 20 August 1988, the Iran-Iraq War was officially over. During Operation EARNEST WILL, the U.S. Navy had escorted 259 ships in 127 convoys over a 14-month period.

Looking back at the burning hulk of an Iranian oil platform from a boat carrying Navy SEALs away from their target. The muzzle of a SEAL's M203 40mm grenade launcher is seen in silhouette to the left.

U.S. Navy

Chapter 60

Panama: JUST CAUSE

The United States had signed a treaty with Panama in 1979 to defend the Panama Canal from outside threats. By 1999, the United States was scheduled to turn over control of the strategically important Panama Canal, the most direct route for shipping between the Atlantic and Pacific Oceans, back to Panama. Before half that time period had expired, the United States would be in Panama—in force.

General Manuel Antonio Noriega had been the de facto ruler of Panama since 1981. The military dictator was deeply involved in the lucrative drug trade from South America to the United States and elsewhere. Since February 1988, Noriega had been under U.S. federal indictment for money laundering and drug trafficking. As the 1980s drew to a close, Noriega stirred the population of Panama to greater and greater resentment of the United States. In late 1989, the situation reached the breaking point.

Democratic elections had been held in Panama on 7 May 1989. Overturning the results of that election, Noriega prepared to set himself up to be the president for life. On 15 December 1989, Panama's national People's Assembly, filled with Noriega appointees, declared a state of war between Panama and the United States. The next day, Panamanian troops shot and killed a U.S. Marine officer who had been driving around with some of his fellow officers looking for a local restaurant. Another Marine officer witnessed the shooting and was quickly arrested, along with his wife who was accompanying him.

This was the last straw as far as President George Bush was concerned. As the Panamanians were beating and torturing the wife and the young officer, long-held plans were put into play that same day. During the Reagan years, Operation BLUE SPOON had been put together as a military operations plan against Panama. Following President Bush's directives, the plan was put into motion as Operation JUST CAUSE. The objectives of the operation would be to neutralize military resistance to U.S. forces, capture Noriega, and return a stable democratic government to the people of Panama.

JUST CAUSE would have a three thousand–man airborne jump into the country to get U.S. troops on the ground. In addition, there were a number of special operations calling for a variety of units. Rangers, Army Special Forces, and Delta Force all had assigned tasks in support of JUST CAUSE. The Navy SEALs also had a number of missions. Naval Special Warfare Group Two deployed SEAL elements to an active combat environment expected in Panama as a Naval Special Warfare Task Group (NSWTG) for the first time.

Task Force White were the SEAL units going in to Panama. Their initial base of operations would be the Rodman Naval Station on the west side of the Panama Canal. The task force had five SEAL platoons, four riverine patrol boats, and two light patrol boats (twenty-two-foot Boston Whalers) as its primary naval assets. The SEAL and Special Boat Unit forces were broken down into three task units, each with a particular objective.

At 62 men, Task Unit Papa was the largest SEAL unit, and it had the largest job. TU Papa was made up of Bravo, Delta, and Golf Platoons from SEAL Team Four. Along with additional assets, they would deny Noriega and his forces use of the Paitilla Airfield. In particular, TU Papa was to destroy Noriega's personal Lear jet stored at the airport in order to prevent the dictator from using it to escape.

Task Unit Whiskey was made up of a single reinforced platoon of twenty-one men from SEAL Team Two. The mission of TU Whiskey would be the first operation of JUST CAUSE as two swimmer pairs of SEALs would go to Pier 18

SEALs aboard an armed Boston Whaler conduct security patrols near the Panama Canal.

U.S. Navy

in Balboa Harbor and destroy the patrol boat *Presidente Porras*. The SEALs would be conducting a swimmer attack and place heavy demolition charges, MK 138 demolition charges each containing twenty pounds of C4 plastic explosive, underneath the hull of the target ship. Their charges would be timed to go off at exactly 0100 hours on 20 December.

Task Units Charlie and Foxtrot were to respectively secure the Atlantic and the Pacific gates to the Panama Canal. At about 2300 hours on 19 December, two rubber boats with the operational crews of TU Whiskey left the Rodman Naval Station on the first leg of their mission. Using Draeger LAR-V rebreathers, the two SEAL swimmer pairs conducted their operation without casualties. At 0100 hours, the *Presidente Porras* blew into the night sky, the victim of the first successful combat swimmer attack by U.S. Navy forces.

TU Whiskey would later assist in the seizure of Noriega's yacht on 20 December as well as the securing of the Balboa Yacht Club the next day. A few days later, on 23 December, TU Whiskey would help repel PDF (Panamanian Defense Force) forces who tried to take over the merchant ship *Emanuel B* in the Panama Canal. Their final mission was the seizure of Noriega's beach house at Culebra on 25 December. The men of the unit returned to the United States on 2 January 1990.

It was Task Unit Papa that went through what turned out to be the most difficult operation the SEALs conducted during JUST CAUSE. Launching from Howard AFB Beach in fifteen rubber boats at 1930 hours local time on 19 December, the SEALs traveled the eight miles to Paitilla, arriving off their target beach at 2330 hours.

Following normal procedures, TU Papa sent out a pair of scout swimmers to recon the landing site and guide the other boats in. With the sounds of distant firing and explosions in the background, TU Papa began landing at 0045 hours on 20 December.

The element of surprise had been lost well before the SEALs reached the airfield. Forming into their platoons after penetrating the fence surrounding the airfield, the SEALs prepared to move up from the southern end of the field. Delta platoon set up a hasty ambush at the midpoint of the runway to respond to reports that Noriega was coming in on a small plane. The other two platoons continued moving up along the west side of the runway.

Arriving in front of the three targeted hangars at 0105 hours, the SEALs of Golf Platoon, which was in the lead, encountered a number of PDF troops guarding the specific hangar that held the Lear jet. Within moments, a savage firefight broke out between the SEALs and the PDF forces.

In less than a few minutes four SEALs were dead and eight more SEALs were wounded, five of them seriously. All the SEALs of TU Papa were involved in the firefight, the sharp reports and green and red tracers fire criss-crossing in the dark. By 0117 hours, the remaining PDF forces withdrew, leaving the hangar and the airfield in SEAL hands.

At 0146 hours, the SEALs were able to report that the airfield was secured. The Lear jet, in spite of last-minute order changes to save it, had been damaged in the firefight. At 0205 hours, a medevac helicopter arrived to take the wounded out for treatment. At 1400 hours on 21 December, CH-47 helicopters arrived at the airfield with the Army Ranger company that was to relieve the SEALs of Task Unit Papa.

Instead of the five hours the mission had been planned for, the SEALs had been operating for thirty-seven hours straight and suffered the worst casualties of any SEAL operation. After conducting some search-and-seizure operations, the unit was released and sent back to the United States on 1 January 1990.

Task Unit Charlie on the Caribbean end of the Canal conducted patrols and prevented shipping from entering the Canal. A firefight broke out between some PDF forces who had apparently taken control of a German merchant ship, the *Asian Senator*. After a few moments of seeing the massive firepower the SEALs had brought to the occasion, the PDF troops surrendered. TU Charlie was deactivated on 26 December.

TU Foxtrot had much the same mission on the Pacific end of the Canal, but without the firefights. The SEALs stopped and searched ships, finding a cargo

A SEAL combat swimmer dressed for land warfare comes ashore during a daylight training operation. Normally, this kind of operation is only conducted under the cover of darkness.

U.S. Navy

of looted electronic equipment aboard a Colombian vessel. The mission of TU Foxtrot ended on 2 January 1990.

Additional smaller SEAL units assisted in the search for Manuel Noriega. The Panamanian dictator was taken prisoner and removed to the United States to face trial and later imprisonment. The government of Panama that had been elected by the people in May 1989 took office in 1990.

Randy Lee Beausoleil, Warrant Officer

Back when I was about nine years old, it was my swimming coach, Coach Cunningham, who first told me about the Navy SEAL Teams. He told me he was an old Frogman from Vietnam and talked all about it. I loved swimming and swam all the way though my high school years. Coach Cunningham basically stayed with me, as he moved from the grade school that I attended to the same high school I went to.

The vision I got from his stories was one of what it was like to be in the jungle as a SEAL, as compared to what it was like to be with an Army unit, or some other large unit. From what he described to me, being with the SEALs in Vietnam sounded like the safest thing you could think of—a small unit of guys who were very well trained. They were in bad-guy territory, but they were 100 percent confident that their abilities could overcome anything in that environment. That, to me, sounded like the way that things should be done.

The one incident Coach Cunningham told me that stuck out was when he got shot in the leg. He kind of sloughed it off as no big deal. Though the particulars of that story have escaped me over time, it stuck out. Obviously, when you get hit, your own mortality kind of creeps in to the picture. You don't want to die doing this job, but that's always a possibility.

Coach Cunningham kept filling my head with stories about the SEALs. He was my mentor while I was competing, and his stories kind of stuck in my head. But when I originally joined the Navy, I didn't enlist to become a SEAL—kind of an odd twist for me. It wasn't until after three years of my enlistment passed that I started looking to volunteer for the Teams. That ended up being the path I took in my Navy career.

In August 1984, I classed up at BUD/S with Class 131, a summer into winter class but officially considered a summer class. When I got into the training, I really liked it, especially when I compared it to the other part of the Navy. In my opinion, you weren't treated like a real man when I first came into the Navy. There was a lot of pettiness, a lot of people who just didn't seem to want to treat you what your age was. When you're twenty years old, you shouldn't be treated like a ten-year-old.

When I got to BUD/S, we were off on the weekends. When we were done with training for the day, we were off-duty. That was great, and a heck of a lot better than being on a ship. I liked it.

I knew I was in trouble during training because I had never run before. That first run we went on was led by a senior chief who later ended up being the Master Chief of BUD/S. He was big and maybe a little overweight, and he took us on a two-mile run through the soft sand. I just about died during that run, so I knew I was in trouble.

But running was the only part of BUD/S I had problems with. All of the swimming events I did pretty good in, and I didn't have any problems with the other evolutions. Then there was Hell Week—that sucked pretty bad. I think that's a good way of putting it.

As a whole, Hell Week is pretty much a blur in my memories. I remember quite a bit about it. One thing I remember is that I didn't hallucinate badly like a lot of the other guys did later in the week. Extreme fatigue was very new to me, but it still didn't get me to the point that I was ready to quit and move on to something else.

Temperature extremes are something a SEAL has to get used to. I've seen some people just quit when the temperature gets extremely cold. Their body just shuts down. You can't allow your body to do that. Mentally, you have to be above that.

When I say extremely cold, it's very difficult, I think, to convey that to somebody in words. But imagine this: your core temperature, the temperature inside where all your major internal organs are, drops. Your body starts to shiver. The shivering is a way for your body to try to generate some heat. After your body shivers for so long, your hip flexors, the large muscles in your hips and the top of your legs, contract.

Now imagine having a cramp, one that runs from your mid-section all the way down to the top of your knees. All those muscles are so tight that when you stand up it's almost like you've got to have somebody straighten you out. The muscles are so cold that they're actually cold to the touch. That's how cold I've gotten in the past.

Lying on a steel pier during Hell Week makes you cold. The instructors have the old rain bird, a lawn sprinkler, running, just spitting, chiit. . . . chiit . . . chiit . . . over us. You're there all night long, in and out of the water. Your core temperature drops.

You get so cold that you can't feel your feet anymore. You can't feel your hands anymore. Your hip flexors hurt so bad that you just want to cut them out of your body. To me, that's what extreme cold is—pain.

One thing I remember about that long week was that, when it was over, when it was finally over, my feet had been cold throughout the week. Class 131 had its Hell Week in October, and I just remember my feet being cold that whole time. When we were secured late in the afternoon on Friday, I remember sticking my feet into the sand, that hot sand that had the Southern California sun beating down on it all day.

I just stood there for a while, trying to warm my feet up in the sand. Finally, Senior Chief Scarborough came by and grabbed me to tell me that I had to take my final med (medical) inspection. I was a little disappointed because my feet had finally started to warm up.

That ended the week with kind of a bang for me. I slept for eighteen hours straight and after that I was fine.

My desire to be a SEAL is what got me through Hell Week. But I never really got to that point where I really wanted to quit. I think that anyone who says that they didn't think about quitting, or how nice it would be if they did quit and go back to a normal life, is fooling themselves. You think about it at some point, but you don't quit. I never got to the point of quitting. For me, everything we did was something that was fun or new. I can't say that I enjoyed that long week, but I did definitely value the experience. That's probably the best way for me to put it.

There really isn't any specific incident that stands out in my mind from my BUD/S training. The one thing that does stand out was that first two-mile run where I realized that I was in trouble. But other than that, nothing really stands out. Everything was all so new to me. In my youth, I had been one of the kids who liked playing with GI Joes, so BUD/S to me was like playing GI Joe for real, and I loved every minute of it. I especially liked BUD/S when we got to the later phases of training, where we learned more of what being a real SEAL was all about.

So for me, BUD/S was all of that. There just wasn't any one event all though those weeks that had any more impact on me that any other event. The day I was done with training, knowing that I had accomplished that feat and was ready to move on to the Teams, was a really good one.

The weapons and demolition phase was the part of BUD/S that stood out to me with the greatest impact. The diving was nice. I had spent my life in the water, so underwater swimming wasn't really that great a change to me. They hadn't really developed a good combat swimming program at that point in BUD/S like they have now, so the diving portion didn't hold as much impact for me as it could have.

When we finally got out to San Clemente Island and started working with demolitions and getting to shoot the Army guns, that was the most fun for me. That was a great time and is something I'll never forget. Plus, I developed some pretty good friendships at BUD/S that have stayed with me over the years.

Not everything was great at San Clemente, though. I had the dubious honor of being the first guy who had to run a "flight" up to the Frog on the top of the hill at the base there. It was myself and my swim buddy, then ensign Herbert, who had to run up the hill with an eight-by-eight steel pallet on our backs, around the Frog, and back down to the starting point. That circuit was a flight, and the pallet on your back were your wings.

That very last day of training, standing on the grinder at graduation, was a tremendous relief for me. I figured the physical pain was over and we would be ready to move on to other things. I didn't realize that when I got to my Team the physical pain was only to continue.

But graduation from BUD/S still gave me a strong feeling of accomplishment. I knew I had finished something that, to me, was a monumental feat that very few people in the world will ever do. That meant a lot to me. My Dad was there at graduation and that also meant a lot. He was a World War II vet and got to see me moving forward. That definitely was a great day for me and is something that still sticks in my mind.

The Trident, the insignia of Naval Special Warfare that I wear on my uniform, signifies everything that I've accomplished. It means to me that I'm part of a small and very special unit. I am very defensive of the Trident. I get very upset when I see somebody wearing one who I feel either hasn't earned it all the way (completed BUD/S and his probationary period) or doesn't deserve to wear it and continues to do so.

My position now is one in which I have to evaluate people. I watch people who show up, and we're very strict on who actually wears a Trident. Once a man shows up at a Team, that doesn't mean he can just put it on his uniform. He has to successfully complete a six-month probationary time. And after that time is completed, we have to evaluate all the training that individual has done and we review all of his records before we put the Trident on him for the first time.

People did that to me, and it meant an awful lot to me. The day I received my Trident was a very, very big event for me. Even though there wasn't anyone there for me to share my feelings with, it meant that I had made it. Since I was nine years old, I had thought about being a Navy SEAL. I was twenty years old when I first received my Trident, so for eleven years I had thought about wearing that thing.

Every time I saw a man who was wearing a Trident, I knew that he was totally different than just about anyone else who walked the planet. Receiving the Trident was a tremendous accomplishment. BUD/S was great. And getting out of there was more of just a physical accomplishment. But receiving my Trident meant that I was recognized by all the other guys who had come before me—thousands of Team guys who had been there and some who still were—as someone who was up to snuff, someone who had earned the right to wear it. And I defend that symbol to this day with a great amount of zeal, I guess you could say.

The Trident connects every Team guy with all those who have come before him. From the guys who started off in World War II in the NCDUs to the guys who are just coming out of BUD/S and the guys who we just gave Tridents to today—they are all connected, all members of the fraternity, the brotherhood, of the Teams. They all have something in common—BUD/S. Even though training has changed some, it hasn't changed all that much where it counts. Everybody can say that they are wearing their Trident because they have accomplished that major feat, completing training.

Everybody I think equates BUD/S to Hell Week. That's definitely a separator during training, but the amount and level of training that a SEAL gets is what separates him more from everybody else out there. That means a great deal.

After I graduated BUD/S and completed Jump School, my first assignment was to SEAL Team Two in Little Creek, Virginia. I arrived there on 10 April 1985, and they pretty much stuck me. There was going to be four or five months yet before I could go through my SEAL Tactical Training, which is the training that every Team gives you to indoctrinate you in the way they do business.

So they stuck me in the air operations department and threw me out of a plane a couple days later in my first free fall. So my four months before I started my tactical training and getting into my platoon was spent jumping. That was a great experience for me.

I did feel a real connection with the old SEALs who had come before

A student from BUD/S Class 83 in 1975 heads for the ground after jumping from the top of an obstacle. Trainees are expected to constantly better their time in completing the BUD/S obstacle course, and continued practice under the watchful eyes of SEAL instructors helps ensure that this happens.

U.S. Navy

me when I arrived at SEAL Team Two. At Team Two, we had a lot of history still walking the deck. We still had Rudy Boesch as our Command Master Chief. Rudy Boesch had been at the Team since the first dinosaur went through BUD/S, and he was just a hell of a guy. He wasn't a great storyteller, but Rudy would go with you to your land warfare training up at Camp A.P. Hill. That's where he would talk to you about Vietnam and tell you stories of what Team Two did there. When he retired, he had more than forty-five years in the Navy, and he had been at Team Two for about twenty-five of those years.

When I saw Rudy Boesch for the first time, I wondered just who this old guy was. I got to the Team in 1984, and I could be mistaken, but I think he was around fifty-seven years old at the time. Here was a guy who had been in the Navy since 1945, near the end of World War II. This guy was our Command Master Chief, the senior enlisted guy at our command, and he ran the physical training program at SEAL Team Two.

Every Monday morning, you went out to quarters and you didn't have a choice. You made a right face and ran out the gate, with Rudy leading the way. We would get out and do forty-five minutes of PT—push-ups, sit-ups, pull-ups, and everything else you could think of. And after that, you would go out on a nice five-mile run.

And it wasn't a five-mile run like I'd thought about, the old Army guys singing a cadence and jogging in formation. No, this was an all-out, gut-wrenching run as fast as you could because if you didn't, you were a turd. And there was Rudy, deep in the thick of it.

Tuesdays was always a swim. When we swam, it wasn't in a pool, it was out in the water whether it was wintertime and twenty-eight degrees or summertime and eighty degrees. And every time, there was Rudy.

Wednesdays was always the o-course day. We did four little obstacle courses and one big obstacle course. They were just different types of o-courses. And there was Rudy, running right through the course along with everyone else.

Thursdays we kinda did our own thing. Fridays was a nice, long, ten-mile run. And there was Rudy. It amazed me. I was thinking that here was a man who was fifty-seven, he was about the age of my dad. My dad is in good health, but this guy was busting it out with all the other SEALs—and this was after nearly forty years in the military already.

Rudy was beating young guys straight out of BUD/S. It was an embarrassment if you were behind Rudy on anything. Quite Frankly, Rudy was always between the middle and the upper part of the pack. It was hard to beat him. That's just mind-boggling.

You would know when you met Rudy Boesch for the first time. Here would be a man with a kind of a tan, a flat-top haircut, and a New Jersey accent. He would be fit and in shape. But when he told you how old he was, you wouldn't think that he looked a day over forty. But he was in his late fifties. He's pretty amazing.

It's not that there's something just about an old Navy SEAL guy. There's nothing about the old guys that really separates them from the new crowd, other than maybe the way they carried themselves. But they did set a standard that you have to work at to reach.

How important is it for the new SEALs to know and remember what the old SEALs and UDT men have done before us? Talking about the old guys, I can look from my father's perspective, and I can look from the perspective of all the older Team guys who have been before me. I have been a member of the Special Operations community for a long time. My dad was Airborne in the Army so he, too, was in a special group of men.

I don't think it's fair for anyone who has not been in the military to talk or make decisions about what happens to people in the military. I come from a military background, and when I look at all the older guys the things that they have done are amazing to me. But they all did it for one reason—because they were called to do it, not because what they did was something they wanted to do. They were called to do it because it was part of their job.

The things I've done in the SEAL Team was all a part of my job. And I look at it that way. I get very defensive about our history. I think it's very important to honor the older guys because they were the ones who paved the way, not only for our country, because a major part of our history has happened in the last fifty years, but also for how I do business today.

If it wasn't for the older guys, and all the sacrifices they made, all the safety we have in training now, all the tactics we use now that have been refined more than fifty years—things that save lives today—we wouldn't have them if it wasn't for those guys who did all of that in the past. Without the older people, especially those men who came through the SEAL Teams, where would we be now? We would be starting over. We would be the old guys, because fifty years down the road the new SEALs will be saying the same things about us—which I hope they do.

We should be setting precedents now to help save lives in the future. The better we do our job, and the better that the United States does its job when it does comes to conflict, the fewer people are going to die. I don't think anybody wants to see people die, although that is part of our job. But more than that, my job is to make sure that nobody who works with me dies. I'd rather the bad guy die for his cause and my guys come back and be able to meet with the old guys.

So when I got to Team Two, we still had Rudy, and there were others—Mikey Boynton, Pierre Birtz, and quite a few of the guys who had been in Vietnam—there to give us their knowledge. They had been in the Teams or the UDTs before that. All those guys were all around us, so it was kind of hard not to be a part of the history. SEAL Team Two has a very thick and proud history to go along with it.

To this day, when people ask me where I'm from, I always mention SEAL Team

Two. I'm at SEAL Team Three now (1998), but my heart's still at SEAL Team Two, and it'll always be there. I hope to get assigned back there some day.

The Vietnam vets in the Teams were guys who we always held up on a pedestal in a way. You've heard all the stories before you even meet the guys. At BUD/S, all the instructors tell all the stories about how great it was for the SEALs back then. I followed through with a habit of mine. I'm the type kind of guy who always looks into things I'm wondering about.

SEAL Team Two had a pretty good history when it came to Vietnam. They lost nine guys who were killed in action; six of those were killed in a situation that might have been preventable. That's a pretty good identifier of just how well SEAL Team Two did its business. And that carried on to the training that I got from my first platoon, for my first deployment, and all the other platoons I did after that.

All the older guys had pretty much set in stone how training was going to happen at Team Two, so you knew that you were getting trained by someone who had twenty years of background and sound tactics behind him. You knew that you were learning something that a lot of guys bled for and that a lot of guys had used many, many times in real combat. That meant a lot to me, so I didn't take anything for granted.

When somebody was talking, especially the old Vietnam vets, you listened. And I brought those men back to the Teams. I had a lot of retired Vietnam vets who I brought back to some of my later platoons when I had become senior and was the LPO (leading petty officer) and later still chief of a platoon. I brought those guys back and paid their way to come to wherever we were at just to talk to the younger guys. We had started losing a lot of those older Vietnam vets who had all that combat experience.

It means a lot to me to have those guys around. And I still draw on that vast well of knowledge. It was a tragedy when Mikey Boynton was lost a few years ago, because he was one of the guys who I brought to just about every training evolution I did.

Mikey Boynton is just one of those guys who seemed to have been around everywhere. You see the old video Men in Green Faces that was used for recruiting into the Teams, and Mikey was one of the guys getting his Silver Star out there on Turner Field. You saw this big, thick-necked guy standing there as they pinned a medal on him, and you wondered just who the heck that guy was. Then you showed up at SEAL Team Two, and there he was. I had been there a couple years before he came back to Team Two and just showed up. I knew automatically who he was.

Going right up to him, I said, "I don't know your name, but I remember you from the video."

He introduced himself and was the most likable guy you'll ever meet in your life. And he knew what he was talking about. Here was a guy who had been through some pretty wild things, which are all in the books now. So when you go through some training and Mikey said, "You'd better listen to that," or "You'd better do that," you did exactly what he said. And he would pull you aside and say, "Hey, I heard about some of the things you guys did. You might want to think about doing it this way . . ." That's a pretty weighty source of advice, so you listened.

Mikey was a great friend up to the time I left Team Two and until he died.

My first actual combat operation was as a combat swimmer attack on Noriega's boat in Panama during Operation JUST CAUSE. My platoon, Hotel Platoon at SEAL Team Two, had been gearing up for what was called a EUCON deployment, which goes to Europe. We had just formed up that July (1989) as a full platoon and had started our pre-deployment training.

For us, the two major blocks of our pre-deployment training were land warfare and combat swimmer. Combat swimmer was basically diving with the closed-circuit Draeger rigs and learning how to navigate underwater in order to get to whatever target you had to.

So those two blocks of instruction were very major, and we started with land warfare training. The officer we started with developed a medical problem so he had to be relieved. Then we got a new officer in the platoon, Lieutenant Ed Coughlin. He and I had gone through BUD/S together; he had been an ensign while I had been an E-5. We knew each other right away, and we just happened to click immediately.

Lieutenant Coughlin had come into the platoon at that time because they (the higher command) knew some things I didn't know. Command knew that the invasion of Panama was probably going to happen soon, and that our platoon was probably going to be the ready platoon at SEAL Team Two for that operation. The ready platoon is the platoon that has been through most of their pre-deployment training and is the next platoon that will head out the door on a deployment.

We were kind of the more senior platoon at the Team in relation to training, not age. We were going to become the ready platoon in December, we knew that. It was finally revealed what was going to happen down in Panama. Because SEAL Team Four's and SEAL Team Two's standard operating procedures were a little different, it was decided that because SEAL Team Two had done most of the training with a fairly major combat swimmer block, and because we had worked with a lot of foreign swimmer units and done a lot of combat swimming, we would be tasked with a special dive op in Panama.

The dive op was strictly to deny Noriega the use of his patrol boats that were going to be docked in Balboa Harbor on the southern part of the canal. Quite frankly, that's about two thousand yards across the canal from the U.S. Naval Special Warfare Unit that was based in Panama at the time.

So we were tasked with that op, and we practiced for that mission. We did a lot of dives, and combat swimming became second nature to everybody in my platoon. We dove so much that diving was as common and natural as breathing or sleeping.

That combat swimmer–type operation is something we're trained to do, that every Team is trained to do. It just so happened that we had worked a little bit more at it.

That dive op was our task, and we knew it inside and out. We had spent six to nine weeks just conducting combat swimmer–type attacks for practice. It was the beginning of December, by the time we got done with all that and we started to wind down as far as training went. Right around 13 December, we were tasked to go down to Florida with a bunch of other people, other units, in order to rehearse for the op we would do in Panama. At the time, we didn't know specifically what the op or the target was. That wasn't made clear to us until later.

During our rehearsal, we tried to keep everything pretty much the same as we would experience on the real op. I was very strict on making sure all the guys who dove that night would be diving with the exact equipment they would be diving with in Panama.

That was kind of hard, because the water in Florida at that time of year was only about 50 degrees, and the water in Panama was over 90 degrees, so we had to find sort of a happy medium. In Florida we were freezing our butts off practicing that dive. Just about all four of us got hyped out—hypothermia—in the Florida water. It was hard to stay warm the three days following that, but the practice paid off.

I like to train people so they're going to do exactly the same thing in training that they will in combat. And if we have an opportunity to rehearse the op, they're going to keep rehearsing until they are so tired of rehearsing that they can do it in their sleep—which is what we did.

Right around 16 December, that particular exercise was over and myself and four other guys were supposed to stay in Florida to do some other training, some follow-on stuff. On the seventeenth, we were recalled and had to drive to Atlanta and then fly to Norfolk, Virginia.

It was in Norfolk that we met up with the rest of our platoon, who were already back and getting prepared. At Team Two, we had a little cover story for what we had been doing. The exercise we had just been on was something all the guys at Team Two knew about but not what it was for. They certainly didn't know that it was practice for a real operation.

Our CO had told the guys at the Team that our platoon had screwed up the exercise so we had to do it again. They threw us into Isolation, a secured area where we have no contact with the outside world and very little contact even with the Team. While we were in Isolation, the rest of the Team was pointing their fingers at us like we were a bunch of bad little boys.

But all the guys in the platoon knew what was going on. Plus we had some additional guys who we augmented the platoon with who were let in on what was really going on. At this point, we all knew that we were going to do the real deal.

So we flew to Panama in the middle of the night of 18 December. We climbed onboard a C-141 with all the guys from SEAL Team Four and all the live ammunition that you never get to see in training, and flew to Panama. We arrived in Panama around 8 o'clock in the morning on December 19, 1989.

Everything was supposed to happen at 0100 hours on the twentieth, so we were getting in the water that night. From 8 o'clock in the morning when we first hit the ground, we were only seventeen hours out. This fast reaction is the same kind of stuff that we train for. For the operation, we had a clock, a timer, and a firing device that nobody had ever seen before. It was real-time clock that you set with the current time and the time you wanted it to go off and it started a countdown.

We got all our charges ready. The target we were going after was an aluminum-hulled Swift boat, made in the USA. The limpet mine we normally use has magnets on it to hold it to the target, but we couldn't use it to secure the limpets to the target. There are some other things we could use, some stud drivers that secure a limpet to the target with an explosively fired nail, but we were worried that on a small craft—the Swift was only a sixty-five foot patrol boat—with the engines not running, the bad guys would hear the studs going off into the hull.

So we decided to use just a regular, standard haversack charge of high explosives. The special clock was attached with a safety and arming device, which is a device that keeps the charge from going off for at least fifteen minutes after it is set. That delay gives you some time to get away in case the clock was to malfunction and go off early.

All of that was stuffed into the haversack, which already held twenty pounds of C-4 plastic explosive. The haversacks were strapped to the swimmer backpacks that we normally carry our training limpet mines on. That's what we dove with.

Our prep work went on in the morning. There was only one target boat in the water. Originally, the platoon was told that there could be up to eight boats that would have to be targeted, but on this day, there was only one so we decided on four divers. Two guys who were picked were myself and Lieutenant Coughlin. We were the most senior guys in the platoon and had done the most diving. Then we picked our dive buddies. My dive buddy was Chris Dye, the most calm, cool, and collected cucumber you could ever find to dive with. Then we picked the other guy who became the lieutenant's swimmer pair because he could drive a compass like nobody's business.

The four of us got our rigs ready, then the wait began. This was a drill we had done a hundred times before, so there wasn't anything new to us. By about 3 or 4 in the afternoon, we were done getting ready. Although you're getting things done, you aren't thinking too much about anything but the job at hand. But after that, you have all that time to rest or get some sleep before your first contest.

All our gear was ready and we just sat. I told all my guys to get some sleep, but it wasn't easy. If you've been in combat before, the wait might have been a little

In the swimming pool during training, a BUD/S student intently watches the indicator on the compass of his attack board. His swim-buddy, to the side and slightly above him, would watch out for obstacles and dangers in the water as his partner "drives" the compass.

easier, but none of us had. That was the most difficult part—the wait for that first dive. The anticipation was killing everybody.

I think we all were very confident about the operation. I was and I know my buddy was. But you never know just how things are going to go. You never know just what branch is going to be turned or what Murphy is going to throw at you.

We were supposed to get in the water that night at 11 o'clock—two hours before H-Hour. Because of all the different fears that were around at the time as far as whether or not the Panamanians knew when H-Hour was, Command didn't want us to get in the water and start diving too early. Once they put us in the water, there was no way of calling us back.

If the commanding general decided that H-Hour was going to change to, say, the next day and we were in the water, that boat was going to blow up that night. So Command had to be sure, and they backed us up a half-hour, which wasn't good for us because we had added in some crunch time on our dive.

By 10:30 the night of the nineteenth, we were across the canal from our target and put our boats in the water. Getting our dive rigs on, we were wearing exactly the same equipment we had on during rehearsal. I knew that once I got into the water, nothing was going to change for me. I would immediately be able to start diving.

Right about 11:15 or so, we decided it was time to be going. Because of the current that came down the Panama Canal when the gates were opened up north, we couldn't just get in the water and start our dive and go across the canal and hit the target. That was a little too chancy, because the current was never consistent. One minute it could be zero, and the next it could be running at five knots.

So we got into two zodiacs, one pair in each boat along with a driver, a communicator (radio operator), and M60 gunner. Driving across the canal, we hid the boats in a mangrove just north of the target. Our CO at the time, Commander Carley, decided at that point that it was time to insert us into the water. It was about 11:30 at night.

At that point, we started motoring over to the insert point, where we were going to get off and enter the water. We started breathing on our rigs before we ever got into the water to make sure we weren't going to have any problems with them.

The boat I was in was having some problems, and the motor wasn't idling all that well. It had been tuned pretty much for the fifty degree water back around Florida. We hadn't had an opportunity to lean them out for the warmer water around Panama. So our boat conked out.

They went ahead with the other boat and inserted the first swimmer pair into the water. Then they came back and took the bow line on our boat and motored us out to where we were going to get into the water, just outside of the mangrove. Myself and Chris just slipped over the side of the boat and immediately went under the water and started diving. There was no wait for us.

At that point, both Chris and I felt very normal. This was something that we were very familiar with. All the anticipation and anxiety immediately went away for me because I was doing exactly what I knew how to do.

We hadn't swum more than a minute or two before we hit a tree that was under the water. It had obviously fallen down at some point and become waterlogged. Chris and I had dove so much together that we knew exactly what to do. Chris climbed up on my back and we drove right through the obstacle, got to the other side, and kept on diving. It was nothing new to us.

That tree was something that might have thrown us off earlier on in our training. We would have been down there wrestling around in the quagmire of branches. But it didn't really affect us because of the amount of training that we had. As we kept on diving, we hit the first big pier that was our first reset point.

Without going into all the sordid details, because of the little things that did happen, Chris and I had decided at that point that diving underneath the pier was the better option for us. What worried us was the large current that would flow through the open area when the gates were opened.

Driving with the compass out in the open water probably wasn't the best way to go for that op, but it was something that we had trained for so Chris and I followed the long pier that led down to our target using the available light to guide us on our way.

The boat was docked on a floating cement pier that had two halves, about seventy-five yards each half. The floating pier was big enough that a six-by (2½ ton) truck could have driven along it. The pier had a big old awning over it, and there were a lot of fluorescent lights underneath it.

All the water within fifty yards of that pier was just like daylight to us, so as we were diving up to the target, we could see it coming. There was a ship parked on the outside of the pier, so we were still diving along the outside of that ship. As soon as the water grew light, we knew we were within about fifty yards of the pier.

We cut in at a forty-five and drove on until we hit that floating cement pier. Once there, we got down underneath it to maintain our concealment and started diving down to where the target was.

Remember, we were running into a time-crunch. When you're driving around a pier underwater, it's not as fast as swimming in the open. We were backed up about a half-hour on our schedule, so that fudge factor we had in our schedule wasn't there any more and now we were worried about time.

Because of the clock on the charge and everything else, we had to arm that thing thirty minutes prior to when we wanted it to go off, which was 1 o'clock in the morning on the twentieth.

We were starting to come up on the time that we really had to get that thing up on the boat. As we continued on, I could hear something that sounded like some-body on top of the pier dropping fifty-five-gallon drums on the cement. I didn't know what it was; it just sounded like somebody was up there working. They were going to be dead in a few minutes anyway.

But we kept on going and got to where the boat was. We could tell we had gotten to the boat because there was a nice big shadow in the water to our right side where the boat was docked, butt-end in against the pier.

Immediately, we went underneath the boat. Chris got all the way underneath the target. I stuck one hand on the boat and one on the pier and kind of let myself up a bit so I could make sure the number on the boat was the proper one.

My head just broke the surface and I could see the number, "P202." It was the right one. It was at that point that I figured out what was going on up on the pier. Somebody was up there, one foot on the boat and one foot on the pier, and he was definitely a bad guy. He had a gun in his hand, and he was frantic about something.

All I did was go right back underneath the boat, and I don't think Chris and I spent more than a minute there. All we did was take off the backpack and clip it onto the boat around a propeller shaft. Then we prepared the clock and armed it. I checked everything, then Chris and I went back under the pier and we started on our way out.

It turned out that the other swimmer pair had gotten into the water about five minutes before we did. But we just happened to get to the target before they did, I think because of the route we selected. They were only maybe a minute behind us.

They got to the target and put their charge on, connected the two, and were on their way out. During the whole dive, I don't think we were more than a hundred yards apart, even though we never saw each other.

On the way out I was pretty much straightforward in the route we chose. Because of the time crunch and because of the way the piers were constructed and our fears about that big current when the gates were opened, we stuck close to the pier on the way out. So it was slow-going again.

Chris and I were maybe five hundred yards down when it came time that the charge would be going off. At that point, he and I got as far back up underneath the piers as we could. You could say we broke a tactic at that point because we surfaced, put our rigs offline, and just sat there. The water was so hot at that point. It was over ninety degrees, and we had been practicing in fifty-degree water, and we were overheating. That made it a good time for us to stop and get something to drink from our canteens and listen for that charge to go off.

The only problem was that everything had started early and it would be hard to hear the shot. With any kind of detonation that goes off in the water, the sound is pretty muffled. Because I had been the one who set the clocks by my watch, I was counting down to the firing time. There was so much stuff going on at that point that I never did hear the shot go off.

Not hearing the shot made me pretty worried. Something was wrong. But what are you going to do? The only thing we could do now was extract, get back, and continue on with the next mission.

It was at that point that my mind started working against me. I started thinking that because that guy on the pier had been so frantic, the other pair of swimmers could have been compromised. If they were, could they have found the charges? That might have been why they didn't go off.

It turned out that I was all wrong. The charges went off exactly on time. There had been some people across the way that had set their watches to mine. They counted it down, and the charge went right off. The boat actually came out of the water and then settled back down. A piece of it landed next to a friend of mine who gave it to me almost three months later. He came back and gave me this piece of the hull and said, "Hey, this is from your boat. It blew up and then this piece landed next to me." I still have it. You keep that kind of stuff.

So Chris and I were stopped underneath the pier. It was a good time to get some water and cool down because we were really hot. Part of our tasking was that we were supposed to have made it farther on and actually called back on a radio to our higher-ups and tell them that the charges were on the boat. But because of the time crunch, that wasn't going to happen. We were still so close to the boat after we had set the charge that we just didn't get far enough away with enough time allowed to call back and let them know the charges were on.

Once we were done and all cooled off, we decided to get going again. We got our rigs back on and started diving back out. When a boat blows up in the water and there are other boats docked near it that might be of questionable origin, boat crews worry about guys like us. There had been some large ships docked along that pier and they started jacking their screws—they started turning their propellers while they were still next to the pier to potentially blow a diver off the bottom of the boat.

I know of one boat that felt like it was doing that to me. But after that, the dive out along that pier was pretty much like standard training. When we got past the end of the pier, we were supposed to dive out and box around an area that had some additional piers where some larger ships were docked in a dry dock area. So we were going to box out around it, make ninety-degree turns to our heading, and go around the area rather than trying to run past underwater lines and whatever else might have been there. We were worried about getting sucked up into the suction intakes underneath one of the boats.

Diving out away from the boats was all part of our plan. It was pretty simple. But the gates must have been finally opened and a good current was heading down the canal at that point. What was supposed to be a twelve-minute leg out that should have put us a few hundred yards out, ended up putting us a lot farther out into the bay.

Both dive pairs, us and the other pair, ended up right in the middle of the canal, because as the current came it pushed us a little bit faster than we had figured. So as we started our westbound leg to get out of that op area, I started hearing a large ship moving through the water.

When you're underwater, ship sounds carry pretty far. When you have a large ship coming, it can get bad. And I've been under some big ships before, aircraft carriers and the like, and I knew that whatever was coming at us was big, so I started going deeper in the water. When you're diving a pure-oxygen rig like we were, the deeper you go, the more toxic oxygen becomes to your system.

We were still within the depth limits of the training that we had done before, so I was very confident that nothing was going to happen to us—but I could still hear that ship coming.

The approaching ship was getting louder and louder. It was dark in that water. There was a lot of bioluminescence in the water when all the little microorganisms glow like little fireflies when you move through them, but I wasn't worried about that showing us up. We were far enough away from the piers for that. But it was still really dark in the water.

We hit about thirty-five feet of depth, and I was thinking to myself that I had no idea of just how deep in the water a big freighter drives, so I wanted to go a little bit deeper. I don't think Chris wanted to go that deep because he was pulling me the other way as I pulled him down deeper. We ended up down around forty-five feet, and that ship above us was extremely loud.

There's a strap that goes around the breathing rig's mouthpiece that's there just in case you go underneath a ship. The noise vibrates you so much that your teeth can't hold the mouthpiece in your mouth. So you cinch that strap down so that the mouthpiece won't come out.

When we were down there at forty-five feet and I heard that boat coming, I reached up to tighten up my straps. Just as I did that, I heard the zip-zip sound of Chris tightening his straps. He tightened them at the same time I was planning to. He had been thinking exactly the same thing that I had been thinking. We definitely were in sync with each other.

It was dark, but when that ship went over the top of us, the water got even darker. It was unbelievably loud and passed right over our heads. We probably were only at that depth for five minutes or so. As soon as that freighter went over the top of us, both Chris and I swayed back and forth a little bit—that meant the screw was over and had already passed. We both were thinking the same thing and headed straight for the surface.

We were not thinking about the bad guys at that point, whether or not there was somebody on the back of that freighter looking for a diver in the wake. I went to the surface so I could take a bearing and figure out which way I wanted to go. What I wanted to do was extract and get picked up by my guys because there was now a war going on around us.

After taking a compass bearing on the extract pier, I went back down, and Chris and I dove as fast as we could to the pier. We ended up getting back to the pier and because all of the work we had done getting there, we decided to stop again, vent ourselves a little bit, and take on some water. That put us a little behind the other swim pair. They had decided not to stop and had just gone on to the extract.

At the end of the pier we were under was another pier. It was at the end of that second pier that our boats were supposed to have been sitting and picked us up.

Because of everything that was going on, that spot was pretty much out in the open. The boats moved to the pier before the planned op, staying away from the bad guys and doing what they were supposed to do.

We got to that point and I was just going to go up and radio that we were late but we were coming. As I ascended, I was still in between the pilings, and I popped out of the water right between two zodiacs.

Like a knucklehead, I went right back down, wondering what the Panamanians were doing underneath the pier in black zodiacs. Then it dawned on me that they probably didn't have black zodiacs and that those had probably been our guys. So I went back up and took a look at the engine without exposing myself above the water. Sure enough, there was a big blue "H" painted on the side of the engine. I surfaced and obviously it was our guys.

I had to splash a little bit in order to let them know I was there. Then we took our rigs off, they pulled us into the boat, and we headed back over to the good guy's side, down by the naval facility across the canal.

All in all, the operation probably took us about five hours, in and out. It was a long op, but it was standard. There was nothing we did that any other SEAL Team couldn't have done. We were just lucky enough that our platoon was there. And I feel that we were the most prepared for that particular job.

The dive went flawlessly. It went just as it should have and exactly as we had planned except maybe for the stops to prevent us from overheating. It turned out to have been a great op for us. And we were rewarded nicely for it.

There aren't any SEALs that I know of who'll pat themselves on the back, because you get humbled every day in SEAL Team. Every day you go to work and although you might think you're the hot thing on the block that day, there's always somebody that's better than you in something. That has a humbling effect.

I go and I work with these guys, and I might think that I'm the greatest at this inside. Then, I meet somebody who's better at it or there's somebody who can teach me something I don't know. So it's kind of hard to feel at all superior when you're in a group of what I perceive to be amazing people. I not saying that there's not a lot of amazing people outside the Teams, but SEALs, in my opinion, are the most amazing people on the planet because of what they do and how they do it. And they go home at the end of the day to the wife and kids, and it's like nothing ever happened that day.

And you also get humbled by the older guys. Some of the stuff we do today, the stuff we think is great, that we did this monumental feat—Hey, I did this great and wonderful thing. Then you hear stories from an old guy that make what you did seem like just eating breakfast. That's pretty humbling. It has a humbling effect to just be around people of the caliber that SEALs are.

I feel gratified that I'm a SEAL. I don't feel lucky, because there was nothing about luck that got me to where I was. It was putting forth effort that got me here. But I do feel gratified that I am here, because every day I get to come to work with people who there isn't a match for anywhere else on the planet. You just can't find people of this caliber. I hear it all the time from guys who retire, get out of the Navy, and go on to other work places. They just say that it's not the same.

That's why we get so many people back at our reunions. That's why we have so many guys get out of the Navy and soon come back in. They go out into what I call the real world and see that there's nothing like what we do every day.

There's a camaraderie there, because when you go to work in the Teams every day, you banter back and forth, call each other names, and do whatever. That doesn't happen anywhere else like it does here. And with us, it's all in fun. Hopefully you don't see all the back-biting and that kind of thing in the SEAL Team as you do in the real world, although I'm not saying that it doesn't happen, but it's at a minimum. It's nothing like what's out there in the rest of the world.

One thing I don't want to see in the future is the core basics of training that everyone has gone through in the past change all that much. I think most of the changes need to be at the Team level. That's what bonds SEALs together, training. Every SEAL, no matter where he's been or what he's done, can always talk about BUD/S.

There's one thing that a SEAL will never forget, and that's his class number. You can always talk about BUD/S. I might have a guy who went through Class 1 and a guy who went through Class 217, and they can both talk about their experiences at BUD/S. What's amazing is, if you're outside the conversation, how a lot of the stories are the same as what you could tell.

The one word I can use to describe what I do and what we do as a group is amazing. I am always astonished at what new thing can come up, and how we will accomplish that new mission or reach that new goal. I think we would be grossly neglecting ourselves or our training if we didn't keep up with the pace of the world around us. Of course, the world is always changing, and the SEALs have to change right along with it.

I don't want to say technology is the wave of the future, but it is something that we will have to use to do our job better. And we have to be on the leading edge of that technology. We need the money and the backing and everything else to make sure that the SEAL of the future is equipped with what he needs to properly go out and do his job.

There's always going to be the basic equipment—knife, gun, explosives, that kind of thing—but there's a lot of technology, a lot of electronics, that we need to have, too. So the SEAL of the future not only has to be a physical specimen in order to go out and do the things we do in and out of the water, but he also has to be smart and educated. We're constantly upgrading our training to keep pace with the technology and all the other things that are happening out there in the world.

If we sit on our laurels and rest, the world's going to pass us by. And just how effective is a group of SEALs going to be if they go out on a mission ill-prepared? They aren't going to be effective at all.

The Hollywood version of a SEAL is this good-looking guy. He's big, buff, and carries a lot of guns that he uses to kill a lot of people. But that's such a small part of our job. I might be six-foot-one and 210 pounds, but I work with guys every day who are five-foot-five and 150, and they're doing exactly the same job I'm doing, they're swimming though the same surf I am. And there are guys in the Teams who are bigger than I am. I've got guys who are six foot six and 260.

The stereotypical SEAL you get in the movies comes nothing close to the guys I work with every day. We've got guys who are single and guys who have five, six, or seven kids. They go home every day to their families and have a normal life, then they come to work and perform on an unbelievable level. It's this diversity that I find intriguing every day I go to work.

You've got guys who have families that they go home to. They can't be in the same mind-set at home as they are at work. They can't be that way with their kids. But when you are at work, you have to be focused. If you're not focused on the task at hand in our job, you're going to die. And you can die any day. That's what's so weird about being a SEAL.

You come to work, but you might not go home the next day. It's the same as it is with police officers, firemen, and other guys who are out there on the edge. One day in the Teams, you might be jumping out of airplanes. The next day, you're diving under water. Any one of the things you do on a daily basis could do you in, so you have to be focused, and you have to be hard. But it's nice to be able to see that guys can differentiate between the two. That's something you probably don't see in the movies.

The other thing you don't see in the movies is how one minute, a SEAL can be sitting at his home base, and the next minute he can be overseas killing bad guys. One thing Hollywood doesn't show you is the hours and hours of packing, palletizing, flying, and waiting at airports for airplanes—the military's airplanes break down just like anybody else's. The negative side of traveling to get to where we have to go to do our job is not something Hollywood will show you.

■ Chapter 61

DESERT SHIELD/DESERT STORM

The end of the Iran-Iraq War allowed shipping to return to relatively normal in the Persian Gulf region. The aftermath of the war left the Iraqi economy in a shambles. The infrastructure of the country was damaged, primary Iraqi port facilities on the Gulf were choked with wreckage and unexploded ordnance, goods were difficult to move, and exports of oil were equally hard to get out of the country.

The Iran-Iraq War resulted in Iraq being deeply in debt to much of the world, especially its neighboring Arab states. The other major result of the war was a militarily weakened Iran and a militarily very powerful Iraq. Saddam Hussein was now in control of military assets that added up to Iraq having the fourth largest standing army in the world after the United States, China, and the Soviet Union. And Saddam's was a bloodied, combat-experienced military with 955,000 troops under arms, 5,500 armored vehicles and tanks, 3,500

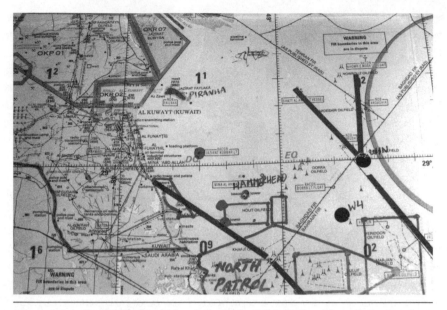

A close-up view of a map of the Kuwaiti shore in the Persian Gulf during Desert Storm. The map was hanging in the ready room of Fighter Squadron 41 (VF-41) aboard the nuclear-powered aircraft carrier USS *Theodore Roosevelt* (CVN-71). At the center of the shoreline on the left side of the map is Kuwait City.

U.S. Navy

pieces of artillery, and 665 combat aircraft. It was by far the largest, fully equipped, modern army in the Middle East.

On 2 August 1990, at 2 A.M. local time (1100 Zulu, 1 August) Saddam Hussein ordered 100,000 troops and tanks across his southeastern border and into Kuwait. There was little prior warning of the invasion detected by the United States or the other countries in the Gulf region. There was even less effective resistance put forward by the limited Kuwaiti forces. The small country was overwhelmed and conquered in less than half a day. Within a week, Hussein declared Kuwait the Nineteenth Province of Iraq.

Under orders from the Commander-in-Chief, President George Bush, the U.S. military immediately put standing plans into effect to reinforce the Saudi Arabian border with Iraq and Occupied Kuwait. The U.S. Central Command (CENTCOM) held the primary U.S. military responsibility for the region. As CENTCOM finalized preparations to send U.S. forces into the area, the special operations component of CENTCOM made ready to put special operations forces into the area as soon as possible.

Within a few days of the invasion, a five-ship amphibious group left Norfolk, Virginia, en route to the Mediterranean. A detachment of SEALs were onboard the ships as part of a normal component of a deployed amphibious group. A stop in North Carolina brought 2,100 Marines onto the amphibious group, which then continued on across the Atlantic. Originally scheduled to go into the Mediterranean for maneuvers, the group now was being deployed to the Persian Gulf and Saudi Arabia.

On the West Coast, a 105-man Naval Special Warfare Task Group (NSWTG-1) assembled from Navy Special Warfare Group One assets in Coronado, arrived in Saudi Arabia on 10 August 1990. A second group of NSWTG-1 personnel arrived incountry almost a month later on 9 September. Operation DESERT SHIELD, the defense of Saudi Arabia, had begun immediately with the first of the U.S. forces being deployed to the Middle East in August.

To establish a "tripwire" warning system, as well as to direct close air support if needed and gather intelligence on Iraqi deployments and movements, SEAL elements were deployed to the Saudi Arabian–Kuwait border on 19 August. The SEALs remained in position, maintaining listening and observation posts dangerously close to the border, until the SEALs began to be gradually relieved by assets from the 5th Special Forces Group beginning on 5 September. The SEALs had been the first U.S. combat forces to directly face Iraqi troops. They had the ability to call in air strikes from the limited U.S. forces available. But if the Iraqis had decided to invade Saudi Arabia, the SEALs could expect to do little more than raise the alarm and attempt to withdraw.

Within days of the Iraqi invasion, the second of many UN resolutions against the situation in Kuwait was made. UN Resolution 661 of 6 August imposed trade sanctions against Iraq and Kuwait. By 25 August, teeth were put into the trade sanctions when UN Resolution 665 went into effect. Resolution 665 allowed the use of limited Naval force to ensure compliance with the embargo of goods to Iraq. The SEALs became a close part of that "limited" naval force.

Visit, Board, Search, and Seizure (VBSS) operations were conducted by various naval elements of the Coalition forces. One of the more common landing parties were Navy SEALs moving in to a stopped ship by small boat, or fast roping down and seizing a ship that refused to stop for inspection. SEALs conducted these VBSS operations at all times and in all kinds of weather. Airborne SEAL snipers in helicopters would circle stopped ships to provide precision fire support to their Teammates aboard the ship. Many of the techniques used were developed or directly adapted from those of SEAL Team Six. The VBSS mission has since become a standard part of the SEAL training and mission parameter.

Missions continued to be conducted by the SEALs task group in support of DESERT SHIELD and in the buildup of native coalition naval special operations units. A few Saudi naval personnel had completed BUD/S in Coronado the years prior to 1990 under the allied personnel exchange program. The

Aboard the USNS *Joshua Humphries*, SEALs from SEAL Team Eight practice Visit, Board, Search, and Seizure (VBSS) operations in a safe environment. This was an almost constant mission for the SEALs as part of the Maritime Interception Force during Desert Shield.

U.S. Navy

Saudi commander had worked with the Navy SEALs during Operation EARNEST WILL in the 1980s. With this as a nucleus, the SEALs initiated the further training of their Saudi counterparts and produced three Saudi SEAL Teams. Special Boat Unit operators instructed Saudi navy personnel in the operation of high-speed boats. Additional Saudi personnel were taught how to conduct general water-borne operations.

In September, NSWTG-1 undertook the assistance of the Kuwaiti navy in the reconstitution of the limited navy assets that had escaped occupied Kuwait. Two Kuwaiti fast-attack craft missiles, the TNC 45 Type Al Sanbouk and the FPB 57 Type Istiqlal along with the motorized coast guard barge *Sawahil*, joined a handful of small patrol craft to make up the Kuwaiti navy in exile. The SEALs trained thirty-five Kuwaiti sailors in seamanship, naval engineering, and small arms. Further training was conducted by instructors from the U.S. Fleet Navy. Kuwaiti naval assets were eventually able to take successful part in combat search-and-rescue exercises. In addition, the *Sawahil* acted as an operational platform for NSWTG-1 assets during DESERT STORM.

It has been reported that assets from SEAL Team Six arrived in the Persian Gulf theater with the intent of performing a water-borne rescue of U.S. Ambassador Nathaniel Howell and his staff who had been held under virtual house arrest at the U.S. Embassy in Kuwait City since shortly after the invasion. The fact that the U.S. Embassy in Kuwait City was only across a street and a few hundred yards from the waters of the Persian Gulf made the possible rescue operation a SEAL responsibility. The sudden release of all foreign hostages by Saddam Hussein in December 1990 eliminated the need for a rescue operation.

Naval Special Warfare Task Group assets included four SEAL platoons, a SEAL fast-attack vehicle (FAV) detachment, a high-speed boat unit, a SEAL delivery vehicle detachment, and a joint communications support element. This gave the task group a great deal of flexibility in carrying out various assignments and tasks during both DESERT SHIELD and DESERT STORM.

Kuwaiti military personnel had been receiving specialized training in unconventional operations by SOCCENT (Special Operations Command-Control) instructors. The intent was for the Kuwaitis to infiltrate across the border to transmit out information and support the Kuwaiti resistance forces. The beginning of the Air War and Operation DESERT STORM on 16 January 1991 changed the plans to infiltrate across the border.

On 18 January, SEALs helped in the attack and capture of Iraqi-held oil platforms in the Durra oil field that had fired shoulder-launched missiles at Coalition aircraft. After an aerial attack by Army OH-58D helicopters, SEALs moved in and landed on the Iraqi installations. Guns, communications gear, and intelligence documents were captured along with twenty-three Iraqis. A

The Fast-Attack Vehicle used by the SEALs in Desert Storm. The modified racing dune buggies were fast-moving gun platforms and transportation in the desert sand. The SEAL at the rear of the FAV is manning a .50 Caliber M2 heavy machine gun.

U.S. Navy

number of small islands were searched and captured on 24 January with the specific mission being to capture maps of the Iraqi Gulf mine fields. The results were much the same as they had been on the oil platforms—intelligence materials and Iraqi personnel were collected up by the SEALs with no casualties on their part.

SEALs supplied swimmers for combat search-and-rescue (CSAR) operations prior to the beginning of the air campaign and DESERT STORM. SEALs would join Navy helicopter crews aboard patrolling Navy ships in the Gulf waters. If a call came in for the rescue of a downed pilot, the helicopters would be launched. Special CSAR crews would normally do the entire operation, but rescue swimmers were in such short supply that the addition of SEAL combat swimmers helped increase the measure of safety and rescue that could be offered pilots going down in the water.

On 23 January, the SEAL/CSAR mission was put to the test when a USAF F-16 pilot was shot and had to bail out into the Gulf. A Navy SH-60B helicopter along with a pair of SEAL swimmers, launched from the USS *Nicholas* immediately on hearing the distress call. The CSAR helicopter crew located the downed pilot quickly, and the SEALs jumped into the water only six miles from the Kuwaiti coast. All three men were quickly retrieved from the water, and the helicopter returned to the *Nicholas*. The whole operation, from launch to landing, had only taken thirty-five minutes.

With the beginning of the air war campaign and DESERT STORM, the Iraqi

An HH-60H Sea Hawk helicopter on a Search and Rescue training flight in California. These helicopters are Navy versions of the Blackhawk.

U.S. Navy

The blasted remnants of an Iraqi concrete aircraft hangar. Targets such as these were destroyed by precision-guided munitions dropped by Coalition aircraft during Desert Storm. Many of the precision bombs were guided by laser lights that illuminated the target invisibly. Some of those laser designators were aimed by special operations troops on the ground.

forces further sealed the Kuwait–Saudi Arabian border to infiltration. On some of the first bombing operations of the air campaign, high-value targets in Iraq and Kuwait were illuminated by compact laser designator devices intended to guide in high-tech bombs. The lasers were operated by SOCCENT assets, including Navy SEALs.

The only viable infiltration routes left to the Coalition forces were by air—a very dangerous option for Kuwaiti operators with limited training—and along the shoreline. The SEALs had already established that they could effectively operate along the shoreline of Kuwait, so they were given the task of getting the Kuwaiti operators into their country.

The SEALs trained thirteen Kuwaitis in maritime infiltration techniques from 14 to 20 February with a dress rehearsal conducted on 21 February. The target beach was south of Kuwait City. The infiltration operation was given the green light and launched on 22 February.

Five Kuwaitis followed SEAL swimmer-scouts into the shoreline of Occupied Kuwait. The specific target of the operation was a pier where the Kuwaitis would rendezvous with local resistance contacts. The meeting with the locals never took place. After waiting on the pier, the Kuwaitis signaled for extraction.

The incoming SEALs met the Kuwaitis, who were swimming out to sea, about five hundred meters from shore.

Later reconnaissance of the beach area after the war was over showed that there had been a much greater concentration of Iraqi troops in the area than had first been estimated. The density of beach fortifications indicated that the Kuwaiti resistance forces might not have been able to ever reach the pier for the planned rendezvous.

SEALs also conducted a great number of hydrographic surveys and other traditional UDT operations off the shores of Kuwait during DESERT SHIELD and up to the beginning of the ground campaign of DESERT STORM. Many of those recons were in support of U.S. Marine and Coalition amphibious forces. The very large Marine presence off-shore of Kuwait—more than 17,000 men and their equipment—made the threat of an amphibious landing in Kuwait a very real one.

Operation SEA SOLDIER I took place on the shores of Saudi Arabia 1 through 5 October 1990. A further exercise, Sea Soldier II, was conducted on 30 October to 8 November. The same forces of Amphibious Ready Group 2 and the 4th Marine Expeditionary Brigade took part in both exercises. Deployed SEALs, a normal component of the amphibious group, conducted their usual recons in support of the exercises.

From 15 to 21 November, Coalition forces conducted IMMINENT THUNDER, a massive amphibious landing exercise. The U.S. Marines as well as Saudi Arabian and other Coalition forces also took part in the exercise. Landings took place only one hundred miles from the Saudi Arabian–Kuwait border, near al-Jubail. IMMINENT THUNDER was a very obvious show of force and intent to the Iraqis. To be certain that they received the message, a number of news services were allowed to observe and broadcast the exercise. It was known that Saddam regularly watched the Western news services.

Continuing reconnaissance missions were conducted by the SEALs along the Kuwaiti shore. Ordered by CENTCOM as part of a deception plan, fifteen separate close-in recon operations were conducted by NSWTG-1 SEALs between 30 January and 15 February 1991. The missions ended with a single, large-scale operation conducted on the night of 23 and 24 February, the eve of the beginning of the ground war to liberate Kuwait.

Foxtrot Platoon of SEAL Team One went in to the Kuwaiti beaches south of Kuwait City aboard two high-speed boats. The SEALs switched to rubber boats for the final paddle in to shore. For the last part of the approach, the SEALs slipped into the water to conduct a classic UDT demolition swim. Each SEAL of the eight-man squad was towing a twenty-pound haversack of C4 explosives. The clocks of the explosive firing trains had been set to a specific time.

Some of the barbed wire and steel hedgehog beach obstacles along the shore of the Persian Gulf south of Kuwait City during Desert Shield/Desert Storm. Interspersed among the obstacles are mines.

Kevin Dockery

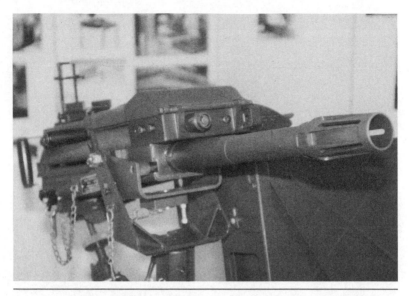

The Mark 19 Mod 3 40m grenade launcher. The MK 19 has been in Navy hands since the Vietnam War and can throw its half-pound high explosive grenades for more than two kilometers. It can be mounted on any facility that can accept a .50 caliber machine gun.

Kevin Dockery

After placing their charges and arming them right under the noses of the Iraqi troops on the beach, the SEALs withdrew to their boats.

When the explosives detonated, the SEALs swept the beaches with automatic weapons fire from 7.62mm and .50 caliber as well as 40mm grenades from Mark 19 grenade launchers. With the massed groups of Marines afloat offshore, backed up by an armada of ships that included battleships complete with their sixteen-inch guns, the Iraqi command was convinced that an invasion was following the SEALs' demolition swim.

Elements of several Iraqi divisions were diverted from their positions to reinforce the beach defenses. That left fewer Iraqi forces to face the real incoming Coalition ground forces, thrusting in from overland.

From 30 January to 15 February, the SEALs and the SDV detachment from SDVT-1 conducted the first operations of their kind. Using the Mark IX SDV and its integral sonar system, SEAL operators conducted six searches for moored sea mines in the Northern Persian Gulf area. The Kuwaiti coast guard barge *Sawahil* acted as a transport and service craft for the SEALs and their SDV. The crane on the barge could move the SDV for launchings and recoveries. This was reportedly the first combat use of the Mark IX SDV, a flat, two-man craft.

Although the SEALs and their SDVs did not locate any mines, the search

NAVY SEALs: A COMPLETE HISTORY

A floating antiship mine in the Persian Gulf. During both the Iran–Iraq War and Desert Shield/Desert Storm, these mines caused tremendous difficulties for shipping in the Gulf. A large amount of Navy resources went into trying to chart, clear, and defeat these old weapons of war. The lead horns sticking up from the mine can easily bend on contact with a ship's hull, breaking a vial of acid within the horn. Electrical current generated by the acid detonates a huge charge of high explosive, more than 250 pounds of TNT in a Soviet M-08/39 model.

U.S. Navy

area was considered a particularly vital one. Searching an area of twenty-seven square miles, the SEALs examined the offshore areas and channels surrounding a number of islands that could be scheduled for future invasion. In addition, the SEALs helped establish cleared channels for Naval assets, including the battleships *Missouri* and *Wisconsin*.

Throughout DESERT SHIELD and DESERT STORM, SEALs assisted in mine clearing and protection operations. SEAL sharpshooters aided in destroying floating mines with precision rifle fire. SEAL and EOD swimmers entered the Gulf waters to approach floating and moored mines. After examining the mines, the swimmers would place demolition charges to safely destroy the floating menaces that could even threaten the thick armor of a battleship.

One of the last SEAL combat missions of the ground war took place on 27 February. Even though the Iraqis had effectively abandoned Kuwait City, precautionary measures had to be taken against possible "stay-behind" forces. When the special operations forces planned a takedown of the U.S Embassy in Kuwait City, the SEALs joined in the operation. Adding the SEAL fast-attack vehicles to the ground convoy, the Embassy compound was quickly encircled. A

This floating contact mine has been prepped for destruction by the demolition charge attached to it. The charge is in the rectangular bag strapped to the right side of the mine. Both the SEALs and the Explosive Ordnance Disposal divers (one is shown here in the photograph) dealt with a number of Iraqi mines in the Gulf using the same methods.

U.S. Navy

search of the buildings by troops fast roping down from helicopters showed there to be no danger from boobytraps or Iraqi soldiers. The U.S. Embassy in a free Kuwait was once more in American hands.

Raymond C. Smith, Rear Admiral, USN (Ret.)

My position as of about one month ago (November 1998) was the Director of Navy Assessment for the Chief of Naval Operations. I joined the Navy on 12 February 1962. Enlisting with a buddy, I joined because I decided I would be able to take advantage of the Service, in terms of what it offered. I wasn't doing well in college at the time, so I enlisted.

The first time I heard about the Underwater Demolition Teams was while I was on a midshipman's cruise. After joining the Navy, I went on to the Naval Academy after receiving an appointment. So I finished my first year at Annapolis, Maryland, and we went on a summer cruise, part of which was to Coronado, California. While

A long area view taken of the beach obstacles at Normandy during World War II. The scale of the obstacles can be seen against the size of the running figures to the left of center in the photo. It was because of obstacles like this that the Naval Combat Demolition Units were founded. Through the NCDUs came the UDTs and then the SEALs.

National Archives

there, I was able to see a demonstration by the ten underwater demolition teams. It was in 1964, and that was the first time I had ever heard of them.

In 1964, there wasn't very much spoken about the SEALs. I suspect that at that time, they were still a classified unit. The UDTs were really the "front-office" units, so to speak, for the Navy Special Operations. At that time, Frogmen were the officers and enlisted men who had worked so hard during World War II to clear the beaches of Normandy and in the Pacific, so they were a common term among the military for the men of the Underwater Demolition Teams.

What attracted me to these Teams was not so much the fact that they were clearing beaches, but the camaraderie that went on in the units. That's the kind of thing I had looked for and was the kind of military unit I wanted to be involved with.

What was unique to the UDTs, and what built such a great bond in the units that existed then, and still today, was the fact that the officers and the enlisted men went through training together. That's really rather unique, and it's a wonderful gift that we in Naval Special Warfare have because we're small enough to get away with it. And it's recognized that, if you can do it, you set yourself up for a community that has great bonding between the men and the officers. So it really was something that attracted me. I also wanted to be involved physically in things. Normally, as a commissioned officer, you don't do that. So those were the kinds of things that attracted me to Naval Special Warfare.

The payoff is that when you graduate from BUD/S training and you go across the street to report to your unit, every one of the enlisted men in that Team know you've done everything they did. Simply put, that's it. You've proven yourself in exactly the same manner as each and every other man in the Teams. There's a great respect for the officers in the Teams for that reason.

Basic Underwater Demolition/SEAL (BUD/S) training is a course for Naval Special Warfare forces that enables the Navy to look at, screen, and grow young men who, as the product of that course, will normally wind up a young man who has proven to be fearless, in the sense that for twenty-five weeks he has been forced to do things he's never done before, he doesn't like to do, and he's afraid of doing. You can't go through the course without confronting those things.

So the product of the BUD/S course is a young man who now has learned that there's almost no limit to what he can do. The only way you can achieve that is by putting a man through stress that constantly upgrades his level of awareness of himself. Coming out of today's society, young men lead a very relaxed life in the sense that there's not a lot of extreme stress. In BUD/S, we train them to be ready to go to combat. The only way you can do that is to push them beyond the limits they expect to be pushed to. That is the gift and the beauty of BUD/S training—it enables us to draw from within, out of the young man's soul. That is the key. I've always said that BUD/S training manifests itself in things physical, but it's all about a man's soul.

If you can capture his soul and make him realize that there's nothing that can prevent him from doing his job, then you got him. The kids who go through training recognize that. Some don't see it until the last day of training, and some see it the first day they're there. But during that twenty-five weeks, all of those who stay the course get it. And once they got it, you have a product that you can depend upon.

The use of the word Teams probably comes from a couple places, one of which is that in BUD/S training, nobody goes through there by themselves. Even on swims, you're with a swim buddy. In almost all cases, those who try to go by themselves don't make it through the course. It's not a course for young men who are individualists, and we inculcate this idea of teamwork throughout BUD/S.

The students hear the word teamwork probably every day for twenty-five weeks. Team, team, team. And so it becomes part of their very being. Combined with the fact that our units are named Teams—whether it was Underwater Demolition Teams or SEAL Teams, the word Teams has become synonymous with what we are. They aren't SEAL people, they're SEAL Teams. I think that underpins the very philosophy SEALs go by.

Naval Special Warfare is synonymous with the name SEAL Teams. Just as a more common term, the SEAL Teams themselves embody what we call maritime special operations. Special operations, by definition, are a host of small unit operations that are not done by conventional forces, whether it be gathering intelligence, conducting raids on small targets, doing counterterrorism work, or any of the things assigned to a special operations force.

The kind of people who make up that force have to have certain kinds of characteristics. First of all, they have to have gone through a vetting process, in our particular case, BUD/S training; in the case of the Green Berets, Army Special Forces school. But in any case, there has to be a vetting where you look at the young man and decide that he's physically capable of doing the job, that he's mentally capable of doing the job, and that he has a great heart and soul. They have to have all three things.

Physical work is easy to see in BUD/S training. For the intellectual part, we do a lot of work in terms of their ability to do diving and conduct diving operations. And finally, we test them for their mettle every day for twenty-five weeks. Every day they finish, they feel they've reached a plateau, but the next day is always harder. The students are constantly reassessing where they are in their life. All of a sudden, they realize that, no matter how hard it gets, it can always be tougher. So what you get is a young man who is totally capable and totally confident of his own abilities. That's the kind of person who has to be in a SEAL Team.

There's no way that you can call time out in combat. As is known in the terms of the Navy SEALs, we have never left a man on the field in combat. That is synonymous with the kind of person we breed, so to speak, in BUD/S training. So the term Team just underscores the whole idea that we are not a "Rambo" organization. When a SEAL platoon is formed, those men become as close as brothers—in fact probably closer than most brothers are, because they rely upon each other for their very lives.

All officers and enlisted men who want to become a Navy SEAL, or in the past a Frogman, have to volunteer. It's a voluntary force. You volunteer in, and you can volunteer out.

I don't know that one looks at a life in the Teams as being fun. I always explain it according to the fact that young men and young women in today's society approach their careers in a lot of different ways. One psychologist named Maslow, in the late 1960s, developed what is called Maslow's Hierarchy of Needs. It explains why people do things in their lives.

In most cases, most people approach careers and life in the sense of gathering security, having friends, and succeeding financially. But at the top of Maslow's pyramid is the term self-actualization. Self-actualization is a term that means doing something for the sake of doing it for the individual himself and for whatever higher authority the individual believes in. That holds true for the men who accept the challenge of the Teams. They do it for themselves.

*   *   *

There were a lot of instructors when I went through BUD/S training who "inspired" me—and I use that term loosely here. They were all remarkable people, the kind of men I wanted to try to be. They were certainly models for me. In the Teams themselves, I thought one man who personified what I thought was a great SEAL was a guy named Frank Perry. He was legendary in our community as a quiet, extraordinarily intense, and extraordinarily competent man. I always put him on a higher level than most. There are several others also, but certainly Frank Perry is one. Most of the men know him. If you knew him, you knew what a great role model Frank was for junior officers and junior enlisted men.

I think the thing that makes SEALs, SEALs is that they're—and I use the term cautiously—humble. They are very content with who they are; they don't need to tell people who they are. I don't really call that humility per se. What I do call it is a human being who is totally at ease and confident with himself, what he's doing in life, and what he's capable of doing. I think that really personifies what makes SEALs so unique. They are very self-satisfied people in terms of they've accounted for something already in their lives, and they don't feel the need to have to advertise about that.

In terms of how young men go through BUD/S training and the transformation that takes place, I do believe that the vast majority of young men who get through that course, are the kind of young men who were just mentioned. That is, solid physically; solid mentally; very, very intense in terms of their ability to focus on things; but also quiet people. There's very few young men who get through BUD/S with the habit of talking about themselves.

The young man who gets through BUD/S training is the kind of man who helps his Teammates and who stays focused on what he's doing. Normally, that's not the kid who's talking about how good he is. Those aren't the kind of people who make it through to graduation. I think what we find is that those kind of young men, and they might be very good, lack the capacity to be team players. That might be because they've always been very successful at, say, a sport or something like that. If they can't subjugate themselves to a higher organization, a Team, then they aren't successful.

So what you get out of that training program is the kind of person who has been talked about, the kind of man who's self-satisfied with what he is doing, but who has also subjugated his own ego to a higher part of society, his Navy SEAL Team.

Between 1981 and 1983, I served as the commander of the BUD/S training course. It was the first time I had returned to BUD/S training since I was a student and now I was a Commander in the Navy. Something struck me shortly after I arrived, was that in the interviews all the students had to write, all their answers about why they were coming to BUD/S training and what they hoped to accomplish all had a common theme that sort of transcended all the young men who showed up here. I think it personified the kind of young men that we have coming in to SEAL training, even today. It's a young man who's looking for goals in his life, who wants to be part of an organization that he knows is successful because he has read about it and appreciates it. So he's coming in with the idea that he wants to be part of this, and he wants to know what it takes to do it, what the rules are, and how to get there. He wants a black-and-white world. He wants to see what it takes and have a shot at it himself.

When I saw that time after time on these papers of students who were not taking these interviews together, it became clear that these young men of America were looking for this kind of thing. I think this underscores some of the things that we have in society today in terms of what our young men and women are looking for in all walks of life. In our particular case, the goal was to become a Navy SEAL, but it was clear that these young people wanted to know how to succeed. They wanted us to show them what needed to be done, and they were going to go after it. That was very reassuring to me.

What I didn't see in those interview answers, almost without exception, were statements like "I want to go out and kill the enemy" or do things like that. That is an understood part of what we do when these young men come to us, but that's not the reason they come. The reasons are organizational and the betterment of their own lives. That knowledge is very satisfying to me.

When I graduated from BUD/S with Class 52, I was married and had two little kids, and that's what was going through my mind at the time. But I was very proud of what I had done. I had been serving on a destroyer for two years after graduating Annapolis, which I did enjoy. I wanted to try something different, so off I went to BUD/S training. Graduation was something that gave me a tremendous feeling of accomplishment and pride. It was one of the great achievements of my life.

I felt the same thing when I first had the Trident, the Naval Special Warfare insignia, pinned to my chest. That established that I had accomplished my goal and had become part of a community as elite as the Navy SEALs. It was certainly another high point of my life.

In terms of our evolution in warfare and the history of our military, the Navy SEALs have grown from 1962 to today. We moved from Vietnam and the very great success we enjoyed there in doing what we could do in a very limited war. As the world moved on, the United States took a different role in being the only superpower in the world and shouldered its burden to have to provide leadership across the world to all the nations, enemies and friends.

The Navy SEAL has evolved with that change. What we see now is definitely changed what we saw ten or twenty years ago, and is most certainly different from the operators of World War II. The young Navy SEAL now is very much akin to the Army Green Berets in the sense that they are much more culturally skilled—many more SEALs have second-language qualifications today. And all these young men are out and about in the world today, doing our nation's work conducting peacetime operations in one hundred and thirty to one hundred and forty nations a year.

We have a State Department that believes in the use of the military to conduct certain parts of its foreign policy. Special Operations, and SEALs in particular, do that—we do those operations for the maritime forces. So what you see are language-qualified young men who are going out, doing operations in small countries, in groups of two, three, five, ten, fifteen, or twenty, on their own, very mature and very capable.

In many cases, these SEALs are working with a U.S. ambassador directly in a nation or the deputy chief of mission. In any case, they are working to help support and progress our foreign policy. That is a much more sophisticated mission than we had, say, thirty or forty years ago.

Accomplishing the new missions requires a young man of extreme maturity, who is very good on his feet, and who is able to understand the politics of the given nation, vis-à-vis America. And so it is a much more complicated environment that our SEALs live in today than they lived in thirty or forty years ago.

Operations DESERT SHIELD and DESERT STORM are both typical examples of what I mean when I say that the role of special operations forces, and SEALs in particular, has expanded. When we were deployed to Saudi Arabia in August 1990, we were sent there basically without a mission per se. We were just told to get to Saudi Arabia and be prepared for follow-on operations.

A SEAL in the early (chocolate chip) pattern of desert camouflage aims his M4 carbine fitted with an M203 40mm grenade launcher. This arrangement is a favorite of the SEALs as it combines the range of the 5.56mm round from the M4 with the high explosive fragmentation of the 40mm grenade.

U.S. Navy

Within nine days of arriving in Saudi Arabia, I had a platoon of SEALs forty kilometers below the border of Kuwait, teaching the Saudi army close-air support. Within another five days, I had more SEALs in the harbor of Jubail conducting harbor patrol operations as the U.S. Marines off-loaded their equipment. Inside of another two weeks—less than a month since we arrived in Saudi Arabia—we had met with the Kuwait navy in exile and began a three-month course to train the Kuwait navy to take back their nation.

It is easy to see the breadth of operations we were confronted with early on in the campaign, not even including the combat operations during DESERT STORM, which is another matter altogether. Throughout DESERT SHIELD we worked training foreign military forces. There were coalition support teams from many of the coalition nations that we assisted. Training was conducted with the Saudi military, and we lived and worked with the Saudis. We had actually planned to work operations with the Saudis.

All these things were done before the war even started, which is really an expansion of what we do. When DESERT STORM came, we were prepared to do combat search-and-rescue. Our primary mission, in fact our only assigned mission, at that time was to rescue downed pilots. General Schwarzkopf believed that we probably would take some pretty good losses and that the SEALs would be in charge of conducting maritime search-and-rescue, but we only did one of those. Only one pilot was shot down over water and we picked him up.

In the scope of DESERT STORM, we conducted more than two hundred and seventy operations—everything from the famous diversion operation that Lieutenant Commander Deitz ran, to scaling oil platforms and capturing the first Iraqis of the war, to conducting intelligence operations and photographing the Iraqis off the stern of one of their now-famous mine-laying vessels. We trained Kuwaiti resistance forces to go in and set up communications in Kuwait City. SEALs captured right away the first piece of territory in Kuwait, Quruh Island, which was held by the Iraqis. We ran the gamut of operations.

The main thing to take away is that those special operations were not conducted in and of themselves for themselves. They were conducted to contribute to the campaign. What I found out shortly after getting to DESERT SHIELD/DESERT STORM was that this was not going to be a special operations campaign—this was going to be a war. And unless special operations forces, i.e., the SEALs or the Army Special Forces, could adapt what they do to support the higher objective of the war, we were going to be left out.

We turned around our entire conduct of operations and went to the Marine Corps and Army and asked them what we could do for them to support their campaign. That was the genesis of the deception operation and all the reconnaissance work we did on the beaches of Kuwait. That was to help the larger-scale forces. That's what I think is the beauty of special forces today. We can adapt to conduct very singular operations or work operations that support the general purpose forces in a large-scale operation.

DESERT SHIELD/DESERT STORM was a campaign. It was a campaign first to come up with a plan to defend Saudi Arabia. And then, the ultimate aim was not only to defend Saudi Arabia, but to return Kuwait to its rightful owners. It was a large-scale campaign with large infusions of conventional forces. That was really what DESERT STORM was all about. The special operations forces (SOF) had very specific and focused missions to support the campaign, and they needed to support it at the operational level, i.e., the level that would affect and benefit the large-scale forces.

General Schwarzkopf did not need us to do very precise tactical operations; he needed us to do operational things. That's what I tried to do in DESERT STORM, to get our forces involved in operations that would benefit the entire campaign. We were very successful in doing that only because the general purpose forces recognized the value of the SOF. They recognized that we could do more than just very singular operations, that we had more to bring to the table than being able to just swim in and take out a small target, for instance.

We could do other things that would benefit the campaign. We were able to do many operations that led to a number of breakthroughs for the campaign. Certainly the capture of two hundred Iraqis early in January 1991, with no opposition, indicated to General Schwarzkopf that this was probably how the war was going to go.

In and of themselves, they were great operations that took courage on the part of our young men. The fact is, when we took it all back and looked at those operations, we very easily deduced that there was more to it than just capturing those men. The fact that they didn't fight—none of them—led us to believe and recommend to General Schwarzkopf that maybe, just maybe, this was what we were going to see when the land assault started. In fact, that is what we saw.

So those kinds of benefits that you can give to a large scale conventional force have great value to the conventional force commanders. And I think it underscores SOFs value in a new era where not only are we able to do small-scale operations, but we can bring benefit with small insertions of forces that we couldn't do in the old days.

There are a number of notable individuals who have served and are serving in the Teams today. I'll never forget the first day I met Rear Admiral Tom Richards. He was an ensign, and he stood out in this field in BUD/S training. He weighed about 240 pounds, most of it in his chest. I looked at this guy and asked to myself, This is the kind of guy I have to train with?

Tom and I are very close friends. He's enormously strong physically and intellectually in all matters. There ought to be a law against somebody that strong. He's fearless and aggressive. He's taken all the hard jobs in our community and has led our community very well.

One of the things that underscores the kind of person Tom Richards is that he's an extraordinary competitor. Tom was the biggest guy in our class, and as most would say, the slowest runner, because he carried so much weight and was such a physically strong guy. I watched him go though that class, and I saw the determination of this guy who really could not deal with the running at BUD/S training.

In order to go through BUD/S, much running is required. Tom was enormously strong in everything we did, and was especially a great swimmer. When we got on the beach, though, it was another matter altogether. Tom took much grief from his instructors, but he would not give up. That just highlights the kind of person he was. To this day, he still runs and he's still a big guy, but his intense focus on what he does drives him to always be better.

The only thing Tom really was not very good at is boxing. Although he was a great wrestler and a great weight-lifter, he was not very skillful with his fists. In those days, we had to box in BUD/S training, and I drew the enviable task of having to box Tom. Having boxed at the Naval Academy, I was a little better at it than he was, so I avoided his swings with great skill and managed to put a few on him, but I could not move him.

I've already mentioned the kind of young man who comes into the SEALs. I think it's a surprise to many people when they meet a young SEAL to see the kind of professional the young man is. Normally, he's a quiet, very competent individual, and I think that underscores the kind of jobs our Navy SEALs are doing now. They're not in the limelight very much and you don't read a lot about them, but every day, throughout the world in fifty, sixty, eighty, one hundred countries, there are groups of SEALs doing things.

There is a definite benefit that accrues just from having a special operations force like the SEALs in the military. Several years ago, we had an operation in the Ivory Coast. The Ivory Coast Navy was having a problem with poaching. They had bought a number of the kind of swamp craft we see in America, the air boats with large fans in the back, but they did not know how to operate them, maintain them, or surveil or approach poachers with them. We sent a platoon of SEALs—a couple of lieutenants and about fourteen enlisted men—over to help deal with this problem.

The SEALs spent three weeks working with the Ivory Coast Navy and Coast Guard. When they left there, after teaching them how to do what they needed, the defense minister of that nation came out himself to wish the best to that platoon. That was just two officers and Navy sailors. What that does for the United States, our embassy, and our relations with the Ivory Coast cannot be quantified. That's the value of a special operations force.

We've had SEALs on the border between Peru and Ecuador for the last four years. Peru and Ecuador have been fighting over that border for more than one hundred years. Who do you put on that kind of border to handle the sensitivity of two nations grappling over this undefined border? You put out Army Special Forces and Navy SEALs. You send men who are language-qualified and understand the culture and the history of the nations and who can deal with the people there. That's the kind of thing you don't hear much about, but it's happening all the time around the world.

Our Navy SEALs are involved heavily in counternarcotics operations throughout Latin America, working with the nation's navies and marine corps to train them to conduct their operations. This is also something you don't see very often in the papers, but they are the kind of forces that have to be able to do that. They have the wisdom, intellect, language, and cultural acclimatization they need so they can talk to these nations' navies and marine corps about how to deal with their problems.

Those are the kind of things we see going on today and that are heavily supportive of the idea of special operations forces and SEALs in particular. There is a need to have a very sophisticated force of small numbers that can deal with small interruptions in our foreign policy around the world. That is the beauty and the value of the Navy SEALs.

As we look at our nation's role in foreign policy today and look at adapting that foreign policy to the world, I think that it's apparent to everyone involved that our nation is the preeminent world power. We have taken it upon ourselves to use that strength and our example to help placate the problems that exist around our world. There's no other nation that can do the things we do in this world. And if we're not involved, if we're not engaged, then the other nations that can support us won't be engaged, either.

Accomplishing that task requires a lot of things. It requires a foreign policy and a foreign service that can do the negotiations and the deliberations. It requires a military that can back us up when we really, really carry through with the threat. Between those two, there's the special operations force.

The SOF stands between the foreign service of our State Department and the large, conventional forces that we use to go to war. They are the scalpel to the hammer of our conventional military. Of the military special operations forces, the Army Special Forces and the Navy SEALs are the preeminent members of those forces, although there are many other ones as well. I believe those two forces probably do the most to deal with supporting our foreign policy around the world.

The Navy SEALs and the Army Special Forces accomplish their support of our foreign policies in part by professionalizing the third-world nations' militaries. That is a very important role in the third world. Their militaries have a preeminent role in their society; in many cases, they run the country. In our particular case, we work very hard, both the SEALs and the Special Forces, to train the militaries that their role as the military force of a nation is to be subservient to the political leadership and the people it represents. That's a very hard concept to bring across in many nations and an even harder one to bring some people to believe in.

Our military, in this case our SEALs, can do that kind of stuff. That is a very sophisticated operation, but it has a big payoff in terms of our foreign policy and the acceptance of our leadership around the world. We see that every day with the reception our SEALs receive all around the world.

Shortly after our nation failed at DESERT ONE in Iran, our military went through a whole reassessing of our special operations forces. That culminated in 1986 in the Goldwater-Nichols Defense Reorganization Act. That act instituted a new organization for special operations forces in our military.

The act decreed that we would create a U.S. Special Operations Command (USSOCOM), commanded by a four-star general or flag officer who would have budgetary authority. He would be able to buy equipment, train his people, and deploy them around the world. And his people would be made up of all the services' special operations forces. That has been a stunning success for special operations forces in our military.

Our Navy SEALs are a key component of USSOCOM. Although while they now wear the Navy uniform and serve proudly in the U.S. Navy, the SEALs are funded and equipped by Special Operations money. It's a totally different approach to how special forces had been handled for thirty or forty years—as a small part of each conventional military force. It has been a great success and has allowed U.S. special operations forces, and SEALs in particular, to actually grow over the last ten years.

Though our conventional military has decreased by almost 40 percent in the last ten years, the Navy SEALs have almost doubled in size. That isn't because we're just nice guys. Our military and political leadership as well as our congress have looked and asked, "What are the kind of forces we need for this nation?"

Well, there are many kinds that we have to have, but certainly special operations forces and the Navy SEALs are the kind of forces that we have to have in today's world and the world of the future. I think that, all things considered, the Navy SEALs are in a great position. They are highly needed around the world, they have been consistently successful during the last ten years in all the operations that they have run, and they have a great record of success. Recruiting is good, and funding is as well. The SEALs are really a military success story today.

To help meet the personnel needs of the SEALs' success, I think every Navy SEAL is a recruiter at heart. We're always out looking for great young men who are willing to take up the challenge the Teams offer. I have done it a hundred times over myself and would do it again in a second if I felt a young man needed guidance and was interested in the program. You have to look at them and get them focused, but I would do that without hesitation, as most SEALs would.

Wearing the Naval Special Warfare insignia, the Trident, is something you don't think about every day when you get up in the morning. But when you stop and think about it, and think about the people you have met in your career, the people who have come and gone, and the young men still coming in, you realize that you are part of a very special group of people. That fills me with a great deal of pride, just to be one of those guys, regardless of rank. I don't care who you are, a young seaman or a four-star admiral, the very fact that you're a part of this, of Naval Special Warfare, the Teams, transcends rank. I am as close to some of my enlisted men as I am to many of the officers. The rank, although it has a great deal of importance to our military society, in the Navy SEALs, the friendships and brotherhood you form transcends rank. So when I wake up in the morning, if I think about it, I tell myself that I'm a lucky guy.

Besides just being in the Teams, I'm also very fortunate to have two sons who have followed me in my career as a Navy SEAL. I'm very proud of that. When most fathers who are SEALs deal with their sons, they always want to know their son's answer to the question, "Why are you doing this?" I can tell you that the PT grinder at BUD/S is littered with the bodies of sons whose fathers were SEALs and who were there for the wrong reason. I didn't want my sons to do the same thing.

Of course I was particularly interested because of my rank. My sons would not be singled out; they would be held to the same standard everyone would be expected to meet. So I quizzed both my sons on their motivations for volunteering for BUD/S. If they were doing it for me or for anyone else, they weren't going to get through the course. They assured me that they weren't, that they joined for their own reasons. They are in the Teams today.

The BUD/S graduations of both of my two sons were unique events. I can't think of too many things in my life where I could be as proud of two young men as I was of my two sons, and of my nephew, who also served as a SEAL. I guess the thing that struck me was the fact that it didn't seem that long ago that I had graduated from BUD/S myself. When my sons graduated, I had to stop and contemplate that twenty-five years had gone by in a flash, which I guess underscores the whole idea that if you do something in your life, have fun doing it. When you're having fun, time goes by fast—it certainly has passed quickly for me.

The value of making sure all the young men coming in to the SEALs today recognize the past warriors who have preceded them, I think, is the same principle that we should apply to our nation as a whole. We should never lose sight of the people who have preceded us in this great nation. If we don't study our history, we're liable to make the same mistakes that have been made in the past. The same thing applies with the SEALs.

Although we all think we know more than our parents and our other predecessors did, the fact is that they were a lot smarter than we give them credit for. I think it's very important that we don't lose sight of the fact that heroism has no hold on any particular generation. Heroism can happen any time at any place, in most cases when you least expect it. So for young men who watch the event horizon, with the amount of time they look ahead, it's very difficult for them to look back and really ponder the heroism of the great men who came before them.

There's great wisdom that comes from studying the past. Our junior officer course brings in retired enlisted and officers to talk to our young officers and make them understand that many of them had been through the same things that the young officers were about to go through. They can give the young men some things to live by that will help them be successful.

I think most of the kind of guys who come into the SEALs are sensitive to the fact that our strength is in the people who have gone before us, so I don't find it surprising at all that the young men coming in to the Teams today believe that they need to really respect the great men who have come before them. They feel that they need to elicit from those men the wisdom that they developed from their experiences.

The young men coming into the SEALs today are very, very smart. If you were to give them college boards exam, I think they all would do very well. We're looking for smart young men, and we're looking for a lot more than just book smarts. I think we're finding that more of the enlisted volunteers today have had some college, many of them, in fact, have college degrees.

Does that matter or not? It only matters in the maturation process. There is a big difference between an eighteen-year-old young man and a twenty-one-year-old man. Having three sons, I can tell you that. So when a kid goes off to college for a couple years, he matures. He grows intellectually and emotionally. That makes him better able to handle the kind of things he's going to be exposed to on his way to becoming a Navy SEAL.

I think that it's great that we're getting this kind of young man to volunteer for the Teams. It is a challenge for us, because young men with a lot of college, and especially those with degrees who are sailors, are certainly looking for upward mobility. So how do we get these young men commissioned if that's what they decide to do? That makes it sort of a good news–bad news story.

It's great to have these bright young guys. But how do we motivate them to stay in? How do we keep upward mobility for them and make sure they stay in the Teams for a career? Answering those questions is a challenge for us, but it's better to have that challenge than not to have it.

The Navy SEALs are very blessed today because we have great equipment. We have the money to buy good equipment, and we have the talent available to be able to use that equipment. But that's not what we do in the Navy SEALs. We don't man the equipment, we equip the man. That's the key thing to realize here. The man is, in fact, the weapon system. The things that adorn his being are all the manifestations of technology. The real factor is the human being underneath all that. That's what really counts.

Some have mentioned that when they went to BUD/S training, they didn't see a lot of big guys there—guys with eighteen-inch biceps and twenty-two-inch necks. The fact is that you will see a few of those, but you'll also see a bunch of guys who aren't very big, aren't very physically impressive—on the outside anyway. But that's not what BUD/S training is all about. It's not about having big guys; it's about having men with soul.

Unfortunately, there's no way we can look into a man's soul when he arrives at BUD/S. You learn of the strength of a man's soul, his commitment to himself and to excellence, only when he goes through the course. At some point in time during that course, his soul will bare itself, and you'll find out what kind of person he is.

Once you see what kind of person he is, you'll see that the kind of man he is has nothing to do with his biceps or how fast he runs, or swims, or completes the o-course. It's the inner strength that comes to some people that we're looking for. That inner strength is what a man's soul is built of.

When you graduate from BUD/S training, that's a great event. That's the good news. The bad news is that you haven't earned your Special Warfare insignia yet. Even after twenty-five weeks of vetting so to speak, that young man reports to a Team after having gone to Jump School at Fort Benning and earning his parachute jump wings. There he begins to prove that, after all those push-ups he did, after as cold as he got in BUD/S training, above all of that, he can still think.

We ask those young men, over the next six months to a year, to go through a thirteen-week course of advanced training. We watch and observe these young men for their maturity, their military behavior, their appearance, and how well they integrate themselves into the Teams. At the end of six months to a year, he earns his Trident. Then he can start to become a SEAL operator.

Many people ask me that now we've left our roots as Frogmen, where pretty much the young Frogman swam in with a pair of swim fins, a knife, and a haversack full of explosives, how do those men relate to the warrior of today? You'll notice that in BUD/S training, the students spend a lot of time doing the same very thing that those Frogmen did. We start with the roots from which we came. There are a lot of long-distance ocean swims with very little on other than maybe a wet suit, a Kabar knife, and a lifejacket. The whole idea is to start at the very basic level of training—that is starting at the level of a Navy Frog, just as he was in World War II, so they never lose that link between our history and tradition of old to where we are at today.

To give an example of the irony of history, after all the years of the Teams going through World War II, to Korea and Vietnam, through the Mayaguez incident,

Grenada, and Panama, we wound up in DESERT STORM with many of our SEALs embarked on U.S. Navy ships. From those ships, they were prepared to go in and swim in to the beaches and do a combat demolition, just as we did during World War II, to enable the Marines to cross the beach.

General Schwarzkopf decided not to do that. But the fact was that after all these years, after all this time had passed and compared to all the sophisticated things we do in the SEALs, doctrinally, our young men are basically Frogmen. We had four to six SEAL platoons sitting out on those ships ready to conduct the same operations as their forefathers did in World War II.

On top of a parade float after the successful conclusion of Desert Storm, this SEAL in full desert combat camouflage and armed with an M60E3 light machine gun shows the American public just who was among the troops that helped liberate Kuwait.

U.S. Navy

Vic Meyer, Lieutenant Commander

Presently, I serve as the Executive Officer of SEAL Team One. My start with the Teams was fairly conventional. I first heard about the Teams while at the Naval Academy. In a lot of ways, I was sort of an underachiever at the Naval Academy. The one thing I was interested in was the physical aspect of the Teams.

There were only five billets offered the year I went through the Naval Academy. My choice was to be a pilot, which appealed to me, but not as much as being a Frogman. My other option was to go into Surface Warfare for two years and qualify for my surface warfare pin. Then I could try and do a lateral transfer into Naval Special Warfare. Ultimately, I chose the Surface Warfare route and went to a destroyer for two years, three months. Finally, I received orders to BUD/S and then on to SEAL Team One after graduation.

I don't really remember when I first heard about the SEAL Teams. My dad was a Naval officer, a submariner. So I was always aware, sometimes on the periphery, sometimes a little more directly, of the Teams. We lived in Virginia Beach and saw guys running up and down the beach all the time. They were SEALs or UDT Frogmen. There was no seminal moment, no epiphany, where all of a sudden I decided the Teams was where I wanted to be.

My decision was made while I was at the Naval Academy. I think, though, that it was more that the Teams sort of found me rather than me finding the Teams. Fortunately, there were some instructors at the Naval Academy who were from the Teams, and they helped get me even more interested in the SEALs. I sort of fit in more with those guys than I did anywhere else and felt very at ease with them.

I was in BUD/S Class 156, a summer class, a very, very warm summer class. In fact, Hell Week was balmy. The water temperature seemed to be around seventy-two degrees, which frustrated the instructors. They really couldn't hammer us by throwing us into the water, so they just ran us back and forth between Imperial Beach and the base all week with rubber boats on our heads.

BUD/S wasn't that difficult for me, in spite of my having been in the surface fleet for several years. As an officer, there was still an inherent degree of professional distance I was able to maintain because I was the class leader. However, I was very comfortable for the line between officers and enlisted men to become blurred during training. There was always that measure of respect for my position, and I think that was accorded me because I showed a great deal of respect for the guys with me.

No where else in the military do you maintain those enduring friendships developed in training, as you do with the guys who go through BUD/S with you. You continue to work with those same people throughout your career in Naval Special Warfare—at least I've certainly found that to be the case.

Constantly on the move at BUD/S, these students move away from the surf zone carrying the rubber boat that has been their constant companion since the beginning of training. While his classmates carry the boat, at the rear of the group is a single student carrying a large outboard motor on his back.

U.S. Navy

The closeness between the officers and the enlisted men in the Teams is one of its strengths. It's much easier to demonstrate your good faith to your Teammates, and the enlisted men know you inside and out. Your reputation as an operator and your reputation as a human being, sort of precedes you wherever you go in the community. The men know your strengths and weaknesses, and the enlisted guys are very demanding and tough. They do not tolerate weaknesses easily. But they are also pretty forgiving and will forgive an officer a mistake if they see a redeeming quality in him.

The officer-students do make a number of mistakes going through BUD/S. That's one of the things that's sort of important. You go through the good times together, and you get hammered together when a mistake is made. That's all just part of being a SEAL.

I found that instructors take a particularly personal interest in the officers going through training—and with good reason. Someday, they could easily have to follow that same officer they're pushing through the mud at BUD/S. It is in their own best interest to make certain that each man who goes through training makes the grade completely, and that goes even more so for the officers.

The things that stand out for me in my experience in training, are somewhat difficult to admit. I found that hate is a very powerful motivator. You get into the dark side of your character, that dark part of you, and pull out what you need to get you through the most difficult parts in BUD/S. That was the single most important quality I noticed. To be able to use that dark side to overcome pain and adversity, extraordinary fatigue, and everything else, and then put it back in its place when it was no longer required, that was probably the thing that helped me the most.

I think we search for those kind of guys in the Teams. We search for guys who thrive on hardship. We search for guys who thrive on chaos. And those men have to be able to manage that chaos, that pain, and overcome it through whatever part of their character they use. I think a lot of those qualities are found in the dark side of the soul.

Hell Week, I will admit, was very physical. But I think the cold is the most debilitating thing about every Hell Week. My class certainly experienced cold out at San Clemente Island. Our Hell Week was so warm the instructors had to hammer us another way. Their technique of running us back and forth until we started to hallucinate worked out for us. Once you start to hallucinate, the hard part's gone. You really just cease to be aware of your surroundings.

I had an advantage in that I had come to BUD/S directly from the fleet. I was not physically broken down and I classed up and went through in one class. When I came out of Hell Week, sure, my feet were swollen and bleeding, and I had difficulty walking around, but I wasn't in the physical shape that some of the other guys were—bleeding from their crotches, swollen testicles, just some extraordinarily painful situations. Some of the new doctors who were at the training center and hadn't worked with Special Warfare before had rarely seen stuff like this. It was pretty incredible.

What got me through Hell Week was creating sort of an image in my mind, almost a mental photo. When everything else sort of closes in on you, and that picture gets real small, you focus on that image and see yourself on the other side of Hell Week.

There's also a great amount of peer pressure to keep going in the class. I was the class leader, and if I quit, I could have taken a number of the other students with me. There was a case where a class leader quit and almost the entire class followed him out of BUD/S. I had an enormous amount of pressure on me to finish the class, and I'd like to think that I rose to the occasion. That might not have been the case, though, because I think I was surrounded by extremely capable, confident, and dedicated people, and we just helped each other succeed. That's one of the things I think makes BUD/S so significant.

I had come from the Surface Fleet. I don't want to cast disparaging remarks on the Surface Fleet, but I never thought of quitting BUD/S. They were going to have to take me out of BUD/S in a body bag before I would quit and go back to the Fleet.

Other than my platoon in the Gulf, the most significant, and rewarding, event of my life, and that includes my diploma from the Naval Academy, is graduating BUD/S and entering the Teams. I place more value on my Trident than I do on my diploma. It really defines who you are to a large extent.

Standing there on the grinder that last day was a little weird. Because the instructors played so many mental games on us, I still refused to believe that training was really over, even at graduation. It wasn't until I had gotten home, grabbed something to eat, and taken the phone off the hook, that I finally didn't expect to see an instructor show up at the front door and send me back to the surf zone. I was always looking over my shoulder for the instructor I knew had to be there. After graduation, I got in the car as quickly as possible and had my girlfriend drive me home.

The Trident on my chest is, most important, representative of a commitment to a legacy and a commitment to those who have gone before. Guys from the Teams in Vietnam, such as Barry Enoch, Mike Thornton, and Don Crawford, had sacrificed a lot. And other guys left their lives back in Vietnam. Guys in the Teams take that very seriously. At SEAL Team One, we have those guys come back and talk to the Teams. They let us know where we came from.

I also think that there's a legacy of leadership in the men who went before us. You have only to look around you to see guys in and out of the Teams who have continued to be leaders, officer and enlisted alike, in civilian life. They continue to be extraordinary men. So it's not only a leadership role to be in the Teams, to be

a SEAL is also a leadership role for the community, the culture at large, and the nation.

BUD/S training creates a guy who is capable of thinking on his feet and acting individually to the maximum of his capacity. But he also knows that he is part of a team effort. In a singular, visceral manner, a BUD/S graduate is able to concentrate on the mission at hand to the exclusion of everything else. It doesn't matter how cold he is, how painful his situation, or how tired or beat up the guy is, he is able to concentrate on the mission. And he is able to do that in part because he knows he is acting in concert with one, six, seven, eight, or sixteen other guys to accomplish that mission.

I don't think there is such a thing as a loner in the Teams. There are guys who are eccentric, guys who are quite different from even the average SEAL, but they all work as part of the Team, part of a platoon. I've had a couple such men in my own platoons. Each platoon has its own dynamic, and each platoon integrates all its parts and brings out the best in those guys. They would not have made it through training if they did not have the raw materials to make it in the Teams. And the most important of those raw materials is the ability to work as a team.

So the teamwork attitude is there. It's innate in every SEAL, but it might not be as obvious in some people as it is in others. So when each platoon develops its own dynamic, it brings out the best in those people, in all its parts, and uses them to its greatest advantage.

It's always been sort of a dichotomy that there's a great deal of individualism in each member of a SEAL platoon. But they all sort of subjugate that individuality and concentrate to develop the dynamic that allows the team to work best together. I think that's an incredibly powerful message about what they are able to do in BUD/S, and it's a very powerful message about what a SEAL platoon can accomplish, to be able to transcend those differences and individuality between its members and become a very effective, functioning team.

My first assignment after BUD/S graduation was to SEAL Team One. Since then, I've moved around a lot, but my operational career has been centered on the West Coast, primarily at SEAL Team One. I was fortunate enough to have two platoons at SEAL Team One, one of which I went to the Gulf War with.

In the Persian Gulf during DESERT SHIELD/DESERT STORM, we were doing primarily reconnaissance missions. We did a reconnaissance and surveillance mission on the border between Kuwait and Saudi Arabia, north of Khafji—which was attacked by the Iraqis on 16 January 1991.

We were tasked with seeing if there were any mine-laying activities, troop movements, or anything of consequence going on up there. We saw quite a few things going on, and we were there on the border the night when the air war was launched and the war actually started. By the time the ground war was launched, we had abandoned our observation post, as the area was no longer tenable.

UDT operators in the Pacific during WWII prepare explosive charges prior to an operation. They are cutting the blocks from M1 tetrytol chains apart to make smaller individual charges. The blocks are further wrapped with a length of cord to secure them to a target. This procedure made the equivalent of a Hagensen pack for use in the hot environment of the Pacific Islands. The men are very comfortable working with this quantity of explosives. So much so that several of the men are sitting on loaded haversacks.

U.S. Navy

Until Khafji, we conducted ground operations as our primary mission. After the Iraqi attack on Khafji, Admiral Ray Smith, the SEAL commander in the Gulf, decided that we could best serve the CinC (Commander-in-Chiefs pronounced sinks) by conducting maritime reconnaissance missions into Kuwait. These were missions conducted well behind Iraqi lines to see if there was a good point for an amphibious landing.

Our operations off the coast of Kuwait were very much like those conducted by the UDTs on enemy-held beaches in the Pacific during World War II. I'd like to think that we were doing the operations as our forefathers had. I have always admired those early Frogmen. The degree of courage it took to go in at daybreak, search for obstacles, place demolitions on them, then blow the demolition—all while under enemy fire—took and extraordinary amount of courage, especially with the losses the NCDU (Naval Combat Demolition Units) took in Normandy.

I'd like to think that the mission we did in the Persian Gulf was still a viable mission. Tom Deitz's platoon succeeded in distracting and diverting a large number of

the Iraqis into a coastal area we had no intention of invading. That was a very successful operation. I have since found out that the diversion operation was very much like the those run by the UDT during World War II and even Vietnam.

The thing that sticks out in my mind about DESERT STORM is the extraordinary character of the guys I worked with, the guys in my platoon. Their sense of humor was great. We still laugh about some of the things that happened today.

It is right around Christmas now (1998), so I think a lot about the season and being there in the Gulf at that time of year. My platoon chief, Randy Palladium, had just missed being in Vietnam, and here he was in the Gulf. He loved that movie Platoon, which had only been released for a couple years then. He had a copy of the soundtrack with us. He would often play that very poignant passage by Samuel Barber, the adagio for strings. Then he would say to us, "If I ever don't come back, you guys know what to do. Give my wife the flag . . ."

It was so melodramatic that we would all laugh about it. "Randy, you're not going to die," we would say. And of course he didn't. We laughed at him then, and we sort of laugh at him now. He is a great operator, but that was a very funny moment to us.

There was another op that we were on in the Gulf. We were about a kilometer from the beach, about twenty kilometers north of the border, and it was pitch black. There were A-6s (intruder strike aircraft) running air strikes into the area where we were inserting for a beach reconnaissance. Three swimmers were to be inserted—myself and Jimmy and Jerry, two members of my platoon. My communicator, Lafe, was on the radio, and he also had the GPS (global positioning system) receiver, so he knew exactly at what point we would put the swimmers in the water.

It was very cold, and the boat was advancing slowly at an idle. It took us quite a while to get from the 2-kilometer point in to the 1,000-meter point where we were going to launch the swimmers. We were still about two kilometers off the beach when Lafe leaned over to Jimmy and nodded his head. Then Jimmy went into the water. Lafe started laughing hysterically because Jimmy was now wet, cold, and miserable—and we were still about an hour from the insert point.

We did see the oil wells in Kuwait, but we didn't see them when they were on fire. We were at a place called Ras al-Mishab, the base from where we launched the high-speed boats, when they were burning. It was very eerie, almost like the movie Bladerunner. There was no day and no night, and it just rained a thick, black oil that accumulated in puddles on the ground. It was almost apocalyptic in the appearance. It was just black and there was nothing but oily water coming out of the sky. It really made you think of Armageddon. That fact wasn't lost on the guys, and they laughed pretty hard about that.

We were extremely busy during the whole of DESERT SHIELD/DESERT STORM. A lot of our staff were involved with the early days of the conflict. Some had been working all through September, October, November, and December. During the air war in January, we were very involved as well. When the ground war finally started in February, it was almost anticlimactic to us.

To a certain extent, that was due to Admiral Raymond Smith. He realized that once there were troops moving in on the ground, advanced force ops were no longer relevant, and our job was basically done. There wasn't anything to be added to the CinC's objectives once the ground war had occurred.

The mission we did have, that we ultimately weren't successful in, was to go and interdict elements of the Iraqi police force that was escaping from Kuwait City on to Bubiyan Island. We were just a little too late and didn't encounter any Iraqis, but we like to think that we were the first ones into Kuwait City proper. We had fast-attack vehicles with the Marines at the airport, but my platoon was actually sitting in the boat basin in Kuwait City when they were fighting it out on the runway. There just wasn't anyone there at that point for us to engage.

One thing we were very concerned with prior to and during the war was the mine threat in the Persian Gulf. We had been listening to the news reports and no one really knew just how capable the Iraqis were in laying sea mines. We had heard reports that the Iraqis had laid the mines but never armed them. Mines, for a Frogman, can be a very pronounced deterrent effect.

We were very worried, it was so pitch black when we were swimming into the beach that I figured that since I couldn't see the Iraqis, I knew they couldn't see me. Or at least I contented myself with that fact. But there was a good degree of apprehension as we went in on our first combat operation. At the same time, there was a high degree of exhilaration. Missions like that, classic SEAL water ops, are very few and far between. And here I was, swimming in on an enemy beach to go do one.

We ran into some problems just moving offshore in our boats after Saddam had ordered the valves opened up in Kuwait, creating the oil spills in the Gulf. Our high-speed boats, the equivalent of cigarette boats, would leave Ras al-Mishab and quickly run into trouble. Oil on top of the water would be so thick that our boat engines would overheat because they were not able to draw in cooling water.

About eight months after the war, I went back to Ras al-Mishab as the platoon commander of another SEAL platoon. I was amazed at how the environment had rebounded from the effects of the oil spills and fires. But I'm sure a lot of the oil just sank to the bottom and caused untold environmental damage that just didn't show on the surface.

Although I did not see the actual oil well fires while they were burning, I experienced some of the results. Black, oily rain falling down on you twenty-four hours a day made the duration of the war no fun.

We're losing some guys on the Teams now. The economy is really good on the outside and private industry does a great job of marketing, so men leave the Teams for the civilian sector. There are still a lot of guys who are staying on, and I think that speaks well of their character. They're just extraordinary guys. I think one of the reasons that guys stay around is that the Teams attract purists. There's no "just in time delivery" or "just good enough to get by" attention on the profit margin.

The men in the Teams are purists doing a very dangerous job to absolute perfection—because there is no margin of error in our line of work. Our mission demands nothing less.

Last night, I went to the airport to greet one of the platoons coming in from the Persian Gulf. The leading petty officer of that platoon was at Khafji. He was one of the three guys who had been able to escape the Iraqi advance and let us know they were coming. We, my platoon, had just left the border about fifteen minutes before that happened, so we had a only fire team in Khafji at the time.

When I greeted him, that man was coming back from his third or fourth Gulf deployment since then. These guys all sort of remind me of Horatio Hornblower at the bridge. They're just extraordinary guys doing an extraordinarily difficult job, and for not too much pay. They're largely underappreciated and forgotten in peacetime. They are men of incredible character, and their degree of self-sacrifice is too high to be measured.

Even if they can't express it very eloquently, I think they all realize that happiness is not achieved through any pursuit of self-indulgence or self-fulfillment. It's really achieved through assiduously pursuing a just cause.

And I think they believe in the cause, as they believe in their Teammates. That's what makes Naval Special warfare so successful—the bond that develops between us. The bond between myself and the guys that I got to work with during the Gulf War remains very strong. I talk to those men on an almost daily basis, and I have served with the few of them who are with SEAL Team One right now. That fact was not lost on me last night when that man came back from the Gulf after a six-month deployment.

A SEAL is someone who is almost perfectly adapted to the aquatic environment and is extremely adept in transitioning from the water to the land. SEALs operate mostly in the littoral area, that area relating to the shore and coastal regions, to accomplish a variety of missions.

The thing that sets us apart from other Special Operations forces is our ability to operate seamlessly in that area. It is the most demanding area that Special Operations is tasked to work in.

The reason we can do that work starts at the Naval Special Warfare Center with the instructors at BUD/S. When I think of the instructors, I'm reminded of a quote from Goethe in which he said something along the lines of, "If you treat a man as he is, he will remain as he is. But if you treat him as he should be, he will become who he should be."

The instructors at BUD/S create an image of themselves, an image of a SEAL as a SEAL should be. I think that is what is so extraordinary about BUD/S and why SEALs come out of BUD/s without necessarily thinking that they have done anything particularly extraordinary. They're proud of their accomplishment, to be sure. But after graduation, it's time to move on, do other things, and get into the work of being a SEAL and actually get into the work where they can utilize the skills they spent so long acquiring.

The road to being a SEAL doesn't end with BUD/S. That's really only just the beginning of training. After graduation, you're qualified to take part in the platoon training cycle—which is extremely demanding. In the Teams, I've been colder than I was in BUD/S, and I've done harder stuff than I did while in BUD/S. But BUD/S is the psychological training that lets you know you can do it. The rule of thumb is that your body can do ten times more than your mind thinks it can do. I didn't believe that before I went to BUD/S, but now I do believe it.

There were runs at BUD/S where I thought my heart was going to come out of my mouth and I was going to turn inside out and die on the beach. But there was always something that got me through it. One of the instructors' favorite things was to do the run, say a four-mile run, and then, just as you thought you were back at the Team, they would continue running down the beach.

The lesson learned was that the op is never over. You never can relax until you are actually back home and the gear is cleaned up. You can never say, "Well, the way the op is planned, we'll be home in four hours."

There is no "four hours", there is no time limit. That's what they try to instill in training, to not get demoralized when the rules change. If you do get demoralized when the rules change, that's the mark of an amateur. The mark of a true professional is to be able to persevere through that, and anything else. That's what they create at BUD/S, the raw material of the professional.

Our last war of consequence was DESERT STORM. In spite of that, I think it's important not to dwell too much on the Gulf War as a milestone in Naval Special Warfare. It certainly taught us some very valuable lessons about boats, our mobility, and our ability to operate in a maritime environment. We also leaned how to better conduct those seamless transitions from the water to the land that are so important to our operations. But as a seminal event in Naval Special Warfare, we're not going to have a compliant enemy like we did in the Gulf ever again.

We're going to have to be able to think on our feet and to deploy much faster with a much more adaptable force package, than we deployed with for DESERT SHIELD/DESERT STORM. We won't have six months to built up and train for the missions we'll have to do. The actions will be now and with what we brought with us.

That's the lesson that might have been learned in the Gulf. We were very well led and very fortunate not to have any casualties. The missions we did supported the CinC but were very justifiable in the amount of risk that was assumed. Those were important factors that were laid out in the beginning by Admiral Smith. He did not take missions that we were not suited to do, and he did not take missions for the SEALs that did not support the CinC's objectives.

That was very clear to us. We knew that lives were not going to be put in danger unnecessarily. SEALs will put their lives at risk, they'll do a mission regardless of the risk—if they know it's not a frivolous mission and if they know that the mission supports the national, or at least the CinC's, objectives.

To concentrate on the Gulf would be a mistake. We need to look toward the future. There were lessons learned during DESERT SHIELD and DESERT STORM, and we need to continue to integrate those lessons into the way we do business now.

I think Vietnam was the crucible in which modern Naval Special Warfare, the SEALs, were formed. We owe an extraordinary debt of gratitude to those guys from Vietnam.

The SEALs who served in Vietnam are very magnanimous about their service in that war. They did what they did for the right reasons. They did it for their country, and they did it for their Teammates.

President Ronald Reagan said that there's no limit to what you can do if you don't care who gets the credit. SEALs are like that. Good SEAL officers realize that it's not their leadership, it's their ability to bring out the best in their men. It's the men who are responsible for all our successes in the Teams. As officers, we provide a minimal amount of guidance and direction, and the guys just exceed themselves at every opportunity. It's very gratifying to watch that. It's also very, very humbling to be around men of that caliber.

I think that's why you find that SEALs—especially those SEALs from Vietnam—don't go around patting themselves on the back. They've faced fire and seen friends die. To walk around and puff themselves up, to pat themselves on the back, would be to desecrate the memory of their fallen comrades.

They should be justifiably proud of what they do. But I think it's also quite understandable why they don't show it. Barry Enoch wrote a great book called Teammates that explains it much better than I ever could.

The guys from Vietnam created a legend. Their stories were around at the Naval Academy. The stories circulate around the Navy, even on my ship. Guys like Mike Thornton are in the community. You run into a guy in the commissary who has ribbons that go from his pocket, over the top of his shoulder, and down his back. You can figure that he has been there and done that.

You see Mike Thornton someplace and you just go, Man, just who is that guy? I want to be like him. When I was younger, I saw the way SEALs were confident and how they carried themselves—poised, articulate, no-nonsense, and no-compromise kind of guys—and that made me want to be with them. They have principles, and they adhere to them. They get a mission, and they do it. That's what appealed to me about the SEALs before I even joined the Teams.

When I did join the Teams, I wasn't surprised at the people I met and worked with. I had found exactly what I was looking for. Working with guys who exude confidence from every pore of their body and are the ultimate professionals at what they do is more than a pleasure. They are purists who won't rest until the job is 100 percent complete—not just "good enough," but 100 percent complete, because they know there's no margin for error in their world.

I think the Hollywood image of the SEALs is excessive. I think the best thing that could happen to Naval Special Warfare is to put up a big, black fence around every SEAL Team with a big sign that says "DO NOT ENTER UNDER PENALTY OF DEADLY FORCE."

That would be our best recruiting poster, too, because we would attract the right kind of guys to the Teams. It's not that we don't now, but there are guys who are attracted to the SEALs because of the Rambo image. They rarely make it through BUD/S. If they are guys who show up that way, but have the character, the innate skills, and most important, the psychological makeup to make it through BUD/S, they will. It was always there in them, they just came for the wrong reasons—but they stayed for the right ones.

What I hope people learn from this is that being a SEAL is very, very hard work. The guys work extremely hard. They spend a lot of time away from home and make extraordinary sacrifices for their chosen jobs. And they do a job that's absolutely essential to our national security. It's very often forgotten around Thanksgiving and Christmas, but those guys are always there, on the edge. They are always vigilant, and they're always downrange and doing that job.

When the rest of us are sleeping or worried about how our stocks are doing, when we're tucking our kids in at night or taking them to child-care in the morning, and when we're just sitting down to eat, there are always those guys who are downrange, doing the job. They have to leave their families far behind. And they do their jobs for not much pay, because they're professionals and they're proud of what they do.

The first word that comes to mind when I think of the SEALs is competence. That word speaks for itself. The level of competence SEALs are able to demonstrate in three different environments—sea, air, and land—is governed by a document that lists the skills we're required to maintain.

The quantum leap in technology that has occurred between Vietnam and today demands a smarter guy. That is to take nothing away from the men who worked in the swamps and rice paddies of Vietnam, but the guys who come into the Teams now are technically proficient. They're brilliant. A full third of the enlisted men who graduate from BUD/S have college degrees.

At SEAL Team One right now, there's a Rhodes Scholar. Another lettered scholar just left a few months ago to study in Paris. These are exceptional people, with exceptional educations and diverse backgrounds. It's been healthy for the Teams to take in that kind of guy. Conversely, those guys who are so talented are also highly sought outside the Navy. Some of them succumb to the temptation and leave, that's sort of the nature of the beast. But the guys in the SEALs are, by and large, extremely competent.

It's so gratifying to work with guys who have achieved the levels of skill, competence, professionalism, and most of all the self-discipline to make the most of their skills. It makes being an officer in the Teams a privilege and a pleasure.

It's trite to say that the world is not becoming any safer. I think it's difficult to realize that unless you go to some other countries. I had the opportunity to live in France for two and a half years. In 1995, on almost a weekly basis, there were bombs going off in Paris subways, killing scores of people. We have not had anything like that, to that degree, here in the United States yet. [Note: This interview took place several years prior to September 11, 2001.]

But the schism between the haves and the have-nots, and the mass migrations of refugees and people seeking a better way of life in the more developed countries, is going to create a great deal of friction. That friction is going to create instability.

SEALs, and special operators in general, thrive in that chaos. There are missions that require us to go to those regions and to monitor that instability, to perhaps aid refugees and decrease that instability. And in some cases, to manage violence for U.S. national objectives.

I mentioned that SEALs thrive in a chaotic environment. They are language-trained, they are operationally savvy, and they're street smart. They are strong, mentally tough, and self-disciplined. They are mature, and they know how to fade in and out of situations in complete silence. The world is not becoming a safer place; instability is going to continue to grow. For that, we have the Teams. As Plato said, "Only the dead have seen the end of war."

Tom Deitz, Commander

When I was deployed to the Persian Gulf, I had to have a mini history lesson on Saddam Hussein. When I first heard that Iraq had invaded Kuwait, my first question was, "Where's Kuwait?" Then we did an intelligence study on Saddam Hussein. Really his persistence was impressive—ten years in the Iran-Iraq War, which resulted in sort of a stalemate, yet he was still in charge.

Special Operations is a group of military personnel from all services who focus in small number on certain missions. Our missions as SEALs are primarily direct action, special reconnaissance, psychological warfare, guerrilla warfare, and foreign internal defense.

The role of Special Operations during DESERT SHIELD was to get in place and to find out exactly what we needed to do in case a war broke out. We did that by working with the Saudi Arabian special forces and doing some training missions with them. While we were doing that, we were also able to look at the coastal bases the Saudi Arabians had, to see if we could possibly use them later in a wartime situation as a forward staging base.

The Saudi Arabian navy special warfare forces at the time were very determined. They were fearful for the fate of their country, therefore they were training harder in case they had to be deployed. They were defending their country, so they were very proud. I've worked with them since, and their equipment and tactics have increased dramatically over time.

I only know of a few, about three, Saudi Arabian naval personnel who went through the full BUD/S course. I don't think we've had any go through since DESERT SHIELD/DESERT STORM, but there are others who would know that much better than I.

A force multiplier is really what Special Operations brings to the table. We are small in number, yet the missions we can conduct have a dramatic impact on the military as a whole.

The biggest advantage the United States had during the Gulf War was our determination. We knew why we were there. We saw the atrocities committed by the Iraqis on the Kuwaiti people. There was really a purpose for us to be there.

The devastation of Kuwait by the Iraqis was horrendous. There really cannot be a reason for a country to do that to another country, much less a neighbor with the same ethnic and religious backgrounds. The atrocities committed by Iraq were truly uncalled for.

On 2 August 1990, it was really a total surprise when the Iraqis came across their border with Kuwait in strength. Looking back, yes, there was some intelligence, and the Iraqis had been gathering near the border. But they had done that many times before. The idea of them actually attacking Kuwait had never been a realistic thought. But they did. They just stormed in.

Militarily, it was a great operation. But the way they treated the Kuwaiti population was excessive. They drove them out of their country. I got to see some of Kuwait City after the cease-fire and the war had ended. It was just devastated.

The Iraqi troops I encountered during my reconnaissance and direct-action mission either weren't paying attention, or we really were as sneaky as we claim to be. We saw a lot of their patrol boats and some personnel back off the beach a little bit, yet they never saw us.

When I was looking at how we would conduct DESERT STORM, if we did move to that phase, I was very confident that America would do it the right way, from President Bush, a World War II veteran, to Generals Schwarzkopf and Powell, both Vietnam-era Army captains. They saw firsthand on the ground in Vietnam what a poorly fought and poorly directed war can do to a country. From my perspective, I was confident that they would not let that happen in DESERT STORM.

My platoon was SEAL Team Five, Foxtrot Platoon, and our mission focus was coastal reconnaissance. We did reconnaissance missions, gathering intelligence all along the Kuwaiti coast. Our missions were not just on the beach itself, but we also looked at what type of patrol boats were being used, what type of navigation aids were out there in the water, and how the Iraqis were manning the water and the coastline.

Looking at the missions we conducted, they were very similar to what the Navy Combat Demolition Teams and Underwater Demolition Teams did in World War II both in the European theater and in the Pacific. We swam in to beaches with explosive charges, then we placed those charges on and near obstacles. Other than the PowerPoint briefings that we had to give via computers, our missions were probably very similar to the missions conducted in World War II.

Part of getting the intelligence from a beach is determining the trafficability. By that I mean determining if the sand is strong enough to hold the vehicles that would be crossing the beach. We were told that we would be going in and doing a deception operation; therefore, getting sand samples really wasn't in our mission area. It was planned to be a deception from the very beginning. I was the platoon commander in charge of the deception operation on the Kuwaiti coast.

The threat of an amphibious invasion by U.S. forces was very clear. I think the Iraqis realized it was a definite option for the U.S. Navy and Marine Corps, and we played along with that idea. There were rehearsal landings in the southern Gulf conducted by the amphibious ships and the Marine Corps.

So the Iraqis were looking at history, and they were looking at CNN. They really thought that there was going to be an amphibious invasion. In addition to the reconnaissance missions, my platoon was tasked with scouting out a beach where it would be feasible to support an amphibious landing.

Even though we were going to be doing it as a deception, we still had to find a beach that was suitable. If you try to deceive someone on a small beach that couldn't handle a landing, they wouldn't take it seriously. The idea behind the deception was really to hold the Iraqi troops on the coast and not have them move inland to try and stop the ground forces from coming in.

The Iraqis in Kuwait had been bombed for upward of forty days and were a little shell-shocked at the time of our deception operation. Twenty-four hours prior to when we were going to blow up the beach, we ceased any air strikes and any naval gunfire in the area of our target beach. We wanted it to be quiet.

We left our base in northern Saudi Arabia in four forty-foot high-speed boats. When we were seven miles off the coast of our target beach, we took to our eighteen-foot rubber zodiac boats, which held my fifteen-man SEAL platoon. The zo-

One of the Soviet-made Iraqi S-60 57mm antiaircraft guns. The weapon is emplaced so that it could sweep the beach and offshore waters with its full-automatic fire of high explosive shells. A number of the four-round clips of ammunition to the gun are stacked along the left side of the weapon.

Kevin Dockery

diacs then moved in to about a thousand yards offshore. That's where six of us got out and swam in to the beach. We left the boats probably around 2215 hours (10:15 in the evening), and swam in so we could be on the beach and pull the pins at 2300 hours (11 P.M.).

Myself and five other SEALs swam in off the zodiacs, each of us towing a twenty-pound haversack of explosives. We spread out to cover two hundred and fifty yards of beach. The timing clocks on the charges we set to go off at 0100 hours; the ground war was scheduled to commence three hours later at 0400 hours. We wanted to give the Iraqis about three hours to react to our deception.

We swam in, placed the charges on the beach, pulled the timers, and came back out and rendezvoused with our boats. The firing runs we were going to make along the beach were to start at 12:30, thirty minutes prior to our explosives going off.

If you had been an Iraqi on the Kuwaiti shore, you hadn't been bombed for about twenty-four hours and you thought the U.S. Marines were going to be coming in to your beach. Then, all of a sudden, in the middle of the night, you were being shot at. You would know it wasn't an airplane, and you would know it wasn't a battleship firing shells at you. If you peeked your head up, you'd see small boats about five hundred yards offshore just hammering your position.

All kinds of fire would be coming in—.50 caliber and 7.62mm machine guns as well as 40mm grenade launchers. An Iraqi on the beach would keep his head up a little bit, but not too much because all our fire would have been coming in strong.

Our boats shot at the beach for about ten minutes. Following that, we threw four pounds of C4 plastic explosive wrapped in plastic over the side of the boat with delay fuses attached. They exploded sporadically over the next fifteen minutes. Again, the Iraqis would be seeing and hearing explosions very close to the beach. Five minutes after that, the six charges went off. Twenty pounds of C4 makes a heck of a noise. We had six charges that size going off in a span of about thirty seconds.

That was the picture the Iraqis would have seen. That was what our deception consisted of, and it worked. The Iraqi forces along the coast stayed there. Additionally, elements of two separate Iraqi armored divisions that had been facing south and waiting for the ground forces to come in began to move toward the coastline in reaction to our deception.

This was the fifth time we had gone north. The first four times had been reconnaissance missions. The adrenaline, especially that first night we went north, was definitely peaked. I think the adrenaline probably pushed down any nervousness we might have been feeling. When we got to the actual mission of swimming in and placing the charges on the beach, knowing the ground war was starting three hours later, the professional side of being a Navy SEAL took over. You become very focused on your mission, and you don't let any outside forces come in on your thoughts. You conduct your mission, pull back out, and they never see you.

The fear of being captured really did not come into play on our ops. Certain Special Operations missions put you more into harm's way. We were in the water or we were in our boats. Yes, there were Iraqi patrol boats out there, but in a small zodiac boat going pretty slow. It was very doubtful that anyone was going to see us. We also had communications directly to the airborne controller. If we needed close-air support, we could call in a plane to help us.

Usually, we would take our own boats and go north on an op. The third night we went, the seas were brutal. The Persian Gulf is usually a picture of calm waters. In the winter, though, it gets very rough. The winds that night were about thirty-five knots, and the seas were running six to seven feet. Our boats just couldn't make it.

That night, we got dropped in by two MH53 Pave Low's from Air Force Special Operations and MH60s from the Army's 160th SOAR (Special Operations Aviation Regiment) flew in as gunship cover. That was a great night because it was true joint special operations mission—an Air Force special operations helicopter dropping in Navy SEALs with Army special operations helicopters flying cover.

The 160th Special Operations Aviation Regiment, better known as the Nightstalkers, are, I would say, the premier combat helicopter pilots in the world. Whenever we can work with them, we will.

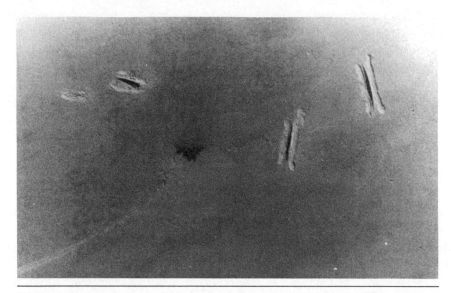

The faint markings of Iraqi Scud missile launcher emplacements in the sands of the desert. The small raised sand berms are for the protection of the missile crews when the weapons are launched. The long black scorch marks in the sand are the only remaining evidence that the long-gone Scud missiles were ever actually there.

U.S. Navy

Obtaining ground truth is having a real person in an area who can come back and debrief the exact intelligence that's there. Satellite coverage can get really tricky, especially in the Gulf with the oil fires creating cloud cover. When someone swims into a beach and comes back and tells you that there are these types of mines, these types of concertina wire, and this amount of personnel activity, there's no doubt that it is exactly what's there.

Today's technology allows detailed satellite coverage—yes, you can read a license plate from space. But when a cloud comes in, a storm rolls in, or there are fires and smoke covers the target, a satellite cannot get through that, so you need people on the ground.

The smoke from the oil fires made working in the Gulf area very eerie. Cloud cover, actually smoke cover, maybe a hundred feet off the deck of the Persian Gulf, acted as almost a sound barrier for some of the explosions that would happen inland, reverberate off the smoke, come down to bounce off the water, then come up to us on the boat. It was a pretty good show.

A direct-action mission is just what the name says: You go in and conduct an action. Special reconnaissance is when you're going in to collect intelligence, and a lot of time that leads to a direct-action mission. Scud hunting is another kind of reconnaissance and was possibly a direct-action mission in the Gulf.

The Naval Special Warfare forces in the Gulf were on search-and-rescue alert twenty-four/seven. We had one SEAL platoon that was out and divided among three ships in the northern Gulf on CSAR (combat search-and-rescue) alert with a helicopter element. We were pier-side with our boats. At any one time we had four personnel with CSAR equipment and ready to go.

There was one Air Force pilot who was shot down and bailed out into the water. Our boats were under way in under five minutes, and the helicopter from the ship with the SEALs onboard was off the deck in under five minutes. From the time the pilot ejected to the time he was back onboard a ship, healthy and recovered, was only thirty-five minutes total.

The importance of recovering pilots is crucial, and it's the American way. You never want to leave anyone behind, you never want to have anyone captured. In reality, some people are going to get captured. But we need to be able to stand by and prevent that from happening whenever possible.

A classmate of mine from the Naval Academy at Annapolis, Lieutenant Jeff Zaun, was in the Gulf. I came down to our office one morning and looked at the list of pilots who had been shot down and saw his name. Three days later, his face was on the cover of Newsweek. That really hit home. The treatment the Iraqis were giving our warriors was uncalled for.

We did no rescue operations on land. That was the job of the PJs, the Air Force Pararescuemen. They were the guys who picked up an F-14 pilot who was shot down over land.

The commander for Naval Special Warfare in the Gulf was Captain Ray Smith, who just retired as a rear admiral. When we went over there, he was discussing our employment with his superiors. He came back and told the SEAL platoon that we were going to keep one foot in the water. By that, he meant that we would be doing work along the coast, on the coast, and maybe a little bit inland from the coast. But we weren't going to get out of our sphere. The water is where SEALs come from. The water is where SEALs go back to. And there's no one who does that better than us.

For a Navy SEAL, water is our element. If we get in trouble, we look for the nearest way to get back to the water. Once we're there, we feel safe.

Everything we do in training and in real-world missions comes from the water. We'll have sixty to seventy pounds of gear we'll take in the water. You look at the normal person and ask him to carry that amount of gear on land, and it will be difficult for him. You tell him to swim three miles with that gear, and that's a much greater level of difficulty. But that's what SEALs do every day.

A psychological operation, psyop, is a method of getting into the mind of the enemy. We were able to do that with CNN showing the Marines and the amphibious forces doing landings in the southern part of the Gulf as rehearsals. Then Newsweek wrote an article saying that the ground war had actually started because Navy SEALs had been swimming in to the beaches. All that built up in the Iraqi mind-set that "Hey, these guys are coming in!" Then our deception operation was one final psychological aspect to help make the Iraqis think that yes, we were going to conduct a major landing.

Doug Waller, who wrote that Newsweek article, also wrote a book called The Commandos. When I told him I read his article, he started laughing. He really thought that we were swimming in. That article had been written some time earlier. I came back the first night I had done a reconnaissance, debriefed, and went out to a Saudi store and bought that Newsweek. There it was written up. I said, "I did the first one, and it hasn't happened yet." But the media were pitching the idea. It was great for us.

The media have a lot of ex-military and a lot of very intelligent analysts, so they can sort of get a good picture of what we might be doing. If that convinces the enemy that yes, we are doing it, so much the better for us.

The deception operation and the rehearsals that helped make it so believable worked. The only people on our side who were unhappy with it were the Marines. When there's a war, the Marines want to go ashore. When they don't get to, they are not happy. The rehearsals were good, but the Marines and the amphibious forces really wanted to do that mission.

The world knew that when the SEALs go in to a beach to blow up obstacle, a landing force isn't far behind. Later, in Somalia in late 1992, the guys who swam in to the beach and faced all the cameras were Marine Force Recon swimmers. The SEALs were a quarter-mile down the beach. They had told the Marines that there was a bunch of press where they wanted to land, and that they didn't want to go in there. The Marines decided to go ahead with their landing reconnaissance anyway and were filmed for the whole world to see.

Navy frogmen emplace demolition charges on beach obstacles. This classic UDT operation was carried forward and assigned to the Navy SEALs today.

U.S. Navy

The deception operation was really what we were focused on, and that was a kind of psyop. The leaflet campaign conducted by Air Force Special Operations was fantastic. Millions of leaflets, designed to help convince the Iraqi soldier to surrender, were dropped over enemy areas. I think it's a tribute to that operation that a lot of Iraqis were holding those pamphlets when they surrendered to U.S. forces.

Psychological operations are not always meant to deceive. They're also meant to tell the truth to people who are not receiving the whole picture. The Iraqis were not being told the truth by their chain of command. When we dropped leaflets saying that we would bomb this area tonight and you need to leave and go to this other area and then actually bomb that area, the soldier on the ground believes us and not his chain of command. That undermines what the enemy is trying to do while we are still telling them the truth.

On a whole, the performance of Special Operations in DESERT STORM was a true success. We went in there and there were Army, Air Force, and Navy Special Operations units. Each of us had our own task to do, and we weren't stepping on each other. Naval Special Warfare went over there with 275 personnel, and we returned with 275 personnel. When everybody comes back and the task is accomplished, it is a success by every measure of the word.

The platoon that was out on the three ships also conducted some hot operations besides CSAR duty. U.S. helicopters came under fire on 18 January from several Iraqi-held oil platforms in the Gulf. SEALs counterattacked and boarded the platforms, capturing weapons and gathering valuable intelligence documents. The Iraqis basically surrendered by the time the SEALs got there, so it wasn't as hostile a takedown as it could have been. The Iraqis had been beaten up pretty good by

Examples of some of the psychological warfare leaflets dropped over Iraqi positions during Desert Storm. Just holding the colorful leaflet overhead was supposed to signal the peaceful surrender of an Iraqi soldier.

Iraqi troops surrendering in a group. The man in the front is holding a surrender leaflet dropped by psyops forces.

the surface Navy before the SEALs went in. In some respects, it was a preview of what the ground war would be.

We left for the States soon after the war was over. We were the first West Coast platoon to return to CONUS. The reaction of the Kuwaiti people to our liberation of their country was phenomenal. I was able to go into Kuwait City after the cease-fire, and they were having spontaneous parades thanking not only the United States, but all the Coalition forces. It was a great feeling to see the American flag being held up and Kuwaitis looking up and being very proud of that.

I don't think Saddam Hussein really expected us to come in the way we did. He probably thought he could wait us out. What President Bush, General Schwarzkopf, and General Powell did was make sure that we had the exact forces needed to do the mission in a timely manner, succeed in the mission, then leave the area.

Probably the best lessons we came away from Desert Storm with was not to underestimate an enemy, and not to move until we were firmly sure in our military and political minds that it is the right thing to do.

Our expectations when we landed in Saudi Arabia on 12 August were really, "Okay, how can we get out of here if the Iraqis come south?" They had the fourth-largest standing army in the world. If they wanted to come south at that time, there would have been nothing to stop them. With the possible nuclear, chemical, and biological weapons they were purported to have, that was a something we really couldn't worry about much. If it happened, there wasn't much we could do.

As DESERT SHIELD went on, it became pretty obvious that the Iraqis weren't go-

ing to come south. If the U.S. and Coalition forces continued to build up as we did, then our fear, our anxiety about the Iraqis, lessened.

As with U.S. intelligence, the Kuwaitis looked at the buildup of the Iraqi troops in the beginning of August 1990 as just another ruse. This was just another bully tactic from Saddam Hussein. The Kuwaiti military forces were taken by surprise as much as we were, and the conquest of Kuwait was relatively easy for the Iraqis. Granted, with the size of the Iraqi army, even if it wasn't by surprise, they would have still been able to take Kuwait. It would have just been a little more difficult and costly for them.

Victory is the only acceptable outcome. Commanding officers are supposed to put together a command philosophy. Some guys write it out as narratives; I made mine "SEAL TEAM FIVE." For every letter I wrote a sentence. When I got to the V in FIVE, I wrote "Victory is the only acceptable outcome."

There's no substitute for real-world operations. Timing is such that a SEAL can go his entire career and never do a real-world mission. The fact that timing was on my side, and we were prepared for it at the time, definitely helps me when I have the young SEALs coming in now. They know that when I was a lieutenant, I was in real-world missions. That gives me a little bit of credibility, but nothing much. If I don't build on that myself, then all it is is history.

All the various units in Special Operations have their purpose, their mission. The Rangers, coming in with the size they have (it's relatively small compared to the Army, but relatively large compared to a SEAL platoon or Special Forces Operational Detachment), come in hard and hit you hard. The Army Special Forces, better known as the Green Berets, are small units like us. Their cultural and language skills allow them to work with almost any nation in the entire world, and they do a great job at it.

■ Chapter 62

Somalia

Somalia is a long, slender country on the east coast of Africa. Roughly bent in the shape of the numeral 7, Somalia makes up the point of what is called the Horn of Africa. If the continent of Africa was a face looking east, Somalia would be the nose.

A national rebellion overthrew the twenty-one-year-old dictatorial Somali government of Siad Barre in early 1991. The elimination of the Barre regime was not replaced by a central government, and the control of Somalia was split up among various groups of feuding military strongmen who proposed themselves as warlords of the country. The warlords took over the extended family clans that made up the clan system that had managed Somalia for decades. The warlords pillaged the country to build up their own power bases and obtain funds, food, and supplies for their men. In the wake of this situation, hundreds of thousands of Somalis faced famine and death by starvation.

Somali warlord fighters destroyed farms and stole foodstuffs sent in by the world's relief organizations. The death by starvation of 100,000 Somalis cause the United Nations to dispatch a humanitarian peacekeeping mission to protect the relief efforts and help stop the severe famine.

In support of the UN relief effort, President George Bush ordered Operation PROVIDE RELIEF initiated. In August, men from the 2nd Battalion, 5th Special Forces Group, deployed to Kenya to provide security for Somalia-bound relief flights. These relief efforts were expanded, and Operation RESTORE HOPE was begun with the intent to secure transportation facilities at Mogadishu, Somalia.

Ordered in by Chairman of the Joint Chiefs of Staff, General Colin Powell, Operation RESTORE HOPE began on 2 December 1992. An amphibious squadron of three ships, the USSs *Tripoli, Juneau,* and *Rushmore* were off the coast of Somalia in December to secure the Mogadishu airport by means of Marine amphibious landings. Onboard the squadron was a Marine Expeditionary Unit, a Special Boat Unit (SBU) detachment, and a platoon of Navy SEALs from SEAL Team One.

Initial operations by the SEALs were dictated by the needs of the intended amphibious landing. No up-to-date charts of the beaches off Mogadishu were available, so the first operation of the SEALs was to be a throwback to the earliest days of the UDT in World War II.

A classic UDT beach recon was conducted by the SEALs, supported by the boats and men of the SBU. The night of 6 December 1992 had twelve SEALs of the deployed platoon conducting a swimmer beach recon, measuring the water's depth with lead lines, a method first developed by Draper Kauffman during World War II. In spite of the passage of almost fifty years, the technique was sufficient for the needs of the SEALs and the cartographers back aboard the *Juneau.*

As the bulk of the SEAL platoon measured and noted the depth of the offshore waters, the balance of the platoon swam ashore and examined the beach proper. Obstacles, the shore gradient, the composition of the beach itself, and the measurements of the beach berm were all taken down for inclusion into charts for the Marine planners. Returning to the *Juneau,* charts were compiled from the SEALs information and the Marine commanders were briefed.

On the night of 7 December, the SEALs swam into Mogadishu Harbor to examine the waters and facilities. The SEALs' mission included locating satisfactory landing sites, assessing any existing threat from warlord or other armed forces, and determing if the port facilities could support the offloading of maritime prepositioned supply ships.

In spite of the relatively simple mission requirements, the conduct of the SEALs recon swim on 7 December was anything but easy. The warm waters of Mogadishu Harbor combined with a strong opposing current exhausted and overheated the SEALs as they conducted their operation.

Another threat, one not foreseen by the SEALs or their planners, were the waters of the harbor itself. Instead of facing enemy fire, the SEALs found themselves facing the heavily contaminated waters of the harbor. Raw sewage filled many areas of the harbor, making even the worst days of BUD/S training and the mud pits pale in comparison. A number of SEALs became sick from the mission.

It was on the night of 8 December, during the actual landing of the Marine forces, that the SEALs faced a very modern threat to special operations forces, one that they had not been trained for. To increase the beach coverage for the amphibious landings, both the SEALs and elements of the Force Recon units from the Marine Expeditionary Unit went in as scout-swimmers ahead of the landing forces. On the beach were a number of media and press corps re-

Sliding through the mud—backward. Students at BUD/S receive extensive familiarization with how to move through mud. It is during evolutions like this one during Hell Week that they also learn even more about the importance of working as a team. Only if the boat crews shown here work together can they move as a unit and not receive further incentive from their ever-present instructors.

U.S. Navy

A SEAL sniper adjusts the Aimpoint sight on his modified M14 rifle. The SEAL sniper will provide precision fire support for his Teammates as they conduct training in VBSS operations for Desert Storm. The vertical front handgrip on the rifle is a personal modification of the weapon by the user.

U.S. Navy

porters, complete with cameramen and bright lights. Caught full on film were a number of the Marine Force Recon operators. The SEALs conducted their part of the pre-landing scout about a quarter-mile away from the reporters.

On television screens across the United States and other parts of the world were live pictures of some very confused and unhappy Force Recon swimmers. When the actual landing force of U.S. Marines started coming in some minutes later, the attention of the media went to them, leaving the Force Recon operators and SEALs to continue with their operations in relative peace.

The SEAL detachment conducted a survey of the port of Kismaayo, operating from the French frigate *Dupleix*. It was during this operation that the SEALs came under fire from Somali snipers. In spite of the sporadic fire, no SEALs were hit and they completed their mission without further incident.

The SEALs provided additional sniper support to the Marines who were coming under fire from warlord forces. Additionally, the SEALs gave personal security to their commander-in-chief when President George Bush visited Somalia to see the difficulties firsthand. The SEALs also conducted joint training operations with further UN forces in Somalia, a unit of Indian naval commandos.

The SEALs of the first platoon in Somalia were relieved by a platoon from SEAL Team Two who came in as part of the Wasp Amphibious Ready Group when they arrived in February 1993. The men from SEAL Team Two also faced a new threat when they conducted their first operation in Somalia, a more active one than their compatriots had found in the harbor waters of Mogadishu.

To gather intelligence on gun-smuggling operations, the SEALs conducted a reconnaissance of the Jubba River in the southern part of Somalia. While gathering their intel, the SEALs found that they had to dodge the crocodiles that infested parts of the river. Natural obstacles aside, U.S. Marine forces were able to conduct two raids on towns along the river based on SEALs intelligence.

A number of operations were conducted by the SEALs during April and May, including further reconnaissance swims of Kismaayo; the clearing of a potential beach landing site south of Mogadishu; recon missions of the Three Rivers region south of Kismaayo, relatively close to the border between Kenya and Somalia; recons of Koyaama Island; and a reconnaissance of Daanai Beach, conducted in very bad conditions and rough seas.

In addition to the SEALs deployed with the Marine Ready Groups, further operators from SEAL Team Six were deployed to Somalia to assist the U.S. special operations forces there. SEAL snipers conducted a number of supporting operations for both Marine and SOCOM units.

U.S. commanders determined that the chaotic situation in Mogadishu could be brought under control if the local warlord leader of the Habr Gedir subclan of the Hawiye clan, Mohamed Aideed, was eliminated as a functional threat. Orders were put out to either capture or kill the elusive and troublesome Aideed. This action served to increase the number of attacks on UN forces, especially those of the U.S. contingent.

In one reported incident, a SEAL sniper with an M88 .50-caliber sniper rifle prevented a number of Marines from becoming possible casualties. The SEAL sniper had seen a Somali gunman duck down behind a rock wall to prepare his

A SEAL sniper, posed for the photograph, takes aim with his McMillan M88 .50-caliber sniper rifle. The massive clamshell muzzle break visible on the end of the barrel helps reduce the recoil of the huge cartridge fired by the weapon. If this was an actual firing position, the sniper would be much more concealed and difficult to locate.

USSOCOM PAO

RPG-7 for firing. RPGs proved to be a very popular weapon among warlord forces for attacking the heavily armed U.S. units.

As the Somali gunner prepared his weapon, the SEAL noted his location and the amount of damage he could do to the Marines before they could be given a warning. The power of the .50-caliber rifle was ably demonstrated when the SEAL sniper punched a 700-grain bullet through the intervening rock wall and dropped the probably astonished Somali gunman.

It was in October 1993 that the U.S. forces in Somalia were involved in the worst and most costly urban firefight since the 1968 Tet Offensive during the Vietnam War. On 3 October 1993, a joint unit of Rangers, specialized Army assets, and SEALs were to conduct an assault on a targeted building on Hawlwadig Road near the Olympic Hotel in Mogadishu.

During the insertion by vehicle to the target area, a SEAL chief was struck by a Somali bullet. The SEAL heard the shot and felt it strike him on the left hip where he sat in the rear of a Humvee. Amazingly enough, the bullet was stopped by the knife the SEAL was wearing on his right hip. The bullet shattered the blade, driving several pieces into the SEAL's hip, but the blade prevented the wound from being life-threatening. After having several blade fragments pulled out of the wound and his leg quickly bandaged, the SEAL continued with the operation.

Later in the op, a Blackhawk helicopter was shot down by a Somali gunner with an RPG-7. During the ensuing battle to rescue the downed crew and passengers of the Blackhawk, the streets of Mogadishu were filled with armed gunmen, U.S. forces, and Somalis caught in the middle of the raging firestorm. When it all was over the next day, eighteen Americans were dead, seventy badly injured, and an estimated one thousand Somalis killed or wounded.

After the incident on 3–4 October, reinforcements to the U.S. military forces in the area were made both in Somalia and neighboring Kenya. AC-130 gunships, starting now in Kenya, flew patrols over Mogadishu. Additional US-SOCOM assets were deployed to the area, including a platoon from SEAL Team Two and a platoon from SEAL Team Eight. The SEALs helped raise the general level of security for all the U.S. forces as well as the UN contingent in Somalia.

Operation UNITED SHIELD, the pullout of all U.S. forces in Somalia, was the final result of the actions that took place in Mogadishu on 3–4 October. SEALs helped maintain security on the beaches of Mogadishu, the same beaches that they had to conduct reconnaissance on to determine their suitability for use by the Marine landing craft and vehicles. By 3 March 1995, the U.S. withdrawal from Somalia was complete.

Chapter 63

Haiti: Operation SUPPORT DEMOCRACY/ Operation UPHOLD DEMOCRACY

Occupying the western half of the Island of Hispaniola, an island it shares with the Dominican Republic to the east, the country of Haiti has had a turbulent past. Periods of military governments put in place by coups were spaced by times of no government whatsoever where simple anarchy ruled. In 1956, a military coup put François Duvalier in charge of the country, ostensibly as an elected president. Any pretensions of democracy were eliminated when in 1964 Duvalier proclaimed himself president for life.

"Papa Doc" Duvalier, previously a medical doctor, ruled with a strange mixture of military force and voodoo rites until his death in 1971. Succeeded by his son, Jean Claude "Baby Doc" Duvalier, the situation remained one of grinding poverty for much of the population. In 1986, Baby Doc was overthrown in a military coup.

The situation was little improved for the Haitian population as a whole as they remained in poverty with little chance for escape. A bright point for the country were the democratic elections held in 1990. The election results put Jean-Bertrand Aristide in the president's office. On 30 September 1991, a military coup removed Aristide from office.

To replace Aristide into office, the United Nations placed economic sanctions in place against Haiti, establishing an embargo against most shipping, on 23 June 1993. The situation went from bad to worse for the people of Haiti, who were leaving the island in droves, mostly traveling on very poor boats to the United States as economic refugees. On 15 October 1993, President William Clinton ordered the U.S. Navy to help enforce the economic embargo against Haiti in an attempt to break the power of the military regime in place.

The combined joint task force (CJTF) 120 was established to plan, lead, and execute Operation SUPPORT DEMOCRACY, a multinational action against Haiti. The more than six hundred U.S. and allied warships of CJTF 120 conducted more than six hundred shipboardings against smugglers and shipping during the first five months of the operation. To escape the reach of the large Navy ships, smugglers turned to smaller craft that could use the shallower waters close to the coast to move embargoed goods between Haiti and the Dominican Republic.

The shallow-water tactics of the smugglers directed the U.S. Navy to put the new Cyclone class patrol boat into action off Haiti. Very new to the fleet and assigned to Naval Special Warfare Group Two in Little Creek, the two first Cyclone-class patrol craft were ordered to CJTF 120 after their crew training and ship certifications were completed. On 24 May, the *Cyclone* (PC-1) and the *Tempest* (PC-2) left Guantanamo Bay, Cuba, for Haiti. Arriving on-station on 27 May, the ships came under the operational control of CJTF 120, and they began active operations three days later.

The patrol craft went into action quickly, under the escort of the Peary-class guided missile frigate USS *Simpson* (FFG 56). The *Simpson* was to familiarize the *Cyclone* with the standard ship-boarding practices of the task force. On the first voyage, a smuggler was encountered who at first refused to stop under the orders of the *Cyclone*. Flares fired over the fleeing boat and the launching of a rigid-hull inflatable boat (RIB) with a crew of SEALs onboard caused the smugglers' ship to try and wait out the larger craft as it came to rest in shallow waters.

The next day, a combined party of SEALs from the *Cyclone* and six Canadian sailors from HMCS *Terra Nova,* a CJTF craft that had come onto the scene, conducted a board-and-search operation very close to those VBSS ops con-

The USS *Tempest* at dockside. The rubber boats that support SEAL operations can be seen at the stern, next to the rear deck that allows the easy recovery of SEALs in the water.

U.S. Navy

ducted during DESERT SHIELD/DESERT STORM. Contraband (embargoed) goods were found aboard the smuggler's ship, and it was impounded and towed to Guantanamo Bay.

The economic situation on Haiti continued to deteriorate, and more refugees tried to come into U.S. waters. The Clinton administration sought for and received approval on 31 July 1994 from the UN Security Council to lead a military invasion of Haiti to reinstate Aristide. Fifteen thousand multinational forces would conduct the invasion, the bulk of them being from the United States.

The threat of Operation UPHOLD DEMOCRACY was first established with the orders given to General Shalikashvili, the Chairman of the Joint Chiefs of Staff, to execute the invasion within ten days of 10 September 1994. Navy SEALs conducted a hydrographic survey of the invasion site along Cap Haitien during the night of 16–17 September. The invasion was prepared and planned to go ahead within days.

On 21 September 1994, a last-minute deal brokered by American politicians and the military rulers of Haiti changed the format of the invasion. The troops landed unopposed and relatively peacefully the morning of 19 September 1994. The patrol craft *Monsoon* (PC-4) became the first U.S. ship to enter the harbor of Port-au-Prince on 19 September. The new patrol craft had proven their worth off the waters of Haiti as both effective military craft and operational SEAL-launching platforms. The patrol craft and deployed SEALs remained off the shores of Haiti for some time after the landings.

On 31 March 1995, Operation UPHOLD DEMOCRACY became RESTORE DEMOCRACY as the UN mission took over in Haiti.

A Rigid Inflatable Boat (RIB) bounces up into the air as it rides the waves with SEALs and crewmen from the Special Boat Teams aboard.

USSOCOM PAO

■ Chapter 64

Bosnia: Operation JOINT ENDEAVOR/ Operation JOINT GUARD

Yugoslavia and the Balkans area in general has suffered through centuries of fragmentation, occupation, and unrest that stretch back to the days of the Roman Empire. In the post–World War II world, Yugoslavia, which had only been named as a country in 1929, was held together and controlled by one man. After the defeat of Nazi Germany and the ousting of its occupying forces from Yugoslavia in 1945, elections were held that WWII leader Joseph Tito won easily with 90 percent of the vote. Very quickly, Tito transformed Yugoslavia into a Communist republic under his solid control.

Tito's death in 1980 caused some serious unrest in Yugoslavia, but it continued to be governed as a Soviet state. The harsh system of Tito's government did continue to be relaxed during the 1980s, with nationalistic tendencies continuing to rise among the separate ethnic peoples of the country. With the general fall of communism and the breaking of the Iron Curtain starting in the late 1980s, Yugoslavia began a final breakup as a country. On 3 March 1992, the Muslim and Serbian population of Bosnia-Herzevinia declared themselves an independent country.

The Bosnian-Serbs soon began an internal armed struggle for control of the newly independent state. The term *ethnic cleansing* took on meaning as the Bosnian-Serbs raised an army and seized more than 70 percent of Bosnia. The resistance of the Muslim-Croatian coalition soon changed the situation in Bosnia to one that was considered an international humanitarian crisis.

A UN protection force was deployed to Bosnia to ensure that aid to the civilian population and the estimated five million displaced persons in the area was not interfered with. Attempts to force a peace settlement on the strife-torn area failed within a year.

U.S. forces airlifted and dropped in supplies to cut-off groups of civilian populations during Operation PROVIDE PROMISE, which ran from 3 July 1992 to 1 October 1994. After thousands of civilian Serbs and Muslims had been killed in the fighting, a formal peace agreement, developed in Dayton, Ohio, in November 1995 and signed in Paris, France, on 14 December that same year, was established. Operation JOINT ENDEAVOR was put forward to implement the terms of the Dayton Peace Accords.

The U.S. Special Operations Command Europe (SOCEUR) had been involved with the peace efforts in Bosnia since February 1993. At that time, the Joint Special Operations Task Force 2 (JSOTF2) was established. The general mission assignments of JSOTF2 included combat search-and-rescue, fire support, air drops, and the VBSS operations necessary to enforce a UN blockade of former Yugoslavian waters to unauthorized ships. The blockade had been conducted as Operation MARITIME GUARD from 1 November 1992 to 14 June 1993 and then as Operation SHARP GUARD from 15 June 1993 to 18 June 1996.

Rumored and unofficially reported SEAL actions in Bosnia included a wide range of missions. Verified SEAL missions include the hydrographic survey of the Sava River in Croatia in December 1995. The operation was conducted by SEALs from Delta and Hotel Platoons of SEAL Team Two, part of SEAL Team Two Task Unit Alpha. The fast-moving river was at the border of Croatia and Bosnia, and U.S. Army engineers wanted to put a pontoon bridge across the fast-moving, very cold waters.

The SEAL detachment conducted the operation in water that gave them zero visibility. The normal dangers of the operation from the cold, muddy, fast-moving waters were increased by the situation in the area and the aftermath of the war. The SEALs remained in body armor and were armed when on the surface and shoreline. That did little to protect them from floating debris in the water, though, including a dead cow that floated by.

The missions of the SEALs at the river included the hydrographic survey as well as taking bottom samples of the riverbed. The three hundred-meter-wide river had a current of three to five knots. The severe current in the river sapped even the SEALs' strength in swimming.

A later repeat of the SEALs' mission to include a search for lost weapons was conducted in late January with the intent being the erection of a permanent causeway. Two M16 rifles had been lost by U.S. forces in the rapidly moving river. Although the SEALs searched, they were unable to find the weapons. The SEALs also later surveyed a partially destroyed bridge at Brcko in Bosnia-Herzegovinia. The SEALs' assistance in providing a gift to the people of Bosnia included an open road in Croatia, and a soon-to-be-in-place bridge courtesy of the U.S. Army.

Other missions were conducted by the SEALs in Bosnia but have yet to be declassified—some of the operations may never be reported to the public at large.

Chapter 65

Afghanistan: Operation ENDURING FREEDOM/ Operation ANACONDA

In the mid-morning hours of 11 September 2001, the people of downtown New York City witnessed what they at first thought was the most horrendous air crash in modern U.S. history. In stunned disbelief, at 8:45 A.M., the normally unshakable New Yorkers watched the Boeing 767 of American Airlines Flight 11 smash into the upper floors of the 1,300-foot-tall North Tower of the World Trade Center.

Such a crash of a large aircraft into a skyscraper hadn't happened since 28 July 1945, when a B-25 bomber plowed into the seventy-eighth floor of the Empire State Building. That accident happened during wartime, and the casualties were relatively light. What the New Yorkers watching the smoke billow out from the North Tower didn't know was that they were seeing the first major attack of a new war.

Eleven minutes after the first plane struck, those same New York people knew that what they had seen was no accident. A second plane, Flight 175, a United Airlines Boeing 767, flying from Boston Airport, smashed into the South Tower of the World Trade Center.

Thousands of pounds of fuel from the two jet aircraft, both filled for a cross-country flight, ignited and burned. The tall towers of the World Trade Center were breached and acted as chimneys, feeding air to the massive fire. Rather than face death by the flames, many individuals who had been trapped above the impact floors chose to jump to their deaths on the concrete hundreds of feet below. A lasting image of one such jumper, who might have been a skydiver, was captured on film. The camera tracked the individual as he maintained perfect form while he hurtled to the ground, smoke trailing from the clothes burning on his back.

The bodies on the cold ground did not have long to wait in the open. At 9:50 A.M., the South Tower collapsed, killing and injuring thousands. A huge billow of smoke and dust roared through the streets of New York, a sight of such magnitude that it had never been seen before outside of Hollywood special effects in a disaster film. Only this was no movie.

The South Tower collapsed almost straight down as its structure gave in to the massive damage and steel-softening fire. At 10:29 A.M., the North Tower collapsed. The steel, glass, and concrete of the upper floors drove down through the building, causing the lower floors to explode outward in their collapse. The tall radio spire on top of the tower remained pointing up as it fell until it descended into the roiling cloud of smoke, dust, and ash.

Earlier, at 9:38 A.M., prior to the collapse of the towers, the Boeing 757 of American Airlines Flight 77 plowed into the northwest side of the Pentagon near Washington, D.C. A fourth plane, the Boeing 757 of United Airlines Flight 93 bound for San Francisco, crashed into the ground near Shanksville, Pennsylvania.

All the flights had been hijacked by terrorist members of al-Qaeda and followers of Osama bin Laden. The passengers of Flight 93 learned about the fate of the other hijacked planes through the cell phones some of the passengers had. They made the fateful decision to try to take back the plane—an action that cost them all their lives but may have saved thousands on the ground.

The people of the United States wanted vengeance. They wanted the leader of al-Qaeda, Osama bin Laden, brought to justice and punished for his crimes. The Taliban government of Afghanistan was harboring bin Laden and refused to surrender him. The Islamic Fundamentalist Talibans had long been known to harbor terrorists and allow them safe haven in the mountains, passes, and caves of Afghanistan. Terrorism was nothing new to them, and its use against non-Muslims was not only allowed, it was sanctified by the Taliban mullahs.

After repeated warnings to give up bin Laden, and the Talibans continual refusal to do so, President George W. Bush initiated Operation ENDURING FREEDOM, the American War on Terrorism in Afghanistan. On 7 October 2001, military targets in Afghanistan began to receive the first of many strikes against them by U.S. aircraft. By 19 October, more than one hundred Rangers landed in Afghanistan for a raid near Kandahar. The campaign against the Taliban and al-Qaeda in Afghanistan had fully begun.

The war in Afghanistan quickly turned into a ground campaign by Special Operations soldiers. The visible military targets of the Taliban and al-Qaeda were quickly eliminated by air strikes, but the majority of the terrorists were hiding in caves and tunnels under the rocky mountains of Afghanistan. The Soviet Union had finally called it quits when they invaded Afghanistan in the 1980s. The United States had no intention of remaining in Afghanistan after the elimination of the Taliban and al-Qaeda as functioning units. That made the people of Afghanistan generally look to the U.S. forces as liberators.

The U.S. Special Operations forces in Afghanistan included elements from the Army, Navy, and Air Force. Navy SEALs were on the ground in the fighting regardless of Afghanistan being a land-locked country and even drinkable water being sometimes hard to find. A twelve-hour mission was planned in Janu-

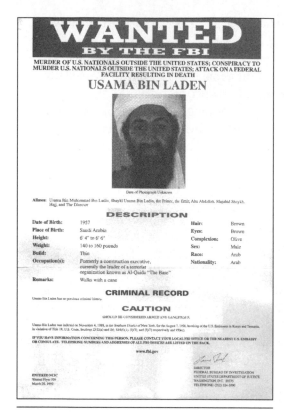

WANTED
BY THE FBI

MURDER OF U.S. NATIONALS OUTSIDE THE UNITED STATES; CONSPIRACY TO MURDER U.S. NATIONALS OUTSIDE THE UNITED STATES; ATTACK ON A FEDERAL FACILITY RESULTING IN DEATH

USAMA BIN LADEN

Date of Photograph Unknown

Aliases: Usama Bin Muhammad Bin Ladin, Shaykh Usama Bin Ladin, the Prince, the Emir, Abu Abdallah, Mujahid Shaykh, Hajj, and The Director

DESCRIPTION

Date of Birth:	1957	Hair:	Brown
Place of Birth:	Saudi Arabia	Eyes:	Brown
Height:	6' 4" to 6' 6"	Complexion:	Olive
Weight:	140 to 160 pounds	Sex:	Male
Build:	Thin	Race:	Arab
Occupation(s):	Formerly a construction executive, currently the leader of a terrorist organization known as Al-Qaida "The Base"	Nationality:	Arab
Remarks:	Walks with a cane		

CRIMINAL RECORD

Usama Bin Laden has no previous criminal history.

CAUTION

SHOULD BE CONSIDERED ARMED AND DANGEROUS.

Usama Bin Laden was indicted on November 4, 1998, in the Southern District of New York, for the August 7, 1998, bombing of the U.S. Embassies in Kenya and Tanzania, in violation of Title 18, U.S. Code, Sections 2(Two) and 3(Three), 844(f)(1), (f)(3), and (f)(7) respectively and 930(e).

IF YOU HAVE INFORMATION CONCERNING THIS PERSON, PLEASE CONTACT YOUR LOCAL FBI OFFICE OR THE NEAREST U.S. EMBASSY OR CONSULATE. TELEPHONE NUMBERS AND ADDRESSES OF ALL FBI OFFICES ARE LISTED ON THE BACK.

www.fbi.gov

DIRECTOR
FEDERAL BUREAU OF INVESTIGATION
UNITED STATES DEPARTMENT OF JUSTICE
WASHINGTON, D.C. 20535
TELEPHONE: (202) 324-3000

ENTERED NCIC
Wanted Flyer 939
March 29, 1999

The official Wanted poster issued by U.S. Department of Justice for Osama bin Laden. This poster was sent out by the FBI several years before the events of 9-11 made bin Laden the most wanted man in the world.

Federal Bureau of Investigation

ary to put special operations forces, led by a SEAL platoon, into the Zawar Kili cave complex to search out the area. On 6 January, the units went in. They didn't come back out until January 14.

The SOCOM operators and SEALs, part of Task Force K-Bar, scoured more than seventy caves during the operation, which covered a three-mile-long ravine near the Pakistani border. They found caches of weapons, ammunition, supplies, and a treasure trove of intelligence information. The intel materials included planning documents, New York City tourist posters, and other landmarks around the United States.

In spite of the success of the operation, the strain on the SEALs and other SOCOM operators was severe. They had been running light in terms of food, water, and shelter equipment. The twelve-hour mission becoming one eight days long forced the operators to face dehydration, hunger, and subfreezing temperatures for two days before additional supplies could be flown in.

To survive as the sleet and snow started coming down in the thin air of their encampment at 6,500 feet, the SOCOM operators moved into three abandoned villages in the ravines around Zawar Kili. Inside the simple mud huts, they found clothes and blankets they were able to use to keep warm. Al-Qaeda supplies were used as a last resort when the food started to run out, but as the SEAL commander suggested, the goat meat they were able to locate was "not good."

The SEALs were in a "boots on the ground" mission, which meant that they would face the Taliban and al-Qaeda forces face-to-face. The SOCOM operators used all the means at their disposal to fight the al-Qaeda forces, including air strikes with heavy bombs that were called in dangerously close to the SO-

COM positions. In the words of the SEAL platoon commander, "We were able to surprise them. They did not surprise us." There were daily firefights, though no SOCOM personnel were hit or wounded. More than a dozen enemy forces were killed with an additional eight subjects detained for further questioning.

SOCOM operators also conducted a ninety-minute raid on a five-building complex at Yaya Kehyl in Paktika Province. There, the intelligence finds included sophisticated satellite phones, operational computers filled with al-Qaeda data, stockpiles of weapons, and two pounds of unrefined opium. At almost every target hit by the SOCOM forces, they found what were being called "terrorist escape kits." The kits were suitcases filled with clothes, small arms, Pakistani currency, passports, and work visas. The materials were packed and ready to be grabbed up by a terrorist operative trying to flee Afghanistan.

In spite of the hardships and danger of their operations, the morale of the SEALs and the special operations forces in general was very good. They were fighting "the good fight," taking the terror to the terrorists and denying them a safe haven. But the situation was anything but safe for the men of the Teams and SOCOM. Casualties were taken by SOCOM and the SEALs.

One of the biggest ground attacks of the Afghan campaign was Operation ANACONDA. Delayed from beginning for twenty-four hours while B-52 heavy bombers and other aircraft strafed and attacked Taliban and al-Qaeda positions, as many as two hundred Taliban and al-Qaeda followers were killed in the first four days of ANACONDA.

The first Navy SEAL killed in action since the Paitilla Airfield action during Operation JUST CAUSE was Aviation Boatswains Mate (Handling) (SEAL) 1st Class Neil Roberts, who was killed on 4 March in eastern Afghanistan. The MH-47E Chinook helicopter Roberts was riding in was operating in support of Operation ANACONDA. At around 3 A.M. on Monday, 4 March 2002, the helicopter that Roberts was riding in was struck by a rocket-propelled grenade just as it touched down.

The helicopter and a second bird in the flight immediately took off from the hot landing zone to fly off and check for damage. What wasn't known was that Neil Roberts had fallen from the MH-47E when the rocket hit and the bird took off.

An unmanned Predator gave the commanders real-time access to a video of the SEAL being captured by al-Qaeda forces. Roberts did not go down without a fight, and his death is being investigated for a possible Congressional Medal of Honor. At least one report has Roberts single-handedly attacking a machine gun nest to prevent it from hitting the helicopters as they escaped.

A large number of SOCOM troops immediately boarded helicopters to go in and rescue Roberts or at least recover his body. The Teams do not leave anyone behind—ever. The resulting twelve-hour battle cost the lives of seven U.S.

servicemen and eleven more were wounded before the helicopters could evacuate the SOCOM forces. Circling AC-130 gunships poured down a hail of steel and high explosives at the approaching al-Qaeda forces as the SOCOM unit extracted.

Roberts had been last seen from the overhead Predator being dragged off by al-Qaeda men. His body was recovered later. Roberts was apparently shot at the hands of his captors.

Later in the month, on 28 March, SEAL Chief Hospital Corpsman Matthew Bourgeois was killed while conducting small-unit training near Kandahar. There was no enemy fire involved, and Bourgeois was killed after apparently stepping on a mine or other piece of unexploded ordnance. The lands of Afghanistan are littered with mines and other ordnance left over from the years of Soviet occupation and fighting and the years of near civil warfare that followed.

In August 2002, two SEALs from the West Coast teams were wounded by enemy gunfire during intelligence gathering operations in the Oruzgan Province of southern Afghanistan. Both SEALs were shot in the legs during the early morning hours. They were able to be medevaced out to a field hospital and later moved on to more permanent medical facilities.

■ Chapter 66

Training: The Building of an Operator

There is no single item that ties the Teams together like the basic training that all operators have to go through to enter the UDTs or the SEALs. No matter what era a SEAL or a Frogman was in, he can share training stories that each man can understand. Whether they went through Underwater Demolition Team Replacement training or Basic Underwater Demolition/SEAL training from the early 1970s to today, every operator in the Teams has shared the common experience of training.

Each training class is known by a number. It isn't any exotic code, simply the consecutive number of the class in the history of training. Classes used to be run on both the East and West Coasts, and Teams would supply instructors for their own replacements training. But with the graduation of the last East Coast class in August 1971, all BUD/S training is done on the West Coast at Coronado, California.

An operator's class number is something that no man will consciously forget. It would take a disease or injury to make a Teammate forget that number that indicated to him the men he first trained with. Along with the number, the names of his Teammates are something a SEAL or Frogman expects to take to the grave with him. And the number of a student's class is not classified by the Navy. It doesn't matter to the Navy who attended BUD/S or UDTR, only if they graduated and where they served afterward. The class numbers are effectively a matter of public record, although the Teams make sure the numbers aren't *that* available to the public at large.

BUD/S is conducted a number of times each year at the Naval Special Warfare Training Command in Coronado. The "Schoolhouse," as it is known in the Teams, is located in sunny, pleasant, Southern California, close to the U.S. border with Mexico with the waters of the Pacific to the West and the protected waters of San Diego Bay a short distance to the east.

The sunny weather the San Diego area is known for does little to warm the Pacific waters off the SEAL Training compound. The California current running close offshore maintains itself with water from Alaska, water that remains close to 55° F throughout the year. The California current waters mix with the warmer waters of the Pacific off California, but the warmth of the water is only relative. BUD/S instructors maintain a close watch on their students as they force them to sit in the cold water. A time chart, stopwatch, and thermometer readings of the water add up to a safety measure against hypothermia—although the miserable, shivering, cold students wouldn't know that or care if they did.

A line of BUD/S students struggle up the sand berms in Coronado, carrying their rubber boats along with them.

U.S. Navy

Training has gotten more sophisticated over the years, and the course has grown longer—it's twenty-six weeks long at the time of this writing (2002). Exercises have changed, as has equipment. As older gear became worn and unavailable, it was replaced with modern components. In some cases, the newer gear, boats, life jackets, etc. are lighter and stronger. Exercises that were found to cause more physical damage than good have been dropped or modified. But one thing has not changed at BUD/S—it hasn't gotten any easier.

The one thing that is easy at BUD/S is quitting. It is intentionally made that way. The basic philosophy is that anyone who is in fairly good shape could get through a week or so of BUD/S. But when the course is twenty-six weeks long, and each week makes even more physical demands on the individual than the week before, it takes a special mental discipline, a drive, to go the distance. This drive is especially important because it is so easy to quit.

A student can DOR, drop on request, at any time during the training. Once he has quit, the ex-student is gone from the training usually within the day. Students wear painted helmet liners during their training, and the color of the liner indicates the phase of training they are in. During the earlier years of UDTR, a student taking off his helmet liner was enough to signify that he was quitting.

Today, there is a brass ship's bell hanging at the northeast corner of the training compound. Ringing that bell three times is the signal that the individual is quitting. Given that some of the individuals at BUD/S have never failed at any real challenge in their young lives before, the walk to that bell can be the longest one they've ever taken.

The individual attitude of a student and their personal resolve to complete the course mean the most toward an individual getting through the training than any other single attribute. Tremendous high school and college athletes, excellent physical specimens, have attended BUD/S and they have failed because they didn't have the drive to complete the course. Any student who completes the physical screening tests to enter BUD/S has the physical necessities to complete the course—if they have the heart and the drive.

There is no single physical type that is an example of a SEAL. The men of the Teams are tall, short, stocky, slender, muscular, and slight. They are never fat, but they can be big. What all the graduates of BUD/S share is a very positive mental attitude. They are fit and in shape, and they are supremely confident that they can do the job, no matter what the job is. If they don't know how to complete a specific task, they will either learn, or find a Teammate who knows how to do it. It is as a Team that the SEALs accomplish their missions. The learning of just what it means to be a Team begins at BUD/S.

Arriving at BUD/S is a bit of a shock to newcomers. The center court of the main building at the training center is a large, square expanse of packed and leveled asphalt. Painted on the surface of the asphalt and facing north are sets

A SEAL demonstrates an unusual rope skill during a demonstration at the UDT-SEAL Museum in Fort Pierce, Florida.

Kevin Dockery

of swim fins. These are where the students will stand as they face the small podium at the northern wall. On that podium, an instructor will stand and run them through calisthenic exercises—lots of exercises. The big square is known as the grinder. On its rough surface, thousands of strong young men have been ground down. What finally stood on the grinder were men on their way to the Teams—SEALs.

There are three phases of training and an introductory or beginning time period. The first weeks of training are referred to as the indoctrination period, the time before a class formally "classes up" and begins training. Now some times referred to as Fourth Phase, the initial time gives the students a chance to learn the basic exercises, skills they will need, and procedures that they will be expected to follow while at BUD/S. More important, it is a time that allows the students who were not sure of why they were at BUD/S, or were insufficiently prepared physically, to drop out of training without being officially counted in the class totals.

There is a large dropout rate at BUD/S. The instructors simply say that the course is not for everyone. Sixty percent of a class dropping out is not unusual. Between one hundred and twenty and one hundred and forty students might start training as a class, and only twenty to thirty will be expected to eventually

A fully equipped SEAL demonstrating the equipment and weapons he would carry during an operation. This is a far cry from the "naked warrior" of the UDT during World War II, but underneath all of the modern gear is the same warrior.

Kevin Dockery

finish. At one point, an entire class disappeared. No one graduated.

After Fourth Phase is completed, the students will have learned their basic combat swimming strokes, the side stroke and the breast stroke. These are used because they expose the absolute minimum parts of a swimmer above the water. The side stroke is also a very useful, maximum-efficiency long-distance stroke—and the students will be doing a lot of long-distance swimming.

About every two to three months, a new BUD/S class begins training at First Phase. Their helmets are painted green with each student's name and their class number stenciled on in white. As the days go on during training, the helmets of the students who dropped out will be lined up next to the bell at the corner of the grinder—mute testimony of those who couldn't make it and a motivation booster for those who remain in training. More than one BUD/S student has heard the bell ring and knew a classmate was gone but that he was still there.

And the students will need every bit of motivation they can get for the rigors of First Phase. Exercises will be conducted several times every day. The physical training, PT, seems more like a constant thing to the harried students. And they are chased, harassed, and needled by their instructors, each one a very qualified SEAL who is trying to make sure that only the best will go on to graduate and join the Teams.

Instructors for BUD/S are more than just impressive; they are very imposing figures, especially those instructors in First Phase. These SEALs are volunteers from the Special Warfare community, all the combined Teams. Only the very top percent of the SEALs qualify to be instructors. They have to be proven operators to begin with. On top of the skills that the instructors bring with them from their experience in the Teams, they are given further training to make certain that they can develop a good, high-quality BUD/S product and that what they do and know how to do is as safe as it can be made. They are consummate professionals at their jobs.

The Teams operate in a very dangerous environment. Just their operations in the open sea are conducted in an environment that can easily kill you if you make a mistake. Meticulous attention to detail prevents accidents. And when an accident does happen, careful and complete analysis of the situation helps prevent that accident from ever happening again. But the SEALs do operate in a dangerous world. If the students get scared of what they are told to do, that's fine with the instructors. You can be scared, that's a normal human reaction to danger. But it is how you act even though you are scared that matters.

And the students can be very scared, or at least apprehensive, of one part of First Phase: Hell Week. That is the fifth week of training, originally officially called Indoctrination Week during the World War II days at Fort Pierce. Listed on the official training schedules as Motivation Week, this time period has been named from almost its very inception as Hell Week.

In spite of the constant reminder that Teamwork is the essence of being a SEAL, students are also asked to put out the maximum possible effort from the individual. Here, a single BUD/S student carries a massive outboard motor over the sand.

U.S. Navy

During the first years of training in World War II, Hell Week was the first week of training. The Team had no time to waste on someone who couldn't cut it as an operator. So Hell Week became the fastest way of getting rid of the dead wood.

Draper Kauffman, the individual who founded the original Naval Combat Demolition Unit training at Fort Pierce and who is considered the father of the UDTs, looked to the most physically demanding course of training in the Navy at that time in 1943. Training at Fort Pierce were the Scouts and Raiders. They had a very demanding course of PT, put together by the best individuals available at that time. Kauffman and his staff took the weeks-long training schedule of the Scouts and Raiders and condensed it to a single week. That was Hell Week.

The concept behind that demanding time is multifold. First, it was Kauffman's opinion that an individual was capable of ten times the physical output that they thought possible. All an individual had to do was learn that the mind could drive the body past what had been considered possible. Second, Hell Week brought out the motivation in the individual, the "won't quit" attitude. Individuals who went through that week would not stop when the going got tough, they proved that. Third, Hell Week exposed an individual to explosions, noise, fear, lack of sleep, and physical exhaustion. It was as close as training could come to simulating the combat environment, especially what it was like on an invasion beach. If a person couldn't hack Hell Week, it was better to find out right at the start rather than later when it could cost men their lives.

Hell Week is a full week, from Sunday night to Saturday, of constant, nonstop activity. Students are scheduled to receive four hours of sleep total for the entire week. Sometimes the students regret even getting that small amount of sleep. It isn't that they aren't exhausted; it's that they have to get up afterward and keep going.

From that first night, the students are wet, cold, and confused. Men who cannot face the cold cannot operate in the water. The value of the rigors of Hell Week have been proven time and time again in combat. Men who have passed Hell Week know they can make it, no matter what obstacles rise up in their way. They know this fact simply because they have completed Hell Week. Very little can compare to it.

The Teams demand the maximum effort an individual can give—and more. But it is as a Team that a class completes Hell Week and BUD/S. Students learn to depend on each other unlike they have ever depended on anyone in their lives. This is one of the reasons that no one ever forgets their Hell Week or the men they survived it with.

Crawling through the mud, exposed to the cold and wet, rocked by explosions and noise, and forced to complete evolutions that look impossible, are all part of Hell Week. An evolution in training is a event. It can be a simple as a period of exercise, a boat drill, or the completion of the obstacle course. Hell Week is considered the biggest single evolution of training, although completing it hardly means that an individual will get though BUD/S.

Valuable students who are injured, but who the instructors consider worthwhile material, can be "rolled back." They are held back to the next class and allowed to heal as needed. If the student who is rolled back has completed Hell Week, he will join the next class after they have completed that evolution. If he hasn't completed Hell Week, or if he only went through part of it before he was injured, the rolled-back student gets to do the whole thing again.

After First Phase comes Second Phase, where the students paint their helmets red and go on to learn diving operations. This is the phase where students must be able to learn complicated dive physics and physiology to continue training. They must be able to operate underwater with very dangerous equipment. The breathing equipment is as safe as it can be made, but without knowing the rules and limitations of the human body underwater, a swimmer can be killed before he ever knows it. Even excellent physical students who could get through First Phase as leaders, bringing their classmates along with them, have failed training because of the academic side of Second Phase.

Third Phase is land warfare, where the students wear a blue helmet and learn the tools of their trade. Basic weapons, explosives, demolitions, tactics, and operations are taught in this phase. At the end of the course, the student will be standing on the grinder one last time to receive his graduation certificate from BUD/S. That is when each man will ring the bell to indicate he is leaving and going on to the Teams. Actually, they will be going on to more training.

After BUD/S graduation, the students will be sent to Fort Benning, Georgia, where they will complete the basic three-week Army Airborne course that will qualify the students as basic paratroopers.

Instead of going on to an assignment to a Team and a six-month probationary period after Fort Benning, students go back to Coronado and complete the SEAL qualification program. The fifteen-week-long program instructs the students in the more advanced skills used in the Teams. They learn combat swimming, further demolitions, and advanced patrolling. After they complete the program successfully, the students receive their Tridents, the Naval Special Warfare insignia, the outward uniform symbol of a Navy SEAL.

Joseph Valderrama, Engineman First Class

I was first exposed to the Teams as a trainee in 1976 until I finally graduated in 1979. Then I went to SEAL Team One. The SEALs were something I first heard about while I was in boot camp when a friend of mine, Mark Scolari, had a buddy in the SEAL Teams. He started to talk to me about his buddy who was a BUD/S trainee, what a crazy man he was, and how he fit in well with the persona of a Navy SEAL.

At the time, being a SEAL wasn't something I wanted to do. While I was standing in the classification line in boot camp, I thought I was going to be a photographer's mate. It ended up that my interest was in photography and I didn't have an A-school. My brothers had told me that if you didn't have an A-school rating in the Navy, you were going to be chipping paint. Through my friend Mark, I found out that if you pass the BUD/S screening test, they'll give you an A-school.

So right there in the classification line, I decided to let the chief behind the counter know that I wanted to be a Navy SEAL. He was asking for my Form 509 or whatever it was, to say that I was qualified for BUD/S. I didn't have any form at all, so I ended up taking the BUD/S screening test right there at boot camp. Out of eighteen people, I was the only one to make it through the screening test.

The screening test gave me a taste of what I would be facing at BUD/S, but it was a small taste. When I finally arrived in Coronado, I was very apprehensive. I knew there were some things to be afraid of, and I knew that there were some things in training that I probably would enjoy. Basically, that information had come from the men who had given me the screening test.

The tester's conversation was with a friend of his while I was taking the test. He was talking about something I wasn't used to hearing as a nineteen-year-old. These things they were talking about let me know that I was going to be getting into something different.

The physical end of training was something I enjoyed. My attitude was that this was something I was going to do for the rest of my life. I fully enjoyed it. There were times when the instructors put us into the surf zone and I was having a good time and the officer in charge came up and told me to knock it off—I was having too much fun and it might project the wrong impression on the instructors.

Hell Week, the first time, was tough, but this was something I wanted to do. So I never thought about quitting. I had been on the ocean my entire life, and I loved it. The instructors who put me through training were men I would do anything for. And Hell Week was just something I had to do to be one of them.

The first incident that really stands out in my mind about that Hell Week was a very valuable lesson. It had to do with an insertion point. When you insert somewhere, you have to make sure that it is the exact spot you were supposed to go in at. The incident had to do with myself and my swim buddy. It was the third day of Hell Week, and everybody was cold. We were all cold and I thought we would swim in to the beach, just turn around, and signal the rest of the guys in without doing a recon of the beach area or anything. We would just get them in because it was cold.

We got to the beach and there was an instructor up on the berm. I figured he was just observing us. Not seeing any reaction from the instructor, we didn't do the recon, spun around, and signaled the boat in. When I turned around, my swim partner was gone. I figured he was maybe scouting the beach, so I didn't really think much about his being missing and kept signaling the boat in.

The boat came in about fifty yards south of where my swim buddy and I had landed. When I turned back around to get my swim buddy so we could rejoin the boat crew, he had reappeared. I was calling his name, but he wouldn't respond. So I picked up some small rocks and threw them at him while saying, "Come on, let's go."

When I turned to go, I was immediately tackled to the sand, spun around, and two hands grabbed my throat. The instructor on top of me said I was dead. Then he proceeded to go down to the boat and kill everybody in my boat crew. After it was all said and done, the instructors took us for a little extracurricular activity. Then we were told about an operation in Vietnam that entailed a whole company of Marines who had been helicoptered in to the wrong insertion point and slaughtered. That wasn't something I have ever forgotten, and insertion points were very important after that.

By the end of Hell Week, things were all kind of a blur when they secured us. We were at Gator Beach, and back then they had beer there. We had a couple beers and I was thinking about getting back to the barracks and crawling in that rack. It was probably the first thought that came to me after I heard those words, "Hell Week is secured." Sleep, that was a good thought right about then.

I had difficulty graduating my first class. I failed the diving physics portion of the diving phase. I was given the opportunity to take a makeup test, took that, and failed it as well. Then, the instructors did something that they normally don't do and gave me a third try. But I failed that one as well and was academically dis-enrolled.

BUD/S training isn't all physical. The most important aspect about going through training, as far as the physical, heart, or mental aspect, I think is the determination. It is your heart, but also, because of the structure of BUD/S, the mental aspect is heavy also. The psychological portion of the training is tough. As far as the instructors go, you have to be mentally strong to overcome the adversity they throw your way.

We did a run on San Clemente Island. It was a long, hard, run as it stood, and the instructor asked, "Who wants to go another two miles?" Well, you're not going to say you don't want to go another two miles. What you're going to say is, "Yes, let's go another two miles."

That's the way I look at training as far as the mental aspect goes. You have to be prepared for that. I guess your heart will follow.

It took two months, but I did get back into a class. Going through BUD/S the second time was harder in that I knew what was coming and I started thinking ahead. The worst thing you can do is to start anticipating. You're wet, cold, and sandy now, and you know you're going to be wet, cold, and sandy tomorrow. Once you start doing that, you've more or less lost the "bubble," the insulated world you withdraw yourself into and just do things as they come. That's when you'll break down.

Diving was the Third Phase when I went through the first class. The time period between my first and second BUD/S class was two months. The time between my second BUD/S class and when I finally graduated was two years. When I was thinking ahead in my second class, that wet, cold, and sandy day after day just caused me to hit the wall and say enough. I DOR'd, dropped on request.

For two years, I was in the Fleet Navy, serving on an LST (Landing Ship, Tank). I knew I wanted to go back when my ship was in Subic in the Philippines and I ran into all the friends I had back in Class 90. I saw what they were doing, which was laying around the pool getting suntans while I was working in the scullery onboard a ship. I was willing to go back and endure another six months of BUD/S so I could lay out by the pool and get a suntan.

I don't know if going through BUD/S three times is an unusual situation, I think there are a lot of guys who have gone through multiple times. Mr. Todd, who was a mustang officer, pulled some strings for me and got me orders back two months later that first return. That was unusual.

By the time I got to the third BUD/S class I attended, I had refocused and had found that same spark I had the first time I went through. I was going to make it. This time through, I was married and I told my wife, "Sorry, but graduating from this training is my number-one priority right now." I ended up graduating with Class 104 in 1979.

I honestly don't remember much of the last Hell Week I went through. I remember more of the Class 90 Hell Week than I do of Class 104's. What I do remember is that during that last try, I never thought about quitting. Finally, it was instilled in me to make sure I studied a lot harder and different than I had the first time.

The center of the BUD/S compound is the grinder, the exercise and parade ground. The SEAL grinder is a big, square piece of asphalt that gets very hot during the summertime. You can burn your hands on its surface. I never really thought about why they called it the grinder before right now. I think it's because we're put into the grinder so to speak, and that's where we conducted most of our physical evolutions, the calisthenics. It ground you up and spit you out, because it's also the last place you stand when you graduate.

Standing on the grinder that last day, we had Admiral Lyons as a guest speaker. (He went on to become the mayor of Oceanside, California.) Standing up there for graduation that beautiful California morning, shaking hands with the admiral, getting my diploma, and having a look around the grinder at all the people there—there were even other BUD/S classes that sang to us—it was a swelling feeling, and it was a relief. Finally, finally, I had made it.

The first place I was assigned was SEAL Team One. Like everyone else, I was in a probationary period for my first six months. I wasn't immediately in a platoon until about four months after my arrival in September. All of us new arrivals were officially on probation as far as our abilities to accomplish the basic skills of a SEAL.

After successfully completing our probation, we were awarded the NEC, Naval Enlisted Code, that says you're a SEAL, and you get your Trident. Pinning the Trident on my uniform added some height and weight to me. It was something I feel was in my blood, and it definitely reflects who I am. It's a nice, big, piece of gold on my uniform that tells everybody that I just completed the toughest training in the world. Receiving it was one of the proudest moments of my life.

My first years in the Teams were spent at SEAL Team One. Then, I was transferred over to the new SEAL Team Three, where I held plankowner status. I didn't look back on the history of the UDTs when they were turned into SEAL Teams in 1983. I had been a SEAL my whole time in the community. There was always that playful animosity between the UDTs and the SEAL Teams. The old saying was that you were just UDT, and we were only a SEAL Team.

What I think about now when I see a Underwater Demolition sticker on a vehicle with Freddie the Frog on it, if it's a young guy behind the wheel, I wonder if he really knows the significance of that emblem. The UDT mission was a lot different from the SEAL mission. It's a shame these young guys don't know more about the UDT.

The connection between myself as a SEAL and that Naked Warrior, the UDT man of World War II, is a tough one to make. I think those World War II guys were just hard as nails. They were absolutely a special breed, the forerunners to the elite unit known as the SEAL Teams. I think that's a legacy that should definitely always be in the present. It's where I came from as a SEAL.

Thinking of the Naked Warrior, I think of a man by the name of Tom Winters, who's one of the toughest men I've ever met in my life. He never wore a wet suit while we were in Korea. He had been a Naked Warrior, an Underwater Demolition Team member. That's no small example to follow.

Even though you leave the Teams, you will never not be a SEAL. There's one thing in common that we all have, and that's the blood and tears that were shed at BUD/S. We've all done it. The only difference are those who have gone on to combat and other accomplishments in the SEAL Teams. That's the only difference between us. But we've all gone through BUD/S. That's the common factor that will be between us forever.

It's funny to think of, but any SEAL who forgets his class number is not a SEAL. I don't know if any class numbers are classified, I've never heard of that. But any SEAL who forgets his class number, isn't a SEAL, and never was.

When I think of the word SEAL, I think of closeness, tight-knit, cohesive, intelligent. The Teams to me are a core group of men who impart the rule that it takes a Team to be successful.

Tom Richards, Rear Admiral, USN (Ret.)

I first showed up at BUD/S training fresh out of Villanova University where I had placed third in the National Collegiate Weightlifting Championships as a heavyweight—that's more than 242 pounds. Afterward, I thought I had trimmed down nicely to about 233 to 235 pounds. But what did I know about going through BUD/S training?

That first day, I was standing out there on "the line," as it's referred to. One of the instructors had seen me at 235 pounds, which was arranged a little bit differently about my person back then. I was standing out there with the rest of the student officers when the instructor asked for the muster report.

The muster report was that we had eight officers and forty-seven enlisted men. But that wasn't what the instructor felt. What he said was that we had seven officers, one gorilla, and the enlisted. Things kind of went downhill from there.

That instructor was Vince Olivera. He said he felt I could go out bear hunting armed with just a switch [stick]. Once he said that, I had an image to maintain at BUD/S.

My Navy career had started without my first thought being to go out for BUD/S. Back in 1964, my father said, "Tom, why don't you go up to the high school and take this Navy ROTC scholarship exam?"

We had discussed my taking up a career in the Navy, where my father had been a petty officer during World War II. My father thought a career as a Naval officer would be a pretty good thing. His impression of an officer in the Navy, and my mother's as well, was that one was not necessarily always down there in the bilges. They used the phrase "three squares and clean sheets."

Well, when I joined the Navy and ended up in Naval Special Warfare, my mother could not exactly understand what it was that her son was doing out in the mud and the blood, getting shot at and all that kind of thing. So although I might have originally gone into the Navy looking for the three squares and clean sheets, that's not exactly what I ended up with.

I first learned about the SEALs while I was still in high school. What I heard about them came from an early article in Reader's Digest. What they said those men did sounded like the kind of thing I wanted to do. Growing up on the southern shore of Long Island, New York, I spent all of my time on the water. If I wasn't on the water—water skiing, boating, or fishing—I was in the water bodysurfing, surfing, or so on. Being in the Navy, small boats and that type of thing is what I thought I was going to be getting in to. So the SEALs sounded about like what I wanted to do.

There's an old expression, "When opportunity knocks, you answer the door." I volunteered for the SEAL Teams because that's what I thought I wanted to do. To be honest, I recognized that I had a different outlook on life. You'll find that everybody in Naval Special Warfare is a risk-taker and an achiever, probably even an overachiever. And that's what I wanted to do—live life to the absolute edge—and so I have.

Whether I was in a summer BUD/S class or a winter one, who cares? The point is that I graduated training. Having been both a student and, later, an instructor, I can tell you that the instructor staff has a way of leveling the pain across the summer and the winter months. I specifically started in the fall (1969) and graduated in the spring (April 1970).

There isn't enough time to talk all about my BUD/S training. It was a great experience. The friendships, the associations that I made during that period of my life, as I overcame some of the most difficult challenges that will ever be presented to me in my life, those associations are the strongest I have had in my life since then.

Training is something that a lot of people know only from what they've seen in the media. There, they talk about how physically challenging SEAL training, specifically Basic Underwater Demolition/SEAL training. They're missing the boat. It isn't about the physical.

Every individual who shows up at BUD/S training today has proven that they have the basic physical skills needed for the course. Everyone who stands tall on the line, day one, week one, has the physical skills to graduate from training. Day one, week one, all that physical stuff is out the door. Now, the question is what do you have between the ears? What kind of guts do you have? What kind of focus do you have? What kind of self-discipline do you have? How far are you willing to go to achieve your goal?

That's not physical, that's all mental. Let me give you a few examples. In my training class, we had a kid who started who had been a junior college runner. He had run a four-minute, fifteen-second mile. By anybody's standard, that's greased lightning. As I remember, they timed my runs using a sun dial; today, they've shifted to a calendar. But I was there at the end, and it didn't matter to me that I was cold, wet, tired, hungry, and miserable. Those are just the facts of life. That's the environment you live in while you go through training. Getting through that is a given that you just have to accept.

This guy, instead of running in his Adidas or his nice little running shorts and a tank top, was running in boots, long pants, and probably a heavy military blouse. And by the way, he's wet.

Have you ever gone running down the beach with a pair of wet boots on? They weigh about five pounds each, so it becomes a given that you're going to run slower. The point is that you're going to run, you're going to keep going and be there at the end. That's what we're looking for in training. We don't need the guy who is the fastest runner or the fastest swimmer. We need the guy who's going to keep swimming, no matter what it takes, to get to where he needs to be.

Mike Thornton was a man in the Teams who is a Medal of Honor recipient. He received that medal because he took the body of Tommy Norris offshore in Vietnam. He was swimming on his E&E (escape and evasion) route, as they had briefed for the mission. He was going to swim until he couldn't swim any longer—and he was going to keep Tommy Norris with him—and that's just what he did. That's the kind of guy we're looking for.

When I went through training, I started with Class 54 and graduated with Class 55. The reason I graduated with Class 55 has been taken care of since then. That is, at the time when I went through training, if you had an injury, you were sort of pushed off to the side—we don't care about this, we don't want to hear about this, and so on. I ended up with a 104-degree temperature from a major infection and was in surgery the day after they admitted me to the hospital. So I wasn't exactly whining.

As a result of my illness, I had to be rolled back from one class to another. So I started with 54, ended with 55, and I have a lot of close friends from both classes.

Just trying to speak about one incident of my Hell Week sort of sells the week short. But one incident I can relate involved an all-night paddle. I believe it was Wednesday night of Hell Week, and I say I believe that was the night because sometime after Monday night of Hell Week, you're no longer completely sure of what day it is.

So there we were that Wednesday night, paddling down the ocean parallel to the Silver Strand south of the training base. We were doing pretty well. "It always pays to be a winner," as they say at BUD/S, so if you're the first boat crew to finish that particular paddle, you get a chance to rest while the other crews are still pad-dling. Then, when they come in, they'll do push-ups or sit-ups, whatever the instruc-tors feel is necessary to remind them that it pays to be a winner.

My boat crew was paddling along, making pretty good time, and we were out ahead of (now) Admiral Ray Smith's boat crew. It was usually his boat crew and mine that tagged for one and two on most of the evolutions. On this paddle, I was having a certain amount of difficulty staying awake. Granted, I'd only been awake for three days, and this situation wasn't unusual among the trainees.

The boat crew officer's job is to steer, so his position was in the rear of the boat as the coxswain, so I was steering as we were going. I noticed myself starting to nod off a bit. One way to stay awake is to engage in a bit of banter with the boys in the crew, so I spoke up and said, "You guys are probably not going to find this funny, but your nice, slow, steady paddling is lulling me to sleep."

I was right, they didn't find any humor in that.

But what I did just to make sure we would be winners, was to move things around. "Okay guys," I said. "What we're going to do is rotate through the coxswain's position. I'm not going to sit back here and rest and try to stay awake. We're going to make sure we come in first."

It might not have been a great idea. Smith beat us on that paddle.

What got me through Hell Week was all between my ears. When I was at Vil-lanova University, I met a corpsman who had served with the Teams. He was work-ing out at the YMCA, and we talked about a lot of things. As a result of our discussions, I decided that there was nothing that another human being had done that I couldn't do.

As instructors, every one of us have done what the students were about to do or about to be asked to do. So I said to myself, if another human being could do it, I could as well. And I'd be damned if I wasn't going to do it. That attitude—and you *have to have an attitude, you need to be positive about everything you do in training—got me through.*

Breaking training down from one event to another helped get me through training. You just can't look at a six-month program that has a fourteen-mile run in boots, a five-mile ocean swim, and Hell Week—with a maximum of six or eight hours of sleep in the course of five days of constantly going—in one piece. You can't look at that elephant and expect to swallow it whole. You take it a bite at a time.

The way I did it was that I said that we had a run, we had a swim, and we had a PT evolution. There's a start and a finish to every one of those evolutions. I was obviously there at the start, and I intended to be there at the finish. Breaking it into manageable chunks like that helped me make my way through it all.

I had been a weight-lifter before going to BUD/S, so I sort of like food. At the end of the morning's evolutions was lunch. At the end of the afternoon's evolution was dinner. And during Hell Week, we got to eat four times a day. I sort of looked forward to those meal times, a self-reward if you will.

After graduation from BUD/S came the assignment to the Teams. With Vietnam still being very active then, the time came for me to go into my first combat. My wife still has the letter I wrote to her following that.

Combat was what I was trained to do. That's something about the Teams. Throughout the years, there have been a number of movies about Vietnam—how screwed up it was, how unfair this was, and how miserable that was. I knew it was going to be miserable. That's why I raised my hand and volunteered, that's why I wanted to do it. I knew I could do it, and I knew the people with me could do it, too.

We were all trained and prepared for what we saw. Okay, this is the environment, these are the conditions, this is the job. Let's go do that. In the Teams we wanted to do that, and we were good at what we did. We took pride in doing what we did well. We took the war to the enemy in his own backyard.

During my first combat tour in Vietnam, we had a couple operations where there was no real contact with the enemy. The first contact we had, being shot at and missed or hit as the situation might be, I had no difficulty with. Several of the people who fell during the course of the engagement fell as a result of my marksmanship. I did my job and did it well. It wasn't that Tom Richards or SEAL Team One said "Hey, let's go fight a war." We were fighting in a conflict that our government was engaged in. You can debate whether you feel the war was right or wrong, but we went over there and did our jobs well.

My first impression of Vietnam came as I stepped off the airplane at Tan Son Nhut air field. It was the hottest place I had ever been in my life. The weather was hot, muggy, and sticky, but there's nothing you can do about that. What I was a bit concerned about was how lax things seemed to be. There was a lack of attention to security in and around the area the base where we were. My impression was that I had gone into a third-world country, and I wasn't exactly sure what to expect next.

I was damned sure not going to be walking around as relaxed as some of the folks were nearby.

Again, going back to our training, for the entire time I was there, and most of the other SEALs who were incountry, we would not lose that focus on our environment. Today, we talk about force protection in the military, the protection of our personnel and equipment in all locations and situations. We were doing force protection back then.

Vietnam gave a lot of other impressions than just the weather. My platoon was assigned down to the very southern tip of IV Corps at the southern end of South Vietnam. When we moved ashore, we actually had some ground water available and set up some showers. That ground water was always at 110 degrees and smelled like sulfur. I don't think Vietnam itself has a different smell than say Barbados or Florida or Hawaii. I didn't pick up anything that really separated it. Yes, Vietnam was primarily an agricultural country at the time, and there were water buffalo in the rice paddies and the farmers used waste products as fertilizer. But once you were there a couple days, you didn't smell anything much any more.

My first tour was with Zulu Platoon, SEAL Team One. We went over were in August 1970 and came back in January 1971. The platoon commander for Zulu Platoon was Lieutenant Grant Telfer, who was later the commanding officer of SEAL Team One [30 March 1974 to 3 April 1976] as was I [7 August 1986 to 1 September 1988].

Vietnam was the experience I trained for. On the many operations we went out on, I did things well. A most memorable one would probably be the prisoner-of-war rescue mission that we executed.

We had intelligence that there were three American pilots being held about fifteen or twenty miles as the crow flies from where we were. Getting to that spot was a different matter.

Taking two platoons, we went out on the operations. Lieutenant Dick Couch was the commander of one platoon, and his platoon had the primary responsibility for the operation. I went in with my squad as his assistant. Unfortunately, we arrived at the POW camp a day late and a dollar short as the saying goes, and didn't find any American prisoners of war. But we freed twenty-one Vietnamese prisoners of war who were being held in cages that you wouldn't keep your dog in.

Just to see how happy those people were to see us Americans and to release those twenty-one prisoners of war was the most rewarding operation I did during the entire period I was over there.

There were two SEALs who influenced me the most during my first tour. One was a guy we referred to as Uncle Dave Schaible. If Uncle Dave hadn't retired before we had our first flag officer selected from the Teams, there's no doubt in my mind that Dave Schaible would have been that man.

Commander Schaible was the commanding officer of SEAL Team One, my first CO. He was an impressive man who believed in leadership by example and could talk to the troops or up the chain of command with equal ease.

The other individual was Leon Rauch. Chief Rauch taught me a lot about operating. He also taught me about dealing with the chain of command. There are some people out there who haven't got a clue about what's going on, who couldn't find first base if they were standing on it. Leon told me that there was a way to deal with those people—you can say no.

There I was, a lieutenant, junior grade, sitting with Leon Rauch and then Lieutenant Grant Telfer, getting a briefing on the mission we had coming up. The target was in the middle of nowhere, no fire support was available to us, and we had no E&E support in case things went to hell in a handbasket. And this Navy captain wanted us to go in to his target and do something.

Leon looked at me, then he looked at Grant, and he said, "We're not going to do this."

"Sounds good to me, Grant," I said. And we didn't do that operation. It would have been absolutely foolhardy to go in under the conditions that had been set up for that operation. Leon taught me a lot about taking a good look at a situation and making the right decision.

Probably a tougher question about the SEALs in Vietnam would be who the most unusual operator I knew there was. The answer to that would just follow the roster for SEAL Team One. That would be a list of the most unusual SEALs. Every SEAL is unique. Every SEAL is an achiever and a risk-taker. We all went out and did such difficult things that people would not believe other human beings could do.

Names come to mind as I think about the question of unusual SEAL. Frank Bomar was a huge E-6 petty officer who carried more ammunition on an op than you could store in an ammo dump. Frank was unusual because, like everyone else in the Teams, there was no "can't do" in his vocabulary.

Leon Rauch would also fit the bill. There was no operation he couldn't figure out a way to carry out. If it was worth doing, if there was a valid mission concept, a reason, and a justification for going after a target, Leon could figure out how to do it.

Mike Thornton is a SEAL who I don't know personally very well, but I do know the operation Mike participated in that resulted in his receiving the Medal of Honor. As I had said earlier, Mike Thornton received his medal for swimming Lieutenant Norris away from an enemy beach. Mike didn't know if he was dead or alive at one point, but he was not going to leave the body behind.

What Mike did personifies the attitude of the SEALs. We, that is the Navy SEALs, have never left anybody behind. We didn't do that—it was a creed of ours. Mike's swimming out to sea for hours, not knowing if Tom was going to survive, but not going to let him go—that tells you an awful lot about Mike Thornton. I don't know Mike well enough other than to say that he was a fantastic SEAL, a hell of a hard worker, and had an attitude that was indomitable. Those are characteristics you will find in every other SEAL.

We recently had a building dedication to Lieutenant Tom Norris, the individual who Mike earned his Medal of Honor for saving. Tom had actually been on an operation that he later received the Medal of Honor for himself. That operation had taken place well before his long swim with Mike Thornton. In Norfolk, Virginia, we dedicated a building to Tom—a highly unusual occurrence given that the honoree was still alive and attended the ceremony.

As Tom made his remarks, one of the things he said was that he had been in the right place at the right time to conduct the action that resulted in his earning the Medal of Honor. Tom looked at the formation of troops made up of today's young SEALs, doing the things he did during his time, and said to them that he had no doubt that any one of those SEALs would have done the same thing given the same situation. That's the kind of people we have in the organization.

Other SEALs have gone farther, literally, than anyone else in the Teams. There ought to be a law about people being as smart as Bill Shepherd is. He's quite an individual. Bill is in the astronaut program, and he worked on the project that we have between the United States and the Russians. He has the mental focus and drive that gets a man through Naval Special Warfare training, and that's exactly the thing that got him into the astronaut program. Bill did not get accepted the first time he applied to the astronaut program, but that was okay for the first time. He figured out what he needed to do to fix that situation, and he reapplied and made it.

Bill was on a training operation back off the Virginia coast during his Team days. A limpet mine, a live limpet mine, did not attach itself solidly to the side of the ship that Bill and his Teammates were attacking. The mine fell away from the side of the target ship before it detonated.

There was now a live, armed piece of explosive ordnance somewhere out there in the Chesapeake. Bill probably has several degrees, but I know that one of them is in naval architecture. He went back to the Team compound and examined the situation. He knew the location of the target ship, what the tide was, its direction, and its speed. He took the shape of the limpet mine, sort of an inverted bowl but not as smooth, and made some calculations.

Shepherd decided that, given the weight of the mine, it would fall at a given rate through the 150 feet or so of water at the target site. That would mean that the mine would be in the water column for a certain amount of time. The current and directions were known, and he determined how far the mine would travel before it reached the bottom. It wasn't a very big mine, and the situation was very much like looking for a needle in a haystack. After just a few dives, the search party found the mine where Bill said it should come to rest—an absolutely incredible demonstration of knowledge and ability.

There is no difference between the SEALs who went through training back in my day and the young men who are going through training today—they are the same. We have exactly the same kind of individual coming into the Teams today as have been coming to the Teams since the days of World War II. These are people looking to accept the challenge we offer, to see what they are made of, among other things. That is absolutely the same for every man ever in the Teams. It's the same focus, the same drive, and the same self-discipline that has always been needed to get through training.

How are these young men today different? When I graduated from Villanova University, Mendel Hall, a science building, was next to John Barry Hall, the Naval ROTC building. The entire basement of Mendel Hall was the computer system at Villanova University. Today, I carry a laptop computer that probably has as much or more capability as that computer in the basement of Mendel Hall.

Our kids coming in to Naval Special Warfare today take things like that for granted. I didn't know anything about computers when I came into the service. I didn't know anything about the technology that we have today. Cars and that kind of thing were what I knew about as a young man. Computers and those types of things are what the youth of today play with when they socialize. That's the difference between the people joining today, their level of experience with technology.

Our missions are changing in the Teams today as well. Instead of trying to find a courier moving along a jungle trail as we did, the couriers of today can be a fiber-optic cable. That's what has to be found and attacked. The vulnerable points of a fiber-optic cable and how it can be attacked and penetrated is something that the young SEALs of today know.

The people who conduct the operations are the same as they have always been. The experiences they have now, that developed them into the individuals in the Teams, are slightly different.

There was an operation we did in Vietnam where we were set up to conduct an ambush against a VC supply route. There was a trail about twelve or fifteen yards in from the river bank we learned about during the op. The VC didn't come down the river in a sampan as we expected, they came down along the trail. We were set up for our ambush facing the river, between the river and the trail.

There was no way we could get up and turn around to reorient the ambush when we heard them start coming down the trail. The VC would have heard us moving about, and we would have been in a particularly vulnerable position. So we had to sit there while the enemy walked by, carrying their mortars and everything, chatting away to each other. They ended up launching a few mortar rounds on our base camp nearby, but there was nothing we could do. We just had to sit there and be quiet. We never did get them.

Trying to rate the three things that get you though training—the heart, the mind, and the body—will give you some consistent answers from all the SEALs you talk to. The priority might be a bit different for individuals, but what gets you through training is drive and focus. Everybody who shows up to start training has proven that they have the basic physical skills to get through training. That's a given. What's next?

What is not only next, but foremost, is that mental drive, that absolute and total focus on the task at hand. Monday morning of a training week through that Friday evening, you are totally focused on going through the training. There's nothing else in the world but that task. As soon as you relax, as soon as you let yourself think about your dog, your car, or whatever, you're done. You have to maintain that total focus.

So I'm going to rate the body as third in importance. The total focus is first. Second, I would put the risk-taking and challenge aspect of the training and the Teams. If you want to get something done, you go in and tell a SEAL Platoon; "You know, I really don't know if this operation can be done, so don't spend too much time on this. If you don't think we can do it, just let me know."

Two hours later, that platoon commander and his men will come in, and they will have a plan. If you want something done, you challenge a SEAL.

The Trident stands for our capabilities. SEAL stands for SEa, Air, and Land. The flintlock pistol on the symbol is for the land activity we do. The sea is the anchor and the Trident. The air is the wings of the eagle. Every SEAL is an excellent marksman, every SEAL is diving-qualified, every SEAL has differing levels of training in demolitions, and every SEAL is jump-qualified. That's what we do.

What does the Trident mean to me? That one's hard to explain. The level of pride I have in wearing the Trident is really difficult to express. What is even more difficult to express is the honor I have to lead a community of 5,000 Naval Special Warfare people. It's mind-boggling. The responsibility I hold, and the faith and trust they have placed in me . . . I just can't put the feelings I have for that in words. I just can't tell you.

In order to get through Naval Special Warfare training, BUD/S, you have to be totally focused on one goal—getting through training. Everything else just goes along with that. There's an expression that we use in the Teams, "Mind over matter—you don't mind, and it don't matter."

Pain is another of those four-letter words. Navy, Boat, SEAL—there's a bunch of four-letter words I live with. Pain is a frame of mind. It's something you're can either accept, or you can blank it out. It is something you're going to have to put up with.

Here's an example of pain. We're cold. I can't tell you how cold. There's no concept of this kind of cold that can be told in terms of degrees. That doesn't matter. We're standing there in line, my class, and I'm vibrating like you would picture a jackhammer operator. You know those guys you see on the street, bouncing about as they handle the heavy jackhammer? They're not even moving in comparison to how badly we're all shaking in that line.

That's a degree of pain. There are more definitions of pain, here's one: We were out on a particular operation in Vietnam where I was shot in the hand, for which I received my Purple Heart. How do I describe the sensation? Well, take your hand and put it on an anvil. Then take one of these, say, four- or five-pound sledgehammers, wind up as hard as you can, and just smack your hand. See what it feels like? That's pain.

That was my definition of pain, and I took it just a little bit further. We've all been to the movies, and some of us have seen John Wayne in Green Berets or his cowboy movies. There he is, standing there with this arrow sticking out of his chest. What does Wayne do? He pulls it out and keeps going.

Heck, I told myself I could do that. I looked down at my hand after I was shot. It kind of looked like some bloody hamburger down there. But I could see the bullet sticking out of the back of my hand. This is a piece of cake, I thought. John Wayne did it, and so could I. So I lifted up my hand, clamped my teeth down on the bullet, and got ready to pull it out of my hand.

Minor complication. My vision at the time wasn't what it could have been. That wasn't a bullet; it was a bone sticking out of the back of my hand. Unfortunately, it was still attached.

I grabbed it, I pulled—and my toes curled.

I told myself I'd worry about that later. That's pain. You can put it out of your mind. I loaded three guys who were shot much worse than I, two in the lungs and one in both legs, into a helicopter with that hand. It was somewhat painful. But pain is something you can accept, deal with, and put out of your mind when you have to.

When you report to a Team, you have to let the rest of the guys know who you are and what you're going to bring to that Team. We SEALs tend to be pretty low-key and don't brag about what we do, especially not to outsiders, but when you arrive at a Team, you're already 90 percent known to those guys. Somewhere between six to nine months or maybe a year later after starting your training, you go before a board. There you get the authority to wear the Special Warfare Insignia, the Trident. Once you're a member of that club, what else do you need? You've been through the hardest military training there is.

When I say that BUD/S is the hardest military training there is, it's because of that combination of mental discipline and focus it takes to get through on top of the physical tasks that have to be accomplished. That's why the guys don't have to brag.

Never is a Teammate, wounded or dead, left behind. It has never happened, and it never will. During training, these BUD/S students have that lesson brought home as they carry one of their classmates along to simulate a wounded man.

U.S. Navy

We don't do Rambo in the Teams. The guy who does Rambo doesn't make it through training. To the guy who comes in and says he's going to do what's in the movies, kill 4,000 enemy single-handed, save the girl, and fly off in the helicopter, we tell him that that's the movies, that's entertainment. It's wonderful entertainment, and I'll go to see that movie again, but that's not real life, and that's not what the SEALs do. We don't want a Rambo.

We have SEAL Teams. There's no "i" in Team, and that's what it's all about. We operate as a Team, always. When the three guys in my squad were wounded—two guys shot through the chest, one in the legs—there was never the thought in their minds that anybody was going to leave them behind just because they couldn't move. That's not part of what we are. Those men knew that they could depend on their Teammates out there in the rice paddy with them. That's what it's about. It isn't Rambo.

If I suddenly had the mission to win the Super Bowl of football with a group of Navy SEALs, that's probably a do-able mission. That is, if I can pick and choose my SEALs.

I was at SEAL Team Two once with Mike Thornton. There was a guy there by the name of Jack Ford, who had been a wide receiver at the Naval Academy. I hadn't played organized football, but I was just big enough that I could keep anyone out of anyone else's way. So we had an interesting crew put together for a football game.

What happened exactly during that game, I don't quite remember. Mike Thorn-

ton had his arm in a splint and I was limping. Unfortunately, Jack Ford had his knee dislocated to a degree that it resulted in his ultimately leaving the Navy. But we won the game, that was the important part. You play the game to win, and you find a way. If we had to play the Super Bowl, we could do that.

SEALs have tenacity. It gets real easy, because it goes back to focus, focus and mission accomplishment. And that's what Naval Special Warfare brings to the equation. We thrive on challenges. What is the mission? What is it we need to do? What is the objective, and what are the obstacles in our way?

We take a look at whatever that mission might be, and we break it down into parts. We examine the parts to see just what could go wrong here or there. We do that so that if something does go wrong, we have an SOP, a standard operating procedure, to deal with that.

Everyone in that platoon is known to everyone else, and their skills and abilities are augmented by their Teammates. There was an event in Southeast Asia I remember. It was in a coconut grove at night. There was no moon, and it was so dark that you couldn't see your hand as you held it in front of your face. But there was a faint outline in front of me. I knew that outline was Jim Roland. I knew that just because of the way that outline carried itself, how he moved. My squad was that well known to me.

Tenacity is, give us this mission, and we will accomplish it. There's no question. That's why we exist. What else is there?

We teach the new SEALs our history. You have to know what your roots are. You have to know what the organization is built on, what it's based on. The SEALs of today came from the Underwater Demolition Teams and the Naval Combat Demolition Units of World War II. We are the water side of Special Operations. The Navy talks about our cornerstone capability of coming from the sea. And that's exactly what we do in Naval Special Warfare—we do special operations from the sea.

Up along the coast of New England, there are beautiful mansions here and there, facing the sea. On the third or fourth story of the mansions, they have a cupola or doorway leading out onto what's called the widow's walk. Back in the days of sailing ships, the families would go up on that widow's walk, and they would look out to sea. They would look out to see if there was any sign of the ships that would be bringing their family members back. Not only when, but if. The sea is a very unforgiving environment. It always has been. And that's the environment that we live and operate in.

The SEALs don't consider an ocean, river, or bay an obstacle. That's what we live and work in. That's the environment we've mastered. And that is why it is so important that the young SEALs of today understand where that mastery came from.

Barry Enoch won his Navy Cross doing operations up and down the rivers of

Southeast Asia. Mike Thornton received his Medal of Honor by swimming out to sea, carrying Tom Norris. Special operations from the sea are what we do, so we had to master that very unforgiving environment.

SEALs are human beings. We're not loners, and we certainly aren't Rambos. We come from the family next door, just like anyone else. I'm not a whole lot different from anyone else who was born in Brightwaters, Long Island. We're part of society, and we're no different from anyone else in that society.

We have something we call "SEAL Pups." We bring together the kids of the SEALs and the Navy Special Warfare Combatant Crewmembers who are assigned to work with us, and we have a sports day for these kids.

During one of these days, I was standing and talking to the mayor of Coronado, who is a former Navy aviator. Standing there, we looked at all the people who were known to the public at large as these hard cases, loners, or whatever. And here was this 220-pound SEAL, on his hands and knees, a target for the water balloons being launched at him by these three four-year-olds. We're just like anyone else.

One thing I could promise that you would find in a SEAL Team is yourself. When you go through training, you have to dig deep, concentrate, and focus to master those challenges. What you learn about yourself is just what challenges you can master.

Anybody knows that you can't just stay up three days, run X number of miles, swim X number of miles, paddle a rubber boat, and do all these other things. Mind over matter. If you are going to do it, you're going to have to pay attention and focus. What you will learn about yourself is that you can do that. And that's what you get out of being a SEAL. You learn what you can do.

And we're a family, we're all accepted. If somebody from Class 54, or Class 55, the class I graduated with, were to call me up and ask me anything, I would stop what I was doing and meet that request. That's an absolute given.

Barry Enoch and I were not in a platoon together, we didn't go through Training together, but we were assigned to SEAL Team One at the same time years ago. But if Barry or Mike Thornton, or any one of my Teammates was to give me a call, I would stop what I was doing to do whatever they need me to do.

A nineteen-year-old BUD/S trainee is probably about as connected to the original Naked Warrior of World War II as you can get. That youngster is about as naked as he can be. He's standing there, freezing his butt off, wearing nothing but a pair of UDT shorts and a coating of water. And he's hoping like hell that he has the guts to stick it out and graduate from training. That's the same person, he has the same core as the first NCDU during World War II. He has the drive, the discipline, and the risk-taking mentality that makes that individual meet whatever challenge you give him.

Joe Maguire, Captain

When this interview was taken in 1998, I'd been in the Teams for twenty-two years. For the first two years of my Navy career, I'd been a surface warfare officer, a rather undistinguished surface warfare officer. After scraping enough paint off the ship, I decided to change and come into the Teams.

Brooklyn, New York, was where I first heard about the Teams. It was while I watched the recovery of the astronauts from the Mercury, Gemini, *and* Apollo *space capsules that I saw the men who jumped from the helicopters and were the first to reach the capsules after splashdown.*

When I was young, a lot of my friends who were watching the shows with me wanted to grow up to be astronauts. But I wanted to be one of those guys in the water who were recovering the space capsule. The news shows always had some human-interest stories about the guys who were recovering the capsules, men from UDT 21. Some of these guys were Olympic swimmers and really impressive men. So I just said to myself that it looked like something I would like to do when I grew up—and here I am.

To get to the Teams, I first had to go through training just like everyone else. To get to Basic Underwater Demolition/SEAL training (BUD/S) was pretty interesting and rewarding. During my first two years in the Navy, I had applied to BUD/S a number of times. When I finally arrived at BUD/S, it had already seemed like an accomplishment just to have gotten here.

I really enjoyed the training. It was twenty-five weeks of very demanding training and hard work. But if being in the Teams is something you want to do, and something you've had to work hard at just to be there, the work is good.

Instead of being aboard ship, I was outside most of the time. There were three meals a day and I was told what to wear, where I had to be, and when I had to be there. There was never a question about what I had to do, and I had no trouble sleeping at night for twenty-five weeks.

As an officer at BUD/S, I had a different experience than enlisted students. It wasn't that the instructors were really any harder on the officers than the enlisted men. Because there were so few officers in comparison to the number of enlisted men in a class, the instructors provided them with a lot more chances to excel than the rest of the guys in a class.

My class, Class 93, had 4 officers and 20 enlisted men graduate in August 1977 from a starting group of 145. So those of us who finished had been scrutinized pretty closely by the time we were done. We officers wore a khaki belt and a stripe on our helmet liner to identify us as the officers in a class. That made us visible to our classmates, as well as the instructors, as we went through training.

What is attempted at BUD/S is to give the officer students leadership opportunities. They clearly have to be just as good operators as the enlisted men, but they also have to be more than that—they have to be leaders. So the instructors give the student officers a lot more of a leadership challenge during their training. We're such as small community in Naval Special Warfare that the officers who go though training one day will very possibly have those same instructors working for them some time down the road, so the instructors are pretty careful about who makes it through BUD/S.

The role between officers and enlisted in the Surface Navy is more formalized than it is in Naval Special Warfare. The relationship between officers and enlisted, in training and what I could see among the instructors, was a lot less formal. There was still a tremendous level of respect between the officers and the enlisted, but the bar that separated the two groups so much in the regular Navy had very much been lowered.

To me, one of the big differences between Naval Special Warfare, the SEAL Teams, the rest of the Navy, and the Department of Defense was the quality of the enlisted people who make up the ranks of the community. Right now, as the commanding officer of the Naval Special Warfare Center, I can say that 35 percent of the enlisted men who graduate from BUD/S have their Bachelor of Science degrees. These are some very high-quality individuals. The rest of the Navy, and the rest of the military, is really not as fortunate to have such a high-caliber enlisted community.

As far as the relationship between the officers and enlisted men in the Special Warfare community goes, it starts at BUD/S. As an officer in training, your swim buddy will most likely be a junior enlisted man. Then, when you get into the SEAL Team, the guy who is swimming alongside of you—the person whose hands you're placing your life in—he's an enlisted guy, too. That gives us a much more fraternal relationship than just a professional one between the officers and the enlisted in the Teams.

The training I underwent at BUD/S was wonderful. It was everything I had hoped it would be, and then some. The initial part trying to get used to life as a trainee was a little bit difficult, but once you finished Hell Week and went on to the diving phase and the land warfare phase, training was wonderful. The thing that really struck me was the image of what the instructors were like, and what SEALs were like when you were a trainee. Comparing them to what the men are actually like in reality is vastly different.

When I went through training in 1977, I would say that 99 percent of my instructors were fairly recently out of Vietnam. The vast majority of them either had the Bronze Star or the Silver Star. I even had the good fortune to have Mike Thornton, a Medal of Honor recipient, as one of my instructors. These were men who had ably demonstrated that they knew what they were doing and had brought the lessons home and were passing them on to us.

The thing that struck me about the instructors I had was their willingness to work with somebody and to be kind to someone who needed it. During my third phase of training, a situation came up for me when I had a stress fracture in my right leg. I really didn't know that I had a stress fracture, but I was running about ten minutes behind the class on most runs when I had earlier been right up there with the pack. The swims and obstacle course were things I could still compete in pretty well, but the pain was getting bad.

One day, I was going to go across the street to the Amphibious base to get my leg x-rayed to find out just what was going on. One of my third-phase instructors was Johnny Johnson, a SEAL corpsman. Chief Johnson came up to me and said, "If you go across the street, you're going to come back with a cast. You've got a broken leg. But if you're willing to stick it out and work with us—I'm not making any promises—but we'll see what we can do for you."

So I continued to fall behind in class in a lot of ways, but they remained my class. But I was able to work through that stress fracture and keep going. It finally did heal. But the point that stuck out to me was that the instructors cared enough that I made it through training. It had been shown over time that the longer you stayed at BUD/S, if you had been rolled back from an earlier class due to an injury or whatever, the less your chances of successfully completing training were.

If you got rolled back, to recuperate from an injury or to work on an academic problem, statistically, you had a lower chance of completing the program than someone who had never been rolled back. You have to be up all the time during training. Every single day during basic Underwater Demolition/SEAL training is game day. For the twenty-seven weeks you are there, you have to put out the maximum you have every day. After a certain period of time, your battery just runs out. You just lose some of that self-motivation and enthusiasm you need to get through the program. And you can't just fake it through BUD/S; you have to be "up" every day.

So if you're at BUD/S just a little too long, you can really get too tired and things can seem to be too much for you. And that can be a terrible waste, because you had to accomplish so much in just getting through the first parts of BUD/S. Once you've completed Hell Week, you've demonstrated that you have the personal drive to get through the program.

I really don't recall much details about Hell Week when I went through it. One thing I do remember was that you really couldn't tell just who would be able to get through it—you still can't even today. We started off with about 145 students. By the time Class 93 had gotten to Hell Week, we were down to around 60 students.

The first guy who quit during Hell Week was somebody who I never would have thought would quit. He had been first in the runs and first in the obstacle course, and he had a tremendous amount of leadership. But he quit on Monday afternoon of Hell Week. When that individual quit, there were about ten men who went with him.

That individual might as well have had a big red "S" on his chest for "Superman" from what the rest of us saw during the first five weeks of training. I think when he quit, a lot of the guys figured that if he couldn't make it, they never would be able to make it through. Even though I was just a trainee going through the same misery myself, I felt that this guy quitting was a bad thing. I went up to him and tried to tell him to hang in there with the rest of us, that things would be fine. But he had just had it, he was done. The fact that when he quit, he took ten guys with him, was very significant to me.

I never really thought about quitting during Hell Week. There was one moment when I was down in the sloughs, the mud flats, near Tijuana, probably about Wednesday night, that things got tight for me. We had set up Camp Swampy, a collection of tents and so forth, near the mud flats. We had been in the mud for seven or eight hours when for some reason I found myself just standing alone in the mud. The cold and exhaustion got to me and I just started shaking uncontrollably. The shakes happen to every student during Hell Week and you usually get through them together. But while I was standing there, I started to think. What I thought about was just how miserable things were and that my situation really stank.

At that point in time, one of the instructors came by, grabbed my life jacket, and threw me back into the mud. Once I was back into the mud, I was back into the game and I was just fine. But that was about as close as I came to considering quitting during my Hell Week.

I was also impressed by the camaraderie the instructors showed. Almost every one of those men had been through Vietnam either as platoon mates or as Teammates in SEAL Team One or Two. They were focused on conducting our training. They knew what was required to get through training, and they kept it demanding and forced us to meet a high standard. That made things hard for those of us who made up the class, but it also made the final result very rewarding. And we had an awful lot of laughs along the way.

Graduation from BUD/S was an interesting day. The thing about graduation was that we were ready to leave BUD/S and go on to the SEAL Teams, and yet we still felt like students. Even on the day of graduation, we still weren't really convinced that we had made it through the program. Up to the morning of graduation day, the instructors were still the instructors, they were still on us, challenging us, and being very demanding on our performance.

I remember being there at graduation when they went up to announce the honor man award for the class. I just assumed that the award would go to one of my classmates. When the commanding officer read my name as the class honor man, I just sat there for a little while. Part of me was still not convinced that I was going to graduate, let alone be the honor man of Class 93. I had thought that there were a lot more men in the class who should have been the honor man rather than me, and no one was more surprised than I was when the announcement was made. Graduation was quite a defining moment for me.

Once you've gone through BUD/S and successfully completed a six-month probationary time with a Team, you are awarded the Naval Special Warfare Breast Device. That symbol you wear on your uniform tells the world that you are a Naval Special Warfare officer or enlisted man.

The thing that is remarkable about the device we wear is that it is the only warfighting insignia in the U.S. Navy that the officers and the enlisted alike wear. That's to signify that we go through training right alongside each other. The officers and enlisted men share the same mud, cold, and wet of BUD/S. In some of the other warfare specialties, there are distinct qualifications as well as training pipelines for officers and enlisted. But as far as the SEALs are concerned, whether you are Admiral Tom Richards, Admiral Tom Steffins, Admiral Ray Smith, or one of the youngest petty officers in a SEAL Team, you all wear the same device.

To me, the Trident doesn't necessarily signify the warfare specialty of the wearer as much as it says the man is a member of a very close fraternity. When I work with somebody who has worn the Trident, they don't even have to have it on. They can be in civilian clothes, but I still know we have a tremendous number of things in common. And what I especially know is that I can count on that individual—if we were in the face of adversity, that individual would not call "time out," no matter what.

The Naval Special Warfare device, the Trident, is made up of several different parts assembled into a single whole. SEAL stands for SEa, Air, and Land, the three environments a SEAL can insert from. The device identifies those three areas of insertion.

The eagle is the largest single part of the device, signifying strength, but also showing that we come from the air. The vertical anchor and horizontal Trident show our heritage and membership as part of the U.S. Navy and the water it operates in. In the right talon of the eagle is a flintlock pistol, cocked and ready to go. That pistol also symbolizes the land warfare side of the SEAL Teams.

Once I had graduated from BUD/S, I had the good fortune of reporting to Underwater Demolition Team 21 on the east coast at Little Creek, Virginia. It was quite a remarkable group of men at UDT 21, both officer and enlisted. There were about thirty officers who were assigned to UDT 21, twenty of whom had been former enlisted men who had served in Vietnam. The men had taken their commissions and become "mustangs," the term we had for prior enlisted officers.

As far as the enlisted men in the Team were concerned, most of them had rotated from SEAL Team Two into UDT 21. With this mixing of personnel, there were a tremendous number of people in UDT 21 who were true warriors with a great deal of combat experience. They were also people who liked to work hard, play hard, and

The sign for the NCDU training base at Fort Pierce during WWII. The octopus is holding a sledgehammer over his head, has a case of TNT in one of the other tentacles, and has secured himself to a horned sculley obstacle under the water.

UDT-SEAL MUSEUM

have a lot of fun getting the job done. I can't think of a better place to have broken in to Naval Special Warfare than UDT 21.

It could have gone either way for me, having all those people around me who had seen so much combat and were so highly decorated. They could have ostracized me as someone who had never faced the challenges of combat. But I really feel that those men took me under their wing, put their arm around me—especially the senior enlisted at UDT 21—and taught me a lot about how to be a Special Warfare operator.

You only get one chance to make a first impression, and the impression I received in UDT 21 was that this was a community. And being a part of that community was something I thought I would like to be for a long, long time.

A little more than the first two years of my career in Naval Special Warfare were spent at UDT 21. Then I left the UDT and went to the Amphibious Force, Seventh Fleet, over in Okinawa for a couple years. Once I came back to Little Creek, I was in SEAL Team Two as a Platoon Commander. While I was at SEAL Team Two, UDT 21 became SEAL Team Four.

The ending of the history of the UDTs, and the continuation of the SEAL history, was something that came up among us. You always have to remember where you came from and just what your origins are. In the SEAL Teams, we certainly have a history, a distinguished history, of the Teams in Vietnam. But the people who were involved in the Underwater Demolition Teams, and the Naval Combat Demolition Units who came before them in World War II, had a long and respectable history themselves.

The UDTs performed heroically during the Korean War and earlier, and they did a number of pioneering actions over the years. It was the guys from the World War II Teams and from Korea, their history and capabilities, that got us the SEALs Teams today. When we changed over from the UDTs to just the SEAL Teams, there was a tremendous sense that we were losing something. I agree with the decision to make the change; it was something we needed to do. And yet it was very difficult to say good-bye to that past. To this day, those of us who were in the UDTs, still pretty much refer to ourselves as Frogmen as opposed to SEALs.

As the Commanding Officer of the Naval Special Warfare Center, I have a number of courses that are conducted under my watch. BUD/S is really the most important course taught at the Center; without BUD/S, we would have no community. At the time of this interview (1998), I have Class 223 getting ready to class up. In a couple days, Captain Bob Gormly will be the guest speaker at the graduation of Class 220.

The changes over time at the Center and at BUD/S have been for the better, in my opinion. We try to train a little smarter and do things a little better than we did in the past. But in essence, BUD/S is the same training that Class 123 received and that Class 23 received.

I graduated in 1977. Since then, there have been tremendous technological advances in weapons systems and communications just in our boats. But BUD/S training has not changed very much over those same years. We've incorporated new weapons systems and have different dive gear today, but for the twenty-seven weeks that the student goes through training, we test their spirit just as hard now as we did in the past.

When a student graduates from BUD/S, they have only finished Basic Underwater Demolition/SEAL training. What we know about them is that their spirit has been tested and proven. When called upon to use the wonderful technological weapons available for the defense of freedom, these guys will do the same fine job today as the SEALs have done in the past.

It is our philosophy, our ethos, in Naval Special Warfare, that it is the spirit of the men who lead and the spirit of the men who follow, not the weapons that achieve victory on the field of battle. So we're still working on the spirit at BUD/S.

To me, the most important factor for a man to become a SEAL, to pass though BUD/S, is clearly his mind. BUD/S is, without a doubt, the most demanding physical program in the Department of Defense. But every single day is game day at BUD/S. You could be a tremendous athlete, but you have to be up and psychologically prepared for this program that will humble anybody.

We have all-Americans, national champions, and other people of extremely high physical caliber who don't make it through the program. The man who does make it through is someone who has made up his mind that being a SEAL is what he wants. That's what it takes, that goal to say, this is where I want to be to be able to make it through. That's what makes it clear to me that the psychological part of BUD/S is much more demanding than the physical part—although they do get their money's worth physically.

The student who starts, and completes, Basic Underwater Demolition/SEAL training is, in many ways, similar to Mike Thornton, Moki Martin, Bob Gormly, and all the other people who have come before them. And in a lot of ways, those same students are vastly different today than their forefathers. Of the enlisted students who complete the program, 35 percent have their Bachelor of Science degrees from major universities. A large number of them have also been accepted into Officer Candidate School, but the wait for OCS ranges from two to two-and-a-half years. These men make the decision that, although they would like to be commissioned officers, they would really rather be SEALs. They forego their commission in order to go through training.

I think we have always had a very high caliber of enlisted man in Naval Special Warfare. Years ago, if a lot of the men in the Teams had been afforded the economic advantages some of the men have now, I think we probably would have had just as many enlisted men with their college degrees as opposed to their high school degrees. But in essence, all the men from then and now still have the same spirit, and that's what we're looking for at BUD/S.

It isn't your academic achievements, or your physical ones, that will get you through BUD/S. It is whether or not you have the spirit, the intelligence, and the wherewithal to not only complete the basic program, but to be highly effective and sophisticated, in challenging missions of national importance. Right now, as in the past, I feel that the student of today is every bit as good as his forefathers were.

So if you want to be a Navy SEAL, there are two ways to go—officer and enlisted. For the officers, the number one source of commissioning is the Naval Academy. Along with the Naval Academy, officers can receive their commissions from the Naval Reserve Officer Training Corps (NROTC), Officer Candidate School (OCS), and some other smaller programs.

This year (1998) we will bring fifty-eight officers into our BUD/S program, but we will receive hundreds of qualified applications for those fifty-eight officer slots. It is much more demanding for an officer to get accepted into the program than it is for an officer to complete the course of training. Accepted officer applicants have to have succeeded in many different things, be at the very top of their graduation class, and just be well above the average.

A large percentage of the enlisted men have completed advanced education. When I went through training in 1977, the average age for an enlisted man at BUD/S was nineteen years of age. Now, the average graduate from BUD/S is almost twenty-five years of age because so many of them have completed college.

Each man, officer or enlisted, has to be able to swim five-hundred meters in a certain period of time. They all have to be able to run a mile and a half in a certain period of time wearing long pants and boots. Push-ups, pull-ups, and sit-ups are all basic and part of the physical standards that have to be met in order to qualify for BUD/S.

The enlisted men have to be able to pass the same physical standards the officers do. And they also have to meet the highest scholastic aptitude scores that the Navy requires for any training. When a young man walks into a Navy recruiter's office and says he wants to be a SEAL, he will take a battery of tests. Scholastically, if he passed the tests and qualifies, he is also a candidate to become a nuclear propulsion technician, and filling those slots is a higher priority for the Navy.

So the individual who comes into the SEAL Team could compete in any category he wants in the whole of the U.S. Navy. We are very fortunate to have that caliber of individual coming to us.

When a man goes through training, he first has two weeks of pre-training and then he has seven weeks of First Phase. The fifth week of First Phase is Hell Week. During that week, we start off on Sunday evening and keep the students up continuously until Friday evening. On the average, the class will receive an hour-and-a-half of sleep on Wednesday and another ninety minutes of sleep on Thursday.

What we do is stress the students during that week. We give them as close as we can to real combat conditions. The reason we give them the rest we do is that our sleep studies have shown that's the minimum amount of rest they need in order to make it through to Friday.

Hell Week is also our highest attrition week. We lose more students during that week than during any other evolution in the training.

Once they've completed the basic phase, First Phase, they go on to Second Phase, the diving phase, for an additional seven weeks. Second Phase is where the students will learn to be basic scuba divers. They will also be exposed to the LAR-V, a closed-circuit pure oxygen breathing rig, and they'll start to become combat swimmers.

When the students are finished with Second Phase, they'll move on to Third Phase, the the land warfare phase, and the final phase of the BUD/S program. During the ten weeks of Third Phase, we conduct a lot of training in the local San Diego country area. Four weeks are spent out on one of the Channel Islands, San Clemente Island, where students are put through rigorous training and are exposed to high explosives and their use. On the island, the students will also put together everything they have learned for a final exercise.

During the course of their training at BUD/S, every week the students have to compete in a two-mile ocean swim, a four-mile timed run, and the obstacle course. When they finish First Phase and go on to Second Phase, the times the students have to complete those competitions decrease. The times decrease again when they go from Second to Third Phase.

A two-mile swim in Third Phase must be ten minutes faster than the two-mile swim in First Phase. We bring these young men to a very high level of physical condition during training. We have to keep raising the bar to keep challenging them, because these are men who need to be challenged.

Once the students have completed our program, they go on to basic airborne

A swimmer pair of BUD/S students. They are wearing the Draeger LAR-V rebreather systems on their chests. With the Draeger system, swimmers have their backs clear to be able to transport additional materials, such as pack-boards carrying limpet mines.

Kevin Dockery

training at Fort Benning. From there, they go into their SEAL Teams, where they will conduct their advanced operator training, SEAL tactical training. After about nine months to a year from having come onboard at BUD/S, they will be designated Naval Special Warfare operators and receive their Tridents.

It takes about four years, two cruises, to get somebody who's really up on step. That's when they are a quite competent as a Naval Special Warfare operator.

When I came in to UDT 21 for the first time, two-thirds of the wardroom were mustang, or prior enlisted, officers. Now, it's rare to have mustangs in the commu-nity. We have a great number of very qualified enlisted men in the Teams who would make good officers, so we have tried to expand the commissioning opportunities in the community for the enlisted men.

We have increased the number of Officer Candidate School quotas for our SEAL enlisted operators. That lets them go on to OCS and come back to the Teams as commissioned officers. We also have the seaman-to-admiral program in the Navy, and last year (1997) we had two of our SEALs selected for that. So there's still up-ward mobility for the enlisted men.

We also have the warrant officer program and the limited duty officer program in the Teams. These are programs where senior enlisted SEALs can apply to be ap-pointed as warrant officer or commissioned as limited duty officers. This is a pro-gram that has been highly successful in Naval Special Warfare during the last several years.

We've had a number of very successful enlisted SEALs become officers. One of these men is Michael Thornton, who I've known since 1977, when he was a first class petty officer and I was a trainee. I would say that Mike is like every other SEAL in that he's reserved, humble, intelligent, and extremely competent.

If you saw Mike, he would strike you as a very physically imposing person. There would be nothing about him that you could pick out from across the room that would cause you to say that he was a Medal of Honor winner, but when Mike was working as a SEAL, he was very competent and one of the most professional people I know.

Other SEALs have been officers who went on to make a name for themselves outside the Teams. Bill Shepherd is a Naval Academy graduate who had extensive experience as a SEAL operator. He went to and received his graduate education from MIT. In the 1980s, Bill applied to become a mission specialist at NASA.

You have to be careful what you wish for. Bill had to leave the Teams when he was picked up by NASA to join the space shuttle program. He went into space on the mission following the Challenger disaster. I believe that after the successful completion of that mission, Bill received an automatic promotion from commander

BUD/S students on San Clemente Island carefully prepare live explosive charges as part of their training. All SEALs, no matter what their individual specialty training may be, know basic and advanced demolition techniques.

U.S. Navy

to captain. Bill has stayed with the space program and has done successful things for NASA and for our country.

It is a real source of pride for those of us in the SEAL community to have a member of the astronaut community among us.

At BUD/S, we really test the spirit of the students. It is a course that has the highest attrition rate of any in the Department of Defense. This is not something we're proud of, because the mission is to graduate men and send them on to the SEAL Teams. And 95 percent of the people who leave the program do so voluntarily; they drop on request (DOR).

We do stress these people, these men, and try to build their confidence and test their spirit. It is our feeling that "that which doesn't kill you, makes you stronger." After their twenty-seven weeks at BUD/S, these men are certainly a lot stronger.

Every day they have to be physically and psychologically up to the challenge. But BUD/S is also the type of thing that you can't do on your own. Getting though the course has to be done by a team effort.

No matter how good you are, one day just won't be your day. And you don't want to have to ask, "Hey, I need some help." When you start falling behind, you just want that hand extended to you, someone lowering the rope down to you and pulling you up without your asking.

So we work on teamwork, and the spirit, that really makes the Teams what they are. The testing of the spirit of the men tells us that when somebody completes Basic Underwater Demolition/SEAL training, they aren't going to call time out.

No matter how difficult the situation you are in, in the Teams, you know you can have confidence in the man to the left of you and the man to the right of you. They are going to be there for you, no matter what. And they can look over at you and realize that you're going to be there for them. That's why we work so hard to prove that the individual has the spirit within them at BUD/S.

I would never talk anyone into becoming a SEAL. This is just something that you have to want, and you have to want it a lot, in order to successfully complete the program. Only three out of every ten students who show up at BUD/S finally graduate. With that high an attrition rate, I personally wouldn't want to be responsible for bringing somebody in and setting them up for a program like this. I would have to be absolutely, thoroughly convinced that they were the right person for the program. As I have said, we've had all-Americans and national champions in BUD/S who just don't make it through the program. You just never know what a man has inside of himself.

On the other hand, the mission of the Naval Special Warfare Center includes the recruiting of students for BUD/S, so I've got to get out there and try to bring

NAVY SEALs: A COMPLETE HISTORY

them in the door. But on a personal level, it's difficult to bring somebody in, knowing what they're going to be put up against.

But if someone wants to come in on their own, we're glad to have them. The Russians have a saying, "you can't tell a man who is warm what it's like to be cold." And our students at Basic Underwater Demolition have a realistic appreciation for what it's like to be cold.

After a couple decades in this business—I've been UDT 21, SEAL Team Two, SEAL Delivery Vehicle Team, Naval Special Warfare Development Group, Special Operations Command Pacific, and Naval Special Warfare Group Two—I've had a lot of experience in a lot of different areas. That experience has shown me that you can pretty much tell who doesn't have the spirit for the Teams. So if I met an individual who had all the tools physically and who qualified academically, but just didn't have what it takes to come in here and make a contribution, to be a part of the Team, he would be someone I would actively discourage from coming to BUD/S. Because SEAL Teams are a Team and the work we do is a team effort, he would be getting himself into the wrong business. The individual who cannot work as part of a team and make a contribution for the common good of everyone really has no business in our community.

Out of all those people who quit the course, the vast majority of them quit because they couldn't come to terms with the cold, and it's best that they realize that now. When you're out there operating in the Teams, you're cold and you're wet—that's the environment we work in, that's the environment we thrive in. So when the cold drives most of them out during training, it's really for the best.

Last year (1997) we brought in close to 800 students—712 enlisted men and about 65 officers. Out of that group we graduated 250 people. There is no way we can predict who will successfully complete the program. An individual might have all the tools necessary to do the job, but if they become weak psychologically, they could quit.

Or an individual might just get a bad break. People break their legs, stress fractures of the lower leg are not uncommon at BUD/S, and we have stress fractures of the femur as well. The femur is a pretty large bone. For that bone to be stressed, it shows we're conducting some pretty demanding training here.

As far as who makes it through, right now we are conducting studies to determine predictability on just who would successfully complete the program. We should be able to identify the people who were studied and compare them to the predictions.

I've been the commanding officer of the Naval Special Warfare Training Center for a little more than sixteen months now, and I wouldn't want to place a bet on who would or wouldn't make it through the program. We keep the standards high—lives and the success or failure of our missions depend on those standards.

As far as describing the Teams, I think the term elite is overused. To me, just SEAL is enough. That says it all for me. I don't consider myself to be elite; I consider myself to be a person who works very hard, who loves what he's doing, and who enjoys his work. I would say that's pretty much the same for everyone I know.

We're fathers, we're sons, we're brothers. We work in the community, and we go to church on Sunday. But when we have to go to work, we do it to the best of our ability. We have tremendous talent in the Teams, and the people of America have given us the best technology and the best equipment available in the world.

With the raw talent and the marvelous technology we have, we can really do the job. To me, the job is wonderful. Blowing things up, shooting machine guns, jumping out of airplanes, locking out of nuclear submarines, driving in the SEAL delivery vehicles—it's all quite interesting. But after twenty-two years, even that can get old.

The thing I find wonderful and highly rewarding in the Teams is the people I get to work with. That's why I get up every morning and put my feet on the floor, and look forward to coming to work. I know there are a lot of people out there in the civilian sector making a lot more money than I am, but I don't think there are many people in our country who enjoy their work as much as I do, and that's because of the people I have the opportunity to work with—it's pretty wonderful.

If you become a SEAL, you'll be exposed to the best people in the world. We are a family; we are a fraternity. You will be challenged every single day—not just during your basic training, but in your job. You'll be challenged with people who enjoy challenging other people.

If you are an officer, you will be given tremendous leadership challenges at a very, very junior position. Even in the platoon, if there was a power vacuum, the caliber of our enlisted people is such that they would fill that vacuum in a nanosecond. It is a rewarding job. But most important, it is working with the most wonderful people in the world that's kept me around and made my career rewarding for twenty-two years.

You might get the impression that, in my opinion, the best part of being a SEAL is the people you have to work with. And that doesn't necessarily mean just the SEALs, because our job is really a team effort. In Basic Underwater Demolition/SEAL training, we conduct 7,500 high-risk evolutions a year. What I have, and what the Naval Special Warfare community has given me, are the best people to go out there and conduct training and look after these young men. These students are quite literally putting their lives on the line every day to go through this basic training.

Those people working here include the physicians. We had a case during a recent Hell Week, where on Thursday night during the evening meal, one of the students came up and told the corpsman that he was having difficulty with his arm. The student could no longer move his fingers, and there was a lot of tenderness and swelling in his arm.

We were fortunate that the student went and talked to the corpsman when he did. He had already invested more than three days in Hell Week, and I'm sure he didn't want to come and point out a problem to the corpsman that might get him rolled out of Hell Week and forced to complete it again with a later class. The nature of the kind of trainee we have, and of SEALs in general, is that they really don't complain about aches and pains. They're always fine.

The corpsman took a look at the student's arm and wasn't quite sure what the problem was. He went to one of our doctors, Dr. Mark Gould, who was one of the physicians with the Hell Week class that evening. Mark took a look at the arm and recognized it as necrotizing fasciatitis, a flesh-eating disease.

These young men are torn down so much during Hell Week, that they are exposed to a lot of different bugs that can take hold where they normally couldn't. Dr. Gould immediately called the hospital, had the student admitted, and operated on him within the hour to attack the bacteria and clear out the site.

Necrotizing fasciatitis was a very fast-moving disease. I asked the people involved to walk me through the timeline of events. Somewhere around 11 to 1 o'clock that day, the student was exposed to the bug. By 5 o'clock in the evening, it started to bother him. About 5:15, the student reported his problem to the corpsman. Several minutes later, Dr. Gould identified the problem as the flesh-eating disease.

We admitted the student to Balboa Hospital within the hour. By 7 o'clock that evening, the operation was ongoing. If the student had not identified and announced the problem when he did, if he had just waited two hours more, he would have lost most of the muscle tissue in his arm. If he had waited a few hours longer, there was a likelihood that he would have lost his arm to the disease.

It's to the credit of somebody like Dr. Mark Gould, who is intelligent enough, experienced enough, and caring enough, to be able to identify something like that and make the immediate decision to get the young man admitted into a hospital.

We will look out for the students to the very best of our ability, but we will also stress them and challenge them every day they are here.

Right now, I'm twenty-two years older than when I went through training. Although I'm a captain, I look on these students a lot like a father would. These young men going through training are somebody's sons. We owe it to the individuals going through training, to their families, and to ourselves, to make sure that we maintain control of the situation at all times. If there's a problem, we identify it. We put these people through tremendous challenges and they excel, but we must maintain control of the program. And it is people like Dr. Gould, as well as all the other instructors, who every single day walk out there and push these young men, who make sure that no harm comes to them.

We control the situation, we're the experts, and we know what's needed to become a SEAL. It's the caring attitude and professionalism of all the instructors on staff that makes my job possible. Whether you're a SEAL, a physician, a special warfare combat crewman, or a data processor, the program is a team effort. In Naval Special Warfare, we really don't judge ourselves as far as how important you are or by how close you get to the target. It's a Team effort.

Joseph Hawes, Quartermaster First Class, USN (Ret.)

Within a few months of now, it will have been twenty-two years since I first came in to the service. The Navy wasn't my first choice of the service; originally I wanted to be in the Marine Corps because I wanted to be a Frogman. One of the recruiters told me, "Hey, we have Frogmen. We could get you here . . . there. . . ." It was just one of those little ploys to get me to enlist so they could fill their quota of recruits.

Later on, the recruiter for the Navy saw that I was disgruntled with the Marine Corps recruiter and he said, "Hey, we have Frogmen. They're called UDT/SEALs, and you would love it."

I said in return that the reason I wanted to be a Frogman was that I wanted to go on the astronaut recovery program. The Navy recruiter told me that they had that, so I decided to go for it. The recruiter did warn me that it would be hard, but I replied, "Whatever it takes."

I did all my enlistment things and finally arrived at BUD/S. Later on, I found out that the astronaut recovery program had gone out the window because of the space shuttle program coming online. But I have never had any regrets about going into the Teams, though, because it's been great.

At BUD/S, I started out originally with Class 104 and graduated with Class 105. This was on the West Coast and the classes were a combination of a summer class and a winter class. It felt like winter every time we went out because the water was cold. Whether it was in the pool or in the ocean, the water was cold. And the things they have you doing—it's always cold for the students.

The cold wasn't the hardest part of training for me. I can deal with cold; I've always dealt with cold; I'm from Connecticut. One time my brother and a few friends carried on a little tradition of ours of breaking the ice at the lake and going swimming. That finally got to me as a kid when I came down with pneumonia, which turned into whooping cough. My brother got a beating because of that.

"Why'd you get sick?" I was asked.

"Well," I said, "Benji and some guys made me jump into the water. . . ."

But we really only wanted to swim. It was just one of those stupid things kids do.

The main thing that bothered me during BUD/S was the mind games. You would look at your classmates and go, Well, they're cold and I'm cold. Are they any better than me? Do I have any special privilege because I'm cold? Do I get a time out?

No, the main thing was that we were together, and we were all cold. If you let the mind games bother you, that's when you start to get weak. You needed to stay strong.

My Hell Week wasn't fun. In those days, it seemed like a free-for-all, with the instructors doing whatever they pleased. What I remember is finding friends in boat crews or in class, clinging to them for strength, praying, and saying that this can't last forever.

Once Hell Week was over, we cried, knowing that we had made it past a big one. Because Hell Week was the main thing, the big stumbling block, we all saw we were on the way to becoming SEALs. First Phase was Hell Week. Second Phase was diving, drownproofing. Third Phase was gun theory, land warfare, and demolitions.

In getting through Hell Week, we knew we had passed the part that causes most people to drop out of training. I really can't pinpoint anything that was particularly hard during the long week. It was something that you can't really describe, but you will never forget.

You get a lot of wannabes that say, "Hey, I was a SEAL." I run into them every day. We sell "I'm a SEAL" T-shirts at the exchange that people buy and wear. Wearing a shirt does not make you a SEAL. It comes from your mind and from your heart. If you don't have the heart of a fighting man who went through BUD/S, you shouldn't claim you're a SEAL.

There are things you'll forget about training. You'll forget those who quit before you. You'll never remember their names. You will remember the classmates who graduated with you. You will remember instructors who put you through all the stuff you had to endure. You won't forget your class numbers, and you won't forget what you had to do. Going through BUD/S is the only way to get to the Teams.

Training is hard, and yes, I did think of quitting during Hell Week, because I had good friends who fell by the wayside. But I kept going. It's just like any other athlete running a marathon, or anybody who goes through a maximum sport. They find their mind telling their body to shut down, they shouldn't have to go through this, there's a better life on the other side. All you have to do is quit.

We had a little saying that the instructors would put out to us when we were in the water. "You guys can get out of the water," an Instructor would holler at us. "All we need is a few quitters."

"Quit, shit!" we would yell out. And that was all we would shout.

In life, we all sometimes want to quit. I don't feel like working here anymore. I don't feel like doing the same old job. It's just human nature to want the change. But I didn't quit. And I didn't because of the embarrassment.

That's just one of the things that go through your mind. The embarrassment of guys in your class seeing you walk away. It's the embarrassment of telling your family that you gave up. It's letting yourself fall short of something you really want to do. And I said there were people in that class who were no better than I was, and if they could keep going, so could I.

We had this thing we did involving holding our breath in the water. Some guys could hold their breath for three minutes, some for two minutes. No one wanted to be the first one to say, "I can't do it," so we all tried and kept going. Being a Team guy means you are competitive, with others and with yourself. So I didn't lose to myself. I didn't quit.

The words "secure from Hell Week" are unbelievable to hear. Tears come to your eyes as you look around you. I think we started out with 126 people; after Hell Week, there were only 30-something left. And the mind games had continued right up to the end.

Before we actually heard the order to secure from Hell Week, we had been told that we were going into Saturday, that there had been a lot of things we hadn't done right. We were marching across the street, over to the base, to go into that water and stay there. Why? Because we had messed up.

We thought the others had secured by now and our Hell Week was going to continue. We were stopped in front of the main building of the base, because the commander of the base had wanted to see us secure. So the instructors stopped us, we faced the building, and we were told that we were secured from Hell Week.

I hugged my friends, I cried, and I was overcome with a feeling I can't describe.

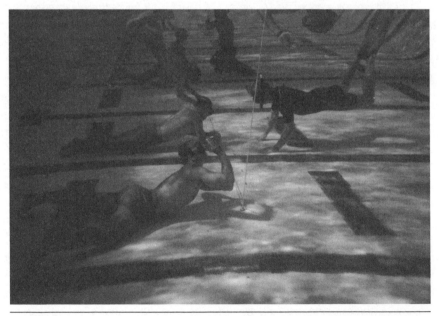

Under the careful eyes of their instructors, BUD/S students practice free-diving and tying knots at the bottom of the training pool. They will do this evolution, a simulation of the UDTs tying demolition charges together during World War II, until the actions become automatic.

U.S. Navy

Even though I was beat down and tore up, I called my mom and told her I had made it. It was great.

I did have problems in training, drownproofing particularly, because I'm negatively buoyant. There are few minorities in the Teams and people always ask, "You're black, how did you get to swim?" or whatever. Kids coming up from the inner cities often don't know how to swim, and neither did their parents. So the parents tend to tell their kids not to go in the water because they'll drown.

I have eight brothers and four sisters. My father's from Jamaica, and we have always swum. It never bothered me to get into the water, and I've been swimming since I was big enough to walk. When I arrived at BUD/S training, I figured I had the swimming part down. I also knew I could run, and I'd played football and other sports. But when the instructors told me we were going to do drownproofing, all I could say was, "What's drownproofing?"

Drownproofing is where the instructors tie your hands and feet together and you have to relax and function in the water. I still didn't have in my mind that this was a secure thing. There are instructors all around the pool, there were safety divers, and all the people conducting the training are skilled in what they wanted us to do. In spite of all of that, the evolution still didn't sit well with me.

They tied my hands and feet and put me in the water. I was so scared that I broke the ropes. So they tied me up again, and I broke the ropes again. We did that three times, my being tied and breaking the ropes, until the instructors came up with some line that could hold me.

Chief Knepper, now retired Master Chief Knepper, instilled in me the absolute knowledge that nothing was going to be allowed to happen to me. The environment was safe at all times, and there were instructors around who were highly skilled and experienced in running that particular evolution. There was no way they were going to allow anything to happen to me, but I had to get that fear out of my system.

That was before the test came for drownproofing. On the test day, I passed with flying colors. That was another hurdle I had to get through, the fear of the unknown, that the Teams helped me get by. I knew what was happening; I knew what was expected of me. And I accomplished the task.

It was great to stand there on the grinder that last day and graduate from BUD/S. Looking around, I could see all my friends who I had started with. And I gave some thought to the people who fell by the wayside. Not all of my family was there, although I wish I could have had the whole herd there to see me graduate. My brother-in-law came down to see me graduate. He was really impressed about what went on. It was kind of upsetting that my mom and dad couldn't be there, but it was good to have one representative of the clan there.

Graduation from BUD/S felt like being on top of the world, and I've stayed on top of the world since I've graduated and gone on to the Teams. There's the respect that we have in being a Team guy, that all the other warriors laid down the roots to before us. I look back at those men who came before me and know that if it wasn't for their courage, skill, and sacrifice, there wouldn't be any of us. That made me feel great about being a a part of such an elite group.

Six months after training, your probationary period is over. If you completed it successfully, you are awarded your Trident. The Trident is a symbol of respect to me. It is also the symbol of great warriors who came before me in the Teams. These men were tasked with jobs that no one else could do—and they accomplished those jobs. Wearing it also means that I'm part of an elite group of people. And most of all, it symbolizes the camaraderie and the brotherhood of the Teams. I'm with a fraternity.

I have a twelve-year-old son, and he loves wearing Teams shirts. He goes to school and says that his dad's a Team guy. They ask him if he's a Team guy, and he says no. But I tell him, "Yes you are. You're my blood, and that makes you a Team guy." But if he wants to wear a Trident as an adult, he had better go through training. And God knows, that if I'm still around, I'm going to tell the guys to make it hard on him.

After I graduated BUD/S, I went to Jump School and then checked in to UDT Twelve. Here I was, a new guy, who didn't know what was going on. All I knew was that I was in the Teams now, and I had no idea what to expect. I hear "Drop" bellowed out from across the grinder, so I immediately dropped to the deck and pushed them out [push-ups] and shouted "Hooyah!"

"Hooyah what?" comes back to me.

"I don't know your names," I said.

It was two guys, one a Master Chief, the man who became my sea daddy. He showed me a lot of how to be an operator in the Teams, and he did a lot for me.

The Master Chief came up to me and said, "I'm Herschel Davis, Master Chief, and this is Roy Dean Matthews. You know what? Recover."

I scrambled up from the ground as Master Chief Davis continued.

"You don't have to drop for us," he said.

"I don't know anything that's going on," I said. "All I know is that I don't want to cause any waves, so I'll do whatever you guys tell me."

Davis started calling me Black Beauty, and that became his and my private joke. That was my introduction to life in the Teams and UDT Twelve. Before too long, I was pulled aside and asked if I would like to be in a platoon. Immediately I agreed, even after they told me that we would be deploying overseas in about a month. I didn't care, and it sounded good to me.

Then I was asked if I would mind carrying a 60 (an M60 machine gun). That was easy enough to answer: I told them that I carried a 60 in BUD/S and that the weapon was fine with me. So I was picked up for that platoon.

It was Lieutenant McTighe, now Captain McTighe, who was the officer in charge of my first platoon. I remember all my guys to this day, and I was on top of the world to be able to deploy with them. All my other friends who had graduated BUD/S with me were still sitting around and going through training. Here I was, the new guy in a platoon, hanging out with the older guys. It was great.

Deploying was so good that I started doing back-to-backs, deploying with the next platoon to get ready to leave as soon as I had come back with another. During my career now, I've had fourteen platoons and thirteen deployments. I'm sorry to see the deployments go, but I'm getting older now and it's time to shut it off.

The "Hooyah" I shouted out for Master Chief Davis is a saying we have in BUD/S and in the Teams in general. It means, "okay," or "right on," or "you got it." It's just one of those things that is said to help build enthusiasm and camaraderie among the trainees. When I was an instructor, hooyah could mean other things, like "Don't get wet, the water's cold," or "You're going to stay out there and sit."

Hooyah can also mean things that can help you feel a little bit warmer, such as "I never liked you and I hate your mother." I hooyah all the time. If you get pulled over by a cop and he wants to give you a ticket, you just go "Hooyah." You know what it means, but he'll probably thinks it means something else.

My first combat deployment was when our first platoon went over during the Iranian Hostage Crisis in the late 1970s. That was really my first look at preparing for war where a hot engagement looked like a really possible thing. My first actual conflict was Desert Storm.

In my first combat platoon, we were called to do ops and practice for ops, because the U.S. Embassy had been taken over in Tehran. We were the platoon on station and got the pep talk about how we might be the guys who were going in. Preparing ourselves for whatever might come up was something we always did. We trained on the ships, shooting outboard, swimming in and swimming out, and sharpening our skills. So it was during the Iranian Hostage Crisis that I had my first taste of getting ready for war. Then there was DESERT STORM.

Between those two events, something took place in the Teams. The UDTs were decommissioned and ended their direct history in 1983. The men went directly into the new SEAL and SEAL Delivery Vehicle Teams that were created at the same time. I never really understood the history of the UDT. When we were broken down into the classes at the end of BUD/S, we were told who would be going to SEAL Team One, who would be assigned to SEAL Team Two, and who would be going to UDT 12, 11, or East Coast Teams.

You kind of felt disappointed if you didn't get picked for a SEAL Team. I hadn't understood the whole aspect of being UDT. The UDTs were the first Naked Warriors to go across the beach and blow open the way for the landing troops during World War II. Before there was a SEAL Team, there were the UDTs.

There's a lot of history that goes along with being UDT that I just didn't understand. Because I hadn't been picked for a SEAL Team, I must be a dirtbag. Then you were teased by guys in your class who said things like, "Aren't you Joe, the

Navy SEAL? Naw, you're just UDT." After a while, I learned just what our history was in the UDTs, and I was very proud to be a member of the real Frogmen and happy that I was a UDT operator.

It was kind of a sad moment when the UDTs went away. But it was more of a misconception when people thought that there were UDTs and SEALs and that they weren't the same. We were the same. The UDTs' primary job was in the water, and their secondary job was on the land. The SEAL Teams' primary mission was on the land, and their secondary job was in the water.

It was a great thing when we all became SEAL Teams, but there was a small feeling of loss when the UDTs were gone. That feeling was relieved when a lot of my friends in the SEAL Teams had to do the recons and the water work that the UDTs had done and hated it. That just made me laugh. Now, I feel privileged that I was part of UDT and SEAL Team.

I was a SEAL Platoon LPO, leading petty officer, the lower senior enlisted in charge of the rest of the guys during DESERT STORM. We went out to the Persian Gulf and trained for missions that the higher-ups had on the planning boards. We also performed our normal duties of keeping in shape, doing physical training, and swimming each and every day on the ship.

On some of the swims, the ship would drop us off three or six miles and then continue on. We would swim back to the ship, escorted by our safety boats. The safety boats were important because the Gulf waters were very warm and you could get overheated easily. The fact that the waters were infested with sharks wasn't lost on us either.

We also worked hand-in-hand with the Marine Reconnaissance Platoons, Marine Recon, who are the Marine equivalent to SEALs just like the Army's Special Forces (Green Berets). We trained with Recon doing ship-boarding and other various joint operations training.

A couple times, when an Iraqi ship or other cargo ship was observed going through our ship's area of responsibility, they were told to stop and prepare to be boarded. The boarding was to see if they were carrying any contraband for Iraq. When they didn't stop, we would do a VBSS (Visit, Board, Search, and Seizure) op.

For a VBSS, we would load into a helicopter equipped with a fast rope system. Then we would fast rope down on the ship while it was moving. There, either the Marines or we would set up security—whoever got to the ship first.

Whoever boarded the ship first would take down the deck and hold security there. The next helicopter would drop off the guys who would take down the engine room and other priority compartments. During all of this, we would have sniper helos circling overhead, off on the side, to make sure that no one was able to come up on us. These operations were done to make sure that the local shipping was in compliance with the UN Resolution 665—enforcing trade sanctions against Iraq.

In spite of the concerns we had about the shark infestation in the Persian Gulf around, and it was dark. You just can't keep your eyes on everyone all the time. I would go in every day at 4:30 to do the 5 o'clock PT. Once I was done PT'ing them for an hour, I would go into the gym for about two hours to work out myself.

One of the talks I gave the guys was to tell them that there were some guys among them who knew they didn't belong here. Now they were hiding in the bunch, but as soon as we weed out the class, they would pop up to the top and we would get rid of them. I told them to stop wasting my time during our 5 o'clock PT, because I already had my Trident, and I was going to get my workout in spite of them. But if they didn't get their workout, they would just fall farther and farther behind and end up getting booted out anyway.

Command Master Chief Chalker came in then to add his part to the talk. He would say that he saw everyone out there on the grinder, and that he wanted to see each one of them standing there on graduation day. They didn't have to do anything to impress him. They just had to be able to look at themselves and say that they had given it everything they had and that would be fine.

Then I told the class officer to move them out and take the class to chow. As they were leaving, one student was already heading over to the bell.

"Hey, bonehead," I said, "come over here. Where are you going?"

"I'm going to quit," he said.

"Why? Because of what Master Chief Chalker or I said?"

"No, Instructor Hawes. I'm just not a morning person."

That floored me. "What?" I practically shouted.

"I'm not a morning person," he repeated.

"I can't believe that you came here and now you want to quit. Didn't you know that we do ops in the morning?"

"Yes."

"Did you know that we do them late at night?"

"Yes, but I just thought you guys could change me."

"Go to chow and think about it," I said. "Then come back and see me."

He came back, and he ended up quitting. But I take my hat off to that guy. The thing he wrote down on his DOR (drop on request) sheet was that he quit because he wasn't a morning person and couldn't take getting up early in the morning. So I give it to him on that. He wasn't fooling himself at all. Besides, taking him in to see Master Chief Chalker and telling him the reason he was quitting was a lot of fun. That must have been a full mouthful of coffee Chalker was drinking when that student told him his reason—at least it looked like a whole mouthful when he sprayed it out of his mouth in surprise.

Because I was assigned as an instructor, I've only missed one Hell Week. My normal shift was from midnight to 8 in the morning. We would take normal eight-hour shifts doing whatever to the students during Hell Week. If I wasn't out there being a bad guy to the students, I was in the truck taking a little nap.

waters, nothing ever happened. In my twenty-two years of swimming out there in the open ocean and looking out for things, I have never had an encounter that bothered me. Yes, there were sharks, but they must have had plenty of natural food, or else they didn't like dark meat and weren't even going to bite me.

But guess what the instructors showed us before we went out and did the five-point, five-mile swim at San Clemente Island—the movie Jaws. Most of us had never seen the movie before, so of course we had to see it the day we had our longest swim. I think I was doing more looking out for sharks than swimming that day, and we were doing a lot of swimming.

Later in my career, I became an instructor at BUD/S. Being a BUD/S instructor was something of a privilege for me. Now I had a first hand on the raw talent we had coming in, questioned what we could make from this raw material, helped make the decision as to whether an individual was salvageable or if he wasn't cut out to be a Frogman. Basically, someone had given me the power to become choose Team guys and add their talent to the SEALs.

The point man in a SEAL formation prep interior hatch during VBSS training, behind him stands ready to open the do gun if necessary.

U.S. Navy

There was no way I could have picked out the ones who would m those who would quit along the way as they came through the door Whether he's skinny, fat, tall, or short, there just isn't any physical g picking out anyone who will make it. It's what they have in their heart the most.

There are a lot of people who I had seen come into training who think had what it took. But they can surprise you. In some way, they b inside themselves something they might not have known they even h decide to prove me wrong.

Time and time again, there were guys who we would tell to sto press the girls by telling them they were going to be a SEAL or that toughest guy around. Those were the guys who we would tell to s and themselves, and just quit.

One time, I had a 5 A.M. PT. There were more than one hu

Sometimes, what I did to the students was mean, and it certainly looked thoughtless at times. But it was all part of making them dig down deep to give me, and the Teams, all they've got.

As far as being an instructor, things could be somewhat hard on you during Hell Week. Typically, a shift was made up by the number of instructors who were needed to manage the class. Because the class size changed so much—always getting smaller—the number of instructors on a shift could change. No matter how many instructors were on a shift, you had to stay sharp all the time. Some of the kids in training were so worried about passing that they disregarded safety, especially as the week went on and they became tired and disoriented.

You could tell a student to get wet, to go dunk his head. He might say to himself that he wanted to impress the instructor by holding his head underwater until he passed out. That's where the instructor had to keep a heads up. And you wouldn't want to push the guys too far, and there might be one or two you would want to keep a particular eye on—not because they weren't putting out, but because they were getting a little wobbly.

Judgment took part in a call on a student as well. One might not look like he was putting his head underneath the boat enough, not carrying his share of the boat. Why? Because a patch of his hair is gone where his hat and the sand rubbed the top of his head raw. You just don't want to be the instructor then. I don't know anyone in the Teams who wants to be an instructor just to go to BUD/S and hurt anybody. Each and every instructor I have ever known wants the same thing—to get the best-quality people for the Teams and get them in a safe manner.

As to list the priorities of what would get a person through training from the heart, mind, or body, for me, it was one—I had to do it from the heart. I had to really want, deep down in my heart, to be a Frogman. After having it in your heart, your heart can tell your mind, that you have everything you need to make it through this training. Then, your mind can tell your body to get in shape.

When you twist an ankle, your ankle hurts, and it sends that signal to your mind. Then your mind says whether it shuts down, gives in to the pain, or keeps going. The heart is the one that says to keep going, because it wants to be where it is. Those are my priorities. And I'm sure if you ask anybody, those are somewhat their priorities, too.

There's an expression at BUD/S, the "fire in the gut." What the expression means is that you set out with that burning desire in your gut to do a job and finish the training, and you did. That fire was never put out. It didn't matter when people talked about your mother, when you were cold, when your wife was home alone, or when your kid was sick and you had duty and couldn't leave the base, or it was Hell Week. That personal fire never went out. That's fire in the gut. And every Team guy who went through training has that same fire. You ask some of the old-timers, and they'll say they still have it.

I never won the fire in the gut award. That's an award they give out at the end of BUD/S, but I don't think it should be given to just one individual. Everybody that's up there grabbing a diploma has earned that award. I still have that fire today, and I'm getting ready to retire. It's one of those things that make you wish you could stay young forever and still do the things we do with each other.

When I was a kid, I played with Army men. I grew up doing the Army man thing, jumping out of planes and swimming in the ocean. But I can't really say I'm doing the Army man now that I did when I was a kid. Actually, I'm not an Army man, I'm better than that. I'm a Frogman. I'm a SEAL. That has made my life more interesting.

That's why you have the guys who pretend. They go into the bars and say, "Hey baby, I'm a SEAL." They know what goes along with that name—the honor, the awareness of people who know what a SEAL is, and what that name stands for. And that's also why we make life very miserable for those phonies when we find one.

Anyone can be hard to the students as an instructor. But you have to have some kind of compassion, you have to put yourself in their place sometimes. I don't try to play the "Billy Bad-Ass" instructor. What I do instead, when I want someone to do something, is to let them know that I did it and that the other instructors and Team guys around all did it as well, and that we aren't trying to make the students do anything different from what we all had to do.

Normally, when I swim, for some reason I don't get very cold in the water. I swim with a hood, fins, and my Speedos on. One day, I was out with the class and we had already swum out through the surf zone. One of the students asked me if I wasn't cold. I told him that was his problem—he worried about being cold. If he worried about doing his job and getting the job accomplished, then good things would come after that.

Finish the swim, complete the job, and a hot shower and meal are waiting for me. Everything from the swim is over, then we start the rest of the day. Nothing can last forever, no matter how bad it is.

So when I was an instructor, I didn't stay down on somebody all the time. Instead, what worked for me was to let up, reward the students, and tell them to hang in there. There were a couple times that I made threats to people while I was an instructor. I told them that if they quit, I was going to look for them and they wouldn't like it. And I said they could tell the skipper, the captain, and I would admit to what I had said, then I would beat them twice as hard for telling on me.

Sometimes, that gave the guys who needed it that extra push. They could see that I would yell at them as if I didn't want them there, but then they could see that I was trying to help them.

When I went through training, the guys in other classes followed a tradition that I never understood. It really made me feel bad that the class ahead of us made more problems for us than the instructors did. But while we were going through Hell

Week, those same students would shout to us to hang in there. They would even leave candy bars underneath our pillows. Those actions touched me, and I never forgot them.

When I became an instructor, if I saw a guy who was doing good, and if I had an extra lunch available, I'd ask him if he wanted more to eat. And I brought candy bars for the students myself. Then one group of guys I gave some candy bars to messed it up for everyone. They had stuffed the Snickers bars in their faces at the wrong time. The senior chief on the shift asked them to turn around and saw that chocolate mess all on their faces.

So when the senior chief roared out that he wanted to know where they had gotten the candy bars, one of the students just flat out told him that Instructor Hawes had given them the candy.

That dime-dropper.

It was just one of those things. Later on, after they had graduated, those students came up to talk to me. They said that they knew I had acted like a real person, and that even though I was just as hard on the class as anyone else when I needed to be, I wasn't like some of the other instructors. I believed that you could be compassionate and still do the job. We don't have to beat anyone into the ground to get them to do what we want them to. You beat them to a point, then let off. I was sometimes known as "Mr. Softy," though.

It was my responsibility to see that there was a level of pain in the training, and I did that just as hard as every other instructor. You push the students until they feel that they can't go on any farther, then you keep pushing them. The ones who can shut it off and keep going are the ones who learn that they can do more than they ever thought they could. The others just fall away.

Everybody has their limitations as to how much pain they can stand, and there are all kinds of pain. When you look at some divorces, or even just breakups between girlfriends and boyfriends, the people involved will say that the other put them through a lot of pain. But if asked if they were beaten, they usually have to say no. It isn't the physical pain, it's the mental and emotional pain they feel. Pain can be mental, or it can be physical. I don't really have a way to describe it. But you can learn to force yourself through the pain and come out the other side.

A good example of pain that can be dealt with happens during the students' 5.5-mile swim. The student swimmer pairs know that it's their last big swim and that the water is icy cold. A pair of swimmers might start off in third place. As they go along, turning over their strokes, all of a sudden, one of the pair starts to fall behind. The swim buddy is starting to become incoherent and can't speak. So the safety boat is called over and they find out that he's going into hypothermia.

So the swim buddy is pulled into the safety boat, and the other swimmer has to stay there in the water and wait for the next swimmer pair to come up so he can swim with them. Trying to just hold position in the water, the swimmer will cup his hands together, but his hands are so cold that he can't lace his fingers together. But he continues to wait and gut out the cold until he can continue the swim.

Three hours later, the swim would finally be over. Only now the student's knees and joints lock up from the cold. He would fall to the ground and not be able to move. A grown man would be forced to ask for help. He couldn't walk by himself, he couldn't even get up off the ground without help. That's pain, not only physical, but mental. That man's dignity and pride are gone, flushed away with the cold that racked his body. That hurts like hell.

But the help he needs is there from his classmates. That's one of the other lessons of BUD/S—no one is ever left behind. That student's classmates, suffering from the cold themselves, would help him get up and move. The ones who can move the best help the ones who can't.

In spite of the fun we have between the services, there's a lot of respect that goes along with the jokes and ribbing. Yeah, we kid each other, make up songs, or whatever, but underlying that is the respect of warriors. The same thing we had to go through to earn our Trident—a very hard course of training—Marine Recon had to go through their own version, as did the Army Rangers and Green Berets. The one thing that stands out is that all our main jobs are different. We SEALs take the jobs that nobody else wants and that nobody else can do.

When you're telling a guy to swim from 4 in the morning until sometime in the afternoon, then get lunch, put on wet rubber, and do some more swimming, a beach recon, or a dive, you can only be talking to a SEAL. There were times I had to do those things in cold water. We were diving for bombs or live shells that were dropped over the side of a ship, or looking for a camera that someone was dumb enough to drop into the water. Things like that happen, and the only people the higher-ups think to get to solve those problems are the SEALs.

That used to bother me, but now it makes me proud. If there's a problem, they think first to give it to the SEALs. It's like we have some kind of big "S" on our chests. I know not to believe that, but it does make me feel good that we're thought of so highly. It makes me proud, and it makes my family proud.

Even saying that, you can't take anything away from the Green Berets, the Rangers, the Air Force PJs, or the Marine Recon. In their communities, they are the top dogs, and their families are just as proud of what they went through and what their accomplishments are. So we have a rivalry amongst ourselves, but it isn't really a rivalry. It's more just something that's traditional and fun.

Twenty-two years in the military and although I didn't make the rank I wanted to, I am still very proud of what I did. I'm proud that I didn't avoid any conflict, that I didn't avoid coming into the military. I'm proud of the guys who I work with and the people who laid down the foundation of the Teams before I actually got there, did the history, and left it for men like me to carry on the story. I'm proud that my family has pride in me.

These things are easy to say after my time in the Teams. Sure, I could have been a high school drop-out, or I could have decided that the military wasn't for me. If I'd have wanted to, I could have been a gang-banger, or even have turned into a statistic in prison. But I had enough pride in myself, instilled by my mom and dad and by my brothers, to make what were the right decisions.

It doesn't matter that time has passed. I might be a great big SEAL, but that doesn't mean I can ever go home and tell my mom that she can't tell me what to do because I'm a grown man. She'll still slap me, and Dad will be right there to knock the hell out of me. And if they didn't do it, I have brothers bigger than me who would show me that disrespect is not to be tolerated.

Wearing the Trident separates me from everybody else. When I go on the base, to the exchange or to take care of business at the personnel office, and I have my cammies (camouflage uniform) or dress uniform on with that Trident on my chest, that tells everyone that I'm someone special. But I can't say I'm someone special just because I wear the Trident; it comes from the whole mannerism that comes from being in the Teams. Your dress uniform is always squared away. In cammies, I always make sure that my boots and pants are properly bloused, my boots are shined, everything is sharp and clean. That tells other people that I'm special.

When they see that Trident, they know I'm a SEAL. And they see a squared-away uniform that tells them the pride I hold in being one. That's always been in my heart, and I try to instill that in the new guys I help train.

Some guys today who get their Tridents have smiles on their faces and tears in their eyes as they receive that symbol of the Teams. Then they'll say they are buying a keg for all their buddies, because they are now one of us, and we'll have a couple drinks at McP's or Danny's in celebration. And that touches you, because you remember being there yourself.

It was twenty-two years ago that I was a young pup like these new guys. And I remember just how good it feels to get that Trident. But the test is not over once you pin it on. You are constantly training, and you have to instill in the new guys how a SEAL has to constantly keep up. Passing the boards and qualifying is just one step. You have to keep on being better and better. That's what separates us from the other guys.

Once I became a SEAL, I cried. I have no problem saying that. People seem to fail to realize that we're people who are SEALs. If you cut me, I bleed. If you kick me, it hurts. We are human and we have emotions just like anyone else. But being a SEAL is a job, and I worked hard to get that job. Having gone through the phases of training does not close off my emotions. Going through BUD/S does not say that now I am a walking, talking machine, that I have no feelings. That is not a SEAL.

A SEAL has feelings. When we go to war and are asked to do things it's not like we can't wait to do those things. We aren't excited about taking lives, we can't wait to do whatever. We look at our job with compassion. Those people who we're going up against have families, too. But that doesn't get in the way of our completing our missions.

We also look at our jobs from another point of view. If we happen to have a mishap with explosives, on a jump, while shooting, or when we go to war, there is every possibility that we're going to die. So those emotions we have inside do have to be kept under solid control. I know I check out everything prior to a jump or any other operation. And I also say, "Please God, let my chute open."

I go through all the planning for a jump. Each action that I'm going to take, I go through step by step in my mind, and once that chute opens, I say, "Thank you, God." When I steer down to the ground and land, I say, "Thank you God, for another successful jump."

If anyone tells you that they were never scared, they are probably lying. Team guys are human, and we get just as scared as the next guy. We just don't let it stop us, or even slow us down. Whether I say it or not, being scared doesn't make me any more, or less, of a man. Most Team guys are secure in themselves. And when you are secure in yourself, you can let your emotions go, and you can let your feelings go. So that's why it doesn't bother me to say that I cried when I first received my Trident.

The first words that come to my mind when I think about the Teams are "camaraderie" and "brotherhood." We are the most elite fighting unit in the world. The camaraderie comes from knowing that you are a Team guy, and that you are with your Teammates. If you are having problems at home, you can always go out with a Team guy, and he will bring up your morale.

During the holiday season, there are a lot of guys who are away from home—some for the first time, some just like every year. They might not have any family to go home to and have to live in the barracks. They don't have to spend the time alone. There's always someone asking them to come over to their house, watch the games on TV while the wife is cooking dinner, and hang out with the kids and watch them open their presents. The Teams are a family unit, and because I have been in the Teams, that's how it has always been.

That's the thing I'm going to miss the most when I retire—the family of the Teams. I grew up in a big family, and leaving the military is like leaving another family. But it doesn't stop there. You can always visit with the Team guys. You can always sit there and partake of a beer, some food, and have some conversation. They will always be there.

■　　■　　■

In front of the UDT-SEAL Museum down in Fort Pierce, Florida, there is a statue of Bronze Bruce, the Naked Warrior, a UDT operator equipped with little more than swim fins, bathing trunks, a face mask, and a knife. I look at that statue and I see a guy who will ask for only the bare minimum, and he will get the job done. He has enough heart and ability, that even given less than the minimum, he will get the job done. If he has to go it alone, he will get the job done. Whatever it takes, the job gets done.

You don't have to have the best equipment. When I first came into UDT, we didn't have all the high-tech stuff we work with today. We had Ingram MAC-10 and M76 submachine guns and .38 revolvers. We really thought we were high-speed then. We didn't even always get a holster; we would put a gun down into our UDT shorts. How roguish is that? But it was what we had and we dealt with it.

Now, the Teams are in an age of different weapons and tools. Now we have MP5 submachine guns, sniper rifles, this, and that. But what we are teaching the students is that you can give a SEAL whatever, and he will survive and get the job done.

Dennis Chalker, Command Master Chief Boatswain's Mate, USN (Ret.)

My career in the Teams spanned about twenty-three years. I finished my tour as the Command Master Chief at the Naval Special Warfare Center. That's where we run BUD/S, SEAL trainers and people who want to be SEALs through training. We run advanced SEAL programs there as well.

My military career started at the age of seventeen when I enlisted in the Army. I served a little over three years with the 82nd Airborne Division. Afterward, I took a break in my service time to try to go to school, because I wanted to be a game warden. Moving to Colorado, I found that I couldn't meet the residency requirements, so I couldn't afford to go to school.

Back during my Jump School days at Fort Benning, I had heard about the Navy SEALs. I even met a few of them there. When I went up to talk to the director of the forestry department in Colorado, he told me that there was a waiting list to be a game warden. When I told him that I was thinking about going into the Navy and try to go through the SEAL program, he told me that if I had my degree and completed that training, it would help jack me to the top of the list for a possible job as a game warden.

Boot camp was nothing. I only had to go through it because I had been out of the Army so long. The boatswain's mate rating was the quickest school to go through and get into BUD/S as fast as possible. Soon enough, I was at BUD/S and joining up with Class 101, graduating March 1979—a winter class—big time.

Training was challenging, which was one of the reasons I went into the program, as I love things that are a challenge. One thing I learned about in training was what

The thumbs-up sign is given by a fully equipped SEAL from SEAL Team Eight during VBSS training aboard the *Joshua Humphries* during Desert Storm. His primary weapon is an MP-5N submachine gun, this one fitted with a removable flash hider and loaded with a doubled set of 30-round magazines. The empty magazine can be removed and the loaded magazine quickly slipped into place with such an arrangement.

U.S. Navy

it meant to work together and be a member of a Team. I learned in the program that there's no room in the Special Warfare community for an individual, what we call an "I." That's the lesson we relate to the students today.

What I learned in training first of all, was that the challenge was not exaggerated. I will admit that there is a time during your training that a little man does come up on your shoulder and works on your head. He asks you if you've had enough, and if you're sure that the program's for you. I know a lot of people say that they never had anything like that happen. Well, I don't think so. I'm not going to call anyone a liar, but I don't think so. The entire time I was at BUD/S, I was wet, cold, and sandy. That's one thing I'll never forget. There were times that were different, but that was only because you were wetter, colder, and covered in more sand.

Hell Week was very challenging, especially the first couple nights, because you're up with no sleep. Now I understand more about Hell Week. It's there for a very specific purpose. It's the most stressful situation you can put an individual through, short of dropping them onto a battlefield.

We use that stress on the students today, just as it was used on me then, to make sure they have what it takes to get through a stressful situation. The instructors try to make it as confusing, physically demanding, and stressful as a combat situation. That's where the fatigue comes in. No sleep.

By the time you hit Wednesday of Hell Week, things become a blur. I don't remember much after that day of my own training. After being Command Master Chief at BUD/S, and seeing the students after Wednesday, you realize you can't hurt them anymore. They just kind of go numb. But those first few nights, those are the ones you can make the most stressful on the students, physically and mentally, because they're entirely cold, wet, and sandy.

Can I describe the cold? All I can say is that it's something that starts from your head and goes through the core of your body. You can feel it through your bones.

You shake, shivering to a point where it exhausts you. That's about all I can remember about being cold.

I think what got me through Hell Week was that first, I put my mind someplace else when I was sitting in the surf zone. Instead of being on that cold, dark, beach, I was on a Caribbean island. Looking up at the moon, I thought about the sun beating down on that island. Then I started humming. That helped out.

What else helped me through Hell Week was working with the other individuals as a Team. At BUD/S, there's that one time that one individual going to sit there and say, "I think I've had enough." His partner is going to look at him and say, "Take one evolution at a time. Hang in there until tomorrow." When tomorrow comes around, the roles have switched. Now the other individual thinks he's had enough and his buddy talks him up.

So the two things that really got me through Hell Week was, first, myself. You go into your mind and decide that you can take it, that you can keep going and push through the limits. The other was my classmates, my future Teammates.

A SEAL will always remember his class number, and he will also remember the Teams he was in. The number is not classified, but it isn't widely known, either. If someone says they were a SEAL and they don't remember their class number—if they haven't had a brain injury—they were never there. The only way into the Teams is through BUD/S. There are no shortcuts, special classes, or transfers in from other services. For a very short time, corpsmen had to go through special training to get into the SEALs, but that has changed now and they all go through BUD/S. It's the only way to become a Teammate.

Graduation day from BUD/S was probably one of the greatest feelings of my life. I had just completed twenty-six weeks of hell, and I felt good about myself. I was physically in the best shape of my life. I went from 200 pounds down to about 175 or 180, but it was hard weight.

But just the feeling of being able to join the ranks of the Teams, to become one of the elite after twenty-six weeks of not torture but really strenuous mental and physical training, was one of the real high points of my life.

After graduating BUD/S, I went straight to SEAL Team One. Like any new meat in the Teams, I was assigned to the Master-at-Arms shack and quickly put to work painting. Gary "Chambo" Chamberlin, who was my sea daddy, picked me up for Kilo Platoon and made me his point man. So my first year and a half in the community was spent at SEAL Team One on the West Coast.

A sea daddy is someone who takes you like a child and puts you under his wing. Pretty much what he does is groom you for the community. He's helping show you the way to be a good operator without stepping on you. Once you get to the community, you need someone like that. Usually, a sea daddy will pick you up and show you the ways of the command and what's expected of you, then let you carry on from there.

A swim buddy is, first of all, somebody you rely on whenever you're doing any type of water work. You swim as a team, you work as a team, and you watch each other. Deep down in your heart, a swim buddy is a brother. Like in training, you and your swim buddy and become close. I talked about being in training and how you have to pick up each other's morale. That's what you and your swim buddy do. You pick each other up, and pull or push as necessary.

The single most important thing about being a good operator and Teammate is teamwork. No one has ever been left behind. That fact is part of the Teams, a reflection of the heart and soul of the brotherhood that is first forged at BUD/S. Years in the Teams only makes that bond stronger.

When you first get to the Teams from training, you're on probation. I was fortunate when I got to Team One that a majority of Kilo Platoon was made up of classmates, or Class 100 guys who had graduated only a few months in front of me. So we had a young platoon. It was only after I had been at the command in Coronado for about six months that the platoon formed up and we deployed. That's deploying fairly early in your career. Back then we did a six-month workup to train and prepare the platoon for deployment.

You hold up to the standards, and you got to pin on the Trident after your probationary period was over, usually six months after graduating BUD/S. That was determined by a board who reviewed your record and talked to those SEALs who worked with you. We were in a platoon, so our board was run by the platoon officer in charge (OIC) and the platoon chief. The administration part of the command back in Coronado also had a say in how an individual's probation was going to turn out.

What the Trident meant was that I had finally earned something that I had been waiting to receive for about a year and a half, since I had joined the Navy. It meant a lot to me, and it brought back to me what I had gone through to earn the Trident. It also made me feel very proud to actually be one of the SEAL community.

Even today, I hold that symbol in high regard. I look at the people who have given their lives while wearing that symbol, or the people who have been with me, or fought alongside me, during my career. Then there are the future guys who are going through training today, and tomorrow, who will earn that same symbol. It all means a great deal to me and every SEAL I've ever known.

We have a connection with those who have gone before us, all the way back to the Naked Warriors of World War II. We're the next generation. There's a connection that goes back to the past through the UDTs, the Naval Combat Demolition Units, and even the Scouts and Raiders before them. I happened to be in the West Coast area when UDT Eleven and UDT Twenty-One converted to SEAL Teams. Then a couple more SEAL Teams were added to each coast. That's a constant history and a direct lineage to the Naked Warrior.

In the late 1970s, there was a new enemy rising up against the United States and the free world—terrorism. When a new SEAL Team was commissioned to fight that new enemy, I was one of the privileged ones to be chosen to be a plankowner for the new Team.

Being a plankowner means that you helped establish a new Team and that you were one of the first people in that new Team. The term comes from the old days, when the Navy used wooden ships. A member of the first crew of a new ship was said to own a plank from the deck.

When I first got a chance to meet Dick Marcinko, he struck me as a man who, once given a task, is going to complete that task whatever it takes. Yes, he has been known to burn a few bridges over the years while getting the job done, but that's to be expected. Dick was tasked with some very hard missions in Navy Special Warfare, and he rubbed some very influential people the wrong way. But he did what he had to do to get the mission completed, and you either like him or you don't like him. That's the type of person he is. I like the man because he took care of me just as he took care of all the guys in the enlisted community under him. That's the biggie right there.

The 1980s started a new era of operating. Dick Marcinko was tasked with the mission given to him by the CNO (Chief of Naval Operations—the boss of the Navy) to combat the new terrorism threat in the world. Before that Team was created, I had gotten out of Kilo Platoon and was in Echo Platoon at SEAL Team One. A lot of people have heard about MOB-Six at SEAL Team Two. On the West Coast, Team One's version of MOB-Six was Echo Platoon.

When Dick Marcinko started collecting the men he wanted for the new SEAL Team, he came out to the West Coast and conducted interviews. He combined men from both coasts in SEAL Team Six on the East Coast. When people ask why it was put on the East Coast, I think it was because it was closer to Washington, D.C., and the commander-in-chief's (CinCs) in that area. A CinC is a commander in charge of a certain area, such as CinCPac—Commander-in-Chief, Pacific.

The guys at SEAL Team Six were top-notch individuals. That's who Dick had to pick in order to get this thing off the ground. He had two years to accomplish what the Army took six years to do. The guys were all tight, and that first year we packed thirty hours of work into twenty-four-hour days. As a result, the bond between us developed into a very close brotherhood.

In the early 1960s, before my time, President Kennedy needed an elite group to work in the riverine environment, and the Army had a hard time filling that requirement. So to meet that need, they went to the UDTs and created the SEAL Teams. In 1972, when I graduated high school, terrorism was starting to affect the country a lot more than it ever had before. So in the 1970s, the planners in the military were taking a hard look at how to combat terrorism.

In the later part of the 1970s, both coasts had to have a Team to answer to terrorist threats or maritime crisis situations. That is a major mission in and of itself.

Instead of a whole SEAL Team being assigned that mission, a platoon in SEAL Team One and a platoon in SEAL Team Two were tasked for counterterrorism. That was how SEAL Team Six evolved, from those two platoons combining to a single new Team with the same mission. And when SEAL Team Six was first manned, I would say we had about sixty guys onboard—the same number of men as were in the first SEAL Teams.

What did it mean to me to be chosen for the new Team? I had to answer this question even in the community. I remember my sea daddies talking about when they formed the first SEAL Teams out of the UDTs. They told me that I would enjoy the new Team and that it would be something different. But one thing that was going to come along with that new challenge would be the factor of getting to do something a different from the rest of the community, which could cause some friction with the operators in the rest of the Community.

But when I was selected for Team Six, I was honored, very honored. I feel that there were a lot of other people who could have been selected for SEAL Team Six. I think that when Dick started the new Team, he was looking for single people because there was going to be a lot of time involved with training. That counted out a lot of married people from the personnel pool.

And to call it like it is, I was in the right place at the right time. I happened to be in Echo Platoon at the time, and we were at the top of the list for the new Team. I was very honored for the opportunity to go there.

Team Six was commissioned in 1980, and our first active combat operation was in October 1983. The kind of unit we had meant that we had the funding to dedicate more time to training to bring us up to speed to face terrorism throughout the world. So for those three years, we trained almost constantly. Dick Marcinko said once that he was going to buy us new toys and buy us new gear—and to believe him that we would be using it. And we certainly did.

My first year at Team Six, I got a half-day off for Thanksgiving and the same for Christmas. Anyone who says there are 365 days a year didn't spend any time at Team Six. On Marcinko's training schedule, there were 465 days in a year. But things got a lot easier the second year, when I got a day off for Thanksgiving and a half-day off for Christmas.

Our first combat operation at Team Six was in Grenada under Captain Robert Gormly. Because it was my first actual combat mission, I will never forget one thing about getting ready to go in. When we were getting our intelligence dump on the operation, Gormly held up a blank sheet of paper and said that was our Intel on the island.

The mission I was involved with was down at the governor-general's mansion where we were going to recover Governor-General Scoon. We were a little bit late going in on the op. Our helicopters were supposed to have inserted us right at sunrise, but instead we ended up arriving in broad daylight. Whether the Grenadians

A Blackhawk helicopter flying in support of a ground operation. In the open doorway is the door gunner aiming a .50 caliber M3 aircraft machine gun. This weapon can be easily interchanged with either a minigun or M60D machine gun, depending on the mission requirements.

were tipped off on the operation or not, I don't know, but we took antiaircraft fire coming in across the island.

In the helo, I remember looking across at all the people we had stuffed onboard. We had three more people onboard the Blackhawk helicopter than we were supposed to have. As the number one, I was going to kick the rope out the doorway when we were over the target. My partner, Rich, was with me, and he had his hand and elbow on the rail that extended out to hold the fast rope clear of the bird.

Looking over at the Vietnam vets we had in the Teams, they were all smiling at us. Then one of them said, "How's it feel to be shot at?"

Hey, not too bad, but we couldn't do anything back. Our M60 gunner had decided to test-fire his weapon across the ocean on our way in. He lifted the aluminum feed tray cover on the gun as we were moving at the helicopter's top speed. The slip stream just ripped the feed cover from the weapon, tearing it away and wrecking the gun for the insertion. So we had no M60 on our side of the bird.

Coming up to the governor-general's mansion, the situation was a little different than our limited intelligence had told us was the case. Most SEALs on the East Coast have spent time down in Puerto Rico and we know the Caribbean. Grenada was the first Caribbean island I saw that had Ponderosa pines, fir trees. And I'm not talking ten-foot trees. These things were forty or fifty feet tall. The gradient at the front of the governor-general's house was greater than a forty-five-degree angle in places.

As the helo came to a hover over the target, I kicked out the rope as the bird was taking fire. Going down the rope with Rich practically on my shoulders and Duke Leonard right above him, I was breaking every branch on one of those big pine trees on the way to the ground. Hitting the ground in a flurry of pine branches, we picked each other up as we stopped rolling down the hill. Now we had to get established and get up to do what we were supposed to do at the mansion.

We had a little trouble with some of the gear because of that fast rope insertion. There came a time when some armored personnel carriers came up to the mansion. They were coming to the gate, and Duke or Bill called down to where I was, saying to get the LAW (Light Antitank Weapon) ready in case we needed it. I looked over at my partner, Foster, and he had this M-72 LAW rocket launcher that looked like a banana. When he fast roped down, he kind of landed on the launcher as he rolled down the hill.

"Denny," Foster said, "you've been in the Army and have fired more of these than I have." And he handed off to me this bent, nasty, rocket launcher.

I actually got the launcher extended properly into its firing configuration, but the back of the weapon, where the rocket was, was bent around a bit. I thought that if I had to use this thing, it worked. Fortunately, I never had to fire it. Once the vehicles backed off, I just folded it back down.

We were supposed to have a bigger punch available to us in Grenada than just the weapons in our hands. There were gunships, AC-130 aircraft, that were supposed to be orbiting overhead and rotate off with each other so one was always there. As it got close to evening, both gunships started being on station at the same time. Sometime in the early hours of the morning of our second day at the mansion, we got the word that more than thirty individuals were coming up to our position. Because our radio's batteries were down, we were very short on radio communications.

Two of the older vets, Johnny Johnson and Tim Prusak, put Rich and me out forward about 50 meters, had us lie down, and told us to wait until they were almost on top of us. Then we were supposed to open up on full automatic and keep our heads down, because they would be behind us with M60 machine guns.

Rich had been wounded in the elbow just before the insertion by some antiaircraft fire. He told me that he didn't think he would be able to reload easily. I told him that I didn't think we would have the time to reload anyway.

While all that was going on with us out on the yard, Ma Bell was taking a hand with the SEALs. Some years later, I remember watching the movie Heartbreak Ridge, and I think they got the idea for a bit in that movie from what happened to us at Grenada.

One of the guys in the mansion used a calling card and got on the phone to Hurbert Field back in Florida and to the operations office there. Over the phone, he ordered a gun run. Both birds overhead were running low on fuel, so only one was able to make one gun run before it had to turn back. That gunship might have saved our butts, even with only one run.

From our "headquarters" inside the mansion, they called in the gunfire and walked in the 40mm gunfire close to our position to eliminate the threat facing us. We were okay as they walked the gunfire in to where we were laying. I remember the area looking like triple-canopy jungle, because the trees were so thick when we came in. The next morning, the area was pretty much open ground. The close explosions of the 40mm cannon shells from that gunship probably contributed more than a little to my losing a bunch of my hearing. But our mission at Grenada, for what we had to do, was a success.

Grenada wasn't the only combat operation I went on while in SEAL Team Six. Most of what we did is still highly classified, but the public does know that we were involved in some very high-profile operations. One of these took place just at the end of the 1980s.

Panama was a joint service, a joint command operation. Everyone knows that we went down there to pull Noriega out of power. As part of SEAL Team Six, our mission was to go and look in different areas, to search out Noriega, and prevent his escape from the country.

For my last assignment of my Navy career, I returned to where it had all started. I received the assignment to be the Command Master Chief at the Schoolhouse, the Training Center Command where all BUD/S training was run. That was a honor for me. I looked at my whole military career, and saw that the Teams have been good to me. What I wanted to do was give something back to the community, and the opportunity to be the Command Master Chief at the center, gave me the opportunity to do that.

I got to take all I had learned from all the veterans before me and all my own experiences to the center and use it to help make sure that we kept up the quality of training. It also helped me make sure that the individuals I was responsible for training would learn the new ways of being a SEAL. It was an honor to go there and have that responsibility. And I finally left, feeling that I did give something back to the community.

My job as Command Master Chief, in my view, was to motivate the individuals going through BUD/S. I used to go in as the new recruits arrived at the command, give my first talk on motivation, then give them a brief history of the Teams themselves. That history alone can motivate people to try to become a part of it.

What I would try to bring out in the individual is to work as part of a team. I would stress to them that teamwork was what it would take for them to get through the program. If they thought they were an individual, they might just have a problem successfully finishing BUD/S.

You cannot tell just by looking at a trainee, whether or not he's going to complete training. Anyone who tells you you can is wrong. The years I was at BUD/S, I would look at certain individuals and try to "see" if they would be among the graduates of a class. The trouble was, often as not, that was the first person to decide that the program wasn't for him. And I looked at other individuals and thought that they might have a problem getting through, but they ended up being the strongest in a class and helped motivate their classmates. Sometimes, a guy I thought wouldn't even make it, ended up as honor man for his class.

It was so funny to see who would and wouldn't make it. There was no standard. Most people think you have to be a football player or athletic star to be a SEAL. SEALs come in all sizes. To be honest with you, football player-types, which is nothing to say against that kind of person, I've played football myself, are usually the first persons to leave the program.

I've even had swimmers and marathon runners come through, but even that one field of expertise in their favor wasn't enough and they dropped. It's that individual who has a basic running pace and maybe a good swimming pace—the ability to pass the screening tests makes sure of that—are the ones who tend to make it through the program.

Mud, mud, and more mud. Such is the life of a BUD/S student during Hell Week, as the face of this student well illustrates.

U.S. Navy

As the Command Master Chief, I had the opportunity to run a couple shifts during training and look at the students from the instructors' standpoint. During Hell Week there were times I would look in an individual's eye and you could see his desire to become a SEAL waver. This particularly happened during the first two nights, because that's when the students are still shaky about what they've let themselves in for.

Tuesday night, when they go into the chow hall (they get four meals a day, mid-rats are at midnight) they've been cold. Now, you've just put them into a warm environment. You know exactly what's going through their heads, because you can see it in their eyes. The motivation goes down.

So you try to pick them up. I used to walk around and add a few jokes to the atmosphere, to try to bring their motivation back up and not let them just sit there and clam up. I also used to explain to the individuals how there was this little man who would show up your shoulder and tell you that you'd had enough. What I used to tell them was to take their fork and just stab the little sucker, to get him off their shoulder.

Sometimes, especially on Tuesday night, I would be walking around and see guys stabbing at their shoulders when they saw me looking. They would smile and I would know that they had won the fight for at least that moment.

You might see a student next to the mud just shaking from the cold. And as an instructor, you could see that he was wavering but was otherwise a good prospect, so you'd toss him back into the mud. People who would see that might not understand. But it's a little bit warmer in that mud than it is standing there in the outside air.

Tuesday night was probably the worst night in Hell Week while I was Command Master Chief, as far as DORs (drop on request) go. If we took that warm chow hall out of the equation and had them eating out in the cold, I don't think we would have quite as many drop-outs. But that's all part of the program.

In spite of all of the testing they've tried, the physical and mental screening, no one has been able to come up with a guide to say who would or would not make it through training. It's the heart, what the guy has inside himself, that counts the most toward graduation and the Teams. You just can't tell by looking at them or talking to them. Who makes it is not determined until the day they graduate.

The purpose of Hell Week, and something I tried to stress when I took over as Command Master Chief, was to prepare the students for a combat situation. Hell Week is the most stressful situation that we get to put the students through to see if they have what it takes. They have to still be able to function in that situation and be productive, and the only way to know that is to put them through it.

I used to compare the students' paddle to a weapon. Their IBS (inflatable boat, small) was their way of insertion and extraction, so they had to take care of it. Their kapoks, or lifejackets, for flotation were their web gear. So if a student was coming through the surf and lost his paddle, he had lost his weapon, and he couldn't be productive to the team without it.

That kind of thing was how I handled Hell Week when I held the position. It was, and still is, a necessary test. There hasn't been anything better than Hell Week to weed out the ones who can't meet the challenge. And the concept of Hell Week has proven itself over time—since the very first days of training back in World War II.

The phrase I used to use in training was: "There is no 'I' in SEAL Team." That phrase means there is no room for individuals. That's not what the Teams are about. It isn't about an individual. You hear stories about certain outstanding people in the Teams, SEALs who have committed incredible acts of bravery. But guess who made that individual? It wasn't just the individual, it was his Teammates.

Sure, everybody gets and deserves personal recognition. One of the biggest things I ever heard one of these outstanding individuals say came from Mikey

Thornton regarding his Medal of Honor. We had a discussion about it once, and I don't think he would mind me repeating what he told me. He said that it wasn't his Medal of Honor; it was the Teams', that the Teams earned it. I highly respect him for that opinion. That's what it's about. That's why there is no room for the individual in the Teams.

To complete BUD/S takes three things: the mind, the heart, and the body. The most important thing from those three factors to successfully get you through BUD/S is, first of all, to have the will inside you. You've got to have the heart, because it will take a lot of heart just to get to BUD/S and it takes heart to adjust to the situations you will face every day and take what's going to be dished out to you. The heart will drive you on when you think you can't take another step. When the cold gets to you and you can't face the icy ocean, the heart will move you into the surf.

The second thing in order of importance is the mind. You have to be able to sit there and mentally take each evolution as it comes. You have to not anticipate, not worry, and block out what you're facing and the misery you're in. And your mind has to be able to tell your body to keep going and how to get the job done, even when it says it can't.

The third thing you need is your body, but that's almost the least of the requirements. Because guess what we're doing at BUD/S? I don't care what you are when you get there or what you did in the past. We're going to physically and mentally break you down. Then, we're going to rebuild you to meet the needs of the Teams as we know them.

So the most important thing you can bring with you to BUD/S is your heart, the desire to be in the Teams more than anything. You will have to have the discipline, your mind, to keep going and to drive yourself forward. Last, you have to prepare your body to complete the screening tests and be able to do what's expected of you. But the instructors will see to it that you get enough exercise to meet that last requirement. We'll take care of that for you.

I wouldn't exactly use the terminology "made intentionally hard" when describing BUD/S. What would be a better question is why do the standards that we hold the students to seem so high? The standards at BUD/S are high because we are trying to get a good-quality person through the program and on to the Teams. Any person who volunteers for the program and steps through that door at the training center can be one of those quality people. It's up to the individual. I think because of the ratio of a graduating class compared to those who started, around 25 percent just for a round number, a lot of people think that it's just a too difficult program.

Don't get me wrong, it is difficult. But it's that way for a reason. It's the only way to test the heart and mind of someone who wishes to be a SEAL. The training has proven itself time and time again. And if it was to fail, Teammates would die in combat.

The money handlers, the bean-counters in the Navy, would see benefits if the standards at BUD/S were lowered. A higher percentage of students graduating would mean less money being wasted on the students who drop out. But the Teams would pay for those lowered standards in the long run. The thing that we get from BUD/S as a final product is a quality student. As Command Master Chief, I didn't like the idea of sacrificing quality to get the quantity. As an operator in the Teams, I couldn't stand that idea.

Making training easier by lowering the standards would save the Navy money in the short run, but it wouldn't benefit the Teams. You would be balancing quality against quantity.

As an operator, I would rather take two quality individuals to the field rather than thirty who met a lower standard. The standards have been set from the earliest days of the UDTs. The demands of BUD/S have not lessened since those days. If anything, they've gotten harder. Being Command Master Chief, I can say that the standards have to stay where they are.

We've gotten smarter since the days I went through training. Medically, we take better care of the students as we've learned more over the years. Some of the older Frogmen, myself included, still have scars from the old gear we wore in the sand. But that's been changed today. We still want an individual to make it through the program, but only if he's good enough. Anything less would hurt the Teams badly, and it would lower their mission profiles.

Who are SEALs? Most people have heard how they use SEALs bare hands as weapons, or that they're all martial artists. Or the SEALs are all weapons experts, spies, or supermen. The term I like to use to describe a SEAL is jack of-all-trades. I didn't say expert-of-all-trades. What you have to do is be aware, be knowledgeable, and be competent in different fields, because SEALs do work in the sea, air, and land.

Once a man gets into the SEAL community, he might become an expert in de-molitions or work in the communications field. Over time, a man might become the guru of Air Ops for his Team. And we do have our own program for close-in fighting skills. But the point I'm trying to make is that the better SEALs are not specific ex-perts in any one field or even in several fields. What makes a very good operator is some skills in a lot of fields.

To any young man who would want to be a SEAL, I would tell to start being more active in your running and swimming. Start working out under proper guidance. To-day, education plays a major factor in a person's career in the Navy, or anywhere, so study hard and learn. Keep your grades up, keep your motivation up, and keep driv-

ing forward. Whatever is telling you right now that you want to be a SEAL, keep that in mind. Don't get carried away by the books and movies you see—those are entertainment. There's no way to test yourself until you get the opportunity to step though the doors at Coronado and get to BUD/S.

Erick Peterson, Ensign

It had been a long haul to make it to the end of BUD/S training. Training was supposed to have been a six-month stretch, but because of an injury, I had turned six months into nine months. But in spite of a medical rollback, I had completed the course. A lot of the men I had been in charge of had been in the same boat as me, and I was as proud of their accomplishments as I was of my own. Completing BUD/S had been hard; the course was trying and difficult. But I had made it.

At the end of my BUD/S training, I had only been in the service for about fourteen months. In October, I had started to attend Officer Candidate School (OCS). By January, I had been commissioned as a ensign. Officially, I had only been in the active Navy for eleven months, and the bulk of that had been spent as a trainee at BUD/S.

It was well before joining the Navy that I had learned about the SEALs and the UDTs from reading books and magazine articles about them. I was thirteen or fourteen years old when I decided that being in the Teams was what I wanted to do. My father had been a fighter pilot and had flown F8s over Vietnam during that war, so I had grown up with the mind-set of being a fighter pilot. We even had a private aircraft when I was growing up and my dad had taught me how to fly. My focus had been on attending the Naval Academy and becoming a pilot after graduation, but when I discovered the SEALs, that all changed.

Swimming was always something I had been inclined to. Water polo was a sport I enjoyed, and spending time at the beach always had appeal to me. Camping and trail running were also some things I had done a lot of. So as strange as it sounds, being down and dirty, wet, and miserable sounded more enjoyable to me than flying some hunk of steel at mach one and passing over the countryside without ever really seeing it.

I sadly disappointed my father because of that but I had made the right decision for myself, and at a young age I focused all my attention and energy on making it to where I am now.

The Navy and my training at OCS hadn't been all that hard. When I first showed up at the BUD/S training center that first day, it was quite a shock. My ideas of incredible professionalism, rigidity, and regimentation pretty much went out the door with my first look at the inside of the training center. When I showed up, there were men running around on crutches while other men were all wet and sandy and doing jumping jacks. Still other guys, in the same wet and sandy condition, were do-

ing push-ups. Some men were running about in camouflage uniforms while still others were wearing greens. And among all this chaos were the instructors yelling orders.

From my point of view, the whole place had a circuslike atmosphere. Later, I learned what was going on and how everything came together in that high level of professionalism I had expected. But my first impression of the BUD/S compound was one of controlled chaos, directed with a lot of yelling and shouting.

All in all, my first impression was that it was going to be a long, hard six months. And I was right, but not for the reasons I had first thought.

The hardest part of my six months of training was during First Phase. That is the initial physical training phase. During the first four weeks of training, we did small boat handling. We were introduced to the IBS, or inflatable boats, small, and we used those inflatable boats to conduct surf passage. It sounded simple—we were going to learn how to row a boat through the surf. It wasn't simple.

When I went through First Phase, it was in February with Class 218. The surf conditions in Southern California were dictated by the El Niño effect, so an average day had four-to-six-foot waves crunching down on the shore, with the occasional eight-footer roaring in as well.

A SEAL Boat crew penetrates the surf zone with their rubber boat during a demonstration.

U.S. Navy

Going though that surf was a nightmare. A lot of my classmates just weren't used to the ocean and quit the course right there because of the surf conditions.

But there were a lot of other activities in First Phase to help weed out the trainees who didn't really want to be there. We had log PT, which was eight guys carrying around a telephone pole. With our poles held overhead, we ran races up and down the sand berms. And there were conditioning runs over long distances in that same sand, only without the telephone poles. Two-mile swims, the obstacle course, and lots of general PT kept us very busy.

The obstacle course was actually kind of fun once you figured it out. But the initial stages of figuring out the course and how to get through the obstacles involves a lot of pain and more than a little heartache. During First Phase, we would be constantly doing physical evolutions, five or six of them a day.

That much exercise and effort breaks down your body. Your body doesn't get a chance to relax, heal, and grow stronger. Instead, you just continually have to force yourself along. It's just a matter of hanging on and staying strong inside yourself. Then there's the fifth week.

The fifth week of First Phase is Hell Week—and it lives up to the hype it receives. That week is just as miserable as it sounds. Somewhere along the way during that week-long period of maximum output and minimum rest, your brain just turns off. The misery stops and you just kind of go into overdrive. Then, things become just a matter of finishing the evolution.

Getting acclimated to being physical from 5 in the morning until 6 or 7 o'clock at night was what made the first four weeks of training so hard for me. As I was an officer, the instructors gave me more attention, but only in that I had to act as a leader to the men under my command. It's unavoidable at BUD/S, that as an officer, you are going to be spotlighted by the instructors from time to time.

As an officer at BUD/S, you are in charge of your boat crew, so whatever the boat crew does, it is a reflection of your leadership. The instructors understand that during First Phase, the officers are learning how to go through training just as the enlisted men are. They don't expect you to be the great leader right from the start, so they don't come down on you more than you can handle—but you do get spotlighted for that extra attention that points out that they will expect a lot from you down the line.

During Second Phase, which was the diving portion of BUD/S for my class, an officer would be put in charge of certain departments. The department I was put in charge of was communications, so whenever we needed radios, or anything to do with communications, if what was needed wasn't there, it was directly my fault. The same situation existed for the other class officers with their departments of diving equipment and such. If the gear wasn't there, it would be some student officer's fault, not the class's fault, and not some enlisted man's fault. The blame would fall squarely on the officer, because he hadn't checked up on it.

A boat crew of students at BUD/S learns the value of teamwork as they struggle to do sit-ups during log PT. The helpful instructor behind them stands ready to shovel on more sand with his boat paddle to help get the students used to working in a sandy environment.

U.S. Navy

In Third Phase, leaders would really get spotlighted. This was the time that the instructors really brought officers forward and expected more of them. In Third Phase, the class was now broken up into squads instead of the boat crews that we had been in for the first two phases.

The same situation extended to the men's uniforms and equipment. It was the duty of the officers in Third Phase to check their men over every day. You had to be sure everyone's boots were polished perfectly, that their uniforms and equipment were all in order, and that knives sharp and clear of any spots of rust. If one of the men in my squad hadn't shaved correctly or had missed a spot—well, that would be my fault because I hadn't checked him correctly.

That situation introduced the junior officers to the level of responsibility that we would encounter when we finally got to the Teams. In a SEAL Team, we would be responsible for men's lives. In training, we would just be responsible for seeing to it that everyone's knives were sharpened. But if you couldn't handle that, it was a lot better to learn it in training rather than later when lives would be on the line. In was a very good introductory phase on just what responsibility actually was.

The attention to detail that was driven into us, from the very first day when we showed up at training, to the very last day, was constant. Even three days before our class graduated, I was yelled at in regards to attention to a detail. That attention would be what would keep you alive in the Teams. If part of your equipment wasn't right during an operation, if you hadn't paid attention to it, you had a chance of not only killing yourself, but also the men who looked to you for leadership. When you cleaned your weapon, every piece had to be perfect. The attention to detail had

FIRE IN THE HOLE! A UDT operator uses a ten-cap electrical blasting machine or "Hell Box" to fire an explosive shot out in the water. A 500-foot reel of firing wire is lying on the sand next to his knee. This training and the live firing of explosives is experienced by BUD/S students for the first time on San Clemente Island off the shores of California.

U.S. Navy

to be there, otherwise things couldn't be expected to work when you needed them to. The point that was ground home from day one was that someone could die because you missed a detail.

It was out on San Clemente Island where the final training for Third Phase is held, that they really drove home the need to pay attention to the details. For the twenty-nine days we spent on San Clemente, we studied and trained with small arms and demolitions.

During that time, the instructors made sure that we all knew just what the attention to detail was for. Making sure the small points were all covered and that everything was ready to go when you had the time to pay attention to it was the bread-and-butter of what we were there to do. It was the little things that could get you killed.

That was the important point brought home during training, but it was only one of the points. The really detailed training didn't come until after you had passed Hell Week. A lot of people never got through that evolution. I went into Hell Week with an injury, and a lot of people thought I wouldn't be able to get through it. The tendon in my left knee was torn and I had a hard time walking. But you didn't do much walking in Hell Week—mostly running.

One of the things that got me through the week was the fact that so many of the instructors and others didn't think I could make it. That helped give me the sheer determination to prove them wrong, that I could make it. At least that was half the reason I wanted so badly to stick it out.

The other half was that I really didn't want to go back to day one of training. There was no way I would go back to week one, day one of First Phase training and do log PT, IBS training, and the four-mile timed runs again. In part, it was the fear of having to go back and do all those things that I just didn't enjoy the first time that helped keep me going.

Of course, there was another way out instead of just getting through that week. To be quite honest, I think most of the guys in my class thought about quitting at one time or another. You thought about it, especially when you would sit down for a meal. That was when the situation would sneak up on you.

At a meal, you would finally be allowed to just sit. You were exhausted, more tired than at any other time in your life, and all you wanted to do was close your eyes. That was when the specter would loom over you, that you could take the easy way out and just quit. We all knew quitting was an option, but most of us never seriously contemplated it. It was an option, but not a viable one. Quitting just wasn't what we were there to do. I didn't go through all it had taken me just to get to BUD/S only to quit.

It was kind of a catch-22 situation. We all thought about quitting at one time or another, but we really didn't acknowledge it as an option.

It was down in the demo pits, about half a mile from the training center, that we heard the phrase that only really means something to a person who has gone through BUD/S. It was next to that stinking pond of muddy water on a Friday that our Command Master Chief secured us from Hell Week.

The instructors were scolding and yelling at us for something we had supposedly done wrong. At that stage of the game, it just becomes accepted that everything we do, no matter what it is, will be wrong.

We were wet, we were sandy, and we were cold—pretty much the standard condition for students during Hell Week. We had been in the surf for a while and then moved back into the sand. Now the instructors had us put our life jackets back on. That meant that we would be getting back in the water and paddle the boats some more.

The instructors told us that we still had a number of hours to go during Hell Week. The morale level plummeted at that point. We stood by in our life jackets and listened to the Command Master Chief scold us, then his words turned around. He started to commend us and congratulate us. Finally, he said that it was his honor and that he was very proud to say that Class 218 was secured from Hell Week.

Men all around me were jumping and screaming, just overwhelmed with joy. I was just pleased it was over with. At that point, my leg was pretty torn up and I was going to be very happy just to get off it for a while. But it was a tremendous feeling of relief and no small amount of pride in myself, that I had eventually accomplished what I had set out to do.

Hell Week is really just a very small portion of the training at BUD/S. But it's what is considered by many to be one of the bigger milestones of the program. And it was a great feeling of relief to have that week behind you. It was another stepping stone toward graduation and the Teams.

There was an expression we learned early on during training, "There is no 'I' in SEAL Team." That meant exactly what it said, that everything you did was for the betterment of the Team and not for yourself. At the end of the day, when you cleaned your equipment, you first cleaned the class's equipment, then the squad's equipment, your swim buddy's equipment, then your own. You, the individual, always came last, and the Team was first. You looked after each other.

The benefit of this philosophy would come up when you were down and hurting, tired, and miserable. The natural thought process would be just to close up, to think about yourself, and to just survive. The idea in the Teams was to think about your buddy. If you were spending all your energy thinking about if your swim buddy was doing well, or if a man in your squad was making it, then it took your mind off your own pain. That helped you; it made your own pain a bit less. And it motivated your buddy to do better. Then he, in turn, motivated you.

If you just sat there thinking about yourself, wrapped in your own misery, then you would miss a detail. If you just worried about your own equipment, you wouldn't get everything ready. But with two, three, four, or eight pairs of eyes on everyone's equipment, everything gets done, and everyone is the better for it. All the equipment gets cleaned and prepared faster, better, and more efficiently. And with that many people paying attention to the details, not much has a chance of being missed. That makes it better for the whole operation as well.

An individual, a person just concentrating on his own situation, could get through a certain part of the training at BUD/S. A number of individuals made it through First Phase, and they even got through Hell Week. But once you got to Second Phase, that's when you had to rely on a swim buddy to get through the evolutions. There was a lot of diving and you could only work with your swim buddy, that other person who was with you on a swim. You had to operate as a team, or you couldn't get the job done.

There are certain aspects of BUD/S that an individual can get through. But the overall aspects of the training prevent that individual from graduating. There just isn't any way to get through training without learning the value of teamwork and just what it means to be in a Team.

During Second Phase, you relied on just one other person. Underwater, your life would literally be in their hands. There's no way to call for help when you get in trouble underwater. In Third Phase, you were relying on seven other individuals. You had to work as a squad. As a group, you had to patrol and do the mission together.

For one individual to do what he wants to do, what he felt was best for himself, that would jeopardize the lot. That kind of behavior is unacceptable in the Teams, and it is gotten rid of in training. The instructors would see it, and the class officer in charge would see it. If that person wanted to be an individual, if he didn't want to become part of the team, he would be singled out and reprimanded accordingly. Or he would just go away.

We were told in training that no SEAL has ever been left behind in the field of combat. That is bred into us from the first day of training. Out at San Clemente Island, my squad went through a fire and movement exercise where we were broken up into two fire teams of four men each. One fire team would give supporting fire to the other fire team as it moved back. The orders somehow got mixed up and one of our fire teams ended up getting "killed," according to the instructors.

That was a simulation, of course; we didn't have students killed just for a training point. But because of that situation, the fire team I was in charge of had to recover the others. We had to run in, under fire, and recover our Teammates and their weapons. Rushing forward, we grabbed up the bodies and the gear, threw them over our shoulders, and carried them out for about a klick and a half or two klicks.

That situation was conducted under training conditions, in a very controlled atmosphere. As soon as we picked up the men and had them on our shoulders, the aggressor squad backed off on their firing and we were allowed to carry our simulated dead away.

That wasn't enjoyable. I didn't like it at all. It hurt to even move, and the area was very hilly and full of potholes. But it gave you the feeling that men's lives depended on you. You would have to carry a man out on your back if anything happened to him. That really drove home the point that you wanted to stay alive—and that there was no way you would ever leave anyone behind. You would bring them back with you.

The BUD/S student of today learns the traditions of the Teams as he goes through training. All the military looks on their traditions, those things that made us what we are today, with pride. In the Teams, the first men who conducted operations against the enemy were the Frogmen of World War II. From what I understand, they've called these ancestors of ours the "Naked Warrior." They went in and conducted their missions on enemy beaches wearing a pair of swim trunks and fins, and very little else. They did their work basically naked, with limited or no weapons and little in the way of even clothing.

These were our ancestors, they were where we came from, and we wanted to hold on to that somehow. Today, we run around in jungle boots and cammies, with thirty pounds of gear on us, but we still have that connection with the Naked Warrior. That UDT man in World War II, in just a pair of shorts, isn't that different from us today.

Often times, our job is to go in "slick," with minimal equipment and as little weapons as possible. What you are carrying with you is what you have, and you aren't going to get any more once you go in. With that, we're doing a job that nobody else can do, that nobody else wants to do. And we're in an environment that few are familiar with—the water.

The SEALs are the best there is in the water. That's our environment. When something has to be done in the ocean, river, or riverine environment, that's when the commands call on us. We look back on those men in a pair of shorts, with maybe a dagger strapped to their leg, and that was all they had to work with. They got the job done, they were our ancestors—could we do any less?

Those are who we look up to, who we want to remember when we go in on an operation. Whether we're loaded for bear or stripped down to our shorts for a basic reconnaissance, we keep the image of the men who have done it before us.

Even though BUD/S training is just about behind us, we still have a way to go before were are really in the Teams. For six months, we'll be watched and tested. Only after our probationary time is completed will we be awarded the Naval Special Warfare Insignia—the Trident.

The Trident means acceptance to me. It is the symbol that you've made it, that your initiation into the brotherhood of the warrior is behind you. To join the Teams, you have to pay your dues, and BUD/S and probation are those dues. The Trident shows that you've earned your right to wear it. It isn't like other military training. You don't just pass classes, do your flights, and boom, there's your pin. You don't just spend time onboard a ship, take a test, and wear a badge. You have to earn the right to wear the Trident.

BUD/S training is considered the hardest military training course in the world. And it's only the basic selection course. All BUD/S does is weed out the men who don't have the heart to do what it takes; it's from there that you go on to advanced training. It's only after you have completed your advanced training that you go on to your probationary period with a Team.

They evaluate you during probation to see if you have learned just what it takes to be in the Teams, and not just that you can do the job, but that you have the heart and mind to continue.

In the Teams, it's a never-ending process of training and evaluation. At the point that it is decided that you have actually proven yourself—and that's a year down the road from when you started in BUD/S—then you receive your Trident. It's a well-earned symbol. It's the Holy Grail for BUD/S students.

Then, once you've received your Trident, the training starts all over again. Now, you're expected to step up to an even higher standard of performance, do even better, keep training, and keep performing. You have to work to stay the best.

Jacob Woroniecki, Operational Specialist Third Class

I've been in the Navy approximately a year and a half, and approximately seven months of that have been at BUD/S. It's a straight-through class for me, no roll-backs. I only want to do this once.

I heard about the Teams from a friend of mine who was a martial arts instructor and an ex-SEAL. I just learned about his lifestyle and was interested for about four or five years. Now, I've gone on from there.

BUD/S was a lot different than I expected when I arrived here. It was a little more regimented than I thought it would be, and it was definitely a stress-shock at first. But you acclimate to the situation very quickly with the rest of the students and hear all the different stories about what you need to do and what you need to not do. You get the scoop on the situation and soon get used to it.

The physical end of BUD/S during First Phase definitely is a stress test. It wears you down both physically and mentally. But if you come in as a regular athlete or someone who has done any kind of physical activity beforehand, it's not as bad. But it doesn't matter what kind of athlete you are or what kind of physical level you are, it definitely will be draining. That is for sure.

The most draining part is the cold water. Cold water takes the most from you simply because it taps as much as it possibly can out of you. The push-ups and the sit-ups and all of that take it from you as well, but nothing like the cold water does. It takes more out of you than anything else.

You remember about the first two and a half days of Hell Week. After that, it starts to become like a daydream. It was stressful, but you just do it. You just keep on going through it. You forget a lot. Even though you're going through it, and your legs are moving one in front of the other, you start to forget. Then it becomes basically like a dream.

I just had to keep going. You don't quit, not because everybody else is, you just keep going because you don't stop. That's part of the training, too, I guess. You just don't stop because you have to keep going, you have to do it.

What got me through it? Well, I have a family, and I knew they were behind me 100 percent of the way. That's always good to have in the back of your mind when it's dark and cold. Even though you have a lot of friends around you, you have to have something inside you. For me, it was my family. The friends I was with helped, too, but it was definitely my family who pulled me through the most.

Every day when my alarm went off, I thought of quitting. If the bell would have been close to my alarm, I'm afraid that would have been ringing just about as much. But the walk to the bell was too far, and much too far in the morning. Everybody who says they don't think about quitting is a liar; they always do, but you just don't—that's the real difference.

The most enjoyable part of training for me probably was Third Phase, where you learn tactics, demolitions, and weapons. The parts you don't like stand out slightly, but they're a good majority of BUD/S. The things you enjoyed and the things you learned that you can use later on, you definitely remember. Those are the things that stand out in my memory the most I think.

Hearing the phrase "secure from Hell Week" is incredible. At first, you don't believe it. The entire week is stress games and more than a little bit of mind games. The first time you hear that phrase, what goes through you is of course doubt and disbelief. Then, when you look around and you see that it's really happening, it's just such a relief. You can finally let down some of that guard you had during Hell Week. You can finally consider sleeping and actually getting some good food. It's just an awesome relief.

I helped a few of my Teammates get through Hell Week. A few of them you can't help. Some guys just want to quit. You can restrain them as much as possible, but when they want to really quit, you can just see it in their eyes and you have to let them go. That's really hard.

But the friends you know can make it just need a little push, a little shove, or a little nudge—mentally or physically. Those are the ones who you definitely remember. And we have a lot of them in our class at this point, guys who didn't want to do it, but they did, and they're so happy that they did.

Everyone helps everybody in BUD/S. Everyone is going to have a lull, a low time and you help them past it. I've been helped before. Just a nudge can do it when you're slightly depressed because the last few days have been really hard, really difficult, and you're mentally and physically drained. That's when someone kind of gives you a mental push, just says "let's go," and you go.

There's an expression, "There is no 'I' in SEAL Team." That expression comes from the fact that you're not necessarily a robot, just going along like everyone else. But it's everything together, everybody together all at once. If one guy gets wet, everybody's going to get wet. If one guy suffers, everyone will suffer. If one guy's behind, everybody's going to be behind. That's true, it goes throughout BUD/S. And I don't know yet, but I'm sure it goes throughout the Teams as well.

We never leave anybody behind. It doesn't matter if it's in training, in PT, on a run, or anywhere. We wait for everybody. Everyone starts and stops together.

Having a swim buddy is something that's drilled into us from the beginning of BUD/S. It's the buddy who watches your back. When you're tired, he's the one watching. When he's tired, you're the one watching. A swim buddy is from the first day of BUD/S until, as I understand it, the last day you're a Frogman. A swim buddy is important. He's covering your back, watching your six behind you and you're watching the front. It's just the most important thing.

The Trident, to me, means accomplishment. Everyone goes into BUD/S, or goes into the SEAL program, for one individual thing, and I'm sure that thing is self-accomplishment, to prove something to themselves. To me, the Trident means accomplishment. It means I've gone through some of the hardest training in the world—and I have more to go—and that I've taken it by the neck and accomplished it.

I've been climbing that hill, but I'm not near the top yet. It's a long road. But after six or seven months of training, you start to realize that patience is so important. I have a feeling getting that bird is going to be better than graduating from BUD/S.

The Naked Warrior is a reference that basically means you don't need all those breathing tanks and all that different armament, you just need yourself. It's the thinking warrior.

There are a lot of different parts of the military that suggest you need a lot of weapons, a lot of equipment, a lot of this and that. But the Naked Warrior, to a lot *of us, means that you are a thinking warrior. You don't need all that, you just need yourself and your brain, and you can get through so much more than the average.*

Who are the men who've been in the Teams before me? Wow, there are so many, so many people who I look up to. All the chiefs, the stories we've heard from our different instructors, you just look up to them for all they've been through, all the training they've done, all the different platoons they've been a part of, and all the deployments they've done. It's amazing just to meet these men.

Why do I want to be a SEAL? Interesting question. Self-accomplishment. It's just another rung on the ladder to being a better person, and being one of the best. That's about it, being the best. Everybody wants to be good, not many get to be the best. Being a SEAL in the military today, you can't do much better than that.

■ Chapter 67

The New Teams and the Future

Since 2002, the organization, deployment, and even the number of SEAL Teams have undergone substantial changes. As it was when the UDTs became SEAL and SDV Teams in 1983, the new changes should significantly enhance the operational capabilities of the SEAL Teams and the Naval Special Warfare Groups. The Teams shall remain a force multiplier, with an effect far greater than their size would dictate, well into the foreseeable future.

Odd-numbered Teams—SEAL Teams One, Three, and Five as well as SDVT-One—are still on the West Coast under the overall command of Special Warfare Group One. Even-numbered Teams—SEAL Teams Two, Four, and Eight as well as SDVT-Two—are on the East Coast at Little Creek, Virginia, and are under the command of Special Warfare Group Two. As of 2002, two new SEAL Teams have been added to the roster, SEAL Teams Seven and Ten.

SEAL Team Seven, part of SpecWarGru-One, was commissioned on 17 March 2002. On the East Coast, SEAL Team Ten was also commissioned on 19 April 2002. Although the newest SEAL Teams add to the overall number of Teams, they do not add significantly to the overall number of active SEALs, which currently stands at about 2,200.

The lack of increase in the number of SEALs is due to the change of size of the Teams themselves. Instead of being made up of eight operational platoons of sixteen men each, SEAL Teams were reduced in size to six platoons. The concept of the smaller Teams fits in with the new idea of deploying SEAL Teams as a whole unit, a squadron, complete with a special boat team and necessary support personnel.

A nuclear submarine moves out on an exercise with the Navy SEALs. Secured to the deck of the submarine, and accessible through a loading hatch, is a Dry Deck Shelter (DDS) capable of transporting an SDV or rubber boat and launching or recovering the same while remaining submerged.

U.S. Navy

The idea of geographical areas of responsibility for each separate Team has changed with the new deployment procedures. Now, a SEAL squadron will deploy for six months as a unit. Each SEAL Team will have an eighteen-month period at their home base between deployments. This allows the SEALs of a particular Team to train for at least six months prior to a deployment with the support people, especially the special boat personnel, who they will be operating with.

New equipment and technology is being adopted by the Teams to meet new challenges. The newest big-ticket item for the Teams, especially the SDV Teams, is the Advanced SEAL Delivery System (ASDS). Instead of being the wet-type of underwater craft that the Teams have been using since the 1950s, exposing the men to the cold of the water, cramped conditions, and the need for breathing equipment, the ASDS is a true mini-submarine.

The inside of the ASDS is dry. SEALs will be able to operate in a shirt-sleeve environment, traveling to their target until it becomes time for them to lock out of the ASDS and continue with their mission. The ASDS is transportable by air, and the new classes of nuclear submarines being developed today are designed with the means to attach the ASDS to their hulls. The nuclear submarines of just a short time from now will have the ability to transport and deploy SEALs, dry deck shelters, or the ASDS from the moment of their launch.

■　■　■

THE SEALs have met every challenge given to them over the years. They have adapted to meet the requirements of their job or of a changing world environment. With the joining of a SEAL to NASA and the space program, they have even gone beyond what they themselves thought possible only a few decades ago. Thanks to Captain William Shepherd, the first commander of *Space Station Alpha*, the SEALs may now be able to change their famous name. Instead of being SEa, Air, and Land, SEALS can now stand for SEa, Air, Land, and Space.

Dave Maynard, Corpsman Second Class

My mother used to read us stories out of Reader's Digest*s, and one day she picked this story about the Navy SEALs. That was where I first heard about them and was really fascinated. I think I was a freshman or so in high school, and the first time I heard the story about the SEALs, I wanted to be one. It was instant, that's what I wanted to be. All the way through high school, I knew I was going to join the Navy and become a SEAL.*

When I was a kid in school, I was a total John Wayne, Audie Murphy wannabe warrior. I wanted to join the military. I probably was going to be a Marine, I just wanted to do that. I felt a calling that I should spend my time serving my country, and that's what I was going to do out of high school. What I specifically was going to go into, I didn't know. But ever since I was a small boy, I knew I was going to be in the military. I just knew it.

My enlistment into the Navy came right out of high school. On the delayed entry program I had six months to report, and the time counted toward my reserve time. That was cool, I thought. The reserve time wouldn't take effect until after I got out. That would be time I wouldn't have to spend in the reserves after I left active duty. It wasn't really much of a deal anyway, but as a high schooler it looked pretty good to me. That was 1971, the year I actually enlisted, but I didn't have to go on to active duty until January 1972.

Believe it or not, I had a Navy recruiter who actually told me the truth. And I got into a special BUD/S guarantee program, which meant I would go straight from boot camp to BUD/S. While in boot camp, I was in a special company for prospective SEALs. So I went through four weeks of regular boot camp, then I was already into a regular SEAL boot camp company. We did special training, our regular boot camp stuff, and trips to Coronado, where we ran on the beaches. We did all kinds of things to make us more prepared for BUD/S.

As long as I stayed qualified, everything would go according to the paperwork. So I did everything my recruiter said, because as far as I was concerned, he was the bible on the subject of my getting to the Teams. That guy told me everything I needed to do, and I went by the book and got there. I went straight from boot camp to BUD/S training.

Class 68 was the BUD/S class I started with, but I broke my arm during about the eighth week of training and finished with Class 69. I didn't have to go through Hell Week twice, but after I broke my arm, I was really afraid that I would be dropped from training. In those days, a rollback was a rare thing. If you got hurt in training, you were usually gone until you could rehabilitate and come back maybe a year or two later. That's what really frightened me, the idea of going to the Fleet. To me, that was worse than dying.

Fortunately, I had managed to impress Scotty Lyon, the officer who was in charge of our phase at the time, along with Chief Kenny Estok. At least I think they thought a lot of me because I was a really motivated trainee. So they rolled me back to the following class and I didn't have to leave while I recuperated. The medical department put a fiberglass cast on my arm, and I continued BUD/S training with this lightweight cast in place.

When you're nineteen years old, it's great to have a mentor, somebody you really look up to. Scotty Lyon had that professional look, he was the consummate professional, and he had a way of motivating me like I've never been motivated in my life. I had some great instructors, but Scotty Lyon really stood out.

It didn't matter what physical condition I was in or how cold or how miserable I was; when Scotty Lyon walked into an evolution, I felt no pain. In his presence, I was unstoppable. If he was to tell me to jump off a tower on my head, I would jump from the tower. I knew he wouldn't want me hurt and would only tell me to do things I needed to do. I had that much trust and faith in him that I wouldn't question any direction of his. It was because that was the kind of people I idolized that meant I could never quit BUD/S. How could you quit BUD/S when you would give your life for this guy? That's the kind of person he emulated to me.

Overall, the cold, the shivering until you felt like you couldn't move anymore, was the hardest part of training for me. It wasn't just the cold, it was being literally fatigued from shivering so much. Parts of my body would ache from the shivering, and there would be the pins-and-needles pain from the cold and the shaking. I would have preferred to be numb from the cold, anything but that complete pain of just shivering. I became so tired of it. My jaw, and my neck muscles would all convulse and twitch. That drove me nuts.

As far as the running and the swimming, I loved running—they couldn't hurt me with running. The swimming I loved because we were moving and I could stay warm. The obstacle course was something I loved. Obstacle course day was something I could look forward to, especially in comparison to some of the other things we could have been doing. The physical part, the physical challenge of BUD/S, was something I loved. When they were trying to make us do things, I was having fun. But it was the cold that really got to me. That was the biggest thing about that training that got to me.

I was so driven that the thought of quitting never even came to my mind during Hell Week. I was going to be a Navy SEAL. Period. End of story. There was never any question of my quitting; it wasn't an option. I was going to make it through. They would have to physically get rid of me or I would have to break something (which I managed to do) or die—but I wasn't going to quit.

The swim buddy concept is basically the two-man rule. Never do anything without your swim buddy. My swim buddy's name was Mike Faketty. I had torn a cartilage in my knee right before Hell Week and when we did the fourteen-mile run, I literally limped the fourteen miles. When I got done with the run, I could barely walk. And we went right from the run, ate chow quickly, and went into a couple-mile swim. As soon as I hit the water, my whole body turned into one giant cramp, and I could not move my legs. The only way I could swim was to crawl along with my arms. Mike hooked into me and started towing me. He towed me for two miles.

The instructors came over in the boat, told me to get out of the water, and told me to quit. I told them to go fly a kite—in gentle terms. They told Mike to stop towing me or he was going to get thrown out of training. He told them to pack sand. And he got me to where I had to be, in spite of my being physically screwed up. I was a handicap, and he towed me anyway, even at the threat of being thrown out of BUD/S. That's a swim buddy.

Maybe I'm twisted, but Hell Week for me was a proving thing. It helped me define myself, to see myself measured against other guys who went through Hell Week, guys who I really looked up to. I was with these guys the whole way; went through what they did. The ending of Hell Week wasn't so much a relief. I could have gone more days, it wouldn't have mattered to me. The bottom line was that it told me I had accomplished something here. And I was damned proud to be next to those guys who I finished Hell Week with.

To be honest with you, graduation from BUD/S wasn't a big up for me. I just didn't want to get out of there. I wanted to get into the Teams. Vietnam was still going on, and I was so motivated that I wanted to go to the jungles and operate. I was dying to operate. I wanted to get graduation over with, get the pins and diploma, and head out of the door. Just let me get to Jump School; I already had my orders for the trip to Fort Benning.

So for me, graduation was a nice thing, but I had my objectives down the road. Graduation had been a long time coming. I had rolled back a class with that broken arm of mine, so I was there a long time—from May to December. Now I was very impatient and glad to be out of there. All I wanted was to be a SEAL, not a BUD/S trainee.

Fort Benning and Jump School were a blast. I have tremendous respect for the Army. They put up with us, and we were a bunch of jerks. We just had to break all the rules, and we pissed them off all the time. On the runs, we would have to have cigars in our mouths just to piss them off. We would do thing to make them drop us for extra push-ups. Because I had broken my arm, I became very proficient at one-armed push-ups. Even though I had a broken arm at BUD/S, I still had to do push-ups.

When they dropped me down once, I had my hand in my pocket, so I banged out ten one-armed push-ups. The Army only dropped for ten push-ups at a time. I'd just gotten out of SEAL training. When we were dropped for push-ups at BUD/S, it was for fifty at a time. I was going to drop for ten push-ups? Oh, hurt me please.

We had to piss off those Army instructors so they would drop us for push-ups a lot, because we needed the workout. It wasn't like they were going to work us out; what they were doing looked like a joke to us. One sergeant would just get pissed at us. When I was doing my push-ups one-handed, he would run up to me and get in my face shouting. It didn't affect me any, because I had been shouted at by BUD/S instructors.

We did have another sergeant who had been to Vietnam, and he loved SEALs. All the other sergeants hated us, but this one thought the world of SEALs. He called me over and told me to drop down and "Do that again." More one-handed push-ups.

"Now do it with the other arm," he said.

No problem. I banged out ten with the other arm.

"Now do twenty."

I just kept banging out push-ups. It didn't matter which arm I used, and he just stood there amazed as the number of push-ups I was doing kept getting higher and higher. I dug it because I was working out.

Later on, that same sergeant called me into his office and told me that he had the world of respect for SEALs. But he had a job to do and just wanted to know if I would play the game. He knew we were the best and he respected us, and just asked me to play by the rules.

When he said that, just by treating me with that respect, I snapped in and played the Army game. I became an Army, squared-away airborne trooper at that point. He gave me respect, and I had a lot of appreciation for that, so I certainly had to give the same respect back.

To be honest about it, while I was going through jump school I was still pretty motivated. Yeah, this was great. I was sitting there with my buddies through two weeks of ground school and jumped from towers, little buildings, and everything. This was going to be great.

As soon as they opened the doors to the plane and I saw Mother Earth and realized I was going to be stepping out into that big wind tunnel outside the plane, I literally freaked. This was a new fear, and I'd never had fear like that before. It blew me away. We were ordered to hook up, and I eventually hooked my static line to the overhead cable. I was shaking just a bit.

Then we checked equipment, and everything was okay. I hoped to God that it was all okay, because I didn't want to meet him right now. I was actually going to do this thing. Motivation wasn't what was on my mind right then—the great big step out that door and down was on my mind. All of a sudden, there was the shout for us all to go, and I see these guys going out the door.

They would jump out the door and—woomp! They would be snatched away by the wind. Everybody was going out the door and the line was getting shorter, and I could swear I heard guys bouncing off the outside of the aircraft. Then it was my turn at the door.

Supposedly, you have this airborne position you're supposed to take as you stand in the door. You jump out and count to four. I went out the door and had my eyes closed tight. My scream was snatched away by the wind, just like I was. I knew I was going to die or get sucked up in the engine or something. As it was, I did end up banging off the side of the aircraft.

Supposed to count to four? Yeah, right. I had my eyes closed and just felt the wind go by. The parachute opened and so did my eyes. Looking up, I had a good, full canopy. I had no idea what the count was when that canopy opened, but it was open and I wasn't going to splat into the ground or gum up the inside of an aircraft engine.

Now, I was right back to being Joe controlled SEAL again. Yeah, this is great. Okay, the landing didn't go badly and I'm alive. No problems. It scared the crap out of me. It took two or three jumps for me to finally get squared away on doing that. But it was good, because it made me face my fear. That was the thing about over-coming fear: it wasn't about not having it; it was about getting past it and doing the job. But it did scare the crap out of me.

Finally, I got to a SEAL Team, and I loved it. I was over there with legends like Mike Thornton and Leon Rauch. Leon Rauch looked like James Coburn, only this guy was for real. James Coburn is an actor who does movie parts; Leon Rauch walked it for real life. And he was just one of many. I got in a platoon where my lead-ing petty officer (LPO) was a SEAL named Wade Puckett. He had six or seven trips to Vietnam or some crazy thing like that and I didn't know it. He didn't even look like a SEAL. He was the quietest, mellowest guy in the world, until we started oper-ating and he was training us.

The first time I saw Wade Puckett tactically move and patrol, I was in awe. I'd never seen a human being move like that. What he taught me was invaluable. He took a liking to me and was training me to become a point man, so I got a lot of per-sonal attention from him.

Another guy in the platoon was Kirby Horrell, a crazy and funny guy. Other guys—Frank Sale, Terry Davis, and more—were just funny. Every evolution we would do was like spending the day with a bunch of Richard Pryors because they were so funny. Until they started operating or serious training that is. Everything would click. All of a sudden they were all these serious, dedicated, knew-what-they-were-doing professionals. Total professionals. But in between, they were the Keystone Cops, and I was very happy to be there.

One thing that really stood out, and this was probably a major event for me, was a training op we did with Wade Puckett when I was all of maybe twenty years old. After a training op, the standard thing is to do a debrief of the op. We were all just standing there, and I was surrounded by these guys who just impressed the hell out of me. I felt lucky that they trusted me enough to let me have a gun, let alone be out there working with them.

Then Wade just floors me during the debrief. He looks at me and asks, "Well, Dave, what did you think?"

He was asking me, airhead of the north, what I thought. And I started putting out what I thought. He took what I thought under consideration, and he listened to what I said. I actually helped developed an SOP for an upcoming event, because Wade developed the SOP from my recommendations right there on the spot. All I could think was, Wow.

That pulled me into the Teams. That took a twenty-year-old kid standing next to these decorated combat veterans and made him an accepted person. I had gone from being a kid in high school, and after a year's training, and was now standing next to men I considered some of the best fighters in the world. Here I am, I thought, I'm home.

After six months of very intense work went by, I had completed my probationary period in the Teams, although I hadn't noticed the time going by. I was called in to the air loft for something. I think I was getting ready to head out to Free Fall school, so I figured they were going to give me another briefing on something.

When I got to the air loft, there were a bunch of the guys from the platoon in there. One of the guys had a Trident in his hand. He said something like, "Hey, we want to give you this award. Here's your Trident." And he stuck it on my chest.

There were three metal prongs, about a quarter-inch long, on the back of the Trident so it could be secured to the uniform. I had no idea what was coming; I was too new to the Teams. After he put it on my chest, he hauled back and slammed his hand down hard onto it. Boom. He stuck it right into my chest.

It actually felt kind of good, after the shock wore off. I looked down and saw that big, gaudy, metal badge on my chest and just said, "Hooyah."

That was a good day. I had to buy the beer, but I was a very proud young man, and I felt very fortunate to be standing there with these men, and to be accepted as one of them. Very fortunate indeed.

For me, the Trident is an emblem of honor. That I could wear something that has represented so much to so many men is humbling. Here I was, just this average

Joe Blow guy, and I'm wearing something that represents to me these heroes who have done all these wonderful things through their history. I was just one of the guys who came along through the flow of time, and I got to wear that. Honor, that's what it means.

One thing that all the guys do is tell Hell Week stories. Joe DiMartino went through kind of a different Hell Week. His Hell Week was actually landing on the beaches in Normandy during the D-Day invasion. He didn't do the five-or six-day no-sleep deal, but going through that qualifies him I think.

In BUD/S, you go through Hell Week to simulate the exhaustion and stress of a battlefield. The mental toughness of that guy and the guys with him to do that landing without being properly prepared, that tells you a lot about that gentleman. That requires a lot of respect.

Some of the operations I did with the Teams included training to go to Vietnam. My platoon was the next one in order to rotate to Vietnam, but we never went. Command shut down deployments to Vietnam just as my platoon was trained up to go.

For me, that was a big let-down. To spend a year and a half to train to go do a job, and then be told no, you can't go do what you were trained to do. That was a tough thing to hear.

At that point, I worked up with two more platoons, going overseas on several different occasions. They were just your typical platoon workup, go overseas, and train foreign troops. There was no combat; all the wars were over and there was no combat left. America's position at that point was definitely no more fighting.

However, I did get recalled for the Gulf War. That was a good opportunity for me to see what the Teams were doing, see the new guys, and watch how they operated. They're still the same as they've always been. Watching the platoon work up, you see the same characters today as were in the Teams back then.

What I do see is a difference between the peacetime platoons and the wartime platoons. With my first platoon I worked up with, I felt honored when they finally came up to you and asked you to be a part of the platoon. That was no small honor that they would trust you to operate with them. The older SEALs would kick guys out of a platoon in a heartbeat if they didn't want to operate with them. There were guys who graduated BUD/S and went over to the SEAL Team who nobody wanted to work with. Boom, they were out in the Fleet.

As time has gone on, things have changed. Without war, you don't get to test the true mettle of the men. So some of the platoons are just made up of a lot of green guys. There is a lack of combat experience today. The newer platoons I was working with during the Gulf War were good, but they just didn't have that combat experience that gives you a greater edge.

That doesn't mean to say that once those new guys got their taste of combat, that they wouldn't be ass-kicking SEALs. You could easily see that they wanted that opportunity. They were eager, and they wanted to go into harm's way very badly.

I had a chance to train some of the platoon for the Gulf War, and it was a great opportunity to work and train with them. Other than that, I wasn't in any special operations that are worth even mentioning.

Is there anything a SEAL can't do? That's one of the biggest issues with SEALs, because you learn what your limitations are. You understand what you can't do. That's why you have to cheat a little. You know if you can't do something, so you figure out what you have to do to get around it and still get the job done.

When you can't do something is the most important lesson to learn, and that's probably what gets more SEALs killed than anything else. There are idiots out there who think that SEALs can do all these weird things like jump at night into high seas with high winds, not prepared for that kind of jump. There's a guy who thinks you can do that—and you can't. Other guys will plan ops where the SEALs have to swim fifteen miles to get to the beach, then patrol for another twenty miles. There is a plain reality about what a SEAL actually can and cannot do. What your limitations are is the first thing you have to realize and it can be a very hard lesson to accept.

When you put a platoon of SEALs together, and they put all their heads together to attack a problem, it will absolutely amaze you what they can come up with. When everybody starts throwing their ideas in, you can come up with some incredibly unique and innovative ways to accomplish the objective.

Say the platoon was ordered to go in and hit these Marines. We did this mission as a reserve unit. Going in, we found that there were some three hundred Marines guarding one target. They had night vision, heat sensors, thermal imagers—all the hi-tech gadgets to try to catch us. We sat and figured out what we were going to do by putting our heads together as a team. In most cases, the officers stood by but just kind of shut up and let the enlisted men figure things out.

With out plan roughed out, we told the officers what we wanted to do and we all worked it out together. The officer did the big planning thing and we prepared to do the op. Going in, we had four different squads hit that target from four different directions. The Marines never knew we were in and out.

When you see stuff like that done by a group of men, it's impressive to watch. Some of the operations we did were sudden actions that took a fast response. When the Mayaguez incident went down and the Khmer Rouge captured the Mayaguez off Cambodia, I happened to be overseas at the time. We were called on to go in and take back the ship. We were supposed to go in unarmed to the beach where the ship was being held, hold up a white flag, and ask for our sailors back. Obviously, we told them to go fly a kite.

We did have one SEAL platoon, Bravo Platoon, that was going to go in and hit the target, recapture the ship, and take back the hostages. My platoon was a backup platoon to support the first one in. We were all locked and loaded and ready to do it. Then Command backed down from sending us in. Instead, a bunch of Marines were sent in, got shot up, and generally didn't have a very good time of it.

We weren't going to go walk in on the beach, like the Marines were directed to do. We would have done it the smart way—sneak in and kill them before they could kill us or the hostages. Command just didn't want us to go.

A result of the incident was that the SEALs received a directive to develop a way to get onboard a ship. So we figured out a way to get onboard a ship from the water. That platoon started the ship-boarding procedure, working from the water where a group of swimmers can get on deck to take back a ship.

That's evolved into quite a large evolution now for ship-boarding and ship take-downs. It's kind of interesting to see how it's grown. That just shows you how people adding their ideas to one idea keeps it growing and growing. We literally used to use a slingshot to shoot a little lead ball up and over a boom that was sticking out over the side of a ship. That lead ball would carry a fishing line up and over the boom that would let us pull a heavier line up after it. Then we could pull up a rope and finally a ladder.

Another way we used to board a ship was by going in with swimmer delivery vehicles, up to a ship underwater, work the ship, get all the way up on deck, and continue on. That worked great. Now they are a lot more scientific about coming up with these ideas.

SEALs spend a lot of time in water. Ocean critters have not been something I've ever had much trouble with, although some of the encounters I had while I went though BUD/S training were interesting. Because I worked as a point man, I was always selected as the swimmer scout, the first man in, on insertions.

My swim buddy and I were swimming in to the beach during training when some sea lions decided they wanted to play with us. The problem is, at night, when big things swim through the water, they make this phosphorescent glow. All you see is this big missile-looking thing swimming around your legs, and you don't know if it's a sea lion or a shark.

I was not having a good time on that insertion. All I was doing was waiting for the crunch of teeth into bone. I didn't know what these things in the water around me were, and I was freaking out. I didn't know they were sea lions until one of them popped up and looked at us. It was just kind of a "Hey, what's happening?" kind of thing on his part, then he was gone.

I was trying to be quiet, but when you see something come up and look at you, and it looks like some kind of sea monster in the dark, you tend to swallow a bit of sea water. I think I put down about three gallons. That was hairy, and swimming at night was not my forte—especially not after seeing that stupid movie Jaws.

Watching Jaws and then doing a night swimmer recon was a dumb thing to do. Real smart. Your imagination tends to run a little wild, and any deep string music from the background would have gotten a very bad reaction from me. So of course my swim buddy starts singing the soundtrack to Jaws. He could see that I was really strung out. To this day, I still think he's an asshole for that.

Other than that problem with my imagination, I never had much in the way of shark encounters. Mostly, I had problems with sea snakes—the most poisonous snakes on earth. We would be out doing operations in the water and I would have some wrap around my feet. Sea snakes aren't aggressive, so if you're careful and play the game with them, they don't give you much trouble. They have really small mouths so it's hard for them to bite, but don't piss them off.

There was another critter encounter several of us had underwater, but this one was done on purpose. We were one of the first groups to be tested for the dolphin program, which was the counterswimmer program where the Navy would use dolphins to locate swimmers around ships.

The testers, a bunch of idiots as it turned out, told us to go and swim in to a designated ship. They told us that there were going to be dolphins in the area and when they tapped us or butted us with their nose, we should swim to the surface. In effect, we were told to surrender to a fish.

I thought this was kind of cool and not much work, so my swim buddy and I were swimming in to the target ship, really hugging the bottom and staying low. We figured that the lower we were, the harder it would be for the dolphin to figure out just what and where we were. Wrong.

The next thing I knew, my swim buddy was knocked into me. This wasn't a tap—his whole body slammed into me from the side. We were just swimming along and then—boom! He was freaked out and pretty close to panic. When I looked at him, all I could see were these two gigantic staring eyeballs filling his face mask. I wondered was just what the hell his problem was. Then I found out.

The dolphin came back around and stopped right between us. That critter looked at us and we could see the meaning in his eyes—You want some more? My swim buddy and I just looked at each other for a moment. We didn't know what to do, and both of us were frozen in place. We were so scared and didn't know what the hell this thing was going to do to us. We didn't know if he was horny, playful, or just mean.

Freaked out is a pretty good description of how my swim buddy and I felt right about then. The dolphin took off and we both knew that he was coming around to hit us again, so we headed to the surface fast—real fast.

Our original plan was to cheat,

Tuffy, one of the first porpoises trained by the Navy as part of their Marine Mammals program.

U.S. Navy

to just ignore the dolphin when he tapped us and just keep going. Well, it wasn't a tap and we didn't ignore him. After we were hit like that, we were on the surface quick. No more of that, no more of those big fish under the water. That's their ocean.

Fortunately for me, when I left the active service, I stayed in the Department of Defense training programs, where I've been able to continuously train with the SEALs, either as a reservist or as a DoD employee. Over the course of the last thirteen or fourteen years, I've had the opportunity to train SEALs in a variety of areas. What I've seen in the younger SEALs is that they are very hungry for knowledge. They want to be SEALs as much as I did, and they have the skills and the physical capabilities to do it all.

I see these guys, and it's really great to watch them as we train them. We do some radical training with these guys today. You watch them at first struggle with the training, then all of a sudden they pick up what's going on and kick in and just blow you away with their capability. I get a chance now to train with S.W.A.T. teams and other special forces and law enforcement units—a lot of different training groups. The SEALs compared to these other people is just night and day.

With working with the history project, and having the opportunity to interview the guys from the World War II Teams and way back when, has solidified the connection I feel with the Naked Warrior of days gone past. When you go through BUD/S, a big part of it is UDT training. You're doing the drop and pickup (cast and recovery), the recons, the swims—you are a Frogman. You're still the Naked Warrior. Even today, the students are still doing BUD/S training as a Naked Warrior. It's a good portion of the curriculum.

And you totally identify with those older Frogs. If you could change time, you could take that guy from 1943 and put him into today's platoon of SEALs, you would have a group of all the same men. I really believe that. Listening to those vets, how they look at life, how they respond—that's the same guy as in the Teams today. I feel totally attached to them, and I feel blessed that those guys learned all those lessons in the past, some at a terrible cost, they were able to pass down to us. They give us all this history to look back on and live up to.

Working with these men on this project, saving their history, their own personal stories, it's just undescribable. Sometimes, you listen to these guys give an interview about say, landing at Normandy. These aren't actors, this isn't a movie, these men did it—they were there on those sands, hearing those explosions, feeling the bullets snapping past, and they did their jobs. Sometimes I have to go outside and take a half-hour walk just to get emotionally back for the next guy.

And you have to be ready for the next guy. You must show that respect. These guys have done so many phenomenal things, and the humility they show about what they did comes across. They give their Teammates credit for the job getting done—not what they did themselves but what they feel they all did. It puts you in your place. It humbles you to a point where you have a hard time accepting the fact that you are privileged to receive the honor of hearing their stories, let alone record them.

It's a high honor just to be able to sit next to these men and listen. We're very lucky.

I want that older generation to be known for what they did, and I want to see the younger generation accept the older. I want them all together to see that they are all uniquely one. They are all the Teams, all the way back. If it wasn't for those guys in World War II, doing what they did, these guys coming out now wouldn't have it. They would have a bunch of good gear and hard training, but they wouldn't have that soul inside. It wouldn't be there.

That training that was created way back in those dark days in World War II has followed through all these years. It's still finding the right guys to come out of the test of training. All the gear, all the high tech doesn't mean a thing without the right guys. And by doing this project, we're going to bring all the guys together.

When these new guys coming out of training go to reunions, they'll see the old guys sitting there, gray hair and not a lot of it, some hardly able to walk. Now they'll realize that those men are legends, that those people built the story of the Teams. They made the legend real with their blood, sweat, and sacrifice. I don't want to see the legends die, and this project will bring the legends to the forefront.

One subject I have studied for years is the mind-set of being prepared for combat. Because I trained to go to Vietnam, I went to sleep every night expecting to go into combat. I was prepared to go into combat, and I wanted to go. When I didn't get that opportunity, I missed out, and that desire to go never left me. The mystery of what combat is like, and how I would react to it, has never left me, either. I've been a student of it ever since.

I do a lot of force-on-force training—that's man-to-man fighting with hands or weapons, or shooting nonlethal projectiles at each other—for years and try to really understand the mind-set, and what's going on inside the heads of the guys who do this work.

What I see with the SEALs is an initial breakdown in their technique. They will make mistakes. But what you constantly see with the SEALs is their commitment to each other. Once you get them focused on their commitment to each other, past the nuts and bolts of what they are trying to learn, that's when they start doing incredible things so that they don't let their buddy down. They are more worried about their buddy getting shot than they are about themselves.

Of everything I've seen from this project, it is these people talking about their combat experiences and how they're bonded with the men they had those experi-

---

enccs with that stands out the most. They were in these hellacious gunfights, where they didn't know whether they would come out alive or not. When the fight was over, they looked to their left and right and saw their buddies still standing there. They fought right alongside each other.

That sends a message. They don't say it out loud. You're not going to hear the words come out of a SEAL's mouth. But there's a message in their actions, a knowledge that each and every SEAL lives with every day. That message is, "I love you so much that I'm willing to die with you. I'll die for you. There's no way I'll leave you in the field, dead or alive. I cannot leave you there." That's a powerful message.

How many people do you know in life that will give his or her life for you? Here you have a whole platoon of these guys working with each other on a day-to-day basis. That's why these guys cannot leave the Teams, because they'll never be with a group of people that care that much about them, that will sacrifice that much with them and for them.

Your Teammate is your brother, somebody you come to care so much about and know so well that you would do anything for—and you know he would do anything for you. You can abuse him physically, get in fights with him, argue with him, and cut him down, but it all actually brings you closer together. Being in the Teams is like having an extended family. When you get into a platoon, you have fourteen new Teammates, and you get very close to those new Teammates. That platoon goes away and you get another platoon, and now you have fourteen new family members. You get very tight with them as well.

The Teammate concept extends even beyond the platoon level. Maybe you'll work with another platoon and perhaps one of the guys you were in BUD/S with, or were in an earlier platoon together with, is there. You ask him what he thinks of another operator, and he tells you he thinks he's a good operator, that he would operate with him. That's probably the ultimate compliment you can get in the Teams: "I'd operate with that guy."

That's saying a lot. That's not just saying that you'd go and work with somebody. Operating with someone means that you trust them, that you can trust them with your life, that you'll risk your life for someone, that you'll go into combat with them. That's what makes it a tremendous compliment.

When you hear that no SEAL has ever been left in the field, a lot of people wonder why, if the guy is dead, would you risk everything to go back for a body? To put it in a more understandable frame, think about yourself as a parent and then think about your kid being hit by a car or something. Would you just leave him there, just laying at the side of the road? You couldn't leave your kid. And because you love your kid so much, whether he was dead or alive, you couldn't ever leave him behind. You'd risk your life for your child. The thought of walking away just couldn't enter your mind. That's loving your brother, your Teammate, so much that you wouldn't ever leave him behind.

That tenacity is what brings the Teams together. That's why they fight so well together, because they will die together. You'll have to kill every one of these guys if you're going to beat them—that's the only way.

Bill Shepherd, Captain, USN (Ret.)

First I was an ensign in UDT Eleven, a lieutenant, junior grade in SEAL Team One, then lieutenant and lieutenant commander in SEAL Team Two. Presently (1997), I'm assigned to NASA on a military detail as an active duty Navy captain. I've been working here at the Houston Space Center for fourteen years and have been on three shuttle flights. Fairly soon, my title is going to be Expedition Commander as I take my position as the first commander of the space station.

In the early 1960s, when the war in Vietnam was fairly active, I heard about the SEALs exploits in the Mekong Delta. Shortly after that, I went to the Naval Academy and there was a lot of insight at the Academy about what the SEALs were doing. We had several presentations at the Naval Academy during the course of my four years there that made me very interested in the Naval Special Warfare program and got me headed that way.

To be honest, I was kind of torn between being a pilot and being a Frogman. It turned out that I couldn't see quite well enough to do the kind of flying I wanted to do so I went to Coronado and became a Frogman.

There's an interesting question about what Hell Week was like for me. There were several classes, from about Class 59 through Class 67 that didn't have a Hell Week. As a member of Class 64, I'm in one of the few groups of Frogs and SEALs to go through BUD/S and never have a Hell Week. An observer from Class 68, the first class to resume Hell Week, watched Classes 66 and 67 and noticed that the instructors well made up for the classes not having a Hell Week. The expression was that they had Hell Month instead.

It's probably something that few SEALs will ever admit, that they never had a Hell Week, but there were very few SEALs who would even have had to admit it. It was a political thing for the most part. They tried to lower the number of people who dropped out of the course, but the numbers stayed the same pretty much throughout all the classes. The instructors just made up for the lack of that traditional week by harassing the students for a couple weeks instead of just one solid week.

One observer from Class 68 remembered watching Class 66 be up all the time. The instructors worked the class hard to be certain that the quality of the graduating students was up to their own exacting standards. Not having a Hell Week actually made training harder for us. We were under the gun until the day we graduated. That would have been different if we had gone through the Hell Week rite of passage.

Some family friends worked with the SEALs and I knew a lot about their activi-

ties before I made my decision to volunteer for training. I thought the Teams would be a real challenge. When I got to Coronado and became involved with the kind of work that Frogmen and SEALs were doing, I found that my original idea of it was very true. I think it's a very individual and very challenging part of the Navy.

I think our training as SEALs is important in a whole range of activities, including being an astronaut. The training teaches you to be responsible, to never underestimate yourself, and to always be a good Teammate. These are things that apply to almost any walk of life. It's helped me a great deal here at NASA with my being an astronaut, and I think the Teams would be a great experience for people in general.

It's kind of hard to say as a student just where you sit in the ranking of the class. I tried to be good at all things, not bad at any of them, and not really a standout. Part of being a good SEALs is being able to do everything at least well, which is what I've tried to do.

Comparing BUD/S training and astronaut training is difficult because you have two completely different groups of people. The difference between BUD/S and astronaut training is that the people who come to NASA to be astronauts have already been really accomplished people in their own careers, either operationally or academically. So you don't need a lot of sorting out or filtering of the people in order to get a good product. That kind of thing is done up front well before they ever reach training.

At BUD/S, it's a very stressful environment because you want to mold people into a certain way of thinking and acting. I think BUD/S is a lot more stressful to the students who attempt it, but I also think it is so stressful for good reason. Only those who can overcome the stress and still achieve the necessary requirements of BUD/S can complete the course. It filters out those people who are not motivated enough or who are just incapable of pushing themselves past their perceived limits.

In 1975, after having been in the Teams for five years, I went through part of the Navy's post-graduate program, which happened to be in Boston at MIT. It was just one of those career moves you don't often get the chance to make, so I jumped on it and did that for a couple years, then went right back to the SEAL community, except now on the East Coast.

I think BUD/S training is great from almost any aspect. There, you learn to accept huge challenges and learn not to limit yourself. We didn't have a lot of cold weather–specific training at BUD/S, but we were certainly made to stay out all night, wet and cold the entire time. That just shows you that your body and your mind can take a lot more than you think they can. That sort of knowledge is very useful in any kind of survival situation.

To me, the most notable guys in the SEAL community were some of the folks I worked with: Bill Foran, who we called fearless, was an incredible personality; Don

Crawford, who's still out in Coronado as a schoolteacher; Mike Fitzgerald, a lieutenant who worked with me a couple times. Mostly the guys who I remember and respect are some of the enlisted and senior enlisted I worked with, even the instructors at BUD/S.

My flight suit is part of my military uniform, and I wear my Trident on it every time I go flying. The outfits you wear here at NASA, either in the training aircraft or the space shuttle, are like a military uniform. The Air Force and the Navy pilots wear their wings, and people who have other military insignia wear them on their flight suits. I wear the Trident. Hopefully, when we're up on the station and doing something that gets televised back to earth, you'll be able to see the Trident up there.

It's kind of interesting what the Trident means, and what it means to me. I'm not sure who designed the Navy Special Warfare Insignia, but I think it's very appropriate for the kind of work we do. I also think it's significant that of all the military insignia on the planet, it's one of the few that's actually a complete animal, as the whole eagle is there.

In the heraldry and business of emblems in the United States, Federal Eagles with their heads erect and up are a sign of peace. When the head of the eagle is looking down, that means you're ready for war. I think that makes it a very fitting insignia for Team guys.

Working with the Russians today really is the last chapter in the Cold War. It's absolutely incredible. When I was an ensign of a junior grade in the Teams, being here and working with these guys was the last thing I thought I would ever be doing. And here we are, not only working together, but having a situation where we fly together in very tight, confined, hazardous environments where we've got to depend on each other. It's a complete turnaround from the roles we all had as military people two decades ago.

Just to give you an example, I've been training in Russia for the better part of two years. All the folks I work with were on the military base outside of Moscow that was set up in the 1960s specifically to provide the Russian military with their corps of cosmonauts. I was there for a long time and people were very curious about what kind of aircraft I flew in my service days before I got to this place called Star City.

"Well, I'm not a pilot. I don't fly airplanes," I said.

"Well, what did you do?" I was asked.

"I was a SEAL," I said. "It's like your special commandos that go underwater and attack things."

The Russians all thought this was absolutely incredible, that in front of them was a guy who, ten years ago, was facing them as their counterpart underwater, somewhere else on the planet. The Russians were very surprised that we were in that situation.

In Russia, I've been in their equivalent of the huge swimming pool we train in for weightless simulation. They had their Navy divers in there. They all support the submarine program and are kind of like a ship's company on a submarine. They're not dedicated diving units separately attached to the cosmonaut program.

The divers knew who and what SEALs are, and they knew the SEAL equivalent in Russia. It took a while for me to establish with them that that was my background, but after they came to know what I had been, we really hit it off well. Those guys thought it was absolutely incredible that a Russian Naval Spetsnaz equivalent from the United States was diving in a pool over there. It took them a while to believe it—it was just such a psychological disconnect that such a situation would be how our two countries would be relating.

Two winters ago, before I started my Russian training at Star City, I went over to do some leg work, some ground work, to see what I was getting in to. I had the privilege to go to Kazakhstan, which is the launch site for the Russian space hardware.

The site is about a thousand miles southeast of Moscow. I went in February, and it was about twenty degrees and blowing snow. I was a guest of the base general, and we went into the compound where their active space crews are isolated the day before their launch takes place. There, I attended a pretty good buffet and party.

As I was leaving, the general took me and another American astronaut aside and we went to the general's apartment and had some vodka. One thing led to another, and we all decided that we had to get up the next morning and go shooting.

It was 7 o'clock the following morning when a bus pulled up and this other astronaut and I got on board and went down to the local police station. There, they had an indoor pistol range set up with about seven firing positions and these 9mm Makarov automatic pistols, a little like an American .380 automatic.

There was a pistol at each position, so we started shooting. Blasting away offhand, I was at the far end of the firing line. We would shoot a magazine, then put the weapons down and go check our targets.

The first target was the general's. Out of eight rounds in the magazine, he had eight of them in the body. The same thing stood for just about everybody as you went go down the line. There were a pretty good set of holes in the target. Then the general looked at my silhouette target down at the end.

The body of the target was clean—there wasn't a mark on it. Right up on the forehead of the target, there was a cluster of holes about the size of a fifty-cent piece. The general looked at that, then he looked at me, then he looked back at the target.

"I see you've done this before." he said.

It was just one of those things. It took a while for the Russians to figure out just where I was coming from.

*   *   *

Back in the Teams, my sea daddies were a couple of guys really. I think my first sea daddy was Tom Lawson, who was the XO of SEAL Team One, when I went from UDT to SEAL Team. He was a great guy, and one of the things I remember most was that on Friday afternoons, we would have a junior officer bull session. There, we would discuss what was going right and what was going wrong with the Team. That was very productive and one of the few opportunities in my military career that we could really air out what was on our minds.

Another sea daddy I had was Chester Stevens, who was an E6 who got out of the Navy and went to work for the government as a civilian. He did a lot of different special activities, and I had a lot of interaction with him. He was a really good guy, and I would certainly rank him as one of my sea daddies who brought me up in the Teams.

There are people I wouldn't put in the sea daddy category, but who were more than a little impressive. Tom Richards is a legend in the Teams and a great guy as well as a tremendous athlete. He's a very level-headed person. I think the Navy did very well to put him in the position he currently holds. We need more people like him. And people such as Ray Smith, who has been one of the standouts in the Teams' officer corps for a long time. I think the Navy is really well served by having him as a flag officer and doing the things he's doing at SOCOM.

Where's the space program going? I'm not sure anybody has a good answer to that question. One of the things we're trying to decide what this space station is about is the place and the role for humans. Are we destined to live only on this planet, or are we going to go somewhere else? We're going to do research and try to solve the problems that will come up, with the space station.

So hopefully, the space station is a way to allow us to go a long distance from planet Earth and view places we haven't seen yet. This is just a first step in that direction. I wish I could tell you how we're going to do that, what's going to happen, and what steps are needed to make that a reality, but that's all yet to be defined. That's really what the space program is about—learning what we have to learn.

What I would like to bring to the space station and the space program is pretty much the kinds of things I did in SEAL Team or in the UDT platoon as a platoon junior officer. I want to have a good team, to have people do their jobs well and know what they are doing. I want to be able to be given a nice, clear mission and get it done.

Being an astronaut was something I thought about as a kid. When the space program really got going in the Mercury days in the late 1950s and early 1960s, it was clear that you had to be an aviator in order to be an astronaut. It wasn't until I was in grad school that it I realized I could be an engineer or some other type of technical person and get into the astronaut program.

For a period of about nine or ten years, between thinking about flying and getting through grad school, I didn't even think about being an astronaut. One day, it just kind of occurred to me to compare scuba diving and space walking. Some of the things we do in space as astronauts and in the water as SEALs are pretty similar. So I decided to see if I could get in to the space program.

When I was told I would be the first commander of the space station, I felt it was a big challenge—I still think that. Being in charge of an expedition that has this multinational character to it is a huge deal. We're under the control of two control centers, one in Moscow and one in Houston. Most of the hardware is Russian. There's a language issue; we have to be able to think and act in Russian as well as in English. It's something way beyond the types of jobs I've been faced with before in the space program. I think I like that it's such a big challenge.

I'm honored and really kind of humbled that other SEALs look up to me as an example of the lack of limits on what a SEAL can do. Their outlook on me is something I think about it a lot. It's very visible here, being an astronaut and being a Team person. A lot of new guys who I never worked with or never even met probably know a lot about what's going on here and what I'm doing. I think that it's very important that I bring a Team outlook to some of the challenges here at the space center.

The kinds of training and the things that SEALs are prepared to do are very ap-

Men from Underwater Demolition Team Eleven make ready an inflatable boat next to a mock-up of the Apollo 14 Command Module during recovery training.

U.S. Navy

propriate to some of the demands of space and what the crews are going to be faced with on the day-to-day operations as well as the hard times in orbit—the bad situations and emergencies. Even though not every SEAL is going to get the chance to fly in space, the average SEAL needs to realize that the training and the things they've been through are very unique.

One of the things I think is really interesting about the SEAL community goes back to one of our best-known symbols, the Frogmen and frogs. Why should frogs even be a mascot? You've got this little animal that jumps in and out of the water all the time. Well, above all else, frogs are very adaptable. One of the virtues of our communities, SEALs and frogs, is that you can put a SEAL in a strange place, like here at the space center, and he'll adapt. That's the way people in our community are trained, and to have people ready to go and adapt to whatever comes along is a very powerful attribute.

Jumping out of the SEAL community and getting into NASA was really kind of strange for me. You apply and go through a lot of screening and selection. You show up at the Houston Space Center and go through interviews, spend an hour before a board made up of a lot of NASA managers, then, you're kind of in the dark for months about whether you made the cut or not.

The first time around, I didn't get in. I waited four years after that and reapplied. This time I was selected. I don't think there's any obvious correlation between being a SEAL and being an astronaut, although a lot of the good things SEALs do and know how to do certainly apply to the job here. I think that was a major factor in my being fortunate enough to begin here.

The Teams: they are always ready, always capable, and always willing.

USSOCOM PAO

In the earliest parts of the space program, we lost a Mercury capsule in 1961 when Gus Grissom was recovered after his flight. After that, NASA decided we needed Frogmen to jump out and put flotation collars around the spacecraft. All the way through the Apollo mission to the moon, UDT people were jumping in and meeting the capsule in the water. But those guys were always on the outside of the hatch. One of the things about the space program now is that we have SEALs on both sides of the hatch. It's kind of an interesting turn of events.

The reason why a SEAL is going into

space, probably the first of many, is that space is a unique place. There is no horizon, no limit, no boundary, to what you can do or what you can think about doing. It's very much the same way SEALs are trained to think when they go through BUD/S. There are no limits to what SEALs can do. There's no place that's too far or too high, and no water that's too cold. That's just the way SEALs are, and that's probably why SEALs will have a place in space for some time in the future.

Index

Page numbers in *italic* indicate illustrations.

American eagle, 256
Amphibious Force development, 4–9, *6*
Amphibious invasion deception (Desert
   Storm), 707–709, 712–713
Amphibious Scout and Raider School
   (Joint), 14, 18–19, 27
Amphibious Training Base (ATB), 13, 26, *27*
"Anchors Aweigh," 105
Anderson, Captain, 490
Anderson, Commander, 442
Anderson, Dick, 341
Anderson, Franklin W. (Lieutenant
   Commander), 282
Anderson, George Jr. (Admiral), 206, 207
Anderson, Lloyd "Andy," 28
Andrews, E.F. "Andy" (Lieutenant), 97–111,
   99
Andrews, James H. "Hoot" (Chief
   Storekeeper, USN (Ret.)), 191–197, 219
AN/PVS-1 (starlight) scope, 315, 320
Antimilitary sentiment, 343, 516–517. *See
   also* Image of SEALs
Anxieties about first combat, 254
"Anywhere, anytime," 217
APDs (Assault Personnel Destroyers), 78, *79*,
   79–80, 86, 90, 187, *328*
Apex boats, 67
Apollo 11 recovery, 98, *98*
Aqualung, 72, 139
AR-15 rifles, 220, 224–225, 313, 317, 318–319
Arctic missions, *180*, 180–182, *182*, 188–189,
   505–506
Aristide, Jean-Bertrand, 721, 723
Army
   Gap Assault Team (GAT), 68
   Rangers, 578, 586, 588, 715, 782
   Scouts and Raiders (S&Rs), 13–14, *14*
   SEALs operations and, 377–378
   Special Forces, 233–234, 319
   support of Navy SEALs creation, 211
   Tarawa Atoll, 45
Army of the Republic of Vietnam (ARVN),
   269–270, 417, 425–426
Artillery fire support, 356, *357*, 411–412
Ashby, Edwin R. (Boatswain's Mate, Second
   Class), 81–92
Ashton, Al, 598
Ashton, Curtis M. (AE1), 429
Asian cultures, 342, 352
Asian Senator, 647
Assault group system, 408
Assault Personnel Destroyers (APDs), 78, *79*,
   79–80, 86, 90, 187, *328*
Astronaut training vs. BUD/S, 825
ATB (Amphibious Training Base), 13, 26, *27*
Atcheson, George (Lieutenant, USN (Ret.)),
   142–152
Athwartships, 362–363

Atomic bomb, feelings about
   Naval Combat Demolition Units
      (NCDUs), 43
   Underwater Demolition Teams (UDTs),
      71, 95, 108, 117, 125
Attention to detail at BUD/S, 810–802
Australian troops, 116
Axis forces, 6

B
Backgrounds of UDTs, 90–91, 111
Bailey, Larry (Lieutenant (j.g.)), 237, 320, 336
Bailey, Sam, 266
Balboa Yatch Club, securing of, 646
Balzarini, Donald (Commander, USN (Ret.)),
   176–185
Bao Dai government, 259–260, 260
Barbey, Daniel E. (Rear Admiral), 33
Barge, "Doc" (Warrant Officer), 51
Barnes, James H. (Lieutenant, USNR), 282,
   567, 568, 572
Barre, Siad, 715–716
Barrett, Eve, 265
Barry, Lee, 528
Basic Underwater Demolition/SEALs
   (BUD/S), 730–809. *See also* Chalker,
      Dennis; Hawes, Joseph; Hell Week
      (Motivation Week); Maguire, Joe;
      Mental discipline; Peterson, Erick;
      Quitting training; Richards, Tom;
      Teamwork importance; Underwater
      Demolition Team Replacement (UDTR)
      training; Valderrama, Joseph;
      Woroniecki, Jacob
   astronaut training vs., 730–809
   attention to detail, 810–802
   cast-and-recovery, 41, 83, 94, 325, *326*,
      405, *406*, 464, 612–613
   casualties, 602, 616–617, 620, 735
   class numbers, 730–731, 741, 787
   cold training, 33, 123, 736, 767, 770,
      786–787, 807, 812
   combat swimming, 529–532, 734
   commonality of training, 578, 730, 782
   demolition, 650–651, 765, *765*, 802, *802*
   drop on request (DOR), 732, 766, 795
   dropout rate, 733–734, 766, 796, 797
   drownproofing, 773
   equipment, 732
   evolution (training event), 736
   fear, dealing with, 735
   First Phase, 734–736, 763, 771, 799–800, 807
   fitness of trainees, 732, 743
   Fourth Phase (indoctrination period), 733
   free-diving and tying knots, 772, *772*
   friendships made during, 743
   graduation from, 730, 737, 758–759,
      773–774, 787, 813

grinder, 730, 732–733, 737, 773
helmet liners and training phase, 732, 734, 736
individual effort, *735*, 735–736
insertions of Teams, 738–739
instructors, 275–280, *299*, 490, 494, 734, 756–757, 758, 769, 777–778, 778–779, 780
intelligence of SEALs, 552–553
last invasion, WWII, 125, 126–127
leadership, 800–801
length of course, 732
mud training, 717, *717*, 794, *794*
obstacle course, 652, *652*, 653
officers vs. enlisted, 552–553, 565–566, 695, 755–756, 762–763, 800–801
pain of, 630, 695–696, 750–751, 781
physical training (PT), 633, 734, 738, 796, 812–813
platoon training cycle, 702
push-ups, 597, *597*
rolled-back students, 574–575, 736, 743–744, 757, 798, 812
rope skills, 733, *733*
rubber boats, 564, *564*, 731, *731*
running training, 649, 650, 653, 687, 702
"Schoolhouse," 731
screening test, 732, 738, 762
SEAL qualification program, 737
Second Phase (diving operations), 736–737, 739, 763, 771, 800
"Secure from Hell Week," 565, 612, 772, 807
situps, 801, *801*
swim buddies, 74, 274–275, 378, 463, 788, 808, 813
tactical training, *627*
Third Phase (land warfare), 656, 737, 763, 771, 801, 807
Battle of Dien Bien Phu, 260
Battle Surveillance System (BASS), 571
Bay of Pigs failure, 205–206
Beach Jumpers, 185–190
   Arctic Circle assignments, 100–109
   Assault Personnel Destroyers (APDs), 187
   Distant Early Warning (DEW) line deployment, 188
   Douglas Fairbanks Jr., 185
   graduation rates, 187
   Iwo Jima exercise, 187–188
   Jet Assisted Take Off (JATO), 189
   missions of, 186
   Operation HUSKY, 185
   Peter C. Dirkx, 185–190
   Pirelli suits, 189
   teamwork importance, 186
Beach jumper units (BJUs), 373
Beach reconnaissance, 157–159, 379, *465*

Beakley, Wallace (Admiral), 203
Beausoleil, Randy Lee (Warrant Officer), 648–667
   adaptability of SEALs, 666
   Basic Underwater Demolition/SEALs (BUD/S), 648–651, 652, *652*, 653
   camaraderie of SEALs, 665–666
   cold-weather operations, 650
   combat swimming, 656–665, *659*
   demolition training, 650–651
   diversity of SEALs, 667
   friendships, 651
   Hell Week, 649, 650, 652
   history of Teams, 652–653, 654–655
   humbling by SEALs, 665
   image of SEALs, 666–667
   Jump School, 652
   land warfare training, 656
   obstacle course, 652, *652*, 653
   Panama experiences, 656–664
   quitting training, 650
   running training, 649, 650, 653
   Tactical Training, 652
   training (advanced), 666
   traveling demands on SEALs, 667
   Trident insignia, 652
   Vietnam vets, 654, 655
Beebe, Bill, 522
Belgian Gate (Element C), 57, *57*
Biak landings, 30
Biet Hai, 293, *294*
Billings, Al (Lieutenant), 521
Bills, Bob, *321*
bin Laden, Osama, 727, 728, *728*
Birtz, Pierre, 340, 654
Bishop, Maurice, 585
Bisset, Andrew (Captain), 125
BJUs (beach jumper units), 373
Black, Robert, 112
"Black Death," 138, *138*
Black Ponies Squadron (OV-10s), 307–311, *308*, *309*, 311, 356, 381, *382*, 580
Black September organization, 533
Blending in with locals, 536–537, *537*
Bliss, Rip (Platoon Leader), 300
"Bloody Omaha," 58, 110
Boat handlers, 68
Boat Pool, 13, 14
Boat support, 554–559
   Boat Support Units (BSU), 554–555, 555–556
   Brown Water Navy, 541, 554
   Combat Rubber Raiding Craft (CRRC), 558
   Dry Deck Shelter (DDS) capability, 558
   High Speed Boats, 558
   light patrol boats, 558
   Mark I/II Patrol Boat, River (PBR), 541, 555, *555*

Felt, Harry D. (Admiral), 332, 333
Ferruggiaro, John, 443
Fietsch, "Killer John," 390
Fifth Amphibious Force, 45, 48
Finley, Jim, 347
Firebolt (PC 10), 558
First aid teaching to teammates, 450
First combat, Vietnam, 238–244
  anxieties about, 254
  "break-in" ops, 238, 241
  Frank Toms, 238–244
  losses from, 243, 244
  maturing from, 242
  Philippines deployment, 241
  prisoners vs. killing, 242
  Stoner machine gun, 239, *239,* 243
  Vietnam War, 241–244
  wounded from, 243, 244
First land combat operations, 142, 145–150
First major amphibious landing, 15
First Navy SEALs CO. *See* Callahan, John
First SEAL. *See* Boehm, Roy
Fitness. *See* Physical fitness
Fitzgerald, Mike, 826
Five Year Defense Plan, 574
Flanagan, Dick, 480
Fleet Landing Exercises (FLEXs), 5
Fleet Training exercises, 289
Flexible capabilities of SEALs, 150
FLEXs (Navy-Marine Corps Fleet Landing
  Exercises), 5
FLINTLOCK exercise, 289, 529–532
"Flying mattresses," 54–55
Flynn, Bill (Lieutenant), 48–49
Flynn, Irish, 573, 591
Foran, Bill, 825
Force multiplier, 706, 809
Ford, Jack, 752–753
Foreign policy and SEALs, 684, 688–689
Forest of Assassins. *See* Rung Sat Special
  Zone (RSSZ)
Fox, Ron, 347
Fraley, Gene, 418
Freddie the Frog insignia, 174–175, *175*
Fredrickson, Delmar "Freddie," 440–441,
  442
Free-diving and tying knots, 772, *772*
Free-fall skills, 629
Free fire zones, 337
French, Todd, 625
French and Vietnam, 257, 259, 260
Friendly fire accident, 395–397
Friendships of SEALs, 651, 694, 743
Frogmen, 33, 126, 559, 561–562, 621
Frogmen, The (movie), 334, 345, 463, 477
Frömandskorpet cross-training, 614
Funding
  SEALs, 229–230, 234, 343, 344–345

U.S. Special Operations Command
  (USSOCOM), 633, 689
Funkhouser, Harlen (Petty Officer First
  Class), 300
Fusco, Arthur, 628
Future of Navy SEALs, 809–831. *See also*
  Maynard, Dave; Shepherd, Bill
  active SEALs, number of, 809
  Advanced SEAL Delivery System (ASDS),
    810–811
  deployment of Teams, changes in, 810
  equipment (new), 810
  even-numbered Teams, 809
  NASA and SEALs, 748, 765–766, 811, 824,
    828–831, 829, *829*
  new Teams, 809
  odd-numbered Teams, 809
  size of Teams, changes in, 809

G
Gallagher, Robert "The Eagle," 219, 315, 347,
  408, 491, 523, 608
Gap Assault Team (GAT) at Normandy,
  68–77
  aqualung, 72
  Army engineers and, 68
  boat handlers, 68
  Dominican Republic, 75
  double-loop snare, 70
  Escape and Evasion (E&E) school, 75
  fear, 70
  formation of, 62, 68
  integrity of team members, 74–75
  intelligence nets, 77
  Joseph D. DiMartino, 69–77, 201, 233
  Korean War, 72
  Lambertson Amphibious Respiratory Unit
    (LARU), 71, *71,* 112, *112*
  Landing Craft, Mechanized (LCMs),
    69
  Landing Craft, Tank (LCTs), 69
  marine hinterland missions, 73
  Omaha Beach, 68
  Operation HIGH JUMP, 71
  Operation NEPTUNE, 68
  Operation OVERLORD, 68
  parachuting, 72
  physical fitness for, 77
  recognition for, 68–69
  Roy Boehm, 73, 74, *74*
  scuba gear training, 71–72
  SEAL Team creation, 73–74
  "sticks," 72
  swim buddies, 74
  teamwork importance, 74
  Tet offensive, 76
  training experiences, 69, 70–71, 72, 74–75
  unknown, fear of, 70

HH-60H Sea Hawks, 672, *672*
Higgins boat, 16, 17, 163, *163*
High altitude, high opening (HAHO), 602
High altitude, low opening (HALO), 569
High Speed Boats, 558
History of Teams. *See also* Today's vs.
    historical Teams
  Dave Maynard, 821–823
  Dennis Chalker, 788–789, 793
  Erick Peterson, 805
  Joe Maguire, 760
  Randy Lee Beausoleil, 652–653, 654–655
  Raymond C. Smith, 683–684, 690–691,
    692–693
  Richard Marcinko, 549–550
  Robert Gormly, 594–595
  Thomas N. Tarbox, 552, 553–554
  Tom Richards "The Hulk," 753–754
  Vic Meyer, 696–697
"Hit-and-run" operation, 114
Hitler, Adolf, 2, 3, 4
HK MP-5N submachine gun, 520, *520*
HMCS *Terra Nova*, 722
Ho Chi Minh (Nguyen Ai Quoc), 259, 260,
    260, 402
Ho Chi Minh Trail, 332, 402
Honduran operations, 623–624
Hooch, *276*
"Hooyah," 377, 502, 775
Horn, Rich, 617
Horrell, Kirby, 815–816
Hospital corpsmen, 439–461. *See also*
    McPartlin, Greg; Salts, Jack
  Geneva Convention, 440
  history of service, 440
  Medal of Honor received by, 440
  "Medcaps," 445–446
  SEALs and, 443–444, 449, 452–453,
    453–454, 460–461
  special operations technician course, 440,
    441, 447–448, 461
Hot war in Vietnam, 298, 299
Howell, Nathaniel, 670–671
HSSC (Heavy SEAL Support Craft), 354, *354*
Huey, Al (Captain), 177, 480
"Huey" (UH-1) helicopters, 354, 367
Humanity of SEALs, 446
Humility of SEALs, 665, 682
Humphries, Harry (Draftsman, First Class),
    404–426
  aftermath of Tet offensive, 425–426
  Agency for International Development
    (AIDs) nurses, rescue of, 412–417
  Army of the Republic of Vietnam (ARVN)
    and Chau Doc, 417, 425–426
  assault group system, 408
  "brushfire" wars, 423
  Chau Doc province, 411–418

enemy, learning from, 425
formative years of SEALs, 407–408
intelligence of Navy SEALs, 425
interservice problems, 419
mental vs. physical aspect, 424–425
Phoenix Program, 420, 421
platoon operations, 410
Provincial Reconnaissance Units (PRUs),
    419–421
selection process concept, 422, 425
Special Operations Forces (SOF), 423
Tactical Operations Center (TOC),
    412–413
Underwater Demolition Team
    Replacement (UDTR) training, 404–405
veterans vs. new men, 410
Viet Cong, similarities with, 410–411
Viet Cong command center operation,
    417–418
Vietnam (post) to present, 422–423, 541,
    545, 547, 549
volunteering of SEALs, 413
Hurricane (PC 3), 557
Hussein, Saddam, 548–549, 639–640,
    667–668, 671, 674, 705, 714, 715
Huth, Doug, 482
Hydrographic reconnaissance, 52–53, 321,
    322, 674, 725

I
IBS (Inflatable Boat, Small), 155, *155*, 177,
    180, *180*, *268*, *294*
Ice demolitions, 160–161, *161*
Image of SEALs, 331, 460, 493, 527, 577,
    595–596, 607, 619, 637, 666–667, 704,
    712, 752
IMMINENT THUNDER exercise, 674
Improvised explosive devices (IEDs), 538
Individual effort in BUD/S, 735, *735*,
    735–736
Indoctrination period at BUD/S, 733
Inflatable Boat, Small (IBS), 155, *155*, 177,
    180, *180*, *268*, *294*
Injuries during UDTR, 509–510
Insertions, 327–328, *329*, 348, *350*, 474,
    579–580, 582–583, 738–739
Inshore Undersea Warfare Group One
    (IUWG-1), 570–571
Insignias. *See also* Trident insignia
  Freddie the Frog, 174–175, *175*
  Seawolves, *356*
Inspections, passing, 507, 518
Instability of world and SEALs, 705
Instructors at BUD/S
  Vietnam era, 275–280, *299*, 490, 494
  Vietnam (post) to present, 734, 756–757,
    758, 769, 777–778, 778–779, 780
Integrity of team members, UDTs, 74–75

Meals of SEALs, 456–457
Medal of Honor, 385–387, 440, 490
Medals, view of, 311, 364, 367
"Medcaps," 445–446
Meder, Frank, Jr. (Machinist's Mate, Second
    Class), 113–119
Media attention in Somalia, 718
Medics. *See* Hospital corpsmen
Medium SEAL Support Craft (MSSC), *353*
Mekong Delta
    deployment to Vietnam, 334
    Garry Bonelli, 513–322
    Mark Schimpf, 367–368
    Richard Marcinko, 347–348
    Robert Gormly, 336–337, *337*
    Vietnam, 261–262, *262*, 264, 426
Melochick, Mel, 201
Men in Green Faces (video), 655
Mental discipline
    BUD/S, 732
    Dennis Chalker, 795, 796
    Joe Maguire, 761, 762
    Joseph Hawes, 779–780
    Joseph Valderrama, 739
    Naval Combat Demolition Units
        (NCDUs), 41, 43, 60
    SEALs, 77, 126
    Tom Richards "The Hulk," 742, 743,
        744–745, 749, 750, 751–752, 754
    Underwater Demolition Teams (UDTs),
        109, 115, 179, 181
Mentality of SEALs
    Mark Stefanich, 615
    Raymond C. Smith, 682–683, 692
    Rudy Boesch, 638
    Steven Scott Helvenston, 627, 628, 630,
        632
    Vic Meyer, 697, 701
    Wellington T. Leonard "Duke," 606, 607,
        609
Mental vs. physical, 424–425, 490–491,
    498–499
Metzel, Jeffrey C. (Captain), 20, 21
Meyer, Vic (Lieutenant Commander),
    693–705
    Basic Underwater Demolition/SEALs
        (BUD/S), 693–697, *694*, 701–702
    camaraderie of SEALs, 701
    combat swimmer operations, 699
    competence of SEALs, 704–705
    confidence of SEALs, 703
    cultural knowledge of SEALs, 705
    dark side of soul as motivator, 695
    Desert Shield/Desert Storm, 697–700,
        702–703
    diversity of SEALs, 704–705
    friendships, 694
    Hell Week, 694, 695–696

history of Teams, 696–697
image of SEALs, 704
instability of world and SEALs, 705
language-qualified SEALs, 705
leadership, 696–697, 703
mentality of SEALs, 697, 701
Naval Combat Demolition Units
    (NCDUs), 698
officers vs. enlisted, 695
pain of training, 695–696
platoon training cycle, 702
professionalism of SEALs, 702, 704, 705
quitting training, 696
running training, 702
teamwork of SEALs, 697
Trident insignia, 696
Vietnam vets, 703
water environment of SEALs, 701
MH-6F Little Birds, 581, *581*, 582, 590, *590*
MH-47E Chinook helicopter, 729
MH-53 Pave Low helicopters, 582, 709
Mike boat (Heavy SEAL Support Craft), 354,
    354
"Military Mafia," 349
Mine clearing operations, 162, 166–167, 168,
    168, 676–677, 678, *678*
Mini-Armored Troop carrier, 557, *557*, 558
Mining of Persian Gulf, 641–642, 675, *675*,
    677, *677*, 700
Minisubs, 34
Mission of Navy SEALs, 132–133, 197, 204,
    204, 205, 206, 211
Mistakes of Tarawa Atoll ("Terrible Tarawa"),
    44–45, 52, 140
Mobile Comm Teams, 571
Mobile support teams (MSTs), 372–373
Mobile Training Teams (MTTs), 237, 238,
    286, 292–293
Mobility Platoon Six (MOB-Six), 534, 601,
    614, 618, 635, 789–790
Moncrief, Frank, 315
Monsoon (PC 4), 557
Monster Mashes, 571
Montgomery, Sir Bernard (Lieutenant
    General), 24
Morale of Teams, 570, 571
Moran, Dick, 598
Moreell, Ben (Rear Admiral), 11
Morris, Stephen Leroy (Hull Technician First
    Class), 587
Mosure, Tom, 551
Motivation Week. *See* Hell Week
Moy, Terry "Mother," 477, 478, 491, 498, 501
MP-5N submachine gun, 556, *556*
MSSC (Medium SEAL Support Craft), *353*
MSTs (mobile support teams), 372–373
MTTs (Mobile Training Teams), 237, 238,
    286, 292–293

MU (Maritime Unit), 92, 93
Mud training, 717, *717*, 794, *794*
Munich Olympics (1972), 533–534
Mustang officers, 228–229, 759, 764

N
Naguers de combat (French combat
    swimmers), 531
"Naked Warrior" (Bronze Bruce), 549–550,
    553, 578, 730, 754, 785, 808–809, 821
Naked Warrior, The (Fane), 133
Nam Meo, 306
Namur invasion, 46
Naple, Vinnie, 532
NASA and SEALs, 748, 765–766, 811, 824,
    828–831, *829*
"Nasty"-class fast patrol boat, *333*
Naval Advisory Group, 494–495
Naval Combat Demolition Units (NCDUs),
    18–43. *See also* Kauffman, Draper
    Admiralty Islands invasion, 39–40
    Amphibious Training Base (FL), 13, 26, *27*
    assignments, 36–43
    atomic bomb, feelings about, 43
    Biak landings, 30
    cast-and-recovery, 41
    closed-circuit rebreathing rigs, 42, *42*
    cold-water training, 33
    DUKW vehicles, 19
    elimination event for, 27–28
    enemy fire, 32, 41
    England assignments, 37
    Ernest J. King, 7, 19, 20
    fear, 32
    Frank Kaine "MacArthur's Frogman," 7,
        28–36, 38
    frogmen, 33
    grouper fish feast, 31, 40
    Hell Week, 27–28, 38, 50
    Japan occupation, 32
    jobs of, 38–39, 40
    John F. Kennedy and, 34
    Kiska invasion, 36
    Landing Craft, Personnel, Large (LCPLs),
        23, 24, 95, 301
    Leyte Gulf operation, 30, 40
    Los Negros operation, 30–31
    mental discipline for, 41, 43, 60
    minisubs, 34
    mission evolution, 35–36
    missions of, 132
    Naval Demolition Unit #1 (NDU), 22–36
    Navy Bomb and Mine Disposal School,
        21–22, 22–23
    obstacle clearance, 19–20, *20*
    officers vs. enlisted, 37–38, 43
    Operation HUSKY, 22, 23–24
    physical fitness for, 38, 49

reconnaissance of beaches and offshore
    waters, 29
Robert P. Marshall, Jr., 25–26
Scouts and Raiders (S&Rs) and, 129
Seabees and, 22–24
selection process for boat crews, 50
Sicily target, 19, 22
Southwestern Pacific assignments, 36
swimming emphasis, 28
teamwork importance, 26–27, 32, 41, 60
training experiences, 37–38, *46–48*, 48–50,
    59–60, 61–62
Underwater Demolition Teams (UDTs)
    vs., 33–34, 35
Vietnam (post) to present, 578, 679, *679*,
    698, 760, *760*
William L. Dawson, 37–43
Naval CT (counterterrorist), 535–537, *537*,
    541–543, 622–623
Naval Demolition Unit #1 (NDU), 22–36
Naval Inshore Warfare Command, 344–345
Naval Intelligence Liaison Officer (NILO),
    303, 431
Naval Special Warfare Groups
    (SpecWarGru), 555–558, 680–681
Naval Special Warfare Master Plan, 572
Naval Special Warfare reorganization,
    559–560
Naval Special Warfare Task Group (NSWTG),
    645, 669, 671
Naval Special Warfare Training Center
    (SWCC), 556
Naval Special Warfare Western Pacific
    Detachment (WESTPAC), 469
Naval Underwater Demolition Training and
    Experimental Base (HI), 45
Naval Warfare Information Publication
    excerpt, 215–216
Navy Bomb and Mine Disposal School,
    21–22, 22–23
Navy Demolition Unit, 16–18
Navy in Scouts and Raiders (S&Rs), 14
Navy-Marine Corps Fleet Landing Exercises
    (FLEXs), 5
Navy Reserves, 503–518. *See also* Bonelli,
    Garry; Sarber, John
    active-duty requirement, 506
    active Teams and Reserves, 508–509,
        517–518, 809
    Desert Storm, 423, 518
    drill weekend, 506
    inspections, passing, 507, 518
    Special Warfare reserves, 507
    training, 504
    uniforms, 507
Navy SEALs, 1. *See also* Navy SEALs creation;
    Navy SEALs Vietnam era; Navy SEALs
    Vietnam (post) to present

Navy SEALs Vietnam (post) to present
(*cont.*)

Operation BRIGHT LIGHT, 462
Operation CHARLESTON, 283
Operation CORONET, 118, 137–138
Operation CRIMSON TIDE, *306*
Operation DEEP CHANNEL, 513
Operation DRAGOON, 58, 127
Operation EAGLE CLAW, 534, 535, 540, 547
Operation EARNEST WILL, 641, 643, 670
Operation ENDURING FREEDOM, 727–729
Operation FIRE MAGIC, 534–535
Operation FISHNET, 166, *166*
Operation FLINTLOCK, 46–47
Operation FORAGER, 47, 53
Operation GALVANIC, 44
Operation GAME WARDEN, 334
Operation HIGH JUMP, 71
Operation HUSKY, 22, 23–24, 185
Operation JACKSTAY, 282, 567–568
Operation JOINT ENDEAVOR, 725
Operation JUST CAUSE, 645–648
Operation MARITIME GUARD, 725
Operation MARKET TIME, 334
Operation NEPTUNE, 68
Operation NIMBLE ARCHER, 642–643
Operation NIMROD, 535
Operation Olympic, 137–138
Operation OVERLORD, 68
Operation PRAYING MANTIS, 643, *643*
Operation PROVIDE PROMISE, 725
Operation PROVIDE RELIEF, 716
Operation RESTORE HOPE, 716
Operations. *See* Navy SEALs operations
Operation SEA SOLDIER, 674
Operation SHARP GUARD, 725
Operation SUPPORT DEMOCRACY, 721–723
Operation THUNDERBALL, 534
Operation THUNDERHEAD, 468, 471–473
Operation TORCH (North Africa), 14–18
    Central Attack Group, 15
    Fedala target, 15
    first major amphibious landing, 15
    Frederick A. Henney, 16, 17
    Henry K. Hewitt, 15
    Higgins boat, 16, 17
    James W. Darroch, 16
    Lloyd Peddicord, 16
    Mahdia/Port Lyautey target, 15, 16–18
    Mark Starkweather, 16, 17
    Navy Demolition Unit, 16–18
    net/cable cutting team, 16–18
    Northern Attack Group, 15, 16
    Office of Strategic Services, 18
    recognition of, 16
    Safi target, 15
    Scouts and Raiders (S&Rs), 14, 15–16
    Southern Attack Group, 15
    Western Naval Task Force (Task Force 34), 15

Operation UNITED SHIELD, 720
Operation UPHOLD DEMOCRACY, 723
Operation URGENT FURY, 585–590, 632
Operation WATCHTOWER, 8
Orange plans, 6
Organization of SEALs, 282, 289–290, *290, 291*
Osborne, Chet, 511
OSS. *See* Office of Strategic Services

P
Pain of BUD/S, 630, 695–696, 750–751, 781
Painter, William (Lieutenant, Junior Grade), 200
Paitilla Airfield, 645, 647
Palladium, Randy, 699
Panama, 644–667. *See also* Beausoleil, Randy Lee
    Atlantic gate, securing of, 646
    Balboa Yatch Club, securing of, 646
    casualties, 647
    combat swimming, 646–647, 648, *648,* 656–665
    Dennis Chalker, 792–793
    Manuel Antonia Noreiga, 644–645, 648
    Naval Special Warfare Task Group (NSWTG), 645
    Operation BLUE SPOON, 645
    Operation JUST CAUSE, 645–648
    Pacific gate, securing of, 646
    Paitilla Airfield, 645, 647
    Presidente Porras destruction, 646
    Task Unit Charlie, 646, 647
    Task Unit Foxtrot, 646, 647–648
    Task Unit Papa, 645, 646–647
    Task Unit Whiskey, 645–646
    Vietnam era, 423
Parachuting skills
    accident, 201
    Gap Assault Team (GAT), 72
    SEALs skills, 213, *213,* 221, 237
    Vietnam (post) to present, 601, *601,* 602
Partying reputation, 457–459
Patrol Boat, River (Mark I/II) (PBR), 555, *555*
Patrol Boat, River (PBRs), *271, 340,* 353–354, *359, 396,* 397, *403, 411*
Patrol boats (PTF-3/PTF-4), *336*
Patrol Ships Coastal Cyclone-class (PCs), 557, 722, 723
Patton, George S., Jr. (Major General), 14, 24
Pearl Harbor attack, 4
Pearls Airport capture, 588
Pechacek, William (LTJG), 283
Peddicord, Lloyd (Lieutenant), 13, 16
Peleliu, 78, 111
Penn, Petty Officer Third Class, 283
Pennsylvania crash, 727
Pentagon attack, 727

Stealth skills, 212, *212*
Stefanich, Mark (Signalman First Class),
    610–623
  adaptability of SEALs, 615
  Basic Underwater Demolition/SEALs
    (BUD/S), 611–613, 619
  buddy system of SEALs, 616
  camaraderie of SEALs, 615–616, 621–622
  cast-and-recovery, 612–613
  casualties during training, 616–617, 620
  Close Quarters Battle (CQB), 617
  counterterrorism, 622–623
  door partners, 616
  "Frogman," 621
  Frömandskorpet cross-training, 614
  Grenada experiences, 617–618
  Hell Week, 611–612
  image of, 619
  Jump School, 613, 619
  leadership, 615, 622
  mentality of SEALs, 615
  Mobility Platoon Six (MOB-Six), 618
  pride of SEALs, 613
  probationary period, 619
  professionalism of SEALs, 619
  quitting training, 612
  "Secure from Hell Week," 612
  Teammates of SEALs, 615–616, 617
  Teammates' view of, 610
  training (advanced), 619–620
  Trident insignia, 619, 621
Stethem, Robert, 552
Stevens, Charles, 828
Stevens, Wally, 605
"Sticks," 72
"Stockholm Syndrome," 552
Stoner machine gun, 239, *239*, 243, 273, *302*,
    342, 400, *401*, *454*, 454–455
Stoner man, 599–600
"Stovepipe commands," 544
Strategic Technical Directorate Assistance
    Team (SDAT), 476
String reconnaissance system, 53
STRONG EXPRESS exercise, 289
Submarine-launched operations, 111–112
Submarines, getting in and out of, 169–170,
    169–170
Support personnel for Korean War, 172–176
Survival, Escape, Resistance, and Evasion
    (SERE), 36, 555, 626
Sutherland, Bill, 236
Swatow gunboat attacks, 333
Swenson, Dick, 182, 183
Swim buddies, 74, 274–275, 378, 463, 788,
    808, 813
Swim fins, 93
Swimmer delivery vehicles (SDVs), 470, 471,
    471, 472

Swimmer Propulsion Units (SPUs), 132, *132*,
    183, *183*, 184
Swimming. *See* Combat swimmer

T
Tactical Operations Center (TOC), 412–413
Tactical Training, *627*, 652
Tafelski, Andy, 532
Taliban, 727, 728, 729
Tarawa Atoll ("Terrible Tarawa"), 44–56
  Army contingent, 45
  Chester W. Nimitz, 45–46
  cohesiveness of teams, 55–56
  enemy fire, 53, 54
  Fifth Amphibious Force, 45, 48
  "flying mattresses," 54–55
  hydrographic reconnaissance, 52–53
  intelligence for, 44
  J.T. Koehler, 46
  Kwajalein invasion, 46–47
  Landing Craft, Personnel, Ramped
    (LCPRs), 49, 53–54
  Landing Craft, Vehicle, Personnel (LCVPs),
    44
  Landing Vehicle, Tracked (LVTs), 44
  Marines contingent, 45
  mistakes, 44–45, 52, 140
  Namur invasion, 46
  Naval Underwater Demolition Training
    and Experimental Base (HI), 45
  Operation FLINTLOCK, 46–47
  Operation FORAGER, 47, 53
  Operation GALVANIC, 44
  Reef Obstacle and Mine Committee, 46
  Richard Conolly, 46
  Richmond Kelly Turner, 8, 44, 45–46
  Robert P. Marshall, Jr., 48–56
  Roi invasion, 46
  Saipan invasion, 54–55
  Seabees contingent, 45
  selection process for boat crews, 50
  sling pickups, 53–54
  string reconnaissance system, 53
  Underwater Demolition Teams (UDTs)
    creation, 1, 45–48
Tarbox, Thomas N. (Captain, USNR (Ret.)),
    550–554
  Basic Underwater Demolition/SEALs
    (BUD/S), 550–551, 552
  Bronze Bruce ("Naked Warrior"), 553
  camaraderie, 554
  equipment for SEALs, 553–554
  Gap Assault Team (GAT) at Normandy, 75
  Hell Week, 550–551
  history of Teams, 552, 553–554
  intelligence of SEALs, 552–553
  leaders and losses in the Teams, 198–202
  officers vs. enlisted, 552–553
